This registration code provides access to selected

documents available at the *Western Civilizations*,

Eighteenth Edition, StudySpace site:

wwnorton.com/web/westernciv18

WCIV-18SP

Western Civilizations

Their History & Their Culture

Joshua Cole

Carol Symes

Western Civilizations

Their History & Their Culture

EIGHTEENTH EDITION

W. W. Norton & Company ▪ NEW YORK ▪ LONDON

W. W. Norton & Company has been independent since its founding in 1923, when William Warder Norton and Mary D. Herter Norton first published lectures delivered at the People's Institute, the adult education division of New York City's Cooper Union. The firm soon expanded its program beyond the Institute, publishing books by celebrated academics from America and abroad. By midcentury, the two major pillars of Norton's publishing program—trade books and college texts—were firmly established. In the 1950s, the Norton family transferred control of the company to its employees, and today—with a staff of four hundred and a comparable number of trade, college, and professional titles published each year—W. W. Norton & Company stands as the largest and oldest publishing house owned wholly by its employees.

Editor: Jon Durbin
Associate editor: Justin Cahill
Editorial assistant: Penelope Lin
Project editor: Melissa Atkin
Managing editor, College: Marian Johnson
Copyeditor: Jude Grant
E-media editors: Steve Hoge, Tacy Quinn
Ancillary editor: Lorraine Klimowich
Assistant editor, E-media: Stefani Wallace
Photo editor: Evan Luberger
Photo research: Rona Tucillo
Marketing manager, History: Sarah England
Production manager, College: Sean Mintus
Design director: Rubina Yeh
Book designer: Judith Abbate / Abbate Design
Composition: Jouve
Cartographers: Mapping Specialists
Manufacturing: Transcontinental

Library of Congress Cataloging-in-Publication Data

Cole, Joshua, 1961–
    Western civilizations : their history & their culture / Joshua Cole and Carol Symes. —Eighteenth edition.
       pages cm
    Includes bibliographical references and index.
    ISBN 978-0-393-92213-4 (hardcover)
    1. Civilization, Western—Textbooks.   2. Europe—Civilization—Textbooks.   I. Symes, Carol.   II. Title.
    CB245.C56 2013
    909'.09821—dc23
                                                                    2013029952

W. W. Norton & Company, Inc., 500 Fifth Avenue, New York, N. Y. 10110
wwnorton.com

W. W. Norton & Company Ltd., Castle House, 75/76 Wells Street, London W1T 3QT

2 3 4 5 6 7 8 9 0

To our families:

Kate Tremel, Lucas and Ruby Cole
Tom, Erin, and Connor Wilson

with love and gratitude for their support.
And to all our students, who have also been
our teachers.

About the Authors

JOSHUA COLE (Ph.D., University of California, Berkeley) is Associate Professor of History at the University of Michigan, Ann Arbor. His publications include work on gender and the history of the population sciences, colonial violence, and the politics of memory in nineteenth- and twentieth-century France, Germany, and Algeria. His first book was *The Power of Large Numbers: Population, Politics, and Gender in Nineteenth-Century France* (Ithaca, NY: Cornell University Press, 2000).

CAROL SYMES (Ph.D., Harvard University) is Associate Professor of History and Director of Undergraduate Studies in the history department at the University of Illinois, Urbana-Champaign, where she has won the top teaching award in the College of Liberal Arts and Sciences. Her main areas of study include medieval Europe, the history of information media and communication technologies, and the history of theater. Her first book was *A Common Stage: Theater and Public Life in Medieval Arras* (Ithaca, NY: Cornell University Press, 2007).

Brief Contents

Contents

Primary Sources

This new edition of *Western Civilizations* sharpens and expands the set of tools we have developed to empower students—our own and yours—to engage effectively with the themes, sources, and challenges of history. It presents a clear and vigorous narrative, supplemented by a compelling selection of primary sources and striking images. At the same time, as the authors of this book's previous edition, we have worked to develop a unified program of pedagogical elements that guide students toward a more thorough understanding of the past, and of the ways that historians reconstruct that past. This framework helps students to analyze and interpret historical evidence on their own, encouraging them to become active participants in the learning process.

Moreover, the wide chronological scope of this book offers an unusual opportunity to trace central human developments (population movements, intellectual currents, economic trends, the formation of political institutions, the power of religious belief, the role of the arts and of technologies) in a region of the world whose cultural diversity has been constantly invigorated and renewed by its interactions with peoples living in other places. Students today have a wide selection of introductory history courses to choose from, thanks to the welcome availability of introductory surveys in Latin American, African, and Asian history, alongside both traditional and innovative offerings in the history of the United States and Europe. Global history has also come into its own in recent years. But our increasing awareness that no region's history can be isolated from global processes and connections has merely heightened the need for a richly contextualized and broad-based history such as that represented in *Western Civilizations*.

As in previous editions, we have attempted to balance the coverage of political, social, economic, and cultural phenomena with extensive treatment of material culture, daily life, gender, sexuality, art, science, and popular culture. And following the path laid out by the book's previous authors, Judith Coffin and Robert Stacey, we have insisted that the history of European peoples must be understood through their interactions with peoples in other parts of the world. Our treatment of this history is accordingly both deep and dynamic, attentive to the latest developments in historical scholarship.

Given the importance of placing human history in a global context, those of us who study the histories of ancient, medieval, and modern Europe are actively changing the ways that we teach this history. For good reasons reflected in the title of this book, few historians today would uphold a monolithic vision of a single and enduring "Western civilization" whose inevitable march to domination can be traced chapter by chapter through time. This older paradigm, strongly associated with the curriculum of early twentieth-century American colleges and universities, no longer conforms to what we know about the human past. Neither the "West" nor "Europe" can be seen as distinct, unified entities in space or time; the meanings attributed to these geographical expressions have changed in significant ways. Moreover, historians now agree that a linear notion of any civilization persisting unchanged over the centuries was made coherent only by leaving out the intense conflicts, extraordinary ruptures, and dynamic changes that took place at the heart of the societies we call "Western." Smoothing out the rough edges of the past does students no favors; even an introductory text such as this one should present the past as it appears to the historians who study it—that is, as complex panorama of human effort, filled with possibility and achievement but also fraught with discord, uncertainty, accident, and tragedy.

We know that current and future users of our text will be enthusiastic to see the efforts made in this new edition to update and reorganize the Late Medieval and Early Modern periods in order to place them in a larger Atlantic World context. The major highlight of this reorganization is a brand new chapter, entitled "Europe in the Atlantic World, 1550–1650." It places the newly integrated space of the Atlantic at the center of the story, exploring the ways, that religious warfare, economic developments, population movements, and cultural trends shaped—and were shaped by—historical actors on this dynamic frontier. Another significant result of the reorganization of these two periods is to provide a clearer chronological framework for the narrative, so that the students can better see how major topics and events emerge from their historical contexts. This, of course, was part of a larger effort begun across the entire text in the previous edition. These revisions demonstrate our dual commitment to keep the book current and up-to-date, while striving to integrate strong pedagogical features that help students build their study and history skills.

New and Revised Pedagogical Features

In our ongoing effort to shape students' engagement with history, this book is designed to reinforce your course objectives by helping students to master core content while challenging them to think critically about the past. In order to achieve these aims, our previous edition augmented the traditional strengths of *Western Civilizations* by introducing several exciting new features. These have since been refined and revised in accordance with feedback from student readers and teachers of the book. The most important and revolutionary feature is the pedagogical structure that supports each chapter. As we know from long experience, many students in introductory survey courses find the sheer quantity of information overwhelming, and so we have provided guidance to help them navigate through the material and to read in meaningful ways.

At the outset of each chapter, the **Before You Read This Chapter** feature offers three preliminary windows onto the material to be covered: *Story Lines*, *Chronology*, and *Core Objectives*. *Story Lines* allow the student to become familiar with the primary narrative threads that tie the chapter's elements together, and the *Chronology* grounds these *Story Lines* in the period under study. *Core Objectives* provide a checklist to ensure that the student is aware of the primary teaching points in the chapter. The student is then reminded of these teaching points upon completing the chapter, in the **After You Read This Chapter** section, which prompts the student to revisit the chapter in three ways. The first, *Reviewing the Core Objectives*, asks the reader to reconsider core objectives by answering a pointed question about each one. The second, *People, Ideas, and Events in Context*, summarizes some of the particulars that students should retain from their reading, through questions that allow them to relate individual terms to the major objectives and story

lines. Finally, *Thinking about Connections*, new to this edition, allow for more open-ended reflection on the significance of the chapter's material, drawing students' attention to issues that connect it to previous chapters and giving them insight into what comes next. As a package, the pedagogical features at the beginning and end of each chapter work together to enhance the student's learning experience, by breaking down the process of reading and analysis into manageable tasks.

A second package of pedagogical features is designed to capture students' interest and to compel them to think about what is at stake in the construction and use of historical narratives. Each chapter opens with a vignette that showcases a particular person or event representative of the era as a whole. Within each chapter, an expanded program of illustrations and maps has been enhanced by the addition of **Guiding Questions** (following these illustrations' and maps' captions) that urge the reader to explore the historical contexts and significance of these features in a more analytical way. The historical value of images, artifacts, and material culture is further emphasized in another feature we introduced in our previous edition, **Interpreting Visual Evidence**. This section provides discussion leaders with a provocative departure point for conversations about the key issues raised by visual sources, which students often find more approachable than texts. Once this conversation has begun, students can further develop their skills by **Analyzing Primary Sources**, through close readings of primary texts accompanied by cogent interpretive questions. The dynamism and diversity of Western civilizations are also illuminated through a look at **Competing Viewpoints** in each chapter, in which specific debates are presented through paired primary-source texts. The bibliographical **Further Readings**, located at the end of the book, has also been edited and brought up-to-date.

In addition to these features, which have proven successful, we are delighted to introduce an entirely new segment with this eighteenth edition. The new **Past and Present** features in the main text prompt students to connect events unfolding in the past with the breaking news of our own time, by taking one episode from each chapter and comparing it with a phenomenon that resonates more immediately with our students. To bring this new feature to life for students, we have also created a new series of **Author Videos**, in which we describe and analyze these connections across time and place. There are a number of illuminating discussions, including, "Spectator Sports," which compares the Roman gladiatorial games with NFL Football; "The Reputation of Richard III," which shows how modern forensics like those we see used on numerous TV shows were recently used to identify the remains of Richard III;

"The Persistence of Monarchies in a Democratic Age," which explains the origins and evolution of our ongoing fascination with royals like Louis XIV and Princess Diana; and "The Internet and the Enlightenment Public Sphere," which compares the kinds of public networks that helped spread Enlightenment ideas to the way the Internet can be used today to spread political ideas in movements such as the Arab Spring and Occupy Wall Street. Through this new feature, not only do we want to encourage students to recognize the continuing relevance of seemingly distant historical moments, but also we want to encourage historically-minded habits that will be useful for a lifetime. If students learn to see the connections among their world and the past, they will be more apt to place unfolding developments and debates in a more informed and complex historical context.

A Tour of New Chapters and Revisions

Our previous edition of *Western Civilizations* featured significant changes to each of the book's first five chapters, and this process of revision has continued in the present edition. In Chapter 1, the challenge of locating and interpreting historical evidence drawn from nontextual sources (archaeological, environmental, anthropological, mythic) is a special focus. Chapter 2 further underscores the degree to which recent archeological discoveries and new historical techniques have revolutionized our understanding of ancient history, and have also corroborated ancient peoples' own understandings of their past. Chapter 3 offers expanded coverage of the diverse polities that emerged in ancient Greece, and of Athens' closely related political, documentary, artistic, and intellectual achievements. Chapter 4's exploration of the Hellenistic world includes an unusually wide-ranging discussion of the scientific revolution powered by this first cosmopolitan civilization. Chapter 5 emphasizes the ways that the unique values and institutions of the Roman Republic are transformed through imperial expansion under the Principate.

With Chapter 6, a more extensive series of revisions has resulted in some significant reshaping and reorganization, so that the book's narrative reflects recent scholarship. The story of Rome's transformative encounter with early Christianity has been rewritten to ensure clarity and also to emphasize the fundamental ways that Christianity itself changed through the Roman Empire and in contact with peoples from northwestern Europe. Chapter 7, which examines Rome's three distinctive successor civilizations, now offers more extensive coverage of the reign of Justinian

and emergence of Islam. Balanced attention to the interlocking histories of Byzantium, the Muslim caliphates, and western Europe has carried forward in subsequent chapters. Chapters 8 contains an entirely new section, "A Tour of Europe around the Year 1000," with coverage of the Viking diaspora, the formation of Scandinavian kingdoms and the empire of Cnute, early medieval Rus' and eastern Europe, and the relationship among Mediterranean microcosms. It also features greatly expanded coverage of economy, trade, and the events leading up to the First Crusade. Chapter 9, which now covers the period 1000–1250, features a new segment on the Crusader States and crusading movements within Europe.

Chapter 10's treatment of the medieval world between 1250 and 1350 is almost wholly new, reflecting cutting-edge scholarship on this era. It includes a fresh look at the consolidation of the Mongol Khanates, new images and maps, some new sources, and a new *Interpreting Visual Evidence* segment on seals and their users. Chapters 11 and 12 have been thoroughly reorganized and rewritten to ensure that the narrative of medieval Europeans' colonial ventures (from the western Mediterranean to the eastern Atlantic and Africa, and beyond) is integrated with the story of the Black Death's effects on the medieval world and the impetus for the intellectual and artistic innovations of the Renaissance. In previous editions of the book, these concurrent phenomena were treated as separate, as though they took place in three separate periods (the later Middle Ages, the Renaissance, and the Age of Exploration). This made the connections among them almost impossible to explain or appreciate. In this eighteenth edition, therefore, the voyages of Columbus are firmly rooted in their historical contexts while the religious, social, and cultural upheavals of the Reformation (Chapter 13) are more clearly placed against a backdrop of political and economic competition in Europe and the Americas.

This program of revisions sets the stage for the most significant new chapter in the book: Chapter 14, "Europe in the Atlantic World, 1550–1650." This chapter, the hinge between the book's first and second halves, resulted from a close collaboration between us. It is designed to function either as the satisfying culmination of a course that surveys the history of Western civilizations up to the middle of the seventeenth century (like that taught by Carol Symes) or to provide a foundation for a course on the history of the modern West (like that taught by Joshua Cole). The chapter illuminates the changing nature of Europe as it becomes fully integrated into the larger Atlantic world that dramatically impacts all of its internal political, social, cultural, and economic development. In addition to greatly enhanced treatment of the transatlantic slave trade and the Columbian

Exchange, it also features new sections on the different models of colonial settlement in the Caribbean and the Americas, as well as expanded coverage of the Thirty Years' War.

The new emphasis on the emergence of the Atlantic world carries over to Chapter 15, which covers the emergence of powerful absolutist regimes on the continent and the evolution of wealthy European trading empires in the Americas, Africa, and Asia. This material has now been reorganized to clarify developments over time, as the early successes of the Spanish empire are gradually eclipsed by the successes of the Dutch, the French, and the British empires. A new document on the Streltsy rebellion, meanwhile, allows students to better understand the contested nature of power under the Russian tsars during the absolutist period. We have retained the emphasis on intellectual and cultural history in Chapter 16, on the Scientific Revolution, and in Chapter 17, on the Enlightenment. In Chapter 16 we have enhanced our treatment of the relationship between Christian faith and the new sciences of observation with a new primary-source document by Pierre Gassendi. In Chapter 17, meanwhile, we have sought to set the Enlightenment more clearly in its social and political context, connecting it more explicitly to the theme of European expansion into the Americas and the Pacific. This helps, for example, in connecting a document like the American Declaration of Independence with the ideas of European Enlightenment thinkers.

Chapters 18–19 cover the political and economic revolutions of the late eighteenth and early nineteenth centuries. Chapter 18 covers the French Revolution and the Napoleonic empires in depth, while also drawing attention to the way that these central episodes were rooted in a larger pattern of revolutionary political change that engulfed the Atlantic world. Chapter 19 emphasizes both the economic growth and the technological innovations that were a part of the Industrial Revolution, while also exploring the social and cultural consequences of industrialization for men and women in Europe's new industrial societies. The *Interpreting Visual Evidence* feature in Chapter 19 allows students to explore the ways that industrialization created new perceptions of the global economy in Europe, changing the way people thought of their place in the world.

Chapters 20–21 explore the successive struggles between conservative reaction and radicals in Europe, as the dynamic forces of nationalism unleashed by the French Revolution redrew the map of Europe and threatened the dynastic regimes that had ruled for centuries. Here, however, we have sought to clarify the periodization of the post-Napoleonic decades by focusing Chapter 20 more clearly on the conservative reaction in Europe after 1815, and the ideologies of conservatism, liberalism, republicanism, socialism,

and nationalism. By setting the 1848 revolutions entirely in Chapter 21 (rather than split between the two chapters as in previous editions) instructors should be able to demonstrate more easily the connection between these political movements and the history of national unification in Germany and Italy in subsequent decades. While making these changes in the organization of the chapters, we have retained our treatment of the important cultural movements of the first half of the nineteenth century, especially Romanticism.

Chapter 22 takes on the history of nineteenth-century colonialism, exploring both its political and economic origins and its consequences for the peoples of Africa and Asia. The chapter gives new emphasis to the significance of colonial conquest for European culture, as colonial power became increasingly associated with national greatness, both in conservative monarchies and in more democratic regimes. Meanwhile, Chapter 23 brings the narrative back to the heart of Europe, covering the long-term consequences of industrialization and the consolidation of a conservative form of nationalism in many European nations even as the electorate was being expanded. The chapter emphasizes the varied nature of the new forms of political dissent, from the feminists who claimed the right to vote to the newly organized socialist movements that proved so enduring in many European countries.

Chapters 24 and 25 bring new vividness to the history of the First World War and the intense conflicts of the interwar period, while Chapter 26 uses the history of the Second World War as a hinge for understanding European and global developments in the second half of the twentieth century. The *Interpreting Visual Evidence* feature in Chapter 24 allows for a special focus on the role of propaganda among the belligerent nations in 1914–1918; and the chapter's section on the diplomatic crisis that preceded the First World War has been streamlined to allow students to more easily comprehend the essential issues at the heart of the conflict. In Chapter 25 the *Interpreting Visual Evidence* feature continues to explore the theme touched on in earlier chapters, political representations of "the people," this time in the context of fascist spectacles in Germany and Italy in the 1930s. These visual sources help students to understand the vulnerability of Europe's democratic regimes during these years as they faced the dual assault from fascists on the right and Bolsheviks on the left.

Chapters 27–29 bring the volumes to a close in a thorough exploration of the Cold War, decolonization, the collapse of the Soviet Union and the Eastern Bloc in 1989–1991, and the roots of the multifaceted global conflicts that beset the world in the first decade of the twenty-first century. Chapter 27 juxtaposes the Cold War with decolonization, showing how this combination sharply diminished the ability of European nations to control events in the international arena, even as they succeeded in rebuilding their economies at home. Chapter 28 explores the vibrancy of European culture in the crucial period of the 1960s to the early 1990s, bringing new attention to the significance of 1989 as a turning point in European history. Finally, extensive revisions to Chapter 29, add to the issues covered in our treatment of Europe's place in the contemporary globalized world. The chapter now includes a new section on efforts to deal with climate change, as well as expanded discussion of the impact of global terrorism, and recent developments in the Arab-Israeli conflict. The discussion on the financial crisis of 2008 and the presidency of Barack Obama has been brought up to date, and two new sections have been added to allow students to think about the Arab Spring of 2011 and the European debt crisis of recent years in connection with the broader history of European democracy, nation building, and colonialism in the modern period.

Media Resources for Instructors and Students

LMS COURSEPACKS WITH STRONG ASSESSMENT AND LECTURE TOOLS

- **Dynamic Author Videos (55 total)** in which the authors discuss two of the main topics or themes in each chapter. New to this edition, illustrations, maps, and other types of media are integrated into the interviews to make them richer and more dynamic. These segments can serve as lecture launchers or as a preview tool for students before and after they read a chapter. (Available in PowerPoint and on Norton StudySpace.)
- **NEW *Past and Present* Author Videos (29 total)** that connect topics across time and place and show why history is relevant to understanding our world today (see further explanation above). Examples include "Spectator Sports," "Medieval Plots and Modern Movies," "Global Pandemics," and "The Atlantic Revolutions and Human Rights" (Available in PowerPoint and on Norton StudySpace.)
- **NEW Guided Reading Exercises** by Scott Corbett (Ventura College) are designed to help students learn how to effectively read a textbook. The reading exercises, which are keyed to each chapter's *People, Ideas, and Events in Context*

questions, instill a three-step Note-Summarize-Assess pedagogy. Exercises are based on actual passages from the textbook (three exercises per chapter). Feedback will provide model responses with direct page references. (Available only in the Norton Coursepack.)

- **NEW 36 Map Exercises** can be assigned for assessment. These activities ask students a series of questions about historical events that must be answered by clicking on the map to record the answer. (Available only in the Norton Coursepack.)
- **NEW Chrono-Quiz** improving on the ever-popular Chrono-Sequencer, the Chrono-Quiz is now available as an assessment activity that will report to the school's native LMS. (Available only in the Norton Coursepack.)
- **NEW *StoryMaps*** break complex maps into a sequence of four to five annotated screens that focus on the *story* behind the *geography*. There are ten StoryMaps that include such topics as The Silk Road, The Spread of the Black Death, and Nineteenth-Century Imperialism. (Available only on wwnorton.com/web/westernciv18/instructors.)

INSTRUCTOR'S MANUAL

Bob Brennan (Cape Fear Community College)
Bruce Delfini (Rockland Community College)
Christopher Laney (Berkshire Community College)
Alice Roberti (Santa Rosa Community College)

The Instructor's Manual for *Western Civilizations*, Eighteenth edition, is designed to help instructors prepare lectures and exams. The Instructor's Manual contains detailed chapter outlines, general discussion questions, document discussion questions, lecture objectives, interdisciplinary discussion topics, and recommended reading and film lists. **This edition has been revised to include sample answers to all of the student-facing comprehension questions in the text.**

TEST BANK

Geoffrey Clark (SUNY Potsdam)
Donna Trembinski (St. Francis Xavier University)

The Test Bank contains over 2,000 multiple-choice, true/false, and essay questions. This edition of the Test Bank has been completely revised for content and accuracy. All test questions are now aligned to Bloom's Taxonomy for greater ease and effectiveness of assessment.

FOR STUDENTS

⊚ wwnorton.com/web/westernciv18
Free and open to all students, Norton StudySpace includes

- **Author Videos (over 80 in all)** for every chapter, including the new *Past and Present* segments that connect topics. Examples include
  - "Medieval Plots and Modern Movies"
  - "Controlling Consumption" (the legalization of controlled substances, from sixteenth-century regulations to contemporary marijuana policy)
  - "The Internet and the Enlightenment Public Sphere"
- **Chapter Outlines and Quizzes.** Quiz feedback is aligned to student learning outcomes and core objectives, along with page references.
- **World History Tours,** powered by Google Earth™, now operate from within the browser, eliminating the need to download third-party applications or files.
- **iMaps** allow students to view layers of information on each map.
- **Map Worksheets** provide each map without labels for offline re-labeling and quizzing.
- **Flashcards** align key terms and events with brief descriptions and definitions.
- Over **400 primary-source documents and images**
- **Ebook links** tie the online text to all study and review materials.

A FEW WORDS OF THANKS

Our first edition as members of *Western Civilizations'* authorial team was a challenging and rewarding one. Our second edition has been equally rewarding in that we have been able to implement a number of useful and engaging changes in the content and structure of the book, which we hope will make it even more student- and classroom-friendly. We are very grateful for the expert assistance and support of the Norton team, especially that of our editor, Jon Durbin. Melissa Atkin, our fabulous project editor, has driven the book beautifully through the manuscript process. Justin Cahill has provided good critiques of the illustrations and the new *Past and Present* features in addition to all the other parts of the project he has handled so skillfully. Evan Luberger and Rona Tucillo did an excellent job finding many of the exact images we specified. Lorraine Klimowich did an expert job developing the print ancillaries. Sean Mintus has efficiently marched

us through the production process. Steve Hoge has done a great job developing the book's fantastic emedia, particularly the new *Past and Present* Author Videos, the new Guided Reading Exercises, and the new StoryMaps. Jude Grant and John Gould were terrific in skillfully guiding the manuscript through the copyediting and proofreading stages. Finally, we want to thank Sarah England for spearheading the marketing campaign for the new edition. We are also indebted to the numerous expert readers who commented on various chapters and who thereby strengthened the book as a whole. We are thankful to our families, for their patience and advice, and to our students, whose questions and comments over the years have been essential to the framing of this book. And we extend a special thanks to, and hope to hear from, all the teachers and students we might never meet—their engagement with this book will frame new understandings of our shared past and its bearing on our future.

REVIEWERS

17th Edition Consultants
Paul Freedman, Yale University
Sheryl Kroen, University of Florida
Michael Kulikowski, Pennsylvania State University
Harry Liebersohn, University of Illinois, Urbana-Champaign
Helmut Smith, Vanderbilt University

17th Edition Reviewers
Donna Allen, Glendale Community College
Ken Bartlett, University of Toronto
Volker Benkert, Arizona State University
Dean Bennett, Schenectady City Community College
Patrick Brennan, Gulf Coast Community College
Neil Brooks, Community College of Baltimore County, Essex
James Brophy, University of Delaware
Kevin Caldwell, Blue Ridge Community College
Keith Chu, Bergen Community College
Alex D'Erizans, Borough of Manhattan Community College, CUNY
Hilary Earl, Nipissing University
Kirk Ford, Mississippi College
Michael Gattis, Gulf Coast Community College
David M. Gallo, College of Mount Saint Vincent
Jamie Gruring, Arizona State University
Tim Hack, Salem Community College
Bernard Hagerty, University of Pittsburg
Paul T. Hietter, Mesa Community College

Paul Hughes, Sussex County Community College
Kyle Irvin, Jefferson State Community College
Llana Krug, York College of Pennsylvania
Guy Lalande, St. Francis Xavier University
Chris Laney, Berkshire Community College
Charles Levine, Mesa Community College
Michael McKeown, Daytona State University
Dan Puckett, Troy State University
Dan Robinson, Troy State University
Craig Saucier, Southeastern Louisiana University
Aletia Seaborn, Southern Union State College
Victoria Thompson, Arizona State University
Donna Trembinski, St. Francis Xavier University
Pamela West, Jefferson State Community College
Julianna Wilson, Pima Community College

18th Edition Reviewers
Matthew Barlow, John Abbott College
Ken Bartlett, University of Toronto
Bob Brennan, Cape Fear Community College
Jim Brophy, University of Delaware
Keith Chu, Bergen Community College

Geoffrey Clark, SUNY Potsdam
Bill Donovan, Loyola University Maryland
Jeff Ewen, Sussex County Community College
Peter Goddard, University of Guelph
Paul Hughes, Sussex County Community
    College
Michael Kulikowski, Penn State University
Chris Laney, Berkshire Community College
James Martin, Campbell University
Derrick McKisick, Fairfield University
Dan Puckett, Troy University
Major Ben Richards, US Military Academy
Bo Riley, Columbus State Community College
Kimlisa Salazar, Pima Community College
Sara Scalenghe, Loyola University Maryland
Suzanne Smith, Cape Fear Community College
Bobbi Sutherland, Dordt College
David Tengwall, Anne Arundel Community
    College
Pam West, Jefferson State Community College
Julianna Wilson, Pima Community College
Margarita Youngo, Pima Community College

Western Civilizations

Their History & Their Culture

STORY LINES

- Historians gather and interpret evidence from a diverse array of sources, many of them environmental, visual, and archaeological.

- All civilizations emerge as the result of complex historical processes specific to a time and place, yet all share certain defining features.

- Prominent individuals can come to power through the use of force, but maintaining power requires legitimacy.

- Those individuals wielding power in ancient Mesopotamia and Egypt responded in different ways to the challenge of establishing legitimacy.

Before You Read This Chapter

CHRONOLOGY

11,000 B.C.E.	Neolithic Revolution begins
7500–5700 B.C.E.	Çatalhöyük flourishes
6800–3000 B.C.E.	Jericho flourishes
4300–2900 B.C.E.	The rise of Uruk in Sumer
c. 3200 B.C.E.	Development of writing
c. 3100 B.C.E.	King Narmer unites Upper and Lower Egypt
2900–2500 B.C.E.	Early Dynastic Period in Sumer
c. 2700 B.C.E.	Reign of Gilgamesh
c. 2686–2160 B.C.E.	Old Kingdom of Egypt
c. 2650 B.C.E.	Imhotep engineers the Step Pyramid for King Djoser
c. 2350 B.C.E.	Sargon of Akkad consolidates power in Sumer
2160–2055 B.C.E.	First Intermediate Period in Egypt
2100–2000 B.C.E.	Ziggurat of Ur constructed
2055–c. 1650 B.C.E.	Middle Kingdom of Egypt
c. 1792–1750 B.C.E.	Reign of Hammurabi

Early Civilizations

CORE OBJECTIVES

- **UNDERSTAND** the challenges involved in studying the distant past.

- **DEFINE** the key characteristics of civilization.

- **IDENTIFY** the factors that shaped the earliest cities.

- **EXPLAIN** how Hammurabi's empire was governed.

- **DESCRIBE** the main differences between Mesopotamian and Egyptian civilizations.

There was a time, the story goes, when all the peoples of the earth shared a common language and could therefore accomplish great things. They developed new technologies, made bricks, and aspired to build a fortified city with a tower reaching to the sky. But their god was troubled by this, so he destroyed their civilization by making it hard for them to understand one another's speech.

We know this as the legend of Babel. It's a story that probably circulated among peoples of the ancient world for thousands of years before it became part of the Hebrew book we call by its Greek name, Genesis, "the beginning." The story lets us glimpse some of the conditions in which the first civilizations arose, and it also reminds us of the ruptures that make studying them hard. We no longer speak the same languages as those ancient peoples, just as we no longer have direct access to their experiences or their beliefs.

Such foundational stories are usually called *myths*, but they are really an early form of history. For the people who told them, myths helped to make sense of the present by explaining the past. The fate of Babel conveyed a crucial message: human beings are powerful when they share a common goal, and what enables human interaction is civilization. To the peoples of the ancient world, the characteristic benefits of civilization—stability and safety, government, art, literature, science—were always products of city life. The very word *civilization* derives from the Latin word *civis*, "city." Cities, however, became possible only as a result of innovations that began around the end of the last Ice Age, about 13,000 years ago, and that came to fruition in Mesopotamia 8,000 years later. The history of civilization is therefore a short one. Within the study of humanity, which reaches back to the genus *Homo* in Africa, some 1.7 million years ago, it is merely a blip on the radar screen. Even within the history of *Homo sapiens*, the subspecies to which we all belong and which evolved about 40,000 years ago, civilization is a very recent development.

The study of early civilizations is both fascinating and challenging. Historians still do not understand why the first-known cities should have developed in the region between the Tigris and the Euphrates Rivers, in what is now Iraq. Once developed, however, the basic patterns of urban life quickly spread to other parts of the Near East, both by imitation and by conquest. A network of trading connections linked these early cities, but intense competition for resources made alliances among them fragile. Then, around the middle of the second millennium B.C.E. (that is, "Before the Common Era," equivalent to the Christian dating system B.C., "Before Christ"), emerging powers began to shape these fiercely independent cities into empires. How this happened—and how we know that it happened—is the subject of Chapter 1.

BEFORE CIVILIZATION

More than 9,000 years ago, a town began to develop at Çatalhöyük (*CHUH-tal-hih-yik*) in what is now south-central Turkey. Over the next 2,000 years, it grew to cover an area of thirty-three acres, within which some 8,000 inhabitants lived in more than 2,000 separate houses. If this seems small, consider that Çatalhöyük's population density was actually twice that of today's most populous city, Mumbai (India). It was so tightly packed that there were hardly any streets. Instead, each house was built immediately next to its neighbor and generally on top of a previous house. People entered their houses by walking across their neighbors' rooftops and climbing down ladders into their own living spaces.

The people of Çatalhöyük developed a highly organized and advanced society. They wove wool cloth; they made

kiln-fired pottery; they painted elaborate hunting scenes on the plaster-covered walls of their houses; they made weapons and tools from razor-sharp obsidian imported from the nearby Cappadocian mountains. They honored their ancestors with religious rites and buried their dead beneath the floors of their houses. As settled agriculturalists, they grew grains, peas, and lentils and tended herds of domesticated sheep and goats. But they also hunted and gathered fruits and nuts, like their nomadic ancestors, and their society was egalitarian—another feature common to nomadic societies: both men and women did the same kinds of work. But despite their relatively diverse food supply, their life spans were very short. Men died, on average, at the age of thirty-four. Women, who bore the additional risks of childbirth, died around age thirty.

The basic features of life in Çatalhöyük are common to all early civilizations. But how, when, and why did such settlements emerge? And how do we have access to information about this distant past? The era before the appearance of written records, which begin to proliferate around 3100 B.C.E., is of far greater duration than the subsequent eras we are able to document—and no less important. But it requires special ingenuity to identify, collect, and interpret the evidence of the very distant past. In fact, historians have only just begun to explore the ways that climatology, neuroscience, and evolutionary biology can further illuminate this period, augmenting the older findings of paleontology, archaeology, and historical anthropology. The following summary of our knowledge may need to be radically revised in the next few years.

Societies of the Stone Age

Primates with human characteristics originated in Africa 4 to 5 million years ago, and toolmaking hominids—species belonging to the genus *Homo*, our distant ancestors—evolved approximately 2 million years ago. Because these early hominids made most of their tools out of stone, all human cultures flourishing before the fourth millennium B.C.E. (that is, the thousand years ending in 3000 B.C.E.) are designated as belonging to the Stone Age. This vast expanse of time is divided into the Paleolithic ("Old Stone") and the Neolithic ("New Stone") Eras, with the break between them falling around 11,000 B.C.E.

Long before modern humans made their appearance, then, recognizable human traits had already begun to leave traces on the landscape. Hominids in Africa were kindling and controlling fire as early as 164,000 years ago, and using it to make tools. The Neanderthals, a hominid species that flourished about 200,000 years ago, made

CAVE PAINTINGS FROM LASCAUX. These paintings, which date to between 10,000 and 15,000 B.C.E., show several of the different species of animals that were hunted by people of the Ice Age. The largest animal depicted here, a species of long-horned cattle known as the *auroch,* is now extinct.

jewelry, painted on the walls of caves, and buried their dead in distinctive graves with meaningful objects such as horns (blown to make music) and, in one case, flowers. Could these hominids speak? Did they have a language? At present, there is no way that archaeology can answer such questions.

However, archaeology has shown that in the last phase of the Paleolithic Era, around 40,000 B.C.E., the pace of human development began to accelerate dramatically. Human populations in Africa expanded, suggesting that people were better nourished, perhaps as a result of new technologies. In Europe, the subspecies *Homo sapiens sapiens* began to produce finely crafted and more effective tools such as fishhooks, arrowheads, and sewing needles made from wood, antler, and bone. The most astonishing evidence of this change was produced by these new tools: cave paintings like those at Lascaux and Chauvet (France)—those at Chauvet were discovered only in 1994—some of which may be 30,000 years old. These amazing scenes were purposefully painted in recesses where acoustic resonance is greatest, and were probably intended to be experienced as part of multimedia musical ceremonies. (Flutes made from bone and ivory, dating to around 33,000 B.C.E., were found in a cave in southern Germany in 2008.) This is almost certain evidence for the development of language.

Despite these extraordinary changes, the basic patterns of human life altered very little during this era. Virtually all human societies consisted of hunter-gatherers, bands of a few dozen people who moved incessantly in search of food. As a result of this constant movement, these groups have left no continuous archaeological record. Yet we can discern some of the social, economic, and political structures that make these subsistence societies different from those that can be called "civilizations." Early humans had no domestic animals to transport goods, so they could have no significant material possessions aside from basic tools. And because they could not accumulate goods over time, the distinctions of rank and status created by disparities in wealth could not develop. Hierarchical structures were therefore uncommon. When conflicts arose among members of a group or resources became scarce, the solution was probably to divide and separate.

Although scholars once assumed that men did the hunting and women the gathering, such gendered presumptions do not reflect the complex realities of modern hunter-gatherer societies and they are probably not applicable to the Paleolithic Period, either. It is more likely that all members of a band (except for the very young and very old) engaged in the basic activity of acquiring food.

THE BUILDING BLOCKS OF CIVILIZATION

What changes allowed some hunter-gatherer societies to settle and build civilizations? Around 11,000 B.C.E., very evident developments brought about by changes in the climate led to the development of managed food production, which in turn fostered settlements that could trade with one another, both locally and over long distances. For the first time, it became possible for individuals and communities to accumulate and store wealth on a large scale. The results were far-reaching. Communities became more stable, and human interactions more complex. Specialization developed, along with distinctions of status and rank. Both the rapidity and the radical implications of these changes have given this era its name: the Neolithic Revolution.

The Neolithic Revolution

The artists who executed the cave paintings at Lascaux and Chauvet were conditioned to survive in harsh climatic conditions. Between 40,000 and 11,000 B.C.E., daytime temperatures in the Mediterranean basin averaged about 60° F (16° C) in the summer and about 30° F (–1° C) in the winter. These are very low compared to today's temperatures in the city of Marseilles, not far from Lascaux, which average about 86° F (30° C) in summer and 52° F (11° C) in winter. Cold-loving reindeer, elk, wild boars, bison, and mountain goats abounded in regions now famous for their beaches and vineyards. But as the glaciers receded northward with the warming climate, these species retreated with them, all the way to Scandinavia. Some humans moved north with the game, but others stayed behind to create a very different world.

Within a few thousand years after the end of the Ice Age, the peoples living in the eastern Mediterranean accomplished the most momentous transformation in human

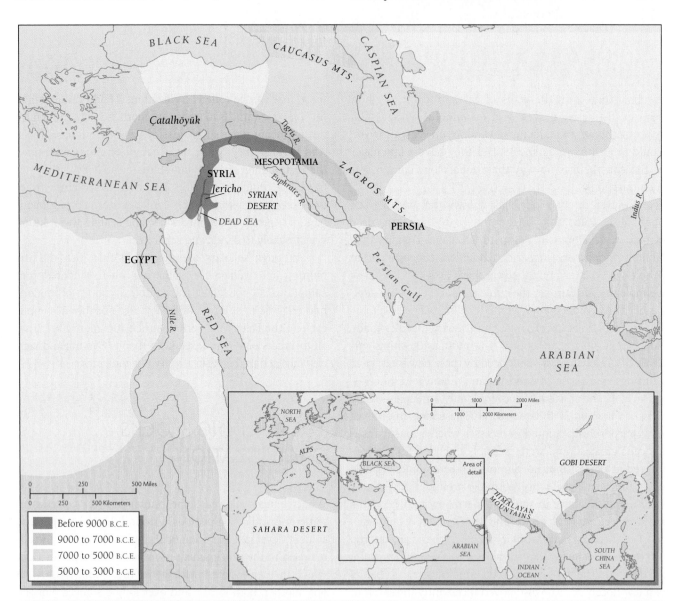

Before 9000 B.C.E.
9000 to 7000 B.C.E.
7000 to 5000 B.C.E.
5000 to 3000 B.C.E.

THE GROWTH OF AGRICULTURE. Examine the chronology of agriculture's development in this region. ■ *What areas began cultivating crops first, and why?* ■ *In what period did agriculture spread the most rapidly, and why?* ■ *How might rivers have played a crucial role in the spread of farming technologies?*

history: a switch from food-gathering for subsistence to food production. The warmer, wetter climate allowed wild grains to flourish, geometrically increasing the food supply and making settlements possible. People then began to domesticate animals and cultivate plants. Stable settlements grew into cities. This process took several thousand years, but it still deserves to be called "revolutionary." In a relatively short time, people living in this area fundamentally altered patterns of existence that were millions of years old.

This revolution produced new challenges and new inequalities—a salutary reminder that not all attributes of a civilization are positive. For example well-nourished women in sedentary communities can bear more children than women in hunter-gatherer groups, and so the women of this new era became increasingly sequestered from their male counterparts, who in turn gave up an equal role in child care. The rapid increase in population was also countered by the rapid spread of infectious diseases, while dependence on carbohydrates resulted in earlier deaths than were typical among hunter-gatherers.

Eventually, increased fertility and birthrates outweighed these limiting factors, and by about 8000 B.C.E. human populations were beginning to exceed the wild food supply. They therefore had to increase the food-growing capacity of the land and to devise ways of preserving and storing grain between harvests. Some peoples had learned how to preserve wild grain in storage pits as early as 11,500 B.C.E., and eventually they discovered that they could use this seed to produce even more grain the following year. The importance of this latter discovery cannot be overstated: once humans began deliberate cultivation, they could support larger populations and could also compensate for disasters (such as flooding) that might inhibit natural reseeding. Even more important, intensified seeding and storage provided humans with the stable and predictable surpluses needed to support domestic animals. This brought a host of additional benefits, not only guaranteeing a more reliable supply of meat, milk, leather, wool, bone, and horn but also providing animal power to pull carts and plows and to power mills. But it also resulted in a pattern of environmental engineering that could have devastating and unsustainable effects.

The Emergence of Towns and Villages

The accelerating changes of the Neolithic Revolution are exemplified by towns like Çatalhöyük and by the simultaneous rise of trade and warfare—sure signs of increased specialization and competition among human societies. Hundreds, and probably thousands, of settlements grew up in the Near East between 7500 and 3500 B.C.E. Some of these can be classified as cities: that is, centers of administration and commerce with a relatively large and diverse population, often protected by walls. Among the earliest of these was Jericho, in the territory lying between modern Israel and Jordan. Jericho emerged as a seasonal, grain-producing settlement, but by 6800 B.C.E. its inhabitants were undertaking a spectacular building program to protect their stored surplus of food. Many new dwellings were built on stone foundations, and a massive dressed stone wall was constructed around the western edge of the settlement. It included a circular tower whose excavated remains still reach to a height of thirty feet, a powerful expression of its builders' wealth, technical prowess, and political ambitions.

This wall and its tower served a growing and now permanent population: Jericho eventually covered at least eight acres and supported 3,000 people, so it was even more densely settled than Çatalhöyük. It was sustained by the intensive cultivation, made possible by irrigation, of recently domesticated strains of wheat and barley. Jericho's inhabitants also produced some of the earliest-known pottery, which allowed them to store grain, wine, and oils more effectively. Pottery's most important benefits, however, were in cooking. For the first time, it was possible

EARLY POTTERY. This ceramic bowl, with its lovely depiction of dancing figures, was fashioned sometime between 5000 and 1700 B.C.E. Although it cannot be dated precisely, distinctive design features such as these make it possible to track the shipment of commodities throughout the ancient world.

to produce nourishing stews, porridges, and ales. (The capacity to produce beer is a sure sign of civilization.) Pottery production was not only vital to ancient civilizations, it is vital to those who study them: as the techniques for making pottery spread throughout the Near East and Asia, identifiable regional styles also developed. By studying the different varieties, archaeologists can construct a reasonably accurate chronology and can also trace the movements of goods and people.

Jericho and Çatalhöyük illustrate the impact that stored agricultural surpluses have on human relations. In these settled societies, significant differences began to arise in the amount of wealth individuals could stockpile for themselves and their heirs. Dependence on agriculture also made it more difficult for individuals to split off from the community when disputes and inequities arose. The result was the emergence of a much more stratified society, with more opportunities for a few powerful people to become dominant. The new reliance on agriculture also meant a new dependence on the land, the seasons, and the weather, which led to new speculations about the supernatural. Different life forces were believed to require special services and gifts, and the regular practice of ritual and sacrifice ultimately produced a priestly caste of individuals or families who seemed able to communicate with these forces. Such spiritual leadership was allied to more worldly forms of power, including the capacity to lead war bands, to exact tribute from other settlements, to construct defenses, and to resolve disputes. Through their command of the community's religious, military, economic, and political structures, certain clans could establish themselves as a ruling class.

Trade was another important element in the development of early settlements. Local trading networks were already established around 9000 B.C.E., and by 5000 long-distance routes linked settlements throughout the Near East. Exotic goods and luxury items were the most frequent objects of exchange, including marine shells and semiprecious stones like turquoise and lapis lazuli. Long-distance trade also accelerated the exchange of ideas and information, and it further increased social stratification: because status was enhanced by access to high-prestige goods, local elites sought to monopolize trade by organizing and controlling the production of commodities within their own communities and by regulating their export. Certain people could now devote at least a portion of their labor to pursuits other than agriculture: making pottery or cloth, manufacturing weapons or tools, building houses and fortifications, or facilitating trade. The elites who fostered and exploited the labor of others eventually became specialized themselves, as full-time speculators and organizers,

with the leisure and resources to engage in intellectual, artistic, and political pursuits. The building blocks of civilization had been laid.

URBAN DEVELOPMENT IN MESOPOTAMIA

The Greeks called it Mesopotamia, the "Land between Rivers." It was a land that received only about eight inches (20 cm) of rainfall per year. Its soils are sandy and summer temperatures exceed 110° F (44° C). The two rivers supplying water—the Tigris and Euphrates—are noted for their violence and unpredictability. Both are prone to flooding, and the Tigris was liable to jump its banks and change its course from year to year. It was in this challenging environment that the first urban society, the civilization of Sumer, flourished.

The Ubaid Culture

The earliest cities of Mesopotamia were founded by the Ubaid peoples, so called because of their settlement at al-Ubaid (now in Iraq), which dates from around 5900 B.C.E. In this era, the headwaters of the Persian Gulf extended at least 100 miles farther inland than they do today, so some Ubaid settlements bordered on fertile marshlands, which enabled them to develop irrigation systems. Although these began as relatively simple channels and collection pools, Ubaid farmers quickly learned to build more sophisticated canals and to line some pools with stone. They also constructed dikes and levees to control the seasonal flooding of the rivers and to direct the excess water into irrigation canals. Despite the hostility of the environment, Ubaid communities were soon producing surpluses sufficient to support specialists in construction, weaving, pottery making, metalwork, and trade: the typical attributes of Neolithic village life.

Yet there is also evidence of something quite new in Ubaid culture: central structures that served religious, economic, and administrative functions, something not found in Çatalhöyük. Starting out as shrines, these structures soon became impressive temples built of dried mud brick, like the bricks described in the story of Babel—and unlike the plentiful stone used at Jericho; the scarcity of stone meant that builders in this region had to be more resourceful. Each large settlement had such a temple, from which a

THE WHITE TEMPLE AT URUK, c. 3400 B.C.E. This temple may have been dedicated to the sky god, An, or designed to provide all the region's gods with a mountaintop home in a part of the world known for its level plains.

priestly class acted as managers of the community's stored wealth and of the complex irrigation systems that would make the civilization of Sumer possible.

Urbanism in Uruk, 4300–2900 B.C.E.

After about 4300 B.C.E., these Ubaid settlements developed into larger, more prosperous, and more highly organized communities. The most famous of these sites, Uruk, is considered the first Sumerian city-state. Its sophistication and scale is exemplified by the White Temple at Uruk, built between 3500 and 3300 B.C.E. This massive sloping platform looms nearly forty feet above the surrounding flatlands, and its four corners are oriented toward the cardinal points of the compass. Atop the platform stands the temple proper, dressed in brick and originally painted a brilliant white.

Such temples were eventually constructed in every Sumerian city, reflecting the central role that worship played in civic life. Uruk in particular seems to have owed its rapid urban growth to its importance as a religious center. By 3100 B.C.E. it encompassed several hundred acres, enclosing a population of 40,000 people within its massive brick walls. The villages and towns of Sumer were also growing rapidly, their teeming economic activity attracting immigrants just as the great cities did. Grain and cloth production grew tenfold. Trade routes expanded dramatically, binding the peoples of Mesopotamia to the Mediterranean and bringing foods from as far away as Scandinavia and China. To manage this increasingly complex economy, the Sumerians invented the technology on which most historians rely: writing.

The Development of Writing

In 4000 B.C.E., the peoples of Mesopotamia were already using clay tokens to keep inventories. Within a few centuries, they developed a practice of placing tokens inside hollow clay balls and inscribing, on the outside of each ball, the shapes of all the tokens it contained. By 3300 B.C.E., priests (or their scribes) had replaced these balls with flat clay tablets

CUNEIFORM WRITING. The image on the left shows a Sumerian clay tablet from about 3000 B.C.E. Here, standardized pictures are beginning to represent abstractions: notice the symbol *ninda* (food) at the top. On the right, carvings on limestone from about 2600 B.C.E. reveal the evolution of cuneiform into more abstract forms. ▪ *Why would such standardized pictograms have been easier to reproduce quickly?*

on which they inscribed symbols representing the tokens. These tablets made keeping the tokens themselves unnecessary, and they could also be archived for future reference or sent to other settlements as receipts or requests for goods.

Writing thus evolved as a practical recording technology to support economic pursuits. And because it existed to represent real things, its system of symbols—called pictograms—was also realistic: each pictogram resembled the thing it represented. Over time, however, a pictogram might be used not only to symbolize a physical object but to evoke an idea associated with that object. For example, the symbol for a bowl of food, a *ninda*, might be used to express something more abstract, such as "nourishment" or "sustenance." Pictograms also came to be associated with particular spoken sounds, or *phonemes*. Thus when a Sumerian scribe needed to employ the sound *ninda*, even as part of another word or name, he would use the symbol for a bowl of food to represent that phoneme. Later, special marks were added to the symbol, so that a reader could tell whether the writer meant it to represent the object itself, or an abstract concept, or a sound used in a context that might have nothing to do with food.

By 3100 B.C.E., Sumerian scribes also developed a specialized tool suited to the task of writing, a durable stylus made of reed. Because this stylus leaves an impression shaped like a wedge (in Latin, *cuneus*), this script is called *cuneiform* (kyoo-NAY-i-form). With it, cuneiform symbols could be impressed more quickly into clay. But because the new stylus was not suited to drawing pictograms that accurately represented things, the symbols became even more abstract; eventually they barely resembled the original pictograms at all. Meanwhile, symbols were invented for every

possible phonetic combination in the Sumerian language, reducing the number of necessary pictograms from about 1,200 to 600. Whereas the earliest pictograms could have been written and read by anyone, writing and reading now became specialized, powerful skills accessible only to a small and influential minority who were taught in designated scribal schools.

Despite the complicated nature of the script, cuneiform proved remarkably durable. For over 2,000 years it remained the principal writing system of the ancient Near East, even in societies that did not speak the Sumerian language. Documents using the script were still being produced as late as the first century C.E. ("Common Era," equivalent to the traditional Christian practice of designating dates by A.D., for *Anno Domini*, "in the Year of the Lord"). By about 2500 B.C.E., Sumerians were using writing for a wide variety of economic, religious, political, and artistic purposes. Tens of thousands of clay tablets still survive and this makes it possible for us to know a great deal more about the Sumerians than we do about any other human society before this time. We can better understand the social structures that shaped their lives, their attitudes toward their gods, and their changing political circumstances.

THE CULTURE OF SUMER

The great centers of Sumerian civilization—the cities of Uruk, Ur, Lagash, Eridu, and Kish—shared a common culture and a common language. They also shared a set of beliefs. However, this common religion did not produce

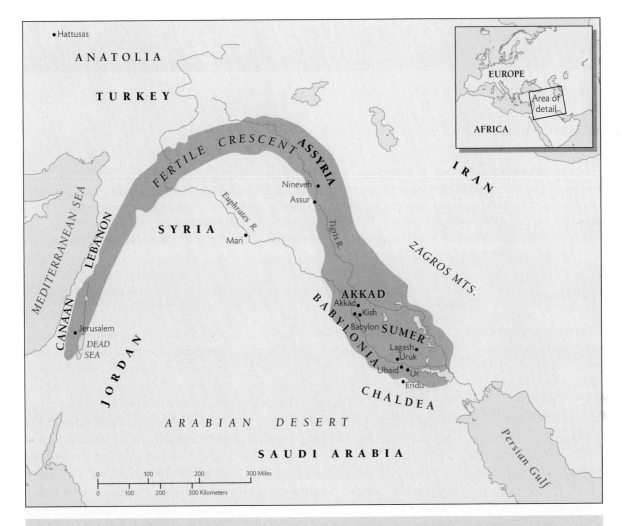

peace. The residents of each city considered themselves to be the servants of a particular god, whom they sought to glorify by exalting their own city above others. The result was intense competition that frequently escalated into warfare. There was also an economic dimension to this conflict, since water rights and access to arable land and trade routes were often at stake.

Much of the economic production of a city passed through great temple warehouses, where priests redistributed the city's produce. During the third millennium, these great temples also began to control the production of textiles, employing thousands of servile women and children. Temple elites also played a key role in long-distance trade, as both buyers and sellers of goods. So for any city-state to surrender its independence would not only offend the conquered city's god, it would jeopardize its entire economy and the power of its ruling class.

Each Sumerian city therefore had its own aristocracy, the group from which priests were drawn. As much as half the remaining population consisted of free persons who held parcels of land sufficient to sustain themselves; but the rest were dependents of the temple who worked as artisans or as agricultural laborers on its lands. Many of these dependents were slaves. Most were prisoners of war from other Sumerian city-states whose bondage was limited to three years, after which time a slave had to be released. But non-Sumerians could be held indefinitely, although a few might manage to buy their freedom. In either case, slaves were the property of their owners. They could be beaten, branded, bought, and sold like any other form of merchandise. Perhaps the only positive thing to say about slavery in antiquity is that it was egalitarian: anyone could become a slave. It was not until the beginning of the modern era that slavery became linked to race (see Chapter 14).

Competing Viewpoints

The Flood: Two Accounts

One of the oldest stories in the world tells of a great flood that decimated the lands and peoples of the earth, an event that can be traced to the warming of the earth's climate at the end of the last Ice Age. Many ancient cultures told versions of this story, and two of these are excerpted below. The first, included in the Epic of Gilgamesh, *was written down during the first half of the third millennium B.C.E., making it at least 1,500 years older than the similar account in the Hebrew Bible. But both are probably the products of much older storytelling traditions. The hero of the Sumerian story is Utnapishtim. The Hebrew story's hero is Noah.*

The Epic of Gilgamesh

Utnapishtim spoke to Gilgamesh, saying: "I will reveal to you, Gilgamesh . . . a secret of the gods. . . . The hearts of the Great Gods moved them to inflict the Flood. Their Father Anu uttered the oath (of secrecy). . . . [But the god] Ea . . . repeated their talk [to me, saying]: 'O man of Shuruppak, son of Ubartutu: Tear down the house and build a boat! . . . Spurn possessions and keep alive living beings! Make all living beings go up into the boat. The boat which you are to build, its dimensions must measure equal to each other: its length must correspond to its width. Roof it over like the Apsu.' I understood and spoke to my lord, Ea: 'My lord, thus is the command which you have uttered. I will heed and will do it.' . . . On the fifth day I laid out her exterior. It was a field in area, its walls were each 10 times 12 cubits in height. . . . I provided it with six decks, thus dividing it into seven (levels). . . . Whatever I had I loaded on it. . . . All the living beings that I had loaded on it. I had all my kith and kin go up into the boat, all the beasts and animals of the field and the draftsmen I had go up.

I watched the appearance of the weather—the weather was frightful to behold! I went into the boat and sealed the entry. . . . All day long the South Wind blew . . . , submerging the mountain in water, overwhelming the people like an attack. . . . Six days and seven nights came the wind and flood, the storm flattening the land. When the seventh day arrived . . . [t]he sea calmed, fell still, the whirlwind and flood stopped up. . . . When a seventh day arrived, I sent forth a dove and released it. The dove went off, but came back to me, no perch was visible so it circled back to me. I sent forth a swallow and released it. The swallow went off, but came back to me, no perch was visible so it circled back to me. I sent forth a raven and released it. The raven went off, and saw the waters slither back. It eats, it scratches, it bobs, but does not circle back to me. Then I sent out everything in all directions and sacrificed (a sheep). I offered incense in front of the mountain-ziggurat. . . .

The gods smelled the savor . . . and collected like flies over a sacrifice. . . . Just then Enlil arrived. He saw the boat and became furious. . . . 'Where did a living being escape? No man was to survive the annihilation!' Ea spoke to Valiant Enlil, saying . . . How, how could you bring about a Flood without consideration? Charge the violation to the violator,

The Early Dynastic Period, 2900–2500 B.C.E.

Around 2900 B.C.E., conflicts among the growing Sumerian city-states became more acute. Competition for resources intensified and warfare became more frequent and destructive, leading to the eradication of many urban centers. During this period, a new type of military leadership began to emerge and eventually evolved into a form of kingship. Historians refer to this phase as the Early Dynastic Period because it was dominated by powerful clans, each headed by a war leader known as a *lugal,* "big man." Unlike the priestly rulers of the Uruk Period, lugals did not see themselves as humble servants of a city's god. Rather, they believed that success in battle had earned them the right to exploit the city's wealth for their own glory. This gave them a new and frightening degree of influence.

charge the offense to the offender, but be compassionate lest (mankind) be cut off, be patient lest they be killed.' Enlil went up inside the boat and, grasping my hand, made me go up. He had my wife go up and kneel by my side. He touched our forehead and, standing between us, he blessed us. . . .''

Source: Maureen Gallery Kovacs, trans., *The Epic of Gilgamesh*, Tablet XI (Stanford, CA: 1985, 1989), pp. 97–103.

The Book of Genesis

The Lord saw that the wickedness of humankind was great in the earth and . . . said "I will blot out from the earth the human beings I have created . . . for I am sorry I have made them." But Noah found favor in the sight of the Lord. . . . God saw that the earth was corrupt and . . . said to Noah, "I have determined to make an end to all flesh. . . . Make yourself an ark of cypress wood, make rooms in the ark, and cover it inside and out with pitch. . . . Make a roof for the ark, and put the door of the ark in its side. . . . For my part I am going to bring a flood on the earth, to destroy from under heaven all flesh. . . . But I will establish a covenant with you, and you shall come into the ark, you, your sons, your wife, and your sons' wives with you. And of every living thing you shall bring two of every kind into the ark, to keep them alive with you. . . . Also take with you every kind of food that is eaten." . . . All the fountains of the great deep burst forth, and the windows of the heavens were opened. . . . The waters gradually receded from the earth. . . . At the end of forty days, Noah opened a window of the ark . . . and sent out the raven, and it went to and fro until the waters were dried up from the earth. Then he sent out the dove from him, to see if the waters had subsided from the face of the ground, but the dove found no place to set its foot, and it returned. . . . He waited another seven days, and again sent out the dove [which] came back to him . . . and there in its beak was a freshly plucked olive leaf, so Noah knew the waters had subsided from the earth. Then he . . . sent out the dove, and it did not return to him anymore. . . . Noah built an altar to the Lord . . . and offered burnt offerings. And when the Lord smelled the pleasing odor, the Lord said in his heart, "I will never again curse the ground because of humankind . . . nor will I ever again destroy every living creature as I have done." . . . God blessed Noah and his sons.

Source: Genesis 6:5–9:1, *The New Oxford Annotated Bible* (Oxford: 1994).

Questions for Analysis

1. What are the similarities and differences between these two accounts?

2. What do these differences or similarities reveal about the two societies that told these stories? Does one seem to derive from the other? Why or why not?

3. How did the geography and climate of Mesopotamia affect the Sumerian version of the story?

The most striking expression of this development is the *Epic of Gilgamesh*, a series of stories recited over many generations and eventually written down on cuneiform tablets: the first literary monument in world history. It recounts the exploits of a lugal named Gilgamesh, who probably lived in Uruk sometime around 2700 B.C.E. Gilgamesh earns his legendary reputation through military conquest and personal heroism, particularly in campaigns against uncivilized—that is, nonurban, non-Sumerian—tribes.

But he becomes so powerful that he ignores his own society's code of conduct: we hear at the start of the epic that his people complain about him because he keeps their sons away at war and shows no respect for the nobles, carousing with their wives and compromising their daughters; he also disrespects the priesthood and commits acts of sacrilege. So the people of Uruk pray to the gods for retribution, and the gods fashion a wild man named Enkidu to challenge Gilgamesh.

The confrontation between Gilgamesh and Enkidu reveals the core values of Sumerian society. Gilgamesh is a creature of the city; Enkidu is a creature of the past, a hunter-gatherer. But then Enkidu has a sexual encounter with a beguiling woman and is unable to return to the wilderness: his urban initiation has civilized him, and this allows him to befriend the lord of Uruk. Together they have many adventures. But Enkidu is eventually killed by the goddess Inanna, who punishes the friends for mocking her powers. Gilgamesh, distraught with grief, searches for a magical medicinal plant that will revive his friend. He finds it at the bottom of a deep pool, only to have it stolen from him by a water snake. In the end, he is forced to confront the futility of all human effort. He becomes "The One Who Looked into the Depths," the name by which his story was known to Sumerians. The larger message seems to be that not even civilization can shield humans from the forces of nature and the inevitability of death.

Sumerian Religion

In the Uruk Period, the Sumerians identified their gods with the capricious forces of the natural world. In the Early Dynastic Period, however, they came to imagine their gods as resembling the lugals who now lorded over their city-states. Like these dynastic rulers, the gods were imagined as having the desire to live in the finest palaces and temples, to wear the costliest clothing and jewels, and to consume the tastiest foods. According to this new theology, which clearly reflects changes in Sumerian society, humans exist merely to provide such luxuries for their gods. This was, indeed, why the gods had created people in the first place; for if

humanity ever ceased to serve the gods, the gods themselves would starve. There was thus a reciprocal relationship between humanity and divinity. The gods depended on their servants to honor and sustain them; and in return, the gods occasionally bestowed gifts and favors on humans.

As the gods' representatives on earth, lugals who reigned as kings bore special responsibilities and also enjoyed special privileges. They were believed to rule by divine sanction and were thus set apart from all other men, including priests. But kings were also obliged to honor the gods through offerings, sacrifices, festivals, and massive building projects; their obligations were greater, just as their power was greater. Kings who neglected these duties, or who exalted themselves at the expense of the gods, were likely to bring disaster on themselves and their people. And even kings could not evade death, when the human body returned to clay and the soul crossed into the underworld, a place of silent darkness.

Science, Technology, and Trade

The Sumerians' worldview was colored by their adversarial relationship with their capricious surroundings. Precisely because neither their gods nor their environment were trustworthy, Sumerians cultivated a high degree of self-reliance and ingenuity. These qualities made them the most technologically innovative people of the ancient world.

For example, despite the fact that their land had no mineral deposits, the Sumerians became skilled metallurgists. By 6000 B.C.E., a number of cultures throughout the Near East and Europe had learned how to produce weapons and tools using copper. Mesopotamia itself has no

SUMERIAN WAR CHARIOTS. The earliest-known representation of the wheel, dating from about 2600 B.C.E., shows how wheels were fashioned from slabs of wood. (For a later Mesopotamian wheel with spokes, see the illustration on page 42.)

copper, but by the Uruk Period (4300–2900 B.C.E.), trade routes were bringing this raw element into Sumer, where it was processed into weapons and tools. Shortly before 3000 B.C.E., perhaps starting in eastern Anatolia (now Turkey), people also discovered that copper could be alloyed with arsenic (or later, tin) to produce bronze. Bronze is almost as malleable as copper, and it pours more easily into molds; when cooled, it also maintains its rigidity and shape better than copper. For almost 2,000 years, until about 1200 B.C.E. and the development of techniques for smelting iron (see Chapter 2), bronze was the strongest metal known to man—the most useful and, in war, the most deadly. Following the ancient Greeks, we call this period the Bronze Age.

Alongside writing and the making of bronze, the invention of the wheel was a fundamental technological achievement of the era. The Sumerians were using potter's wheels by the middle of the fourth millennium B.C.E. and could produce high-quality clay vessels in greater quantity than ever before. By around 3200 B.C.E., the Sumerians were also using two- and four-wheeled chariots and carts drawn by donkeys. (Horses were unknown in the Near East until sometime between 2000 and 1700 B.C.E.). Chariots were another new and deadly military technology, giving warriors a tremendous advantage over armies on foot: the earliest depiction of their use, dating from 2600 B.C.E., shows one trampling an enemy. At the same time, wheeled carts dramatically increased the productivity of the Sumerian workforce.

The use of the wheel in pottery making may have suggested its use for vehicles, but such a connection is not inevitable. The ancient Egyptians, too, were using the potter's wheel by at least 2700 B.C.E., but they did not use the wheel for transport until a millennium later, when they learned the technique from Mesopotamia. In the Western Hemisphere, wheeled vehicles were unknown until the sixteenth century C.E., although the Incas had a sophisticated system of roads and probably used iron rollers to move huge blocks of stone for use in building projects. These two points of comparison help to explain why the wheel was probably invented by nomadic peoples living on the steppes of what is now Russia: sedentary civilizations that can rely on the manpower of thousands, or that can transport heavy cargo by water, do not feel the same necessity for invention.

The Sumerians can also be credited with innovations that made the most of their scarce resources. An example is the seed drill, in use for two millennia before it was depicted on a stone tablet of the seventh century B.C.E. Strikingly, this was a technology unknown to any other Western civilization until the sixteenth century C.E., when Europeans adopted it from China, and it would not be in general use until the nineteenth century of our era. Other impressive Sumerian inventions derived from the study of mathematics. In order

to construct their elaborate irrigation systems, the Sumerians had developed sophisticated measuring and surveying techniques as well as the art of mapmaking. Agricultural needs may also lie behind the lunar calendar they invented, which consisted of twelve months, six lasting 30 days and six lasting 29 days. Since this produced a year of only 354 days, the Sumerians eventually began to add a month to their calendars every few years in order to predict the recurrence of the seasons with sufficient accuracy. The Sumerian practice of dividing time has lasted to the present day, not only in our notions of the 30-day month (which corresponds approximately with the phases of the moon) but also in our division of the hour into sixty minutes, each comprising sixty seconds. Mathematics also contributed to Sumerian architecture, allowing them to build domes and arches thousands of years before the Romans would adopt and spread these architectural forms throughout the West.

Sumerian technology depended not only on ingenuity but also the spread of information and raw materials

A SUMERIAN PLOW WITH A SEED DRILL. Seed drills control the distribution of seed and ensure that it falls directly into the furrow made by the plow. By contrast, the method of sowing seed practiced elsewhere in the world—and as late as the nineteenth century in Europe and the Americas—was to broadcast the seed by throwing it out in handfuls. Such plows were developed during the third millennium B.C.E. and were still being used in the seventh century B.C.E., when this black stone tablet was engraved.
■ *Based on what you have learned about the Sumerians and their environment, why would they have developed this technology?*

through trade. Because their homeland was almost completely devoid of many natural resources, Sumerian pioneers traced routes up and down the rivers and into the hinterlands of Mesopotamia, following the tributaries of the Tigris and Euphrates. They blazed trails across the deserts toward the west, where they interacted with and influenced the Egyptians. By sea, they traded with the peoples of the Persian Gulf and, directly or indirectly, with the civilizations of the Indus Valley (modern Pakistan and India). And, along with merchandise, they carried ideas: stories, art, the use of writing, and the whole cultural complex that arose from their way of life. The elements of civilization, which had fused in their urban crucible, would thus come together in many other places throughout the world.

THE FIRST EMPIRES

Evidence shows that competition among Sumerian city-states reached a new level around 2500 B.C.E., as ambitious lugals vied to magnify themselves and their kingdoms. This aggrandizement of royal power was made possible by the growing complicity of the aristocracy and the priesthood, and also by the growing marginalization of commoners, whose lives and property were increasingly exploited.

It was also facilitated by the new technologies discussed above.

The Royal Tombs of Ur showcase the wealth of the city's ruling families during this period. The dazzling armor and jewelry uncovered by excavations also reveal a shift in Sumerian ideas about the afterlife, since they presuppose a belief that one could enjoy such goods in perpetuity. The tombs further demonstrate how powerful the lugals had become. Still, it seems that no Sumerian lugal ever attempted to create an empire by imposing centralized rule on the cities he conquered. As a result, Sumer remained a collection of interdependent but mutually hostile states whose rulers were unable to forge any lasting structures of authority. This pattern would ultimately make the people of Sumer vulnerable to a new style of imperial rulership imposed on them from the north, in the person of Sargon the Akkadian.

Sargon and the Akkadian Empire, 2350–2160 B.C.E.

The Akkadians were the predominant people of central Mesopotamia. Their Sumerian neighbors to the south had greatly influenced them, and they had adopted cuneiform script along with many other elements of Sumerian culture.

OBJECTS FROM THE ROYAL TOMBS AT UR. On the left is a helmet made from an alloy of gold and silver. Its cloth lining would have been attached through the holes visible around the edges of the helmet. On the right is a queen's headdress made of gold leaf, lapis lazuli, and carnelian.

Yet the Akkadians preserved their own Semitic language, part of the linguistic family that includes Hebrew, Arabic, Aramaic, Ethiopic, and Assyrian. Sumerians tended to regard these peoples as uncivilized, but in the case of the lugal whom the Akkadians called "great king," this probably meant that Akkadians were not bound by the conventions of Sumerian warfare. For Sargon initiated a systematic program of conquest designed to subject all the neighboring regions to his authority. By 2350 B.C.E., he had conquered the cities of Sumer and then moved to establish direct control over all of Mesopotamia.

From his capital at Akkad, Sargon installed Akkadian-speaking governors to rule the cities under his control, ordering them to pull down existing fortifications, collect taxes, and impose his will. Sargon thus transformed the independent city-states of Sumer and Akkad into a much larger political unit: the first-known empire, a word derived from the Latin *imperium*, "command." This enabled him to manage and exploit the network of trade routes crisscrossing the Near East. So although his political influence was felt only in Mesopotamia, his economic influence stretched from Ethiopia to India. Sargon's capital became the most splendid city in the world, and he exercised unprecedented power for a remarkable fifty-six years.

Sargon's imperialism also had an effect on Sumerian religion. To unite the two halves of his empire, Sargon merged the Akkadian and Sumerian divinities, so that (for example) the Akkadian fertility goddess Ishtar became identified with the Sumerian goddess Inanna. He also tried to lessen the rivalry of Sumerian cities by appointing a single Akkadian high priest or priestess, often a member of his own family, to preside over several temples. His own daughter Enheduanna (*en-he-doo-AH-nah*) was high priestess of both Uruk and Ur, and her hymns in honor of Ishtar/Inanna are the earliest surviving works by a named author in world history. The precedent she and her father established would continue even after their Sargonid dynasty finally fell: for several centuries thereafter, the kings of Sumer continued to appoint their daughters as high priestesses of Ur and Uruk.

Sargon's successor, his grandson Naram-Sin, extended Akkadian conquests and consolidated trade, helping to stimulate the growth of cities throughout his dominion and binding them more closely together. By 2200 B.C.E., most people in central and southern Mesopotamia would have been able to converse in the language of either the Sumerians or the Akkadians. Indeed, the two civilizations became virtually indistinguishable except for these different languages.

The Dynasty of Ur and the Amorites, 2100–1800 B.C.E.

After Naram-Sin's death, Akkadian rule faltered. For a brief period, evidence shows that invaders from the Iranian plateau gained control of the region, which once again

THE ZIGGURAT OF UR. Built around 2100 B.C.E., this great temple is the best-preserved structure of its kind. It is located at Nasiriyah, in what is now Iraq. Archaeological investigations (see diagram) reveal that its central shrine, the most sacred part of the temple, was reached by climbing four sets of stairs and passing through a massive portal.

dissolved into a collection of rival city-states. Around 2100 B.C.E., however, a new dynasty came to power in Ur under a king called Ur-Nammu and his son Shulgi. Ur-Nammu was responsible for the construction of the great ziggurat at Ur, which originally rose seventy feet above the surrounding plain, and for many other architectural marvels. Shulgi continued his father's work, subduing the lands up to the Zagros Mountains northeast of Ur and demanding massive tribute payments from them; one collection site accounted for 350,000 sheep per year. Shulgi built state-run textile-production facilities to process the wool. He promulgated a code of law, calling for fair weights and measures, the protection of widows and orphans, and limitations on the death penalty for crimes. He also pursued military conquests, the centralization of government, commercial expansion and consolidation, and the patronage of art and literature.

Shulgi established a pattern of rule that influenced the region for centuries to come, and that could even survive the much less competent rule of his grandson, Ibbi-Sin, who was eventually deposed by his own general. This man, Ishbi-Irra, was a chieftain of Amorite descent. The Amorites, like the Akkadians, were a Semitic people. Until this period they had largely been nomads and warriors, but now they came to control the ancient cities of Mesopotamia. For the next 200 years, they used these cities as bases for the wars they fought among themselves.

The Empire of Hammurabi

In 1792 B.C.E., a young Amorite chieftain named Hammurabi (*hah-muh-RAH-bee*) became the ruler of Babylon, an insignificant city in central Mesopotamia. By this time, Babylon was precariously wedged among a number of powerful Amorite kingdoms. Its site on the Tigris and Euphrates had great potential; but it was also dangerous, because it lay in the path of mighty antagonists.

Hammurabi turned this situation to advantage. Indeed, he may have been the first ruler in history to understand that power need not be based on force. He recognized that military intelligence, diplomacy, and strategic planning might accomplish what his small army could not. A rich archive of tablets found at the city of Mari (which eventually fell under his rule) testifies to his talents and cleverness, for Hammurabi used writing itself as a weapon. He did not try to confront his mightier neighbors directly. Rather, through letters and embassies, double-dealing and cunning, he induced his stronger counterparts to fight each other. While other Amorite kings exhausted their resources in costly wars, Hammurabi fanned their mutual hatred and skillfully portrayed himself as a friend and ally to all sides. Meanwhile, he quietly strengthened his kingdom, built up his army, and, when the time was right, fell on his depleted neighbors. By such policies, he transformed his small state into what historians call the Old Babylonian Empire.

Under Hammurabi's rule, Mesopotamia achieved an unprecedented degree of political integration. Ultimately, his empire stretched from the Persian Gulf into Assyria. The southern half of the region, formerly Sumer and Akkad, would henceforth be known as Babylonia. To help unify these territories, Hammurabi introduced another innovation, promoting the worship of the little-known patron god of Babylon, Marduk, and making him the ruler-god of his entire empire. Although he also paid homage to the ancient gods of Sumer and Akkad, Hammurabi made it clear that all his subjects now owed allegiance to Marduk.

The idea that political power derives from divine approval was nothing new, but Hammurabi's genius was to use Marduk's supremacy over all other gods to legitimate his own claim to rule, in Marduk's name, because he was king of Marduk's home city. Hammurabi thus became the first-known ruler to launch wars of aggression justified in the name of his primary god. This set a precedent for colonial expansion that would become a characteristic feature of Near Eastern politics, as we will see in Chapter 2—and that lies behind nearly all imperial ventures down to the present day.

Yet Hammurabi did not rely solely on religion to bind his empire together. Building on the precedents of past rulers, he also issued a collection of laws, copies of which were inscribed on stone and set up in public places throughout his realm. The example that survives is an eight-foot-tall *stele* (*STEH-leh*) made of gleaming black basalt, erected in the central marketplace of Babylon. The upper portion shows Hammurabi consulting with Shamash, the god of justice. The phallic form on which the laws were inscribed would have been immediately recognizable as a potent symbol of Hammurabi's authority, obvious even to those who could not read the laws themselves. (It still makes a strong impression on visitors to the Louvre museum in Paris.)

It is impossible to overemphasize the importance of Hammurabi's decision to become a lawgiver. By collecting and codifying legal precedents, like those of Shulgi, Hammurabi declared himself to be (as he stated in the code's preamble) "the shepherd of the people, the capable king"—not a lugal ruling through fear and caprice. This was setting a new standard of kingship, and expressing a new vision of empire as a union of peoples subject to the same laws.

WOMEN AND TEXTILES. Women were the predominant producers of textiles throughout the ancient world. Even upper-class women were almost continuously engaged in spinning thread and weaving cloth for their households. Here, a servant fans an elegant lady at work with her spindle.

Law and Society under Hammurabi

The code of Hammurabi reveals a great deal about the structure and values of Babylonian society. The organization of its 282 pronouncements offers insight into the kinds of litigation that Hammurabi and his officials regularly handled, and also suggests the relative importance of these cases. It begins with legislation against false testimony (fraud or lying under oath) and theft; followed by laws regulating business deals; laws regulating the use of public resources, especially water; laws relating to taverns and brothels, most of which appear to have been run by women; laws relating to debt and slavery; many laws dealing with marriage, inheritance, divorce, and widows' rights; and finally laws punishing murder, violent assault, and even medical malpractice. What emerges is a fascinating picture of a complex urban society that required more formal legislation than the accumulated customs of previous generations.

Most of these laws appear to be aimed at free commoners, who made up the bulk of the population. Above them was an aristocratic class, tied to the king's court and active in its bureaucracy, who controlled a great deal of the community's wealth: these were the palace officials, temple priests, high-ranking military officers, and rich merchants. Indeed, even legally free individuals were probably dependents of the palace or the temple in some way, or leased land from the estates of the powerful. They included laborers and artisans, small-scale merchants and farmers, and the minor political and religious officials. At the bottom of Babylonian society were the slaves, and these were far more numerous than they had been in the older civilizations of Sumer or Akkad. Many, indeed, had become slaves not because of war but through trade: either sold as payment for debts or to the profit of a family with too many children, or because they had been forced to sell themselves on the open market. Others had been enslaved in punishment for certain offenses. Slaves in the Old Babylonian Empire were treated much more harshly than in previous civilizations and were more readily identifiable as a separate group: whereas free men in Babylonia wore long hair and beards, male slaves were shaved and branded.

The division among classes in this society was marked. As Hammurabi's code indicates, an offense committed against a nobleman carried a far more severe penalty than did the same crime committed against a social equal or against a dependent or slave; nobles were also punished more severely than were commoners for crimes they committed against other nobles. Marriage arrangements also reflected class differences, with bride-prices and dowries depending on the status of the parties involved. That said, Hammurabi's code also provides evidence as to the status of women in Babylonian society, and shows that they enjoyed certain important protections under the law, including the right to divorce abusive or indigent husbands. If a husband divorced a wife "without cause," he was obliged to

Analyzing Primary Sources

The Code of Hammurabi

The laws of Hammurabi, published on the authority of this powerful king and set up in central places throughout Old Babylonian Empire, were influenced both by the needs of an urban society and by older ideas of justice and punishment common among Semitic peoples. In its entirety, the code comprises 282 laws, beginning and ending with statements of Hammurabi's devotion to the gods, his peacekeeping mission, and his sense of his duties as king. The following excerpts are numbered so as to show the order in which these provisions appear on the stele that publicizes them.

When the god Marduk commanded me to provide just ways for the people of the land in order to attain appropriate behavior, I established truth and justice as the declaration of the land. I enhanced the well-being of the people.

* * *

1. If a man accuses another man and charges him with homicide but cannot bring proof against him, his accuser shall be killed.

2. If a man charges another man with practicing witchcraft but cannot bring proof against him, he who is charged with witchcraft shall go to the divine River Ordeal, he shall indeed submit to the divine River Ordeal; if the divine River Ordeal should overwhelm him, his accuser shall take full legal possession of his estate; if the divine River Ordeal should clear that man and should he survive, he who made the charge of witchcraft against him shall be killed; he who submitted to the divine River Ordeal shall take full legal possession of his accuser's estate.

   If a man comes forward to give false testimony in a case but cannot bring evidence for his accusation, if that case involves a capital offense, that man shall be killed.

* * *

6. If a man steals valuables belonging to the god or to the palace, that man shall be killed, and also he who received the stolen goods from him shall be killed.

7. If a man should purchase silver, gold, a slave, a slave woman, an ox, a sheep, a donkey, or anything else whatsoever, from a son of a man or from a slave of a man without witnesses or a contract—or if he accepts the goods for safekeeping—that man is a thief, he shall be killed.

8. If a man steals an ox, a sheep, a donkey, a pig, or a boat—if it belongs either to the god or to the palace, he shall give thirtyfold; if it belongs to a commoner, he shall replace it tenfold; if the thief does not have anything to give, he shall be killed.

* * *

15. If a man should enable a palace slave, a palace slave woman, a commoner's slave, or a commoner's slave woman to leave through the main city-gate, he shall be killed.

* * *

53. If a man neglects to reinforce the embankment of the irrigation canal of his field and then a breach opens and allows the water to carry away the common irrigated area, the man in whose embankment the breach opened shall replace the grain whose loss he caused.

* * *

104. If a merchant gives a trading agent grain, wool, oil, or any other commodity for local transactions, the trading agent shall collect a sealed receipt for each payment in silver that he gives to the merchant.

* * *

128. If a man marries a wife but does not draw up a formal contract for her, she is not a wife.

129. If a man's wife should be seized lying with another male, they shall bind them and throw them into the water; if the wife's master allows his wife to live, then the king shall allow his subject (i.e., the other male) to live.

* * *

142. If a woman repudiates her husband, and declares, "You will not have marital relations with me"—her circumstances shall be investigated by the authorities of her city quarter, and if she is circumspect and without fault, but her husband is wayward and disparages her greatly, that woman will not be subject to any penalty; she shall take her dowry and she shall depart for her father's house.

Source: Martha T. Roth, ed., *Law Collections from Ancient Mesopotamia and Asia Minor* (Atlanta, GA: 1995), pp. 76–135 (excerpted).

THE CODE OF HAMMURABI.
The laws of Hammurabi survive on an eight-foot column made of basalt. The top quarter of the column depicts the Babylonian king (standing, at left) being vested with authority by Shamash, the god of justice. Directly below one can make out the cuneiform inscriptions that are the law code's text.
■ *How would the very format of these laws send a powerful message about Hammurabi's kingship?*

Questions for Analysis

1. Based on these excerpts, what conclusions can you draw about the values of Old Babylonian society? For example, what types of crimes are punishable by death, and why?

2. In what ways does the code of Hammurabi exhibit the influences of the urban civilization for which these laws were issued? What are some characteristics and consequences of urbanization? What, for example, do we learn about economic developments?

3. Examine the photographs of the *stele* preserving the code. What is the significance of the image that accompanies the laws, Hammurabi's conference with the enthroned god Marduk? What is the significance of the *stele* itself as the medium that conveyed these laws to the people?

provide financial support for her and their children. However, a wife who went around the city defaming her spouse was subject to severe punishment; and a woman would risk death, as would her lover, if she were caught in adultery. The sexual promiscuity of husbands, by contrast, was protected under the law.

Hammurabi's Legacy

Hammurabi died around 1750 B.C.E. Although some contraction of the Babylonian Empire followed under his successors, his administrative efforts created a durable state in Mesopotamia. For another two centuries, the Old

Babylonian Empire played a significant role in the Near East, until invaders from the north sacked the capital and occupied it. But even for another thousand years thereafter, Babylon remained the region's most famous city.

Hammurabi's legacy also extended well beyond the borders of his own kingdom. His success in achieving political stability was instrumental in shaping conceptions of kingship in the ancient world. After Hammurabi, unifying state religions would play an increasingly important role in the techniques that kings used to annex and subjugate diverse territories and peoples. Hammurabi had also demonstrated the effectiveness of writing as a political tool. Diplomacy and the keeping of archives would be essential to all subsequent empires. So too would the claim that rulers should be the protectors of the weak and the arbiters of justice.

THE DEVELOPMENT OF CIVILIZATION IN EGYPT

At about the same time that Sumerian civilization was transforming Mesopotamia, another civilization was taking shape in a very different part of the world and in very different ways. Unlike the Sumerians, the Egyptians did not have to wrest survival from a hostile and unpredictable environment. Instead, their land was renewed every year by the flooding of the Nile River. The fertile black soil that was left behind every summer made theirs the richest agricultural region in the entire Mediterranean world.

The distinctiveness of Egyptian civilization rests on this fundamental ecological fact. It also explains why ancient Egypt was a narrow, elongated kingdom, running along the Nile north from the First Cataract (a series of rocks and rapids near the ancient city of Elephantine) toward the Mediterranean Sea for a distance of more than 600 miles (1,100 km). Outside this narrow band of territory—which ranged from a few hundred yards to no more than 14 miles (23 km)—lay uninhabitable desert. This contrast—between the fertile Black Land along the Nile and the dessicated Red Land beyond—deeply influenced the Egyptian worldview, in which the Nile itself was the center of the cosmos and the lands beyond were hostile and beyond the pale of habitation.

In many respects, ancient Egyptian civilization enjoyed a remarkable continuity. Its roots date back to 5000 B.C.E. at least, and Egypt would continue to thrive as an independent and distinctive entity even after it was conquered by Alexander the Great in 331 B.C.E. (see Chapter 4), until its assimilation into the Roman Empire after 30 B.C.E. (see Chapter 5). From about 3000 B.C.E., the defining element of this civilization would be the pervasive influence of a powerful, centralized, bureaucratic state headed by pharaohs who were regarded as living gods. No other civilization in world history has ever been governed so steadily, for so long, as ancient Egypt.

For convenience, historians have traditionally divided ancient Egyptian history into distinctive "kingdoms" and "periods." Following ancient Egyptian chroniclers, modern historians have also tended to portray these Old, Middle, and New Kingdoms as characterized by unity and prosperity, punctuated by chaotic interludes when central authority broke down: the so-called Intermediate Periods. Like all attempts at periodization, these divisions do not capture the complexities of human experience or even the real pace of historical development. In essence, the periodization still used by historians reflects the conservative perspective of the ancient Egyptian state, which prized continuity and feared change. As we will see, though, the "First Intermediate Period" in particular looks like a positive development if viewed from the perspective of individual communities and commoners, rather than from the viewpoint of the pharaoh's court.

Predynastic Egypt, c. 10,000–3100 B.C.E.

The phrase *Predynastic Egypt* refers to the period before the emergence of the pharaohs and their royal dynasties, an era for which archaeological evidence is difficult to find and interpret. Many predynastic settlements were destroyed long ago by the waters of the Nile and are now buried under innumerable layers of silt. Furthermore, the very abundance of naturally occurring foodstuffs in the Nile Valley made the need for settlement and cultivation less pressing than in the Fertile Crescent, where (as we have seen) Mesopotamian peoples were already living together in villages during the eighth millennium B.C.E. In Egypt, by contrast, a growing population was able to sustain itself by hunting and gathering until the fifth millennium B.C.E.

The first-known permanent settlement in Egypt, situated at the southwestern edge of the Nile Delta (near the modern town of Merimde Beni Salama) dates to approximately 4750 B.C.E. It was a farming community that may have numbered as many as 16,000 residents, and this number (based on burial remains) suggests that some Egyptian communities were much larger than those of a comparable period in Mesopotamia. Thereafter, evidence shows that

ANCIENT EGYPT AND THE NEAR EAST. Notice the peculiar geography of ancient Egypt and the role played by the Nile River. Identify the Nile on the map. ▪ *In what direction does the Nile flow?* ▪ *How did the lands on either side help to isolate Egyptian culture from outside influences?* ▪ *Consider how the Nile helped forge Egypt into a unitary state under a powerful centralized government. Yet how might Egypt's relationship to the Nile be potentially hazardous as well as beneficial?*

the Egyptian economy rapidly became more diversified: by around 3500 B.C.E. the residents of Ma'adi, just three miles away from Merimde Beni Salama, had extensive commercial contacts with the Sinai Peninsula, the Near East, and the upper reaches of the Nile some several hundred miles to the south. Copper was a particularly vital import, since it enabled residents to replace stone tools with metal ones.

Many other Neolithic farming centers have also been discovered in or near the Nile Delta, where a degree of cultural cohesiveness was already developing, fostered by shared interests and trade. In later centuries, this northern area would be known as Lower Egypt, so called because

it was downstream. Comparable developments were also occurring upstream. By the end of this Predynastic Period, Egyptian culture was more or less uniform from the southern edge of the delta to the First Cataract, a vast length of the Nile known as Upper Egypt.

Although towns in Lower Egypt were more numerous, it was in Upper Egypt that the first Egyptian cities developed. By 3200 B.C.E.—when the Sumerian city of Uruk had been thriving for a thousand years—important communities such as Nekhen, Naqada, This, and Abydos had all developed high degrees of occupational and social specialization. They had encircled themselves with sophisticated

Past and Present

Engineering Nature

Humans have been manipulating our planet's environment since the Neolithic Revolution. The image on the left shows the irrigation canals that enabled ancient Egyptians to channel the Nile's life-giving waters into the desert. The image on the right shows a storm-surge barrier in the Netherlands, which protects reclaimed land from rising sea levels (ironically) caused by the cumulative results of man-made climate change.

 Watch related author interview on StudySpace
wwnorton.com/web/westernciv18

fortifications and had begun to build elaborate shrines to honor their gods. Indeed, the establishment of permanent sites of public worship may be key to explaining the growth of these towns into cities. As in Mesopotamia, a city's role as the center of a prominent religious cult attracted travelers and encouraged the growth of industries. Yet travel in Upper Egypt was relatively easy compared to Mesopotamia. The Nile bound cities together, and the lack of competition for resources fostered peace.

It was due to the Nile, therefore, that the region south of the delta was able to forge a cultural and eventually a political unity, despite its enormous length. The Nile fed Egypt and was a conduit for people, goods, and ideas. Centralizing rulers could project their power quickly and effectively up and down its course. Within a remarkably short time, just a century or two after the first cities' appearance in Upper Egypt, they had banded together in a confederacy under the leadership of This. The pressure

exerted by this confederacy in turn forced the towns of Lower Egypt to adopt their own form of political organization. By 3100 B.C.E., the rivalry between these competing regions had given rise to the two nascent kingdoms of Upper and Lower Egypt.

The Power of the Pharaoh, c. 3100–c. 2686 B.C.E.

With the rise of powerful rulers in these two kingdoms, Egyptian history enters a new phase, one that can be chronicled with unusual precision. The system for numbering the ruling dynasties that emerged in this era—known as the Archaic Period—was actually devised nearly 3,000 years later by an historian named Manetho (*mahn-EH-thoh*), who wrote in the third century B.C.E. By and large, Manetho's work has withstood the scrutiny of modern historians and archaeologists, although recent research has added a "Zero Dynasty" of early kings who were instrumental in bringing about the initial unification of Egypt.

Manetho did not record these rulers because he didn't know about them; we know them almost exclusively from archaeological evidence. Among them was an Upper Egyptian warlord known to us as King Scorpion, because the image of a scorpion accompanies engravings that assert his authority over most of Egypt. Another warlord, King Narmer, appears to have ruled both Upper and Lower Egypt. His exploits, too, come down to us in powerful pictures (see *Interpreting Visual Evidence* on page 26). Both of these kings probably came from Abydos in Upper Egypt, where they were later buried. Their administrative capital, however, was at Memphis, the capital city of Lower Egypt and an important center for trade with the Sinai Peninsula and the Near East.

Following the political unification of Upper and Lower Egypt, the basic features of Egypt's distinctive centralized kingship took shape along lines that would persist for the next 3,000 years, down to Manetho's own day. The title used to describe this kingship was *pharaoh*, a word that actually means "great household" and thus refers not only to an individual king but to the whole apparatus that sustains his rule. This fact, in turn, helps to explain the extraordinary stability and longevity of Egyptian civilization, which could survive even a dynastic takeover by Macedonian Greeks in the century before Manetho wrote his chronicle. Indeed, it is comparable to some modern forms of government—none of which has yet lasted nearly so long. As we have seen, kingship in Mesopotamia tended to be a form of personal rule, dependent on the charisma of a particular individual; the empires of Sargon and Ur-Nammu scarcely survived another generation or two after their deaths. But in Egypt, the office of the pharaoh was durable enough to survive the deaths of many individual successors, facilitating the peaceful transition of power to new rulers and withstanding the incompetence of many.

This was accomplished, as we shall see, by the efficiency of palace bureaucracy, but it was also a function of the pharaoh's close identification with the divine forces credited with renewing Egypt every year. Like the seasons, the pharaoh died only to be born again, renewed and empowered. Egyptian rulers thus laid claim to a sacred nature quite different—and much more benign—than that governing Sumeria. And they were more powerful than any Sumerian lugal, who was never more than a mortal who enjoyed (an all too temporary) divine favor.

How the earliest kings of Egypt came to be distinguished as pharaohs and to establish their claims to divinity is still not well understood. We do know, however, that legitimating their rule over Egypt was difficult. Local civic and religious loyalties remained strong, and for centuries Lower Egyptians would continue to see themselves as distinct in some respects from their neighbors to the south. Efforts to create a united Egyptian identity began very early, however, as the Narmer Palette may indicate. Indeed, it seems probable that the centralization of government in the person of the pharaoh, and his association with divinity, were related approaches to solving the problem of political unity. Together, they had astonishing success. By the end of the Second Dynasty, which coincides with the end of the Archaic or Early Dynastic Period (2686 B.C.E.), the pharaoh was not just the ruler of Egypt, he *was* Egypt: a personification of the land, the people, and their gods.

The Old Kingdom, c. 2686–2160 B.C.E.

Because so few written documents of the Old Kingdom survive, historians have to rely on surviving funerary texts from the tombs of the elite in order to reconstruct the achievements of particular individuals. These sources are hardly representative, and they have tended to convey the impression that Egyptians were obsessed with death; they also tell us little about the lives of ordinary people. Further complicating the historian's task is the early Egyptians' own belief in the unchanging, cyclical nature of the universe. In this early period, there appears to have been little interest in maintaining a record of key events arranged in chronological order. This makes it difficult for us to reconstruct ancient Egyptian history in detail.

However, the surviving inscriptions, papyri, and art of the Third Dynasty (c. 2686–2613 B.C.E.) do tell us a great deal about the workings of the "great household" that undergirded individual rulers' power. This power was vast because the pharaoh, as the embodiment of Egypt, was considered to be the intermediary between the land, its people, and their gods. Hence, all the resources of Egypt belonged to him. Long-distance trade was entirely controlled by the pharaoh, as were systems for imposing taxation and conscripting labor. To administer these, the pharaohs installed provincial governors, known to the Greeks as *nomarchs*, many of whom were members of the pharaoh's own family.

Old Kingdom pharaohs kept tight control over the nomarchs and their armies of lesser officials, in order to prevent them from establishing local roots in the territories they administered. Writing was therefore critical to internal

The Narmer Palette

The Narmer Palette (c. 3100 B.C.E.) is a double-sided carving made of green silt-stone. Palettes were used to grind pigments for the making of cosmetics, but the large size (63 cm, over 2 feet) of this one is unusual. It was discovered in 1897 by archaeologists excavating a temple dedicated to the god Horus at Nekhen, the capital of Upper Egypt. Found nearby were other artifacts, including the so-called Narmer Macehead, thought to depict the marriage of Narmer, king of Upper Egypt, to a princess of Lower Egypt.

On the left, dominating the central panel, Narmer wears the White Crown of Upper Egypt (image A). He wields a mace and seizes the hair of a captive kneeling at his feet. Above the captive's head is a cluster of lotus leaves (a symbol of Lower Egypt) and a falcon representing the god Horus, who may be drawing the captive's life force (ka) from his body. The figure behind Narmer is carrying the king's sandals; he is depicted as smaller because he is an inferior. The two men in the lower panel are either running or sprawling on the ground, and the symbols above them indicate the name of a defeated town. On the right, the other side of the palette shows Narmer as the chief figure in a procession (image B). He now wears the Red Crown of Lower

A. Namer wearing the White Crown of Egypt.

B. Namar wearing the Red Crown of Egypt.

Egypt and holds a mace and a flail, symbols of conquest. Behind him is the same servant carrying his sandals, and in front of him are a man with long hair and four standard-bearers. There are also ten headless corpses. Below, the entwined necks of two mythical creatures (serpopards, leopards with serpents' heads) are tethered to leashes held by two men. In the lowest section, a bull tramples the body of a man whose city he is destroying.

Questions for Analysis

1. This artifact has been called "the first historical document in the world," but scholars are still debating its meanings. For example, does it represent something that actually happened, or is it political propaganda? In your view, is this proof that Narmer has united two kingdoms? Why or why not?

2. Do the two sides of the palette tell a coherent story, and if so, on which side does that story begin?

3. What might be significant about the site where the palette was found? Should the palette be interpreted as belonging with the mace, found nearby? If so, how might that change your interpretation of the palette's significance?

communication and the management and exploitation of Egypt's vast wealth. This gave rise to a whole class of scribal administrators who enjoyed the power, influence, and status that went along with literacy, a skill few people could command—especially in Egypt, since few could master the intricacies of hieroglyphic reading or writing. Even a child just beginning his scribal education was considered worthy of great respect because the training was so difficult. But it carried great rewards. Indeed, the scribal author of a document from the Middle Kingdom called "The Satire of the Trades" exhorted the beginning student to persevere by reminding him how much better off he would be than everyone else.

The Power of Writing

Among the many facets of Egyptian culture that have fascinated generations of scholars is the Egyptian system of pictographic writing. Called *hieroglyphs* (HI-eroh-glifs) or "sacred carvings" by the Greeks, these strange and elaborate symbols remained completely impenetrable and mysterious to modern scholars until the nineteenth century, when a Frenchman named Jean François Champollion deciphered them with the help of history's most famous decoding device, the Rosetta Stone. This *stele* preserves three versions of the same decree issued by one of the Ptolemaic rulers of Egypt in 196 B.C.E. (see Chapter 3), written in ancient Greek, demotic (a later Egyptian script), and hieroglyphics—still in use after more than three thousand years. Because he could read the text in Greek, Champollion was eventually able to translate the demotic and hieroglyphic texts as well. From this beginning, generations of scholars have added to and refined the knowledge of ancient Egyptian language.

The development of hieroglyphic writing in Egypt dates to around 3200 B.C.E., about the time when pictograms begin to appear in Mesopotamia. But the two scripts are so different that they probably developed independently; and the uses of writing for government and administration developed far more quickly in Egypt than in Sumer. But unlike Sumerian cuneiform, Egyptian hieroglyphics never evolved into a system of phonograms. Instead, the Egyptians developed a faster, cursive script for representing hieroglyphics, called *hieratic*, which they employed for the everyday business of government and commerce. They also developed a shorthand version of hieratic that scribes could use for rapid note taking. Little of this hieratic script remains, however, owing to the perishable nature of the medium on which it was usually written: papyrus. Produced by hammering, drying, and processing river reeds, papyrus was much lighter, easier to write on, and more transportable than the clay tablets used by the Sumerians. When sewn together into scrolls, papyrus also made it possible to record and store large quantities of information in very small packages. Production of this versatile writing material remained one of Egypt's most important industries and exports throughout antiquity and into the Middle Ages. Yet even in the arid environment of Egypt, which has preserved so many ancient artifacts that would have perished in wetter, colder climates, papyrus is fragile and subject to decay.

THE ROSETTA STONE. This famous stone, carved in 196 B.C.E., preserves three translations of a single decree in three different forms of writing: hieroglyphs (top), demotic Egyptian (middle), and classical Greek (bottom). ▪ *Why would scholars be able to use the classical Greek text to decipher the hieroglyphic and demotic scripts?*

EGYPTIAN WRITING. Egyptian scribes used a variety of scripts: hieroglyphs for inscriptions and religious texts (top), a cursive hieratic script for administrative documents (middle), and a more informal shorthand for note taking (bottom). ▪ *What are the relationships among these three forms of writing?*

Compared to the huge volume of papyrus documents that would have been produced, therefore, the quantity that survives is small, and this significantly limits our understanding of Old Kingdom Egypt.

The origins of the ancient Egyptian language in which these texts were written has long been a matter of debate, and it can be plausibly linked to both the Semitic languages of the Near East and a number of African language groups. Some historical linguists have postulated that early Egyptian might represent the survival of a root language from which the other languages of the Afro-Asiatic group evolved. The movements of people through the Nile Valley makes this theory a distinct possibility. Whatever its origins, the Egyptian language has enjoyed a long history. Eventually, it became the tongue known as Coptic, which is still used today in the liturgy of the Coptic Christian church in Ethiopia.

STEP PYRAMID OF KING DJOSER. This monument to the pharaoh's power and divinity was designed by the palace official Imhotep around 2650 B.C.E.

Imhotep and the Step Pyramid

One of the greatest administrative officials in the history of Egypt exemplifies both the skills and the possibilities for advancement that the consummate scribe could command. Imhotep (*im-HO-tep*) rose through the ranks of the pharaoh's administration to become a sort of prime minister, the right-hand man to Djoser (*ZOH-ser*), a pharaoh of the Third Dynasty (c. 2686–2613 B.C.E.). Imhotep's expertise embraced medicine, astronomy, theology, and mathematics; but above all, he was an architect. Earlier pharaohs had already devoted enormous resources to their burial arrangements at Abydos. It was Imhotep, however, who designed the Step Pyramid, the first building in history constructed entirely of dressed stone. It was not only to be the final resting place of Djoser but an expression of his transcendent power as pharaoh.

Built west of the administrative capital at Memphis, the Step Pyramid towers over the desert to a height of 200 feet. Its design was based on an older form of burial monument, the *mastaba*, a low rectangular structure built entirely of brick with a flat top and sloping sides. Imhotep probably began with the mastaba pattern in mind, but he radically altered it by stacking one smaller mastaba on top of another and constructing each entirely of limestone. Surrounding this structure was a huge temple and mortuary complex, perhaps modeled after Djoser's palace. These buildings served two purposes. First and foremost, they would provide Djoser's *ka*, his spirit or life force, with a habitation and sustenance in the afterlife. Second, the design of the buildings, with their immovable doors and labyrinthine passageways, would (it was hoped) thwart tomb robbers, a chronic problem as pharaonic burials became more elaborate and more tempting to thieves.

Imhotep set a precedent to which all other Old Kingdom pharaohs would aspire. The pyramids on the plain of Giza, built during the Fourth Dynasty (2613–2494 B.C.E.), are a case in point. The Great Pyramid itself, built for the pharaoh Khufu (*KOO-foo*, called Cheops by the Greeks), was originally 481 feet high and 756 feet along each side of its base, constructed from more than 2.3 million limestone blocks and enclosing a volume of about 91 million cubic feet. In ancient times, the entire pyramid was encased in gleaming white limestone and topped by a gilded capstone, as were the two massive but slightly smaller pyramids built for Khufu's successors. During the Middle Ages, the Muslim rulers of nearby Cairo had their builders strip off the pyramid's casing stones and used them to construct and fortify their new city. (The gold capstones had probably disappeared already.) But in antiquity these pyramids would have glistened brilliantly by day and glowed by night, making them visible for miles in all directions. The Greek historian Herodotus (*heh-RAH-duh-tuhs*), who toured Egypt more than 2,000 years after the pyramids were built, estimated that it must have taken 100,000 laborers 20 years to build the Great Pyramid. This is probably an exaggeration, but it is a measure of the impression these monuments made.

Once thought to have been the work of slaves, the pyramids were in fact raised by tens of thousands of peasant

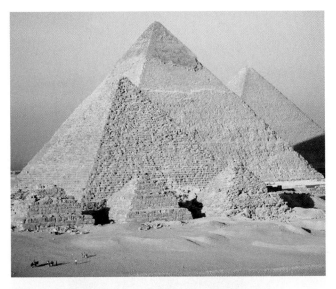

PYRAMIDS AT GIZA. The Great Pyramid of Khufu (Cheops) is in the center and was completed c. 2560 B.C.E.

workers, who labored most intensively on the pyramids while their fields were under water during the Nile's annual flood. Some workers may have been conscripts, but most probably participated willingly, since these projects glorified the living god who served as their link to the cosmic order. Still, the investment of human and material resources required to build the great pyramids put strains on Egyptian society. Control over the lives of individual Egyptians increased and the number of administrative officials employed by the state grew ever larger. So too did the contrast between the lifestyle of the pharaoh's splendid court at Memphis and that of Egyptian society as a whole. At the same time, a gap was opening between the pretensions of the pharaohs and the continuing loyalties of Egyptians to their local gods and local leaders.

The End of the Old Kingdom

For reasons that are not entirely clear, the Fifth and Sixth Dynasties of the Old Kingdom (2494–2181 B.C.E.) witnessed the slow erosion of pharaonic power. Although pyramid construction continued, the monuments of this period are less impressive in design, craftsmanship, and size, perhaps mirroring the diminishing prestige of the pharaohs who ordered them built. Instead, the priesthood of Ra at Nekhen, which was the center of worship for the god Horus and the place where Narmer's unification of Egypt was memorialized, began to assert its own authority over that of the pharaoh. Ultimately, it declared that

the pharaoh was not an incarnation of Horus or Ra, but merely the god's earthly son. This was a blow to the heart of the pharaoh's political theology. More practically threatening was the growing power of the pharaoh's nomarchs, whose increased authority in the provinces allowed them to become a hereditary local nobility: precisely what the vigorous kings of earlier dynasties had refused to permit. These nobles became so influential that one Sixth Dynasty pharaoh, Pepy I, even married into their ranks and produced half-caste successors by these marriages.

Scholars are uncertain as to how certain priests and local officials were able to take power away from the pharaonic center. It may be that the extraordinarily costly building efforts of the Fourth Dynasty had overtaxed the economy, while the continued channeling of resources to the royal capital at Memphis increased shortages and resentments in the provinces. Other evidence points to changing climatic conditions that may have disrupted the regular inundations of the Nile, leading to famine in the countryside. Meanwhile, small states were beginning to form to the south in Nubia, perhaps in response to Egyptian aggression. With better organization and equipment, the Nubians may have restricted Egyptian access to precious metal deposits in and around the First Cataract, further crippling the Egyptian economy.

As a result of these developments, the pharaoh's power diminished. Local governors and religious authorities began to emerge as the only effective guarantors of stability and order. By 2160 B.C.E., which marks the beginning of what historians call the First Intermediate Period, Egypt had effectively ceased to exist as a united entity. The central authority of the pharaoh in Memphis collapsed, and a more ancient distribution of power reemerged: a northern center of influence based at Herakleopolis was opposed by a southern regime headquartered at Thebes, with families from each region claiming to be the legitimate pharaohs of all Egypt.

Compared to the centralized authority of the Old Kingdom, this looks like chaos. But redistribution of power always leads to the opening of new opportunities in any society. In Egypt, wealth became much more widely and evenly diffused than it had been, as did access to education, means for the creation of art, and possibilities for personal advancement. Resources that the pharaoh's court at Memphis had once monopolized now remained in the provinces, enabling local elites to emerge as both protectors of society and as patrons of local artisans. The result was a much wider and more rapid dispersal of cultural forms and goods throughout Egyptian society than had been possible under the old regime. Many of these arts and luxuries—including elaborate rites for the dead—had been developed originally at the pharaoh's court, and limited to it. Now, however, they became available to Egyptian society at large.

EGYPTIAN CULTURE AND SOCIETY

As we noted above, the special environment of Egypt and the special benefits it conferred on its inhabitants were construed as divine gifts, renewed each year through the mediation of the pharaoh. From what we can discern, this meant that Egyptians saw themselves as superior to all other civilizations. A person was either an Egyptian or a foreigner, and the lines between the two were absolute. For Egyptians, it was simply self-evident that their country—nurtured by the Nile and guarded by the deserts and seas that surrounded it—was the center of the universe.

Religion and Worldview

Although the Egyptians told a variety of stories that dealt with the creation of their world, these were not greatly concerned with how humanity came to exist. Rather, what mattered was the means by which all life was created and re-created in an endless cycle of renewal. Unlike the peoples of Mesopotamia, who were constantly faced by new and terrible challenges, both environmental and political, Egyptians experienced existence as predictably repetitive, and this was mirrored in their perception of the cosmos. At the heart of Egyptian religion lay the myth of the gods Osiris and Isis, not only brother and sister but husband and wife, two of the gods most fundamental to Egyptian belief. Osiris was, in a sense, the first pharaoh: the first god to hold kingship on earth. But his brother, Seth, wanted the throne for himself. So Seth betrayed and killed Osiris, sealing his body in a coffin. But his loyal sister Isis retrieved the corpse and managed to revive it long enough to conceive her brother's child, the god Horus. Enraged by this, Seth seized Osiris's body and hacked it to pieces, spreading the remains all over Egypt. (All of Egypt could therefore claim to be part of Osiris, a belief witnessed by shrines dedicated to him throughout the land.) Still undeterred, Isis sought the help of Anubis, the god of the afterlife. Together, they found, reassembled, and preserved the scattered portions of Osiris's body, thus inventing the practice of mummification. Then Horus, with the help of his mother, managed to

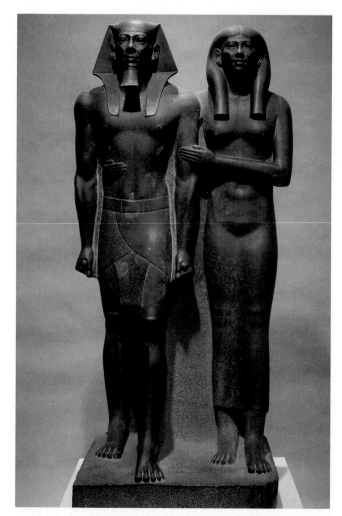

PHARAOH MENKAURE AND HIS QUEEN, KHAMERERNEBTY II. A sculpture from the Fourth Dynasty, c. 2500 B.C.E., shows this queen as her husband's royal partner.

defeat Seth. Osiris was avenged and revived as god of the underworld. Like Egypt itself, he could not be killed, and the cycle of his death, dismemberment, and resurrection was reflected in the yearly renewal of Egypt itself.

Life and Death in Ancient Egypt

In addition to embodying Egypt's continual regeneration, Osiris exemplified the Egyptian attitude toward death, which was very different from the Sumerians' rather bleak view. For the Egyptians, death was a rite of passage, a journey to be endured on the way to an afterlife that was more or less like one's earthly existence, only better. To be sure, the journey was full of dangers. After death, the individual body's ka would have to roam the Duat, the underworld, searching for the House of Judgment. There, Osiris and

The Instruction of Ptah-Hotep

Egyptian literature often took the form of "instructions" to or from important personages, offering advice to those in public life. This document declares itself to be the advice of a high-ranking official of the Old Kingdom to his son and successor, perhaps composed around 2450 B.C.E. However, the earliest surviving text dates from the Middle Kingdom period.

Be not arrogant because of your knowledge, and be not puffed up because you are a learned man. Take counsel with the ignorant as with the learned, for the limits of art cannot be reached, and no artist is perfect in his skills. Good speech is more hidden than the precious greenstone, and yet it is found among slave girls at the millstones.

. . . If you are a leader commanding the conduct of many seek out every good aim, so that your policy may be without error. A great thing is *ma'at*, enduring and surviving; it has not been upset since the time of Osiris. He who departs from its laws is punished. It is the right path for him who knows nothing. Wrongdoing has never brought its venture safe to port. Evil may win riches, but it is the strength of *ma'at* that endures long, and a man can say, "I learned it from my father." . . . If you wish to prolong friendship in a house which you enter as master, brother, or friend, or anyplace that you enter, beware of approaching the women. No place in which that is done prospers. There is no wisdom in it.

A thousand men are turned aside from their own good because of a little moment, like a dream, by tasting which death is reached. . . . He who lusts after women, no plan of his will succeed. . . . If you are a worthy man sitting in the council of his lord, confine your attention to excellence. Silence is more valuable than chatter. Speak only when you know you can resolve difficulties. He who gives good counsel is an artist, for speech is more difficult than any craft.

Source: Nels M. Bailkey, ed., *Readings in Ancient History: Thought and Experience from Gilgamesh to St. Augustine*, 5th ed. (Boston, MA: 1995), pp. 39–42.

Questions for Analysis

1. According to Ptah-Hotep, what are the most important attributes of a man engaged in public life? What are the most dangerous pitfalls and temptations he will encounter?

2. Why does Ptah-Hotep emphasize the importance of acting in accordance with *ma'at*? How does this idea of *ma'at* compare to that in "the Prophecies of Neferty"?

3. Based on what you have learned about the changes in Egyptian politics and society, what might indicate that Ptah-Hotep lived during the time of the prosperous Fifth Dynasty of the Old Kingdom? How might these instructions have resonated differently with later readers of the Middle Kingdom?

---

forty-two other judges would decide the ka's fate. Demons and evil spirits might try to frustrate the ka's quest to reach the House of Judgment, and the journey might take some time. But if successful and judged worthy, the deceased would enjoy immortality as an aspect of Osiris.

Egyptian funerary rites aimed to emulate the example set by Isis and Anubis, who had carefully preserved the parts of Osiris's body and enabled his afterlife. This is why the Egyptians developed their sophisticated techniques of embalming, whereby all of the body's vital organs were removed and then treated with chemicals—except for the heart, which played a key role in the ka's final judgment.

A portrait mask was then placed on the mummy before burial, so that the deceased would be recognizable despite being wrapped in hundreds of yards of linen. To sustain the ka on his or her journey, food, clothing, utensils, weapons, and other items of vital importance would be placed in the grave along with the body.

"Coffin texts," or books of the dead, also accompanied the body and were designed to speed the ka's journey. They contained special instructions, including magic spells and ritual incantations, that would help the ka travel through the underworld and prepare it for the final test. They also described the "negative confession" the ka would

FOOD FOR THE JOURNEY OF THE KA. These wooden models show peasants plowing, grinding grain, baking bread, brewing beer, and slaughtering a steer. Bread and beer were the staple foods of ancient Egypt; beef was too expensive for ordinary consumption, but cattle were frequently sacrificed as funeral offerings. Such models were placed in Middle Kingdom tombs to provide food for the afterlife.

make before the court of Osiris, a formal denial of offenses committed in life. The god Anubis would then weigh the deceased's heart against the principle of *ma'at*: truth, order, justice. Because ma'at was often envisioned as a goddess wearing a plumed headdress, a feather from this headdress would be placed in the scales, along with the heart, at the time of judgment; only if the heart was light (empty of wrongdoing) and in perfect balance with the feather would the ka achieve immortality.

Throughout the era of the Old Kingdom, the privilege of undergoing these preparations (and thus of ensuring immortality) was reserved for the royal family alone. By the time of the Middle Kingdom, however, it was becoming possible for most Egyptians to ensure that their bodies would participate in these rituals, too.

As noted above, this careful manner of confronting death has often led to the erroneous assumption that ancient Egyptians were pessimistic, but in actuality their practices and beliefs were inherently life affirming, bolstered by confidence in the resilience of nature and the renewal of creation. Binding together this endless cycle was ma'at, the serene order of the universe with which the individual must remain in harmony, and against which each person's ka would be weighed after death. And embodying ma'at on earth was the pharaoh, the earthly manifestation of all gods. For most of the third millennium, thanks to a long period of successful harvests and peace guaranteed by Egypt's geographic isolation from the outside world, the Egyptians were able to maintain their belief in this perfectly ordered paradise and the pharaoh that ensured it. But when that order broke down, so too did their confidence in the pharaoh's power.

Egyptian Science

Given the powerful impression conveyed by their monumental architecture, it may seem surprising that the ancient Egyptians lagged far behind the Sumerians and Akkadians in science and mathematics, as well as in the application of new technologies. Only in the calculation of time did the Egyptians make notable advances, since their close observation of the sun for religious and agricultural reasons led them to develop a solar calendar that was far more accurate than the Mesopotamian lunar calendar. Whereas the Sumerians have bequeathed to us their means of dividing and measuring the day, the Egyptian calendar is the direct ancestor of the Julian Calendar adopted for Rome by Julius Caesar in 45 B.C.E. (see Chapter 5) and later corrected by Pope Gregory XIII in 1582 C.E.: this is the calendar we use today. The Egyptians also devised some effective irrigation and water-control systems, but they did not adopt such labor-saving devices as the wheel until much later than the Sumerians, perhaps because the available pool of peasant manpower was virtually inexhaustible, so that the necessity for such innovations was not felt.

The Social Pyramid

The social pyramid of Old Kingdom Egypt was extremely steep. At its apex stood the pharaoh and his extended family, whose prestige and power set them entirely apart from all other Egyptians. Below them was a class of nobles, whose primary role was to serve as priests and officials of the pharaoh's government; scribes were usually recruited and trained from among the sons of these families. All of these Egyptian elites lived in considerable luxury. They owned extensive estates, exotic possessions, and fine furniture. They kept dogs and cats and monkeys as pets, and hunted and fished for sport.

Beneath this tiny minority was everyone else. Most Egyptians lived in crowded conditions in simple mud-brick dwellings. During a period of prosperity, master craftsmen—jewelers, goldsmiths, and the like—could improve their own conditions and those of their families by fulfilling the needs of the wealthy, but they did not constitute anything like a middle class. Other skilled professionals—potters, weavers, masons, bricklayers, brewers, merchants, and schoolteachers—also enjoyed some measure of respect as well as a higher standard of living. The vast majority of Egyptians, however, were peasants who provided the labor for agriculture and construction. Beneath them were slaves, typically captives from foreign wars rather than native Egyptians.

Yet despite the enormous demands the pharaohs placed on Egypt's wealth, this Egyptian social hierarchy does not appear to have been particularly oppressive. Commoners' belief in the pharaoh's divinity made them willing subjects, as did the material benefits of living in a stable, well-governed society. Even slaves had certain legal rights, including the ability to own, sell, and bequeath personal property.

Unfortunately, though, the written laws and other documentary practices produced by the lugals of Mesopotamia do not have any Old Kingdom parallels. The Egyptians of this era apparently had no need for written laws beyond what was customary in their communities or what was proclaimed as law by their pharaoh. This makes it difficult for historians to reconstruct their lives in any detail.

The Status of Women

Despite the absence of formal law codes, there is evidence that Egyptian women enjoyed unusual freedoms by the standards of the ancient world. Female commoners were recognized as persons in their own right and were allowed to initiate lawsuits (including suits for divorce), to defend

FUNERARY PAPYRUS. This scene, inscribed on a papyrus scroll dating from the Twenty-First Dynasty (c. 1000 B.C.E.), shows the heart of the princess for whom this book was prepared being weighed in a balance before the god Osiris. On the other side of the balance are the symbols for life (the *ankh*) and the feather of the goddess Ma'at.

themselves and act as witnesses, to possess property of their own, and to dispose of it: all without the sanction of a male guardian or representative, as was typically required in other ancient societies—and in most modern ones until the twentieth century. Women were not allowed to undergo formal scribal training, but surviving personal notes exchanged between high-born ladies suggest that some could read and even write.

Normally, women were barred from holding high office, apart from that of priestess and also, importantly, queen. Indeed, queens are often represented as the partners of their royal husbands and were certainly instrumental in ruling alongside them: note the proud, confident bearing of Queen Khamerernebty II (*kah-mehr-en-EB-tee*, see image on page 30). And occasionally, a woman from the royal family might assume pharaonic authority for a time, as did Queen Khasekhemwy (*kah-sehk-KEM-wee*, d. 2686 B.C.E.) on behalf of her son Djoser before he came of age. Some women may even have ruled in their own right; this was certainly the case under the New Kingdom (see Chapter 2).

Among the peasantry, gender divisions were less clearly defined. Peasant women often worked in the fields during the harvest alongside men and carried out a number of vital tasks in the community. The limitations of our sources, however, means that we can only glimpse the lives of these people through the eyes of their social superiors. Whatever their status, it seems that women did not enjoy sexual equality. While most Egyptians practiced monogamy, wealthy men could and did keep a number of lesser wives, concubines, and female slaves; and any Egyptian man, married or not, enjoyed freedoms that were denied to women, who would be subject to severe punishments under the law if they were viewed as guilty of any misconduct.

The Widening Horizons of the Middle Kingdom (2055–c. 1650 B.C.E.)

After the disruption of Old Kingdom authority around 2160 B.C.E., warfare between two competing pharaonic dynasties would continue for over a century. Then, in 2055 B.C.E., the Theban king Mentuhotep (*men-too-Ho-tep*) II conquered the northerners and declared himself the ruler of a reunited Egypt. His reign marks the beginning of Egypt's Middle Kingdom and the reestablishment of a central government—but this time based in Thebes rather than Memphis. The head of this new government was Men-

tuhotep's chief supporter, Amenemhet (*ah-meh-NEHM-het*), who actually seized power after the king's death and established himself and his descendants as Egypt's Twelfth Dynasty.

This succession of remarkable pharaohs remained in power for nearly 200 years, and under them Egyptians began to exploit more thoroughly the potential for trade. They secured their border with Nubia and began to send mounted expeditions to the land they called Punt, probably the coast of Somalia. By the middle of the nineteenth century B.C.E., Nubia was firmly under Egypt's control. Meanwhile, diplomatic relations with the smaller states and principalities of Palestine and Syria led to decisive Egyptian political and economic influence in this region. Yet these lands were not incoroporated into Egypt; instead, Amenemhet constructed the Walls of the Prince in Sinai to guard against incursions from the Near East.

The huge fortifications built along Egypt's new frontier demonstrate the great resourcefulness of the Twelfth Dynasty and their very different ways of allocating resources and expressing ambition. As such, they also dis-

SESOSTRIS III (1870–1831 B.C.E.). This powerful Twelfth Dynasty pharaoh led military campaigns into Nubia, constructed massive, garrisoned fortresses along the Nile, and dug new waterways near Aswan. More than a hundred portrait busts of Sesostris survive, all with similar features. His overhanging brow, deep-set eyes, and drawn-down mouth are intended to communicate the enormous burden of responsibility the pharaoh bore as the ruler of all Egypt.

The Prophecies of Neferty

This text presents itself as a prophecy foretelling the disasters that would strike Egypt during the First Intermediate Period. In fact, it was composed during the Middle Kingdom, shortly after the death of the pharaoh Amenemhet I, the founder of the Twelfth Dynasty. By contrasting the disorders that preceded Amenemhet's reign with the peace that he established, the document seeks to justify Amenemhet's usurpation of the throne and perhaps to legitimize his son's succession.

Arise, oh my heart! Weep for this land wherein you were born! Falsehood is as the flood, and behold, evil is spoken with impunity.... The land perishes, and there is no one who cares for it. There is no one who speaks out, no one who makes lament.... Perished and gone are those joyful places, the fish ponds where dwell fish-eating birds, ponds alive with fish and fowl. All joy has been driven out, and the land is plunged into anguish by those voracious Asiatics who rove throughout the land. Foes have appeared in the east, Asiatics have entered Egypt. We have no (border) fortress, for foreigners now hold it, and there is no one to heed who the plunderers are. One may expect attack by night, the fortress will be breached and sleep driven from all eyes.... The land is destitute, although its rulers are numerous, it is ruined, but its taxes are immense. Sparse is the grain, but great is the measure, for it is distributed as if it were abundant.

But then there shall come a king from the south. His name will be Ameny, justified. He will be the son of a woman of Ta-Sety [Nubia], an offspring of the royal house of Nekhen. He shall receive the White Crown, he shall wear the Red Crown, he shall unite the Two Powers.... The people of his time will rejoice, for this son of a man will establish his name for ever and eternity.... The Asiatics will fall before his sword, the Libyans will fall before his fire, rebels will fall before his wrath, and enemies will fall through awe of him....

Then Ma'at will return to her throne, and Chaos will be driven off. Joyful will he be who will see (these things), he who will serve the king.

Source: William Kelly Simpson, ed., *The Literature of Ancient Egypt: An Anthology of Stories, Instruction, Stelae, Autobiography, and Poetry*, 3rd ed. (New Haven, CT: 2003), pp. 214–220.

Questions for Analysis

1. In what ways does the "Prophecies of Neferty" highlight the anxieties felt by Middle Kingdom Egyptians? What caused these anxieties?

2. Why would the author of this document choose to present it as a prophecy about the future, rather than as a description of current events?

---

play a marked shift in the Egyptian outlook on the world. The placid serenity epitomized by ma'at, and the shared devotion to the pharaoh that had built the pyramids, had been challenged. Egyptians could no longer be dismissive of outsiders or disregard the world beyond their borders. Unlike their Old Kingdom ancestors, the Egyptians of the Middle Kingdom were not turned inward. Their attitude to the pharaoh also seems to have changed. Although he continued to enjoy a special position as a divine representative, his authority did not derive solely from this source. Rather, the pharaohs of the Middle Kingdom represented themselves in a new light, as good shepherds, tenders of their flock. Only by diligently protecting Egypt from a hostile outside world could a pharaoh provide the peace,

prosperity, and security desired by his subjects; his alignment with ma'at was now clearly conditional, and it had to be earned.

Portraits of the great pharaohs of the Twelfth Dynasty mirror this anxious outlook on the world. The literature of the Middle Kingdom also expresses the general change in attitude. Among the most popular of the new literary forms were manuals ostensibly written by or for kings, detailing the duties and perils of high office and offering advice for dealing with difficult situations. These include the *Instruction of Amenemhet*, which purports to be life lessons handed down by this pharaoh to his son from beyond the grave, and *The Instruction of Ptah-Hotep* (see **Analyzing Primary Sources** above), an example of Egyptian "wisdom literature" attributed to a court official of the Old Kingdom, which achieved a wider readership in this new era—much as Machiavelli's *The Prince* (see Chapter 12) has become a "self-help" book for business executives and politicians in our own time. Ptah-Hotep's teaching is upbeat and practical; by contrast, the examples of this genre produced under the Middle Kingdom are bleakly pragmatic. A pharaoh must trust no one: not a brother, not a friend, not intimate companions. He must crush the ambitions of local nobles with ruthless ferocity. He must always be on the lookout for potential trouble. In return for his exertions on behalf of his people, he should expect neither gratitude nor reward; he should expect only that each year will bring new dangers and more pressing challenges. Reading between the lines, we discern that Egyptians' sense of their own superiority—a product of their former isolation and their comparatively benign environment—had been shattered. They saw themselves being drawn into a much wider world, and in the course of the next millennium they would become more fully a part of it.

CONCLUSION

While the story of Babel records the legendary loss of a shared language, this chapter shows that people of the distant past can still communicate with us. The marks they have left on the landscape, the remains of their daily lives, their written

After You Read This Chapter

Visit StudySpace for quizzes, additional review materials, and multimedia documents. **wwnorton.com/web/westernciv18**

REVIEWING THE OBJECTIVES

- The study of the distant past is challenging because written sources are rare. What other sources of information do historians use?
- All civilizations require the same basic things and share certain characteristics. What are they?
- The cities of Mesopotamia remained largely independent from one another yet shared a common culture. Why was this the case?
- Hammurabi's empire created a new precedent for governance in Mesopotamia. How did he achieve this?
- The civilizations of ancient Mesopotamia and Egypt differ in profound ways. What were the major causes of their differences?

records, and their very bodies make it possible for historians to piece together evidence and to make sense of it. And every year new sources come to light, meaning that we have to be ready to revise—constantly—our understanding of what happened in the past.

Although this chapter has emphasized the differences between the early civilizations of Mesopotamia and Egypt, it is worth noting some significant similarities. Both developed the fundamental technologies of writing at about the same time, and this facilitated political alliances, long-distance trade, and the transmission of vital information to posterity. During the third millennium, both underwent a process of political consolidation, an elaboration of religious ritual, and a melding of spiritual and political leadership. Both engaged in massive building and irrigation projects, and both commanded material and human resources on an enormous scale. At the same time, each of these civilizations cultivated an inward focus. Although they had some contact with each other, and some transfers of information and technology probably took place, there were few significant political or cultural interactions. For the most part, they inhabited separate worlds. This relative isolation was about to change, however. The next millennium would see the emergence of large-scale, land-based empires in the Near East that would transform life in Mesopotamia, Egypt, and the lands that lay between them. These are the developments we examine in Chapter 2.

PEOPLE, IDEAS, AND EVENTS IN CONTEXT

- What fundamental changes associated with the **NEOLITHIC REVOLUTION** made early civilizations possible?
- What new technologies allowed the **SUMERIANS** to master the environment of **MESOPOTAMIA**, and how did these technologies contribute to the development of a new, urbanized society?
- By contrast, why did the Nile River foster a very different civilization and enable the centralized authority of the **PHARAOH**?
- How do the differences between **CUNEIFORM** and **HIEROGLYPHS** reflect the different circumstances in which they were invented and the different uses to which they were put?
- In what ways are the *EPIC OF GILGAMESH* and the *CODE OF HAMMURABI* rich sources of information about the civilizations of Sumer and **BABYLON**?
- How do the **ZIGGURATS** of Mesopotamia and the pyramids of Egypt exemplify different forms of power, different ideas about the gods, and different beliefs about the afterlife?
- Why was the worldview of ancient Egyptians, which was strongly reflected in the concept of **MA'AT** during the **OLD KINGDOM**, altered in significant ways by the time of the **MIDDLE KINGDOM**?

THINKING ABOUT CONNECTIONS

- How do the surviving sources of any period limit the kinds of questions that we can ask and answer about the distant past? In your view, are there sources for this early era that have been undervalued? For example, if writing had not been developed in Mesopotamia and Egypt, what would we still be able to know about the civilizations of these two regions?
- What features of ancient civilizations do modern civilizations share? What might be the implications of these shared ideas, social structures, and technologies?
- In particular, what lessons could we draw from humans' tendency to manipulate their environment? How should knowledge of the distant past influence current debates over sustainability and climate change?

Before
You
Read
This
Chapter

Peoples, Gods, and Empires: 1700–500 B.C.E.

CORE OBJECTIVES

- **DESCRIBE** the impact of new migrations and settlements on the ancient Near East.

- **DEFINE** the differences between Egypt's New Kingdom and the previous Old and Middle Kingdoms.

- **EXPLAIN** the workings of transnational networks in the late Bronze Age.

- **IDENTIFY** the new empires and kingdoms that emerged in the Iron Age.

- **UNDERSTAND** the historical importance of monotheism.

A ccording to Hesiod, a Greek poet who flourished during the eighth century B.C.E., all of human history falls into five ages. The dawn of time was a golden age, when men lived like gods. Everything was good then, food was plentiful, and work was easy. The next age was silver, when men took gods for granted, killed one another, and lived in dishonor. So the gods destroyed them, sending a mighty flood that spared only the family of Deucalion, the son of wily Prometheus, who built an ark. Then came the age of bronze, when everything was made of bronze— houses and armor and weapons and tools—and giants fought incessantly from huge strongholds, causing destruction so great that no man's name survives. The time following was short but bright, a heroic age, the time of men who ventured with Theseus and fought with Achilles and sailed with Odysseus, men whose names will live forever. But Hesiod's own age was iron—a dull age, a time of tedium and strife and bickering and petty feuds.

Hesiod's periodization captures an understanding of history that had evolved with humanity itself and that reflects actual developments. The stories he knew told of a time before cities and the need for agriculture. They recalled a time when the harmony between gods and men broke down, and the human race was saved by one man's ingenuity: the Sumerian Utnapishtim, the Hebrew Noah, or the Greek Deucalion. These stories chronicled the wars of the age we still call Bronze, when the enormous abandoned palaces still visible in Hesiod's day were built. And they remembered the race of heroes whose glory was measured by their abiding fame, and who bequeathed to us a further round of stories. Thanks to new archaeological finds, new linguistic discoveries, and new efforts at decoding the historical record, we can both confirm and correct Hesiod's perspective on the past.

In the second millennium B.C.E., the ancient Near East was transformed by the arrival of new peoples and by the emergence of extensive land-based empires built up through systematic military conquest. These migrations and conquests caused upheaval, but they also led to cultural contact and economic integration that encompassed not only the Mediterranean but even extended from Scandinavia to China. The last few centuries of the Bronze Age (1500–1200 B.C.E.) were a period of intense diplomacy, trade, and exchange. By the thirteenth century B.C.E., peoples from the southern Balkans to the western fringes of Iran had been drawn into a wide-ranging web of relationships.

Yet this extraordinary system proved more fragile than its participants could have imagined. Around 1200 B.C.E., a wave of mysterious invasions led to the destruction of nearly every established Mediterranean civilization. As a result, around the turn of the first millennium B.C.E., we enter a world organized along profoundly different lines. In this Iron Age, iron would slowly replace bronze as the primary component of tools and weapons. New and more brutal empires would come to power, while new ideas about the divine and its relationship to humanity would emerge. Two of the Western world's most enduring religious traditions—Judaism and Zoroastrianism (*zoh-roh-AHS-tree-nism*)—were born, fundamentally altering conceptions

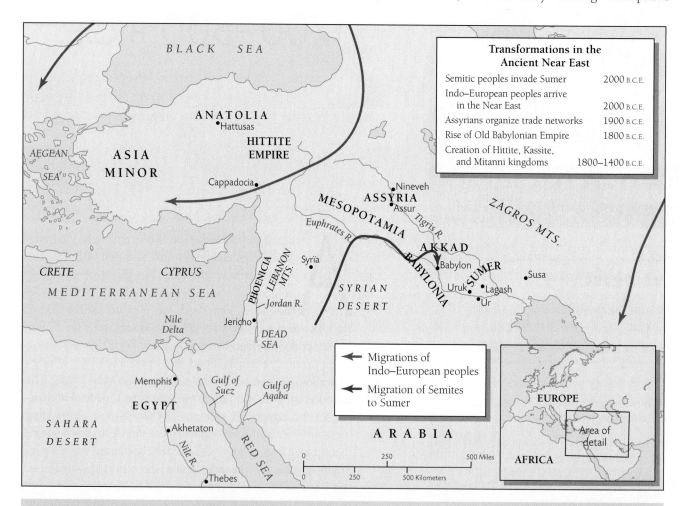

Transformations in the Ancient Near East

Semitic peoples invade Sumer	2000 B.C.E.
Indo–European peoples arrive in the Near East	2000 B.C.E.
Assyrians organize trade networks	1900 B.C.E.
Rise of Old Babylonian Empire	1800 B.C.E.
Creation of Hittite, Kassite, and Mitanni kingdoms	1800–1400 B.C.E.

← Migrations of Indo–European peoples

← Migration of Semites to Sumer

THE BRONZE AGE NEAR EAST, 2000–1400 B.C.E. Notice the geographical relationship among the older centers of Mesopotamia and Egypt, and among newer civilizations such as Babylonia, Assyria, Phoenicia, and the Hittite Empire. ▪ *Which of these emerging cultures would be most likely to come into contact with Egypt, and why?* ▪ *Where did the Indo-European peoples come from?* ▪ *What was the impact of Indo-European settlements?*

of ethics, politics, and the natural world. This age would prove a fateful historical crossroads, as elements both old and new combined to reconfigure the ancient world.

INDO-EUROPEAN LANGUAGES AND PEOPLES

In 1786, a British judge serving in India made a discovery that transformed the prevailing understanding of history. Turning his spare time to the study of Sanskrit, the ancient language of South Asia, Sir William Jones discovered that it shares the same grammar and vocabulary as ancient Greek and Latin, to an extent inexplicable by sheer coincidence. His interest piqued, he then examined the early Germanic and Celtic languages of Europe and the Old Persian language of the Near East and found that they also exhibit marked similarities. He concluded that all of these languages must have evolved from a common source. Within another generation, the ancient language whose existence Jones had hypothesized, and the later languages derived from it, would be labeled Indo-European, reflecting a wide distribution from India to Ireland. The biblical story of mankind's shared language, the story of Babel, turns out to be partly true.

Since then, scholars have greatly enlarged our understanding of Indo-European languages and their speakers. Yet much remains controversial. Was an original form of the language spoken by a single population at some point in time? If so, when and where? How did it spread? Can the diffusion of its speakers be determined archaeologically, by tracing characteristic pottery types and burial rites, or are such practices distinct from language? At the moment, we have no clear answers to any such questions. It is certain, however, that Indo-European linguistic forms began to appear in the Near East and eastern Mediterranean shortly after 2000 B.C.E. Around this same time, a group of Indo-European speakers also moved into the Aegean basin, where the resulting language became an early form of Greek. Other Indo-European speakers went east; some may have reached western China.

These were not the only new peoples moving into the Near East. As we noted in Chapter 1, Semitic-speaking peoples were also making their mark, beginning with the Akkadians and the Amorites, from whose ranks Hammurabi came. The Assyrians, the Phoenicians, and the Canaanites would also become prominent. These newcomers did not wipe out existing cultures; rather, they built on established patterns of urban life and organization. But their collective impact was enormous.

New Settlers in Anatolia

By 1900 B.C.E., the nomadic Assyrians had become caravan merchants whose extensive trade networks stretched across Anatolia and Mesopotamia. They did not seek military dominance over the region; instead, they relied on the protection of local rulers and, in turn, they made these rulers rich. They also served as advisers and officials, and married into important urban families. In the process, they carried Mesopotamian civilization and its trappings into far-flung regions of the world.

In the wake of Assyrian-assisted urbanization, new population groups were attracted to Anatolia, northern Syria, and Mesopotamia. The most formidable of these were the Hittites, an Indo-European-speaking people who arrived around 2000 B.C.E. In contrast to the Assyrians, the Hittites were military conquerors and colonists who imposed themselves and their language on the peoples they vanquished. By 1700 B.C.E., they had integrated many Hittite-dominated city-states into a larger kingdom. About fifty years later, they captured a strategic mountain stronghold, Hattusas, from which their king took a new name, Hattusilis.

Under Hattusilis and his successors, the Hittites' warrior aristocracy fielded the most fearsome army of the Bronze Age. They were quick to adopt the latest technologies, including the chariot and (eventually) the use of iron for weaponry. But the Hittites also adopted the more peaceful practices of those they conquered, using cuneiform to record their own language and laws. They also sought to control trade routes, particularly the overland trade in copper and arsenic, the raw materials for making bronze. By 1595 B.C.E., they had moved southeastward into Mesopotamia, capturing and sacking Babylon.

A century later, the Kassites, another new people, moved into the devastated city and took control of it. For the next 500 years, they presided over a largely peaceful and prosperous Babylonian realm. The Hittites, however, continued to destabilize the region, until they were themselves checked by the arrival of a people known as the Mitannians, who moved into Syria around 1550 B.C.E. The Mitannians' initial advantage was their use of horses, hitherto unknown outside the steppes of Asia. Their light, horse-drawn chariots became terrifying death-machines, transporting archers rapidly around the battlefield. The Mitannians also pioneered cavalry tactics which devastated the foot soldiers of their rivals. Eventually, however, the Mitannians' opponents borrowed these same technologies, and the Hittites once again achieved the advantage. By the mid-fourteenth century, they had subjugated the Mitannians and were turning their attention to Egypt.

A NEAR EASTERN WAR CHARIOT. A light, spoke-wheeled chariot, developed for warfare, is here being used for lion hunting by the Assyrian king Assurnasirpal II (883–859 B.C.E.), whose reign is discussed on page 59.

THE NEW KINGDOM OF EGYPT

As we have seen, Egypt's Middle Kingdom had been reshaped by the many internal changes of the First Intermediate Period, chiefly the redistribution of wealth and power. Now it was further transformed by external forces, through the dynamic movement of new peoples from western Asia and Nubia. Some of these came to Egypt as immigrants; others were hired as mercenaries. And for a while, a strategy of accommodation preserved Egypt from large-scale armed attack and fostered commercial exchange with neighboring regions. But around 1700 B.C.E., Egypt was invaded for the first time since the unification of the Upper and Lower Kingdoms. The invaders' origins and identity remain mysterious; the Egyptians called them simply Hyksos (*HIHK-sohs*), "rulers of foreign lands." From their power base in the eastern delta of the Nile, the Hyksos began to project their authority over most of Lower Egypt.

With this conquest, the central authority of the pharaoh once again dissolved and Egypt entered what historians call the Second Intermediate Period (c. 1650–1550 B.C.E.). Significantly, however, the Hyksos did not destroy the machinery of pharaonic government in Lower Egypt but took steps to legitimize their rule in accordance with Egyptian precedents. Some Hyksos rulers even incorporated the name of the sun-god Ra into their own names. In Upper Egypt, by contrast, Hyksos power was weak. Here, a native pharaonic regime maintained a tenuous independence at the traditional capital of Thebes, although it sometimes had to acknowledge the suzerainty of the foreigners to the north.

This relatively short period of Hyksos domination was regarded by later Egyptians as the greatest shame of their history. Although the Hyksos established Lower Egypt as the most significant power in the Near East, filling the temporary power vacuum left by the Hittites, their conquest also weakened the dominion of Upper Egypt over the Nubians, who eventually founded an independent kingdom called Kush. This Nubian kingdom posed a much greater threat to the native dynasty at Thebes than to the Hyksos in Lower Egypt—but it also provided an additional incentive to southern pharaohs determined to oust the Hyksos usurpers and reunify Egypt. Ultimately, they succeeded. By the end of the sixteenth century B.C.E., the pharaoh Ahmose had driven out the Hyksos, establishing the Eighteenth Dynasty and the New Kingdom of Egypt.

The Pharaohs of the Eighteenth Dynasty

Under the Eighteenth Dynasty, Egyptian civilization reached the height of its magnificence and power, which it now exercised more widely than ever before. Although many Egyptian traditions were renewed and strengthened, the dynamism of the New Kingdom—particularly its new focus on imperial expansion—changed the very fabric of Egyptian life, which had never before looked beyond the narrow world of the fertile Nile Valley.

The Eighteenth Dynasty ruled Egypt for more than two and a half centuries, and striking developments took place during this period. Most important was the rise of an aristocracy whose wealth was acquired through warfare and the winning of lands (with slaves to work them) which they received from the pharaoh as rewards for service. The Eighteenth Dynasty itself was forged in battle, something that had not been true of a ruling family since the time of King Narmer, over a millennium and a half earlier (see Chapter 1). Ahmose, the man who expelled the Hyksos, had been reared by the warrior queen Ahhotep, who had ruled Upper Egypt in her own right. His eventual successor, Thutmose I (c. 1504–1492 B.C.E.), was the son of an unknown warrior who married Amhose's daughter.

Under Thutmose's leadership, the Egyptians subdued the Nubians to the south, seizing control of their gold mines and securing the wealth needed to finance expanded commerce in the Near East. They also penetrated beyond their northeastern frontier, driving deep into Palestine and Syria.

By the time of his death, Thutmose could claim to rule the land from beyond the Nile's Fourth Cataract in the south to the banks of the Euphrates in the north. Never had Egypt held sway over so much territory, or so clearly declared its imperial ambitions. Nor was this success fleeting. The Egyptians would sustain a strong military presence in the Near East for the next 400 years, using the new horse-powered battle chariots to devastating effect against their enemies.

The Legacy of Hatshepsut

The early death of Thutmose's son and successor could have resulted in a crisis for the Eighteenth Dynasty. Instead, it led to one of the most remarkable reigns in Egypt's history, for Thutmose II (1492–1479 B.C.E.) passed the power of

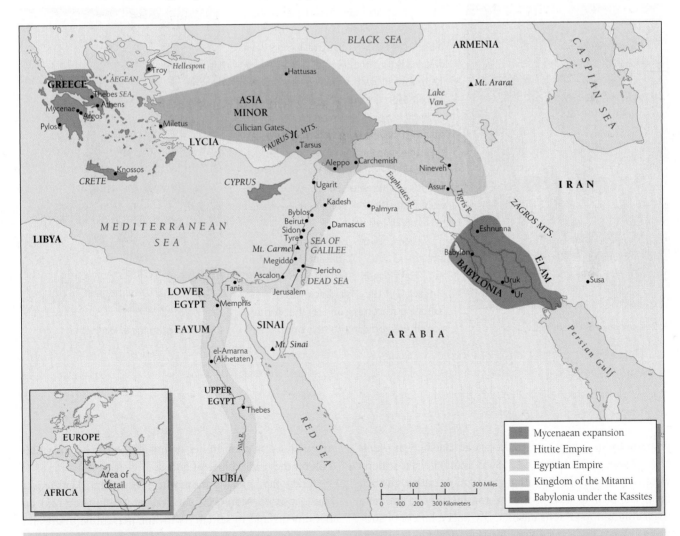

EGYPT AND ITS NEIGHBORS, C. 1400 B.C.E. ▪ *What is the major change on this map compared to the previous map of the Bronze Age Near East (page 40)?* ▪ *What factors appear to shape patterns of conquest and settlement in the Mediterranean?* ▪ *What developments would have enabled trade to flourish during this period?*

Interpreting Visual Evidence

Remembering Hatshepsut

he pharaohs of Egypt's New Kingdom were obsessed with self-representation and they carefully controlled their public images. The visual language they used was highly symbolic, an iconogra-phy (vocabulary of images) intended to make each successive pharaoh look as much like his royal predecessors as possible: godlike, steadfast, virile, authoritative—even when the pharaoh was a woman, Hatshepsut (1479–1458 B.C.E.). So many statues and portraits of her survive that nearly every major museum in the world has at least one (the Metropolitan Museum of Art in New York has a whole room set aside for them). But many of these images show signs of having been defaced during the reign of her successor, Thutmose III, who was also her nephew and stepson (images A and B). Until very recently, scholars assumed that Hatshepsut must have usurped his powers, and that this was his revenge. Yet the evidence clearly shows that Hatshepsut was Egypt's legitimate ruler. Why, then, would Thutmose III or his heirs have tried to efface to her memory?

These two unblemished *steles* (images C and D) depict Hatshepsut and Thutmose III. In the *stele* on the left (image C), they sit back-to-back on matching thrones, under the protection of the gods. In the *stele* on the right (image D), Thutmose III wears a warrior's crown, while Hatshepsut wears the double crown of Upper and Lower Egypt and wields a mace.

A. Defaced head of Hatshepsut.

B. Undefaced statue of Hatshepsut.

pharaoh to his sister, wife, and co-ruler Hatshepsut (*haht-SHEHP-soot*, 1479–1458 B.C.E.). Such brother-sister unions were common in the Egyptian royal family, although they do not appear to have been the routine way to produce royal children: pharaohs customarily kept a harem of subsidiary wives and concubines for this purpose. However, Thutmose II and Hatshepsut did conceive at least one child together, Neferure (*neh-feh-RUH-reh*); in fact, she may have been their designated heir. For twenty-one years, Hatshep-sut ruled as pharaoh in her own right, while her daughter took on the usual duties of queen.

Like her great-grandmother, Ahhotep, Hatshepsut was a warrior. Moroever, she was routinely protrayed on monuments and in statuary with the masculine figure and ceremonial beard characteristic of pharaohs. She did not pretend to be a man; inscriptions almost always indicate her gender, and she herself claimed to be the most beautiful woman in the world. But it was important to Egyptians that

Questions for Analysis

1. Bearing in mind that few Egyptians could read the hieroglyphs accompanying these images, how might they have "read" the relationship between these two royal relatives? Does this evidence support the hypothesis that Thutmose was slighted by Hatshepsut?

2. What can these images tell us about gender roles? What else would we need to know before making a judgment about masculine and feminine characteristics in ancient Egypt?

3. Given that Hatshepsut was Egypt's legitimate pharaoh, what might have motivated either Thutmose III or his son Amenhotep II to deface her image many years after her death?

C. *Stele* of Hatshepsut and Thutmose.

D. *Stele* of Thutmose and Hatshepsut from the Red Chapel at Karnak.

she use the conventional iconography of power to locate herself firmly within a long history of dynastic rule.

Hatshepsut's statecraft proved crucial to the continuing success of Egypt. With her stepson/nephew, Thutmose III (son of one of her brother's lesser wives), she launched several successful military campaigns and extended trade and diplomacy. The arts also flourished, setting standards that would be emulated for a thousand years. Indeed, Hatshepsut was one of the most ambitious builders in Egyptian history, which is saying something. Her own mortuary temple, which housed the remains of her father and herself, was probably the first tomb constructed in the Valley of the Kings, the New Kingdom's answer to the pyramids.

Yet after Hatshepsut's death in 1458 B.C.E. her legacy was called into question. At some point late in her nephew's reign, attempts were made to remove her name from inscriptions and to destroy her images (see **Interpreting**

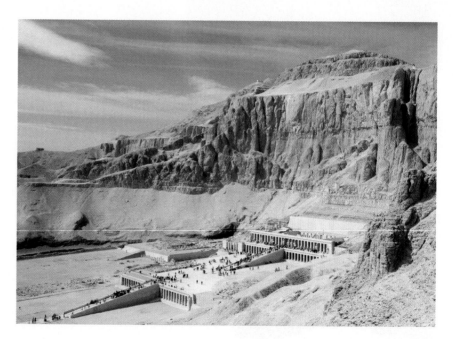

THE MORTUARY TEMPLE OF HATSHEPSUT. Unlike the pharaohs of the Old Kingdom, those of the Eighteenth Dynasty chose to be buried in specially built temples rather than in separate pyramids. The innovative architecture of Hatshepsut's temple, which was built into a hillside and set off by rows of columns, was widely imitated by her successors.

Visual Evidence on pages 44–45). Scholars used to assume that Thutmose himself was responsible, because he resented his stepmother/aunt's power over him. But more recent research has suggested that the culprit was his son, Amenhotep II (1427–1400 B.C.E.), who was thereby blocking the claims of royal rivals, possibly the descendants of Hatshepsut or her daughter Neferure. In either case, the near erasure of Hatshepsut's legacy caused her to be neglected by historians until the late twentieth century.

Religious Change and Political Challenge

The great conquests of the Eighteenth Dynasty brought mind-boggling riches to Egypt. Much of this wealth went to the glorification of the pharaoh in the form of grand temples, tombs, and other monuments, including the thousands of steles that provide us with so much information about this era. Another significant portion of the plunder went to the military aristocracy that made such conquests possible. But the lion's share went to the gods as offerings of thanks for Egypt's success. As the temples became wealthy and powerful, so too did their priests. But no temple complex was so well endowed as that of Amon at Thebes.

Thebes was not only the capital of New Kingdom Egypt, it was also the capital of the Eighteenth Dynasty and the place most sacred to Amon (or Amun), the god of creation.

He therefore played an important role in the dynasty's self-image, and he is evoked in the dynastic name Amenhotep ("Amon Is Pleased"). But Amon was more than a local god. He had come into prominence when the political center of gravity shifted to Thebes during the Middle Kingdom, and his cult had steadily increased in status and popularity. By 1550 B.C.E., he had become identified as another manifestation of the sun god Ra, and as Amon-Ra he was believed to be the divine force behind the Eighteenth Dynasty's triumph over the Hyksos. This accounts for the favor shown to his priests at Thebes, who became a formidable political and economic force. Eventually, the priesthood of Amon surpassed even the military aristocracy in importance and influence. And since the dynasty's prestige was intertwined with that of Amon, the priests had seemingly gained the controlling voice in Egypt.

The Reign of Akhenaten (1352–1336 B.C.E.)

All of these factors are important when we consider the reign of Amenhotep IV, who inherited the vast, well-governed kingdom assembled by his predecessors. This young pharaoh showed an early inclination toward the worship of the sun—but not as an aspect of Amon. Instead, Amenhotep exalted Ra as a discrete divinity and he laid aside the traditional iconography of this god as a falcon (or a falcon-headed man), replacing it with the symbol *Aten*, the hieroglyph representing the sun's rays. He then went further, changing his own name to Akhenaten (*AH-keh-NAH-ton*), "He Who Is Profitable to the Aten," and building a new capital to honor the god. Located halfway between Memphis in the north and Thebes in the south, it was called Akhetaten ("The Horizon of the Aten").

Although the priesthood of Amon exalted Amon-Ra, it had continued to recognize all the other gods of the Egyptian pantheon. Akhenaten's theology, by contrast, was closer to monotheism: unlike traditional Egyptian deities, the Aten could not be imagined as taking on human or animal form. As if this were not controversial enough, Akhenaten also celebrated his new religion by representing himself in a very unconventional way. In a complete departure from the divine virility of his ancestors—which even his ancestor Hatshepsut had emulated—Akhenaten had himself pictured as a normal human being with distinctive features and as a family man enjoying the company of his wife, Nefertiti, and their children. This emphasis on his own humanity might have been an extension of his theology, which honored the life force within every being. But it was very dangerous to the ideology of royal power. The pharaoh was not supposed to be approachable and affable, a man with quirky personality. He was supposed to be god's son on earth.

Akhenaten's spiritual revolution therefore had enormous political implications. Indeed, some scholars have suggested that it was part of a cunning attempt to undermine the influence of Amon's priests, to the pharaoh's benefit. Whatever the motives behind it, Akhenaten did not succeed in converting many Egyptians to his new religion. Not surprisingly, the priesthood of Amon also put up strenuous resistance. To make matters worse, Akhenaten did not balance his theological enthusiasm with attention to Egypt's security or interests abroad. This cost him the support of his nobility and may even have led to his deposition. He was ultimately succeeded by one of his younger sons, Tutankhaten ("Living Image of Aten"), a child of nine whose name was quickly changed to reflect his advisers' rejection of Akhenaten's beliefs and the restoration of the god Amon and his priesthood to a position of power. He thus became Tutankhamun (1333–1324 B.C.E.), the famous boy king whose sumptuous tomb was discovered in 1922. After his early death, he was succeeded by a general called Horemheb, a man unrelated to the royal family who nonetheless reigned as the last pharaoh of the Eighteenth Dynasty and managed to maintain stability for nearly three decades. When he died, he passed his office to another general. This was Ramses, the founder of the Nineteenth Dynasty, who would restore Egypt to glory in the Near East.

AKHENATEN, HIS WIFE NEFERTITI, AND THEIR CHILDREN. The Aten is depicted here as a sun disk, raining down power on the royal family. ■ *What messages might this image have conveyed to contemporary Egyptians?* ■ *How does this depiction of the pharaoh differ from earlier precedents?*

THRONE OF TUTANKHAMUN. Dating from about 1330 B.C.E., this relief in gold and silver is part of the back of the young pharaoh's throne. Although the reign of the boy king marked the rejection of Akhenaten's theology, the informal artistic style favored by his father is still detectable here in the relaxed, lounging position of the pharaoh and the intimate, confiding gesture of his queen, Ankhesenamen.

TRANSNATIONAL NETWORKS OF THE LATE BRONZE AGE

After 1500 B.C.E., Bronze Age history must be understood within the context of what we might call international relations. Yet it is more accurate to call the political and economic networks of this period *transnational*, because this web of alliances and relationships transcended any idea of national identity or national boundaries.

This Late Bronze Age was an age of superpowers. The great pharaohs of the Eighteenth Dynasty had transformed Egypt into a conquering state, and the Hittites had created an empire out of the disparate city-states and kingdoms of Anatolia. The Assyrians controlled Near Eastern trade, and the Kassite kingdom of Babylonia remained a significant force in economic and military relationships. In addition to these imperial entities, numerous smaller states also flourished and extended their influence westward into the Mediterranean. Holding it all together was a network of trade routes that created an interdependent Afro-Eurasian world.

Transnational Diplomacy

Although warfare remained the fundamental mode of interaction in the late Bronze Age, a balance of power among the larger empires gradually helped to stabilize the region and encourage trade. The archives discovered by archaeologists at Akhenaten's abandoned capital of Akhetaten (modern el-Amarna) provide us with a clear picture of this process. By the fourteenth century B.C.E., a wide-ranging correspondence was forging alliances and promoting a set of mutual goals and understandings among rulers and elites. This is reflected in the letters' vocabulary: the most powerful rulers address one another as "brother," while lesser princes and chieftains show their deference to the pharaoh, the Hittite king, and other sovereigns by using the term "father." Breach of this protocol could cause great offense. When a thirteenth-century Assyrian king presumed to address the Hittite ruler as "brother," he received a stern rebuke: "What is this you keep saying about 'brotherhood'? Were you and I born of the same mother? Far from it! Just as my father and grandfather were not in the habit of writing about 'brotherhood' to the king of Assyria, so should you stop writing to me about 'brotherhood!'"

Rulers of this period also exchanged lavish gifts and entered into marriage contracts with each other. Professional envoys journeyed back and forth between the centers of power, conveying gifts and handling politically sensitive missions. Some of these emissaries were also merchants, sent to explore the possibility of trading opportunities as well as to cement alliances.

Transnational Trade

Indeed, it was trade that allowed smaller communities to become integral parts of this transnational network. Seaside centers became powerful merchant city-states and centers for the exchange of dazzling commodities. A single vessel's cargo might contain scores of distinct items originating anywhere from the interior of Africa to the Baltic Sea, as demonstrated by the contents of a merchant ship discovered at Uluburun off the Turkish coast in 1982. At the same time, the region was supplied with goods brought in over land, via contacts reaching into India and the Far East.

Long-distance trade was not only the basis for a new economy but also the conduit for art, ideas, and technology. In the past, such influences had spread slowly and unevenly; now, though, the societies of the late Bronze Age could keep abreast of all the latest developments. Egyptians delighted in Canaanite glass, Greeks prized Egyptian amulets, and the merchants of Syria admired Greek pottery and wool. Examples of avid desire for the products of other cultures could be endlessly enumerated.

This trend was particularly marked in large coastal towns. At Ugarit, on the coast of modern-day Syria, the swirl of commerce and the multiplicity of languages spoken by traders even propelled the development of a simpler form of written communication than the cuneiform still current throughout most of the Near East. The Ugaritic alphabet consisted of about thirty symbols representing the sounds of consonants. (Vowels had to be inferred.) This system was far more easily mastered and more flexible than cuneiform, and it would become the model for the development of all modern alphabets.

The search for markets, resources, and trade routes also promoted greater understanding among cultures. After a great battle between Egyptians and Hittites near Kadesh (c. 1275 B.C.E.), the pharaoh Ramses II realized that more was to be gained through peaceful relations with his northern neighbors than through warfare. The treaty he established with the Hittites fostered geopolitical stability in the region and allowed further economic exchanges to flourish. But greater integration also meant greater mutual dependence. If one economy suffered, the effects of that decline were sure to be felt elsewhere. And the farther this transnational system spread, the more fragile it became. Many of the new markets depended on emerging societies in regions far less stable, where civilization was new.

AEGEAN CIVILIZATION: MINOAN CRETE, MYCENAEAN GREECE

Like Hesiod, many ancient Greek poets described a heroic age when great men mingled with gods and powerful kingdoms contended for wealth and glory. For a long time, modern scholars dismissed these stories as fables. Tales of Theseus and the Minotaur, the Trojan War, and the wanderings of Odysseus were not regarded as reflecting any historical reality. Greek history was assumed to begin in 776 B.C.E., when the first recorded Olympic Games occurred. Greece in the Bronze Age was considered a primitive backwater that played no significant role in the Mediterranean world or in the later, glorious history of classical Greece.

But in the late nineteenth century, an amateur archaeologist named Heinrich Schliemann became convinced that these legends were really historical accounts. Using the epic poems of Homer as his guide, he found the site of Ilium (Troy) near the coast of northwest Anatolia. He also identified a number of once-powerful citadels on the Greek mainland, including the home of the legendary king Agamemnon at Mycenae (*MY-seh-nee*). Soon afterward, the British archaeologist Sir Arthur Evans took credit for discovering the remains of a great palace at Knossos (*Kuh-NAHS-ohs*) on the island of Crete, a vast complex that predated any of the major citadels on the Greek mainland. He dubbed its magnificent culture—which no modern person had known to exist—"Minoan," after King Minos, the powerful ruler whom the ancient Greeks had described as dominating the Aegean, and the man for whom the legendary engineer Daedalus had designed the Labyrinth. Although some of their conclusions have proven false, the discoveries of Schliemann and Evans forced scholars to revise, entirely, the early history of Western civilizations. It is now clear that Bronze Age Greece—or, as it is often termed, Mycenaean Greece—was an important player in this integrated Mediterranean world during the second millennium B.C.E.

MYCENAEAN DEATH MASK, C. 1550–1500 B.C.E. When the archaeologist Heinrich Schliemann discovered this gold funeral mask in a burial shaft at Mycenae, he immediately declared it to be that of Agamemnon. Although it is certainly royal, this mask is too old to have been made for that legendary king, who would have lived several centuries later.

The Minoan Thalassocracy

In the fifth century B.C.E., the Athenian historian Thucydides wrote that King Minos of Crete had ruled a *thalassocracy*, an empire of the sea. We now know that he was correct, that a very wealthy civilization began to flourish on the island of Crete around 2500 B.C.E. Thereafter, for about a millennium, the Minoans controlled shipping around the central Mediterranean and the Aegean and may have exacted tribute from many smaller islands. At its height between 1900 and 1500 B.C.E., Minoan civilization was the contemporary of Egypt's Middle Kingdom and the Hittite Old Kingdom. And unlike them, it was virtually unassailable by outside forces, protected by the surrounding sea. Astonishingly, neither the great palace at Knossos nor the other palaces on the island were fortified so secure were they from attack.

Thanks to its strategic position, Crete was not only a safe haven but also a nexus of vibrant economic exchange. In this it resembled its counterparts in the Near East because it acted as a magnet for the collection of resources which were then redistributed by its rulers and their emissaries. Knossos was also a production center for textiles, pottery, and metalwork. Minoan merchants traded these with Egypt, southwest Anatolia, and Cyprus for a range of exotic goods. Through Cyprus, the Minoans had further contacts with the Levantine coast of modern-day Lebanon and Syria. Artistic influences also traveled along these routes; among much else, Minoan-style paintings from this period appear regularly in the Nile Delta and the Levant.

Traces of the bright colors and graceful lines of these paintings are still evident on the ruined walls of the palace

MINOAN FRESCO, C. 1500 B.C.E. A stylized representation of bull-leaping, painted into the plaster of a wall at Knossos. ▪ *Is this likely to represent real practices?* ▪ *Why or why not?*

at Knossos. Endowed with indoor plumbing, among other luxuries, it covered several acres and comprised hundreds of rooms joined by an intricate network of winding hallways that surely inspired the famous story of the Labyrinth, where the terrible Minotaur lurked in the center. These legends, too, reflect historical evidence: the Minoans probably worshiped a god in the form of a bull or bull-man, and they appear to have devised an elaborate ritual sport known as bull-leaping, similar to bull-fighting but involving an element of athletic dance. There is also some evidence that they practiced human sacrifice (possibly facilitated by the dangers of bull-dancing) as a religious rite.

Despite all these fascinating remains, Minoan culture remains mysterious because its language has yet to be decoded. Its script is called Linear A, to distinguish it from Linear B, used in Mycenaen Greece—a script that *has* been deciphered. Although Linear A and Linear B represent different languages, the formal relationship between them reflects the fact that Minoan commercial activity engaged the mainland of Greece. The presence of a wide variety of Minoan objects on the Greek mainland corroborates this.

Yet the dynamics of the relationship between Minoans and Mycenaeans remains debatable. Before 1600 B.C.E., the

Minoans were clearly much more sophisticated and may have dominated their Greek neighbors. One story told of Theseus describes how the young hero was sent to Crete as a hostage, intending to free Athens from the heavy tribute imposed by King Minos. Given what we have already learned about the close relationship between myth and history, it is probable that this story preserves ancient memory, just as the story of Daedalus, the brilliant inventor and engineer, is an attempt to explain the technological marvels of the palace at Knossos.

Mycenaean Greece

In the early 1950s, the Englishmen Michael Ventris and John Chadwick joined their linguistic skills to expertise gained during the Second World War, when many classically trained scholars were employed in cracking enemy codes. Their efforts resulted in the decoding of Linear B. Analysis of the texts written in this script forced scholars to reconsider the history of ancient Greece, and proved that it stretched well back into the Bronze Age. Since then, new

LINEAR B TABLET FROM KNOSSOS. Unlike cuneiform, whose characters are formed using the wedge-shaped tip of a reed, the scripts of Linear B used a sharp stylus that incised fine lines in clay or soft stone.

research shows that the Indo-Europeans whose language became Greek entered the region in several waves after the turn of the second millennium, dominating and displacing the indigenous inhabitants. By 1500 B.C.E., huge citadels dotted the Greek landscape, ruled by warriors whose epitaphs boast of their martial prowess and who were buried with their weapons. The power of these rulers was based on their leadership and their ability to reward followers with plunder. The most successful of them gained control of strategic sites from which they could exploit major trade routes, engaging in both trade and piracy. (The line between these two pursuits has always been fine.)

Over time, and perhaps under the influence of Minoan culture, the Mycenaean citadels developed into complex societies. They served as both centers of government and warehouses for the storage and redistribution of goods and agricultural surpluses, of which they kept careful records. (Thousands of Linear B tablets have survived to testify to this.) By the thirteenth century B.C.E., some rulers had carved out territorial kingdoms with as many as 100,000 inhabitants, dwarfing the city-states of the later classical age; Hesiod imagined them to have been built by giants.

Indeed, these palace centers were adapted from Near Eastern models and their massive size was not ideally suited to the Greek landscape. In war also, Mycenaean imitation of Near Eastern examples had its limits. For example, Mycenaean kings cherished the chariots used by their contemporaries on the plains of Anatolia, yet such chariots were highly impractical on Greece's rocky terrain.

Despite these and other differences from their Mediterranean neighbors, the Mycenaean Greeks played a central role in Bronze Age networks. By about 1400 B.C.E., they had subjugated Crete, taking over Knossos and making it as a Mycenaean center. When the pharaoh Amenhotep III mentions a place called "Keftiu" in his correspondence, he is probably negotiating with Crete's Mycenaean conquerors. In western Anatolia, not far from fabled Troy, at least one Mycenaean king exercised enough influence for a Hittite ruler to address him as "my brother." This evidence suggests that the Mycenaeans earned prestige as warriors and mercenaries, just as the Greeks' heroic poems attest.

The basic political and commercial unit of the Mycenaean world—a powerful king and war leader, a warrior aristocracy, a palace bureaucracy, a complex economy, large territorial kingdoms—differs markedly from the tiny, self-contained Greek city-state of the later classical age (see Chapter 3). However, we can trace some features

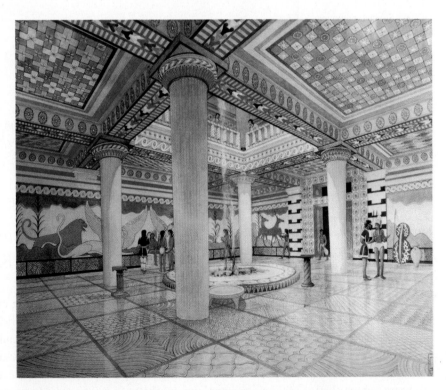

AN ARTIST'S RECONSTRUCTION OF THE GREAT HALL AT PYLOS. Located on the western coast of the Greek Peloponnesus, Pylos was excavated in 1952 by the archaeologist Carl Blegen and his team. The principal feature of its Bronze Age palace was a large, brightly painted "great room" (*megaron*) with a central hearth.

MYCENAEAN GREECE. ▪ *What stands out about the geography of Greece?* ▪ *How might this dry, mountainous country surrounded by the sea determine the nature of Greek civilization and economic interests?* ▪ *How might geography have allowed Mycenaean culture able to spread so widely?*

of this later civilization back to the Mycenaeans, including the Greek language. Linear B tablets speak of a social group with considerable economic and political rights, the *damos*; this may be the precursor of the *demos*, the urban population that sought political empowerment (*democracy*) in many Greek cities. The tablets also preserve the names of several gods familiar from the later period, such as Zeus, Poseidon, and Dionysus. Indeed, the later Greeks believed themselves to be descended from these legendary forebears, whom they credited with superhuman achievements. Although later Greeks like Hesiod knew little about these Mycenaean ancestors in fact, the impact of what they imagined about them was considerable.

The Sea Peoples and the End of the Bronze Age

The civilization of Mycenaean Greece seems to have collapsed around the end of the thirteenth century B.C.E. What triggered this cannot be determined with any certainty: drought, famine, disease, and social unrest have all been posited. But the consequences of the collapse are clear. Because Mycenaean Greece was an integrated part of a transnational network, the effects of its demise were felt throughout the Near East. Thereafter, a wave of devastation swept from north to south, caused by a group of people so

The Diplomacy of the Mycenaeans and the Hittites

Around 1260 B.C.E., the powerful Hittite king Hattusilis III sent the following letter to a "King of Ahhiyawa," identifiable as a leader of the Mycenaean Greeks, who often called themselves Akhaiwoi, Achaeans. This fascinating document exemplifies the tangle of close ties that bound powerful men together within the transnational system of the Late Bronze Age, as well as the problems and misunderstandings that could arise from the misbehavior of men under their command. The events referenced here all occur in western Anatolia (Turkey), a region controlled partly by the Hittites and partly by the Greeks, the same region in which Troy (Ilium) was located. (See the map on page 52.)

 have to complain of the insolent and treacherous conduct of one Tawagalawas. We came into contact in the land of Lycia, and he offered to become a vassal of the Hittite Empire. I agreed, and sent an officer of most exalted rank to conduct him to my presence. He had the audacity to complain that the officer's rank was not exalted enough; he insulted my ambassador in public, and demanded that he be declared vassal-king there and then, without the formality of an interview. Very well: I order him, if he desires to become a vassal of mine, to make sure that no troops of his are found in Iyalanda when I arrive there. And what do I find when I arrive in Iyalanda?—the troops of Tawagalawas, fighting on the side of my enemies. I defeat them, take many prisoners . . . scrupulously leaving the fortress of Atriya intact out of respect for my treaty with you. Now a Hittite subject, Piyamaradus by name, steals my 7,000 prisoners, and makes off to your city of Miletus. I command him to return to me: he disobeys. I write to you: you send a surly message unaccompanied by gift or greeting, to say that you have ordered your representative in Miletus, a certain Atpas, to deliver up Piyamaradus. Nothing happens, so I go fetch him. I enter your city of Miletus, for I have something to say to Piyamaradus, and it would be well that your subjects there should hear me say it. But my visit is not a success. I ask for Tawagalawas: he is not at home. I should like to see Piyamaradus: he has gone to sea. You refer me to your representative Atpas: I find that both he and his brother are married to daughters of Piyamaradus; they are not likely to give me satisfaction or to give you an unbiased account of these transactions. . . . Are you aware, and is it with your blessing, that Piyamaradus is going round saying that he intends to leave his wife and family, and incidentally my 7,000 prisoners, under your protection while he makes continual inroads on my dominion? . . . Do not let him use Achaea [in Greece] as a base for operations against me. You and I are friends. There has been no quarrel between us since we came to terms in the matter of Ilios [the territory of Troy]: the trouble there was my fault, and I promise it will not happen again. As for my military occupation of Miletus, please regard it as a friendly visit. . . . [As for the problems between us], I suggest that the fault may not lie with ourselves but with our messengers; let us bring them to trial, cut off their heads, mutilate their bodies, and live henceforth in perfect friendship.

Source: Adapted from Denys Page, *History and the Homeric Iliad* (Berkeley, CA: 1959), pp. 11–12.

Questions for Analysis

1. Reconstruct the relationship between Hattusilis III and the Achaean king, based on the references to people and places in this letter. What picture emerges of their interactions and of the connections between the Hittite Empire and Mycenaean Greece?

2. Why is Hattusilis so concerned about the disrespect shown to him by the Achaeans? Reading between the lines, what do you think he wanted to accomplish by sending this letter?

3. Based on this letter, what you can you deduce about the standards of behavior expected of civilized participants in the transnational system of the Late Bronze Age? Within this code of conduct, what sanctions or penalties could be imposed on individuals or their nations?

thoroughly destructive that they obliterated everything in their path.

We might know nothing at all about them were it not for a narrow victory by the pharaoh Ramses III around 1176 B.C.E. In the *stele* set up to commemorate his triumph near the modern city of Luxor on Egypt's West Bank, Ramses III referred to these invaders as the "Sea Peoples" and named several groups as part of a coalition. Some were familiar to the Egyptians, who had employed them as mercenaries. From Ramses' description of their battle gear, it seems that many were from the Aegean. Most notable were the Philistines who, after their defeat, withdrew to populate the coast of the region named after them: Palestine.

Because the Sea Peoples' arc of annihilation started in the north, it may have been one of the factors contributing to the collapse of Mycenaean Greece. Disruption of northern commercial networks would have devastated the Mycenaean kingdoms, which could not support their enormous populations without trade. Suddenly faced with an apocalyptic combination of overpopulation, famine, and violence, bands of desperate refugees would have fled the Aegean basin. Meanwhile, the damage to commerce had a domino effect and devastated the economy of the Hittites, whose ancient kingdom rapidly disintegrated. Along the Mediterranean coast we find other clues. The king of Ugarit wrote a letter to a "brother" king on the island of Cyprus, begging for immediate aid because he had sent all his own warriors to help the Hittites. Poignantly, however, we have his letter only because the clay tablet on which it was written baked hard in the fire that destroyed his palace. The letter was never sent.

In the end, the Sea Peoples destroyed the civilizations that had flourished in the Near East and Mediterranean for over two thousand years. The devastation was not total; not all cities disappeared, and trade did not cease entirely. But the Hittite Empire was eradicated, leaving behind it many weak, short-lived principalities. The great cosmopolitan cities of the eastern Mediterranean lay in ruins, and new groups—sometimes contingents of Sea Peoples like the Philistines—populated the coast. The citadels of Mycenaean Greece were depopulated by as much as 90 percent over the next century, and Greece entered into a period of cultural and economic isolation that would last for 250 years.

The victorious Egyptians survived; but with their major trading partners diminished or dead, their civilization suffered. The Assyrians, the original architects of the networks that had undergirded the transnational system, had to fight for their very existence. In Babylon, the peaceful and prosperous rule of the Kassites withered. In the vacuum left behind, new political configurations took shape and a new metallurgical technology began to supplant the use of bronze. Out of the ashes arose the culture of the Iron Age.

THE STATES OF THE EARLY IRON AGE

With the destruction of transnational networks, the geopolitical map of the Near East changed significantly. In Anatolia, a patchwork of small kingdoms grew up within the territories once controlled by the Hittites. Similar developments took place in the Levant: the eastern Mediterranean coastline that today comprises Israel, Lebanon, and parts of Syria. For centuries, this region had been controlled either by the Egyptians or the Hittites. With the collapse of these empires, new states began to emerge there, too. They were small, but they had a huge impact on the history of Western civilizations.

The Phoenicians

One of the most influential peoples of this period are usually called by their name: the Greek Phoenicians. They are also known as Canaanites, and were speakers of a Semitic language closely related to Hebrew, Amorite, and Ugaritic. Each Phoenician city on the coast of the Levant had its own hereditary royal government, and every Phoenician's first loyalty was to his or her own city. In the Phoenicians' overseas colonies, however, a new type of political system emerged in which power was shared among a handful of elite families. This aristocratic form of government would become a model for many other Western societies, including those of classical Greece and Rome (see Chapters 3 and 5).

During the late Bronze Age, most Phoenician cities had been controlled by Egypt. But the erosion of Egyptian imperial power after 1200 B.C.E. gave these cities the opportunity to forge a new independence and to capitalize on their commercial advantages. One Phoenician city, Gubla, was a clearing house for papyrus, the highly prized Egyptian writing material. This explains why the Greek name for this city, Byblos, became the basis for the Greek word *biblion*, meaning "book." (The Bible is so called from the plural *biblia*, "the books.") Another valuable commodity came to be associated with the Phoenicians and gave them their name a rare purple dye derived from the shells of snails culled from seabeds off the Levantine coast. As far as the Greeks were concerned, those who supplied this rich dye were *phoinikeoi*, "purple people." Phoenician textiles commanded a high price everywhere. So did timber from the Levant, especially cedar, and Canaanite glass. The Phoenicians also became expert metalworkers, ivory carvers, and shipbuilders.

Phoenician Colonies and Cultural Influence

The Phoenicians became famous as merchants and seafarers, but they were also aggressive colonists. By the end of the tenth century B.C.E., they had planted settlements from one end of the Mediterranean to the other and their merchants had begun to venture out into the Atlantic Ocean. We have good evidence that they traveled as far as Cornwall (southwest Britain) during this period. The Greek historian Herodotus later claimed that Phoenician merchant-explorers even circumnavigated Africa. At the end of the ninth century B.C.E., Phoenicians from the city of Tyre established Carthage in modern-day Tunisia (North Africa). Carthage would ultimately become the preeminent power in the western Mediterranean, bringing it into conflict with Rome centuries later (see Chapter 5).

The widespread colonial and mercantile efforts of the Phoenicians meant that they influenced cultures across the Mediterranean. Among their early overseas trading partners were the Greeks, and the Phoenicians may have played an important role in reintroducing urban life to Greece after the collapse of the Mycenaean citadels. They also brought with them a number of Near Eastern artistic and literary influences. Without question, however, the most important contribution of the Phoenicians was their alphabet.

As we noted earlier, a thirty-character alphabet had evolved at Ugarit by the end of the Bronze Age. Around 1100 B.C.E., the Phoenicians refined this writing system to twenty-two characters. This simpler system further facilitated trade and accounting, and the Phoenicians may have wanted to encourage similar practices among their partners, to safeguard their own interests. The Greeks certainly remained aware of their debt to the Phoenicians: their legends ascribe the invention of the alphabet to Cadmus, a Phoenician who settled in Greece. Their debt is also clear in the close relationship between the names of letters in Greek (alpha, beta, gamma, delta . . .) and Phoenician letter names (aleph, bayt, gimel, dalet . . .), and from the obvious similarities in letter shapes.

PHOENICIAN COLONIZATION. Compare this map to the more detailed one of the Hebrew kingdoms on page 59. ▪ *What part of the Mediterranean serves as the homeland for the Phoenician city-states, and where did Phoenicians establish colonies?* ▪ *Why would overseas colonization be of such crucial importance to Phoenician city-states?* ▪ *What does their westward colonization imply about the Phoenicians' aims and about the different opportunities available in the western Mediterranean, as compared to the New East?*

Phoenician	Hebrew	Classical Greek	Modern Alphabetic
𐤀	א	A	A
𐤁	ב	B	B
𐤂	ג	Γ	G
𐤃	ד	Δ	D
𐤄	ה	E	E
𐤅	ו	Y	V
𐤆	ז	Z	Z
𐤇	ח	H	H
𐤈	ט	Θ	T
𐤉	י	I	Y
𐤊	כ	K	K
𐤋	ל	Λ	L
𐤌	מ	M	M
𐤍	נ	N	N
𐤎	ס	Ξ	S
𐤏	ע	O	O
𐤐	פ	Π	P
𐤑	צ		TZ
𐤒	ק	φ	Q
𐤓	ר	P	R
𐤔	ש	Σ	S
𐤕	ת	T	T

THE EVOLUTION OF THE ALPHABET. This table shows how the shapes of letters changed as the Phoenician alphabet was adapted by the Hebrews, the Greeks, and eventually the Romans (from whom our modern alphabet derives).

The Philistines

Southward along the Levantine coast from Phoenicia lay the land of the Philistines, descendants of the Sea Peoples defeated by Ramses III. Their reputation is the result of their dominance over their pastoral neighbors, the herdsmen known as the Hebrews, who used writing as an effective weapon: the Philistines thus became the great villains of the Hebrew scriptures, and the word *philistine* has accordingly come to mean a boorish, uncultured person. Unfortunately, the Philistines do not appear to have made use of the same powerful technology to record their own outlook on the world, and almost everything we know about them comes from the work of archaeologists, or has to be sifted through the bad press of their detractors.

The Philistines occupied a unique position in the Levant and retained a separate identity for several generations; each new archaeological discovery roots this identity more firmly in their Aegean past. We know little about their language, but their material culture, behavior, and organization all exhibit close affinities with Mycenaean Greece. For example, the Philistines introduced grapevines and olive trees to the Levant from the Aegean basin. With the profits from these industries, they created powerful armies that dominated the region in the twelfth and eleventh centuries B.C.E. They also established a monopoly over metal smithing, making it virtually impossible for their enemies to forge competitive weaponry.

Philistine power was based in five great strongholds, the so-called Pentapolis (Greek for "five cities"): Gaza, Ashkelon, and Ashdod on the coast, and the inland cities of Ekron and Gath. (Again, these citadels are strikingly similar to the fortified palaces of Mycenaean civilization, and they appear to have served many of the same functions). From these strongholds, the Philistines dominated the surrounding countryside by organizing agricultural production and controlling trade routes. An independent lord ruled over each citadel, and no doubt tensions and rivalries existed among them. But much like the heroes of Greek epic, the Philistines could set aside differences when facing a common enemy.

Because we see the Philistines primarily through the eyes of their Hebrew enemies, we must be careful about drawing conclusions about them from the stories of Goliath's brutality or Delilah's sexual treachery, to name the two most infamous Philistines of the Hebrew scriptures. Yet the Hebrews had good reason to fear the Philistines, whose pressure on the Hebrew hill country was constant and who threatened the Hebrews' holy sanctuary at Shiloh, where the sacred Ark of the Covenant was said to contain the original tablets of the law given to Moses on Mount Sinai. In Hebrew tradition, the tribes of Israel had once carried the Ark before them into battle against the Philistines, only to lose it in the fray and to witness thereafter the destruction of Shiloh. The Philistines then established garrisons throughout the land of the Hebrews and exacted tribute, denied them access to weapons, and engaged in the typical abuses of an occupying people.

The Hebrews and Their Scriptures

The central feature of Hebrew culture, their conception of and relationship to their god, will be discussed at greater length toward the end of this chapter. In this section, we focus our attention on the development of Hebrew society in the Iron Age Levant—while at the same time acknowledging that religion is always related to politics, as well as to economic conditions and the concerns of everyday life. Indeed the Hebrews, like all ancient peoples and many people today, could not have distinguished among these phenomena.

In reconstructing the early history of the Hebrews, we are indebted to an unusual textual source already mentioned: a series of scriptures (literally "writings") that comprise mythology, laws and ritual practices, genealogical records, books of prophecy, proverbs, poetry, and royal chronicles. These are collectively known as the Hebrew Bible or (among Christians) as the Old Testament. These books are full of information about cultural practices and key events, and they are also a guide to the intellectual unfolding of the most influential religious tradition of the West. They do not, however, constitute a unified history. The books of the Bible were assembled over many centuries, mostly by unknown authors, copyists, and editors. Like other historical sources, they have to be treated as artifacts produced by particular historical circumstances, which also governed the way that certain texts were preserved and put together.

The first five books of the Hebrew Bible are traditionally attributed to the Hebrew leader Moses, but most of the materials in these books were borrowed from other Near Eastern cultures, including the stories of the creation and the flood, which parallel those of Sumer (as we saw in Chapter 1). The story of Moses's childhood draws on a legend told about the Akkadian king Sargon the Great. The laws and rituals of the patriarchs can be found in other traditions, too. Meanwhile, the story of the exodus from Egypt is fraught with contradictions. Although the later Book of Joshua claims that the Hebrews who returned from Egypt conquered and expelled the native Canaanites, archaeological and linguistic evidence suggests that the Hebrews were essentially Canaanites themselves. They may have merged with scattered refugees from Egypt in the aftermath of the Sea Peoples' invasions, but for the most part they had been continuously resident in Canaan for centuries. In sum, the first five books of the Bible constitute a retrospective history whose purpose was to justify Hebrew traditions and claims to power.

Among the other writings included in the Hebrew Bible are a group of texts which record events of the more recent past, those of the period we are considering now. These "historical books" are more straightforwardly verifiable, even if many details are difficult to confirm. According to the Book of Judges, the Hebrews were herdsmen who had just begun to establish permanent settlements around the time of the Philistines' arrival in the Levant. They had organized themselves into twelve tribes—extended clan units whose families owed one another mutual aid and protection in times of war, but who frequently fought over cattle and grazing rights. Each tribe was ruled by a patriarch known as a judge, who exercised the typical functions of authority in a clan-based society: war leadership, high priesthood, and dispute settlement. By the middle of the twelfth century B.C.E., these tribes occupied two major territories, with those settled in the south calling themselves the tribes of Judah, and those in the north the tribes of Israel.

The Struggle for Hebrew Identity

The Hebrew tribes of this period had few occasions to work together as a group and little experience of organized activity. This made them highly vulnerable, especially when the Philistines conquered the Levantine coast, around 1050 B.C.E. Faced with the threat of extinction, the Hebrews appear to have put up desperate resistance from their bases in the hilly interior. To counter the Philistine threat effectively, however, they needed a leader. Accordingly, around 1025 B.C.E., an influential tribal judge called Samuel selected a king to lead the Hebrew resistance against the Philistines. His name was Saul. However, Saul proved to be an ineffective war-leader. Although he blocked Philistine penetration into the hill country, he could not oust the Philistines from the valleys or coastal plains. So Samuel withdrew his support from Saul and threw it behind a young warrior in Saul's entourage, Saul's son-in-law David. Waging his own independent military campaigns, David achieved one triumph after another over the Philistines. By contrast, the armies of Saul met frequent reverses—that is, according to the chroniclers responsible for the historical books of the Bible, who wrote their accounts under David's patronage.

These same books reveal that David was not initially motivated by patriotism. He was a man on the make; and when Saul finally drove him from his court, he became an outlaw on the fringes of Hebrew society and then a mercenary in Philistine service. It was as a Philistine mercenary, in fact, that David fought against Saul in the climactic battle in which Saul was killed. Soon thereafter, David himself became king, first over the tribes of Judah, his home territory, and later over Saul's territory of Israel as well.

The Consolidation of the Hebrew Kingdom

After David's victory around 1000 B.C.E., he strove to strengthen his authority within and beyond his kingdom. He took advantage of the opportunity afforded by Egypt's decline to expand his territory southward, eventually confining the Philistines to an inconsequential strip of coastal land. David also defeated the neighboring Moabites and Ammonites, extending his control to the Dead Sea. By the time of his

Past and Present

The Fragility of Global Networks

In the late Bronze Age, the destruction of transnational commercial networks had a domino effect on the interlocking civilizations of the West, plunging many into a "dark age" of isolation and impoverishment. The global economic crisis of our own day was caused by a similar phenomenon: the collapse of mutually dependent financial systems that proved more fragile than anyone had anticipated.

 Watch related author interview on StudySpace
wwnorton.com/web/westernciv18

death in 973 B.C.E., his kingdom stretched from the middle Euphrates in the north to the Gulf of Aqaba in the south, and from the Mediterranean coast eastward into the Syrian deserts. Israel was now a force to be reckoned with, although it owed that status to the temporary weakness of its imperial neighbors, Egypt and Assyria.

As David's power and prestige grew, he was able to impose on his subjects a highly unpopular system of taxation and forced labor. His goal was to build a glorious capital at Jerusalem, a Canaanite settlement that he designated as the central city of his realm. It was a shrewd choice. As a newly conquered city, Jerusalem had no previous affiliation with any of Israel's twelve tribes and so stood outside the ancient rivalries that divided them. Geographically, too, Jerusalem was a strategic choice, lying between the southern tribes of Judah (David's people) and the northern tribes of Israel. David also took steps to exalt the city as a religious

center by making Jerusalem the resting place of the sacred Ark of the Covenant and elevating the priesthood of the Hebrew god, Yahweh. By these measures, he sought to forge a new collective identity centered on his own family and its connections to Yahweh. To this end, he also encouraged the writing of histories and prophecies that would affirm this identity and his central role in forging it.

The Reign of King Solomon (973–937 B.C.E.)

Continuing his father's policies, but on a much grander scale, David's son Solomon built a great temple complex at Jerusalem to house the Ark. Such visible support of Yahweh's cult was approved by the chroniclers whose works are included in the Bible, and which portray Solomon's reign as a golden age. Despite his proverbial wisdom, however, Solomon was a ruthless and often brutal ruler whose promotion of Yahweh coincided with a program of despotism. According to his own histories, Solomon kept an enormous harem of some 300 wives and 700 concubines, many of them drawn from subject or allied peoples. His palace complex—of which the Temple was a part—allowed him to rule in the grand style of ancient Near Eastern potentates. To finance his expensive tastes and programs, Solomon instituted oppressive taxation and imposed customs duties on the lucrative caravan trade that passed through his country. With the help of the Phoenician king of Tyre, Solomon constructed a commercial fleet whose ships plied the waters of the Red Sea and beyond, trading—among other commodities—the gold and copper mined by Solomon's slaves.

Israel's new wealth was bought at a high price. Solomon maintained a large standing army of unwilling conscripts from his own people, equipped with chariot and cavalry squadrons and powered by horses purchased abroad. To undertake his ambitious building projects, Solomon also required many of his subjects to perform forced labor four months out of every year. This level of oppression was too much for many Israelites, and the northern tribes seethed with rebellion against the royal capital. Within a decade or so of Solomon's death, in fact, the fragile monarchy split in two. The dynasty descended from David continued to rule the southern kingdom of Judah with its capital at Jerusalem, but the ten northern tribes banded together as the kingdom of Israel, with their capital at Shechem. Archaeology combined with other accounts included in the Bible reveal that the cult of Yahweh was not yet dominant in either the north or the south, so major religious differences made reunification even more difficult. In the meantime, the changing political situation of the Near East made the Hebrew kingdoms increasingly vulnerable.

THE REVIVAL OF THE ASSYRIAN EMPIRE

As we have already seen, the Assyrians had long played an important role in spreading trade and promoting urban settlements. But like the other great powers of the Near East, their civilization had been devastated by the Sea Peoples. For several centuries afterward they struggled for survival. Then, in the ninth century B.C.E., a brilliant but brutal ruler laid the foundations of what historians call the Neo-Assyrian Empire. Under the leadership of Assurnasirpal II (*ah-sur-NAH-sur-PAHL*, 883–859 B.C.E.), the Assyrians began to conduct aggressive military campaigns against their neighbors on an annual basis. Those whom they defeated either had to pay tribute or face the full onslaught of the Assyrian war machine, which under Assurnasirpal acquired a deserved reputation for savagery.

Despite their military successes, Assurnasirpal and his son, Shalmeneser III (*SHAHL-meh-NEE-zehr*, 853–827 B.C.E.), also inspired stiff resistance. The northern kingdom of Israel formed an alliance with other small states to halt Assyrian expansion. This coalition ultimately forced Shalmeneser III to settle for smaller victories against the Armenians to his northwest and the Medes to his northeast, until a great revolt within Assyria itself ended his reign. Thereafter, a usurper named Tiglath-Pileser III seized the Assyrian throne in 744 B.C.E. and immediately demanded

Two Accounts of Saul's Anointing

> When the charismatic judge Samuel chose Saul as the first king of the Hebrews, he opened a new chapter in the political history of Israel. But Saul's kingship was not a success, and Samuel ultimately turned against him, supporting Saul's rival (and son-in-law), David. These two quite different accounts of Samuel's anointing of Saul reflect the tensions that later arose between them—and were probably written down during the later kingship of David, Saul's challenger and successor. The first account also suggests the ambivalence some Hebrews felt about having a human king at all, doubts which may have been shared by Saul himself.

1 Samuel 8:4–22, 10:20–25

All the elders of Israel gathered together and [said to Samuel]: "You are old and your sons do not follow in your ways; appoint for us, then, a king to govern us, like other nations." But the thing displeased Samuel [who] prayed to the Lord, and the Lord said to Samuel, "Listen to the voice of the people in all that they say to you; for they have not rejected you, but they have rejected me from being king over them. Just as they have done to me, from the day I brought them up out of Egypt to this day, forsaking me and serving other gods, so they are also doing to you. Now then, listen to their voice; only—you shall solemnly warn them, and show them the ways of the king who shall reign over them." So Samuel reported all the words of the Lord to the people who were asking for a king. "These will be the ways of the king who will reign over you: he will take sons and appoint them to his chariots . . . he will take your daughters to be perfumers and cooks and bakers . . . he will take one-tenth of your grain and your vineyards and give it to his officers and courtiers . . . and one-tenth of your flocks, and you shall be his slaves." But the people refused to listen, and Samuel said to the people, "Each of you return to his home."

Then Samuel brought all the tribes of Israel near, and the tribe of Benjamin was chosen by lot. He brought the tribe of Benjamin near, [organized] by its families . . . and Saul the son of Kish was chosen by lot. But when they sought him, he could not be found. So they inquired again of the Lord . . . and the Lord said, "See, he has hidden himself among the baggage." Then they ran and brought him from there. When he took his stand among the people, he was head and shoulders taller than any of them. Samuel said, "You see the one whom the Lord has chosen? There is no one like him among the people." And the people all shouted, "Long live the king!" Samuel told the people the rights and duties of the kingship; and he wrote them in a book and laid it up before the Lord.

---

tribute from various kingdoms that had not paid up for generations. Those who refused fell victim to his armies.

When Tiglath-Pileser III died in 727 B.C.E., many of these recently conquered states rebelled, but Tiglath-Pileser's son, Shalmeneser V, energetically crushed them. When he died in battle, he was quickly replaced by one of his military commanders, who took the name Sargon II (722–705 B.C.E.) and claimed to be the direct successor of Sargon of Akkad, the great king of Sumer and the first great king in Mesopotamian history, nearly 1,500 years earlier (see Chapter 1). Like the Hebrews, then, Sargon

and his successors skillfully deployed history as a political tool. Eventually, they extended the frontiers of the Assyrian Empire from western Iran to the shores of the Mediterranean. Briefly, they even subjugated parts of Egypt. Sargon himself put an end to the kingdom of Israel in 722, enslaving and deporting most of the population, and he terrified the southern kingdom of Judah into remaining a loyal and quiet vassal. The ancient kingdom of Elam on the Iranian plateau—a civilization almost as old as Sumer—also fell during this period. By the seventh century B.C.E., Assyria was the unrivaled power of the ancient Near East.

1 Samuel 9:1–10:1

There was a man of Benjamin whose name was Kish . . . [who] had a son whose name was Saul, a handsome young man . . . he stood head and shoulders above everyone else. Now the donkeys of Kish had strayed. So Kish said to his son Saul, "Take one of the boys with you; go and look for the donkeys." . . . As they were entering [a] town, they saw Samuel coming out toward them on his way up to the shrine. Now the day before Saul came, the Lord revealed to Samuel, "Tomorrow about this time I will send you a man from the land of Benjamin, and you shall anoint him to be ruler over my people Israel. He shall save my people from the hand of the Philistines; for I have seen the suffering of my people, because their outcry has come to me." . . . Saul approached Samuel inside the gate and said, "Tell me please, where is the house of the seer?" Samuel answered Saul, "I am the seer, go up before me to the shrine. . . . As for your donkeys that were lost three days ago, give no further thought to them, for they have been found. And on whom is all Israel's desire fixed, if not on you and your ancestral house?" Saul answered, "I am only a Benjaminite, from the least of the tribes of Israel, and my family is the humblest of all the families of the tribe of Benjamin. Why then have you spoken of me this way?" . . . As they were going down to the outskirts of town, Samuel said to Saul, "Tell the boy to go on before us . . . that I may make known to you the word of God." Samuel took a vial of oil and poured it on [Saul's] head and kissed him; he said: "The Lord has anointed you ruler over his people Israel. You shall reign over the people of the Lord and you will save them from the hand of their enemies all around."

Source: *The New Oxford Annotated Bible* (Oxford: 1994) (slightly adapted, source for both documents).

Questions for Analysis

1. Do these two accounts fit together? How do they differ? Why would both have been preserved in the Book of Samuel?

2. What view of kingship emerges in the first account? What are the attributes of a king, and what is the relationship between the king, his god, and the priest anointing him? What is the role of the people in his selection?

3. The writers of Jewish scripture judged kings by their observance of the law, their zeal in fighting against competing religious cults, and their support of centralized worship at the temple in Jerusalem. How did this form of theocracy in ancient Israel compare to that in Egypt and Mesopotamia?

Neo-Assyrian Government and Administration

The Neo-Assyrian Empire was a military dictatorship, built on the ability of its army to spread terror and oppress both enemies and subjects alike. At its head was a hereditary monarch regarded as the earthly representative of the Assyrians' patron god, Assur. When his army was not in the field, the king's time was taken up with elaborate sacrifices and rituals to appease the "great god." Divination and the consultation of oracles were central features of this religion, because the Neo-Assyrian king—as chief priest—had to be able to discern the will of Assur through the portents of nature.

Supporting the empire's centralized authority was an extensive bureaucracy of governors, high priests, and military commanders—professions by no means mutually exclusive. These administrators formed the highest class in Neo-Assyrian society and exercised local authority on

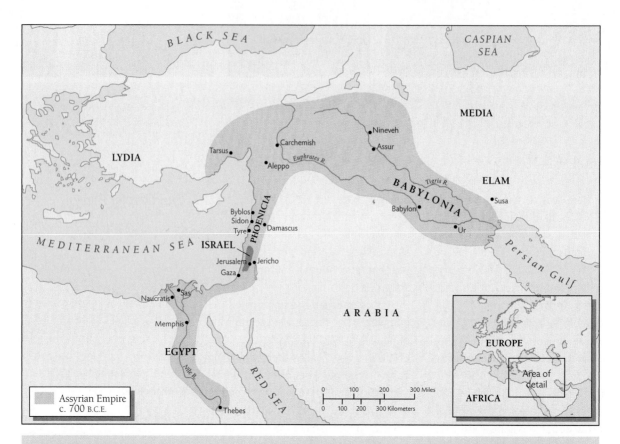

THE NEO-ASSYRIAN EMPIRE, C. 700 B.C.E. ▪ *What were the territorial boundaries of the Neo-Assyrian Empire?* ▪ *Why would the Assyrians concentrate their efforts in the river valleys and along the coast, neglecting the Syrian interior?* ▪ *Notice the location of the Neo-Assyrian capitals of Nineveh and Assur; how was their situation in Mesopotamia likely to affect the Assyrians' sense of their own historical identity?* ▪ *Consider the position of Egypt. Why might the Assyrians find it difficult to subjugate Egypt permanently?*

behalf of the king. They maintained lines of transport and communication, which were the engines of imperial hegemony, and they oversaw construction of an extensive network of roads across the Near East that served these needs for centuries. The Neo-Assyrian state also deployed a system of spies and messengers to report to the royal court on the activities of subjects and provincial governors.

These provincial governors collected tribute, recruited for the army, and administered the king's law. Not surprising for a people so mindful of historical precedent, the Assyrians modeled their laws on the code of Hammurabi, though many of their penalties were more severe. The harshest punishments were reserved for practices deemed detrimental to human reproduction; the penalties for homosexuality and abortion were particularly harsh. Neo-Assyrian law was also rigidly patriarchal, which entailed substantial revision of Hammurabi's code: now only husbands had the power of divorce, and they were legally permitted to inflict a variety of penalties on their wives, ranging from corporal punishment to mutilation and death.

The Assyrian Military-Religious Ethos

The Assyrians' new religious, political, and military ideology had taken shape during the long centuries when they fought for survival, and it then became the foundational ethos for their empire's relentless conquests. Its two fundamental tenets were the waging of holy war and the exaction of tribute through terror.

The Neo-Assyrians were convinced that their god demanded the constant expansion of his worship through military conquest. Essentially, their army belonged to Assur, and all who did not accept Assur's supremacy were, by that fact alone, enemies of Assur's people. Ritual humiliation of a defeated city's gods was therefore a regular feature of conquest. Statues of conquered gods would be carried off to the Neo-Assyrian capital, where they would remain as hostages at the court of Assur. Meanwhile, an image of Assur himself—usually represented as a sun disk with the head and shoulders of an archer—would be installed in the defeated city, and the conquered people would be required to worship him. Although conquered peoples did not have to abandon their previous gods altogether, they were made to feel their gods' inferiority. The Assyrians were therefore strict henotheists, meaning that they acknowledged the existence of other gods but believed that one god should be the supreme deity of all peoples.

For the Neo-Assyrians, "receiving tribute" meant the taking of plunder. Rather than defeating their foes once and imposing formal obligations, the Assyrians raided even their vanquished foes each year. This strategy kept the Neo-Assyrian military machine primed for battle, but it did little to inspire loyalty among subject peoples, who often felt that they had nothing to lose through rebellion. Moreover, annual invasions toughened the forces of the Neo-Assyrians' subjects. To counter them, imperial battle tactics became notoriously savage—even by the standards of ancient warfare, which regarded the mutilation of prisoners, systematic rape, and mass deportations as com-monplace. Neo-Assyrian artwork and inscriptions often celebrate the butchering and torture of their enemies. Smiling archers are shown shooting fleeing enemies in the back while remorseless soldiers impale captives on stakes.

The Neo-Assyrian army was not a seasonal army of part-time warriors or peasant conscripts, but rather a massive standing force of more than 100,000 soldiers. Because the Assyrians had mastered iron-smelting techniques on a large scale, they could equip their fighting men with high-quality steel weapons that overwhelmed opponents still reliant on bronze. The organization of this army also contributed to its success. At its core were heavily armed and armored shock troops, equipped with a variety of thrusting weapons and bearing tall shields for protection. They were the main force for crushing enemy infantry in the field and for routing the inhabitants of an enemy city once inside. To harass enemy infantry and break up their formations, the Assyrians deployed light skirmishers with slings and javelins, and they combined archery and chariotry as never before. They also developed the first true cavalry force in the West, with individual warriors mounted on armored steeds, wielding bows and arrows or heavy lances. They even trained a highly skilled corps of combat engineers to undermine city walls and to build catapults, siege engines, battering rams, and battle towers.

NEO-ASSYRIAN ATROCITIES. Judean captives whose city has fallen to the Neo-Assyrian king Sennacherib (704–681 B.C.E.) are shown being impaled on stakes. This triumphal carving comes from the walls of Sennacherib's palace at Nineveh. ▪ *What would be the purpose of advertising these captives' fates?*

The Legacy of Neo-Assyrian Power

The successors of Sargon II continued these military policies while devoting great energy to promoting an Assyrian cultural legacy. Sargon's immediate successor Sennacherib (*sen-AH-sher-ib*, 704–681 B.C.E.) rebuilt the ancient Assyrian city of Nineveh, fortifying it with a double wall for a circuit of nine miles. He constructed an enormous palace there, raised on a giant platform decorated with marble, ivory, and exotic woods; and he ordered the construction of a massive irrigation system, including an aqueduct that carried fresh water to the city from thirty miles away. His son rebuilt the conquered city of Babylon along similar lines, and was also a patron of the arts and sciences. His grandson Assurbanipal (*ah-sur-BAHN-en-pahl*, r. 669–627 B.C.E.) was perhaps the greatest of all the Neo-Assyrian kings. For a time, he ruled the entire delta region of northern Egypt. He also enacted a series of internal reforms, seeking ways to govern his empire more peacefully.

By Neo-Assyrian standards, Assurbanipal was an enlightened ruler, and one to whom we owe a tremendous debt. Like Sargon II before him, he had a strong sense of the rich traditions of Mesopotamian history and laid claim

ASSURBANIPAL FEASTING WITH HIS WIFE IN A HANGING GARDEN. Even in this peaceful, domestic scene, the severed head of the king's recently defeated enemy, the king of Elam, can be seen hanging from the pine tree on the left.

to it. But he did this much more systematically: he ordered the construction of a magnificent library at the great capital of Nineveh, where all the cultural monuments of Mesopotamian literature were to be copied and preserved. This library also served as an archive for the correspondence and official acts of the king. Fortunately, this trove of documentation has survived. Our knowledge of history, not to mention all modern editions of the *Epic of Gilgamesh*, derive from the library at Nineveh.

When Assurbanipal died in 627 B.C.E., the Neo-Assyrian Empire appeared to be at its zenith. Its borders were secure, the realm was largely at peace with its neighbors, its kings had adorned their capitals with magnificent artwork, and the hanging gardens of Babylon were already famous: these were artificial slopes whose cascading flowers and trees were fed by irrigation systems that pumped water uphill, an amazing marriage of engineering and horticulture. The collapse of this empire is therefore all the more dramatic for its suddenness. Within fifteen years of Assurbanipal's reign, Nineveh lay in ruins. An alliance had formed between the Indo-European Medes of Iran and the Chaldeans, a Semitic people who controlled the southern half of Babylonia. By 605 B.C.E., the Chaldeans had occupied Babylon and destroyed the last remnants of Neo-Assyrian power on the upper Euphrates, becoming the predominant imperial power in Mesopotamia and the Levant. In 586 B.C.E., they captured Jerusalem, destroyed the Temple, and deported the population of Judea to Babylon. Meanwhile, the Medes retired to the Iranian Plateau to extend their suzerainty there.

THE RISE OF THE PERSIANS

In the sixth century B.C.E., the Persian Empire emerged as the successor state to the Neo-Assyrian kings. This was after the region had been ruled for a few decades by the Chaldean Empire (612–539 B.C.E.) and the Lydian kingdom. Once the Persians had thrown off the Chaldeans' dominance, they would in turn construct the largest empire known to the world until that time.

The Persian Empire of Cyrus the Great

The Persians came to power relatively suddenly, under an extraordinary prince named Cyrus who succeeded to the rule of a single Persian tribe in 559 B.C.E. Shortly thereafter, Cyrus made himself ruler of all the Persians and then, around 549 B.C.E., challenged the lordship of the Medes and began to claim dominion over lands stretching from the Persian Gulf to the Halys River in Asia Minor.

This brought the Persians into close contact with the kingdom of Lydia. The Lydians had attained great prosperity as producers of gold and silver specie and as intermediaries for overland commerce between Mesopotamia and the Aegean. Most important, they were the first people in the ancient Near East to use precious-metal coinage as a medium of exchange for goods and services. When Cyrus came to power, their king was Croesus (*CREE-suhs*), a man whose reputation as the possessor of untold riches survives in the expression "rich as Croesus." Distrusting his new neighbor, Croesus decided to launch a preventive strike against the Persians in order to preserve his own kingdom from conquest. According to the Greek historian Herodotus, he took the precaution of asking the oracle of Apollo at Delphi whether this strategy was a good one, and was told that if he attacked the Persians he would destroy a great nation. The oracle's pronouncement was both ambiguous and true: the nation Croesus destroyed was his own. Cyrus defeated his forces in 546 B.C.E.

Cyrus then invaded Mesopotamia in 539 B.C.E., striking so quickly that he took Babylon without a fight. Once he was in Babylon, the entire Chaldean Empire was his for the taking, though his own imperial policies proved very different from those of his predecessors in that region. Cyrus freed the Hebrews who had been held captive in Babylon since 586 B.C.E. and sent them back to Jerusalem, helping them to rebuild their temple and allowing them to set up a semi-independent vassal state. Cyrus also allowed other conquered peoples considerable self-determination, especially with respect to cultural and religious practices— a marked reversal of Neo-Assyrian and Chaldean policies. When Cyrus died in battle in 530 B.C.E., Persian expansion continued and his son even conquered Egypt in 525 B.C.E. Two hundred years later, a young Macedonian king, Alexander, would emulate many of Cyrus's policies and build an empire sustained by many of the same strategies (see Chapter 4).

AN EARLY LYDIAN COIN. Probably struck during the reign of Croesus, this coin was one of many that facilitated long-distance trade by making wealth portable.

The Consolidation of Persian Rule

Cyrus's son Cambyses II was a warrior king like his father, but after his death he left the Persian Empire a cumbersome and poorly organized collection of rapid conquests. After a short period of civil war, the aristocratic inner circle that had served both him and his father settled on a collateral member of the royal family as the new king. This was Darius, whose long reign of thirty-five years (521–486 B.C.E.) consolidated his predecessors' military gains by improving the administration of the Persian state. Darius divided the empire into provinces, each of which was administered by an official called a *satrap*. Although satraps enjoyed extensive powers and considerable political latitude, they owed fixed tributes and absolute loyalty to the central government, as did vassal states such as the technically autonomous Hebrew kingdom.

Adhering to the tolerant policy of Cyrus, Darius allowed the various peoples of the empire to retain most of their local institutions while enforcing a standardized central currency and a system of weights and measures. Beyond this, he had little interest in imposing onerous taxes, martial law, or the Persians' own religious practices on subject peoples. After centuries of Neo-Assyrian and Chaldean tyranny, the light hand of Persian rule was welcomed throughout the empire's far-reaching lands.

Darius was also a great builder. He erected a new royal residence and ceremonial capital which the Greeks called Persepolis ("Persia City"). He ordered a canal dug from the Nile to the Red Sea to facilitate trade with the Egyptian interior, and installed irrigation systems on the Persian plateau and on the fringe of the Syrian desert to increase agricultural production. Darius also expanded the existing Assyrian road system to enhance trade and communications throughout his huge realm. The most famous artery was the Royal Road, stretching 1,600 miles from Susa, near the Persian Gulf, to Sardis (the former Lydian capital) near the Aegean. Government couriers along this road constituted the first postal system, carrying messages and goods in relay stages from one post to another. Each post was a day's horseback ride from the next, where a fresh horse and rider would be ready to carry the dispatches brought by the postman before him. An extensive imperial spy network also used this postal system and was famed throughout Persia as "the eyes and ears of the king."

Darius was an extraordinarily gifted administrator, but as a military strategist he made an enormous mistake when he attempted to extend Persian hegemony into Greece. Cyrus's conquest of Lydia had made Persia the ruler of some long-established Greek-speaking cities on the western coast of Asia Minor, a region called Ionia. But these cities resisted

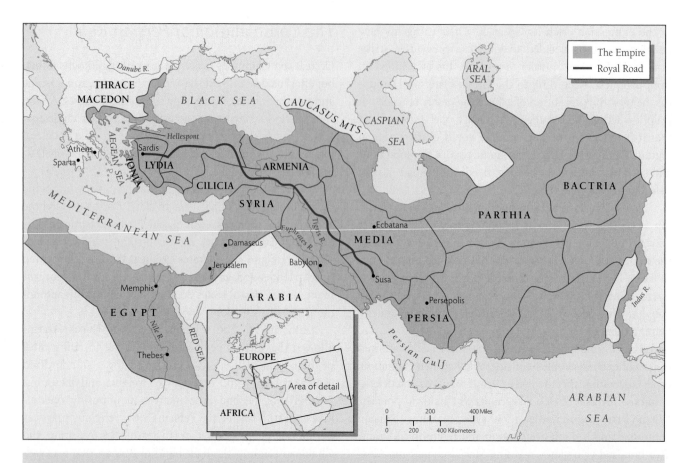

THE PERSIAN EMPIRE UNDER DARIUS I, 521–486 B.C.E. Consider the location of the Persian heartland and the four administrative centers of Persepolis, Susa, Ecbatana, and Sardis. ▪ *What older kingdoms and empires did the Persian Empire contain?* ▪ *Why is the Royal Road especially noted on this map?* ▪ *How did Darius I successfully rule such a large and complex empire?*

even the easy terms of Persian rule, desiring instead to model themselves on the self-governing city-states that had come into being across the Aegean. Consequently, between 499 and 494 B.C.E., the Greeks of Asia waged a war for independence and briefly gained the support of troops from Athens, who joined the Greeks of Ionia in burning the Persian administrative center at Sardis. Darius quelled this uprising and then decided to send a force to punish Athens and serve notice of Persian dominion over all Greek states. But at the battle of Marathon in 490 B.C.E., the Athenians dealt Darius the only major setback of his reign. And when his son and successor, Xerxes (ZEhRK-zees), attempted to avenge this humiliation in 480 B.C.E., a resistance led by both Athens and Sparta forced him to retreat and abandon his plans a year later. (We will discuss these events at greater length in Chapter 3.)

The Persians were thus compelled to recognize that they had reached the westward limits of their expansion. Thereafter, they concentrated on their Asian possessions and used money and diplomacy to keep the Greeks in check. This was not difficult, because the Greeks' hasty union in the face of Persian hegemony was short-lived, and they were too

embroiled in wars with one another to pose any threat to Persia.

The richness of their culture and the general tolerance they exhibited served the Persians well in maintaining their enormous empire. Unlike the Neo-Assyrian or Chaldean rulers, the Persians could count on the loyalty and even the affection of their subjects. In fact, their imperial model— the accommodation of local institutions and practices, consistent administration through a trained bureaucracy, and rapid communications between center and periphery— would be the one adopted by the great and lasting empires of all subsequent Western civilizations.

The Legacy of Zoroastrianism

The Persians' political and cultural achievements were paralleled by a spiritual one: Zoroastrianism. This important religion was one of the three major universal faiths known to the world before Christianity and Islam, along with Buddhism and Judaism. Its founder was Zarathustra, known

A CYLINDRICAL SEAL OF DARIUS THE GREAT (522–486 B.C.E.). Seals were used in place of signatures to authenticate documents and correspondence. The cylindrical matrix (right) was rolled in soft wax to create an impression. This finely wrought example shows the king in a chariot, hunting lions with a bow. A winged representation of the god Ahura-Mazda rises above the scene.

to the Greeks as Zoroaster, a Persian who probably lived shortly before 600 B.C.E. Zarathustra sought to reform the traditional customs of the Persian tribes by eradicating polytheism, animal sacrifice, and magic. That is, he wanted to redefine religion as an ethical practice common to all people, rather than a set of rituals and superstitions that caused divisions among people.

Zoroastrianism teaches that there is one supreme god in the universe, whom Zarathustra called Ahura-Mazda, "Wise Lord." Ahura-Mazda is the essence of light, truth, and righteousness; there is nothing wrathful or wicked about him, and his goodness extends to everyone, not just to one people or tribe. How, then, can there be evil and suffering in the world? Because, Zarathustra posited, there is a counter-deity, Ahriman, treacherous and malignant, who rules the forces of darkness. Yet Zarathustra also posited that Ahura-Mazda must be vastly stronger than Ahriman. Later teachers and priests of Zoroastrianism, the magi, placed greater emphasis on the dualism of these divine forces: they insisted that Ahura-Mazda and Ahriman are evenly matched, engaged in a desperate and eternal struggle for supremacy. According to them, light will not triumph over darkness until the Last Day, when the forces of Ahura-Mazda vanquish those of Ahriman forever. This vision of the universe would prove enormously influential, informing the developing theologies of Christianity

and Islam—not to mention the plots of much modern science fiction, fantasy literature, and film.

The devotion of the Persian imperial dynasty to Zarathustra's teachings made Zoroastrianism important to the conduct of Persian government and helps to explain the tolerance of Persian rule. Unlike the Neo-Assyrians, the Chaldeans, or even the Egyptians, the Persian kings saw themselves as presiding over an assemblage of different nations whose customs and beliefs they were prepared to tolerate. Whereas Mesopotamian potentates characteristically called themselves "true king," Persian rulers took the title "king of kings" or "great king," implying that they recognized the legitimacy of other kings who ruled under their canopy. This same spirit is reflected in Persian architecture, which drew freely and creatively on Sumerian, Babylonian, Assyrian, Egyptian, and Greek influences yet nonetheless created a distinctively Persian style.

Unlike other ancient religions, then, Zoroastrianism did not exalt the power of a godlike king or support any particular political regime. It was a personal religion, making private, spiritual demands as opposed to public, ritual ones. Its Wise Lord supports neither tribes nor states but only individuals who serve the cause of truth and justice. These individuals possess free will and can choose to sin or not to sin; they are not compelled by an array of conflicting gods to act in particular ways. Zoroastrianism thus urges its adherents

Two Perspectives on Imperial Rule

> These two inscriptions exemplify two very different attitudes toward imperial power and two very different methods of achieving it. The first glorifies the victories of the Assyrian king Esarhaddon in Syria and is one of the most important records of his reign (681–669 B.C.E.). The second commemorates the taking of Babylon by the Persian king Cyrus the Great (c. 559–530 B.C.E.), whose empire came to encompass and surpass that of the Assyrians.

The *Stele* of King Esarhaddon at Senjirli, c. 680 B.C.E.

To Assur, father of the gods, lover of my priesthood, Anu mighty and preeminent, who called me by name, Ba'al, the exalted lord, establisher of my dynasty, Ea, the wise, all-knowing . . . Ishtar, lady of battle and combat, who goes at my side . . . all of them who determine my destiny, who grant to the king, their favorite, power and might . . . the king, the offering of whose sacrifices the great gods love . . . their unsparing weapons they have presented him as a royal gift . . . [he] who has brought all the lands in submission at his feet, who has imposed tribute and tax upon them; conqueror of his foes, destroyer of his enemies, the king, who

as to his walk is a storm, and as to his deeds, a raging wolf; . . . the onset of his battle is powerful, he is a consuming flame, a fire that does not sink: son of Sennacherib, king of the universe, king of Assyria, grandson of Sargon, king of the universe, king of Assyria, viceroy of Babylon, king of Sumer and Akkad. . . . I am powerful, I am all-powerful, I am a hero, I am gigantic, I am colossal, I am honored, I am magnified, I am without an equal among all kings, the chosen one of Assur . . . the great lord [who], in order to show to the peoples the immensity of my mighty deeds, made powerful my kingship over the four regions of the world and made my name great.

. . . Of Tirhakah, king of Egypt and Kush, the accursed . . . without cessation I slew multitudes of his men, and him I smote five times with the point of my javelin, with wounds, no recovery. Memphis, his royal city, in half a day . . . I besieged, I captured, I destroyed, I devastated, I burned with fire. . . . The root of Kush I tore up out of Egypt and not one therein escaped to submit to me.

Source: Daniel David Luckenbill, ed., *Ancient Records of Assyria and Babylonia*, Vol. 2 (Chicago: 1926–27), pp. 224–27.

Inscription Honoring Cyrus, c. 539

He [the god Marduk] scanned and looked (through) all the countries, searching for a righteous ruler who would lead him. (Then) he pronounced the name of Cyrus, king of Anshan [Persia], declared him to be the leader of the world. . . . And he (Cyrus) did always endeavor to treat according to justice the black-headed [people] whom he (Marduk) made him conquer. Marduk, the great lord, a protector of his people/worshipers, beheld with pleasure his good deeds and his upright mind, (and therefore) ordered

him to march against his city Babylon. He made him set out on the road to Babylon, going at his side like a real friend. His widespread troops—their number, like the water of a river, could not be established—strolled along, their weapons packed away. Without any battle, he made them enter his town Babylon, sparing Babylon any calamity. He delivered into his hands Nabonidus, the king who did not worship him. All the inhabitants of Babylon as well as of the entire country of Sumer and Akkad, princes and governors (included), bowed to him

and kissed his feet, jubilant that he (had received) the kingship, and with shining faces. Happily they greeted him as a master through whose help they had come (again) to life from death (and) had all been spared damage and disaster, and they worshiped his name.

I am Cyrus, king of the world, great king, legitimate king, king of Babylon, king of Sumer and Akkad, king of the four rims (of the earth), son of Cambyses, great king, king of Anshan, grandson of Cyrus, great king, king of Anshan, descendent of Teipes, great king, king of

Anshan, of a family (which) always (exercised) kingship; whose rule Bel and Nebo love, whom they want as king to please their hearts.

When I entered Babylon as a friend and (when) I established the seat of the government in the palace of the ruler under jubilation and rejoicing.... My numerous troops walked around Babylon in peace, I did not allow anybody to terrorize (any place) of the (the country of Sumer) and Akkad. I strove for peace in Babylon and in all his (other) sacred cities....I abolished the...[yoke] which was against their (social) standing, I brought relief to their dilapidated housing, putting (thus) an end to their (main) complaints.... All the kings of the entire world from the Upper to the Lower Sea, those who are seated in throne rooms, (those who) live in other (types of buildings as well as) all the kings of the West living in tents, brought their heavy tributes and kissed my feet in Babylon.

Source: Excerpted from James B. Pritchard, ed. *Ancient Near Eastern Texts Relating to the Old Testament*, 3rd ed. (Princeton, NJ: 1969), pp. 315–16.

Questions for Analysis

1. Both of these inscriptions constitute propaganda, but of different kinds. How do they differ? What audience(s) are they addressing? What function(s) does each inscription serve?

2. Each of these rulers claims to have a close relationship with the divine. How do those relationships differ, and what do those differences reveal about their attitudes to kingship and its sources of power?

3. Both of these kings boast of their royal lineage and their connections to past rulers. How different or similar are these perspectives? What do they reveal about these kings' awareness of history?

to choose good over evil, to be truthful, to love and help one another to the best of their powers, to aid the poor, and to practice generous hospitality. Those who do so will be rewarded in an afterlife, when the dead are resurrected on Judgment Day and consigned either to a realm of joy or to the flames of despair. In the scriptures of the Zoroastrian faith, known as the Avesta (compiled, like the Bible, over the course of many centuries), the rewards for righteousness are great but not immediate. They are spiritual, not material.

THE DEVELOPMENT OF HEBREW MONOTHEISM

Of all the important developments that we have traced in our study of the Iron Age Near East, perhaps none is of greater significance than monotheism: the belief in a single god, the creator and ruler of all things. This development is traditionally associated with the Hebrews, but even the Hebrews were not always monotheists. Those who argued for the exclusive worship of Yahweh were a minority within Hebrew society, albeit a vocal and assertive one. How the Hebrews came to regard Yahweh as the only divine being in the universe, and to root their identity in such an exclusive religious outlook, is a phenomenon that can only be understood within its historical context.

From Monolatry to Monotheism

For those who later advocated the exclusive worship of Yahweh, the early history of the Hebrews was full of embarrassments. Even the Hebrew scriptures reveal their propensity for the worship of many gods. Yahweh himself, in commanding that his people "have no other gods before me," clearly acknowledged the existence of other gods. The older, polytheistic Hebrew religion honored nature spirits such as Azazel and the Canaanite deity El, whose name is an important element in many Hebrew place-names (for example, Bethel) and soon became a synonym for "god." The temple built by Solomon at Jerusalem had even included altars dedicated to Ba'al and his wife Asherah, a fertility goddess. Later Hebrew kings continued such practices, overriding the protests of religious purists devoted to Yahweh.

By the beginning of the first millennium, however, the Hebrews living under the rule of David began to promote monolatry, meaning that they exalted one god without denying the existence of others. Although the legendary prophet Moses is often credited as the first promoter of Yahweh's cult, sometime around the middle of the second millennium B.C.E., the ascendancy of Yahweh really took place much later, under the influence of the Levites, a tribe who claimed unique priestly authority over Yahwah's worship and sought to enhance their own power and prestige by discrediting other gods.

The success of their campaign rested on the Levites' access to writing. As we have frequently noted, the written word was especially potent in the ancient world because the skills necessary for its mastery were rare. In an age of constant threats to Hebrew religious and political sovereignty, the literacy of the Levites thus helped to preserve and promote Yahweh's worship. So did the political supremacy of David's dynasty, which bolstered its own legitimacy by allying itself with the Levites. The result was a centralized cult situated in the new royal capital of Jerusalem, which attempted to link the political and the religious identity of the Hebrews to the acknowledgment of Yahweh as the supreme god.

Nevertheless, the worship of other Hebrew gods actually increased in the eighth and seventh centuries B.C.E., perhaps in reaction to the austere morality demanded and imposed by the Yahwists. One of these, Jeremiah (c. 637–587 B.C.E.), railed against "foreign" cults and warned of the disastrous consequences that would arise if Yahweh's people did not remain faithful to him. For the Yahweh of this era was still imagined as a conventional god. He was understood as possessing a physical body and was often portrayed as capricious and irascible. Further, he was not omnipotent; his power was largely confined to the territory occupied by the Hebrews.

Still, some of the Hebrews' most important contributions to subsequent Western religions crystallized during this period. One was a theology of Yahweh's transcendence: the teaching that God is not part of nature but exists outside of it. God can therefore be understood, in purely intellectual or abstract terms, as entirely separate from the operations of the natural world. Complementing this principle was the belief that Yahweh had appointed humans to be the rulers of nature by divine mandate. In the book of Genesis, when Yahweh orders Adam and Eve to "replenish the earth and subdue it, and have dominion over . . . every living thing," his injunction stands in striking contrast to other accounts of creation in which humans are made to serve the gods. Finally, Hebrew religious thought was moving in this period toward the articulation of universal ethics—a universal theory of justice and righteousness. According to the Babylonian flood story, for example, a particularly petulant god destroys humanity because their noise deprives him of sleep.

In Genesis, by contrast, Yahweh sends a flood in punishment for human wickedness but saves Noah and his family because "Noah was a just man."

The Hebrews honored Yahweh during this era by subscribing to certain moral precepts and taboos. The Ten Commandments as they now appear in Exodus 20:3–17 may not yet have existed in that exact form, but they certainly reflect earlier ethical injunctions against murder, adultery, lying, and greed. In addition, the Hebrews observed an array of ritual practices unusual in the ancient world, such as infant circumcision, adherence to strict dietary laws, and refraining from labor on the seventh day of the week.

Yet the moral standards imposed by Yahweh on the Hebrew community were not binding when the Hebrews dealt with outsiders. Lending at interest, for example, was not acceptable among Hebrews but was quite acceptable between a Hebrew and a non-Hebrew. Such distinctions applied also to more serious issues, such as the killing of

THE GODDESS ASHERAH. The Canaanite fertility goddess, Asherah, was the wife of the god Ba'al (or his father, El), but she also figures in some inscriptions as the wife of the Hebrew god Yahweh. One Hebrew king placed an image of her in the temple of Yahweh at Jerusalem. ■ *Why would this be viewed as controversial?*

civilians in battle. When the Hebrews conquered territories in Canaan, they took "all the spoil of the cities, and every man they smote with the sword . . . until they had destroyed them." Far from having any doubts about such a brutal policy, the Hebrews believed that Yahweh had inspired the Canaanites to resist so that the Hebrews could slaughter them: "For it was the Lord's doing to harden their hearts that they should come against Israel in battle, in order that they should be utterly destroyed, and should receive no mercy but be exterminated" (Joshua 11:20).

With the political fragmentation of the Hebrew kingdoms after Solomon's death, important regional distinctions arose within Yahweh's cult. As mentioned above, the rulers of the northern kingdom discouraged their citizens from participating in ritual activities at Jerusalem, thereby earning the disapproval of the Jerusalem-based Yahwists who shaped the biblical tradition. The erosion of a cohesive Hebrew identity was further accelerated by the Neo-Assyrians, who under Sargon II absorbed the northern kingdom as a province and enslaved nearly 28,000 Hebrews. The southern kingdom of Judah survived, but political collaboration with the Neo-Assyrians also meant acceptance of the god Assur.

This Neo-Assyrian threat was the whetstone on which the Yahwist prophets sharpened their demands for an exclusive monotheism that went beyond monolatry. Hebrew prophets were practical political leaders as well as religious figures, and most of them understood that military resistance to the Neo-Assyrians was futile. So if the Hebrews were to survive as a people, they had to emphasize the one thing that separated them from everyone else in the known world: the worship of Yahweh and the denial of all other gods. The prophets' insistence that Yahweh alone should be exalted was thus an aggressive reaction to the equally aggressive promotion of Assur by the Neo-Assyrians.

The foremost Hebrew prophets of this era were Amos and Hosea, who preached in the kingdom of Israel before it fell to the Neo-Assyrians in 722 B.C.E.; Isaiah and Jeremiah, who preached in Judah before its fall in 586 B.C.E.; and Ezekiel and the "second Isaiah" (the Book of Isaiah had at least two different authors), who continued to preach "by the waters of Babylon" during the Hebrews' exile there. Despite some differences in emphasis, these prophets' messages consistently emphasize three core doctrines.

RECONSTRUCTION OF THE ISHTAR GATE. This is a reconstruction of one of the fifty-foot-high entrance gates built into the walls of Babylon by King Nebuchadnezzar around 575 B.C.E. About half of this reconstruction in the Pergamon Museum of Berlin, is original.

1. Yahweh is the ruler of the universe. He even makes use of peoples other than the Hebrews to accomplish his purposes. The gods of other nations are false gods. There has never been and never will be more than this one god.
2. Yahweh is exclusively a god of righteousness. He wills only the good, and evil in the world comes from humanity, not from him.
3. Because Yahweh is righteous, he demands ethical behavior from his people. Over and above ritual and sacrifice, he requires that his followers "seek justice, relieve the oppressed, protect the fatherless, and plead for the widow."

The prophet Amos summarized these teachings when he expressed Yahweh's resounding warning in the eighth century B.C.E.:

I hate, I despise your feasts, and I take no delight in your solemn assemblies. Even though you offer me your burnt offerings and cereal offerings, I will not accept them, and the peace offerings of your fatted beasts I will not look upon. Take away from me the noise of your songs; to the melody of your harps I will not listen. But let justice roll down like waters, and righteousness like an ever-flowing stream. (Amos 5:21–24)

Judaism Takes Shape

Through their insistence on monotheism as the cornerstone of Hebrew identity, the Yahwists made it possible for the Hebrews to survive under Neo-Assyrian domination. And as this threat receded in the late seventh century B.C.E., so the Yahwists triumphed religiously and politically. The king of Judah during the waning years of the Neo-Assyrian Empire, Josiah (621–609 B.C.E.), was a committed monotheist whose court employed prominent prophets, including Jeremiah. With his own power increasing, Josiah found himself in a position to pursue significant reforms. He presided over the redrafting and revision of the "Law of Moses" to bring it into line with current policies, and it was during his reign that the Book of Deuteronomy was "discovered" and hailed as Moses's "Second Law." Deuteronomy is the most stridently monotheistic book of the Hebrew Bible, and it lent weight to this new political program.

But within a generation of King Josiah's death, the Chaldeans under Nebuchadnezzar conquered Jerusalem, destroyed the Temple, and carried thousands of Hebrews off to Babylon in 587/586 B.C.E. This Babylonian Captivity brought many challenges, paramount among them the maintenance of the Hebrews' hard-won religious identity. The leading voices in defining that identity continued to be the patriotic Yahwists, the same people who would later spearhead the return to Palestine after Cyrus captured Babylon and liberated the Hebrews two generations later. Among the Yahwists, the prophet Ezekiel stressed that salvation could be found only through religious purity, which meant ignoring all foreign gods and acknowledging only Yahweh. Kingdoms and states and empires came to nothing in the long run, Ezekiel said. What mattered for those living in exile was the creature God had made in his image—man—and the relationship between God and his creation.

This period of captivity and exile was therefore decisive in forging a universal religion that transcended politics. Just as Yahweh existed outside creation, so the people who worshiped him could exist outside of a Hebrew kingdom. In Babylon, the worship of Yahweh therefore became something different; it became Judaism, a religion that was not tied to any particular political system or territory—for after 586 B.C.E., there was neither a Hebrew ruling class nor a Hebrew state. Outside of Judah, Judaism paradoxically flourished. This was an unparalleled achievement in the ancient world: the survival of a religion that had no political power to back it and no holy place to ground it.

After 538 B.C.E., when Cyrus permitted the Hebrews of Babylon to return to their lands and to rebuild the Temple, Jerusalem became once again the central holy place of Hebrew religious life. But the new developments that had fashioned Judaism during captivity would prove lasting, despite the religious conflicts that soon erupted. These conflicts led to ever more specific assertions about the nature of Judaism, and to religious teachings that focused on ethical conduct as an obligation owed by all human beings toward their creator, independent of place or political identity. The observance of ritual requirements and religious taboos would continue,

After You Read This Chapter

Visit StudySpace for quizzes, additional review materials, and multimedia documents. **wwnorton.com/web/westernciv18**

REVIEWING THE OBJECTIVES

- The settlement of Indo-European peoples in the Near East had marked effects on the older civilizations there. What were some major consequences?

- Egypt's New Kingdom differed profoundly from the Old and Middle Kingdoms that preceded it. Why was this the case?

- The civilizations of the late Bronze Age were bound together by transnational networks. What were the strengths and fragilities of these relationships?

- What kingdoms and empires emerged in the Near East after the devastation caused by the Sea Peoples?

- Monotheism was a significant historical development of the first millennium B.C.E. Why is it so important?

but not as the essence of religious life; rather, they would be symbolic of the special relationship binding Yahweh to the Hebrews. Eventually, the transcendental monotheism that emerged from these historical processes would become common to the worldview of all Western civilizations.

CONCLUSION

The centuries between 1700 and 500 B.C.E. were an epoch of empires. While the two great powers of the second millennium were New Kingdom Egypt and the Hittite Empire in Anatolia, a host of lesser empires also coalesced during this period, including Minoan Crete, Mycenaean Greece, and the trading empire of the Assyrians. All were sustained by a sophisticated network of trade and diplomacy. But between 1200 and 1000 B.C.E. the devastation wrought by the Sea Peoples destroyed this integrated civilization. These invasions cleared the way for the emergence of many new, small states, including those of the Phoenicians, the Philistines, the Hebrews, and the Lydians. Many crucial cultural and economic developments were fostered by these small states, including alphabetic writing, coinage, mercantile colonization, and monotheism. But the dominant states of the Iron Age continued to be great land empires centered in western Asia: first that of the Neo-Assyrians, then briefly the Chaldeans, and finally the Persians.

Yet the empires of the early Iron Age were quite different from those that had dominated the Near East a thousand years before. These new empires were much more highly unified. They had capital cities, centrally managed systems of communication, sophisticated administrative structures, and ideologies that justified their aggressive imperialism. They commanded armies of unprecedented size, and they demanded from their subjects a degree of obedience impossible for any Bronze Age emperor to imagine or enforce. Their rulers declared themselves the chosen instruments of their god's divine will.

At the same time, we can trace the emergence of more personalized religions. Zoroastrian dualism and Hebrew monotheism added an important new emphasis on ethical conduct, and both pioneered the development of authoritative written scriptures that advanced religious teachings. Zoroastrianism, despite its radical re-imagining of the cosmos, proved fully compatible with imperialism and became the driving spiritual force behind the Persian Empire. Judaism, by contrast, was forged in the struggle to resist the imperialism of the Neo-Assyrians and Chaldeans. Both systems of belief would exercise enormous influence on future civilizations. In particular, they would provide the models on which Christianity and Islam would ultimately erect their own traditions, just as models of imperial governance forged in this period would become the template for future empires. In Chapter 3, we will look at the ways in which the city-states of ancient Greece both built on and departed from these models.

PEOPLE, IDEAS, AND EVENTS IN CONTEXT

- How did the Hittite Empire integrate the cultures of **INDO-EUROPEANS** with the older civilizations of this region?
- What do the reigns of **HATSHEPSUT** and **AKHENATEN** tell us about the continuities and limitations of pharaonic power?
- What factors produced the transnational networks of the Late **BRONZE AGE**?
- How did the civilizations of **MINOAN CRETE** and **MYCENAEAN GREECE** differ from one another and from the neighboring civilizations of the Near East?
- In what ways do the **PHOENICIANS**, the **PHILISTINES**, and the **HEBREWS** exemplify three different approaches to state-building at the beginning of the first millennium B.C.E.?
- What was new about the **NEO-ASSYRIAN EMPIRE**? How do its methods of conquest and its military-religious ethos compare to the **PERSIAN EMPIRE** that followed it?
- How and why did monotheism develop in the Hebrew kingdoms? In what ways might **JUDAISM** have been influenced by **ZOROASTRIANISM**?

THINKING ABOUT CONNECTIONS

- In the religions of Akhenaten, the Persians, and the Hebrews, we see a rejection of polytheism. What cultural factors may have contributed to this? What would you consider to be the long-term effects of montheism as a motivating force in history?
- What patterns of success or failure appear to be emerging when we consider the empires that flourished in the Iron Age, particularly those of the Assyrians and the Persians? Are similar patterns visible in other periods of history, including our own?

Before You Read This Chapter

The Civilization of Greece, 1000–400 B.C.E.

CORE OBJECTIVES

- **DESCRIBE** the factors that led to the emergence of the Greek polis.

- **EXPLAIN** the importance of hoplite warfare and its effects on democracy.

- **DEFINE** the key differences among the poleis of Athens, Sparta, and Miletus.

- **IDENTIFY** the ways in which Athenian culture, philosophy, and art reflect democratic ideals.

- **UNDERSTAND** the impact of the Persian and Peloponnesian Wars on Greek civilization.

n the fifth century B.C.E., a Greek-speaking subject of the Persian Empire began to write a book. He had been to Egypt and along the African coast, to the Greek colonies of Italy, the cities of Persia, the wilds of Thrace and Macedonia, and all over the Aegean. He had collected stories about peoples and places even farther afield: Ethiopia, India, the Black Sea. We have already met this intrepid traveler, Herodotus (c. 484– c. 425 B.C.E.), who marveled at the pyramids of Giza (see Chapter 1) and who told how the king of Lydia lost his power to the Persians (see Chapter 2). His reason for compiling this information was timely: he wanted to write a history of recent events. As he put it, "Herodotus of Halicarnassus here sets forth the results of his research, with the aim of preserving the remembrance of what men have done, and of preventing the great and wonderful deeds of both Greeks and barbarians from losing their glory; and in particular to examine the causes that made them fight one another."

Herodotus's fascination with the Persians, Phoenicians, and Egyptians underscores the extent to which all Greek-speakers regarded themselves as different from other ancient peoples.

75

THE ACROPOLIS OF ATHENS AND THE PARTHENON. Many Greek cities were built upon mountain strongholds, but the most famous of these is the acropolis of Athens. First settled in the Neolithic Period, it was a fortified palace during the Bronze Age—allegedly that of the hero Theseus—and then a precinct sacred to the goddess Athena, for whom the city was named. The Parthenon, its most important surviving structure, was built on the site of an older temple after the Athenian victory over the Persians at Marathon in 490 B.C.E. It was then rebuilt after the Persians sacked Athens ten years later. Most of the damage it sustained thereafter occurred during modern wars. ▪ *Why was this site the focal point of so much activity?* ▪ *What does its longevity tell us about the relationship between place and identity in Greece?*

Indeed, they had responded very differently to the Bronze Age collapse. While they struggled to cooperate politically, they were able to forge a common language and culture, and they cherished values that were distinct from those of the people they called *barbarians*: peoples whose speech, to Greek ears, sounded like jibberish ("bar-bar-bar"). They celebrated individual liberty, participatory government, artistic innovation, scientific investigation, and confidence in the creative powers of the human mind. Although the practical implementation of these ideals would prove problematic—and continues to be so—our own civilization would be unimaginable without the political experiments and cultural achievements of ancient Greece.

FROM CHAOS TO POLIS

By the end of the twelfth century B.C.E., Mycenaean civilization had vanished. Except at Athens, the great citadels that had crowned the heights of mainland kingdoms were destroyed. But even at Athens the population steadily declined, with severe effects on the economy and on social organization. Settlements shrank in size and moved inland, away from vulnerable coastlines, thus cutting themselves off from trade and communication. Indeed, the use of writing declined to such an extent that the knowledge of the system known as Linear B disappeared (see Chapter 2). Archaeological evidence suggests a world in stasis, isolated from the centers of civilization that were re-emerging in the Near East.

The material realities of life in this era profoundly shaped the civilization that emerged from it. This civilization would emphasize political equality and modest display, the importance of domestic economy and self-sufficiency: these were the principles that formed the basis of early democracies. At the same time, this new historical reality had similar long-term effects on religion and philosophy; the hardships of daily life, which contrasted sharply with the stories of a heroic and opulent past, made the Greeks suspicious of their gods. They came to rely far more on the power of individual human beings than on divine intervention in human affairs. They also developed an awareness that excessive pride in one's own accomplishments could be dangerous, because such *hubris* attracted the adverse attention of the gods. While the gods favored those who showed initiative and daring, they would punish the hubris of those who failed to acknowledge their own limitations.

Homer and the Heroic Tradition

By the year 1000 B.C.E., the chaotic conditions that had contributed to the isolation of Greece were alleviated by a period of relative peace. The standard of living improved, artisans developed their crafts, and increased contact among individual settlements fostered trade. Greek pottery, in particular, became a sophisticated and sought-after commodity, which Greek merchants could exchange for luxury goods from abroad.

As trade became an increasingly important feature of the new economy, the personal fortunes of those who engaged in trade increased accordingly, leading to a new kind of social stratification based on wealth. The men who controlled that wealth were aware that their status was not founded on warfare or noble birth, as had been the case in the distant past. Instead, they began to justify their preeminence as a reflection of their own superior qualities as "best men" (*aristoi*). Wealth was one sign of this superiority, but it was not sufficient in itself as a claim to aristocracy, which literally means "the rule of the best." Those who aspired to this status were also expected to emulate, as far as possible, the heroes of old, whose stories lived in the prodigious memories and agile voices of the singers of tales.

These singers, the guardians of a rich oral history that had never been written down, were part poets in their own right and part *rhapsodes*, "weavers of songs." The most famous of these is Homer, the poet credited with having woven together the mesh of stories that we know as the *Iliad* and the *Odyssey*. They appear to have crystallized around 800 B.C.E., at about the same time that Hesiod was working on a series of much shorter lyrics that capture a more contemporary perspective (see Chapter 2). By contrast, the epics ascribed to Homer are vast encyclopedias of lore set at the end of the Bronze Age, the time Hesiod called "the Age of Heroes." These were the days when Agamemnon had ruled in Mycenae and launched a vast expedition to conquer Troy, where the prince Paris had taken Helen, the ravishing wife of Agamemnon's brother, Menalaus; it was the age of Achilles and his Trojan rival, Hector; it was the age of Odysseus.

Like the much older epic of *Gilgamesh* (see Chapter 1), these epics preserve long-standing traditions. But over centuries of retelling, the social and political relationships portrayed in the poems changed to reflect the assumptions and agendas of later ages. As a result, the Homeric epics are of tremendous value to historians. They also offer significant analytical challenges. For although the great events and many of the material objects described in them date from the late Bronze Age, the society they reflect is that of Homer's contemporaries, half a millennium later. Treating these epics as historical sources, therefore, requires the historian to work like an archaeologist, carefully peeling back layers of meaning and sifting through the accumulated sediment of generations.

For example, Homer depicts a world in which competition and status are of paramount importance to the warrior elite, just as they were of vital concern to the aristocrats of his own day. Through the exchange of expensive gifts and hospitality, men aspiring to positions of power sought to create strong ties of guest friendship (*xenia*, zeh-NEE-ah) with one another, and thus to construct networks of influence that would support their economic, social, and political ambitions. Indeed, it is almost impossible to overestimate the importance of guest friendship as a sacred institution, something that is well illustrated by the encounter between the Trojan warrior Glaucus and the Greek Diomedes in the *Iliad* (see page 78). It suggests that aristocrats in the Greek world conceived of themselves as having more in common with each other than they did with the local societies they dominated, something that is also reflected in the essential similarity of Trojans and Greeks in the *Iliad* and the lack of perceived differences among various Greek tribes.

However, the practice of guest friendship and the shared sense of a common culture among artistocratic households did not lessen the competition that frequently led to violence. (The Trojan War, after all, is supposed to have begun when Paris violated the holy ties of hospitality by seducing the wife of Menalaus while he was a guest of the Spartan king.) It also led to competition over the epic past, as fledgling aristocratic clans vied to claim descent from one or another legendary hero. A hero cult might begin when an important family claimed an impressive Mycenaean tomb as that of their own famous ancestor, someone named in the *Iliad* and said to come from that place. They would then develop a pious tradition of practicing dutiful sacrifices and other observances at the tomb. This devotion would extend to their followers and dependents; eventually, an entire community might come to identify itself with the famous local hero. The heroic ideal thus became a deeply ingrained feature of Greek society, as did the stories that the epics preserved and propagated.

Greek Guest Friendship and Heroic Ideals

Before the emergence of the Greek poleis, relations among communities depended largely on the personal connections made among leading families of different settlements. Often founded on the exchange of gifts or hospitality, the resulting bonds of guest friendship imposed serious obligations on those involved in such relationships—and on their heirs. Honoring these ties was an important part of the heroic ideal, even among those fighting on opposing sides. In this episode from the Iliad (Book VI), the fierce Greek warrior Diomedes encounters Glaucus of Lykia, fighting for Troy, on the field of battle.

hen Glaucus, son of Hippolochus,
   Met Diomedes in
   no-man's-land.
   Both were eager to
fight, but first Tydaeus' son
Made his voice heard above the battle
   noise:
"And which mortal hero are you? I've
   never seen you
Out here before on the fields of glory,
And now you're here ahead of
   everyone,
Ready to face my spear. Pretty bold.
I feel sorry for your parents . . ."
And Glaucus, Hippolochus' son:
"Great son of Tydaeus, why ask me
   about my lineage? . . .
But if you really want to hear my
   story,
You're welcome to listen. Many men
   know it.
Ephyra, in the heart of Argive horse
   country,
Was home to Sisyphus, the shrewdest
   man alive,
Sisyphus son of Aeolus. He had a son,
   Glaucus,
Who was the father of faultless
   Bellerophon,
A man of grace and courage by the gift
   of the gods. . . .
[Here, Glaucus relates the adventures of his
   grandfather, Bellerophon, and how he
   came to Lykia and fought many battles
   for its king.]
When the king realized that
   Bellerophon had divine blood,

He kept him there and gave him his
   daughter,
And half his royal honor. . . .
His wife, the princess, bore him three
   children,
Isander, Hippolochus, and
   Laodameia. . . .
His son Isander was slain by Ares,
As he fought against the glorious
   Solymi,
And his daughter was killed by Artemis
Of the golden reins. But Hippolochus
Bore me, and I am proud he is my
   father.
He sent me to Troy with strict
   instructions
To be the best ever, better than all the
   rest,
And not to bring shame on the race of
   my fathers. . . .
This, I am proud to say, is my lineage."
Diomedes grinned when he heard all
   this.
He planted his spear in the bounteous
   earth
And spoke gently to the Lykian prince:
"We have old ties of hospitality!
My grandfather Oeneus long ago
Entertained Bellerophon in his halls
For twenty days, and they gave each
   other
Gifts of friendship. Oeneus gave
A belt bright with scarlet, and
   Bellerophon
A golden cup, which I left at home.
I don't remember my father Tydeus,
Since I was very small when he left for
   Thebes

In that great war that killed so many
   Achaeans.
But that makes me your friend and you
   my guest
If ever you come to Argos, as you are
   my friend
And I your guest whenever I travel to
   Lykia.
So we can't cross spears with each
   other. . . .
And let's exchange armor, so everyone
   will know
That we are friends from our fathers'
   days."
With this, they vaulted from their
   chariots,
Clasped hands, and pledged their
   friendship.

Source: Excerpted from the *Iliad* of Homer, trans. Stanley Lombardo (Indianapolis, IN: 1997), pp. 115–18 (vv. 120–241).

Questions for Analysis

1. Why would Glaucus and Diomedes place such emphasis on lineage and on the stories of their ancestors?

2. What are the attributes of heroism in this passage? Why is respect for the sacred ties of hospitality so important?

3. Why do these two men exchange armor? What might be the symbolic significance of this action? What might be its consequences on the battlefield?

The Rise of the Polis

The ninth century B.C.E. saw dramatic changes throughout the Aegean basin. Contacts between Greeks and Phoenicians intensified. Most crucially, the Greeks adopted the Phoenician alphabet, which replaced the forgotten Linear B of the Myceneans (Chapter 2). Indeed, the Greeks adopted this alphabet to better serve their own language by assigning some unneeded consonantal symbols to vowels. They also incorporated into their culture many artistic and literary traditions of the Near East, reshaping them to suit their own purposes.

At the same time, the example of the Phoenicians pointed the way to the revival of a lost art among the Greeks: seafaring. After the devastation of the late Bronze Age, Greek vessels no longer ventured out into the Mediterranean, but hugged the shoreline and traveled only short distances. Most Greek traders waited at home for the Phoenicians to come to them. By the tenth century, however, Greeks were copying Phoenician designs for merchant vessels, which allowed them to launch trading enterprises of their own. As commercial activity increased, significant numbers of Greeks began to move back to the shores of the mainland, to outlying islands, and to the coast of Anatolia.

These developments were accompanied by a dramatic expansion of the Greek population. Around Athens, the population may have quadrupled during the ninth and early eighth centuries. Such rapid growth placed heavy demands on the resources of Greece, a mountainous country with limited agricultural land. As smaller villages grew into towns,

THE ATTIC PENINSULA. This map highlights the numerous poleis that dotted the Attic peninsula. It also shows the surrounding territories of Euboea, Boeotia, and Megaris. Consider the scale of the map and the geography of the peninsula.
- *Where is Athens located?* - *How do natural boundaries appear to affect patterns of settlement?* - *Why would citizens of the other Attic poleis be regarded as citizens of Athens also, even though they did not live in the city itself?*

inhabitants of rival communities came into more frequent contact with each other. Soon, some degree of economic, political, and social cooperation among the inhabitants of these towns became necessary. But the values that had developed during centuries of isolation did not make such cooperation easy. Each local community treasured its autonomy and independence, celebrated its own rituals, and honored its own heroes. On what basis could such communities unite?

The Greek solution to this challenge was the *polis*, the root from which we derive the words *politics* and *political*. Yet Greeks considered the polis to be a social collectivity, first and foremost—not a state. For this reason, our sources speak of groups of people—"the Athenians," "the Spartans," or "the Thebans"—rather than places (Athens, Sparta, Thebes). The formation of *poleis* (the plural of *polis*) came to be considered so essential to Greek identity that Aristotle would later define man as "a political animal," someone who participates in the life of the polis and who cannot survive outside it.

Most poleis combined both formal legal institutions and informal social and cultural customs that could differ widely according to the size of the population and its material and historical circumstances. They were usually organized around a social center known as the *agora* ("central marketplace"), where markets and meetings were held and where the business of the polis was conducted in the open air. Surrounding this was the urban settlement, the *asty*, and beyond this was the *khora*, "land." The khora of a large polis might support several other towns or smaller poleis, as well as numerous villages; for example, all the residents of the entire territory of Attica were considered to be citizens of Athens. Thus the vast majority of Athenian citizens were farmers, who might come to the asty only at certain times of the year to participate in the affairs of their polis or to exchange goods in the agora.

The Greeks described this early process of urbanization as the "bringing together of dwellings" (*synoikismos*, synoecism). Polis formation could come about through the conquest of one settlement by another and/or through the gradual alliance of neighboring communities. Some poleis took shape around fortified hilltops, such as the Athenian acropolis, which suggests that the initial impetus may have been defensive. Other communities may have borrowed a Near Eastern (and particularly Phoenician) practice of orienting the urban center around a temple precinct. In Greece, however, the main temple of a polis was not always located within the city's walls; at Argos, for example, the massive temple to Hera was located several miles away from any sizable settlement. In many Greek cities, moreover, temple building may have been a consequence of polis formation rather than a cause, as elites competed with one another to exalt their poleis and glorify themselves.

THE CULTURE OF ARCHAIC GREECE, 800–500 B.C.E.

Scholars date the Archaic Period of Greek history to the emergence of the polis and the return of writing, which the Greeks would put to a wide variety of practical, artistic, intellectual, and political uses. The Athenians, in particular, used writing as a way of establishing their cultural dominance over other Greek poleis, by controlling the inscription of the Homeric canon, promoting the work of contemporary poets, and fostering the writing of prose histories, which allowed them to pass on a narrative of Greek history in which they themselves played the central role. It is therefore important to bear in mind that much of what we know about this early period derives from the work of later authors who wrote from this Athenian perspective: these include the Ionian-born Herodotus, who spent much of his later life in Athens; the historians Thucydides (c. 460–c. 395 B.C.E.) and Xenophon (430–354); and the philosophers Plato (c. 428–348) and his pupil Aristotle (384–322).

Colonization and Panhellenism

In the eighth and seventh centuries B.C.E., small-scale Greek trading ventures and settlements had gradually developed into a full-fledged colonial enterprises which, like their mercantile efforts, followed the example of the Phoenicians. Many larger poleis competed with one another to establish colonies that functioned as trading posts, with Athens and Corinth being particularly successful. Although each new colony was technically an independent entity, it sustained familial and emotional ties to its mother polis; so even if it had no formal obligations to that city, it was often called upon to support the polis and could become entangled in the political and military affairs of the mainland. At the same time, these scattered Greek colonies were united by their shared language and heritage, which was being exported to far-flung reaches of the known world, eventually creating a Panhellenic ("all-Greek") culture that stretched from the Black Sea (parts of modern Romania, Ukraine, and Russia) to the southern coastlines of modern France and Spain.

This process of Greek colonization permanently altered the cultural geography of the Mediterranean world. The western shores of Anatolia (modern Turkey) would remain a stronghold of Greek culture for the next 2,000 years (see Chapter 12). So many Greeks settled in southern Italy that later Romans called the region Magna Graecia, "Greater Greece"; Greek-speaking enclaves would survive there into

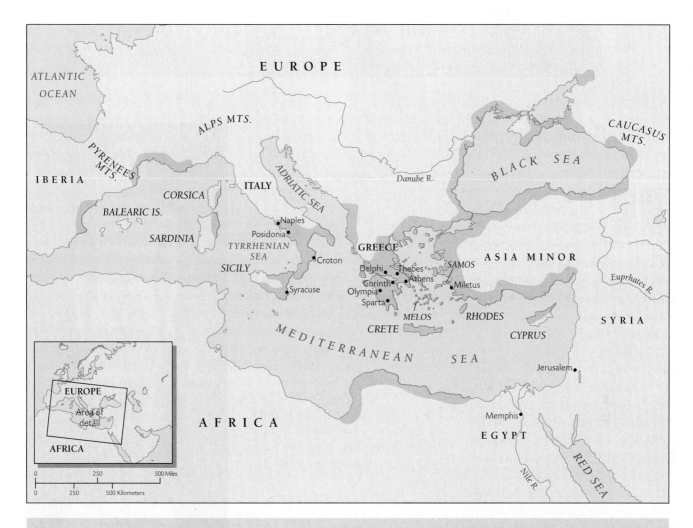

GREEK COLONIZATION, C. 550 B.C.E. Compare this map with that on page 55. ▪ *How do you account for the differences in Greek and Phoenician patterns of colonization?* ▪ *Were Greek colonies likely to compete with Phoenician colonies?* ▪ *Where were such conflicts most likely to erupt?*

the twentieth century of our era. By the fourth century B.C.E., more Greeks lived in Magna Graecia than in Greece itself.

Motives for colonization varied. A polis such as Corinth was blessed by its strategic location on the land bridge between Attica and the Peloponnesus (*pel-oh-poh-NEE-suhs*; the large peninsula of mainland Greece) but cursed by the poverty of its land. Trade therefore became the lifeblood of this polis and of the ruling aristocracy who bankrolled the ambitious planting of colonies up the coast of the Adriatic and into Sicily during the eighth century B.C.E. Other poleis, confronted by the pressures of growing populations and political unrest, sponsored new colonies as outlets for undesirable elements or unwanted multitudes. These colonial projects parallel, in many ways, those of modern nation-states.

Colonial expansion intensified Greek contacts with other cultures. Phoenician pottery brought new artistic motifs and mythological figures into Greece, while Egyptian artists profoundly influenced early Greek sculptural representations of the human form (see **Interpreting Visual Evidence** on page 82). However, intensified contact with other cultures also sharpened Greeks' awareness of their own identity as Hellenes (the Greeks' name for themselves). Such self-conscious Hellenism did not necessarily lead to greater political cooperation, but it did encourage the establishment of Panhellenic festivals, such as the Olympic Games, and holy sites. The most important of these was the temple of Apollo at Delphi, home to the oracle of the sun god and situated on the slope of the sacred mountain of Parnassus. People from all over the Greek world (and beyond) came to seek advice from the prophetic spirit embodied in Apollo's priestess, who lived in a state of trance induced by fumes rising from a fissure in the earth and enhanced by the chewing of eucalyptus leaves. Suppliants who sought

The Ideal of Male Beauty

The Greek word *kouros* ("young man" or "youth") is now applied to a whole series of life-sized statues from the Archaic Period. The one shown here comes from Anavyssos in Attica, and was made between 540 and 515 B.C.E. (It is now in the National Archaeological Museum of Athens.) Although scholars used to believe that such statues were meant to represent the god Apollo, further research has shown that most were made to commemorate the dead, especially young warriors who had fallen in battle. This one appears to be walking forward, smiling, but his eyes are closed. The accompanying inscription reads: "Stop and show your pity here for Kroisos, now dead, who once fighting in the foremost ranks of battle was destroyed by raging Ares."

Questions for Analysis

1. What aspects of the body does the kouros emphasize? If this is intended to be a model of Greek manhood, what values would it convey to contemporary youths?

2. Is this a representation of the young man as he was when living or in death? How do your conclusions about the ideal of male beauty change if this is a glorification of death?

3. Compare this image to the values expressed in the verses by Tyrtaeus of Sparta on "The Beautiful and the Good" (page 84). How do these two perspectives complement one another?

---

to have their questions answered by the oracle would offer gifts to the shrine and then wait while the god spoke through the priestess, whose mysterious answers would be translated by an attending priest into enigmatic Greek verse. The resulting advice was essentially a riddle that called for further interpretation on the part of the recipient—who often misconstrued it: as we noted in Chapter 2, Croesus of Lydia thought that he was following the advice of the oracle when he attacked the Persians, but the great nation he destroyed turned out to be his own.

At the Olympic Games, Greeks honored the king of the gods, Zeus, near the giant temple dedicated to him at Olympia. The Greeks took great pride in these athletic competitions, and Greek historians dated events by Olympiads, the four-year periods between games, traditionally believed to have begun in 776 B.C.E. Only Hellenes were permitted to participate in these sacred contests, and all wars among Greeks ceased while they took place. A victory in the games brought great prestige to the victor, who could be catapulted to a position of social and political power within his polis. These games did little to alleviate rivalry among the poleis; in fact, they often increased it. Yet they further strengthened the Greeks' awareness of their common culture, an awareness that could be harnessed when they faced a common threat.

Hoplite Warfare

In the centuries immediately following the calamities of the late Bronze Age, the defense of surviving Greek communities rested with the few elite warriors who had the

HOPLITE INFANTRY ADVANCING INTO COMBAT. This Corinthian vase, dating from around 650 B.C.E., displays the earliest-known depiction of hoplites fighting in a phalanx formation.

resources to invest in armor, chariots, and weaponry—and the leisure to emulate the heroic ideals of the past. Commoners fighting on foot played a very secondary role. This monopoly on military prowess gave the aristocracy tremendous political and social leverage. As a result, aristocrats dominated political offices and priesthoods in the poleis, as well as economic life.

But during the Archaic Period, a revolution in military tactics brought aristocratic military dominance to an end. It came about because the effective defense of a polis increasingly required that it be able to call on a standing militia, not just an ad hoc band of elite warriors. Accordingly, ablebodied citizens began to equip themselves for battle and to train alongside one another. These citizen-soldiers became known as *hoplites*, from the large round shield (*hoplon*) carried by each, which was the chief element in a panoply (*hoplite outfit*) weighing as much as seventy pounds, which also consisted of spear, short sword, breastplate, helmet, and sometimes leather greaves and wrist-guards. In battle, hoplites stood shoulder to shoulder in a close formation called a *phalanx*, several columns across and several rows deep, with each hoplite carrying his shield on the left arm to protect the unshielded right side of the man standing next to him. In his right hand, each hoplite carried a thrusting weapon, a spear or sword, so that an approaching phalanx presented a nearly impenetrable wall of armor and weaponry to its opponents. If a man in the front rank fell, the one behind him stepped up to take his place; indeed, the weight of the entire phalanx was literally behind the front line, with each soldier aiding the assault by leaning with his shield into the man in front of him.

This tight formation required only one shared skill: the ability to stay together. As long as the phalanx remained intact, it was a nearly unbeatable formation. But like the polis itself, it could fall apart if its men were not committed to a common goal. The "hoplite revolution" was therefore bound up with a parallel revolution in politics. As a polis came increasingly to draw upon the resources of more and more citizens, it was forced to offer them a larger share in political power. By the seventh century B.C.E., every polis needed a hoplite force to protect its independence, so any town-dweller or farmer who could afford the requisite panoply became a man with political and social standing. Together, these citizen-soldiers formed a new hoplite class, which could demand a share in decision making and thereby challenge the dominance of old elites. Sometimes, though, they could be co-opted by an aristocratic faction or persuaded to throw support behind an aspiring tyrant.

Aristocracy, Tyranny, and Democracy

For the better part of the seventh and sixth centuries B.C.E., aristocrats continued to control the Greek poleis. Struggles for influence among competing families were commonplace, and factions often attempted to checkmate rivals by passing new laws which favored their interests, or by sponsoring building projects or colonial expeditions. These rivalries affected polis government at every level, not least because aristocrats were the only members of society who

"The Beautiful and The Good"

The poet known as Tyrtaeus of Sparta flourished during the middle of the sixth century B.C.E. He may originally have come from Athens, but whatever his origins he expressed ideas of honor, beauty, and virtue that were universal among the hoplite warriors of the new poleis. The key terms he uses in the following verses cannot be adequately translated into English, since these short Greek adjectives are freighted with ancient meanings: kalos *(beautiful, honorable),* agathos *(good, brave, manly). They stand in opposition to the term* aischros *(shameful, ugly, mean).*

 alos it is for an *agathos* warrior to die, fallen among the foremost fighters, in battle for his native land; but to leave his polis and rich fields and beg—that is most painful of all, as he wanders with his dear mother and aged father, his small children and his wedded wife. Detested he will be in the eyes of all those to whom he comes, constrained by need and hateful poverty. He shames his birth and belies his glorious appearance; dishonor and misery are his companions. If no account is taken of a warrior who is a wanderer, if there is no respect for him or his family in the future, then let us fight with all our hearts for this land and die for our children, no longer hesitating to risk our lives. Young men, stand firm beside each other and fight. Do not begin shameful flight or fear. Rather, cre- ate a mighty, valorous spirit in your breasts, and show no love for your lives when you are fighting. Do not flee, abandoning the older men, whose knees are no longer nimble. For *aischros* it is for an older warrior to fall among the foremost fighters and lie out ahead of the young men—a man whose hair is already white and his beard grey—as he breathes out his valorous spirit in the dust, holding his bloody guts in his own hands, his body laid bare. *Aischros* is this to the eyes, and a cause of resentment to look upon. But to the young men all is seemly, while the glorious flower of lovely youth is theirs. To men the young man is admirable to look upon, and to women lovable while he lives and *kalos* when he lies among the foremost fighters. So let a man take a firm stance and stand fast, with both feet planted upon the ground, biting his lip with his teeth.

Source: Excerpted and modified from *The Greek Polis*, eds. W. H. Adkins and Peter White (Chicago: 1986), pp. 23–24.

Questions for Analysis

1. How does Tyrtaeus characterize defeat? How does this poem exemplify the values and tactics of hoplite warfare?

2. Why is so much emphasis placed on physical beauty and youth? What other qualities are associated with the word *kalos*? Why is old age potentially *aischros*?

3. How does this ideal of male beauty compare with that made visible in the kouros of Anavyssos (page 82)? How does it compare to the heroic ideal expressed in the exchange between Diomedes and Glaucus (page 78)?

---

could afford to hold unpaid and time-consuming political offices.

The aristocrats of this period pursued not only wealth, power, and fame; they also cultivated a distinctive lifestyle. Participating in politics and holding office was part of this lifestyle. So too was the *symposium*, literally a "drinking party," an intimate gathering at which elite men would enjoy wine, poetic competition performances by trained dancers and acrobats, and the company of *hetaeras* (courtesans) who provided witty conversation, music, and the promise of sex. Respectable women were excluded from such meet- ings, as they were from most other aspects of social and political life (see below). So too were non-aristocratic men. The symposium was thus an arena for the display of aristo- cratic masculinity.

The glorification of male sexuality was another impor- tant aspect of this homosocial aristocratic culture and was regulated by social custom. Typically, a man in his late twenties to late thirties, who had just begun to make his career in political life, would take as his lover and protégé an aristocratic youth in his early to mid-teens. The two would form an intimate bond in which sexual intercourse played a role. This personal and social intimacy benefited both partners and their families and allowed the younger partner to learn the workings of politics while making valuable connections and alliances. Many later philosophers, including Plato, argued that true love could exist only between two such lovers, because only within such a relationship could a man find a partner worthy of his affections. Other types of sexual relationships were considered illicit, including those between men of unequal social status.

A complex system of values, ideas, practices, and assumptions thus shaped aristocratic identity in this era. As a result, it was difficult for those outside this elite world to participate fully in the public life of the polis. Eventually, in many poleis, the circle of the aristocratic elite tightened further as smaller and smaller groups came to dominate higher offices. This meant that even many aristocrats were left on the outside of their own culture, looking in.

For these men, one remedy lay close at hand: they could form an alliance with the rising class of hoplites, who had complaints of their own about exclusion from political power. And occasionally, a single aristocrat with the backing of the hoplites would succeed in setting up an alternative form of government, a *tyranny*. The word *tyrannos* was actually foreign to the Greeks, and had been borrowed from the Lydians; it signified someone who ruled outside the traditional framework of the polis.

But a tyrant in Archaic Greece was not necessarily an abusive ruler. Indeed, tyranny often led the way to wider political enfranchisement. This is because a would-be tyrant who had sought the support of the hoplite class would then have to appease that class by extending further rights of political participation, while all the time striving to keep the reins of power in his own hands. This was an inherently unstable state of affairs, because after the original tyrant had fulfilled the wishes of the hoplites, the continuance of tyranny became an obstacle to even greater power for this segment of the population, which would work to overthrow it. For this reason, tyrannies rarely lasted for more than two generations and could drive a transition from aristocracy to a more broadly participatory form of government: democracy.

It is important to stress that our notion of democracy is quite different from that of the Greeks. In fact, the philosopher Aristotle denigrated this form of government as "mob rule," because it gave too much power to the *demos*, a word meaning "neighborhood" or "affinity group." He saw it as a system too easily controlled by a particular faction. Our ideal of democracy is closer to what Aristotle would have called a polity, governance by the polis as a whole.

The Power of Poetry

Although the aristocracies of this period were deeply invested in the heroic ideals enshrined in the epics of an earlier age, they also strove to express their unique culture and outlook in newer poetic forms. The most characteristic of these is the lyric, a series of rhythmic verses sung to the music of the lyre. Because these songs would have been composed orally, or even improvised, relatively few survive. But those that do are valuable historical sources because they concentrate on themes of immediate interest to poets and their audiences: beauty, love, sorrow, ambition, or important life events. And because they were the focus of entertainment at gatherings, lyrics are often politically charged, sexually explicit, or daringly subversive of accepted norms. For example, the poet Archilochus of Paros (c. 680–640 B.C.E.) flouts the conventions of epic poetry by mocking his own failures on the battlefield: "Some barbarian hefts my shield, since I had to abandon it / . . . but I escaped, so it scarcely matters / . . . I can get another just as good." So much for the heroic ideal of returning either with one's shield or on it! In another lyric, Archilochus castigates his faithless (female) lover and his even more faithless (male) lover with whom she has an affair.

AN ARISTOCRATIC MAN AND HIS YOUNG LOVER. An illustration from a red-figure drinking cup, c. 480 B.C.E. ■ *As suggested by this image, what are the differences between these two male lovers?* ■ *What relationship(s) are being depicted here?*

Songs of Sappho

Although Sappho of Lesbos (c. 620–550 B.C.E.) was a prolific poet and skilled musician, we know very little about her life, and only a few examples of her extraordinary verse survive. Of the nine books collected in the third century B.C.E., we now have just one complete lyric and a series of fragments, some consisting of only two or three words, often preserved because they were quoted admiringly by other authors. Astonishingly, though, a papyrus scroll containing a previously unknown part of a poem was identified as recently as 2004.

Fragment 16

Some say thronging cavalry, some say
    foot soldiers,
others call a fleet the most beautiful of
sights the dark earth offers, but I say it's
    whatever you love best.

And it's easy to make this understood by
everyone, for she who surpassed all
    human
kind in beauty, Helen, abandoning her
    husband—that best of

men—went sailing off to the shores of
    Troy and
never spent a thought on her child or
    loving
parents: when the goddess seduced her
    wits and left her to wander,

she forgot them all, she could not
    remember
anything but longing, and lightly straying
aside, lost her way. But that reminds me
    now: Anactória,

she's not here, and I'd rather see her
    lovely

step, her sparkling glance and her face
    than gaze on
all the troops in Lydia in their chariots
    and glittering armor.

Source: Translated by Jim Powell, *The Poetry of Sappho* (New York: 2007), pp. 6–7.

The New Fragment (2004)

Live for the gifts the fragrant-breasted
    Muses
send, for the clear, the singing, lyre, my
    children.
Old age freezes my body, once so lithe,
rinses the darkness from my hair, now
    white.
My heart's heavy, my knees no longer
    keep me
up through the dance they used to
    prance like fawns in.
Oh, I grumble about it, but for what?
Nothing can stop a person's growing
    old.
They say that Tithonus was swept away
in Dawn's passionate, rose-flushed arms
    to live

forever, but he lost his looks, his youth,
failing husband of an immortal bride.

Source: Translated by Lachlan Mackinnon, *Times Literary Supplement*, July 15, 2005.

Questions for Analysis

1. How does Sappho use stories from the older tradition she has inherited to address her own concerns? How does the perspective of the female poet transform masculine ideas about heroism, beauty, warfare, aging?

2. What are the challenges of working with such fragmentary sources as these? If these were the only pieces of evidence to survive from Archaic Greece, what conclusions could you draw about the society and its values?

Given the male domination of Greek culture, it is surprising that the most famous poet of this age was not a man. Rather, it was Sappho (*SAF-foh*, c. 620–550 B.C.E.), who lived in the polis of Mytilene on the island of Lesbos. Revered by her contemporaries as the Tenth Muse, Sappho composed songs for a wide array of occasions and a range of moods: songs of courtship and marriage, longing and desire, loss, old age, and death. Sometimes her lyrics seem to be addressed to men, but more often they are passionately dedicated to women: both the women whom Sappho loved and the historical women who occupy the margins of masculine epic. Frequently, her verses take some image or incident from that inherited tradition and give it a distinctive spin. In one song, Sappho compares herself to Agamemnon, who was only able to return from Troy after he prayed to Hera, a goddess worshiped at Lesbos; Sappho now prays that her beloved will arrive safely with the goddess's help. In another, she imagines a scene not included in the *Iliad*, the joyous wedding of the Trojan Hector and his bride, Andromache. Like later tragedies, the poignancy of this bridal song (just like the ones Sappho herself would have sung at the marriage feasts of her friends) derives from the listeners' foreknowledge of the legendary couple's terrible fate: Hector's death at the hands of Achilles, Andromache's enslavement at the hands of the victorious Greeks, and the murder of their infant son. The intimacy of lyric thus reveals something that few other sources from antiquity are able to convey: the distinctive feelings and desires of individuals who were often at odds with the dominant culture of their time.

PORTRAITS OF THREE POLEIS

The poleis of the Archaic Period developed in very different ways. To illustrate this diversity, we examine three particularly interesting examples: Athens, Sparta, and the Ionian city of Miletus. None of these, however, can be considered typical. There were approximately 1,000 poleis in Greece, and about most of them we know almost nothing. But at least we can survey some of the features that, with variations, made each polis unique—and yet comparable, in some ways, to its neighbors.

Athens

The Athenians liked to boast that their city had been a great metropolis since the Bronze Age described by Hesiod: a claim integral to their identity and their sense of self-importance within the larger Greek world. But although Attica had long been a populous and prosperous region, Athens itself was of no great significance during the Mycenaean Era. Moreover, it continued throughout the Archaic Period to be overshadowed by Corinth, the leading commercial city; Sparta, the preeminent military power; and the leading cultural centers of the Aegean islands and the coast of Anatolia.

When Athenians first came together to form a polis, theirs was a distinctly agricultural economy. Whatever profits aristocrats acquired through trade, they reinvested in land on the Attic Peninsula. Indeed, Athenian elites

OSTRACISM. This political practice takes its name from the pot shards (in Greek, *ostraka*) on which the names of candidates for political exile were scratched. Many of the ballots have survived. Here we see the names of Aristeides, Kimon, and Themistocles: prominent citizens of the fifth century B.C.E. who had fallen out of favor.

came to regard commerce as a disreputable means of earning a living, a mentality that persisted even when the city's excellent harbors and orientation toward the Aegean made Athens famous as a mercantile polis.

In the Archaic Period, aristocratic dominance over the polis rested on monopolization of elected offices and control of the city's council, the Areopagus (*ah-ree-OP-ah-guhs*), which was composed of former office-holders. It took its name from the rocky outcrop where the council met, just below the Acropolis, a site that afforded a panoramic view of the whole city. By the early seventh century B.C.E., an even smaller group of aristocratic officials wielded executive authority in Athens: the *archons* or "first men." Ultimately, nine archons presided over the entire governance of the polis, including its military, judicial, and religious affairs. Although each served for only one year, all became lifetime members of the Areopagus. And because the Areopagus appointed the archons, it could therefore control its own future membership. It also served as a kind of high court, with tremendous influence over the hearing of cases.

As power was consolidated by this small group, deep economic and social divisions developed in Athenian society. A significant proportion of the population fell into slavery through debt, while struggles among aristocratic families destabilized the government and fomented cycles of revenge killings. This situation eventually inspired Athenians' first attempt to promulgate a set of written laws. In 621 B.C.E., an aristocrat named Drakon was charged with this task, and he sought to control civic violence through harsh punishments: hence our term *draconian* to describe

THE ATHENIAN PNYX, WITH A VIEW OF THE ACROPOLIS. The Athenian assembly, the *ekklesia*, met on the sloping hill of the Pnyx. A speaker standing on the *bema* ("stepping-stone," to the right) would have to make himself heard by all the citizens gathered in front of this platform, and all proceedings would have been plainly visible to noncitizens and foreigners in the agora at the foot of the hill (to the left). Overlooking it all was the temple of the city's patron goddess, Athena, on the crest of the Acropolis. ■ *How is the relative openness and accessibility of Athenian democracy symbolized by this chosen site?*

any severe penalty, policy, or regime. Drakon's attempt failed, but its effects ultimately led both aristocrats and hoplites to an agreement. In 594 B.C.E., they elected one man, the poet Solon, as the sole archon for one year, and they gave him broad legislative powers. Solon was an aristocrat, but he had made his fortune as a merchant and did not hold that vocation in contempt; this meant that he was not allied with any single interest.

Solon's legendary political and economic reforms laid the foundations for the later development of Athenian democracy. He forbade the practice of debt slavery and set up a fund to buy back Athenian slaves who had been sold abroad. He encouraged the cultivation of olives and grapes, thus spurring cash-crop farming and urban industries such as oil and wine production, and the manufacture of pottery storage jars and decorative drinking cups. He also broadened rights of political participation and set up courts in which a range of citizens served as jurors and to which any Athenian might appeal. He based eligibility for political office on property qualifications, thus making it possible for someone not born into the aristocracy to gain access to power. Moreover, he convened an Athenian assembly, the *ekklesia* (*eh-KLAY-see-a*) and gave it the right to elect archons. Now all free-born Athenian men over the age of eighteen could participate in government. Even those who were not eligible for citizenship were able to see the workings of government for themselves, since the assembled citizens met on the slopes of the Pnyx (*pNIX*), a hill visible from the central marketplace and overlooked by the sacred precincts of the Acropolis.

However, Solon's reforms were not immediately accepted. The aristocracy thought them too radical; the people of the demos, not radical enough. In the resulting generation of turmoil, an aristocrat named Peisistratos (*pi-SIS-trah-tohs*) succeeded in establishing himself as tyrant in 546 B.C.E. Somewhat ironically, Peisistratos then proceeded to institute Solon's reforms, and he also launched a massive campaign of public-works projects, including the collection and codification of Homer's epics. But the apparent mildness of his rule was undergirded by the quiet, persistent intimidation of Athenian citizens by foreign mercenaries and the ruthlessness with which he crushed any dissent. Still, by enforcing Solon's laws, he strengthened the political role of the demos and remained a popular ruler until his death. His sons, however, were less able to control the various factions that threatened their rule. One was assassinated and the other was ousted with the help of the Spartans in 510 B.C.E.

The following period of Spartan-sponsored oligarchy ("rule of the few") was very brief. Two generations of increasing access to power had left the Athenian demos with a taste for self-government, and for the first time in recorded history, a group of commoners can be credited with the overthrow of a regime: they rallied behind Cleisthenes (CLIE-sthen-ees), an aristocrat who championed the cause of the demos. Once voted in as archon in 508/7 B.C.E., Cleisthenes took steps to limit aristocratic power. By reorganizing the Athenian population into ten voting districts, he suppressed traditional loyalties tied to certain aristocratic families. He further strengthened the Athenian assembly and extended the machinery of democratic government to the local level throughout Attica. He also introduced the practice of ostracism, whereby Athenians could decide each year whether they wanted to banish someone for a decade and, if so, whom. With this power, Cleisthenes hoped that the demos could prevent the return of a tyrant and quell factional strife if civil war seemed imminent.

By 500 B.C.E., the political struggles of the sixth century had given Athens a far more populist character than any other Greek polis and had strengthened its institutions of government. In the meantime, Athens had become the principal exporter of olive oil, wine, and pottery in the Greek world. It was poised to assume the role it would claim for itself during the fifth century B.C.E. as the exemplar of Greek culture and the proponent of democracy.

Sparta

Located in the southern part of the Peloponnesus, the polis of the Spartans represented everything that Athens was not. Athens was sophisticated, outward looking, and creative; Sparta was practical, defensive, and conservative. Depending on one's point of view, either set of adjectives might indicate admiration or criticism.

Sparta took shape when four villages (and ultimately a fifth) combined to form a single polis. Perhaps as a relic of the unification process, Sparta retained a dual monarchy throughout its history, with two royal families and two lines of succession. Although seniority or ability usually determined which of the two ruling kings had more influence, neither was technically superior to the other, a situation that often led to political in-fighting among their respective supporters.

According to traditional accounts, Spartan control over the surrounding region of Laconia began with the conquest of Messenia, one of Greece's few agriculturally rich territories. Around 720 B.C.E., the Spartans subjugated and enslaved the indigenous people there, the *helots*, who now became an unfree population forced to work under Spartan lordship. Around 650 B.C.E., however, the helots revolted, gaining support from several neighboring poleis and briefly threatening Spartan hegemony with annihilation. Eventually, Sparta triumphed; but the shock of this rebellion brought about a permanent transformation.

Determined to prevent another uprising and to protect its superior position, Sparta became the most militarized polis in Greece. Within a few generations, everything was oriented to the maintenance of its hoplite army—a force so superior that Spartans confidently left their city unfortified. At a time when Athenian society was becoming more democratic and when citizens spent more time legislating than fighting, Spartan society was becoming increasingly devoted to an older aristocratic ideal of perpetual warfare, with personal freedom mattering less than the collective honor and security of the polis.

The Spartan system made every male citizen a professional soldier of the phalanx. At birth, every Spartiate child was therefore examined by officials who determined whether it was healthy enough to raise; if not, the infant was abandoned in the mountains. This was a custom observed elsewhere in the ancient world, but only in Sparta was it institutionalized by the state. If deemed worthy of upbringing, the child was placed at age seven in the polis-run educational system. Boys and girls trained together until age twelve, participating in exercise, gymnastics, and other physical drills and competitions. Boys then went to live in barracks, where their military training would commence in earnest. Girls continued their training until they became the mates of eligible Spartiate males, usually when the girls were around the age of eighteen and the men were often much older. This was not a domestic partnership: no such thing was possible under the Spartiate system, or even desirable, for such a marriage would merely create a new set of loyalties and interests that would compete with the Spartan state.

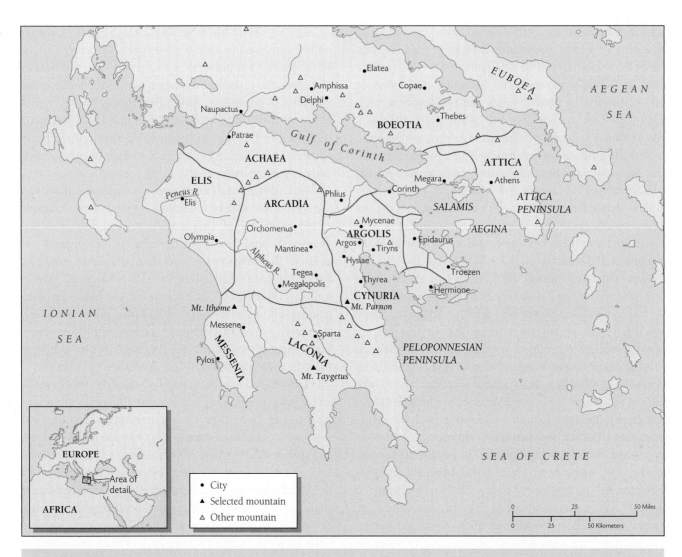

THE PELOPONNESUS. Located on the Peloponnesian peninsula, the highly militarized society of Sparta dominated the region known as Laconia. ▪ *Where is Sparta located?* ▪ *How might Sparta's location have influenced its outlook on foreign affairs?* ▪ *Did geography make conflict between Athens and Sparta inevitable?*

Barracks life was rigorous, designed to accustom youths to physical hardship. At age eighteen, the young man who survived this training would try for membership in a brotherhood whose sworn comrades lived, ate, and fought together. Failure to gain acceptance would mean that the young man could not become a full Spartiate and would lose his rights as a citizen. If accepted, however, he remained with his brotherhood until he was thirty years of age. Between the ages of twenty and thirty he was also expected to mate with a Spartiate woman—but occasions for this were few, a fact that partially accounts for the low birthrate among Spartan citizens. After age thirty, a Spartiate male could opt to live with his family, but he was still required to remain on active military duty until he was sixty.

All Spartiate males over the age of thirty were members of the citizens' assembly, the *apella*, which voted on matters proposed to it by a council consisting of twenty-eight elders (the *gerousia*, "assembly of elders") and the two kings. This gerousia (*gher-oo-SEE-ah*) was the main policy-making body of the polis and also its primary court. Its members were elected for life but had to be over the age of sixty before they could stand for office. Meanwhile, five *ephors* (overseers), elected annually, supervised the educational system and acted as guardians of Spartan tradition. In the latter role, ephors could even remove an ineffectual king from command of the army while on campaign. The ephors also supervised the Spartan "secret service," the *krypteia*, recruiting agents from among the most promising young Spartiates. Agents spied on citizens, but their main job was to infiltrate the helot population and identify potential troublemakers.

This Spartan polity hinged on the precarious relationship with the helots, who outnumbered the Spartiates ten to one. Messenia routinely seethed with revolt. In wartime, helots accompanied the Spartans on campaign as shield bearers, spear carriers, and baggage handlers. At home, however, the helots were a constant security concern. Every year the Spartans ritually declared war on them as a reminder that they would not tolerate dissent. Moreover, the constant threat of unrest at home meant that the polis was notoriously reluctant to commit its army abroad. So helot slavery made the Spartan system possible, but Sparta's reliance on a hostile population of slaves was also a serious limitation.

This system also limited Spartans' contact with the outside world. Spartiates were forbidden to engage in trade or commerce, because wealth might distract them from the pursuit of martial glory. Nor did Spartiates farm their own lands, as many Athenians did. Economic activity in the Spartan state fell either to the helots or to the free residents of other Peloponnesian cities who were known as *perioikoi*, "those dwelling round about." The perioikoi (*per-ee-OY-koi*) enjoyed certain rights and protections within Spartan society, and some grew rich handling its business concerns. But unlike the residents of Attica, in the hinterland of Athens, the perioikoi exercised no political rights within the Spartan polis. Spartiates who lost their rights as citizens also became perioikoi.

The Spartans self-consciously rejected innovation or change. They styled themselves as the protectors of the "traditional customs" of Greece, by which they meant aristocratic regimes and a strict observance of older heroic ideals. In this role, Sparta tried to prevent the establishment of tyrannies in neighboring states and moved to overthrow them

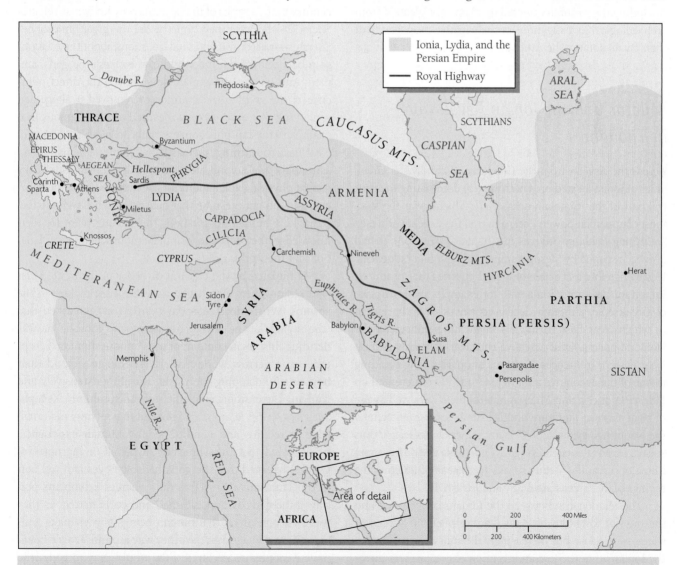

IONIA, LYDIA, AND THE PERSIAN EMPIRE. During the seventh and sixth centuries B.C.E., the Greek cities of the Ionian coast were the cultural and commercial leaders of Greece. But during the fifth century B.C.E., after the Persians conquered Lydia, they lost this position to Athens. ■ *Where are Ionia, Lydia, and Miletus on this map?* ■ *How does Ionia's geographical position help to explain the change in its fortunes?* ■ *How might this change have influenced Ionian attitudes toward the Persian Empire?*

when they arose: hence their willing intervention in the affairs of Athens under the Peisistratids. Indeed, Sparta's stern defense of tradition made it an object of admiration throughout the Greek world, even though few Greeks had any desire to live as the Spartans did.

The fatal flaw in the Spartan system was demographic. There were many ways to fall from the status of Spartiate, but the only way to become one was by birth—and the Spartan birthrate simply could not keep pace with the demand for trained warriors. As a result, the number of full Spartiates declined from perhaps as many as 10,000 in the seventh century to only about 1,000 by the middle of the fourth century B.C.E. Another flaw is historical: because the Spartans placed little value on the written record of their traditions, almost everything we know about them (including the summary offered here) must be gleaned from archaeological investigations or the negative propaganda of their rivals notably the Athenians.

Miletus and the Ionian Revolution in Thought

Across the Aegean from the Greek mainland lay the Greek cities of Ionia, located on a narrow strip dominating the central part of the Anatolian coast. Here, Miletus was the foremost commercial power. Long a part of the Greek world (see **Analyzing Primary Sources** in Chapter 2, page 53), it had also been shaped by Mesopotamian and Egyptian influences. It was therefore a crucible of hybrid cultures that produced important art forms. Ionia was, for example, the birthplace of Greek epic, although debate continues over the extent to which Near Eastern models might have influenced the Homeric poems. Other creative endeavors certainly exhibit Near Eastern influences. Fantastic animals, a long-standing theme of the decorative arts, were frequently represented on Milesian pottery; and Milesian intellectuals were well aware of Near Eastern literature and learning. Some even echoed the vaunting rhetoric of Persian imperial decrees ("thus speaks Darius the Great King. . . .") to make their own, more ironic observations ("thus speaks Hecataeus of Miletus: the sayings of the Greeks are many and foolish").

The relationship between the Ionians of the coast and the interior kingdom of Lydia—and its Persian successor state—were close but increasingly difficult. It was through the Ionians that the Lydian invention of coinage was introduced to the Greek world, where it revolutionized trade, made wealth portable for the first time there, and introduced a host of new philosophical and ethical problems. The Ionians, in turn, played a crucial role in Hellenizing

Asia Minor while at the same time insisting on their independence from it. Under the pressure of the Lydians—who sought the excellent ports of the Anatolian coast for themselves—the major cities of Ionia ultimately banded together to form the Ionian League, a political and cultural confederation of poleis pledged to support each other. This was the first such organization known in the Greek world.

The Milesians founded many colonies, especially in and around the Black Sea. They were also active in Egypt, where the main Greek trading outposts were Milesian foundations. These colonial efforts, combined with its advantageous position for trade with the rest of Asia Minor, brought Miletus extraordinary wealth. At the same time, it also became a center for speculative thinking, what the Greeks called *philosophia*, "the love of wisdom." Beginning in the sixth century B.C.E., a series of intellectuals now known as the pre-Socratics—because they came before the great philosopher Socrates—raised new and vital questions about the relationship between the natural world (the *kosmos*), the gods, and men. And often, their explanations moved the direct influence of the gods to the margins or removed it altogether, something that other Greeks regarded as blasphemous. For example, Milesian philosophers built on older traditions of Near Eastern learning, such as Babylonian mathematics and astronomy, but complicated many older conclusions. They sought physical explanations for the movements of the heavens, and did not presume that heavenly bodies were divine. By making human observations the starting point for their knowledge, they began to formulate more scientific explanations for the working of the universe.

Stimulated by the cultural diversity of their city, Milesian philosophers also began to rethink their place in the cosmos. When Hecataeus (*heck-ah-TAY-us*) remarked that "the sayings of the Greeks are many and foolish," he was deriding his own contemporaries' unquestioning acceptance of a narrow worldview. He set out to expand their horizons by mapping the world, traveling extensively and studying the customs and beliefs of other cultures. Xenophanes (*zee-NOFF-uh-nees*) also posited that all human knowledge is relative and conditioned by human experience: he observed that the Thracians (a people living north of Greece) believed that the gods had blue eyes and red hair as the Thracians themselves did, whereas Ethiopians portrayed the gods as dark skinned and curly haired, as they were. He concluded that human beings always make gods in their own image, not the other way around. If oxen could pray, Xenophanes declared, they would pray to gods who looked like oxen.

Such theories would become a distinctive strand in later Greek philosophy, yet they would continue to be regarded as disturbing and dangerous—dangerous enough to warrant the execution of Socrates in Athens, where the struggle between religion and philosophy would ultimately be fought more than a hundred years after Xenophanes' bold proclamation. By that time, the Persian conquest of Lydia had made Miletus and its sister cities subject to that great empire. Indeed, Ionian resistance to Persian rule would ultimately trigger the greatest clash the Greek world had yet known.

THE CHALLENGE OF THE PERSIAN WARS

The two major wars fought between the uneasily unified Greeks and the vast empire of the Persians were construed as defining events by those who witnessed and looked back on them. From the first, the contest was unequal. Persia was the largest and most efficient state the world had ever seen, capable of mustering over a million armed men. The Greeks, by contrast, remained a collection of disparate communities, fiercely competitive and suspicious of one another. An exceptionally large polis, such as Athens or Sparta, might put 10,000 hoplites in the field; but the vast majority of Greek states could only provide a few hundred each. So the threat of Persian conquest loomed large on the Greek horizon, after which the experience of international warfare changed the Greek world immeasurably.

A MODERN REPLICA OF AN ATHENIAN TRIREME. These versatile warships were much more powerful than the old 50-oared pentakonters that had been in use for centuries. As the name suggests, a trireme featured three banks of oars on each side, 170 oars in total. These were manned by citizen rowers seated on benches at three different levels in the vessel's hold. In battle, rowers could help power a ship forward, turn it, and keep it on course in a chase, even when sailing into the wind. In favorable winds, sails could be used to add speed. ▪ *How does this new military technology build on some of the same strategies as hoplite warfare?*

The Ionian Revolt (499–494 B.C.E.)

For the first time in the history of Western civilizations, we can follow the unfolding of these events through the narrative of a contemporary historian: Herodotus, the first person who self-consciously set out to write an account of his own times in careful, unambiguous prose—rather than in the form of heroic poetry or the boastful language of victorious inscriptions. And luckily for us, Herodotus was uniquely qualified to probe the long-term and more immediate causes of the Persian Wars. Raised in the Ionian polis of Halicarnassus, he was a product of the hybrid culture discussed above. He was also a keen observer of human nature and human diversity. He regarded both the Greeks and the Persians as great peoples. Yet, as a Greek himself—albeit one born within the Persian dominion—he was not impartial. Indeed, his surviving account reflects many of the intellectual currents of mid-fifth-century Athens, where he spent the better part of his career, as well as many Athenian prejudices. This is something that must be borne in mind when reading his work.

Herodotus wanted to show that the war between the Persians and Greeks had ancient roots and could be traced back to long-standing cultural differences, but his narrative also shows that the catalyst was a political conflict in Miletus. In 501 B.C.E., the city was governed by Aristagoras (*EHR-is-STAG-or-uhs*), a tyrant who owed his power to the backing of the Persian emperor, Darius (Chapter 2). But apparently, Aristagoras came to believe that his days as the emperor's favorite were numbered. So he turned abruptly from puppet to patriot, rousing the Milesians and the rest of Ionia to revolt against Persian rule. As a safeguard, he also sought military support from the sympathetic poleis on the Greek mainland. The Spartans refused to send their army abroad, but Athens and Eretria (*er-eh-TREE-uh*), on

Past and Present

Political Satire

In the fifth century B.C.E., the playwright Aristophanes took an older form of comedy, the satyr play, and turned it into a vehicle for what we still call satire. Instead of gently mocking the gods, he lampooned the politics, popular culture, and current events of his own day—and so made his fellow citizens take a fresh look at themselves. If he were alive today, he might be working for *The Daily Show*.

 Watch related author interview on StudySpace
wwnorton.com/web/westernciv18

the island of Euboea (*you-BOY-ah*), agreed to send twenty-five ships and crews. This small force managed to capture the old Lydian capital of Sardis (by then a Persian administrative center) and burn it to the ground. Then the Athenians and Eretrians went home, leaving the Ionians to their own devices. In 494 B.C.E., the rebellious poleis were finally overwhelmed by the vastly superior might of Persia.

Darius realized, however, that so long as his Greek subjects in Asia Minor could cast a hopeful eye to their neighbors across the Aegean, they would forge alliances with them. He therefore decided to launch a preemptive strike against Athens and Eretria, to teach these upstart poleis a lesson. In the summer of 490 B.C.E, a punitive expedition of 20,000 soldiers under two of Persia's finest generals crossed the Aegean and landed on the coast of Euboea. Their forces sacked and burned Eretria to the ground, sending its population into captivity in Persia. They then crossed the narrow strait to Attica, landing on the plain of Marathon, approximately twenty-six miles from Athens.

Marathon and Its Aftermath

When the Persians landed in Attica, the Athenians quickly sought help from the only polis that could conceivably help them forestall annhilation: Sparta. But the Spartans responded that they were unable to assist—they were celebrating a religious festival. Only the small, nearby polis of Plataea offered the Athenians aid. The Athenian and Plataean hoplites would have to engage the mighty Persians on their own.

Heavily outnumbered and without effective cavalry to counter that of the Persians, the Athenian phalanx took a position between two hills blocking the main road to the polis. After a standoff of several days, the Athenian general Miltiades (*mil-TIE-uh-dees*) received word that the Persians were watering their horses and that the Persian infantry was vulnerable to attack. So Miltiades led a charge that smashed the Persian force and resulted in crippling losses. Almost unbelievably, the Athenians had defeated the world's major imperial power, and they had done it without Spartan help. It was a vindication of hoplite tactics and a tremendous boost to Athenian confidence.

Yet the Athenian politician Themistocles (the-MIS-toh-klees) warned that the Persians would not suffer such humiliation quietly and that they would retaliate with an even larger force. So when the Athenians discovered a rich vein of silver ore in the Attic countryside a few years later, Themistocles persuaded them not to divide the windfall among themselves (the customary practice) but to finance a fleet of 200 triremes, state-of-the-art warships. Athens thereby transformed itself into the preeminent naval power of the Greek world, just in time to confront a new Persian onslaught.

Xerxes' Invasion

Darius the Great died in 486 B.C.E. and was succeeded by his son Xerxes, who almost immediately began preparing a massive overland invasion of Greece designed to conquer the entire territory, thus eradicating any future threats to Persian imperial expansion while avenging his father's shame. Supported by a fleet of 600 ships, this grand army (which numbered at least 150,000 men and may have been as large as 300,000) set out from Sardis in 480 B.C.E., crossing the Hellespont (literally "bridge to Greece"), the narrow strait separating Europe from Asia. Unlike his father, who had dispatched talented generals against Athens, Xerxes led this campaign himself.

THE PERSIAN WARS WITH GREECE. Imagine that you are the Persian emperor Xerxes, planning the conquest of Greece in 480 B.C.E. ■ *What are the two possible routes that you could take to attack Greece?* ■ *What geographical considerations would dictate your military strategy?* ■ *Bearing in mind that Xerxes' attempt failed, what would you do differently?*

Many Greek poleis capitulated immediately. But Athens, Sparta, Corinth, and some thirty others refused to surrender. Instead, they hastily formed the Hellenic League, an unprecedented alliance in the face of an unprecedented external threat. In August of 480, a major Persian offensive was held at bay when the outnumbered Greek allies, under the military leadership of Sparta, confronted Xerxes at the mountain pass of Thermopylae (ther-MO-puh-lie). For three days, they valiantly held off the Persian multitude, whose way through the narrow pass was effectively blocked. Meanwhile, a Greek fleet led by Athens and guided by Themistocles engaged a Persian flotilla off the Attic coast. The Spartans' defense of Thermopylae ultimately failed, but their sacrifice allowed the new Athenian warships to inflict heavy losses on the Persians.

However, these engagements left Athens without any men to defend the city. Themistocles therefore persuaded the entire population to abandon Athens for the island of Salamis. From there, the Athenians watched the Persians torch their city. Time, however, was on their side. Xerxes' massive army depended on his damaged fleet for supplies, and the Persians' military tactics—which included a heavy reliance on cavalry and chariots—were not adapted for the rocky terrain of Greece. Bad weather also made sailing the Aegean in autumn a risky business; the Persians were now desperate to force a decisive battle and return home before the season turned against them.

In late September, the numerically superior Persian fleet sailed into the straits of Salamis, believing that the Athenians were preparing to flee the island. The report turned out to be false, but so confident was Xerxes that he had a throne placed on the headland above the bay, where he would have a good view of his victory. Instead, he watched as the battle-ready Athenian triremes demolished the Persian fleet. This was the turning point of the war. Xerxes retreated with the majority of his army to Persia, while an elite force stayed behind. But when the allied Greek army met the Persians on favorable terrain the next spring—an open plain near Plataea, which had been razed the year before—the Greeks prevailed. Against all odds, the small, fractious poleis had defeated the mightiest army of the known world.

THE GOLDEN AGE OF CLASSICAL GREECE

In the half century after the Persian Wars, Athens enjoyed a meteoric rise in power and prestige, becoming the premier naval power of the eastern Mediterranean and the military rival of Sparta. Athens also emerged as leader of the Delian League, a group of poleis whose representatives met on the sacred island of Delos and pledged to continue the war against Persia, which was now being fought in the Aegean. As the league's leader, Athens controlled its funds and resources. This era simultaneously witnessed the greatest achievements in Athenian culture and politics. These were complicated, however, by the increasingly awkward relationship of Athens with its allies, who began to feel more like Athenian subjects than free poleis.

Periclean Athens

In the decades before the Persian Wars, political reforms in Athens had continued to encourage further experiments in democracy, including the practice of selecting major officeholders by lot. Only one key position was now filled by traditional voting: the office of *strategos*, or general. And because a man could be elected strategos year after year, this office became the career goal of Athens' most ambitious figures. Themistocles had been strategos, as was Cimon (KEY-mohn), who led the Delian League to victories over Persia in the 470s and 460s B.C.E. But Cimon also used the league

GREEK FORCES DEFEAT PERSIANS. This detail from a bowl commemorating the defeat of Xerxes' army depicts an Athenian hoplite poised to strike a death-blow to his Persian opponent. The artist has carefully delineated the differences between the enemies' dress and weaponry. To the Greeks, the Persian preference for trousers over short tunics seemed particularly barbaric and effeminate.

to punish poleis who tried to opt out of membership, even suppressing revolts in these cities by force of arms and so turning the league into an instrument of Athenian policy.

By then, the political mood in Athens was changing. New voices were demanding a greater role in government; most prominent were the *thetes* (THAY-taes), the lowest class of free men and the class that provided the triremes' rowers: the backbone of the all-important Athenian fleet. Like the hoplites of the Archaic Period, who had achieved citizenship because they were indispensable to the defense of the poleis, the thetes wanted higher status and equal representation. The man who emerged to champion their cause was Pericles (PEHR-eh-klees), an aristocrat from one of Athens' most prestigious families.

Pericles made the enfranchisement of the thetes the main plank of his political platform, and also advocated a foreign policy that was oriented away from cooperation with Sparta. In 462–461 B.C.E. he was elected strategos and immediately used his position to secure the ostracism of his rival, Cimon. He then pushed through reforms that gave every Athenian citizen the right to propose and amend legislation, not just to vote yes or no in the citizen assembly. And by paying an average day's wage for attendance, he made it easier for poorer citizens to participate in the assembly and in courts of justice. Through such measures, the thetes and other free men of modest means became a dominant force in politics—and loyal to the man who had made that dominance possible.

In keeping with the ambitions of Pericles, this populist program glorified Athens through an ambitious scheme of public building and lavish festivals honoring the gods, especially Athena. Personally, too, Pericles was a generous patron of the arts and sciences, attracting the greatest minds and talents of the day to Athens. His popularity, combined with his charisma and his promotion of the Athenians' sense of superiority, ensured his reelection as strategos for the next three decades. During these years Athens flourished, but it also alienated much of the Greek world by its arrogance and aggression.

Athenian Literature and Drama

Athens was not the only city to produce great works of art during this period, but our knowledge of classical Greek culture is dominated by the dramas produced at its great religious festivals. The most important of these was the Dionysia, a great spring feast devoted to the god Dionysus, which became a celebration of Athenian exceptionalism and democratic ideals. From the beginning, therefore, drama was closely connected to the political and religious life of the state that sponsored it. Indeed, the very format of classical tragedy replicates the tensions of democracy, with its complex cast of characters and its conflict among opposing perspectives. This format was perfected under the great tragedian Aeschylus (AY-skihl-uhs, 525–456 B.C.E.) and his younger contemporary, Sophocles (496–406 B.C.E.). Their dramas made use of two or eventually, three professional actors, each of whom could play numerous roles, and a chorus of Athenian citizens which represented collective opinion and could comment on the action.

Although Aristotle would later declare that the purpose of tragedy was to inspire pity and fear and so to purge these emotions through a process called *katharsis* ("purification"), this definition does not capture either the variety or impact of Athenian tragedy. Tragedies were almost always set in the distant or mythical past, but they were intended to address the cutting-edge issues of their day. Indeed, the very earliest of all surviving tragedies, Aeschylus' *The Persians*, represents events of the playwright's own lifetime; we know for certain that he fought at Marathon, because he had this fact proudly recorded on his tomb. Performed for the first time in 472, this contemporary tragedy tells the story of the great Athenian victory at Salamis—but through the eyes of the defeated Xerxes, who thus becomes its tragic hero.

Even when its subject matter was derived from the epics of Homer, the fundamental themes of tragedy—justice, the conflicting demands of personal desire and public duty, the unforeseen consequences of human actions, the brutalizing effects of power—addressed problems of immediate concern to Athenians. For example, Aeschylus' trilogy the *Oresteia* (458 B.C.E.) is ostensibly about the legendary family of the Mycenaean king Agamemnon, and traces the long-term consequences of the king's sacrifice of his daughter, Iphigenia; his subsequent murder at the hands of his grieving wife, Clytemnestra; and the vengeance taken by the couple's son, Orestes, on his own mother. But the court of law which eventually tries Orestes is actually that of Periclean Athens, and the plays' debates over the rational application of law are debates that resonated with Aeschylus' contemporaries. *Oedipus at Colonus*, one of Sophocles' later tragedies, used the story of the mythical king of Thebes to comment bitterly on Athens' disastrous war with Sparta (see below). Similarly, the *Trojan Women* of Euripides (485–406 B.C.E.), presented in 415, marks the tragic turning point in the Athenians' march toward defeat in this war. By looking back at the capture, rape, and enslavement of Troy's defeated women, Athenians were forced to look at the dreadful consequences of their own imperial policies.

Comedy was even more obviously a genre of political commentary and social satire, and could deal openly with the absurdities and atrocities of current events. Not

THE THEATER AT EPIDAUROS. Greek dramas were invariably presented in the open air, usually at dawn. Since these were civic spectacles, theaters had to be large enough to accommodate all citizens. Most, like this one at Epidauros (right), took advantage of the natural slope of a hill. The plan for the theater is shown above (left). The acting area would have been backed by a high wall, the *skene*, which housed stage machinery and enhanced the acoustics. A trained actor standing in the *orchestra* would have been plainly audible even to those seated in the top tier. ▪ *How would the size and setting of such a theater enhance the political character of the plays performed within it?*

only was it unconstrained by any formal poetic framework, comedy—then as now—could be effectively and safely deployed to deal with issues that were too hot to handle in any other medium: sexual scandals, political corruption, moral hypocrisy, intellectual pretension, popular fads. Aristophanes (*EHR-ih-STOFF-ah-nees*, c. 446–386 B.C.E.), the greatest of the Athenian comic playwrights, lampooned everything from the philosophy of Socrates to the tragedies of his contemporary Euripides, and was an especially outspoken critic of Athenian warmongers and their imperialist aims. He regularly savaged the powerful figures whom he saw as leading Athens to its doom, and he was repeatedly dragged into court to defend himself against the demagogues he attacked. But the power and popularity of comic theater was such that politicians never dared to shut it down for long. It was too much an expression, and outcome, of Athenian ideals.

Periclean Athens was also fertile ground for the development of new literary forms. Even though the Greeks of this age were becoming more dependent on writing for legal and commercial transactions, they valued highly the arts of memory and oral debate; and intellectuals had long been used to expressing themselves through poetry, which was always intended to be sung and enjoyed in performance, not to be read. (The Milesian philosophers had conveyed their ideas in verse, and Solon had used poetry in justifying his political reforms). In the course of this century, though, the rise of functional literacy in Athens encouraged the emergence of prose as a distinct literary form. Herodotus found

a ready market for his histories in Athens. His younger contemporary Thucydides (*thoo-SID-ih-dees*) followed suit, using his time in exile to write a masterful—and scathingly critical—history of the war between his polis and Sparta, in which he himself had unsuccessfully fought.

Between them, these two historians developed a new approach to the study of the past, emphasizing the need to collect and interpret multiple sources and focusing on human agency as the driving force of history (rather than divine intervention or divine will). Although in different ways, both conceived the historian's role as distinct from that of a storyteller. The word *historia* would continue to mean both "story" and "history" in Greek, but for Herodotus and Thucydides the historian's task was to investigate and critically reflect on the events of his own time, as well as to illuminate those of the past. These methods and goals would increasingly come to inform other prose genres, including the philosophical writings of Plato and Aristotle (see Chapter 4).

Art and Architecture

The visual artists of fifth-century B.C.E. Greece revealed the same range of talents in the visual arts as poets did in their dramas. Their comic gift is exhibited in vessels made for festive use at symposia, which often depict the delights of sensuality, sexual encounters, and scenes from bawdy tales. By contrast, the heroic but humane mode of tragedy corresponds to the marble statues and sculptured reliefs made for temples and public places. Athenian sculptors in particular were drawn to the challenges of representing the human form accurately, while at the same time celebrating an ideal of physical beauty.

Perhaps the most striking development in fifth-century Greek sculpture was the new attention paid to the crafting of naturalistic figures, both clothed and nude. This happened first in Athens. Nothing like it had ever been seen before, although it is a trend already discernible in the figure of the kouros examined on page 82 and in the successive refinements of the sculptor's art made in the previous century. What hastened the acceptance of naturalism in art is a matter of intense debate, but scholars have long wanted to link this innovation to the triumphant victories over the Persians in those key decades. Greeks tended to

regard the Persian male's modesty of dress, preference for trousers, fondness for jewelry, and luxurious long hair as proofs of effeminacy (see the bowl on page 96), whereas Greek men took pride in sculpting their physiques, exercising and participating in athletic contests in the nude. A Greek might have said that only barbarians bowed down to their rulers like slaves and covered their shameful bodies in constricting clothes; free men celebrate their individuality not only in politics but in the care of the body and its representation.

The Athenians also made exceptional contributions to architecture in this period. All Greek temples sought to create an impression of harmony, but the Parthenon of Athens, built between 447 and 438 B.C.E., is generally considered the finest example. Construction of this stunning, expensive, and structurally ambitious building was urged on the

APOLLO OF TENEA, APOLLO OF PIOMBINO, AND THE CRITIAN BOY. These three statues, dating from about 560, 500, and 480 B.C.E., respectively, display the development of Greek statuary art. The first rather stiff and symmetrical statue (left) is imitative of Egyptian sculpture. Roughly a half century later, the second representation (middle) of Apollo begins to display motion, not unlike the kouros on page 82. The last figure (right), showing a boy standing in a relaxed posture with his weight resting on one leg, displays even greater naturalism.

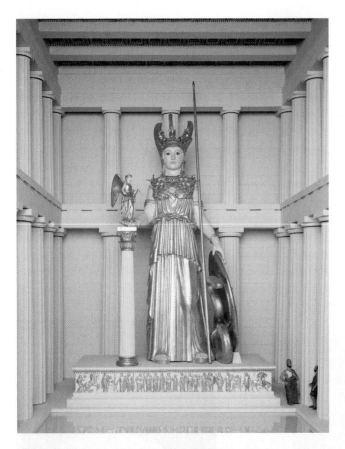

THE SHRINE OF ATHENA IN THE PARTHENON. This is a replica of the statue of Athena that once stood inside the Parthenon dedicated to her (see also the image on page 76). Made of gold and ivory and designed by the great sculptor Phidias, who was updating a more archaic style, the statue stood forty feet high and was visible to viewers oustide the temple and some distance away. Its image would have been reflected in a shallow pool of water located in front of the statue.

Athenians by Pericles as a tribute to their patron goddess, Athena Parthenos ("Athena the Virgin"), and as a symbol of their own power, confidence, and genius.

The Daily Life of Athens: Men, Women, and Slaves

Toward the end of his famous funeral oration, which Thucydides quotes in his history, Pericles addresses only a few brief remarks to the women of Athens who mourn their fallen fathers, husbands, and sons at the end of the first year of the disastrous war with Sparta. He urges them to do three things: rear more children for the support of Athens and its wars, show no more weakness than is "natural to their sex," and attract no attention to themselves. For as he says, the greatest glory of a woman is not to be spoken of at all, whether for good or ill. His remarks reveal widely held

attitudes toward women in classical Greece, although they may not reflect complex historical realities.

The growth of democracy did not lead to greater equality between the sexes; in fact, it had the opposite result. In the Bronze Age of Mycenaean Greece, women were viewed as possessing extraordinary funds of courage and wisdom, as well as beauty and virtue. They were prized for their shrewd advice on political and military matters, and they played an active role in the world. Sometimes, elite women ruled kingdoms in their own right. Indeed, this was still the case in the northern territories of Macedon and Epirus, as we shall see (Chapter 4), as well as in some Ionian poleis.

But as aristocratic ideals gave way to more democratic ones, Greek women increasingly spent their lives in the confinement of the home. On the one hand, the importance of the hoplite infantry and its spirit of shared purpose encouraged men to train together and to develop close relationships, something that was also sanctioned by the political system. On the other hand, that spirit of equality discouraged the political agency of women. Instead, the production of children to supply the infantry became the female imperative. Public spaces were largely restricted to male activities, while domestic spaces were reserved for female endeavors, such as child care and weaving. Respectable women lived largely in the seclusion of a house's inner courtyard, rarely venturing forth from their homes.

In Athens, girls could be legally married at age fourteen to husbands more than twice their age. (Younger men were supposed to devote themselves to war.) A girl's father arranged her marriage and provided a dowry that her husband could use for her support. Shortly after a wife entered her new home, a regular schedule of childbirth would begin. Typically, the interval between births was two to four years, meaning that the average young wife would bear between four and six children before she died, usually around the age of thirty-five. Her place might then be taken by another, younger woman.

Because women seldom went out of doors or ventured beyond their immediate neighborhood, since it was thought immodest for them to be seen by men other than those in their families, slaves did whatever shopping or marketing the household required. Even at home, women were expected to withdraw into private rooms if visitors arrived. But they were not supposed to sit around idly, and their main occupation—this was true of all women, from royalty to slaves—was the spinning and weaving of cloth. And since women's work was basically menial, men looked down on them for it, even though their own livelihoods and comfort depended on it. Some evidence even suggests that husbands were not encouraged to form emotional attachments to their wives, although many certainly

WOMEN AND WEAVING. Wool-working and weaving were gender-specific activities throughout the ancient world, in which women of all social ranks were expected to participate. On this red-figure vase, dating from 460–450 B.C.E., we see the woman on the left carding wool, and the two women on the right preparing fibers for spinning into threads, which could then be woven into cloth.

did. In a revealing passage, Herodotus reports of a certain Lydian king that he "fell in love with his own wife, a fancy that had strange consequences." By contrast, an Athenian orator remarked that "we have prostitutes for pleasure, concubines for daily physical needs, and wives to bear us legitimate children and be our faithful housekeepers." But these perspectives are offset by a range of archaeological and material evidence that testify to women's valued social roles, the affection of their husbands and children, and even their wider economic and legal powers.

In addition to depending on the labor and fertility of women, Athenians were as reliant on slaves as Spartans were on helots. Without slavery, none of the Athenian accomplishments in politics, thought, or art would have been possible. The Athenian ideal of dividing and rotating governmental duties among all free men depended on slaves who worked in fields, businesses, and homes while free men engaged in politics. In fact, the Athenian democratic system began to function fully only with the expansion of Athenian mining and commerce around 500 B.C.E., which enabled the Athenians to buy slaves in larger numbers. Freedom and slavery were thus an inescapable contradiction of this democracy—much as they would be many centuries later in the United States, prior to the Civil War.

Although widespread, Athenian slavery was modest in scale. Slaves did not ordinarily work in teams or in factories; the only exceptions were the state-owned silver mines, where large numbers of slaves toiled in miserable conditions. Most slaves were owned in small numbers by a wide range of Athenian families, including the relatively poor. As domestic servants and farm laborers, slaves might even be considered trusted members of the household, although their masters were legally empowered to beat them or abuse them; concubines were often drawn from among this class of slaves. Yet slaves could never be entirely dehumanized, as they were in modern slaveholding societies: the misfortune of becoming a slave through debt was a reality of Athens' recent past, and the real possibility of being enslaved in war would become a widespread consequence of Athens' overreaching ambitions.

"THE GREATEST WAR IN HISTORY" AND ITS CONSEQUENCES

In more ways than one, Athenian freedom rested on the servitude of others. Slaves performed much of the labor at home, while Athens' allies in the Delian League provided the resources that supported Athenian greatness. Without the surplus wealth flowing into Athens from the league, none of the projects Pericles undertook—pay for political participation, massive building projects, the patronage of Athenian drama—would have been possible. These projects kept Athens rich, its democracy vibrant, and Pericles in power. But ultimately, Athens' foreign policy and imperial ambitions undermined these achievements.

Since the 470s, as we noted above, Athens had begun crushing those allies who attempted to break from its control. By the early 440s, its only rival for supremacy in the Greek world was Sparta. Rather than attempting to maintain a balance of power, however, Pericles determined on a more aggressive policy. In order to ensure that available military resources would be directed toward any future Spartan opposition, he made formal peace with Persia. Yet this undermined the sole purpose of the Delian League, which had been the defense of Greece against Persian aggression. Athens now had no justification for compelling its members to maintain their allegiance. Many remained loyal nonetheless, paying their contributions and enjoying the economic benefits of warm relations with Athens. Others, however, did not, and Athens found itself increasingly having to force its reluctant allies back into line, often installing Athenian garrisons and planting Athenian colonists—who retained their Athenian citizenship—to ensure continued loyalty.

In the context of recent history and longstanding Greek values, such behavior was disturbing. The Delian League had been established to preserve Greek independence. Now Athens itself was becoming an oppressive, imperial power. Foremost among its critics were the Corinthians, whose own economic standing was threatened by Athenian dominance. The Corinthians were close allies of the Spartans, who in turn were the dominant power in what historians call the Peloponnesian League. (The Greeks called it simply the "Spartans and their allies.") When war finally erupted between Athens and Sparta, Thucydides—himself an Athenian—ascribed it to the growing power of Athens and the anxiety this inspired in other poleis. No modern historian has improved on Thucydides' thesis. Yet for the Athenians and their leaders, there could be no question of relinquishing their empire, or the dream of dominating the Mediterranean world. For Sparta and its allies, meanwhile, the prospect of relinquishing their own culture and independence was equally unthinkable. Two very different ideas of Greek superiority were about to fight to the death.

The Peloponnesian War Begins

When the Athenians and Spartans found themselves at war with one another in 431 B.C.E., both sides believed a conclusion would come quickly—a delusion common to many of history's pivotal wars. Instead, the war dragged on for twenty-seven years. Thucydides, writing about it in exile, recalled that he knew from the time of its outbreak that it was going to be "the greatest war in history," amounting to the first world war, because by the time it was over it would involve the entire Mediterranean. He also meant that it was the worst, so devastating to both sides that it partially destroyed the Greeks' proud heritage of freedom. By the time Athens was forced to concede defeat, all the poleis were weakened to such an extent that they would never again be able to withstand outside threats.

From the beginning, Athens knew that it could not defeat Sparta on land; and neither Sparta nor its allies had a fleet capable of facing the Athenians at sea. Pericles therefore developed a bold strategy: he would pull the entire population of Attica within the walls of Athens and its harbor, and not attempt to defend the countryside against Sparta. For sustenance, Athens would rely on supplies shipped in by its fleet, which would also be deployed to ravage the coasts of the Peloponnesus.

The Spartans duly plundered the farms and pastures of Attica, frustrated that the Athenians would not engage them in battle. Meanwhile, the Athenians inflicted significant destruction on Spartan territory in a series of raids and by successfully encouraging rebellion among the helots. The advantage appeared to be on Athens' side, but in 429 B.C.E. the crowded conditions of the besieged city gave rise to a typhus epidemic that killed over a third of the population, including the aged Pericles. Pericles' death revealed that he had been the only man capable of managing the political forces he had unleashed. His successors were mostly dema-

gogues, ambitious men who played to the worst instincts of the demos. The most successful of these was Cleon, a particular target of Aristophanes' ridicule, who refused a Spartan offer of peace in 425 B.C.E. and continued the war until his own death in battle four years later. It was under Cleon that Thucydides was given the impossible task of liberating a city under Spartan control; his failure in 423 led to his exile.

After the death of Cleon, a truce with Sparta was negotiated by an able Athenian leader named Nikias. But Athenians continued to pursue a "dirty war" by preying on poleis that it feared might support the Spartans. This led to atrocities like the destruction of Melos, an island that had been colonized by the Spartans but had maintained its neutrality since the beginning of the war. When the inhabitants of Melos refused to compromise this position by accepting Athenian rule, Athens had the entire male population slaughtered and every woman and child sold into slavery. Thereafter, Athens' policy of preemptive warfare proved destructive to itself. In 415 B.C.E., a charismatic young aristocrat named Alkibiades (al-kih-BY-uh-dees) convinced the Athenians to attack the powerful Greek city of Syracuse in Sicily, which was allegedly harrying Athenian allies in the western Mediterranean. The expedition failed disastrously, ending with the death or enslavement of thousands of Athenian warriors.

News of the Syracusan disaster shattered the Athenians. Many political leaders were driven from the polis as scapegoats, and in 411 B.C.E. a hastily convened assembly of citizens voted democracy out of existence, replacing it with an oligarchy ("rule of the few") consisting of 400 members, many of whom had been present at this vote. The remains of the Athenian fleet, then stationed at Samos on the Ionian coast, responded by declaring a democratic government in exile under the leadership of none other than Alkibiades. The oligarchy proved to be brief, and democracy was restored to Athens by 409. But a pattern of self-destruction had been established, making it difficult for anyone in Athens or outside it to believe in the possibility of restored greatness.

THE FAILURE OF ATHENIAN DEMOCRACY

The Spartans, too, despaired of bringing the war to an end. Even in its weakened condition, the Athenian fleet was still invincible. Finally, Sparta turned to the Persians, who were glad to avenge themselves on Athens and agreed to supply the gold and expertise necessary to train an effective

THE PELOPONNESIAN WAR. This map shows the patchwork of colonies and alliances that bound together the supporters of Sparta and Athens at the outbreak of the Peloponnesian War. ▪ *Which side had the geographical advantage?* ▪ *Which neutral powers might have been able to tip the balance by entering the war on one side or the other?* ▪ *What strategic and military choices did geography impose on the two combatants and their allies?*

Spartan navy. Meanwhile, Athenians were turning against each other and making the Spartans' task easier. In 406, a rare Athenian naval victory at Arginusae (*ar-geh-NOO-si*) ended in a sudden storm, which prevented Athenian commanders from rescuing the sailors whose ships had been wrecked. A firestorm of protest was fanned by demagogues who insisted on making an example of those generals brave enough to return to Athens. One of these was Pericles' son Pericles, who was executed, thereby dying a victim of his father's policies. Through such measures, the Athenians killed or exiled the last of their able commanders.

The result was tragic. The poorly led Athenian fleet was destroyed in 404 B.C.E. Without ships, the Athe-

nians could neither feed themselves nor defend their city. The Spartans sailed the Aegean unopposed, installing pro-Spartan oligarchies to rule former Athenian allies. Finally, they besieged Athens, which surrendered. Corinth and Thebes, remembering the ruthless treatment of Melos, called for Athens' annihilation. The Spartans refused, but imposed harsh terms: the dismantling of Athens' defensive walls, the scrapping of its fleet, and the acceptance of an oligarchy under Spartan supervision. These so-called Thirty Tyrants confiscated private property and murdered their political opponents. Their excesses drove committed democrats to plan a desperate coup, a bloodbath averted only through the intervention of the Spartan kings. By the end

Competing Viewpoints

Two Views of Socrates

Socrates as a Sophist

Most people regard Socrates as the sage thinker who challenged the prevailing prejudices of his day. During his own time, however, he was not so universally admired. In Aristophanes' comedy The Clouds, *the protagonist, Strepsiades, goes to Socrates and his "Thought Shop," asking that Socrates make him and his son, Pheidippides, orators capable of winning lawsuits and growing rich. Aristophanes implies throughout that Socrates is a charlatan who teaches word games and tricks for hire.*

STREPSIADES: See that he [Pheidippides] learns your two Arguments, whatever you call them—oh yes, Right and Wrong—the one that takes a bad case and defeats Right with it. If he can't manage both, then at least Wrong—that will do—but that he must have.

SOCRATES: Well, I'll go and send the Arguments here in person, and they'll teach him themselves.

STREPSIADES: Don't forget, he's got to be able to argue against any kind of justified claim at all.

RIGHT: This way. Let the audience see you. . . .

WRONG: Sure, go wherever you like. The more of an audience we have, the more soundly I'll trounce you.

RIGHT: What sort of trick will you use?

WRONG: Oh, just a few new ideas.

RIGHT: Yes, they're in fashion now, aren't they, [*to the audience*] thanks to you idiots. . . . [*to Pheiddipides*] You don't want to be the sort of chap who's always in the agora telling stories about other people's sex lives, or in the courts arguing about some petty, filthy little dispute. . . .

WRONG: People here at the Thought Shop call me Wrong, because I was the one who invented ways of proving anything wrong, laws, prosecutors, anything. Isn't that worth millions—to have a really bad case and yet win? . . . Suppose you fall in love with a married woman—have a bit of fun—and get caught in the act. As you are now, without a tongue in your head, you're done for. But if you come and learn from me, then you can do whatever you like and get away with it . . . and supposing you do get caught with someone's wife, you can say to him. . . . "What have I done wrong? Look at Zeus; wasn't he always a slave of his sexual passions? And do you expect a mere mortal like me to do any better than a god?" . . .

STREPSIADES [*to Socrates*]: I wonder if you'd accept a token of my appreciation? But my son, has he learned that Argument we were listening to a moment ago?

SOCRATES: Yes, he has.

STREPSIADES: Holy Fraud, how wonderful!

SOCRATES: Yes, you'll now be able to win any case at all.

Source: Aristophanes, *The Clouds*, trans. Alan H. Sommerstein (New York: 1973), pp. 148–50, 154, 159–60 (slightly revised).

Socrates and the Laws of Athens

According to his pupil Plato, Socrates spent the last days of his life in conversation with his friends and followers, some of whom urged him to escape from captivity and live in exile. In the dialogue Crito, *a young aristocrat of that name argues that the very laws that have condemned Socrates are unjust, and that by choosing to obey them Socrates is giving them a legitimacy they do not deserve. Halfway through the debate, Socrates turns the tables on him.*

SOCRATES: I should like you to consider whether we are still satisfied on this point: that the really important thing is not to live, but to live well.

CRITO: Why, yes.

SOCRATES: And that to live well means the same thing as to live honorably, or rightly?

CRITO: Yes.

SOCRATES: Then in light of this agreement we must consider whether or not it is right for me to try to get away without an official pardon. If it turns out to be right, we must make the attempt; if not, we must let it drop. . . .

CRITO: I agree with what you say, Socrates. . . .

SOCRATES: Well, here is my next point, or rather question. Ought one to fulfill all one's agreements, provided they are right, or break them?

CRITO: One ought to fulfill them.

SOCRATES: Then consider the logical consequence. If we leave this place without first persuading the polis to let us go . . . are we or are we not abiding by our just agreements?

CRITO: I can't answer your question, Socrates. I am not clear in my mind.

SOCRATES: Look at it this way. Suppose that while we were preparing to run away (or however one should describe it), the Laws of Athens were to come and confront us with this question: "Now, Socrates, what are your proposing to do? Can you deny that by this act which you are contemplating you intend, so far as you have the power, to destroy us, the Laws, and the whole polis as well? Do you imagine that a city can continue to exist and not be turned upside down, if the legal judgments which are pronounced in it have no force but are nullified and destroyed by private persons?"—How shall we answer this question, Crito, and

others of the same kind? . . . Shall we say, "Yes, I do intend to destroy the laws, because the polis has wronged me by passing a faulty judgment at my trial"? Is this to be our answer, or what?

CRITO: What you have just said, by all means, Socrates.

SOCRATES: Then supposing the Laws say, "Was there provision for this in the agreement between you and us, Socrates? Or did you pledge to abide by whatever judgments the polis pronounced? . . . [I]f you cannot persuade your country you must do whatever it orders, and patiently submit to any punishment it imposes, whether it be flogging or imprisonment. And if it leads you out to war, you must comply, and it is right that you should do so; you must not give way or retreat or abandon your position. Both in war and in the law courts you must do whatever your city and your country commands."

Source: Plato, *Crito*, excerpted (with modifications) from *The Last Days of Socrates*, trans. Hugh Tredennick (New York: 1969), pp. 87–91.

Questions for Analysis

1. Socrates actually refused to teach the art of "making the weaker argument defeat the stronger." But in *The Clouds*, Aristophanes shows him teaching how "to win any case at all." Why were the powers of persuasion considered potentially dangerous in democratic Athens? Why would Aristophanes choose to represent Socrates in this way?

2. How do the arguments of Plato's Socrates compare to those of Aristophanes' character?

3. How does Socrates' sense of honor and his duty toward the polis compare to that of Tyrtaeus of Sparta (page 84)?

---

of 401 B.C.E., Athens had restored a semblance of democratic governance, but it was never more than a shadow of its former self.

With its victory, Sparta succeeded Athens as the arbiter of the Greek world. But this was a thankless job, made worse by the losses the Spartans themselves had suffered during the war, and by the fact that they were even more aggressive in their control of the Aegean than the Athenians had been. In fact, the Spartans found themselves in a position they had avoided throughout their history, because their far-flung interests now sapped their manpower and undermined their control over the helots. They also faced a reinvigorated Persian Empire, which took advantage of the Greeks' fratricidal struggles to increase its naval presence in the Aegean.

These were the circumstances in which the Athenian philosopher Socrates (469–399 B.C.E.) attempted to reform his city's ethical and political traditions. To understand something of his accomplishments, and to assess the reasons for his tragic death, we must trace briefly the history of philosophical speculation in the half century before his birth.

The Pythagoreans and the Sophists

After the Persian conquest of Ionia, many Milesian philosophers fled to southern Italy. Philosophical speculation thus continued in the Greek "far west." A major proponent was Pythagoras, who founded a philosophical community in the Italian city of Croton. Pythagoras and his followers regarded the speculative life as the highest good, but they believed that one must be purified of fleshly desires in order to achieve this. Just as the essence of life lay in the mind,

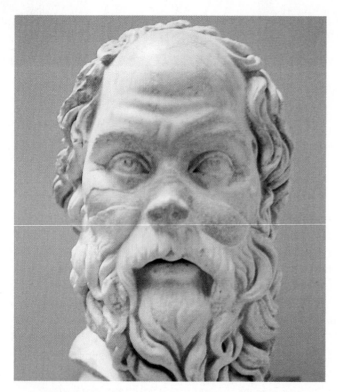

SOCRATES. According to Plato, Socrates looked like a goatman but spoke like a god.

other words, values are not moral imperatives, established by the gods. Instead, Protagoras declared that no one could know whether the gods existed or, if they did, what they wanted. He thus concluded that there could be no absolute standards of right and wrong. Empirical facts, established by the perception of the senses, were thus the only source of knowledge. And because each man experienced the world in a different way, there could be only individual truths valid for the individual knower.

Such teachings struck many Greeks as dangerous. Sophists like Protagoras made everyday life a subject for philosophical discussion, but their relativism could too easily degenerate into a conviction that the wise man (or the wise state) is the one best able to manipulate others and gratify individual desires. Both personally and collectively, this conviction could rationalize monstrous acts of brutality—like those committed by Athens in the case of Melos. Indeed, the lessons of the Peloponnesian War went a long way toward demonstrating the disastrous consequences of this self-serving logic: if justice is merely relative, then neither individual morality nor society can survive. This ethical conviction led to the growth of a new philosophical movement grounded on the theory that absolute standards do exist, and that human beings can determine what these are through the exercise of reason. The initiator of this trend was Socrates.

The Life and Thought of Socrates

Socrates was not a professional teacher, as the Sophists were. He may have trained as a stonemason, and he certainly had some sort of livelihood that enabled him to maintain his status as a citizen and hoplite. Having fought in three campaigns as part of the Athenian infantry during the war with Sparta, he was both an ardent patriot and a sincere critic of Athenian policy. His method of instruction was conversation: through dialogue with passers-by, he submitted every presumed truth to rigorous examination in order to establish a firm foundation for further inquiry. Everything we know about Socrates' teachings comes from the writings of younger men who considered themselves his pupils, and who participated in these conversations. The most important of these followers was Plato.

According to Plato, Socrates sought to show that all supposed certainties are merely unexamined prejudices inherited from others. Socrates always said that he himself knew nothing, because this was a more secure place from which to begin the learning process. He sought to base his speculations on sound definitions of key concepts—justice, virtue,

they believed that the essence of the universe was to be found not in the natural world but in the study of abstracts, and so they concentrated on mathematics and musical theory. The Pythagoreans established the key properties of odd and even numbers and also proved an old Babylonian hypothesis in geometry, known today as the Pythagorean theorem. Even though they shunned the material world, they still exhibited the characteristic Greek quest for regularity and predictability in that world.

Meanwhile, philosophy as it developed in mainland Greece was more attuned to questions of ethics and politics than mathematics. The increasing power of individual citizens begged the question of how a man should conduct himself, in public and private life, so as to embrace "the beautiful and the good"—or at least to advance himself by the use of his wits. To answer this latter need were a new group of teachers known as Sophists, a term simply meaning "wise men."

Unlike the Milesian philosophers or the Pythagoreans, however, the Sophists made a living by selling their knowledge. Their teachings are best exemplified by Protagoras (*pro-TAG-or-ahs*), an older contemporary of Socrates. His famous dictum, "man is the measure of all things," means that goodness, truth, and justice are relative concepts, adaptable to the needs and interests of human beings. In

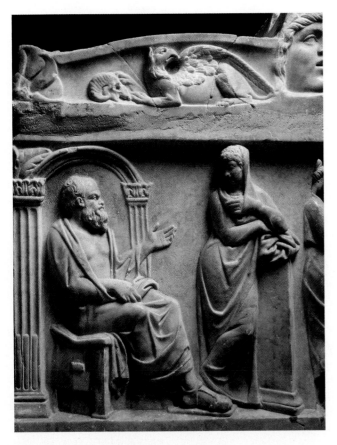

SOCRATES AS THE IDEAL EDUCATED MAN. This image of Socrates features a Roman funerary monument known as the Sarcophagus of the Muses, made in the second century C.E. The Sarcophagus advertises its owner-occupant's desire to be viewed (even in death) as a highly cultivated man: the companion of the Nine Muses of Greek mythology and the companion of Socrates, who taught that the practice of philosophy helped to prepare the soul for immortality.

beauty, love—which he and his pupils could arrive at only by investigating their own assumptions. And he focused his attention on practical ethics rather than the study of the physical world (as the Milesians did) or mathematical abstractions (like the Pythagoreans). He urged his listeners to reflect on the principles of proper conduct, both for their own sakes and for that of society as a whole. One should consider the meaning and consequences of one's actions at all times, he taught, and be prepared to take responsibility for them. According to one of his most memorable sayings, "the unexamined life is not worth living."

It is bitterly ironic that such a man, the product of Athenian democracy, should have been put to death by democratic processes. Shortly after the end of the Peloponnesian War, in 399 B.C.E., when Athens was reeling from both the shock of defeat and violent internal upheavals, a democratic faction decided that Socrates was a threat to the state. A democratic court agreed, condemning him to death for denying the gods, disloyalty to the polis, and "corrupt-

ing the youth." Although his friends made arrangements for him to flee the city and thus evade punishment, Socrates insisted on abiding by the laws and remaining in prison, thus proving himself true to his own principles and setting an example for future citizens. He died calmly by the prescribed method, self-administered poison.

According to Socrates, the goal of philosophy is to help human beings understand and *apply* standards of absolute good, rather than to master a series of mental tricks that facilitate personal gain at the expense of others. The circumstances of his death, however, show that it is difficult to translate this philosophy into principles that can be widely accepted. This would be the task of Plato, who would lay the groundwork for all subsequent Western philosophy (see Chapter 4).

CONCLUSION

There are many striking similarities between the civilization of ancient Greece and our own—and many stark differences. Perhaps the most salient example of both is the concept of democracy, which the people of ancient Greece would have defined as rule by a class of privileged male citizens supported by slavery. In theory and in practice, this amounted to only a small percentage of the population in Athens, whereas in Sparta the vast majority were subject to the rule of an even smaller class of Spartiates. Moreover, the growth of Athenian power meant, increasingly, the exploitation of other poleis and the spread of imperialism, a ruinous policy of preemptive warfare, and increased intolerance and paranoia. Socrates was not the only man put to death for expressing his opinions. Finally, the status of women in this "golden age" was lower than it had been in earlier periods of Greek history, and women had fewer personal rights than in any of the ancient societies we have studied so far.

And yet the profound significance of Greek experiments with new forms of governance and new ideas about the world is undeniable. This can be seen with particular clarity if we compare the Greek poleis with the empires and kingdoms of the Bronze Age. The typical political regime of the ancient Near Eastern world was, as we have seen, that of a monarch supported by a powerful priesthood. In this context, cultural achievements were mainly instruments to enhance the prestige of rulers, and economic life was controlled by palaces and temples. By contrast, the core values of the Greeks were the primacy of the human male and the principles of competition, individual achievement, and human freedom and responsibility. (The very word for freedom—*eleutheria*—cannot be translated into any ancient Near Eastern language, not even Hebrew.) In his history,

Herodotus records a conversation between a Greek (in this case a Spartan) and a Persian, who expresses surprise that the Greeks should raise spears against the supposedly benign rule of his emperor. The Spartan retorts, "You understand how to be a slave, but you know nothing of freedom. Had you tasted it, you would advise us to fight not only with spears but with axes." How the Greeks came to turn those spears on one another within a few generations of their united victory is a story worthy of one of their own tragedies.

Another way of appreciating the enduring importance of Greek civilization is to recall the essential vocabulary we

After You Read This Chapter

Visit StudySpace for quizzes, additional review materials, and multimedia documents. **wwnorton.com/web/westernciv18**

REVIEWING THE OBJECTIVES

- The Greek polis was a unique form of government. What factors led to its emergence?
- Hoplite warfare had a direct effect on the shaping of early democracy. Why?
- Poleis could develop in very different ways. What are some of the reasons for this?
- In what ways did Athenian culture, philosophy, and art reflect democratic ideals?
- The Persian and Peloponnesian Wars affected Greek civilization in profound ways. Describe some of the consequences of Athens' victory in the former and its defeat in the latter.

have inherited from it: not only the word *democracy* but *politics, philosophy, theater, history*. How would we think without these concepts? The very notion of humanity comes to us from the Greeks. For them, the fullest development of one's potential should be the aim of existence: every free man is the sculptor of his own monument. This work of growing from childishness to personhood is what the Greeks called *paideia*, from which our term *pedagogy* is derived; the Romans called it *humanitas*. How this and other ideas came to be disseminated beyond Greece, to be adopted by the peoples and places of a much wider world, is the subject of Chapter 4.

PEOPLE, IDEAS, AND EVENTS IN CONTEXT

- How did the epics of **HOMER** transmit the values of the Bronze Age to the **ARISTOCRACY** of the new Greek **POLEIS**?
- How did the spread of Greek culture transform the Mediterranean, even as the adoption of **HOPLITE** military tactics transformed Greek politics?
- Compare and contrast the historical circumstances that led to the development of **ATHENS**, **SPARTA**, and **MILETUS**. What were the main differences among them?
- What were the different motives for the invasions of **DARIUS** and **XERXES**? By what methods did the Greek poleis manage to emerge victorious from the **PERSIAN WARS**?
- What were the triumphs and limitations of **DEMOCRACY** in **PERICLEAN ATHENS**?
- How did the **PELOPONNESIAN WAR** transform Athens and affect the balance of power in the Mediterranean?

THINKING ABOUT CONNECTIONS

- The trial and execution of Socrates can be seen as a referendum on the relationship between the individual and the state. What does this incident reveal about the limitations of personal power and individual rights? To what degree was this incident a product of Athenian losses during the Peloponnesian War? To what extent does it reflect long-term trends in the Greek world?
- We like to think that we can trace our democratic ideals and institutions back to Athens, but does this mean that the failings of Athenian democracy also mirror those of our own? What parallels can you draw between the cultures of fifth-century Athens and today's United States? What are some key differences?

STORY LINES

- After the Peloponnesian War, divisions within and among the Greek poleis eventually made them vulnerable to the imperial ambitions of King Philip II of Macedonia and his son, Alexander the Great.

- Alexander's conquest of the Persian Empire and Egypt united the civilizations of antiquity under Greco-Macedonian rule. Even after his untimely death, a shared language and culture continued to bind these civilizations together in a new Hellenistic ("Greek-like") world.

- Ease of travel, trade, and communication throughout this Hellenistic world fostered urbanization on an unprecedented scale. The resulting cosmopolitan culture challenged traditional social, economic, and political norms, giving rise to new social classes, forms of wealth, and technological innovations.

- The unique art forms and intellectual inquiries of Greece were thus disseminated throughout this world, and transformed by it.

CHRONOLOGY

404 B.C.E.	Sparta defeats Athens in the Peloponnesian War
401 B.C.E.	Xenophon and the Ten Thousand begin their Persian expedition
395–338 B.C.E.	The struggle for Greek dominance (Thebes, Athens, Sparta)
371 B.C.E.	Epaminondas of Thebes defeats the Spartans at Leuctra
356 B.C.E.	Philip II becomes king of Macedonia
338 B.C.E.	Macedonia defeats Thebes and Athens at Chaeronea
336–323 B.C.E.	Reign and campaigns of Alexander
323–c. 275 B.C.E.	Formation of the Hellenistic kingdoms
323–c. 225 B.C.E.	The Greek diaspora
c. 300 B.C.E.	Formation of the Aetolian and Achaean Leagues
300–270 B.C.E.	Rise of Stoicism and Epicureanism
c. 300–200 B.C.E.	The Hellenistic scientific revolution
203–120 B.C.E.	Lifetime of the historian Polybius

Before
You
Read
This
Chapter

The Greek World Expands, 400–150 B.C.E.

CORE OBJECTIVES

- **EXPLAIN** the reasons for Macedonia's rise to power and its triumph over the Greek poleis.

- **DESCRIBE** Alexander's methods of conquest, colonization, and governance.

- **IDENTIFY** the three main Hellenistic kingdoms and their essential differences.

- **DEFINE** the main characteristics of the Hellenistic world.

- **UNDERSTAND** how new philosophies and artistic movements reflect historical changes.

W hen the young Alexander of Macedonia set out for Persia in 334 B.C.E, he brought along two favorite books. The first was a copy of the *Iliad*, which his teacher Aristotle had given him. The second was the *Anabasis*, "The Inland Expedition," by an Athenian called Xenophon (*ZEN-oh-fon*, 430–354 B.C.E). Both choices are significant. The *Iliad* recounts the story of a much earlier Greek assault on Asia, and its protagonist is the hero Achilles—a figure with whom Alexander identified: consummate warrior, favorite of the gods, a man who inspired passionate loyalty. It is also full of information useful to someone planning a long campaign in foreign lands against a formidable enemy, with a fractious army drawn from all parts of Greece and little prospect of bringing them home safely or soon. The *Anabasis* was an even more practical choice. Its author had been one of 10,000 Greek mercenaries hired by a Persian prince to overthrow his older brother, the Great King. The attempted coup failed, but Xenophon's book made the prince, Cyrus, another role model for Alexander. It also told, in detail, how Persians fought, how they lived, how they were governed, and what the terrain of their vast empire was like. Moreover, it showed what

111

a dedicated army of hoplites could accomplish on Persian soil. This book would be Alexander's bible for the next ten years as he cut a victorious swath through the ancient civilizations of the Near East.

An avid student of history, Alexander recognized that the golden age of the Greek polis had ended in the war of attrition between Athens and Sparta (discussed in Chapter 3). The fifty years prior to his own birth in 356 B.C.E. had merely continued this trend on a smaller scale, as the dominant poleis—first Sparta, then Thebes, then Athens—jockeyed for prominence. Meanwhile, social and economic problems were mounting. Faith in the old ideals of democracy were compromised by the vast gulf which now opened up between the rich and the poor. Increasingly, the wealthy withdrew from politics altogether, while free citizens were reduced to debt slavery. As the values of the polis decayed, a new generation of intellectuals argued about what had gone wrong, and they tried to imagine how Greece could be saved. One of these philosophers was Aristotle, pupil of Plato and Alexander's own tutor.

Under the circumstances, no one would have been able to predict that the era of greatest Greek influence lay ahead. For rather suddenly, the stalemate of the weakened poleis was shattered by the rise to prominence of a tiny kingdom on their northern borders. Beginning in the reign of King Philip II, Macedonia came to control the Greek mainland. Then, under Philip's remarkable son, a united Greek and Macedonian army extended Greek culture and Greek governance from Egypt to the frontiers of India.

This personal empire, the empire of Alexander, could not last. But a cultural empire built upon it did. For a thousand years, a Hellenistic ("Greek-like") civilization united the disparate lands and peoples of a vast region, forming the basis of the more lasting Roman Empire and mirroring, in uncanny ways, the cosmopolitan world of our own time. How this happened is the subject of Chapter 4.

THE DOWNFALL OF THE GREEK POLIS

The Peloponnesian War had left Sparta as the dominant power in the Greek world, but the Spartans showed little talent for their new preeminence. At home, Spartan politicians remained deeply divided over the wisdom of sending forces beyond their frontiers; abroad, Spartan armies showed even less restraint than the Athenians had done in subduing cities that should have been their allies. In 395, a significant portion of Greece—including such sworn enemies as Athens, Argos, Corinth, and Thebes—accordingly aligned

themselves against Sparta in the so-called Corinthian War (395–387 B.C.E.). After years of stalemate, the Spartans could win the war only by turning once again to Persia, as they had done in the final stages of the Peloponnesian War. The Persians brokered a peace which they were also prepared to enforce, one which left Sparta in control of Greece. This pattern of Greek-on-Greek violence, temporarily halted by the intervention of Persia, was repeated time and again over the next fifty years, during which the advantage shifted steadily toward Persia.

The Struggle for Dominance

After the Corinthian War, the Spartans punished the most dangerous of their rivals, Thebes, by occupying the city for four years. This subjugation to a military garrison was intended and received as an act of humiliation, and when

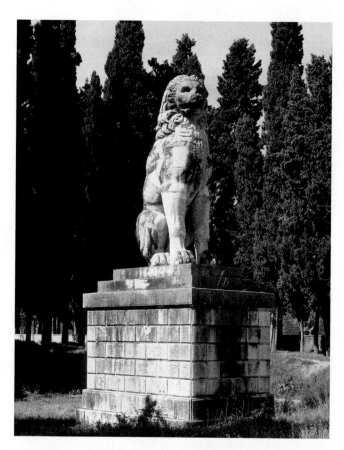

HONORING THE THEBAN SACRED BAND. According to ancient historians, all 300 of the Band's sworn lovers fell at the Battle of Chaeronea in 338 B.C.E., when Thebes was defeated by Macedonian forces led by King Philip II and his son, Alexander. An excavation undertaken at this site in 1890 uncovered the remains of only 254 warriors, but it is possible that some were buried elsewhere. This monument is a modern reconstruction of the one originally erected by the citizens of Thebes toward the end of the fourth century B.C.E.

the Thebans regained their autonomy they elected as their leader a fierce patriot who was also a military genius, Epaminondas (*eh-pa-min-OHN-das*, c. 410–362 B.C.E.).

For decades, various poleis had been experimenting with the basic form of the hoplite phalanx, adding light skirmishers and archers to enhance its effectiveness. Epaminondas now went further. In imitation of the Spartan system, he formed an elite hoplite unit known as the Theban Sacred Band, made up of 150 male couples, sworn lovers who had pledged to fight to the death for their polis and for each other's honor. Epaminondas also trained a corps of lighterarmed, fast-moving infantry. By the early 370s, he was ready for another trial of strength with the Spartans.

The Theban and Spartan armies met at Leuctra in 371 B.C.E. Epaminondas defied convention by placing his best troops (the Sacred Band) on the left-hand side of his formation, and by stacking this phalanx fifty rows deep, making

a narrow wedge of ten men abreast whose hidden depth of strength he further disguised under a cover of arrows and javelin attacks. When the two sides met, the weight of the Theban left drove through the Spartan right flank, breaking it in two and collapsing it. Epaminondas followed his victory by marching through Messenia and freeing the helots. Spartan power—and the unique social system that had supported it—was at an end. Almost overnight, Epaminondas had reduced Sparta to a small, provincial polis and launched what has often been called the Theban Hegemony.

But as Theban power grew, so did the animosity of the other Greek poleis. In 371, Athens had supported Thebes against Sparta, its ancient enemy, but when the Thebans and Spartans squared off again in 362 at the Battle of Mantinea, the Athenians allied themselves with the weaker Spartans. Although the Theban army again carried the day, the brilliant Epaminondas fell in battle, crippling Thebes'

THE INLAND EXPEDITION OF THE TEN THOUSAND. This map shows the route taken by Xenophon and his fellow Greek mercenaries during their Persian campaigns, when they supported the failed coup of Cyrus against his brother Artaxerxes II and then fought their way home through enemy territory (as the *Anabasis* records). Follow Xenophon's route with your finger. ▪ *Where did it start and end?* ▪ *Compare this route with that of Alexander on page 125. How closely was Alexander following it?* ▪ *When and how did he diverge from it?* ▪ *Why would this journey of Greek mercenaries have provided Alexander with an important model?*

Xenophon Describes an Ideal Leader

In his history of "The Inland Expedition" undertaken by the Ten Thousand, Xenophon (430–354 B.C.E.) mourns the death of Cyrus the Younger, whom he believes would have made a better Great King of Persia than the brother he challenged, Artaxerxes II. The following description of the prince's character and leadership became very famous in its time, often circulating as a separate booklet. It is likely to have influenced the young Alexander.

hus then died Cyrus, a man who, of all the Persians since Cyrus the elder, was the most princely and the most worthy of rule, as is agreed by all who appear to have had personal knowledge of him. In the first place, while he was yet a boy, and when he was receiving his education with his brother and other youths, he was thought to surpass them all in everything. For all the sons of the Persian nobles are educated at the gates of the king, where they may learn many a lesson of virtuous conduct, but can see or hear nothing disgraceful. Here the boys see some honored by the king, and others disgraced, and hear of them, so that in their very childhood they learn to govern and to obey.

Here Cyrus, first of all, showed himself most remarkable for modesty among those of his own age, and for paying more ready obedience to his elders than even those who were inferior to him in station; and next, he was noted for his fondness for horses, and for managing them in a superior manner. They found him, too, very desirous of learning, and most assiduous in practicing, the warlike exercises of archery, and hurling the javelin. When it suited his age, he grew extremely fond of the chase, and of braving dangers in encounters with wild beasts. On one occasion, he did not shrink from a she-bear that attacked him, but, in grappling with her, was dragged from off his horse, and received some wounds, the scars of which were visible on his body, but at last killed her. The person who first came to his assistance he made a happy man in the eyes of many.

When he was sent down by his father, as satrap of Lydia and Great Phrygia and Cappadocia, and was also appointed commander of all the troops whose duty it is to muster in the plain of Castolus, he soon showed that if he made a league or compact with anyone, or gave a promise, he deemed it of the utmost importance not to break his word. Accordingly the states that were committed to his charge, as well as individuals, had the greatest confidence in him; and if anyone had been his enemy, he felt secure that if Cyrus entered into a treaty with him, he should suffer no infraction of the stipulations. When, therefore, he waged war against Tissaphernes, all the cities, of their own accord, chose to adhere to Cyrus in preference to Tissaphernes, except the Milesians; but they feared him, because he would not abandon the cause of the exiles; for he both showed by his deeds and declared in words that he would never desert them, since he had once become a friend to them, not even though they should grow still fewer in number, and be in a worse condition than they were.

Whenever anyone did him a kindness or an injury, he showed himself anxious to go beyond him in those respects; and some used to mention a wish of his that he desired to live long enough to outdo both those who had done him good, and those who had done him ill, in the requital that he should make. Accordingly to him alone of the men of our days were so great a number of people desirous of committing the disposal of their property, their cities, and their own persons.

Source: Excerpted from Xenophon, *Anabasis*, ed. M. I. Finley in *The Portable Greek Historians* (New York: 1959), pp. 383–84.

Questions for Analysis

1. According to Xenophon, what are the attributes of a great leader? How would Alexander have applied these to his own situation?

2. What seems to be Xenophon's attitude toward the Persians? How might his portrayal of them have been influenced by his travels among them? How might it have been colored by his attitude toward his own countrymen?

3. In what ways does Cyrus the Younger appear to have followed the example of his ancestor, Cyrus the Great (Chapter 2, page 64)?

leadership. Athens then attempted to fill the vacuum by establishing a naval confederacy, organized more equitably than the Delian League had been. But the Athenians quickly reverted to manipulating and abusing their allies, and the confederacy dissolved in rebellions. Greece was thus reduced to a constellation of petty warring states, increasingly debilitated by their struggles with one other.

Social and Economic Crises

Meanwhile, individual poleis were also riven by internal turmoil. Athens was spared the political revolutions many other cities suffered, mostly because the memory of the Thirty Tyrants had discredited the cause of oligarchy there; but elsewhere in the Greek world, strife between democrats and oligarchs worsened. Incessant warfare, combined with these political struggles, profoundly affected the Greek world's economic and social infrastructures. Many ordinary people were driven from their homes or reduced to slavery. Country towns had been ravaged, some repeatedly, as had farmlands throughout Greece. The destruction of orchards and vineyards was particularly devastating because of the long time it takes grapevines and olive trees to mature: 40 or 50 years in the latter case. So when an invading army cut down an olive grove, it was destroying a staple crop for two generations. Even arable land was exhausted and less productive than it had been earlier. As a result, prices rose around 50 percent while standards of living declined because wages remained more or less stagnant. Taxes increased. In Athens, the wealthiest private citizens now became the sponsors of public theaters and buildings, as well as the patrons who maintained roads and warships. Even so, the kind of ambitious civic spending undertaken by the tyrants or by Pericles was unknown in the fourth century B.C.E.

Unemployment was also widespread, especially among the growing population of the cities, which were swollen with refugees from the political collapse of the countryside and overseas colonies. During wartime, men might find employment as rowers or soldiers in the service of their city; but when their city was at peace, many turned instead to mercenary service. The Greek states of Sicily and Italy began to hire mercenaries from the mainland, as did Sparta to supplement its own campaigns. As we have already noted, the brother of the Persian emperor Artaxerxes II, Cyrus, even hired a Greek mercenary force of 10,000 men in an attempt to seize the throne in 401 B.C.E.—although he did not reveal this aim until the army was deep in Persian territory and suddenly confronted with an enemy far more formidable than the tribal bands it had originally agreed to fight. Cyrus was killed in battle, and shortly thereafter, the Ten Thou-

sand's Spartan general was murdered by agents of Artaxerxes. The army—marooned in a hostile country—had to fight its way out under elected leaders, one of whom was Xenophon, who later wrote his account of these adventures. Finally, the veterans reached the Black Sea and made their way back to Greece, where many (including Xenophon) settled in Sparta. Despite all these hardships, this episode was a stunning demonstration of what a professional Greek army could achieve, and it would fire the imagination of Alexander.

REIMAGINING THE POLIS: THE ARTISTIC AND INTELLECTUAL RESPONSE

399 B.C.E., the year of Socrates' execution, might be taken to mark the end of an era: that of the polis. This basic engine of Greek life had continued to drive innovation and cultural production even during the Peloponnesian War, both in support of the war and in opposition to it. In Athens alone, the historians Herodotus (in his final years) and Thucydides were at work, as were the tragic poets Sophocles and Euripides, the comic playwright Aristophanes, and scores of talented statesmen, poets, sculptors, and artisans. But it's hard not to see the death of Socrates as symbolic of democracy's failure. Thereafter, the evident breakdown of society during the fourth century had a profound impact on the arts, philosophy, and political thought.

The Arts of the Fourth Century

As we observed in Chapter 3, the painters and sculptors of the fifth century B.C.E. were already working to achieve a heightened appearance of realism. This experimentation continued in the fourth century, especially in the relatively new art of portraiture. In this era, painters and sculptors tried to render both objects and people as they actually looked—for better or for worse—and to convey the illusion of movement, trends that would continue in subsequent centuries. They also grew bolder in their use of tricky techniques, like the casting of full-size statues in bronze, a technology that combined high levels of artistry with sophisticated metallurgy. This was a medium in which the era's most famous sculptor, Praxiteles, excelled. Praxiteles (*prak-SIT-el-ees*) was bold, too, in his choice of subjects, and he is widely regarded as the first artist to create full-size

Reconstructing an Ideal of Female Beauty

The lost statue known as the Aphrodite of Knidos was considered the most beautiful in the ancient world, but we can only study it by looking at later copies. It was the work of the fourth century's most renowned sculptor, Praxiteles, who was reputed to have modeled it after the Athenian courtesan known as Phryne, a renowned beauty who inspired several contemporary artists and a whole series of apocryphal stories. The most reliable of these tales concerns the riches she accrued: apparently she became so wealthy that she offered to finance the rebuilding of Thebes in 336—on the condition that the slogan "destroyed by Alexander, restored by Phryne the Courtesan" be prominently displayed on the new walls. (Her offer was rejected.)

Praxiteles' original statue is thought to have been the first monumental female nude fashioned in antiquity. According to one authority, Praxiteles had initially received a commission from the island of Kos, for which he fashioned both clothed and naked versions of Aphrodite. Apparently, the scandalized citizens approved only the draped version and refused to pay for the nude. It was purchased instead by the city of Knidos on Cyprus, where it was displayed in an open-air temple so that it could be seen from all sides. It quickly became a tourist attraction and was widely copied and emulated. Two of the more faithful replicas, made by later artists working in Rome, are pictured here.

Questions for Analysis

1. As we have seen, the male nude was a favorite subject of Greek artists from the Archaic Period onward. Based on your knowledge of contemporary Greek culture and society, why was it only in the fourth century B.C.E. that a life-size female nude could be publicly displayed? Are there any precedents for statues like this?

2. Compare and contrast the ideal of female beauty suggested by the Knidian Aphrodite with the male ideals discussed in Chapter 3. What can you conclude about the relationship between these ideals and the different expectations of male and female behavior in Greek society? Why, for example, would ancient sources insist that the model for this statue was a courtesan?

3. Among the Romans, a statue like the Knidian Aphrodite was called a *Venus pudica*, a "modest Venus" (image A). Yet the citizens of Kos were allegedly shocked by its indecency, while old photographs of the copy in the Vatican Museum (image B) show that it was displayed until 1932 with additional draperies made of tin. How do you account for these very different standards of decency? To what degree do they suggest that concepts of "beauty" or "modesty" are historically constructed?

A. Roman copy of the Aphrodite of Knidos.

B. Second century C.E. copy of the Aphrodite of Knidos.

female nudes, an innovation that sparked controversy in his own day and in other eras as well (see **Interpreting Visual Evidence** on page 116).

The forms and functions of drama also changed considerably. In large part, this was because tragedy and comedy were no longer mounted as part of publicly funded festivals but were instead paid for by private individuals who could exercise greater control over the content of performances. As a result, fourth-century playwrights did not have the freedom to use drama as a vehicle for political and social critique. Nor did the comic genius of Aristophanes have any true fourth-century successors. His biting, satirical wit gave way to a milder, less provocative style that bears some resemblance to early

BRONZE YOUTH. This lithe statue, dating from the years 340–330 B.C.E., was found in the sea near Marathon and has been identified as a work by the master sculptor Praxiteles (or one of his pupils). Compare this male nude to those discussed in Chapter 3. ■ *How might changes in the style of sculpture parallel cultural changes in society at large?*

television sitcoms. It was this "New Comedy" that laid the groundwork for comedy as it developed over the next several centuries: it came to rely more and more on mistaken identities, tangled familial relationships, humorous misunderstandings, and breaches of etiquette. The most famous comic playwright of this age was Menander (c. 342–292 B.C.E.), whose work survives today only in fragments but who directly inspired the comedians of the Roman theater, who in turn inspired medieval and then early modern playwrights like Shakespeare. Similar trends toward escapism and frivolity are also apparent in a new literary genre that emerged during the fourth century: the prose novel, in which star-crossed lovers undergo extraordinary trials and perilous adventures before reuniting happily after a long separation. These pleasant fictions targeted an increasingly literate audience, including (like modern romance novels) an audience of women.

Philosophy after Socrates: The Schools of Plato and Aristotle

The intellectual and political work undertaken by Socrates was carried forward by his most talented student, Plato. Born in Athens to an aristocratic family around 429 B.C.E., Plato joined Socrates' circle as a young man and witnessed at first hand the persecution, trial, and death of his mentor. For the next fifty years, to the time of his own death around 349 B.C.E., he usually shunned direct political involvement and strove instead to vindicate Socrates by constructing a philosophical system based on his teacher's unwritten precepts. Socrates had taught through dialectical conversation and by example; he mistrusted writing and resisted developing a coherent set of principles. Plato's mission was therefore to transmit his legacy in a way that captured the liveliness and charm of the Socratic method but within a more structured framework.

He did this in two ways: first by founding an informal school called the Academy (which had no tuition or set curriculum) and later by writing a series of dialogues that wrapped weighty philosophical content in a witty and accessible dramatic format, with Socrates as the central character. Most dialogues are known by the names of Plato's contemporaries, the original students who had engaged Socrates in discussion (such as Crito, whose imagined dialogue with Socrates is excerpted in Chapter 3). One dialogue, the *Symposium*, actually re-creates the conversation at a drinking party, where a tipsy Socrates, the comedian Aristophanes, and other Athenian worthies debate the nature of love.

PLATO AND ARISTOTLE. Although many artistic representations of Plato and Aristotle were made in antiquity, the image that best captures the essential difference between their philosophies is this one, the focal point of a fresco by the Renaissance painter Raphael Sanzio (1483–1520 C.E., to be discussed further in Chapter 12). Plato is the older man to the viewer's left, who points with his right hand to the heavens; Aristotle is the younger man, gesturing with an open palm to the earth. ▪ *How does this double portrait reflect these philosophers' teachings and perspectives?*

The longest and most famous of Plato's dialogues is now known by its Latin title, the *Republic*. In Greek, it is the *Politeía* ("Polis-governance" or even "Policy"), the first treatise on political philosophy written in the West. In it, Plato argues—through the character of Socrates—that social harmony and order are more important than individual liberty or equality. He imagines an ideal polis in which most of the people—farmers, artisans, traders—are governed by a superior group of "guardians" chosen in their youth for their natural attributes of intelligence and character. These prospective guardians would serve the polis first as soldiers, living together without private property. Those found to be the wisest would then receive more education, and a few would ultimately become "philosopher-kings." These enlightened rulers would in turn choose the next generation of guardians.

This utopian system actually bears an intriguing resemblance to the social order of Sparta, as well as containing elements of a benign tyranny, and is clearly a response to the failures of Athenian democracy in Plato's youth. But whether Plato himself believed in this system—he never voices his own opinion—is open to interpretation. Indeed, the students of Socrates who are represented as discussing it with him voice many objections. The most obvious of these is "Who will guard the guardians?" For such a system presumes that properly educated rulers will never be corrupted by power or wealth: a proposition that has yet to be sustained in practice.

The more practical applications of philosophy would be the preoccupation of Plato's own student, Aristotle (384–322 B.C.E.). Aristotle, the son of a physician, learned from his father the importance of observing natural phenomena. Although receptive to Plato's training, Aristotle's own philosophical system was geared toward understanding the workings of the world through the rational analysis of empirical knowledge—that is, information gained through sensory experience. In contrast to Plato, who taught that everything we see and touch is an untrustworthy reflection of some intangible ideal, Aristotle advocated the rigorous investigation of real phenomena, in order to uncover the natural order of the universe and of human beings' place within it. His method of instruction was also different. Unlike Socrates and Plato, whose dialogues were often playful, Aristotle delivered lectures on which his students took detailed notes, and eventually these notes became the basis of separate but interrelated treatises on politics, ethics, logic, metaphysics, and poetics. Aristotle also established rules for the syllogism, a form of reasoning in which certain premises inevitably lead to a valid conclusion, and he developed precise categories that could be used to further philosophical and scientific analysis.

With respect to ethics, Aristotle taught that the highest good consists in the harmonious functioning of the individual human mind and body. Since humans differ from animals by virtue of their rational capacities, he argued, they find happiness by exercising these capacities appropriately. Good conduct is therefore rational conduct, and consists in acting moderately: showing courage rather than rashness or cowardice, temperance rather than excessive indulgence or self-denial. And whereas Plato conceived of politics as a means to an end which could never be achieved in this life, Aristotle thought of politics as an end in itself: the collective exercise of moderation.

But Aristotle also took it for granted that some people—like barbarians—are not fully human, and so are intended by nature to be slaves. He also believed that women were not endowed with a full measure of humanity and so could never achieve the good life, either as individuals or as participants in the public sphere of the polis. So when Aristotle asserted that "man is by nature a political animal" (or, to be more faithful to the Greek, "a creature of the polis"), he meant only Greek males of privileged status. Nor did he believe that the best form of government is a democracy. Like Plato, Aristotle saw that as a "debased" form of government. What he preferred was the polity, in which monarchical, aristocratic, and democratic elements are combined by means of checks and balances. Only this form of government, he posited, would allow free men to realize their rational potential.

Men of Thought and Action

For all their brilliance and originality, Plato and Aristotle offered few prescriptions for reforming their own societies. Both imagined the perfect polis as one made up of a few thousand households, largely engaged in agriculture and living together in a single community. Although Greek civilization had begun in such a world, the realities of fourth-century political life were very different. Plato and Aristotle recognized this, to an extent, yet for both the answer was a reorganization of existing institutions, not something entirely new.

But there were other intellectuals at this time who were considering more radical alternatives. One was Xenophon, that veteran of the Ten Thousand, who was actually another product of the Socratic tradition and an exact contemporary of Plato. After his return from Persia, he went on to fight for the Spartan king Agesilaus (*ah-geh-si-LA-uhs*), who became a trusted friend. Thoroughly disillusioned by the failures of Athenian democracy, Xenophon spent most of his adult life in exile, and it is mostly thanks to his admiring account that we know anything about the Spartiate system described in Chapter 3. He intended his description to be a rebuke to Athens. We also have his own view of Socrates' teaching, which he related in a series of memoirs and treatises on kingship and household management (the *Oikonomikos*, the root of our word *economics*). He also loved horses and dogs, and wrote a treatise on training them for the hunt. All the while, he watched as the Theban leader Epaminondas crippled the state he so admired, Sparta. (Xenophon hated him so much that he refused to mention his name in the history he was compiling).

The Athenian orator Isocrates (436–338 B.C.E.) was another direct contemporary of Plato and was also convinced that something had gone horribly awry as a result of the Peloponnesian War. Rather than imagining that a solution lay in the reform of the polis, he proposed instead that the Greeks rediscover their lost unity by staging a massive invasion of Persia. This assault, he prophesied, would be led by a man of vision and ability, someone who could unite the Greek world behind his cause. Isocrates spent most of his life casting about to find such a leader. Finally, he began to think that the man for the job was someone whom most Greeks considered no Greek at all: the king of Macedonia, Philip II.

THE RISE OF MACEDONIA

Iscocrates had a point. By the middle of the fourth century, the Greek poleis had become so embroiled in military, political, and socioeconomic turmoil that they barely noticed the powerhouse on their northern frontier. Until the fourth century, Macedonia (or Macedon) had been a weak kingdom, regarded as a throwback to the "dark ages" before the

Aristotle's Justification of Slavery

Like The Republic *of his teacher, Plato, Aristotle's treatise on* Politics *attempts to define and rationalize various methods of governance. Early in this work, Aristotle must grapple with the fact that all ancient societies were highly dependent on slave labor, and he must answer objections that the forcible subjugation of some men to the will of others goes against the laws of nature and the ideals of his own society.*

ut is there anyone thus intended by nature to be a slave, and for whom such a condition is expedient and right, or rather is not all slavery a violation of nature? There is no difficulty in answering this question, on grounds both of reason and of fact. For that some should rule and others be ruled is a thing not only necessary, but expedient; from the hour of their birth, some are marked out for subjection, others for rule. . . .

But that those who take the opposite view have in a certain way right on their side, may be easily seen. For the words *slavery* and *slave* are used in two senses. There is a slave or slavery by law as well as by nature. The law of which I speak is a sort of convention—the law by which whatever is taken in war is supposed to belong to the victors. But this right many jurists impeach, as they would an orator who brought forward an unconstitutional measure: they detest the notion that, because one man has the power of doing violence and is superior in brute strength, another shall be his slave and subject.

Even among philosophers there is a difference of opinion. The origin of the dispute, and what makes the views invade each other's territory, is as follows: in some sense virtue, when furnished with means, has actually the greatest power of exercising force; and as superior power is only found where there is superior excellence of some kind, power seems to imply virtue, and the dispute to be simply one about justice (for it is due to one party identifying justice with goodwill while the other identifies it with the mere rule of the stronger). If these views are thus set out separately, the other views have no force or plausibility against the view that the superior in virtue ought to rule, or be master. Others, clinging, as they think, simply to a principle of justice (for law and custom are a sort of justice), assume that slavery in accordance with the custom of war is justified by law, but at the same moment they deny this. For what if the cause of the war be unjust?

And again, no one would ever say he is a slave who is unworthy to be a slave. Were this the case, men of the highest rank would be slaves and the children of slaves if they or their parents chance to have been taken captive and sold. Wherefore Hellenes [Greeks] do not like to call Hellenes slaves, but confine the term to barbarians. Yet, in using this language, they really mean the natural slave of whom we spoke at first; for it must be admitted that some are slaves everywhere, others nowhere.

The same principle applies to nobility. Hellenes regard themselves as noble everywhere, and not only in their own country, but they deem the barbarians noble only when at home, thereby implying that there are two sorts of nobility and freedom, the one absolute, the other relative. . . .

We see then that there is some foundation for this difference of opinion, and that all are not either slaves by nature or freemen by nature, and also that there is in some cases a marked distinction between the two classes, rendering it expedient and right for the one to be slaves and the others to be masters: the one practicing obedience, the others exercising the authority and lordship which nature intended them to have. The abuse of this authority is injurious to both; for the interests of part and whole, of body and soul, are the same, and the slave is a part of the master, a living but separated part of his bodily frame. Hence, where the relation of master and slave between them is natural they are friends and have a common interest, but where it rests merely on law and force the reverse is true.

Source: Excerpted from Aristotle, *Politics*, Book I: v–vi, trans. Benjamin Jowett (Oxford: 1920), pp. 32–37.

Questions For Analysis

1. According to Aristotle, how does one become a slave? Why is the question of slavery's justice related to that of the just war?

2. Aristotle posits that some people are slaves by nature, others by some unfortunate circumstances (such as being captured in battle). For example, he says that Hellenes (Greeks) do not admit that they can be slaves; that is possible only for barbarians. What are the implications of this argument?

emergence of enlightened poleis, ruled by a royal dynasty barely strong enough to control its own nobility and beset by intrigue and murderous ambition. As recently as the 360s, Macedonia had teetered on collapse, nearly succumbing to the even smaller kingdoms and predatory tribes that surrounded it.

Despite the efforts of a few Macedonian kings to add a gloss of Hellenic culture to their court—one had successfully invited Euripides and Sophocles to his palace—the Greeks considered them nearly as barbaric as their northern neighbors. It is still not known whether the ancient Macedonians were Greek-speaking during this period, although the royal family and nobility would at least have spoken Greek as a second language; and Macedonians seem to have participated in the Olympic Games, which were open only to Greeks. But they were definitely perceived as dangerous outsiders. Therefore, when a young and energetic king named Philip consolidated the southern Balkans under his rule, many Greeks saw it as a development no less troubling than the approach of the Persians in the fifth century.

The Reign of Philip II (359–336 B.C.E.)

Philip II of Macedonia was not supposed to be its ruler. Born in 382, he was the third and youngest son of King Amyntas III, and was considered so dispensable that he was sent to Thebes as hostage when he was fourteen, at the time of the Theban Hegemony. This turns out to have been the making of him: he became the protégé of the brilliant Epaminondas and may even have trained alongside the general Pelopidas (*pel-OH-pi-das*) in the Theban Sacred Band. By the time he returned to the Macedonian capital of Pella in 364, three years later, he had received a more thorough education in Greek culture and military tactics than any Macedonian before him.

He was also ambitious, and may already have laid great plans for the future. So when both of his older brothers died in battle, one after the other, Philip was not content with the role of regent for an infant nephew. By 356, he had supplanted this nephew and was reigning as king, the same year that his queen, Olympias, bore him an heir. The boy was given the dynastic name Alexandros, meaning "a leader of men."

The first problem of Philip's reign was the fragility of Macedonia's northern borders. Through a combination of warfare and diplomacy, he subdued the tribes of the southern Balkans and incorporated their territory into his kingdom—losing an eye in the process. His success in this had much to do with his reorganization of Macedonian warriors into a hoplite infantry along Theban lines. The mineral resources to which he now had access also helped, since Philip used that new wealth to pay and equip

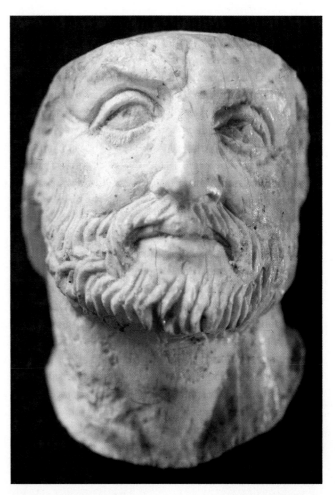

PHILIP II OF MACEDONIA. This tiny ivory head was discovered in a royal tomb at Vergina and is almost certainly a bust of the king himself. Contemporary sources report that Philip the Great had his right eye blinded by a catapult bolt, a deformity visible here—and testimony to the unflinching realism of Greek portraiture in the fourth century B.C.E.

a standing professional army; just one of his gold mines produced as much in one year as the Delian League at its height had collected annually.

Philip also organized an elite cavalry squad—the Companions—who fought with and beside the king, an innovation that may have been designed to emulate the esprit de corps of the Sacred Band, and was further intended to counter the Persian reliance on cavalry. These young men were drawn exclusively from the nobility, and Philip thereby hoped to inspire their deeper loyalty; in fact, under the guise of recruiting future Companions, he gained valuable young hostages to ensure the good conduct of aristocratic rivals. Their sons were now being brought up alongside Alexander and sharing his lessons with Aristotle, who had arrived at the Macedonian court in 343 B.C.E. Through a series of strategic marriages, Philip also managed to gain the good will and alliance of many neighboring kingdoms—although his frank polygamy was, in Greek eyes, another barbarity that called to mind the harems of Persia.

Eventually, the increasing strength of Macedonia began to impinge on the consciousness of some Greeks, most notably the Athenians. But whereas Isocrates saw in Philip a potential savior of Greece, many Athenians believed that Philip's ultimate aim was to conquer and subjugate them. They may have misunderstood Philip's goals: his northward expansion was designed to secure his frontiers and the resources necessary to support an invasion of Persia, not of Greece. From 348 B.C.E. on, he was actually trying to forge an alliance with Athens, whose fleet could facilitate such an invasion by sea; in return, Philip promised to support Athens' old claim to hegemony over Greece. But the Athenians took the advice of an orator called Demosthenes, and refused to cooperate with Philip.

This miscalculation would prove disastrous. Philip's inability to reach a peaceful understanding with Athens, despite strenuous diplomatic efforts, ultimately led to war, which sent the Athenians scrambling to ally with their former enemy, Thebes, and a number of smaller poleis. Their fate was sealed at the battle of Chaeronea (*kie-ROH-nee-ah* in 338 B.C.E., when an army led jointly by Philip and Alexander (aged eighteen) won a narrow victory, decimating the Athenian forces and destroying the Theban Sacred Band. In the aftermath, Philip called delegates from around mainland Greece to Corinth, where he established a new political federation. The main purpose of this federation, the League of Corinth, was to provide forces for the invasion of Persia and to maintain peace among the rival poleis.

Philip never realized his dream of Persian conquest. Two years later, in 336 B.C.E., he was assassinated during a festival at Pella, purportedly by a vengeful favorite. The kingship now fell to Alexander. Among the Greeks, he would be known as Alexander, the Sacker of Cities. To the Romans, impressed by his ruthless military genius, he was Alexander the Great.

THE CONQUESTS OF ALEXANDER (336–323 B.C.E.)

By the time of Alexander's early death at the age of thirty-two, a monumental legend had already built up around him. This makes it all the more ironic and frustrating that no contemporary account of his life and achievements survives. The great library assembled in his capital of Alexandria in Egypt—the repository of all ancient Greek learning and literature—was destroyed centuries later, and with it a great portion of assembled knowledge. So when we try to reconstruct the history of Alexander, we are depending on the writings of men who lived and worked under the Roman Empire, notably Plutarch (46–120 C.E.) and Arrian (c. 86–160 C.E.), both of whom were separated from their subject by a distance of 400 years. Luckily, there is good reason to believe that they were basing their histories on sources derived from two firsthand accounts, one written by Alexander's general (and alleged half brother) Ptolemy (*TOHL-eh-mee*, c. 367–c. 284 B.C.E.), who founded a new dynasty of Egyptian pharaohs, and another by Æschines Socraticus (c. 387–322 B.C.E.), an Athenian statesman. Nevertheless, it is a salutary reminder of how fragile the historical record of antiquity is, that sources for the life of the era's most famous man are so hard to come by.

The Conquest of Persia

When Alexander succeeded his father in 336 B.C.E., he could not begin to carry out his plans of conquest until he had put down the revolts that erupted immediately after Philip's death—notably at Thebes, an uprising that he punished by destroying its famous walls. Two years later, he was crossing the Hellespont at the head of a hoplite army to challenge the Great King of Persia, Darius III.

From the beginning, Darius was no match for Alexander. He was a minor member of the royal family who had taken the dynastic name when he was placed on the throne after a palace coup, at the relatively old age of forty-five, in the same year that Alexander himself became king at age twenty. Darius and his advisers failed to take the Macedonian threat seriously, despite the Persians' past history of defeat at the hands of Greek armies—even on Persian soil and within living memory. Perhaps they assumed that the enormous forces they could rally in defense of their empire would easily overwhelm a comparatively small army of 42,000; perhaps they misunderstood Alexander's aims, which would

MACEDONIAN PHALANX. Philip of Macedonia's hoplite infantry—the model for Alexander's—was armed with two-handed pikes of graduated lengths, from thirteen to twenty-one feet, and was massed in squares sixteen rows deep and wide. Members of the phalanx were trained to wheel quickly in step formation and to double the width of their front rank as needed, by filing off in rows of eight. The reach of their spears, called *sarissas*, extended the phalanx's fighting range.

reveal themselves over time to be far-reaching indeed. In any event, the Persian army of Darius III was made up of mercenaries or poorly paid conscripts under the command of inexperienced generals.

Alexander achieved a series of extraordinary victories, beginning in northwest Anatolia, near the epic field of Troy, and continuing down the Ionian coastline. In 333 B.C.E., Darius was persuaded to engage Alexander personally, at the head of a force that significantly outnumbered that of his opponent. But the chosen site, on the banks of a river near Issus, favored Alexander's fast-moving infantry, not the heavy cavalry and chariots of the Persians, which had no room to maneuver and were hampered by mud. No warrior himself, Darius disrespectfully fled the battlefield, abandoning not only his army but his entire household, which included his wife and his mother. They were captured by Alexander's troops, and treated by him with great respect.

Darius spent the remainder of his life running from Alexander's advancing army, until his decisive defeat at Gaugamela (near Mosul in modern Iraq) in 331, when he was killed by a local chieftain who hoped to win Alexander's favor. Instead, Alexander—acting as the new Great King—had the chieftain executed for treason against his former enemy and predecessor. The next spring, Alexander destroyed the royal capital of Persepolis, lest it serve as a rallying point for Persian resistance.

Meanwhile, in the two years that had passed since Darius's humiliation at Issus, Alexander had completed his conquest of Asia Minor. One by one, the cities of Syria and Palestine surrendered after Alexander made a powerful statement by destroying the wealthy Phoenician capital at Tyre. Following the example of Cyrus the Great, whose tactics he came increasingly to emulate, Alexander developed a policy of offering amnesty to cities that submitted peacefully—but dealing mercilessly with those that resisted. The forti-

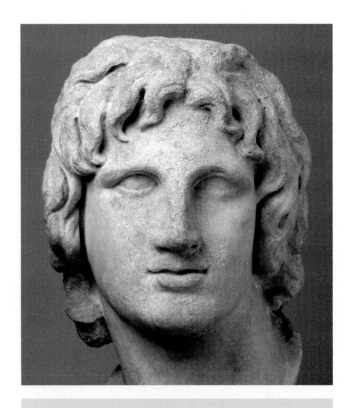

MARBLE HEAD OF ALEXANDER. Alexander the Great was reported to have been very striking in appearance, although sources vary in their assessment of his physical beauty. This portrait bust was made in 180 B.C.E., about 150 years after his death. ■ *Given the trends in sculpture during that period (see page 139), is this likely to have been an accurate portrait?*

fied city of Gaza, the last Persian stronghold on the Egyptian border, provides an example: its commander, Batis, not only refused to surrender but seemed determined to fight to the death, inflicting severe losses on the troops besieging his city and seriously wounding Alexander himself. When the fortress was finally taken, Alexander's troops slew all the adult

ALEXANDER DEFEATS KING DARIUS OF PERSIA AT THE BATTLE OF ISSUS (333 B.C.E.). This Roman mural, discovered at Pompeii, shows Darius fleeing from the battlefield in his chariot (right), pursued by Alexander, the mounted figure on the far left. Note the reflection of Alexander and his horse in Darius's large round shield.

males and enslaved the women and children. According to a later Roman historian, Alexander also dragged the body of Batis around the city's walls behind his chariot, imitating Achilles' treatment of his fallen rival Hector.

Alexander in Egypt

After this, Alexander marched into Egypt unopposed. In fact, he was welcomed as a liberator: Egypt had been governed as a Persian satrapy (principality) since 525 B.C.E., when Cambyses, son of Cyrus the Great, had deposed the last pharaoh of the reigning dynasty (see Chapter 2). Now Alexander himself was hailed as pharaoh and given the double crown of Upper and Lower Egypt, becoming the latest in a succession of rulers reaching back 3,000 years to the time of King Narmer (see Chapter 1).

Something about this feat seems to have amazed even Alexander himself. The "barbarian" chieftain of a backwater kingdom in the Balkan foothills had become pharaoh of the oldest civilization on earth and heir to its immense riches and extraordinary history—a history that the Greeks knew, thanks to the writings of Herodotus. While the Persians and (before them) the Medes had long been the Greeks' traditional enemies, the Egyptians had always been too far away to pose a threat; indeed, they were an object of awe and source of inspiration.

This may help to explain Alexander's response to the oracle of Ammon, the name the Greeks gave to the Egyptian sun god Amun-Ra, whom they identified with Zeus. At the oracle's desert oasis of Siwa, Alexander was reportedly told that he was "son of Ammon" and a god himself, a pronouncement that gave weight to a story already in circulation among his men, that he had been fathered not by Philip but by Zeus. Alexander, ever mindful of historical precedent and the historical significance of his own actions, seems to have decided at this point that Egypt should be the capital of his new empire. Persia had been the goal, and it still remained to be conquered, piece by piece; but it was in Egypt that he would build his shining new city of Alexandria. In the end, he had time only to lay out a plan for the streets and central spaces before he marched north to the reckoning with Darius at Gaugamela. When he finally returned, he was in his sarcophagus.

Alexander's Final Campaigns

Over the ensuing five years, Alexander campaigned in the far reaches of the Persian Empire, in the mountainous regions that had been only loosely yoked together with

ALEXANDER'S WORLD. This view of the world, modeled on maps made in antiquity, represents what intellectuals of Alexander's own time knew about geography. ▪ *Comparing it to the map of Alexander's campaigns on page 125, how do you think this worldview affected the planning of his route?* ▪ *Based on available knowledge, why would he have traveled down the Indus river (near the marking* **India***) and traveled overland to Susa?* ▪ *What similarities and differences do you find more generally, comparing this ancient map with the other maps that appear in this book?*

the more settled lands of Mesopotamia. This is the region encompassed today by Afghanistan, a terrain famous for defeating every attempt at conquest or control. There, in the mountains of Bactria, Alexander and his army experienced the hardest fighting of their long campaign. Indeed, they never succeeded in getting more than a tenuous hold on the territory, despite Alexander's marriage to Roxane, daughter of a local Bactrian chieftain. Thereafter, Alexander moved down through what is now Pakistan to the Indus Valley, meeting stiff resistance from its warlords but eventually defeating their leader, Porus, at the Battle of Hydaspes (*heed-AH-spes*) in 326 B.C.E.

This was to be the last major battle of his career, and the one in which his famous warhorse, Bucephalus, was killed. (He was buried nearby, and a city was founded in his name.) And it was here in India that Alexander's exhausted army refused to go on, thousands of miles and eight years from home. He was forced to turn back, and

THE CAMPAIGNS OF ALEXANDER. The conquests of Alexander the Great brought Greek culture to the vast expanse of the former Persian Empire, as far east as the Indus River. Trace Alexander's route with your finger. ▪ *Where did he start and end?* ▪ *What was the farthest point east that he traveled on his conquests?* ▪ *Why might Alexander have chosen to found so many cities named after him, and what can you conclude about the purposes of these cities, based on their locations?*

rather than attempting to recross the mountains of the Hindu Kush or the foothills of the Himalayas, he pressed southward to the shores of the Arabian Sea—what was then known as Ocean, and the end of the world. The ensuing march through the Gedrosian Desert, combined with a decade of continuous fighting, weakened him and his army considerably.

But Alexander still had great plans for the future, and when he reached the royal palace of Susa he took steps that indicate how he would have tried to combine his Greco-Macedonian Empire with that of Persia, had he lived. He announced that he would begin training Persian youths to fight alongside Greeks and Macedonians, so as to begin an integration of the two armies. He arranged a mass marriage between hundreds of his officers and a corresponding number of Persian noblewomen, and he made

an example of men who had been caught desecrating the nearby tomb of Cyrus the Great. Most controversially, he showed respect for his Persian subjects by adopting Persian dress—considered by Greeks to be symbolic of their enemies' barbarism—and by encouraging those around him to perform the ritual of *proskynesis* (*pros-kin-EE-sis*).

According to Herodotus, who gave the practice its Greek name, this was a gesture of bodily submission performed by those of lesser social standing when they met their superiors, and by all Persians—even those of royal rank—to honor the Great King. The person paying homage would bow deeply and kiss his hand to the emperor, in some cases prostrating himself entirely. To the Greeks, this practice was not only humiliating but blasphemous: it suggested that the Persians worshiped their emperor as a god. To Alexander and his close advisers, *proskynesis* may

LESSER KINGS OF PERSIA APPROACH THE GREAT KING TO PERFORM THE *PROSKYNESIS.* ▪ *Why would Alexander's Greek and Macedonian soldiers have balked at the suggestion that they show their solidarity with Persians by performing this ritual?*

have seemed an appropriate tribute to his status as "son of Ammon," but it was more likely intended to level cultural differences between Persians and Greeks. In any case, it was not a success, and it fueled a mutiny among the Macedonians, which Alexander himself had to quell.

Alexander's Death

Apart from these attempts to create cross-cultural cohesion, which he was not able to pursue fully, Alexander took no realistic steps to create an administration for his vast empire. How he planned to govern it effectively and bequeath it intact remains a mystery; he seems to have fixed his sights more clearly on further conquests, perhaps in Arabia, perhaps toward "Greater Greece"—Italy and Sicily. We will never know. In late May of 323 B.C.E., he began to show signs of what may have been malarial fever. Some ancient sources suggest he was poisoned; his closest friend and longtime lover, Hephaistion, had died the year before at Ecbatana, leaving Alexander without his most able and vigilant bodyguard. (Emulating Achilles' passionate grief at the death of Patroclus, the mourning Alexander is reported to have built an enormous funeral pyre and "sacrificed" the residents of a nearby town to appease Hephaistion's ghost.) But Alexander ignored the advice of his doctors and continued to play the part of a Homeric hero, drinking late into the night and exerting himself

incautiously. His condition worsened, and he died on June 10 or 11, 323 B.C.E., in the palace built by the Chaldean king Nebuchadnezzar in Babylon, the ancient capital of Hammurabi. He was not yet thirty-three years old.

THE HELLENISTIC KINGDOMS

According to one account—by a later Roman historian—Alexander's friends and officers gathered around his bed as he lay dying and asked to whom he wished to leave his empire. He had replied, "To the strongest." According to Plutarch and Arrian, though, he was actually incapable of speech. According to still other late sources, he silently gave his signet ring to a Macedonian general called Perdiccas, the leader of his cavalry.

It was certainly Perdiccas who attempted to arrange a settlement among all the possible claimants to Alexander's imperial power, albeit unsuccessfully. Alexander's own son and heir was born to Roxane after his death, and eventually it was decided that the baby, Alexander IV of Macedonia, should rule jointly with Alexander's half brother, Philip, the son of Philip II by one of his lesser wives, who may have been both mentally and physically disabled. This solution proved impractical, and eventually both the child and his uncle were murdered, as was Perdiccas.

Analyzing Primary Sources

Alexander Puts Down a Mutiny

The following account comes from the history of Alexander's campaigns by the Greek-speaking Roman historian Arrian (c. 86–160 C.E.), who lived in the Roman province of Bythinia in northern Anatolia. This is the closest thing we have to a primary source, since histories written by Alexander's own contemporaries have not survived. The following passage describes Alexander's response to a mutiny among his troops after his return from India, in 324 B.C.E.

y countrymen, you are sick for home—so be it! I shall make no attempt to check your longing to return. Go wherever you will; I shall not hinder you. But if go you must, there is one thing I would have you understand—what I have done for you, and in what coin you have repaid me. . . .

"[M]arching out from a country too poor to maintain you decently, [I] laid open for you at a blow, and in spite of Persia's naval supremacy, the gates of the Hellespont. My cavalry crushed the satraps of Darius, and I added all Ionia and Aeolia, the two Phrygias and Lydia to your empire. . . . I took them and gave them to you for your profit and enjoyment. The wealth of Egypt and Cyrene, which I shed no blood to win, now flows in your hands; Palestine and the plains of Syria and Mesopotamia are now your property; Babylon and Bactria and Susa are yours; you are the masters of the gold of Lydia, the treasures of Persia, the wealth of India—yes, and the seas beyond India, too. You are my captains, my generals, my governors of provinces.

"From all this that I have labored to win for you, what is left for me myself except the purple and the crown? I keep nothing for my own. . . . Perhaps you will say that, in my position as your commander, I had none of the labors and

distress which you had to endure to win me what I have won. . . . Come now—if you are wounded, strip and show your wounds, and I will show mine. There is no part of my body but my back which does not have a scar; not a weapon a man may grasp or fling, the mark of which I do not carry on me . . . and all for your sakes: for your glory and your gain. Over every land and sea, across river, mountain, and plain, I led you to the world's end, a victorious army. I marry as you marry, and many of you will have children related by blood to my own. . . . But you all wish to leave me. Go then! And when you reach home, tell them that Alexander your king, who vanquished the Persians and Medes and Bactrians . . . tell them, I say, that you deserted him and left him to the mercy of barbarian men, whom you yourselves conquered. . . ."

On the Macedonians, the immediate effect of Alexander's speech was profound. . . . But when they were told [three days later that] . . . command was being given to Persian officers, foreign troops drafted into Macedonian units, a Persian corps of Guards called by a Macedonian name, Persian infantry units given the coveted title of Companions . . . every man of them hurried to the palace . . . and [they] swore they would not stir from the spot until Alexander took pity on them.

Source: Arrian, *The Campaigns of Alexander*, trans. Aubrey de Selincourt (New York: 1958), pp. 360–65 (slightly modified).

Questions for Analysis

1. What qualities of leadership does Alexander display in this speech? How do these qualities compare to those of Cyrus the Younger, in Xenophon's description of him (page 114)?

2. Given the circumstances that precipitated this mutiny, why does Alexander use the term *barbarians* to describe the Persians and other conquered peoples? What does he hope to convey by using this word and then by reorganizing his forces to replace Macedonians with Persians?

3. Histories written well into the nineteenth century of our era feature speeches that were allegedly spoken by historical characters on momentous occasions. How closely do you think Arrian's reconstruction of this speech reflects historical reality? How might you go about arguing that it is, in fact, an accurate reflection of what Alexander actually said?

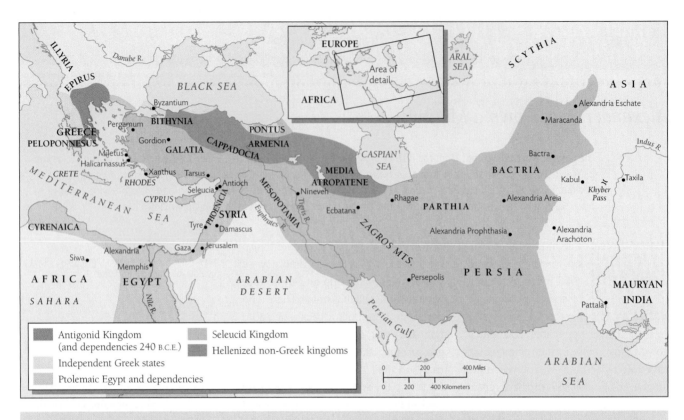

THE HELLENISTIC WORLD. Each of the three successor kingdoms to Alexander's empire was based in one of the three major civilizations we have studied so far: Egyptian, Mesopotamian, and Greek. ▪ *Based on the map above, what were the names of the three main successor states and where were they located?* ▪ *What might the division of Alexander's empire along such lines suggest about the lasting cultural differences among these regions?* ▪ *What might it suggest about the likelihood of forging a united empire, had he lived?*

Meanwhile, the Persian satrapies that had been allotted to various leaders of Alexander's armies became the bases from which they attempted to seize control. The turmoil lasted for two generations. By about 275 B.C.E., however, three separate axes of military and political power had emerged, each with a distinctive character but all headed by a Greco-Macedonian ruling class that shared a similar background. Indeed, a striking feature of this period is the renewal of ancient political patterns. But more striking is the fact that a common culture continued to unite Alexander's fragmented empire, which is why the era after his death is called Hellenistic, "Greek-like."

Ptolemaic Egypt

By far the most stable of the three successor states was Egypt, thanks in large part to the canny governance of Alexander's former general Ptolemy, possibly an illegitimate son of Philip II and certainly one of Alexander's most trusted advisers. Ptolemy decided to withdraw from the contest over the larger empire and asked only to be given Egypt as his satrapy. This might have been construed as a modest request by potential rivals, but Ptolemy had ulterior motives. Clearly, he recognized Egypt's virtual invulnerability to attack. He also seems to have appreciated, as Alexander did, its historical cachet. And he may already have been planning to make Egypt an independent monarchy and a shrine to Alexander's memory.

It was thanks to Ptolemy, in fact, that Alexander's embalmed body was returned to Egypt in 323 B.C.E. It was supposed to have gone to the royal burial ground of Aigai in Macedonia, but Ptolemy hijacked the funeral cortege and brought it to the holy city of Memphis. Later, his son Ptolemy II moved the sarcophagus to a tomb in Alexandria, where it became a pilgrimage site and an object of veneration, especially by Romans with imperial ambitions of their own (see Chapter 5).

The Ptolemies ruled for the next 300 years, until Egypt became a Roman province in 30 B.C.E. This dynasty, the thirty-second since the unification of the Upper and Lower Nile in the fourth millennium B.C.E., would be the last. The male heirs of the line all took the name Ptolemy (hence the term Ptolemaic Egypt). Many of their sisters were called Cleopatra, the name of Alexander's own sister and a dynastic name among Macedonian royal women.

Beginning in the reign of Ptolemy II Philadelphus ("sibling-lover"), the Ptolemies even began to follow ancient Egyptian custom by marrying their siblings. And in many other ways, they showed reverence for the culture of their kingdom while at the same time bringing it within the ambit of the wider Hellenistic world.

TWO PORTRAITS OF PTOLEMY I OF EGYPT. The Ptolemaic rulers of Egypt represented themselves as pharaohs to their Egyptian subjects (as in this bust) and as Greeks to their Macedonian and Greek subjects (as on this gold coin). ▪ *Why would it have been important to project these two very different images?*

They achieved this, in part, by ruling from the new city of Alexandria on the Mediterranean coast, rather than from the older pharaonic capitals. In Alexandria, they acted as Macedonian kings toward their Greek and Macedonian citizens; outside of Alexandria, they played the role of pharaohs, surrounding themselves with the trappings and symbols of Egypt's heritage. But only the last Ptolemaic ruler, Cleopatra VII (69–30 B.C.E.), bothered to learn the Egyptian language—although, as the Rosetta Stone attests (see Chapter 1), the Ptolemies surrounded themselves with able administrators who could communicate effectively with their multilingual and multicultural subjects.

For the Ptolemies, as for the ancient pharaohs, all of Egypt was basically crown land, to be exploited for the benefit of the royal house. Supporting this tradition was the Macedonian idea that conquered land—land won by the spear—was plunder, to be used for personal enrichment and glorification. Accordingly, the Ptolemies exploited the wealth of the Egyptian countryside to the fullest. Most of this wealth ended up in Alexandria, which became the dazzling hub of the Hellenistic world. But there was little interest in improving the lives of the Egyptian peasantry whose bread-winning labors made their rulers rich. So although the third century was a prosperous and relatively peaceful one in Egypt, future pharaohs would face regular and dangerous revolts from the native populations of the countryside.

Nevertheless, Ptolemaic Egypt remained the most successful of the Hellenistic kingdoms. It was also the most influential, not only in its own day but for posterity, because of its key role in preserving and transmitting the accumulated heritage of the civilizations that had preceded it: Egyptian, Mesopotamian, and Greek. The Ptolemies used their wealth to patronize science and the arts, and they established a great Museum ("home of the Muses") and library, which attracted the greatest minds of the Hellenistic world and eventually displaced Athens as an intellectual and artistic center. Many breakthroughs in astronomy, mechanical engineering, and physics occurred in Alexandria. In particular, the study of medicine advanced greatly under Ptolemaic rule: freed from the taboos of their homeland, Greek researchers were permitted to perform autopsies on the bodies of dead criminals and vagrants, making it possible for anatomy to become a scientific discipline in its own right. It was also here that the texts of Greek poetry, drama, history, and philosophy were copied and preserved in the forms in which we know them, and here that the Hebrew scriptures were translated into Greek for a wider audience.

Seleucid Asia

The vast possessions that Alexander had accumulated in Asia—both within the Persian Empire and outside of it—eventually fell to another Macedonian, Seleucus (*seh-LOO-kus*). Seleucus had not been a senior officer during Alexander's lifetime, but he had navigated the turmoil after Alexander's death successfully and cleverly exploited the connections he made through his Persian wife. At his death in 281 B.C.E., his half-Persian son Antiochus (*an-TYE-oh-kuhs*) inherited an expansive realm; but despite his best efforts he could not extend it beyond the city named after him, Antioch, into Egypt.

Throughout its history, the Persian dynasty founded by Seleucus (known as the Seleucids) struggled with the problem of keeping the disparate parts of their realm together. Their hold on the easternmost provinces was especially tenuous, but Seleucus solved part of this problem by ceding much of the Indus Valley to the great Indian warrior-king Chandragupta, in exchange for peace and a squad of war elephants. By the middle of the third century B.C.E., the Seleucids had also lost control of Bactria, where a series of Indo-Greek states were emerging with a uniquely complex culture of their own. (One Greco-Bactrian king, Menander, is memorialized in Buddhist tradition. The Seleucid heartland became northern Syria, parts of Anatolia, Mesopotamia, and the western half of Persia: still a great, wealthy kingdom but far less than what Alexander had left.

Like the Ptolemies, the Seleucids presented two faces to their subjects, one looking to ancient Near Eastern tradition, another looking to Greece. In his proclamations, Antiochus used terms reminiscent of Sargon, Hammurabi, and Cyrus: "I am Antiochus, Great King, legitimate king . . . king of Babylon, king of all countries." But on his coins, he wore his hair short in the fashion of the Greeks and styled himself *basileus*, the Greek word for "king." Although the Seleucids' bureaucracy was less organized than that of the Ptolemies, even haphazard tax collection could reap huge rewards in an empire of 30 million inhabitants. However, the Seleucids did not convert their gains into public-works projects or capital investments. Instead, they hoarded their wealth in great state treasuries. All the same, they had more than enough cash to defend their borders through the third century, a period of regular warfare with Egypt. It was not until the second century, when Antiochus III lost a costly war with the Romans, that he had to plunder temples and private wealth to pay off the indemnity imposed on him.

Antigonid Macedonia and Greece

The Macedonian homeland did not possess the vast wealth of the new kingdoms carved from Alexander's conquests in Egypt and the Near East. It also remained highly unstable from the time of Alexander's death until 276 B.C.E., when a general named Antigonus (*an-TIG-on-uhs*) was finally able to establish his rule over the area and his own dynasty (known as the Antigonids). Thereafter, Macedonia drew its strength from considerable natural resources and from its influence over Aegean trade, as well as its status as overlord of Greece. The Macedonians also continued to field the most effective army of any of the successor states, and these warriors had coveted bragging rights as the heirs of Alexander's unconquered army.

Antigonus was influenced by a philosophical outlook called Stoicism (discussed later in this chapter) and viewed kingship as a form of noble servitude, an office to be endured rather than enjoyed. This perspective, combined with his modest resources, convinced him not to compete with the Seleucids and Ptolemies for dominance. Instead, Antigonid policy was to keep these other two powers at war with one another and away from the Macedonian sphere of influence. Antigonus and his successors thus pursued a strategy more reminiscent of Philip II than of his son. They secured the northern frontiers, maintained a strong, standing army, and kept the divided Greeks at heel.

The Greeks, however, were restive under the Antigonids, and two emergent powers within the Greek world served as rallying points for those who resented "barbarian" rule. These two forces, the Aetolian League and the Achaean League, represent a new form of Greek political organization. Unlike the defensive alliances of the classical period, each of these two leagues constituted a real political unification, with some centralization of governance. Citizens of the member poleis participated in councils of state that dealt with foreign policy and military affairs, trials for treason, and the annual election of a league general (also the chief executive officer) and his deputy. New members were admitted on an equal footing with existing members, and all citizens of the various poleis enjoyed joint citizenship throughout the league. The same laws, weights and measures, coinage, and judicial procedures also applied throughout each federation. So impressive was this degree of cooperation that James Madison, John Jay, and Alexander Hamilton employed the Achaean League as one of their models in advocating federalism in the United States.

FROM POLIS TO COSMOPOLIS

So what became of the polis, that building block of classical Greek civilization? As we have seen, the changes of the fourth century B.C.E. were already disrupting the traditional patterns of social and political life well before Alexander's conquests. But these conquests hastened the process of transformation, and they also opened up a wider world—a world that, within a few generations, came to admire all things Greek. By 300 B.C.E., a common Hellenistic culture encompassed the eastern Mediterranean and western Asia, transcending political and geographical boundaries. It was fueled by the hundreds of thousands of adventurers who joined the Greek *diaspora* ("dispersion") and whose emigration reduced the population of the Greek mainland by as much as 50 percent in the century between 325 and 225 B.C.E.

This exciting, urbane world was made up of interconnected cities whose scale dwarfed anything imaginable in Periclean Athens. In the fifth century B.C.E., direct participation in government had meant that every male citizen of a Greek polis had some share and stake in his society, its institutions, its gods, its army, and its cultural life. If we transpose this outlook onto the cosmopolitan Hellenistic city, which would have been at least three times larger, we can appreciate the magnitude of the change: two centuries later, all these ways of defining oneself were no longer rele-

Past and Present

Assimilation and Difference

The Greek diaspora ("dispersion") that bound the Hellenistic kingdoms together would eventually lead to the emergence of distinctive new hybrid cultures. The mosaic on the left comes from an ancient synagogue and shows Jewish ritual objects (including a menorah and a shofar) accompanied by a Greek inscription. The image on the right shows one manifestation of the modern Turkish diaspora: a clothing store in a district of Berlin called "Little Istanbul," where many German "guest workers" settled in the 1960s.

 Watch related author interview on StudySpace
wwnorton.com/web/westernciv18

vant. The individual male's intimate connection with the political life of the state was broken, as was his nexus of social and familial relationships. An average Greek in one of the Hellenistic cities might have only his immediate family to rely on, if that. Very often, he was alone. What resulted was a traumatic disjunction between the traditional values and assumptions of Greek life and the social and political realities of the day—and a host of entirely new opportunities.

Commerce and Urbanization

The Hellenistic world was prosperous, owing to the freedom of long-distance trade, the development of financial networks, and the enormous growth of cities. Alexander's conquests had opened up a vast trading area stretching from Egypt to the Persian Gulf, dominated by Greek-speaking rulers and well-established merchant communities. These conquests also stimulated the economy by putting into circulation hoards of Persian gold and silver coins, jewelry, and other commodities acquired through plunder. Industries also benefited, because autocratic rulers found manufacturing to be a further means of increasing their revenues through trade and taxation.

New trading ventures were particularly encouraged in Ptolemaic Egypt and the area of western Asia ruled over by the Seleucid monarchs, the heartland of which was Syria. Every facility was provided by the Ptolemies and the Seleucids for the encouragement of commerce. Harbors were improved, warships were sent out to police the seas, roads and canals were built. The Ptolemies even employed geographers to discover new routes to distant lands and thereby opened up valuable markets. As a result of such methods, Egypt developed a flourishing commerce in the widest

HELLENISTIC EARRINGS. These exquisite pieces of jewelry illustrate the enormous wealth and extraordinary craftsmanship available to the elites of the Hellenistic world.

variety of products obtainable. Into the port of Alexandria came spices from Arabia, gold from Ethiopia and India, tin from Britain, elephants and ivory from Nubia, silver from Spain, fine carpets from Asia Minor, and even silk from China. Profits for the government and for some of the merchants were often as high as 20 or 30 percent.

The rapid growth of cities had both political and economic causes. Greek rulers imported Greek officials and especially Greek soldiers to maintain their control over non-Greek populations, making many new Greek settlements necessary. Alexander himself had founded some 70 cities as outposts of imperial domination; in the next two centuries, his successors founded about 200 more. Urbanization also increased due to the expansion of commerce and industry, as well as the proliferation of government offices.

But the most significant factors contributing to urban expansion were the Greek diaspora and the migration of workers from rural areas. Population growth in some centers was explosive. At Antioch, the population quadrupled during a single century. Seleucia on the Tigris grew from nothing to a metropolis of several hundred thousand in less than two centuries. Alexandria in Egypt had a half-million inhabitants. Only imperial Rome would have surpassed it in size, and it would not be until the eighteenth century of our era that European cities like London and Paris were as large. Alexandria was not only populous, it was magnificent and spacious—which Rome never was. Its wide streets were paved and laid out in an orderly grid. It had splen-

did public buildings and parks, the great museum, and the famous library containing a half-million books. It was the storehouse and showcase of Greek culture.

Despite the overall growth of the Hellenistic economy, not everyone enjoyed prosperity. Agriculture remained the major occupation and primary source of wealth, and small farmers in particular suffered severely from exploitative taxation. Although industrial production increased, it continued to be based on manual labor by individual artisans, most of whom lived in poverty. Among the teeming populations of Hellenistic cities, unemployment was a constant concern. Those who could not find work were forced to beg, steal, or prostitute themselves to survive.

Even those who prospered in the new economy were often subject to drastic fluctuations in their fortunes, owing to the precarious nature of mercantile endeavors. A trader who did very well selling a luxury cloth might invest heavily in it, only to find that tastes had changed or that a ship full of his wares had sunk. Merchants were also vulnerable to the boom-and-bust syndrome all too familiar to us today: an investor, thinking he could make a fortune during an upward price spiral, might go into debt to take advantage of the trend, only to find that supply in the commodity he traded suddenly exceeded demand, leaving him nothing with which to pay back his creditors. The economic landscape of the Hellenistic world was therefore one of contrasting extremes. In many ways, this was also the case with respect to its culture.

HELLENISTIC WORLDVIEWS

Life in the Hellenistic boomtowns produced new perspectives on the world and new philosophies that differed significantly from those of Plato and Aristotle. Two opposing trends ran almost parallel with one another. The first, exemplified by Stoicism (*STOH-iss-ism*) and Epicureanism (*eh-pi-CURE-ee-an-ism*), promoted rational thought as the key to alleviating the anxieties of modern life. This trend was a manifestation of Greek influence, although a major departure was the new separation of philosophy from scientific inquiry, which now became its own field of study. The second trend, exemplified by the Skeptics and various religious cults, tended to deny the possibility of attaining truth through the exercise of human reason alone and in some cases turned toward mysticism and reliance on divine revelation. Despite these stark differences, however, both philosophers and religious teachers were motivated by the same thing: the need to make human existence meaningful in a new age that lacked traditional civic structures and social values.

Two Paths to Tranquility: Stoicism and Epicureanism

The two strains of philosophy that dominated the Hellenistic world both originated in Athens around 300 B.C.E. Their promoters were Epicurus (c. 342–270 B.C.E.) and Zeno (fl. after 300 B.C.E.), and their teachings had several features in common. Both were concerned with the well-being of the individual, not with the welfare of society as a whole. Both were also firmly rooted in the material world, denying the existence of any purely spiritual phenomena; even the soul was considered to be part of the mortal body. Stoicism and Epicureanism also responded to the new cosmpolitan age by promoting universal values: both taught that people are the same the world over, and both recognized no distinctions between Greeks and the peoples hitherto known as "barbarians."

But in other ways the two systems were radically different. The Stoics who followed Zeno of Citium (c. 335–c. 263 B.C.E.)—they took their name from the *stoa* ("colonnade") in which he regularly taught—believed that the cosmos is an ordered whole in which all contradictions are resolved for ultimate good. Evil is not absolute but relative; this means that the particular misfortunes that befall individual human beings are merely incidents that will lead to the final perfection of the universe. Everything that happens is therefore predetermined, which means that no individual is master of his or her fate. People are free only in the sense that they can accept fate or rebel against it; that is, one is free to choose *how to respond* to adversity or prosperity. By freely submitting to the workings of the universe, and by acknowledging that whatever happens must be for the best, one can attain true happiness: tranquility of mind. Through the exercise of reason and emotional restraint, Stoics strove to adjust their expectations to the workings of fate and to purge their souls of all bitterness or regret.

The Stoics' theory of ethics and social responsibility grew out of this personal philosophy. Believing that the highest good is serenity of mind, they emphasized self-discipline and the fulfillment of one's duties. They taught tolerance and forgiveness, and they also urged participation in public affairs as a special responsibility for those with able minds. They condemned slavery and violence, although they took no real actions against these evils because they saw them as inevitable—and because extreme social change might be worse.

With some later modifications, Stoic philosophy became the driving force behind the values of the Roman Republic and even influenced early Christianity; it can be considered one of the most important products of the Hellenistic Age. Even today, those who do not consciously embrace its tenets or its perspective may find that they have been influenced by its egalitarian and humanitarian ethos.

The second main philosophical trend in this era derives from teachings of Epicurus (341–270 B.C.E.). Epicurius, in turn, was influenced by the atomic theory of an earlier Greek philosopher called Democritus (*dem-OH-kree-tuhs*), who lived in the latter part of the fifth century B.C.E. and who is often called "the father of modern science." According to his central thesis, the universe is made up entirely of atoms, infinite in number, indestructible, and indivisible. Every individual object or organism is therefore the product of a combination of atoms.

Studying Democritus's writings, Epicurus and his followers reached a conclusion exactly opposite to that of the Stoics: they interpreted the atomic theory to mean that there is no ultimate purpose in the workings of the universe, that these workings are entirely random. So the highest good cannot come of submitting oneself stoically to the endurance of hardship, because no hardship is part of a larger plan; it is merely the chance by-product of random atomic actions. The highest good, then, must be pleasure: the moderate satisfaction of bodily appetites, the intellectual pleasure of contemplating excellence and remembering past enjoyments, and serenity in the face of death. Indeed, an individual who understands that the soul itself is material and will not survive the death of the body, that the universe operates at random, and that no gods intervene in human affairs should have no fear of death or any other supernatural phenomena. The Epicureans thus came by a very different route to the same general conclusion as the Stoics: nothing is better than tranquility of mind.

The moral teachings and political goals of the Epicureans reflected this worldview. In contrast to the Stoics, however, they did not insist on virtue as an end in itself or on the fulfillment of one's duties. For an Epicurean, the only duty a person has is to the self, and the only reason to act virtuously is to increase one's own happiness. Similarly, Epicureans also denied that there is any such thing as justice: laws and political institutions are "just" only insofar as they contribute to the welfare of the individual. Yes, certain rules have been found necessary in every society for the maintenance of order, but these rules should be obeyed solely because that is to one's advantage. The state is, at best, a mere convenience, and the wise man should take no active part in politics. Instead, he should withdraw to study philosophy and enjoy the fellowship of a few congenial friends. Modern libertarian movements share many characteristics with Epicureanism.

Extreme Doubt: Skepticism

The most pessimistic philosophy generated by the Hellenistic era was propounded by the Skeptics, whose name derives from a Greek word meaning "those on the lookout" or "the spies." Skepticism reached the zenith of its popularity in the second century under the influence of Carneades (*kar-NEE-ah-dees*, c. 214–129 B.C.E.), a man born in the Greek city of Cyrene, in North Africa, who spent his youth in Athens. The chief source of his inspiration was the teaching (filtered through Aristotle) that all knowledge is based on sense perception and is therefore limited and relative. From this, the Skeptics concluded that no one can truly know or prove anything. Because the impressions of our senses can deceive us, we cannot even be certain about the truth of whatever empirical knowledge we think we have gained by observation of the world. All we can say is that things *appear* to be such and such; we do not know that they really *are* that way. It follows, furthermore, that we can have no definite knowledge of the supernatural, of the meaning of life, or of right and wrong.

The only sensible course for the Skeptic is therefore to suspend judgment: this alone can lead to happiness. If a person abandons the fruitless quest for truth and ceases to worry about good conduct and the existence of evil, he can at least attain a certain peace of mind—the highest satisfaction that an uncertain life affords. Needless to say, the Skeptics were even less concerned than the Epicureans with political and social problems, from which they felt wholly alienated. Their ideal was one of escape from an incomprehensible world. In some key respects they anticipated modern existentialism and nihilism.

The Varieties of Religion

Like Epicureanism and Skepticism, Hellenistic religion tended to offer vehicles of escape from political commitments. When we think back to how close was the link between Greek selfhood and politics down to the middle of the fourth century B.C.E.—"man is a creature of the polis"—we can begin to appreciate what a radical change had occurred in just a few generations. In the classical age of the polis, as in all the societies we have studied so far, religion was wholly interconnected with politics. Divine worship centered on the gods who protected a community and furthered its interests. Hence, the most serious of the charges brought against Socrates was that he had "denied the gods of the polis" and thus committed treason. Religious crimes were political crimes, and piety was the same as patriotism.

Although this sense of a vital connection between a place and its gods persisted to a certain extent during the Hellenistic period, civic-oriented worship was compromised by the rootless multiculturalism of the third and second centuries B.C.E. In its place, some elite members of society gravitated toward one of the philosophies discussed above. Ordinary people, though, were more likely to embrace religious cults that offered emotional gratification or the diversion of colorful rituals, as well as some assurance of an afterlife, which the new philosophies did not.

In Greek-speaking communities especially, cults that stressed extreme methods of atonement for sin, ecstatic mystical union with the divine, or contact with supernatural forces attracted many followers. Among these mystery religions—so called because their membership was select and their rites secret—one of the most popular was the cult of Dionysus, which celebrated the cyclical death and resurrection of that Greek god. The Egyptian cult of Isis, drawing on the story of Osiris (see Chapter 1), also revolved around rituals of death and rebirth. So too did Zoroastrianism (see Chapter 2), which became increasingly dualistic: its magi taught that the material world was entirely evil and urged believers to adopt ascetic practices that would purify their souls and prepare them for ethereal joy in the afterlife.

Like the peoples who worshiped them, the gods of the Hellenistic world were often immigrants from other lands. Temples to Greek gods and goddesses were dedicated throughout the Near East and Egypt; conversely, temples to Near Eastern divinities were constructed in the cities of the Greek homeland. In Alexandria, scholars of religion collected Egyptian and Near Eastern mythologies, which were recorded and reformulated for Greek-speaking audiences. Throughout the Hellenistic world, there was a dazzling variety of religious choices.

Even among the Jews of Palestine, who resisted assimilation and the adoption of foreign customs, Hellenistic culture put down deep roots. This was especially true among Jewish elites and Jews living outside Palestine, who outnumbered the Palestinian population by a considerable margin by the end of the second century B.C.E. To meet the needs of these Greek-speaking Jews, and to satisfy the curiosity of Gentiles interested in Jewish beliefs, scholars working in Alexandria produced a Greek version of the Hebrew scriptures. It is still known as the Septuagint, from the Greek word meaning "the seventy": legend has it that seventy scribes, each working independently, produced individual translations from Hebrew to Greek that were identical in every respect. This story conveyed the message that the Septuagint was no less a product of divine inspiration than the original books that made up the Hebrew Bible, and could be treated as an authoritative text in its own right. For Jews concerned about their social and cultural standing vis-à-vis their Greek neighbors, it was also proof of their cultivation and their acceptance of Hellenistic values—although, ironically, many of the Jewish scriptures that were now written in Greek disapproved strongly of those values.

Analyzing Primary Sources

A Jewish Response to Hellenization

Greek culture became a powerful force throughout the Hellenistic world, even in Israel. In the second century B.C.E., the Hellenized ways of the Jewish elites in Jerusalem led to a revolt by a native Hebrew dynasty known as the Maccabees, who decried the effects of Hellenization on Jewish life. These events are recorded in two apocryphal books of the Hebrew Bible. In the passage that follows, note that even the High Priest of the Temple bears a Greek name, Jason.

n those days, lawless men came forth from Israel and misled many, saying, "Let us go and make a covenant with the Gentiles [Greeks] round about us, for since we separated from them many disasters have come upon us." . . .

[This happened when] Antiochus [IV, 175–164 B.C.E.] who was called Epiphanes had succeeded to the kingdom, [and] Jason the brother of Onias obtained the high priesthood by corruption. . . . [H]e at once shifted his countrymen over to the Greek way of life . . . and he destroyed the lawful ways of living and introduced new customs contrary to the law. For with alacrity he founded a gymnasium right under the citadel, and he induced the noblest of the young men to wear the Greek hat [and not the traditional head covering]. There was such an extreme of Hellenization and increase in the adoption of foreign ways . . . that the priests were no longer intent upon the services of the altar. Despising the sanctuary and neglecting the sacrifices, they hurried to take part in the unlawful proceedings in the wrestling arena after the signal for the discus-throwing, disdaining the honors prized by their ancestors and putting the highest value upon Greek forms of prestige. . . . When the quadrennial games were being held at Tyre and the king was present, the vile Jason sent envoys . . . to carry three hundred silver drachmas for the sacrifice to Heracles. . . .

Not long after this, the king sent an Athenian senator to compel the Jews to forsake the laws of their fathers and cease to live by the laws of God, and also to pollute the temple in Jerusalem and call it the temple of Olympian Zeus. . . . Harsh and utterly grievous was the onslaught of evil. For the temple was filled with debauchery and reveling by the Gentiles, who dallied with prostitutes and had intercourse with women within the sacred precincts, and besides brought in things for sacrifice that were unfit. The altar was covered with abominable offerings that were forbidden by the laws. A man could neither keep the Sabbath nor observe the feasts of his fathers, nor so much as confess himself to be a Jew.

Source: Excerpted from 1 Maccabees 1:11; 2 Maccabees 4:10–18 and 6:1–6, in *The New Oxford Annotated Bible* (Oxford: 1973).

Questions for Analysis

1. Given the history of the Hebrew kingdoms (see Chapter 2), why would Hellenistic culture be particularly threatening to the Jews?

2. What, specifically, are the offensive actions and activities described here? Why, for example, would the building of a gymnasium (a Greek academy and athletic facility) in Jerusalem be problematic?

THE SCIENTIFIC REVOLUTION OF ANTIQUITY

The Hellenistic period was the most brilliant age in the history of science before the seventeenth century of our era. There are three major reasons for this. First, there was the enormous stimulus to intellectual inquiry caused by the fusion of Mesopotamian and Egyptian science with the philosophical methods of the Greeks. Second, as in the more famous scientific revolution of modernity (see Chapter 16), the use of a common language (in the seventeenth century it was Latin) and the ease of communication facilitated by quick, affordable travel also made the circulation of knowledge and sharing of ideas easier (in the seventeenth century, ease of communication was increased by the printing press and an international postal system). Finally, as in the seventeenth century, the competition among patrons of science was intense, which ensured the availability of ample funding. Every Hellenistic autocrat wanted to be thought enlightened

Debating the Education and Role of Women

The drastic political, social, and economic changes of the fourth century led philosophers to reimagine the traditional structures of the polis and to debate the proper role of women within these structures. Meanwhile, the cosmopolitan culture of the expanding Hellenistic world made it increasingly difficult to limit women's access to public spaces. The following excerpts represent two philosophical responses to these problems. The first comes from Plato's treatise on "Polis-matters" (Politeía), known to us as The Republic, *the longest of his philosophical dialogues and the most influential work of political thought in history. Its conceptual narrator and protagonist is Socrates, who engages in a series of debates with his pupils. The second excerpt is taken from a philosophical treatise attributed to a female follower of Pythagoras (see Chapter 3), but it was really written around 200 B.C.E. in Hellenistic Italy, and by a man.*

Plato, *The Republic*, c. 380 B.C.E.

SOCRATES: For men born and educated like our citizens, the only way, in my opinion, of arriving at a right conclusion about the possession and use of women and children is to follow the path on which we originally started, when we said that the men were to be the guardians and watchdogs of the herd.

GLAUCON: True.

SOCRATES: Let us further suppose the birth and education of our women to be subject to similar or nearly similar regulations; then we shall see whether the result accords with our design.

GLAUCON: What do you mean?

SOCRATES: . . . The education which was assigned to the men was music and gymnastic[s].

GLAUCON: Yes.

SOCRATES: Then women must be taught music and gymnastic[s] and also the art of war, which they must practice like the men?

GLAUCON: That is the inference, I suppose.

SOCRATES: I should rather expect . . . that several of our proposals, if they are carried out, being unusual, may appear ridiculous.

GLAUCON: No doubt of it.

SOCRATES: Yes, and the most ridiculous thing of all will be the sight of women naked in the palaestra, exercising with the men, especially when they are no longer young; they certainly will not be a vision of beauty, any more than the enthusiastic old men who in spite of wrinkles and ugliness continue to frequent the gymnasia. . . . . [Yet] not long ago, as we shall remind them, the Hellenes were of the opinion, which is still generally received among the barbarians, that the sight of a naked man was ridiculous and improper; and when first the Cretans and then the Lacedaemonians [Spartans] introduced the custom, the wits of that day might equally have ridiculed the innovation.

GLAUCON: No doubt. . . .

SOCRATES: First, then, whether the question is to be put in jest or in earnest, let us come to an understanding about the nature of woman: Is she capable of sharing either wholly or partially in the actions of men, or not at all? And is the art of war one of those arts in which she can or cannot share? That will be the best way of commencing the enquiry, and will probably lead to the fairest conclusion. . . .

GLAUCON: I suppose so. . . .

SOCRATES: And if . . . the male and female sex appear to differ in their fitness for any art or pursuit, we should say that such pursuit or art ought to be assigned to one or the other of them; but if the difference consists only in women bearing and men begetting children, this does not amount to a proof that a woman differs from a man in respect of the sort of education she should receive; and we shall therefore continue to maintain that our guardians and their wives ought to have the same pursuits.

GLAUCON: Very true.

SOCRATES: Next, we shall ask . . . how, in reference to any of the pursuits or arts of civic life, the nature of a woman differs from that of a man? . . .

GLAUCON: By all means.

SOCRATES: . . . [W]hen you spoke of a nature gifted or not gifted in any respect, did you mean to say that one man will acquire a thing easily, another with difficulty; a little learning will lead the one to discover a great deal; whereas the other, after much study and application, no sooner learns than he forgets? Or again, did you mean, that the one has a body which is a good servant to his mind, while the body of the other is a hindrance to him? Would not these be the sort of differences which distinguish the man gifted by nature from the one who is ungifted?

GLAUCON: No one will deny that.

SOCRATES: And can you mention any pursuit of mankind in which the male sex has not all these gifts and qualities in a higher degree than the female? Need I waste time in speaking of the art of weaving, and the management of pancakes and preserves, in which womankind does really appear to be great, and in which for her to be beaten by a man is of all things the most absurd?

GLAUCON: You are quite right . . . in maintaining the general inferiority of the female sex: although many women are in many things superior to many men, yet on the whole what you say is true.

Source: Excerpted from Plato, *The Republic*, Book V, trans. Benjamin Jowett (New York: 1982), pp. 170–76.

Treatise attributed to Phintys, Third/Second Century B.C.E.

Now some people think that it is not appropriate for a woman to be a philosopher, just as a woman should not be a cavalry officer or a politician. . . . I agree that men should be generals and city officials and politicians, and women should keep house and stay inside and receive and take care of their husbands. But I believe that courage, justice, and intelligence are qualities that men and women have in common. . . . Courage and intelligence are more appropriately male qualities because of the strength of men's bodies and the power of their minds. Chastity is more appropriately female.

Accordingly, a woman must learn about chastity and realize what she must do quantitatively and qualitatively to be able to obtain this womanly virtue. I believe that there are five qualifications: (1) the sanctity of her marriage bed, (2) the cleanliness of her body, (3) the manner in which she chooses to leave her house, (4) her refusal to participate in secret cults . . . , (5) her readiness and moderation in sacrificing to the gods.

Of these, the most important quality for chastity is to be pure in respect of the marriage bed, and for her not to have affairs with men from other households. If she breaks the law in this way she wrongs the gods of her family and provides her family and home not with its own offspring but with bastards. . . .

She should also consider the following: that there is no means of atoning for this sin; no way she can approach the shrines or the altars of the gods as a pure woman. . . . The greatest glory a freeborn woman can have—her foremost honor— is the witness her own children will give to her chastity toward her husband, the stamp of the likeness they bear to the father whose seed produced them. . . .

As far as adornment of her body is concerned . . . [h]er clothes should not be transparent or ornate. She should not put on silken material, but moderate, white-colored clothes. In this way, she will avoid being over-dressed or luxurious or made-up, and not give other women cause to be uncomfortably envious . . . She should not apply imported or artificial coloring to her face—with her own natural coloring, by washing only with water, she can ornament herself with modesty. . . .

Women of importance leave the house to sacrifice to the leading divinity of the community on behalf of their husbands and their households. They do not leave home at night nor in the evening, but at midday, to attend a religious festival or to make some purchase, accompanied by a single female servant or decorously escorted by two servants at most. . . . They keep away from secret cults . . . particularly because these forms of worship encourage drunkenness and ecstasy. The mistress of the house and head of the household should be chaste and untouched in all respects.

Source: From Mary R. Lefkowitz and Maureen B. Fant, eds. *Women's Life in Greece & Rome: A Source Book in Translation*, 2nd ed. (Baltimore, MD: 1992), pp. 163–64.

Questions for Analysis

1. Follow the steps of the argument made by Socrates. How does he go about proving that women and men are different and should have different roles in society? Are there flaws in this argument? What are they?

2. How does the author of the treatise seem to define "chastity," and why does she (or he) say that it corresponds to more masculine qualities of courage and intelligence? Why would this author have wanted to attribute these reflections to female members of the community founded by the philosopher Pythagoras (c. 570–c. 495), three centuries earlier? How might this treatise be responding to the changes brought about by the expansion of the Greek world in the fourth and third centuries B.C.E?

3. What are main points on which these two perspectives agree? How might ideas like those expressed here have influenced contemporary ideas of female beauty (see **Interpreting Visual Evidence**, page 116)?

and to be associated with new discoveries. And it might even be profitable to subsidize research that led to the development of new technologies, especially ones with military applications. But most of all, the rulers who financed scientific endeavors did so primarily for motives of prestige and competition: they could show off a scientific gadget just as they could show off a sculpture. Even purely theoretical advances were so much admired that a Hellenistic prince who had bankrolled such a breakthrough would share the glory of it.

The arts were also transformed by the economic and political conditions of the Hellenistic world. Writers and artists working in various media strove to demonstrate their mastery of difficult techniques and so to attract the notice of potential patrons. New markets for art also changed *what* was being made, how, and for whom. In all of the civilizations we have studied so far, artists worked directly for royal or civic patrons, who were often very particular in their demands. In the Hellenistic world, art became commodified. Sometimes a piece would be made expressly for a particular patron, but many works of art were fashioned for the open market. They were also designed to suit the tastes and lifestyles of urbane men and women, especially those of the merchant classes and the elite who had disposable income and wanted to increase their social standing through conspicuous consumption. This was as true of literature as of sculpture or the decorative arts: we know the names of over a thousand Hellenistic authors, either because their work survives in multiple copies sold in bookshops, or because they are mentioned in other writings (letters, pamphlets) as being in fashion. Indeed, the number of texts and *objets d'art* that exist from this period is huge compared to earlier eras.

Measuring and Mapping: Astronomy, Geography, and Mathematics

Hellenistic scientists took a major interest in measurements and mapmaking, whether of the heavens (astronomy) or the earth (geography) and the forms occuring in nature (geometry). The most renowned—and most wronged—of the Hellenistic astronomers was Aristarchus of Samos (310–230 B.C.E.), whose major discovery anticipated that of Copernicus by 1,700 years: he deduced that the earth and other planets revolve around the sun. Unfortunately, however, his heliocentric model was not accepted by many of his contemporaries or successors because it conflicted with the teachings of Aristotle and with the Greek conviction that humanity, and therefore the earth, must be at the center of the universe.

The sad fate of his discovery was sealed in the second century C.E., when the Alexandrian scholar Claudius Ptol-

emaeus (also known as Ptolemy) published an astronomical treatise called the *Almagest*, which unequivocally argued that Aristotle was correct, and that all heavenly bodies revolve around the earth. This misinformative book was then handed down to posterity as the authoritative work of ancient astronomy. It would not be overturned until a much later scientific revolution occurred two-thousand years later—and after the condemnation of theories advanced by Copernicus and Galileo that were identical to that of Aristarchus.

Closely allied with astronomy were geography and mathematics, especially geometry. The most influential Hellenistic mathematician was Euclid, whose *Elements of Geometry* (c. 300 B.C.E.) codified the work of others, including pre-Socratic philosophers like Pythagoras (see Chapter 3). It remained the basic textbook for the study of that subject until the twentieth century of our era. Euclid's successor Hipparchus (second century B.C.E.) then laid the foundations of both plane and spherical trigonometry.

In the field of geography—and in a host of other pursuits, too—the most original thinker was Eratosthenes of Alexandria (*air-ah-TOS-then-ees*, c. 276–c. 196 B.C.E.). Not only did he accurately calculate the circumference of the earth (within a tiny margin of error, less than 200 miles), he also developed a system of latitude and longitude, and he was the first to suggest the possibility of reaching eastern Asia by sailing west. In addition, he founded the science of chronology by attempting to establish the dates of major events reaching back to the siege of Troy. Students of history are forever in his debt.

Medicine and Mechanics: The Sciences of Physiology and Physics

Before the third century B.C.E., physics had been a branch of philosophy. It became a separate, experimental science thanks to the single-handed genius of one man, Archimedes of Syracuse (*ar-ki-MEE-dees*, c. 287–212 B.C.E.). It was he who discovered the law of floating bodies, or specific gravity, now known as "Archimedes' principle." According to legend, the idea came to him quite suddenly when he was in his bath, pondering possible theories. The stunning insight so excited him that he leaped from the water and dashed out naked into the street, shouting "*Eureka!*" ("I found it!"). He also established the principles of the lever, the pulley, and the screw, and he invented both a compound pulley and a propeller. All of these discoveries had numerous practical uses in the construction of buildings, ships, and military machinery.

Other extaordinary advances of Hellenistic science were made in the field of medicine. Especially significant was the work of the Alexandrian scholar Herophilus of Chalcedon (c.335–c.280 B.C.E.), the greatest anatomist of antiquity and probably the first to practice human dissection. Many of his discoveries directly challenged the orthodoxy of Aristotelian teaching—and rightly, since Aristotle's understanding of physiology (like his knowledge of astronomical and natural science) has not stood the test of time so well as his grasp of logic and politics. Herophilus's achievements included a detailed description of the brain, which allowed him to prove that the brain was the engine of human intellect (Aristotle thought this was the heart), as well as the discovery that the arteries contain blood alone (not a mixture of blood and air, as Aristotle had taught), and that their function is to carry blood from the heart to all parts of the body. He also understood the significance of the pulse and its use in diagnosing illness.

His colleague Erasistratus (*ehr-ah-sis-STRAH-tus*) made allied discoveries, establishing that the heart was a pump and not an organ of emotion, explaining the working of its valves, and distinguishing between motor and sensory nerves. Erasistratus also rejected the widely held theory of the physician Hippocrates (c. 460–c. 370), who had posited that the body consists of four "humors" which need to be kept in balance through bloodletting and other invasive practices. Unfortunately, this discovery went the way of the heliocentric universe posited by Aristarchus: another encyclopedist of the second century C.E., Galen, preferred the erroneous theory of Hippocrates. His baleful influence, and the practice of bloodletting, thus persisted into the nineteenth century of our era.

SURGICAL INSTRUMENTS. Tools like these were used by both Hellenistic and Roman doctors to perform surgical procedures, but they also had a variety of nonmedical uses. Shown here are a grinding stone, spoons, probes, depressors, and tongs. The large, flat-headed tool may have been used for cauterizing wounds. The inscription visible on the stone in the upper left-hand corner is probably a recipe for eye medicine.

Urban Architecture and Sculpture

Hellenistic architecture drew on Greek models, but it was also influenced by standards and tastes more characteristic of Egypt and Persia. Two examples (both of which no longer survive) are the great lighthouse of Alexandria, which rose to a height of nearly 400 feet and which was daringly composed of three diminishing stories topped by eight slender columns supporting the light; and the citadel of Alexandria, built of stone and covered with blue-tinted plaster, described by a contemporary as seeming to float in mid-air. The best-surviving example, though, comes from Pergamon, a city on the coast of Anatolia that became the capital of a new kingdom wrested from the control of the Seleucids in the second century B.C.E. It boasted an enormous altar dedicated to Zeus that crowned the heights of the city, below which an open-air theater was built into the steep slope of the hill. In Ephesus, not far away, the streets were not only paved, but paved with marble.

Perhaps the most influential of all Hellenistic arts was sculpture, which represents a further movement away from classical ideals and even more emphasis on realism than the fourth-century sculptures discussed earlier in this chapter. Sculptors now prided themselves on faithfully reproducing facial furrows, muscular distensions, and complex folds of drapery. Awkward human postures offered the greatest technical challenges, to the degree that sculptors might prefer to show people stretching themselves or balancing on one leg in ways that hardly ever occur in real life.

Because monumental sculpture of this kind was executed for wealthy private patrons, it is clear that the goal was to create something unique in both conception and craftsmanship—something a collector could show off as the only one of its type. It is not surprising, therefore, that complexity came to be admired for its own sake, and extreme naturalism sometimes teetered on the brink of distortion. To our eyes, such works frequently appear familiar because of the influence they exerted on later sculptors like Michelangelo (see Chapter 12) and Auguste Rodin. Three of the most famous examples are pictured here, each exhibiting different aesthetic qualities and artistic techniques: the *Dying Gaul*, made in Pergamon around 220 B.C.E.; the *Winged Victory of Samothrace*, dating from around 200 B.C.E.; and the *Laocoön* group, from the first century B.C.E.

Literary Fantasy and Historical Reality

In the sixth century B.C.E. it was the lyric, in the fifth century it was tragedy, and in the fourth century it was the novel; but in the Hellenistic era, the new literary genre was pastoral verse.

THE CITADEL OF PERGAMON. An artist's reconstruction of Pergamon in the second century B.C.E., based on the work of nineteenth-century German archaeologists. High atop the hill is the massive altar of Zeus (now in the Pergamon Museum in Berlin) and below it slope the tiers of the theater. Other features include fortifications, terraces, and artificial landscaping for public gardens. ▪ *How does this complex of buildings compare to that of another citadel, the Acropolis of Athens (see page 76)?*

These poems tapped into a strong vein of nostalgia for rural pastimes and simple pleasures, a make-believe world of shepherds and wood nymphs. The most important pastoral poet of the age was Theocritus (*thee-AW-krit-uhs*), who flourished around 270 B.C.E. in the big-city environment of Alexandria. Theocritus was a merchant of escapism. In the midst of urban bustle and within sight of overcrowded slums, he celebrated the charms of country life and lazy summer afternoons, putting into the mouths of his rustic characters unlikely sentiments expressed in ornate language. He thereby founded an enduring tradition that would be taken up by poets from the Roman Virgil to the Englishman (and classical scholar) A. E. Housman, and that has continuously provided a wealth of themes for the visual arts. Musical composers like Beethoven and Debussy also owe a debt to Theocritus.

By contrast, Hellenistic prose literature was dominated by historians and biographers who consciously modeled their work on earlier pioneers, especially Thucydides. By far the most important was Polybius (*pol-LIB-ee-uhs*, c. 203–120 B.C.E.), a well-born Greek from the mainland whose father was a prominent politician active in the Achaean League. Polybius himself was trained as a horseman and cavalry officer, and both his vocation and his family connections gave him ample opportunity to observe the workings of government, diplomacy, and military strategy. This was at a time when the Achaean League was trying to position itself favorably in ongoing wars between the rising republic of Rome and the various warring kingdoms of northern Greece, notably Macedonia and Epiros. In 168 B.C.E., the Romans became suspicious of the Achaeans' declared neutrality and demanded that a thousand noble hostages be sent from Greece to Rome as a guarantee of the League's good behavior.

Polybius was one of those hostages, and he spent the next seventeen years living in Rome. There, he became a fervent admirer of Roman customs and especially of Rome's unique form of government. He also formed warm friendships with

THE MARBLE STREETS OF EPHESUS. Ephesus was already a splendid city when it was incorporated into the Persian Empire, along with other Greek settlements in Ionia. In the Hellenistic era, it became more splendid still.

display can contrast strikingly with the more austere tastes of the fifth century B.C.E. Yet Hellenistic civilization had its own achievements that the classical age could not match, achievements that make it in some ways more familiar to us. Most Hellenistic cities offered a greater range of public facilities than any Greek cities of the previous period, and the numerous advances in science and technology are astonishing when compared to anything that came before or even after.

But the most important contribution of the Hellenistic era to subsequent historical developments was its role as an intermediary between the nascent empire of Rome and the older civilizations of Mesopotamia, Egypt, and Greece. The example set by Alexander, in particular, was one that the Romans would emulate, and the economic and political infrastuctures that were put in place after his conquests would form the framework of Roman imperial government. The Romans would also take advantage of the common language and cultural expectations that bound the far reaches of the Greek-speaking world together. Their own Latin language would only become acceptable for cultivated conversation and literary expression toward the

high-ranking Roman families, including the descendants of Scipio Africanus, a prominent Roman general. He kept up these contacts after his release, traveling to North Africa during the Third Punic War and witnessing firsthand the destruction of Carthage in 146 B.C.E. (see Chapter 5).

The result of this colorful career was a series of histories that glorified the achievements of Rome and its political system. Polybius also attempted to account for the patterns that he discerned in the history of Greece since the Peloponnesian War. He argued that historical developments follow regular cycles, and that nations pass inevitably through stages of growth and decay. Hence, it should be possible to predict exactly where a given state is heading if one knows what has happened to it in the past. Yet he also argued that the special character of Rome's constitution would allow it to break free from this cycle, because it combined all of the different forms of government that Aristotle had outlined in his *Politics*. This view of history galvanized the framers of the U.S. Constitution, directly influencing their conception of our own political institutions.

CONCLUSION

Judged from the perspective of classical Greece, Hellenistic civilization seems strange. The autocratic governments of the age that followed Alexander's conquests would probably appear repugnant to a staunch proponent of Athenian democracy, and the Hellenistic love of extravagance and

DYING GAUL. The original (now lost) statue on which this Roman copy was based was sculpted in Pergamon around 220 B.C.E. The sculptor clearly wished to exhibit skill in depicting an unusual subject: the Gauls were a Celtic people about whom very little was known in this era. ■ *How does this sympathetic representation of a "barbarian" express the new values of Hellenistic philosophy?*

***THE WINGED VICTORY OF SAMOTHRACE* (left).** This marble sculpture of the goddess Nike (Victory) may originally have been displayed on the prow of a monumental ship. It formed part of a temple complex on the island of Samothrace in the northern Aegean, and dates to around the year 200 B.C.E. It is now in the Louvre museum, Paris. ***LAOCOÖN AND HIS SONS* (right).** In sharp contrast to the serene and confident *Winged Victory* is this famous sculpture group from the first century B.C.E. According to legend, Laocoön warned the Trojans not to accept the wooden horse sent by the Greeks and was accordingly punished by the sea-god Poseidon, who sent two serpents to kill him and his sons. The intense physicality of this work was an important influence on Michelangelo, a millennium and a half later. It is now in the Vatican museum, Rome.

After You Read This Chapter

Visit StudySpace for quizzes, additional review materials, and multimedia documents. **wwnorton.com/web/westernciv18**

REVIEWING THE OBJECTIVES

- Macedonia's successful conquest of the Greek poleis can be attributed to several factors. What are they?
- Alexander the Great's imperial policies were influenced by his own upbringing, the different cultures he encountered, and some key historical precedents. Give at least one example of each type of influence.
- Explain how the three Hellenistic kingdoms reflect the differences among the three main civilizations we have studied so far.
- Why is the Hellenistic world described as "cosmopolitan"? How did this urban culture differ from that of the Greek poleis?
- The philosophies of Plato and Aristotle both derive from the teachings of Socrates, but they diverge in some important ways. What are those main differences?

very end of the first century B.C.E., and it would never supplant Greek as the preeminent language of scholarship and administration in the eastern portions of their empire.

The Hellenistic era must also be recognized as the bridge that connects us to the earlier ages of antiquity: most of what is contained in the first four chapters of this book is known to us only because older texts and inscriptions and artifacts were collected and copied by the scholars of Alexandria and other Hellenistic cities. This era also bridges the gap between the tastes and ideals and customs of classical Greece and those that would be more characteristic of Rome. It was Hellenistic art and architecture, Hellenistic city planning and civic culture that the Romans strove to emulate and export to their own colonies, not those of Periclean Athens. The same can be said of drama and poetry.

For us, two further aspects of Hellenistic culture deserve special mention: its cosmopolitanism and its modernity. The word *cosmopolitan* itself comes from a Greek word meaning "universal city," and it was the Greeks of the Hellenistic period who came closest to turning this ideal of globalization into reality. Around 250 B.C.E. a Greek tourist could have traveled from Sicily to the borders of India—the two known ends of the earth—and never have found himself among people who did not speak his language or share his basic outlook. Nor would this tourist have identified himself in ethnic or nationalist terms, or felt any exclusive loyalty to a city-state or kingdom. He would have considered himself a citizen of the world. He would also have considered himself a modern man, not bound by the old prejudices and superstitions of the past. It is for these reasons that Hellenistic civilization seems so closely related to our own. It was a world of stark contrasts and infinite possibilities, where economic instability, extremism, and authoritarian regimes existed side by side with unprecedented prosperity, rational inquiry, and extraodinary freedoms. In Chapter 5, we will see how this world adapted itself to the dominion of a single Italian city.

PEOPLE, IDEAS, AND EVENTS IN CONTEXT

- In what ways were the military strategies of **PHILIP II** variations on older forms of hoplite warfare? How did the rise of mercenary armies and of Thebes further change military strategies in the fourth century?
- How did the philosophies of **PLATO** and **ARISTOTLE** respond to the crisis of the polis?
- To what degree did the conquests of **ALEXANDER THE GREAT** unite Mesopotamia, Egypt, and Greece?
- Why and how did the three **HELLENISTIC KINGDOMS** emerge? How were the **AETOLIAN AND ACHAEAN LEAGUES** new models for governance and cooperation in Greece?
- In what ways were **STOICISM, EPICUREANISM**, and other new philosophies a response to **COSMOPOLITANISM** and the breakdown of traditional societies and values?
- What were the driving forces behind the **SCIENTIFIC REVOLUTION OF ANTIQUITY**? What were its main achievements?
- What are some essential characteristics of **HELLENISTIC ART**? In what ways did it differ from that of the fifth century B.C.E. (see Chapter 3)?

THINKING ABOUT CONNECTIONS

- "The history of the world is but the biography of great men": so the Scottish historian Thomas Carlyle (1795–1881) summarized the impact of figures like Alexander the Great. How would you construct an argument in support of this proposition, using what you've learned in this chapter? How would you refute it?
- In what ways do Alexander's actions demonstrate his own knowledge of history as well as a capacity to apply that knowledge to his own circumstances? Can you identify leaders of our own day who have mobilized their understanding of history in similar ways?
- In your view, which civilization more resembles our own: classical Athens or the Hellenistic world? Why? What characteristics make an era seem "modern"?

STORY LINES

- Romans were proud of their unique history, especially the legend that they had overthrown their kings. They clung to this story even when individual men came to wield kingly powers.

- Roman identity, religion, and politics were intimately bound up in the worship of ancestors, especially male ancestors. As a result, fathers (living and dead) wielded extraordinary power in early Rome.

- Roman women enjoyed many more freedoms than women of ancient Greece, but they were still subject to the authority of their male relatives.

- Paradoxically, the Romans celebrated their farming heritage even as they built a highly urbanized society. At the same time, they regarded Greek culture as both superior and dangerous.

- The Roman army had unprecedented strength and importance in this civilization, but the army's relationship to Roman politics and society changed drastically as Rome's empire grew.

CHRONOLOGY

753 B.C.E.	Legendary founding of Rome
c. 509 B.C.E.	Roman Republic established
c. 450 B.C.E.	Law of the Twelve Tables
287 B.C.E.	"Struggle of the Orders" ends
264–146 B.C.E.	Punic Wars
134–104 B.C.E.	Slave revolts in Sicily
133–122 B.C.E.	Reforms of the Gracchi
107–86 B.C.E.	Consulship of Marius
82–79 B.C.E.	Dictatorship of Sulla
73–71 B.C.E.	Rebellion of Spartacus
52–48 B.C.E.	Struggle of Pompey and Caesar
48–44 B.C.E.	Dictatorship of Casaer
44–30 B.C.E.	Rivalry of Octavian and Antony
27 B.C.E.–14 C.E.	Principate of the Emperor Augustus
27–180 C.E.	Flowering of the *Pax Romana*
79 C.E.	Eruption of Mount Vesuvius destroys (and preserves) Pompeii
117 C.E.	Roman Empire reaches its greatest territorial extent under Trajan

Before
You
Read
This
Chapter

The Civilization of Ancient Rome

CORE OBJECTIVES

- **IDENTIFY** the factors that influenced the formation of the Roman Republic.

- **UNDERSTAND** the basic elements of Roman identity.

- **DEFINE** the classes of people who struggled for power in Rome.

- **DESCRIBE** the impact of territorial expansion on Roman society.

- **TRACE** the events leading up to the establishment of the Principate.

"Could anyone be so indifferent or slow-witted as not to care how, and under what system of government, the Romans managed to bring nearly the whole inhabited world under their rule? Can anything be more important than understanding this?" So the Greek soldier Polybius (c. 203–120 B.C.E.) addresses Greek readers in a history celebrating the achievements of the Roman Republic. Polybius had witnessed some of these firsthand: on the battlefield, in Rome itself as a hostage and a guest, and on a visit to newly conquered Carthage. What better testament could there be to the success of a small Italian city than the admiration of a cultivated Greek aristocrat who, having been subjected to Roman authority, wholeheartedly embraced it? None, unless we cite the equally enthusiastic endorsement of the same Jews who had rebelled against Greek influence in 164 B.C.E. They, too, could not say enough in praise of the Romans, and they willingly placed themselves under Roman protection:

> Those whom they wish to help and to make kings, they make kings, and those whom they wish they depose; and they have been greatly exalted. Yet for all that, not one of

them has put on a crown or worn purple as a mark of pride, but they have built for themselves a senate chamber and every day three hundred and twenty senators constantly deliberate concerning the people, to govern them well. (1 Maccabees 8:12–15)

The only people who could say more in praise of Rome were the Romans themselves. To them, the enormous success of their empire meant that they were divinely chosen to colonize the world. This was the message conveyed by the poet Virgil (70–19 B.C.E.), commissioned by the emperor Augustus to tell the story of Rome's rise to glory in a manner imitating the epics of Homer. In one key passage of this monumental poem, the father of Aeneas, Virgil's epic hero, "foretells" the future and addresses posterity: "Remember, Roman, you whose power rules / all peoples, that these are your arts: plant peace, / make law, spare subjects, and put down the proud" (*Aeneid*, Book VI, lines 851–53).

While the Greeks struggled against the Persians and against each other, a new civilization had emerged beyond the far fringes of the Greek world, on the banks of the river Tiber in central Italy. By 300 B.C.E., Rome was the dominant power on the Italian peninsula. Two centuries later, it had conquered Greece itself. For the next three centuries after that—an unprecedented period of sustained expansion—its power steadily increased. In the first century of our era, it ruled the former Hellenistic kingdoms as well as a vast region that Greek culture had never touched: northwestern Europe. Eventually, Rome's empire united the entire Mediterranean world and most of Asia Minor, while at the same time embracing provinces that are now parts of France, Spain, Portugal, Britain, Belgium, Germany, Switzerland, and the Balkan states. Rome thus built a historical arch that enabled Europe to share in a rich heritage reaching back to ancient Mesopotamia and Egypt, and which gives meaning to the concept of "western civilization." Without Rome, European culture as we know it would not exist, and neither would the political and legal institutions that formed the United States. To echo Polybius: "Can anything be more important than understanding this?"

THE TIME OF THE KINGS

Romans looked back uneasily on their early history, for this was the time when they were ruled by kings. It may have been necessary in those days: Romans had never been peaceful settlers, and their land did not yield an easy living. Although Italy had sizable forests and much more fertile land than Greece, it has few mineral resources aside from excellent supplies of marble. Its extensive coastline boasts only a few good harbors, and most of these are on the western side, away from the commercial hubs of Greece and the Near East. Nor does the length of this coastline offer secure natural defenses. In short, Italy was rich enough to be attractive but not rich enough to be easily defended. So the Romans were a warlike people from the first, continually forced to defend their hard-won lands against other invaders and needing strong leaders to spearhead their efforts.

Early Influences

When the Romans arrived in Italy, the dominant inhabitants of the peninsula were a people whom the Greeks called Tyrrhenians. To the Romans, they were Etruscans; and to us they remain mysterious, despite the rich archaeological record they left behind. This is because their language (not a branch of Indo-European) has never been fully deciphered, even though the Etruscans used an alphabet borrowed from the Greeks, with whom they were in frequent contact. By the sixth century B.C.E., the Etruscans had established a confederation of independent city-states in north-central Italy. They were skilled metalworkers, artists, and architects, from whom the Romans later took their knowledge of the arch and the vault, among much else, including the bloody sport of gladiatorial combat and the practice of foretelling the future by studying the entrails of animals and the flight of birds.

The two most important foundation myths told by the Romans were also derived from Etruscan tradition: the story of Aeneas's escape from Troy, which became the basis of Virgil's *Aeneid*; and also the story of the infant twins Romulus and Remus, abandoned at birth and then raised by a maternal wolf, afterward founding a city on the slopes of the Palatine Hill. Both legends would be mined by Rome's politicians and historians for their metaphorical significance, and further details would be added to increase their relevance for a changing audience. For example, the story of Aeneas's seduction and abandonment of Dido, queen of Carthage, reflected Rome's defeat of that powerful North African civilization. And for many Roman commentators, the murder of Remus at the hands of his brother Romulus encapsulated an all-too-familiar pattern in Roman politics.

One aspect of Etruscan culture was of more limited influence. In marked contrast to Greek society, Etruscan women enjoyed a very high status and played important roles in public life. They participated in politics and sporting events, they attended dramatic performances and athletic competitions (forbidden to Greek women), and they danced

The Romans also borrowed ideas from the Greek settlers who had begun to colonize southern Italy and Sicily in large numbers during the eighth century B.C.E. From them, Romans derived their alphabet, many of their religious beliefs, and much of their art. But the Romans downplayed Greek influence in their founding mythology, preferring to emphasize their alleged descent from Trojans and also tracing their ancestry back to an Italic people called the Sabines, from whom (according to legend) Romulus and his men had forcibly abducted their women. This was a practice Romans would continue, in one form or another, as the legions planted new colonies and intermarried with indigenous populations from the Persian Gulf to the lowlands of Scotland.

The Founding of Rome

The real founders of Rome were a tribe called the Latins, descendants of a cluster of Indo-European-speaking peoples who crossed the Alps into Italy during the second millennium B.C.E. Recent archaeological research has pushed the origins of the city back to at least the tenth century, several centuries earlier than 753 B.C.E., which the Romans themselves calculated as the year of their city's foundation.

Rome's position on the Tiber was advantageous. Trading ships (but not large war fleets) could navigate the river as far as the city, but no farther; Rome could thus serve as a commercial port but was not threatened by attack from the sea. Rome also sat astride the first good ford across the Tiber, making it a major crossroads. This was particularly important in its early years, when all roads did *not* lead to Rome and the city was just a trading post on the frontier between Latium (the territory of the Latins) and Etruria (the Etruscan homeland). There were also strategic advantages to the seven hills that ringed the settlement, among which Rome was nestled. Eventually, its central marketplace—the *forum* or "open space"—would become the beating heart of the world's most populous and powerful city, with approximately a million people crowded into an area of five square miles.

The topography of Latium—a broad, flat plain with few natural obstacles—also influenced the way the Romans dealt with neighboring communities, because it was not a terrain with defensible natural boundaries. At an early date, they negotiated a series of agreements with their neighbors which were collectively known as the Latin Right: a trading pact called the *commercium*, provisions for intermarriage called the *connubium*, and the *migratio* that allowed a Latin resident of one settlement to emigrate to another and, after a year's residence, to have the full rights of a citizen there. These privileges contrast strongly with the rigid isolationism and mutual suspicion that divided the city-states of

AN ETRUSCAN COUPLE. This sarcophagus lid dates from the middle of the fourth century B.C.E. and depicts a deceased couple as they lie together in bed, emphasizing by their intimate embrace the closeness of their marital bond.

in ways that shocked both Greeks and Romans. Etruscan wives also ate meals with their husbands, another departure from both Greek and Roman custom, and reclined with them on the same couch at banquets. After death, these devoted couples were buried together in the same mortuary vaults, and their tombstones and sarcophagi often emphasize their mutual affection. Etruscan families even traced their descent through the female line. Some of these practices certainly affected the Romans, since Roman women were less sequestered than their Greek counterparts. Yet they did not enjoy the same freedoms as Etruscan women until very late in Roman history, and by then these freedoms were condemned as signs of Rome's decadence.

ancient Mesopotamia or Greece. Indeed, the Romans' later willingness to extend the Latin Right far beyond Latium was a key factor in the success of their empire.

According to their own legends, the Romans' early government was a monarchy that mirrored the structure of Roman households, with a patriarchal king who exercised power that was checked only by a council of elders, the Senate (a word derived from the Latin *senex*, "old man"). Seven kings, including Romulus, are said to have ruled in succession. The last, Tarquinius Superbus (Tarquin the Arrogant), is reputed to have been an Etruscan who paved the way for Rome's imperial expansion by dominating Latium and the agriculturally wealthy district of Campania to the south. But his power came at the price of Roman freedom and dignity, as was made clear when Tarquin's son allegedly raped a virtuous Roman wife, Lucretia, around 510 B.C.E. When she committed suicide to avoid dishonor, the Romans—led by Lucretia's kinsman, Lucius Junius Brutus—rose up in rebellion, overthrowing not only the Etruscan dynasty but rejecting the very idea of monarchy as a legitimate form of government. Henceforth, any claim to royal authority in Rome was considered anathema, and the very word *rex* ("king") was a term of insult. The Brutus who would be instrumental in the assassination of Julius Caesar nearly five centuries later was a descendant of that same Brutus who had driven out the Tarquin kings, something he and his contemporaries never forgot.

THE TRIUMPH OF THE EARLY REPUBLIC

The story of Lucretia's defilement and death, whether or not it occurred as it was remembered, remained a rallying theme of patriotic myth and was also a potent statement of Roman attitudes toward female chastity and family honor. And it coincided with a radical change in Roman governance. This change was so radical, in fact, that it did not match any of Aristotle's political categories (see Chapter 4), but instead combined elements of them all. The Romans themselves didn't know what to call their political system: they spoke of it merely as *res publica*, "the public thing."

The Territorial Expansion of Rome

The early Roman republic was marked by almost constant warfare, initially defensive but soon aimed at stitching together a patchwork of valuable territories that could sup-port Rome's growing population. Gradually, Romans came to control all of the Latin hinterland and the valuable port of Ostia at the mouth of the Tiber, about twenty miles from their city. They also pushed northward toward Etruscan territory, and southward to Naples, another good port. By 300 B.C.E., Romans had absorbed or allied themselves with all of central Italy and had begun to look even further south, to the wealthy Greek colonies of Sicily.

Their rapid success is remarkable when compared to the patterns familiar to us from our study of classical Greece, the only corollary (and not a close one) being Philip II of Macedonia's subjugation of the poleis earlier in that same century. What was the secret of it? For one thing, the Romans did not impose heavy burdens of taxation and tribute on the settlements they conquered. More often, they demanded that their allies contribute only soldiers to the Roman army. Rome also extended the Latin Right to many of these conquered territories, giving them a further stake in its continued political and military expansion.

Rome thus gained for itself nearly inexhaustible reserves of fighting men. By the middle of the third century B.C.E., its army may have counted as many as 300,000—a huge force even by modern standards, and all the more formidable due to the soldiers' rigorous training. As we have seen, the Greeks had eventually turned to paid soldiering out of economic necessity, but they fought in smaller numbers; Xenophon's army was 10,000 and Alexander's 100,000. The Great King of Persia, at the height of his powers, could claim to muster a million men, but these were private or tribal armies commanded by his satraps, not a standing army loyal to him. The Romans, by contrast, devoted themselves to the discipline of warfare in ways the Greeks (except for the Spartans) and the Persians did not. In this, although not in their tactics, they resemble the Hittites of the late Bronze Age and the Neo-Assyrians of the eighth century B.C.E. (see Chapter 2).

Although the Romans originally used the phalanx formation borrowed from the Greeks, they quickly replaced it with smaller, more flexible divisions that could adjust to the varied geographical conditions of central Italy. While the major unit of the Roman army was always the legion (5,000 men), the basic combat unit was the *maniple* ("handful"), a group of about 120 infantrymen who trained together and who often performed specialized tasks or used special weaponry. The Greek Polybius could not say enough in praise of this system, which made the army adaptable to climate, terrain, and the deployment of new military technologies.

The republic's early history reinforced not only the military character of the Roman state but its commitment to agriculture as the only proper peacetime employment for a Roman. The acquisition of new lands made it possible

ROMAN EXPANSION TO 218 B.C.E.

- Roman and Latin territory in 298 B.C.E.
- Roman allies in 298 B.C.E.
- Roman and Latin acquisitions from 298–263 B.C.E.
- Roman allies from 298–263 B.C.E.
- Roman acquisitions from 241–218 B.C.E.
- Roman acquisitions from the Second Punic War 218–201 B.C.E.
- Kingdom of Syracuse
- Allies of Syracuse

ROMAN EXPANSION IN ITALY, 485–265 B.C.E. This map illustrates early Roman expansion in the peninsula. ▪ *What is the geographical relationship between Roman and Etruscan territory?* ▪ *What seem to have been the most attractive avenues for Roman expansion?* ▪ *What powers might have threatened Rome after its transformation into the dominant power on the peninsula after 265 B.C.E.?*

for needy citizens to maintain themselves as farmers in the new colonies around Rome. By accommodating an increasing population in this way, Romans were able to remain staunchly agricultural for a surprisingly long time. As a result, they developed an interest in shipping and commerce fairly late when compared with the Greeks or Phoe-

nicians. And they would continue—even at the height of their empire—to valorize rural life over that of the city.

The paragon of Roman heroism in this era was Lucius Quinctius Cincinnatus (519–c. 430 B.C.E.), a stout-hearted citizen-farmer who reluctantly accepted political office when Rome was threatened by attack. According to legend, he

The Constitution of the Early Republic

CINCINNATUS THE STATESMAN-FARMER. This bronze statue of Cincinnatus is prominent in Cincinnati, Ohio, which was named after the Roman hero (and in honor of George Washington) in 1790. In his right hand he holds the *fasces*, symbolizing his powers as dictator. In his left, he grasps the handle of a plow. ▪ *Why would this figure have fired the imagination of Americans after their War of Independence?*

was found plowing his fields when a delegation of senators arrived to bring him to Rome. Arriving in the city, he found that he had been named *dictator*: a word that originally (like *tyrant* in Greece) had neutral connotations. This was a position of power to which the Romans elected one man during times of crisis. And as the term implies, the dictator's job was to tell everyone what they should do in a tough situation requiring decisive leadership. As legend has it, Cincinnatus dutifully performed this role, led Rome in its wars with hostile neighbors—and then went back to his farm. If Lucretia was the Roman epitome of matronly fortitude, Cincinnatus was the paradigm of manly virtue: willing to put his hand to politics or warfare, but preferring to put it to the plow. George Washington was frequently compared to him, to his own satisfaction.

During this period of expansion, Rome's political system evolved accordingly. Initially, the overthrow of the monarchy had resulted in only moderate changes; instead of a king, the government was headed by two elected officers called *consuls*. Although the consuls of the infant republic were supposedly chosen by all citizens, the Roman assembly of this period actually voted in affiliated blocs with shared interests, economic or territorial. And since groups consisting of the wealthiest citizens voted first, a majority could be reached even before the votes of the poorer groups were cast.

Consequently, the consuls were inevitably members of aristocratic families, known in Rome as *patricians* because they traced descent from a famous ancestor or "father" (*pater*). During his term of office, which lasted for one year, each consul exercised essentially the same power as a king: dealing justice, making law, and commanding the army. The only limit on consular power was the right of each consul to veto the actions of the other, which often led to stalemate or violent conflict. In such cases, the Senate might have to arbitrate. In times of grave emergency (like that resulting in Cincinnatus's election), a dictator might be appointed for a term not longer than six months.

Within a generation after the establishment of the republic, patrician dominance of the government began to be challenged by the *plebs* ("people"). This was the first stage in a centuries-long contest known as the Struggle of the Orders. The plebeian classes made up nearly 98 percent of the Roman population, and they were a diverse group. Some had grown wealthy through trade or agriculture, but most were smallholding farmers, artisans, or the urban poor. Their causes for grievance were numerous. Although they were forced to serve in the army, they were nevertheless excluded from holding office. They were also the victims of discriminatory decisions in judicial trials, which were judged by patricians. They did not even know what legal rights they were supposed to enjoy, because Rome had as yet no established laws: there were only unwritten customs and practices whose meaning was interpreted by the patricians to their own advantage. The plebeians were also, like the poorer citizens of Greek poleis, threatened with debt slavery.

These wrongs prompted a rebellion in the early fifth century B.C.E., when plebeians refused to join in the military defense of Rome and instead seceded from the city, camping out on the Aventine hill (see the map of Rome on page 174). This general strike of military labor forced the patricians to allow the people to elect their own officers, who were known as *tribunes* (tribal leaders). The job of each tribune was to protect his constituents from patrician injustice. Moreover, the plebeians guaranteed the safety of these officers by vowing to kill any person who hindered them in the exercise of their powers.

The plebs' victory led to the codification of the Law of the Twelve Tables, issued around 450 B.C.E. and inscribed on wooden tablets (hence "tables"). Although this law would be regarded by later Romans as a charter of liberties, it was really a perpetuation of ancient custom. Nevertheless, the fact that the law was now *defined* made it a significant improvement. Plebeians were also made eligible to hold elected offices and they gradually gained access to the Senate. A further victory came in 287 B.C.E., when the plebeians succeeded in passing a law that made decisions enacted in their own assembly, the *concilium plebis*, binding on the Roman government—whether the Senate approved them or not. It was at this time that the phrase *Senatus Populusque Romanum* came into regular use, abbreviated *SPQR* and designating any decree or decision made by "the Senate and People of Rome." (Visitors to Rome will still find *SPQR* emblazoned on everything from public buildings to the manhole covers of Rome's sewers.)

These reforms had several important consequences over the long term. Successful plebeians could now work their way into the upper reaches of Roman society, which loosened the hold of patrician families on the exercise of power. At the same time, laws preventing wealth from becoming a controlling factor in Roman politics barred senators from engaging directly in commerce. This restriction had the effect of creating a new social order, that of the equestrians ("horsemen" or knights): men who chose a life of business rather than politics and whose wealth made it possible for them to own and equip warhorses and thus to

SENATUS POPULUSQUE ROMANUM. The proud stamp of "the Senate and People of Rome" can be found even on public works and buildings in modern Rome. It is displayed here on a manhole cover.

provide Rome's cavalry. But the equestrians and the senators were never wholly distinct. Often, some members of an important family would stay aloof from politics while underwriting the political careers of their brothers and cousins. Those families who managed to win election by such means, generation after generation, became increasingly prestigious and influential. Meanwhile, patricians who chose politics over wealth became impoverished and resentful. By the first century B.C.E., many such men felt excluded from political influence and were tempted to pursue their private agendas by styling themselves champions of the people (see below).

Later Roman patriots would regard this as a golden age of shared government, but Rome was never a democracy. A republic differs from a monarchy only because power is exercised by officers who are in some way responsible to citizens and whose offices are not (at least in theory) hereditary. It is essentially a system for reserving power to an oligarchy or privileged group. This is what the republic had been founded to achieve: kings were driven out, but patricians reigned. The constitution that emerged in these key centuries therefore broadened and stabilized oligarchy by the balance it struck between competing governmental institutions: the assembly, the Senate, and executive officeholders. Thanks to this distribution of powers, no single individual or clique could become overwhelmingly strong; but neither could direct expressions of the popular will (that is, democracy) affect Roman policy.

For the Greek historian Polybius, this was an ideal system because it combined elements of a monarchy (executive officeholders, the consuls), an aristocracy (the Senate), and a polity (the people's assembly and the tribunes). For the framers of the U.S. Constitution, it was a model for the three branches of a new government designed to *prevent* the vast majority of Americans from participating directly in politics, while allowing some citizens (originally, white men with sufficient property) a say in choosing their representatives. Polybius prophesied that such a system would break the political cycle that had destroyed the Greek poleis and that it would last forever. He was wrong.

THE ESSENCE OF ROMAN IDENTITY

The slow unfolding of the early republic ensured, in part, its success: Romans were conservatives who accepted new things reluctantly but then preserved them fiercely. The prevailing principle behind their institutions was the *mos maiorum* (MOHSmy-OR-um), "the code of the elders" or "the custom of the ancestors" or even—to use the word derived from the Latin *mos*—"morality." This unwritten code was sacrosanct and essential to Roman identity. It accounts for the remarkable coherence of Roman culture, religion, and law, all of which rested on ancestor worship. The Latin word *pietas* ("piety") meant reverence for family traditions and for one's fathers—living and dead. What made the legendary Aeneas "pious Aeneas" was his devotion to his father, Anchises (*an-KIE-sees*), whom he carried to safety on his back while Troy burned. Metaphorically, this meant that Aeneas was the carrier of tradition, a man willing to shoulder the burdens of his ancestors and carry them forever.

This helps to explain why the Romans, in the ensuing centuries of their world domination, continued to identify so strongly with their homeland and its customs. To a Roman, "going native" in a foreign place was a terrible betrayal of the *mos maiorum*; patriotism, after all, is dedication to the fatherland. It also explains the extraordinary maxim of *patria potestas* (*PAH-tree-apoh-TEST-as*, "fatherly power") upheld by the Twelve Tables. A Roman father, no matter what his social class, had absolute authority within his household, including the powers of life and death. If he was too poor to raise a child, he could expose it (leaving it to perish or to charity) or sell it into slavery. If his wife or child dishonored him, he could kill with impunity. It was upheld in theory and in legends like that of Lucretia: had she not killed herself, her father could have killed her with his own hands.

These values set the Romans apart from everyone in the Hellenistic world. The Greeks, for example, never condoned anything like *patria potestas*: when fathers kill their children in Greek mythology, they are inevitably killed in revenge by another member of their own family or by the gods. And while pride in one's ancestry is a very human attribute, and patriarchy common to every known civilization, the Romans' contemporaries were awed by their extreme devotion to these principles. It was one of the things that made the Romans so admirable in the eyes of those Jews disgusted by the loose morals of Hellenistic civilization (see Chapter 4). For the Greek Polybius, it was the key to Roman success. In addition to describing the workings of the Roman government and army in minute detail, he reports (with anthropological interest) on the conduct of Roman funeral processions and the Romans' practice of wearing the death-masks of their ancestors, which on other days would be hung in special household shrines.

In some respects, Rome's public religion resembled that of the Greeks: Jupiter corresponded to Zeus as god of the skies, Neptune to Poseidon as god of the seas, Venus to Aphrodite as goddess of beauty and sexuality, Mars to Ares as god of war. But in keeping with the Roman equation of religion with family, this entire pantheon functioned

A ROMAN PATRICIAN OF THE FIRST CENTURY B.C.E. This man, who wears the toga of an aristocrat, displays his piety by holding the busts of his ancestors. Busts, like the funerary masks described by Polybius (see page 153), commemorated the dead and served as the focus for family worship in household shrines. ▪ *How does the Roman attitude toward age and death differ from that of the Greeks (see the image on page 82)?* ▪ *What do these differences suggest about the broader values of these two societies?*

Analyzing Primary Sources

Polybius Describes the Romans' Worship of Their Ancestors

The Law of the Twelve Tables forbade excessive display at funerals, especially displays of wealth and grief on the part of women. Instead, funerals were supposed to be occasions for the display of family piety. In the following passage, the Greek historian Polybius—who had spent a formative fourteen years of his life in Rome—describes Roman burial customs and these rites' relationship to the strength of republican ideals.

quote just one example to illustrate the pains taken by the Roman state to produce men who will endure anything to win a reputation for valor in their country. Whenever one of their celebrated men dies . . . his body is carried with every kind of honor into the Forum, . . . sometimes in an upright position so as to be conspicuous, or else, more rarely, recumbent. The whole mass of the people stand round to watch, and his son, if he has one of adult age who can be present, or if not some other relative, then . . . delivers an address which recounts the virtues and successes achieved by the dead man during his lifetime. By these means the whole populace . . . are involved in the ceremony, so that when the facts of the dead man's career are recalled . . . their sympathies are so deeply engaged that the loss seems . . . to be a public one which affects the whole people. Then, after the burial of the body and the performance of the customary rites, they place the image of the dead man in the most conspicuous position in the house, where it is enclosed in a wooden shrine. This image consists of a mask which is fashioned with extraordinary fidelity . . . to represent the features of these dead men. On occasions when public sacrifices are offered, these masks are displayed and decorated with great care. And when any distinguished member of the family dies, the masks are taken to the funeral, and are worn by men who are considered to bear the closest resemblance to the original, both in height and their general appearance and bearing. . . .

It would be hard to imagine a more impressive scene for a young man who aspires to win fame and practice virtue. For who could remain unmoved at the sight of the images of all these men who have won renown in their time, now gathered together as if alive and breathing? What spectacle could be more glorious than this?

Source: Polybius, *The Rise of the Roman Empire*, trans. Ian Scott-Kilvert (New York: 1979), pp. 346–47.

Questions for Analysis

1. Why does Polybius place so high a premium on the Romans' conduct at funerals? How can such rites be related to republican ideals?

2. Compare this analysis of Roman funerary rites to the image of a Roman patrician and his ancestors on page 152. How do they complement one another?

as family gods of the Roman state. The republic was essentially a giant, timeless household run by "elders" (senators) and "father figures" (patricians), some of whom traced their ancestry back to gods; the mother of Aeneas was Venus. Like a Roman household, the Roman state could flourish only if these father- and mother-gods lent their continuing and active support to its enterprises. Committees of priests therefore functioned as branches of the government and tended to the worship of the city's temples. And in stark contrast to other ancient societies, these priests were not full-time professionals who formed a special caste, but prominent men who rotated in and out of office while serving as leaders of the Senate. Their dual roles made religion even more integral to political life in Rome than it had been in Greece—similar in some ways to the integration of religion and politics in ancient Mesopotamia (see Chapter 1).

The Roman man's primary duty to honor his ancestors also bolstered the prestige of the Roman army, because soldiers were supposed to sacrifice themselves for the public good and to fear disgrace above all things. The all-important sense of ancestral duty is further reflected in Roman naming practices, another custom that separated them from other ancient cultures. Most free men in antiquity were known by a given name and their father's name only: Alexander, before he was "the Great," was "son of Philip." A free-born Roman, by contrast, had at least two names. The name by which he was known—the name that mattered—was the name of his earliest ancestor, the man from whom his family descended. Gaius Julius Caesar, to take a famous example, would have entered public life as Julius, a member of the family of the Julii, who claimed ancestry from Iulus, the son of Aeneas. His forename, Gaius, was the most common name in Rome, the equivalent of "Joe" or "John," and he would never be addressed by this name in public, except perhaps by very intimate friends or family members. His third name, Caesar, was a nickname he acquired in the course of his career: "Hairy" (probably a joke). And because it was the most distinctive of his names—the name he didn't share with an ancestor or with average Romans—it became the name by which he was universally known. The same goes for Marcus Tullius Cicero (Cicero means "chickpea"). The illustrious Cincinnatus was actually "Curly."

What's in a name? Everything, if you were a Roman man. And nothing, at least nothing of personal significance, if you were a Roman woman. Lucretia's name was not her own but her father's—or forefather's: the feminine version of Lucretius. If she had a sister, they would both be called Lucretia, differentiated only as Major and Minor ("big/elder" and "little/younger") Lucretia. If there were two more girls, they would be Tertia and Quarta ("Third" and "Fourth") Lucretia, and so on. The only people in Rome who had personal names were slaves (who were named by their masters, like pets) or very low-born Romans and immigrants who had no lineage that mattered.

FROM REPUBLIC TO EMPIRE

For more than two centuries after the founding of the republic, warfare and agriculture remained the chief occupations of most Romans. A few artisans could be found in cities, and some minor attempts were made to establish trading networks. But the fact that Rome had no standard system of coinage until 289 B.C.E suggests strongly that commerce was an insignificant component of its economy. Apparently, Romans didn't rely on portable wealth; when they weren't fighting, they wanted to be home on the farm, not gadding about the world. If they had money, they put it into real estate: land or slaves.

All of this changed rapidly when Romans began to look beyond Italy. In 265 B.C.E., they completed their absorption of Etruscan territory and could claim to control most of the peninsula. A year later, they were already embroiled in a war overseas. For a home-loving people who had now secured ample resources for their own support, this seems paradoxical. Indeed, historians continue to argue about the motives for Roman expansion. Did Rome constantly seek to extend its rule as a matter of policy, to feed a collective appetite for warfare and plunder? Or was it an accidental empire, built up in a series of reactions to changing pressures at home as well as in response to threats—real and imagined—from abroad? No definitive answer is yet possible, but it is in this crucial period that the Roman Republic began to transform Western civilizations and to transform itself into the Roman Empire.

The Punic Wars, 264–146 B.C.E

In 265 B.C.E., Roman territory extended to the tip of Italy's "boot," but there it ended. Just off its coast, the large islands of Corsica and Sardinia and the western half of Sicily were part of another state, much older and far wealthier. This was the great maritime empire of Carthage, which stretched along the northern coast of Africa from modern-day Tunisia through the Straits of Gibraltar and into modern Spain. Carthage itself was a vital port city at the northeastern tip of Africa, founded around 800 B.C.E. as a Phoenician colony (see Chapter 2) but now independent and powerful. It had the largest and most effective navy of its day, and it commanded the vast resources of commercial networks that reached as far north as Britain and deep into Egypt and the Near East. In almost every respect but one it was far superior to Rome. Yet that one factor was decisive: while the Carthaginian fleet was unrivaled, Carthage had no standing army. It relied on mercenaries bankrolled by the enormous profits of its merchants.

The epic struggle between Rome and Carthage for dominance of the Mediterranean lasted well over a century. It crystallized in three periods of concentrated warfare known as the Punic Wars, because the Romans called their enemies Poeni, "Phoenicians." The first of these wars began in 264 B.C.E., when Rome sent a garrison to occupy the independent city of Messina (originally a Greek colony) on the eastern tip of Sicily, directly across from the Italian mainland. Carthage, in response, took advantage of the local enmity between Messina and Syracuse, another Greek city, and sent warships to protect Syracuse from what it saw as Roman aggression. Twenty-three years of bitter fighting ensued, protracted because the Carthaginians only needed to suffer one defeat in a land battle before resolving to engage the Romans solely at sea. There, they had the advantage—until the Romans built their own navy, virtually from scratch. In 241 B.C.E., Carthage was beaten down and forced to cede all of her Sicilian lands to Rome and to pay a large indemnity. Sicily thus became Rome's first overseas province. It was shortly followed by Corsica and Sardinia, which the Roman Senate contrived to seize on the grounds that Carthage had defaulted on the payment of reparations.

Thereafter, the Carthaginians had ample reason to harbor resentment against Rome, while the Romans were determined not to let Carthage revive its maritime power. So when Carthage attempted to expand its presence in Spain, leaders of the Senate interpreted this as a threat to Roman interests and declared a new war that lasted for sixteen years: the Second Punic War. This time, however, Rome was thrown entirely off its guard by the brilliant exploits of the Carthaginian commander Hannibal (247–183 B.C.E), who very nearly defeated the Romans at their own game and on their own soil. No one had imagined that a Carthaginian attack could come by land, from the north. But daringly, Hannibal raised an army in Spain, heavily manned by cavalry in order to counter the superior infantry of Rome, and equipped it with dozens of war elephants and siege engines. He then led this entire force across the Pyrenees into Gaul (now southern France) and then over the Alps into Italy. There, he harried Roman forces in their own territories for nearly sixteen years, from 218 to 202 B.C.E.

In the end, Hannibal was challenged more by the rigors of campaigning and the difficulty of supplying his army in hostile terrain than by the Romans themselves (he had lost many of his elephants and some important equipment in the icy mountain passes of the Alps). He also seems to have counted on winning the support of the Italian territories that Rome had conquered, but Rome's generous treatment of its Latin allies kept them loyal. As a result, Rome could call on vast human resources while Hannibal had only his exhausted army, and no reserves forthcoming from Carthage. Nevertheless, he won several amazing victories in Italy before retreating—technically undefeated—in 202 B.C.E. He also won the admiration of the Romans themselves, whose own histories frankly acknowledge his tactical genius. Indeed, this phase of warfare ended only when a Roman general, Publius Cornelius Scipio, took a leaf out of Hannibal's book. He had been campaigning in Spain against the army of Hannibal's brother, Hasdrubal, and having seized a number of key Carthaginian strongholds he crossed into Africa and met Hannibal at Zama, near Carthage, in 201 B.C.E. Scipio's victory ended the Second Punic War and won him a new name, "Africanus," in honor of his conquest.

Carthage was now compelled to abandon all of its possessions except the city itself and its immediate hinterlands, and to pay an indemnity three times greater than the already crippling reparations demanded after the First Punic War. Yet Roman suspicion of Carthage remained obsessive, and warmongers in the Senate read every sign of its recovery as a threat. By the middle of the second century, some hardliners were urging a preemptive strike. Among the most vocal was an elderly patrician called Marcus Porcius Cato, famous for his stern obedience to Roman custom and his virulent xenophobia. Cato ended every speech he gave—no matter what the topic—with the words: "And furthermore, I strongly advise that Carthage be destroyed." This won him the nickname Cato the Censor, from the Latin verb meaning "to advise."

Eventually, the Senate was persuaded. In 149 B.C.E., it seized on a minor pretext to demand that the Carthaginians abandon their city and settle at least ten miles from the coast, where they would have no access to the sea. Of course, this absurd mandate amounted to a death sentence for a city dependent on commerce, and it was refused—as the Romans knew it would be. The result was the Third Punic War and the siege of Carthage, which ended in 146 B.C.E. when the Romans breached the walls and butchered the population.

CARTHAGINIAN COIN. This coin was issued by Hannibal's family around 230 B.C.E. and circulated in the Carthaginian colonies of Spain. Its face shows the Carthaginian god Melqart in the guise of Hercules (notice the club over his shoulder). The reverse features a war elephant with a mounted rider, like the ones that would be used by Hannibal against Rome.

Those who survived the massacre were sold into slavery, and their once-magnificent city was razed to the ground. The legend that the Romans sowed the land with salt (to make it infertile) is not a real tactic but a poetic way of describing the successful eradication of an entire civilization. It would stand as a warning to Rome's other potential enemies.

Roman Control of the Hellenistic World

Rome's victories over Carthage enormously increased Roman territory, leading to the creation of new colonial provinces in Sicily, North Africa, and Hispania (Spain).

This not only brought Rome great new wealth (above all, access to Sicilian and African grain supplies and to the silver mines of the Iberian Peninsula), but it was also the beginning of the westward expansion that became Rome's defining influence on the history of Europe.

At the same time, Rome's overseas expansion brought it into conflict with eastern Mediterranean powers, paving the way for further conquests. During the Second Punic War, Philip V of Macedonia had entered an alliance with Carthage; soon afterward, he moved aggressively into Greece and was rumored to have designs on Egypt. Rome sent an army to stop him, and later foiled the plans of the Achaean League (see Chapter 4). This was when Polybius was sent to Rome as a hostage, and became a guest-friend in the family descended from Scipio Africanus, and later

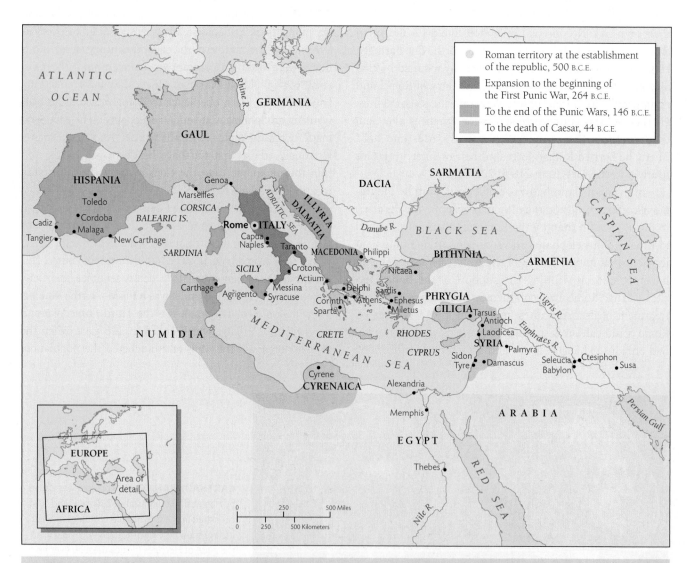

THE FURTHER EXPANSION OF ROME, 264–44 B.C.E. The rapid increase of Rome's territories opened up new opportunities and challenges.
▪ *Looking at the phases of expansion on this map, in what directions did Roman dominion move?* ▪ *Why was this the case?* ▪ *What particular problems might have been created by the eventual extension of Roman rule into Gaul, well beyond the "Roman lake" of the Mediterranean?*

witnessed the destruction of Carthage. Rome also thwarted similar efforts by the Seleucid monarch Antiochus III. In neither of these cases did Rome set out to conquer the eastern Mediterranean on purpose. By 146 B.C.E., however, both Greece and Macedonia had become Roman provinces, Seleucid Asia had lost most of its territories, and Ptolemaic Egypt had largely become a pawn of Roman commercial and political interests.

THE CONSEQUENCES OF IMPERIALISM

Rome's seemingly inadvertent conquest of Greece and Asia Minor transformed the economic, social, and cultural life of the republic. New wealth poured in, increasing the inequalities within Roman society and challenging traditional values of frugality and self-sacrifice. Small farmers left the land and swelled the impoverished urban population, unable to compete with the huge new plantations owned by aristocrats and worked by gangs of slaves. Slaves also played an increasing role in Roman cities as artisans, merchants, and household servants. Roman rule over the Hellenistic world had a particularly pervasive impact on cultural life—so much so that many Romans considered themselves to have been intellectually "conquered" by Greece. Hitherto self-assured and self-satisfied, they now felt their own language, history, and customs to be uncouth and barbaric compared to those of their cultivated colonial subjects.

Economic Change and Social Upheaval

Like all peoples of the ancient world, Romans took slavery for granted. But nothing in Rome's earlier experience prepared it for the huge increase in the number of slaves that resulted from its western and eastern conquests. In 146 B.C.E., 55,000 Carthaginians were enslaved after the destruction of their city; not long before, 150,000 Greek prisoners of war had met the same fate. By the end of the second century B.C.E., there were a million slaves in Italy alone. Rome's became one of the most slave-based economies in history, rivaling ancient Egypt or the antebellum American South.

The majority of Roman slaves worked as agricultural laborers on the vast (and growing) estates of the Roman aristocracy. Some of these estates were the result of earlier Roman conquests within Italy itself. But others were consolidated by aristocrats buying up the holdings of peasant farmers. Soldiers in particular, who might be required to serve for years at a time on foreign campaigns, often found it impossible to maintain their farms. Instead, they moved to the city—where there was no way for free men to sustain themselves except through trade or violence. With abundant, cheap slaves to do all the rough work, moreover, there was no impetus for technological innovation. Meanwhile, expensive slaves did the specialized jobs: they were secretaries, bookkeepers, personal assistants, playwrights, musicians, sculptors, artists. There was almost no incentive to employ paid labor at all or even to train oneself in these arts, as the Greeks had. By the first century B.C.E., as a result, a third of Rome's 1 million inhabitants were receiving free grain from the state, partly to keep them alive and partly to keep them quiet. The poet Juvenal (see page 171) would later satirize the plebs as needing only "bread and circuses" to stay satisfied and docile.

As we have seen, the Roman economy had remained fundamentally agrarian until the mid-third century B.C.E. During the following century, however, Rome's eastern conquests brought it fully into the sophisticated commercial hub of the Hellenistic world. The principal beneficiaries of this were the equestrian class. As overseas merchants, they profited handsomely from Rome's voracious appetite for foreign luxury goods. And as representatives of the Roman government in the provinces, they operated mines, built roads, and collected taxes, always with an eye toward their own profits. They were also the principal moneylenders to the Roman state and to distressed individuals. Interest rates were high, and when the state could not pay its bills, it would often allow the moneylenders to repay themselves by exploiting the populations of the provinces.

Commoners who lost their lands suffered from these economic changes, but the principal victims of Rome's transformation were its slaves. Even though some were cultivated foreigners—mainly Greek-speaking—taken as prisoners of war, the standard policy of their owners was to get as much work out of them as possible until they died of exhaustion or were "freed" in old age to fend for themselves. The same irascible Cato the Censor who had demanded the destruction of Carthage even wrote a "how-to" book on this subject. The ready availability of slaves also made Roman slavery a far more impersonal and brutal institution than it had been in many other ancient civilizations. Of course, there were exceptions. Some domestic slaves were treated as trusted family members, and slave secretaries vital to the business of Roman governance and literature could even win fame or earn enough to buy their freedoms. Some slave artisans were permitted to run their own businesses, keeping some of the profits.

But the general lot of slaves was horrendous. Some businessmen owned slaves whom they trained as gladiators, to be mauled by wild animals or by other gladiators

Past and Present

Spectator Sports

Like the Romans' love for gladiatorial combat, Americans' love of football is inextricably tied to a sense of shared identity and fascination with violence and warfare. Although American football is not a bloodsport in a technical sense, part of its allure stems from the very great physical risks taken by its players, whose careers are often cut short by injury. Both pastimes form the core of far-reaching entertainment economies that would be dismantled by any attempts at reform: concessions, advertising, merchandising, and an array of other money-making activities.

 Watch related author interview on StudySpace
wwnorton.com/web/westernciv18

for the amusement of a paying public. The luxurious lifestyles of the wealthy meant that dozens of slaves in every household were trapped in a cycle of menial tasks, as doorkeepers, litter-bearers, couriers, valets, wet-nurses, and child-minders. In some great households, designated slaves had no other duties than to rub down the master after his bath or to keep track of the mistress's social engagements. It was a life that debased both slave and owner, according to many Roman critics, and thereby undermined the values of the republic.

New Money, New Values

In the early republic, as we have seen, Roman men had nearly absolute powers over their individual households. During the second century B.C.E., however, two innovations greatly altered

this pattern of patriarchal control. One was the introduction of new laws that allowed married women to manage their own property instead of handing that wealth over to their husbands; if a married woman died, her possessions would then revert to her father or her father's heirs if she had no children of her own. Alongside this new law came more liberal laws that allowed women to initiate divorce proceedings.

These changes were intended to safeguard family wealth, but they eventually resulted in greater independence for women. A woman now had much more authority within the household because she contributed to its upkeep. If her husband did not show respect, she could leave him and deprive him of income. Ironically, the growth of Rome's slave system also gave women greater freedom, for slaves took over the traditional work of child rearing, household maintenance, and the endless tasks of spinning and weaving. Women from well-to-do families now spent more time away from the home and began to engage in a range of social, intellectual, and artistic activities. Indeed, women were among the chief consumers of the new Hellenistic fashions, commodities, and ideas available in Rome.

In earlier centuries, Romans had taken pride in the simplicity of their lives, their language, and their moral code. Now, however, elite Romans began to indulge in creature comforts and to cultivate Hellenistic habits as proof of their refinement. Bilingualism became increasingly common, and Greek literature became the standard against which Roman authors measured themselves. For Latin was not yet a literary language. It was fine for business or politics or farming, but if one wanted to express lofty or beautiful thoughts one did so in Greek, which was far more flexible and sophisticated.

Well-educated Greek slaves were therefore at a premium: to lend social cachet, to act as secretaries and personal assistants, and to tutor Roman children. The popularity of Greek plays, mostly comedies, was such that they quickly spawned Latin imitations, like those of Plautus (257?–184 B.C.E.) and Terence (195/185–159 B.C.E.). Terence's career path is suggestive of a larger pattern: a Greek-speaker of Libyan descent, he was sold as a slave-boy in Carthage and bought by a wealthy Roman called Terentius, who took him back to Rome and cultivated his talents, which he marketed under his own name. Six of Terence's Latin adaptations of Greek comedies survive, and they enjoyed enormous popularity well into the Middle Ages, eventually influencing the plays of Shakespeare.

In short, many Romans nursed an inferiority complex with respect to Greek culture. But others (including Cato) regarded these foreign influences with disgust. For them, the good old ways of paternal authority and stern military discipline were giving way to effeminacy and the decadence of soft living. Accordingly, conservative politicians deplored these new trends and passed laws that would restore "family values" and regulate the conspicuous consumption of luxuries, especially by women. These measures were ineffectual. Rome was being irreversibly transformed from a republic of self-reliant farmers into a complex metropolitan empire reliant on foreign slaves, foreign grain, and foreign luxuries, in which the gap between rich and poor was widening and where traditional behavioral constraints were giving way to new morals and ideas.

Philosophy and Spirituality in the Late Republic

The late republic was deeply influenced by Hellenistic philosophy, and both Epicureanism and Stoicism found strong adherents in Rome. The former was popularized by Lucretius (98–55 B.C.E.), author of a book-length philosophical poem, *On the Nature of Things*. But more congenial to Roman values was Stoicism, which soon numbered among its converts many powerful public figures. The most influential of these was Cicero (106–43 B.C.E.), famous in his day as an orator, statesman, and staunch defender of republican values. Cicero based his ethical teachings on the Stoic

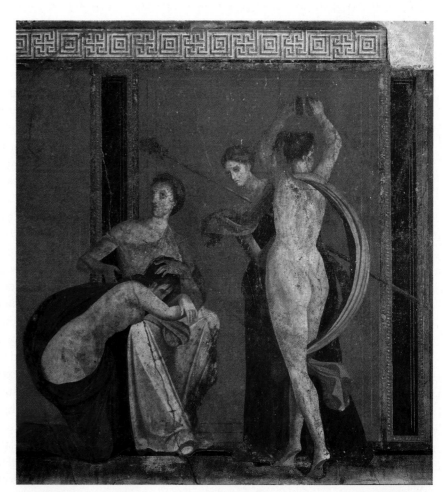

ROMAN MYSTERY RITES. One of the Roman houses preserved at Pompeii features an astonishing cycle of wall paintings, executed around 50 B.C.E., which give the house its name: Villa of the Mysteries. The exact meaning of these images is still debated, but some scholars have argued that they depict a succession of ritual practices. Here a young woman is being whipped, perhaps as part of an initiation ceremony, while another woman performs a dance.

premises that virtue is happiness and tranquillity of mind the highest good. The ideal man is therefore rational and indifferent to sorrow and pain. Yet Cicero diverged from the Stoics in his approval of the active, political life. He became an advocate for the revival of Roman tradition through service to the state. His elegant prose style also advanced the use of Latin as a language of eloquence and became the standard model for Latin composition: students learning Latin today still learn to read with Cicero.

The religious practices of Rome also changed markedly in this era. The most pronounced innovation was the spread of exotic mystery cults, which satisfied a need for more emotionally intense spiritual experiences than did traditional forms of Roman worship—again, especially for women, who were largely excluded from the rites of the patriarchal state religion. From Egypt came the cults of Isis and Osiris, while from Asia came the worship of the Great Mother, all emphasizing the power of female sexuality and reproduction. Despite the attractions of these new cults, Romans continued to honor their traditional gods alongside these new deities. Roman polytheism could absorb them all, so long as the ancestor gods of the household and of the city were paid due reverence.

"RESTORING THE REPUBLIC": THE STRUGGLE FOR POWER

In Rome itself, the period from the end of the Third Punic War in 146 to about 30 B.C.E. was one of turbulence. Politically motivated murders, bloody competition among rival dictators, wars, and insurrections were common occurrences. Slave uprisings also added to the general disorder. In 134 B.C.E., some 70,000 slaves defeated a Roman army in Sicily before being put down by emergency reinforcements. Slaves ravaged Sicily again in 104 B.C.E. But the most threatening revolt of all was led by Spartacus, a Thracian captive who was being trained as a gladiator. Along with a band of 200 fellow slaves from a gladiatorial training camp—they had all been bought by a wealthy entrepreneur—they escaped from Capua (near Naples; see the map on page 149), heavily armed, to the slopes of Mount Vesuvius, where their cause attracted a huge host of other fugitives.

From 73 to 71 B.C.E., this desperate army defeated trained Roman forces of as many as 10,000 men, and they overran much of southern Italy before Spartacus himself was killed. The Senate, terrified of the precedent set by the near victory of the rebels, ordered 6,000 of the captured slaves to be crucified along the length of the road from Capua to Rome (about 150 miles) as a warning to future insurgents. Crucifixion was a form of punishment reserved for slaves and non-Roman rebels, and it meant a slow, terrible, and public death from gradual suffocation and exposure.

The Reforming Efforts of the Gracchi

Meanwhile, these waves of rural rebellion were being mirrored by urban unrest in various forms, and the poorer classes were finding new champions among some progressive aristocrats. In 133 B.C.E., a grandson of Scipio Africanus, Tiberius Gracchus, was elected a tribune of the people. He took his office seriously and proposed to alleviate social and economic stress by instituting major reforms, chiefly the redistribution of property. As we have noted, small farmers had been losing their lands to patricians and equestrians whose new wealth allowed them to amass giant estates. To counter this, Tiberius Gracchus invoked old laws that had, under the early republic, limited the amount of land that could be held by a single person.

His motives were not entirely populist. There was a grave manpower shortage in the Roman army, which had been forced to expand its presence in the far reaches of the world and had left Rome itself prey to uprisings like that of Spartacus. Since a man had to meet certain property qualifications to serve in the Roman army, the available pool of citizen soldiers was contracting. So Tiberius Gracchus also aimed to refresh the reserves by creating new citizens.

With the support of his brother Gaius, Tiberius Gracchus proposed a law that would restrict estates to a maximum of 300 acres per citizen, plus 150 acres for each child in his family, with the excess land to be divided among poor settlers. Not surprisingly, most senators stood to lose from this legislation and so engineered its veto by Gracchus's fellow tribunes. But Gracchus retaliated, arguing that tribunes who opposed the people's interests were betraying their offices, and he announced plans to stand for reelection when his term expired. A conservative faction in the Senate then alleged that Gracchus had his sights set on a dictatorship, and with this excuse they attacked and murdered him and his supporters on the day of the elections.

Ten years later, Gaius Gracchus renewed his older brother's struggle after being elected to the same office. Although a version of Tiberius's land reforms had finally been enacted by the Senate, Gaius believed that the campaign had to go further. In 123 B.C.E., he enacted several laws for the benefit of the poor, stabilizing the price of grain in Rome by building public granaries along the Tiber and checking the administrative abuses of the senatorial class by giving the equestrians greater powers. He also imposed controls on provincial governors suspected of exploiting their subjects for personal gain. Most controversially, Gaius proposed to extend full Roman citizenship to all the allied states of Italy, a move that would have kept the army well supplied with new soldiers but which would also alter the political landscape of Rome to the detriment of the existing elite. Accordingly, the Senate proclaimed Gaius Gracchus an outlaw and authorized its consuls to deal ruthlessly with his supporters. In the ensuing conflict, Gaius and about 3,000 of his followers became the victims of a violent political purge.

Rivalry among Rome's Generals

Although the reforms of the Gracchi were ultimately unsuccessful, they exposed the weakness of the Senate and increased the power of the plebs, whose favor was now courted by a succession of ambitious men. Most of these were professional soldiers who controlled one or more legions of the Roman army and who traded on military victories abroad to win the confidence of the people and access to power.

The first of these was Gaius Marius, a man from an obscure provincial family who fought a successful campaign against Jugurtha of Numidia, whose small kingdom threatened Rome's hard-won supremacy in North Africa. In 107 B.C.E., Marius's popularity catapulted him to the consulship, despite the protests of the Senate's aristocracy, and he would be elected to that office six more times in the course of his life.

Marius was no statesman. But he set a powerful precedent by demonstrating how easily a general with an army behind him could override opposition—and that an army command could be an alternative path to political power. He also influenced the future of Rome by reorganizing and expanding the army. Desperate for more men to fight in Africa and in Gaul, which Rome was slowly infiltrating, Marius abolished the property qualification that had hitherto limited military service; the potential pool of soldiers now included the urban poor and landless peasants. As a result, a career as a Roman legionnaire became an end in itself, and a soldier's loyalty was directed toward his commander (whose success would win rewards for his men) rather than to an abstract ideal of patriotism or service to the state. Moreover, this change meant that factional fighting could lead to full-blown civil war, as legions loyal to one general were pitted against those of another.

This happened in Marius's own lifetime. The aristocratic general Lucius Cornelius Sulla had fought with distinction in the so-called Social War of 91–88 B.C.E., a conflict between Rome and her Italian allies that resulted in the extension of Roman citizenship throughout the peninsula. Thereafter, Sulla seemed the likely person to lead Rome's army to war in Asia Minor. Marius, however, did not agree; he forced the Senate to deny Sulla's claim. Sulla's response was to rally the five victorious legions that had just fought under his command and, with a Roman army at his back, to march on Rome.

This was a disturbing move, since strong taboos had long prevented any armed force from entering the city limits. But Sulla argued that his actions were in keeping with the *mos maiorum*, which Marius and the Senate had betrayed. He was then given the coveted army command in Asia Minor, after which Marius again seized control of the city. When Marius died soon afterward, a conservative backlash led the aristocracy to appoint Sulla to the office of dictator—but not for the traditional six months. Instead, Sulla's term had no limits, and he used this time to exterminate his opponents. He extended the powers of the Senate (whose ranks, depleted by civil war, he packed with men loyal to himself) and curtailed the authority of the peoples' tribunes. Then, after three years of rule, he decided that his job was done and retired to a life of luxury on his country estate.

Caesar's Triumph—and His Downfall

The purpose and effect of Sulla's dictatorship was to empower the aristocracy and terminally weaken the power of the plebs. Soon, however, new leaders emerged to espouse the people's cause, once again using the army as their tool of influence. The most prominent of these were Gnaeus Pompeius Magnus (106–48 B.C.E.) and Gaius Julius Caesar (100–44 B.C.E.). Initially, they cooperated in a plot to gain control of the government and to "restore the republic" by forming an alliance with a third general, Marcus Junius Crassus, the man credited with finally defeating Spartacus. This alliance was known as a *triumvirate* (tri-UM-vir-et), meaning "rule of three men," but it soon dissolved into open rivalry. Pompey (as generations of English-speaking historians have called him) had won fame as the conqueror of Syria and Palestine, while Caesar devoted his energies to a series of campaigns in Gaul. It was under his authority that the territories encompassing modern France, Belgium, and western Germany were added to the Roman Empire, extending its northern border along the length of the Rhine.

Caesar himself advertised these conquests in a series of self-congratulatory dispatches published in book form— *On the War in Gaul*—which secured his reputation at home and cemented the loyalty of his army. These victories also put him in a strong political position. It had become accepted that the best general should be the leader of Rome, and the example of Sulla had made it possible for that leader to be a dictator for life, a king in all but name. But it was Pompey, not Caesar, who was actually in Rome and in a position to influence the Senate directly. Indeed, in the face of tremendous popular protest and even some opposition from the aristocracy, Pompey had managed to get himself elected sole consul. Essentially, this meant that he could act as dictator. Using this authority, he declared that Caesar, who was still stationed in Gaul, was an enemy of the republic and that his ambition was to make himself king.

The result was a pervasive and deadly civil war. In 49 B.C.E. Caesar took up Pompey's challenge and crossed the Rubicon River, the northern boundary of Rome's Italian territories, thereby signaling his intention to take Rome by force. Pompey fled to the east in the hope of gathering an army large enough to confront Ceasar's legions. Caesar pursued him, and in 48 B.C.E. the two Roman armies met at Pharsalus in Greece. Pompey was defeated and fled to Alexandria, where he was murdered by a Roman officer attached to the court of Ptolemy XIII (62/61–47? B.C.E.).

This young pharaoh, a descendant of Alexander's general Ptolemy, was then about fourteen years old and engaged in a civil war of his own—against his elder sister and co-ruler, Cleopatra VII (69–30 B.C.E.). He must have thought that he could curry favor with Caesar by encouraging the murder of Pompey; but instead Caesar threw his support on the side of the twenty-one-year-old queen. The two must have become lovers soon after their first meeting, since their son Caesarion ("Little Caesar") was born just nine months later. After a brief struggle, Ptolemy was defeated and mysteriously drowned in the Nile. Cleopatra then took as consort her even younger brother, known as Ptolemy XIV, but she ruled as pharaoh of Egypt in her own right, much as Hatshepsut had done nearly a millennium and a half before (see Chapter 2).

After that, Caesar returned to Rome in triumph—literally. A *triumph* was a spectacular honor awarded to a victorious Roman general by the Senate and was the only legal occasion on which (unarmed) soldiers were allowed to parade in the streets of Rome. Triumphs had been celebrated since the earliest days of the republic, and they featured columns of prisoners and spoils of war, chained captives (often enemy kings) led in humiliation to their public executions, floats featuring live tableaux commemorating the achievements of the triumphant man, and thousands upon thousands of cheering Romans, who received extra rations of grain and gathered up coins thrown by the handful. Through it all, Caesar would have ridden in a chariot with a golden wreath held above his head while a slave stood behind him, murmuring in his ear the words *Memento mori*, "Remember: you will die." A triumph was so glorious and—under the republic—so rarely granted that those thus honored might forget their own mortality.

Caesar may well have done so. His power seemed absolute. In 46 B.C.E. he was named dictator for ten years; two years later, this was changed to a lifetime appointment. In addition, he assumed nearly every other title that could augment his power. He obtained from the Senate full authority to make war and peace and to control the revenues of the state. He even governed the reckoning of time, something that was regarded as controversial. In imitation of the Egyptian calendar (slightly modified by a Greek astronomer) he revised the Roman calendar so as to make a 365-day year with an extra day added every fourth year. This Julian calendar (as adjusted by Pope Gregory XIII in 1582) is still observed, and the seventh month is still named after Julius.

Caesar also took important steps toward eliminating the distinction between Italians and provincials within the empire by conferring citizenship on residents of Hispania

BUST OF JULIUS CAESAR. Caesar's nickname meant "Hairy," but it has come to be synonymous with imperial rule. It was the title preferred by modern German rulers, who called themselves *kaisers*, and by the tsars of Russia. In classical Latin, the "C" sound is hard, which means that the pronunciations of *caesar, kaiser,* and *tsar* are very similar.

CLEOPATRA VII AS EGYPTIAN PHARAOH AND HELLENISTIC RULER. Like her ancestor, Ptolemy I, Cleopatra represented herself as both enlightened Greek monarch and as pharaoh. It was perhaps owing to her example that Julius Caesar was the first Roman leader to issue coins impressed with his own image. ▪ *How does Cleopatra's self-representation compare to that of Hatshepsut (see page 44) or Ptolemy (see page 129)?*

(Spain) and the newly annexed provinces in Gaul. By settling many of his army veterans and some of the urban poor in these lands, moreover, he relieved economic inequities and furthered colonization. Even more important was Caesar's farsighted resolve to focus his efforts in northwestern Europe. Whereas Pompey, and before him Alexander, went East to gain fame and fortune, Caesar followed only the Phoenicians in recognizing the potential of the wild West. By incorporating Gaul into the Roman world he brought in a much-needed source of food and natural resources and created a new outlet for the spread of Roman settlement and culture.

In the eyes of many contemporaries, however, Caesar's achievements were signs that he actually did intend to make himself king: a hateful thought to those who still cherished the *mos maiorum* and glorified the early days of the republic. Indeed, it was around a descendant of Lucretia's avenger, Lucius Junius Brutus, that a faction of the Senate crystallized into an assassination conspiracy. On the Ides of March in 44 B.C.E.—the midpoint of the month, according to his own calendar—Caesar was attacked on the floor of the Senate's chamber and stabbed to death by a group of men. His body would later be autopsied, the first such examination in recorded history. It was found that he had sustained twenty-three wounds.

IDES OF MARCH COIN. This coin celebrates the assassination of Julius Caesar by Marcus Junius Brutus. Brutus is shown on the face; on the reverse, a cap of liberty (customarily worn by freed slaves) is flanked by two daggers. Below is the legend *EID-MAR*, the Latin abbreviation for "the Ides of March." ▪ *Given that Caesar drew criticism for depicting himself on Roman coinage, what do you think is the significance of using Brutus's image in this way?*

THE PRINCIPATE AND THE *PAX ROMANA*, 27 B.C.E.–180 C.E.

In his will, Caesar had adopted his grandnephew Gaius Octavius (or Octavian, 63 B.C.E.–14 C.E.), then a young man of eighteen serving in Illyria, across the Adriatic Sea. On learning of Caesar's death, Octavian hastened home to claim his inheritance and to avenge his slain "father," whose name he took: he now called himself Gaius Julius Caesar the younger. He soon found that he had rivals among those supporters of Caesar who had not been implicated in the plot to kill him, most notably Marcus Antonius (or Mark Antony, 83–30 B.C.E.), who had served under Caesar's command in Gaul and who was ambitious to make himself governor of that whole province.

Octavian engineered his own election to the office of consul (though he was far too young for this honor) and used his powers to have Caesar's assassins declared outlaws. He then pursued Antony to Gaul, at the head of an army. Antony's forces were overwhelmed, and in 43 B.C.E. he and Octavian reconciled and formed an alliance, bringing in a third man, a senator called Marcus Aemilius Lepidus, to make up a second triumvirate. They then set about crushing the political faction responsible for Caesar's murder.

The methods they employed were brutal: prominent members of the opposition were hunted down and their property confiscated. The most notable of these victims was Cicero, who was murdered by Mark Antony's hired thugs. (This was a revenge killing: Cicero had actively sought to undermine Antony and had branded him a public enemy.) Meanwhile, the masterminds behind Caesar's assasination, Brutus and Gaius Cassius, left Rome and raised an army of legions from Greece and Asia Minor. But they were defeated by the united forces of Antony and Octavian on a battlefield near the Macedonian town of Philippi (founded by Alexander's father, Philip II) in 42 B.C.E. There, both Brutus and Cassius committed suicide.

With their mutual enemies effectively destroyed, tensions mounted between Antony and Octavian, whose friendship had never been firm. Antony went to Egypt and made an alliance with Cleopatra, plotting to use the resources of her realm against Octavian. Octavian, meanwhile, reestablished himself in Rome, where he skillfully portrayed Antony as having been seduced and emasculated by his foreign lover, reminding people that the Egyptian queen's son, Caesarion, threatened Octavian's position as Caesar's rightful heir.

For ten years, Antony played the king in Egypt, fathering three of Cleopatra's children and making big plans for annexing Rome's eastern provinces. Eventually, Octavian had him declared a traitor while the Senate declared war on Cleopatra—not on Antony, lest Octavian be accused of starting another civil war. In 31 B.C.E., Octavian's superior forces defeated those of Antony and Cleopatra in the naval battle of Actium, off the coast of Greece. Soon afterward, both Antony and Cleopatra committed suicide. Their children were taken back to Rome—Caesarion promptly disappeared—and although their lives were spared, they were paraded through the streets as captives. This marked the end of Egypt's long independence: Cleopatra had been its last pharaoh. After more than 3,000 years of self-rule, Egypt was now another province in Rome's empire.

The Government of Augustus

The victory at Actium ushered in a new period of Roman history. The new Gaius Julius Caesar was the only claimant to power left standing, and with no rivals left he had no further need for political purges. For the first time in nearly a century, Rome was not embroiled in civil war.

But it was no longer a republic, even though Octavian maintained the fiction that he was governing as a mere citizen. For four years, he ruled as sole consul, until he accepted the titles of *imperator* (emperor) and *augustus*. Although these honorifics had been in use under the republic—*imperator* meant "victorious general" and *augustus* meant "worthy of honor"—they now became attached to the person of the sole ruler. So although Rome had been an empire for centuries, it was only now that it had a single emperor. To avoid confusion, historians therefore refer to this phase of Rome's history as the Principate, from the title Augustus himself preferred: *princeps*, "prince" or "first man."

Because Augustus was determined not to be regarded as a tyrant or (worse) a king, he left most of Rome's republican institutions in place—but gradually emptied them of their power. In theory, the emperor served at the will of "the Senate and People of Rome," *SPQR*. In practice, though, he controlled the army, which meant that he also controlled the workings of government. Fortunately, Augustus was an able ruler. He introduced a range of public services, including a police force and fire brigade; he reorganized the army; and he allowed cities and provinces more substantial rights of self-government than they had enjoyed before. He instituted a new system of coinage throughout the empire, and he abolished the old, corrupt system of taxation, whereby tax collectors were compensated by being allowed to keep a portion of the monies they collected, which inevitably encouraged them to collect more than were legally due. Instead, Augustus appointed his own representatives as tax collectors, paid them regular salaries, and kept them under

Analyzing Primary Sources

Antony and Cleopatra

In his Parallel Lives, *the Greek intellectual Plutarch (c. 46–120 C.E.) paired the biographies of famous Greeks with those of famous Romans, always to the disadvantage of the latter; for example, Julius Caesar suffers in comparison to Alexander the Great, as Romulus does when set up against Theseus. The following excerpt is from Plutarch's* Life of Mark Antony, *in which the Hellenistic ruler of Egypt, Cleopatra, plays a starring role.*

Caesar and Pompey knew Cleopatra when she was still a girl, and ignorant of the world, but it was a different matter in the case of Antony, because she was ready to meet him when she had reached the time of life when women are most beautiful and have full understanding. So she prepared for him many gifts and money and adornment, of a magnitude appropriate to her great wealth and prosperous kingdom, but she put most of her hopes in her own magical arts and charms. . . . For (as they say), it was not because her beauty in itself was so striking that it stunned the onlooker, but the inescapable impression produced by daily contact with her: the attractiveness in the persuasiveness of her talk, and the character that surrounded her conversation was stimulating. It was a pleasure to hear the sound of her voice, and she tuned her tongue like a many-stringed instrument expertly to whatever language she chose, and only used interpreters to talk to a few foreigners. . . . She is said to have learned the languages of many peoples, although her predecessors on the throne did not bother to learn Egyptian, and some had even forgotten how to speak the Macedonian dialect.

She took such a hold over Antony that, while his wife Fulvia was carrying on the war in Rome against Octavian on his behalf, and the Parthian army . . . was about to invade Syria, Antony was carried off by Cleopatra to Alexandria, and amused himself there with the pastimes of a boy . . . and whether Antony was in a serious or a playful mood she could always produce some new pleasure or charm, and she kept watch on him by night and day and never let him out of her sight. She played dice with him and hunted with him and watched him exercising with his weapons and she roamed around and wandered about with him at night when he stood at people's doors and windows and made fun of people inside, dressed in a slave-woman's outfit; for he also attempted to dress up like a slave. He returned from these expeditions having been mocked in return, and often beaten, although most people suspected who he was. But the Alexandrians got pleasure from his irreverence . . . enjoying his humor and saying that he showed his tragic face to the Romans and his comic one to them.

Source: Plutarch, *Life of Marcus Antonius,* cc. 25–29, excerpted in *Women's Life in Greece and Rome: A Sourcebook in Translation,* eds. Mary R. Lefkowitz and Maureen B. Fant (Baltimore, MD: 1992), pp. 147–49.

Questions for Analysis

1. How do Cleopatra's behavior and accomplishments, in Plutarch's description of her, compare to those of Roman women?

2. Given what you have learned about the values of the Roman Republic, how would a Roman reader respond to this description of Antony's behavior under the influence of the Egyptian queen? What do you think were Plutarch's motives in portraying him in this light?

---

strict supervision. He simultaneously conducted a census of the empire's population for this purpose, and it was during one of these "enrollments" that the birth of Jesus is said to have taken place, according to the gospel of Luke (see Chapter 6). Augustus also established new colonies in the provinces, encouraging the emigration of Rome's urban and rural poor, thereby removing a major source of social tension and promoting the integration of the Roman heartland and its far-flung hinterland.

Although his rule had definitively ended the republic, Augustus represented himself as a stern defender of the *mos maiorum* and traditional Roman virtues. He rebuilt many of the city's ancient temples and prohibited the worship of foreign gods. In an attempt to increase the birthrate of

Rome's citizens, he penalized men who failed to marry, required widows to remarry within two years of their husbands' deaths, and rewarded women who gave birth to more than two children. He also introduced laws punishing adultery and making divorces more difficult to obtain. To hammer the message home, Augustan propaganda portrayed the imperial family as a model of domestic virtue and propriety. Yet these portrayals were only moderately successful because the emperor's own extramarital affairs were notorious, while the sexual promiscuity of his daughter Julia finally forced Augustus to have her exiled.

Meanwhile, more land was gained for Rome in the lifetime of Augustus than ever before. His generals advanced into central Europe, conquering the territories that are now Switzerland, Austria, and Bulgaria. Only in Germania did Roman troops meet defeat, when three legions were slaughtered in the Teutoburg Forest in 9 C.E., a devastating setback that convinced Augustus to hold the Roman borders at the Rhine and Danube Rivers.

Subsequently, though, the emperor Claudius would begin the conquest of Britain in 43 C.E., while the emperor Trajan (91–117 C.E.) would push beyond the Danube to add Dacia (now Romania) to the empire. Trajan also conquered territories in the heartland of Mesopotamia, but in so doing aroused the enmity of the Parthians, who now ruled in Persia. His successor, Hadrian (117–138 C.E.), accordingly halted Rome's expansion and embarked on a defensive policy epitomized by the construction of Hadrian's Wall in northern Britain. The empire had now reached its greatest extent (see the map on page 173); in the third century, as we shall see (see Chapter 6), the tide would turn and these limits would recede.

When Octavian died in 14 C.E., he was not only Caesar, Imperator, and Augustus; he was *pontifex maximus* (high priest) and "father of the country" (*pater patriae*). He was even deified by the Senate, which had also deified Julius Caesar at Augustus's urging. These titles would be passed on to his successors, as would the system of government he had devised. And even those who mourned the passing of the republic and loathed these displays of imperial hubris had to admit that the system worked. Rome enjoyed nearly two centuries of peace, prosperity, and stability because of it.

The true test of any political institution is its capacity to survive incompetent officeholders. Aside from one brief period of civil war in 68 C.E., the transition of power between emperors was generally peaceful and the growing imperial bureaucracy could manage affairs competently even when individual emperors proved vicious or ineffectual, as did Caligula (37–41 C.E.). Nevertheless, the fact that Rome had become an autocratic state became harder and harder to conceal. Many of Augustus's successors were heavy-handed and had difficult relationships with the Sen-

OCTAVIAN. Caesar's adopted heir was later granted the title "Augustus" by the Senate, and was also known as *princeps,* "first man." He would come to be worshiped as a god in Rome's provinces, and idealized statues like this one would be erected in temples and public places throughout the empire.

ate; and because the historians of this era were invariably members of the senatorial elite, they had a vested interest in sullying the reputations of these emperors. Hence the skilled administrators Tiberius (14–37 C.E.) and Claudius (41–54 C.E.) were accused by their biographers of sexual perversion on the one hand and idiocy on the other. Nero (54–68 C.E.) and Domitian (81–96 C.E.) were also reviled by the aristocracy but popular among the Roman people

HADRIAN'S WALL. Stretching 73.5 miles across northern England, this fortification (begun in 122 C.E.) marked the frontier of the Roman province of Britannia as established by the emperor Hadrian. (A later wall, built further north by Antoninus Pius in 142, was quickly abandoned.) Long stretches of the wall still exist, as do many of the forts built along it. The tree in this photograph stands on the site of a "mile castle," one of the smaller watchtowers built at intervals of a Roman mile and garrisoned by sentries.

Occasionally, the Roman Peace was broken. In Britannia, Roman legions had to put down a rebellion led by the Celtic warrior queen Boudica (d. 60/61 C.E.), which ended in a massacre of indigenous tribes; thousands of Britons lost their lives. Another rebellion was violently quashed in Judea, the most restive of all Roman provinces, leading to the destruction of the Temple at Jerusalem in 70 C.E. In 135 C.E., a second rebellion completed the destruction of the city. Although it was refounded by Hadrian as Aelia Capitolina, a colony for veterans of Rome's army, Jews were forbidden to settle there (see Chapter 6).

Such rebellions were not the norm, however. Although the Roman Empire had been gradually achieved by conquest, it was not maintained by force. Instead, Rome controlled its territories by offering incentives to assimilation. Local elites were encouraged to adopt Roman modes of behavior and dress in order to gain entrance to political office. Local gods became Roman gods and were adopted into the Roman pantheon of divinities. Cities were constructed on a Roman model of urban planning, and the amenities of urban life were introduced: baths, temples, amphitheaters, aqueducts, and paved roads (see ***Interpreting Visual Evidence*** on pages 174–75). Rights of citizenship were extended, and able provincials could rise far in the imperial government. Some, like the emperors Trajan and Hadrian—both raised in Hispania—came to control it.

Meanwhile, tens of thousands of army veterans were settled in the provinces, marrying local women and putting down local roots. It was common for soldiers born in Syria or North Africa to end their days peacefully in northern Gaul or Germania. In Camulodunum (now Colchester, England), the gravestone of a legionnaire called Longinus sketches a typical career: born in Serdica (modern Sofia, in Bulgaria) to a local man named Szdapezematygus, he rose through the ranks to become sergeant of the First Thracian Cavalry under Claudius and one of the first Roman colonists of Britannia.

Even the outer fringes of the empire need to be understood as part of Rome's orbit. Although historians speak of the empire's "borders" for the sake of convenience, these were in fact frontiers: highly fluid and permeable zones of intensive interaction. Roman influence reached far beyond these zones,

and in the provinces; indeed, Domitian's needed reforms of provincial government and his blatant disregard for senatorial privilege account for both the Senate's hostility and his subjects' approval.

The height of the Augustan system is generally considered to be the era between 96 and 180 C.E., often known as the reign of the "Five Good Emperors": Nerva (96–98 C.E.), Trajan (98–117 C.E.), Hadrian (117–138 C.E.), Antoninus Pius (138–161 C.E.), and Marcus Aurelius (161–180 C.E.). All were capable politicians, and since none but the last had a son that survived him, each adopted a worthy successor—a wise practice that allowed this generation of rulers to avoid the messy family dysfunctions that absorbed Augustus and his immediate heirs. They also benefited from the fact that Rome had few external enemies left. The Mediterranean was under the control of a single power for the first (and only) time in history. On land, Roman officials ruled from Britain to Persia. A contemporary orator justly boasted that "the whole civilized world lays down the arms which were its ancient burden, as if on holiday. . . . [A]ll places are full of gymnasia, fountains, monumental approaches, temples, workshops, schools." The continual bloodshed of civil wars and of Augustus's reign of terror had abated. Now was the time of the *Pax Romana*, the Roman Peace.

Two Views of Augustus's Rule

Augustus Speaks for Himself

The emperor Augustus was a master propagandist with an unrivaled capacity for presenting his own actions in the best possible light. This list of his own deeds was written by Augustus himself and was displayed on two bronze pillars set up in the Roman forum.

Below is a copy of the accomplishments of the deified Augustus by which he brought the whole world under the empire of the Roman people, and of the moneys expended by him on the state and the Roman people. . . .

1. At the age of nineteen, on my own initiative and at my own expense, I raised an army by means of which I liberated the Republic, which was oppressed by the tyranny of a faction.

2. Those who assassinated my father I drove into exile, avenging their crime by due process of law.

3. I waged many wars throughout the whole world by land and by sea, both civil and foreign. . . .

5. The dictatorship offered to me . . . by the people and by the Senate . . . I refused to accept. . . . The consulship, too, which was offered to me . . . as an annual office for life, I refused to accept.

6. [T]hough the Roman Senate and people together agreed that I should be elected sole guardian of the laws and morals with supreme authority, I refused to accept any office offered me which was contrary to the traditions of our ancestors.

7. I have been ranking senator for forty years. . . . I have been *pontifex maximus*, augur, member of the college of fifteen for performing sacrifices, member of the college of seven for conducting religious banquets, member of the Arval Brotherhood, one of the *Titii sodales*, and a *fetial* [all priestly offices].

9. The Senate decreed that vows for my health should be offered up every fifth year by the consuls and priests. . . . [T]he whole citizen body, with one accord, . . . prayed continuously for my health at all the shrines.

17. Four times I came to the assistance of the treasury with my own money . . . providing bonuses for soldiers who had completed twenty or more years of service.

20. I repaired the Capitol and the theater of Pompey with enormous expenditures on both works, without having my name inscribed on them. I repaired . . . the aqueducts which were falling into ruin in many places . . . I repaired eighty-two temples . . . I reconstructed the Flaminian Way. . . .

34. [H]aving attained supreme power by universal consent, I transferred the state from my own power to the control of the Roman Senate and people. . . . After that time I excelled all in authority, but I possessed no more power than the others who were my colleagues in each magistracy.

35. At the time I wrote this document I was in my seventy-sixth year.

Source: "Res Gestae Divi Augusti," in *Roman Civilization, Sourcebook II: The Empire*, eds. Naphtali Lewis and Meyer Reinhold (New York: 1966), pp. 9–19.

into the heartland of Germania and lands far to the East. By the middle of the third century C.E., when some frontier garrisons were withdrawn to take part in civil wars within the empire itself, many of these peoples moved into the empire's settled provinces, sometimes as plunderers but more often as aspiring Romans (see Chapter 6).

The Entertainments of Empire

The cultural and intellectual developments that began in Rome during the late republic came to fruition during the Principate, and are richly reflected in its literature. For the first time in its already long history, Latin began to replace

The Historian Tacitus Evaluates Augustus's Reign

Writing in the first decades of the second century C.E., the senatorial historian Tacitus (c. 56–117) began his chronicle of imperial rule, the Annals, *with the death of Augustus a century earlier.*

Intelligent people praised or criticized Augustus in varying terms. One opinion was as follows. Filial duty and a national emergency, in which there was no place for law-abiding conduct, had driven him to civil war—and this can be neither initiated nor maintained by decent methods. He had made many concessions to Antony and to Lepidus for the sake of vengeance on his father's murderers. When Lepidus grew old and lazy, and Antony's self-indulgence got the better of him, the only possible cure for the distracted country had been government by one man. However, Augustus had put the State in order not by making himself king or dictator but by creating the Principate. The empire's frontiers were on the ocean, or on distant rivers. Armies, provinces, fleets, the whole system was interrelated. Roman citizens were protected by the law. Provincials were decently treated. Rome itself had been lavishly beautified. Force had been sparingly used—merely to preserve peace for the majority.

The opposite view went like this. Filial duty and national crisis had been merely pretexts. In actual fact, the motive of Octavian, the future Augustus, was lust for power. Inspired by that, he had mobilized ex-army settlers by gifts of money, raised an army—while he was only a half-grown boy without any official status—won over a consul's brigade by bribery, pretended to support Sextus Pompeius [the son of Pompey], and by senatorial decree usurped the status and rank of a praetor. Soon both consuls . . . had met their deaths—by enemy action; or perhaps in the one case by the deliberate poisoning of his wound, and in the other at the hand of his own troops, instigated by Octavian. In any case, it was he who took over both their armies. Then he had forced the reluctant Senate to make him consul. But the forces given him to deal with Antony he used against the State. His judicial murders and land distributions were distasteful even to those who carried them out. True, Cassius and Brutus died because he had inherited a feud against them; nevertheless, personal enmities ought to be sacrificed to the public interest. Next he had cheated Sextus Pompeius by a spurious peace treaty, Lepidus by spurious friendship. Then Antony, enticed by treaties and his marriage with Octavian's sister, had paid the penalty of that delusive relationship with his life. After that, there had certainly been peace, but it was a bloodstained peace. . . . And gossip did not spare his personal affairs—how he had abducted [Livia] the wife of Tiberius Claudius Nero, and asked the priests the farcical question whether it was in order for her to marry while pregnant. Then there was the debauchery of his friend Publius Vedius Pollio. But Livia was a real catastrophe, to the nation, as a mother and to the house of the Caesars as a stepmother.

Source: Tacitus, *Annals* i.9–10. Based on *Tacitus: The Annals of Imperial Rome*, trans. Michael Grant (New York: 1989), pp. 37–39.

Questions for Analysis

1. How does Augustus organize his list, and why? What does he leave out and what does he choose to emphasize?

2. Tacitus presents two contrasting views of Augustus's motives. Which does he himself seem to believe? How does his account complement or undermine that of Augustus himself?

3. Could you write a new account of Augustus's life making use of both sources? How would you strike a balance between them? What would your own conclusion be?

Greek as a language of learning and poetry. Roman literature of this era is conventionally divided into two periods, the Golden Age of writings produced under the more or less direct influence of Augustus, and the Silver Age of the first and early second centuries C.E. Most Golden Age literature is, not surprisingly, propagandistic: its purpose was to advertise and justify Augustus's achievements. The poetry of Publius Virgilius Maro (Virgil, 70–19 B.C.E.) is typical, and we have already noted his strategic use of "prophecy" to link the reign of Augustus to the story of Aeneas (see page 146). Other major poets of this age were Quintus Horatius Flaccus (Horace, 65–8 B.C.E.) and Publius Ovidius Naso

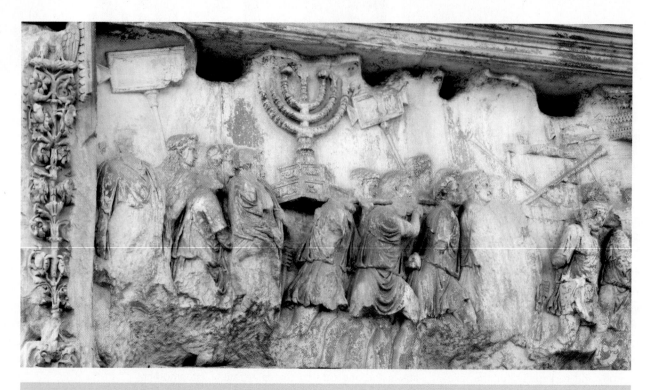

SPOILS FROM JERUSALEM. A bas-relief inside the triumphal Arch of Titus in the Roman Forum shows plundered treasures of the Temple at Jerusalem, including the menorah, being carried in triumph through Rome after the quashing of a Jewish rebellion in 70 C.E.
- *What message(s) would this image convey to viewers?*

(Ovid, 43 B.C.E.–17 C.E.): the former a master of the lovely, short lyric and the latter our major source for Greek mythology, which he retold in a long poem called the *Metamorphoses* ("Transformations"). Ovid was also a satirist, and his frank advice to his readers on the best way to attract women at the race course and his own (probably fictional) strategy for conducting an adulterous affair with the wife of a senator are exemplary of the writings that resulted in his banishment.

After Augustus's death, Roman authors had more license and became incisive cultural critics. The tales of Petronius and Apuleius describe the more bizarre and sometimes sordid aspects of Roman life, and the satirist Juvenal (60?–140 C.E.) wrote with savage wit about the moral degeneracy he saw in his contemporaries. A similar attitude toward Roman society characterizes the writings of Tacitus (55?–117? C.E.), an aristocratic historian who describes the events and people of his age largely for the purpose of passing judgment on them. His *Annals* offer a subtle but devastating portrait of the political system constructed by Augustus and ruled by his heirs; his *Germania* contrasts the manly virtues of northern barbarians with the effeminate vices of decadent fellow Romans. Like Juvenal, Tacitus was a master of ironic wit. Referring to Rome's conquests, he has a barbarian chieftain say, "They create a wilderness and call it peace."

To many people today, the most repellant—or most fascinating and familiar—aspect of Roman culture during the Principate was its spectacular cruelty, exhibited (literally) in the public arenas erected in every Roman town. Gladiatorial contests were not new, but they were now presented in ampitheaters built to hold thousands. Everyone, even emperors, attended these events, and they became increasingly bloody and brutal as people demanded more and more innovative violence. Individual gladiators fought to the death with swords or the exotic weapons of their homelands. Teams of gladiators fought pitched battles, often simulating historic Roman victories. Occasionally, a wealthy entrepreneur would fill an arena with water and stage a naval battle. Hundreds of men and women would die in these organized slaughters. On other occasions, hundreds of half-starved animals imported from Africa, India, or the forests of Germania would tear one another (or their human victims) apart. When a fighter went down with a disabling wound, the crowd would be asked to decide whether to spare his life or to kill him. If the arena floor became too slippery with blood, the action would stop—but only so that a fresh layer of sand could be spread over the gore for the performance to continue.

Roman Art, Architecture, and Engineering

Like Latin literature, Roman art assumed a distinctive character during the Principate. Before this time, most artworks

Rome's Party Girls

The Satires *of the poet Juvenal circulated around the year 100 C.E. and attacked everything from the general erosion of public morality to the effete tastes of the elite. Some of his most pointed criticism was directed at contemporary women.*

hat conscience has Venus, when she is drunk? Our inebriated beauties can't tell head from tail at those midnight oyster suppers when the best wine's laced with perfume, and tossed down neat from a foaming conch-shell, while the dizzy ceiling spins round, and the tables dance, and each light shows double. Why, you may ask yourself, does the notorious Maura sniff at the air in that knowing, derisive way as she and her dear friend Tullia pass by the ancient altar of Chastity? And what is Tullia whispering to her? Here, at night, they stagger out of their litters and relieve themselves, pissing in long hard bursts all over the goddess's statue. Then, while the Moon looks down on their motions, they take turns to ride each other, and finally go home. So you, next morning, on your way to some great house, will splash through your wife's piddle. Notorious, too, are the ritual mysteries of the Good Goddess, when flute-music stirs the loins, and frenzied women, devotees of Priapus, sweep along in procession, howling, tossing their hair, wine-flown, horn-crazy, burning with the desire to get themselves laid. . . . So the ladies, with a display of talent to match their birth, win all the prizes. No make-believe here, no pretense, each act is performed in earnest, and guaranteed to warm the age-chilled balls of a Nestor or a Priam.

Source: Juvenal, *Sixth Satire* 301–26; based on *Juvenal: The Sixteen Satires*, trans. Peter Green (New York: 1974), pp. 138–39 (modified).

Questions for Analysis

1. Compare Juvenal's account of female behavior to the legend of Lucretia, on the one hand, and Plutarch's description of Cleopatra, on the other. What can you conclude about attitudes to women and to sexual morality? Why and on what grounds would men living under the Principate hold women responsible for society's ills?

2. In your view, what are the benefits and the drawbacks of the *Satires* as a historical source?

---

displayed in Roman homes and public places were imported from Hellenistic capitals. Conquering armies also brought back wagonloads of statues, reliefs, and marble columns as plunder from Greece and Asia Minor. These became the property of the wealthy, and as demand for such works increased, hundreds of copies were made by Roman artisans. In many cases, these copies proved more durable than their originals: in Chapter 4, we were able to examine the lost Aphrodite of Knidos, courtesy of Roman sculptors.

Encouraged by the patronage of Augustus and his successors, artists began to experiment with more distinctively Roman styles and subjects. The relief sculpture of this period is particularly notable for its delicacy and naturalism, and sculptors also became adept at portraiture. On their coins, emperors were portrayed very much as they looked in real life; and since the matrices for coins were recut annually, we can trace on successive issues a ruler's receding hairline or his advancing double chin.

Painting and mosaic, however, were the Romans' most original and most intimate arts. Romans loved intense col-

ors, and those who could afford it surrounded themselves with brilliant wall paintings and mosaics made of tiny fragments of glass and stone, which were often set into the floors of houses and public baths or which formed the centerpieces of gardens. Lavish mosaics have been found in the remains of Roman villas in all the territories of the empire, and similar design features indicate that many were mosaic "kits" that could be ordered from a manufacturer, who would ship out all the necessary components along with a team of workmen to assemble them.

Augustus liked to boast that he had found Rome a city of clay and left it a city of marble. It is certainly true that ambitious public works projects were initiated under the Principate, but in reality marble was too precious to be used in common construction. Instead, marble panels or ornaments were added to the facings of buildings that were otherwise built of concrete. For the Romans had discovered how to make a hard and reliable building material from a mixture of quicklime, volcanic ash, and pumice, and it was this— along with superior engineering skills—that allowed them

THE COLOSSEUM. Constructed between 75 and 80 C.E., this was the first ampitheater in Rome purposely built to showcase gladiatorial combats. Prior to this, gladiators would often fight in improvised arenas in the Forum or in other public places. ■ *How does this fact change your perception of Roman history?*

banquet hall revolved day and night like the heavens. "At last," said Nero on moving day, "I can live like a human being."

The Reach of Roman Law

As impressive and ingenious as Roman architecture and engineering are, the most durable and useful of this civilization's legacies was its system of law. Over the course of several centuries, the primitive legal code of the Twelve Tables was largely replaced by a series of new precedents and principles. These reflect the changing political climate of Rome and the needs of its diverse and ever-growing population. They also reveal the influence of new philosophies, especially Stoicism; the decisions of specific judges; and the edicts of magistrates called *praetors*, who had the authority to define and interpret law in particular cases, and to issue instructions to judges.

The most sweeping legal changes occurred during the Principate. This was partly because the reach of Roman law had to match the reach of the empire, which now extended over a much wider field of jurisdiction. But the major reason for the rapid development of Roman legal thinking during these years was the fact that Augustus and his successors

to build massive structures like the Colosseum, which could accommodate 50,000 spectators at gladiatorial combats.

Roman engineers also excelled in the building of roads and bridges, many of which were constructed by Rome's armies as they moved into new territories. Like the Persian Royal Road of the sixth century B.C.E.—or the German Autobahn of the 1930s and the interstate highways of the United States begun in the 1950s—roads have always been, first and foremost, a device for moving armies and then, secondarily, for moving goods and people. Many of these Roman roads still survive or form the basis for modern European highways. In Britain, for example, the only major thoroughfares before the building of the high-speed motorways were Roman roads, to which the motorways now run parallel.

The inhabitants of Roman cities also enjoyed the benefits of a public water supply. By the early decades of the second century C.E., eleven aqueducts brought water into Rome from the nearby hills and provided the city with 300 million gallons per day, for drinking and bathing and for flushing a well-designed sewage system. These amenities were common in cities throughout the empire, and the homes of the wealthy even had indoor plumbing and central heating. Water was also funneled into the homes of the rich for private gardens, fountains, and pools. The emperor Nero built a famous Golden House with special pipes that sprinkled his guests with perfume, baths supplied with medicinal waters, and a pond "like a sea." In addition, a spherical ceiling in the

FEMALE GLADIATORS. Like men, enslaved women also fought as gladiators. This marble relief commemorates the freeing of two such fighters, "Amazon" and "Achillia," presumably as a reward for their successes in the arena.

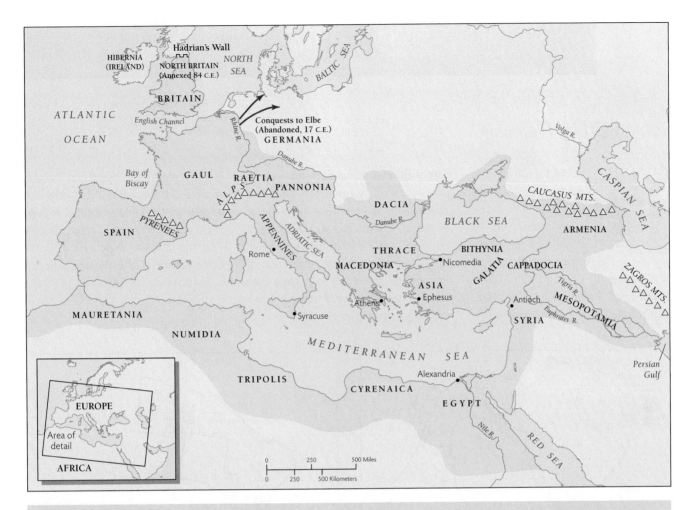

THE ROMAN EMPIRE AT ITS GREATEST EXTENT, 97–117 C.E. ▪ *How much farther north and west does the empire now reach compared to its earlier extent (see map on page 156)?* ▪ *How did geography influence the process of expansion?* ▪ *How did it dictate its limits?* ▪ *For example, what role do major river systems seem to play?*

appointed a small number of eminent jurists to deliver opinions on the issues raised by cases under trial in the courts. The five most prominent of these jurists flourished in the second century C.E.: Gaius (only this most common of his names is known), Domitius Ulpianus (Ulpian), Modestinus, Aemelianus Papinianus (Papinian), and Paulus. Although most of them came to hold high offices, they gained their reputations primarily as lawyers and commentators. Taken together, their legal opinions constitute the first philosophy of law and the foundation for all subsequent jurisprudence, a word derived from the Latin phrase meaning "legal wisdom."

As it was developed by the jurists, Roman law comprised three great branches or divisions: civil law, the law of nations, and natural law. Civil law was the law of Rome and its citizens, both written and unwritten. It included the statutes of the Senate, the decrees of the emperor, the edicts of magistrates, and ancient customs that had the force of law (like the *mos maiorum*). The law of nations was not specific to Rome but extended to all people of the world regardless

of their origins and ethnicity: it is the precursor of international law. This law authorized and regulated slavery; protected the private ownership of property; and defined the mechanisms of purchase and sale, partnership, and contract. It was not superior to civil law but supplemented it, and it applied especially to those inhabitants of the empire who were not citizens, as well as to all foreigners.

The most interesting (and in many ways the most important) branch of Roman law was natural law, a product not of judicial practice but of legal philosophy. Roman Stoics, following in the footsteps of Cicero, posited that nature itself is rationally ordered and that careful study will reveal the laws by which the natural world operates, including the nature of justice. They affirmed that all men are by nature equal and that they are entitled to certain basic rights that governments have no authority to transgress. "True law," Cicero had said, "is right reason consonant with nature, diffused among all men, constant, eternal." Accordingly, no person or institution has the authority to infringe on this

Roman Urban Planning

Prior to Roman imperial expansion, most cities in the ancient world were not planned cities—with the exception of the new settlements established by Alexander the Great, notably Alexandria in Egypt. Rome itself was not carefully planned, but grew up over many centuries, expanding outward and up the slopes of its seven hills from the nucleus of the Forum. By the time of Augustus, it was a haphazard jumble of buildings and narrow streets. Outside of Rome, however, the efficiency of Roman government was in large part due to the uniformity of imperial urban planning. As their colonial reach expanded, Romans sought to ensure that travelers moving within their vast domain would encounter the same amenities in every major city. They also wanted to convey, through the organization of the urban landscape, the ubiquity of Roman authority and majesty.

A. Imperial Rome

B. Roman settlement in Aelia Capitolina (Jerusalem) after 135 C.E.

law, repeal it, or ignore it. This law supersedes any state or ruler; a ruler who transgresses it is a tyrant.

Although the jurists did not regard the philosophical concept of natural law as an automatic limitation on the workings of civil law, they did uphold it as an ideal. The practical law applied in local Roman courts often bore little resemblance to the law of nature, yet the development of a concept of abstract justice as a fundamental principle was one of the noblest achievements of Roman civilization. It has given us the doctrine of human rights—even if it has not ended abuses of those rights.

CONCLUSION

The resemblances between Rome's history and that of Great Britain and the United States have often been noted. Like the British Empire, the Roman Empire was founded on conquest and overseas colonization intended to benefit both the homeland and Britain's colonial subjects, who were seen as beneficiaries of the metropolis' "civilizing mission." Like America's, the Roman economy evolved from agrarianism to a complex system of domestic and foreign

Questions for Analysis

1. Looking closely at the map of Rome (map A), how have topographical features—like the river Tiber and the seven hills—determined the shape and layout of the city? What are the major buildings and public areas? What were the functions of these spaces, and what do they reveal about Roman society and values?

2. Compare the plan of Rome to those of Roman London (map C) and Roman Jerusalem (map B). What features do all three have in common, and why? What features are unique to each place, and what might this reveal about the different regions of the empire and the needs of the different cities' inhabitants?

3. Given that all Roman cities share certain features, what message(s) were Roman authorities trying to convey to inhabitants and travelers through urban planning? Why, for example, would they have insisted on rebuilding Jerusalem as a Roman city after the rebellion of 135 C.E.?

C. London under the Romans, c. 200 C.E.

markets, problems of unemployment, gross disparities of wealth, and vulnerability to financial crisis. And like both the British and the American empires, the Roman Empire justified itself by celebrating the peace its conquests allegedly brought to the world.

Ultimately, however, such parallels break down when we remember that Rome's civilization differed profoundly from any society of the modern world. It was not an industrialized society. Its government never pretended to be representative of all its citizens. Roman class divisions are not directly comparable to ours. The Roman economy rested on slavery to a degree unmatched in any modern state. As a result, technological advances were not encouraged, social stratification was extreme, and gender relations were profoundly unequal. Religious practice and political life were inseparable.

Nevertheless, the civilization of ancient Rome continues to structure our everyday lives in ways so profound that they can go unnoticed. Our days are mapped onto the Roman calendar. The Constitution of the United States is largely modeled on that of the republic, and Roman architecture survives in the design of our public buildings. Roman law forms the basis of most European legal codes and American judges still

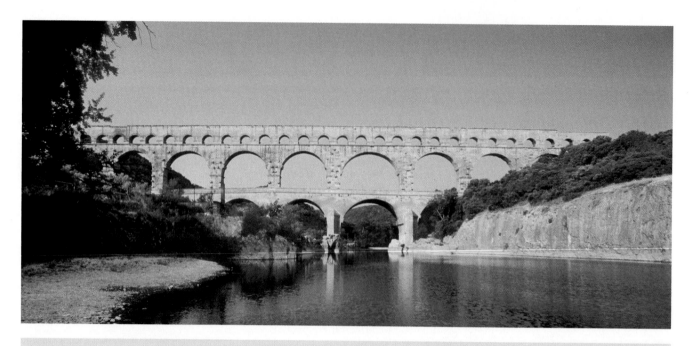

ROMAN AQUEDUCT IN SOUTHERN GAUL (PROVENCE). Aqueducts conveyed water from mountains and lakes to the larger cities of the Roman Empire. The massive arches shown here span the river Gardon (in southern France) and were originally part of a thirty-one-mile-long complex that supplied water to the city of Nemausus (Nîmes). It is now known as the Pont du Gard (Bridge of the Gardon), reflecting the use to which it was put after the aqueduct ceased to function, some eight centuries after its construction in the first century C.E. Some Roman aqueducts remained operational into the modern era: the one at Segovia, Spain, was still in use at the end of the twentieth century. ▪ *What does the magnitude and longevity of such projects tell us about Roman power and technology?*

After You Read This Chapter

REVIEWING THE OBJECTIVES

- The founding of the Roman Republic was both a cherished myth and a series of events. What factors contributed to this unique system of government?
- The shared identity and values of the Roman people differed in many ways from those of other ancient civilizations. What were some of these major differences?
- Rome's population was divided among classes of people who often struggled with one another for power. Identify these classes and their points of contention.
- The expansion of Rome's empire had a profound impact on Roman society. Why?
- The establishment of the Principate ushered in a new era in the history of Rome. What events led to this?

A ROMAN FLOOR MOSAIC. This fine mosaic from the Roman city of Londinium (London) shows Bacchus (Dionysus), the god of wine and revelry, mounted on a tiger. Tigers, native to India, were prized by animal collectors and were also imported for gladiatorial shows.

cite Gaius and Ulpian. Virtually all modern commemorative sculpture is inspired by Roman sculpture, and Roman authors continue to set the standards for prose composition in many Western countries. Indeed, most European languages are either derived from Latin—Romance languages are so called because they are "Roman-like"—or have borrowed Latin grammatical structures or vocabulary (German, for example). As we shall see in the following chapters, the organization of the modern Roman Catholic Church can be traced back to the structure of the Roman state: even today, the pope bears the title of Rome's high priest, *pontifex maximus*.

Perhaps the most significant of all Rome's contributions was its role as mediator between Europe and the civilizations of the ancient Near East and Mediterranean. Had Rome's empire not come to encompass much of Europe, there would be no such thing as the concept of Western civilization and no shared ideas and heritage to link us to those distant places and times. Although we shall pursue the history of Rome's fragmentation and witness the emergence of three different civilizations in the territories once united by its empire, we shall see that they all shared a common cultural inheritance. In that sense, at least, the Roman Empire did not collapse. But it was transformed, and the factors driving that transformation will be the subject of Chapter 6.

PEOPLE, IDEAS, AND EVENTS IN CONTEXT

- In what ways were the early Romans influenced by their **ETRUSCAN** neighbors and by their location in central Italy?
- What were the components of the **ROMAN REPUBLIC**'s constitution? What was the relationship between **ROMAN CITIZENSHIP** and the **ROMAN ARMY** in this era?
- How do the stories of **AENEAS, LUCRETIA,** and **CINCINNATUS** reflect core Roman values? How did those values, summarized in the phrase *MOS MAIORUM*, set the Romans apart from the other civilizations we have studied?
- Why did the Romans come into conflict with **CARTHAGE**? How did the **PUNIC WARS** and Rome's other conquests change the balance of power in the Mediterranean?
- How did imperialism and contact with **HELLENISTIC CULTURE** affect the core values of Roman society, its economy, and its political system? What role did **SLAVERY** play in this civilization?
- What were the major crises of the late republic, and what were the means by which ambitious men achieved power? How did **JULIUS CAESAR** emerge triumphant, and why was he assassinated?
- In what ways did the **PRINCIPATE** differ from the **ROMAN REPUBLIC**? What were the new powers of the **EMPEROR**, and how did **AUGUSTUS** exemplify these?
- How did the Romans consolidate their **EMPIRE** during the *PAX ROMANA*? By what means did they spread Roman culture?

THINKING ABOUT CONNECTIONS

- Polybius believed that the Roman Republic would last forever, because it fused together aspects of monarchy, aristocracy, and polity. What were the chief factors that led to its demise in the first century B.C.E.? Could these have been avoided—and if so, how?
- In what ways does the Roman Empire share the characteristics of earlier empires, especially that of Alexander? In what ways does it differ from them?
- The Roman Empire could be said to resemble our own civilization in different ways. What features does today's United States share with the republic? With the Principate? What lessons can we draw from this?

CONSTANTINVS MINOR IMPERATOR
HERACLII ET TIBERII IMPERATOR

AR
COP
VS

PRIVILEGIA

Before
You
Read
This
Chapter

The Transformation of Rome

CORE OBJECTIVES

- **IDENTIFY** the historical factors that shaped early Christianity.

- **DESCRIBE** the pressures on Roman imperial administration during the third century.

- **TRACE** the ways that Christianity changed after it became a legal religion.

- **EXPLAIN** how barbarian migrations affected the empire.

- **UNDERSTAND** the difference between traditional Roman and Christian worldviews.

I n the year 203 C.E., a young woman called Vivia Perpetua was brought before the Roman governor at Carthage. She was twenty-two years old, well educated, from a respectable family. At the time of her arrest she had an infant child who was still nursing. She also had two brothers (one of whom was arrested with her) and a father who doted on her. She must, one presumes, have had a husband, but he is conspicuously absent from the firsthand account of her experiences. Perpetua herself says nothing about him, though she says a great deal about her father's grief and the efforts he made to intercede on her behalf. Not only did he beg the judge for mercy, he begged his daughter to confess so that her life could be spared. He admitted to having loved her more than her brothers and blamed himself for the liberal education he had given her. Clearly, he had failed as a father: a Roman *paterfamilias* should never suffer humiliation through the conduct of a daughter; he should kill her with his own hands if she disgraced the family. For Perpetua's crime was terrible. It was not only treason against the Roman state but an act of gross impiety toward her father, her family, and her ancestors. Worse, it was punishable by a death so debasing that it was reserved for slaves, barbarian

179

prisoners, and hardened criminals. It was inconceivable that a respectable Roman matron would be stripped naked before a holiday crowd and mauled by wild beasts in the arena of her own city. But that was the death Perpetua died. Perpetua was a Christian.

Early Christianity posed a challenge to the Roman Empire and its core values at almost every level, a challenge exemplified by Vivia Perpetua. To be a Christian was to be, by definition, an enemy of Rome, because Christians refused to venerate the emperor as the embodiment of Rome's gods; denying his association with divinity meant denying his authority. Moreover, the Christ whom Christians worshiped had himself been declared a criminal, a political insurgent,

and had been duly tried and put to death by the Roman state. Also disturbing was the way that Christians flouted the conventions of Roman society. Perpetua was young, yet she was disobedient to her father and ancestors. She was well born, yet she chose to endure the filth of a common jail. She was a woman, yet she denied the authority of men and renounced her femininity, dying in the dust like a gladiator. If this was what it meant to be a Christian, then being a Christian was incompatible with being a Roman.

How, then, did a Roman emperor become a Christian just a few centuries after Christ's death—and just a century or so after Perpetua's? What changes did both Rome and Christianity have to undergo in order for this to happen? And what other forces were at work, within the empire and beyond its borders, that helped bring this about?

The Rome in which Perpetua was raised stretched from central Asia to the British Isles, from the Rhine to her own province of North Africa. But as we shall see, the governance of this enormous state and its diverse population was straining the bureaucracy that had been built on the foundations of the old republic. By the end of the third century, it was increasingly obvious that Rome's western and eastern provinces could not be controlled by a single centralized authority. In the fourth century, Rome itself ceased to be the capital and hub of the empire; it now shared prestige with the new city of Constantinople, named by the Christian emperor who founded it. At the same time, Rome's settled provinces were coming under increased pressure from groups of people who had long lived along its borders but who were now moving from the periphery to the center. These peoples, too, would challenge what it meant to be Roman and would contribute to the transformation of the Roman world.

JUDEA AND GALILEE IN THE TIME OF JESUS. ▪ What are the major cities in first-century C.E. Judea? ▪ What do they indicate about the effects of Roman occupation on the lives of Jews? ▪ Given what you have learned about their history, why would some Jews resist Roman rule?

THE CHALLENGE OF CHRISTIANITY

Even faiths have histories. Like the Hebrew monotheism that undergirds Judaism or the central tenets of Zoroastrianism (see Chapter 2), Christianity was (and is) the product of historical processes. It began with the teachings of Jesus, who lived and worked among his fellow Jews in rural Judea and Galilee around the year 30 C.E. It took root, however, in the Hellenistic world we studied in Chapter 4: the cosmopolitan, Greek-speaking cities around the eastern Mediterranean, which had now been absorbed into the Roman Empire.

The Career of Jesus

Yeshua bar Yosef (Joshua, son of Joseph), known to the Greeks as Jesus, is one of the few figures of the ancient world—certainly one of the few commoners—about whose life we know a great deal. The earliest writings that mention Jesus specifically are the letters of his follower Paul of Tarsus, a Hellenized Jew who was active during the 50s and 60s C.E. These epistles are closely followed by many different narratives of Jesus's life and teachings, most written between c. 70 and 100 C.E. Four such accounts were eventually included in the New Testament, a collection of Christian scriptures appended to the Greek text of the Hebrew Bible around the third century C.E. In their original Greek, these accounts were called *evangelia* ("good messages"); we know them as *Gospels*, an Old English word that means the same thing.

Jesus was born around the year 4 B.C.E., a generation or so after Augustus came to power in Rome. (He was not born precisely in the first year of the Common Era as we now reckon it. When the monk Dionysius Exiguus first calculated time "in the year of Our Lord" during the sixth century, he made some mistakes.) When Jesus was around thirty years old, he was endorsed by a Jewish preacher of moral reform, John the Baptist, whom some considered to be a prophet. Thereafter, Jesus traveled widely around the rural areas of Galilee and Judea, preaching and displaying unusual healing powers. He accumulated a number of disciples, some of whom had political ambitions.

Around the year 30 C.E., Jesus staged an entry into Jerusalem during Passover, a major religious holiday that brought large and excitable crowds to the city. This move was interpreted as a bid for political power by both the Roman colonial government and the high-ranking Jews of the Temple. Three of the Gospel accounts say that Jesus also drew attention to himself by attacking merchants and moneychangers associated with the Temple. The city's religious leaders therefore arrested him and turned him over to the Roman governor, Pontius Pilatus (Pilate), for sentencing.

Pilate's main concern was to preserve peace during a volatile religious festival. He knew that his authority depended on maintaining good relations with local Jewish elites and with Herod, a recent convert to Judaism who ruled the province of Galilee in collaboration with Rome, as a client king of the empire. Because Jesus was a resident of Galilee, not a citizen of Roman Judea, Pilate sent Jesus to Herod for sentencing. But Herod sent him back to Pilate, politely indicating that dealing with Jesus fell under Roman jursidiction. So Pilate chose to make an example of Jesus by condemning him to death by crucifixion, the standard criminal penalty for those judged guilty of sedition. It had been rumored that Jesus planned to lead a rebellion, and something similar had happened in the second century B.C.E., when the Maccabees overthrew Seleucid rule. Indeed, the Roman occupation of the region had only begun in 67 B.C.E. and was still resented by many Jews. Pilate would have been mindful of all this.

That might have been the end of the story. But soon after Jesus's execution, his followers began to assert that he had risen from the dead before being taken up into heaven. Moreover, they said that Jesus had promised to return again at the end of time. Meanwhile, he had promised spiritual support to his followers in their own preaching missions. His entire career now had to be rethought and reinterpreted by his followers: in life, he had been a teacher and healer; in death, he had been revealed as something more. The evidence of this reinterpretation has come down to us in the letters of Paul and in the Gospel narratives.

Jesus and Judaism

In 1947, an extraordinary cache of parchment and papyrus scrolls was discovered in a cave near Qumran on the shores of the Dead Sea. Over the course of the next decade, eleven more caves were found to house similar texts dating from the first century C.E. Only since the mid-1980s, however,

JESUS. This depiction of Jesus is from a third-century C.E. stone inlay.

have the texts of these Dead Sea Scrolls been widely available to scholars. Written in Hebrew, Greek, and Aramaic at various times between 100 B.C.E and 70 C.E., they have revolutionized our understanding of Judaism in the lifetime of Jesus, a period known as "Second Temple" Judaism. What these documents show, overwhelmingly, is the diversity of religious practice in this period, and the intense competition among groups of Jewish believers.

When Jesus was born, Roman rule in this region was still inspiring extreme responses. While many Jews were content to live under Rome's protection—especially the urban elite, who reaped the rewards of participation in the Roman economy and administration—there was talk of rebellion among rural communities and the urban poor. Many of those disadvantaged by Roman rule hoped for a messiah, an inspired leader who would establish Jewish autonomy and a new Jewish kingdom. The most extreme of these were the Zealots, whose activities eventually led to two disastrous revolts. The first, between 66 and 70 C.E., ended in the Romans' destruction of the Temple that had been rebuilt when Cyrus the Great released the Jews from captivity in Babylon, 600 years earlier (see Chapter 2). The second, in 132–35 C.E., caused the destruction of Jerusalem itself and prompted the Romans to expel the entire Jewish population.

Whereas the first exile of the Jews had ended after fifty years, this new diaspora would not be reversed until the controversial establishment of the modern state of Israel in 1948. For over 500 years, Jerusalem even ceased to exist; on its ruins the Romans built the colony of Aelia Capitolina (see Chapter 5). It was only in 638, when the Islamic Caliphate established Arab rule in the region and restored Jerusalem as a holy site, that Jews were allowed to settle there (see Chapter 7).

This political and religious context is essential to understanding the circumstances of Jesus's death and the different messages conveyed by his words and actions. The Dead Sea Scrolls reveal that significant divisions had arisen among Jewish communities, and that Jesus participated in several key debates. In his lifetime, the hereditary Temple priesthood was controlled by a group known as the Sadducees, elite Jews who collaborated closely with Rome; the high priest of the Temple was even appointed by the Roman Senate. As a result of their overt political agenda, the Sadducees were regarded with suspicion by many. Their chief rivals were the Pharisees, preachers of religious doctrine who were heirs to the prophetic tradition of the "First Temple" period of the sixth century B.C.E. In contrast to the Sadducees, who claimed the right to control the interpretation of the Torah, the five books attributed to Moses, the Pharisees argued that Yahweh had given Moses an oral Torah as well as a written one, which explained how these books should be

PAUL OF TARSUS. Many ancient images of Paul survive, and all depict him with the same features: a gaunt face, balding head, pointed black beard, and intense dark gaze. In the summer of 2009, archaeologists working in the catacombs of Thekla (named after a holy woman and follower of Paul) discovered this faded fresco. It has been identified as the oldest known portrait of this formative Christian figure and can be dated to the fourth century C.E.

applied to daily life. This oral tradition had been handed down from teachers to students and was now claimed as the special inheritance of the Pharisees.

The Pharisees were accordingly quite flexible in the practical application of religious law. For example, in order to allow neighbors to dine together on the Sabbath (when Jews were forbidden to work and could not even carry food outside their homes), the Pharisees ruled that an entire neighborhood could constitute a single household. They also believed in a life after death, a day of judgment, and the damnation or reward of individual souls. They actively sought out converts through preaching and looked forward to the imminent arrival of the Messiah whom God (through the prophets) had long promised. In all these respects they differed significantly from the Sadducees, who interpreted the Torah more strictly, who considered Judaism closed to anyone who had not been born a Jew and who had a vested interest in maintaining the political status quo. Even more radical than the Pharisees was a faction known as the Essenes, a quasi-monastic group that hoped for spiritual deliverance through repentance, asceticism, and sectarian separation from their fellow Jews.

Although some scholars see Essene influence behind the career of Jesus, his Jewish contemporaries probably saw him as some sort of Pharisee: Jesus's emphasis on the ethical requirements of the law rather than its literal interpretation is reflected in many of his teachings. Jesus's apparent belief in life after death and the imminent coming of "the kingdom of God" also fits within a Pharisaic framework, as does his willingness to reach out to people beyond the Jewish community. Nevertheless, he seems to have carried these principles considerably further than did the Pharisees.

For most Jews at this time, Judaism consisted of going up to the Temple on holy days; paying the annual Temple tax; reciting the morning and evening prayers; and observing certain fundamental laws, such as circumcision (for men), ritual purity (especially for women), and prohibitions on the consumption of certain foods. Jesus deemphasized such observances, and it may have seemed to some that he

wished to abolish them. But what made him most controversial was his followers' claim that he was the Messiah sent to deliver Israel from its enemies.

After Jesus's death, such claims grew more assertive, yet they never persuaded more than a small minority of Jews. But when Jesus's followers began to preach to non-Jewish audiences, they found many willing listeners. They began to represent Jesus in terms that made sense to the Greek-speaking communities of the Hellenistic world. Jesus, his followers now proclaimed, was not merely a messiah for the Jews. He was the "anointed one" (in Greek, *Christos*), the divine representative of God who had suffered and died for the sins of all humanity. He had now risen from the dead and ascended into heaven, and he would return to judge all the world's inhabitants at the end of time.

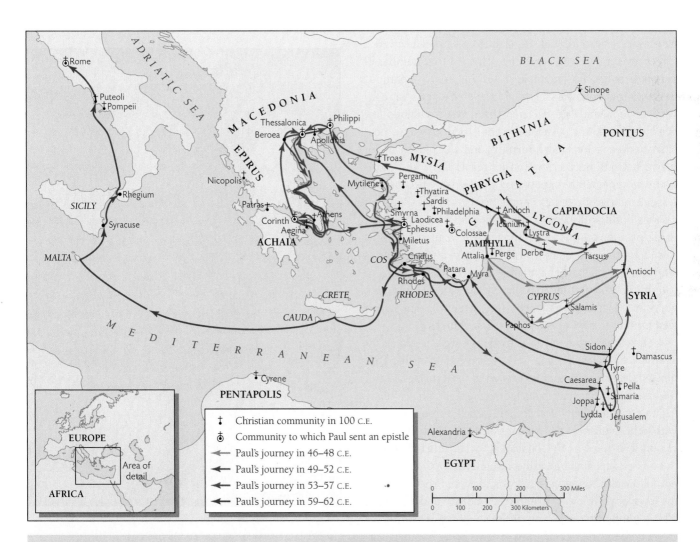

PAUL'S MISSIONARY JOURNEYS. Quite apart from its theological importance, Paul's career offers fascinating glimpses into the life of a Hellenized Roman citizen from one of the empire's eastern provinces. ▪ *What were the main phases of Paul's travels in the eastern Mediterranean?* ▪ *How were his itineraries shaped by geography and by various modes of transport?* ▪ *What conclusions about his mission can you draw from the extent of his travels and his major destinations?*

Christianity in the Hellenistic World

The key figure to develop this new understanding of Jesus's divinity was his younger contemporary, Paul of Tarsus (c. 10–c. 67 C.E.). Named Saul when he was born in the capital city of the Roman province of Cilicia (now south-central Turkey), he was the son of a Pharisee and staunchly sympathetic to that cause. The Acts of the Apostles, the continuation of Luke's Gospel and a major source for Saul's early life, says that he was dedicated to stamping out the cult that had grown up around the crucified Jesus. But at some point in his mid-twenties—a few years after Jesus's death—he underwent a dramatic conversion experience, changed his name to Paul, and devoted the rest of his life to spreading the new faith to Greek-speaking, mainly non-Jewish communities.

Unlike Peter and some other early apostles (from the Greek word meaning "one who is sent forth"), Paul had never met Jesus. Instead, he claimed to have received a direct revelation of his teachings. This led to a number of major disputes. For example, Peter and his companions believed that followers of Jesus had to be Jews or converts to Judaism. Paul declared that Jewish religious law was now irrelevant; Jesus had made a new covenant possible between God and humanity, and the old covenant between God and the Jews no longer applied. This position was vehemently opposed by the Jewish Christians of Jerusalem, a group led by Jesus's brother, James. But after a series of difficult debates that took place around 49 C.E., Paul's position triumphed. Although some early Christians would continue to obey Jewish law, most of the converts who swelled the movement were Gentiles. Paul began to call this new community of believers an ekklesia, the Greek word for a legislative assembly (see Chapter 3). The Latinized form of this word is translated as "church."

The earliest converts to Christianity were attracted for a variety of reasons. Some were Hellenized Jews like Paul himself. Jewish communities existed in most major cities of the eastern Mediterranean, including Rome, and had already begun to adapt their lifestyles and beliefs through contact with other cultures. Christianity also appealed to groups of non-Jews known as "God-fearers," who gathered around these Greek-speaking Jewish communities. God-fearers did not follow all the precepts of Jewish law, but they admired the Jews for their loyalty to ancestral tradition and their high ethical standards. Christianity was also attractive to ordinary cosmopolitan Greeks. Some saw Jesus as living by Stoic principles (Chapter 4) or as the embodiment of Ahura-Mazda, the good god of Zoroastrianism (Chapter 2). Others were already devotees of mystery religions, like the very old cult of the Egyptian goddess Isis (Chapter 1) or the newer worship of the warrior-god Mithras, popular among Rome's professional soldiers. Both of these religions also revolved around stories of sacrifice, death, and regeneration and would have prepared their adherents to embrace the worship of Jesus. It was largely for the benefit of these converts that Christians began to practice elaborate initiation ceremonies such as baptism, a ritual purification common to many ancient religions and exemplified among Jews in the ministry of John the Baptist.

At the same time, there were significant differences between Christianity and these other religions. Most mystery cults stressed the rebirth of the individual through spiritual transformation, but Christianity emphasized the importance of community. By the middle of the second century, the Christian church at Rome had a recognizable structure, headed by a bishop (in Greek, *episcopos* or "overseer") and lesser officeholders, including priests, deacons, confessors, and exorcists. Women were extremely prominent in these churches, not only as patrons and benefactors

A FRECSO FROM THE CATACOMBS OF ROME. This image shows a catachumen (Greek for "instructed one") being baptized by the Holy Spirit in the form of an eagle. It is one of many paintings to be found in the ancient catacombs around Rome: subterranean burial and meeting places where Christians also hid during times of persecution. ■ *Why would such images have been important?*

A CHRISTIAN LOVE FEAST. This fresco, another image from the catacombs, shows Christians celebrating a feast. The inscription above it reads, "I join with you in love."
▪ *How would a Roman viewer interpret this scene?* ▪ *How might this interpretation differ from that of a Christian?*

More Christians could have responded as did Marcion, a second-century Christian scholar who declared that Jewish religious practices and the entire Hebrew Bible could be ignored. Most Christians, however, refused to abandon their religion's Jewish foundation. For them, the heroes of Jewish scripture prefigured Jesus, while the major events of Hebrew history could be read, allegorically, as Christian paradigms. Christ was the new Adam, reversing man's original sin: wood from the fateful Tree in Eden became the wood of the Cross on which he died. Christ, like Abel, had been slain at the hands of a brother and his blood continued to cry out from the ground. Christ was the new Noah, saving creation from its sins. Christ was prefigured in Isaac, in Joseph, in Moses. Furthermore, according to Christians, all the words of the Hebrew prophets point to Jesus, as do the Psalms and the Proverbs.

In short, Christian theologians argued that the Christian church is the true Israel and that when the Jews rejected Jesus, God rejected the Jews and made Christians his new chosen people. The Hebrew Bible was henceforth the Old Testament, vital to understanding Christianity but superseded by the New Testament. At the end of time, the Jews would see the error of their ways and convert. Until then, their only reason for existing was to testify to the truth of Christianity. From a Christian perspective, the Jews' own impiety had caused their exile from the Holy Land and would continue to bring suffering down on their descendants.

(a role Roman women often played in religious cults) but also as officeholders.

This high status accorded to women was unusual: in other ancient religions, women could be priests and officeholders—but only in cults open solely to women; they never took precedence over men. Many cults, like Mithraism, denied them access entirely. The fact that Christianity drew its adherents from a broad range of social classes also distinguished it from other cults, which were accessible mainly to those with money and leisure. In time, these unusual features were distorted by Christianity's detractors, who alleged that Christians were political insurgents like the Jesus they worshiped, that they engaged in illict acts during "love feasts," or that they practiced human sacrifice and cannibalism.

As both Christianity and Judaism redefined themselves during the second and third centuries, they grew further apart. Judaism was adapting to the Romans' destruction of the Temple and the mass exile of Jews from Jerusalem and surrounding provinces. By and large, the scholars who reshaped it during these difficult years ignored Christianity. It simply did not matter to them, any more than did the cults of Mithras or Isis. Christians, however, could not ignore Judaism. Their religion rested on the belief that Jesus was the savior promised by God to Israel in the Hebrew Bible. The fact that so few Jews accepted this claim was a standing rebuke to their faith, one that threatened to undermine the credibility of the Christian message.

Christianity and the Roman State

As long as Christianity remained a minority religion within the Roman Empire, such attitudes had no effect on the position of Jews under Roman rule. Judaism remained a legally recognized religion and many Jews were further protected by their Roman citizenship. Indeed, the biblical book known as the Acts of the Apostles represents Paul as a Roman citizen who could not be summarily put to death (as the noncitizen Jesus had been) when brought up on charges of treason. Instead, Acts follows his progress through the Roman judicial system, until he is finally brought to trial at Rome and executed (by beheading) under Nero. Even after their rebellion, the Jews of the diaspora were allowed to maintain the special status they had always had under Roman rule and were not required, as other subject peoples were, to offer sacrifices to the emperor.

The Prosecution of a Roman Citizen

The Acts of the Apostles *was written by the same author as Luke's Gospel and was intended as a continuation of that book. It recounts the adventures and ministry of Jesus's original disciples and also follows the career of Paul, a Hellenized Jew who became a missionary to Gentiles throughout the Roman world. It offers fascinating glimpses into the workings of the Roman legal system because Paul, depicted here as a Roman citizen, would have had special rights under Roman law (as Jesus had not). In this passage, Paul has been accused of treason against the emperor by a group of Pharisees and has been sent to Felix, the governor of Judea. These events took place between 57 and 59 C.E.*

So the soldiers, according to their instructions, took Paul and brought him by night to [the city of] Antipatris. The next day, they let the horsemen go on with him, while they returned to the barracks. When they came to Caesarea and delivered the letter to the governor, they presented Paul also before him. On reading the letter, he asked what province he belonged to, and when he learned that he was from Cilicia he said, "I will give you a hearing when your accusers arrive." Then he ordered that he be kept under guard in Herod's headquarters.

Five days later, the high priest Ananias came down with some elders and an attorney, a certain Tertullus, and they reported their case against Paul to the governor. When Paul had been summoned, Tertullus began to accuse him, saying: "Your Excellency, because of you we have long enjoyed peace, and reforms have been made for this people because of your foresight. We welcome this in every way and everywhere with utmost gratitude. But, to detain you no further, I beg you to hear us briefly with your customary graciousness. We have, in fact, found this man a pestilent fellow, an agitator among all the Jews throughout the world, and a ringleader of the sect of the Nazarenes. He even tried to profane the temple, and so we seized him. By examining him yourself you will be able to learn from him concerning everything of which we accuse him." The Jews also joined in the charge by asserting that all this was true.

When the governor motioned to him to speak, Paul replied: "I cheerfully make my defense, knowing that for many years you have been a judge over this nation. As you can find out, it is not more than twelve days since I went up to worship in Jerusalem. They did not find me disputing with anyone in the temple or stirring up a crowd either in synagogues or throughout the city. Neither can they prove to you the charge that they now bring against me. But this I admit to you, that according to the Way, which they call a sect, I worship the God of our ancestors, believing everything laid down according to the law or written in the prophets. I have hope in God—a hope that they themselves also accept—that there will be a resurrection of both the righteous and the unrighteous. Therefore I do my best always to have a clear conscience toward God and all people. . . ."

But Felix, who was rather well informed about the Way, adjourned the hearing with the comment, "When Lysias the tribune comes down, I will decide your case." Then he ordered the centurion to keep him in custody, but to let him have some liberty and not to prevent any of his friends from taking care of his needs.

When some days later Felix came with his wife Drusilla, who was Jewish, he sent for Paul and heard him speak concerning faith in Christ Jesus. And as he discussed justice and self-control and future judgment, Felix was alarmed and said, "Go away for the present; when I have an opportunity I will summon you." At the same time he hoped that money would be given him by Paul. So he sent for him often and conversed with him. But when two years had elapsed, Felix was succeeded by Porcius Festus; and desiring to do the Jews a favor, Felix left Paul in prison.

Source: Acts of the Apostles 23:31–24:27, in *The New Oxford Annotated Bible,* New Revised Standard Version, eds. Bruce M. Metzger and Roland E. Murphy (New York: 1994).

Questions for Analysis

1. Based on this account, what legal procedures are in place for dealing with any Roman citizen accused of a crime?

2. What seems to be the relationship between the Jewish elite of Judea and the Roman governor? What is the role of their spokesman, Tertullus?

3. What is the nature of the accusation against Paul, and how does he defend himself?

As we have seen, nothing was more important to the Romans than *pietas* and respect for one's ancestors, and the Romans understood the Jews' traditions as a form of ancestor worship.

Christianity, by contrast, was a novelty religion. It carried neither the patina of antiquity nor the sanction of tradition—quite the contrary. It raised suspicions on many levels: it encouraged women and slaves to hold office and therefore to rise above their proper stations; it revolved around the worship of a criminal condemned by the Roman state; its secret meetings could be breeding grounds for rebellion. Nevertheless, the official attitude of the Roman state toward Christians was largely one of indifference. There were not enough of them to matter, and few of them had any political power. During the first and second centuries C.E., therefore, Christians were tolerated by Roman officials, except when local magistrates chose to make an example of someone who flagrantly flouted authority.

THE CHALLENGE OF IMPERIAL EXPANSION

The emergence of Christianity within the Roman Empire coincided with the empire's most dramatic period of growth and, as a result, with a growing variety of challenges. For a long time, Rome's emperors and administrators clung to the methods of governance that had been put in place under Augustus, methods which were based on a single centralized authority. The reality, however, was that Rome's empire was no longer centered on Rome, or even on Italy. It embraced ecosystems, linguistic groupings, ethnicities, cultures, economies, and political systems of vastly different kinds. More and more people could claim to be Roman citizens, and more and more people wanted a share of Rome's power. This placed enormous stress on the imperial administration, as the centrifugal forces of Rome's own making constantly pulled resources into her far-flung provinces, where cities had to be built, people governed, and communications maintained. The fact that the empire had few defensible borders was another problem. Hadrian had attempted to establish one after 122, by building a wall between Roman settlements in southern Britannia and the badlands of northern tribes (see Chapter 5); but this act was more symbolic than effective.

For much of the second century, such stresses were masked by the peaceful transfer of power among the so-called "Five Good Emperors": Nerva, Trajan, Hadrian, Antoninus Pius, and Marcus Aurelius. This harmonious state of affairs was partly accidental. None of these first four rulers had a surviving male heir, and so a custom developed whereby each adopted a young man of a good family and trained his successor in the craft of government. This sensible practice changed with the death of Marcus Aurelius in 180 C.E. Although he was the closest Roman equivalent to Plato's ideal of the philosopher-king, Marcus was not wise enough to recognize that his own son, Commodus, lacked the capacity to rule effectively. After his father's death, Commodus alienated the army by withdrawing from costly wars along the Danube. This move was also unpopular with the Senate, as were Commodus's violent tendencies and his scorn for the traditional norms of aristocratic conduct, including an alleged appearance as a gladiator in the Colosseum. In 192, a conspiracy was hatched inside his own palace, where he was strangled by his wrestling coach.

The Empire of the Severan Dynasty

Because Commodus had no obvious successor, the armies stationed in various provinces of the empire raised their own candidates. Civil war ensued, as it had during the crises of the late republic and in 68 C.E., when three men had struggled for imperial power. In this case, there were five major contenders. The eventual victor was a North African general called Septimius Severus (r. 193–211 C.E.).

Under Severus (*SEH-ver-uhs*) and his successors, the administration of Rome's empire changed to a greater extent than it had since the time of Augustus. In many respects, these changes were long overdue. Even the "Five Good Emperors" had been somewhat insulated from the realities of colonial rule. Many of them were able commanders, but they were not professional soldiers as Severus was. Another major difference was the fact that Severus had been born and raised in the North African town of Leptis Magna (now in Libya) and identified strongly with his father's Punic ancestors, seemingly more so than with his mother's patrician family. Unlike Trajan and Hadrian, who had also grown up in the provinces, Severus did not regard Rome as the center of the universe, and the time he spent in the imperial capital as a young man seems to have convinced him that little could be accomplished there.

In fact, Severus represents the degree to which the Roman Empire had succeeded in making the world Roman—succeeded so well that Rome itself was becoming practically irrelevant. One could be as much a Roman in Britannia or Africa as in central Italy. Severus's second wife, Julia Domna, exemplifies this trend in a different way. Descended from the Aramaic aristocracy who ruled the Roman client kingdom of Emesa (Syria), her father was the high priest of its sun-god, Ba'al. She was highly educated and proved an effective governer during her husband's almost perpetual absence from Rome.

The Development of an Imperial Policy toward Christians

> *It was not until the third century that the Roman imperial government began to initiate full-scale investigations into the activities of Christians. Instead, the official position was akin to a policy of "don't ask, don't tell." Local administrators handled only occasional cases, and they were often unsure as to whether the behavior of Christians was illegal or criminal. The following letter was sent to the emperor Trajan by Gaius Plinius Caecilius Secundus (Pliny the Younger), the governor of Bithynia-Pontus (Asia Minor), around 112 C.E. Pliny was anxious to follow proper procedures in dealing with the new sect and wanted advice about this. His letter indicates what Romans did and didn't know about early Christian beliefs and practices.*

From Pliny to Trajan

It is my regular custom, my lord, to refer to you all questions which cause me doubt, for who can better guide my hesitant steps or instruct my ignorance? I have never attended hearings concerning Christians, so I am unaware what is usually punished or investigated, and to what extent. . . . In the meantime, this is the procedure I have followed in the cases of those brought before me as Christians. I asked them whether they were Christians. If they admitted it, I asked them a second and a third time, threatening them with execution. Those who remained obdurate I ordered to be executed, for I was in no doubt . . . that their obstinacy and inflexible stubbornness should at any rate be punished. Others similarly lunatic were Roman citizens, so I registered them to be sent back to Rome.

Later in the course of the hearings, as usually happens, the charge rippled outwards, and more examples appeared. An anonymous document was published containing the names of many. Those who denied that they were or had been Christians and called upon the gods after me, and with incense and wine made obeisance to your statue . . . and who moreover cursed Christ . . . I ordered to be acquitted.

Others, who were named by an informer, stated that they were Christians and then denied it. They said that they had been, but had abandoned their

---

Severus largely ignored the politics of the Senate and slighted what remained of its powers. He preferred to rule through the army, which he reorganized and expanded. Two of his reforms had long-term consequences. The first was a drastic raise in army pay, probably as much as 100 percent, which had the effect of securing the soldiers' absolute loyalty and diminishing their need to augment their wages through plunder. The other was a relaxation of the long-standing rule forbidding soldiers to marry while still in service. This dispensation encouraged men to put down roots in local communities, but it also made them reluctant to move when their legion was called up. On the one hand, this domesticated the army (hitherto a highly mobile fighting machine) and may have made it less effective. On the other, it gave the army a stake in the peaceful governance of Rome's colonies and further contributed to the decentralization of power.

Severus spent most of his imperial career with his army. He died at Eboracum (York) in 211, after conducting a series of successful negotiations with Pictish tribes north of Hadrian's Wall. On his deathbed, he is reported to have said to his sons, "Get along together, keep the soldiers rich, and don't bother about anyone else." His elder son, Caracalla, didn't heed the first of these injunctions for long: by the end of the year, he had assassinated his brother, Geta. He then attempted to erase his brother from the historical record by declaring a *damnatio memoriae* (literally, "a condemnation of memory") that banned the mention of Geta's name and defaced his image on public monuments. The second of his father's orders he obeyed in a certain sense, by extending the rights of Roman citizenship to everyone in the empire. This not only included the entire army in the franchise but increased the tax base. This was beneficial in some respects, allegiance some years previously.... They maintained, however, that all that their guilt or error involved was that they were accustomed to assemble at dawn on a fixed day, to sing a hymn antiphonally to Christ as God, and to bind themselves by an oath ... to avoid acts of theft, brigandage, and adultery.... When these rites were completed, it was their custom to depart, and then reassemble again to take food, which was, however, common and harmless. They had ceased, they said, to do this following my edict, by which in accordance with your instructions I had outlawed the existence of secret brotherhoods. So I thought it all the more necessary to ascertain the truth from two maidservants [i.e., slaves], who were called deaconnesses, even by employing torture. I found nothing other than a debased and boundless superstition....

From Trajan to Pliny

You have followed the appropriate procedures, my Secundus.... [N]o general rule can be laid down which would establish a definite routine. Christians are not to be sought out. If brought before you and found guilty, they must be punished, but in such a way that a person who denies that he is a Christian, and demonstrates this by his action ... may obtain pardon for his repentance, even if his previous record is suspect. Documents published anonymously must play no role in any accusation, for they give the worst example, and are foreign to our age.

Source: Excerpted from *Pliny the Younger: The Complete Letters*, trans. P. G. Walsh (Oxford: 2006), pp. 278–79 (X.96–97).

Questions for Analysis

1. How does Pliny's treatment of Christians differ according to their social class? How does it differ from Felix's treatment of Paul (p. 186)?

2. Why would Trajan insist that anonymous accusations, like those discussed by Pliny, should not be used as evidence? Why is this "foreign to our age"?

3. What do you conclude from this exchange about the relationship between religion and politics under the Roman Empire?

but it may also have cheapened Roman citizenship, which was no longer a prize to be won through service or the adoption of Roman values and manners. Another indication of his populism was Caracalla's sponsorship of the largest public baths ever constructed in Rome, an enormous complex that would rival St. Peter's Basilica had it survived (the sprawling remains can still be seen). His father's final piece of advice helped to shorten Caracalla's reign significantly, since it exacerbated his already pronounced tendency to alienate everyone who disagreed with him. He was assassinated in 217.

Caracalla's true successor was his mother's sister, Julia Maesa, who ruled through his nominal heir and cousin, her adolescent grandson. This youth was known as Heliogabalus (or Elagabalus, r. 218–22) because of his devotion to Ba'al. But when Heliogabalus caused controversy by attempting to replace Jupiter, Rome's patron god, with a Latinized

THE EMPRESS JULIA DOMNA. This Roman coin, dating from about 200 C.E., is one of several issued in the name of Severus's powerful wife. As the coin's legend shows, she ruled as "Julia Augusta," names associated with the imperial family since the time of Augustus Caesar.

version of this eastern deity, Sol Invictus ("Invincible Sun"), his own grandmother engineered his assassination. Another of her grandsons, Alexander Severus (r. 222–35 C.E.), took his place. Alexander, in turn, was ruled by his mother Julia Mamea, the third in a succession of strong women behind the Severan dynasty, who even traveled with her son on military campaigns. This eventually proved fatal. The new prominence of the army made Rome's legions engines of political advancement even more so than under the dictators of the late republic. Many aspiring generals could harness this power, and with it the support of their legions' provincial bases. In 235, in consequence, Alexander and his

THE EMPEROR SEPTIMIUS SEVERUS. This statue, carved during the emperor's lifetime, emphasizes his career as a military commander, showing him in the standard-issue uniform of a Roman legionnaire. How does this image of Severus compare to that of Augustus (see Chapter 5, page 166)? ▪ *What do these differences suggest about the emperor's new role in the third century?*

mother were murdered at Moguntiacum (Mainz) in Upper Germania, when the army of the region turned against them. Nearly fifty years of civil unrest ensued.

The Test of Rome's Strength

From 235 to 284 C.E. there were no fewer than twenty-six "barracks emperors" in Rome: military commanders who, backed by a few loyal legions, struggled with one another and an array of problems. This period is sometimes called the "Third-Century Crisis" and interpreted as a time when the Roman Empire was nearly destroyed. It is more accurately interpreted as a time when the consequences of Roman imperialism made themselves acutely felt. Those aspects of the empire that were strong survived. Those that had always been fragile were further strained.

For example, the disruptions of the mid-third century exposed weaknesses in economic and administrative infrastructures. Inflation, caused by the devaluation of currency under Severus, nearly drained Roman coinage of its value. Meanwhile, aspiring emperors levied exorbitant taxes on civilians in their provinces, as warfare among rival claimants and their armies destroyed crops and interrupted trade, causing food shortages. Because Rome itself was almost entirely dependent on Egyptian grain and other goods shipped in from the East, its inhabitants suffered accordingly. Poverty and famine even led to a new form of slavery in Italy, as free artisans, local businessmen, and small farmers were forced to labor on the estates of large landholders in exchange for protection and food.

In 251, a terrible plague, probably smallpox, swept through the empire's territories and recurred in some areas for almost two decades. A similar plague had ravaged Rome a century earlier, but its effects had been mitigated by sound governance. Now, with an estimated 5,000 people dying every day in the crowded city, people sought local scapegoats. Christians were among those targeted. Beginning in the short reign of Decius (r. 249–51), all Roman citizens were required to swear a public oath affirming their loyalty to Rome, which meant worshiping Rome's gods. Those who did so received a certificate testifying to this fact, which they had to produce on demand. Large numbers of Christians were implicated when this edict was put into effect. The enlightened policies of earlier emperors were abandoned.

The Reorganized Empire of Diocletian

As it happens, the most zealous persecutor of Christians was also responsible for reining in these destructive forces. Diocletian (*die-oh-KLEE-shan*, r. 284–305) was a cavalry officer from the Roman province of Dalmatia (modern Croatia) who had risen through the ranks. He could have been another "barracks emperor," but he was determined not to be a victim of the cycle. Instead, he embraced the reality of Rome as a multicultural entity that could not be governed from one place by one person with one centralized bureaucracy. He appointed a fellow officer, Maximian, as co-emperor, putting him in charge of the western half of the empire and retaining the wealthier eastern half for himself. In 293, he delegated new authority to two junior emperors or "caesars," Galerius and Constantius. The result was a tetrarchy, a "rule of four," with each man governing a quarter of the empire, further subdivided into administrative units called *dioceses*. This system not only responded to the challenges of imperial administration, it was designed to secure a peaceful transfer of power, since the two young "caesars" were being groomed to take the place of the two senior "augusti."

Diocletian apparently recognized that disputes over succession had been a fatal flaw of the Augustan system. Also unlike Augustus, who had cloaked the reality of his personal power in the trappings of the republic, Diocletian presented himself as an undisguised autocrat. His title was not *princeps* ("first man"), but *dominus* ("lord"). In fact, his style of imperial rule borrowed more from the Persian model than it did from the Roman. Gone were the days of republican simplicity and the scorn of kingly pomp. Diocletian wore a diadem and a purple gown of silk interwoven with gold, and he introduced Persian-style ceremonies at his court. Under the Principate, the emperor's palace had been run like the household of any well-to-do Roman, only on a large scale. Diocletian, however, remained physically removed behind a maze of doorways, rooms, and curtains. Those lucky enough to gain an audience with him had to prostrate themselves, while a privileged few could kiss his robe. Too much familiarity with their soldiers had bred contempt for the "barracks emperors." As a soldier-turned-emperor himself, Diocletian was able to avoid this mistake.

Although Diocletian retained close personal control over the army, he took steps to separate military from civilian chains of command; never again would Roman armies make and unmake emperors. To control the devastatingly high rates of inflation that were undermining the economy, Diocletian stabilized the currency and attempted to fix prices and wages. He reformed the tax system. He even moved the administrative center of the empire from Italy to Nicomedia in the Roman province of Bithynia (modern Turkey). Rome remained the symbolic capital of the empire, not least because the Senate continued to meet there. But Diocletian had little need for the Senate's advice. The real power lay elsewhere.

THE CONVERSION OF CHRISTIANITY

By the beginning of the fourth century, the number of Christians living within the jurisdiction of Rome was statistically insignificant, probably no more than 5 percent of the total population in the West and possibly 10 percent of the Greek-speaking East. Still, it was making an impact, and one of Diocletian's methods for promoting unity within the empire was to take a proactive stance against any group perceived as subversive. This meant reviving the policies of Decius and Valerian, but taking an even harder line. Those who could not show proof of their loyalty to Rome's gods were stripped

THE TETRARCHY: DIOCLETIAN AND HIS COLLEAGUES. This grouping, carved from a valuable purple stone called porphyry, shows the two augusti, Diocletian and Maximian, embracing their younger caesars, Galerius and Constantius. ▪ *Why do you think that these rulers are portrayed with identical facial features and military regalia?* ▪ *What message does this convey?*

of their rights as citizens. Christians who had been serving in the army or in government offices were dismissed. So were Manicheans, followers of the Persian prophet Mani (c. 216–276), whose teachings paralleled Zoroastrianism by positing an eternal struggle between the forces of good and evil. Indeed, Christianity and Manichaeism must have seemed very similar to outsiders, and both were implicated in a full-scale purge of religious dissidents in 303. This was the Great Persecution, a time when many Christians became martyrs—a Greek word meaning "witnesses"—to their faith.

Christianity and Neoplatonism

Ironically, the very crises that prompted Diocletian's Great Persecution were contributing to a growing interest in Christianity. Its message of social justice and equality before God was attractive to those suffering from the breakdown of political, economic, and social structures. It also appealed to followers of a new and influential philosophical system called Neoplatonism ("New Platonism"), which drew upon the more mystical aspects of Plato's thought (Chapter 4). Its founder was Plotinus (204–270 C.E.), a Hellenistic philosopher from Egypt who had many followers among the Roman upper classes.

Plotinus taught that everything has its source in a single supreme being. The material world, too, is part of this creation, but it is merely the residue of the divine, from which all spirituality has been drained. Human beings are thus composed of matter (bodies) and emanations of the divine (souls). This means that the individual soul, originally a part of God, is now separated from its divine source by the fact of its embodiment. The highest goal of life is therefore to attain spiritual reunion with the divine, through contemplation and acts of self-denial that will help to liberate the soul from its earthly bondage. Asceticism (from the Greek word meaning "exercise" or "training") was therefore a major focus. Plotinus and his followers believed that the body could be tamed by

DIOCLETIAN'S DIVISION OF THE EMPIRE, C. 304 C.E. ▪ *What areas did each of the four divisions of the empire cover?* ▪ *What seems to be the strategy behind the location of the four major capitals, both within their respective quarters and in relation to one another?* ▪ *What is the status of Rome itself, according to this map?*

fasting and other forms of self-denial and thus made a more fitting vessel for the soul.

Neoplatonism became so popular in Rome that it almost supplanted Stoicism. (Although the two philosophies shared some fundamental characteristics, Stoicism did not hold out the hope of union with the divine.) Neoplatonism also struck a blow at traditional Roman precepts, including the worship of ancestors and the devotion to the empire's gods. It was thus a natural ally of Christianity, and many important Christian theologians would be influenced by it, while many educated Romans found their way to Christianity because of it. This was not, however, the path by which Christianity's first imperial convert reached the new faith.

Constantine's Vision

In 305, Diocletian built a palace near his hometown of Split on the Adriatic coast and retired there to raise cabbages—the first time a Roman ruler had voluntarily removed himself from power since Sulla had resigned his dictatorship, nearly four hundred years earlier (see Chapter 5). Diocletian obliged Maximian to retire at the same time, and the two caesars Galerius and Constantius moved up the ladder of succession, becoming augusti of the East and West, respectively. But the transfer of power was not as orderly as Diocletian had intended. One of the candidates to fill the vacant post of caesar was Constantius's son, Constantine, who was being trained at Galerius's court. But he was passed over, perhaps so that Galerius could pursue his own imperial agenda. So Constantine left the court at Nicomedia and joined his father in Gaul. From there, father and son went to Britannia and campaigned on the northern borders until 306, when Constantius died and named Constantine as his successor. This infuriated Galerius, but with Constantine in control of a large army (the legions of Gaul and the Rhineland, as well as Britannia) he was forced to concede.

Meanwhile, war broke out among several other claimants to imperial authority, reducing Diocletian's tetrarchy to rivalry. Constantine remained aloof from this struggle, waged mostly in Italy, and concentrated on securing his quarter of the empire. Beginning around 310, he also began to promote himself as a favored devotee of the sun-god Sol Invictus, whose cult had been revived by the emperor Aurelian (r. 270–75). This was a smart move. Increasingly, the "Invincible Sun" was associated not only with the Roman gods of light and war, Apollo and Mars, but also with Mithras, whose cult was popular with soldiers. It was increasingly popular in Rome as well, where the feast long dedicated to the sky-god Saturn, the Saturnalia, was now being celebrated as the rebirth of the sun after the winter solstice, on December 25.

From the worship of Sol Invictus to the worship of Christ was, at least for Constantine, a small step (see **Interpreting Visual Evidence** on page 194). In 312, Constantine decided to march on Italy, which was now in the hands of a man called Maxentius, who had declared himself emperor in the West and was trying to build up a coalition of supporters. Among them was the Christian community of Rome. It may have been this that gave Constantine the idea of currying favor in the same way, or it may have been another kind of inspiration that led him to emblazon Christian symbols on his banners and the shields of his soldiers the night before a major battle north of Rome, at the Milvian Bridge over the Tiber. According to later legend, Constantine had seen a vision of two intertwined Greek letters inscribed on the sky, the first two letters in the name of Christ, and was told that "In this sign, you will conquer." He did.

In gratitude for his victory, Constantine showered benefits on the Christian clergy of Rome and patronized the construction of churches throughout the empire. He also forced Licinius, the augustus of the East, to join him in promoting religious tolerance when they met at Milan in 313. Their Edict of Milan guaranteed freedom of worship to all Rome's citizens, Christian and non-Christian. But it was apparent that Christianity was the favored faith of the imperial family and thus the pathway for anyone with political ambitions. Almost overnight, then, Christians ceased to be members of an illegal and often despised cult and became affiliates of a prestigious and profitable religion, one that was suddenly attractive to the ruling classes. The entire basis of Christianity's appeal had changed.

From Illegal Sect to Imperial Institution

In his letters, Paul of Tarsus had addressed small Christian assemblies that he called churches (*ekklesiae*). Sometimes he had even spoken of the whole Christian community as a church. But it is doubtful that Paul could have imagined a day when representatives of an official Church could meet openly, or a time when his letters to separate churches in Corinth, Ephesus, Rome, and elsewhere would be gathered together in a single book.

Early Christianity had grown organically; it had not been designed as a religious system. It had no absolute teachings, apart from the words of Jesus reported in the Gospels, which do not always agree on those teachings. And not all Christian communities had access to the same scriptures. Some churches had a few of Paul's letters; others had none. Some had bishops, priests, deacons, and other officeholders; others had only a handful of believers. Some counted women as their leaders; others disapproved of women in authority. Some had come under the influence of

The Power of the Invincible Sun

Roman emperors often linked their power with those of Rome's traditional gods, and they were also worshiped as gods in their own right. Look carefully at the following images and consider the visual language of power that came to be associated with Sol Invictus, "the Invincible Sun," and eventually with Jesus Christ.

Questions for Analysis

1. How did Constantine invoke the iconography of Sol Invictus (image A)? What messages does this image convey?

2. How might Constantine's use of this imagery—after his initial conversion to Christianity—have been interpreted by Christians? How might it have been interpreted by followers of Rome's other religions? Do you think it was designed to be ambiguous?

3. Scholars dispute both the dating and the significance of this mosaic found beneath St. Peter's Basilica in Rome (image B). Is it likely that this is a representation of Jesus as Sol Invictus? If not, how would you explain the later association of this pagan deity with the Christian God?

A. This gold medallion was issued by Constantine in 313, a year after his victory at the Battle of the Milvian Bridge. The legend calls him "Invincible Constantine."

B. This mosaic comes from a necropolis (cemetery) found beneath St. Peter's Basilica in Rome. Its precise dating is in dispute, but it was made sometime between the mid-third and mid-fourth century.

Neoplatonism or Manichaeism; others considered Neoplatonism and Manichaeism to be perversions.

In every respect, then, the Christianity that emerged after Constantine's conversion had to reinvent itself. Rituals and doctrines that had been formulated to suit the needs of small, scattered communities now had to be reconciled. Members of this new Church needed to agree on a shared set of beliefs. They needed a shared set of scriptures. They needed a chain of command. All of these fundamental structures had to be hammered out in a painful process that never quite managed to forge a common understanding. Historically speaking, this is hardly surprising. The varieties of Christianity had been too separate for too long, and they were the products of the same diversity that made the Roman Empire hard to govern. Indeed, the degree to which the Christians of the fourth century were able to agree on so many things is remarkable, given these challenges.

The Hierarchy of the Church

When it came to organization, Rome's imperial administration provided practical models. Because the empire's basic unit of governance was the city, the city became the basic

CONSTANTINE'S CHRISTIAN SYMBOL. This fourth-century fresco shows the chi-rho symbol that Constantine claimed to have seen in the sky before his victory at the Milvian Bridge. Chi and rho are the first two letters in the Greek word *Christos*. Flanking this monogram are the first and last letters of the Greek alphabet, alpha and omega, which also refer to Jesus, "the beginning" and "the end."

unit of ecclesiastical administration, too. Each major city now had a bishop who oversaw all the churches and also the rural areas of his diocese, a term borrowed from Diocletian's reorganization of the empire. Bishops of the largest cities were called *metropolitans*, and those who ruled over the oldest and most prestigious Christian communities were called *patriarchs*. These patriarchal cities also jockeyed for preeminence: among the main contenders were Rome, whose inhabitants longed to be at the center of the world again; Alexandria, the capital of the Hellenistic world; and Constantinople, a new city founded by Constantine on the Hellespont between Europe and Asia.

Which of these Roman cities should be the capital of the Roman Church? The patriarch of Rome's claim rested on several foundations. Rome had long been venerated as the place where both Peter and Paul were martyred. And according to one of the Gospels (Matthew 16:18–19), Jesus had designated Peter as his representative on earth. Peter's successors, the subsequent bishops of Rome, thus claimed to exercise the same powers. Rome's bishop also enjoyed some political advantages over other patriarchs. Unlike the bishop of the new imperial capital at Constantinople, he could act with more freedom because he didn't have to deal directly with the emperor. But as far as eastern bishops were concerned, the patriarch of Constantinople should be the one to exercise control over the entire Church. This division of opinion—the product of cultural differences and contemporary politics—would continue to affect the development of Christian institutions. In

time, it would lead to a very real division within Christianity, one that has never been resolved.

Orthodoxy, Heresy, and Imperial Authority

Christianity's new prominence also raised the stakes of disputes over its basic teachings. While followers of Jesus had disagreed about such matters almost since the time of his death, these disagreements were of little political consequence so long as Christianity remained an illegal movement. Under Constantine, however, doctrinal disputes had the potential to ignite riots and to undermine the credibility of the emperor. It was imperative, therefore, that these disputes be resolved through active imperial intervention.

The most divisive theological issue of the early Church concerned the nature of God. Jesus had taught his followers that he was the Son of God and that after his death he would leave behind him a comforting spirit that would also be an emanation of God. Accordingly, many Christians believed that God encompassed a Trinity of equal persons: Father, Son, and Holy Spirit. But other Christians, influenced by Neoplatonism, rejected the idea that Jesus could be equal with God. Instead, they maintained that Jesus was part of God's creation and shared in his divine essence; but he was not equal to God, or eternal. This latter school of thought was called Arianism, after the Christian teacher Arius who espoused it. (It should not be confused with Aryanism, a modern racial concept.) After protracted struggles, Arianism was condemned as a heresy, a word that comes from the Greek verb meaning "to choose for oneself" and which became the Church's term for false beliefs punished with damnation. Yet many Christians continued to adhere to the Arian view.

This new emphasis on orthodoxy (Greek for "correct teaching") was another major consequence of Christianity's conversion. The beliefs of early Christians had been fairly simple: there is one God; Jesus is the anointed one who suffered and died for the sins of mankind and who was raised from the dead; in order to be saved, his followers must renounce sin. But beginning in the fourth century, Christian theology would become ever more complex. Christian intellectuals had to demonstrate that their beliefs could withstand intense philosophical scrutiny and that Christianity was superior to Hellenistic philosophy. Just as there were many different schools of Greek and Roman thought, so there arose many different interpretations of Christian doctrine. Before Christianity became a legal religion, any doctrinal disputes could only be addressed informally, by small groups of bishops meeting at local councils that had no power to enforce their decisions. In the fourth century, doctrinal disputes had real political consequences.

As a result, the Roman state became increasingly enmeshed in the governance of the Church. Constantine began this process in 325 C.E., when he summoned Christian representatives to the first ecumenical ("worldwide") meeting of the Christian community, the Council of Nicea, where Arianism was condemned and discrepancies over the canon of the Christian Bible were resolved. Constantine's successors carried this intervention much further. Gradually, they claimed to preside over Church councils as Christ's representatives on earth, which entitled them to decide what Christian doctrine should be. Some even violently suppressed Christian groups who refused to accept imperial mandates, labeled them heretical, and subjected them to ecclesiastical penalties—condemnation and excommunication from the Church—and to criminal penalties, too. Essentially, these imperial interventions were an extension of Augustan policies, which had made the emperor *pontifex maximus,* Rome's high priest. In the fourth century, it began to look as though this trend would continue, and that secular and spiritual authority would be combined in the person of the emperor. But this would change in later centuries, as we shall see.

New Attitudes toward Women and the Body

Women were conspicuously absent from the new hierarchy of the Church and were also barred from the decision-making process at Nicea. Even though they had long been deacons and may even have performed priestly duties, women were now firmly and completely excluded from any position of power.

This was an enormous change, more fundamentally so than any other aspect of Christianity's conversion. Jesus had included many women among his close followers, yet one of the early gospels now rejected from the biblical canon was ascribed to Mary Magdalene. Paul had relied on women to organize and preside over churches and to finance his missionary journeys; he had declared in one letter (Galatians 3:28) that there should be no distinctions of gender, rank, or ethnicity among Christians. Women had been leaders of many early churches. Women like Perpetua were prominent among the martyrs and were often regarded as prophets. These strong roles had always been

controversial because they set Christianity apart from the traditional values of Roman society. But that had also been one of Christianity's main attractions.

What accounts for this drastic change? Three factors can be clearly identified. When Christianity was absorbed into the staunch patriarchy of Rome, it could no longer promote the authority of women effectively. As the Church came to mirror the imperial administration, it replicated the structures of governance that had been the province of men since the founding of the republic. The Church now had the capacity to exclude or censor writings that represented women as the companions of Jesus and founders of the religion based on his teachings. These efforts were so successful that it was not until the very end of the nineteenth century that a gospel attributed to Mary Magdalene (among other writings) was known to exist.

The second factor leading to the marginalization of women was the growing identification of Christianity with Roman cults that emphasized masculinity, particularly the worship of Sol Invictus and the soldier-god Mithras. This was a deliberate strategy on the part of the Church. It is easier to convert people to a new religion if that religion is not wholly new, and embraces elements of other religions. In common with these two cults, as well as with many of the other religions we have studied (like the worship of Osiris in Egypt), Christianity emphasized the heroic suffering and death of a male god and his eventual victory over death itself. Christ was increasingly identified with Sol Invictus and his birthday came to be celebrated on December 25, which marked the passing of the winter solstice and the return of lengthening days.

The third factor contributing to women's exclusion from power was the Christian emphasis on asceticism ("self-denial"), which changed attitudes toward the body. As we noted above, Neoplatonism taught that the goal of life was to liberate the soul from the tyranny of bodily desires, a teaching that it shared with Stoicism. None of this was emphasized in the teachings of Christ. Quite the contrary: the body was celebrated as God's creation, and Christ himself had encouraged feasting, touching, bathing, and marriage. His followers insisted that he had been bodily resurrected, and that the bodies of all the faithful would be resurrected, too. Although early Christians had to be willing to sacrifice their lives for their faith, if need be, they were not required to renounce pleasures.

After Christianity became legal, however, there were few opportunities to "bear witness" to the faith through martyrdom. Instead, some Christians began to practice asceticism as an alternative path to sanctity. This meant renunciation of the flesh, especially sex and eating, activities both associated with women, who were in charge of

Past and Present

Resisting Imperialism

Attempts at conquest are always met with resistance. In the Roman province of Britannia, a Celtic warrior queen named Boadicea led an armed uprising against the imperial army that is still celebrated as a proud example of British independence—as this modern statue in London indicates. A more peaceful uprising against American imperialism took place in Manila on the eve of President Barack Obama's first inauguration in 2008.

 Watch related author interview on StudySpace
wwnorton.com/web/westernciv18

any household's food supply and who were (obviously) sexual partners. A new spiritual movement called monasticism also took hold, providing an alternative lifestyle for men who wanted to reject the world entirely; the word for this movement comes from the Greek word *monos*, "alone." Early monks lived as hermits and practiced extraordinary feats of self-abasement. Some grazed in the fields like cows; others penned themselves into small cages; still others hung heavy weights around their necks. A monk named Cyriacus would stand for hours on one leg, like a crane. Another, Simeon "the Stylite," lived on top of a high pillar for thirty-seven years, punishing his lice-infested flesh while crowds gathered below to marvel.

This extreme denial of the body was a departure not only from most previous Christian practices but from the practices of many civilizations up to this point—not to mention the realities of human existence. Ancient religions often celebrated sexuality as a delight, as well as a necessity.

Even Roman religion had a place for priestesses and female prophets. Moreover, marriage was so important a marker of social respectability that unmarried men were objects of deep suspicion. Furthermore, Romans had regarded citizens' bodies as being at the service of the state: men as soldiers and fathers, women as mothers and wives. Now, however, some Christians were asserting that their bodies belonged not to the state but to God, and that to serve God fully meant no longer serving the state—or posterity—by bearing children.

Virginity for both men and women was accordingly preached as the highest spiritual standard, with celibacy for those who had once been married valued almost as highly. Marriage remained acceptable for average people, the laity, but was often represented as a second-best option whose purpose was to prevent weak-minded people from being consumed by desire. Moreover, because pseudo-scientific theories stemming back to Aristotle posited that women were inherently more lustful than men, the denigration of sexuality had a disproportionately negative effect on attitudes toward women.

Christians and Pagans

The urban focus of Christianity is reflected in the Latin word referring to a non-Christian: *paganus*, meaning someone who lives in the countryside. The implication is that only someone with a hopelessly rustic outlook would cling to the old Roman religion and so spoil his chances of advancement in society. As Christians came to occupy positions of power within the empire, men with political ambitions were increasingly forced to convert—or at least conform—to Christian norms.

Constantine had retained both pagan and Christian officials in his court, and was careful to speak in terms that embraced a non-Christian audience. But his successors were less inclined to tolerate competing faiths. An interesting exception was Julian "the Apostate" (r. 360–63), Constantine's nephew, who abandoned Christianity and attempted to revive traditional Roman piety. But when Julian was killed in a battle with the Persians, his pro-pagan edicts were allowed to lapse. By 391, the emperor Theodosius (r. 379–95 C.E.) had prohibited pagan worship of any sort within the empire. This meant that within three generations, Christianity had gone from being a persecuted faith to a persecuting religion. Theodosius even removed the sacred altar of the goddess Victory from the Senate chamber in Rome, prompting pagan loyalists to prophesy the end of the empire. Fifteen years later, Rome fell to a barbarian army.

SHIFTING CENTERS AND MOVING FRONTIERS

In 324, Constantine broke ground for the capital city he named after himself. It was built on the site of a settlement called Byzantium, chosen for its strategic location at the mouth of the Black Sea and at the crossroads between Europe and Asia: the Hellespont (literally "the bridge to Greece"). This site gave Constantinople commanding advantages as a center for communications and trade. It also made the city readily defensible, because it was surrounded on three sides by water and protected on land by walls. It would remain the political and economic center of the Roman Empire until 1453, when the city was conquered by the Ottoman Turks (see Chapter 11).

East or West?

The founding of Constantinople epitomizes the shift in Rome's center of gravity from Italy and western Europe to the eastern Mediterranean. It also signaled Constantine's intention to abandon the political precedents set by Diocletian, including the institution of the tetrarchy. Instead, the imperial succession became hereditary. Constantine thus embraced a principle of dynastic monarchy that Romans had rejected 800 years earlier. Even more ominously, he divided

SAINT SIMEON THE STYLITE. This gold plaque dating from the sixth century depicts the exertions of the ascetic saint who defied the devil (shown as a huge snake) by abusing his own body. Admirers wishing to speak to the saint could climb the ladder shown on the left. ▪ *What do you make of the relationship between the luxurious medium of this image (gold) and the message it conveys?*

the empire among his three sons. Civil war ensued, made more bitter because each of these men represented a different faction within the Christian Church. In the meantime, the empire became more and more fragmented. The last ruler who could claim to govern a united Rome was the same Theodosius who outlawed its venerable religion. Then he, too, divided the empire between his sons.

As we have seen, there had always been linguistic and cultural differences between the Greek- and Latin-speaking peoples under Roman rule. Now, however, these differences became heightened. The eastern empire was becoming more populous, more prosperous, and more central to imperial policy; the western provinces were becoming poorer and more peripheral. Many western cities now relied on transfers of funds from their eastern counterparts, and they suffered when these funds dried up, when trade or communication failed, or when Roman legions were transferred elsewhere. Rome itself, which had been demoted to provincial status under Diocletian, now lost even that nominal position: the Italian city of Ravenna on the Adriatic coast became the new capital of the region and a more convenient stopping place for emperors and ambassadors traveling from Constantinople to the administrative centers of Milan and Trier. Only two of Constantine's successors ever visited Rome itself, and none of them lived there.

Internal and External Pressures

The shifting center of the empire and the widening gap between the eastern and western provinces were not the only fault lines emerging in this period. There were secessionist movements among many residents of Britannia, Gaul, Hispania, and Germania. The residents of Egypt were particularly affected by high levels of taxation, which targeted their rich agricultural lands. Meanwhile, North Africans and other citizens living in the empire's interior regions were increasingly ignored by authorities. Italians resented their new status as provincial subjects of Constantinople. Beneath the surface of imperial autocracy, the fourth-century empire was slowly dissolving into its constituent parts.

The empire was also coming under renewed pressure from its borders. Since the third century, the growing power of a new Persian dynasty, the Sassanids, had prompted a shift of Roman military weight to the eastern frontier, reducing the number of troops stationed elsewhere. Partly as a result of this, the northwestern territories suffered a devastating series of raids along the porous frontier of Germania. During the fourth century, relations between assimilated Romans and their barbarian neighbors were generally peaceful. But starting in the early fifth century, a new wave of settlers moved into the empire's oldest provinces, permanently altering their histories and cultures.

From the Periphery to the Center

In the eyes of many Romans, the tribes that lived along the empire's northern frontiers were barbarians in the pure sense of that (Greek) term: they did not speak either of the empire's civilized languages and they did not live in cities. But in no sense were they savage peoples. They were sophisticated agriculturalists and metalworkers who had enjoyed trading relationships with the Roman world for centuries. Many had been settled within Roman provinces for generations as farmers and craftsmen. Legionnaires from the hinterlands of Germania were core components in Roman armies. In some frontier areas, entire tribes had become Roman *foederati*: allied troops who reinforced Roman garrisons or took their places when legions were withdrawn. By the end of the fourth century, many of these tribes had even adopted the form of Christianity preached by disciples of Arius. Although this made them heretics from the perspective of the institutional Church, it also tied them more closely to Roman civilization. One general of mixed descent, Flavius Stilicho (359–408), was the military leader of the western empire under Theodosius.

What altered this relatively peaceful coexistence? Our study of many previous civilizations has prepared us to answer this question: the arrival of new peoples and the subsequent struggle for land and resources. During the mid-fourth century, a group of nomadic herdsmen known as the Huns began to migrate westward from central Asia, into the region north and east of the Black Sea. Around 370, their arrival forced a number of other groups, notably the Goths, to migrate south and west—and in a hurry. Within a few years, they had reached the Roman frontier along the Danube River. The Goths had been clients of the Roman state for several centuries. But now they were refugees and too numerous and too desperate to repel by force. The Romans therefore permitted them to cross the Danube and settle within the empire. In return for food and other supplies, they were to guard the region against other migrant groups.

Local officials, however, failed to uphold their end of the bargain. Instead, they forced the starving Goths to sell themselves and their children into slavery in return for food. In 378, the Goths revolted and the Roman army sent to suppress them was defeated at the battle of Adrianople. Peace was restored by accommodating the Goths' demands for goods and farmland and by enrolling them in the Roman army under their own military leaders. But when Theodosius divided the

A Senator Defends the Traditional Religion of Rome

In 382, the Emperor Theodosius ordered the removal of the ancient altar dedicated to the goddess of Victory (Nike) from the Senate chamber in Rome, as part of his efforts to make Christianity the dominant religion in the empire. This controversial move sparked heated debate and elicited strong protests from Rome's senatorial elites. The following statement of their case was made by Quintus Aurelius Symmachus (c. 345–402), who was at that time prefect of the city of Rome. It is principally addressed to the young western emperor, Valentinian.

o what is it more suitable that we defend the institutions of our ancestors, and the rights and destiny of our country ... than to the glory of these times, which is all the greater when you understand that you may not do anything contrary to the custom of your ancestors? We demand then the restoration of that condition of religious affairs which was so long advantageous to the state. ... Who is so friendly with the barbarians as not to require an Altar of Victory? ... But even if the avoidance of such an omen were not sufficient, it would at least have been seemly to abstain from injuring the ornaments of the Senate House. Allow us, we beseech you, as old men to leave to posterity what we received as boys. The love of custom is great. ... Where shall we swear to obey your laws and commands? By what religious sanction shall the false mind be terrified, so as not to lie in bearing witness? All things are indeed filled with God, and no place is safe for the

perjured, but to be urged in the very presence of religious forms has great power in producing a fear of sinning. That altar preserves the concord of all, that altar appeals to the good faith of each, and nothing gives more authority to our decrees than that the whole of our order issues every decree as it were under the sanction of an oath. ...

Let us now suppose that Rome is present and addresses you in these words: "Excellent princes, fathers of your country, respect my years to which pious rites have brought me. Let me use the ancestral ceremonies, for I do not repent of them. Let me live after my own fashion, for I am free. This worship subdued the world to my laws, these sacred rites repelled Hannibal from the walls, and the Senones [Gauls] from the capitol. Have I been reserved for this, that in my old age I should be blamed? I will consider what it is thought should be set in order, but tardy and discreditable is the reformation of old age." We ask, then, for peace for the gods of our fathers and of our country. It is just that all worship should be considered as

one. We look on the same stars, the sky is common, the same world surrounds us. What difference does it make by what pains each seeks the truth? We cannot attain to so great a secret by one road; but this discussion is rather for persons at ease, we offer now prayers, not conflict.

Source: Excerpted from *A Select Library of the Nicene and Post-Nicene Fathers,* 2nd Series, Vol. X, (New York: 1896), pp. 411–14.

Questions for Analysis

1. How does Symmachus's defense exemplify the traditional values of the Roman Republic?

2. How does Symmachus justify the coexistence of Christianity and Rome's state religion? How would a Christian refute his position?

3. Less than a decade after the altar's removal, Theodosius outlawed all religions but Christianity. Based on your reading of this letter, how would that edict have affected Romans like Symmachus?

empire between his two young sons, their military advisers—including Stilicho, father-in-law of the emperor Honorius, the de facto ruler—constantly undermined one another. This provided an opening for Alaric, a young leader of the Goths, to advance his own agenda. Targeting the wealthier eastern provinces, he led his army into Greece, looting or capturing many ancient cities, including Athens.

In a desperate attempt to halt these incursions, Alaric was offered a Roman military command and encouraged to move into Italy: meaning that the price of peace in the eastern empire was Rome itself. Meanwhile, the Huns had arrived in the region corresponding to modern-day Hungary, forcing several other peoples westward toward the Rhine. On New Year's Eve in the year 406, a people known as the Vandals crossed the frozen Rhine and invaded Gaul. To repulse them, Stilicho (whose own father had been a Vandal) made an alliance with Alaric and his Goths. But Stilicho fell from imperial favor just a few months later, and the imperial government could no longer exercise any restraint on Alaric's actions.

Like Stilicho, Alaric seems to have wanted to win a permanent place for himself in the imperial hierarchy. But unlike Stilicho—and many Roman generals before him—he did not understand how to use violence as a means toward that end. His assault on Rome did not make him Rome's conqueror, it made him its destroyer. In 410, after a protracted period of siege, Alaric's army captured and sacked the city. But by now, Rome had little to offer in the way of either food or spoils. So many of the Goths moved on, eventually settling in southern Gaul and Hispania, where they established what came to be known as the Visigothic kingdom. Others, later labeled as the Ostrogoths, remained in Italy. The Vandals set out for the Iberian Peninsula, too, but ultimately crossed the Strait of Gibraltar to settle in North Africa. Other tribes, including the Franks and the Burgundians, followed the Vandals across the Rhine into Gaul and established kingdoms of their own.

A generation later the Huns—whose migrations had set all of these gears in motion—themselves invaded Roman territory under the leadership of their warlord, Attila. Britannia, meanwhile, had been abandoned by its remaining legions which were hastily withdrawn in 410. There, a mixed population of Romans and Celts eventually intermingled with invaders from northwestern Germania and Scandinavia: Angles, Saxons, and Jutes. These tribes were so efficient that they dominated all but the westernmost and northern portions of the island within a few generations. Many Celts retreated to the regions where Celtic languages are still spoken today, including Wales and Scotland. The rest of Britain would become Angle-land: England.

The last western Roman emperor was an ineffectual usurper derisively known as Romulus Augustulus ("Little Romulus Augustus"). In 476, he was deposed by Odovacar, a chieftain who headed a mixed band of barbarians, Huns, and disgruntled Romans. Viewed from the perspective of Constantinople, this event was decisive: now it was not only "New Rome," it was the only viable capital. And the best way for its imperial agenda to be carried forward in the western provinces was through a strong barbarian ruler. Luckily, the emperor Zeno (r. 474–91) knew just the man: Theodoric, the son of a Gothic king, who had been sent to Constantinople as a hostage and raised in the civilized surroundings of the imperial court. After a decade of fierce fighting, Theodoric and his imperially equipped Gothic army managed to drive the Huns from Italy and establish a kingdom based in Ravenna, which he ruled (with imperial support) until his death in 526.

The Impact of the Fifth-Century Migrations

The events of the fifth century widened the porousness of the empire's northern frontiers and penetrated to its core provinces: Italy, Gaul, Hispania, North Africa. Yet the groups that moved through these territories were small. They were joined by refugees and desperados, but they were never more than war bands. So why couldn't long-established imperial cities sustain themselves?

By the beginning of the fifth century, many Roman armies were already weakened. The best legions had been withdrawn from frontier provinces to protect richer eastern ones. Those that remained tended to be integrated into local civilian populations, staffed by married men who grew their own food and lived with their families, making it difficult to move troops even in an emergency. Furthermore, there was no mechanism for increasing the revenues needed to support the army. And even if the citizens of Rome's western provinces had been able to maintain a crack fighting force on the frontier, there would have been little reason for them to think that such expenditure was necessary. Their "barbarian" neighbors hadn't seemed threatening for generations. Many were so Romanized that differences between the groups are difficult to detect in surviving archaeological evidence.

In the eastern Roman Empire, by contrast, a thriving economy made it easier to equip and maintain a strong fighting force. Cities remained centers of commerce and industry,

THEODORIC THE OSTROGOTH. This coin shows the king in Roman dress but with the long hair characteristic of a barbarian nobleman. The inscription reads *Rex Theodericvs pivs princis,* "King Theodoric, pious prince." ■ *How does this image compare to that of Constantine (see page 194)?*

THE MIGRATIONS OF ROME'S FRONTIER PEOPLES. ▪ *What do the routes followed by these different peoples suggest about their destinations and motives?* ▪ *Why did so many converge on Rome, even though the city was no longer the capital even of the western Roman Empire?* ▪ *Why did the Romans refer to them as "barbarians"?*

which meant that citizens possessed greater taxable wealth and could sustain the burdens of the imperial bureaucracy more easily. Moreover, potential invaders could be bought off or bribed to direct their attention elsewhere—as Alaric had been. For all these reasons, the eastern empire prospered during the fifth century, while the western empire floundered. After the fifth-century migrations, these differences were exacerbated. Every territory that was plundered or occupied represented tax revenues lost, and the scale of these losses was enormous. Ten years after the Goths sacked Rome, the area was capable of producing only 15 percent of

the revenues it had generated in 407. Similar reductions in revenues resulted from attacks on Gaul and Hispania. After 420 or so, as the newcomers began to set up their own kingdoms, these areas ceased to pay any taxes at all to imperial authorities. When the Vandals captured North Africa in 439, the richest of all Rome's western provinces was lost.

The consequences of these structural changes were far-reaching. In the year 400, the economy of the western Roman Empire was characterized by the mass production of low-cost, high-quality consumer goods that circulated in massive quantities. Although regional and local systems of exchange continued after 500, long-distance trade in bulk goods could be sustained only in the Mediterranean. As markets disappeared in northwestern provinces, skilled artisans had to find other ways to make a living, or had to emigrate. Standards of living gradually declined, and so did the overall population. Indeed, it is likely that the population of western Europe did not return to its fourth-century levels for a thousand years, until just before the Black Death (see Chapter 10).

Other aspects of Roman life in these regions changed, too, but almost imperceptibly. Roman bureaucracies often survived, although the proceeds from taxes now went into the purses of the new barbarian rulers or Christian bishops. Roman agricultural patterns continued in most areas, frequently under the same landlords. Local Roman elites continued to dominate civic life, and Roman cities continued to dominate their surrounding regions, especially in southern Gaul and Hispania. Nor did the invasions bring an end to Roman culture or to the influence of Roman values. As King Theodoric the Goth was fond of remarking: "An able Goth wishes to be like a Roman; but only a poor Roman would want to be like a Goth."

THE SHAPING OF A NEW WORLDVIEW

Throughout this time of change, Christian intellectuals were formulating a new outlook on the world that would remain dominant for over a thousand years. As the empire sustained attack from external forces and began to fragment along old fault lines, it seemed clearer than ever that a new age was beginning. Christ had promised to come again at the end of time, when all human souls would be judged. How, then, should Christians live in this new world and prepare for that imminent event? The men who forged answers to this question were contemporaries who knew and influenced one another, though they did not always agree. They are now regarded as saints and "fathers" of the Church: Jerome (c. 340–420), who came from the northeastern edge of Italy, near the port of Aquilea; Ambrose (c. 340–397), who grew up in Trier and was eventually named bishop of Milan; and Augustine (354–430), born and raised in North Africa, where he became a bishop in later life.

Jerome: Translating the Christian Message

Jerome's signal contribution to the culture of the Roman West was his translation of the Bible from Hebrew and Greek into Latin. Known as the Vulgate or "common" version, it was not the first attempt to produce a Latin Bible—but it quickly became the standard, and remained so until the sixteenth century (see Chapter 13). Jerome's translation is vigorous, colloquial, and clear; its powerful prose and poetry would influence Latin authors for centuries. Jerome was also an influential commentator on the Bible's interpretation, encouraging readings that emphasized a passage's symbolic or allegorical significance, as well as its literal or historical meaning.

Jerome was not a notably original thinker, but he was an eloquent and effective translator of others' ideas as well as of others' words. He was among the first to argue that pagan learning could and should be studied by Christians as long as it was thoroughly adapted to Christian aims. The perennial problem, of course, was that one was always tempted to appreciate classical literature for its own sake, and not for the light it shed on Christian truths. Jerome himself never succeeded in subordinating his love for classical authors, especially Cicero, to his love for God. He liked to tell a story about a dream he'd experienced, in which he arrived at the gates of heaven and was asked by God if he was a Christian. When he replied that he was, God retorted, "You're not a Christian; you're a Ciceronian." Perhaps in an effort to compensate for this, Jerome became a rigorous ascetic and a fervent promoter of monasticism. He also held a narrow view of women's roles that exercised a strong influence on some later Christian teachers.

Ambrose and the Authority of the Church

Jerome was primarily a scholar. Ambrose, by contrast, was an aristocrat and man of the world who helped to define the relationship between the sacred authority of the Church and the secular authority of worldly rulers. As patriarch of the imperial administrative capital at Milan, he fearlessly rebuked the pious emperor Theodosius for a mismanaged massacre of innocent civilians in the Greek city of Thessalonian. Theodosius may have been the emperor, but until he did penance for his sins Ambrose refused to admit him into his church. On matters of faith, he declared, "The emperor is within the Church, not above the Church." Eventually, Theodosius capitulated and begged forgiveness of God's representative, Ambrose, in his cathedral at Milan.

Ambrose was also an admirer of Cicero—but because of his Stoicism, not his prose. He wrote an ethics handbook, *On the Duties of Ministers*, which drew heavily on Cicero's treatise *On Duties*, written nearly four centuries earlier for the senatorial elite of the Roman republic. Unlike Cicero, however, Ambrose argued that the motive and goal of human conduct should be reverence for God, not social or political advancement. Even more fundamentally, Ambrose argued that God assists all Christians by sharing with them the power of divine grace, but extends more grace to some Christians than to others. Ambrose's emphasis on the necessity and mystery of grace (Why does God give more grace to some than to others?) would be refined and amplified by his disciple, Augustine.

The Salvation of Saint Augustine

Apart from Jesus, Augustine is often considered the greatest of all Christianity's founders. He may be the most important Christian thinker of all time. His theology is essential to the doctrine of the medieval Church and thus to modern Catholicism, and it also had a profound effect on Martin Luther and on the development of Protestant Christianities (see Chapter 13). In our own twenty-first century, many Christian philosophers of various denominations describe themselves as neo-Augustinians.

Augustine's understanding of Christianity was the result of a long process of self-discovery, which he described in a remarkable book, the *Confessions*, a series of autobiographical reflections addressed to God. Augustine was not, as Jerome and Ambrose were, a confident Christian from the cradle. His father was not a Christian, and although his mother was, he scorned her influence and refused baptism. Full of ambition and eager to make his mark, he left North Africa for Italy as a young man, winning early fame as a teacher and charismatic orator. All the while, he gravitated from one philosophical system to another without finding intellectual or spiritual satisfaction. He regarded Christianity as a religion for fools, and only his increasing doubts about the alternatives (notably Manichaeism) and the appeal of Ambrose's teachings drove him to enquire further. After a spiritual epiphany described in his *Confessions*, Augustine decided to embrace Christianity at the significant age of thirty-three (the age when Jesus died). Yet his struggle to grasp and explain its paradoxes occupied him for the rest of his life. His skills as a preacher and commentator led to his rapid advancement in the Church hierarchy, and he returned to North Africa as the bishop of Hippo Regis in 395.

Although he led an extremely active life—when he died in 430, he was defending Hippo against the Vandals—Augustine still found time to write more than a hundred profound, complex, and powerful treatises analyzing the problems of Christian belief. All of these grapple with a basic question: if humanity is the creation of an omnipotent God whose nature is entirely good, why are human beings so profoundly sinful? Augustine was convinced of humans' innate capacity for evil, and he believed this tendency was evident even in babies. He adduced himself as a supreme example. In the *Confessions*, he remembers that he and a few other boys once stole some pears from a neighbor's garden, not because they were hungry or even because the pears were beautiful, but simply for the sake of doing something bad. He also recounted his many sexual adventures as a young man and recalled that rather than asking God's help in suppressing his desires he prayed, "O God, give me chastity—but not just now!" In short, he argued that the human inclination toward evil is innate. But how, if we are the creatures of a good God?

Augustine traced the origin of evil back to the Garden of Eden, where God had given Adam and Eve, the first human couple, the freedom either to follow his will or their own. Thereafter, God simply left Adam and Eve's descendants to do the same, by withdrawing from human beings the divine power (grace) by which they might overcome their own wills in order to follow his. All the evils that plague the world are thus the result of the human propensity to place one's own desires ahead of God's. This fact alone would justify God's condemnation of all mankind. But because God is merciful, he chose instead to save some human beings through the sacrifice of his son, Jesus.

Why only some? Because human beings are inherently sinful, Augustine reasoned, they cannot achieve salvation on their own; they need to be led to accept Jesus by an act of God's grace—hence the power of Augustine's own transformative experience, which led him to embrace Christianity *against his own will* but in accordance with God's. God alone makes this choice, and by granting grace to some and not to others he predestines a portion of the human race to salvation and sentences the rest to be damned. If this seems unfair, Augustine would answer that strict fairness would condemn everyone to hell. Moreover, he would say that the basis for God's choice is a mystery shrouded in his omnipotence—far beyond the realm of human comprehension.

Defending the City of God

Augustine's audience consisted of converted Christians and intelligent skeptics like himself. And after the sack of Rome in 410, he knew that some staunchly traditional Romans blamed Christianity for it. According to them, the attack on their city was the consequence of gross impiety, exemplified by the removal of the altar of Victory from the Senate chamber. In response, Augustine wrote one of his most famous works, *On the City of God*, a new interpretation of human history. He argued that mankind has always been divided into two opposing societies: those who live for the world and those who seek eternal life. The former belong to the City of Man, and their rewards are the riches, fame, and power they may win on earth, all of which are tainted by sin. Only those predestined to salvation, members of the City of God, will be saved on Judgment Day.

Although Augustine is the architect of much Christian theology, he believed that he was doing no more than drawing out truths from the Bible. But he also knew that many biblical texts are obscure and that a certain amount of education is needed to understand them. In consequence, he approved of some Christians' acquiring a classical education, as he himself had done, as long as they directed their learning toward its proper end: the study of the Bible. Along with Jerome, Augustine thus formulated the rationale for Christianity's preservation of the pagan past.

CLASSICAL LEARNING AND THE CHRISTIAN LIFE

Jerome, Ambrose, and Augustine were members of the first generation to grow up in a world where Christianity was legal, even normal. For three centuries there had been no such thing as a Roman Christian: this was a contradiction in terms. Now, however, many Romans *were* Christians. How could these identities be reconciled? As we have seen, none of these influential teachers wanted to discard the heritage of the past. But for all of them it posed serious challenges. Many new converts thought they could embrace both Christian and pagan beliefs simultaneously—and why not? Since the time of Socrates, philosophy had been characterized by its capacity to absorb and blend many competing ideas. Christian intellectuals wanted to be regarded as philosophers, but they also wanted to replace the doctrines of pagan philosophy with the doctrine of Christ. To do this, they needed to make classical learning applicable to a Christian way of life.

Preserving and Recycling the Classics

Reinterpreting classical culture for a Christian audience involved careful selection, something made easier by the fact that a gradual winnowing of Greek texts had already occurred in Alexandria and continued in Rome. Roman readers had little interest in the scientific works of an earlier age, and by the third century many extraordinary advances made by Hellenistic scientists (see Chapter 4) were ignored, simplified, or suppressed by popular authors like Galen and

THE CITY OF MAN. This image illustrating a late-medieval manuscript of Augustine's *City of God* displays the violence that characterizes the City of Man by showcasing one example from the Old Testament and another from Roman mythology: Cain kills his brother, Abel, while Romulus murders his brother, Remus. Its message is that all human forms of government are the product of human sin.

Ptolemy. Nor did the Romans have much interest in Greek philosophy, drama, or epic. Later Roman tastes ran toward comedies, novels, and pastiches of Latin classics. One favorite pastime consisted of rearranging the verses of Virgil's *Aeneid* so that they described sexual exploits. Christians, too, could play at this game. In the fourth century, Faltonia Betitia Proba (c. 322–c. 370), the wife of a Roman senator, used Virgil's poetry to replace Aeneas with Christ.

Those pagan authors whose works were most immediately useful to Christians, like Cicero and Virgil, therefore enjoyed continued celebrity. Those texts that had long educated students in the liberal arts were also preserved, alongside major classics of Latin poetry as well as histories that recorded the errors of Rome's pagan past. But texts that could not be readily adapted to Christian purposes were subjected to careful editing. One of the men who undertook this task was Anicius Manlius Severinus Boethius (*boh-EE-thee-uhs*, c. 480–524), an aristocrat attached to the court of Theodoric. He is often described as the "last of the Romans," and his goal was to preserve the best aspects of ancient learning by compiling a series of handbooks and anthologies which packaged and explained classical texts in ways appropriate for Christian readers.

Roman or Barbarian?

These two letters from Sidonius Apollinaris (c. 430–c. 480) illustrate the ways in which cultural assimilation was rapidly blurring the distinctions between "Roman" and "barbarian" in the West. Sidonius was himself the descendant of an illustrious Roman provincial family in Gaul. He was one of the most admired Latin stylists of his day, and although he eventually became a bishop and was regarded as a saint, his letter collection (from which these extracts are taken) tells us much more about the literary culture of Romano-Visigothic Gaul than it does about his Christianity. His two correspondents also exemplify this new hybrid culture. Arbogastes (ahr-go-BAHS-tees) was the Frankish governor of the Roman city of Trier (in what is now Germany). Syagrius (sigh-AG-ree-uhs) was from an ancient Roman family and became, effectively, the king of a large region now corresponding to northern France and Belgium.

Letter 4:17: Sidonius to his Friend Arbogastes

My honored Lord, your friend Eminentius has handed me a letter written by your own hand, a really literary letter, replete with the grace of a three-fold charm. The first of its merits is certainly the affection which prompted such condescension to my lowly condition, for if not a stranger I am in these days a man who courts obscurity; the second virtue is your modesty. . . . In the third place comes your urbanity, which leads you to make a most amusing profession of clumsiness, when as a matter of fact you have drunk deep from the spring of Roman eloquence and, dwelling by the Moselle, you speak the true Latin of the Tiber: you are intimate with the barbarians but are innocent of barbarisms, and are equal in tongue, as also in strength of arm, to the leaders of old, I mean those who were wont to handle the pen no less than the sword. Thus the splendor of the Roman speech, if it still exists anywhere, has survived in you, though it has long been wiped out from the Belgian and Rhenic lands: with you and your eloquence surviving, even though Roman law has ceased at our border, the Roman speech does not falter. For this reason . . . I rejoice greatly that at any rate in your illustrious breast there have remained traces of our vanishing culture. If you extend these by constant reading you will discover for yourself as each day passes that the educated are no less superior to the unlettered than men are to beasts.

Boethius devoted special attention to logic, translating several of Aristotle's treatises from Greek into Latin. Because Roman philosophers had never been much interested in logic, Boethius thus forged a crucial link between classical Greek thought and the new intellectual culture of Christianity. This is most evident in *The Consolation of Philosophy*, which he wrote in prison after Theodoric condemned him to death for treason. (The justice of the charge is unclear.) In this treatise, Boethius concludes that happiness is not found in earthly rewards such as riches or fame but in the "highest good," which is God. Yet he comes to this realization not through any reference to Christian revelation but through a series of imaginary conversations with "Lady Philosophy," the embodiment of wisdom. For the next millennium, Boethius's *Consolation* was one of the most read and imitated books in the West: the ultimate example of classical philosophy's absorption into the Christian worldview.

Monastic Education

The vital work of preserving selected classics and interpreting their meaning was increasingly done by monks, whose way of life had undergone some significant changes during the fourth century. Leaders of the monastic movement recognized that few men were capable of ascetic feats, and some disapproved of such showmanship. Rather, they advocated a more moderate approach and emphasized the benefits of communal life. In the Roman East, the most important figure in this new monasticism was Basil of Caesarea (c. 330–379). Basil's guidelines prohibited monks from engaging in prolonged fasts or extreme discipline of the flesh. Instead, he encouraged useful work and silent meditation.

In the Roman West, the most influential proponent of the monastic movement was a contemporary of Boethius,

Letter 5:5: Sidonius to his Friend Syagrius

You are the great-grandson of a consul, and in the male line too—although that has little to do with the case before us; I say, then, you are descended from a poet, to whom his literary glory would have brought status had not his magisterial glories done so . . . and the culture of his successors has not declined one whit from his standard, particularly in this respect. I am therefore inexpressibly amazed that you have quickly acquired a knowledge of the German tongue with such ease.

And yet I remember that your boyhood had a good schooling in liberal studies and I know for certain that you often declaimed with spirit and eloquence before your professor of oratory. This being so, I should like you to tell me how you managed to absorb so swiftly into your inner being the exact sounds of an alien race, so that now after reading Virgil under the schoolmaster's cane and toiling and working the rich fluency of [Cicero] . . . you burst forth before my eyes like a young falcon from an old nest.

You have no idea what amusement it gives me, and others too, when I hear that in your presence the barbarian is afraid to perpetrate a barbarism in his own language. The bent elders of the Germans are astounded at you when you translate letters, and they adopt you as umpire and arbitrator in their mutual dealings. . . . And although these people are stiff and uncouth in body and mind alike, they welcome in you, and learn from you, their native speech combined with Roman wisdom.

Only one thing remains, most clever of men: continue with undiminished zeal, even in your hours of ease, to devote some attention to reading; and, like the man of refinement that you are, observe a just balance between the two languages: retain your grasp of Latin, lest you be laughed at, and practice the other, in order to have the laugh of them. Farewell.

Source: Reprinted by permission of the publishers and the Trustees of the Loeb Classical Library from *Sidonius: Volume II–Letters,* Loeb Classical Library, Volume 420, prepared by W. H. Semple and E. H. Warmington from material left by W. B. Anderson, pp. 127–29, 181–83, Cambridge, MA: Harvard University Press, copyright © 1965 by the President and Fellows of Harvard College. Loeb Classical Library® is a registered trademark of the President and Fellows of Harvard College.

Questions for Analysis

1. For what qualities does Sidonius praise Arbogastes? What might have been the motive behind his extravagant compliments?

2. For what different qualities does Sidonius praise Syagrius? Given that Syagrius controlled much of the former Roman province of northern Gaul, what would have been his reasons for learning the local language?

Benedict of Nursia (c. 480–c. 547), the son of a Roman aristocrat. Benedict founded a monastery at Monte Cassino, southeast of Rome, where he urged his followers to adopt "a simple rule for beginners." Adapted from a much harsher set of precepts called *The Rule of the Master,* Benedict's *Rule* is notable for its brevity, flexibility, and practicality. It established a carefully defined cycle of daily prayers, lessons, and communal worship. It laid down guidelines for what monks should eat (a sufficiency of simple food, a small amount of wine, meat only for the sick or on special occasions), and how the work of the monastery should be performed. Physical labor was encouraged—idleness, Benedict declared, was "an enemy of the soul"—but there was also time for private study and contemplation. In all such matters, Benedict left much to the discretion of the leader of the monastery, whom all the monks were expected to obey without hesitation. This man was the abbot, from the Syriac word *abba,* "father."

Cassiodorus and the Classical Canon

Benedict was no admirer of classical pagan culture, but he did believe that monks must study the Bible in order to perform their daily cycle of prayers properly and to participate fully in a life of worship. This meant that they had to be educated along the lines prescribed by Augustine. And because many monks entered religious life as children, the monastery would need to provide schooling. Through this somewhat roundabout path, classical learning entered the monastic curriculum.

The man largely responsible for this was Flavius Magnus Aurelius Cassiodorus Senator (c. 490–c. 583), a younger contemporary of Benedict. Like Boethius, Cassiodorus (*cass-ee-oh-DOHR-uhs*) was attached to Theodoric's court and was for many years the secretary in charge of the king's correspondence. He also wrote a *History of the*

CASSIODORUS. This frontispiece from a Bible, produced in a monastery in Britain around the year 700, depicts Cassiodorus as a copyist and keeper of books. Monasteries were instrumental in changing the form of the book from the ancient scroll to the modern codex. Because their parchment pages were heavy, codices were customarily stored in cupboards, lying flat, as we see them here.

Goths, which depicted Theodoric's people as part of Rome's history. After Theodoric's death, Cassiodorus founded an important monastery at Vivarium in southern Italy. There, he composed commentaries on the Psalms as well as his most influential work, the *Institutes*.

Inspired by Augustine and his own classical education, Cassiodorus believed that study of classical literature was an essential preliminary to a proper understanding of the Bible. The *Institutes* is essentially a syllabus, a list of readings arranged so that a monk would begin with simpler, straightforward works of pagan literature before moving on to more difficult works and finally to the demanding study of theology. Cassiodorus thereby defined a classical canon that formed the basis of Christian education in the Roman West.

In order to ensure that his monks had access to the necessary readings, Cassiodorus encouraged the copying of books. He argued that this was precisely the sort of manual labor that Benedict had advocated. Under his influence, monasteries thus became engines for the collection, preservation, and transmission of knowledge. It is worth noting that nearly all the Greek and Latin texts on which we rely for our study of western civilizations survive because they were copied in monasteries.

Monasteries also developed and disseminated an important new information technology: the codex. For millennia, the book had been a scroll, a clumsy format that made searching for a particular passage difficult and con-

After You Read This Chapter

Visit StudySpace for quizzes, additional review materials, and multimedia documents. **wwnorton.com/web/westernciv18**

REVIEWING THE OBJECTIVES

- A number of historical factors shaped the way that Jesus's teachings were received. Describe the most important of these.
- The expansion of Rome and the strain on its central government posed significant challenges in the third century. How did Roman emperors respond?
- Christianity's acceptance as a legal religion changed it in profound ways. Why was this?
- In the fourth and fifth centuries, a new wave of migrations penetrated to the very heart of the empire. What made this possible?
- The differences between traditional Roman and Christian cultures were gradually reconciled through the efforts of Christian intellectuals. Why was this considered necessary?

fined the reader to one passage at a time. The codex facilitates indexing (from the Latin word for "finger") because a reader can flip back and forth among various pages and keep a finger in one place while looking at another. Codices also store information more safely and efficiently, because they compress many hundreds of pages within protective bindings. They are less wasteful, too, because texts can be copied on both sides of a page. They even make finding a given book easier, since titles can be written on the codex's spine. It's arguable, in fact, that the invention of the codex was more revolutionary than the invention of printing a thousand years later. Unless you are scrolling through a digital version, your copy of *Western Civilizations* is a codex.

CONCLUSION

Since the English historian Edward Gibbon published the first volume of *The Decline and Fall of the Roman Empire* in 1776 (a year when Britain's own empire suffered a setback), more has been written about "the fall of Rome" than on the passing of any other civilization. Gibbon himself blamed Christianity, depicting it as a debilitating disease that sapped the empire's strength. Others have accused the barbarians whose movements put pressure on Rome's frontiers. But even in the time of Julius Caesar, Roman moralists had already declared that Rome was in decline. Indeed, any self-respecting Roman republicans would say that Rome fell when Augustus came to power.

More recent scholarship has influenced the narrative offered in this chapter, which views transformation as a more accurate way of understanding this period. No civilization is static and unchanging; civilizations, like human beings, are living organisms. Indeed, any evidence of Rome's decline can also be read as evidence of its adaptability. The imperial policies of Septimius Severus and Diocletian responded to the realities of Rome's size and diversity. The settlement of frontier peoples in Rome's western provinces gave rise to hybrid polities that found new uses for Roman buildings, political offices, and laws. Through Christianity, the language, administrative structures, and culture of ancient Rome were preserved and extended. The flexibility of the Roman political system made this possible, because it was inclusive to a degree no modern empire has ever matched.

Still, this transformation changed what it meant to be Roman, to the extent that historians now call this period "late antiquity" to distinguish it from the classical world that preceded it. By the seventh century, indeed, so much had changed that the contours of three distinctive civilizations can be discerned, each one exhibiting different aspects of Roman influence and crystallizing around different regions of the former empire. We will explore each of these civilizations in Chapter 7.

PEOPLE, IDEAS, AND EVENTS IN CONTEXT

- What were the main differences between **JESUS** and other Jewish leaders of his day?
- How did **PAUL OF TARSUS** reach out to the peoples of the Hellenistic world? How did his teachings influence the development of early Christianity?
- In what ways did **DIOCLETIAN**'s division of the empire and his institution of the **TETRARCHY** respond to longstanding problems?
- How and why was Christianity changed under **CONSTANTINE**? What effects did this have on attitudes toward women and their role in the church?
- How did the relocation of the imperial capital to **CONSTANTINOPLE** contribute to the growing divide between the **GREEK EAST** and the **LATIN WEST**? How did the mass migrations of frontier peoples then transform the Latin West?
- What were the key contributions of **JEROME, AMBROSE**, and **AUGUSTINE** to the development of a specifically Christian outlook by the end of the fourth century?
- How did **BOETHIUS, BENEDICT**, and **CASSODORUS** reshape classical culture in the fifth century?

THINKING ABOUT CONNECTIONS

- In your opinion, which phenomenon had a more profound impact on Rome: the overextension of imperial power or the mass migration of peoples from Rome's frontier? Why?
- Few historians would now agree with the judgment of Edward Gibbon, who posited that Christianity destroyed the Roman Empire. But to what extent did Christianity alter the traditional values and infrastructure of the Roman state? Were these alterations inevitable?

Before You Read This Chapter

Rome's Three Heirs, 500–950

CORE OBJECTIVES

- **EXPLAIN** why Justinian's efforts to reunite the Roman Empire proved destructive.

- **DEFINE** the distinctive features of Byzantine culture.

- **IDENTIFY** the reasons for Islam's rapid expansion.

- **DESCRIBE** the relationship between monasticism and secular power in early medieval Europe.

- **UNDERSTAND** the importance of the Carolingian Empire.

Around the year 600, Anglo-Saxon tribes settled on the island of Britain were approached by missionaries sent from Rome. These Latin-speaking evangelists faced an enormous challenge: they had to find a way to convert tribal leaders and also to translate the central ideas of their faith into languages and concepts that made sense in a new cultural context. They also needed to look for ways to meld Roman practices with Anglo-Saxon ones, building churches on sacred sites and gradually turning the worship of pagan gods into the rituals of Christianity. An account of these negotiations comes down to us in a remarkable book written several generations later. In *The History of the English Church and People*, a monk named Bede (c. 672–735) described how Celtic and Anglo-Saxon peoples were uneasily united under the Roman Church and came to adopt Latin as a language of learning and worship. But he also shows how Roman Christian ideals were changed and adapted in the process, in order to meet new needs and express a new worldview.

This is but one example of the ways in which Rome's legacy was transmitted and transformed during the pivotal period known as the Middle Ages. This term is a vague one, and it doesn't begin to express the diverse realities—or perceptions—of the generations of people who lived during this thousand-year period. For the idea of "the Middle Ages" is really a modern invention: in the seventeenth century, intellectuals began to argue that an intermediate, "medieval period" (*medium ævum*) separated their own "modern age" from the glorious accomplishments of classical Greece and the empire of ancient Rome, which many European states were trying to emulate by establishing empires of their own. But in fact, it is arguable that the period between 500 and 1500 was the beginning of that "modern age." In this era, the foundations of modern political institutions were laid. In this era, the relationships among Judaism, Christianity, and Islam were first articulated—relationships that continue to affect our daily lives. In this era, three new civilizations became heirs of the Western civilizations formerly encompassed by the Roman Empire: the New Rome of Byzantium, the new empire of Islam, and the western European territories that looked increasingly to the Roman Church for leadership. Each of these interlocking civilizations preserved and modified different aspects of their shared Roman inheritance. Our world is still being shaped by the interactions among them.

JUSTINIAN'S IMPERIAL AMBITIONS

As we observed in Chapter 6, the eastern and western territories of Rome's empire were becoming divided along linguistic, cultural, and economic lines. By the end of the fourth century, this division also became political. The Ostrogothic conquest of Italy under Theodoric (r. 493–526)—which was supported by the imperial government—briefly placed Constantinople in a position to influence affairs in the old Roman

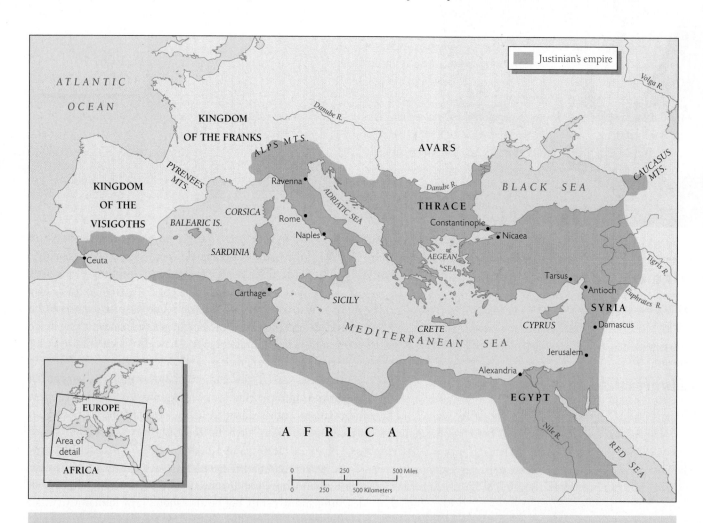

THE MEDITERRANEAN WORLD UNDER JUSTINIAN, 527–565. Compare this map with the one on page 192. Here, the green shading represents those regions controlled by Justinian. ▪ *What was the geographical extent of Justinian's empire?* ▪ *Which areas of the former Roman Empire did Justinian not attempt to reconquer?* ▪ *What may have been the strategy behind these campaigns?*

heartland. But none of Theodoric's short-lived successors was able to rule this territory effectively, and in 535 the Ostrogothic kingdom was overthrown in an attempt to reunify the Roman Empire.

The man responsible for this was Justinian (r. 527–65), the most ambitious emperor since Constantine. Although the empire that he ruled was largely Greek-speaking, Justinian himself came from the Latin-speaking province of Dardania (now Serbia). A student of history, he saw himself as the heir to the Principate established by Augustus, and like Augustus he was aided by an astute and determined wife, Theodora, who played an influential role in his reign. Although his efforts ultimately failed, they had a lasting influence on the entire Mediterranean world.

Justinian's Attempted Reconquest

Justinian's initial efforts to strengthen and reunite the Roman Empire seemed successful. In 533, his general Belisarius conquered the Vandal kingdom of northwest Africa, thereby facilitating campaigns in Ostrogothic Italy and Visigothic Spain. By 536, Belisarius appeared poised to occupy Rome's old homeland, where he was welcomed as a savior by some former subjects of the Ostrogoths. But these early victories were illusory. Although the Mediterranean was under Roman control, the human and financial costs of these campaigns drastically strained imperial resources. Belisarius's army in Italy was overextended, and Justinian's need to levy soldiers led to oppressive taxes on vitally important regions like Egypt and Syria, which undermined support for his imperial project. The Romans of Italy and North Africa, meanwhile, resented the costs their own "liberation" imposed on them.

Justinian's campaigns also distracted attention from dangers closer to Constantinople: in particular, the developing strength of Persia under the Sassanid dynasty. To respond to the Persians' advances, Justinian's successors were eventually forced to withdraw their troops from Italy and North Africa. This left both regions dangerously exposed to further invasions and yet still failed to guarantee the safety of the eastern frontier. Only a heroic reorganization of the empire's resources after 610 (see below) saved Constantinople, but it put an end to Justinian's dream of reunification.

The pressure and perils of warfare during this period were further exacerbated by a pandemic known as the Justinianic Plague, which broke out in 541–42 and which even afflicted Justinian himself (though he recovered). It was probably caused by the same bacteria that spawned the terrible Black Death of the fourteenth century (see Chapter 10), and it may have been just as deadly. Although the plague appears to have devastated the urban region around Constantinople with particular ferocity, it has recently been confirmed to be a global phenomenon, affecting regions from China (where it appears to have originated) to Scandinavia and reaching down into Africa and the Indian Ocean. It is estimated to have killed a large percentage of the world's population at that time, some 25 million people; and it would recur in some places every generation or so for the next 200 years. It certainly assisted in weakening Justinian's bid for extended imperial power, while at the same time strengthening the disruptive force of barbarian and Arab war-bands on the empire's frontiers. And ironically, it spread so rapidly and so far because of the very efficient infrastructures (roads, bridges, trading networks) that bound the Roman Empire together and linked it to its neighbors.

Justinian's Impact on the West

Justinian's wars proved more devastating to Italy than the previous incursions of barbarian peoples, almost as devastating as the plague named for him. Around Rome, the vital supply lines of the aqueducts were cut and the elaborate system of conduits, drainage ditches, and reservoirs was destroyed. Parts of the Italian countryside returned to marshland, and some areas would not be drained again until the twentieth century. In 568, a new people, the Lombards, took advantage of the chaos to conquer the northern third of the peninsula. Thereafter, Italy would be divided between Lombard territories in the north and imperial territories in the southeast, with Rome and its region precariously sandwiched between them. The controlling forces within these territories would change greatly over time, but this tripartite division remained the essential political configuration of Italy until the nineteenth century. In fact, it still divides Italian politics to this day.

Constantinople's control over North Africa lasted only a few generations longer. Weakened by religious conflict and heavy taxation, this area fell easily to invading Muslims in the seventh century, along with Egypt and the rest of Roman Africa (see below). When it did, Christianity in North Africa largely disappeared, although a vibrant Christian community continued to flourish in Ethiopia. Meanwhile, tensions between Arian Visigoths and their Latin subjects continued even after the Visigothic king officially converted in 587. This mutual hostility would subsist until the Visigothic kingdom, too, was largely absorbed by Islam. By the end of the eighth century, Christian rulers controlled only the northernmost parts of the Iberian Peninsula, and Al-Andalus (Muslim Spain) became part of a wider Islamic world.

The Codification of Roman Law

Justinian's most positive and lasting accomplishment was his codification of Roman law. This was a necessary project, and long overdue: since the time of the third-century jurists (see Chapter 5), the number of imperial statutes and legal decisions had multiplied, and the resulting body of law was both massive and self-contradictory. Moreover, conditions had changed so radically within the empire that many legal principles could no longer be applied. When Justinian came to power in 527, one of his first initiatives was to bring existing precedents into harmony with actual historical conditions and thereby to restore the prestige and power of the imperial office.

To carry out this work, Justinian appointed a team of lawyers under the supervision of a jurist called Tribonian. Within two years, this commission published the first result of its labors: the Code, a systematic compilation of imperial statutes which was later supplemented by another book, the Novels (*Novellae*, "new laws"), containing the legislation of Justinian and his immediate successors. By 532, the commission had also completed the Digest, a summary of the writings of Rome's great legal authorities, including the jurists of the Principate. Its final product was the *Institutes,* a textbook of legal principles. Together, these four volumes constitute the *Corpus Juris Civilis,* the "body of civil law."

Justinian's *Corpus* was a brilliant achievement. In the eastern Roman Empire, it immediately became the foundation on which all subsequent legal developments would rest. Although little known in western Europe for centuries, it eventually influenced the legal systems of many nations. The nineteenth-century Napoleonic Code—still the basis of law in France, Spain, much of Latin America, and the state of Louisiana—is essentially based on the *Corpus* of Justinian.

The *Corpus* also had a profound impact on political philosophy. Starting from the maxim that "what pleases the prince has the force of law," it granted unlimited powers to the emperor and was therefore adopted by early modern rulers as a foundation for absolutism (see Chapter 15). But the *Corpus* also provided some support for constitutional forms of government, because it maintained that a sovereign's powers are delegated to him by the people and that what

JUSTINIAN AND THEODORA. These sixth-century mosaics from the Church of San Vitale in the imperial capital of Ravenna (Italy) show the emperor and empress processing toward the main altar of the church carrying the holy vessels used for the consecration of bread and wine. ▪ *What do these images convey about the sacred and secular powers of both figures?*

is mandated by the people can also be taken away by them. Equally important is the fundamental principle that the state is a corporate body, not the extension of an individual's private property. The modern conception of the state as a public entity derives from the legal maxims of the *Corpus*.

THE ROMAN EMPIRE OF BYZANTIUM

With the failure of Justinian's project of imperial reunification, the history of the eastern Roman Empire can be said to enter a new phase. Indeed, many historians regard it as essentially a new entity, the Byzantine Empire, a name derived from the ancient port where Constantinople was situated. Byzantium thus became *one* of Rome's three heirs—not the sole heir of Roman authority, as Justinian had hoped. But according to the citizens of this empire, it never ceased to be Rome, and they were never anything but Romans. They saw themselves as carrying forward Roman traditions, values, and institutions under new circumstances.

As a result of Justinian's policies, however, this new Rome was struggling for survival. By 610, the Greek-speaking imperial dynasty that began with Heraclius (r. 610–41) was unable to extend its influence farther west than the Adriatic. Meanwhile, the Persians had conquered almost all of the empire's eastern and southern territories in Syria and Palestine. They had even plundered Jerusalem and carried off a precious relic believed to be part of the original cross on which Jesus had been crucified. With an enormous effort, Heraclius rallied his remaining military powers and routed the Persians, recapturing Jerusalem and retrieving the relic in 627.

But these gains were short-lived. Arab armies, inspired by the new religion of Islam, were able to profit from the empire's exhaustion. They soon occupied the recently reconquered Byzantine territories and claimed Jerusalem as a holy site for Muslims, too. They also absorbed the entire Persian Empire and rapidly made their way westward to North Africa. They then took to the sea, and in 677 attempted a naval conquest of Constantinople. Repulsed, they made another attempt in 717 by means of a concerted land and sea operation. This new threat was countered by the emperor Leo III (r. 717–41). Deploying keen strategy and a secret incendiary mixture known as "Greek fire" (of course, the Byzantines called it "Roman fire"), Leo's forces were able to defeat the Arabs. Over the next few decades, moreover, Byzantium reconquered most of Asia Minor, which remained the imperial heartland for the next 300 years.

Sources of Stability

In many ways, the internal politics of the Byzantine Empire were as tumultuous as the history of its changing neighborhood. Because all power was concentrated in the imperial court at Constantinople and because emperors followed their predecessors in claiming autonomous rule, opposition usually took the form of intrigue, treason, and violence. Indeed, Byzantine politics is now so famous for its cloak-and-dagger complexity that the word *byzantine* has come to denote devious machinations or elaborate systems of courtship and bureaucracy. In reality, though, many able rulers wielded their powers very effectively in Constantinople, where a centralized government continued to function even in times of upheaval. No polity in western Europe had anything resembling such effective mechanisms of government until a much later period.

Strong, self-perpetuating political institutions thus constituted a major source of stability in Byzantium and offer an explanation for the extraordinary longevity of the empire's core provinces: nearly a thousand years. The imperial bureaucracy in Constantinople regulated prices and wages, maintained systems of licensing, and controlled exports and trade. Its highly educated officials also supervised many aspects of social and cultural life, overseeing schools, the organization of the Orthodox Church, and the observance of religious rites and holidays. Even the popular sport of chariot racing—New Rome's exciting answer to gladiatorial combat—fell under strict supervision, as did the regulation of the various teams' fiercely competitive fans. Established bureaucracies also regulated the army and navy, the courts, and the diplomatic service, endowing these agencies with organizational strengths incomparable for their time.

Another source of stability was Byzantium's sound and well-managed economy, which was far superior to that of western Europe. Commerce and cities continued to flourish as they had done in late antiquity. Constantinople became a central emporium for Far Eastern luxury goods and western raw materials. The empire also nurtured and protected its own industries, most notably the manufacture and weaving of silk, and it was renowned for its stable gold and silver coinage. Nor was Constantinople the only great urban center. The Hellenistic capital Antioch and the bustling cities of Thessalonica and Trebizond were very large and prosperous. Any one of them would have dwarfed any western European city; Constantinople may have had a population of close to a million. In the West at this time, Paris was a village and Rome may have had a few thousand people living among the ruins.

THE SECRET WEAPON OF BYZANTIUM: "GREEK FIRE." This depiction of Greek fire in action illustrates a chronicle by John Skylitzes, a Byzantine historian who flourished in the eleventh century. This manuscript was copied in Sicily during the twelfth century and is now preserved in the Biblioteca Nacional de España in Madrid.

This emphasis on Byzantine trade and industry is justified because both were advanced and both provided most of the surplus wealth that sustained the state. But agriculture lay at the heart of the Byzantine economy, so much so that peasant farmers struggled to maintain their independence from large estates owned by wealthy aristocrats and monasteries. And as in the final centuries of the Roman republic, they were only able to do so with the help of legislation. When the aristocracy eventually gained control during the eleventh century, however, free peasants were transformed into impoverished tenant-farmers, as had been the case in Italy during the third century C.E. This was one of the less fortunate ways in which Byzantium resembled its ancient predecessor.

Orthodoxy, Iconoclasm, and Identity

Law, strong governance, and a thriving economy: viewed from our perspective, these seem to be the basis of Byzantine civilization. Yet the inhabitants of New Rome seem to have cared more about religious orthodoxy. On the one hand, their intense preoccupation with questions of doctrine could be a catalyst for political and social dissension; on the other hand, it endowed the empire's inhabitants with a sense of shared purpose and a shared identity. In old Rome, the *mos maiorum* had undergirded Roman pride and superiority (Chapter 5); in New Rome, Orthodox Christianity occupied the same fundamental place. The stakes of Byzantine doctrinal disputes were further heightened by the fact that emperors took an active role in them.

The most contentious issue, and one that came to a head in the eighth century, was a violent clash over the meaning and use of religious images, known as the Iconoclast ("image-breaking") Controversy. As we saw in Chapter 6, Christians had long been accustomed to expressing their devotion to Christ and the saints through the making and veneration of images. There was even a legend that the author of Luke's Gospel had been a painter, the maker of the first icon. At the same time, however, there was always an awareness that any representation of a holy person came close to being a form of idolatry, something that Jewish tradition strongly condemned and something that made Christians look like idol-worshipers in the eyes of their religious rivals, especially Muslims. Although both Latin and Orthodox Christians insisted that images were only *aids* to worship, not *objects* of worship, the line between the two was very fine.

In Byzantium, where the veneration of icons was an especially potent part of daily devotion, any suggestion that such images should be suppressed or destroyed was bound to be contentious. But that is precisely what the Iconoclasts advocated. They argued that honoring images was blasphemous because nothing made by human beings should be worshiped, an injunction expressed in the Ten Commandments given to Moses (Exodus 20:4). Moreover, they contended that Christ's divinity could not be represented artistically; it was beyond the power of even the most skilled craftsman. For their part, traditionalists retorted that the images themselves were never objects of worship; rather, icons were windows through which a glimpse of Heaven might be granted to human beings on earth.

The Iconoclast movement was initiated by the same Emperor Leo III who had saved Constantinople from invasion by Muslims, and it is even possible that the icono-clasm so central to Islamic belief (Qur'an, V. 92) played an influential role in his thinking. In other words, cracking down on icons may have been his attempt to answer one of Islam's greatest criticisms of Christianity. There may also have been political and financial considerations behind the campaign: by proclaiming a radical new religious movement, the emperor may have intended to strengthen his control over the Orthodox Church and thus to combat the growing power of monasteries. And indeed, the great monasteries of Byzantium were major producers of icons as well as books: the manufacture of both was considered a labor especially suited to the monastic life. So when the monasteries rallied to the cause of images, they were bitterly suppressed by Leo's successors, who took this opportunity to confiscate much of their wealth.

The Iconoclast Controversy was resolved toward the end of the eighth century in favor of the promoters of religious imagery, the Iconodules ("image servants"). But it had some long-lasting effects. One was the destruction of many artworks produced or preserved in Byzantium, by previous imperial edict. This means that examples of Christian artistry from the first eight centuries after Jesus's death are very rare and can be found mainly in Italy, Palestine, or Egypt, which were beyond the reach of the Iconoclast emperors. A second consequence was the widening of a religious and political breach between the Greek East and the Latin West. Prior to Emperor Leo's iconoclastic initiatives, the patriarch of Rome—known familiarly as "papa" in Latin slang—had often been a close ally of Byzantium's rulers. But iconoclasm called into question not only the veneration of images but the cult of the saints, and by extension the claims of papal primacy that were based on the Roman patriarch's claim to be Saint Peter's successor (see Chapter 6).

The ultimate defeat of iconoclasm crystallized some aspects of belief and practice that came to be characteristic of Byzantine identity. One was a renewed emphasis on the Orthodox faith of the empire as the key to its political unity and military success. Defense of religious tradition became the touchstone of political legitimacy, and vice versa. This emphasis on tradition helped Greek orthodoxy gain new adherents in the ninth and tenth centuries, but it subsequently enforced the hegemony of Constantinople's own Christian traditions, marginalizing those of Syria and Armenia. Fear of heresy also tended to inhibit freedom of thought and not just in religious matters. Although the Byzantine emperors eventually founded a university in Constantinople, its students and faculty were discouraged from expressing dissenting opinions or engaging in any significant degree of intellectual speculation—in marked contrast to the freewheeling intellectual atmosphere cultivated by the universities of western Europe (see Chapters 8 and 9).

DEVOTIONAL IMAGE—OR DANGEROUS IDOL? This icon of *Christos Pantokrator* ("Christ the Almighty") was painted in the sixth century and is one of the oldest such images in existence. It is preserved at the Orthodox monastery of St. Catherine on Mount Sinai (Egypt). ▪ *According to the proponents of iconoclasm, why would such an image be considered blasphemous?*

Competing Viewpoints

Debating the Power of Icons

The Iconoclast Controversy of the eighth century divided Byzantine society and was a factor in the growing division between the Latin Church of Rome and the Greek Orthodox Church. The excerpts below are representative of the two main arguments voiced at the time. The first is from a treatise by John of Damascus (c. 675–749), a Christian in the service of the Muslim Umayyad caliphs. The second is an official report issuing from the synod convened by the emperor Constantine V (r. 741–75) in 754. Constantine was carrying forward the iconoclastic policies of his father, Leo III.

John of Damascus, *On Holy Images*

Now adversaries say: God's commands to Moses the law-giver were, "Thou shalt adore the Lord thy God, and thou shalt worship him alone, and thou shalt not make to thyself a graven thing that is in heaven above, or in the earth beneath." . . .

These injunctions were given to the Jews on account of their proneness to idolatry. Now we, on the contrary, are no longer in leading strings . . . We have passed the stage of infancy, and reached the perfection of manhood . . . and know what may be imaged and what may not. . . . An image is a likeness of the original with a certain difference, for it is not an exact reproduction of the original. Thus, the Son is the living, substantial, unchangeable Image of the invisible God, bearing in Himself the whole Father, being in all things equal to Him, differing only in being begotten by the Father. . . . That which is divine is immutable; there is no change in Him, nor shadow of change. . . . God has noted and settled all that He would do, the unchanging future events before they came to pass. In the same way, a man who wished to build a house, would first make and think out a plan. Again, visible things are images of invisible and intangible things, on which they throw a faint light. Holy Scripture clothes in figure God and the angels. . . . If, therefore, Holy Scripture, providing for our need, ever putting before us what is intangible, clothes it in flesh, does it not make an image of what is thus invested with our nature, and brought to the level of our desires, yet invisible? . . . For the invisible things of God since the creation of the world are made visible through images. We see images in creation which remind us faintly of God, as when, for instance, we speak of the holy and adorable Trinity, imaged by the sun, or light, or burning rays, or by a running fountain, or a full river, or by the mind, speech, or the spirit within us, or by a rose tree, or a sprouting flower, or a sweet fragrance. . . .

Source: Excerpted from *St. John Damascene on Holy Images*, trans. Mary H. Allies (London: 1898), pp. 6–12.

Tradition and Innovation

Although Orthodox religion was central to the identity of Romans in Byzantium, so was their direct link with the Hellenistic past and the heritage of ancient Greece. Byzantine schools based their instruction on classical Greek literature to a degree that might seem surprising given the more tentative attitude toward classical learning in western Europe (see Chapter 6). Educated people around the Byzantine court who quoted only a single line of Homer could expect their listeners to recognize the entire passage from which it came. In the English-speaking world, only the King James Bible has ever achieved the same degree of cultural saturation. For the Romans of Byzantium, indeed, Homeric epics were a kind of sacred text: a literary model, an instructional textbook, and a guide to personal morality and wisdom.

Byzantine scholars also studied the philosophy of Plato and the historical prose of Thucydides intensively. By contrast, Aristotle's works were less well known, while many other philosophical traditions of antiquity were deemed

Canons of the Synod of 754

❝It is the unanimous doctrine of all the holy Fathers and of the six Ecumenical Synods, that no one may imagine any kind of separation or mingling in opposition to the unsearchable, unspeakable, and incomprehensible union of the two natures in the one *hypostasis* or person. What avails, then, the folly of the painter, who from sinful love of gain depicts that which should not be depicted—that is, with his polluted hands he tries to fashion that which should only be believed in the heart and confessed with the mouth? He makes an image and calls it Christ. The name *Christ* signifies *God and man*. Consequently it is an image of God and man, and consequently he has in his foolish mind, in his representation of the created flesh, depicted the Godhead which cannot be represented, and thus mingled what should not be mingled. Thus he is guilty of a double blasphemy—the one in making an image of the Godhead, and the other by mingling the Godhead and manhood . . .

like the Monophysites, or he represents the body of Christ as not made divine and separate and as a person apart, like the Nestorians.

The only admissible figure of the humanity of Christ, however, is bread and wine in the holy Supper. This and no other form, this and no other type, has he chosen to represent his incarnation. Bread he ordered to be brought, but not a representation of the human form, so that idolatry might not arise. And as the body of Christ is made divine, so also this figure of the body of Christ, the bread, is made divine by the descent of the Holy Spirit; it becomes the divine body of Christ by the mediation of the priest who, separating the oblation from that which is common, sanctifies it. . . .

Source: Excerpted from *The Seven Ecumenical Councils of the Undivided Church*, trans. H. R. Percival, in *Nicene and Post-Nicene Fathers*, 2d Series, eds. P. Schaff and H. Wace (repr. Grand Rapids, MI: 1955), pp. 543–44.

Questions for Analysis

1. To what other phenomena does John of Damascus compare the making of images? How do these comparisons help him to make his argument in favor of them?

2. To what phenomena do the theologians of the synod compare the making of images? Why do they declare the bread and wine of the Eucharist to be the only legitimate representations of Christ?

3. What is the significance of the fact that John of Damascus did not fall under the jurisdiction of the emperor of Byzantium but that of the Muslim Umayyad caliph? What conclusions can you draw about the relative freedoms in these two realms?

---

dangerous to orthodox belief. Paradoxically, Justinian, who had presided over the codification of ancient Roman (and thus pagan) law, registered his distrust of philosophy by shutting down the Athenian academies that had existed since Plato's day. Eventually, the emperor Alexius Comnenus (d. 1118) would ban the teaching of Aristotelian logic. The traditions of Greek scientific inquiry and the advances of Hellenistic science were also neglected. Tradition was more highly prized than originality, as was preservation over innovation. The benefit of this, for posterity, is that

Byzantium rescued Greek and Hellenistic writings for later ages. The vast majority of ancient Greek texts known today survive only because they were copied by Byzantine scribes.

In further contrast to western Europe, as we shall see, Byzantine classicism and learning were the products of an educational system that extended to the laity and was open to women as well as to men. Byzantine commitment to the formal education of women was especially unusual. Although most girls from aristocratic or prosperous families were educated at home by private tutors, they nevertheless mingled freely with their male counterparts at court or on social occasions, and many female intellectuals were praised for being able to discourse like Plato or Pythagoras. There were even female physicians in the Byzantine Empire, another extraordinary departure both from ancient tradition and from the practices of western Europe until the latter part of the nineteenth century.

Byzantine achievements in the realms of architecture and art are also remarkable. The finest example of both may be the church of Hagia Sophia (Greek for "Holy Wisdom") in Constantinople, constructed at enormous cost under the patronage of Justinian. It quickly came to define an architectural style unique to Byzantium. Its purpose was not to express pride in human accomplishment but rather to symbolize the mysteries of the Christian religion and the holy knowledge imparted by Christ to the soul of the believer. For this reason, the architects paid little attention to the external appearance of the building. The interior, however, was decorated with richly colored mosaics, gold leaf, colored marble columns, and bits of tinted glass set on edge to refract rays of sunlight like sparkling gems. Light appeared to be generated from within. The magnificent dome over its central square represented an unprecedented engineering feat and was upheld by four great arches springing from pillars at the four corners of the square. The result was an architectural framework that is marvelously strong but delicate. Its effect is heightened by the many windows placed around the dome's rim, which convey the impression that it floats in mid-air.

Many aspects of Byzantine arts and learning exerted strong influence on the craftsmen and scholars of western Europe through its continued economic and cultural contact with New Rome. The basilica of San Marco in Venice (c. 1063) reflects this influence distinctly, as do medieval mosaics in such cities as Ravenna and Palermo. Greek-speaking monasteries in southeastern Italy maintained especially close ties with their counterparts in the eastern empire, and many were allowed to practice the rituals of the Orthodox Church. Greek books—including the comedies of Aristophanes (Chapter 4)—were copied and preserved there. But much of the heritage of Western civilizations that was cultivated in Byzantium was largely inaccessible elsewhere in Europe, because the knowledge of Greek became increasingly rare.

HAGIA SOPHIA. This great monument to the artistry, engineering skill, and spirituality of Byzantium was built during the reign of Justinian. The four minarets at its corners were added in 1453, after Constantinople was absorbed into the empire of the Ottoman Turks. Hagia Sophia is now a mosque and a museum.

MUHAMMAD AND THE TEACHINGS OF ISLAM

In many ways, the civilization that formed around the religion of Islam mirrors the Roman Empire in its global reach and longevity; in this, it is truly one of Rome's heirs. Islam (Arabic for "submission") also resembles the early republic of Rome in that it demands from its followers not just adherence to common forms of worship but also to certain social and cultural norms. But whereas the Roman Empire came to undergird Christianity, and elevated it to the status of a major faith by legalizing it, the Islamic faith was itself the engine of imperial expansion. Indeed, Islam is unique among the major religions in the way it has *created* political empires rather than depending on them.

The Revelations of Muhammad

Islam had its beginnings in Arabia, a desert land considered so forbidding that neither the Romans nor the Persians sought to conquer it. Arabian society was tribal and did not revolve around urban settlements. Many Arabs were herdsmen, living off the milk of their camels and the produce

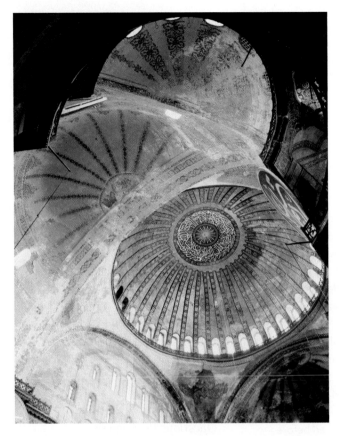

INTERIOR OF HAGIA SOPHIA. The revolutionary structure of the church, shown here, made it appear as if the enormous dome floated on light and air.

of desert oases. But like the Hittites in the second millennium B.C.E. (Chapter 1), their very mobility, ingenuity, and pioneering spirit made them excellent explorers and long-distance traders. In the second half of the sixth century, when protracted wars between Byzantium and Persia made travel dangerous for merchants, the Arabs quickly established themselves as guides, couriers, and guardians of transit routes between Africa and Asia.

As part of this process, towns began to emerge. The most prominent of these was Mecca, an ancient sacred site that lay at the crossroads of major caravan routes. Mecca was home to the Kaaba (*KAH-ah-bah*), a shrine housing the Black Stone worshiped by many Arabian tribes. (It may be a meteorite, and hence of celestial origin.) The tribe that controlled this shrine, the Quraish (*kur-AYSH*), thus came to dominate the economic and religious life of the whole region, forming an aristocracy of traders and entrepreneurs.

Muhammad, the founder of Islam, was a member of this tribe. He was born in Mecca about 570. Orphaned early in life, he entered the service of a rich widow whom he later married, thereby attaining financial security.

Until middle age he lived as a prosperous trader, little different from his fellow townsmen. But around 610, he experienced a spiritual epiphany. At this time, the Arab tribes worshiped many gods. Yet like the ancient Hebrews, they also acknowledged one god as more powerful. For the Hebrews, God was Yahweh; for the Arabs, Allah. But whereas the Hebrews' embrace of monotheism was a long and gradual process, Muhammad's conversion was sudden, the immediate consequence of revelation. Thereafter, Muhammad received further revelations that became the basis for his teachings, and by which he was persuaded to accept the calling of a prophet and to proclaim the new faith to his tribe.

At first, he was not very successful in gaining converts. In Mecca, tribal leaders probably feared that his teachings would diminish the importance of the Kaaba. The town of Yathrib to the north, however, had no such concerns. Its representatives invited Muhammad to live among them and to serve as judge and arbiter in local rivalries. Muhammad and a few loyal friends accepted this invitation in 622. Because this migration—in Arabic, the Hijrah (*HIJ-ruh*)—marks the beginning of Muhammad's wider influence, Muslims regard it as the beginning of time. Just as Christians date all events according to the birth of Jesus (see Chapter 6), so Muslims begin their dating system with the Hijrah.

Muhammad changed the name of Yathrib to Medina ("City of the Prophet") and established himself as the town's ruler. In so doing, he consciously organized his followers into a political community held together by shared economic ambitions as well as by a shared set of beliefs and rituals. Yet he did not abandon his desire to exercise political and prophetic authority among his own people, the Quraish. Accordingly, he and his followers began raiding Quraish caravans traveling beyond Mecca. The Quraish defended themselves, but they could not continue to operate an extensive commercial enterprise in the face of such violent threats. By 630, Muhammad had worn down the opposition and was invited back to Mecca. His kinsmen submitted themselves to his authority and accepted his teachings. Muhammad, for his part, ensured that the Kaaba's shrine was revered as Islam's holiest place, a status it maintains today. And because Mecca had long been a pilgrimage site and gathering place for tribes throughout Arabia, many people were exposed to Muhammad's teachings. At the time of his death in 632, Islam had become an established faith.

Muhammad and the Qur'an

As its name indicates, the faith of Islam calls for absolute submission to Allah, the same God worshiped by Jews and

A Sura from the Qur'an

The Qur'an *preserves the teachings of Muhammad in a series of* suras, *or chapters. Composed in verse forms that draw on much older traditions of Arabic poetry, they are meant to be sung or chanted. Indeed, the word* Qur'an *means "recitations," referring both to Muhammad's method of revealing divine truths and to the Muslim practice of memorizing and repeating portions of this sacred scripture.*

Sura 81: The Overturning

In the Name of God the Compassionate
the Caring

When the sun is overturned
When the stars fall away
When the mountains are moved
When the ten-month pregnant
    camels are abandoned
When the beasts of the wild
    are herded together   5
When the seas are boiled over
When the souls are coupled
When the girl-child buried alive
is asked what she did to deserve
    murder
When the pages are folded out   10
When the sky is flayed open
When Jahím [the Day of Reckoning]
    is set ablaze

When the garden is brought near
Then a soul will know what it
    has prepared
I swear by the stars that slide,   15
stars streaming, stars that sweep
    along the sky
By the night as it slips away
By the morning when the fragrant
    air breathes
This is the word of a messenger
    ennobled,
empowered, ordained before
    the lord of the throne,   20
holding sway there, keeping trust
Your friend [Muhammad] has
    not gone mad
He saw him on the horizon clear
He does not hoard for himself
    the unseen
This is not the word of a satan
    struck with stones   25

Where are you going?
This is a reminder to all beings
For those who wish to walk straight
Your only will is the will of God lord
    of all beings

Source: From *Approaching the Qur'an: The Early Revelations*, trans. Michael Sells (Ashland, OR: 1999), pp. 48–50.

Questions for Analysis

1. What impressions of Arab culture emerge from this sura? What does the litany of unlikely or mystical events reveal about the values of Muhammad's contemporaries?

2. How does Muhammad speak of himself and his role in society?

Christians. Hence, the Muslim saying "there is no god but Allah" is more accurately translated as "there is no divinity but God." For Muslims, the history and prophecies of the Hebrews are important components of their religion, as are the teachings of Jesus, who is venerated as a great prophet. But they consider Muhammad to be the last and greatest prophet, and the closest to God.

Muhammad's teachings are so essential because they established the rituals and practices that help to ensure salvation of all Muslims. These teachings are preserved in the sacred scripture of Islam, the Qur'an (*kuhr-AHN*), an Arabic word meaning "recitations." This is because Muhammad recited his revelations to his listeners, and these were eventu-

ally gathered together and transcribed, a process that continued after Muhammad's death. Unlike the Christian Gospels, which offer different perspectives on Jesus's ministry and which were recorded a generation or two after his death, the Qur'an is considered a direct link with Muhammad. It is also unlike most books of the Bible because it takes the form of poetry, drawing on ancient genres of Arabic song.

Like Christianity, Islam teaches that a day of judgment is coming—and soon. On this day, the righteous will be granted eternal life in a paradise of delights, but wrongdoers will be damned to a realm of eternal fire. Every person is therefore offered a fundamental choice: to begin a new life of divine service or to follow their own scholar qualified to comment on matters of faith, who may also act as a judge in disputes (as Muhammad had done in Medina). Although Muslims value the opportunity to come together for prayer, there is no prescribed liturgy as in the Roman and Orthodox Churches. Like Judaism, Islam emphasizes the inextricable connection between religious observance and daily life, between spirituality and politics. There is no opposition of sacred and secular authority, as in Christianity. But in marked contrast to Judaism, Islam is a religion that aspires to unite the world in a shared faith. This means that Muslims, like Christians, consider it their duty to engage in the work of conversion. This further means that there will inevitably be competition between the followers of these faiths, as both try carry out this mission.

THE WIDENING ISLAMIC WORLD

As we have frequently noted, the death of any charismatic leader precipitates a series of crises. Muhammad and Alexander the Great represent very different types of leadership, but both created communities whose very survival seemed to depend on that leadership. Neither designated his own successor, and both left behind a number of close followers who disagreed as to the proper uses of the power they had inherited. Although the very survival of Islam seemed unlikely after Muhammad's death, within a generation it had come to encompass much of the ancient Near East.

The Arabic Conquest of the West

Muhammad's closest followers were his father-in-law, Abu-Bakr (ah-boo-BAHK-uhr), and an early convert named Umar. After Muhammad's death, these two men took the initiative by naming Abu-Bakr *caliph*, a word meaning "deputy" or "representative." In this capacity, Abu-Bakr began a campaign to subdue various tribes that had been loyal to Muhammad but were not willing to accept his own authority as Muhammad's successor. In the course of this, Abu-Bakr's forces began to move northward beyond the borders of Arabia, where they met only minimal resistance from Byzantine and Persian armies.

When Abu-Bakr died two years later, he was succeeded as caliph by Umar, who continued to direct his growing warrior bands against Byzantium and Persia. In the following years, Arab victories were virtually continuous. In 636, the Arabs routed a Byzantine army in Syria and then

THE KAABA. This holy shrine remains the focus of worship for all Muslims, especially during the annual pilgrimage to Mecca. According to legend, Muhammad resolved a dispute among several tribes as to which should have the honor of lifting the Black Stone into place when the Kaaba was rebuilt. Muhammad's solution was to invite representatives of the tribes to hold the four corners of a carpet and to lift the stone together while he himself directed its placement. ▪ *What is the significance of this story?* ▪ *What message does it convey about the Prophet's important role in his own society?*

path. If they choose to follow God, they will be blessed; if they do not, God will turn away from them. Thus the only sure means of achieving salvation is observance of the Five Pillars of the faith: submission to God's will as described in the teachings of Muhammad, frequent prayer, ritual fasting, the giving of alms, and an annual pilgrimage to Mecca (*Hajj*).

Unlike Christianity, Islam is a religion without sacraments or priests. It more closely resembles Judaism as it developed after the Diaspora, when Jews no longer had access to the Temple and no need for a Temple priesthood but instead gathered around a master teacher (*rabbi*). Similarly, Muslims often rely on a community leader (*imam*) or quickly swept over the entire area, occupying the leading cities of Antioch, Damascus, and Jerusalem. In 637, they destroyed the main army of the Persians and took the Persian capital of Ctesiphon. The rest of the realm offered little resistance. By 651, the Arabian conquest of the entire Persian Empire was virtually complete.

Islamic forces now turned westward toward North Africa, capturing Byzantine Egypt by 646 and extending their control throughout the rest of North Africa during the following decades. Attempts to capture Constantinople in 677 and 717 were not successful, as we noted earlier, but in 711 the Arabs crossed from North Africa into Visigothic Spain and quickly absorbed most of that territory, too. Within less than a century, followers of Islam had conquered the ancient Near East and much of the Roman Mediterranean; in the process, the desert-dwelling Arabs had transformed themselves into the world's most daring seafarers.

How can we explain this prodigious achievement? On a basic level, what motivated the Arabs had motivated the Sumerians, the Neo-Assyrians, the Greeks, the Macedonians, and the Romans: the search for richer territory and new wealth. There is little evidence that Arab Muslims attempted to convert subject peoples to the faith of Islam at this time. Instead, they aimed to establish themselves as a superior ruling class. Yet religious enthusiasm certainly played a crucial role in forging a shared identity among tribes hitherto at war with one another. This identity and sense of superiority must have been further strengthened by the absence of any serious opposition. Indeed, many of the local populations living within the Persian and Byzantine empires were restive and exhausted by the demands of these far-reaching imperial bureaucracies. To them, conquest brought deliverance. The Arabs did not demand that Jews or Christians convert to Islam, and because they exacted fewer taxes than the Byzantines and the Persians, they were often

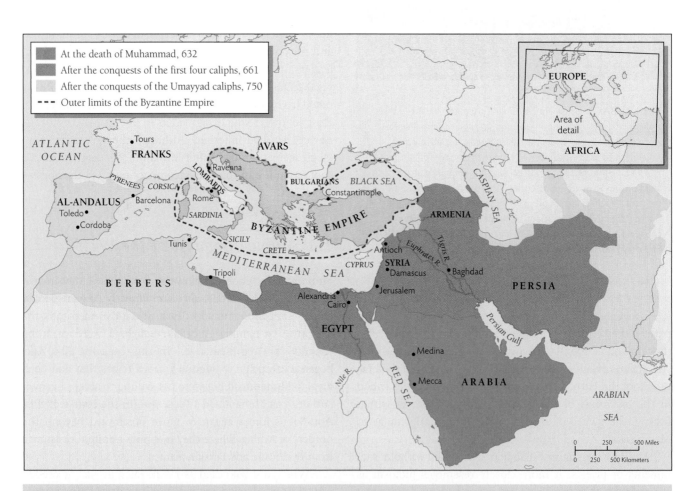

THE EXPANSION OF ISLAM TO 750. This map shows the steady advance of Islam, through Arab conquests, from the time of Muhammad to the middle of the eighth century. ▪ *What was the geographical extent of Islam in 750?* ▪ *What role did the Byzantine Empire play in the expansion of Islam?* ▪ *What conclusions can you draw regarding the period of especially rapid expansion in the generation after Muhammad's death?*

preferred to the old rulers. For all these reasons, Islam quickly spread over the territory between Egypt and Iran, and has been rooted there ever since.

The Shi'ite–Sunni Schism

As these Arab conquests widened the world of Islam, disputes continued to divide the Muslims of Mecca. When the caliph Umar died in 644, he was replaced by a member of the Umayyad (oo-MY-yad) family, a wealthy clan that had resisted Muhammad's authority. Opponents of this new caliph, Uthman, rallied instead around Muhammad's cousin and son-in-law, Ali, whose family ties to Muhammad made him seem a more appropriate choice. When Uthman was murdered in 656, Ali's supporters declared him the new caliph. But Uthman's powerful family refused to accept this. Ali was murdered and another member of the Umayyad family replaced him. From 661 to 750, this Umayyad dynasty ruled the Islamic world, establishing its capital at Damascus in Syria.

THE GREAT UMAYYAD MOSQUE AT DAMASCUS. This mosque was built by Caliph al-Walid between 705 and 715. Byzantine influence is apparent in its arched colonnades, its mosaics, and its series of domes, all of which were replicated in much subsequent Islamic architecture. The mosaic over the central doorway, shown here, indicates that the visitor is entering paradise. The mosque was constructed on the foundations of a Roman temple and also incorporates a later Christian shrine dedicated to Saint John the Baptist. ■ *Why would the caliph have chosen this site for his mosque?*

Ali's followers, however, did not accept defeat. They formed a separate group known as the Shi'ites (from *shi'a*, the Arabic word for "faction"). The Shi'ites insisted that only descendants of Ali and his wife, Muhammad's daughter Fatimah, could legitimately rule the Muslim community. Moreover, the Shi'ites did not accept the customary religious practices (*sunna*) that had developed under the first two caliphs who succeeded Muhammad— his father-in-law Abu-Bakr and his disciple Umar. Hence those Muslims who supported the Umayyad family and who *did* regard these customs as binding were called Sunnis. This division between Shi'ites and Sunnis has lasted until the present day. Often persecuted by the Sunni majority as heretics, Shi'ites consider themselves the only true exponents of Islam. Today, Shi'ites predominate in Iran and are the largest single Muslim group in Iraq, yet they constitute only one-tenth of the world's Muslims.

The Umayyad and Abbasid Dynasties

The political triumph of the Umayyads in 661 and the military conquests of their supporters created a strong state centered on Damascus, formerly an administrative capital of the Roman Empire. And in many ways, the Umayyad Caliphate functioned as a Roman successor state; it even continued to employ Greek-speaking bureaucrats trained in the techniques of Byzantine governance. Through these means, the Umayyads dominated the Mediterranean for several generations.

But the failure of their two massive attacks on Constantinople checked their power, which was also being challenged by a rival dynasty, the Abbasids, who claimed descent from one of Muhammad's uncles and who regarded the Umayyads as usurpers. In 750, the Abbasids led a successful rebellion with the help of the Persians, forcing the Umayyads to retreat to their territories in Al-Andalus (Spain). In contrast with the Umayyads, the Abbasid Caliphate stressed Persian elements over Roman ones. Symbolic of this change was the shift in capitals from Damascus to Baghdad, where the second Abbasid caliph, al-Mansur (r. 754–75), built a new city near the ruins of the old Persian capital. The Abbasid caliphs also modeled their behavior on that of Persian princes and their administration on the autocratic rule of the former Persian Empire, imposing heavy taxation to support a large professional army and presiding over an extravagantly luxurious court. This is the world described in the *Arabian*

Nights, a collection of stories written in Baghdad under the Abbasids. The dominating presence in these stories is Harun al-Rashid, who ruled from 786 to 809. His reign marked the height of Abbasid power.

Meanwhile, the Umayyad dynasty continued to rule in Spain and continued to claim that it was the only legitimate successor of Muhammad. Relations between the Umayyads of Al-Andalus and Abbasids of Persia were therefore very cold; but because their realms were far apart, the hostility between them rarely erupted into war. Instead, the two courts competed for preeminence through literary and cultural patronage, much as the Hellenistic kingdoms had done. Philosophers, artists, and especially poets flocked to both. The *Arabian Nights* was one product of this rivalry in Baghdad. Not to be outdone, the caliphs at the Spanish capital of Córdoba amassed a library of more than 400,000 volumes—at a time when a monastery in western Europe that possessed 100 books qualified as a major center of learning. Nothing remotely comparable had been seen in the Mediterranean since the time of the Ptolemies in Alexandria.

ARABIC CALLIGRAPHY. Muslim artists experimented with the art of calligraphy to make complex designs, sometimes abstract but often representing natural forms. This ink drawing on paper actually incorporates Arabic words. It dates from the seventh century, and also represents the Muslim mastery of papermaking.

Islamic Commerce and Industry

Alongside its political and military triumphs, the transformation of tiny settlements into thriving metropolitan commercial centers is one of Islam's most remarkable achievements. So is the Arabs' capacity to adapt themselves to life in highly urbanized regions and to build on the long-established commercial infrastructures of Egypt, Syria, and Persia. Conversion to Islam further increased the economic reach of this infrastructure as trading contacts grew in tandem with the growth of the Islamic world. By the tenth century, Arab merchants had penetrated into southern Russia and equatorial Africa and had become masters of the caravan routes that led eastward to India and China. Ships from the Muslim world established new trade routes across the Indian Ocean, the Persian Gulf, and the Caspian Sea, and for a time dominated the Mediterranean as well.

The growth of Muslim commerce in this period was driven and sustained by a number of important new industries. Mosul, in Iraq, was a center for the manufacture of cotton cloth; Baghdad specialized in glassware, jewelry, pottery, and silks; Damascus was famous for its fine steel and for its woven-figured silk known as "damask"; Morocco and portions of Al-Andalus were both noted for leatherworking; Toledo also produced excellent swords. Drugs, perfumes, carpets, tapestries, brocades, woolens, satins, metal goods, and a host of other products turned out by skilled artisans were carried throughout the Mediterranean world. They were also carried into central Asia, along the network of roads to China that came to be known as the Silk Road, after the most prized commodity for which these goods were traded. With them went the Islamic faith, which took root among some peoples of modern India, Pakistan, and Afghanistan.

One commodity in particular deserves special mention: paper. Muslim Arabs and Persians learned papermaking from the Chinese and became masters of the art in their own right. By the end of the eighth century, Baghdad alone had more than a hundred shops where blank paper or books written on paper were sold. Paper was cheaper to produce, easier to store, and far easier to use than papyrus or parchment. As a result, paper replaced papyrus in the Muslim world by the early eleventh century—even in Egypt, the heartland of papyrus production for almost 4,000 years.

The ready availability of paper brought about a revolution. Many of the characteristic features of Islamic civilization—bureaucratic record keeping, high levels of literacy and book production (especially copies of the Qur'an), even the standard form of cursive Arabic script known as Kufic—would have been impossible without the widespread availability of paper. Only in the thirteenth century would western Europeans master papermaking, but they would still continue to rely on the more durable parchment made from animal hides for the copying of most books and documents. It was not until the advent of print that paper began to replace parchment as the reading and writing material of western Europe (see Chapter 12).

Mobility, Opportunity, and Status

As the reach of Islam extended through conquest and commerce, so Muslim culture became highly cosmopolitan, blending Arab customs with the civilizations of Byzantium and Persia, which were themselves the heirs of ancient empires stretching back to the time of Hammurabi's Babylon. The preeminence of trade and ease of travel also increased geographical mobility, and therefore social mobility. Muhammad's teachings further encouraged social mobility because the Qur'an stressed the equality of all Muslim men. At the courts of Baghdad and Córdoba, therefore, careers were open to men of talent, regardless of birth or wealth. Because literacy was remarkably widespread, many could rise through education and achieve top offices through enterprise and skill.

For those men wishing instead to embrace the religious life alone, Islam offered two main alternatives. One was that of the *ulama*, a learned man whose studies qualified him to offer advice on aspects of religious law and practice. These men often exerted great influence on the conduct of public life. Complementary to them were the Sufis, mystics who might be equated with Christian monks were it not for the fact that they seldom withdrew from the life of the community. While the ulama stressed adherence to religious law, the Sufis stressed individual contemplation and the cultivation of spiritual ecstasy. Some Sufis were "whirling dervishes," so known in the West because of their mystical dances; others were *faqirs*, associated in the West with snake charming; still others were quiet, meditative men. Sufis were usually organized into brotherhoods and eventually made many successful efforts to convert the peoples of Africa and India to Islam. Sufism also provided a channel for the most intense religious impulses. The ability of the ulama and the Sufis to coexist is testimony to the cultural pluralism of the Islamic world.

The absence of comparable careers for religious women, even comparable to those available to Christian nuns, is a reminder of the limits often imposed by gender. There are significant exceptions, of course. For example, Muhammad's favored wife, Aisha (*ah-EE-sha*, d. 678), was revered as a scholar and played an important role in the creation and circulation of *hadith* (Arabic for "narrative"): stories and sayings that shed light on the Prophet's life and teachings. But in general, women did not benefit from Muslim egalitarianism and opportunity. They were considered valuable but mostly as indicators of a man's wealth and status. The Qur'an allowed any Muslim man to marry as many as four wives, which often meant that the number of women available for marriage was far smaller than the number of men who desired to marry. This made for intense competition, and those men who had wives and daughters needed to ensure that their prized assets were safeguarded. So women were usually kept from the sight of men who were not members of the family, or trusted friends. Along with female servants and the concubines also owned by a wealthy man, they were housed in a segregated part of the residence called the *haram* ("forbidden place"), guarded by eunuchs (men, usually sold as slaves, who had been castrated prior to adolescence). Within these enclaves, women vied with one another for precedence and worked to advance the fortunes of their children. But this was often the only form of power they could exercise.

Islam's Neighbors

For the inhabitants of Byzantium, the triumph of the Abbasid Caliphate in the eighth century released the Mediterranean from the pressures of Umayyad expansion. Farther west, the Franks of Gaul also benefited from the advent of the Abbasids. Because an Umayyad dynasty still controlled Al-Andalus, the great Frankish ruler Charlemagne (*SHAHR-leh-mayn*, r. 768–814) could counter these neighboring Muslims' power by maintaining strong diplomatic and commercial relations with the more distant Abbasid Caliphate. The most famous symbol of this connection was an elephant called Abul Abbas, a gift from Harun al-Rashid to Charlemagne. More important, however, was the flow of silver that found its way from the Abbasid Empire north through Russia and the Baltic into the Rhineland, where it was exchanged for Frankish exports of furs, wax, honey, leather, and especially slaves—Europeans, often Slavic peoples, who were captured and sold for profit by other Europeans. Through these channels, jewels, silks, spices, and other luxury goods from India and the Far East also flowed north and west into Frankish territory. These trading links with the Abbasid world helped fund the extraordinary achievements of Charlemagne's own empire, which had a lasting effect on the culture and politics of Europe.

Past and Present

The Meanings of Medievalism

The people who lived during the thousand-year period that we call the Middle Ages didn't think of themselves as "medieval." And indeed, this modern term tends to be used to describe modern phenomena—whether things that we seek to condemn (terrorism, persecution) or that we wish to glorify. The romantic image of Joan of Arc, on the left, was used to rally Americans to the cause of France and its allies during World War I. The image on the right shows warfare as imagined by the game called *Arthur II*.

 Watch related author interview on StudySpace
wwnorton.com/web/westernciv18

THE CONVERSION OF NORTHWESTERN EUROPE

At the end of the sixth century, the Frankish chronicler Gregory of Tours (c. 538–594) considered himself to be a Roman, living in a Roman world of towns, trade, and local administration. Gregory was proud of his family's senatorial status and took it for granted that he and his male relatives should be bishops who ruled, by right of birth and status, over their cities and the surrounding countryside. Like others of his class, Gregory still spoke and wrote Latin—a rather different Latin from the polished prose of Cicero but a Latin that would certainly have been comprehensible to the Romans of the republic. Although Gregory was aware that the western territories of the Roman Empire were now ruled by Frankish, Visigothic, and Lombard kings, he regarded at least some of these kings as Roman succes-

sors because they ruled in accordance with Roman models. In the case of the Franks, the king even ruled with the approval of the Roman emperor in Constantinople. It was also a source of satisfaction to Gregory that all these barbarian kings had converted to Roman Christianity and no longer embraced the heresy of Arianism. This, too, reinforced their *romanitas* and lent legitimacy to their rule.

Two hundred years later, the greatest of all Frankish kings, Charlemagne (742–814), was crowned as a new kind of Roman emperor in the West. By this time, there was no longer a sense of direct continuity with the earlier Roman world or a sense of obligation to the Roman emperor in Byzantium. When intellectuals at Charlemagne's court set out to reform the political, religious, and cultural life of their time, their goal was to revive a Roman Empire from which they considered themselves estranged. They sought a *renovatio Romanorum imperii*, "a renewal of the empire of the Romans." This awareness of a break with the Roman past developed during the seventh century, and was the consequence of profound economic, religious, and cultural changes.

Economic and Political Instability

Even though the economy of the Roman Empire had become increasingly regionalized from the third century C.E. onward (see Chapter 6), the Mediterranean remained a crucial nexus of trade and communication. Gold coinage continued to circulate in both the eastern and the western provinces; a luxury trade in silks, spices, swords, and jewelry continued to move west; and slaves, wine, grain, and leatherwork still moved east from Gaul, Hispania, and North Africa toward Constantinople, Egypt, and Syria. By about 650, however, this Mediterranean world became more disintegrated. This was partly a result of Justinian's failed efforts to reconquer the empire's western territories, but imperial overtaxation of agricultural land, especially in Egypt and North Africa, also played a role. So did the temporary disruptions to traditional trade routes caused by Arab raiders—temporary, because Muslim merchants and rulers would soon do much to reconstruct and encourage patterns of commerce.

But the most significant causes of economic instability in northwestern Europe were internal, not external. The cities of Italy, Gaul, and Hispania could no longer maintain their walls, their public buildings, and their urban infrastructures as they had done under the Roman Empire. Although Christian bishops and their aristocratic kinsmen still governed from these cities and continued to provide a market for certain kinds of luxury goods, barbarian kings and their nobles were moving to the countryside during the seventh century, living as much as possible from the produce of their own estates rather than purchasing their supplies in the marketplace. At the same time, much agricultural land was passing out of cultivation. The slaves or servile peasants who had farmed the large plantations for hundreds of years had no efficient Roman state to enforce their obedience. They were able to become more independent—yet they were also less effective, working just a few acres by themselves. Productivity declined, as did revenues from tolls and taxes.

The systems of coinage that circulated in western Europe were also breaking down, which meant that wealth ceased to be readily portable, hindering long-distance exchange. The Arab conquests may have further reduced the supply of gold available in western Europe, because it was now being channeled eastward. But in any case, gold coins were too valuable to be useful in a local market economy. When we find evidence of such coins in western Europe at this time, they are more likely to have been plundered, hoarded, or given as gifts rather than used to facilitate commerce. By the 660s, those rulers who were still in a position to mint coins and guarantee their value had shifted from a gold to a silver coinage. Indeed, Europe would remain a silver-based economy for the next thousand years, until the supply of gold from European conquests in Africa and America once again made a gold standard viable (see Chapter 12).

As a result of these processes, western Europe came to rely on a two-tier economy of a kind that had not been necessary in any Western civilization since the Lydians introduced a standardized currency in the sixth century B.C.E. (see Chapter 2). Gold, silver, and luxury goods circulated among the very wealthy, but most people relied on barter and various substitute currencies to facilitate transactions. Lords collected rents from their peasants in food or labor, but then found it difficult to convert these in-kind payments into the weapons, jewelry, and silks that brought prestige in aristocratic society. This was problematic not only for social reasons but for political ones: the power of lords depended on their ability to bestow rich gifts on their followers (see *Interpreting Visual Evidence* on pages 230–31). When they could not acquire these items through trade, they had to win them through plunder and extortion. Either way, the process led to violence.

The successful chieftains of this era therefore tended to be those whose areas of influence adjoined wealthy but poorly defended territories that could be easily attacked or blackmailed. Such "soft frontiers" provided warlords and kings with land and booty which they could then distribute to their followers. Successes of this sort would bring more followers to a lord's service, allowing him to further extend his influence; and as long as more conquests were made, the process of amassing power and wealth would continue. But power acquired through plunder and conquest was inherently unreliable. A few defeats might speedily reverse the fortunes of the lords reliant on it, leaving their followers to seek plunder elsewhere.

Another factor contributing to the instability of power in this world was the difficulty of ensuring its peaceful transfer. The barbarian rulers who established themselves during the mass migrations of the fifth and sixth centuries did not come from the traditional royal families of their peoples, and thus they faced opposition from many of their own warriors. Moreover, the groups who took possession of territories within the western Roman Empire during these years were rarely (if ever) composed of a single affinity group; they were usually made up of many different tribes, including a sizable number of displaced Romans. Such unity as they possessed was largely the creation of the charismatic chieftain who led them, and this charisma was not easily passed on by inheritance.

Interpreting Visual Evidence

The Ship Burial of Sutton Hoo

The two most impressive finds in the history of British archaeology have been made by amateurs. The most recent, in the summer of 2009, was the largest hoard of worked gold and silver ever found in one place (more than 5 kilograms of gold and 2.5 kilograms of silver; image A), discovered by a man in Staffordshire walking over a neighbor's farm with a metal detector.

The hoard's extraordinary value and range of artifacts—and their historical implications—can only be guessed at now; even the dating is inconclusive.

The other find, made in 1939, was a royal gravesite dating from the seventh century (image B), which many scholars believe to be the tomb of King Redwald of East Anglia, described by Bede as a baptized Christian who refused to give up the worship of his ancestral gods. The king's body was placed in a wooden

structure in the middle of a ninety-foot-long ship that had been dragged to the top of a bluff (a *hoo*), eleven miles from the English Channel. The ladder in the photograph of the original excavation reaches into the burial chamber.

The contents of the grave included:

- a lamp and a bronze bucket that had been suspended from a chain

- a ceremonial helmet (image C) modeled on those worn by Roman cavalry officers

A. The Straffordshire hoard, found in 2009.

B. The original excavation of the burial chamber at Sutton Hoo, 1939.

The Prosperous Kingdom of the Franks

Of all the groups that set up kingdoms in western Europe during the fifth and sixth centuries, only the Franks succeeded in establishing a single dynasty from which leaders would be drawn for the next 250 years.

This dynasty reached back to Clovis (r. c. 481–511), a warrior-king who established an alliance between his family and the powerful bishops of Gaul by converting to Roman Christianity—emulating the example of Constantine on many levels. Clovis's family came to be known as the Merovingians, after his legendary grandfather just before the withdrawal of the legions from Britain in 410—but decorated like helmets found in eastern Sweden

- a sword and a large, circular shield, resembling those found in Swedish burial sites

- exquisitely crafted belt buckles and shoulder clasps (image D), made of gold and garnet, and worked with designs

- a pair of silver spoons with long handles, possibly crafted in Byzantium, and inscribed in Greek with the names PAULOS and SAULOS (Paul and Saul)

- a large silver dish (72 cm in diameter) made in Byzantium between 491 and 518

- a bronze bowl from the eastern Mediterranean

- a six-stringed lyre in a bag made of beaver skin, similar to lyres found in Germany

- a purse containing thirty-seven gold coins, each from a different Merovingian mint, the most recent datable to the 620s

- heaps of armor, blankets, cloaks, and other gear

Questions for Analysis

1. What do these artifacts, and the context in which they were found, reveal about the extent of Anglo-Saxon contact with the rest of the world? Which regions are represented, and why?

2. Based on this evidence, what conclusions can you draw about Anglo-Saxon culture and values?

3. Do any of these graves' goods indicate that the occupant was a Christian king? Why or why not?

C. A Sutton Hoo helmet.

D. Sutton Hoo buckles.

Merovech, who was said to have been fathered by a sea monster (meaning, in effect, that no one really knew who Clovis's grandfather was). Clovis's own name proved even more long-lasting than the dynasty he founded. As the language of the Franks merged with the Latin of Gaul to become French, the name "Clovis" lost its hard *C* while the pronunciation of the *V* was softened. Thus "Clovis" became "Louis," the name borne by French kings up to the time of the French Revolution over a millennium later (see Chapter 18).

The Merovingians were not the only noble family in Gaul with a claim to kingship, but they were more successful

ABBEY CHURCH, ISLAND OF IONA. This tiny island off Scotland's west coast is the site of many Iron Age forts and has been home to a monastic community since the sixth century. Missionaries from Iona were instrumental in converting the Celtic tribes of northern Britain to Christianity.

in defending it than their counterparts in Visigothic Spain, Lombard Italy, and both the Anglo-Saxon and Celtic territories of Britain. In part, this was due to their capacity to transfer power from one generation to another. In medieval Europe, as at other times and places, the right of inheritance was not limited to the eldest male claimant of each competing royal family. When it came to property or power, all the sons of a king—and frequently all his male cousins and nephews, and even his daughters—could consider themselves rightful heirs. So even when the rule of any family was not threatened by outsiders, the transfer of power was almost always bloody.

In Gaul, however, the often brutal conflicts between rival Merovingian kings did not materially disrupt the strength and sophistication of their governance. Many elements of late Roman local administration survived throughout this period. Latin literacy, fostered by a network of monasteries linked to the Frankish court, remained an important element in this administration, providing a foundation on which Charlemagne would later build. Even the cultural revival associated with the reign of Charlemagne (see below) really began in the late seventh century at the monastic foundations fostered by members of the Merovingian family and other powerful lords.

Such monasteries grew remarkably during the seventh century and became the engines that made Merovingian Gaul wealthier and more stable than other regions of northwestern Europe. Approximately 550 monasteries were thriving by the year 700, more than 300 of which had been established in the preceding century alone. Frankish bishops also prospered along with their cities, amassing most of

their landed possessions by the end of the seventh century, possessions from which their successors would continue to profit until the time of the French Revolution.

This massive redistribution of wealth reflected a fundamental shift in the economic gravity of the Frankish kingdom. In the year 600, the wealth of Gaul was still concentrated in the south, where it had been throughout the late Roman period. By the year 750, however, the economic center of the kingdom lay north of the Loire, in the territories that extended from the Rhineland westward to the North Sea. It was here that most of the new monastic foundations of the seventh century were established.

Behind this shift in prosperity lay a long and successful effort to bring under cultivation the rich, heavy soils of northern Europe. This effort was largely engineered by the new monasteries, which harnessed the peasant workforce and pioneered agricultural technologies adapted to the climate and terrain. The most important invention was a heavy, wheeled plow capable of cutting and turning grassland sod and clay, soils very different from those of the Mediterranean. This innovation in turn necessitated the development of more efficient devices for harnessing animals (particularly oxen) to these plows. Gradually warming weather also improved the fertility of the wet northern soils, lengthening the growing season and so making possible more efficient crop-rotation systems. As food became more plentiful, the population began to expand. Although much of Frankish Gaul remained a land of scattered settlements separated by dense forests, it was far more populous by 750 than it had been in the time of Clovis. All these developments would continue during the reign of Charlemagne, and beyond.

Analyzing Primary Sources

From Anglo-Saxon Slave Girl to Frankish Queen

The Anglo-Saxon Saint Balthild rose to prominence as the wife of the Merovingian king Clovis II (r. 639–57), but she began life as a slave. After the king's death, she was left in a precarious position at the Frankish court as regent for her son, Clothar III, and was eventually forced to enter the convent she had founded at Chelles, near Paris. The following excerpt from her Latin vita *("life") describes her speedy ascent to a position of power. It was probably written by a nun of Chelles.*

Praise should first be sung of Him Who made the humble great and raised the pauper from the dunghill and seated him among the princes of his people. Such a one is the woman present to our minds, the venerable and great lady Balthild the queen. Divine Providence called her from across the seas. She, who came here as God's most precious and lofty pearl, was sold at a cheap price. Erchinoald, a Frankish magnate and most illustrious man, acquired her and in his service the girl behaved most honorably.... For she was kind-hearted and sober and prudent in all her ways, careful and plotting evil for none.... And since she was of the Saxon race, she was graceful in form with refined features, a most seemly woman with a smiling face and serious gait. And she so showed herself just as she ought in all things, that she pleased her master and

found favor in his eyes. So he determined that she should set out the drinking cup for him in his chamber and, honored above all others as his housekeeper, stand at his side always ready to serve him.... She gained such happy fame that, when the said lord Erchinoald's wife died, he hoped to unite himself to Balthild, that faultless virgin, in a matrimonial bed....

[But] when she was called to the master's chamber she hid herself secretly in a corner and threw some vile rags over herself so that no one could guess that anyone might be concealed there.... She hoped that she might avoid a human marriage bed and thus merit a spiritual and heavenly spouse.... Thereafter it happened, with God's approval, that Balthild, the maid who escaped marriage with a lord, came to be espoused to Clovis, son of the former king Dagobert. Thus by virtue of her humility she was raised to a higher rank....

Source: Excerpted from *Sainted Women of the Dark Ages,* ed. and trans. John E. Halborg, Jo Ann McNamara, and E. Gordon Whatley (Chapel Hill, NC: 1992), pp. 268–70.

Questions for Analysis

1. Based on what you have learned about the prevalence of the slave trade in ancient and early medieval civilizations, what might you speculate about Balthild's actual role in Erchinoald's household?

2. Balthild would have been a contemporary of the king buried at Sutton Hoo. Is it likely that she would have been a Christian when she was sold into slavery in England? Why or why not?

3. In light of Balthild's later status as a queen and regent for her son, why would her biographer stress that she was "careful and plotting evil for none"? To what allegations or incidents might the author of this life be responding?

The Power of Monasticism

As we just noted, the seventh century witnessed a rapid increase in the foundation of monastic houses all over northwestern Europe. Although monasteries had existed in Gaul, Italy, and Hispania since the fourth century, most were located in highly Romanized areas. In the fifth century, a powerful monastic movement began in Ireland as

well, and eventually spread to the Celtic regions of Britain and from there to the Continent. The Irish missionary Columbanus (540–615), for example, was the founder of Merovingian monasteries at Luxeuil and Fontaine. Important monasteries were also established on the island of Iona, off the western coast of what is now Scotland, and at Lindisfarne, off Britain's northeastern coast. In all of these cases, close ties were forged between monks and local tribal leaders or powerful families, much to the political and economic gain of all parties.

Most monastic foundations of the seventh century were deliberately located in rural areas but at strategic trading crossroads, where they played a crucial role. Indeed, the material advantages of monastic innovation were a powerful incentive toward Christian conversion in the communities directly affected by the improved living conditions they fostered. Prosperity was also a powerful advertisement for authority: a lord or chieftain who had the support of a monastery and the beneficent Christian God was obviously worthy of loyalty. Because monasteries played such a key role in economic development and political order, lords often granted them special privileges, helping to free them from the control of local bishops and giving them jurisdiction over their own lands. Thus, monasteries became politically powerful not only because they had been founded by powerful men, but because they were lordships in their own right.

Frequently, these new foundations were double monasteries that accommodated women as well as men. Often they were established for women only. In either case, they were often ruled by abbesses drawn from noble or royal families. Monasticism thus became a road to political power for women. It also gave women—commoners as well as queens—freedoms they did not have elsewhere, or at any other time in history up to this point. Within the monastery, women had more control over their own minds and bodies. They could also wield enormous influence, promoting their families' diplomatic and dynastic interests but without the dangers and uncertainties of pregnancy. And they were guaranteed salvation, at a time when salvation outside the cloister seemed a perilously uncertain prospect. Moreover, the prayers of holy women were regarded as particularly effective in securing divine support or retribution. This further enriched convents through donations of land and wealth, although it could not always safeguard them from violence, or their inhabitants from abduction and rape.

Monasteries for women also served the interests of men, which is why kings and lords supported them. They were dynamic repositories of prayer, regarded as essential to furthering the ambitions of their male benefactors and protecting them from harm. They provided a dignified place of retirement for inconvenient but politically powerful women, such as the sisters and daughters of rivals or the widow of a previous ruler. And by limiting the number of powerful women who could reproduce, female monasteries also reduced the number of male claimants to power. Establishing aristocratic and royal women in such convents was thus an important way of controlling successions and managing political disputes.

Monasticism played an important role in missionary activity, too. As noted above, the work of Irish monks was crucial to the spread of Christianity in northern parts of Britain and in other areas of northern Europe virtually untouched by the Roman Empire. Missionaries were also sponsored by the fledgling papacy in Rome and by the Merovingian royal family—especially its women. The best example of this is the conversion of Britain's Anglo-Saxon tribes, which we glimpsed in the opening paragraph of this chapter. In 597, a group of forty Benedictine monks were sent by Pope Gregory I (r. 590–604) to the southeastern kingdom of Kent, where their efforts were assisted by Frankish translators—and by the fact that the local king, Æthelbehrt (*EH-thel-behrt*), had married a Frankish princess who was already a Christian. This pattern of influence repeated itself all over southern and eastern Britain. Writing a hundred years later in the monastery of Monkwearmouth in Northumbria, the historian Bede could claim that the tribes of England were now united in their shared allegiance to the Roman Church and its English archbishop, whose seat was the cathedral in Æthelbert's capital at Canterbury. Bede credited the Roman pope for initiating this remarkable feat, and the monastic rule under which he himself lived for bringing it to fruition.

The Papacy of Gregory the Great

Pope Gregory I, also known as Gregory the Great, was the first bishop of Rome to envision a new role for the papacy in northwestern Europe. We have seen that the Roman *papa* had begun to assert his superiority over other patriarchs throughout the Christian world; but in reality, he was subordinate to the emperors in Constantinople and to the greater prestige of its patriarch. As Byzantine power in Italy declined, however, Gregory sought to create a more autonomous Latin Church by focusing attention on the untapped resources of the wild West. An influential theologian, he is considered the intellectual successor of Jerome, Ambrose, and Augustine (see Chapter 6) because he greatly extended the applicability of their teachings to the world outside the Romanized Mediterranean.

Among Gregory's doctrinal contributions were an emphasis on the necessity of penance for the forgiveness of sins and the concept of Purgatory as a place where the soul could be purified before it was admitted into heaven—instead of being sent immediately to perpetual damnation. Alongside this emphasis on penance, Gregory emphasized the importance of pastoral care: the proper instruction, encouragement, and control of the laity. He also sought to

THE LINDISFARNE GOSPELS. This page from one of the astonishing illuminated ("light-filled") books produced by the monastery at Lindisfarne shows the opening of the Gospel of John. ▪ *Why would monastic scribes have devoted so much time, energy, and skill to the decoration of a text? How do these artistic motifs compare to those featured on the metalwork found at Sutton Hoo (pages 230 and 231)?* ▪ *What conclusions can you draw from these similarities?*

THE COVER OF THE LINDAU GOSPELS. This book, bound in gilded silver and encrusted with jewels and ivory cameos, was presented by Pope Gregory the Great to a Lombard queen around the year 600. ▪ *Given what you have learned about the economic and cultural circumstances of northern Europe, what is the significance of this rich gift?* ▪ *What would Gregory have been attempting to achieve by giving it?*

increase the affective power of Christian worship by promoting the performance of music. Song has always been essential to religious ritual, but Gregory encouraged it to such a degree that the very style of singing that emerged in this period is known as "Gregorian chant."

Gregory was also a statesman and leader in the model of his Roman forebears. Within Italy, he ensured the survival of the papacy against Lombard invaders by clever diplomacy and expert management of papal estates and revenues. He maintained good relations with Byzantium while asserting his authority over the other bishops of the Latin Church. His support of communities living under the *Rule* of Saint Benedict (see Chapter 6) helped make Benedictine monasticism the predominant monastic force in the West. Yet Gregory's influence was not always benign. He was the first

prominent theologian to articulate the Church's official policy toward Jews, which became increasingly negative. Building on Gregory's example, later popes would insist that the Jews' alleged role in Christ's crucifixion and their denial of his divinity had deprived them of their rights in a Christian world.

THE EMPIRE OF CHARLEMAGNE

Toward the end of the seventh century, tensions among noble families in the Merovingian heartland of Neustria and those in the Frankish border region of Austrasia were increasing. The Austrasian nobles had profited from their steady push into the "soft frontier" east of the Rhine,

The map includes the following labels:

- IRELAND
- ENGLAND
- London
- NORTH SEA
- BALTIC SEA
- SLAVS
- POLES
- ATLANTIC OCEAN
- SAXONIA
- Aachen, Cologne
- AUSTRASIA
- NEUSTRIA
- Tours
- Poitiers
- Regensburg
- AQUITAINE
- BURGUNDY
- Danube R.
- AVARS
- KINGDOM OF ASTURIAS
- PROVENCE
- CATALONIA
- ITALY
- Toledo, UMAYYAD CALIPHATE (AL-ANDALUS)
- Cordoba
- CORSICA
- SARDINIA
- BALEARIC ISLANDS
- Rome
- ADRIATIC SEA
- SERBS
- BULGARS
- DUCHY OF BENEVENTO
- SICILY
- BYZANTINE EMPIRE
- MEDITERRANEAN SEA
- BLACK SEA
- CASPIAN SEA
- Constantinople
- Tigris R.
- Euphrates R.
- Baghdad
- Persian Gulf
- Nile R.
- RED SEA
- CALIPHATE OF BAGHDAD UNDER THE ABBASIDS

Inset map: The Division of the Carolingian Empire under Charlemagne's Grandsons, 840
- TO CHARLES (WEST FRANCIA)
- TO LOUIS (EAST FRANCIA)
- TO LOTHAR

Legend:
- The empire of Charlemagne, 814
- Tributary peoples
- Byzantine Empire
- Abbasid Caliphate

THE EMPIRE OF CHARLEMAGNE IN 814. When Charlemagne died in 814, he had created an empire that embraced a large portion of the lands formerly united under the western Roman Empire. ▪ *What were the geographical limits of his power?* ▪ *How were these limits dictated by the historical forces we have been studying?* ▪ *Along what lines was Charlemagne's empire divided after his death?*

acquiring wealth and military power in the process. The Merovingians, settled in Neustria, had no such easy conquests at their disposal. Moreover, a considerable portion of their land had been given to monasteries in the course of the seventh century, which decreased their wealth and their capacity to attract followers. A succession of short-lived kings then opened the door to a series of civil wars, and finally to a decisive challenge to the dynasty.

Kings and Kingmakers

In 687, an Austrasian nobleman called Pepin (635/45–714) succeeded in forcing his way into power by making himself the Frankish king's right-hand man. He took the title *maior domus*, "great man of the house," and began to exercise royal authority while maintaining the fiction that he

was merely a royal servant. He did this effectively for more than twenty-five years. After his death, his illegitimate son Charles Martel ("the Hammer," 688–741) further consolidated control over both the Merovingian homeland and the Frankish royal administration. For two generations, the Merovingian kings were largely figureheads in a realm ruled by Charles Martel and his sons.

Charles Martel is sometimes considered the second founder (after Clovis) of the Frankish kingdom. His claim to this title is twofold. First, in 733 or 734 he repelled a Muslim force that had ventured into Frankish territory, meeting them in battle at Tours, some 150 miles from the Merovingian stronghold at Paris. Although the Arab-led contingent was a raiding party rather than a full-scale army, this incursion may have been regarded as an attempted conquest on the part of the Umayyad dynasty of Al-Andalus; in any case, Charles's victory won him great prestige. More important, Charles had developed an alliance with Benedictine missionaries from England, who were attempting to convert the Low Countries and central Germany to Christianity. Charles's family had long been active in the drive to conquer and settle these areas, and he understood clearly how missionary work and Frankish expansion could go hand in hand. Charles assisted these conversion efforts. In return, the leader of the English Benedictines, Boniface (c. 672–754), brought him into contact with the papacy and assisted his efforts to control Frankish churches.

Although Charles never sought to become king himself, he was so clearly the effective ruler of Gaul that the Franks did not bother to choose a new king when the reigning Merovingian died in 737. But then Charles himself died in 741, and his sons Carloman and Pepin were forced to allow the election of a new king while they continued to exercise power behind the scenes. This compromise did not last long, however; in 750, Carloman withdrew from public life by entering a monastery, and Pepin decided to seize the throne for himself. This turned out to be harder than he may have expected. Even though the reigning king was ineffectual, Frankish identity was bound up with loyalty to Clovis's descendants; although tribal leaders had the power to elect a new king, they were reluctant to do so. Pepin therefore turned to the Frankish bishops, who were unwilling to support him without backing from the pope. To gain this, Pepin was able to trade on his family's support of the Benedictines. The pope, for his part, saw that a powerful leader of the Franks could be a potential ally in his political struggle with the Byzantine emperors over iconoclasm (which the papacy opposed) and in his military struggle against the Lombard kings for control of central Italy.

So Boniface, acting as papal emissary, anointed Pepin king of the Franks in 751. This was a new ritual, but it had a powerful biblical precedent: the ceremony by which the prophet Samuel had made Saul the first king of Israel, by anointing him with holy oil (see Chapter 2). Indeed, the significance of the Old Testament association would grow under Pepin's son Charlemagne (associated with David) and his grandson Louis the Pious (associated with Solomon). To contemporary observers, however, the novelty of these proceedings underscored the uncertainty of the process by which a legitimate king had been deposed and a new king created. And as we will see, this king-making process was the first step on a long road that would ultimately limit the power of later medieval kings and modern constitutional monarchs alike: the principle that kingship is an office and can be occupied, at least theoretically, by anyone—and that if a ruler is ineffectual or tyrannical, he can be deposed and replaced by a new officeholder.

The Reign of Charlemagne

Pepin's position as king was a tenuous one, and when he died it seemed likely that the Frankish kingdom would break up into mutually hostile regions: Austrasia, Neustria, and (to the southwest) Aquitaine. That it did not was the work of Pepin's son, Charles, known to the French as Charlemagne and to the Germans as Karl der Grosse—"Charles the Great." It is from him, as well as from his grandfather Charles Martel, that this new Frankish dynasty takes the name "Carolingian" (from *Carolus*, the Latin form of "Charles").

When Charlemagne came to power in 768, he managed to unite the Franks by the tried and true method of attacking a common, outside enemy. In a series of conquests, the Franks succeeded in annexing the Lombard kingdom of northern Italy, most of what is now Germany, portions of central Europe, and Catalonia (in southeastern Spain). These conquests seemed to set a seal of divine approval on the new Carolingian dynasty. More important, they provided the victorious Franks with spoils of war and vast new lands that enabled Charlemagne to reward his closest followers.

Many of the peoples whom Charlemagne conquered were already Christians. In pagan Saxony, however, Charlemagne's armies campaigned for twenty years before subduing the inhabitants and forcing their conversion. This created a precedent with momentous consequences, because it linked military conquest with conformity of belief. In time, the assumption that the subjugation of a vanquished people should be accompanied by their religious conversion would become ingrained in the philosophy and practice of most Western civilizations.

To rule his new empire, Charlemagne enlisted the help of the Frankish warrior class he had enriched and elevated to positions of prominence. These counts (in Latin, *comites*, "followers") supervised local governance within their territories. Among their many duties was the administration of justice and the raising of armies. Charlemagne also established a network of other local officials who convened courts, established tolls, administered royal lands, and collected taxes. To facilitate transactions and trade, he created a new coinage system based on a division of the silver pound into units of twenty shillings, each worth twelve pennies—a system that would last in parts of continental Europe and in Britain into the 1970s (when it was replaced by a decimal-based currency). As we noted

Analyzing Primary Sources

The Capitularies of Charlemagne

Charlemagne's careful governance of his domains would set a high standard for other rulers far into the future. One of the means by which this governance was carried out was through capitularies (from a Latin word denoting a document divided into chapters), which contained instructions issued by the central administration of the court to local counts and other authorities. The following are directives addressed in 785 to the administrators of Saxony, a region recently conquered by Charlemagne, whose inhabitants were forcibly converted to Christianity.

Capitulary Concerning the Parts of Saxony

1. Decisions were taken first on the more important items. All were agreed that the churches of Christ which are now being built in Saxony and are consecrated to God should have no less honor than the temples of idols had, but rather a greater and more surpassing honor.

2. If anyone takes refuge in a church, let no one presume to drive him out of that church by force; rather let him be in peace until he is brought to plead his case, . . . and after this let him be brought to the presence of our lord the king. . . .

3. If anyone makes forcible entry to a church, and steals anything from it by violence or stealth, or if he sets fire to the church, let him die.

4. If anyone in contempt of the Christian faith should spurn the holy Lenten fast and eat meat, let him die; but let the priest enquire into the matter, lest it should happen that someone is compelled by necessity to eat meat.

* * *

6. If anyone is deceived by the devil, and believes after the manner of pagans that some man or some woman is a witch and eats people, . . . let him pay the penalty of death.

7. If anyone follows pagan rites and causes the body of a dead man to be consumed by fire, . . . let him pay with his life.

8. If there is anyone of the Saxon people lurking among them unbaptized, and if he scorns to come to baptism, . . . let him die.

9. If anyone sacrifices a man to the devil, . . . let him die.

* * *

12. If anyone rapes the daughter of his lord, he shall die.

13. If anyone kills his lord or his lady, he shall be punished in the same way.

* * *

18. On Sundays there are to be no assemblies or public gatherings, except in cases of great need or when an enemy is pressing; rather let all attend church to hear the word of God. . . .

* * *

33. With regard to perjury, the law of the Saxons is to apply.

34. We forbid the Saxons to come together as a body in public gatherings, except on those occasions when our *missus* [messenger] assembles them on our instructions; rather, let each and every count hold court and administer justice in his own area. And the clergy are to see to it that this order is obeyed.

Source: From *The Reign of Charlemagne: Documents on Carolingian Government*, ed. and trans. H. R. Loyn and John Percival (New York: 1975), pp. 31–34.

Questions for Analysis

1. What types of behavior does this capitulary attempt to regulate? What seem to be the major challenges faced by Charlemagne's administrators in this new territory?

2. In only one case does this capitulary mention the law of the Saxon people themselves, in the clause relating to perjury (number 12). Why would Charlemagne's administrators consider it advisable to punish this particular crime in accordance with Saxon custom?

3. How would you characterize Charlemagne's method of dealing with a conquered people? In your estimation, is this policy likely to be effective?

above, much of the silver for this new coinage originated in the Abbasid Caliphate and was payment for furs, cloth, and especially slaves captured in Charlemagne's wars, who were now being transported to Baghdad. The silver, in turn, circulated as far north as Scandinavia, Russia, and the Baltic Sea.

Like Carolingian administration generally, this new monetary system depended on the regular use of written records, which means that the sources supporting historical research on Charlemagne's empire are numerous. But Charlemagne did not rely on the written word alone to make his will felt. Periodically, his court sent special messengers, known as *missi*, on tours through the countryside to relay his instructions and report back on the conduct of local administrators. This was the most thorough system of governance known in Europe since the height of the Roman Empire, reaching many parts of the Continent that the Romans had never occupied. It set a standard for royal administration that would be emulated and envied for centuries.

Christianity and Kingship

In keeping with the traditions established by his father and grandfather, Charlemagne took his responsibilities as a Christian king seriously. As his empire expanded, moreover, he came to see himself as the leader of a unified Christian society, Christendom, which he was obliged

CHARLEMAGNE'S IMAGE OF AUTHORITY. A silver penny struck between 804 and 814 in Mainz (as indicated by the letter *M* at the bottom) represents Charlemagne in a highly stylized fashion, as a Roman emperor with a military cloak and laurel wreath. The inscription reads *Karolus Imp Avg* (Charles, Emperor, Augustus). Charlemagne's portrait is closely modeled on both Hellenistic and Roman coins.

to defend. Like his contemporaries in Byzantium and the Muslim world—as well as his Roman predecessors—he recognized no distinction between religion and politics. Indeed, he conceived kingship as a sacred office created by God to protect the Church and promote the salvation of his Christian people. Religious reforms were therefore no less central to proper kingship than were justice and defense. In some ways, indeed, a king's responsibilities for his kingdom's spiritual welfare were more important than his other, secular responsibilities.

These ideas were not new in the late eighth century, but they took on a new importance because of the extraordinary power Charlemagne wielded. Like other rulers of this period, Charlemagne was able to appoint and depose bishops and abbots, just as he did his counts and other officials. He extended his authority by changing the liturgy of Frankish churches, reforming the rules of worship in Frankish monasteries, declaring the tenents of Christian belief, ruthlessly prohibiting pagan practices, and forcibly imposing basic Christian observances on the conquered peoples of Saxony. As the dominant political power in central Italy, Charlemagne was also the protector of the papacy. Although he acknowledged the pope as spiritual leader of Christendom, Charlemagne dealt with the bishop of Rome much as he did with other bishops in his empire. He supervised and approved papal elections, and he also protected the pope from his many enemies. To Charlemagne, such measures were clearly required if God's new chosen people, the Franks, were to avoid the fate that befell biblical Israel whenever Hebrews turned away from obedience to God.

The Carolingian Renaissance

Similar political motivations lay behind the phenomenon known as the Carolingian Renaissance, a cultural and intellectual flowering that took place around the Carolingian court. Like their biblical exemplars David and Solomon, Charlemagne and his son Louis the Pious considered it a crucial part of their role to be patrons of learning and the arts. In doing so, they created an ideal of the court as an intellectual and cultural center that would profoundly influence western European cultural life until the First World War (see Chapter 24).

Behind the Carolingians' support for scholarship was the conviction that learning was the foundation on which Christian wisdom rested and that such wisdom was essential to the salvation of God's people. Charlemagne therefore recruited intellectuals from all over Europe to further the cause of scholarship. Foremost among these was the

ROMAN HISTORY IN CAROLINGIAN MINISCULE. The very survival of Livy's history of the Roman Republic, originally written during the reign of Augustus Caesar, is a product of the Carolingian Renaissance. Furthermore, the clear layout and beautifully formed script of this manuscript copy helped readers without detailed knowledge of Latin to make out the words. For example, the first two words of the heading near the bottom are *Incipit Liber* ("[Here] begins the book") and the sentence following it begins with a reference to the Carthaginian general Hannibal.

Anglo-Saxon monk Alcuin, whose command of classical Latin established him as the intellectual leader of Charlemagne's court. Under Alcuin's direction, Carolingian scholars produced much original Latin poetry and an impressive number of theological and pastoral tracts. But their primary efforts were devoted to collating, correcting, and recopying ancient Latin texts, including, most importantly, the text of the Latin Bible, which had accumulated many generations of copyists' mistakes in the 400 years since Jerome's translation (see Chapter 6).

To detect and correct these errors, Alcuin and his associates gathered as many different versions of the biblical text as they could find and compared them, word by word. After determining the correct version among all the variants, they made a new, corrected copy and destroyed the other versions. They also developed a new style of handwriting, with simplified letter forms and spaces inserted between words, reduce so as to the likelihood that subsequent copyists would misread the corrected texts. Reading was further facilitated by the addition of punctuation. This new style of handwriting, known as Carolingian miniscule, is the foundation for the typefaces of most modern books—including this one.

The Revival of the Western Roman Empire

On Christmas Day in the year 800, Charlemagne was crowned emperor by Pope Leo III. Centuries later, popes would cite this epochal event as precedent for the political superiority they claimed over the ruler of the "Holy Roman Empire," as it came to be called (see Chapter 9). In the year 800, however, Pope Leo was entirely under Charlemagne's thumb. Yet Charlemagne's biographer, Einhard, would later claim that the coronation was planned without the emperor's knowledge. For one thing, it was certain to anger the imperial government in Byzantium, with which Charlemagne had strained relations. Nor did the imperial title add much to Charlemagne's position; he was already a de facto emperor in his own right. Why, then, did he accept the title and, in 813, transfer it to his son Louis?

Historians are still debating this question. What is clear, in any case, is the symbolic significance of the action. Although the Romans of Byzantium no longer influenced western Europe directly, they continued to regard it (somewhat vaguely) as an outlying province of their empire. Moreover, the emperor in Constantinople claimed to be the political successor of Caesar Augustus. Charlemagne's assumption of the title was therefore a clear slight to the reigning empress Irene (r. 797–802), whose occupation of the imperial throne was controversial because she was a woman; and it deepened Byzantine suspicion of his cordial relationship with Byzantium's enemy, Harun al-Rashid, the Abbasid caliph in Baghdad. But for Charlemagne's followers—and for all the medieval rulers who came after him—the assumption of the imperial title was a declaration of independence and superiority. With only occasional interruptions, western Europeans would continue to crown Roman emperors until the nineteenth century, while territorial claims and concepts of national sovereignty continued to rest on Carolingian precedent. Whatever his own motives may have been, Charlemagne's revival of the western Roman Empire was crucial to the developing self-consciousness of western Europe.

DISPUTED LEGACIES AND NEW ALLIANCES

When Charlemagne died in 814, his empire descended intact to his only surviving son, Louis the Pious. Under Louis, however, the empire disintegrated, and it was divided among his three sons in 840. Western Francia (the core of modern France) went to Charles the Bald; eastern Francia (which became key principalities of Germany) went to Louis the German; and a third kingdom (stretching from the Rhineland to Rome) went to Lothair, along with the imperial title. But when Lothair's line died out in 856, this fragile compromise dissolved into open warfare, as the East and West Franks fought over Lothair's former territories and the imperial power that went with them. The heartland of this disputed domain, known to the Germans as Lotharingia and to the French as Alsace-Lorraine, would continue to be a site of bitter contention until the end of the Second World War (see Chapter 26).

The Collapse of the Carolingian Empire

Louis faced an impossible situation of a kind we have studied many times before: the task of holding together an artificial constellation of territories united by someone else. Charlemagne's empire had been built on successful conquest. By 814, however, Charlemagne had pushed the borders of his empire beyond the practical limits of his administration. To the southwest, he now faced the Umayyad rulers of Al-Andalus; to the north, the pagan inhabitants of Scandinavia; and in the east, his armies were too preoccupied with settling the territories they had already conquered to secure the Slavic lands that lay beyond. At the same time, the pressures that had driven these conquests—the need for land and plunder to cement the allegiance of followers—had become ever more pronounced as a result of their very success. The number of counts had tripled, from approximately 100 to 300, and each of them wanted more wealth and power.

Frustrated by their new emperor's inability to reward them, the Frankish aristocracy turned against him and

on each other. Smoldering hostilities among Austrasians, Neustrians, and Aquitanians—which Charlemagne had stifled by directing their energies elsewhere—flared up again. As centralized authority broke down, the vast majority of the empire's free inhabitants found themselves increasingly dominated by local lords who treated them as if they were serfs. At the same time, internal troubles in the Abbasid Empire caused a breakdown in the commercial system through which Scandinavian traders brought Abbasid silver into Carolingian domains. Deprived of their livelihood, these traders turned to raiding, which is what the Norse word *viking* means. Under these combined pressures, the Carolingian Empire fell apart, and a new political map of Europe began to emerge.

The Impact of the Viking Invasions

Scandinavian traders were already familiar figures in the North Sea and Baltic ports of Europe when Charlemagne came to power. They had begun to establish strategic settlements from which they navigated down the rivers to Byzantium (through the Black Sea) and the Abbasid Caliphate (through the Caspian Sea). But when the power of the Abbasids declined, Viking raiders turned to plunder, ransom, tribute collection, and slaving. At first, these were small-scale operations. But soon, some Viking attacks involved organized armies numbering in the thousands. The small tribal kingdoms of the Anglo-Saxons and Celts made the British Isles easy targets, as were the divided kingdoms of the Franks.

By the tenth century, the Vikings controlled independent principalities in eastern England, Ireland, the islands of Scotland, and the region of France that is still called "Norseman-land," Normandy. A Viking people known as the Rus' established the beginnings of a kingdom that would become Russia. At the end of the tenth century, Vikings ventured farther west and colonized Iceland, Greenland, and a distant territory they called Vinland (Newfoundland, Canada). In 1016, a Viking army placed a Danish king on the English throne.

The threat of Viking attacks began to lessen with Scandinavia's conversion to Christianity, which proceeded rapidly from the late tenth century onward. But it was more effectively mitigated by the fact that Viking populations quickly assimilated into the cultural and political world of northwestern Europe. By 1066, when the "Norsemen" of Normandy conquered England, the English—many of whom were descended from Vikings themselves—perceived them to be French. Driving this rapid assimilation may have been the raids of the Magyars,

PATTERNS OF VIKING ACTIVITY AND SETTLEMENT, c. 800–1100. The Vikings were instrumental in maintaining commercial contacts among northern Europe, Byzantium, and Islam until the eighth century, when changing historical forces turned them into raiders and colonists. ▪ *What area was the original homeland of the Vikings?* ▪ *What geographic region did the Vikings first conquer, and why?* ▪ *The areas marked in green show territories that were later targeted by pillagers. Why would the Vikings have avoided settlement in these areas?*

a non-Indo-European people who crossed the Carpathian Mountains around 895 and carried out a number of devastating campaigns throughout continental Europe before settling in what is now Hungary. The disparate inhabitants of the new Viking colonies may have been forced to unite against this common enemy and thus have come to share a sense of common identity.

The overall effect of the Vikings on Europe continues to be a matter of scholarly controversy. The destruction they caused is undeniable, and many of the monasteries of Frankish, Anglo-Saxon, and Celtic lands were destroyed—along with countless precious books and historical artifacts. Yet the Vikings were not the only source of disorder in the ninth and tenth centuries. The civil wars and local political rivalries that had replaced the centralized states of Charlemagne

and the Islamic caliphates contributed mightily to the chaos of the post-Carolingian world and made the Vikings' successes easily won. Nor were the Vikings a source of disorder alone. In Ireland and eastern England, Vikings founded a series of new towns. As long-distance traders, Vikings transported large quantities of silver into western Europe, fueling the European economy.

In those few regions where people did succeed in fending off Viking attacks, the unifying force of victory was strong. The best example of this phenomenon is England, which had never been part of Charlemagne's empire and which had remained divided into small kingdoms at war with one other—despite Bede's wishful history of "an English church and people." Yet in a direct response to the Viking threat, a loosely unified kingdom emerged for the

The manuscript illumination shows Latin text:

Post canis igitur. magni caluda sed
conflitata e. qua fabule poecam mtasfta
mi nerua que primi ea excogitasse
murium fuerat honum b. pau
habet autein stellas
mo mali m fabeari na

ftellariu ordinem uduii
collocata dicant. pp
dicit ecmaie qdante
nduali ingenio fecisse
ui mlaxere v. mfam
v sunt. vvii.

A tednis addla uda serpens plabitur argo .
Conuecans pse uortans cumlumine puppim.

first time under Alfred the Great (r. 871–99). His success in defending his own small kingdom from Viking attacks, combined with the destruction of every other competing royal dynasty, allowed Alfred and his heirs to assemble effective armed forces, institute mechanisms of local government, found new towns, and codify English laws. In addition, Alfred established a court school and fostered a distinctive Anglo-Saxon literary culture. While the Anglo-Saxon vernacular had been a written language since the time of the Roman missions, it now came to rival Latin as a language of administration, history, scholarship, and spirituality. Moreover, oral traditions of poetic composition and storytelling were preserved and extended, as exemplified by the epic *Beowulf*. Until the eleventh century, Anglo-Saxon was the only European vernacular used for regular written communication.

The Disintegration of the Islamic World

As we noted above, the declining power of the Abbasid dynasty in Persia was one of the forces that contributed to the escalation of Viking raids. A major cause of this decline was the gradual impoverishment of the Abbasids' economic base, the agricultural wealth of the ancient Tigris-Euphrates basin, which resulted from ecological crises and a devastating revolt by the enslaved African workforce there. Tax

revenues from the Abbasid Caliphate were also declining, as provincial rulers in North Africa, Egypt, and Syria retained larger and larger portions of those revenues for themselves. As their sources of income became depleted, the Abbasids were unable to support either their large civil service or the mercenary army on which they relied for defense. This army was manned largely by slaves and hired troops whose loyalties lay with the individual rulers who employed them, not with the caliphs. Massively expensive building projects, including the construction of the new Abbasid capital at Baghdad, further exacerbated the fiscal, military, and political crisis.

Behind the Abbasid collapse lay two fundamental developments of great significance for the future of the Islamic world: the growing power of regional rulers and the sharpening religious divisions between Sunnis and Shi'ites, and among the Shi'ites themselves. In 909, regional and religious hostilities came together when a local Shi'ite dynasty known as the Fatimids seized control of the Abbasid province of North Africa. In 969, the Fatimids succeeded in conquering Egypt also. Meanwhile, another Shi'ite group, rivals of both the Fatimids and the Abbasids, attacked Baghdad in 927 and Mecca in 930, seizing the Kaaba. Although an Abbasid Caliphate would continue to exist in Baghdad until 1258, when invading Mongol armies dispatched it (see Chapter 10), its empire had effectively disappeared by the 930s. In its place a new order began to emerge in the eastern Mediterranean, centered around an independent Egyptian kingdom and a new Muslim state based in Persia.

In Al-Andalus, disputes over succession within the Umayyad dynasty were matched by new external pressures. Beginning in the mid-ninth century, the small Christian kingdoms of northern and eastern Iberia began to encroach on Muslim territory, increasing the internal difficulties of the Umayyad caliphate. By the opening years of the eleventh century, the caliphate had dissolved, to be replaced by a host of smaller kingdoms, some of which paid tribute to the Christian rulers of the north.

The fractured political unity of the Islamic world deepened the divisions that had always existed among Muslim groups. While Islamic rulers were extremely tolerant of religious and cultural differences when dealing with Jews and Christians, dissent within Islam itself was another matter. Under the strong rule of the caliphates, some different groups had learned to coexist; but with the disappearance of these centralized states it would be difficult to reconcile the ideal of universality with the realities of regional and ethnic differences.

CONCLUSION

The three civilizations that emerged as Rome's heirs each exhibit aspects of Roman civilization, which was itself a product of older civilizations. Which was Rome's true successor? It depends on the criteria used to make this evaluation. If imperial Rome's most fundamental characteristics were the maintenance of legal and political institutions, the answer is Byzantium. If one is looking for a

After You Read This Chapter

Visit StudySpace for quizzes, additional review materials, and multimedia documents. **wwnorton.com/web/westernciv18**

REVIEWING THE OBJECTIVES

- Justinian's attempted reunification of the Roman Empire proved destructive. What were its effects in the East? In the West?
- Byzantine culture was distinctive in many ways. What are some of its important features?
- The rapid expansion of Islam can be explained with reference to several historical factors. What were they?
- What accounts for the close relationship between monasticism and secular power in early medieval Europe?
- What was the Carolingian Empire, and why is it important?

civilization that combines the rich legacies of the ancient Near East, Egypt, and the Hellenistic world, the answer is Islam, which also emulated Rome in promoting commerce and cultural exchange. If one associates Rome chiefly with the city itself and the Latin language of the first Romans, or with the Christian patriarch of Rome, the answer is northwestern Europe.

There are also many connections to be drawn among these three successors. All took on their defining characteristics in the sixth and seventh centuries and, by the eighth century, had developed unique strengths and weaknesses. Moreover, they had fruitful—if uneasy—relationships with one another, and many mutual dependencies. Italian traders were active in Constantinople, and Muslim traders were common in the ports of southern Italy and Gaul. Anglo-Saxon merchants were regular visitors to the Mediterranean. Jewish merchants in the Rhineland were carrying on an active trade with the communities of Muslim Egypt, while Viking traders had opened trade routes from the Baltic through Russia to the Black Sea and were busily founding cities from Novgorod to Dublin.

But developments of the ninth and tenth centuries would disrupt these networks and created new centers of power. Western Europeans began to share a sense of common Christian identity: within the vast territory that extended from the Baltic to the Mediterranean, and from the Pyrenees to Poland, every ruler was (or would soon be) looking to the Roman Church for spiritual guidance and to his fellow rulers for aid and alliance. At the same time, western Europe became a society mobilized for war to a degree unmatched in either Byzantium or the Islamic world. In the centuries to come, this militarization was to prove a decisive factor in the shifting relationship among Rome's heirs.

PEOPLE, IDEAS, AND EVENTS IN CONTEXT

- In what ways do **JUSTINIAN'S CODE OF ROMAN LAW** and the building of **HAGIA SOPHIA** reflect his desire to revive the glories of ancient Rome?
- What were **BYZANTIUM**'s sources of stability, and of dissent? What effect did the **ICONOCLAST CONTROVERSY** have on Byzantine society?
- What factors contributed to **MUHAMMAD**'s rise to power? What are the **FIVE PILLARS OF ISLAM**, and what is the role of the **QUR'AN**?
- To what extent were the **UMAYYAD** and **ABBASID CALIPHATES** heirs of Rome? What made Islamic culture of this period distinctive?
- How did the **MEROVINGIAN** kings of the Franks acquire and hold power? How did **BENEDICTINE MONASTICISM** contribute to the economy of western Europe, and how was it linked to politics?
- How did **CHARLEMAGNE** build an empire, and how did the **CAROLINGIAN RENAISSANCE** revive and extend **CLASSICAL LEARNING**?
- How did the **VIKINGS** contribute to the developments of the ninth and tenth centuries?

THINKING ABOUT CONNECTIONS

- Arguably, each of these three civilizations could claim the mantle of the Roman Empire. In your view, which one has the strongest claim to carrying forward the legacies of the classical past?
- How do the historical circumstances in which Islam emerged compare to those that shaped early Christianity? What are some key similarities and differences?

Before
You
Read
This
Chapter

The Expansion of Europe, 950–1100

CORE OBJECTIVES

- **EXPLAIN** the reasons for the fragmentation of political power throughout most of Europe in this period.

- **IDENTIFY** the most important outcomes of the medieval agricultural revolution.

- **DESCRIBE** the effects of the reforming movement with the Church.

- **UNDERSTAND** the motives behind the Crusades.

- **TRACE** the political, economic, social, religious, and cultural effects of the Crusades.

In the version of history popularized by medieval minstrels, Charlemagne and his knights are able to defeat an Islamic army on enemy soil, in the mountainous borderlands of Spain. They then face only one remaining obstacle: the castle of a Muslim king whose stalwart courage commands the Christians' respect. So when ambassadors from the king promise his conversion in exchange for the safety of his people, Charlemagne readily agrees. One of his men must now negotiate the terms of surrender. Roland, Charlemagne's noblest knight, suggests that his stepfather Ganelon be the chosen messenger. But Ganelon is furious, certain that the mission will end in his death. Secretly, he resolves to betray both his stepson and his liege lord: he convinces the Muslim king that Charlemagne intends to trick him, and thus incites the king to attack the Christian warriors as they travel homeward through the mountain passes of the Pyrenees. Because Roland is the bravest knight, Ganelon knows that he will volunteer to command the rear guard.

And so it happens. Roland's men are ambushed and his sworn companion, Olivier, urges him to call for help. But Roland refuses: he will never endanger his lord by any such dishonorable deed. Instead, he will fight to the death and,

247

with his last ounce of strength, break his sword, Duran-dal. For it would never do to have this sacred gift of Charlemagne—made holier still by the relic in its pommel—fall into the hands of heathens. As Roland reminds Olivier, "We must not be the theme of mocking songs." The worst thing imaginable is shame; the best, to become the hero of just such an epic.

Like Homer's *Iliad*, the *Song of Roland* is the product of an oral storytelling tradition that took shape over hundreds of years. Written down around the year 1100, it reflects the many ways in which the world had changed since the time of Charlemagne. Its very language exemplifies one such change: the language we call French, no longer the Frank-ish tongue of Charlemagne. In Charlemagne's time, more-over, there was no such thing as knighthood or chivalry, there were no major castles, there was no holy war against Muslims. All of these features were added to the story over time, to mirror a new reality and, most immediately, the ethos of the First Crusade (1095–99).

In this chapter, we will begin to trace the processes that transformed western Europe from an economic backwater and political patchwork into the premier power among the three successor civilizations of the Roman Empire. With the increased authority and prestige of the Roman Church, European Christendom came to embrace the for-merly outlying provinces of Scandinavia, Hungary, Poland, and Bohemia. Christian colonists and missionaries would also push eastward into Prussia, Lithuania, Livonia, and the Balkans. Allied Christian armies would come to domi-nate Muslim Spain and Constantinople. They would also establish (and eventually lose) a Latin kingdom centered on Jerusalem and come to control commerce in the Mediter-ranean as well as trade routes to Central Asia and China. This expansion would be accompanied by a revolution in agricultural production, significant urbanization, a rising standard of living, and a growing population. It would fos-ter the growth of territorial monarchies, create a wealthy but highly stratified new social order, and spur remarkable intellectual and cultural achievements.

A TOUR OF EUROPE AROUND THE YEAR 1000

The mapmakers of antiquity (see Chapter 4) had used the term Europe to refer to one of three known continents, and they divided it from Asia by the river Don and from Africa by the Straits of Gibraltar. We have seen that many of Europe's territories were gradually brought into the orbit of Western civilizations through trade, imperial conquest, the Jewish diaspora, and the spread of Chris-tianity and Islam. Meanwhile, waves of immigration from the steppes of Asia increased the already rich ethnic and cultural diversity of Europe, as did the movements of the Vikings and their interactions with both newer and more established groups. So while Charlemagne (see Chapter 7) had tried to promote an idea of a Europe as unified and coterminous with Christendom, Europe was not (and could never be) wholly Christian; and it was certainly not unified. So what was it?

This chapter is entitled "The Expansion of Europe" for two main reasons: because the very idea of Europe gains increasing coherence during this pivotal period and because Europeans' forceful annexation of territories along the Continent's eastern frontiers and throughout the Medi-terranean is a crucial development. Indeed, some influ-ential historians argue that Europe was really invented in this era, through an ongoing process of internal and external colonization. That is, new kingdoms and com-munities were being created by conquest and settlement within Europe— complicating ethnic identities, kinship networks, and tribal loyalties—but also well beyond it. Europeans were becoming the agents of imperialism, not its targets. This is a striking change. The West's center of gravity had always been the Mediterranean and its adja-cent lands in Anatolia, the Near East, and North Africa; it was from there that influences flowed to the less civilized lands of the farther West. The movements of peoples, too, had usually been westward. But now that trajectory was being reversed.

Viking Initiatives

In the aftermath of the Viking invasions, new politi-cal entities began to emerge in Europe. Some, on the far-flung fringes of the known world, were formed when the Vikings themselves became colonists: Iceland, Greenland, and (briefly) Newfoundland. Indeed, Iceland can claim to be Europe's oldest state and the world's first parliamentary democracy. Its political institutions date back to the year 930, when settlers formed a legislative assembly called the Althing, a Norse word with the same meaning as the Latin *res publica*. Icelanders would build one of the most cultur-ally distinctive polities of the Middle Ages and would pro-duce a fascinating and influential body of poetic forms and literary entertainments, notably the *sagas*: sprawling family histories that unfold over generations, feature diverse casts of characters, and range from the hilarious to the ruthless (often both at once). Modern action films and epics are heavily indebted to the sagas and their historical contexts.

In regions where Vikings settled among more established groups—throughout the British Isles, Scandinavia, and the Low Countries—they both absorbed and affected these cultures. In Normandy, for example, the descendants of Vikings maintained marriage alliances and ties of kinship with the rest of the Norse world while at the same time intermarrying with the Franks and adopting their language.

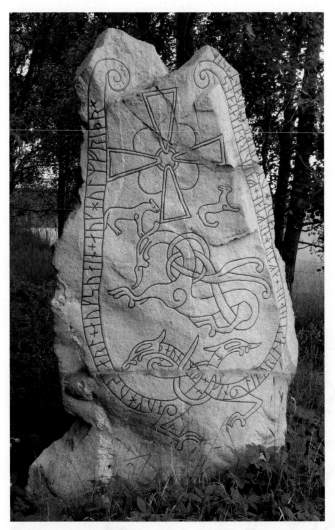

LINGSBERG RUNESTONE. This is one of two commemorative runestones erected at Lingsberg, Sweden, at the beginning of the eleventh century. The runic inscription records that a woman named Holmfríðr had it placed here in memory of her husband, Halfdan, whose father had been a Viking raider in England. Runic alphabets were in use among Germanic-speaking peoples of the North prior to the adoption of the Latin alphabet. Some runic letters survive in Anglo-Saxon and Old Norse, including the *edh*, the letter ð in the name of Holmfríðr, which is pronounced *th* as in *the*.

The Rise of Rus' and the Kingdoms of Eastern Europe

One group of Vikings would establish an important kingdom on the broad steppes of Eurasia, at the heart of a region that still bears their name: Russia. Originally from Sweden, the Rus' were active raiders and traders in the Baltic region, where they came to dominate the Finns and Slavic peoples who lived along the seaboard. According to their earliest chronicle, they were invited to rule over these warring tribes and so extended their reach through the navigation of Eurasian waterways while also moving further inland, to Novgorod. By the year 1000, they had conquered the fortress of Kiev.

This was a key outpost of the frontier region controlled by the Khazars, a Turkic people who had established an empire along the Silk Road to China and whose effective practices of assimilation extended their influence still further (many had embraced a form of Judaism centuries before). From Kiev, on the shores of the river Dneiper, the Rus' had easy access to the Black Sea and thence to Constantinople and Baghdad. They were thus in a position to trade directly with the eastern Roman Empire in Byzantium, and with Arabic, Persian, and Turkic peoples who also had access to China. Through a series of strategic intermarriages, moreover, they forged further connections with many of the royal and aristocratic dynasties of western Europe. This placed Kievan Rus' at the heart of economic and political activity in the medieval world.

Meanwhile, the dominion of the Rus' over northern Slavic peoples was countered by the crystallization of Slavic kingdoms farther to the south: Serbia and Croatia on the Adriatic, which grew up within long-settled provinces of the old Roman Empire, and Poland. The ruling families of Croatia embraced the Latin Christianity of Rome in this period; so did those of Poland. The Serbians, however, were drawn more into the orbit of Byzantium, and with it Greek Orthodoxy. Sandwiched between them, and on the borders of Rus', was Hungary, comprising the old Roman province of Pannonia and stretching eastward toward the Carpathian mountains. It had been conquered by the Huns in the late fourth century and had since attracted numerous other immigrants. The most recent arrivals were the Magyars, a nomadic people from the region of the Urals whose language, like that of the Finns, was non-Indo-European (Chapter 7). The Magyars were expert herdsmen and horsemen. They also served as mercenaries fighting for various warring kings in western Europe and for the emperor in Byzantium. Around 895, they united under a leader called Arpád and took control of the fertile land of the Danube river basin, where they became farmers and cattle ranchers. Arpád's descendants would later embrace Latin Christianity and would work to integrate the kingdom of Hungary into western Europe through dynastic marriage and diplomacy.

New Scandinavian Kingdoms and the Empire of Cnut the Great

While Rus' was on the rise, other groups of Vikings were establishing territorial control over parts of their Scandinavian homeland—by borrowing forms of governance that drew on Carolingian and Byzantine models and by embracing Latin Christianity as a way of legitimizing their rule. Around the year 1000, three strong kingdoms had emerged: Norway, Sweden, and Denmark. Each built on the legacy of powerful Viking forebears who had already established strong Norse settlements in the lands of the Franks, the Anglo-Saxons, and the Irish: their kings' reputation for fearlessness in battle and generosity afterward, their capacity to dominate seas and riverways and thereby to supply the lifeblood (silver and gold currency) of the medieval economy, and their canny practices of adaptation and intermarriage.

What made these new states special was their rulers' very deliberate manipulation of this heritage, blended with the strategic decision to convert their followers to Christianity and to the political conventions of the Continent. They simultaneously glorified their own distinctive culture and economic achievements while tying them to newer models of government. For these reasons, scholars have often spoken of this as Europe's "Viking Age," and it exemplifies the cross-currents of colonial enterprise mentioned above. For on the one hand, older western civilizations can be said to have colonized Scandinavia; on the other hand, it was really Scandinavians who were doing the colonizing.

The empire forged by King Cnut (*kuh-NOOT*) of Denmark is a good example of this. At the time of his death in 1035, Cnut the Great ruled over Norway, much of Sweden, and England as well as his native Denmark; he had a controlling interest in large parts of Ireland and portions of the Low Countries, too. He also had diplomatic and family ties to the independent principalities of Flanders and Normandy, the new kingdom of Poland (through his mother, a Polish princess), and to the imperial family of Germany (through his daughter, who became empress). Although his was, in many ways, a personal empire and (like that of Alexander) came apart after his death, it had long-term effects on the political organization of northwestern Europe. Most notably, it set the stage for the Norman Conquest of England (see **Interpreting Visual Evidence** on page 262). Cnut's empire could only have been brought together as a result of the initiatives that had made raiding Vikings into settled kings who were still able to exploit the far-flung networks of trade, influence, and kinship that had allowed their forebears to flourish in earlier times.

Mediterranean Microcosms

The dynamism of the new states of eastern Europe, Rus', and Scandinavia stands in contrast to the very different

MAGYAR HORSEMAN. This tenth-century wall painting from Aquileia (on the Adriatic coast of northern Italy) illustrates the superior horsemanship and dexterity that made Hungarian warriors sought-after mercenaries.

EUROPE, c. 1000. This map shows the patchwork of political power in western Europe after the millennium, although it cannot accurately illustrate the degree of fragmentation within these major territories, especially those of the Holy Roman Empire. ▪ *What factors account for the close relationship between Italy and the German principalities?* ▪ *How are they related to the northwestern regions of the Continent and the British Isles?* ▪ *Which geopolitical entities would you expect to emerge as dominant in the following centuries?*

dynamics that governed relations in an older part of western civilizations: the Mediterranean. If the map above struggles to capture the patchwork of principalities and polities of Europe's mainland, it fails utterly to convey the contours of political, religious, cultural, and economic interactions in this maritime world. It is useful, in fact, to imagine the Mediterranean coastal regions and islands as interlocking components of a different zone entirely, and to further imagine that a community on the shores

of North Africa—say, Muslim Tunis—would have more in common, and more contact, with Christian Barcelona than with another African Muslim community farther inland.

Indeed, it is extremely tricky (and probably futile) to pin down the identity and allegiances of any one group or individual in this zone. The medieval Mediterranean was a complex organism made up of diverse microcosms whose contours and interrelationships were more determined by geography,

EMPEROR OTTO THE GREAT. In this opening from a deluxe set of Gospels he commissioned for himself, Otto is shown seated on a throne and vested with the regalia of imperial and royal authority, surrounded by clerical and secular counselors, and receiving tribute from a procession of deferential women representing the four regions of his domain: Slavinia, Germania, Gallia, and Roma. Compare this image to that of Emperor Justinian on page 214 (Chapter 7). ▪ *In what ways is Otto making use of similar iconography?* ▪ *What claims to power does he make thereby?*

prevailing winds, trading patterns, and climate than by the vaunted control of a particular ruler. In many places, it made little difference who the ostensible rulers were, especially since the persons and forms of rule changed so often.

Take Sicily, for example: the first overseas colony of Rome (Chapter 5), it had been part of the Phoenician maritime empire of Carthage and, before that, a major Greek settlement (Chapters 2 and 3). All of those elements would still have been part of Sicily's historical DNA when it was invaded by the Vandals in the fifth century and afterward by the Goths. It was then reconquered by Justinian and became part of Byzantium—so important a part, in fact, that one Byzantine emperor tried to move the capital from Constantinople to Palermo. In the course of the tenth century, it became an emirate of the Fatimid Caliphate based in Egypt. In the eleventh, it was progressively infiltrated by Norman mercenaries who eventually succeeded in establishing a Norman (but only nominally Christian) kingdom there in 1072. So who were the Sicilians? More important, who did they think they were—and how stable was that identity over this long period of continual change? These are not easy questions to answer.

In any such case, it is better to think in terms of influences, connections, and orbits of exchange than about sta-

ble borders or identities; this holds true of many areas of Europe in this period but is especially true when speaking of regions joined by water. Gaining "control" of any constellation of Mediterranean communities—constantly in flux—meant harnessing its inherent complexity and commercial power, something not best done through violent conquest or military occupation. Indeed, an exemplary light-handed interference was what enabled the Venetians to build a successful and long-lived trading empire in the Adriatic and then in the eastern Mediterranean and Aegean Seas. The Venetians opened up the sea lanes and ports that would be crucial to the implementation of a more military form of European expansion: the Crusades.

The Heirs of Charlemagne

What of Europe's heartland, which had become the empire of Charlemagne (Chapter 7)? The most powerful monarchs on the Continent were the Saxon kings of eastern Francia (in what is now Germany). Like the Anglo-Saxon kings of England, they modeled themselves on Charlemagne, but they drew on different aspects of his rule. While England was becoming an effective administrative monarchy, with centralized financial and judicial systems, royal power on the Continent rested on the profits of continual expansion. So just as the Carolingians had built their power on the conquest of Saxony in the eighth century, the Saxon kings now built theirs on the conquests of Slavic lands to the east. They also nurtured their image as guardians of Christendom: in 955, King Otto I of Saxony defeated the then-pagan Magyars while carrying a sacred lance that had belonged to Charlemagne.

This victory established Otto as a dominant power and, by extension, as Charlemagne's worthy successor. In 962, accordingly, he went to Rome to be crowned emperor by Pope John XII, who hoped Otto would help him defeat his own enemies. But Otto turned the tables on the pope, deposing him and selecting a new pope to replace him. Otto thereby laid the foundation for his successors' claims to imperial autonomy, in imitation of the Byzantine emperors. He also advertised his inheritance of Carolingian and Roman power through his patronage of arts and learning. Under Otto's influence, the Saxon court became a refuge for men and women of talent. The first known female playwright, Hrotsvitha of Gandersheim (c. 935–c. 1002), was raised there, and grew up hearing the works of classical authors read aloud. When she entered a royal convent, she wrote plays blending Roman comedy with the stories of early Christian martyrs for the entertainment and instruction of her fellow nuns. Otto also presided over the establishment of cathedral schools and helped the bishops of his domain turn their own courts into cultural centers.

However, Otto could not control either the papacy or the independent towns of northern Italy unless he maintained a permanent presence there. And if he remained in Italy too long, his authority in Saxony broke down. Balancing local realities with imperial ambitions thus presented a dilemma that neither he nor his successors were able to solve. The result was a gradually increasing rift between local elites and the king in his guise as Holy Roman Emperor. This alienation would accelerate in the eleventh century, when the imperial crown passed to a new dynasty, the Salians, centered not in Saxony but in neighboring Franconia. By the 1070s, when the Salian emperor Henry IV attempted to assert control over Saxony, he touched off a war that was to have momentous repercussions (see below).

Aspects of Charlemagne's legacy also survived in the Mediterranean world. In Catalonia, counts descended from Carolingian appointees continued to administer justice in public courts of law throughout the tenth century, and to draw revenues from tolls and trade. The city of Barcelona grew rapidly as both a long-distance and a regional market under the protection of these counts. In Aquitaine also, the counts of Poitiers and Toulouse continued to rest their authority on Carolingian foundations.

In Charlemagne's own Frankish kingdom, however, Carolingian rule collapsed under the combined weight of Viking raids, economic disintegration, and the growing power of local lords. A few Carolingian institutions—such as public courts and a centrally minted coinage—survived in some regions, but they were used to build up new, autonomous principalities such as Anjou and Flanders. The Norse-Frankish rulers of Normandy also used these techniques effectively. But in the Franks' traditional heartland, however, even this modicum of Carolingian authority disappeared. The Franks still had a king, but this king was no longer a descendant of Charlemagne. Moreover, his domain had been reduced to the tiny region around Paris: the only territorial remnant that the local count, Hugh Capet, had managed to defend against the Vikings. In 987, this modest feat earned him the title King of the Franks. Marooned on this Ile de France (literally, "island of France"), the Capetian kings clung to the fiction that they were the heirs of Charlemagne's greatness. It would be another 200 years before one of them made this fiction a political reality (see Chapter 9).

AN AGRICULTURAL REVOLUTION

Like all economies prior to the nineteenth century, the medieval economy rested largely on agriculture. Although agricultural innovation tends to occur slowly, it is still appropriate to call the profound changes that took place in this period revolutionary. Indeed, it is arguable that this medieval agricultural revolution was more important than that of the modern era.

New Technologies

As we noted in Chapter 7, the driving force behind this agricultural boom was technological. The new heavy-wheeled plow, fitted with an iron-tipped coulter and dragged by a team of oxen or horses, could cut and turn the rich soil of northern Europe far more effectively than traditional Mediterranean plows. Related improvements in collars and harnesses enhanced the efficiency of plow animals and made it possible for them to pull heavy loads without choking themselves. The development of iron horseshoes (around 900) and the tandem harnessing of paired teams (around 1050) also made the use of horses more effective, not only in the field but for the transport of agricultural surpluses to new markets.

LIGHT PLOW AND HEAVY PLOW. Compare these two contemporary depictions of plowing: the one at left is taken from a Greek manuscript copied in Byzantium and shows the light plow in use throughout the Mediterranean and Near East since antiquity; the other shows the heavy wheeled plow adapted to northern Europe. Note that the peasant using the light plow has to press his foot on it to give it added weight. Another major innovation of the heavy European plow was the long moldboard, which turned over the ground after the plowshare cut into it. The padded horse collar allowed horses to throw their full weight into pulling.

Labor-saving devices further increased productivity. Since most work was done by individuals using hand tools, the more widespread use of iron for hoes, forks, shovels, and scythes made work faster and easier. The wheelbarrow was a crucial invention, as was the harrow, a tool drawn over the field after plowing to level the earth and mix in the seed. Watermills represented another major innovation. The Romans had relied mainly on human- and animal-powered wheels to grind grain into flour, even though they had known about the use of running water as a power source. But the need for greater efficiency and the lack of slave labor led medieval engineers—usually monks—to experiment with various ways of harnessing water power. Secular landowners followed suit, recognizing the mill as a source of economic and political power to which they could control access through the imposition of tolls.

Mills were also adapted to a variety of purposes beyond the grinding of grain: they drove saws for lumber, processed cloth, pressed olive oil, provided power for iron forges, and crushed pulp for manufacturing paper. The importance of mills cannot be overstated: they would remain the world's only source of mechanical power for manufacturing until the invention of the steam engine powered the Industrial Revolution (see Chapter 19).

New Conditions for Growth

Although many of these technologies had been invented in the eighth century, it was only in the eleventh that they became sufficiently widespread as to have a decisive impact.

Climate change certainly played a role in this. Starting in the eighth or ninth century, average temperatures in Europe gradually rose by about 1° or 2°C (3.6°F)—the same increment that has led to global warming today. Eventually, these higher temperatures made it possible to raise crops as far north as Greenland and to produce wine in southern England. Moreover, the warming climate benefited northern Europe by drying the soil and lengthening the growing season, while hotter summers and diminishing rainfall hurt Mediterranean agriculture in equal measure.

These new technologies also became more widespread after the settlement of Viking and Magyar peoples decreased the threat of invasion and the consequent disruption of planting cycles and damage to crops. Left in relative peace, monasteries could develop and implement the tools described above, which were then copied by local lords who saw the benefits of managing their own lands more efficiently, rather than raiding others'. It became clear to entrepreneurial peasants, too, that investment in agricultural improvements would yield surpluses and result in profits. Productivity was also linked to increased population, fundamental changes in patterns of settlement, and the organization of the peasant workforce.

Harnessing People

In the centuries after the fragmentation of Roman imperial power, most farmers in northern Europe lived on individual plots of land worked by themselves and their families. Starting in the ninth century, however, many of these individual holdings merged into large, common fields that could be farmed collectively by the inhabitants of entire villages. The resulting complex is sometimes called a *manor* (from the Latin verb *manere*, meaning "to dwell").

In many cases, the impetus for the consolidation of manors came from the peasants themselves. Large fields could be farmed more efficiently than small fields. Investment costs were lower and could be shared equally: a single plow and a dozen oxen might suffice for an entire village, obviating the need for every farmer to maintain his own plow and team. Common fields were potentially more productive, too, allowing villagers to experiment with new crops and to support larger numbers of animals on common pastures. In time, prosperous peasants might be able to establish a parish church, a communal oven, a blacksmith, a mill, and a tavern. They could also converse, socialize, and assist their neighbors. In a difficult and demanding natural environment, these were important considerations.

In other cases, a manor could be created or co-opted by a local lord or a monastery acting as a lord. Manors were attractive because their greater productivity meant that lords could take a larger share of the peasants' surplus; it was also easier to control and exploit peasants who lived together in villages and who were bound to one another by ties of kinship and dependence. Over time, some lords were therefore able to reduce formerly free peasants to the status of serfs who could not leave the land without permission. Like slaves, serfs inherited their servile status; but unlike slaves, they were not supposed to be sold apart from the lands they worked. Practically speaking, there may have been little difference between a serf and and a free peasant—indeed, some serfs may have been better off. But as we have seen, social mobility is often tied to geographical mobility; and the inability of serfs to move freely would prevent them from achieving the liberties of those workers who could (see below).

The Conquest of the Land

The manor's organization of labor opened up more land for cultivation and made that cultivation more efficient. For centuries, farmers had known that if they sowed the same crop in the same field year after year, they would eventually exhaust the soil. The traditional solution was to divide one's land, planting half in the fall to harvest in the spring, and leaving the other half to lie fallow. In the dry, thin soils of the Mediterranean, this remained the most common cropping pattern throughout the Middle Ages. In the more fertile soils of northern Europe, however, farmers slowly discovered that a three-field crop-rotation system could produce a sustainable increase in overall production. One-third of the land would lie fallow or be used as pasture, so that manure would fertilize the soil; one-third would be planted with winter wheat or rye, sown in the fall and harvested in the early summer; and one-third would be planted in the spring with another crop to be harvested in the fall. These fields were then rotated over a three-year cycle.

This system increased the amount of land under cultivation from 50 to 67 percent, while the two separate growing seasons provided some insurance against loss due to natural disasters or inclement weather. The system also produced higher yields per acre, particularly if legumes or fodder crops like oats were a regular part of the crop-rotation pattern and replaced the nitrogen that wheat and rye leach out of the soil. Both humans and animals could eat oats, and legumes provided a source of protein to balance the intake of carbohydrates from bread and beer, the two main staples of the peasant diet in northern and central Europe. Additional fodder supported more and healthier animals, increasing the efficiency of plow beasts, diversifying the economy of the manor, and providing an additional source of protein through meat and milk. The new crop-rotation system also helped spread labor more evenly over the course of the year.

THE GROWTH OF TOWNS AND TRADE

As we observed in Chapter 7, the urban infrastructure of the western Roman Empire was weakened in the course of the fifth and sixth centuries. A few Roman cities continued to thrive under the lordship of bishops, but many—including Rome itself—began to crumble as their depleted populations could no longer maintain public buildings, services, and defensive walls. In most areas, monasteries replaced cities as the nuclei of civilization in northwestern Europe. Then, under Charlemagne and his imitators, towns came to be planted by royal initiative, as centers for markets and administration. In Anglo-Saxon England, too, King Alfred and his successors established new towns in strategic locations while at the same time reviving older Roman cities. They also issued a reliable and well-regulated currency that encouraged commerce.

Fostering Commerce

Although many towns were devastated by the Viking raids of the tenth century, the agricultural revolution helped to revitalize them—as did the influx of silver and gold set in circulation by the Vikings themselves. The rapid urbanization of

1. Cathedral
2. Alt St. Thomas
3. Alt St. Peter
4. Jung St. Peter
5. St. Nikolaus
6. St. Johann
7. St. Wilhelm
8. St. Stephen

0 50 100   200   300m

☐ Roman fortification, the 'city'

▦ Frankish settlement, called 'New City', walled at end of ninth century

▢ Extension of Frankish settlement before 1200 to include Alt St. Peter's parish

▥ Jung St. Peter's parish, walled 1202–1220

▨ St. Nikolaus parish, walled thirteenth and fourteenth centuries

▦ St. Johann Parish, walled 1374–1390

▄▄▄ St. Wilhelm parish, walled 1387–1441

THE METAMORPHOSIS OF A MEDIEVAL CITY. The city of Strasbourg, on the long-disputed border between modern Germany and France, exemplifies the multilayered dynamics of urban change throughout the Middle Ages. It began as a Roman settlement, which became the nucleus for an episcopal see—hence the cathedral (1) located in the ancient precinct. It was fortified with new walls at the end of the ninth century, as the Carolingian Empire was collapsing and the Vikings were on the move. It then responded to the renewed prosperity of the eleventh and twelfth centuries, far outgrowing its original bounds, and continued to expand for several centuries thereafter. ▪ *Note the scale of the map. What can you conclude from this about the density of settlement in a medieval city?*

Europe in the eleventh and twelfth centuries was also fostered by the initiatives of monasteries and secular lords who saw the economic advantages to be gained from providing safe havens for travelers and trade. This was especially true in the principalities of the Rhineland, the Low Countries, and the independent counties of Flanders and Champagne. Many towns grew up around monasteries, which provided protection and encouraged innovation. In southwestern Europe, existing towns prospered from their status as ports or their location along the overland routes connecting the Mediterranean with the Atlantic. In Italy, which had been decimated by five centuries of warfare and invasion, the growth of towns gave rise to especially dramatic changes.

Initially, the renewed prosperity of Italy depended on the Byzantine emperors' suppression of piracy in the eastern Mediterranean. Hence, the most successful cities around the turn of the millennium were situated in the

Byzantine-controlled areas of the peninsula: Venice in the north and Amalfi, Naples, and Palermo in the south. These were the trading posts that brought silks, spices, and other luxuries from the East into western Europe. In the eleventh century, however, the Norman invasions of southern Italy frequently disrupted this trade, while Turkish invasions of Asia Minor turned Byzantium's attention to the empire's eastern frontier. This opened new opportunities to the northern ports of Genoa and Pisa, whose merchant navies took over the task of policing the eastern Mediterranean.

From Italy and other Mediterranean ports, exotic goods flowed northward to the towns of Flanders and to the organized system of fairs—international markets convened at certain times of the year—that enriched the county of Champagne. Flemish towns, in turn, kept up a brisk trade with England, processing English wool

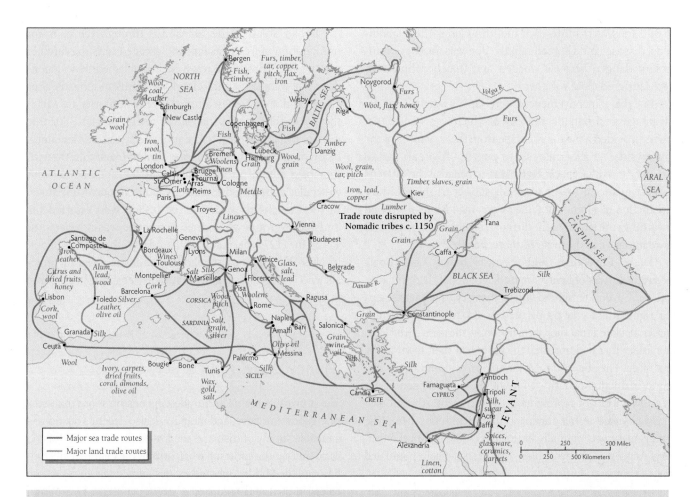

MEDIEVAL TRADE ROUTES. ▪ *What does this map reveal about the relationship between waterways and overland routes during the eleventh and twelfth centuries?* ▪ *Which regions appear to be most extensively interconnected, and why?* ▪ *How does the trade in certain specialized goods create certain commercial patterns?*

into the cloth which, alongside wheat and wine, was the staple commodity of medieval Europe. Eventually, merchants would succeed in opening up a direct route by sea between Italy and the Atlantic ports of northern Europe, after which it became practical to import raw wool directly from England to towns like Florence, which began producing its cloth.

It would be misleading, however, to overemphasize the role of long-distance trade in the urbanization of medieval Europe. Some towns that were dependent on such commerce, like Venice and Genoa, attracted populations approaching 100,000 by 1300. But others that grew to be as large, including Paris and London, drew primarily on the wealth of their surrounding hinterlands for food, raw materials, and the bulk of their population. Furthermore, towns large and small existed in a symbiotic relationship with the countryside, providing

markets for the food surplus of outlying farms and transforming raw materials into marketable goods through manufacturing.

"Town Air Makes You Free"

To modern eyes, most medieval towns would still have seemed half rural. (Indeed, New York City would have seemed so until the end of the nineteenth century.) Streets were often unpaved, houses had gardens for raising vegetables, and animals were everywhere: in the early twelfth century, the heir to the throne of France was killed when his horse tripped over a pig running loose in the streets of Paris. Sanitary conditions were poor, and the air reeked of excrement, both animal and human. (Even in 1900, this was also true of New York, where 150,000 horses produced

45,000 tons of manure each month.) Under these conditions, disease could spread rapidly. Fire was another omnipresent danger, because wooden and thatched buildings were clustered close together.

But these inconveniences were far outweighed by the advantages of urban life, not least of which was the fact that towns provided a means of escape from the strictures of the countryside. As a German adage puts it, "Town air makes you free" (*Stadtluft macht Frei*). This is because the citizens of most medieval towns were not subject to the arbitrary jurisdiction of a lord—or if they were, the lord realized that rewarding initiative with further freedoms fostered still more initiative and produced more wealth.

Many Catalonian and Flemish towns accordingly received charters of liberty from the counts of these regions, and were given the right to govern themselves. Others seized that right: in 1127, the people of Arras, on the Franco-Flemish border, declared that they were no longer the serfs of the local monastery that had nurtured the growth of their town in the first place. They banded together to form a commune, swearing to maintain solidarity with one another and setting up their own form of representative government. The monastery was forced to free them and then free to tax them. The arrangement was mutually beneficial: by the end of the century, Arras was the wealthiest and most densely populated town in northern Europe.

CHRISTIAN BANKERS AND THEIR CLIENTS. As long-distance trade expanded in the Middle Ages, merchants developed new methods of financing their ventures. Many of these practices conflicted with the official policy of the medieval Church, which decried these new investments as usury. This Italian manuscript depicts the seven vices associated with moneylending, but also makes it clear that the people involved in this practice are Christians. (Compare their attire to that of the Jews pictured on page 298 in Chapter 9.)

Urban areas further expanded through the constant immigration of free peasants and escaped serfs in search of a better life. For once a town had established its independence, newcomers could claim the status of citizens after a year and a day; thereafter, the only authority to which they were subject was that of the town's officials. For this reason, some powerful lords and rulers resisted the efforts of towns to claim independence. Almost inevitably, though, they paid a high price for this. In Rome, the pope's claim to secular authority over the city led to frequent uprisings. In the French city of Laon, the bishop who asserted his lordship over a newly formed commune was murdered in 1112. In 1127, the count of Flanders, Charles the Good (r. 1119–27), was assassinated by a family of powerful officials who resented his claims that they were, in fact, his serfs.

Portable Wealth: Money and Credit

The growth of towns and trade depends on more than surplus goods, initiative, and mobility. It also depends on money: a reliable supply of cash and the availability of credit. It is no accident that the earliest participants in the commercial revolution of the Middle Ages were cities located in regions whose rulers minted and regulated a strong currency: Byzantium, Al-Andalus, and the Christian kingdoms of Spain, the old Roman region of Provence (southern France), Anglo-Saxon England, and Flanders. Yet precisely because there were so many currencies in circulation, the economy also depended on moneychangers and bankers who could extend credit to merchants, thus obviating the need to travel roads and waterways with bags full of cash.

Most of the sophisticated financial mechanisms for extending credit and making investments had long been in place throughout the Islamic world and Byzantium, but in western Europe much of this crucial activity was carried forward by Jewish bankers situated within the network of close-knit Jewish communities that connected cities like Constantinople, Baghdad, and Córdoba to the burgeoning cities of the north. In many regions, Jews had a virtual monopoly on these activities, because Christians were technically forbidden to lend money at interest or to make a profit from investments. This practice was called *usury* (from the Latin word for "interest"), and Christian theologians cited various passages from the Old and New Testaments that seemed to condemn it. But in practice, the Roman Church turned a blind eye to such practices. Indeed, many prominent churchmen, including bishops, made fortunes lending money, as did many laymen—especially in towns like Arras and Florence.

Still, the moral stigma attaching to this necessary practice meant that Jews were often the ones targeted at times of crisis, just as they were the people to whom rulers would turn most readily when they needed funds—helping to explain why many kings, princes, and bishops protected the Jewish communities in their realms and often extended special privileges to them in exchange for money. The unfortunate result of this Christian hypocrisy was the circulation of conspiracy theories harmful to Jews, who were perceived as exercising control over Christians through secret channels of communication and a stranglehold on finance. Jewish communities' reliance on the protection of powerful men also made them vulnerable when those men withdrew their support or were incapable of controlling the violence unleashed by their own policies.

VIOLENCE, LORDSHIP, AND MONARCHY

The new wealth of western Europe fostered social mobility, yet it also created a more stratified society. In the Carolingian period, the nobility had comprised a relatively small number of ancient families who counted one another as equals and married among themselves. During the tenth and eleventh centuries, however, new families began to emerge as territorial lords and princes, rivaling and sometimes surpassing the old aristocracy in power and wealth. Some of these new families were descended from lesser officeholders in the Carolingian administration, men who had established independent powers after the empire collapsed and who used their public offices for private gain. Others were successful interlopers who seized control of undefended manors and sustained warbands of treasure-hungry young men.

Tools of Power: Castles and Knights

The predatory lords who emerged in this period protected their territories, their families, and their followers by building strongholds: castles, from the Latin word *castellum*, "little fortress." These structures, seldom known in Europe before the Viking invasions, came to dominate the landscape in the eleventh and twelfth centuries. The castle was both defensive and offensive. It rendered its owner more secure from arson and attack—though it was vulnerable to siege—and it enabled him to dominate the surround-

ing countryside. Indeed, castles often formed the nucleus of a new town by providing protection for the peasants and merchants who clustered their dwellings close to its walls. In case of attack, these outliers could move inside.

Although most early castles were modest structures built of wood, situated on earthwork mounds surrounded by a ditch or moat, stone walls and keeps (fortified towers) soon replaced wooded palisades as the level of competitive violence increased. In Italy, rival families even built castles and towers in the middle of towns. Eventually, some castellans ("castle-holders") acquired enough power and booty to challenge more established lords, laying claim not only to property and influence but to rank. These new lords didn't descend from Roman senators or Carolingian counts; instead, they boasted of lineages reaching back to successful warlords like Rollo the Viking, whom the Normans claimed to be their first duke (from the Latin word *dux*, "leader").

In addition to castle-holding, both the older aristocracy and these self-made lords needed the help of warriors to enforce their claims to power. Accordingly, each lord maintained a private army of men heavily equipped with the new weaponry and armor that the widespread availability of iron—and new techniques for smelting it—made possible. These men fought on horseback, and were therefore called "horsemen": in French, *chevaliers*, and in English, *knights*.

Knighthood was a career that embraced men of widely varying status. Some eleventh-century knights were the younger sons of lords who sought to increase their chances of winning wealth by attaching themselves to the households of greater lords. Others were youths recruited from the peasantry, mounted and armed. All that bound them together was their function, which was the violent prosecution of their lord's interests. Gradually, though, knights also came to regard themselves as belonging to a special military caste with its own rules of conduct. The beginnings of this process are discernible in the *Song of Roland*, and further developments would transform the meaning of chivalry from "horsemanship" to something very different (see below).

Kings, Lords, and Vassals

Despite the emergence of self-governing cities and predatory lordships, the idea of kingship was still a powerful one in continental Europe. For example, the weak Capetian rulers of Paris kept alive the pretense that everyone dwelling in the lands once ruled by more powerful Frankish kings still owed allegiance to them, while the Ottonians claimed

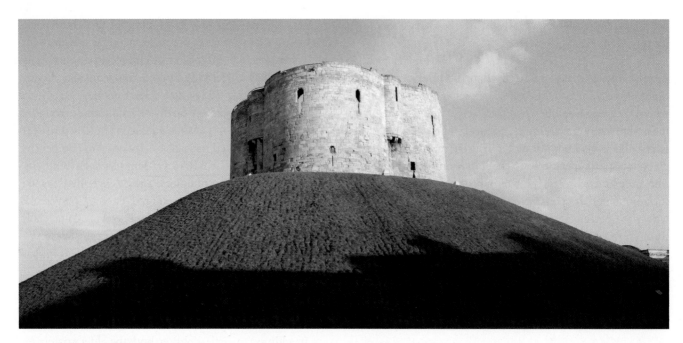

YORK CASTLE (ENGLAND). This fortification exemplifies some of the major phases of medieval castle-building. The large mound is the remains of an earthwork erected on the orders of William the Conqueror in 1068, when it would have been crowned by a wooden palisade: this most basic type of construction is called a motte-and-bailey castle. York's castle remained a wooden tower until it was destroyed by fire and rebuilt in stone after 1245. It is now known as Clifford's Tower, after a rebel leader called Sir Roger Clifford, who was held prisoner there prior to his execution in 1322.

to be kings in northern Italy as well as in their own Saxon domain. In practice, however, neither was able to control the territories they claimed to rule. Effective political and military power lay in the hands of dukes, counts, castellans, and knights, all of whom channeled the increasing wealth of the countryside into their own hands. From their castles, these lords (*domini*) constructed dominions: lordships within which they exercised not only property rights but also the rights to mint money, judge legal cases, raise troops, wage war, collect taxes, and impose tolls.

The Problem of "Feudalism"

This highly diffused distribution of power is conventionally known as "feudalism." But this vague term is unsatisfactory, for several reasons. First and foremost, it is a modern concept not used in the period of history we are discussing. Moreover, it has been used by different people to mean many different things. For example, scholars influenced by the work of Karl Marx (1818–1883, see Chapter 20) use the term *feudalism* to describe an economic system in which wealth is entirely agricultural and cities have not yet formed; as we have seen, this does not reflect the histori-

cal reality of the eleventh and twelfth centuries. For other scholars, feudalism has been construed as an aristocratic social order in which propertied men are bound together by kinship and shared interests; again, this does not explain the varieties of power wielded in this period. Still others have spoken of feudalism as a system of landholding in which lesser men hold land from greater men in return for services of various kinds; but it was not always the greater men who held the most land. Meanwhile, the term has also been used to refer to a system whereby great lords and kings grant land in order to raise troops.

Because all of these definitions of "feudalism" are anachronistic, most recent historians of the Middle Ages have abandoned the use of the term altogether. If, however, we look for a common denominator, we can say that "feudalism" denotes the abuse of official privileges for personal gain: making use of public resources or institutions for private purposes. In this case, there is general agreement that such practices took shape in Frankish lands after the Carolingian Empire had disintegrated and later spread to other areas of Europe, changing as they were adapted to different circumstances. In some regions, these customs fed a developing ideology that justified new kinds of dominion by which kings were supposed to be able to subordinate other powerful men. In this sense, "feudalism" legitimated royal power and helped to lay the groundwork for the emergence of European nation-states.

Although the people living at this time would never have heard the term "feudalism," they would have understood the word at its root: *feudum*, usually translated as "fief" (FEEF). A fief is a gift or grant that creates a kind of contractual relationship between the giver and receiver. This gift could be land, but it could also be the revenues from a toll or a mill, or an annual sum of money. In return, the recipient owed the giver loyalty or services of some kind. In many cases, the gift implied that the recipient was subordinate to the giver and had in fact become the giver's *vassal*, from a Celtic word meaning "boy." This relationship was dramatized in an act of *homage*, a powerful ceremony that made the vassal "the man" (in French, *homme*) of his lord. Typically, the vassal would kneel and place his hands together in a position of prayer, and the lord would cover the clasped hands with his own. He would then raise up his new "man" and exchange a kiss with him. The symbolic importance of these gestures is clear: the lord (*dominus*) was literally the dominating figure. He could protect and raise up his man—but could also discipline him. The role of the vassal, meanwhile, was to support the lord and do nothing to incur his displeasure.

In regions where no centralized authority existed, such personal relationships were essential to creating and maintaining order. However, these relationships were not understood in the same ways all over Europe. Many castellans and knights held their lands freely, owing no service whatsoever to the count or duke within whose territories their lands lay. Nor were these relationships neatly hierarchical. "Feudalism" created no "feudal pyramids," in which knights held fiefs from counts, and counts held fiefs from kings, all in an orderly fashion. Sometimes, kings would insist that the world *should* be structured this way, but they were seldom able to ensure or enforce this.

A New Type of Monarchy: England

The first place where we can begin to observe the efforts of a particular line of kings to establish a monarchy that dominated other powerful lordships is England. In 1066, Duke William of Normandy claimed that he was the rightful successor of the English king, Edward, who had just died. But the English elected a new king, Harold, ignoring William's claim. So William crossed the English Channel to take the kingdom by force, defeating Harold at the Battle of Hastings (see **Interpreting Visual Evidence** on page 262). Now, however, William had to subjugate all of the other chieftains who held power in England, many of whom also aspired to be king.

William accomplished this, first, by asserting that he was king by imperial conquest as well as by succession, and that all the land of England thereby belonged to him. Then William rewarded his Norman followers with fiefs: extensive grants of land taken from their English holders, which the Norman lords were allowed to exploit and subdue. In return, William received their loyalty and a share of their revenues.

The Norman conquerors of England were already accustomed to holding land in return for service to their duke, back in Normandy. But in England, their subordination to the king was further enforced by the effective machinery of the Anglo-Saxon state and by longstanding customs that had the force of law. As king of England, therefore, William was able to exercise a variety of public powers that he could not have enjoyed in Normandy. In England, only the king could coin money and only the king's money was allowed to circulate. As kings of England, William and his successors also inherited the right to collect a national land tax, the right to supervise justice in royal courts, and the right to raise an army. They also retained the Anglo-Saxon officers of local government, known as sheriffs, to help them administer and enforce their rights.

William was thereby able to insist that all the people of England owed ultimate loyalty to the king, even if they did not hold a scrap of land directly from him. William's kingship thus represented a powerful fusion of Carolingian-style traditions of public power with the new forms of lordship that had grown up in the tenth and eleventh centuries, bolstered by indigenous Anglo-Saxon forms of governance. It was a new type of monarchy.

The Struggle for Imperial Power

We can contrast the wide-ranging powers of the new Anglo-Norman kings of England with those of Germany. No German king could claim to rule more than a single principality, and his imperial authority over a host of other rulers was only maintained through a close alliance with the Church. For this reason, the emperor relied heavily on ecclesiastical leaders: his chief administrators were archbishops and bishops whom the emperor himself had appointed and installed in their sacred offices, just as Charlemagne had done. Even the pope was frequently an imperial appointee. The fact that leading churchmen were often members of the imperial family also helped to counter the power of regional rulers.

But in the latter half of the eleventh century, this close cooperation between sacred and secular authority was fractured, and so was the ultimate power of the German monarch.

Interpreting Visual Evidence

The Graphic History of the Bayeux Tapestry

One of the most famous historical documents of all time is not a document at all: it is an embroidered strip of linen 231 feet long (originally much longer) and 20 inches wide. It is also not an actual tapestry, as its name misleadingly implies, but an elaborate exercise in needlepoint. It tells the story of the Norman Conquest of England and the events leading up to it. The circumstances of its making remain mysterious, but it was certainly commissioned by someone close to William the Conqueror (1027–1087), the Norman duke who claimed the throne of England in 1066. Indeed, its purpose was to demonstrate the truth of William's claim and to justify his invasion of England when Harold Godwinson (c. 1022–1066), was crowned king of England in his place (image B). One likely patron is Queen Edith of England, the widow of the late King Edward (r. 1042–66) and sister of Harold, who became a friend and adviser to William. Edith was noted for her skill in embroidery as well as for her political acumen, and she would have been able to oversee the making of this visual history by the women of her household. Two of its evocative scenes, with translations of accompanying Latin texts, are reproduced here.

A. Here Harold Sails the Sea. In this scene from the first portion of the Tapestry, Harold has been sent on an embassy by King Edward. He feasts with friends in a hall on the English coast before crossing the Channel.

B. Here is Seated Harold, King of the English. Although Harold may have promised to relinquish his claim to the English throne in William's favor, the central scene of the tapestry is his coronation. Stigant, the archbishop of Canterbury, stands on his right. Outside the cathedral, the people of London look on curiously. Some appear to be surprised or alarmed.

Questions for Analysis

1. Like a graphic novel or a comic strip, the Bayeux Tapestry tells its story through images; words (in very simple Latin) play a minor role. What do the Tapestry's artists choose to express exclusively through visualization? When do they choose to state something verbally? What might be the motivation behind these choices? What is left out of the story, or left ambiguous? What might be the reason(s) for this?

2. In addition to being a source for political and military historians, the Bayeux Tapestry provides us with fascinating glimpses into the daily life and material culture of the Middle Ages. What, for example, can you conclude about the necessary preparations for a voyage by sea? About the history of clothing, or weaponry, or animals?

3. If Queen Edith is responsible for making the Tapestry, it would constitute one of the few surviving historical accounts by a woman prior to the twentieth century. Would the fact of the creator's gender change your perception of this artifact or of these particular scenes? Why or why not?

REX·ROGAT ABBATEM· MATHILDIM SUPPLICAT ATQ;

MATILDA OF TUSCANY MEDIATES BETWEEN EMPEROR AND POPE. Matilda was one of the most powerful rulers in eleventh-century Europe, controlling many strategic territories in northern Italy. Fluent in German as well as Latin and Italian, she was a key mediator in the struggle between the emperor and the pope and a supporter of the reforming movement within the Church. The Latin inscription accompanying this manuscript miniature reads: "The King entreats the Abbot [i.e., the pope] and even humbles himself before Matilda." ▪ *How does this image represent the relationships among these figures?* ▪ *Which appears to be the most powerful, and why?*

In 1056, the six-year-old Henry IV (1050–1106) succeeded his father as king and emperor; and as we will frequently note, political competition among the advisers of underage rulers often escalates into larger conflicts. In this case, the German princes of various regions—led by the disenfranchised Saxon nobility—tried to gain control of the royal government at the expense of Henry's regents. When Henry began to rule in his own right, in 1073, these hostilities escalated into a civil war. At the same time, the newly elected pope, Gregory VII (r. 1073–85), began to insist that no laymen—not even royal ones—should have any influence within the Church. (This would become a core contention in a movement toward increased papal power, to be discussed in the next section.)

King Henry, of course, resisted any initiative that would prohibit him from selecting his own bishops and abbots: for these were the key players in the administration of his realm. So Pope Gregory allied himself with the rebellious Saxon nobility and together they moved to depose Henry. In order to save his crown, Henry was therefore forced to acknowledge the pope's superiority by begging forgiveness. Crossing the Alps into Italy in 1077, in the depths of winter, he found Gregory installed at the castle of Canossa under the protection of one of Europe's most powerful rulers, Matilda of Tuscany. Encouraged by Matilda, who interceded on his behalf, Henry performed an elaborate ritual of penance, standing for three successive days outside the gates of the castle, barefoot, stripped of his imperial trappings, clad in the sackcloth of a supplicant.

This performance of subjection and servitude forestalled Henry's deposition, but it did not resolve his dispute with the nobility of German lands. And it also symbolically reversed the relationship between secular power and religious power. Since the time of Constantine, popes had been dependent on the rulers who protected them. Now an emperor had been bested by the pope. For the other kings and lords of Europe, Henry's humiliation was a chilling example of what could happen when a king let himself be made a vassal.

RELIGIOUS REFORM AND PAPAL POWER

The increased power of the papacy in the eleventh century was a result of the processes we have been surveying in this chapter, but it was also a development that would have been hard to foresee at the time of Charlemagne's death. In the wake of the Viking invasions and the redistribution of power within the former Carolingian Empire, no ruler could maintain Charlemagne's hold on the Church. Many parish churches had been abandoned or destroyed, while those that survived were often regarded as the personal property of some local family, whose responsibility for protecting parishioners could become an excuse to oppress them. Bishoprics, too, were co-opted by families who regarded Church lands and offices as their private property. Monasteries underwent a further process of privatization, becoming safe havens for aristocratic younger sons and daughters with little inclination for religious life. Meanwhile, the holders of papal office were its worst abusers. Most were incompetent or corrupt, the sons or tools of powerful Roman families. Many fathered sons who themselves succeeded to high ecclesiastical office, including that of pope. As the guardian of the tombs of Peter and Paul, the bishop of Rome had long occupied a privileged position. Now, however, the papacy's credibility had been severely compromised.

The Monastic Reform Movement

The first successful attempts to restore the spiritual authority of the Roman Church can be traced to the founding of a new kind of monastery in Burgundy (now southeastern France). In 910, a Benedictine abbey called Cluny freed itself from any obligation to local families by placing itself under the direct protection of the papacy. And although it had a wealthy benefactor, that benefactor relinquished control over Cluny's property; instead, Duke William of Aquitaine and his family gained the spiritual support and prayers of the monks, whose intercessions might help to save warlike men from eternal damnation.

This arrangement would set a new precedent for the relationship between monasteries and powerful families for centuries to come, as Cluny began to sponsor other monasteries on the same model. Indeed, the foundation of these daughter houses was another innovation: prior to this, all Benedictine monasteries had been independent of one another, united only by their observance of Benedict's *Rule*. Now Cluny established a network of Cluniac clones across Europe, all of which remained subordinate to the mother house. By 1049, there were sixty-seven such Cluniac priories (as the daughter monasteries were called), each one performing the same elaborate round of prayer and worship for which Cluny became famous, and each one entirely free from the control of local lords who hoped to reap spiritual rewards from their support of the pious monks.

Cluniac influence was strongest in the former Frankish territories and in Italy, where the virtual absence of effective kingship allowed monastic reforms to thrive unchecked. In Germany and England, by contrast, fostering monastic reform emerged as an essential responsibility of Christian rulers whose role model was the pious Charlemagne. These rulers, too, followed Cluniac example by insisting on the strict observance of poverty, chastity, and obedience within the monastery, and on the performance of liturgical prayer. Yet because they were the guarantors of the monasteries' freedom from outside interference, it was they who appointed the abbots, just as they also appointed the bishops of their kingdoms. As a result of this trend, and the concurrent Norman conquest of England, future kings of England would have more direct control over Church lands than other European rulers. In Germany, a prince's right to appoint spiritual leaders would be the central cause of strife with the papacy (see below).

Despite the differences in sponsorship, these parallel reforming movements made monasticism the dominant spiritual model for Latin Christianity. The peaceful, orderly round of daily worship in monasteries and convents was regarded as mirroring a perfect celestial harmony, and monastic prayers were considered uniquely effective because of nuns' and monks' holy way of life. Monasteries also had an important influence on the piety of ordinary people, because many monastic communities maintained parishes that ministered directly to the laity. The spiritual practices that had been unique to monks and nuns in earlier centuries therefore came to influence daily life outside the cloister.

THE ABBEY CHURCH AT CLUNY. Its extraordinary wealth and power made Cluny a major target during the French Wars of Religion and again during the French Revolution, when locals who had been subjected to its lordship for centuries razed most of the buildings to the ground (see Chapters 14 and 18). This artist's reconstruction shows the vast abbey church as it might have looked by the twelfth century, after several extensive building campaigns. In its day, Cluny was one of the largest structures in Europe and a quintessential example of the architectural style known as Romanesque.

2. CLUNY (NO).

Analyzing Primary Sources

A Miraculous Reliquary

Although pilgrimages had been a part of Christian religious practice for centuries, they became much more central elements of popular piety from the tenth century on. Pilgrims brought money and spiritual prestige to the monasteries and cathedrals that housed miracle-working relics, and competition among monastic houses sometimes led one house to steal the relics of another. But some critics worried that these newly popular shrines were encouraging idolatry. Bernard of Angers (c. 960–1028) was one such critic. His account of a visit to the shrines of several saints, including that of Sainte Foy ("Saint Faith") at Conques, reveals the negative impression that ornate reliquaries made on him—and the power of wonder-working relics to correct that impression.

t is an ancient custom in all of Auvergne, Rodez, Toulouse, and the neighboring regions that the local saint has a statue of gold, silver, or some other metal . . . [that] serves as a reliquary for the head of the saint or for a part of his body. The learned might see in this a superstition and a vestige of the cult of demons, and I myself . . . had the same impression the first time I saw the statue of Saint Gerard . . . resplendent with gold and stones, with an expression so human that the simple people . . . pretend that it winks at pilgrims whose prayers it answers. I admit to my shame that turning to my friend Bernerius and laughing, I whispered to him in Latin, "What do you think of the idol? Wouldn't Jupiter or Mars be happy with it?" . . .

Three days later we arrived at [the shrine of] St. Faith. . . . We approached [the reliquary] but the crowd was such that we could not prostrate ourselves like so many others already lying on the floor. Unhappy, I remained standing, fixing my view on the image and murmuring this prayer, "St. Faith, you whose relics rest in this sham, come to my assistance on the day of judgment." And this time I looked at my companion . . . because I found it outrageous that all of these rational beings should be praying to a mute and inanimate object. . . .

Later I greatly regretted to have acted so stupidly toward the saint of God.

This was because among other miracles [that] Don Adalgerius, at that time dean and later . . . abbot [of Conques], told me [was] a remarkable account of a cleric named Oldaric. One day when the venerable image had to be taken to another place, . . . he restrained the crowd from bringing offerings and he

The Reliquary of Saint Faith, Early Tenth Century.

insulted and belittled the image of the saint. . . . The next night, a lady of imposing severity appeared to him: "You," she said, "how dare you insult my image?" Having said this, she flogged her enemy with a staff. . . . He survived only long enough to tell the vision in the morning.

Thus there is no place left for arguing whether the effigy of St. Faith ought to be venerated since it is clear that he who reproached the holy martyr nevertheless retracted his reproach. Nor is it a spurious idol where nefarious rites of sacrifice or of divination are conducted, but rather a pious memorial of a holy virgin, before which great numbers of faithful people decently and eloquently implore her efficacious intercession for their sins.

Source: Bernard of Angers, "The Book of the Miracles of St. Faith," in *Readings in Medieval History*, 3rd ed., ed. and trans. Patrick J. Geary (Peterborough, Ont., Canada: 2003), pp. 333–34 (slightly modified).

Questions for Analysis

1. Why does Bernard initially object to the display of relics in ornate reliquaries? Why would he consider this practice blasphemous? How does he become reconciled to it?

2. Can you think of present-day practices that resemble the medieval fascination with collecting, displaying, and venerating relics? What do such practices reveal about any society?

Relics and Pilgrims

One potent example of this new popular spirituality is the growing devotion to relics. Monasteries were often the repositories of cherished objects associated with saints, such as fragments of bone or pieces of cloth cut from the garments of some holy person. These souvenirs were believed to possess special protective and curative powers. Hence, a relic was usually buried beneath the altar of a church during the ceremony of its consecration, in order to render the church building sacrosanct. Relics were also collected and displayed in elaborate reliquaries made of precious metals and studded with jewels, casings that reflected and augmented the value of the holy objects contained within them.

Indeed, relics were so valuable that monasteries and cathedrals competed with one another for their acquisition and even plotted the "holy theft" of a particularly prized treasure. For instance, the relics of Nicholas, a fourth-century bishop of Myra (in Turkey), were stolen from the saint's tomb during the eleventh century. These were brought to Bari in southeastern Italy, where Benedictine monks built a magnificent church to house them. It became a major—and lucrative—attraction for pilgrims.

The possession and display of relics thus became a way for monasteries to attract attention and generate revenue, since those who sought cures or favors at the shrine of a saint would often make a donation to the monastery in the saint's honor. If a saint was especially famous for a particular type of miracle, pilgrims might travel thousands of miles to visit a shrine. Saint Nicholas was famous for increasing the wealth of his suppliants, and for bestowing gifts—hence his later incarnation as Santa Claus. The relics of Sainte Foy ("Saint Faith") of Conques (southern France) were renowned for their power to rectify injustices, restore order, and heal the maladies that afflicted the poor. Those of the apostle James at Compostela (northern Spain) became the chief destination on a major pilgrimage route, rivaling even the holy sites of Rome and Jerusalem in its popularity. Pilgrimage was another of the important ways in which the new patterns of Christian piety that developed in monasteries began to spread to the laity.

The Reform of the Secular Clergy

By the eleventh century, the movement toward spiritual renewal in the monasteries of Europe began to embrace the sees of bishops. This was a major change: bishops and the priests who served in their dioceses were secular clergy, living in the world (*saeculum* in Latin); it had long been expected that they would share some of the worldly preoccupations and lifestyles of their parishioners. But as the values and priorities of monasticism began to spread outward, abbots were more often appointed to episcopal office. Meanwhile, even nonmonastic bishops were forced to adopt stricter standards of personal conduct. Bishops also began to rebuild and expand their cathedral churches to make them more suitable reflections of divine majesty, in accordance with Cluniac example.

As their influence grew, the monasteries under the sway of Cluny began to lobby for even larger reforms, amounting to a fundamental dismantling of customs that reached back to the organization of the Church under Constantine, seven centuries earlier. They centered their attacks on the practice of simony (*SIGH-mony*), a term describing any use of ecclesiastical office for personal gain, including the purchase or sale of a bishopric or a priest's living (i.e., house, goods, and annual salary). In other words, the reform movement targeted the very structure of the Church as a network of independent lordships held by powerful men in trust for their families.

Even more radical was the reformers' demand that secular clergy share the lifestyles of monks, taking vows not only of personal poverty but of celibacy. Although some early councils of the Church had attempted to regulate the marriage of bishops and priests, none had been successful. And for good reason: the task of ministering to the laity was very different from the monk's task of perpetual prayer and communal life. For a thousand years, it had been conceded that the demands of priestly celibacy were unreasonable, and would deprive a priest's parishioners of an additional resource and ministry—that of his wife. In the year 1000, therefore, the vast majority of parish priests all across Europe were married, and in the eastern Orthodox Church they would remain so. Married bishops were rarer, but not unknown. In Brittany, the archbishop of Dol and his wife publicly celebrated the marriages of their daughters, endowing them with lands belonging to the bishopric; in Milan, the archbishops flatly rejected reformers' calls for celibacy, declaring that their patron saint, Ambrose (see Chapter 6), had been married, too.

The Reform of the Papacy

In Rome, the most powerful bishopric of all remained resolutely unreformed until 1046, when the German emperor Henry III deposed three rival Roman nobles who claimed to be pope and appointed in their place his own relative, a monk who adopted the name Leo IX (r. 1049–54). Leo and his supporters took control of the papal court and began to promulgate decrees against simony and clerical marriage. They then took steps to enforce these decrees by traveling throughout the Continent, disciplining and removing from office clerics deemed guilty of simony or obstinately

Past and Present

Ideas of Crusade

The launching of the First Crusade was the beginning of a trend that decisively shaped the relations between western Europeans and their neighbors, and that continues today. The very use of the word "crusade" is apt to cause trouble—as when President George W. Bush spoke of "this crusade, this war on terrorism" to which he pledged the United States after September 11, 2001.

 Watch related author interview on StudySpace
wwnorton.com/web/westernciv18

---

determined not to "put away" their wives—whom the reformers insisted on calling "concubines" as a way of discrediting these respectable relationships.

Implicit in Leo's reforming efforts was a new vision of the Church as a type of monarchy, with the pope at the apex of a spiritual pyramid: an ideal difficult for any secular ruler to realize and one that would severely limit the power of other ecclesiastical officeholders. Not surprisingly, therefore, Leo and his successors met with considerable opposition from powerful leaders within the Church itself, and they could only enforce their claims in regions where they had the support of secular rulers. Chief among these was the pious emperor Henry III, whose protection insulated papal reformers from the Roman nobility, who would otherwise have deposed or assassinated them.

But when Henry III died in 1056, the regents of his child heir Henry IV (whose reign we discussed above) were neither able nor willing to stand behind the reform-

ing movement. In 1058, the Roman aristocracy seized this opportunity to install one of their own number on the papal throne. By this time, however, the reform movement had gathered momentum; a year later, a new pope had been installed and was determined to counter any interference from either the German or Italian nobility. To this end, Nicholas II (r. 1059–61) created a new legislative body, the College of Cardinals (from the Latin for "collection" of "hinges"). Hitherto, local bishops around Rome had served the papacy as advisers and assistants, but now the College became the nexus for the creation of papal policy. It also ensured the continuity of the papal office by overseeing the selection of new popes, a role it still plays today.

Needless to say, this novel arrangement infuriated the advisers of the young Henry IV, since it removed the emperor's prerogative to oversee the process of papal elections himself. And it set the stage for the confrontations that were to follow.

The Investiture Conflict

A few years after Henry IV began to rule in his own right, the new College of Cardinals selected as pope a zealous reformer called Hildebrand, a Cluniac monk of Tuscan origins who had been a protégé of Leo IX. He took the name Gregory VII. Initially, pope and emperor treated one another with deference. Henry IV's position in Germany had been weakened by his wars with the Saxon nobility, and he needed papal backing to restore his authority. In his letters to the new pope, he therefore blamed the advisers of his youth for the troubles that had arisen between his own court and that of Rome, and he promised to make amends. Gregory, in turn, spoke of pope and emperor as the two eyes of a single, Christian body. On the surface, it appeared that harmonious relations might be restored.

Two year later, however, relations between papacy and empire were riven by a conflict that would permanently alter the relationship between spiritual and temporal leaders in western Europe. Superficially, the issue that divided Gregory and Henry was that of investiture, the right to appoint bishops and to equip them with the trappings of office. Since the time of the Carolingians, this had been the prerogative of the emperor—as it was in Byzantium. But to Gregory, this practice smacked of simony, since a lay lord would obviously choose bishops who would be politically useful to him, regardless of their spiritual qualifications.

The issue, however, was not the political power of bishops; it was the control of that power. For paradoxically, the papal reform movement as it developed under Gregory was predicated on liberating the Church from powerful worldly influences in order that the Church itself might become more worldly and powerful. This was the principle that lay behind the discouraging of clerical marriage, too: Church offices and Church property had to be protected by the Church for the Church. Allowing priests to marry might encourage the handing down of offices to sons, just as allowing rulers to appoint bishops encouraged these bishops to act as the rulers' agents. These practices tainted the austere authority that the pope was trying to cultivate, and it also threatened to alienate property and power that the papacy wanted to harness for its own purposes.

Gregory therefore took the reform movement to a new level, insisting that adherence to these principles was not just a matter of policy but a matter of religious dogma, a term defined as "a truth necessary for salvation." When Henry IV refused to accept this and proceeded to invest the new archbishop of Milan, Gregory reminded him that, as the successor of Saint Peter and the representative of Christ on earth, he himself had the power to save or damn all souls. To drive the point home, Gregory excommunicated a number of Henry's advisers, including several of the bishops who had participated in the investiture at Milan. Henry thereupon renounced his obedience to Gregory, calling on him to resign. Gregory responded by excommunicating Henry, along with his supporters.

In itself, the excommunication of a king was not terribly unusual. Gregory, however, went much further by equating excommunication with deposition, declaring that since Henry was no longer a faithful son of the Church, he was no longer the king of Germany and his subjects had a sacred duty to rebel against him. It was this that occasioned Henry's humiliating stand before the castle at Canossa in January of 1077. But the story does not end there, because Henry used his restored powers to crush his Saxon opponents and eventually to drive Gregory himself from Rome. In 1085, the aged pope died in exile in southern Italy. By then, however, he had established the principles on which papal governance would be based for the remainder of the Middle Ages.

In 1122, the conflict over investiture was provisionally resolved through compromise at the Concordat of Worms (VOHRMS) in Germany. Its terms declared that the emperor was forbidden to invest prelates with the *religious* symbols of their office but was allowed to invest them with the symbols of their rights as *temporal* rulers, in his capacity as their overlord. In practice, then, the rulers of Europe retained a great deal of influence over ecclesiastical appointments. But they also had to acknowledge that bishops were now part of a clerical hierarchy headed by the pope, and that they were supposed to be loyal to the Church in Rome and not to the ruler of the region in which they lived.

CRUSADING CAUSES AND OUTCOMES

Gregory VII's equation of excommunication with deposition had given the pope a powerful new weapon to use against wayward rulers. Indeed, according to a series of pronouncements issued in his name, Gregory insisted that the pope has the power to judge all men but cannot himself be judged by any earthly authority. Moreover, he has the power to free any man from his obligations to his lord because every Christian owes ultimate loyalty to the pope, the arbiter of eternal life or death. These were big claims. How could they be realized? Gregory's immediate successors would soon be driven to great lengths in their efforts to establish the credibility of the newly reformed and powerful papacy. In the end, it took the appeal of a Byzantine emperor and the preaching of a crusade against Islam to unite western Christendom under the papal banner.

The Expansion and Limitations of Byzantium

As Europe expanded and changed, the eastern Roman Empire was undergoing its own series of transformations. The decline of the Abbasid Caliphate in Baghdad had relieved some of the pressures on its borders in the course of the ninth century. But at the same time, Byzantium was facing some new threats. In the mid-ninth century, Muslims from North Africa captured the Byzantine islands of Sicily and Crete. Meanwhile, the migration of pagan Slavs into the Balkans was rapidly undermining Byzantine control of that region; and a formidable power had emerged in the north, as the Viking Rus' established themselves along the river systems that fed into the Black and Caspian Seas. The Rus's most important trading partner was the Abbasid Caliphate, with which they exchanged slaves, honey, wax, and furs for silver, Indian spices, and Chinese silks. But the Rus' knew their way to Constantinople, too. In 860, while the Byzantine emperor and his army were busy on the eastern frontier, a fleet of them sailed into the Black Sea and sacked the capital.

The best that the emperor in Byzantium could do was to make these newer enemies their allies. Greek-speaking missionaries began the process by converting some of the Balkan Slavs to Orthodox Christianity, devising for them a written language known as Old Church Slavonic and creating the Cyrillic alphabet still used today in Bulgaria, Serbia, and Russia. As we have often seen, domination went hand in glove with conversion: the Byzantines also established a military and commercial alliance with the kingdom centered around Kiev, and in 911 hundreds of Rus' served with the Byzantine navy in an attack on Muslim Crete. Diplomatic relations were also established: in 957, a Kievan princess named Olga was lavishly entertained on a state visit to Constantinople. And in 989, the emperor Basil II turned to

THE BYZANTINE EMPIRE, c. 1025. ■ *According to the map, what political challenges faced the Byzantine Empire in the eleventh century?* ■ *How was the long-standing influence of Muslims in the Near East likely to affect the character of Byzantine culture?* ■ *How did the domain of Kievan Rus' potentially create additional economic and military pressure on Byzantium, directly as well as indirectly?*

Vladimir, prince of Kiev, for the troops he needed to win a civil war against an imperial rival. In return for Vladimir's help, Basil married him to his sister Anna; and Vladimir, along with his people, accepted baptism into the Orthodox Church. (Russia has remained strongly Orthodox to this day, despite Soviet efforts to dismantle the Russian Orthodox Church in the twentieth century.)

In the tenth century, the eastern Roman Empire further strengthened its position by launching a series of successful campaigns against the Abbasids, reconquering territories that had been lost since the seventh century. But although most of the peoples of this region had remained Christian through three centuries of Islamic rule, the Armenians and the Syrians in particular had their own distinctive Christian traditions that were at odds, both doctrinally and linguistically, with the Greek-speaking church at Constantinople. Reincorporating these "heretics" into the empire strained the limits of Orthodoxy to a considerable degree, and these efforts also created a center of power that lay outside the imperial capital at Constantinople. Accordingly, rivalries divided the eastern nobility and the imperial court, eventually erupting into warfare after one aristocratic family attempted a coup.

Meanwhile, projects of reconquest and expansion were overextending the Byzantine military and its treasury. In an effort to raise cash, some emperors in the mid-eleventh century began to debase the gold coinage that had kept the empire competitive with the Islamic Caliphate, thus undermining Byzantine commerce at the very moment when Venice, Genoa, and Pisa were consolidating their control in the eastern Mediterranean and taking over the lucrative trade between Muslim North Africa (including Egypt) and western Europe.

A failing economy, ongoing dynastic civil war, the weakened condition of the army, and uneasy relations with the new kingdoms of the Balkans (especially Hungary) proved nearly fatal to Byzantine sovereignty. And then the empire was confronted with yet another threat. The Seljuq Turks, a powerful dynasty of Sunni Muslims who were building their own empire based in Persia, began to move westward in the latter part of the eleventh century. In 1071, they captured Armenia and moved swiftly into the Byzantine heartland of Anatolia (Turkey), where they destroyed a Byzantine army sent to deflect them.

At a blow, the wealthiest and most productive part of the empire fell into Muslim hands—and not those of the Abbasids with whom the Byzantines had contended for centuries. In the same year, the Seljuqs captured Jerusalem, which had been part of a Shi'ite caliphate based in Egypt, ruled by the Fatimids. By 1081, when the eastern nobility of Byzantium finally emerged triumphant in their ongoing bid

for the imperial throne, the new emperor Alexius Comnenus (r. 1081–1118) found himself at the head of a crippled state.

The Call for a Crusade

Alexius was an able emperor. In the first decade of his rule, he managed to shore up the failing economy and secure his hold over Bulgarian territory in the Balkans. He then began to plan a campaign against the Seljuqs. But with what forces? The Byzantine army had been decimated in Greece by a far superior cavalry of Norman knights in 1085. For by this time, the Normans had established independent principalities in southern Italy and Sicily and were moving farther east, taking advantage of the perpetual power vacuum in the Mediterranean and showcasing the effective tactics of chivalry. As it happened, this encounter between the Byzantine emperor and western

ROLAND AS A CRUSADING KNIGHT. The association between knighthood and crusading helped to raise the social status of knights and contributed to the refinement of a chivalric ethos. Here, a crusading knight, dressed head to foot in expensive chain mail, is shown kneeling in homage to his lord, God.

Europe's most formidable warriors was historically significant. It convinced Alexius that such heavily armed horsemen would be successful if pitted against the lightly armored Seljuqs.

It was in the hopes of recruiting a mercenary force, therefore, that Alexius approached Pope Urban II (r. 1088–99). This was a move that played into the hands of the reformed papacy. Urban was trying hard to realize some of the powerful claims that his recent predecessors had made on behalf of papal authority, and this seemed like a golden opportunity. By coming to the aid of the eastern Roman Empire, he would show the restive princes of western Europe that the papacy was a force to be reckoned with. At the same time, he hoped to show that Latin military and spiritual might was greater than that of the weakened Greeks, thereby healing the schism between Orthodox and

Latin Christianities and realizing the centuries-old dream of a universal Christian Church based in Rome, with the pope at its head. In addition, Urban would thereby show support for another reforming effort that had gained momentum in recent years: a peace movement that was attempting to quell the endemic violence unleashed by competitive bands of knights and their rapacious lords. What better way to defuse the situation than to ship those violent energies overseas, deploying them against a common enemy?

So Alexius received a favorable reply, but he got far more than he had asked for—or wanted. He had needed a modest contingent of a few thousand troops, to help him reconquer Anatolia. What he got was a vast army of 100,000 men, charged by Urban II to retake the holy city of Jerusalem for Christendom. For Urban decided to interpret Alexius's

THE ROUTES OF THE CRUSADERS, 1096–1204. Compare the routes followed by participants in the first three Crusades. ▪ *What were the three main routes followed by crusaders?* ▪ *What geographical and political factors appear to be determining these trajectories?* ▪ *Why was the Fourth Crusade so different?*

Competing Viewpoints

Preaching the First Crusade: Two Accounts

> We owe the following account of Urban II's call for a crusade to Fulcher of Chartres, a priest who was present at the Council of Clermont in 1095 and who later served as a chaplain to the first Norman king of Jerusalem, Baldwin. It forms part of Fulcher's contemporary chronicle of the First Crusade. The second account of the motives behind the crusade comes from a biography of the Byzantine emperor Alexius Comnenus, written by his daughter Anna (1083–1153), who also lived through these events.

Pope Urban II's Call at Clermont, November 1195

Most beloved brethren: Urged by necessity, I, Urban, by the permission of God chief bishop and prelate over the whole world, have come into these parts as an ambassador with a divine admonition to you, the servants of God. . . .

Although, O sons of God, you have promised more firmly than ever to keep the peace among yourselves and to preserve the rights of the Church, there remains still an important work for you to do. Freshly quickened by the divine correction, you must apply the strength of your righteousness to another matter which concerns you as well as God. For your brethren who live in the east are in urgent need of your help, and you must hasten to give them the aid which has often been promised them. For, as most of you have heard, the Turks and Arabs have attacked them and have conquered the territory of Romania [the Byzantine Empire] as far west as the shore of the Mediterranean and the Hellespont. . . . They have occupied more and more of the lands of those Christians, and have overcome them in seven battles. They have killed and captured many, and have destroyed the churches and devastated the empire.

If you permit them to continue thus for a while with impunity, the faithful of God will be much more widely attacked by them. On this account I, or rather the Lord, beseech you as Christ's heralds to publish this everywhere and to persuade all people of whatever rank, footsoldiers and knights, poor and rich, to carry aid promptly to those Christians and to destroy that vile race from the lands of our friends. I say this to those who are present, but it is meant also for those who are absent. Moreover, Christ commands it.

All who die by the way, whether by land or by sea, or in battle against the pagans, shall have immediate remission of sins. This I grant them through the power of God with which I am invested. O what a disgrace, if such a despised and base race, which worships demons, should conquer a people which has the faith of omnipotent God and is made glorious with the name of Christ! With what reproaches will the Lord overwhelm us if you do not aid those who, with us, profess the Christian religion!

Let those who have been accustomed to wage unjust private warfare against the faithful now go against the infidels and end with victory this war which should have been begun long ago. Let those who for a long time have been robbers now become knights. Let those who have been fighting against their brothers and relatives now fight in a proper way against the barbarians. Let those who have been serving as mercenaries for small pay now obtain the eternal reward. Let those who have been wearing themselves out in both body

request very loosely. Speaking before an assembled crowd at an ecclesiastical council at Clermont (central France) in 1095, he announced that he fully supported the peace movement. He said, furthermore, that any knights who wished to fight, pillage, and wreak havoc could do so for a just and Christian cause by liberating the Holy Land from its Muslim captors. At home, said Urban, most knights were riffraff and marauders, destined for hellfire and damnation; abroad, they would be crusaders, which meant that anyone fighting or dying in the service of Christ would win absolution for his sins. By taking up the cross (*crux*, hence "crusade"), a warrior stood to win glory, booty, and salvation.

This was an irresistible trifecta for many pious, ambitious, or opportunistic men. Consequently, the ultimate and soul now work for a double honor. Behold! On this side will be the sorrowful and poor, on that, the rich; on this side, the enemies of the Lord, on that, his friends. Let those who go not put off the journey, but rent their lands and collect money for their expenses; and as soon as winter is over and spring comes, let them eagerly set out on the way with God as their guide.

Source: S. J. Allen and Emilie Amt, eds., *The Crusades: A Reader* (Peterborough, ON, Canada: 2003), pp. 39–40.

Anna Comnena Describes the Beginnings of the First Crusade

[A]lexius] had no time to relax before he heard a rumour that countless Frankish armies were approaching. He dreaded their arrival, knowing as he did their uncontrollable passion, their erratic character and their irresolution, not to mention . . . their greed for money. . . . So far from despairing, however, he made every effort to prepare for war if need arose. What actually happened was more far-reaching and terrible than rumour suggested, for the whole of the West and all the barbarians who lived between the Adriatic and the Straits of Gibraltar migrated in a body to Asia, marching across Europe country by country with all their households. The reason for this mass-movement is to be found more or less in the following events. A certain Kelt, called Peter [the Hermit] . . . left to worship at the Holy Sepulchre and after suffering much ill-treatment at the hands of the Turks and Saracens who were plundering the whole of Asia, he

returned home with difficulty. Unable to admit defeat, . . . he worked out a clever scheme. He decided to preach in all the Latin countries. A divine voice, he said, commanded him to proclaim to all the counts in France that all should depart from their homes, set out to worship at the Holy Shrine, and . . . strive to liberate Jerusalem. . . . Surprisingly, he was successful. . . . Full of enthusiasm and ardour they thronged every highway, and with these warriors came a host of civilians, outnumbering the sand of the sea shore or the stars of heaven, carrying palms and bearing crosses on their shoulders. There were women and children, too, who had left their own countries. . . .

The upheaval that ensued as men *and* women took to the road was unprecedented within living memory. The simpler folk were in very truth led on by a desire to worship at Our Lord's tomb and visit the holy places, but the more villainous characters . . . had an ulterior purpose, for they hoped on their

journey to seize the capital [Jerusalem] itself, looking upon its capture as a natural consequence of the expedition. . . .

Source: Excerpted from Anna Comnena, *The Alexiad*, trans. E. R. A. Sewter (New York: 1969), pp. 308–11.

Questions for Analysis

1. Given Urban II's explanation of the problems confronting the Byzantine Empire, how do you account for the fact that the Crusades were directed toward the Holy Land and not to the relief of Byzantium?

2. How does Anna Comnena represent the motives of Peter the Hermit and the crusaders? What distinctions does she make among the participants?

3. Are there points of comparison between these two accounts? On what do they agree? How would you explain the differences between them?

response to Urban's call exceeded all expectations. Indeed, his message was amplified by other preachers, including a zealous priest called Peter the Hermit, who claimed (falsely) that he had been prevented by the Seljuqs from visiting the Holy Land. Within a year, tens of thousands of warriors and a large number of women and children from all over western Europe were on the march toward Constantinople,

where they intended to gather before departing for Jerusalem. As with any large enterprise, the participants' motives must have varied. A few might have hoped to win principalities for themselves. Others were drawn by the prospect of adventure. Many were the dependents of greater men, who had no choice but to accompany their lords; some hoped to free themselves from dependence by fighting. Most probably had no idea how long the journey would be or knew anything about the places for which they were destined.

But the dominant motive for joining this First Crusade was religious. Except for a few of the greatest lords—mostly Normans from Sicily and southern Italy—the prospect of winning new lands was both unlikely and undesired. Indeed, one of the greatest challenges facing the Christian kingdom that was established in Jerusalem after 1099 was the fact that crusaders so rarely wanted to stay. After fulfilling their vows, the vast majority went home. So why did they go in the first place? The risks of dying on such a journey were high; the costs of embarking were enormous. Crusading knights needed a minimum of two years' revenues in hand to finance the journey. To raise such sums, most were forced to mortgage lands and borrow heavily from family, friends, monasteries, and merchants. They then had to find some way to pay back these loans if and when they returned home. By any rational assessment, the Crusade was a fool's errand.

The seeming irrationality of this endeavor underscores the importance of reckoning with the crusaders' piety, and even their desire to emulate legendary heroes like Roland. Crusading was the ultimate pilgrimage, the holy places of Jerusalem the ultimate Christian shrines. If anyone could receive special blessings by traveling to Compostela, Conques, or Bari, how much more blessed would be those who fought through to the Holy Land! Urban II made this point explicit at Clermont, promising that crusaders would be freed from all penances imposed by the Church. Some zealots went even further, promising that crusaders would be entirely freed from otherworldly punishments for all sins committed up to that point in their lives, and that the souls of those who died on crusade would go straight to heaven.

Crusade preaching also emphasized the vengeance that Christ's soldiers should exact on his pagan enemies. So to some crusaders, it seemed absurd to wait until they arrived in the Holy Land to undertake this aspect of their mission. Muslims might hold Jesus's property at Jerusalem, but Christian theology held Jews responsible for the death of Jesus himself. Assaults against Jewish communities therefore began in the spring of 1096 and quickly spread eastward with the crusaders. Hundreds of Jews were killed in the German towns of Mainz, Worms, Speyer, and Cologne, and hundreds more were forcibly baptized as the price for escaping death at the hands of crusading knights. Many individual churchmen attempted to prevent these attacks, among them the bishops in whose dioceses Jews lived. But the Church's own negative propaganda thwarted these efforts, and pogroms against Europe's Jews would remain a regular and predictable feature of Christian crusading and its modern manifestations.

The Christian Conquest of Jerusalem

Surprised by the nature and scale of the response to his appeal, Emperor Alexius did his best to move the crusaders quickly through Constantinople and into Asia Minor. But differences in outlook between the crusaders and the Byzantine emperor quickly became apparent. Alexius had little interest in an expedition to Jerusalem, and insisted that the crusaders promise to restore any territory they captured to him; from his standpoint, the crusader army was a threat, not least because it was headed by several of the Norman knights who had attempted to infiltrate his empire only ten years earlier. To the crusaders—whose mission had been shaped by Pope Urban's policies (not those of Alexius)—this seemed like treachery. The crusaders, furthermore, did not understand the Byzantine emperor's willingness to make alliances with some Muslim rulers (the Shi'ite Fatimids of Egypt and the Abassids of Baghdad) against other Muslim rulers (the Sunni Seljuqs). They ignorantly concluded that the Byzantines were working to undermine the crusading effort, perhaps even supporting the Muslims against them. Such suspicions contributed to their growing conviction that the eastern Roman Empire was itself an obstacle to the successful recovery of Jerusalem.

Viewed from the perspective of Alexius, the Crusade was a disaster. But from that of the papacy and the crusaders themselves, it was a triumph. In 1098, crusaders captured the old Hellenistic city of Antioch and with it most of the Syrian coast. At the end of 1099, they took Jerusalem, indiscriminately slaughtering its Muslim, Jewish, and Christian inhabitants. Their quick success stemmed mainly from the fact that their Muslim opponents were at that moment divided among themselves: the Fatimids had in fact recaptured Jerusalem just months before the crusaders arrived, and the defeated Seljuqs were at war with one another. Western military tactics, in particular the dominance of heavily armored knights, also played an important role in the crusaders' success. Equally critical was the naval support offered by Genoa and Pisa, whose merchant adventurers hoped to control the Indian spice trade that passed through the Red Sea and on to Alexandria in Egypt if the papacy's cause was successful. The Crusade thereby contributed to the further decline of Byzantine commerce and decisively altered the balance of power between Byzantium and western Europe.

The Consequences of Crusade

For Byzantium, the consequences of the crusading movement were clearly tragic. On the Muslim world, however, the impact was more modest. The crusader kingdoms

Analyzing Primary Sources

An Arab Aristocrat Encounters the Crusaders

Usama ibn Munqidh (1095–1188) was an Arab Muslim from Syria, whose family maintained a prominent place in the local administration even after the conquests of the Seljuqs and the Christian crusaders. He traveled widely and worked in various Islamic cities as a diplomat and scholar. He ended his life in the service of Salah ad-Din (Saladin), the great Muslim leader who reconquered Jerusalem the year before Usama's death. The following excerpt is from Usama's memoir, which he called The Book of Contemplation. *The Templars mentioned in the account are the Christian military order of the Knights of the Temple, who dedicated themselves to protecting pilgrims in Jerusalem and guarding the holy sites. Their headquarters were in the main mosque of the city, which stood on the Temple Mount.*

 nyone who is recently arrived from the Frankish lands is rougher in character than those who have become acclimated and have frequented the company of Muslims. Here is an instance of their rough character (may God abominate them!):

Whenever I went to visit the holy sites in Jerusalem, I would go in and make my way up to the al-Aqsa Mosque, beside which stood a small mosque that the Franks had converted into a church. When I went into the al-Aqsa Mosque—where the Templars, who are my friends, were—they would clear out that little mosque so that I could pray in it. One day, I went into the little mosque, recited the opening formula 'God is great!' and stood up in prayer. At this, one of the Franks rushed at me and grabbed me and turned my face towards the east, saying, 'Pray like *this*!'

A group of Templars hurried towards him, took hold of the Frank and took him away from me. I then returned to my prayers. The Frank, that very same one, took advantage of their inattention and returned, rushing upon me and turning my face to the east, saying, 'Pray like *this*!'

So the Templars came in again, grabbed him and threw him out. They apologized to me, saying, 'This man is a stranger, just arrived from the Frankish lands sometime in the past few days. He has never before seen anyone who did not pray towards the east.'

'I think I've prayed quite enough,' I said and left. I used to marvel at that devil, the change of his expression, the way he trembled and what he must have made of seeing someone praying towards Mecca.

Source: Usama ibn Munqidh, *The Book of Contemplation: Islam and the Crusades*, trans. Paul M. Cobb (New York: 2008), p. 147.

Questions for Analysis

1. What does Usama's account reveal about the variety of relationships among Christians and Muslims in the crusader kingdom of Jerusalem?

2. Who is the true outsider in this scenario? What does Usama's treatment by the Templars suggest about the policy of Christian leaders toward the city's Muslim residents?

---

established by victorious Norman and Frankish warlords were never more than a sparsely settled cluster of colonies along the coastline of Syria and Palestine. Because the crusaders did not control the Red Sea, the main routes of Islamic commerce with India and the Far East were unaffected by the change in Jerusalem's religious allegiance.

In any case, those crusaders who remained to settle in the region did not *want* to interfere with the overland caravan routes that wound through their new territories. Trade brokered by Arab, Persian, and Jewish merchants therefore continued despite periodic interruptions. The greatest economic gains for western Europeans therefore went to the Italian maritime republics of Venice and Genoa, and to the western markets now open to Muslim merchants for their goods. Both sides also gained in military terms: western Europeans learned new techniques of fortification, and Muslims learned new methods of siege warfare and new respect for the uses of heavy cavalry.

The larger impact of the Crusades on western Europe is more difficult to assess. From one standpoint, the establishment of the short-lived crusader states represents the limits of Europe's expansion during this otherwise extraordinary period of growth. Trade with the Islamic world, and beyond it with India and the Far East, brought enormous prosperity to some, but these trading links had existed before the Crusades and continued long after they ended.

Of course, the most long-lasting consequence of the First Crusade has also proved the most deadly in the long run. Both Christian and Islamic doctrines of holy war—which had been developed in earlier centuries—continue to be so destructive in the twenty-first century. Almost immediately, crusading rhetoric would dictate the terms of western Europeans' attitudes toward the wider world and even toward one another, as we shall see in the following chapters. It fostered a new political and religious ethos that would inform the "reconquest" of the Iberian Peninsula by the Christian rulers of Spain and lead to the massacre or forced conversion of Muslims and Jews. Crusading rhetoric underlay English wars against the Welsh and the Scots, and its language justified the massacre and dispossession of "heretics" in southern France by northern French imperialists. It justified the conquest of the Baltic region and, later, the subsequent conquest of the Americas and the colonization of Asia, Africa, and Australia. And it has continued to exacerbate global animosities to this day.

Even Christian theology was transformed by contact with Islam. For one thing, Muslim scholars were the ones who had inherited, preserved, and developed not only Hellenistic medicine and science but the philosophy of Aristotle, which would form the basis of a new Christian philosophy in the twelfth and thirteenth centuries (see Chapter 9). For another, Europeans had been almost entirely ignorant of Muslim beliefs prior to the Crusades, assuming that Muslims were pagans who worshiped a god called Mahomet or Mahoun. But by 1143, a scholar called Robert of Ketton (c. 1100–c. 1160), originally from a small town in England, had completed a Latin translation of the Qur'an, working in Spain with the encouragement of the abbot of Cluny. In the 1130s, he and a friend, Hermann of Carinthia (in Slovenia), had traveled to Byzantium and the crusader kingdoms, where they became students of Arabic. They exemplify the world of possibilities that had been opened up to northwestern Europeans as a result of the processes we have been studying in this chapter.

Muslim Philosophy and Christian Theology

The scholars of Byzantium took a conservative approach to Greek philosophy, in every sense of the word (see Chapter 7).

THE CULTURE OF THE MUSLIM WEST

It would be misleading to assert that all the consequences of the Crusades were negative. The positive outcomes were hugely important, too. Increased intellectual and cultural contact between the Latin West and the Islamic world had an enormous impact on western European learning, literature, music, and art. Perhaps most importantly, the study and practical applications of mathematics were revolutionized when Europeans adopted Arabic numerals and the concept of zero—first promoted beyond the Islamic world, not surprisingly, by the son of a Pisan merchant who grew up in Algeria, Leonardo Fibonacci (c. 1170–c. 1250).

ARISTOTLE TEACHING ARAB ASTRONOMERS. In this Arabic manuscript from the thirteenth century, Aristotle is represented as a contemporary of the astronomers he is instructing. ■ *What does this suggest about Muslims' attitude toward Greek philosophy?*

The dialogues of Plato and some works of Aristotle were copied and studied, but the latter's ideas were so hard to reconcile with Orthodox theology that Emperor Alexius Comnenus eventually banned the teaching of Aristotelian logic altogether. Ironically, then, the cultures that provided the most direct access to Greek learning were Arabic-speaking, and it was through Arabic translations that western European intellectuals became acquainted with these ideas—thanks to the labor of Arabists like Robert and Hermann.

Even before the rise of Islam, a number of Greek philosophical texts had been translated into Syriac, a Semitic language closely related to Arabic. Arabic translations soon followed, many sponsored by the Abbasid court at Baghdad, which established a special school for this purpose known as the House of Wisdom. By the end of the tenth century, Arabic translations of Plato, Aristotle, Plotinus, and other Greek authors were widely available and intensively studied throughout the Muslim world. Even in the remote Persian city of Bukhara, the great Muslim philosopher and physician Avicenna (Ibn Sīnā, 980–1037) was able to read all of Aristotle's works before he reached the age of eighteen.

Like their counterparts in Byzantium, Muslim philosophers strove to reconcile Greek and Hellenistic philosophical traditions with each other and with the tenets of Islamic theology. Reconciling Aristotelianism and Neoplatonism was the easier task. Many of the translations and commentaries of Aristotle from which Muslim philosophers worked had already been filtered through the philosophical traditions of Alexandria and Rome. Moreover, Aristotle and the Neoplatonists shared a number of common assumptions, including the eternity of the world and the capacity of the human mind to understand the rational principles that govern the world's workings. Both traditions also stressed the freedom of individual humans to choose between good and evil.

Combining Greek philosophy with Islamic theology was more difficult. Like Judaism and Christianity, Islam holds that a single omnipotent God created the world as an act of pure will and that the world will continue to exist only so long as God wills it. This runs counter to the classical Greek view of the world as eternal. Moreover, both Christian and Islamic theology rest on the immortality of the individual human soul, another doctrine flatly in conflict with Aristotelian and Neoplatonic thought. There were also conflicts over the concept of free will; and again, Muslims and Christians had more in common with one another on this head than with ancient Greek tradition. Although medieval theologians strongly emphasized the individual responsibility of believers to choose between good and evil, virtually all Muslims—like most Christians—believed that nothing good could occur unless God actively willed it. Islamic philosophers adopted an array of different intellectual tactics to deal with these challenges and, in doing so, laid the groundwork for the Christian theologians who relied on them (see Chapter 9).

Muslim Science, Medicine, and Mathematics

Many Muslim philosophers were also distinguished physicians and scientists. The study of philosophy could bring a man renown (or censure) but few tangible rewards, whereas successful physicians and astrologers might rise to positions of wealth and power. Both astrology and medicine were applied sciences that relied on careful, accurate observation of natural phenomena. Muslim observations of the heavens were so accurate, indeed, that some astronomers corroborated the findings of Hellenistic scientists (see Chapter 4) that the earth must rotate on its axis and revolve around the sun. But

IVORY PYXIS FROM AL-ANDALUS. Fashioned in the tenth century, this little round box is made from a segment of elephant tusk and would have had a matching lid (now lost). Such boxes usually held spices or incense. Its decorative motifs are echoed in Islamic architecture on a larger scale, reminding us that medieval Islam did not prohibit the representation of natural and fanciful figures, as is often supposed.

because these theories conflicted with the (mistaken) assumptions of Aristotle—that the earth remained stationary with the sun and planets revolving around it—they were not generally accepted in the Islamic world or in Europe. Yet they may have influenced Nicolaus Copernicus (1473–1543), who is usually credited as the first to suggest that the earth orbited the sun (see Chapter 16).

Muslim accomplishments in medicine were equally remarkable. Avicenna discovered the contagious nature of tuberculosis, described pleurisy and several varieties of nervous ailments, and noted that diseases could spread through contaminated water and soil. His *Canon of Medicine* would remain an authoritative textbook in the Islamic world and in western Europe until the seventeenth century. Later Islamic physicians would learn the value of cauterization and of styptic agents, diagnose cancer of the stomach, prescribe antidotes in cases of poisoning, and make notable progress in treating eye diseases. They recognized the infectious character of bubonic plague, pointing out that it could be transmitted by clothing.

Muslim physicians were also pioneers in organizing hospitals and licensing medical practitioners. At least thirty-four great hospitals were located in the principal cities of Persia, Syria, and Egypt, each with separate wards for particular illnesses, a dispensary for giving out medicine, and a library. Chief physicians and surgeons lectured to students and graduates, examined them, and issued licenses to practice medicine. Even the owners of leeches (used for bloodletting, a standard medical practice of the day) had to submit their medicinal worms for inspection at regular intervals.

Islamic scientists made important advances in optics and chemistry, as well as mathematics. Using Arabic numerals—which Muslim scholars actually adopted from the Hindus—mathematicians developed a decimal arithmetic based on place values and hinged on the concept of the zero. Their work enabled fundamental advances in entirely new areas, both of which bear Arabic names: algebra and algorithms. Building on Greek geometry and their own astronomical observations, they also made great progress in spherical trigonometry.

Muslim mathematicians thus brought together and pushed forward all the areas of mathematical knowledge that would later be adopted and developed in western Europe from the sixteenth century on. And they made an indispensible contribution to the burgeoning European economy, since the sophisticated accounting systems that supported commerce would have been impossible if merchants and bankers had continued to use the clumsy numbers adopted by the Romans. (Try balancing your checking account in Roman numerals!) Thanks to Arabic mathematics, western Europeans could now add, subtract, divide, and multiply quickly and accurately, with or without the help of another Muslim invention, the abacus.

Muslim Literature and Art

Poetry was integral to Muslim culture. It had been a highly developed art form long before the emergence of Islam, and then it became even more important to the development and dissemination of Muslim identity because it was the form in which Muhammad framed the Qur'an (see Chapter 7).

Like medicine and astronomy, poetry was also a route to advancement. Not all poetry was composed in Arabic; particularly around the Abbasid court, poets writing in Persian enjoyed great renown. The best known of these is Umar Khayyam (d. 1123), whose *Rubaiyat* was turned into a popular English verse cycle by the Victorian poet Edward Fitzgerald (1809–1883). Although Fitzgerald's translation

MUSLIM ARCHITECTURE AND GARDEN DESIGN Both images display how Muslim architects and designers borrowed features from many cultures but combined them in distinctively graceful ways.

Analyzing Primary Sources

A Hebrew Poem from Muslim Spain

In the courts of tenth- and eleventh-century Muslim Spain, Jewish poets began to write a new style of Hebrew verse closely modeled on contemporary Arabic examples. Samuel the Nagid was perhaps the most remarkable of this group of poets. He became the military leader of the Muslim kingdom of Granada as well as the head of the Jewish community there. In addition to his three volumes of poetry, he also wrote treatises on Hebrew grammar and religious law.

our debt to God is righteously to live,
　　And His to you, your recompense to give.
　　　Do not wear out your days in serving God;
　Some time devote to Him, some to yourself.
　To Him give half your day, to work the rest;
　But give the jug no rest throughout the night.

Put out your lamps! Use crystal cups for light.
　Away with singers! Bottles are better than lutes.
　No song, nor wine, nor friend beneath the sward—
　These three, O fools, are all of life's reward.

Source: Raymond P. Scheindlin, ed. and trans., *Wine, Women, and Death: Medieval Hebrew Poems on the Good Life* (Philadelphia, PA: 1986), p. 47.

Questions for Analysis

1. What values does this poem express? What is its perspective on the relationship among devotion to God, duty, and pleasure?

2. What does the career of Samuel the Nagid—poet, general, scholar—suggest about Jewish identity in this place and time? What does it suggest about the relations between Jewish and Muslim communities in medieval Spain?

---

distorts much, the lush sensuality of Umar's poetic imagery ("a jug of wine, a loaf of bread—and thou") faithfully reflects themes that were common to much Muslim poetry. Much of this poetry was addressed by men to other men, a fact that occasioned no concern within the elite circles in which it was composed and performed. Jews also participated in this elite literary world, especially in Al-Andalus, where they wrote similarly sensuous, playful lyrics in both Hebrew and Arabic, praising wine, sexual intimacy, and their own songs. Muslim Spain also saw a great flowering of Jewish intellectual life, which paralleled and intersected with that of the Muslim society around them.

Perhaps the most distinctive of Islamic arts are architectural and decorative, the arts that created the spaces in which poets and scientists interacted with their patrons. Many characteristic elements of Muslim architecture (the dome, the column, and the arch) were adapted from Byzantine models, but were then combined with the intricate tracery and ambitious scale of Persian buildings to form a new architectural vocabulary. Building styles were further inflected by the many different cultures that embraced Islam, from Spain to Egypt to India and beyond. Muslim artistry was also expressed in the magnificent gardens and fountains that adorned palaces and in the more portable magnificence of gorgeous carpets, tooled leather, brocaded silks and tapestries, inlaid metalwork, enameled glassware, and painted pottery—all decorated with Arabic script, interlacing geometric designs, plants, fruits, flowers, and fantastic animal figures (another Persian influence). These complex designs can often seem strikingly modern, precisely because they anticipate the abstract forms that were considered new in the twentieth century. Indeed, they were the product of a culture that increasingly frowned upon the realistic depiction of natural forms.

The Islamic Influence on Western Europe

Prior to the contacts facilitated by the Crusades, the cultural, economic, intellectual, and political achievements of Islamic civilization had completely overshadowed those of Latin Christian Europe. Even thereafter, the new Europe that emerged in the twelfth century would rely heavily on what it had learned from the Islamic world. This is reflected in the large number of Arabic and Persian words that passed into European languages. Essential words for commerce and trade include *traffic, tariff, alcohol, muslin, orange, lemon, alfalfa, saffron, sugar, syrup,* and *musk,* to name just a few. The word *admiral* also comes from Arabic (from the title *emir*), as do words that tell the story of Europe's reliance on Muslim science and technology: *alchemy, algebra, algorithm, alkali, almanac, amalgam, cipher, soda, magazine,* and *zero*— not to mention the names of stars, such as Aldebaran and Betelgeuse.

The Muslim world also had an enormous influence on the imagination and the self-perception of Christian Europe. Byzantine civilization was at once too closely linked to Latin Christendom and, from the eleventh century on, too weak to compel western Europeans to take much account of it. Western Christians tended to look down on the Byzantine Greeks, but they respected and feared Muslims. And they were right to do so, for Islamic civilization at its zenith (to use another Arabic word) was one of the world's greatest. It brought Arabs, Persians, Turks, Egyptians, Africans, Indians, and Asians together in a common cultural and religious system, creating a diverse society and a splendid legacy of original discoveries and accomplishments that continue to shape the world today. The expanding Europe of the Middle Ages reaped the benefits of its interactions with this rich culture.

CONCLUSION

Before the year 1000, western Europe was the least powerful, least prosperous, and least sophisticated of the three civilizations that had emerged out of the Roman world. A hundred

After You Read This Chapter

Ⓢ Visit StudySpace for quizzes, additional review materials, and multimedia documents.
wwnorton.com/web/westernciv18

REVIEWING THE OBJECTIVES

- The fragmentation of power in the ninth and tenth centuries created a world very different from that of Charlemagne. Describe some of the key changes. What were their causes?
- The agricultural revolution of the Middle Ages had far-reaching economic, social, and political consequences. What were they?
- The reforming movement with the Church changed the relationship between the papacy and the secular rulers of Christendom. Explain why.
- The motives behind the Crusades were political as well as religious. Why was this the case?
- The Crusades had profound effects on western Europe, Byzantium, and Islam, as well as on the relationships among different groups within these societies. In what ways were these three civilizations transformed?

years later, it was a force to be reckoned with. This metamorphosis rested on economic foundations: increasingly efficient agriculture, a growing population, and expanding trade. These changes produced a dynamic, expansionist, self-confident, and mobile society in which individuals cast off old roles and took on new ones with bewildering speed. No less important, however, were the political and military changes that began to alter the map of Europe in these centuries. By 1100, the heavily armored, mounted knight had emerged as the most formidable military weapon of the day, and new conceptions of power—both spiritual and temporal—were being articulated and contested within Europe, and on crusade.

But it was not yet possible either for Europe's rulers to control the energies of the workers, town-dwellers, merchants, knights, and scholars whose endeavors were transforming their world. A new approach to political organization was needed. Up to this point, the civilizations of the West had rested on two basic types of government: city-states and empires. City-states were more capable of mobilizing the loyalty of their citizens; as a result, they could sometimes win extraordinary victories against more-powerful imperial rivals, as the Greeks did against the Persians. But city-states were frequently divided by internal economic and social rivalries; and in the long run, they were not strong enough to defend themselves against foreign conquerors. Empires, by contrast, could win battles and maintain powerful administrative bureaucracies, but they were generally too far-flung to inspire deep loyalties among their subjects.

Where, then, do the emerging kingdoms of medieval Europe fit into this picture? How would the struggle for the control of western Europe's expanding resources be carried forward in the wake of the Crusades? And what cultural, spiritual, social, and intellectual innovations would result? These are the questions we address in Chapter 9.

PEOPLE, IDEAS, AND EVENTS IN CONTEXT

- How was Europe affected by **VIKING** raids and settlements? Which territorial rulers imitated **CAROLINGIAN** models in the wake of these initiatives?
- What new technologies drove the **AGRICULTURAL REVOLUTION** of the Middle Ages? Why did the organization of labor on **MANORS** sometimes lead to **SERFDOM**?
- What conditions led to the growth of medieval **TOWNS** and why did the formation of urban **COMMUNES** foster new types of liberty? How were money and credit essential to medieval commerce?
- Why is **FEUDALISM** a problematic concept? How did the ceremony of **HOMAGE** symbolize the relationship between a **VASSAL** and his lord?
- What were the causes of the **INVESTITURE CONFLICT**?
- Why did **ALEXIUS COMNENUS** ask **POPE URBAN II** for assistance? Why did the pope use this as a pretext for urging the **FIRST CRUSADE**?
- How and why did **MUSLIM LEARNING AND CULTURE** exercise a profound influence on western Europeans?

THINKING ABOUT CONNECTIONS

- In what ways does the Investiture Conflict reflect the unique historical circumstances of the late eleventh century, and in what ways can it be viewed as an extension of longer-term phenomena?
- Based on what we have learned about the relationship between political power and religious power in previous chapters, would you say that the clash between the papacy and the Holy Roman Empire was inevitable?
- Given the many negative aspects of the crusading movement—and its eventual failure—how might you explain the continuing appeal of crusading rhetoric down to the present day?

Before
You
Read
This
Chapter

The Consolidation of Europe, 1100–1250

CORE OBJECTIVES

- **IDENTIFY** the differences among Europe's emerging monarchies.

- **DESCRIBE** the ongoing effects of crusading.

- **UNDERSTAND** the connections between new religious movements and the power of the papacy.

- **DEFINE** scholasticism and trace its development.

- **EXPLAIN** the changing meaning of *chivalry*.

At the turn of the twelfth century, the eldest son of a nobleman did something unusual: he traded lordship for scholarship. His name was Peter Abelard. In his own estimation, he was the smartest man in the world, and the most attractive. He was certainly one of the most ambitious. After leaving his father's lands in Brittany and besting all the established teachers in Paris, he was appointed to the position of master in the cathedral school, one of the highest academic posts then available. There he met Heloise, the niece of a priest called Fulbert.

Heloise had received an excellent education in a nearby convent, but the normal path of intellectual advancement—Abelard's school—was closed to her. So Fulbert arranged for her to become Abelard's private pupil. She soon became more than that: his intellectual partner, his lover, and his wife. This last step was particularly problematic, because marriage was no longer an option for clerics and would therefore ruin Abelard's chances of a brilliant career in the Church. So it remained a secret, as did Heloise's subsequent pregnancy and the birth of their son. But her uncle eventually found out and took revenge on Abelard, sending some local thugs to castrate him.

283

Heloise and Abelard lived out the remainder of their lives in isolation from one another, and most of what we know about their relationship comes from letters they exchanged years later, when Heloise was the leader of a new religious community and Abelard was laying the intellectual foundations of the first university.

The developments of the twelfth and thirteenth centuries altered Europe in profound and lasting ways, affecting individuals, communities, and entire regions. This period witnessed the emergence of large-scale territorial monarchies and the papacy as dominant forces, while cathedral schools and universities turned out larger and larger cohorts of the professional men needed to run the bureaucracies that supported secular and religious authority. New opportunities for social advancement and new spiritual practices transformed daily life, many of these the direct and indirect consequences of the Crusades. Also as a result of the Crusades, both ancient

ABELARD AND HELOISE. This image from a thirteenth century manuscript shows Abelard in a scholar's gown and cap and Heloise wearing a nun's habit; their gestures indicate that they are engaged in heated debate. The story of their fervent attraction and doomed marriage was already famous during their lifetimes, and by the time this manuscript was copied, theirs had become the ultimate example of star-crossed love.

texts and novel ideas generated the intellectual revolution in which Abelard and Heloise participated. Artistic and technological influences were galvanizing forces, too, financed by prelates and kings, princely courts and wealthy towns engaged in an integrated and far-reaching economy. Moreover, new literary forms took shape as the spoken vernaculars of Europe came to challenge Latin, becoming languages of learning, devotion, and entertainment. By the middle of the thirteenth century, the political institutions and cultural identities that still define Europe had been formed.

THE MAKING OF MEDIEVAL MONARCHIES

As we learned in Chapter 8, traditional forms of power were challenged by significant trends in the tenth and eleventh centuries. Independent towns and lords often refused to acknowledge royal authority, and kings could no longer rely on close-knit kin groups or the broad imperial powers wielded by a ruler like Charlemagne. How, then, did some European rulers build the foundations of states that continue to exist today? For crucially, the *idea* of a national state—a state that consolidates its people's sense of a shared identity and destiny—was an idea forged in the twelfth and thirteenth centuries. It would endure to become the basis on which the political system of the modern world is still constructed.

But not all attempts at state transformation were equally successful. For example, the France that emerged in the twelfth century would almost collapse 200 years later (see Chapter 10). Other monarchies would not be consolidated until the nineteenth century (Germany is the best example) and, even then, *political* unification could not hide the continued fact of cultural and linguistic disintegration (as evident in Italy, Belgium, and Switzerland to this day). Yet it became so vital for modern European states to trace their origins to the medieval past that those states without a medieval pedigree would eventually be obliged to invent one.

England: From Conquest to Consolidation

The conquest of England in 1066 allowed the first Norman king, William, to experiment with a new type of kingship. In theory, he commanded the allegiance of every person dwelling in his kingdom, over and above the allegiance owed to kin, a local lord, or even the Church. In practice, however, William needed to impose his will on his new subjects, and this often took the form of violence. It was also expressed through the highly effective administrative structures of his Anglo-Saxon predecessors, which he adapted to his own needs.

This process was carried forward by his son Henry I (r. 1100–35), whose approach to kingship was unusual in its focus on effective governance rather than warfare. Henry strengthened the Anglo-Norman system of local administration and instituted a system of traveling judges to administer royal justice in the countryside. His biggest innovation was the introduction of a method of financial accounting carried out by an office known as the Exchequer, so called because clerks moved counters around on a checkered cloth to calculate receipts and expenditures.

Henry's hands-on approach to royal lordship was both new and unpopular. Then, as now, those opposed to "big government" could react violently against it, and after Henry's death those reactions provoked a civil war that lasted throughout the reign of his cousin and successor, Stephen (r. 1135–54)—until the people of England began to long for a king who would bring back the good old days of centralized rule.

The Reign of Henry II

They found such a king in Henry's grandson Henry of Anjou (b. 1133, r. 1154–89), who at the age of twenty-one was already the duke of Normandy and the lord of two other independent French counties, Anjou and Maine. He also controlled the Aquitaine, thanks to his recent alliance with its powerful and brilliant ruler, Eleanor (1122–1204), who had annulled her first marriage to the French king Louis VII in order to marry Henry. As a result, England found itself integrated into the political and cultural world of the Continent in unprecedented ways.

Henry II restored his grandfather's administration and began, steadily, to extend its reach. He ordered juries (from the Latin *jus*, meaning both "law" and "oath") of reliable local men to report every major crime that occurred in their districts, and also empowered them to investigate civil cases. These innovations stand at the origin of our modern legal system. Henry II also made it easier for common people to seek justice in the royal courts. All of these measures brought an unprecedented number of average people into the exercise of government and thus increased their sense of loyalty to the king and their personal investment in his rulership.

But these innovations also brought Henry into conflict with the Church, because the extension of royal justice impinged on that of ecclesiastical courts: tribunals overseen by bishops that claimed the exclusive right to try and sentence clergy accused of committing crimes—even capital crimes like murder. Henry, by contrast, declared that clerics convicted of serious crimes in church courts should lose their clerical status and be handed over to the royal court for sentencing. The principle underlying this was one that aimed to promote a sense of shared identity and accountability: clients should be English subjects before they were servants of the Roman Church.

Opposition to this policy came from an unexpected quarter: Thomas Becket, a longtime friend and supporter of Henry's, who was now the archbishop of Canterbury. Thomas was a self-made man, the son of immigrants who had benefited from the social mobility of town life (he grew up in London) to obtain an education and thereby rise through the ranks of the Church. He saw the advantages to be gained from maintaining the independence of ecclesiastical procedures, and feared that Henry's goal was to undermine the power of the clergy.

THE MURDER OF THOMAS BECKET. In this illumination from a thirteenth-century prayer book, one of the knights has struck the archbishop so violently that he has broken his sword. ▪ *How might a contemporary viewer have interpreted this symbolism?*

Legend

- Angevin Empire under Henry II, c. 1180
- French Royal domain, 1180
- Disputed frontier, 1180
- Holy Roman Empire, 1180

France at the Death of Philip Augustus 1223

- Royal domain
- Under English rule

ENGLAND
ATLANTIC OCEAN
Paris
FRANCE
Bay of Biscay
AQUITAINE
Compostela
LÉON

0 100 200 300 Miles
0 300 Kilometers

SCOTLAND
NORTH SEA
Edinburgh
Carlisle
Durham
Stamford Bridge
York

IRELAND
Dublin

WALES
ENGLAND
Hereford
Gloucester
Ely
Cambridge
Oxford
London
Runnymede
Winchester
Southampton
Canterbury
Calais

English Channel

ATLANTIC OCEAN

Bruges
Antwerp
Ypres
Brussels
Lille
FLANDERS
Arras
Amiens
VERMANDOIS
Bayeux
Rouen
Beauvais
Rheims
Verdun
Caen
St. Denis
Mont-St. Michel
NORMANDY
Paris
CHAMPAGNE
LORRAINE
BRITTANY
MAINE
Chartres
ILE DE FRANCE
Brétigny
Troyes
ANJOU
BURGUNDY
Nantes
TOURAINE
Bourges
Poitiers
Dijon
POITOU
Autun

HOLY ROMAN EMPIRE

Bay of Biscay
AQUITAINE
Geneva
Lyon
Bordeaux
Angoulême
Perigueux
GASCONY
Albi
PROVENCE
Avignon
TOULOUSE
Montpellier
Aigues-Mortes
Marseilles
NAVARRE
LANGUEDOC
Narbonne
ARAGON
MEDITERRANEAN SEA
CORSICA
CATALUNYA

0 100 200 Miles
0 100 200 Kilometers

EUROPE
Area of detail
AFRICA

HENRY II'S ANGEVIN EMPIRE AND THE KINGDOM OF FRANCE, 1180–1223. ▪ *What areas did Henry II's empire control in 1180?* ▪ *What advantages would the king of France have when challenging English control over continental territories—even though his own power was confined to the "island" (Ile) of France around Paris?*

Henry responded by exiling Thomas from England for several years. When Thomas returned in 1170, he was assassinated in his own cathedral by four of Henry's knights. Thomas was quickly proclaimed a martyr and a saint, and his tomb at Canterbury became one of the most important pilgrimage sites of the Middle Ages. Henry, for his part, was compelled to appear as a barefoot pentitent at this tomb and ask the saint's forgiveness for his sins.

In the long run, Henry II did not win the right to sentence clerics in royal courts, but he did retain the right to nominate clerics to high office and thereby to exercise a large measure of control over those courts' personnel. The most concrete proof of Henry II's success is that his government continued to work efficiently even after his death, to the extent that his crusading son Richard "the Lionheart" (r. 1189–99) could rule his father's empire for ten years *in absentia*, spending only about six months in England during all that time.

The Meaning of Magna Carta

When Richard was killed by a crossbow bolt while besieging a castle, he was succeeded by his brother John (r. 1199–1216), an efficient administrator but a far less enthusiastic warrior. By 1204, military and legal losses forced John to cede nearly all of his father's Continental possessions to the powerful young king of France, Philip II; only the Aquitaine, the inheritance of his mother Eleanor, remained. This was politically disastrous for John. Not only did it deplete his resources, it angered the most powerful lords of England, nearly all of whom were of Norman descent and who thus lost their ancestral lands when John lost Normandy. John's response was to attempt a recovery of lost territories by raising taxes to equip an army, thereby angering the nobility further. In 1215, they forced John to set his seal to Magna Carta, a "great charter" that defined the barons' rights while limiting those of the king.

Magna Carta established some important general principles that would continue to shape the laws of England and, eventually, her North American and Australian colonies. It stipulated that the king could levy no taxes without the consent of the kingdom at large, that no free man could be punished until he had been judged guilty by a jury of his peers in accordance with the law, that no one could be arrested and imprisoned without a warrant, and that no unqualified or ignorant person should hold public office. The charter also provided for the establishment of a representative body of barons: Parliament (a word derived from the French "talking together"). Above all, Magna Carta expressed the extraordinary idea that a king is bound by the law.

We have frequently noted the achievements of the various powerful lawgivers whose contributions have been essential to Western civilizations, starting with Hammurabi (see Chapter 1). But for the most part, those lawgivers held themselves to be above the law. Although medieval monarchs—in England and elsewhere—attempted to behave as though this were true for them as well, they would ultimately be forced to concede the rule of law itself.

Magna Carta thus contributed to the slow process that transformed the inhabitants of England into people with a common national identity and shared values. It also normalized the idea that strong, centralized government was a good thing: when the barons of England revolted again in the reign of John's son, Henry III (r. 1216–72), they did so because Henry's rule was not effective enough.

In time, Parliament became a legislative body that could help run the kingdom and authorize new expenditures. Since Magna Carta had demanded that no taxation be imposed without the common consent of the realm, kings had to convene Parliament to explain why such taxation was necessary and to secure such consent. Meetings of Parliament were also used to take advice about pressing concerns, to hear judicial cases, to review local administration, to hear complaints from the countryside, and to promulgate new laws. Gradually, England was changing from a conquered territory within a larger Norman empire into a constitutional monarchy grounded in representative government and ruled by law.

The Emergence of France

Compared to the Anglo-Saxon and Anglo-Norman kings of England, the king of the Franks presided over a miniscule kingdom over which he exercised little control. After the dissolution of Carolingian royal authority, the kings who succeeded Hugh Capet (987–96) had trouble making good on any claim to lordship beyond the immediate hinterland of Paris. Most of Charlemagne's institutions of governance had collapsed and been further weakened by Viking raids or by ongoing pressure from the Viking state of Normandy. When the Angevin Empire of Henry II was at its height, therefore, the kingdom of Louis VII (r. 1137–80)—who had lost both his wife Eleanor and her lands to that same Henry—was tiny and insignificant.

But in many ways the Capetian dynasty was fortunate. Against all biological odds, they managed to produce an unbroken line of able male heirs for over 300 years (from 987 to 1328), without interruption—men who were also long lived. On average, each Capetian king ruled for 30 years, which contributed greatly to political stability. And this kingdom, though small, was a rich center of agriculture and trade, which provided a steadily increasing source of income. The prestige of the Capetians was also enhanced by their patronage of the new University of Paris founded by Abelard, which made the royal capital the intellectual capital of Europe (see below). Beyond all this, the Capetians proved to be shrewd politicians, carefully husbanding their strengths while more powerful enemies overreached themselves.

The epitome of these strengths was Philip II (r. 1180–1223), a man who styled himself "Augustus" and who was the first to use the title "king of France": king of a sovereign state (rather than "king of the Franks," a loose agglomeration of people). Philip came to the throne at the age of eighteen, having witnessed the struggles of his father Louis VII against the superior strength of Henry II. He understood that he could not win a direct confrontation with either Henry or his son Richard. John, however—known to his detractors as "Soft Sword"—was another matter. Philip declared that John owed him homage and allegiance in return for Normandy and its adjacent territories, and then took advantage of his position as John's overlord to undermine John's control over these lands. When John objected, Philip declared all John's lands to be forfeit to the French crown and backed this declaration with armies that won decisive victories in 1204 and 1214.

With Normandy and the other Angevin territories of northern France added to his domain, Philip now had the resources to build an effective system of local administration. He wisely chose to maintain the bureaucratic structures put in place there by generations of Anglo-Norman rule, but he also appointed royal overseers, known as bailiffs, who had full judicial, administrative, and military authority. Philip drew these men from among the needy knights and lesser nobility of his own domain and rotated them frequently from region to region. This ensured their loyalty to Philip and also prevented them from developing personal ties to the regions they governed.

Philip's administrative pattern, which recognized regional diversity while promoting centralized royal control, would continue to characterize French government down to the time of the French Revolution (see Chapter 18). Philip's son, Louis VIII (r. 1223–26), would extend this strategy to newly conquered territories in the southeast. His son, Louis IX (r. 1226–70), would deepen and legitimize it by his devotion to justice at home and crusading abroad. Even in his lifetime, Louis IX would be celebrated as the paragon of good kingship, and soon after his death he would be canonized as Saint Louis. His successors would draw on that legacy for centuries to come. (See Chapter 10.)

But the French Parlement (later known as the Estates General) never played the crucial role in French government that Parliament did in England. There are many reasons for this, but the most fundamental was the French nobility's successful claim to exemption from taxation, something that would remain a political problem until the French Revolution. Other significant points of comparison between England and France continue to mark the intertwined history of these two states. England, a far smaller country, was much more tightly unified at a much earlier date. English nobles could and did rebel against their kings, but could rarely draw sustained support from regional resentments. In France, however, regional separatism remained (and still remains) a significant force, to the extent that ambitious insurgents have long capitalized on regional animosity toward the French government when making bids for power.

England and France were also governed in different ways. English kings could rely on local men to do much of the work of local government without pay. This made English administration inexpensive, and it also meant that royal policies had to be popular in order to be implemented. French kings, by contrast, ruled through salaried officers who had little connection to local communities. They had less need to summon representative assemblies and, as a result, lacked effective mechanisms for mobilizing public support. In the eigtheenth century, these features would be the undoing of the French monarchy.

German Kingship and the Holy Roman Empire

We have seen (in Chapter 8) that the struggles between the German emperor Henry IV and the papacy ultimately led to the weakening of imperial authority. But in the middle of the twelfth century, a newly elected emperor made an ambitious attempt to restore the power of the German monarchy and to free it from papal control. This was Frederick, later known as Barbarossa ("Red Beard," r. 1152–90), who coined the term "Holy Roman Empire" to describe his realm—thereby asserting that its holiness derived from the blessing of God and did not necessarily depend on the intervention of the pope.

Frederick forged a close alliance with other German princes by supporting their efforts to control their own territories. In exchange, he exacted their support of his efforts to reassert imperial control over the wealthy cities of northern Italy. This strategy worked, but it sparked a series of destructive wars. Led by Milan and sanctioned by the pope, the cities of northern Italy formed an alliance, the Lombard League, which put up a staunch resistance to Frederick's rule and finally forced him to guarantee their political independence in return for large cash payments. Meanwhile, Frederick attempted to bypass the power of the papacy by supporting a series of papal pretenders, or "antipopes." This move was successfully countered by the reigning pope, Alexander III (r. 1159–81), who drove a shrewd bargain with Frederick:

THE HOLY ROMAN EMPIRE AND ITS NEIGHBORS, c. 1200. ▪ *How would the borders of the Holy Roman Empire have been defined during the Middle Ages?* ▪ *Why were the German states not able to unify during this period?* ▪ *Why would the prospect of a single heir to the Holy Roman Empire and to the kingdom of the Two Sicilies have been a threat to the papacy?*

if Frederick would concede the sovereignty of the pope's rule within Rome and its adjacent territories—lands that came to be known as the Papal States—then Alexander would concede the emperor's sovereignty within his domains and even his overlordship of the Church within those domains. Frederick eventually agreed, thereby gaining the pope's support for his rule in northern Italy.

When Frederick left for the Holy Land in 1189—joining Richard the Lionheart of England and Philip Augustus of France on a (failed) crusade to reconquer Jerusalem—he left his realm in a powerful position. Although he died on that venture, his careful planning bore fruit in the reign of his son, Henry VI, who succeeded to his father's throne without opposition and enjoyed a huge income from the north Italian towns; he ultimately became the king of Sicily, too. This strengthened the empire's position even further, for now the Papal States were surrounded by the lands of a single powerful ruler. However, Henry VI died in 1197 at the age of thirty-two, leaving only a three-year-old son, the future Frederick II, as his heir apparent.

ON THE ART OF HUNTING WITH BIRDS. This beautifully illuminated manuscript of Frederick II's famous treatise on falconry was commissioned by his son, Manfred, shortly after his father's death in 1250. It is now in the Vatican Library, Rome.

Frederick II, often called "the Great," is one of the most fascinating of all medieval rulers. Having grown up in Sicily, at the heart of the multicultural Mediterranean, he spoke Arabic and Italian as well as Latin, German, and French. He was both a patron of learning and a scholar in his own right, the author of an important treatise on falconry that is still considered a model of scientific investigation. He maintained a menagerie of exotic animals, a troop of Muslim archers, and a harem of veiled and secluded women, all of whom traveled with him on his journeys. But despite this appearance of exoticism, he was devoted to pursuing his grandfather's policies, supporting the territorial princes in Germany while enforcing imperial rights in Italy.

Much had changed, however, as a result of the two decades' civil war that followed his own father's death. In Germany, the princes had become so entirely autonomous that there was little Frederick could do except to recognize their privileges in exchange for their loyalty. In Italy, the cities of the Lombard League had ceased to pay their taxes and were striving for independence; meanwhile, the powerful administrative structure of Sicily had fallen into chaos.

Frederick tackled all these problems and eventually restored control over the disparate territories of his empire. In 1237, though, he made the mistake of asserting a right to rule the northern Italian cities directly, bypassing their own independent governments. The result was another Lombard League and another lengthy war, which continued until Frederick's death in 1250. The papacy took every advantage of this situation, even excommunicating Frederick and, after his death, denying the rights of his heirs. When Frederick's last legitimate son died in 1254, the prospect of effective imperial rule died with him. For the next 500 years, until the founding of the modern German and Italian states, political power in the lands of the Holy Roman Empire would be divided among several hundred territorial princes.

The "Reconquest" of Spain

Although the Christian kingdoms clustered to the north and east of the Iberian Peninsula were even more distinct from one another than were the principalities of Germany, a unified kingdom of Spain would emerge as the most powerful monarchy in Europe and the wider Atlantic world by the end of the Middle Ages (a process we will continue to trace in future chapters). The key to this extraordinary development lay in the successful alliances forged among the peninsula's Christian rulers and their eventual defeat of neighboring Muslim kingdoms. This process is somewhat misleadingly termed "the Reconquista," the "reconquest" of Christian lands. In reality, the Roman province of Hispania had been only nominally Christian when the Visigoths settled there in the fifth century (see Chapter 6), and the Visigoths themselves had barely converted to Latin Christianity before the Muslims arrived in 711 (see Chapter 7). But conceptualizing this struggle as a holy war to "reconquer" Christian territory allowed Christian propagandists to cast it as another Crusade and, on those grounds, to earn support for their efforts.

By the middle of the twelfth century, there were four major Christian kingdoms in Iberia. In the far north and west were the states of Navarre, which straddled the Pyrenees, and León-Castile, governed as a united kingdom after 1037. Beyond these kingdoms' southern frontier lay a broad swathe of Muslim territory. Farther to the east was the Crown of Aragon, formed in 1137 when the count of Barcelona, who ruled the independent principality of Catalonia, married the queen of Aragon. Farthest west was the new kingdom of Portugal, which had been the first territory gained by Christian conquests in the ninth century and which won independence from León-Castile in 1139.

Like their counterparts elsewhere in Europe, the kings of Spain struggled to control the power of great lords. Centuries of warfare between Muslims and Christians and among competing Christian clans had left the landscape sown with enormous castles, and even those that were nominally

THE "RECONQUEST" OF SPAIN, 900–1250. ▪ *Where were the frontiers of the Christian kingdoms in 900? 1150? 1250?* ▪ *What geographical factors might have helped to sustain these small kingdoms?* ▪ *Why might Castile have become the largest of the Christian kingdoms over time?* ▪ *How could Aragon and Catalonia have maintained important positions as wealthy and significant powers?*

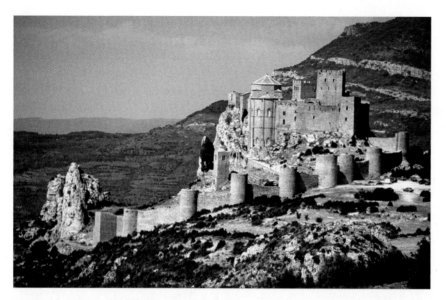

LOARRE CASTLE, ARAGON. No single photograph can capture the size or setting of this massive castle complex in the foothills of the Pyrenees. Initially fortified in the eleventh century as a base for Christian expansion into Muslim territory, it was further enlarged in the twelfth century. The encircling wall and towers were added in the thirteenth and fourteenth centuries.

keep either kingdom from achieving supremacy for the next 200 years, until the marriage of Ferdinand of Aragon and Isabella of Castile joined the two in a unified Spanish monarchy which also included Navarre. In 1492, their united army captured Granada while an Italian adventurer named Christopher Columbus set sail under their flag. The first event completed the "reconquest," while the second began Spain's successful conquest of a new and hitherto undreamed-of world (see Chapter 12).

controlled by kings were in fact the property of castellans who used them as power bases. A ruler seeking to establish sovereignty thus had to use a combination of force and cunning to bring these rival powers to heel. Indeed, the kings of this region came to deploy a combination of tactics that we have already seen at work in England: a mixture of violent conquest and the development of effective administrative structures that made royal power a fact of everyday life.

This is best exemplified by King Alfonso II of Aragon (r. 1162–96), who was also the count of Barcelona and the first to rule the united Crown of Aragon. Alfonso used documentation as the ultimate tool of power, presiding over the compilation of a richly illuminated "big book of fiefs" (*Liber feudorum maior*) between 1192 and 1194 (see **Interpreting Visual Evidence** on page 293). This book recounted property transactions and family lineages dating back centuries, citing documents in the royal archives. Alfonso thereby grounded his authority on his command of history and written records.

Throughout the remainder of the twelfth century and into the thirteenth, Christian influence in Spain continued to spread southward until all that remained of Muslim dominion was the small kingdom centered on Granada in the extreme southwest. Castile became by far the largest kingdom in area, but it was rivaled in wealth and consequence by the more urbanized and commercially connected Aragon. Indeed, wars between Castile and Aragon would

Papal Dominion and Canon Law

Like their secular counterparts, the popes of this era were attempting to establish greater authority by building up bureaucratic structures that increased the visibility of papal power. Specially commissioned papal legates ("legal representatives") began to be sent out from Rome to convey and enforce papal commands, many of which arose from the hundreds (and eventually thousands) of legal cases that poured into Rome as the pope sought to establish a reputation for justice. This extension of the papacy's jurisdiction required the development of a systematic body of law by which such cases could be judged. A crucial step in this development was the codification of papal decrees and decisions of Church councils reaching back to the second century: a thousand years. These formed a body of legal precedents known as canons, from the Greek word meaning "rules" or "supports." The problem, though, was that these precedents often contradicted one another, and so any usable compilation had to determine which was most authoritative.

The resulting *Concordance of Discordant Canons*, first redacted around 1139 and later known as the *Decretum*, is attributed to a jurist known only as Gratian, who was active in the study and teaching of law in Bologna. Significantly, Gratian's codification was influenced by the *Corpus Juris Civilis* codified under Justinian (Chapter 7). This is because another outcome of the Crusades, and of western Europe's increased contact with Byzantium, was the revitalized study of Roman law and the tradition of legal commentary associated with the great jurists of the

Picturing Legal Transactions

Between the years 1192 and 1194, King Alfonso II of Aragon (r. 1162–96) and his court scribes compiled a remarkable book. The codex known today as "the big book of fiefs" (*Liber feudorum maior*) may have been made to assist Alfonso and his descendants in legitimizing their authority over the many areas they controlled. But it was also a way of expressing that authority: its very existence represented a new claim to royal power. In its original form, it consisted of 888 parchment folios (1,776 pages) on which 903 separate documents were copied.

This "big book" represents a new trend in Europe. In most places, claims to property were made on the basis of custom and memory, not on documentation. When property changed hands, the chief witnesses were people, and when questions arose it was these people (or their heirs) whose testimony proved ownership. In Catalonia, the habit of documenting things had a long history, and it was not unusual for individual families to keep archives of documents. At the same time, however, documentation was never sufficient on its own: verbal exchanges of agreement and the public performance of transactions constituted legally binding ceremonies meaningful to the entire community, and the validity of these actions was not dependent on the making of a written record.

With all this in mind, it is striking that seventy-nine of the documents copied into the book are accompanied by images that convey important messages about documentation and its limitations.

On the book's opening frontispiece (image A), King Alfonso consults with his chief archivist, Ramón de Caldes. Ramón discusses one of the charters taken from a large pile at his elbow, while a scribe makes copies behind him—perhaps to aid in the compilation of the "big book." The king is backed by men who look on approvingly.

One of the charters copied into the "big book" is accompanied by the second image (B). It records that the viscount of Nîmes betrothed his daughter, Ermengarde of Carcassone, to the count of Roussillon. Ermengarde, her flowing hair uncovered as a sign of her maidenhood, stands between her bearded father and her seated mother, Cecilia of Provence.

Questions for Analysis

1. Why would a book designed to document property transactions contain images, too? What functions could they have served?

2. Why would the artist of the "big book" have depicted the king consulting his archivist in the very first image? How does he depict the relationship between them? Why does he include a group of men as witnesses to their discussion?

3. Women figure prominently in many of the book's images, including the one below. On what basis could you argue that their active presence is crucial to the transactions being described?

A. King Alfonso and Ramón de Caldes.

B. Betrothal of Ermengarde to the Count of Roussillon.

later Roman Empire (Chapter 5). The *Decretum* was also made possible by the new intellectual trends that were simultaneously giving rise to the universities of Europe (see below).

The *Decretum* claimed ecclesiastical jurisdiction for all sorts of cases, including such matters as marriage, inheritance, and bequests. Although these cases were supposed to be heard in local ecclesiastical courts overseen by bishops, popes increasingly insisted that they alone could issue dispensations exempting certain petitioners from established precedents—such as the annulment of Eleanor's marriage to Louis VII—and moreover that the papal court should function as a final court of appeals in all cases touching the Church.

Thinking back to the dispute between Henry II of England and Archbishop Thomas Becket, we can better understand what was at stake: both secular and ecclesiastical rulers now defined their power in terms of law, and they had to defend their rights against encroachment by others. And just as kings had to become more skillful administrators, so the popes of this era were almost invariably trained as canon lawyers, which was a real departure from the monastic origins of the reforming movement discussed in Chapter 8.

One example of this new breed of popes was Alexander III, who dealt so skillfully with Frederick Barbarossa. Another was Innocent III (r. 1198–1216), who combined an expertise in canon law with a zeal for continuing the work of the Crusades, even within Europe.

CONTINUING THE CRUSADES

When Pope Urban II urged the quarrelsome knights of northwestern Europe to take up the cross against the enemies of Christ in 1095, he was responding to the Byzantine emperor's request for reinforcements in his war with the Seljuq Turks, with the aim of recapturing imperial territories in Anatolia. But the pope's own conception of the crusaders' mission was broader and extended beyond the frontiers of Byzantium to the great cities of Antioch and Jerusalem, which had been in the hands of Muslims after centuries. And as we saw in Chapter 8, many crusaders acted on a still broader interpretation of their mission by attacking "enemies of Christ" in the Rhineland: the Jewish communities of Mainz, Speyer, and Worms.

So from the first, both the reason for crusading and the target of Christian aggression were apt to change. Like a weapon forged for a specific purpose whose uses could not be controlled, the crusading ethos could be copied and

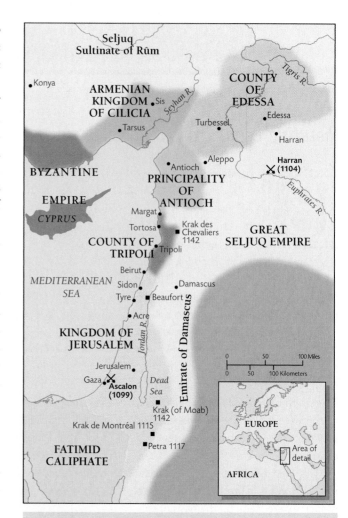

THE CRUSADER STATES. This map shows the fragile colonies known as the Crusader States at their greatest extent, around 1100. ■ *What geographical, political, and military factors would make these states vulnerable?*

disseminated more widely, directed at other targets and for other motives. In the eyes of the Byzantine emperor, some Muslims were valued allies; for the crusaders themselves, who did not understand the politics of the eastern Mediterranean, this was a distinction that made no sense. And even though the papacy never officially sanctioned violence against Jews, individual popes would, in the centuries following the First Crusade, authorize the use of force against many different kinds of people who could be construed as "enemies of Christ" because they stood in opposition to the Roman Church. While historians, for convenience, often speak of the Crusades as divided into seven or more distinct phases (the Second Crusade, the Third Crusade, etc.), the people of the time—both aggressors and victims—experienced crusading as a continuous, snowballing movement. It was (and is still) a powerful and deadly force.

Crusader States and Crusading Orders

The military successes of the First Crusade were due not only to the might of the crusaders but to the diversity of (and divisions among) the many peoples who inhabited the coastline of the eastern Mediterranean. This is an area we have been studying since Chapter 1, and that had been formed by successive waves of colonization over the course of many millennia. The fragile principalities known as "the Crusader States" should therefore be understood as laying a thin veneer of western European influence on top of a deep, complex culture that would withstand any superficial changes.

Those Europeans who stayed and flourished here were those who were able to adapt themselves, and their expectations. Most probably retained some aspects of their former identities—as Normans or Franks, as loyal to the Roman Church—but they and their descendants became intertwined with the local populations, intermarrying and adopting their fashions, food, and outlook. In time, they had more in common with their immediate neighbors (Syrian and Armenian Christians, adherents of Greek Orthodoxy, Shi'ite and Sunni Muslims) than with their distant families "back home." Second- and third-generation settlers might never visit western Christendom in the course of their lives.

Because of all these factors, the four main Crusader States were very different from the territorial monarchies that were being consolidated in parts of Europe at this time. They were more like the loosely configured and combative lordships of the tenth and eleventh centuries than like burgeoning bureaucratic kingdoms. As such, they were mostly short-lived. The largest, the inland county of Edessa founded in 1098, stretched as far east as the Tigris River and had to be heavily fortified against constant internal uprisings and external threats. Its Latin Christian population was always a tiny minority, and by 1150 it had been mostly subsumed into the Seljuq Empire, with some portions reverting to Byzantium.

Edessa's position was made even more precarious because its Frankish rulers had friendlier relations with their Armenian subjects (with whom they largely intermarried) than with the crusader principality of Antioch to the west, which comprised parts of what is now Syria and Turkey. Although Antioch was named a patriarchate of the Roman Church, it also had a tiny Latin Christian population. And, after the fall of Edessa, it was largely dependent on Constantinople, and later Armenia, for protection from the Seljuq Turks. It ceased to exist in 1268, when its lands became part of a vast new empire, that of the Mongols (see Chapter 10).

The third major state, the county of Tripoli, was founded in 1109 and linked these two northern states with the kingdom of Jerusalem. Its strategic commercial position exposed it to constant raids and threats of invasion, which led its rulers to entrust most of the frontier to one of the military orders dedicated to perpetual pursuit of the crusading effort: the Knights Hospitaller. Originally charged with care of pilgrims in the Hospital of St. John at Jerusalem, founded in 1023, members of this religious order became militarized after 1099 and came to control the islands of Rhodes and Malta as well as many strategic fortifications in the eastern Mediterranean. Their massive *Krak des Chevaliers* ("Knights' Castle," in a mixture of Arabic and French) survives as a monument to their might. In fact, the Hospitallers long outlived the Crusader States, maintaining a sovereign presence in the region into the early nineteenth century; the order is now headquartered in Rome.

The Kingdom of Jerusalem and the Conquest of Saladin

The kingdom of Jerusalem, the fourth and most symbolically important of the Crusader States, was really a network of cities and fortresses that constantly changed hands, as much the target of rival crusaders as of any Muslim raiders. Its cosmopolitan population was a testament to the number of peoples who claimed the Holy Land for their own, with major concentrations of Muslims (both Sunni and Shi'a) and Orthodox Christians (Greek and Syrian) alongside smaller communities (Jews, Samaritans)—all of whom dwarfed the Latin Christian population of the region. As a result, those

KRAK DES CHEVALIERS. The necessity of securing hand-won territory in the Holy Land led to the construction of enormous castles like this one, built by the Knights Hospitaller in the early twelfth century when crusading movements were launched in Europe itself. Similar castles would be built to subjugate peoples deemed rebellious or heretical.

who claimed kingship in Jerusalem were heavily dependent on support from other Crusader States as well as from various European princes; yet the cachet of Jerusalem was such that any contingent of reinforcements sent by an ambitious ally could be attempting to seize power there. Defense of the kingdom therefore came to rest heavily on another of the new crusading orders, the Knights Templar. Founded during the reign of King Baldwin II (r. 1118–31), the Templars were based in a wing of the captured Al-Aqsa Mosque, which was now the royal palace and thought to be part of King Solomon's original Temple complex: hence the order's name.

Although the kingdom of Jerusalem persisted in theory until 1291, it ceased to have any purchase on Jerusalem itself after 1187. In this year, a remarkable Kurdish chieftain called Salāh ad-Dīn (c. 1138–1193), who had become the Sunni sultan of both Egypt and Syria, rallied Muslim opposition to the occupying crusader forces and succeeded in recapturing the Holy City. He became the target of a renewed crusading effort (the Third Crusade, 1189–92), which spurred three kings to take the cross: England's Richard the Lionheart, France's Philip Augustus, and the Holy Roman Empire's Frederick Barbarossa. But Frederick was killed, Philip left early, and Richard was captured on the way home. Meanwhile, the victorious Saladin (as he was known in Europe) became celebrated not only among Muslims but also among crusaders, who considered him a paragon of chivalry. Richard even considered arranging a marriage between his sister, Joan of Sicily, and Saladin's brother, thereby establishing allied rule in Jerusalem. But this never happened, and Jerusalem remained in Muslim hands. The city of Acre (Akko, in northern Israel) then became the new capital of the Christian kingdom, until its fall in 1291 marked the end of any viable western European presence in the region—until the short-lived conquests of Napoleon at the end of the eighteenth century (see Chapter 18).

The Extension of Crusading Ideas into European Colonial Projects

Once unleashed, the crusading ethos could not be contained by efforts to liberate the Holy Land. The promise that those who killed "the enemies of Christ" with papal approval would be absolved of their sins and win eternal salvation, while potentially winning lands and riches in the process, was soon applied to a host of other initiatives—especially those that could open new lands for settlement and bring more peoples into the orbit of the Roman Church. Beginning in the 1160s, accordingly, the rulers of Denmark and the German duchy of Saxony began to colonize the Baltic coast and lands between the Elbe and Oder Rivers.

This was represented as a missionary movement, but it was also an attempt to control trading and raiding activities in that region. And it was not carried forward peacefully; the missionary monks who spearheaded it (literally) were members of the military crusading order of the Teutonic Knights. In 1204, they managed to carve out a new bishopric around Riga (present-day Latvia), where they set about converting the indigenous inhabitants. But when they mounted a biblical drama featuring some battle scenes from the Old Testament, the new "converts" fled in terror at the sight of armed actors: it was all too real.

Meanwhile, the English were launching crusades against the "infidel" Irish and Welsh (who were actually Christian), justifying this on the grounds that the Celts were barbarians who would benefit from the civilizing influence of their superior overlords. It had been a short step from the calling of crusades against foreigners to those aimed at fellow Europeans.

The Crusade against Constantinople and the Revenge of Venice

The First Crusade had begun as an attempt to aid Constantinople. The Fourth Crusade (1202–4) ended in its destruction. The object of this expedition, which had been called by Pope Innocent III at the time of his election in 1198, was Egypt, where Saladin's successors continued to rally Muslim opposition to European colonial efforts. This meant launching an attack by sea, since the remaining crusader outposts had become too weak and scattered to enable the movement of armies by land. The natural embarkation point was Venice.

A major player in maritime trade since the ninth century, Venice had already benefited enormously from the Crusades, supplying the ships and supplies that transported and sustained the waves of aspiring conquerors while reaping the benefits of closer ties with Byzantium, with which the Italian city shared many interests. But relations with Constantinople worsened throughout the twelfth century, as the Crusades increasingly damaged Byzantine trade and threatened its security. In 1182, popular anticrusading sentiment had led enraged citizens of Constantinople to massacre enclaves of Italian merchants and seamen; those who were not killed were banished, the Venetians among them.

The Venetians therefore had a reason to resent the Byzantines. And they were now overrun by an army of eager and impoverished crusaders who could not pay for the passage to Cairo; it would cost the Venetians enormously in time, money, and men to ship them there. So in the end, the crusaders paid the Venetians with the services they could render. Rather than sailing for Egypt, the crusading expedition

Past and Present

Medieval Plots and Modern Movies

From westerns to science fiction to action movies to romantic comedies, most of the films that draw big audiences today are based loosely or closely on literary genres that were popularized during the Middle Ages: tales of chivalry and heroism, forbidden love, supernatural events, and magical adventures.

 Watch related author interview on StudySpace
wwnorton.com/web/westernciv18

was diverted to Zara on the Dalmatian coast of the Adriatic, a former Venetian port that had rebelled and sought the protection of the king of Hungary. Despite the fact that Hungary was loyal to Rome, the city was attacked and taken.

From there, the crusaders moved on to Constantinople. After a terrible siege, the city was savagely overrun and sacked in 1204, its people killed or left homeless, its churches and public buildings severely damaged, and its books and artworks consigned to flames or seized as loot (like the porphyry statue of the Roman tetrarchs shown in Chapter 6 on page 191, which is still in Venice). In the aftermath, the Venetians were able to colonize the city itself, controlling the shipping in and around Constantinople as well as the island of Crete and many cities on the Greek mainland. Only in 1261 was Byzantine rule reestablished in the capital; but by that time, the empire had shrunk to a fraction of its former size. Meanwhile, crusading efforts continued within western Christendom.

Innocent III's Crusade for a Unified Christendom

Although Pope Innocent III expressed alarm at the turn taken by the Crusade he had called, he accepted the spoils of war that were offered to him and set his seal of approval on the Latin occupation of Greek territory. He was an ambitious man. Elected to the papal dignity at the age of thirty-seven (probably the youngest holder of the office in history), his goal was to unify all Christendom—and the wider world—under papal hegemony. Unlike Gregory VII (Chapter 8), Innocent never questioned the right of kings and princes to rule in their own secular spheres. Instead, he saw the pope's role as regulatory and disciplinary, which meant that when rulers sinned they should be reprimanded or excommunicated by the pope—who could thereby call into question the legitimacy of their rule. And Innocent

THE JEWISH BADGE. The distinctive apparel that marked Jews as different from their Christian neighbors varied from region to region. In some places it was a pointed hat like the one worn by the Old Testament Jews in this manuscript illumination from a fourteenth-century French vernacular Bible. This hat would later become associated with witchcraft or idiocy, as in the dunce's cap or the witch's peak. In other regions, Jews wore a distinctive patch on their clothing, often colored yellow to make it more visible.

bly of the western Church, the Fourth Lateran Council of 1215 (so called because it was held in the Roman palace of St. John Lateran). This council defined the central dogmas of Latin Christianity and made one of them the acknowledgment of papal supremacy. Since a dogma is defined as "a truth necessary for salvation," this meant that all Christians had to acknowledge the pope's ultimate power; those unwilling to do so (including the Christians of Byzantium) were, by definition, heretics—and as heretics, they could be prosecuted and punished.

In a further effort to achieve unity and uniformity within Christendom, the Fourth Lateran Council took an unprecedented interest in the religious education and habits of every Christian. It responded to the urbanization of Europe by establishing free primary schools (for boys) in all the major cities, requiring bishops to recruit effective preachers, and outlawing all kinds of misbehavior on the part of the clergy. It also sought to increase the distance between Christians and their Muslim and Jewish neighbors by discouraging social relationships, economic exchanges, and intermarriage. Most disturbingly, Innocent's council mandated that "infidels" be visibly distinguished from Christians by the wearing of distinctive clothing, the origins of the infamous "Jewish badge" (see Chapter 26).

The Crusade against Heresy

Innocent's reign achieved the height of papal power, but it also fomented violence and sowed seeds of dissent. Future popes continued to centralize the government of the Church, but they also became involved in protracted political and military struggles that compromised the papacy's credibility. Because the Papal States bordered on the kingdom of Sicily, Innocent's successors quickly came into conflict with Emperor Frederick II, who became an inveterate opponent of papal monarchy. But instead of excommunicating him and calling for his deposition, as Innocent might have done, they called a crusade against him. Yet Innocent himself had paved the way for this by launching a series of Crusades against heretics, now defined as any group or individual who did not fall into line with the papacy's policies—and who were, by association, "enemies of Christ." The most notorious of these campaigns was the Albigensian Crusade, launched in 1209 and ostensibly directed against a heretical sect called the Cathars, but which really justified the colonization of what is now southern France by land-hungry knights from northern France. Although the Albigensian Crusade can be said to have ended by 1255, it created lasting tensions within the forcibly enlarged French kingdom that would lead the

was even more insistent than his predecessors on the obligation of every Christian to obey the pope as Jesus Christ's representative on earth.

Innocent sought to achieve this goal in many different ways. He made the papacy financially and politically independent by expanding and consolidating papal territories in central Italy. (Vatican City is now the last surviving remnant of these territories, and it continues to function as an independent state within Rome and Italy.) He loudly proclaimed his power as kingmaker and king-breaker by brokering the selection of the Holy Roman Emperor, and he also disciplined both Philip Augustus of France (for marital misconduct) and John of England, who was at one point compelled to grant England itself to the papacy, as a fief. Innocent further claimed, with varying degrees of success, a comparable lordship over Aragon, Sicily, and Hungary. He even levied the first income tax on the clergy, in order to support the Crusade that brought Orthodox Christians to heel.

The crowning achievement of Innocent's pontificate was the ratification of his agenda at a representative asseminhabitants of this devastated region to ally with the English during the Hundred Years' War (see Chapter 10) and make southern France particularly susceptible to violent religious warfare during and after the Reformation (see Chapter 13). Indeed, the language, culture, and political orientation of southern France are still very different from that of Paris and its environs. In order to understand how this happened, we must turn to some larger religious developments within Europe.

UNITY AND DISSENT IN THE WESTERN CHURCH

The Investiture Conflict (Chapter 8) engaged both clergy and laity in debates over the essential meaning of Jesus Christ's life and teachings. In many regions of western Europe, the papacy's claim to supremacy was supported, but in others there was marked resistance to its encroachment on centuries-old practices and social networks. After all, bishops had been members of the aristocracy since the time of Constantine, and it was customary for bishoprics to be controlled by certain families. Meanwhile, priests had been married men since the establishment of the first Christian churches; and the wives of priests were not only their husbands' partners, they were also ministers to the communities in which they lived. When the papacy preached against "fornicating priests" and their "concubines," it was delegitimizing relationships that had been essential to local communities for generations. No wonder, then, that nothing else was talked about "even in the women's spinning rooms and the artisans' workshops," as one contemporary reported.

On the one hand, then, the reforms of Pope Gregory VII and his successors gave the common people an important role to play, by urging them to reject certain practices and urging retaliation against offenders. Combined with the fervor that had been whipped up by the Crusades, the result was more-widespread interest in spiritual matters and increased participation in religious life—as well as increased violence. On the other hand, however, the reforming movement severely limited the ways in which the laity were allowed to express their spirituality or to participate meaningfully in the life of the Church.

The New Monasticism

One of the first manifestations of the new popular piety was the growth and diversification of monastic move-ments. The abbey of Cluny had revived the observance of Benedict's *Rule* in the course of the tenth century and, at the same time, had kept Cluny and its daughter houses independent of local lords. As a result, these monasteries became lordships in their own right, acquiring extensive lands and enormous wealth. Those seeking to reject worldliness, therefore, had to look elsewhere. The result, beginning in the late eleventh century, was the founding of new monastic orders.

The one that became most widespread was founded at the monastery of Cîteaux in 1098. Cistercian monks followed Benedict's *Rule*, but in the purest and most austere way possible, and they founded new monasteries in wildernesses and remote areas, far from worldly temptations. They also shunned all unnecessary decoration and elaborate liturgical rites. Instead, they practiced contemplation and private prayer, and they committed themselves to hard manual labor. Under the charismatic leadership of Bernard of Clairvaux (1090–1153), a spellbinding preacher and one of the most influential personalities of his age, the Cistercian order grew exponentially, from 5 houses in 1115 to 343 by 1153. This astonishing increase meant that many more men and women were becoming professional religious. It also meant that still more pious people were donating funds and lands to support monasteries and thereby participating indirectly in their life of devotion.

Another manifestation of popular piety was a new focus on the sacrament of the Mass, the liturgical reenactment of Christ's last meal with his disciples. This celebration, the Eucharist, had always been an important part of Christian religious and social practice (see Chapter 6), but only in the twelfth century did it become the central act of worship in the western Church. Bernard of Clairvaux was instrumental in making it so, by developing and preaching the doctrine of transubstantiation. According to this doctrine, every Mass is a miraculous event, because the priest's blessing transforms the bread and wine on the altar into the body and blood of Christ: hence the term *transubstantiation*, since earthly substances thereby become the substance of Christ's divine body.

Popular reverence for the Eucharist became so great that the Church initiated the practice of elevating the consecrated bread, known as the Host, so that the whole congregation could see it. Not incidentally, this new theology of the Eucharist further enhanced the prestige of the priesthood by seeming to endow it with wonder-working powers. In later centuries, the Latin words spoken at the consecration of the Host, *Hoc est corpus meum* ("This is my body"), were understood as a magical formula: *hocus pocus*.

Analyzing Primary Sources

The Canons of the Fourth Lateran Council

In 1215, Innocent III presided over an ecumenical assembly of Church leaders in the papal palace and church of Saint John Lateran in Rome. The resulting canons both reaffirmed older legislation and introduced a number of new laws that responded to widespread social, economic, and cultural changes. Published in the same year as Magna Carta, they too became a standard set of principles and continued to be applied within the Church until they were modified by the Council of Trent in the sixteenth century.

Canon 1

... There is one Universal Church of the faithful, outside of which there is absolutely no salvation. In which there is the same priest and sacrifice, Jesus Christ, whose body and blood are truly contained in the sacrament of the altar under the forms of bread and wine; the bread being changed (*transsubstantiatio*) by divine power into the body, and the wine into the blood, so that to realize the mystery of unity we may receive of Him what He has received of us. And this sacrament no one can effect except the priest who has been duly ordained in accordance with the keys of the Church, which Jesus Christ Himself gave to the Apostles and their successors. . . .

•••

Canon 3

We excommunicate and anathematize every heresy that rises against the holy, orthodox, and Catholic faith ... condemning all heretics under whatever names they may be known, for while they have different faces they are nevertheless bound to each other by their tails, since in all of them vanity is a common element. Those condemned, being handed over to the secular rulers of their bailiffs, let them be abandoned, to be punished with due justice, clerics being first degraded from their orders.

•••

Canon 9

Since in many places within the same city and diocese there are people of different languages having one faith but various rites and customs, we strictly command that the bishops of these cities and dioceses provide suitable men who will, according to the different rites and languages, celebrate the divine offices for them, administer the sacraments of the Church and instruct them by word and example.

Canon 10

... It often happens that bishops, on account of their manifold duties or bodily infirmities, or because of hostile invasions or other reasons, to say nothing of lack of learning, which must be absolutely condemned in them and is not to be tolerated in the future, are themselves unable to minister the word of God to the people, especially in large and widespread dioceses. Wherefore we decree that bishops provide suitable men, powerful in work and word, to exercise with fruitful result the office of preaching; who in place of the bishops, since these cannot do it, diligently visiting the people committed to them, may instruct them by word and example. . . .

Canon 11

Since there are some who, on account of the lack of necessary means, are unable to acquire an education or to meet opportunities for perfecting themselves, the Third Lateran Council in a salutary decree provided that in every cathedral church a suitable benefice be assigned to a master who shall instruct *gratis* the clerics of that church and other poor students, ... we, confirming the aforesaid decree, add that, not only in every cathedral church but also in other churches where means are sufficient, a competent master be appointed ... who shall instruct *gratis* and to the best of his ability the clerics of those and other churches in the art of grammar and in other branches of knowledge.

•••

Canons 14–16

That the morals and general conduct of clerics may be better, let all strive to live chastely and virtuously, particularly those in sacred orders, guarding against every vice of desire . . .

... All clerics shall carefully abstain from drunkenness. . . .

We forbid hunting and fowling to all clerics; wherefore, let them not presume to keep dogs and birds for these purposes. . . .

Clerics shall not hold secular offices or engage in secular and, above all, dishonest pursuits. They shall not attend the performances of mimics and buffoons, or theatrical representations. They shall not visit taverns except in case of necessity, namely, when on a journey.

They are forbidden to play games of chance or be present at them. They must have a becoming crown and tonsure and apply themselves diligently to the study of the divine offices and other useful subjects. Their garments must be worn clasped at the top and neither too short nor too long. They are not to use red or green garments or curiously sewed-together gloves, or beak-shaped shoes . . .

• • •

Canon 68

In some provinces a difference in dress distinguishes the Jews or Saracens from the Christians, but in certain others such a confusion has grown up that they cannot be distinguished by any difference. Thus it happens at times that through error Christians have relations with the women of Jews or Saracens, and Jews and Saracens with Christian women. Therefore, that they may not, under pretext of error of this sort, excuse themselves in the future for the excesses of such prohibited intercourse, we decree that such Jews and Saracens of both sexes in every Christian province and at all times shall be marked off in the eyes of the public from other peoples through the character of their dress. . . .

Moreover, during the last three days before Easter and especially on Good Friday, they shall not go forth in public at all, for the reason that some of them on these very days, as we hear, do not blush to go forth better dressed and are not afraid to mock the Christians who maintain the memory of the most holy Passion by wearing signs of mourning. . . .

Source: Excerpted from H. J. Schroeder, *Disciplinary Decrees of the General Councils: Text, Translation and Commentary* (St. Louis, MO: 1937), pp. 236–96.

Questions for Analysis

1. Based on this selection of canons, how would you characterize the main concerns of the Fourth Lateran Council? What is it attempting to regulate, and why? What changing historical circumstances do the canons reflect?

2. In what ways do the canons distinguish between clergy and laity? How does legislation work to maintain those distinctions?

3. Why do the canons place so much emphasis on clothing and appearance? Why would it be important for both clerics and "infidels" (Jews and Muslims) to dress in distinctive ways?

Holy Women, Human and Divine

Popular devotion to the Eucharist was matched by another new and hugely influential religious practice: the veneration of Jesus's mother, Mary. In this development, too, Bernard of Clairvaux played an important role, traveling around Europe to promote a theology that made Mary central to Christianity, the very embodiment of the Church. Eventually, Catholic teaching would hold that Mary had not only given birth to Jesus while still a virgin but that she remained a virgin even after Jesus's birth— and, more radically, that she herself had been conceived without sin. This made Mary the exact opposite of Eve, the woman whose disobedience had (according to Judeo-Christian tradition) brought sin into the world for the first time; for through God's grace, Mary had given birth to Christ, a second Adam, whose obedient sacrifice of himself atoned for that original sin.

New doctrines also raised Mary from the position of God's humble handmaid to that of heaven's queen, with the power to intercede on behalf of all, even the worst sinners. Her soaring reputation as a miracle worker and advocate is amply testified by the thousands of devotional images created during this period, the many stories and hymns celebrating her virtues and miracles, and the fact that practically all the magnificent new cathedrals of the age were dedicated to "Our Lady." This explains the many churches of Notre Dame in France, the Frauenkirchen of Germany, and so on.

The burgeoning cult of the Blessed Virgin had two contradictory effects. On the one hand, it elevated a female figure to a prominent place in the official Church for the first time, and it thereby celebrated virtues associated with femininity: motherhood, healing, nourishment, mercy, kindness. On the other hand, it made Mary an unobtainable, paradoxical model of female perfection: she alone could be both virgin and parent, Christ's mother and bride, God's maidservant and queenly consort. No real woman could begin to emulate her, and thus real women were increasingly compared to Eve and perceived as weak, deceitful, and disobedient. Moreover, the veneration of a

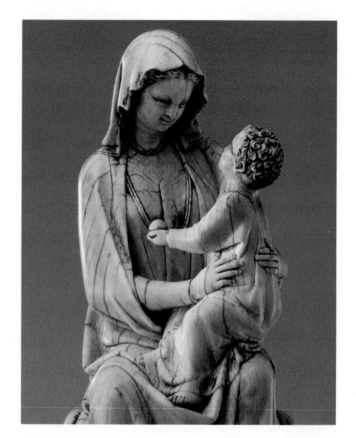

VIRGIN AND CHILD. This exquisite ivory sculpture (just over seven inches high) was carved in Paris in the mid to late thirteenth century, as an aid to private devotion and prayer. The mother of Jesus, Mary, was also regarded as the mother of all humanity, the *alma mater* ("nourishing mother") who could be relied on to protect and heal those who asked for her help.

THE MYSTERY OF THE MASS. In this manuscript illumination, the visionary Hildegard of Bingen (see below) illustrates the doctrine of transubstantiation. In the lower register, the bread and wine of the Mass have been placed on the altar and are being transformed into the body and blood of the crucified Christ, depicted in the upper register. Paired scenes from Christ's life (his birth and death, his ministry and resurrection) emphasize the fact that earthly substances—bread and wine—participate in a divine cycle of regeneration. Note that Hildegard does not imagine the mediating figure as a priest, but as the (female) Church, represented as a crowned queen and associated with the Virgin Mary. ▪ *What might be the significance of this choice?*

single, idealized woman coincided exactly with the suppression of most real women's access to positions of power within the Church; as the cult of the Blessed Virgin grew, so the opportunities for aspiring holy women shrank.

This did not go unremarked at the time. As we noted above, the career of Heloise (c. 1090–1164) exemplifies both the avenues of advancement for women and also the successful blocking of those avenues by new constraints on women's activities. Heloise's exact contemporary, Hildegard of Bingen (1098–1179), was even more creative in her efforts to make a place for herself and her female followers, and more outspoken than Heloise in her criticism of attempts to thwart them. Like Heloise, she was an abbess and a highly original thinker. But she was not, like Heloise, a scholar; she was a mystic who claimed to receive regular revelations from God.

Hildegard expressed these visions in her own version of Latin, writings that were later transcribed and illustrated under her close supervision. She also composed hymns and ambitious musical dramas for her nuns—music now widely available on CD, MP3, and the Internet—and prepared

HILDEGARD OF BINGEN'S DIVINE INSPIRATION. This portrait of Hildegard and her male secretary, Volmar, appears in her book *Scivias* ("Know the Ways"). It shows Hildegard as the recipient of a divine vision (represented by tongues of heavenly fire) which she transcribes onto a wax tablet using a stylus—a common method for creating the first draft of a written work. Volmar is placed outside the frame in which her vision occurs, but he is prepared to copy it onto parchment. ▪ *What does this image tell us about medieval ideas of authorship and authority?* ▪ *What does it suggest about the relationship and status of the two figures?*

treatises on subjects as diverse as cosmology and medicine. Her advice was frequently sought by religious and secular authorities, including Bernard of Clairvaux and Frederick Barbarossa, and she even received a special papal dispensation that allowed her to preach publicly.

Despite all this, Hildegard had to fight constantly for her rights and those of her nuns during her lifetime, and after her death efforts to have her recognized as a saint were thwarted by the papacy. Indeed, she was one of the first candidates for whom a new canonization process was instituted in the papal curia, as a way of controlling the popular veneration of charismatic figures whom the Church consid-

ered threatening. So while many high-ranking clergy of her own day recognized her holiness, the papal courts of subsequent centuries would not acknowledge it. The standards of acceptable female behavior had become too narrow to contain her. It would take 800 years for Hildegard to be officially canonized as a saint, in 2012.

Heresy or Piety?

Christianity has been successfully transmitted to many different civilizations because it is relatively open-ended and absorbent of new influences. In this era, however, the medieval Church began to lose its capacity to respond inclusively to new challenges, preferring instead to crack down on "heresies" that undermined its power. This trend would eventually lead to a reforming movement so intense that it could not be contained within the Church: the Protestant Reformation (see Chapter 13). For the more the Church claimed the right to control every aspect of belief and practice, the more it made itself vulnerable to those who challenged its enforcement. This resulted in large-scale movements of popular opposition to centralized authority, and also to more Crusades aimed at harnessing popular piety to that same authority.

The best way to understand this is through Innocent III's very different responses to rather similar popular movements. On the one hand, the pope resolved to crush all disobedience; on the other, he wanted to support idealistic groups that could be made to acknowledge papal authority, so as not to frustrate all dynamic spirituality. Thus, Innocent labeled as heretical a religious movement that began in southern France, that of the Cathars (from the Greek word for "purity"). He accused Cathars of beliefs that resemble Zoroastrianism (see Chapter 2) and Manichaeism (see Chapter 6), alleging that they held all material creation to be evil, and even that they believed the power of God to be opposed by that of a malevolent deity associated with Satan or the fallen angel Lucifer. The fact that many Cathar leaders were women made the movement heretical by definition.

More typical of twelfth-century religious dissent was Waldensianism, so called because it is said to have originated with the teachings of a merchant called Waldes. Waldensians were laypeople who wished to imitate the life of Christ to the fullest. They were active in the vernacular translation and study of the Gospels and dedicated to lives of poverty and preaching. None of this contradicted any contemporary doctrines, and for a while the Church did not interfere with Waldensians' ministry. But when

Competing Viewpoints

Two Conversion Experiences

> *Both Peter Waldo (or Waldes), later branded as a heretic, and Francis of Assisi, later canonized as a saint, were moved to take up a life of preaching and poverty after undergoing a process of conversion. These experiences exhibit some striking similarities, despite the different fates of these two men. The first account is that of an anonymous chronicler in Peter's home town of Lyons; the second is by Francis's contemporary and hagiographer, Thomas of Celano (c. 1200–c. 1260/70).*

The Conversion of Peter Waldo

At about this time, in 1173, there was a citizen of Lyons named Peter Waldo, who had made a great deal of money by the evil means of usury. One Sunday he lingered by a crowd that had gathered round a traveling storyteller, and was much struck by his words. He took him home with him, and listened carefully to his story of how St. Alexis had died a holy death in his father's house. Next morning Waldo hastened to the schools of theology to seek advice about his soul. When he had been told of the many ways of coming to God he asked the master whether any of them was more sure and reliable than the rest. The master quoted to him the words of the Lord, "If thou wilt be perfect go sell what thou hast and give it to the poor and thou shalt have treasure in heaven. And come follow me."

Waldo returned to his wife and gave her the choice between having all his movable wealth or his property in land.... She was very upset at having to do this and chose the property. From his movable wealth he returned what he had acquired wrongly, conferred a large portion on his two daughters, whom he placed in the order of Fontevrault without his wife's knowledge, and gave a still larger amount to the poor.

At this time a terrible famine was raging through Gaul and Germany.... Waldo generously distributed bread, soup and meat to anyone who came to him. On the [Feast of the] Assumption of the Virgin [August 15] he scattered money among the poor in the streets saying, "You cannot serve two masters, God and Mammon." The people around thought he had gone out of his senses. Then he stood up on a piece of high ground and said, "Friends and fellow-citizens, I am not mad as you think.... I know that many of you disapprove of my having acted so publicly. I have done so both for my own sake and for yours: for my sake, because anybody who sees me with money in future will be able to say that I am mad; for your sake, so that you may learn to place your hopes in God and not in wealth."...

1177 Waldo, the citizen of Lyons whom we have already mentioned, who had vowed to God that he would possess neither gold nor silver, and take no thought for the morrow, began to make converts to his opinions. Following his example they gave all they had to the poor, and willingly devoted themselves to poverty. Gradually, both in public and in private they began to inveigh against both their own sins and those of others....

1178 Pope Alexander III held a council at the Lateran palace.... The council condemned heresy and all those who fostered and defended heretics. The pope embraced Waldo, and applauded the vows of voluntary poverty which he had taken, but forbade him and his companion to assume the office of preaching except at the request of the priests. They obeyed this instruction for a time, but later they disobeyed, and affronted many, bringing ruin on themselves.

Source: Excerpted from *Chronicon universale anonymi Laudunensis*, ed. and trans. Robert I. Moore in *The Birth of Popular Heresy* (London: 1975), pp. 111–13 (slightly modified).

The Conversion of Francis of Assisi

There was a man by the name of Francis, who from his earliest years was brought up by his parents proud of spirit, in accordance with the vanity of the world....These are the wretched circumstances among which the man whom we venerate today as a saint, for he is truly a saint, lived in his youth; and almost up to the twenty-fifth year of his age,...he outdid all his contemporaries in vanities and he came to be a promoter of evil and was more abundantly zealous for all kinds of foolishness.... And while, not knowing how to restrain himself, he was ... worn down by a long illness, [he] began to think of things other than he was used to thinking upon. When he had recovered somewhat and had begun to walk about the house with the support of a cane to speed the recovery of his health, he went outside one day and began to look about at the surrounding landscape with great interest. But the beauty of the fields, the pleasantness of the vineyards, and whatever else was beautiful to look upon, could stir in him no delight. He wondered therefore at the sudden change that had come over him.... From that day on, therefore, he began to despise himself....

Now since there was a certain man in the city of Assisi whom he loved more than any other because he was of the same age as the other, and since the great familiarity of their mutual affection led him to share his secrets with him; he often took him to remote places, places well-suited for counsel, telling him that he had found a certain precious and great treasure. This one rejoiced and, concerned about what he heard, he willingly accompanied Francis whenever he was asked. There was a certain grotto near the city where they frequently went and talked about this treasure. The man of God, who was already holy by reason of his holy purpose, would enter the grotto, while his companion would wait for him outside; and filled with a new and singular spirit, he would pray to his Father in secret....

One day, however, when he had begged for the mercy of God most earnestly, it was shown to him by God what he was to do.... He rose up, therefore, fortified himself with the sign of the cross, got his horse ready and mounted it, and taking with him some fine cloth to sell, he hastened to the city called Foligno. There, as usual, he sold everything he had with him ... and, free of all luggage, he started back, wondering with a religious mind what he should do with the money.... When, therefore, he neared the city of Assisi, he discovered a certain church ... built of old in honor of St. Damian but which was now threatening to collapse because it was so old.... And when he found there a certain poor priest, he kissed his sacred hands with great faith, and offered him the money he had with him, ... begging the priest to suffer him to remain with him for the sake of the Lord....

When those who knew him ... compared what he was now with what he had been ... they began to revile him miserably. Shouting out that he was mad and demented, they threw the mud of the streets and stones at him.... Now ... the report of these things finally came to his father ... [who] shut him up mercilessly in a dark place for several days ... It happened, however, when Francis' father had left home for a while on business and the man of God remained bound in the basement of the house, his mother, who was alone with him and did not approve of what her husband had done, spoke kindly to her son.... and loosening his chains, she let him go free....

He [the father] then brought his son before the bishop of the city, so that, renouncing all his possessions into his hands, he might give up everything he had.... Indeed, he [Francis] did not wait for any words nor did he speak any, but immediately putting off his clothes and casting them aside, he gave them back to his father. Moreover, not even retaining his trousers, he stripped himself completely naked before all. The bishop, however, sensing his disposition and admiring greatly his fervor and constancy, arose and drew him within his arms and covered him with the mantle he was wearing....

Source: Excerpted from Thomas of Celano, "The First Life of Saint Francis" in *Saint Francis of Assisi: Writings and Biographies*, ed. Marion A. Habiq (Chicago: 1973), pp. 229–41.

Questions for Analysis

1. How do the conversions of Peter and Francis reflect the social and economic changes of the twelfth century? What new sources of tension and temptation are evident?

2. How do these two accounts describe these new converts' relationship(s) with their families, communities, and Church authorities? What are the similarities and differences, and why would these be important factors in determining the sanctity of either?

3. The story of Peter's conversion is written by an anonymous chronicler of Lyons, that of Francis by his follower and official biographer. How do these different perspectives shape these two accounts? Which is the more reliable, and why?

they began to preach without authorization they were condemned as heretics. In response, they began to articulate a more radical opposition to the established hierarchy. Many of their leaders, too, were women.

At the same time, however, Innocent embraced two other popular movements and turned them into two new religious orders, the Dominicans and the Franciscans. Like the Waldensians, the friars ("brothers") of these orders imitated the life of Jesus and his apostles by wandering through the countryside and establishing missions in Europe's growing towns, preaching and offering spiritual and material assistance to the poor. They also embraced poverty and begged for a living, hence their categorization as *mendicants*, from the Latin verb *mendicare*, "to beg." In the end, the only thing that separated them from the Waldensians was their willingness to subject themselves to papal authority.

The Dominican order, formally known as the Order of Preachers, was founded by the zealous Dominic of Osma (1170–1221), a Castilian theologian. Approved in 1216, it was particularly dedicated to the prosecution of heretics and to the conversion of Jews and Muslims. At first, the Dominicans hoped to achieve these ends by preaching and public debate; and to further these goals, many of its members pursued academic careers in the nascent universities and thus contributed to the development of philosophy and theology (see below). The most influential intellectual of the Middle Ages, Thomas Aquinas (1225–1274), was a Dominican. But the Dominicans soon became associated with the use of other persuasive techniques through the administration of the Inquisition, which became formalized in the thirteenth century. (It is now called the Congregation for the Doctrine of the Faith and is still staffed by members of the order.)

The Franciscans, formally known as the Order of the Friars Minor ("Little Brothers"), were committed less to doctrine and discipline than to the welfare of the poor and the cultivation of personal spirituality. Whereas Dominic and his earliest followers were ordained priests, the founder of the Franciscans was the ne'er-do-well son of an Italian merchant, Francis of Assisi (1182–1226), who eventually rebelled against the materialistic values of his father. Stripping himself (literally) of all his worldly possessions, he put on the tattered garb of a beggar and began to preach salvation in town squares. Unlike Dominic, Francis did this without official approval, thereby risking papal censure. Indeed, the pope might well have rejected Francis as a heretic. But when he showed himself willing to profess obedience in 1209, Innocent granted Francis and his followers permission to preach.

Although the rapid growth of the Franciscan order would eventually necessitate more administrative stability and doctrinal training for all its members, many Franciscans continued to engage in revivalistic outdoor preaching and to offer a model for apostolic living. This was not, however, an approved religious lifestyle for women. Francis's most important female follower, Clare of Assisi (1194–1253), wanted to found an order along the same lines, but members of the Order of Poor Ladies (also known as the Poor Clares) were not allowed to work directly among the people, as men did, but instead lived in cloistered convents supported by charitable donations. Their counterparts in northern Europe were the Beguines, communities of laywomen who lived in loosely organized communal quarters and ministered directly to the poor. Their relationship with Church officials was strained, because the Beguines embraced many of the precepts and practices associated with the Waldensians, including the unauthorized translation and study of the Bible. The fact that they were women made them even more suspect.

Christians against Jews

Although violence and exploitation continued to prey on Europe's Jewish communities, the Church's official position never explicitly endorsed the views that Jews posed a threat to Christians, yet it did little to combat such attitudes, either. As a result, many ordinary people came to believe that their Jewish neighbors were agents of evil who routinely crucified Christian children, consumed Christian blood, profaned the body of Christ in the Eucharist, and spread disease in Christian communities by poisoning wells. Fanciful stories of Jewish wealth added an economic element to the development of anti-Semitism, as did the fact that the Jews' social and cultural networks were the engine of the medieval economy. From this fact, conspiracy theorists inferred the existence of organized Jewish plots to undermine Christian society, which were regularly cited as justifications for mass executions and other atrocities.

The precarious position of Europe's Jews worsened throughout the twelfth and thirteenth centuries as both secular and ecclesiastical authorities devised more systematic mechanisms for policing undesirable segments of society: not only heretics but the indigent poor, prostitutes, "sodomites," and lepers. The canons of the Fourth Lateran Council had mandated that Jews be exposed through the wearing of the Jewish badge, and this made them easier targets in times of unrest. At the same time, the protections which Europe's rulers had once extended

THE BURNING OF JEWS. This manuscript account, written in the German vernacular, records an incident in which Jews were accused of poisoning the wells in a Christian town—and shows the punishment meted out to them. The wooden enclosure may represent the walls of the Jewish ghetto. As in the image on page 298, the Jews are identified by their distinctive conical hats.

to their Jewish subjects were gradually withdrawn. In Spain, the "Reconquista" had absorbed many of the Muslim kingdoms in which Jews had enjoyed a measure of tolerance, and they were not easily accommodated within the emerging monarchies of Christian Spain. Starting in the 1280s, rulers elsewhere in Europe began to expel their Jewish subjects from their kingdoms altogether, in most cases because they could no longer pretend to repay the enormous sums they had extorted from Jewish money-lenders: this was the case in the kingdoms of Sicily (1288), England (1290), and France (1306). Further expulsions followed during the fourteenth century in the Rhineland, and in 1492 from Spain. By 1500, only northern Italy and various eastern European regions (encompassed today by Poland, Belarus, and Ukraine) were home to sizable Jewish communities. They would survive there until the more efficient persecutions of the Nazi Holocaust eradicated them (see Chapter 26).

AN INTELLECTUAL REVOLUTION

The Fourth Lateran Council responded to the growing urbanization of Europe by mandating the education of the laity and insisting on more rigorous training for all clergy. These measures responded to a number of factors that were working to transform the cultural landscape of Europe and to open up new opportunities for advancement through education. The growth of towns had led to the growth of schools in those towns, for the most part founded by local bishops or monasteries. Meanwhile, the Crusades became conduits for the transmission of Muslim learning and, through Muslim mediation, the precepts of ancient Greek philosophy. The infusion of these new ideas created an extraordinary new forum for intellectual endeavor: the university. In much the same way that ease of travel and communication had fostered a scientific revolution in the cities of the Hellenistic world (see Chaper 4), so the conditions that gave rise to the university mark the beginning of a revolution in the intellectual history of Europe.

Access to Education

Around 800, Charlemagne had ordered that primary schools be established in every city and monastery of his realm. But it was not until the economic revival of the late eleventh century that educational opportunities were more widely available. By 1179, Pope Alexander III decreed that all cathedrals should set aside income for at least one schoolteacher, whose task would be to accept all comers, rich or poor, without fee. He predicted, correctly, that this measure would increase the number of well-trained clerics and administrators, supplying the growing bureaucracy of the Church. The recently martyred Thomas Becket had been an early beneficiary of such schooling.

At first, cathedral schools existed almost exclusively for the training of parish priests, but their curriculum was soon broadened as the growth of both ecclesiastical and

TWO CONCEPTIONS OF ELEMENTARY EDUCATION. In the lefthand illumination from a fourteenth-century manuscript, a master of grammar points to the day's lesson in a book while simultaneously keeping order with a cudgel. On the right, a later woodcut represents education as more benign: Lady Wisdom shows an eager schoolboy how to learn his letters while unlocking the door of knowledge, a multi-tiered tower where scholarly men representing the different branches of learning smile out at him.

secular governments escalated demand for trained men with more sophisticated skills. The most fundamental elements of this curriculum were known as the *trivium*, "the three ways": grammar, logic, and rhetoric. This meant a thorough grounding in Latin through the study of classical Roman authors, such as Cicero and Virgil, and training in the formulation and expression of sound arguments. Students who mastered the trivium were fit to perform basic clerical tasks, but those who wanted to achieve the reputation and advantages of scholars had to master the remaining branches of learning. These were arithmetic, geometry, astronomy, and music: the *quadrivium* or "four ways." Together, these seven liberal arts—so called because they liberated those who acquired them from menial labor—were the prerequisites for advanced study in philosophy, theology, law, and medicine.

Until about 1200, most students in urban schools would have belonged to the minor orders of the clergy. This means that they took vows of obedience and were immune from prosecution by secular authorities, but they were not required to remain celibate—unlike priests

and bishops, who were in major orders. Even those who hoped to become lawyers or bureaucrats usually found it advantageous to "take orders" in case powerful ecclesiastical offices became open to them: Heloise tried to discourage Abelard from marrying her for this very reason, because it would destroy his chances of being appointed a bishop or papal legate. Abelard, a nobleman's son, is by no means typical of the men who rose to prominence in this era through education. His contemporary and rival, Suger, is more representative. An orphan of obscure origins, he became abbot of the royal monastery of Saint-Denis and *de facto* chancellor of France.

By the thirteenth century, most boys who entered schools were not members of the clergy and never intended to be. Some were children of wealthy families, who regarded Latin literacy as a badge of status and a practical necessity. Others were future notaries, estate managers, and merchants who needed to be literate and numerate in order to succeed in these careers. Many alternative schools were eventually established to cater to these vocational students, and would become largely independent of ecclesiastical control. In many cases, Latin ceased to be the language of instruction in these schools and was replaced by the vernacular language of the region.

Formal schooling remained restricted to males. Yet many girls and women became highly educated, especially those reared in convents or princely courts. Heloise had an unusual degree of access to the educational milieu of Paris, but the fact remains that she had clearly received excellent preparatory training in the convent before she began her studies with Abelard. Most laywomen were taught at home, sometimes by private tutors but more often by other women. In fact, laywomen were more likely to be literate than laymen, and it is for this reason that women were often the patrons of poets and the primary readers and owners of books. Significantly, the effigy that Eleanor of Aquitaine commissioned for her own tomb shows her lying awake till Judgment Day, reading, flanked by her sleeping husband and son.

The Development of Scholasticism

The educational revolution that began in the eleventh century led to the development of new critical methods for framing and resolving complex theological and philosophical problems. These methods are collectively known as *scholasticism*, because they had their origins in the pedagogy of medieval schools. Scholastic methods are highly systematic and highly respectful of authority, but they also rely on rigorous questioning and argumentation. They therefore place great emphasis on evidence derived from reason. Indeed, scholasticism can be defined as a way of reconciling various forms of knowledge through logical debate, often called *dialectic*.

The earliest practitioner of the scholastic method is often considered to be Anselm of Canterbury (1033–1109), a Benedictine monk from northern Italy who became archbishop of Canterbury. The central premise of Anselm's teaching was that the human mind can combine knowledge gained through education and experience with divine revelation—as long as one has faith in God and careful scholastic training. As he put it, "I believe in order to understand," so that belief can be enriched and strengthened by understanding.

Building on the writings of Augustine and Boethius (see Chapter 6), and so (indirectly) on the teachings of Plato (see Chapter 4), Anselm developed various rational proofs for the underlying truths of Christian doctrine. The most famous of these is his proof for the existence of God, known as the ontological proof ("proof from the fact of existence") because it reasons that human beings could not have ideas of goodness or truth or justice unless some higher being had instilled these ideas in us. He further reasoned that God, as the essence of all ideals, must be "that than which nothing greater can be conceived" and as such must exist, or else God could not be the greatest thing conceivable.

Anselm's writings were influential, but the philosopher who popularized the scholastic method was Abelard. It was largely thanks to him that Paris became the intellectual capital of Europe. As a cathedral town and seat of the French monarchy, it already boasted a number of schools, but it was only after Abelard was appointed to the schoolmaster's chair at Notre-Dame that Paris became a magnet for ambitious young men, many of whom were attracted to Abelard's unorthodox teaching style. We can glimpse it through the audacious treatise called the *Sic et Non* ("Yes and No" or "So and Not So"). In this book, Abelard

THE TOMB OF ELEANOR OF AQUITAINE. Eleanor probably commissioned the effigies for the tombs representing herself, her husband Henry II, and her son Richard the Lionheart—both of whom died years before she did. She was eventually buried alongside them in the vault of the convent of Fontevrault in Anjou, where she spent the last years of her life. ■ *Notice that Eleanor's effigy shows her reading a book. How does this reinforce or challenge what we have learned about women's access to education?*

Peter Abelard Critiques Theological Contradictions

In 1120, Abelard published the Sic et Non, "So and Not So," a pioneering work of dialectic theology and a model for the development of later scholastic methods. In it, he arranged passages from Scripture as well as writings of the Church Fathers that had bearing on important doctrinal issues and that appeared to offer contradictory views. His eventual aim, as the prologue to this work indicates, was to reconcile these differences through the use of critical analysis.

here are many seeming contradictions and even obscurities in the innumerable writings of the church fathers. Our respect for their authority should not stand in the way of an effort on our part to come at the truth. The obscurity and contradictions in ancient writings may be explained upon many grounds, and may be discussed without impugning the good faith and insight of the fathers. A writer may use different terms to mean the same thing, in order to avoid a monotonous repetition of the same word. Common, vague words may be employed in order that the common people may understand; and sometimes a writer sacrifices perfect accuracy in the interest of a clear general statement. Poetical, figurative language is often obscure and vague. . . .

Doubtless the fathers might err; even Peter, the prince of the apostles, fell into error; what wonder that the saints do not always show themselves inspired? The fathers did not themselves believe that they, or their companions, were always right. Augustine found himself mistaken in some cases and did not hesitate to retract his errors. He warns his admirers not to look upon his letters as they would upon the Scriptures, but to accept only those things which, upon examination, they find to be true.

All writings belonging to this class are to be read with full freedom to criticise, and with no obligation to accept unquestioningly; otherwise the way would be blocked to all discussion, and posterity be deprived of the excellent intellectual exercise of debating difficult questions of language and presentation. But an explicit exception must be made in the case of the Old and New Testaments. In the Scriptures, when anything strikes us as absurd, we may not say that the writer erred, but that the scribe made a blunder in copying the manuscripts, or that there is an error in interpretation, or that the passage is not understood. The fathers make a very careful distinction between the Scriptures and later works. They advocate a discriminating, not to say suspicious, use of the writings of their own contemporaries.

In view of these considerations, I have ventured to bring together various dicta of the holy fathers, as they came to mind, and to formulate certain questions which were suggested by the seeming contradictions in the statements. These questions ought to serve to excite tender readers to a zealous inquiry into truth and so sharpen their wits. The master key of knowledge is, indeed, a persistent and frequent questioning. Aristotle, the most clear-sighted of all the philosophers, was desirous above all things else to arouse this questioning spirit, for in his *Categories* he exhorts a student as follows: "It may well be difficult to reach a positive conclusion in these matters unless they be frequently discussed. It is by no means fruitless to be doubtful on particular points." By doubting we come to examine, and by examining we reach the truth.

Source: Peter Abelard, prologue to the *Sic et Non*, trans. James Harvey Robinson in *Readings in European History*, 2 vols. (Boston, MA: 1904), vol. 1, pp. 450–51.

Questions for Analysis

1. On what grounds can religious authorities be challenged, according to Abelard? What distinctions does he make between criticism of the Scriptures and of other authorities, and why?

2. Abelard did not attempt, in this work, to resolve the contradictions among his sources. Based on what you have learned, why would his project have seemed threatening to the authority of the Church?

gathered a collection of seemingly contradictory statements from the Church Fathers, organized around 150 key theological problems. Like his contemporary Gratian, the codifier of canon law, his ultimate ambition was to show that these divergent authorities could be reconciled—in this case, through the skillful use of dialectic.

Yet Abelard did not propose any solutions in the Sic et Non, and the work therefore caused grave concern. More inflammatory still were Abelard's meditations on the doctrine of the Trinity, which circulated in a book of lectures that was denounced and burned in 1121. Twenty years later, Bernard of Clairvaux had Abelard brought up on another charge of heresy at the Council of Soissons, where he was condemned a second time. Bernard's own mystic spirituality stood in direct opposition to Abelard's tireless quest for reasoned understanding. Abelard, for his part, found no solace in the monastic life beloved of Bernard: teaching was the activity that nurtured his faith. Luckily, teaching also expanded his fame and allowed him to train many pupils who eventually vindicated his teachings. After Abelard's death, his student Peter Lombard would ask the same fundamental questions that his master had done, but he took care to resolve the tensions which the Sic et Non had left open-ended. His great work, known as the Sentences, became the standard theological textbook of the medieval university, on which all aspirants to the doctorate were required to comment.

The Nature of the University

The emergence of the university—a unique public forum for advanced study, the questioning of received ideas, and the resolution of critical problems—was the natural extension of Abelard's teachings. His reputation and that of his students attracted many other intellectuals to Paris, and together they began to offer more varied and advanced instruction than anything obtainable in the average cathedral school. By 1200, this loose association of teachers had formed themselves into a universitas ("corporation" in Latin), and the resulting faculty began to collaborate in the higher academic study of the liberal arts, with a special emphasis on theology. At about the same time, the students of law based in Bologna came together in a universitas whose speciality was law.

Paris and Bologna provided the two basic models on which all medieval universities were based. In southern Europe, such universities as Montpellier, Salamanca, and Naples were patterned after Bologna, where the students themselves constituted the corporation: they hired the teachers, paid their salaries, and fined or discharged them for poor instruction. The universities of northern Europe, were like that of Paris: guilds of teachers who governed themselves and established fees for tuition and rules of conduct. They eventually embraced four faculties—liberal arts, theology, law, and medicine—each headed by a dean. By the end of the thirteenth century, the northern universities also expanded to include separate, semi-autonomous colleges, which usually provided housing for poorer students and were often endowed by a private benefactor. Over time, these colleges became centers of instruction as well as residences. The universities of Oxford and Cambridge still retain this pattern of organization: the colleges of which they are composed are semi-independent educational units.

Most of the academic degrees granted in our modern universities derive from those awarded in the Middle Ages, even though the actual courses of study are very different. No university curriculum included history or vernacular languages or anything like the social sciences prior to the nineteenth century. The medieval student was assumed to know Latin grammar thoroughly before entrance into a university; he had learned it in the primary (or "grammar") schools discussed above. On admission, he was required to spend about four years studying the basic liberal arts, which meant doing advanced work in Latin rhetoric and mastering the rules of logic. If he passed his examinations, he received the preliminary degree of bachelor of arts (the prototype of our BA). But to ensure himself a place in professional life he had to devote additional years to the pursuit of an advanced degree, the master of arts (MA) or the doctor of laws, medicine, or theology. This was accomplished by reading and commenting on standard texts such as Peter Lombard's Sentences (theology), Gratian's Decretum (law), or Aristotle's Physics (medicine). The requirements for the degree of doctor of philosophy (PhD) included even more specialized training, and those for the doctorate in theology were particularly arduous: by the end of the Middle Ages, it took twelve or thirteen years to earn this degree, over and above the eight years required to earn the MA. University degrees of all grades were recognized as standards of attainment and became pathways to a variety of careers.

Student life in medieval universities was rowdy. Because many students began their studies between the ages of twelve and fifteen, they were working through all the challenges of adolescence and early adulthood as they worked toward their degrees; this helps to explain the many injunctions against drunkenness, gambling, and other pursuits

The map shows the geographical distribution of Europe's major universities, with markers indicating the century each was founded.

Locations labeled on the map include:

Norway, Sweden (Uppsala), Scotland (Aberdeen, St. Andrews, Glasgow), Denmark (Copenhagen), England (Cambridge, Oxford), Poland (Warsaw, Cracow), Holy Roman Empire (Greifswald, Rostock, Frankfurt, Wittenburg, Erfurt, Leipzig, Prague, Cologne, Trier, Mainz, Heidelberg, Würzburg, Ingolstadt, Tübingen, Louvain), France (Caen, Paris, Angers, Orléans, Nantes, Bourges, Poitiers, Bordeaux, Cahors, Toulouse, Montpellier, Lyons, Grenoble, Valence, Orange, Avignon, Aix, Besançon, Dôle, Freibourg, Perpignan), Austria (Vienna, Basel), Switzerland, Hungary (Buda, Pressburg, Fünfkirchen), Venetian Empire (Treviso, Padua, Vercelli, Pavia, Piacenza, Ferrara, Turin), Papal States (Florence, Arezzo, Siena, Perugia, Rome, Reggio, Bologna), Spain (Palencia, Valladolid, Huesca, Lérida, Salamanca, Saragossa, Barcelona, Avila, Siguenza, Toledo, Valencia, Palma), Portugal (Coimbra, Lisbon, Seville), Kingdom of Two Sicilies (Naples, Salerno, Palermo, Catania).

CENTURY UNIVERSITY WAS FOUNDED

- ■ Twelfth century
- ■ Thirteenth century
- □ Fourteenth century
- ■ Fifteenth century
- —— Boundaries c. 1500

THE SPREAD OF UNIVERSITIES. This map shows the geographical distribution of Europe's major universities and indicates the dates of their foundation. ▪ *Where were the first universities founded, and why?* ▪ Notice the number and location of the universities founded in the fourteenth and fifteenth centuries. ▪ *What pattern do you see in these later foundations?* ▪ *What might explain this?*

included among the canons of the Fourth Lateran Council. Moreover, university students generally believed that they constituted an independent and privileged community, apart from the local communities in which they lived. This often led to riots or even pitched battles between "town" and "gown."

That said, the time devoted to actual study was very intensive. Because books were prohibitively expensive, the primary mode of instruction was the lecture (Latin for "reading") in which a master would read an authoritative work aloud to his students and comment on it while the students took notes. As students advanced in their disciplines, they were expected to develop their own skills of analysis and interpretation in formal, public disputations. Advanced disputations could become extremely complex and abstract; sometimes they might last for days. Often they sparked public debates of great magnitude. The Ninety-five

Theses posted by Martin Luther in 1517 were actually a set of debating points organized along these lines (see Chapter 13).

Classical Thought, Arabic Learning and Scholastic Theology

The intellectual revolution of the Middle Ages was hugely indebted to the intellectual legacy of Islam, which was filtering into Europe via the Crusades. As we saw in Chapter 8, Muslim philosophers had been honing an array of different techniques to deal with the challenge of reconciling classical thought with Islamic belief, and these techniques contributed fundamentally to the development of Christian theology.

The most influential of these Muslim philosophers was Ibn Rushd, known to his Christian disciples as Averroès (*ah-VER-oh-ayz*, 1126–1198). Born in the Andalusian capital of Córdoba, in Muslim Spain, Averroès single-handedly advanced the study of Aristotelian logic by publishing a series of careful commentaries that sought to purge the Greek philosopher's works of all later (and confusing) influences and thus to allow for their proper analysis and interpretation. Soon translated from Arabic into Latin, these commentaries were received in western Christendom alongside new translations of Aristotle's texts (conveyed to Latin readers via Arabic) and so fundamentally influenced the way all subsequent European scholars understood Aristotle. The prestige of Averroès was so great that Christian intellectuals called him simply "the Commentator," just as they called Aristotle, "the Philosopher"—as if there were no others.

Ultimately, Averroès's learning was suppressed by the new Muslim dynasty that came to power in his lifetime, the Almohads, who demanded that all philosophical inquiry be subordinated to orthodox Muslim belief. After burning several of Averroès's works, they exiled him to Morocco. Thereafter, Islamic philosophy may have had more impact on Europe than in some Islamic kingdoms.

The greatest Jewish scholar of this period, Moses Maimonides (*my-MAHN-eh-dees*, c. 1137–1204), was also driven into exile by the Almohads; he traveled first to North Africa and then to Egypt, where he became famous as a teacher, jurist, and physician. Also like Averroès, he exercised great influence on Christian theologians through his systematic exposition of Jewish law in the *Mishneh Torah*, which earned him the nickname "the second Moses."

Because many aspects of the rabbinic tradition, Greek philosophy, and Arabic learning were not readily compatible with Christian faith, they therefore had to be filtered through

THE INFLUENCE OF AVERROÈS. This portrait of the Muslim polymath Averroès is featured in a fourteenth-century fresco celebrating the achievements of the Christian theologian Thomas Aquinas (c. 1225–1274). ■ *What does his inclusion in this context indicate about the relationship between Muslim and Christian intellectual traditions?*

the dialectical methods pioneered by Abelard and his pupils. By far the greatest accomplishments in this endeavor were made by Thomas Aquinas (1225–1274), who became the leading theologian at the University of Paris. As a member of the Dominican order, Thomas was committed to the defense of Catholic Christianity. But he also believed that the study of the physical world was a legitimate way of gaining knowledge of the divine, because God had created both the world and the many ways of knowing it. Imbued with a deep confidence in the value of both human reason and human experience, Thomas worked quietly and steadily on his two great summaries of theology, the *Summa contra Gentiles* (a compendium of the arguments for refuting non-Christian religions) and the comprehensive *Summa Theologiae*. The theology of the modern Roman Catholic Church still rests on Thomistic methods, doctrines, and principles.

COURTS, CITIES, AND CATHEDRALS

In the eleventh century, it was still possible to describe European society as divided among "those who worked, those who prayed, and those who fought." By 1200, such a description no longer bore much relationship to reality. New elites had emerged in the burgeoning cities of Europe. The wealthiest members of society were merchants and bankers, and aristocrats either had to best them (by engaging in trade themselves) or join them through strategic intermarriage. The aristocracy still fought, but so did upwardly mobile knights, urban crossbowmen, longbowmen, citizen militias, and peasant levies. Meanwhile, such lines as existed between town and countryside were easily crossed. And the pupils of the new schools made up a growing professional class that further defied neat categorization. We have noted that careers in the Church or royal bureaucracies were particularly open to self-made, educated men. But medieval courts and cities also provided opportunities for advancement.

From Chevalerie to Chivalry

The ennoblement of chivalry and the emergence of medieval court culture were connected to the growing wealth of Europe, the competition among monarchies, and contemporary developments in military technology exhibited

by the Crusades. In 1100, a knight could get by with a woolen tunic and leather corselet, a couple of horses, a groom, and a sword. A hundred years later, a knight needed full-body armor made of iron, a visored helmet, a broadsword, a spear, a shield, and several warhorses capable of carrying all this gear. By 1250, a knight also had to keep up appearances at tournaments, which meant maintaining a string of horses, sumptuous silk clothing for himself and caparisons for his steeds, and a retinue of liveried squires and servants. As the costs of a warrior's equipment rose, the number of men who could personally afford it declined dramatically, which made knightly display something increasingly prized by the nobility and upstart merchants alike. Knights who did not inherit or

MAKING A KNIGHTLY APPEARANCE. The costs of maintaining a chivalric lifestyle mounted steeply in the twelfth and thirteenth centuries, not only because a knight needed the most up-to-date equipment but because he was expected to cut a gallant figure at tournaments and to dazzle female spectators. This image is one of many sumptuous full-page illuminations in the Manesse Codex, made in Zurich in the early fourteenth century and preserving the compositions of earlier courtly poets.

gain sufficient property to support themsleves had to seek wealthy brides or the protection of a lord who could afford to equip them.

There were still other factors contributing to the prestige of knighthood. As part of a larger effort to control the violent competition for land and wealth, both secular and ecclesiastical rulers had begun to promote a new set of values that would come to redefine chivalry: bravery, loyalty, generosity, and civility. This new chivalry appealed to knights because it distinguished them from all the other "new men" who were emerging as powerful in this period, especially merchants and clerics. It also appealed to the nobility, whose status in this socially mobile world no longer depended on descent from high-born ancestors; families who *did* have such ancestors did not necessarily have the wealth to maintain a noble lifestyle, while many families who lived as "nobility" did not have prestigious ancestors.

What, then, was "nobility"? Was high status a matter of birth or was it the result of individual achievement? The amalgamation between knighthood and nobility offered something to those on both sides of the question. To the older aristocracy, it was a visible sign of good breeding. To professional warriors like many crusaders, and to the merchants and bureaucrats who later adopted its language and customs, chivalry offered a way of legitimizing social positions attained through bravery or skill. As a result, mounted combat—whether on the battlefield, in tournaments, or in the hunt—would remain the defining pastime of European gentlemen until the end of the First World War (see Chapter 24).

The Culture of the Court

Closely linked to this new ideology of chivalry was a new emphasis on *courtoisie*, "courtliness," the refined behavior appropriate to a court. This stemmed in part from practical necessity. Those great lords who could support a knightly retinue would have households full of energetic, lusty young men whose appetites had to be controlled. Hence, the emerging code of chivalry encouraged its adherents to view noble women as objects of veneration who could only be wooed and won by politesse, poetry, and valiant deeds; they had to be courted. Non-noblewomen, though, were fair game and could be taken by force if they did not yield willingly to the desires of a knight.

Whole new genres of poetry, song, and storytelling emerged in the twelfth century to celebrate the allied cultures of chivalry and courtliness. These genres stand in marked contrast to the older entertainments of Europe's warrior class, the heroic epics that are often the earliest literary artifacts of various vernacular languages: the Anglo-Saxon *Beowulf*, the *Song of Roland*, the Norse sagas, the German *Song of the Nibelungs*, and the Spanish *Poem of the Cid*. These epics portray a virile, violent society. Gore flows freely; skulls are cleaved; manly valor, honor, and loyalty are the major themes. If women are mentioned, it is often as prizes to be won in battle.

The courtly entertainments introduced in the twelfth century are very different in style, subject matter, and authorship. Many of them were addressed to, and commissioned by, women. In some cases, they were even composed by women or were composed in close collaboration with a female patron. An example of the former is the collections of *lais* (versified stories) of Marie de France, who was active during the reigns of Henry II and Eleanor of Aquitaine, and who may have been an abbess as well as a member of the Anglo-Norman aristocracy. An example of the latter is one of the Arthurian tales composed by Marie's contemporary, Chrétien de Troyes (*KRAY-tyan duh TWAH*, fl. 1165–90), who spent some time working under the patronage of Eleanor's daughter (by her first husband, Louis VII), Marie of Champagne.

Romances were engaging tales of love and adventure, often focusing on the exploits of King Arthur and his knights or some other heroic figure of the past, like Alexander the Great. But they were also attuned to the interests and concerns of women: threats to women's independence, enforced or unhappy marriages, disputed inheritances, fashion, fantasies of power. The heroine of one anonymous romance is a woman who dresses as a knight and travels the world performing valiant deeds. Other heroines accompany their husbands on Crusades or quests, or defend their castles against attack, or have supernatural powers. Following in Chrétien's footsteps, the German poets Wolfram von Eschenbach and Gottfried von Strassburg vied to produce romances that retained the scope and complexity of heroic epics while featuring women in strong, central roles: Wolfram's *Parzival*, the story of the search for the Holy Grail, and Gottfried's *Tristan*, which retold the Celtic story of the adulterous love between Tristan and Isolde. Both inspired the operatic reconceptions of Richard Wagner (1813–1883).

The poetic tradition initiated by the southern French troubadours and northern French trouvères (terms deriving from the verbs *trobar/trouver*: "to discover, to invent") also contributed to the culture of chivalry and inspired the work of German *minnesänger* ("love singers"). Much troubadour poetry displays sensitivity to feminine beauty and the natural world, and pays eloquent tribute to the political and sexual power of women. Take, for example, a lyric of Bernart de Ventadorn (c. 1135–1195), one of Eleanor's protégés:

> When leaves and grass are lush with renewed growth
> The beauty of my Lady blossoms forth . . .
> I am her slave, her vassal, she my lord;
> I pay her homage, hope to have a word
> Of kindness, or of love, exchanged for mine
> But she is cruel: she will not make a sign.

Other troubadour songs celebrated old-fashioned warlike virtues, as in the verses of Bernart's contemporary, Bertran de Born (c. 1140–1214), a friend of Eleanor's son Richard the Lionheart:

> It pleases me to hear the mirth and song
> Of birds, filling the wood the whole day long.
> But more it pleases me to see the fields
> All planted thick with tents, to see the shields
> And swords of my companions ranged for war,
> To hear the screams, to see the blood and gore.

To what extent do the entertainments of the court reflect the reality of noblewomen's status? Certainly, there were women throughout this period who wielded tremendous power, particularly in Scandinavia and parts of southern Europe, where women could inherit property, rule in their own right, and were treated as lords in fact and in name (as in Bernart's song). Queen Urraca ruled the combined kingdom of León-Castile from 1109 until 1126. Ermengarde of Narbonne (c. 1127–1197) ruled her strategically placed county from early adolescence to the time of her death. Eleanor remained sole ruler of Aquitaine throughout her long life, and she played a crucial role in the government of England at various times. The strong-willed Blanche of Castile (1188–1252), Eleanor's granddaughter, ruled France during the minority of her son Louis IX and again when he went on crusade.

Queens are not, of course, typical, but their activities in this period reflect some of the opportunities open to other well-born women—and the freedoms that set most western European women apart from their counterparts in the Byzantine and Muslim worlds. A striking symbol of this is the figure of the queen in the game of chess. In the Muslim courts where the game originated, the equivalent of the queen was a male figure, the king's chief minister, who could move only diagonally, and only one square at a time. In twelfth-century Europe, however, this piece became the queen. Eventually, she was the only figure powerful enough to move all over the board.

Urban Opportunities and Inequalities

In 1174, a cleric called William FitzStephen wrote a biography of his former employer, Thomas Becket, who had recently been canonized. In it, William went out of his way to extoll the urban culture of London that had produced this saintly man and other "men of superior quality," as well as all the splendid sights and pastimes to be had there: feasting, churchgoing, ice skating, bear baiting, plays, sports—and of course the pleasures of moneymaking. Towns were crucibles of activity, and as such became cultural powerhouses as well as economic ones. They were launching pads for the careers of ambitious men.

As we noted in Chapter 8, many of the towns that emerged in the eleventh century were governed by associations of citizens who undertook a wide variety of civic responsibilities. But urban governance was also apt to fall into the hands of oligarchs, a trend that became increasingly marked during the thirteenth century when the enormous wealth generated by some forms of commerce led to marked social inequalities, much as in the Greek poleis (see Chapter 3). In Italy, some cities even sought to control the resulting violence by turning to an outsider who would rule as a dictator for a (supposedly) limited term. Other cities adopted the model of Venice and became formal oligarchies, casting off all pretense to democracy. Some cities remained republics in principle, like Florence, but became increasingly oligarchical in practice. Aristocratic families lived in fortified towers surrounded by the houses of their supporters, and their rivalries often produced a violent culture of vendetta.

But even in places where town governance was controlled by a powerful few, there were many meaningful opportunities for collective activity. Urban manufacturing was regulated by professional associations known as guilds or (in some regions) confraternities. Guilds promoted the interests of their members by trying to preserve monopolies and limit competition. To these ends, terms of employment and membership were strictly regulated. If an apprentice or a journeyman worker (from the French *journée*, meaning "day" and, by extension, "day's work") wished to become a master, he had to produce a "masterpiece" to be judged by the masters of the guild. If the market was considered too weak to support additional master craftsmen, even a masterpiece would not secure a craftsman the coveted right to set up his own shop and thus earn enough to marry.

Illicit Love and the Code of Chivalry

Little is known about Marie de France, author of a series of popular verse tales that are among the earliest chivalric romances, but she may have been a nun or abbess living in the Anglo-Norman realm of Henry II and Eleanor of Aquitaine. The following excerpt is from her Lais, *adapted from stories told in the Franco-Celtic county of Brittany (Abelard's home).*

he Bretons, who lived in Brittany, were fine and noble people. In days gone by these valiant, courtly and noble men composed lays for posterity and thus preserved them from oblivion. . . . One of them, which I have heard recited, should not be forgotten. It concerns Equitan, a most courtly man, lord of Nantes, justiciary and king.

Equitan enjoyed a fine reputation and was greatly loved in his land. He adored pleasure and amorous dalliance: for this reason he upheld the principles of chivalry. Those who lack a full comprehension and understanding of love show no thought for their lives. Such is the nature of love that no one under its sway can retain command over reason. Equitan had a seneschal, a good knight, brave and loyal, who took care of his entire territory, governing it and administering its justice. Never, except in time of war, would the king have forsaken his hunting, his pleasures or his river sports, whatever the need might have been.

As his wedded wife the seneschal had a woman who was to bring great misfortune to the land. She was a lady of fine breeding and extremely beautiful with a noble body and good bearing. Nature had spared no pains when fashioning her: her eyes sparkled, her face and mouth were beautiful and her nose was well set. She had no equal in the kingdom, and the king, having often heard her praised, frequently sent her greetings and gifts. . . . He went hunting in her region on his own and on returning from his sport took lodging for the night in the place where the seneschal dwelt, in the very castle where the lady was to be found. He had ample occasion to speak with her, to express his feelings and display his fine qualities. He found her most courtly and wise, beautiful in body and countenance. . . .

That night he neither slept nor rested, but spent his time reproaching and reprimanding himself. "Alas," he said, "what destiny brought me to this region? Because of this lady I have seen, my heart has been overwhelmed by a pain so great

that my whole body trembles. I think I have no option but to love her. Yet, if I did love her, I should be acting wrongly, as she is the seneschal's wife. I ought to keep faith with him and love him, just as I want him to do with me. . . ."

Source: From "Equitan," in *The Lais of Marie de France*, trans. Glyn S. Burgess and Keith Busby (Harmondsworth, UK: 1985), pp. 56–57.

Questions for Analysis

1. Despite the king's initial misgivings, he and the seneschal's wife eventually have an affair and plot to murder her husband, only to be caught in their own trap. Given this outcome, how would you interpret Marie's remarks about courtliness and "the code of chivalry"? What are the tenets of this code, according to the king?

2. What social tensions does this story reflect, and how might it shed light on historical realities? What moral might contemporary readers draw from it?

Most guilds were closed to Jews and Muslims and they also restricted the opportunities available to women, who had little influence over the terms and conditions under which they worked.

Guilds and confraternities were therefore instruments of economic control, but they were also important social, political, and cultural institutions. Most combined the functions of religious association, drinking club, and benevolent society, looking after members and their families in hard times, supporting the dependents of members who died, and helping to finance funerals. Guilds also empowered their members in much the same way that unions do today, providing them with political representation and raising their social status. In the wealthy town of Arras, there was even a guild of professional entertainers, the confraternity of jongleurs, which became the most powerful organization in the town by 1250.

The Varieties of Vernacular Entertainment

Like courts, towns fostered new kinds of vernacular entertainment in the twelfth and thirteenth centuries. Even the genres of Latin poetry, song, and drama produced in this period can be considered "vernacular" because they made use of vernacular elements (like rhyme, not a feature of classical Latin poetry), dealt with current events, and were popular with a wide audience. In one of Heloise's letters to Abelard, she recalls that he was so renowned for the beauty of his love songs that "every street and tavern resounded with my name." It's possible that some of Abelard's songs were sung in French but more probable that they used the edgy, colloquial Latin popular among the student singer-songwriters known as "goliards," which means something like "daredevils." Their lyrics celebrated the carefree life of the open road, the pleasures of drinking and dice, the joys of love, and the agonies of poverty.

Perhaps the genre most representative of urban culture is the fabliau, a "fable" or short story with a salacious, irreverent, or satirical twist. Fabliaux drew attention to the absurdities of urban life and lampooned the different types of people who were striving to reinvent themselves in the permissive world of the town: the oafish peasant, the effete aristocrat, the corrupt priest, the sex-starved housewife, the wily student, the greedy merchant, the con man. Gender-bending and reversals of fortune are common themes. In one fabliau, a young noble woman is forced by her impoverished father to marry a buffoonish

ROMANESQUE AND GOTHIC. Some distinguishing features of the Romanesque and Gothic styles are exhibited in these two churches, both dedicated to the Virgin Mary and built within a century of one another. On the left is the west front of the Church of Notre-Dame-la-Grande in Poitiers, the ancestral domain of Eleanor of Aquitaine. Constructed between 1135 and 1145, it featured rounded arches, strong stone walls, massive supporting pillars, and small windows. On the right is the cathedral of Notre-Dame at Reims in Champagne, built between 1220 and 1299. The emphasis on stolid, horizontal registers is here replaced by soaring, vertical lines. The gabled portals, pointed arches, and bristling pinnacles all accentuate the height of this structure, while the multitude of stained-glass windows—chiefly the enormous rose window—flood the vast interior with colored light.

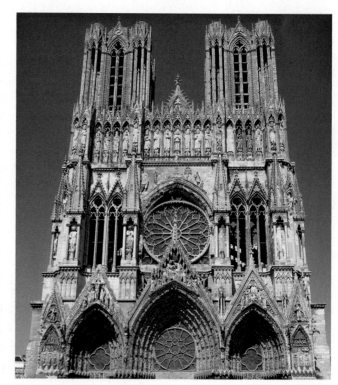

shopkeeper who thereby gains a knighthood. To shame him, she dresses herself as a knight and beats her husband in a jousting match. In another, a priest tricks a poor peasant out of his cow by promising that God will reward him by doubling his "investment" in the work of the Church. When the cow breaks out of the priest's pasture and runs for home, she brings the priest's cow, too, and the peasant is delighted by the fulfillment of the promised miracle.

The Medieval Cathedral

The cathedrals constructed in Europe's major cities during this period exemplify the ways in which the cultural communities of the court, the schools, and the town came together. For although any cathedral-building campaign would have been spearheaded by a bishop looking to glorify his episcopal see, it could not be completed without the support of the nobility, the resources of the wealthy, the learning of trained theologians, and the talents of urban craftsmen. And cathedrals were not merely edifices: they were theaters for the performance of liturgy, music, drama, and preaching.

Cathedrals were not, in themselves, new: the seat of a bishop had long been known as his *cathedra*, his throne, and the church that housed it was the principal church of the diocese. But the size, splendor, and importance of cathedrals increased exponentially in the twelfth and thirteenth centuries alongside the growing power of the Church, the population of cities, and the wealth and knowledge necessary for their construction. Indeed, the cathedrals of this period are readily distinguishable from their predecessors by their architectural style, which came to be called "Gothic," while the style of earlier buildings is known as "Romanesque."

As the term suggests, Romanesque buildings use the basic elements of public architecture under the Roman Empire: the rounded arch, massive stone walls, and sturdy supporting columns. These features convey regularity and stability, and they also made churches places of refuge that could be fortified and defended in troubled times. By contrast, the structural elements of Gothic architecture are the pointed arch, groined and ribbed vaulting, and the flying buttress, an external support that strengthened the much thinner stone walls and enormous stained-glass windows whose light illuminated elaborate decorative programs that made the cathedral a microcosm of the medieval world and an encyclopedia of medieval knowledge.

These new Gothic cathedrals were not buildings that could be defended in wartime and, it was thought, would never have to be: they were manifestations of urban pride, expressions of practical and intellectual genius, and symbols of a triumphant and confident Church. Their builders would have been dismayed to learn that the modern term *Gothic* was actually intended to be derogatory, the name for art forms that Renaissance artists—who favored Roman models—considered barbaric (see Chapter 12). They would have been still more shocked to learn that cathedrals were among the first monuments targeted for destruction during the Reformation, the revolutions of the eighteenth and nineteenth centuries, and the wars of the twentieth. One of the prime examples of Gothic architecture, the cathedral dedicated to the Virgin Mary at Reims (shown on page 318), was largely destroyed during World War I; what the visitor sees today is a reconstruction.

CONCLUSION

A century ago, the American medievalist Charles Homer Haskins described the intellectual, religious, and cultural changes of this era as "the Renaissance of the twelfth century" and the beginning of northwestern Europe's enduring cultural prestige. A generation later, his student Joseph Strayer located "the medieval origins of the modern state" in this same period and, with them, the modern ideas of national sovereignty and national identity. In recent decades, the British medievalists R. I. Moore and Robert Bartlett have also argued that this era marks the beginning of the modern world, but not in positive ways. Moore sees the growth of strong institutions like the Church and the state as leading to "the formation of a persecuting society" in which governmental bureaucracies are used to identify, control, and punish groups of people deemed threatening to those in power through a never-ending "war on heresy." Bartlett views this era as the key phase in a brutal process of "conquest and colonization" visible in the eastern expansion of the Holy Roman Empire, the Norman conquest of England, the growth of papal power, the Crusades, and other movements.

Common to all of these paradigms is a recognition that the expansion of European power and influence that began around the year 1000 continued into the twelfth century and was consolidated in the thirteenth. By 1250, Europe had taken on the geographic, political, linguistic, and cultural characteristics that continue to define it today.

Whether or not a direct line runs between the developments of this period and the world in which we live, many European nations look to these centuries for their origins and for the monuments of their cultural heritage. Magna Carta is still cited as a foundational document of English law and the English constitutional monarchy, while the territories united under the rule of the French kings still form the nation of France. The doctrines crystallized in medieval canon law and scholastic theology have become the core doctrines of the Roman Catholic Church, and devotion to the Virgin Mary is still central to the piety of millions. The religious orders that emerged to educate and

After You Read This Chapter

Ⓢ Visit StudySpace for quizzes, additional review materials, and multimedia documents. **wwnorton.com/web/westernciv18**

REVIEWING THE OBJECTIVES

- The emerging monarchies of Europe shared certain features but differed from one another in significant ways. What were the major similarities and differences of kingship in England, France, and Iberia?
- How did the meaning and purposes of crusading change in the twelfth and thirteenth centuries?
- The growth of papal power made religion an important part of daily life for all Christians in unprecedented ways, but it also limited lay spirituality and the rights of non-Christians. How?
- Scholasticism was the method of teaching and learning fostered by medieval schools but it was also a method of debating and resolving problems. How did scholasticism assist in the reconciliation of classical and Christian thought?
- Why did the meaning of chivalry change in the twelfth century? What new literary genres and art forms of the High Middle Ages were fostered by courts, universities, and towns?

curb a burgeoning medieval population continue their ministries. The daughter houses of medieval monastic orders continue to proliferate in lands unknown to medieval people: Japan, Australia, New Zealand, the Americas. Students still pursue the degrees first granted in medieval universities, and those who earn them wear the caps and gowns of medieval scholars. Meanwhile, poets still aspire to the eloquence of troubadours, singers record the music of Hildegard, and Hollywood films are based on chivalric romances and the tragic love of Abelard and Heloise. It is difficult to tell where the Middle Ages end and the modern world begins.

PEOPLE, IDEAS, AND EVENTS IN CONTEXT

- What was at stake in the clash between **HENRY II** of England and **THOMAS BECKET**?
- What was **MAGNA CARTA** and why was it made? How did **PHILIP AUGUSTUS** consolidate royal authority in France, and why were the German emperors unable to do so?
- Why were the **CRUSADER STATES** short-lived and fragile? How did the **RECONQUESTA** continue the Crusades?
- What were the main goals of **INNOCENT III**? How did the **FRANCISCANS** and **DOMINICANS** advance his agend?
- How do the **CULT OF THE VIRGIN** and the careers of **HILDEGARD OF BINGEN** and **HELOISE** exemplify the ideals and realities of women's roles in the Church?
- What is **SCHOLASTICISM**? How did **THOMAS AQUINUS** respond to the influence of Classical and Muslim philosophies?
- Why were **PETER ABELARD**'s teachings condemned by the Church? In what sense can he be considered the founder of the **UNIVERSITY OF PARIS**?
- How did noblewomen like **ELEANOR OF AQUITAINE** contribute to the emergence of a new vernacular culture? What types of entertainment are characteristic of medieval cities?

THINKING ABOUT CONNECTIONS

- The growth of towns, monarchies, and the Church increased the degree of control that those in power could exercise; but this growth also increased access to education and new forms of social mobility. Is this a paradox, or are these two phenomena related?
- The U.S. Constitution is based on the legal principles and institutions that emerged in medieval England, but it also drew on Roman models. Which do you consider to be more influential, and why?
- Some historians have argued that the extent and methods of persecution discernible in the Middle Ages are unprecedented in the history of Western civilizations. How would you support or refute this thesis? For example, does the persecution of Jews in medieval Europe differ from their treatment under the neo-Assyrians and Chaldeans, or under the Roman Empire? Why or why not?

STORY LINES

- The Mongol Empire widened channels of communication, commerce, and cultural exchange between Europe and the Far East. At the same time, Europeans were extending their reach into the Atlantic Ocean.

- Western civilizations' integration with this wider medieval world led to new ways of mapping, measuring, and describing that world.

- Despite these broadening horizons, most Europeans' lives were bounded by their communities and focused on the parish church.

- Meanwhile, the growing strength of the kings of France and England drew them into terminal disputes that led to the Hundred Years' War.

- As global climate change affected the ecosystems of Europe and caused years of famine, the integrated networks of the medieval world facilitated the rapid transmission of the Black Death.

CHRONOLOGY

1206–1260	Rapid expansion of the Mongol Empire under Genghis Khan and his heirs
1240	Kievan Rus' is taken by the Mongols; Khanate of the Golden Horde established
1260–1294	Reign of Kublai Khan, Great Khan and emperor of China
1271–1295	Travels of Marco Polo
1309	"Babylonian Captivity" of the papacy in Avignon begins
1315–1322	The Great Famine in Europe
1320	The Declaration of Arbroath proclaims Scotland's independence from England
1326–1354	The travels of Ibn Battuta
1337	Beginning of the Hundred Years' War
1347–1353	Spread of the Black Death
1352	Mandeville's *Book of Marvels* is in circulation

Before
You
Read
This
Chapter

The Medieval World, 1250–1350

When Christopher Columbus set out to find a new trade route to the East, he carried with him two influential travel narratives written centuries before his voyage. One was *The Book of Marvels*, composed around 1350 and attributed to John de Mandeville, an English adventurer (writing in French) who claimed to have reached the far horizons of the globe. The other was Marco Polo's *Description of the World*, an account of that Venetian merchant's journey through the vast Eurasian realm of the Mongol Empire to the court of the Great Khan in China. He had dictated it to an author of popular romances around 1298, when both men (Marco Polo and his ghostwriter) were in prison—in Columbus's own city of Genoa, coincidentally. Both of these books were the product of an extraordinary era of unprecedented interactions among the peoples of Europe, Asia, and the interconnected Mediterranean world. And both became extraordinarily influential, inspiring generations of mercantile adventurers, ambitious pilgrims, and armchair travelers. Eventually, they would fuel the imaginations of those future mariners who launched a further age of discovery (see Chapter 12).

323

In many ways, these narratives were as fantastical as they were factual. That makes them problematic sources for historians to use, but it also makes them representative of an era that seemed wide open to every sort of influence. This was a time when ease of communication and commercial exchange made Western civilizations part of an interlocking network that potentially spanned the globe. Although this network would prove fragile in the face of a large-scale demographic crisis, the Black Death, it created a lasting impression of infinite possibilities. Indeed, it was only *because* of this network's connective channels that the Black Death was able to wreak such devastation in the years around 1350. Looking back, we can see the century leading up to this near-global crisis as the beginning of a new global age.

Europeans' integration with this widening world not only put them into contact with unfamiliar cultures and commodities, it opened up new ways of looking at the world they already knew. New artistic and intellectual responses are discernible in this era, as are a host of new inventions and technologies. At the same time, involvement in this wider world placed new pressures on long-term developments within Europe: notably the growing tensions among large territorial monarchies, and between these secular powers and the authority of the papacy. By the early fourteenth century, the papal court would literally be held hostage by the king of France. A few decades later, the king of England would openly declare his own claim to the French throne. The ensuing struggles for sovereignty would have a profound impact on the balance of power in Europe, and further complicate Europeans' relationships with one another and with their far-flung neighbors.

THE MONGOL EMPIRE AND THE REORIENTATION OF THE WEST

In our long-term survey of Western civilizations, we have frequently noted the existence of strong links between the Mediterranean world and the Far East. Trade along the network of trails known as the Silk Road can be traced far back into antiquity, and we have seen that such overland networks were extended by Europe's waterways and by the sea. But it was not until the late thirteenth century that Europeans were able to establish direct connections with India, China, and the so-called Spice Islands of the Indonesian archipelago. For Europeans, these connections would prove profoundly important, as much for their impact on the European imagination as for their economic significance. For the peoples of Asia, however, the more frequent appearance of Europeans was less consequential than the events that made these journeys possible: the rise of a new empire that encompassed the entire continent.

The Expansion of the Mongol Empire

The Mongols were one of many nomadic peoples inhabiting the vast steppes of Central Asia. Although closely connected with the Turkish populations with whom they frequently intermarried, the Mongols spoke their own distinctive language and had their own homeland, located to the north of the Gobi Desert in what is now known as Mongolia. Essentially, the Mongols were herdsmen whose daily lives and wealth depended on the sheep that provided shelter (sheepskin tents), woolen clothing, milk, and meat. But the Mongols were also highly accomplished horsemen and raiders. Indeed, it was to curtail their raiding ventures that the Chinese had fortified their Great Wall, many centuries before. Primarily, though, China defended itself from the Mongols by attempting to ensure that they remained internally divided, with their energies turned against each other.

In the late twelfth century, however, a Mongol chief named Temujin (c. 1162–1227) began to unite the various tribes under his rule. He did so by incorporating the warriors of each defeated tribe into his own army, gradually building up a large and terrifyingly effective military force. In 1206, his supremacy over all these tribes was reflected in his new title: Genghis Khan, from the Mongol words meaning "universal ruler." This new name also revealed wider ambitions, and in 1209 Genghis Khan began to direct his enormous army against the Mongols' neighbors. Taking advantage of the fact that China was then divided into three warring states, he launched an attack on the Chin Empire of the north, managing to penetrate deep into its interior by 1211. These initial attacks were probably looting expeditions rather than deliberate attempts at conquest, but the Mongols' aims were soon sharpened under Genghis Khan's successors. Shortly after his death in 1227, a full-scale invasion of both northern and western China was under way. In 1234, these regions also fell to the Mongols. By 1279, one of Genghis Khan's numerous grandsons, Kublai Khan, would complete the conquest by adding southern China to this empire.

For the first time in centuries, China was reunited, and under Mongol rule. It was also connected to western and central Asia in ways unprecedented in its long history, since Genghis Khan had brought crucial commercial cities and Silk Road trading posts (Tashkent, Samarkand, and Bukhara) into his empire. One of his sons, Ögedei (*EHRG-*

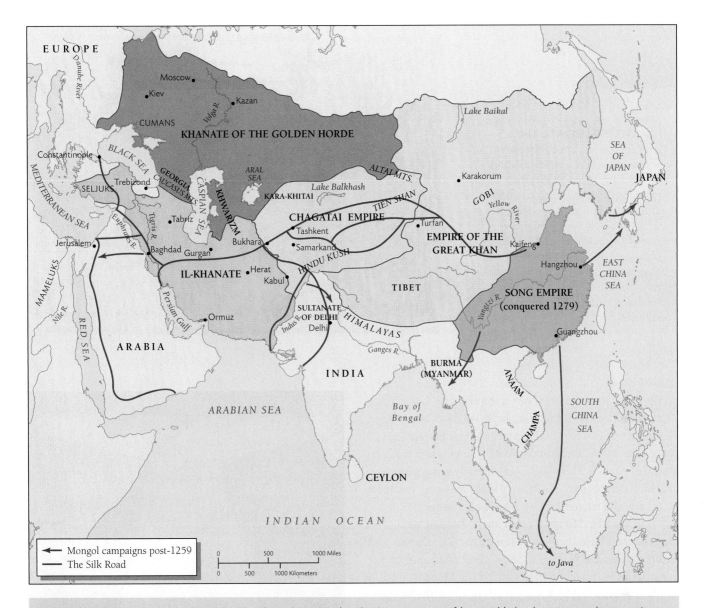

THE STATES OF THE MONGOL EMPIRE. Like Alexander's, Genghis Khan's empire was swiftly assembled and encompassed vast portions of Europe and Asia. ■ *How many different Mongol khanates were there after 1260, when Kublai Khan came to power, and were these domains mapped onto older divisions within Western civilizations?* ■ *How might the Mongol occupation of the Muslim world have aided the expansion of European trade?* ■ *At the same time, why would it have complicated the efforts of crusader armies in the Holy Land?*

uh-day), building on these achievements, laid plans for an even more far-reaching expansion of Mongol influence. Between 1237 and 1240, the Mongols under his command conquered the Russian capital at Kiev and then launched a two-pronged assault directed at the rich lands of the eastern European frontier. The smaller of the two Mongol armies swept through Poland toward Germany; the larger army went southwest toward Hungary. In April of 1241, the smaller Mongol force met a hastily assembled army of Germans and Poles at the battle of Liegnitz, where the two sides fought to a bloody standstill. Two days later, the larger Mongol army annihilated the Hungarian army at the river

Sajo. It could have moved even deeper into Europe after this important victory, but it withdrew when Ögedei Khan died in December of that same year.

Muscovy and the Mongol Khanate

As we have seen in previous chapters, the Russian capital at Kiev had fostered crucial diplomatic and trading relations with both western Europe and Byzantium, and with the Islamic Caliphate at Baghdad. That dynamic changed with the arrival of the Mongols, who shifted the locus of hic pugnae dux hennis · filius sce hedwigis cum thartaris in campo qd dicitur wolstat

hic woellat iste dux hennens filius sce hedwigis athartais cui anima suscepta est mcelum ab angelis

THE BATTLE OF LIEGNITZ, 1241.
This image from a fourteenth-century chronicle shows heavily armored knights from Poland and Germany (at right) confronting the swift-moving mounted archers of the Mongol cavalry. Mongol warriors often had the advantage over Europeans because their smaller, faster horses carried lighter loads and because the warriors themselves could shoot down their opponents at long range. ▪ *Which army appears to be gaining the upper hand here?*

power from Kiev to their own camp on the lower Volga River. This became known as the Khanate of the Golden Horde, an integral part of the larger Mongol Empire for 150 years. Its magnificent name evokes the impression made by tents that shone with wealth, some literally hung with cloth of gold. It derives from the Mongol word meaning "encampment" and the related Turkish word *ordu* ("army").

Initially, the Mongols ruled their Russian territories directly, installing their own administrative officials and requiring Russian princes to show their obedience to the Great Khan by traveling in person to the Mongol court in China. But after Kublai Khan's death in 1294, the Mongols began to tolerate the existence of several semi-independent principalities from which they demanded regular tribute. Kiev never recovered its dominant position, but one of these newer principalities would eventually form the core of a Russian state called Muscovy, centered on the duchy of Moscow. As the tribute-collecting center for the Mongol Khanate, Moscow received some protection against attack. Its dukes were even encouraged to absorb neighboring territories in this region, in order to increase Moscow's security. But this also meant that the Muscovite dukes could extend their powers even further without attracting too much attention from their Mongol overlords, whose power base was far away.

Compared to Kiev, Moscow's location was less advantageous for forging commercial contacts with the Baltic and Black Sea regions. Its direct ties with western Europe were also less developed, but this had little to do with geography. The Moscovites were staunchly loyal to the Orthodox

A MONGOL ROBE IN CLOTH OF GOLD. The majestic term *Khanate of the Golden Horde* captures both the power and the splendor of the Mongol warriors who conquered Rus' and many other lands. The robe depicted here dates from the late thirteenth or early fourteenth century and was made from cloth of gold: silk woven with gold (and sometimes silver) thread, a precious but surprisingly durable material that was also used for banners and even tents. A robe similar to this one was sold at auction in 2011, for nearly a quarter of a million dollars.

Church of Byzantium and had watched relations between the Latin West and the Greek East deteriorate drastically during the Crusades. They became openly hostile to western Europeans after Constantinople was captured and sacked by crusaders in 1204 (see Chapter 9), an event that led Moscovites to see themselves as the last remaining protectors of the Orthodox Roman Church. Eventually, as we shall see in Chapter 12, they would claim to be the rightful heirs of Roman imperial power.

The Making of the Mongol Ilkhanate

As Ögedei Khan moved into the lands of Rus' and eastern Europe, Mongol armies were also sent to subdue the vast territory that had been encompassed by the former Persian Empire, then by the empires of Alexander and Rome. Indeed, the strongest state in this region was known as the sultanate of Rûm, the Arabic word for "Rome." This was a Sunni Muslim sultanate that had been founded by the Seljuq Turks in 1077, just prior to the launching of the First Crusade, and which consisted of Anatolian provinces formerly belonging to the eastern Roman Empire. It had successfully withstood waves of crusading aggression from Latin Christendom while capitalizing on the further misfortunes of Byzantium, taking over several key ports on the Mediterranean and the Black Sea while cultivating a flourishing overland trade as well. But in 1243, the Seljuqs of Rûm were forced to surrender to the Mongols, who had already succeeded in occupying what is now Iraq, Iran, portions of Pakistan and Afghanistan, and the Christian kingdoms of Georgia and Armenia.

Thereafter, the Mongols easily found their way into regions weakened by centuries of Muslim infighting and Christian crusading movements. Byzantium, as we noted in Chapter 9, had been fatally weakened by the Fourth Crusade: Constantinople was now controlled by the Venetians, and Byzantine successor states centered on Nicaea (in Anatolia) and Epirus (in northern Greece) were hanging on by their fingertips. The capitulation of Rûm left

THE MONGOL RULER OF MUSLIM PERSIA, HIS CHRISTIAN QUEEN, AND HIS JEWISH HISTORIAN. The *Compendium of Chronicles* by the Jewish-born Muslim polymath Rashid al-Din (1247–1318) exemplifies the pluralistic culture encouraged by Mongol rule: written in Persian (and often translated into Arabic), it celebrates the achievements of Hulagu Khan (1217–1265), a grandson of Genghis and brother of Kublai, who consolidated Persia and its neighboring regions into the Ilkhanate. But it also embeds those achievements within the long history of Islam. This image depicts Hulagu with his wife, Dokuz Khatun, who was a Turkic princess and a Christian. ■ *Why would Rashid al-Din have wanted to place the new Mongol dynasty in this historical context?*

remaining Byzantine possessions in Anatolia without a buffer, and most of these were absorbed by the Mongols. In 1261, the emperor Michael VIII Peleologus (r. 1259–82) managed to regain control of Constantinople and its immediate hinterland, but the depleted empire he ruled was ringed about by hostile neighbors. The crusader principality of Antioch, which had been founded in 1098, finally succumbed to the Mongols in 1268. The Mongols themselves were only halted in their drive toward Palestine by the Mamluk Sultanate of Egypt, established in 1250 and ruled by a powerful military caste of non-Arab Muslims.

All of these disparate territories came to be called the Ilkhanate, the "subordinate khanate," meaning that its Mongol rulers paid deference to the Great Khan. The first Ilkhan was Hulagu, brother of China's Kublai Khan. His descendants would rule this realm for another eighty years, eventually converting to Islam but remaining hostile toward the Mamluk Muslims, who remained their chief rivals.

The Pax Mongolica and Its Price

Although the Mongols' expansion of power into Europe had been checked in 1241, their combined conquests made them masters of territories that stretched from the Black Sea to the Pacific Ocean: one-fifth of the earth's surface, the largest land empire in history. Within this domain, no single Mongol ruler's power was absolute. Kublai Khan (1260–1294), who took the additional title khagan, or "Great Khan," never claimed to rule all Mongol khanates directly. In his own domain of China and Mongolia, his power was highly centralized and built on the intricate (and ancient) imperial bureaucracy of China; but elsewhere, Mongol governance was directed at securing a steady payment of tribute from subject peoples, which meant that local rulers could retain much of their power.

This distribution of authority made Mongol rule flexible and adaptable to local conditions—in this, it resembled the Persian Empire (see Chapter 3) and could also be regarded as building on Hellenistic and Roman examples. But if their empire resembled those of antiquity in some respects, the Mongol khans differed from most contemporary Western rulers in being highly tolerant of all religious beliefs. This was an advantage in governing peoples who observed an array of Buddhist, Christian, and Muslim practices, not to mention Hindus, Jews, and the many itinerant groups and individuals whose languages and beliefs reflect a melding of many cultures.

This acceptance of cultural and religious difference, alongside the Mongols' encouragement of trade and love of rich things, created ideal conditions for some merchants and artists. Hence, the term *Pax Mongolica* ("Mongol Peace") is often used to describe the century from 1250 to 1350, a period in many ways analogous to that fostered by the Roman Empire at its greatest extent (see Chapter 5). No such term should be taken at face value, however: this peace was bought at a great price. Indeed, the artists whose varied talents created the gorgeous textiles, utensils, and illuminated books prized by the Mongols were not all willing participants in a peaceful process. Many were captives or slaves subject to ruthless relocation. During more settled years, the Mongols would often transfer entire families and communities of craftsmen from one part of the empire to another, encouraging a fantastic blend of artistic techniques, materials, and motifs. The result was an intensive period of cultural exchange that might combine Chinese, Persian, Venetian, and Russian influences (among many others) in a single work of art. These objects encapsulate the many conflicting legacies of the Mongols' empire.

The Mongol Peace was also achieved at the expense of many flourishing Muslim cities that had preserved the heritage of even older civilizations and that were devastated or crippled during the bloody process of Mongol expansion. The city of Heràt, situated in one of Afghanistan's few fertile valleys and described by the Persian poet Rumi as "the pearl in the oyster," was entirely destroyed by Genghis Khan in 1221 and did not fully recover for centuries. Baghdad, the splendid capital of the Abbasid Caliphate and a haven for artists and intellectuals since the eighth century (Chapter 8), was savagely besieged and sacked by the Mongols in 1258. Amid many other atrocities, the capture of the city resulted in the destruction of the House of Wisdom, a library and research center where Muslim scientists, philosophers, and translators preserved classical knowledge (including the works of Plato and Aristotle) and advanced cutting-edge scholarship in such fields as mathematics, engineering, and medicine. Baghdad's destruction is held to mark the end of Islam's golden age, since the establishment of the Mongol Ilkhanate in Persia eradicated a continuous zone of Muslim influence that had blended cultures stretching from southern Spain and North Africa to India.

Bridging East and West

To facilitate the movement of people and goods within their empire, the Mongols began to control the caravan routes that led from the Mediterranean and the Black Sea through Central Asia and into China, policing bandits and making conditions safer for travelers. They also encouraged and streamlined trade by funneling many exchanges through the Persian city of Tabriz, on which both land and sea routes from China converged. These measures accelerated and intensified the contacts possible between the Far East and the West. Prior to Mongol control, such commercial networks had been inaccessible to most European merchants. The Silk Road was not so much a highway as a tangle of trails and trading posts, and there were few outsiders who understood its workings. Now travelers at both ends of the route found their way smoothed.

Among the first travelers from the West were Franciscan missionaries whose journeys were bankrolled by European rulers. In 1253, William of Rubruck was sent by King Louis IX of France as his ambassador to the Mongol court, with letters of introduction and instructions to make a full report of his findings. Merchants quickly followed. The most famous of these are three Venetians: the brothers Niccolò and Matteo Polo, and Niccolò's son, Marco (1254–1324). Marco Polo's account of his travels (which began when he was sev-

enteen) includes a report of his twenty-year sojourn in the service of Kublai Khan and the story of his journey home through the Spice Islands, India, and Persia. As we noted above, this book had an enormous effect on the European imagination; Christopher Columbus's copy still survives.

Even more impressive in scope than Marco's travels are those of the Muslim adventurer Ibn Battuta (1304–1368), who left his native Morocco in 1326 to go on the sacred pilgrimage to Mecca—but then kept going. By the time he returned home in 1354, he had been to China and sub-Saharan Africa as well as to the ends of both the Muslim and Mongolian worlds: a journey of over 75,000 miles.

Yet the window of opportunity that made such journeys possible was relatively narrow. By the middle of the fourteenth century, hostilities among and within various components of the Mongol Empire were making travel along the Silk Road perilous. The Mongols of the Ilkhanate, who dominated the ancient trade routes that ran through

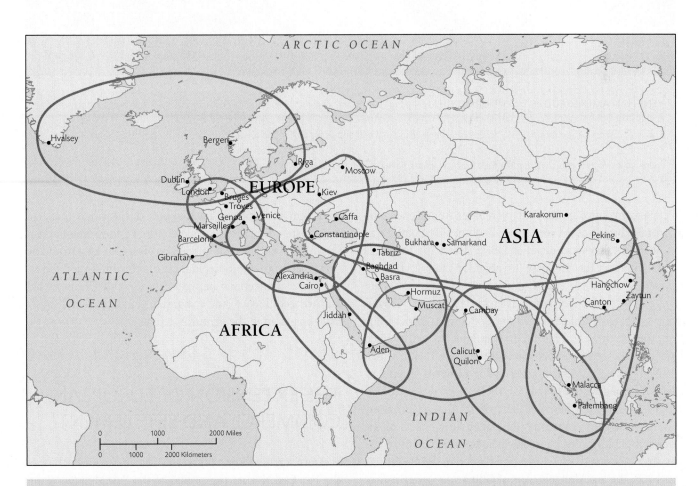

THE MEDIEVAL WORLD SYSTEM, c. 1300. At the turn of the fourteenth century, Western civilizations were more closely connected to one another and to the rest of the world than ever before: waterways and overland routes stretched from Greenland to the Pacific coast of Southeast Asia. ▪ *How has Europe's relationship with its neighbors changed as a result of its integration into this wider world?* ▪ *How might we need to see seemingly marginal territories (like Rus' or Hungary, Scotland or Norway) as central to one or more interlocking components of this system?*

VENETIAN AMBASSADORS TO THE GREAT KHAN. Around 1270, the Venetian merchants Niccolò and Matteo Polo returned to Europe after their first prolonged journey through the empire of the Great Khan, bearing with them an official letter to the Roman pope. This image, from a manuscript of Marco Polo's *Description of the World*, shows his father and uncle at the moment of their arrival in the Great Khan's court, to which they have seemingly brought a Christian cross and a Bible. ▪ *Based on what you've learned about the Mongols and the medieval world, is it plausible that the Polo brothers would have carried these items with them?*

Persia, came into conflict with merchants from Genoa who controlled trade at the western ends of the Silk Road, especially in the transport depot of Tabriz. Mounting pressures finally forced the Genoese to abandon Tabriz, thereby breaking one of the major links in the commercial chain forged by the Mongol Peace. Then, in 1346, the Mongols of the Golden Horde besieged the Genoese colony at Caffa on the Black Sea. This event simultaneously disrupted trade while serving as a conduit for the Black Death, which passed from the Mongol army to the Genoese defenders, who returned with it to Italy (see below).

Over the next few decades, the European economy would struggle to overcome the devastating effects of the massive depopulation caused by plague, which made recovery from these setbacks slower and harder. In the meantime, in 1368, the last Mongol rulers of China were overthrown. Most Westerners were now denied access to its borders, while the remaining Mongol warriors were restricted to cavalry service in the imperial armies of the new Ming dynasty. The conditions that had fostered an integrated trans-Eurasian cultural and commercial network were

no longer sustainable. Yet the view of the world that had been fostered by Mongol rule continued to exercise a lasting influence. European memories of the Far East would be preserved and embroidered, and the dream of reestablishing close connections between Europe and China would survive to influence a new round of commercial and imperial expansion in the centuries to come.

THE EXTENSION OF EUROPEAN COMMERCE AND SETTLEMENT

Western civilizations' increased access to the riches of the Far East during the period of the Pax Mongolica ran parallel to a number of ventures that were extending Europeans' presence in the Mediterranean and beyond it. These endeavors were both mercantile and colonial, and in many cases resulted in the control of strategic trade routes or islands by representatives of a single adventurous state.

The language of crusading, with which we have become familiar, now came to be applied to these economic and political initiatives, whose often violent methods could be justified on the grounds that they were supporting papally sanctioned Christian causes. To take one prominent example, the strategic goal of the Crusades that targeted North Africa in this era was to cut the economic lifelines that supported Muslim settlements in the Holy Land. Yet the only people who stood to gain from this were the merchants who dreamed of controlling the commercial routes that ran through Egypt, not only those that connected North Africa to the Silk Road but the conduits of the sub-Saharan gold trade.

The Quest for African Gold

The European trade in African gold was not new. It had been going on for centuries, facilitated by Muslim middlemen whose caravans brought a steady supply from the Niger River to the North African ports of Algiers and Tunis. In the early thirteenth century, rival bands of merchants from Catalonia and Genoa had established trading colonies in Tunis to expedite this process, exchanging woolen cloth from northern Europe for both North African grain and sub-Saharan gold.

But the medieval demand for gold accelerated during the late thirteenth and fourteenth centuries and could not be satisfied by these established trading relationships. The luxuries coveted by Europeans were now too costly to be bought solely with bulk goods, which were in any case a cumbersome medium of exchange. Although precious textiles (usually silk) were a form of wealth valued by the Mongols, the burgeoning economy of the medieval world demanded a reliable and abundant supply of more portable currency. Silver production, which had enabled the circulation of coinage in Europe, fell markedly during the 1340s as Europeans reached the limits of their technological capacity to extract silver ore from deep mines. This shortfall would lead to a serious cash-flow problem, since more European silver was moving east than could now be replenished from extant sources.

Gold therefore represented an obvious alternative currency for large transactions, and in the thirteenth century some European rulers began minting gold coins. But Europe itself had few natural gold reserves. To maintain and expand these currencies, new sources of gold were needed. The most obvious source was Africa, especially Mali and Ghana—which was called "the Land of Gold" by Muslim geographers.

Models of Mediterranean Colonization: Catalonia, Genoa, and Venice

The heightened European interest in the African gold trade, which engaged the seafaring merchants of Genoa and Catalonia in particular, coincided with these merchants' creation of entrepreneurial empires in the western Mediterranean. During the thirteenth century, Catalan adventurers conquered and colonized a series of western Mediterranean islands, including Majorca, Ibiza, Minorca, Sardinia, and Sicily. Except in Sicily, which already had a large and diverse population that included many Christians (see Chapter 8), the pattern of Catalan conquest was largely the same on all these islands: expulsion or extermination of the existing population, usually Muslim; the extension of economic concessions to attract new settlers; and a heavy reliance on slave labor to produce foodstuffs and raw materials for export.

These Catalan colonial efforts were mainly carried out by private individuals or companies operating under royal charters; they were not actively sponsored by the state. They therefore contrast strongly with the established colonial practices of the Venetian maritime empire, whose strategic ventures were focused mainly on the eastern Mediterranean, where the Venetians dominated the trade in spices and silks. Venetian colonies were administered directly by the city's rulers or their appointed colonial governors. These colonies included long-settled civilizations like Greece, Cyprus, and the cities of the Dalmatian coast, meaning that Venetian administration laid just another layer on top of many other economic, cultural, and political structures.

The Genoese, to take yet another case, also had extensive interests in the western Mediterranean, where they traded bulk goods such as cloth, hides, grain, timber, and sugar. They too established trading colonies, but these tended to consist of family networks that were closely integrated with the peoples among whom they lived, whether in North Africa, Spain, or the shores of the Black Sea.

From the Mediterranean to the Atlantic

For centuries, European maritime commerce had been divided between this Mediterranean world and a very different northeastern Atlantic world, which encompassed northern France, the Low Countries, the British Isles, and Scandinavia. Starting around 1270, however, Italian merchants began to sail through the Straits of Gibraltar and

Two Travel Accounts

> Two of the books that influenced Columbus and his contemporaries were travel narratives describing the exotic worlds that lay beyond Europe: worlds that may or may not have existed as they are described. The first excerpt below is taken from the account dictated by Marco Polo of Venice in 1298. The young Marco had traveled overland from Constantinople to the court of Kublai Khan in the early 1270s, together with his father and uncle. He became a gifted linguist, and remained at the Mongol court until the early 1290s, when he returned to Europe after a journey through Southeast Asia, Indonesia, and the Indian Ocean. The second excerpt is from the Book of Marvels attributed to John de Mandeville. This is an almost entirely fictional account of wonders that also became a source for European ideas about Southeast Asia. This particular passage concerns a legendary Christian figure called Prester ("Priest") John, who is alleged to have traveled to the East and become a great ruler.

Marco Polo's Description of Java

Departing from Ziamba, and steering between south and south-east, fifteen hundred miles, you reach an island of very great size, named Java. According to the reports of some well-informed navigators, it is the greatest in the world, and has a compass above three thousand miles. It is under the dominion of one king only, nor do the inhabitants pay tribute to any other power. They are worshipers of idols.

The country abounds with rich commodities. Pepper, nutmegs, spikenard, galangal, cubebs, cloves and all the other valuable spices and drugs, are the produce of the island; which occasion it to be visited by many ships laden with merchandise, that yields to the owners considerable profit.

The quantity of gold collected there exceeds all calculation and belief. From thence it is that . . . merchants . . . have imported, and to this day import, that metal to a great amount, and from thence also is obtained the greatest part of the spices that are distributed throughout the world. That the Great Khan [Kublai] has not brought the island under subjection to him, must be attributed to the length of the voyage and the dangers of the navigation.

Source: *The Travels of Marco Polo*, trans. William Marsden, rev. and ed. Manuel Komroff (New York: 1926), pp. 267–68.

John de Mandeville's Description of Prester John

This emperor Prester John has great lands and has many noble cities and good towns in his realm and many great, large islands. For all the country of India is separated into islands by the great floods that come from Paradise, that divide the land into many parts. And also in the sea he has many islands. . . .

on up to the wool-producing regions of England and the Low Countries. This was a step toward the extension of Mediterranean patterns of commerce and colonization into the Atlantic Ocean. Another step was the discovery (or possibly the rediscovery) of the Atlantic island chains known as the Canaries and the Azores, which Genoese sailors reached in the fourteenth century.

Efforts to colonize the Canary Islands, and to convert and enslave their inhabitants, began almost immediately. Eventually, the Canaries would become the focus of a new wave of colonial settlement sponsored by the Portuguese, and the base for Portuguese voyages down the west coast of Africa. They would also be the jumping-off point from which Christopher Columbus would sail

This Prester John has under him many kings and many islands and many varied people of various conditions. And this land is full good and rich, but not so rich as is the land of the Great Khan. For the merchants do not come there so commonly to buy merchandise as they do in the land of the Great Khan, for it is too far to travel to. . . .

[Mandeville then goes on to describe the difficulties of reaching Prester John's lands by sea.]

This emperor Prester John always takes as his wife the daughter of the Great Khan, and the Great Khan in the same way takes to wife the daughter of Prester John. For these two are the greatest lords under the heavens.

In the land of Prester John there are many diverse things, and many precious stones so great and so large that men make them into vessels such as platters, dishes, and cups. And there are many other marvels there that it would be too cumbrous and too long to put into the writing of books. But of the principal islands and of his estate and of his law I shall tell you some part.

This emperor Prester John is Christian and a great part of his country is

Christian also, although they do not hold to all the articles of our faith as we do. . . .

And he has under him 72 provinces, and in every province there is a king. And these kings have kings under them, and all are tributaries to Prester John.

And he has in his lordships many great marvels. For in his country is the sea that men call the Gravelly Sea, that is all gravel and sand without any drop of water. And it ebbs and flows in great waves as other seas do, and it is never still. . . . And a three-day journey from that sea there are great mountains out of which flows a great flood that comes out of Paradise. And it is full of precious stones without any drop of water. . . .

He dwells usually in the city of Susa [in Persia]. And there is his principal palace, which is so rich and so noble that no one will believe the report unless he has seen it. And above the chief tower of the palace there are two round pommels of gold and in each of them are two great, large rubies that shine full brightly upon the night. And the principal gates of his palace are of a precious stone that men call sardonyxes [a type of onyx], and the frames and the bars are made of ivory.

And the windows of the halls and chambers are of crystal. And the tables upon which men eat, some are made of emeralds, some of amethyst, and some of gold full of precious stones. And the legs that hold up the tables are made of the same precious stones. . . .

Source: *Mandeville's Travels*, ed. M. C. Seymour (Oxford: 1967), pp. 195–99 (language modernized from Middle English by R. C. Stacey).

Questions for Analysis

1. What does Marco Polo want his readers to know about Java, and why? What does this suggest about the interests of these intended readers?

2. What does Mandeville want his readers to know about Prester John and his domains? Why are these details so important?

3. Which of these accounts seems more trustworthy, and why? Even if we cannot accept one or both at face value, what insight do they give us into the expectations of Columbus, and the other European adventurers who relied on these accounts?

westward across the Atlantic Ocean in the hope of reaching Asia (see Chapter 12).

There was also a significant European colonial presence in the northern Atlantic, and had been for centuries. Viking settlers had begun to colonize Greenland in the late tenth century, and around 1000 had established a settlement in a place they called Vinland: the coast of Newfoundland in

present-day Canada. According to the sagas that tell the story of these explorations, written down in the late twelfth and thirteenth centuries, a band of adventurers led by Leif Eiriksson had intended to set up a permanent colony there. Numerous expeditions resulted in the construction of houses, a fortification, and even attempts to domesticate livestock transported from Scandinavia. Yet North America

THE CHURCH AT HVALSEY, GREENLAND. Located on the southern tip of Greenland, Hvalsey was originally a farmstead established in the late tenth century by the uncle of Eirik the Red, father of the explorer Leif. The church at Hvalsey, pictured here, was built in the twelfth century and would have been roofed with turf. It was the site of the last documented event in the history of Norse settlement on the island, a wedding that took place in 1408. By that time, the population had largely died out due to starvation and disease.

did not become home to a permanent European population at this time; the sagas report that relations with indigenous peoples were fraught, and there may have been other factors hindering settlement.

However, Norse settlers did build a viable community on Greenland, which eventually formed part of the kingdom of Norway. This was facilitated by the warming of the earth's climate between 800 and 1300—the same phenomenon that partly enabled the agricultural revolution discussed in Chapter 8. For several centuries, these favorable climatic conditions made it possible to sustain some farming activities on the southern coastline of that huge island, supplemented by fishing, hunting, and foraging. But with the gradual cooling of the climate in the fourteenth century, which caused famines even in the rich farmlands of Europe, this fragile ecosystem was gradually eroded and the Greenlanders died out.

WAYS OF KNOWING AND DESCRIBING THE WORLD

The success of European commercial and colonial expansion in this era both drove and depended on significant innovations in measuring and mapping. It also coincided with intellectual, literary, and artistic initiatives that aimed to capture and describe the workings of this wider world, and to imagine its celestial (or infernal) counterparts.

Economic Tools: Balance Sheets, Banks, Charts, and Clocks

The economic boom that resulted from the integration of European and Asian commerce called for the refinement of existing business models and accounting techniques. New forms of partnership and the development of insurance contracts helped to minimize the risks associated with long-distance trading. Double-entry bookkeeping, widely used in Italy by the mid-fourteenth century, gave merchants a much clearer picture of their profits and losses by ensuring that both credits and debits were clearly laid out in parallel columns, a practice that facilitated the balancing of accounts. The Medici family of Florence established branches of their bank in each of the major cities of Europe and were careful that the failure of one would not bankrupt the entire firm, as earlier branch-banking arrangements had done. Banks also experimented with advanced credit techniques borrowed from Muslim and Jewish financiers,

DEVIL WITH EYEGLASSES. Spectacles were most commonly worn by those who made a living by reading and writing, notably bureaucrats and lawyers. In this conceptualization of hell, the devil charged with keeping track of human sin wears eyeglasses.
■ *What might this image reveal about popular attitudes toward record-keeping and the growing legal and administrative bureaucracies of the later Middle Ages?*

allowing their clients to transfer funds without any real money changing hands—and without endangering their capital by carrying it with them. Such transfers were carried out by written receipts: the direct ancestors of the check, the money order, and the currency transfer.

Other late medieval technologies kept pace in different ways with the demands for increased efficiency and accuracy. Eyeglasses, first invented in the 1280s, were perfected in the fourteenth century, extending the careers of those who made a living by reading, writing, and accounting. The use of the magnetic compass helped ships sail farther away from land, making longer-distance Atlantic voyages possible for the first time. And as more and more mariners began to sail waters less familiar to them, pilots began to make and use special charts that mapped the locations of ports. Called *portolani*, these charts also took note of prevailing winds, potential routes, good harbors, and known perils.

Among the many implements of modern daily life invented in this era, the most familiar are clocks. Mechanical clocks came into use shortly before 1300 and proliferated immediately thereafter. They were too large and expensive for private purchase, but towns vied with one another to install them in prominent public buildings, thus advertising municipal wealth and good governance. Mechanical timekeeping had two profound effects. One was the further stimulation of interest in complex machinery of all sorts, an interest already awakened by the widespread use of mills in the eleventh and twelfth centuries (see Chapter 8).

More significant was the way that clocks regulated daily life. Until the advent of clocks, time was flexible. Although days had been *theoretically* divided into hours, minutes, and seconds since the time of the Sumerians (see Chapter 1),

PORTOLAN CHART. Accurate mapping was essential to the success of maritime colonial ventures in the thirteenth and fourteenth centuries. The chart shown here is the oldest surviving example of a map used by mariners to navigate between Mediterranean ports. (The word *portolan* is used to describe such charts.) It dates from the end of the thirteenth century, and its shape clearly indicates that it was made from an animal hide. Although parchment was extremely durable, it would have slowly worn away owing to prolonged exposure to salt water and other elements—hence the rarity of this early example.

there had never been a way of mapping these temporal measurements onto an actual day. Now, clocks relentlessly divided time into exact units, giving rise to new expectations about labor and productivity. People were expected to start and end work "on time," to make the most of the time spent at work, and even to equate time with money. Like the improvements in bookkeeping, timekeeping made some kinds of work more efficient, but it also created new tensions and obsessions.

Knowledge of the World and of God

In the mid-thirteenth century, Thomas Aquinas had constructed a theological view of the world as rational, organized, and comprehensible to the inquiring human mind (see Chapter 9). Confidence in this picture began to wane in the fourteenth century, even before the Black Death posed a new challenge to it. Philosophers such as William of Ockham (d.c. 1348), an English member of the Franciscan order, denied that human reason could prove fundamental theological truths such as the existence of God. He argued that human knowledge of God, and hence salvation, depends entirely on what God himself has chosen to reveal through scripture. Instead, Ockham urged humans to investigate the natural world and to better understand its laws—without positing any necessary connection between the observable properties of nature and the unknowable essence of divinity.

This philosophical position, known as nominalism, had its roots in the philosophy of Plato (see Chapter 4) and has had an enormous impact on modern thought. The nominalists' distinction between the rational comprehensibility of the real world and the spiritual incomprehensibility of God encourages investigation of nature without reference to supernatural explanations: one of the most important foundations of the modern scientific method (see Chapter 16). Nominalism also encourages empirical observation, since it posits that knowledge of the world should rest on sensory experience rather than abstract theories. The philosophical principles laid down by these observers of the medieval world are thus fundamental to modern science.

Creating God's World in Art

Just as a fascination with the natural world informed developments in medieval science, the artists of this era were paying close attention to the way plants, animals, and human beings really looked. Carvings of leaves and flowers were increasingly made from direct observation and are clearly recognizable to modern botanists as distinct

Analyzing Primary Sources

Vikings Encounter the Natives of North America

Although Norse voyagers had explored and settled the coast of Newfoundland around the year 1000, written accounts of these exploits were not made or widely circulated until the thirteenth century. The excerpt below comes from one of these narrative histories, the Grænlendinga Saga *("Greenlanders' Saga"). Its hero is Thorfinn Karlsefni, a Norwegian adventurer who arrives in Greenland and marries Gudrid, the twice-widowed sister-in-law of the explorer Leif Eiriksson. Leif had established the original colony of Vinland, but had since returned to Greenland.*

here was still the same talk about Vinland voyages as before, and everyone, including [his wife] Gudrid, kept urging Karlsefni to make the voyage. In the end he decided to sail and gathered a company of sixty men and five women. He made an agreement with his crew that everyone should share equally in whatever profits the expedition might yield. The took livestock of all kinds, for they intended to make a permanent settlement there if possible.

Karlsefni asked Leif if he could have the houses in Vinland; Leif said that he was willing to lend them, but not to give them away.

They put to sea and arrived safe and sound at Leif's Houses and carried their hammocks ashore. Soon they had plenty of good supplies, for a fine big rorqual* was driven ashore; they went down and cut it up, and so there was no shortage of food.

The livestock were put out to grass, and soon the male beasts became very frisky and difficult to manage. They had brought a bull with them.

Karlsefni ordered timber to be felled and cut into lengths for a cargo for the ship, and it was left out on a rock to season. They made use of all the natural resources of the country that were available, grapes and game of all kinds and other produce.

The first winter passed into summer, and then they had their first encounter with Skrælings,† when a great number of them came out of the wood one day. The cattle were grazing near by and the bull began to bellow and roar with great vehemence. This terrified the Skrælings and they fled, carrying their packs which contained furs and sables and pelts of all kinds. They made for Karlsefni's houses and tried to get inside, but Karlsefni had the doors barred against them. Neither side could understand the other's language.

Then the Skrælings put down their packs and opened them up and offered their contents, preferably in exchange for weapons; but Karlsefni forbade his men to sell arms. Then he hit on the idea of telling the women to carry milk out to the Skrælings, and when the Skrælings saw the milk they wanted to buy nothing else. And so the outcome of their trading expedition was that the Skrælings carried their purchases away in their bellies, and left their packs and furs with Karlsefni and his men.

After that, Karlsefni ordered a strong wooden palisade to be erected round the houses, and they settled in.

species. Statues of humans also became more realistic in their portrayals of facial expressions and bodily proportions. According to a story in circulation around 1290, a sculptor working on a likeness of the German emperor allegedly made a hurried return trip to study his subject's face a second time, because he'd heard that a new wrinkle had appeared on the emperor's brow.

This trend toward naturalism extended to manuscript illumination and painting. The latter was, to a large extent, a new art. As we saw in Chapter 1, wall paintings are among the oldest forms of artistic expression in human history, and throughout antiquity and the Middle Ages artists had decorated the walls of public and private buildings with frescoes (paintings executed on "fresh"—wet—plaster). But in addition to frescoes, Italian artists in the thirteenth century began to adapt the techniques used by icon painters in Byzantium, making freestanding pictures on pieces of wood or canvas using tempera (pigments mixed with water and natural gums). Because these altarpieces, devotional images, and portraits were portable, they were also more commercial. As long as artists could afford the necessary materials, they did not have to wait for specific commissions. This meant that they had more freedom to choose their subject matter and to put an individual stamp on their

About this time Karlsefni's wife, Gudrid, gave birth to a son, and he was named Snorri.

Early next winter the Skrælings returned, in much greater numbers this time, bringing with them the same kind of wares as before. Karlsefni told the women, 'You must carry out to them the same produce that was most in demand last time, and nothing else.' . . .

[B]ut a Skræling was killed by one of Karlsefni's men for trying to steal some weapons. The Skrælings fled as fast as they could, leaving their clothing and wares behind . . .

'Now we must devise a plan,' said Karlsefni, 'for I expect they will pay us a third visit, and this time with hostility and in greater numbers. This is what we must do: ten men are to go out on the headland here and make themselves conspicuous, and the rest of us are to go into the wood and make a clearing there, where we can keep our cattle when the Skrælings come out of the forest. We shall take our bull and keep him to the fore.'

The place where they intended to have their encounter with the Skrælings had the lake on one side and the woods on the other.

Karlsefni's plan was put into effect, and the Skrælings came right to the place that Karlsefni had chosen for the battle. The fighting began, and many of the Skrælings were killed. There was one tall and handsome man among the Skrælings and Karlsefni reckoned that he must be their leader. One of the Skrælings had picked up an axe, and after examining it for a moment he swung it at a man standing beside him, who fell dead at once. The tall man then took hold of the axe, looked at it for a moment, and then threw it as far as he could out into the water. Then the Skrælings fled into the forest as fast as they could, and that was the end of the encounter.

Karlsefni and his men spent the whole winter there, but in the spring he announced that he had no wish to stay there any longer and wanted to return to Greenland. They made ready for the voyage and took with them much valuable produce, vines and grapes and pelts. They put to sea and reached Eiriksfjord safely and spent the winter there.

*A kind of whale, the largest species of which is a blue whale.

†A Norse word meaning "savages," applied to the different indigenous peoples of Greenland and of North America.

Questions for Analysis

1. What policies do the Norse settlers adopt toward the native peoples they encounter on the coast of Newfoundland? How effective are they?

2. Given their extensive preparations for colonization and the success of their early efforts, why do you think that Karlsefni and his companions abandoned their settlement in North America? Are there clues discernible in the text?

3. Compare this encounter to the sources describing other interactions between Europeans and the indigenous inhabitants of the New World after 1492 (see Chapters 12 and 14). How do you account for any similarities? What are some key differences?

work—one of the reasons why we know the names of many more artists from this era.

One of these, Giotto di Bondone of Florence (c. 1267–1337), painted both walls and portable wooden panels. Like some of his contemporaries, Giotto (*gee-OHT-toh*) was preeminently an imitator of nature. Not only do his human beings and animals look lifelike, they seem to do natural things. When Christ enters Jerusalem on Palm Sunday, boys climb trees to get a better view; when Saint Francis is laid out in death, someone checks to see whether he has really received the *stigmata*, the marks of Christ's wounds; and when the Virgin's parents, Joachim and Anna, meet after a long separation, they embrace and kiss one another tenderly. Although many of the artists who came after Giotto moved away from naturalism, this style would become the norm by 1400. It is for this reason that Giotto is often regarded as the first painter of the Renaissance (see Chapter 11).

A Vision of the World We Cannot See

One of Giotto's exact contemporaries had a different way of capturing the spiritual world in a naturalistic way, and he worked in a different medium. Dante Alighieri (1265–1321)

Seals: Signs of Identity and Authority

For much of human history, applying a seal to a document was the way to certify its legality and to identify the people who had ratified it. During antiquity and the early Middle Ages, this meant only powerful men—kings, bishops, heads of monasteries—and occasionally powerful women. But as participation in documentary practices became more and more common, corporations (like universities and crusading orders), towns, and many individual people also came to use seals. The devices (images) and legends (writing) on these seals were carefully chosen to capture central attributes of their owners' personality or status. Seals were made by pressing a deeply incised lead matrix onto hot wax or resin, which would quickly dry to form a durable impression. The images reproduced here are later engravings that make the features of the original seals easier to see.

A. Seal of the town of Dover, 1281. Dover has long been one of the busiest and most important port cities of England because of its strategic proximity to France; indeed, the Dover Strait that separates this town from Calais, just across the English Channel, is only twenty-one miles wide. In 1281, when this seal was used, ferries and other ships like the one depicted here (in a later engraving) would have made this crossing several times a day. The legend around the edges of the seal reads (in Latin): "Seal of the commune of barons of Dover." It reflects the extraordinary status accorded to the freemen of Dover by the English crown: because of their crucial role in the economy and defense of the kingdom, they were considered a corporate body and entitled to representation in Parliament alongside individual barons.

B. Personal seal of Charles II, king of Naples and Sicily, 1289. Charles II (b. 1254, r. 1285–1309) was the son and heir of Charles of Anjou, who became King Charles I of Sicily in 1266 and died in 1285. This means that Charles II had succeeded his father and had reigned as king for four years before he used this seal to ratify an agreement to his own daughter's marriage in 1289. Yet the seal in image B was clearly made for him when he was a young man—probably when he was first knighted. It depicts him as count of Anjou (see the heraldic fleur-de-lys) and gives him his other princely titles, including "Son of King Charles of Sicily." Although he was thirty-five-years old, a king in his own right, and a father, he was still using this older seal!

Questions for Analysis

1. Medieval towns represented themselves in a variety of ways on their seals: sometimes showing a group portrait of town councilors, sometimes a local saint, sometimes a heraldic beast, sometimes distinctive architectural features. Why would Dover choose this image? What messages does this seal convey?

2. Think carefully about the mystery of Charles II's seal. Usually, an important agreement like a marriage contract (with the son of the French king, no less!) would have carried a king's official, royal seal. What are all the possible reasons why Charles would still have been using this outdated seal? What are the possible ramifications of this choice? In your role as historian-detective, how would you go about solving this mystery?

3. The seals of medieval women were almost always shaped like almonds (pointed ovals— the technical term is *vesica-shaped*). Yet Ingeborg's seal is round, like the seals of men and corporations. Why might that be the case?

4. In general, what are the value of seals for the study of history? What are the various ways in which they function as sources?

C. Seal of Ingeborg Håkansdotter, duchess of Sweden, 1321. Ingeborg (1301–1361) was the daughter of King Håkon V of Norway and was betrothed to a Swedish duke, Erick Magnusson, when she was only eleven years old. After a dramatic series of events that left her a young widow, she became the regent for her son, Magnus was elected king of both Norway and Sweden in 1319. Ingeborg herself was barely eighteen at the time. The legend on her seal (image C) reads "Ingeborg by the Grace of God Duchess of Norway"—her official title.

THE MEETING OF JOACHIM AND ANNA BY GIOTTO.
According to legend, Anna and Joachim were an aged and infertile couple who were able to conceive their only child, Mary, through divine intervention. Hence, this painting may portray the moment of her conception—but it also portrays the affection of husband and wife. ▪ *What human characteristics and values does it convey to the viewer?*

of Florence pioneered what he called a "sweet new style" of poetry in his native tongue, which was now so different from the Latin of Roman Italy that it had become a language in its own right. Yet as a scholar and devotee of classical Latin verse, Dante also strove to make this Italian vernacular an instrument for serious political and social critique. His great work, known in his own day as the *Comedy* (called by later admirers the *Divine Comedy*) was composed during the years he spent in exile from his beloved city, after the political party he supported was ousted from power in 1301.

The *Comedy* describes the poet's imaginary journey through hell, purgatory, and paradise, a journey beginning in a "dark wood": a metaphor for the personal and political crises that threatened Dante's faith and livelihood. In the poem, the narrator is led out of this forest and through the first two realms (hell and purgatory) by the Roman poet Virgil (see Chapter 5), who represents the best of classical culture. But he can only be guided toward knowledge of the divine in paradise by his deceased beloved, Beatrice, who symbolizes Christian wisdom. In the course of this visionary pilgrimage, Dante's narrator meets the souls of many historical personages and contemporaries, questioning them closely and inviting them to explain why they met their sev-

eral fates: this is his ingenious way of commenting on current events and passing judgment on his enemies. In many ways, this monumental poem represents the fusion of classical and Christian cultures, Latin learning and vernacular artistry.

PAPAL POWER AND POPULAR PIETY

Dante's *Comedy* responded creatively to the political turmoil that engulfed Italy during his lifetime, a situation that was transforming the papacy in ways that he condemned. Indeed, many of the men whom Dante imaginatively placed in Hell were popes or men who had held high office in the Church, or foreign rulers who sought to subjugate Italian territories (like the Holy Roman Emperor), or rapacious Italian princes and factional leaders who fought among themselves, creating a state of permanent warfare among and within cities (like Dante's native Florence). But despite the weakening authority of the papal office, which caused violent divisions within the Church, popular piety arguably achieved its strongest expressions during this era.

The Legacy of Innocent III

As we saw in Chapter 9, Innocent III's reign marked the height of papal power, but it also sowed seeds of disaster. The popes of the thirteenth century continued to centralize the government of the Church, as Innocent had done, but they simultaneously became involved in protracted political struggles that compromised the papacy's credibility.

For example, because the Papal States bordered on the kingdom of Sicily—which comprised the important city of Naples and southern Italy, too—subsequent popes came into conflict with its ruler, the emperor Frederick II, who proved a fierce opponent. And instead of excommunicating him and calling for his deposition, as Innocent might have done, the reigning pope called a crusade against him—a cynical admission of crusading's overtly political motives. To implement this crusade, the papacy became preoccupied with finding a military champion to advance their cause. They found him in Charles of Anjou, the youngest brother of the French king Louis IX (see below). But Charles made matters worse by antagonizing his own subjects, who offered their allegiance to the king of Aragon. The pope then made Aragon the target of another crusade, which resulted in the death of the new French king, Philip III (r. 1270–85). In the wake of this debacle, Philip's son, Philip IV, resolved to punish the papacy for misusing its powers.

The Limits of Papal Propaganda

In 1300, Pope Boniface VIII (r. 1294–1303) celebrated a papal jubilee in Rome and offered a full crusader's indulgence to every pilgrim: the promise of absolution from all sins. It was a tacit recognition that Rome, not Jerusalem, was now the center of the Christian world—and also a tacit admission that the Crusades of the past two centuries had failed.

But just nine years after this confident assertion of Rome's unassailable status, Rome had become obsolete. The new capital of Christendom was in France, because King Philip IV had challenged Boniface to a political duel and won. The pretext was unimpressive: Boniface had protested against Philip's plan to bring a French bishop to trial on a charge of treason—thus violating the bishop's ecclesiastical immunity. Philip, who had probably anticipated this objection, accused Boniface of heresy and sent a troop of knights to arrest him. At the papal residence of Anagni in 1303, Boniface (then in his seventies) was so mistreated by Philip's thugs that he died a month later. Philip then pressed his advantage. He forced the new pope, Clement V, to thank him publically for his zealous defense of the faith and then, in 1309, moved the entire papal court from Rome to Avignon (*AH-vee-nyon*), a city near the southeastern border of his own realm.

The papacy's capitulation to French royal power illustrates the enormous gap that had opened up between rhetoric and reality in the centuries since the Investiture Conflict (see Chapter 8). Although Boniface was merely repeating an old claim, that kings ruled only by divine approval as recognized by the Church, the fact was that the Church now exercised its authority only by bowing to the superior power of a particular king.

The Babylonian Captivity of the Papacy

The papacy would remain in Avignon for nearly seventy years, until 1378 (see Chapter 11). This period is often called the "Babylonian Captivity" of the papacy, recalling the Jews' exile in Babylon during the sixth century B.C.E. (see Chapter 2). Even though the move was probably supposed to be temporary, it was not reversed after Philip IV's death in 1314, perhaps because many found that doing business in Avignon was easier than doing business in Rome. Not only was it closer to the major centers of power in northwestern Europe, it was now far removed from the tumultuous politics of Italy and was safe from the aggressive attentions of the German emperors.

All of these considerations were important for a succession of popes closely allied with the aims of the French monarchy. In time, Avignon began to feel like home; in fact it *was* home for all of the popes elected there, who were natives of the region, as were nearly all the cardinals whom they appointed. This further cemented their loyalty to the French king. And the longer the papacy stayed, the larger its bureaucracy grew and the harder it was to contemplate moving it.

Although the papacy never abandoned its claims to the overlordship of Rome and the Papal States, making good on these claims required decades of diplomacy and a great deal of money. The Avignon popes accordingly imposed new taxes and obligations on the wealthy dioceses of France, England, Germany, and Spain. Judicial cases from ecclesiastical courts also brought large revenues into the papal coffers. Most controversially, the Avignon popes

THE PAPAL PALACE AT AVIGNON. This great fortified palace was begun in 1339 and symbolizes the apparent permanence of the papal residence in Avignon. ▪ *Why would it have been constructed as a fortress as well as a palace?*

claimed the right to appoint bishops and priests to vacant offices anywhere in Christendom, directly, therefore bypassing the rights of individual dioceses and allowing the papacy to collect huge fees from successful appointees.

By these and other measures, the Avignon popes further strengthened administrative control over the Church. But they also further weakened the papacy's moral authority. Stories of the court's unseemly luxury circulated widely, especially during the reign of the notoriously corrupt Clement VI (r. 1342–52), who openly sold spiritual benefits for money (boasting that he would appoint a jackass to a bishopric if he thought it would turn a profit) and insisted that his sexual transgressions were therapeutic. His reign coincided with the Black Death, whose terrifying and demoralizing effects were not alleviated by the quality of his leadership.

Uniting the Faithful: The Power of Sacraments

Despite the centralizing power of the papacy, which came to fruition under Innocent III, most medieval Christians accessed the Church at a local level, within their communities. Somewhat paradoxically, this was another of Innocent III's legacies: because he had insisted that all people should have direct access to religious instruction, nearly all of Europe was covered by a network of parish churches by the end of the thirteenth century. In these churches, parish priests not only taught the elements of Christian doctrine, they administered the sacraments ("holy rites") that conveyed the grace of God to individual Christians, marking significant moments in the life cycle of every person and significant times in the Christian calendar.

Medieval piety came to revolve around these seven sacraments: baptism, confirmation, confession (or penance), communion, marriage, extreme unction (last rites for the dying), and ordination (of priests). Baptism, a ceremony of initiation administered in the early centuries of Christianity to adults (see Chapter 6), had become a sacrament administered to infants as soon as possible after birth, to safeguard their souls in case of an early death. The confirmation of adolescents reaffirmed the promises made on a child's behalf at baptism by parents and godparents. Periodic confession of sins to a priest guaranteed forgiveness by God; for if a sinner did not perform appropriate acts of penance, atonement for sins would have to be completed in purgatory—that netherworld between heaven and hell explored by Dante, whose existence was made a matter of Church doctrine

for the first time in 1274 (though its existence had been posited by Pope Gregory the Great centuries earlier—see Chapter 7).

Marriage was a relatively new sacrament, increasingly emphasized but very seldom practiced as a ceremony; in reality, marriage in this period required only the exchange of solemn promises and was often formed simply by an act of sexual intercourse or the fact of cohabitation. Extreme unction refers to the holy oil with which the priest anointed the forehead of a dying person, signifying the final absolution of all sins and thus offering a final assurance of salvation. Like baptism, this rite could, in an emergency, be administered by any Christian believer. The other sacraments, however, could be administered only by a properly ordained priest— or, in the case of confirmation and ordination, by a bishop. Ordination was therefore the only sacrament reserved for the small percentage of Christians who became priests, and it conveyed to the priest the special authority to share God's grace through the sacraments: a power that could never be lost, even by a priest who led an immoral life.

This sacramental system was the foundation on which the practices of medieval popular piety rested. Pilgrimages, for example, were a form of penance and could lessen one's time in purgatory. Crusading was a kind of extreme pilgrimage that promised the complete fulfillment of all penances the crusader might owe for all the sins of his (or her) life. Many other pious acts—saying the prayers of the rosary, for example, or giving alms to the poor—could also serve as penance for one's sins while constituting good works that would help the believer in his or her journey toward salvation.

The Miracle of the Eucharist

Of these sacraments, the one was most central to the religious lives of medieval Christians was the communion ceremony of the Mass, also known as the Eucharist. As we noted in Chapter 9, the ritual power of the Mass was greatly enhanced in the twelfth century, when the Church began promoting the doctrine of transubstantiation. Christians attending Mass were taught that when the priest spoke the ritual words "This is my body" and "This is my blood," the substances of bread and wine on the altar were miraculously transformed into the body and blood of Jesus Christ. To consume one or both of these substances was to ingest holiness; and so powerful was this idea that most Christians received the sacramental bread just once a year, at Easter. Some holy women, however, attempted to sustain themselves by consuming only the single morsel of bread consecrated at daily Mass.

The Pursuit of Holiness

The fundamental theme of preachers in this era, that salvation lay open to any Christian who strove for it, helps to explain the central place of the Mass and other sacraments in daily life. It also led many to seek out new paths that could lead to God. As we noted in Chapter 9, some believers who sought to achieve a mystical union with God (through rigorous prayer, penance, and personal sacrifice) were ultimately condemned for heresy because they did not subordinate themselves to the authority of the Church. But even less radical figures might find themselves treading on dangerous ground, especially if they published their ideas. For example, the German preacher Master Eckhart (c. 1260–1327), a Dominican friar, taught that there is a "spark" deep within every human soul and that God lives in this spark. Through prayer and self-renunciation, any person could therefore retreat into the inner recesses of her being and access divinity. This conveyed the message that a layperson might attain salvation through her own efforts, without the intervention of a priest or any of the sacraments he alone could perform. As a result, many of Eckhart's teachings were condemned. But views like these would find support in the teachings of popular preachers after the Black Death, when close-knit communities revolving around the parish church were broken up or weakened (see Chapter 11).

STRUGGLES FOR SOVEREIGNTY

When the French king Philip IV transplanted the papal court from Rome to Avignon, he was not just responding to previous popes' abuse of power: he was bolstering his own. By the middle of the thirteenth century, the growth of strong territorial monarchies, combined with the increasing sophistication of royal justice, taxation, and propaganda, had given some secular rulers a higher degree of power than any western European ruler had wielded since the time of Charlemagne (see Chapter 7).

Meanwhile, monarchs' willingness to support the Church's crusading efforts not only yielded distinct economic and political advantages, it also allowed them to assert their commitment to the moral and spiritual improvement of their realms. Although a king still needed to be anointed with holy oil at the time of his coronation in order to claim that he ruled "by the grace of God"—a rite that required a bishop and, by extension, papal support—a king's authority in his own realm rested on the acquiescence of the aristocracy and on popular perceptions of his reputation for justice, piety, and regard for his subjects' prosperity. On the wider stage of the

"THIS IS MY BODY": THE ELEVATION OF THE HOST.
This fresco from a chapel in Assisi was painted by Simone Martini in the 1320s. It shows the moment in the Mass when the priest raises the eucharistic host so that it can be seen by the faithful. The Latin phrase spoken at this moment, *Hoc est corpus meum* ("This is my body"), came to be regarded as a magical formula because it could transform one substance into another: *hocus pocus.* ▪ *Since medieval Christians believed that the sight of the host was just as powerful as ingesting it, how would they have responded to this life-size image of the elevation?* ▪ *What does the appearance of angels (above the altar) signify?*

Yet, to share in the miracle of the Eucharist, one did not have to consume it. One had only to witness the elevation of the host, the wafer of bread raised up by the priest, which "hosted" the real presence of Jesus Christ. Daily attendance at Mass simply to view the consecration of the host was therefore a common form of devotion, and this was facilitated by the practice of displaying a consecrated wafer in a special reliquary called a monstrance ("showcase"), which could be set up on an altar or carried through the streets. Believers sometimes attributed astonishing properties to the eucharistic host, feeding it to sick animals or rushing from church to church to see the consecrated bread as many times as possible in a day. Some of these practices were criticized as superstitious. But, by and large, these expressions of popular piety were encouraged and fervently practiced by many.

medieval world, it also rested on his successful assertion of his kingdom's sovereignty.

The Problem of Sovereignty

Sovereignty can be defined as inviolable authority over a defined territory. In Chapter 9, we noted that Philip Augustus was the first monarch to call himself "king of France" and not "king of the French." In other words, he was defining his kingship in geographical terms, claiming that there was an entity called France and that he was king within that area.

But what was France? Was it the tiny "island" (Île-de-France) around Paris, which had been his father's domain? If so, then France was very small—and very vulnerable, which would make it hard to maintain a claim to sovereignty. Was it, rather, any region whose lord was willing to do homage to the French king, like Champagne or Normandy? In that case, the king would need to enforce these rights of lordship constantly and, if necessary, exert his rule directly—as Philip did when he took Normandy away from England's King John in 1214.

But what if some of France's neighboring lords ruled in their own right, as did the independent counts of Flanders, thus threatening the security of France's borders? In that case, the king would either need to forge an alliance with these borderlands or negate their independence. He would need to assert his sovereignty by absorbing these regions into an ever-growing kingdom.

This is the problem: a claim to sovereignty is only credible if it can be backed up with real power, and a state's or ruler's power must never seem stagnant or passive. The problem of sovereignty, then, is a zero-sum game: one state's sovereignty is won and maintained by diminishing that of other states. Although many French citizens today would assert that France has, in some mystical way, always existed in its present form, the fact is that France and every other modern European state was being cobbled together in the medieval period through a process of annexation and colonization—just as the United States was assembled at the expense of the empires that had colonized North America (the British, French, and Spanish), not to mention the killing or displacement of autonomous native peoples.

The process of achieving sovereignty is thus an aggressive and often violent one, affecting not only the rulers of territories but their peoples, too. In Spain, the "Reconquest" of Muslim lands, which had accelerated in the twelfth century, continued apace in the thirteenth and fourteenth, to the detriment of these regions' Muslim and Jewish inhabitants. German princes continued to push northward into the Baltic, where native peoples' resistance to colonizing efforts was met with brutal force. Meanwhile, the Scandinavian kingdoms that had been forming in the eleventh and twelfth centuries were warring among themselves and their neighbors for the control of contested regions and resources. Italy and the Mediterranean became a constant battleground, as we have observed. Among all these emerging states, the two most strident and successful in their assertion of sovereignty were France and England.

The Prestige of France: The Saintly Kingship of Louis IX

After the death of Philip Augustus in 1223, the heirs to the French throne continued to pursue an expansionist policy, pushing the boundaries of their influence out to the east and south. There were significant pockets of resistance, though, notably from the southwestern lands that the kings of England had inherited from Eleanor of Aquitaine (see Chapter 9) and from the independent towns of Flanders that had escaped conquest under Philip Augustus. In 1302, citizen militias from several of these towns, fighting on foot with farming implements and other unconventional weapons, even managed to defeat a heavily armed French cavalry. This victory at the Battle of Courtrai (Kortrijk) is still celebrated as a national holiday in Belgium (although, ironically, its ultimate meaning is currently at the center of a divisive controversy between French- and Flemish-speaking Belgians).

This defeat was a setback for Philip IV of France, but we have already observed that Philip had other ways of asserting the power of French sovereignty. Much of that power derived from his grandfather, Louis IX (r. 1226–70), who would probably have been horrified by the ways his grandson used it. Louis was famous for his piety and for his conscientious exercise of his kingly duties. Unlike most of his fellow princes, he not only pledged to go on crusade—he actually went. And while both of his campaigns were notorious failures (he died on the second, in 1270) they cemented Louis's saintly reputation and political clout.

First, Louis's willingness to risk his life (and that of his brothers) in the service of the Church would give him tremendous influence in papal affairs—a key factor in making his youngest brother, Charles of Anjou, the king of Naples and Sicily. Second, the necessity of ensuring the good governance of his kingdom during his years of absence prompted Louis to reform or invent many key aspects of royal governance, which made France the bureaucratic rival of England for the first time. Third, Louis's first crusading venture was

A CONTAINER FOR THE CROWN OF THORNS. The Sainte-Chapelle, built by Louis IX, was a giant reliquary for the display of this potent artifact and symbol that Christ's divine majesty, which increased the prestige of king of France.

seen as confirmation that the king of France had inherited the mantle of Charlemagne as the protector of the Church and the representative of Christ on earth. Although it was a military fiasco, this crusade found lasting artistic expression in the Sainte-Chapelle (Holy Chapel), a gorgeous jewel box of a church that Louis built in Paris for his collection of Passion relics—that is, artifacts thought to have been used for the torture and crucifixion of Christ. The most important of these was the Crown of Thorns, intended by Pilate as a mocking reference to "the king of the Jews" (see Chapter 6). Now that this holy crown belonged to Louis and was housed in Paris, it could be taken as a sign that Paris was the new Jerusalem.

Widely regarded as a saint in his lifetime, Louis was formally canonized in 1297—by the same Pope Boniface VIII brought down by Philip IV. Indeed, Boniface partly intended this gesture as a rebuke to the saint's grandson. Philip himself, however, turned it to his advantage. He even used his grandfather's pious reputation as a cloak for his frankly rapacious treatment of the Knights Templar, whose military order he suppressed in 1314 so that he could confiscate its extensive property and dissolve his own debts to the order. He had expelled the Jews from his realm in 1306 for similar reasons.

Castles and Control: Edward I and the Expansion of English Rule

The expulsion of Jews who depended on a king's personal protection had actually been a precedent set by Philip's contemporary and kinsman, Edward I of England

(r. 1272–1307). Unlike Philip, Edward had to build up the sovereignty of his state almost from scratch. His father, Henry III (1216–1272), had a long but troubled reign. Inheriting the throne as a young boy, shortly after his father John's loss of Normandy and capitulation to Magna Carta (see Chapter 9), Henry had to contend with factions among his regents and, later, the restive barons of his realm who rose against him on several occasions. His son Edward even sided with the rebels at one point, but later worked alongside his father to suppress them. When Edward himself became king in 1272, he took steps toward ensuring that there would be no further revolts on his watch, tightening his control on the aristocracy and their lands, diffusing their power by strengthening that of Parliament, reforming the administration of the realm, and clarifying its laws.

Having seen to the internal affairs of England, Edward looked to its borders. Since Welsh chieftains had been major backers of the barons who had rebelled against his father, Edward was determined to clean up the border region and bring "wild Wales" within the orbit of English sovereignty. He initially attempted to do this by making treaties with various Welsh princes, but none of these arrangements were stable or gave Edward the type of control he wanted. He accordingly embarked on an ambitious and ruthless campaign of castle-building, ringing the hilly country with enormous fortifications on a scale not seen in most of Europe; they were more

CAERNARVON CASTLE. One of many massive fortifications built by Edward I, this castle was the birthplace of the first English "Prince of Wales" and the site where the current Prince of Wales, Charles, was formally invested with that title in 1969. ▪ *Castles of this size and strength had been constructed in the Crusader States and on the disputed frontiers of Muslim and Christian Spain but never before in Britain (see the photos on pages 292 and 295 of Chapter 9).* ▪ *What does their construction reveal about Edward's attitude toward the Welsh?*

A Declaration of Scottish Independence

In April of 1320, a group of powerful Scottish lords gathered at the abbey of Arbroath to draft a letter to Pope John XII in Avignon. The resulting "Declaration of Arbroath" petitioned the exiled pope (a Frenchman loyal to the French king) to recognize the Scots as a sovereign nation and to support their right to an independent kingdom that would be free from encroachment by the English. The Scots' elected king, Robert the Bruce, had been excommunicated by a previous pope, who had also upheld English claims to lordship in Scotland. The letter therefore makes a number of different arguments for the recognition of the Scots' right to self-governance.

We know, most holy father and lord, and have gathered from the deeds and books about men in the past, that . . . the nation of the Scots has been outstanding for its many distinctions. It journeyed from the lands of Greece and Egypt by the Tyrrhenian Sea and the Pillars of Hercules, . . . but could not be subdued anywhere by any peoples however barbaric. . . . It took possession of the settlements in the west which it now desires, after first driving out the Britons and totally destroying the Picts, and although often attacked by the Norwegians, Danes and English. Many were its victories and innumerable its efforts. It has held these places always free of all servitude, as the old histories testify.

One hundred and thirteen kings of their royal lineage have reigned in their kingdom, with no intrusion by a foreigner.

If the noble qualities and merits of these men were not obvious for other reasons, they shine forth clearly enough in that they were almost the first to be called to his most holy faith by the King of Kings and Lord of Lords, our Lord Jesus Christ, after his Passion and Resurrection, even though they were settled on the most distant boundaries of the earth. . . .

Thus our people lived until now in freedom and peace . . . , until that mighty prince Edward [I] king of England (the father of the present king) in the guise of a friend and ally attacked our kingdom in hostile fashion, when it had no head and the people were not harbouring any evil treachery, nor were they accustomed to

wars or attacks. His unjust acts, killings, acts of violence, pillagings, burnings, imprisonments of prelates, burnings of monasteries, robbings and killings of regular clergy, and also innumerable other outrages, which he committed against the said people, sparing none on account of age or sex, religion or order—no one could write about them or fully comprehend them who had not been instructed by experience.

From these countless ills we have been set free, with the help of Him who follows up wounds with healing and cures, by our most energetic prince, king and lord Sir Robert [the Bruce, r. 1306–29]. . . . By divine providence his succession to his right according to our laws and customs which we intend to maintain to the death, together with the due consent

like crusader castles, and Edward certainly treated the Welsh (who were actually his fellow Christians) as infidels. Indeed, he treated conquered Wales like a crusader state, making it a settler colony and subjecting the Welsh to the overlordship of his own men. When his son, the future Edward II, was born in 1284 at the great castle he had built at Caernarvon, he gave the infant the title "Prince of Wales," a title usually borne by a Welsh chieftain.

Edward then turned to Scotland, England's final frontier. Until now, control of Scotland had not been an English concern: the Scottish border had been peaceful for many years, and the Scottish kings did homage to the English king for some of their lands. In 1290, however, the succession to the Scottish throne was disputed among many rival

claimants, none of whom had enough backing to secure election. Edward intervened, pressing his own claim to the kingdom and seemingly prepared to take Scotland by conquest. To avoid this, the Scots forged an alliance with the French, but this did not prevent Edward's army from fighting its way through to Scone Abbey in 1296.

Scone was a symbolic target: the site of the Stone of Destiny on which Scottish kings were traditionally enthroned. So Edward seized this potent symbol, brought it back to Westminster Abbey in London, and embedded it in the coronation chair of his namesake, Edward the Confessor, the last Anglo-Saxon king of England (see Chapter 8). Save for a brief hiatus in 1950 (when the stone was stolen from the abbey by Scottish nationalists, students and assent of us all, have made him our prince and king. . . . But if he should give up what he has begun, seeking to subject us or our kingdom to the king of the English, . . . we would immediately strive to expel him as our enemy and a subverter of his right and ours, and we would make someone else our king, who is capable of seeing to our defence. For as long as a hundred of us remain alive, we intend never to be subjected to the lordship of the English, in any way. For it is not for glory in war, riches or honours that we fight, but only for the laws of our fathers and for freedom, which no good man loses except along with his life.

Therefore, most holy father and lord, we implore your holiness with all vehemence in our prayers that you . . . look with paternal eyes on the troubles and difficulties brought upon us and the church of God by the English. And that you deign to admonish and exhort the king of the English, who ought to be satisfied with what he has (since England was formerly enough for seven kings or more), to leave us Scots in peace, living as we do in the poor country of Scotland beyond which there is no dwelling place, and desiring nothing but our own. . . .

It is important for you, holy father, to do this, since you see the savagery of the heathen raging against Christians (as the sins of Christians require), and the frontiers of Christendom are being curtailed day by day, and you have seen how much it detracts from your holiness's reputation if (God forbid!) the church suffers eclipse or scandal in any part of it during your time. Let it then rouse the Christian princes who are covering up their true motivation when they pretend that they cannot go to the assistance of the Holy Land on account of wars with their neighbours. The real reason that holds them back is that in warring with their smaller neighbours they anticipate greater advantage to themselves and weaker resistance. . . .

But if your Holiness too credulously trusts the tales of the English fully, or does not leave off favouring the English to our confusion, then we believe that the Most High will blame you for the slaughter of bodies. . . . Dated at our monastery at Arbroath in Scotland 6 April 1320 in the fifteenth year of our said king's reign.

Questions for Analysis

1. On what grounds does this letter justify the political independence of the Scots? What different arguments does it make? Which, in your view, is the most compelling one?

2. Why does this letter mention crusading? What are the Scottish lords implying about the relationship between Europe's internal conflicts and the ongoing wars with external adversaries?

3. Imagine that you are an adviser to the pope. Based on your knowledge of the papacy's situation at this time, would you advise him to do as this letter asks? Why or why not?

at the University of Glasgow) it would remain there until 1996, as a sign that the sovereignty of Scotland had yielded to that of England. (It will be temporarily returned to London when the next English monarch is crowned.)

Edward considered the subjugation of Scotland to be England's manifest destiny: he called himself "the Hammer of the Scots," and when he died he charged his son Edward II (r. 1307–1327) with the completion of his task. But Edward, unlike his father, was not a ruthless and efficient advocate of English expansion. And he had to contend with a rebellion led by his own queen, Isabella of France, who also engineered his abdication and murder. Their son, Edward III (r. 1327–1377), would eventually renew his grandfather's expansionist policies—but his main target would be France, not Scotland. He would thus launch Europe's two strongest monarchies into a war that lasted over a hundred years.

The Outbreak of the Hundred Years' War

The Hundred Years' War was the largest, longest, and most wide-ranging military conflict since Rome's wars with Carthage in the third and second centuries B.C.E. (see Chapter 5). Although England and France were its principal antagonists, almost all of the major European powers became involved in it at some stage. Active hostilities began in 1337 and lasted until 1453, interrupted by truces of varying lengths.

The most fundamental source of conflict, and the most difficult to resolve, was the fact that the kings of England held the duchy of Gascony as vassals of the French king; this had been part of Eleanor of Aquitaine's domain, added to the Anglo-Norman Empire in 1154 (see Chapter 9). In the twelfth and thirteenth centuries, when the French kings had not yet absorbed this region into their domain, this fact had seemed less of an anomaly. But as Europe's territorial monarchies began to claim sovereignty based on the free exercise of power within the "natural" boundaries of their domains, the English presence in "French" Gascony became more and more problematic. That England also had close commercial links, through the wool trade, with Flanders—which consistently resisted French imperialism—added fuel to the fire. So did the French alliance with the Scots, who continued to resist English imperialism.

Complicating this volatile situation was the disputed succession of the French crown. In 1328, the last of Philip IV's three sons died without leaving a son to succeed him: the Capetian dynasty, founded by the Frankish warlord Hugh Capet in 987 (see Chapter 8), had finally exhausted itself. A new dynasty, the Valois, came to the throne—but only by insisting that women could neither inherit royal power nor pass it on. For otherwise, the heir to France was Edward III of England, whose ambitious mother, Isabella, was Philip IV's only daughter. When his claim was initially passed over, Edward was only fifteen and in no position to protest. In 1337, however, when the disputes over Gascony and Scotland erupted into war, Edward raised the stakes by claiming to be the rightful king of France, a claim that subsequent English kings would maintain until the eighteenth century.

Although France was richer and more populous than England by a factor of at least three to one, the English crown was more effective in mobilizing the entire population, for reasons that we discussed in Chapter 9. Edward III was therefore able to levy and maintain a professional army of seasoned and well-disciplined soldiers, cavalry, and archers. The huge but virtually leaderless armies assembled by the French proved no match for the tactical superiority of these smaller English forces. English armies pillaged the French countryside at will, while civil wars broke out between embattled French lords. A decade after the declaration of war, French knights were defeated in two humiliating battles, at Crécy (1346) and Calais (1347). The English seemed invincible. Yet they were no match for an adversary approaching from the Far East.

FROM THE GREAT FAMINE TO THE BLACK DEATH

By 1300, Europe was connected to Asia and the lands in between by an intricate network that fostered commerce, communication, and connections of all kinds. Yet Europe was also reaching its own ecological limits. Between 1000 and 1300, the population had tripled, and a sea of grain

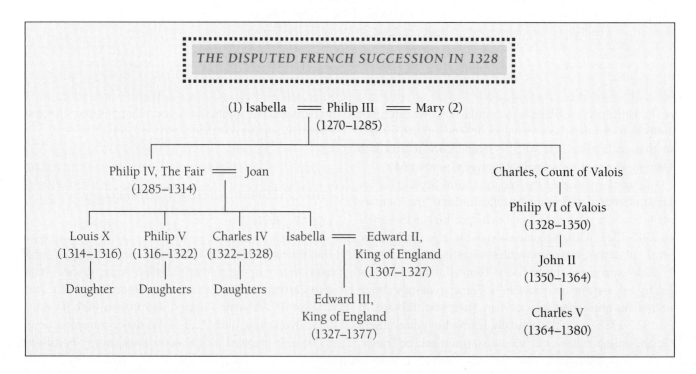

THE DISPUTED FRENCH SUCCESSION IN 1328

(1) Isabella ═══ Philip III ═══ Mary (2)
(1270–1285)

Philip IV, The Fair ═══ Joan   Charles, Count of Valois
(1285–1314)

Louis X   Philip V   Charles IV   Isabella ═══ Edward II,   Philip VI of Valois
(1314–1316) (1316–1322) (1322–1328)   King of England   (1328–1350)
                                       (1307–1327)

Daughter   Daughters   Daughters   John II
                            Edward III,   (1350–1364)
                          King of England
                          (1327–1377)   Charles V
                                         (1364–1380)

Past and Present

Global Pandemics

The image on the left shows citizens from the town of Tournai (now in Belgium) marching in a procession to ward off the plague. They are praying and doing penance for their sins by beating their own bodies with whips, a practice called *flagellation*. On the right, citizens of Mumbai (India), wearing protective masks to ward off infection, stand in line to receive testing for the swine flu virus.

 Watch related author interview on StudySpace
wwnorton.com/web/westernciv18

fields stretched, almost unbroken, from Ireland to the Ukraine. Forests had been cleared, marshes drained, and pastureland reduced by generations of peasants performing lifetimes of backbreaking labor. But still, Europe was barely able to feed its people. At the same time, the warming trend that had begun in the late eighth century reversed itself. Even a reduction of one or two degrees centigrade is enough to cause substantial changes in rainfall patterns, shorten growing seasons, and lessen agricultural productivity. So it did in Europe, with disastrous consequences.

Evil Times: The Seven Years' Famine

Between the years 1315 to 1322, the cooling climate caused nearly continuous adverse weather conditions in northern Europe. Winters were extraordinarily severe: in 1316, the Baltic Sea froze over and ships were trapped in the ice. Rains prevented planting in spring or summer, and when a crop did manage to struggle through it would be dashed by rain and hail in autumn. In the midst of these natural calamities, dynastic warfare continued in the sodden wheatfields, as the princes of Scandinavia and the Holy Roman Empire fought for supremacy and succession. In the once-fertile fields of Flanders, French armies slogged through mud in continued efforts to subdue the Flemish population. On the Scottish and Welsh borders, uprisings were ruthlessly suppressed and the paltry storehouses of the natives were pillaged to feed the English raiders.

The result was human suffering more devastating than that caused by any famine affecting Europe since that time: hence the acceptance of the name "Great Famine" to describe this terrible crisis. Weakened by years of malnutrition and relentless efforts to counteract the climactic effects on the landscape, between 10 and 15 percent of the population of northern Europe perished. Many starved, and others

The Code of Chivalry: Putting Honor before Plunder

The Hundred Years' War between England and France pitted these two countries' warrior aristocracies against one another. Yet these knights had a great deal in common: they all spoke French, many were closely related, and they were supposed to share a common set of values. The following excerpt is taken from The Book of Chivalry *written in French by Geoffroi de Charny, a French nobleman and veteran of this war's first major battles who ultimately died in combat at Poitiers in 1356. Because the war was fought almost entirely on French soil, Geoffroi was keenly aware of the toll it took on the land and its people. In the following passage, he addresses the problem of how a knight can sustain his honor when he is driven to acquire booty for himself through the theft of others' property.*

Those Who Are Brave but Too Eager for Plunder

now need to consider yet another category of men-at-arms, who deserve praise, who are strong and skillful, bold and sparing no effort, some of whom always want to be at the forefront, riding as foragers to win booty or prisoners or other profit from the enemies of those on whose side they fight. And they know well how to do it skillfully and cleverly; and because they are so intent on plunder, it often happens that on the entry into a town won by force, those who are so greedy for plunder dash hither and thither and find themselves separated from those of their companions who have no thought for gain but only for completing their military undertaking. And it often happens that such men, those who ride after and hunt for great booty, are killed in the process—frequently it is not known how, sometimes by their enemies, sometimes through quarrels in which greed for plunder sets one man against another. It often occurs that through lack of those who chase after plunder before the battle is over, that which is thought to be already won can be lost again and lives or reputations as well. It can also happen in relation to such people who are very eager for booty that when there is action on the battlefield, there are a number of men who pay more attention to taking prisoners and other profit, and when they have seized them and other winnings, they are more anxious to safeguard their captives and their booty than to help to bring the battle to a good conclusion. And it may well be that a battle can be lost in this way. And one ought instead to be wary of the booty which results in the loss of honor, life, and possessions. In this vocation one should therefore set one's heart and mind on winning honor, which endures for ever, rather than on winning profit and booty, which one can lose within one single hour. And yet one should praise and value those men-at-arms who are able to make war on, inflict damage on, and win profit from their enemies, for they cannot do it without strenuous effort and great courage. But again I shall repeat: he who does best is most worthy.

Questions for Analysis

1. How does Geoffroi justify the act of plundering? What insights into contemporary military tactics does this passage provide?

2. Given that Geoffroi would have seen Englishmen pillaging French lands, do you find his justification of this activity surprising? Why or why not?

fell victim to epidemic diseases that affected both animals and people. In southern Europe, around the shores of the Mediterranean, the effects of climate change were more muted, and there were also different channels through which food could be distributed. Nonetheless, the overall health of this region suffered from the disruption of trade and the shortage of some staple goods, as well as from the highly unstable political situation we have already discussed.

As food grew scarcer, prices climbed unpredictably. Plans for future crops, which kept hope alive, would be dashed when spring arrived and flooded fields prevented seeds from germinating. Cold summers and autumns were spent foraging for food. Hunting was restricted to the nobility, but even those who risked the death penalty for poaching found little game. Wages did not keep pace with rising costs, and so those who lived in towns

Plague-stricken towns and areas
Progress of plague at certain dates
Towns and areas not stricken by the plague

THE PROGRESS OF THE BLACK DEATH, FOURTEENTH CENTURY. ▪ *What trajectories did the Black Death follow once it was introduced into Europe?* ▪ *How might the growth of towns, trade, and travel have contributed to the spread of the Black Death?* ▪ *Would such a rapid advance have been likely during the early Middle Ages or even in the ancient world?*

and depended on markets had less to spend on scarce provisions. Only a year after the famine began, townspeople were dying of ailments that would not have been fatal in good years.

The effects of the famine were especially devastating for children, since even those who survived would be highly susceptible to disease, owing to the severe impairment of their immune systems. It may have been the Great Famine, then, that paved the way for the more transient (if more horrific) destruction of the Black Death.

A Crisis of Connectivity: Tracking the Black Death

The Black Death is the name given to a deadly pandemic that spread from China to Mongolia, northern India, and the Middle East during the 1330s and 1340s. By 1346, the plague had reached the Black Sea, where it was transmitted to the Genoese colonists at Caffa (as we noted above). From there, in 1347, Genoese ships inadvertently

Responses to the Black Death

Many chroniclers, intellectuals, and private individuals have left accounts of the plague in which they attempt to understand why it had occurred, how it spread, and how communities should respond to it.

The Spread of the Plague According to Gabriele de' Mussi (d. 1356), a Lawyer in Piacenza (Northern Italy)

Oh God! See how the heathen Tartar races, pouring together from all sides, suddenly infested the city of Caffa [on the Black Sea] and besieged the trapped Christians there for almost three years. . . . But behold, [in 1346] the whole army was affected by a disease which overran the Tartars and killed thousands upon thousands every day. It was as though arrows were raining down from heaven to strike and crush the Tartars' arrogance. All medical advice and attention was useless; the Tartars died as soon as the signs of disease appeared on their bodies: swellings in the armpit or groin caused by coagulating humours, followed by a putrid fever.

The dying Tartars, stunned and stupefied by the immensity of the disaster brought about by the disease, and realising that they had no hope of escape, lost interest in the siege. But they ordered corpses to be placed in catapults and lobbed into the city in the hope that the intolerable stench would kill everyone inside. What seemed like mountains of dead were thrown into the city, and the Christians could not hide or flee or escape from them, although they dumped as many of the bodies as they could in the sea. And soon the rotting corpses tainted the air and poisoned the water supply. . . . Moreover one infected man could carry the poison to others, and infect people and places with the disease by look alone. No one knew, or could discover, a means of defence.

Thus almost everyone who had been in the East . . . fell victim . . . through the bitter events of 1346 to 1348—the Chinese, Indians, Persians, Medes, Kurds, Armenians, Cilicians, Georgians, Mesopotamians, Nubians, Ethiopians, Turks, Egyptians, Arabs, Saracens and Greeks. . . .

* * *

As it happened, among those who escaped from Caffa by boat were a few sailors who had been infected with the poisonous disease. Some boats were bound for Genoa, others went to Venice and to other Christian areas. When the sailors reached these places and mixed with the people there, it was as if they had brought evil spirits with them. . . .

* * *

Scarcely one in seven of the Genoese survived. In Venice, where an inquiry was held into the mortality, it was found that more than 70 percent of the people had died. . . . The rest of Italy, Sicily and Apulia and the neighbouring regions maintain that they have been virtually emptied of inhabitants. . . . The Roman Curia at Avignon, the provinces on both sides of the Rhône, Spain, France, and the Empire cry up their griefs. . . .

* * *

Everyone has a responsibility to keep some record of the disease and the deaths, and because I am myself from Piacenza I have been urged to write more about what happened there in 1348. . . .

brought it to Sicily and northern Italy. From Italy, it spread westward along trade routes, first striking seaports, then turning inland with the travelers who carried it. It moved with astonishing rapidity, advancing about two miles per day, summer or winter. By 1350, it had reached Scandinavia and northern Russia, then spread southward again until it linked up with the original waves of infection that had brought it from Central Asia to the Black Sea. It continued to erupt in local epidemics for the next 300 years; some localities could expect a renewed outbreak every decade. The last Europe-wide instance occurred between 1661 and 1669, although there were

I don't know where to begin. Cries and laments arise on all sides. Day after day one sees the Cross and the Host being carried about the city, and countless dead being buried.... The living made preparations for their [own] burial, and because there was not enough room for individual graves, pits had to be dug in colonnades and piazzas, where nobody had ever been buried before. It often happened that man and wife, father and son, mother and daughter, and soon the whole household and many neighbours, were buried together in one place....

A Letter from the Town Council of Cologne to the Town Council of Strasbourg (Germany), 12 January 1349

Very dear friends, all sorts of rumours are now flying about against Judaism and the Jews prompted by this unexpected and unparalleled mortality of Christians.... Throughout our city, as in yours, many-winged Fame clamours that this mortality was initially caused, and is still being spread, by the poisoning of springs and wells, and that the Jews must have dropped poisonous substances into them. When it came to our knowledge that serious charges had been made against the Jews in several small towns and villages on the basis of this mortality, we sent numerous letters to you and to other cities and towns to uncover the truth behind these rumours, and set a thorough investigation in train....

If a massacre of the Jews were to be allowed in the major cities (something which we are determined to prevent in our city, if we can, as long as the Jews are found to be innocent of these or similar actions) it could lead to the sort of outrages and disturbances which would whip up a popular revolt among the common people—and such revolts have in the past brought cities to misery and desolation. In any case we are still of the opinion that this mortality and its attendant circumstances are caused by divine vengeance and nothing else. Accordingly we intend to forbid any harassment of the Jews in our city because of these flying rumours, but to defend them faithfully and keep them safe, as our predecessors did—and we are convinced that you ought to do the same....

Source: From Rosemary Horrox, ed. and trans., *The Black Death* (Manchester: 1994), pp. 16–21, 219–20.

Questions for Analysis

1. How does Gabriele de' Mussi initially explain the causes of the plague? How does his understanding of it change as he traces its movements from East to West—and closer to Italy?

2. Why does the Council of Cologne wish to quell violence against the Jews? How does this reasoning complement or challenge what we have learned so far about the treatment of Jews in medieval Europe?

3. In your view, do these two perspectives display a rational approach to the horrors of the Black Death? Why or why not?

sporadic outbreaks in Poland and Russia until the end of the eighteenth century.

What caused the Black Death? In 2011, scientists were able to confirm that it can be traced to the deadly microbe *Yersinia pestis*, and that it did indeed originate in China. *Y. pestis* actually causes three different kinds of contagion: bubonic plague and its even deadlier cousins, septicemic plague and pneumonic plague. In its bubonic form, this microbe is carried by fleas that travel on the backs of rats; humans catch it only if they are bitten by an infected flea or rat. Bubonic plague attacks the lymphatic system, producing enormous swellings (buboes) of the lymph nodes in the groin, neck, and armpits. Septicemic plague occurs when an infected flea introduces the microbe directly into the human bloodstream, causing death within hours, often before any symptoms of the disease can manifest themselves. Pneumonic plague, perhaps the most frightening variation, results when *Y. pestis* infects the lungs, allowing the contagion to spread silently and invisibly, in the same ways as the common cold.

One of the things that made the Black Death so terrifying, therefore, was that it manifested itself in several different ways. Those afflicted by the hideous bubonic plague might actually recover, while others—seemingly untouched—might die suddenly, mysteriously. Immediate reactions understandably ranged from panic to resignation. Observers quickly realized that the plague was contagious, but precisely how it spread remained enigmatic. Some believed that it was caused by breathing "bad air" and so urged people to flee from stricken areas, which caused the disease to spread even faster.

Others looked for scapegoats and revived old conspiracy theories that implicated Jews in the poisoning of wells. Scores of Jewish communities were attacked and thousands of their inhabitants massacred in the Rhineland, southern France, and Christian Spain. (No such attacks are known to have occurred in Muslim areas of Spain or elsewhere in the Muslim world.) The papacy and some local authorities tried to halt these attacks, but these admonitions came too late. Another response to the plague was the flagellant movement, so called because of the whips (*flagella*) with which traveling bands of penitents lashed themselves in order to appease the wrath of God. But the unruly and sometimes hysterical mobs that gathered around the flagellants aroused the concern of both ecclesiastical and secular authorities, and the movement was suppressed by papal order.

CONCLUSION

The century between 1250 and 1350 was a time of significant change within all Western civilizations. The growing power of some monarchies led to encroachments on territories and cities that had once been independent, and that fueled resistance to these internal acts of colonization. The papacy, whose power had seemed so secure at the turn

After You Read This Chapter

Visit StudySpace for quizzes, additional review materials, and multimedia documents. **wwnorton.com/web/westernciv18**

REVIEWING THE OBJECTIVES

- The conquests of the Mongols had a significant impact on Europe. How?
- The expansion of commerce and communication between Eastern and Western civilizations created a new world system. What were some key characteristics of this system? What kinds of exchange did it enable?
- What were the short- and longer-term causes for the papacy's loss of prestige? Why was the papal court moved to Avignon?
- What is sovereignty? What were the effects of competition for sovereign among European rulers?
- What caused the Black Death? In what sense can it be seen as a product of the new world system that began with the Mongol conquests?

of the thirteenth century, would itself become a pawn in the keeping of the French king by the beginning of the fourteenth. Rome thereby lost its last source of authority while the New Rome, Constantinople, struggled to rebuild its prestige in the face of Mongol expansion. Yet for the Mongol khans and the merchants they favored, for seafaring civilizations like Venice and Genoa, for ambitious students at the universities, and for men on the make, the opportunities for advancement and mobility were great.

And there were still other factors at play during this era. Even in good times, Europe's population had outgrown its capacity to produce food, and when the climate grew cooler, years of cold summers and heavy rainfall took an enormous toll. Those regions most closely tied to the new global networks were also densely settled and urban, which made the shortage of food and the spread of disease more acute there. In short, the benefits and drawbacks of increased globalization were already beginning to manifest themselves in the early fourteenth century—700 years ago. The Black Death can be understood as the ultimate example of medieval connectivity and also as a modern phenomenon.

The scale of mortality caused by this pandemic is almost unimaginable, to us as to those who survived it. At least a third, and probably half, of Europe's people died between 1347 and 1353. In the countryside, entire villages disappeared. Cities and towns, overcrowded and unsanitary, were particularly vulnerable to plague and, thereafter, to outbreaks of violence. The immediate social consequences were profound, and so were the economic ones. Crops rotted in the fields, manufacturing ceased, and trade came to a standstill in affected areas. Basic commodities became scarcer and prices rose, prompting ineffectual efforts to control prices and to force the remaining able-bodied laborers to work.

These were the short-term effects. How did the Black Death matter to those who survived it—including ourselves? According to Ibn Khaldun (1332–1406), a Muslim historian who is considered one of the founders of modern historical methods, it marked the end of the old world and the beginning of a new one, which would require new systems of government, bodies of knowledge, and forms of art. Was he right? We will begin to answer that question in Chapter 11.

PEOPLE, IDEAS, AND EVENTS IN CONTEXT

- What accounts for the success of **GENGHIS KHAN** and his successors? What circumstances enabled **MARCO POLO**'s travels to China? To what extent does the term *PAX MONGOLICA* describe this era in history?

- How did seafaring communities like that of **GENOA** rise to prominence in this era? Why were new navigational aids like **PORTOLAN CHARTS** necessary?

- How do the paintings of **GIOTTO** capture contemporary attitudes toward the world? How does **DANTE**'s artistry respond to the religious and political trends of his day?

- What was at stake in the controversy between **BONIFACE VIII** and **PHILIP IV**? Why is the papacy's residency at **AVIGNON** called the **BABYLONIAN CAPTIVITY**? What is a **SACRAMENT**, and why were these rites so important?

- In what different ways did **LOUIS IX** of France and **EDWARD I** of England contribute to the sovereignty of their respective kingdoms? What was the relationship between claims to sovereignty and the causes of the **HUNDRED YEARS' WAR**?

- How did climate change contribute to the outbreak of the **GREAT FAMINE?**

- What were the long-term and short-term causes of the **BLACK DEATH**?

THINKING ABOUT CONNECTIONS

- If the Mongol khan Ögedei had not died in 1241, the Mongols could conceivably have continued their westward movement into Europe. Given what you have learned about Mongol rule, how might this have changed the history of the world?

- How do the patterns of conquest and colonization discussed in this chapter compare to those of earlier periods, particularly those of antiquity? How many of these developments were new in 1250–1350?

- We live in a world in which the global circulation of people, information, goods, and bacteria is rapid. How does the medieval system compare to ours? What features seem familiar?

STORY LINES

- The Black Death altered Europe in profound ways. The opportunities and challenges of this era are dynamically reflected in an array of developments.

- Some of these developments are associated with a new artistic and cultural movement known as the Renaissance, which began in Italy.

- Here, renewed appreciation of the classics and of Greek was facilitated by the flight of Greek-speaking intellectuals from Byzantium, as the Ottoman Turks absorbed the remaining lands of the eastern Roman Empire.

- Meanwhile, the competing territorial claims of Europe's sovereign powers led to large-scale warfare.

- Even after the papacy's return to Rome from Avignon, the failure of internal reform efforts led to the decline of papal credibility. Consequently, a number of influential religious leaders sought more radical reforms.

CHRONOLOGY

1304–1374	Lifetime of Petrarch
1351	Black Death at its height
	The English Parliament passes the Statute of Laborers
1377	The papacy returns to Rome from Avignon
1378	The Great Schism begins
1381	Rebellions culminate in the English Peasants' Revolt
1414–1418	The Council of Constance is convened to end the Great Schism; Jan Hus burned at the stake in 1415
1429–1431	The career of Joan of Arc
1431–1449	The Council of Basel fails to check papal power
1440	Lorenzo Valla debunks "The Donation of Constantine"
1453	The Hundred Years' War ends
	Constantinople falls to the Ottoman Turks

Before You Read This Chapter

Rebirth and Unrest, 1350–1453

CORE OBJECTIVES

- **TRACE** the economic and social effects of the Black Death.

- **EXPLAIN** the relationship between the Middle Ages and the Renaissance.

- **DESCRIBE** the intellectual, cultural, and technological innovations of this era.

- **DEFINE** the concept of national monarchy and summarize its implications.

- **UNDERSTAND** the significance of the conciliar movement and its defeat by the papacy.

n June 1381, thousands of laborers from the English countryside rose up in rebellion against local authorities. Most were peasants or village craftsmen who were dismissed as ignorant by contemporary chroniclers. Yet the revolt was carefully coordinated: Plans were spread in coded messages circulated by word of mouth and by the followers of a renegade Oxford professor, John Wycliffe, who had called for the redistribution of Church property and taught that common people should be able to read the Bible in their own language. The rebellion's immediate catalyst had been a series of exorbitant taxes levied by Parliament for the support of the ongoing war with France. But its more fundamental cause was an epidemic that had occurred thirty years earlier. The Black Death had reduced the entire population of Europe by 30 to 50 percent and had drastically altered the world of those who survived it. In this new world, workers were valuable and could stand up to those who paid them poorly or treated them like slaves. In that fateful summer of 1381, the workers of England even vowed to kill representatives of both the Church and the government—to kill (as they put it) all the lawyers—and to destroy all the documents that had been used to keep them in subjection. It was a revolution, and it partly succeeded. Although the leaders were eventually captured and executed, the rebellion had made the strength of the common people known to all.

The fourteenth century is often seen as a time of crisis in the history of Western civilizations. Famine and plague cut fearful swaths through the population; war was a brutally recurrent fact of life; and the papacy spent seventy years in continuous exile from Italy, only to see its prestige decline further after its return to Rome. But this was also a time of extraordinary opportunity and achievement. The exhausted land of Europe recovered from centuries of overfarming, while workers gained the economic edge; eventually, some even gained social and political power. Meanwhile, popular and intellectual movements sought to reform the Church. A host of intellectual, artistic, and scientific innovations contributed to all of these phenomena.

This era of rebirth and unrest has been called by two different names: the later Middle Ages and the Renaissance. The latter refers to an intellectual and artistic movement that began in northern Italy, where the citizens of warring city-states desperately sought new models of governance and cultural cohesion by looking back to the older civilizations of Greece and Rome. But these are not two separate historical periods; rather they reflect two different ways of looking back at an era that is considered to be the immediate precursor of modernity. To understand it, we need to study it holistically. And we need to begin with a survey of Western civilizations after the Black Death.

LIFE AFTER THE BLACK DEATH

By 1353, when the bubonic plague began to loosen its death grip on Europe, the Continent had lost nearly half of its population. This happened suddenly, within a half century, owing to a combination of famine and disease (see Chapter 10). In the following century, recurring outbreaks of the plague and frequent warfare in some regions would result in further drastic reductions. In Germany, some 400,000 villages disappeared. Around Paris, more than half of the farmland formerly under cultivation became pastureland. Elsewhere, abandoned fields returned to woodland, increasing the forested areas of Europe by about a third.

Life after the Black Death would therefore be radically different for those who survived it, because this massive depopulation would affect every aspect of existence, from nutrition to social mobility to spirituality.

First and foremost, it meant a relative abundance of food. The price of grain fell, which made it more affordable.

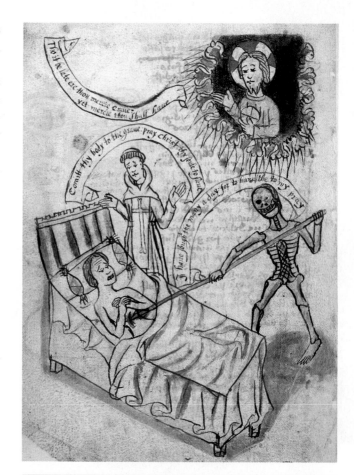

THE PLAGUE CLAIMS A VICTIM. A priest gives last rites to a bedridden plague victim as a smiling devil pierces the dying man with a spear and as Christ looks mercifully down from heaven.
■ *What are the possible meanings of this image?* ■ *What does it reveal about contemporary attitudes toward death by plague?*

At the same time, the scarcity of workers made peasant labor more valuable: wages rose and work became easily obtainable. With wages high and food prices low, ordinary people could now afford more bread and could also spend their surplus cash on dairy products, meat, fish, fruits, and wine. As a result, the people of Europe were better nourished than they had ever been—better than many are today. A recent study of fifteenth-century rubbish dumps has concluded that the people of Glasgow (Scotland) ate a healthier diet in 1405 than they did in 2005.

The Rural Impact

In the countryside, a healthier ecological balance was almost immediately reestablished in the wake of the plague. And gradually, with the lessened demand for fuel and building materials, forests that had almost disappeared began to recover and expand. Meanwhile, the declining demand for grain allowed many farmers to expand their livestock herds. By turning arable land into pastureland, farmers reduced the need to hire so many workers and they also improved the fertility of the soil through manuring. Some farmers were even able to enlarge their holdings, because so much land had been abandoned.

Most of these innovations were made by small farmers because many great lords—individuals as well as monasteries—were slower to adjust to the changing circumstances. But some large landholders were quick to seize the advantage, responding to the shortage of workers and the rising cost of wages by forcing their tenants to perform additional unpaid labor. In parts of eastern Europe, many free peasants became serfs for the first time as a result. In Castile, Poland, and Germany, too, lords succeeded in imposing new forms of servitude.

In France and the Low Countries, by contrast, peasants remained relatively free, although many were forced to pay a variety of new fees and taxes to their lords or to the king. In England, where peasant bondage had been more common than in France, serfdom eventually disappeared altogether. Although the Peasants' Revolt of 1381 was ultimately unsuccessful, increased economic opportunity allowed English serfs to vote with their feet, either by moving to town or to the lands of a lord who offered more favorable terms: lower rents, more animals, fewer work requirements, and greater personal freedoms. Geographical mobility and social mobility are, as we have often noted, intertwined.

The Urban Impact

Mortality rates were high in the crowded cities and towns of Europe, but not all cities were equally affected by the plague and many recovered quickly. In London and Paris, for example, large-scale immigration from the countryside reversed the short-term declines caused by the plague. Many of these newcomers were women, whose economic opportunities (usually very limited) were greatly enhanced by urban labor shortages. Other urban areas suffered more from internal violence or warfare than from disease. In Florence, for example, the population rebounded quickly after the Black Death but was eventually depleted by civil unrest: by 1427, it had dropped from around 300,000 to about 100,000. In Toulouse (southwestern France), the population remained fairly stable until 1430, when it was reduced by a staggering 75 percent as a result of the ravages of the Hundred Years' War.

So while the overall population of Europe declined drastically because of the plague, it is noteworthy that a far larger percentage of all people were living in towns by 1500: approximately 20 percent as opposed to 10 or 15 percent prior to the Black Death. Fueling this urban growth was the increasing specialization of the late-medieval economy. With farmers under less pressure to produce grain in bulk, land could be devoted to livestock, dairy farming, and the production of a more diverse array of fruits and vegetables; and these could now be exchanged more efficiently on the open market.

Towns with links to extant trading networks benefited accordingly. In northern Germany, a group of entrepreneurial cities formed a coalition to build an entirely new mercantile corporation, the Hanseatic League, whose members came to control commerce from Britain and Scandinavia to the Baltic. In northern Italy, the increased demand for luxury goods—which even some peasants and urban laborers could now afford—brought renewed wealth to the spice- and silk-trading city of Venice and also to the fine-cloth manufacturers of Milan and the jewelers of Florence. Milan's armaments industry also prospered, supplying its warring neighbors and the armies of Europe.

Of course, not all urban areas flourished. The Franco-Flemish cities that had played such a large role in economic and cultural life since the eleventh century suffered a serious economic depression, exacerbated by incessant wars in the region. But, on the whole, surviving Europeans profited from the plague. A century afterward, they were poised to extend their commercial networks farther into Africa, Asia, and (ultimately) the Americas (see Chapter 12).

Popular Revolts and Rebellions

Although the consequences of the Black Death were ultimately beneficial for many, Europeans did not adjust easily to this new world; established elites, in particular, resisted the demands of newly powerful workers. When these demands were not met, violence erupted. Between 1350 and 1425, hundreds of popular rebellions challenged the status quo in many regions of Europe. In 1358, peasants in northeastern France rose up violently against their lords, destroying property, burning buildings and crops, and even murdering targeted individuals. This incident is known as the Jacquerie Rebellion, because all French peasants were caricatured by the aristocracy as "Jacques" ("Jack").

In England, as we have already noted, a very different uprising occurred in June of 1381, far more organized and involving a much wider segment of society. Thousands of people marched on London, targeting the bureaucracies of the royal government and the Church, capturing and killing the archbishop of Canterbury, and meeting personally with the fourteen-year-old king, Richard II, to demand an end to serfdom and taxation and to call for the redistribution of property. It ended with the arrest and execution of the ringleaders. In Florence, workers in the cloth industry—known as the Ciompi (*chee-OHM-pee*)—protested high unemployment and mistreatment by the manufacturers who also ran the Florentine government. They seized control of the city, demanding relief from taxes, full employment, and political representation. They maintained power for a remarkable six weeks before their reforms were revoked.

The local circumstances that lay behind each of these revolts were unique, but all of them exhibit certain common features. First of all, they were not bread riots spurred by destitution: those who took part in them were not protesting starvation wages, they were empowered by the new economic conditions and wanted to leverage their position in order to enact even larger changes. Some rebellions, like the English Peasants' Revolt, were touched off by resistance to new and higher taxes. Others, like the Jacquerie and the revolt of the Ciompi, took place at moments when unpopular governments were weakened by factionalism and military defeat. The English revolt was also fueled by the widespread perception of corruption within the Church and the royal administration.

Behind this social and political unrest, therefore, lies not poverty and hunger but the growing prosperity and self-confidence of village communities and urban laborers who were taking advantage of the changed economic circumstances that arose from the plague. For the most part, the rebels' hopes that they could fundamentally alter the conditions of their lives were frustrated. Kings, aristocrats, and urban oligarchs sometimes lost their nerve in the middle of an uprising, but they were almost always successful, after a time, in reasserting dominance. Yet this tradition of popular rebellion would remain an important feature of Western civilizations. It would eventually fuel the American War of Independence and the French Revolution (see Chapter 18), and it continues to this day.

Aristocratic Life in the Wake of the Plague

Although the urban elites and rural aristocracies of Europe did not adapt easily to "the world turned upside down" by the plague, this was hardly a period of crisis for those in power. Quite the contrary: many great families became far wealthier than their ancestors had ever been. Nor did the plague undermine the dominant position they had established. It did, however, make their situations substantially more complex and uncertain, at a time when the costs of maintaining a fashionable lifestyle were escalating rapidly.

Across Europe, most noble families continued to derive much of their revenue from vast land holdings. Many also tried to increase their sources of income through investment in trading ventures. In Catalonia, Italy, Germany, and England, this became common practice. In France and Castile, however, direct involvement in commerce was regarded as socially demeaning and was, therefore, avoided by established families. Commerce could still be a route to ennoblement in these kingdoms; but once aristocratic rank was achieved, one was expected to abandon these employments and adopt an appropriate way of life: living in a rural

A HUNTING PARTY. This fifteenth-century illustration shows an elaborately dressed group of noblemen and noblewomen setting out with falcons, accompanied by their servants and their dogs. Hunting, an activity restricted to the aristocracy, was an occasion for conspicuous consumption and display.

castle or urban palace surrounded by a lavish household, embracing the values and conventions of chivalry (engaging in the hunt, commissioning a family coat of arms), and serving the ruler at court and in war.

What it meant to be "noble" became, as a result, even more difficult to define than it had been during the twelfth and thirteenth centuries. In countries where noble rank entailed clearly defined legal privileges—such as the right to be tried only in special courts—proven descent from noble ancestors might be sufficient to qualify a family as noble in the eyes of the law. Legal nobility of this sort was, however, a somewhat less exclusive distinction than one might expect. In fifteenth-century Castile and Navarre, 10 to 15 percent of the total population had claims to be recognized as noble on these terms. In Poland, Hungary, and Scotland, the legally privileged nobility was closer to 5 percent, whereas in England and France fewer than 2 percent could plausibly claim the legal privileges of noble status.

Fundamentally, however, nobility was expressed and epitomized by an individual's lifestyle. Hereditary land ownership, political influence, deference from social inferiors, courtly manners, and the ostentatious display of wealth— these combined to constitute a family's honor and hence to mark it as noble. This means that, in practice, the social distinctions between noble and non-noble families were very hard to discern. And even on the battlefield, where the mark of nobility was to fight on horseback, the supremacy of the mounted knight was being threatened by the growing importance of professional soldiers, archers, crossbowmen, and artillery experts. There were even hints of a more radical critique of the aristocracy's claims to innate superiority. As the English rebels put it in 1381: "When Adam dug and Eve spun, Who then was a gentleman?" In other words, all social distinctions are entirely artificial.

Precisely because nobility was contested, those who claimed it took elaborate measures to assert their exclusive right to this status through conspicuous consumption. This accounts, in part, for the extraordinary number, variety, and richness of the artifacts

and artworks that survive from this period. Aristocrats— or those who wanted to be classed as such—vied with one another in hosting lavish banquets, which required numerous costly utensils, specially decorated dining chambers, legions of servants, and the most exotic foods attainable. They dressed in rich and extravagant clothing: close-fitting doublets and hose with long pointed shoes for men, multilayered silk dresses with ornately festooned headdresses for women. They maintained enormous households: in France, around 1400, the Duke of Berry had 400 matched pairs of hunting dogs and 1,000 servants. They took part in elaborately ritualized tournaments and pageants, in which the participants pretended to be the heroes of chivalric romances. Aristocrats also emphasized their tastes and refinement by supporting authors and artists and some-

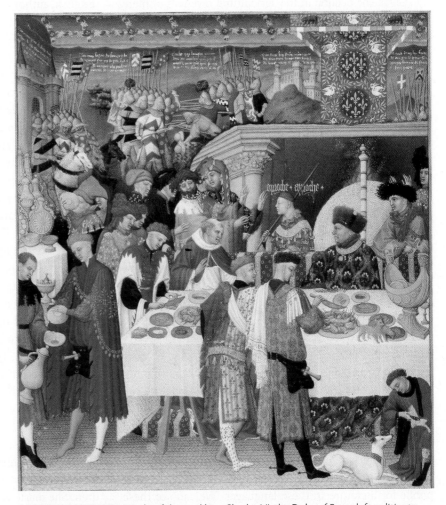

A NOBLE BANQUET. Uncle of the mad king Charles VI, the Duke of Berry left politics to his brothers, the Duke of Burgundy and the Duke of Anjou. In return, he received enormous subsidies from the royal government, which he spent on sumptuous buildings, festivals, and artworks, including the famous Book of Hours (prayer book), which includes this image. Here, the duke (seated at right, in blue) gives a New Year's Day banquet for his household, who exchange gifts while his hunting dogs dine on scraps from the table. In the background, knights confront one another in a tournament.

times by becoming accomplished artists themselves. Nobility existed only if it was recognized, and to be recognized noble status had to be constantly reasserted and displayed.

Rulers contributed to this process; indeed, they were among its principal supporters and patrons. Kings and princes across Europe competed in founding chivalric orders such as the Knights of the Garter in England and the Order of the Star in France. These orders honored men who had demonstrated the idealized virtues of knighthood, virtues celebrated as characteristic of the nobility as a whole. By exalting the nobility as a class, then, chivalric orders helped cement the links that bound the nobility to their kings and princes. These bonds were further strengthened by the gifts, pensions, offices, and marriage prospects that kings and princes could bestow on their noble followers.

Given the decline in the agricultural revenues of many noble estates, such rewards of princely service were critically important to maintaining noble fortunes. Indeed, the alliance that was forged in the fifteenth century between kings and their noble supporters would become one of the most characteristic features of Europe's ruling class. In France, this "Old Regime" (*ancien régime*) alliance lasted until the French Revolution of 1789. In Germany, Austria, and Russia, it would last until the outbreak of World War I. In England, it persisted in some respects until World War II.

Capturing Reality in Writing

The writings of literary artists who survived the Black Death, or who grew up in the decades immediately following it, are characterized by intense observations of the real world—and by appeals to a far larger and more diverse audience than their predecessors. We have noted that vernacular languages were becoming powerful vehicles for poetry and narrative in the twelfth century (see Chapter 9). Now they were being used to express some of the most innovative and critical perspectives on changing social mores, political developments, and philosophical outlooks. Behind this phenomenon lie three interrelated developments: the growing identification between vernacular language and the community of a realm, the still-increasing accessibility of education, and the emergence of a substantial reading public for literature in these languages. We can see these influences at work in three of the major authors who flourished during this period: Giovanni Boccaccio, Geoffrey Chaucer, and Christine de Pisan.

Boccaccio (*bohk-KAHT-chee-oh*, 1313–1375) is best known for *The Decameron*, a collection of prose tales about sex, adventure, and trickery. He presents these stories as being told over a period of ten days (hence the title of the book, which means "work of ten days"), by and for a sophisticated party of young women and men who have taken up residence in a country villa outside Florence in order to escape the ravages of the Black Death. Boccaccio borrowed the outlines of many of these tales from earlier sources, especially the fabliaux discussed in Chapter 9, but he couched them in a freely colloquial Italian. Whereas Dante had used the same Florentine dialect to evoke the awesome landscape of sacred history in the exquisite verse of his *Divine Comedy* (Chapter 10), Boccaccio used it to capture the foibles of human beings and their often graphic sexual exploits in plainspoken prose.

The English poet Geoffrey Chaucer (c. 1340–1400) is similar in many ways to Boccaccio, whose influence on him was profound. Chaucer was among the first generation of English authors whose compositions can be understood by modern readers of that language with relatively little effort. By the late fourteenth century, the Anglo-Saxon (Old English) tongue of England's preconquest inhabitants had mixed with the French dialect spoken by their Norman conquerors, to create the language which is the ancestor of our own: Middle English.

Chaucer's masterpiece is *The Canterbury Tales*. Like *The Decameron*, this is a collection of stories held together by a framing narrative. In this case, the stories are told by an array of people traveling together on a pilgrimage from London to the shrine of Saint Thomas Becket at Canterbury. But there are also significant differences between *The Decameron* and *The Canterbury Tales*. Chaucer's stories are in verse, for the most part, and they are recounted by people of all different classes—from a high-minded knight to a poor university student to a lusty widow. Each character tells a story that is particularly illustrative of his or her own occupation and outlook on the world, forming a kaleidoscopic human comedy.

This period, a generation or so after the Black Death, also saw the emergence of professional authors who made their living through the patronage of the aristocracy and the publication of their works. One of the first was a woman, Christine de Pisan (c. 1365–c. 1434). Although born in northern Italy, Christine spent her adult life in France, where her husband was a member of the king's household. When he died, the widowed Christine wrote to support herself and her children. She mastered a wide variety of literary genres, including treatises on chivalry and warfare, which she dedicated to King Charles VI of France. She also wrote for a larger and more popular audience. For example, her imaginative *Book of the City of Ladies* is an extended defense of the character, capacities, and history of women, designed to help female readers refute their male detractors. Christine also took part in a vigorous pamphlet campaign that condemned the misogynistic claims made by influential (male) authors like Boccaccio. This debate was ongoing for several hundred years and became so famous that it was given a name: the *querelle des femmes*, "the debate over women." Remarkably, Christine also wrote a song in praise of Joan of Arc. Sadly, she probably lived long enough to learn that this other extraordinary woman had been put to death for behaving in a way that was considered dangerously unwomanly (see below).

Visualizing Reality

Just as the desire to capture real experiences and convey real emotions was a dominant trait of the literature produced after the Black Death, so it was in the visual arts. This is evident both in the older arts of manuscript illumination and also in the new kinds of sculpture we discussed in Chapter 10.

CHRISTINE DE PISAN. One of the most prolific authors of the Middle Ages, Pisan used her influence to uphold the dignity of women and to celebrate their history and achievements. Here she is seen describing the prowess of an Amazon warrior who could defeat men effortlessly in armed combat.

A further innovation in the fifteenth century was the technique of painting in oils, a medium pioneered in Flanders, where artists found a ready market for their works among the nobility and wealthy merchants.

Oil paints were a revolutionary development: because they do not dry as quickly as water-based pigments, a painter can work more slowly and carefully, taking time with more difficult aspects of the work and making corrections as needed. Masterful practitioners of this technique include Rogier van der Weyden (c. 1400–1464), who excelled at communicating both deep spiritual messages and the minute details of everyday life (see **Interpreting Visual Evidence** on page 366). Just as contemporary saints saw divinity in material objects, so too an artist could portray the Virgin and Child against a background vista of ordinary life, with people going about their business or a man urinating against a wall. This was not blasphemous. To the contrary, it conveyed the message that the events of the Bible are constantly present, here and now: Christ is our companion, such artworks suggest, not some distant figure whose life and outlook are irrelevant to us.

The same immediacy is also evident in medieval drama. Plays were often devotional exercises that involved the efforts of an entire community, but they also celebrated that community. In the English city of York, for example, an annual series of pageants reenacted the entire history of human salvation from the Creation to the Last Judgment in a single summer day, beginning at dawn and ending late at night. Each pageant was produced by a particular craft guild and showcased that guild's special talents: "The Last Supper" was performed by the bakers, whose bread was a key element in their reenactment of the first Eucharist, while "The Crucifixion" was performed by the nail makers and painters, whose wares were thereby put on prominent display in the depiction of Christ's bloody death on the cross. In Italy, confraternities competed with one another to honor the saints with songs and processions. In Catalonia and many regions of Spain, there were elaborate dramas celebrating the life and miracles of the Virgin, one of which is still performed every year in the Basque town of Elche: it is the oldest European play in continuous production. In northern France, the Low Countries, and German-speaking lands, civic spectacles were performed over a period of several days, celebrating local history or the place of the community in the sacred history of the Bible. But not all plays were pious. Some honored visiting kings and princes. Others celebrated the flouting of social conventions, featuring cross-dressing and the reversal of hierarchies. They were further expressions of the topsy-turvy world created by the Black Death.

Why a Woman Can Write about Warfare

Christine de Pisan (c. 1365–c. 1434) was one of the West's first professional writers, best known today for her Book of the City of Ladies *and* The Treasure of the City of Ladies, *works that aimed to provide women with an honorable and rich history and to combat generations of institutionalized misogyny. But in her own time, Christine was probably best known for the work excerpted here,* The Book of the Deeds of Arms and of Chivalry, *a manual of military strategy and conduct written at the height of the Hundred Years' War, in 1410.*

s boldness is essential for great undertakings, and without it nothing should be risked, I think it is proper in this present work to set forth my unworthiness to treat such exalted matter. I should not have dared even to think about it, but although boldness is blameworthy when it is foolhardy, I should state that I have not been inspired by arrogance or foolish presumption, but rather by true affection and a genuine desire for the welfare of noble men engaging in the profession of arms. I am encouraged, in the light of my other writings, to undertake to speak in this book of the most honorable office of arms and chivalry. . . . So to this end I have gathered together facts and subject matter from various books to produce this present volume. But inasmuch as it is fitting for this matter to be discussed factually, diligently, and sensibly . . . and also in consideration of the fact that military and lay experts in the aforesaid art of chivalry are not usually clerks or writers who are expert in language, I intend to treat the matter in the plainest possible language. . . .

As this is unusual for women, who generally are occupied in weaving, spinning, and household duties, I humbly invoke . . . the wise lady Minerva [Athena], born in the land of Greece, whom the ancients esteemed highly for her great wisdom. Likewise the poet Boccaccio praises her in his *Book of Famous Women,* as do other writers praise her art and manner of making trappings of iron and steel, so let it not be held against me if I, as a woman, take it upon myself to treat of military matters. . . .

O Minerva! goddess of arms and of chivalry, who, by understanding beyond that of other women, did find and initiate among the other noble arts and sciences the custom of forging iron and steel armaments and harness both proper and suitable for covering and protecting men's bodies against arrows slung in battle—helmets, shields, and protective covering having come first from you—you instituted and gave directions for drawing up a battle order, how to begin an assault and to engage in proper combat. . . . In the aforementioned country of Greece, you provided the usage of this office, and insofar as it may please you to be favorably disposed, and I in no way appear to be against the nation from which you came, the country beyond the Alps that is now called Apulia and Calabria in Italy, where you were born, let me say that like you I am an Italian woman.

Source: From *The Book of the Deeds of Arms and of Chivalry,* ed. Charity Cannon Willard and trans. Sumner Willard (University Park, PA: 1999), pp. 11–13.

Questions for Analysis

1. Christine very cleverly deflects potential criticism for her "boldness" in writing about warfare. What tactics does she use?

2. The Greco-Roman goddess Athena (Minerva) was the goddess of wisdom, weaving, and warfare. Why does Christine invoke her aid? What parallels does she draw between her own attributes and those of Minerva's?

THE BEGINNINGS OF THE RENAISSANCE IN ITALY

Rummaging through some old books in a cathedral library, an Italian bureaucrat attached to the papal court at Avignon was surprised to find a manuscript of Cicero's letters—letters that no living person had known to exist. They had probably been copied in the time of Charlemagne, but had then been forgotten for hundreds of years. How many other works of this great Roman orator had been lost to posterity? Clearly, thought Francesco Petrarca (1304–1374), he was living in an age of ignorance. A great gulf seemed to open up between his own time and have written to you long ago," he said in a Latin letter to the Greek poet Homer (dead for over 2,000 years), "had it not been for the fact that we lack a common language."

Petrarch was famous in his own day as an Italian poet, a Latin stylist, and a tireless advocate for the resuscitation of the classical past. The values that he and his followers began to espouse would give rise to a new intellectual and artistic movement in Italy, a movement strongly critical of the present and admiring of a past that had disappeared with the fragmentation of Rome's empire and the end of Italy's greatness. We know this movement as the Renaissance, from the French word for "rebirth" that was applied to it in the eighteenth century and popularized in the nineteenth, when the term *medieval* was also invented. It has since become shorthand for the epoch *following* the Middle Ages—but it was really part of that same era.

Renaissance Classicism

Talking about "the Renaissance," then, is a way of talking about some significant changes in education and artistic outlook that transformed the culture of northern Italy from the late fourteenth to the early sixteenth centuries and that eventually influenced the rest of Europe in important ways. The term has often been taken literally, as though the cultural accomplishments of antiquity had ceased to be appreciated and therefore needed to be "reborn." Yet we have been tracing the enduring influence of classical civilization for many chapters, and we have constantly noted the reverence accorded to the heritage of antiquity, not to mention the persistence of Roman law and Roman institutions.

That said, one can certainly find distinguishing traits that make the concept of "renaissance" newly meaningful in this era. For example, there was a significant quantitative difference between the ancient texts available to scholars in the first thousand years after Rome's fragmentation and those that became accessible in the fourteenth and fifteenth centuries. The discovery of "new" works by Livy, Tacitus, and Lucretius expanded the classical canon considerably, supplementing the well-studied works of Virgil, Ovid, and Cicero. More important was the expanded access to ancient Greek literature in western Europe. In the twelfth and thirteenth centuries, as we have seen in Chapters 8 and 9, Greek scientific and philosophical works became available to western Europeans thanks to increased contact with Islam, via Latin translations of Arabic translations of the original Greek.

Still, no Greek poems or plays were yet available in Latin translations, and neither were the major dialogues of Plato. Moreover, only a handful of western Europeans could

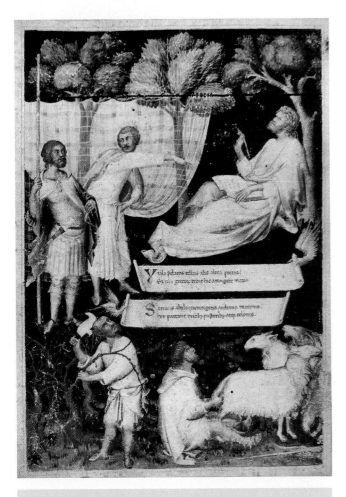

PETRARCH'S COPY OF VIRGIL. Petrarch's devotion to the classics of Roman literature prompted him to commission this new frontispiece for his treasured volume of Virgil's poetry. It was painted by the Sienese artist Simone Martini, who (like Petrarch) was attached to the papal court at Avignon. It is an allegorical depiction of Virgil (top right) and his poetic creations: the hero Aeneas (top left, wearing armor) and the farmer and shepherd whose humble labors are celebrated in Virgil's lesser-known works. The figure next to Aeneas is the fourth-century scholar Servius, who wrote a famous commentary on Virgil. He is shown drawing aside a curtain to reveal the poet in a creative trance. The two scrolls proclaim (in Latin) that Italy was the country that nourished famous poets and that Virgil helped it to achieve the glories of classical Greece. ▪ *How does this image encapsulate and express Petrarch's devotion to the classical past?*

that of the ancients: a middle age that separated him from those well-loved models.

For centuries, Christian intellectuals had regarded "the dark ages" as the time between Adam's expulsion from Eden and the birth of Christ. But now, Petrarch (the name by which English-speakers call Petrarca) redefined that concept and applied it to his own era. According to him, the Middle Ages was not the pagan past but the time that separated him from direct communion with the classics. Yet this did not stop him from trying to bridge the gap. "I would

Realizing Devotion

These two paintings by the Flemish artist Rogier van der Weyden (*FAN-der-VIE-den*, c. 1400–1464) capture some of the most compelling characteristics of late medieval art, particularly the trend toward realistic representations of holy figures and sacred stories. On the left (image A), the artist depicts himself as the evangelist Luke, regarded in Christian tradition as a painter of portraits; he sketches the Virgin nursing the infant Jesus in a town house overlooking a Flemish city. On the right (image B), van der Weyden imagines the entombment of the dead Christ by his followers, including the Virgin (left), Mary Magdalene (kneeling), and the disciple John (right). Here, he makes use of a motif that became increasingly prominent in the later Middle Ages: Christ as the Man of Sorrows, displaying his wounds and inviting the viewer to share in his suffering. In both paintings, van der Weyden emphasizes the humanity of his subjects rather than their iconic status (see Chapter 7), and he places them in the urban and rural landscapes of his own world.

Questions for Analysis

1. How are these paintings different from the sacred images of the earlier Middle Ages (see, for example, pages 214 and 217)? What messages does the artist convey by setting these events in his own immediate present?

2. In what ways do these paintings reflect broad changes in popular piety and medieval devotional practices? Why, for example, would the artist display the dead and wounded body of Christ—rather than depicting him as resurrected and triumphant, or as an all-seeing creator and judge?

3. In general, how would you use these images as evidence of the worldview of the fifteenth century? What do they tell us about people's attitudes, emotions, and values?

A. Saint Luke drawing the portrait of the Virgin.

B. The Deposition.

read the language of classical Greece. But as the Mongols and, after them, the Ottoman Turks put increasing pressure on the shrinking borders of Byzantium (see below), more and more Greek-speaking intellectuals fled to Italy, bringing their books and their knowledge with them.

Thanks to these developments, some Italian intellectuals not only had increased access to more classical texts, they also used these texts in new ways. For centuries, Christian scholars had worked to bring ancient writings and values into line with their own beliefs (see Chapter 6). By contrast, the new reading methods pioneered by Petrarch and others fostered an increased awareness of the conceptual gap that separated the contemporary world from that of antiquity. This awakened a determination to recapture truly ancient worldviews and value systems, and it would eventually be expressed in visual terms, too. In the second half of the fifteenth century, especially, classical models contributed strikingly to the distinctive artistic style that is most strongly associated with the Renaissance (something we will address in Chapter 12).

Another distinguishing feature of this new perspective on the classical past was the way that it became overtly materialistic and commercialized. The competition among and within Italian city-states fostered a culture of display that used the symbols and artifacts of ancient Rome as pawns in an endless power game. Meanwhile, the relative weakness of the Church contributed to the growth of claims to power based on classical models—even by Italian bishops and Church-sponsored universities. When the papacy was eventually restored to Rome, it too had to compete in this Renaissance arena, by patronizing the artists and intellectuals who espoused these aesthetic and political ideals.

Renaissance Humanism

The most basic feature of this new intellectual and political agenda is summarized in the term *humanism*. This was a program of study that aimed to replace the scholastic emphasis on logic and theology—which would continue to be central to the curriculum of medieval universities like Paris and Oxford—with the study of ancient literature, rhetoric, history, and ethics. That is, the goal of a humanist education was the understanding of the human experience as viewed through the lenses of the classical past, and devoted to the fulfillment of human potential in the present. By contrast, a scholastic education filtered human experience through the teachings of scripture and the Church fathers, with human salvation as the ultimate goal.

Moreover, some intellectuals like Petrarch believed that the university curriculum concentrated too much on abstract speculation, rather than the achievement of virtue and ethical conduct in the here-and-now. He felt that the true Christian thinker must cultivate literary eloquence and so inspire others to do good through the pursuit of beauty and truth. And according to him, the best models of eloquence were to be found in the classics of Latin literature, which were also filled with ethical wisdom. Petrarch dedicated himself, therefore, to rediscovering such texts and to writing his own poems and moral treatises in a Latin style modeled on classical authors.

Humanists accordingly preferred ancient writings to those of more recent authors, including their own contemporaries. And although some humanists wrote in Italian as well as Latin, most regarded vernacular literature as a lesser diversion suitable only for the uneducated; serious scholarship and praiseworthy poetry could be written only in Latin or Greek. Proper Latin, moreover, had to be the classical Latin of Cicero and Virgil (Chapter 5), not the evolving language common to universities, international diplomacy, the law, and the Church. Renaissance humanists therefore condemned the living Latin of their day as a barbarous departure from classical (and therefore "correct") standards of Latin style. And ironically, their determination to revive this older language actually killed the lively Latin that had continued to flourish in Europe. By insisting on outmoded standards of grammar, syntax, and diction, they turned Latin into a fossilized discourse that ceased to have any direct relevance to daily life. They thus contributed, unwittingly, to the ultimate triumph of the various European vernaculars they despised, as well as to the demise of Latin as a common medium of communication.

Because humanism was an educational program designed to produce virtuous citizens and able public officials, it largely excluded women because women were largely excluded from Italian political life. Here again there is a paradox: as more and more Italian city-states fell into the hands of autocratic rulers, the humanist educational curriculum lost its immediate connection to the republican ideals of ancient Rome. Nevertheless, humanists never lost their conviction that the study of the "humanities" (as the humanist curriculum came to be known) was the best way to produce political leaders.

Why Italy?

These new attitudes toward education and the ancient past were fostered in a northern Italy for historically specific reasons. After the Black Death, this region was the most densely populated part of Europe; other urban areas, notably northeastern France and Flanders, had been decimated by the Great Famine as well as the plague. This region also differed from the rest of urbanized Europe because aristocratic families customarily lived in cities rather than in rural castles and consequently became more fully involved in public affairs than their counterparts north of the Alps. Moreover, many town-dwelling aristocrats were engaged in banking or mercantile enterprises, while many rich mercantile families imitated the manners of the aristocracy. The Florentine ruling family, the Medici, originally made their fortune in banking and commerce and yet were able to assimilate into the nobility.

These developments help to explain the emergence of the humanist ideals described above. Newly wealthy families were not content to have their sons learn only the skills necessary to becoming successful businessmen; they sought teachers who would impart the knowledge and finesse that would enable them to cut a figure in society, mix with their noble neighbors, and speak with authority on public affairs. Consequently, Italy produced and attracted a large number of independent intellectuals who were not affiliated with monasteries, cathedral schools, or universities—many of whom served as schoolmasters for wealthy young men while acting as cultural consultants and secretaries for their families. These intellectuals advertised their learning by producing political and ethical treatises and works of literature that would attract the attention of wealthy patrons or reflect well on the patrons they already had. As a result, Italian schools and private tutors turned out the best-educated laymen in all of Europe, men who constituted a new generation of wealthy, knowledgeable patrons ready to invest in the cultivation of new ideas and new forms of literary and artistic expression.

A second reason why late-medieval Italy was the birthplace of the Renaissance movement has to do with its vexed political situation. Unlike France and England, or the kingdoms of Spain, Scandinavia, and eastern Europe, Italy had no unifying political institutions. Italians therefore looked to the classical past for their time of glory, dreaming of a day when Rome would be, again, the center of the world. They boasted that ancient Roman monuments were omnipresent in their landscape and that classical Latin literature referred to cities and sites they recognized as their own.

Italians were particularly intent on reappropriating their classical heritage because they were seeking to establish an independent cultural identity that could help them oppose the intellectual and political supremacy of France. The removal of the papacy to Avignon had heightened antagonism between the city-states of Italy and the burgeoning nation-state beyond the Alps. This also explains the Italians' rejection of the scholasticism taught in northern Europe's universities and their embrace of intellectual alternatives. As Roman literature and learning took hold in the imaginations of Italy's intellectuals, so too did Roman art and architecture, for Roman models could help Italians create an artistic alternative to the dominant French school of Gothic architecture, just as Roman learning offered an intellectual alternative to the scholasticism of Paris.

Finally, this Italian Renaissance could not have occurred without the underpinning of Italian wealth gained through the commercial ventures described in Chapter 10. This wealth meant that talented men seeking employment and patronage were more likely to stay at home, fueling the artistic and intellectual competition that arose from the intensification of urban pride and the concentration of individual and family wealth in urban areas. Cities themselves became the primary patrons of art and learning in the fourteenth century.

The Renaissance of Civic Ideals

Petrarch's personal goal was a solitary life of contemplation and asceticism. But subsequent Italian intellectuals, especially those of Florence, developed a different vision of life's true purpose. For them, the goal of classical education was civic enrichment. Humanists such as Leonardo Bruni (c. 1370–1444) and Leon Battista Alberti (1404–1472) agreed with Petrarch on the importance of eloquence and the value of classical literature, but they also taught that man's nature equips him for action, for usefulness to his family and society, and for serving the state—ideally a city-state after the Florentine model. In their view, ambition and the quest for glory are noble impulses that ought to be encouraged and channeled toward these ends. They also refused to condemn the accumulation of material possessions, arguing that the history of human progress is inseparable from the human dominion of the earth and its resources.

Many of the humanists' civic ideals are expressed in Alberti's treatise *On the Family* (1443), in which the nuclear family is presented as the fundamental unit of the city-state and, as such, to be governed in such a way as to further the city-state's political and economic goals. Alberti accordingly argued that the family should mirror the city-state's organization. He therefore consigned women—who, in reality, governed the household—to childbearing, child rearing, and subservience to men even within this domestic realm. He asserted, furthermore, that women should play no role whatsoever in the public sphere. Although such dismissals of women's abilities were fiercely resisted by actual women, the humanism of the Renaissance was characterized by a pervasive denigration of them—a

Analyzing Primary Sources

A Renaissance Attitude toward Women

Italian society in the fourteenth and fifteenth centuries was characterized by marriage patterns in which men in their late twenties or thirties customarily married women in their mid- to late teens. This demographic fact probably contributed to the widely shared belief that wives were essentially children, who could not be trusted with important matters and who were best trained by being beaten. Renaissance humanism did little to change such attitudes. In some cases, it even reinforced them.

 fter my wife had been settled in my house a few days, and after her first pangs of longing for her mother and family had begun to fade, I took her by the hand and showed her around the whole house. I explained that the loft was the place for grain and that the stores of wine and wood were kept in the cellar. I showed her where things needed for the table were kept, and so on, through the whole house. At the end there were no household goods of which my wife had not learned both the place and the purpose....

Only my books and records and those of my ancestors did I determine to keep well sealed.... These my wife not only could not read, she could not even lay hands on them. I kept my records at all times . . . locked up and arranged in order in my study, almost like sacred and religious objects. I never gave my wife permission to enter that place, with me or alone....

[Husbands] who take counsel with their wives . . . are madmen if they think true prudence or good counsel lies in the female brain.... For this very reason I have always tried carefully not to let any secret of mine be known to a woman. I did not doubt that my wife was most loving, and more discreet and modest in her ways than any, but I still considered it safer to have her unable, and not merely unwilling, to harm me.... Furthermore, I made it a rule never to speak with her of anything but household matters or questions of conduct, or of the children.

Source: Leon Battista Alberti, "On the Family," in *The Family in Renaissance Florence*, ed. and trans. Renée N. Watkins (Columbia, SC: 1969), pp. 208–13, as abridged in Julie O'Faolain and Lauro Martines, eds., *Not in God's Image: Women in History from the Greeks to the Victorians* (New York: 1973), pp. 187–88.

Questions for Analysis

1. For what reasons did Alberti argue that a wife should have no access to books or records?

2. Would you have expected humanism to make attitudes to women more liberal and "modern"? How do views like Alberti's challenge such assumptions?

3. Compare Alberti's view of women to that of Christine de Pisan (page 364). How do you think Christine would have responded to this passage?

---

denigration often mirrored in the works of classical literature that these humanists so much admired.

The Emergence of Textual Criticism

The humanists of Florence eventually surpassed Petrarch in their knowledge of classical literature and philosophy, especially that of ancient Greece. In this, they were aided by a number of Byzantine scholars who had migrated to Italy in the first half of the fifteenth century and who gave instruction in the ancient form of their own native language. Wealthy, well-connected Florentines increasingly aspired to acquire Greek masterpieces for themselves, which often involved journeys back to Constantinople. In 1423, one adventurous bibliophile managed to bring back 238 manuscript books, among them rare works of Sophocles, Euripides, and Thucydides. These were quickly paraphrased in Latin and thus made accessible to western Europeans for the first time.

This influx of new classical texts spurred a new interest in textual criticism. A pioneer in this activity was Lorenzo Valla (1407–1457). Born in Rome and active primarily as a secretary to the king of Naples and Sicily, Valla had no allegiance to the republican ideals of the Florentine humanists. Instead, he turned his skills to the painstaking analysis of Greek and Latin writings in order to show how the historical study of language could discredit old assumptions and even unmask some texts as forgeries. For example, some papal propagandists argued that the papacy's claim to secular power in Europe derived from rights granted to the bishop of Rome by the emperor Constantine in the fourth century, enshrined in a document known as "The Donation of Constantine." By analyzing the language of this spurious text, Valla proved that it could not have been written in the time of Constantine because it contained more recent Latin usages and vocabulary.

This demonstration not only discredited more traditional scholarly methods, it made the concept of anachronism central to all subsequent textual study and historical thought. Indeed, Valla even applied his expert knowledge of Greek to elucidating the meaning of Saint Paul's letters, which he believed had been obscured by Jerome's Latin translation (see Chapter 6). This work was to prove an important link between Italian Renaissance scholarship and the subsequent Christian humanism of the north, which in turn fed into the Reformation (see Chapter 13).

THE END OF THE EASTERN ROMAN EMPIRE

The Greek-speaking refugees who arrived in Italy after the Black Death were self-appointed exiles. They were responding to the succession of calamities that had reduced the once-proud eastern Roman Empire to a scattering of embattled provinces. As we've noted, when Constantinople fell to western crusaders in 1204, the surrounding territories of Byzantium were severed from the capital that had held them together as constituent parts of that empire (see Chapter 9). When the Latin presence in Constantinople was finally expelled in 1261, imperial power had been so weakened that it extended only into the immediate hinterlands of the city and to parts of the Greek Peloponnese. The rest of the empire had become a collection of small principalities that existed in precarious alliance with the Mongols and indeed depended on the Pax Mongolica for survival (see Chapter 10). Then, with the coming of the Black Death, the imperial capital suffered the loss of half of its inhabitants and

shrunk still further. Meanwhile, the disintegration of the Mongol Empire laid the larger region of Anatolia open to a new set of invaders.

The Rise of the Ottoman Turks

Like the Mongols, the Turks were originally a nomadic people whose economy depended on raiding. When the Mongols arrived in northwestern Anatolia, the Turks were already established there and were being converted to Islam by the resident Muslim powers of the region: the Seljuq Sultanate of Rûm and the Abbasid Caliphate of Baghdad. But when the Mongols toppled these older powers, they eliminated the two traditional authorities that had kept Turkish border chieftains in check. Now they were free to raid, unhindered, along the soft frontiers of Byzantium. At the same time, they remained far enough from the centers of Mongol authority to avoid being destroyed themselves. One of their chieftains, Osman Gazi (1258–1326), established his own independent kingdom. Eventually, his name would characterize the Turkish dynasty that controlled the most ancient lands of Western civilizations for six centuries: the Ottomans.

By the mid-fourteenth century, Osman's successors had solidified their preeminence by capturing a number of important cities. These successes brought the Ottomans to the attention of the Byzantine emperor, who hired a contingent of them as mercenaries in 1345. They were extraordinarily successful—so much so that the eastern Roman Empire could not control their movements. They struck out on their own and began to extend their control westward. By 1370, their holdings stretched all the way to the Danube. In 1389, they defeated a powerful coalition of Serbian forces at the battle of Kosovo, which enabled them to begin subduing Bulgaria, the Balkans, and eventually Greece. In 1396, the Ottoman army even attacked Constantinople itself, although it withdrew to repel an ineffectual crusading force that had been hastily sent by the papacy.

In 1402, another attack on Constantinople was deflected—this time, by a more potent foe who had ambitions to match those of the Ottomans. Timur the Lame (Tamerlane, as he was called by European admirers) was born to a family of small landholders in the Mongol Khanate of Chagatai (named for its first ruler, the second son of Genghis Khan). Although Timur may have been a Turk himself, he acted as the spiritual heir of the Mongol Empire. While still a young man, he rose to prominence as a military leader and gained a reputation for tactical genius. He was no politician, though, and never officially assumed the title of khan in any of the territories he dominated. Instead, he moved ceaselessly from conquest to conquest, becoming the master of lands stretching

THE HEAD OF TIMUR THE LAME. This bust of the Mongol leader known in the West as Tamerlane is based on a forensic reconstruction of his exhumed skull.

from the Caspian Sea to the Volga River, as well as most of Persia. For a time, it looked briefly as if the Mongol Empire might be reunited under his reign. But Timur died in 1405, on his way to invade China, and his various conquests fell into the hands of local rulers. Mongol influence continued in the Mughal Empire of India, whose rulers claimed descent from the followers of Genghis Khan. But in Anatolia, the Ottoman Turks were once again on the rise.

The Fall of Constantinople

After the death of Timur, Ottoman pressure on Constantinople resumed and escalated. During the 1420s and 1430s, monasteries and schools that had been established since the fourth century found themselves in the path of an advancing army, and a steady stream of fleeing scholars strove to salvage a millennium's worth of Byzantine books—many of them preserving the heritage of ancient Greece and the Hellenistic

world. Then, in 1451, the Ottoman sultan Mehmet II turned his full attention to the conquest of the imperial city. In 1453, after a brilliantly executed siege, his army succeeded in breaching its walls. The Byzantine emperor was killed in the assault, the city itself was plundered, and its remaining population was sold into slavery. The Ottomans then settled down to rule their new capital in a style reminiscent of their Byzantine predecessors.

The Ottoman conquest of Constantinople administered an enormous shock to European rulers and intellectuals—and, indeed, the latter would profit mightily from this event. Yet its actual political and economic impact was minor. Ottoman control may have reduced European access to the Black Sea, but the bulk of the Far Eastern luxury trade with Europe had never passed through Black Sea ports in the first place. Europeans got most of their spices and silks through Venice, which imported them from Alexandria and Beirut, and these two cities did not fall to the Ottomans until the 1520s. Moreover, as we saw in Chapter 10, Europeans already had colonial ambitions and significant trading interests in Africa and the Atlantic that connected them to far-reaching networks.

But if the practical effects of the Ottoman conquest were modest where western Europe was concerned, the effects on the Turks themselves were transformative. Vast new wealth poured into Anatolia, which the Ottomans increased by carefully tending to the industrial and commercial interests of their new capital city, Constantinople, which they also called Istanbul—the Turkish pronunciation of the Greek phrase *eis tan polin* "in (or to) the city." Trade routes were redirected to feed the capital, and the Ottomans became a naval power in the eastern Mediterranean as well as in the Black Sea. As a result, Constantinople's population grew rapidly, from fewer than 100,000 in 1453 to more than 500,000. By 1600, it was the largest city in the world outside of China.

Slavery and Social Advancement in the Ottoman Empire

Despite the Ottomans' careful attention to commerce, their empire continued to rest on the spoils of conquest. To manage its continual expansion, the size of the Ottoman army and administration grew exponentially, drawing more and more manpower from conquered territories. And because both army and bureaucracy were largely composed of slaves, the demand for more soldiers and administrators could best be met through further conquests that would capture yet more slaves. Those conquests, however, required a still larger army and an even more extensive bureaucracy—and so the cycle continued. It mirrors, in many respects, the

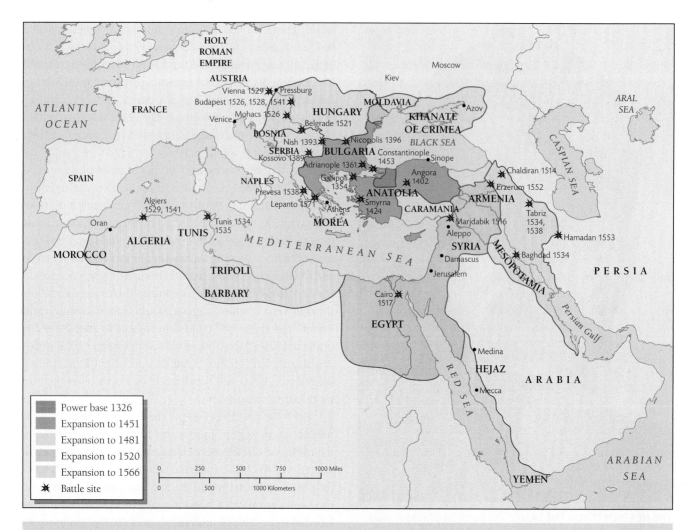

THE GROWTH OF THE OTTOMAN EMPIRE. Consider the patterns of Ottoman expansion revealed in this map. ▪ *Where is Constantinople, and how might the capture of Constantinople in 1453 have facilitated further conquests?* ▪ *Compare the extent of the Ottoman Empire in 1566 with that of the Byzantine Empire under Justinian (see the map on page 212). How would you account for their similarities?*

dilemma of the Roman Empire in the centuries of its rapid expansion beyond Italy (see Chapter 5), which created an insatiable demand for slaves.

Not only were slaves the backbone of Ottoman government, they were also critical to the lives of the Turkish upper class. One of the important measures of status in Ottoman society was the number of slaves in one's household. After the capture of Constantinople, new wealth would permit some elites to maintain households in the thousands. By the sixteenth century, the sultan alone possessed more than 20,000 slave attendants, not including his bodyguard and elite infantry units, both of which also comprised slaves.

Where did all of these slaves come from? Many were captured in war. Many others were taken on raiding forays into Poland and Ukraine and sold to Crimean slave merchants, who shipped their captives to the slave markets of Constantinople. But slaves were also recruited (some willingly, some by coercion) from rural areas of the Otto-

man Empire itself. Because the vast majority of slaves were household servants and administrators rather than laborers, some men willingly accepted enslavement, believing that they would be better off as slaves in Constantinople than as impoverished peasants in the countryside. In the Balkans especially, many people were enslaved as children, handed over by their families to pay the "child tax" the Ottomans imposed on rural areas too poor to pay a monetary tribute. Although an excruciating experience for families, this practice did open up opportunities for social advancement. Special academies were created at Constantinople to train the most able of the enslaved male children to act as administrators and soldiers, some of whom rose to become powerful figures in the Ottoman Empire.

For this reason, slavery carried relatively little social stigma. Even the sultan himself was most often the son of an enslaved woman. And because Muslims were not permitted to enslave other Muslims, the vast majority of Ottoman

SULTAN MEHMET II, "THE CONQUEROR" (r. 1451–81).
This portrait, executed by the Ottoman artist Siblizade Ahmed, exhibits features characteristic of both Central Asia and Europe. The sultan's pose—his aesthetic appreciation of the rose, his elegant handkerchief—are indicative of the former, as is the fact that he wears the white turban of a scholar and the thumb ring of an archer. But the subdued coloring and three-quarter profile may reflect the influence of Italian portraits. ▪ *What did the artist achieve through this blending of styles and symbols?* ▪ *What messages does this portrait convey?*

slaves were Christian—although many eventually converted to Islam. And because so many of the elite positions within Ottoman government were held by these slaves, the paradoxical result was that Muslims, including the Turks themselves, were effectively excluded from the main avenues of social and political influence in the Ottoman Empire. Avenues to power were therefore remarkably open to men of ability and talent, most of them non-Muslim slaves.

Nor was this power limited to the government and the army. Commerce and business also remained largely in the hands of non-Muslims, most frequently Greeks, Syrians, and Jews. Jews in particular found in the Ottoman Empire a welcome refuge from the persecutions and expulsions that had characterized Jewish life in late-medieval Europe. After their expulsion from Spain in 1492 (see Chapter 12), more than 100,000 Spanish (Sephardic) Jews ultimately immigrated to the territories of the Ottoman Empire.

Because the Ottoman sultans were Sunni Muslims, they often dealt harshly with other Muslim sects. But they were extremely tolerant of non-Muslims. They organized the major religious groups of their empire into legally recognized units and permitted them considerable rights of self-government. They were especially careful to protect and promote the authority of the Greek Orthodox patriarch of Constantinople over the Orthodox Christians of their empire. As a result, the Ottomans enjoyed staunch support from their Orthodox Christian subjects during their wars with the Christians of western Europe.

Russia: "The Third Rome"

The Orthodox Church also received staunch support from the Russian people, whose own Church had been founded by Byzantine missionaries in the tenth century (see Chapter 8) and whose written language was based on the Greek alphabet and Greek grammar. Indeed, the emerging duchy of Muscovy (see Chapter 10) saw itself as the natural protector and ally of the eastern Roman Empire, and its alienation from western Europe increased as Byzantium grew weaker and the responsibility for defending Orthodox Christianity devolved onto the Russian Church.

But when the patriarch of Constantinople agreed to submit to the authority of Rome in 1438, in the desperate hope that the papacy would rally military support for the besieged city, Russian clergy refused to follow suit. After Constantinople fell to the Turks—predictably, without any help from Latin Christendom—the Russian Church emerged as the only surviving proponent of Orthodox Christianity.

Its sense of isolation was increased by developments on its western borders. In the thirteenth century, the small kingdom of Poland had struggled to defend itself from absorption by German princes. But when the Holy Roman Empire's strength waned after the death of Frederick the Great (see Chapter 9), Poland's situation grew more secure. In 1386, its reigning queen, Jadwiga, subsequently enabled its dramatic expansion when she married Jagiello, the duke of neighboring Lithuania, thus doubling the size of her kingdom. Lithuania had begun to carve out an extensive territory stretching from the Baltic to modern-day Belarus and Ukraine, and this expansionist momentum increased after its union with Poland. In 1410, a combined Polish and Lithuanian force defeated the Teutonic Knights at the Battle of Tannenberg, crushing the military order that controlled a crucial region lying between the allied kingdoms. Thereafter, Poland-Lithuania began to push eastward toward Muscovy.

Although many of Lithuania's aristocratic families were Orthodox Christians, the established church in Poland was loyal to Rome. Thus, when the inhabitants of Muscovy started to feel threatened by Poland-Lithuania, one way of constructing a shared Muscovite identity was to direct hostility toward Latin Christendom. Another was to take up the imperial mantle that had been abandoned when Constantinople fell, and to declare the Muscovite state the divinely appointed successor to Rome. To drive the point home, Muscovite dukes began to take the title of tsar, "caesar." "Two Romes have fallen," said a Muscovite chronicler, "the third is still standing, and a fourth there shall not be."

WARFARE AND NATION BUILDING IN EUROPE

War has always been an engine for the development of new technologies. This is something we have noted since Chapter 1, but in the era after the Black Death the pace and scale of warfare was escalated to an unprecedented degree—and so was the deployment of new weapons. Although explosives had been invented in China, and originally used in displays of fireworks, they were first put to devastating and destructive effect in Europe. In fact, the earliest cannons were as dangerous to those who fired them as to those who were targeted. But by the middle of the fifteenth century, they were reliable enough to revolutionize the nature of warfare. In 1453, heavy artillery played a leading role in the outcomes of two crucial conflicts: the Ottoman Turks breached the ancient defenses of Constantinople with cannon fire and the French captured the English-held city of Bordeaux, bringing an end to the attenuated conflict known as the Hundred Years' War.

Thereafter, cannons made it more difficult for rebellious aristocrats to hole up in their stone castles and so consequently aided in the consolidation of national monarchies. Cannons placed aboard ships made Europe's developing navies more effective. A handheld firearm, the pistol, was also invented in the fourteenth century, and around 1500 the musket ended forever the military dominance of heavily armored cavalry, giving the advantage to foot soldiers recruited from the ranks of average citizens.

This suggests that there is a symbiotic relationship between warfare and nation building as well as between warfare and technology. Because Europeans were almost constantly at war from the fourteenth century to the middle of the twentieth, governments claimed new powers to tax their subjects and to control their subjects' lives. Armies became larger, military technology deadlier. Wars became more destructive, society more militarized. As a result of these developments, the most successful European states were aggressively expansionist and aggressively engaged in creating an idea of national identity that would bind people together against a common enemy.

The Hundred Years' War Resumes

The hostilities that make up the Hundred Years' War can be divided into three main phases (see the maps on page 000). The first phase dates from the initial declaration of war in 1337 (see Chapter 10), after which the English won a series of startling military victories before the Black Death put a temporary halt to the hostilities. The war then resumed in 1356, with another English victory at Poitiers. Four years later, in 1360, Edward III decided to leverage his strong position: he renounced his larger claim to the French throne, and in return he was to be guaranteed full sovereignty over a greatly enlarged duchy of Gascony and the promise of a huge ransom for the king of France, whom he held captive.

But the terms of the treaty were never honored, nor did it resolve the underlying issues that had led to the war itself, namely the problem of making good on any claim to sovereignty in contested territory and the question of the English king's place in the French royal succession. The French king continued to treat the English king as his vassal, while Edward and his heirs quickly renewed their claim to the throne of France.

Although there were no pitched battles in France itself for two decades after this, a destabilizing proxy war developed during the 1360s and 1370s, which spread violence to neighboring regions. Both the English troops (posted in Gascony) and the French troops (eager to avenge their losses) were reluctant to settle down. Many organized into "Free Companies" of mercenaries and hired themselves out in the service of hostile factions in Castile and competing city-states in northern Italy. By 1376, when the conflict between England and France was reignited, the Hundred Years' War had become a Europe-wide phenomenon.

England's Disputed Throne and the Brief Victory of Henry V

In this second phase of the war, the tide quickly shifted in favor of France. The new king, Charles V (r. 1364–80), imposed a series of taxes to fund the raising of an army,

A FIFTEENTH-CENTURY SIEGE WITH CANNONS. Cannons were an essential element in siege warfare during the Hundred Years' War.

restored order by disbanding the Free Companies, and hired the leader of one of these bands as the commander of his army. He thereby created a professional military that could match the English in discipline and tactics. By 1380, English territories in France had been reduced to a core area around the southwestern city of Bordeaux and the port of Calais in the extreme northeast.

Meanwhile, the aging Edward III has been succeeded by his nine-year-old grandson, Richard II (r. 1377–99), who was too young to prosecute a claim to the French crown. This was problematic, because the war had been extremely popular in England. Indeed, its mismanagement by Richard's advisers was one of the issues that triggered the Peasants' Revolt in 1381. And when Richard came of age and showed no signs of martial ambition, many of his own aristocratic relatives turned against him. Richard retaliated against the ringleader of this faction, his cousin Henry of Lancaster, by sending him into exile and confiscating his property. Henry's supporters used this as pretext for rebellion. In 1399, Richard was deposed by Henry and eventually murdered.

As a usurper whose legitimacy was always in doubt, Henry IV (r. 1399–1413) struggled to maintain his authority in the face of retaliatory rebellions and other challenges to his kingship. The best way to unite the country would have been to renew the war against France, but Henry was

frequently ill and in no position to lead an army into combat. But when his son Henry V succeeded him in 1413, the new king immediately began to prepare for an invasion. His timing was excellent: the French royal government was foundering owing to the insanity of the reigning king, Charles VI (r. 1380–1422). A brilliant diplomat as well as a capable soldier, Henry V sealed an alliance with the powerful Duke of Burgundy, who was allegedly loyal to France but stood to gain from its defeat at the hands of the English. Henry also made a treaty with the German emperor, who agreed not to come to France's aid.

When he crossed the Channel in the autumn of 1415, Henry V's troops thus faced a much-depleted French army that could not rely on reinforcements. Although it was still vastly larger and boasted hundreds of mounted knights, it was undisciplined. It was also severely hampered by bad weather and deep mud when the two armies clashed at Agincourt on October 25 of that year—conditions that favored the lighter English infantry. Henry's men managed to win a crushing victory.

Then, over the next five years, Henry conquered most of northern France. In 1420, the ailing Charles VI was forced to recognize him as heir to the throne of France, thereby disinheriting his own son. (This prince bore the ceremonial title of *dauphin*, "the dolphin," from the heraldic device of the borderland province he inherited.) Henry sealed the deal by marrying the French princess, Catherine, and fathering an heir to the joint kingdom of England and France.

Joan of Arc's Betrayal and Legacy

Unlike his great-grandfather Edward III, who used his claim to the French throne largely as a bargaining chip to secure sovereignty over Gascony (see Chapter 10), Henry V honestly believed himself to be the rightful king of France. And his astonishing success in capturing the kingdom seemed to put the stamp of divine approval on that claim. But Henry's successes in France also transformed the nature of the war, turning it from a profitable war of conquest and plunder into an extended and expensive military occupation. It might have been sustainable had Henry been as long-lived as many of his predecessors. But he died early in 1422, just short of his thirty-sixth birthday. King Charles VI died only a few months later.

The new king of England and France, Henry VI (r. 1422–61), was only an infant, and yet the English armies under the command of his regents continued to press southward into territories held by the dauphin. Although it seemed unlikely that English forces would ever succeed

JOAN OF ARC. A contemporary sketch of Joan was drawn in the margin of this register documenting official proceedings at the Parlement of Paris in 1429.

in dislodging him, confidence in the dauphin's right to the throne had been shattered by his own mother's declaration that he was illegitimate. It might have happened that England would once again rule an empire comprising much of northern France, as it had for a century and a half after the Norman conquest.

But this scenario fails to reckon with Joan of Arc. In 1429, a peasant girl from Lorraine (a territory only nominally part of France) made her way to the dauphin's court and announced that an angel had told her that he, Charles, was the rightful king, and that she, Joan, should drive the English out of France. The fact that she even got a hearing underscores the hopelessness of the dauphin's position, as does the extraordinary fact that he gave her a contingent of troops. With this force, Joan liberated the strategic city of Orléans, then under siege by the English, after which a series of victories culminated in Charles's coronation in the cathedral of Reims, the traditional site for the crowning of French kings.

But, despite her miraculous success, Joan was an embarrassment whose very charisma made her dangerous: a peasant leading aristocrats, a woman leading men, and a commoner who claimed to have been commissioned by God. When, a few months later, the Burgundians captured her in battle and handed her over to the English, the king she had helped to crown did nothing to save her. Accused of witchcraft, condemned by the theologians of Paris, and tried for heresy by an English ecclesiastical court, Joan was burned to death in the market square at Rouen in 1431. She was nineteen years old.

The French forces whom Joan had inspired, however, continued on the offensive. In 1435, the duke of Burgundy withdrew from his alliance with England, and when the young English king, Henry VI, proved first incompetent and then insane, a series of French military victories brought hostilities to an end with the capture of Bordeaux in 1453. English kings would threaten to renew the war for another century, and Anglo-French hostility would last until the defeat of Napoleon in 1815. But after 1453, English control over French territory would be limited to the port of Calais, which eventually fell in 1558.

The Long Shadow of the Hundred Years' War

The Hundred Years' War challenged the very existence of France. The disintegration of that kingdom, first during the 1350s and 1360s, and again between 1415 and 1435, glaringly revealed the fragility of the bonds that tied the king to the nobility, and the royal capital Paris to the kingdom's

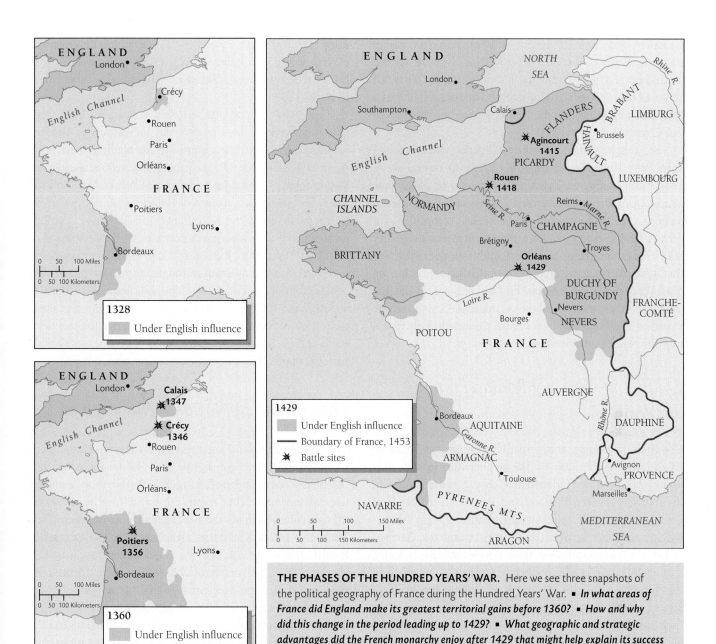

THE PHASES OF THE HUNDRED YEARS' WAR. Here we see three snapshots of the political geography of France during the Hundred Years' War. ■ *In what areas of France did England make its greatest territorial gains before 1360?* ■ *How and why did this change in the period leading up to 1429?* ■ *What geographic and strategic advantages did the French monarchy enjoy after 1429 that might help explain its success in recapturing the French kingdom from the English?*

outlying regions. Nonetheless, the king's power was actually increased by the war's end, laying the foundations on which the power of early modern France would be built.

The Hundred Years' War also had dramatic effects on the English monarchy. When English armies in France were successful, the king rode a wave of popularity that fueled an emerging sense of English identity. When the war turned against the English, however, defeats abroad undermined support for the monarch at home. Of the nine English kings who ruled England between 1307 and 1485, five were deposed and murdered by factions.

This was a consequence of England's peculiar form of kingship, whose strength depended on the king's ability to

mobilize popular support through Parliament while maintaining the support of his nobility through successful wars. Failure to maintain this balance was even more destabilizing in England than it would have been elsewhere, precisely because royal power was so centralized. In France, the nobility could endure the insanity of Charles VI because his government was not powerful enough to threaten them. In England, neither the nobility nor the nation could afford the weak kingship of Henry VI. The result was an aristocratic rebellion against the king that led to a full-blown civil war: the Wars of the Roses, so called—by the novelist Sir Walter Scott (1771–1832)—because of the floral emblems, red and white, adopted by the two competing noble families

Lancaster and York. It ended only when a Lancastrian claimant, Henry Tudor (r. 1485–1509), resolved the dynastic feud by marrying Elizabeth of York, ruling as Henry VII and establishing a new Tudor dynasty whose symbol was a rose with both white and red petals. His son was Henry VIII (see Chapter 13).

So, despite England's ultimate defeat, the Hundred Years' War strengthened English identity in several ways. First, it equated national identity with the power of the state and its king. Second, it fomented a strong anti-French sentiment that led to the triumph of the English vernacular over French for the first time since the Norman conquest over 300 years earlier: the first English court to speak English was that of Richard II, a patron of Geoffrey Chaucer. And having lost its continental possessions, England became, for the first time, a self-contained island nation that looked to the sea for defense and opportunity—not to the Continent. This would later prove to be an advantage in many ways.

Conflict in the Holy Roman Empire and Italy

Elsewhere in Europe, the perpetual warfare that began to characterize the history of Western civilizations in this period was even more destructive than it proved to be in the struggle between England and France. In the lands of the Holy Roman Empire, armed conflict among territorial princes, and between these princes and the German emperor, weakened all combatants significantly. Periodically, a powerful emperor would emerge to play a major role, but the dominant trend was toward the continuing dissolution of power, with German princes dividing their territories among their heirs while free cities and local lords strove to shake off the princes' rule. Between 1350 and 1450, near anarchy prevailed in many regions. Only in the eastern regions of the empire were the rulers of Bavaria, Austria, and Brandenburg-Prussia able to strengthen their authority, mostly by supporting the efforts of the nobility to subject their peasants to serfdom and by conquering and colonizing new territories on their eastern frontiers.

In northern and central Italy, the last half of the fourteenth century was also marked by incessant conflict. With the papacy based in Avignon, the Papal States collapsed and Rome itself was riven by factional violence. Warfare among northern city-states added to the violence caused by urban rebellions in the wake of the plague. But around 1400, Venice, Milan, and Florence had succeeded in stabilizing their differing forms of government. Venice was now ruled by an oligarchy of merchants; Milan by a family of despots; and Florence was ruled as a republic but dominated by the influence of

a few wealthy clans, especially the Medici banking family. Having settled their internal problems, these three cities then began to expand their influence by subordinating other cities to their rule.

Eventually, almost all the towns of northern Italy were allied with one of these powers. An exception was Genoa, which had its own trading empire in the Mediterranean and Atlantic (see Chapter 10). The papacy, meanwhile, reasserted its control over central Italy when it was restored to Rome in 1377. The southern kingdom of Naples and Sicily persisted as a separate entity but a constantly unstable one, riven by local warfare and poor government. After 1453, when the Hundred Years' War had ended and Ottoman expansion had been checked at Constantinople, an uneasy peace was achieved in Italy. But diplomacy and frequently shifting alliances did little to check the ambitions of any one state for further expansion, and it could not change the fact that none of these small-scale states could oppose the powerful national monarchies or empires that surrounded Italy.

The Growth of National Monarchies

In France and England, then, as well as in smaller kingdoms like Scotland and Portugal, the later Middle Ages saw the emergence of European states more cohesive than any that had existed before. (In Chapter 12, we will see how powerful this cohesion made the new united kingdom of Spain.) The basic political patterns established in the formative twelfth and thirteenth centuries had made this possible, yet the active construction of a sense of national identity in these territories, and the fusion of that identity with kingship, were new phenomena. Forged by war and fueled by the growing cultural importance of vernacular languages, this fusion produced a new type of political organization: the national monarchy.

The advantages of these national monarchies when compared to older forms of political organization—such as the empire, the principality, or the city-state—would become very evident. When the armies of France or Spain invaded the Italian peninsula at the end of the fifteenth century, neither the militias of the city-states nor the far-flung resources of Venice were a match for them. Germany and the Low Countries would suffer similar invasions only a few generations later and, along with Italy, would remain battlegrounds for competing armies until the middle of the nineteenth century. But the new national monarchies brought significant disadvantages, too. They guaranteed the prevalence of warfare in Europe as they continued their struggle for sovereignty and territory, and they would eventually transport their rivalry to every corner of the globe in the late nineteenth and early twentieth centuries.

Analyzing Primary Sources

The Condemnation of Joan of Arc by the University of Paris, 1431

After Joan's capture by the Burgundians, she was handed over to the English and tried for heresy at an ecclesiastical court set up in Rouen. It was on this occasion that the theology faculty of Paris pronounced the following verdict on her actions.

You, Joan, have said that, since the age of thirteen, you have experienced revelations and the appearance of angels, of St. Catherine and St. Margaret, and that you have very often seen them with your bodily eyes, and that they have spoken to you. As for the first point, the clerks of the University of Paris have considered the manner of the said revelations and appearances . . . Having considered all . . . they have declared that all the things mentioned above are lies, falsenesses, misleading and pernicious things and that such revelations are superstitions, proceeding from wicked and diabolical spirits.

Item: You have said that your king had a sign by which he knew that you were sent by God, for St. Michael, accompanied by several angels, some of which having wings, the others crowns, with St. Catherine and St. Margaret, came to you at the chateau of Chinon. All the company ascended through the floors of the castle until they came to the room of your king, before whom the angel bearing the crown bowed. . . .

As for this matter, the clerks say that it is not in the least probable, but it is rather a presumptuous lie, misleading and pernicious, a false statement, derogatory of the dignity of the Church and of the angels. . . .

Item: you have said that, at God's command, you have continually worn men's clothes, and that you have put on a short robe, doublet, shoes attached by points, also that you have had short hair, cut around above the ears, without retaining anything on your person which shows that you are a woman, and that several times you have received the body of Our Lord dressed in this fashion, despite having been admonished to give it up several times, the which you would not do. You have said that you would rather die than abandon the said clothing, if it were not at God's command, and that if you were wearing those clothes and were with the king, and those of your party, it would be one of the greatest benefits for the kingdom of France. You have also said that not for anything would you swear an oath not to wear the said clothing and carry arms any longer. And all these things you say you

have done for the good and at the command of God. As for these things, the clerics say that you blaspheme God and hold him in contempt in his sacraments; you transgress Divine Law, Holy Scripture, and canon law. You err in the faith. You boast in vanity. You are suspected of idolatry and you have condemned yourself in not wishing to wear clothing suitable to your sex, but you follow the custom of Gentiles and Saracens.

Source: Carolyne Larrington, ed. and trans., *Women and Writing in Medieval Europe* (New York: 1995), pp. 183–84.

Questions for Analysis

1. Paris was in the hands of the English when this condemnation was issued. Is there any evidence that its authors were coerced into making this pronouncement?

2. On what grounds was Joan condemned for heresy?

3. In what ways does Joan's behavior highlight larger trends in late medieval spirituality and popular piety?

THE TRIALS OF THE ROMAN CHURCH

Although the century after the Black Death would witness the papacy's return to Rome, it would also witness changes in the Church that would have far-reaching consequences in the centuries to come. Like other large landowners, the monasteries of Europe suffered from the economic changes brought about by the new world order, as did the Church's bishops, who confronted the same dilemmas as the secular nobility. But no ecclesiastical institution suffered more severe trials than the papacy, which endured almost seventy years of exile from Rome followed by a debilitating forty-year schism. It then faced a protracted battle with reformers who sought to reduce the pope's role in Church governance. Even though the papacy won this battle in the short term, the renewed abuse of papal power would, in the long run, bring about the permanent schism caused by the Reformation of the sixteenth century (see Chapter 13).

The Great Western Schism

In the decades that were transforming European society in so many other ways, calls for the papacy's return to Rome grew more insistent. It was eventually brought about by the letter-writing campaign of the nun and mystic Catherine of Siena (1347–1380), whose teasing but pious missives to Gregory XI (r. 1370–78) alternately shamed and coerced him. In 1377, he was persuaded to make the move.

But the papacy's restoration was short lived. A year after Gregory's return to Rome, he died. His cardinals—many of them Frenchmen—struggled to interpret the wishes of the volatile Romans, whose habit of expressing themselves through violence was unsettling to outsiders. Later, the cardinals would claim to have capitulated to the Roman mob when they elected an Italian candidate, Urban VI. When Urban fell out with them soon afterward, the cardinals fled the city and, from a safe distance, declared his selection invalid because it had been made under duress. They then elected a new pope, a Frenchman who took the name Clement VII. Urban retaliated by naming a new and entirely Italian College of Cardinals and by refusing Clement access to the city. The French pope and his cardinals withdrew ignominiously to the papal palace in Avignon, while the Italian pope remained in Rome.

The resulting rift is known as the Great Schism, or the Great Western Schism (to distinguish it from the Great East–West Schism between the Latin and Orthodox Churches). Between 1378 and 1417, the Roman Church was divided between two (and, ultimately, three) competing papacies, each claiming to be legitimate and each denouncing the heresy of the others.

Not surprisingly, Europe's religious allegiances fractured along the political lines drawn by the ongoing Hundred Years' War: France and her allies Scotland, Castile, Aragon, and Naples recognized the pope in Avignon; whereas England, Germany, northern Italy, Scandinavia, Bohemia, Poland, and Hungary recognized the Roman pope. Nor was there any obvious way to end this embarrassing state of affairs. The two rival Colleges of Cardinals continued to elect successors every time a pope died, perpetuating the problem. Finally, in 1409, some cardinals from both camps met at Pisa, where they ceremoniously declared the deposition of both popes and named a new one from among their number. But neither of the popes reigning in Rome and Avignon accepted that decision, so there were now three rival popes excommunicating one another instead of only two.

The Council of Constance and the Failure of the Conciliar Movement

This debacle was ultimately addressed between 1414 and 1418 at the Council of Constance, the largest and longest ecclesiastical gathering since the Council of Nicea, over a thousand years before (see Chapter 6). Its chief mission was to remove all rival claimants for papal office before agreeing on the election of a new pope: an Italian who took the name Martin V. But many of the council's delegates had even more far-reaching plans for the reform of the Church, ambitions that stemmed from the legal doctrine that gave the council power to depose and elect popes in the first place.

This doctrine, known as conciliarism, holds that supreme authority within the Church rests not with the pope but with a representative general council—and not just the council convened at Constance but any future council. The delegates at Constance thus decreed that general councils should meet regularly to oversee the governance of the Church, and to act as a check on the unbridled use of papal power.

Had conciliarism triumphed, the Reformation of the following century might not have occurred. But, predictably, Martin V and his successors did everything they could to undermine this doctrine, precisely because it limited their power. When the next general council met at Siena in 1423, Pope Martin duly sent representatives—who then turned around and went back to Rome. (The Council of Constance had specified that councils must meet frequently but had not specified how long those meetings should last.) The following year, the delegates to a general council at Basel took steps to ensure that the pope could not dismiss it, after which a lengthy struggle for power ensued between the advocates of papal monarchy and the conciliarists. Twenty-five years later, in 1449, the Council of Basel dissolved itself, bringing to an end a radical experiment in conciliar government—and dashing the hopes of those who thought it would lead to an internal reformation thorough enough to keep the Roman Church intact.

Spiritual Challenges

We have noted that the spiritual and social lives of medieval Christians were inextricably intertwined; indeed, any distinction between the two would have made little sense to

Past and Present

Replacing "Retired" Popes

When Benedict XVI decided to retire from papal office in February 2013, pundits and theologians alike struggled to find a precedent for this extraordinary decision. Most reached back to the year 1417, when Pope Martin V was elected at the Council of Constance (left) to replace the "retired" Gregory XII. But in this case, the retirement was not voluntary—and it was accompanied by the enforced resignation of an additional rival pope and the excommunication of yet another. The installation mass of Pope Francis in March 2013 (right) was much more universally celebrated and much more public than that of his medieval predecessor.

Watch related author interview on StudySpace
wwnorton.com/web/westernciv18

the people of this era. The parish church stood literally at the center of their lives. Churchyards were communal meeting places, sometimes even the sites of markets, and church buildings were a refuge from attack and a gathering place for parish business. The church's holidays marked the passage of the year, and the church's bells marked the hours of the day. The church was holy, but it was also essential to daily life.

Yet, in the wake of the Black Death, when many parishes ceased to exist and many communities were decimated, an increasing number of medieval Christians were not satisfied with these conventional practices and developed forms of piety that were distinctly controversial. Many are regarded today as saints, but this was not necessarily the case in their lifetimes. Indeed, the distinction between the superhuman powers of a saint and those of a witch could be difficult to discern. As Joan of Arc's predicament reveals, medieval women found it particularly challenging to find outlets for their piety that would not earn

them the condemnation of the Church. (Executed as heretic, Joan would be officially exonerated a generation later, but she would not be canonized as a saint until 1920, when belief in her intercession during World War I gained wide support and was considered a decisive factor in the victory of France and its allies.)

Many women therefore internalized their devotional practices or confined them to the domestic sphere—sometimes to the inconvenience of their families and communities. For example, the young Catherine of Siena (who later convinced the papacy to return to Rome) refused to help with the housework or to support her working-class family; instead, she took over one of the house's two rooms for her own private prayers, confining her parents and a dozen siblings to the remaining room. Julianne of Norwich (1342–1416) withdrew from the world into a small cell built next to her local church, where she spent the rest of her life in prayer and contemplation. Her

Council or Pope?

> The Great Schism spurred a fundamental and far-reaching debate about the nature of authority within the Church. Arguments for papal supremacy rested on traditional claims that the popes were the successors of Saint Peter, to whom Jesus Christ had delegated his own authority. Arguments for the supremacy of a general council had been advanced by many intellectuals throughout the fourteenth century, but it was only in the circumstances of the schism that these arguments found a wide audience. The following documents trace the history of the controversy, from the declaration of conciliar supremacy at the Council of Constance (Haec Sancta), to the council's efforts to guarantee regular meetings of general councils thereafter (Frequens), to the papal condemnation of appeals to the authority of general councils issued in 1460 (Execrabilis).

Haec Sancta Synodus (1415)

This holy synod of Constance . . . declares that being lawfully assembled in the Holy Spirit, constituting a general council and representing the Catholic Church Militant, it has its power directly from Christ, and that all persons of whatever rank or dignity, even a Pope, are bound to obey it in matters relating to faith and the end of the Schism and the general reformation of the church of God in head and members.

Further, it declares that any person of whatever position, rank, or dignity, even a Pope, who contumaciously refuses to obey the mandates, statutes, ordinances, or regulations enacted or to be enacted by this holy synod, or by any other general council lawfully assembled, relating to the matters aforesaid or to other matters involved with them, shall, unless he repents, be . . . duly punished. . . .

Source: R. L. Loomis, ed. and trans., *The Council of Constance* (New York: 1961), p. 229.

Frequens (1417)

The frequent holding of general councils is the best method of cultivating the field of the Lord, for they root out the briars, thorns, and thistles of heresies, errors, and schisms, correct abuses, make crooked things straight, and prepare the Lord's vineyard for fruitfulness and rich fertility. Neglect of general councils sows the seeds of these evils and encourages their growth. This truth is borne in upon us as we recall times past and survey the present.

Therefore by perpetual edict we . . . ordain that henceforth general councils shall be held as follows: the first within the five years immediately following the end of the present council, the second within seven years from the end of the council next after this, and subsequently

younger contemporary, the housewife Margery Kempe (c. 1372–c. 1439), resented the fact that she had a husband, several children, and a household to support, and thus could not take such a step. In later life, she renounced her wifely duties and devoted her life to performing acts of histrionic piety, which alienated many of those who came into contact with her. For example, she was so moved by the contemplation of Jesus's sufferings on the cross that she would cry hysterically for hours, disrupting the Mass. When on pilgrimage in Rome, she cried at the sight of babies that reminded her of the infant Jesus, or young men whom she thought resembled him.

The extraordinary piety of such individuals could be inspiring, but it could also threaten the Church's control over religious life and the links that bound individuals to their communities. It could, therefore, be dangerous. More safely orthodox was the practical mysticism preached by Thomas à Kempis, whose *Imitation of Christ* (c. 1427) taught readers how to appreciate aspects of the divine in their everyday lives. Originally written in Latin, *The Imitation* was quickly every ten years forever.... Thus there will always be a certain continuity. Either a council will be in session or one will be expected at the end of a fixed period. ...

Source: R. L. Loomis, ed. and trans., *The Council of Constance* (New York: 1961), pp. 246–47.

Execrabilis (1460)

An execrable abuse, unheard of in earlier times, has sprung up in our period. Some men, imbued with a spirit of rebellion and moved not by a desire for sound decisions but rather by a desire to escape the punishment for sin, suppose that they can appeal from the Pope, Vicar of Jesus Christ—from the Pope, to whom in the person of blessed Peter it was said, "Feed my sheep" and "whatever you bind on earth will be bound in heaven"—from this Pope to a future council. How harmful this is to the Christian republic, as well as how contrary to canon law, anyone who is not ignorant of the law can understand. For ... who would not consider it ridiculous to appeal to something which does not now exist anywhere nor does anyone know when it will exist? The poor are heavily oppressed by the powerful, offenses remain unpunished, rebellion against the Holy See is encouraged, license for sin is granted, and all ecclesiastical discipline and hierarchical ranking of the Church are turned upside down.

Wishing therefore to expel this deadly poison from the Church of Christ, and concerned with the salvation of the sheep committed to us ... with the counsel and assent of our venerable brothers, the Cardinals of the Holy Roman Church, together with the counsel and assent of all those prelates who have been trained in canon and civil law who follow our Court, and with our own certain knowledge, we condemn appeals of this kind, reject them as erroneous and abominable, and declare them to be completely null and void. And we lay down that from now on, no one should dare ... to make such an appeal from our decisions, be they legal or theological, or from any commands at all from us or our successors. ...

Source: Reprinted by permission of the publisher from Gabriel Biel, *Defensorium Obedientiae Apostolicae et Alia Documenta*, ed. and trans. Heiko A. Oberman, Daniel E. Zerfoss, and William J. Courtenay (Cambridge, MA: 1968), pp. 224–27. Copyright © 1968 by the President and Fellows of Harvard College.

Questions for Analysis

1. On what grounds does *Haec Sancta* establish the authority of a council? Why would this be considered a threat to papal power?

2. Why was it considered necessary for councils to meet regularly (*Frequens*)? What might have been the logical consequences of such regular meetings?

3. On what grounds does *Execrabilis* condemn the appeals to future councils that have no specified meeting date? Why would it not have condemned the conciliar movement altogether?

translated into many vernacular languages and is now more widely read than any other Christian book except the Bible.

Popular Reform Movements

For the most part, the threat of heretical movements was less dangerous to the Church than the corruption of the papacy. But in the kingdoms of England and Bohemia (the modern Czech Republic), some popular movements did pose serious challenges. The key figure in both cases was John Wycliffe (c. 1330–1384), an Oxford theologian and powerful critic of the Church. A survivor of the Black Death, Wycliffe lived at a time when the authority and integrity of the papacy were at a particularly low ebb. Indeed, he concluded that the empty sacraments of a corrupt Church could not save anyone. He therefore urged the English king to confiscate ecclesiastical wealth and to replace corrupt priests and bishops with men who would live according to apostolic standards of poverty and piety.

THE GREAT SCHISM, 1378–1417. During the Great Western Schism, the various territories of Europe were divided in their allegiances.
▪ *According to the map key, who were they choosing between?* ▪ *What common interests would have united the supporters of the Avignon pope or of the Roman pope?* ▪ *Why would areas like Portugal and Austria waver in their support?*

Some of Wycliffe's followers, known to their detractors as Lollards (from a word meaning "mumblers" or "beggars"), went even further, dismissing the sacraments as fraudulent attempts to extort money from the faithful. Lollard preachers also advocated for direct access to the scriptures and promoted an English translation of the Bible sponsored by Wycliffe himself.

Wycliffe's teachings played an important role in the Peasants' Revolt of 1381, and Lollardy gained numerous adherents in the decades after his death. The movement was even supported by a number of aristocratic families; certainly the idea of dissolving the Church's wealth would have been attractive to many of those who stood to gain from it. But, after a failed Lollard uprising in 1414, both the movement and its supporters went underground in England.

In Bohemia and eastern Europe, however, Wycliffe's ideas lived on and struck even deeper roots. They were adopted by Jan Hus (c. 1373–1415), a charismatic teacher at the royal university in Prague. In contrast to the Lollards, crated bread but also the consecrated wine, which was usually reserved solely for priests. This demand became a rallying cry for the Hussite movement. Influential nobles also supported Hus, partly in the hope that the reforms he demanded might restore revenues they had lost to the Church over the previous century.

Accordingly, most of Bohemia was behind him when Hus traveled to the Council of Constance to publish his views and to urge the assembled delegates to undertake sweeping reforms. But rather than giving him a hearing, the other delegates to the council convicted Hus of heresy and

who had scornfully dismissed the Mass and thereby lost much popular support, Hus emphasized the centrality of the Eucharist to Christian piety. Indeed, he demanded that the laity be allowed to receive not only the consehad him burned at the stake. Back home, Hus's supporters raised the banner of open revolt, and the aristocracy took advantage of the situation to seize Church property. Between 1420 and 1424, armed bands of fervent Hussites resoundingly defeated several armies, as priests, artisans, and peasants rallied to pursue Hus's goals of religious reform and social justice.

These victories increased popular fervor, but they also made radical reformers increasingly volatile. In 1434, accordingly, a more conservative arm of the Hussite movement was able to negotiate a settlement with the Bohemian church. By the terms of this settlement, Bohemians could receive both the bread and wine of the Mass, which thus placed them beyond the pale of Latin orthodoxy and effectively separated the Bohemian national church from the Church of Rome.

Lollardy and Hussitism exhibit a number of striking similarities. Both began in the university and then spread to the countryside. Both called for the clergy to live in simplicity and poverty, and both attracted noble support, especially in their early days. Both movements were also strongly nationalistic, employing their own vernacular languages (English and Czech) and identifying themselves with the English or Czech people in opposition to a "foreign" Church. They also relied on vernacular preaching and social activism. In all these respects, they established patterns that would emerge again in the vastly larger currents of the Protestant Reformation (see Chapter 13).

CONCLUSION

The century after the Black Death was a period of tremendous creativity and revolutionary change. The effects of the plague were catastrophic, but the resulting food surpluses, opportunities for expansion, and labor shortages encouraged experimentation and opened up broad avenues for enrichment. Europe's economy diversified and expanded, and increasing wealth and access to education produced new forms of art and new ways of looking at the world. Hundreds and perhaps thousands of new schools were

After You Read This Chapter

Visit StudySpace for quizzes, additional review materials, and multimedia documents. **wwnorton.com/web/westernciv18**

REVIEWING THE OBJECTIVES

- The Black Death had short-term and long-term effects on the economy and societies of Europe. What were some of the most important changes?
- The later "Middle Ages" and "the Renaissance" are often perceived to be two different periods, but the latter was actually part of the former. Explain why.
- What were some of the intellectual, cultural, and artistic innovations of this era in Italy and elsewhere in Europe?
- How were some European kingdoms becoming stronger and more centralized during this period? What are some examples of national monarchies?
- The conciliar movement sought to limit the power of the papacy. How? Why was this movement unsuccessful?

established, and scores of new universities would emerge as a result. Women were still excluded from formal schooling but nevertheless became active—and in many cases dominant—participants in literary endeavors, cultural life, and religious movements. Average men and women not only became more active in cultivating their own worldly goals, they also took control of their spiritual destinies at a time when the institutional Church provided little inspiring leadership.

Meanwhile, some states were growing stronger and more competitive while other regions remained deeply divided. The rise of the Ottoman Empire eventually absorbed many of the oldest territories of Western civilizations, including the venerable Muslim caliphate at Baghdad, the Near Eastern portions of the former Mongolian Empire, the Christian Balkans and Greece, and—above all—the surviving core of the eastern Roman Empire at Constantinople. Greek-speaking refugees streamed into Italy, many bringing with them classics of Greek philosophy and literature hitherto unknown in Europe. Fueled by new ideas and a fervid nostalgia for the ancient past, Italians began to experiment with new ways of reading ancient texts, advocating a return to classical models while at the same time trying to counter the political and artistic authority of the more powerful kingdoms north of the Alps.

In contrast to Italy, these emerging national monarchies cultivated group identity through the promotion of a shared vernacular language and allegiance to a strong, more centralized state. These tactics would allow smaller kingdoms like Poland and Scotland to increase their territories and their influence and would lead France and England into an epic battle for sovereignty and hegemony. The result, in all cases, was the escalation of armed conflict as incessant warfare drove more powerful governments to harvest a larger percentage of their subjects' wealth through taxation, which they proceeded to invest in ships, guns, and the standing armies made possible by new technologies and more effective administration.

In short, the generations who survived the calamities of famine, plague, and warfare seized the opportunities their new world presented to them. In the latter half of the fifteenth century, they stood on the verge of an extraordinary period of expansion and conquest that enabled them to dominate the globe.

PEOPLE, IDEAS, AND EVENTS IN CONTEXT

- Compare and contrast the **BLACK DEATH**'s effects on rural and urban areas.
- In what ways do rebellions like the **ENGLISH PEASANTS' REVOLT** reflect the changes brought about by the plague? How do the works of **GIOVANNI BOCCACCIO**, **GEOFFREY CHAUCER**, and **CHRISTINE DE PISAN** exemplify the culture of this era?
- What was **HUMANISM**? How was it related to the artistic and intellectual movement known as the **RENAISSANCE**?
- How did the **OTTOMAN EMPIRE** come to power? What were some consequences of its rise?
- On what grounds did **MUSCOVY** claim to be "the third Rome"? What is the significance of the title **TSAR**?
- What new military technologies were in use during the **HUNDRED YEARS' WAR**? How did this conflict affect other parts of Europe, beyond England and France? What role did **JOAN OF ARC** play?
- How did the **COUNCIL OF CONSTANCE** respond to the crisis of the **GREAT SCHISM**?
- Why did **CONCILIARISM** fail? How did **JOHN WYCLIFFE** and **JAN HUS** seek to reform the Church?

THINKING ABOUT CONNECTIONS

- In the year 2000, a group of historians was asked to identify the most significant historical figure of the past millennium. Rather than selecting a person (e.g., Martin Luther, Shakespeare, Napoleon, Adolf Hitler), they chose the microbe *Yersinia pestis,* which had caused the Black Death. Do you agree with this assessment? Why or why not?
- In your view, which was more crucial to the formation of the modern state: the political and legal developments we surveyed in Chapter 9 or the emergence of national identities we discussed in this chapter? Why?
- Was the conciliar movement doomed to failure, given what we have learned about the history of the Roman Church? How far back does one need to go, in order to trace the development of disputes over ecclesiastical governance?

Before
You
Read
This
Chapter

Innovation and Exploration, 1453–1533

CORE OBJECTIVES

- **UNDERSTAND** the relationship between Renaissance ideals and the political and economic realities of Italy.

- **IDENTIFY** the key characteristics of Renaissance arts and learning during this period.

- **DEFINE** the term *Reconquista* and its meaning in Spain.

- **DESCRIBE** the methods and motives of European colonization during this period.

- **EXPLAIN** why Europeans were able to dominate the peoples of the New World.

What if exact copies of an idea could circulate quickly, all over the world? What if the same could be done for the latest news, the oldest beliefs, the most beautiful poems, the most exciting—and deadly—discoveries? It would be doing for knowledge what the invention of coinage did for wealth: making it portable, easier to use and disseminate. Indeed, it's no accident that the man who developed such a technology, Johannes Gutenberg of Mainz (c. 1398–1468), was the son of a goldsmith who made coins for the bishop of that German city. Both crafts were based on the same principle and used the same basic tools. Coins are metal disks that have each been stamped with identical words and images, impressed on them with a reusable matrix. The pages of the first printed books—and later newspapers, leaflets, and pamphlets—were stamped with ink spread on rows of movable type (lead or cast-iron letter forms and punctuation marks) slotted into frames to form lines of words. Once a set of pages was ready, a press could make hundreds of copies in a matter of hours, many hundreds of times faster than the same page could be copied by hand. Afterward, the type could be reused.

A major stimulus for this invention was the more widespread availability of paper, a trend that had begun in the late thirteenth century. Parchment, northern Europe's chief writing material since the advent of the codex (see Chapter 6), was extremely expensive to manufacture and required special training on the part of those who used it—one reason why writing remained a specialized skill for much of the Middle Ages, while the ability to read was common. Paper, made from rags turned into pulp by mills, was both cheaper and far easier to use; accordingly, books became cheaper and written communication became easier and more widespread. Growing levels of literacy led to a growing demand for books, which in turn led to experimentation with different methods of book production—and to Gutenberg's breakthrough of the 1450s. By 1455, his workshop had printed multiple copies of the Latin Bible, of which forty-eight complete or partial volumes survive. Although printing never entirely replaced traditional modes of publication via manuscript, it made the cost of books affordable and revolutionized the spread of information.

In fact, the printing press played a crucial role in many of the developments that we will study in this chapter. The artistic and intellectual experiments that contributed to an Italian Renaissance were rapidly exported to other parts of Europe, and specifications for innovative weapons would be printed on the same presses that churned out humanist biographies. News of Columbus's first voyage and the subsequent conquests of the Americas would spread via the same media as critiques of European imperialism there. Printing not only increased the volume and rapidity of communication, it made it more difficult for those in power to censor dissenting opinions.

But at the same time as it created new forms of agency, the printing press also become an indispensable tool of more traditional powers, making it possible for rulers to govern growing empires abroad and increasingly centralized states at home. The "reconquest" of Spain and the extension of Spanish imperialism to the New World were both facilitated by the circulation of printed propaganda. The widespread availability of reading materials even helped to standardize national languages, by enabling governments to promote one official printed dialect over others. Hence the "king's English," the variety of the language spoken around London, was imposed as the only acceptable literary and bureaucratic language throughout the English realm, contributing to the growth of a common linguistic identity among readers. For these reasons, among others, many historians consider the advent of print to be both the defining event and the driving engine of modernity, and

it coincided with another essentially modern development: the discovery of a "New World."

RENAISSANCE IDEALS— AND REALITIES

The intellectual and artistic movement that had begun in Italy during the fourteenth century was, as we noted in Chapter 11, characterized by an intense interest in the classical past and by a new type of educational program known as humanism. These Renaissance ideals—and the realities that both undergirded and complicated them—would be extended and diversified in the later fifteenth century through the medium of the printing press. By the time the Ottoman conquest of Constantinople was complete, just a year before Gutenberg's workshop began to produce pages of the Bible, decades of uncertainty and warfare had propelled hundreds of refugees from the eastern Roman Empire into Italy. Many carried with them precious manuscripts of Greek texts that had long been unavailable in western Europe: the epics of Homer, the major surviving works of Athenian dramatists, the dialogues of Plato. Prior to the invention of print, such manuscripts could be owned and studied by only a very few, very privileged men. Now printers in Venice and other European cities rushed to produce cheap editions of these texts as well as Greek grammars and glossaries that could facilitate reading them.

Within a few decades, so many men were engaged in the study of Plato that an informal "Platonic Academy" had formed in Florence. There, the work of intellectuals like Marsilio Ficino (1433–1499) and Giovanni Pico della Mirandola (1463–1494) was fostered by the patronage of the wealthy Cosimo de' Medici. Based on his reading of Plato, Ficino's philosophy moved away from the focus on ethics and civic life that had been such a feature of earlier humanist thought. He taught instead that the individual should look primarily to the salvation of his immortal soul, to free it from its "always miserable" mortal body: a very Platonic idea that was also compatible with much late-medieval Christian piety. His disciple Pico likewise rejected the everyday world of public affairs but took a more exalted view of man's intellectual and artistic capacities, arguing that man (but not woman) can aspire to union with God through the exercise of his unique talents. Ficino's great achievement was his translation of Plato's works into Latin, which made them widely accessible in Europe for the first time—again, thanks to the medium of print.

NORWAY

SWEDEN

Stockholm
1483

BALTIC SEA

SCOTLAND

NORTH
SEA

Edinburgh
1507

Copenhagen
1490

DENMARK

Odense
1482

POLAND

Dublin
1551

ENGLAND

London
1492

Westminster
1476

Utrecht
1470

Brussels
1475

Cologne
1465

Leipzig
1481

HOLY ROMAN EMPIRE

Eltville
1467

Mainz
1450

Bamberg
1460

Pilsen
1468

Paris
1470

Strasbourg
1458

Nuremberg
1470

ATLANTIC
OCEAN

Basel
1468

Beromünster
1470

SWITZERLAND

Augsburg
1468

Danube R.

Vienna
1482

AUSTRIA

HUNGARY

FRANCE

Lyons
1473

Milan
1471

Venice
1469

VENETIAN EMPIRE

ADRIATIC SEA

Florence
1482

PAPAL
STATES

CORSICA

Rome
1467

Naples
1471

PORTUGAL

SPAIN

Valencia
1474

SARDINIA

KINGDOM
OF TWO
SICILIES

Lisbon
1489

Seville
1478

BALEARIC ISLANDS

MEDITERRANEAN
SEA

0   100   200   300 Miles

0   100   200   300 Kilometers

THE SPREAD OF PRINTING
■ Up until 1470   ■ 1471–1500

THE SPREAD OF PRINTING. This map shows how quickly the technology of printing spread throughout Europe between 1470 and 1500.
▪ *In what regions were printing presses most heavily concentrated?* ▪ *What factors would have led to their proliferation in the Low Countries,
northern Italy, and Germany—as compared to France, Spain, and England?* ▪ *Why would so many have been located along waterways?*

Printing, Patriotism, and the Past

> The printing press helped to create new communities of readers by standardizing national languages and even promoting patriotism. And while it enabled authors of new works to reach larger audiences, it also allowed printers to popularize older writings that had previously circulated in manuscript. The two sources presented here exemplify two aspects of this trend. The first is the preface to a version of the legend of King Arthur, which was originally written by an English soldier called Sir Thomas Malory, who completed it in 1470. It was printed for the first time in 1485, when it quickly became a best seller. The author of this preface was also the printer, William Caxton of London, who specialized in publishing books that glorified England's history and heritage. The second excerpt is from the concluding chapter of Machiavelli's treatise The Prince. Like the book itself, these remarks were originally addressed to Lorenzo de' Medici, head of Florence's most powerful family. But when The Prince was printed in 1532, five years after Machiavelli's death, the author's passionate denunciation of foreign "barbarians" and lament for Italy's lost glory would have resonated with a wider Italian-speaking public.

William Caxton's preface to Thomas Malory's *Le Morte d'Arthur* ("The Death of Arthur"), 1485

AFTER I had accomplished and finished diverse histories, both of contemplation and of other historical and worldly acts of great conquerors and princes, . . . many noble and diverse gentlemen of this realm of England came and demanded why I had not made and imprinted the noble history of the Holy Grail, and of the most renowned Christian king and worthy, King Arthur, which ought most to be remembered among us Englishmen before all other Christian kings. . . . The said noble gentlemen instantly required me to imprint the history of the said noble king and conqueror King Arthur, and of his knights, with the history of the Holy Grail . . . considering that he was a man born within this realm, and king and emperor of the same: and that there be, in French, diverse and many noble volumes of his acts, and also of his knights. To whom I answered that diverse men hold opinion that there was no such Arthur, and that all such books as have been made of him be feigned and fables, because some chronicles make of him no mention. . . . Whereto

they answered, and one in special said, that in him that should say or think that there was never such a king called Arthur might well be accounted great folly and blindness. . . . For in all places, Christian and heathen, he is reputed and taken for one of the Nine Worthies, and the first of the three Christian men. And also, he is more spoken of beyond the sea, and there are more books made of his noble acts than there be in England, as well in Dutch, Italian, Spanish, and Greek, as in French. . . . Wherefore it is a marvel why he is no more renowned in his own country. . . .

Then all these things aforesaid alleged, I could not well deny but that there was such a noble king named Arthur, reputed one of the Nine Worthies, and first and chief of the Christian men. And many noble volumes be made of him and of his noble knights in French, which I have seen and read beyond the sea, which be not had in our maternal tongue. . . . Wherefore, among all such [manuscript] books as have late been drawn out briefly into English I have . . . undertaken to imprint a book of the noble histories of the said

King Arthur, and of certain of his knights, after a copy unto me delivered—which copy Sir Thomas Malory did take out of certain books of French, and reduced it into English. And I, according to my copy, have done set it in print, to the intent that noble men may see and learn the noble acts of chivalry, the gentle and virtuous deeds that some knights used in those days, by which they came to honor, and how they that were vicious were punished and oft put to shame and rebuke; humbly beseeching all noble lords and ladies (with all other estates of what estate or degree they be) that shall see and read in this said book and work, that they take the good and honest acts to their remembrance, and follow the same. . . . For herein may be seen noble chivalry, courtesy, humanity, friendliness, hardiness, love, friendship, cowardice, murder, hate, virtue, and sin. Do after the good and leave the evil, and it shall bring you to good fame and renown.

Source: Sir Thomas Malory, *Le Morte d'Arthur* (London: 1485), (text and spelling slightly modernized).

From the conclusion of Niccolò Machiavelli's *The Prince* (completed 1513, printed 1533)

Reflecting in the matters set forth above and considering within myself where the times were propitious in Italy at present to honor a new prince and whether there is at hand the matter suitable for a prudent and virtuous leader to mold in a new form, giving honor to himself and benefit to the citizens of the country, I have arrived at the opinion that all circumstances now favor such a prince, and I cannot think of a time more propitious for him than the present. If, as I said, it was necessary in order to make apparent the virtue of Moses, that the people of Israel should be enslaved in Egypt, and that the Persians should be oppressed by the Medes to provide an opportunity to illustrate the greatness and the spirit of Cyrus, and that the Athenians should be scattered in order to show the excellence of Theseus, thus at the present time, in order to reveal the valor of an Italian spirit, it was essential that Italy should fall to her present low estate, more enslaved than the Hebrews, more servile than the Persians, more disunited than the Athenians, leaderless and lawless, beaten, despoiled, lacerated, overrun and crushed under every kind of misfortune.... So Italy now, left almost lifeless, awaits the coming of one who will heal her wounds, putting an end to the sacking and looting in Lombardy and the spoliation and extortions in the Realm of Naples and Tuscany, and cleanse her sores that have been so long festering. Behold how she prays God to send her some one to redeem her from the cruelty and insolence of the barbarians. See how she is ready and willing to follow any banner so long as there be someone to take it up. Nor has she at present any hope of finding her redeemer save only in your illustrious house [the Medici] which has been so highly exalted both by its own merits and by fortune and which has been favored by God and the church, of which it is now ruler....

This opportunity, therefore, should not be allowed to pass, and Italy, after such a long wait, must be allowed to behold her redeemer. I cannot describe the joy with which he will be received in all these provinces which have suffered so much from the foreign deluge, nor with what thirst for vengeance, nor with what firm devotion, what solemn delight, what tears! What gates could be closed to him, what people could deny him obedience, what envy could withstand him, what Italian could withhold allegiance from him? THIS BARBARIAN OCCUPATION STINKS IN THE NOSTRILS OF ALL OF US. Let your illustrious house then take up this cause with the spirit and the hope with which one undertakes a truly just enterprise....

Source: Niccolò Machiavelli, *The Prince,* ed. and trans. Thomas G. Bergin (Arlington Heights, IL: 1947), pp. 75–76, 78.

Questions for Analysis

1. What do these two sources reveal about the relationship between patriotism and the awareness of a nation's past? Why do you think that Caxton looks back to a legendary medieval king, whereas Machiavelli's references are all to ancient examples? What do both excerpts reveal about the value placed on history in the popular imagination?

2. How does Caxton describe the process of printing a book? What larger conclusions can we draw from this about the market for printed books in general?

3. Why might Machiavelli's treatise have been made available in a printed version, nearly twenty years after its original appearance in manuscript? How might his new audience have responded to its message?

The Politics of Italy and the Philosophy of Machiavelli

But not all Florentines were galvanized by Platonic ideals. Indeed, the most influential philosopher of this era—and one of the most widely read authors of all time—was a thoroughgoing realist who spent more time studying Roman history than Greek philosophy: Niccolò Machiavelli (1469–1527). Machiavelli's political writings reflect the unstable political situation of his home city as well as his wider aspirations for a unified Italy that could revive the glory of ancient Rome. We have observed that Italy had been in political disarray for centuries, a situation exacerbated by the "Babylonian Captivity" of the papacy and the controversies raging after its return to Rome (see Chapters 10 and 11). Now Italy was becoming the arena in which bloody international struggles were being played out. The kings of France and Spain both had imperial ambitions, and both claimed to be the rightful champions of the papacy. Accordingly, both sent invading armies into the peninsula while they busily competed for the allegiance of the various city-states, which in turn were torn by internal dissension.

In 1498, Machiavelli became a prominent official in the government of a new Florentine republic, set up four years earlier when a French invasion of the region had led to the expulsion of the ruling Medici family. His duties largely involved diplomatic missions to other Italian city-states. While in Rome, he became fascinated with the attempt of Cesare Borgia, son of Pope Alexander VI, to create his own principality in central Italy. He noted with approval Cesare's ruthlessness and his complete subordination of personal ethics to political ends. He remembered this example in 1512, when the Medici returned to overthrow the Florentine republic and Machiavelli was deprived of his position, imprisoned, tortured, and exiled. He now devoted his energies to the articulation of a political philosophy suited to the times and to the tastes of the family that had ousted him from his job.

On the surface, Machiavelli's two great works of political analysis appear to contradict each other. In his *Discourses on Livy*, which drew on the works of that Roman historian (see Chapter 5), he praised the ancient Roman Republic as a model for his own contemporaries, lauding constitutional government, equality among citizens, and the subordination of religion to the service of the state. There is little doubt, in fact, that Machiavelli was a committed believer in the free city-state as the ideal form of human government. But Machiavelli also wrote *The Prince*, "a handbook for tyrants" in the eyes of his critics, and he dedicated this work to Lorenzo, son of Piero de' Medici, whose family had overthrown the Florentine republic that Machiavelli had served.

THE STATES OF ITALY, c. 1494. This map shows the divisions of Italy on the eve of the French invasion in 1494. Contemporary observers often described Italy as being divided among five great powers: Milan, Venice, Florence, the Papal States, and the united Kingdoms of Naples and Sicily. ▪ *Which of these powers would have been most capable of expanding their territories?* ▪ *Which neighboring states would have been most threatened by such attempts at expansion?* ▪ *Why would Florence and the Papal States so often find themselves in conflict with each other?*

Because *The Prince* has been so much more widely read than *Discourses*, it has often been interpreted as an endorsement of power for its own sake. Machiavelli's real position was quite different. In the political chaos of early-sixteenth-century Italy, he saw the likes of Cesare Borgia as the only hope for revitalizing the spirit of independence among his contemporaries, and so making Italy fit, eventually, for self-governance. However dark his vision of human nature, Machiavelli never ceased to hope that his contemporaries would rise up, expel French and Spanish occupying forces, and restore ancient traditions of liberty and equality. He regarded a period of despotism as a necessary step toward that end, not as a permanently desirable form of government.

Machiavelli continues to be a controversial figure. Some modern scholars, like many of his own contemporaries, represent him as disdainful of conventional morality, interested solely in the acquisition and exercise of power. Others see him as an Italian patriot. Still others see him as a realist influenced by Saint Augustine (see Chapter 6), who understood that, in a fallen world populated by sinful people, a ruler's good intentions do not guarantee that his policies will have good results. Accordingly, Machiavelli insisted that a prince's actions must be judged by their consequences and not by their intrinsic moral quality. He argued that "the necessity of preserving the state will often compel a prince to take actions which are opposed to loyalty, charity, humanity, and religion." As we shall see in later chapters, many subsequent political philosophers would go even further than Machiavelli in arguing that the preservation of the state—and the avoidance of political chaos—does indeed warrant the exercise of absolute power on the part of the ruler (see Chapters 14 and 15).

The Ideal of the Courtier

Machiavelli's political theories were informed by years of diplomatic service in the courts of Italy, and so was his engaging literary style. Indeed, he never abandoned his interest in the literary arts of the court and continued to write poems, plays, and adaptations of classical comedies. In this he resembled another poet-courtier, Ludovico Ariosto (1474–1533), who undertook diplomatic missions for the Duke of Ferrara and some of Rome's most powerful prelates. His lengthy verse narrative, *Orlando Furioso* (The Madness of Roland), was a retelling of the heroic exploits celebrated in the French *Song of Roland* (see Chapter 8)—but without the heroism. Although very different in form and tone from *The Prince*, it shared that work's skepticism of political or chivalric ideals. Instead, it emphasized the comedy of its lovers' passionate exploits and sought to charm an audience who sought consolation in pleasure and beauty.

Thus a new Renaissance ideal was born, one that promoted the arts of pleasing the powerful secular and ecclesiastical princes who were in a position to employ clever men like Machiavelli and Ariosto: the ideal of the courtier. The components of this ideal were embodied by their contemporary, the diplomat and nobleman Baldassare Castiglione (1478–1529), who would later write a manual for those who aspired to acquire these skills. If *The Prince* was a forerunner of modern self-help books, *The Book of the Courtier* was an early handbook of etiquette; and both stand in sharp contrast to the treatises on public virtue composed in the previous century. Whereas Bruni and Alberti (see Chapter 11) had taught the sober virtues of strenuous service on behalf of the city-state, Castiglione taught how to attain the elegant and seemingly effortless skills necessary for advancement in princely courts.

More than anyone else, Castiglione articulated and popularized the set of talents still associated with the "Renaissance man": one accomplished in many different pursuits, witty, cultured, and stylish. And in many ways, this new ideal actually represents a *rejection* of the older ideals associated with the Renaissance as a rebirth of classical education for public men. Castiglione even rejected the misogyny of the humanists by stressing the ways in which court ladies could rise to influence and prominence through the graceful exercise of their womanly powers. Widely read throughout Western civilizations, his *Courtier* set the standard for polite behavior until the First World War.

The Dilemma of the Artist

Without question, the most enduring legacy of the Italian Renaissance has been the contributions of its artists, particularly those who embraced new media and new attitudes toward the human body. We have already noted (see Chapter 11) the creative and economic opportunities afforded by painting on canvas or wood, which freed artists from having to work on site and entirely on commission: such paintings are portable—unlike wall paintings—and can be displayed in different settings, reach different markets, and be more widely distributed. We also saw that the use of oil paints, pioneered in Flanders, further revolutionized painting styles. To these benefits, the artists of Italy added an important technical ingredient: mastery of a vanishing (one-point) perspective that gave to painting an illusion of three-dimensional space. They also experimented with effects of light and shade, and studied intently the anatomy and proportions of the human body. These techniques also influenced the sculptors of this age.

New Illusions and the Career of Leonardo

THE IMPACT OF PERSPECTIVE. Masaccio's painting *The Trinity with the Virgin* illustrates the startling sense of depth made possible by observing the rules of one-point perspective.

Behind all of the beautiful artworks created in this era, which led to the glorification of the artist as a new type of hero, lie the harsh political and economic realities within which these artists worked. Increasing private wealth and the growth of lay patronage opened up new markets and created a huge demand for buildings and objects that could increase those grappling for prestige. Portraiture was a direct result of this trend, since princes and merchants alike sought to glorify themselves and their families and to compete with their neighbors and rivals. An artist therefore had to study the techniques of the courtier as well as the new artistic techniques in order to succeed in winning a patron. He also had to be ready to perform other services for which he had to cultivate other talents: overseeing the building and decoration of palaces; designing tableware, furniture, fanciful liveries for servants and soldiers; and even decorating guns. Some artists, like Leonardo da Vinci, were prized as much for their capacity to invent deadly weapons as for their paintings and sculptures.

For much of the fifteenth century, the majority of the great painters were Florentines who followed in the footsteps of the precocious Masaccio (1401–1428), who had died prematurely at the age of twenty-seven. His lasting legacy was the pioneering use of one-point perspective and dramatic lighting effects. Both are evident in his painting of the Trinity, where the body of the crucified Christ appears to be thrust forward by the impassive figure of God the Father, while the Virgin's gaze directly engages the viewer. Masaccio's most obvious successor was Sandro Botticelli (1445–1510), who excelled in depicting graceful motion and the sensuous pleasures of nature. He is most famous today for paintings that evoke classical mythology and that seem to be devoid of any Christian frame of reference.

The most adventurous and versatile artist of this period was Leonardo da Vinci (1452–1519). Leonardo personifies the Renaissance ideal: he was a painter, architect, musician, mathematician, engineer, and inventor. The illegitimate son of a notary, he set up an artist's shop in Florence by the time he was twenty-five and gained the patronage of the Medici ruler, Lorenzo the Magnificent. Yet Leonardo had a weakness: he worked slowly, and he had difficulty finishing anything. This naturally displeased Lorenzo and other Florentine patrons, who regarded artists as craftsmen who worked on specific projects, and on their patrons' time—not their own. Leonardo, however, strongly objected to this view; he considered himself to be an inspired, independent innovator. He therefore left Florence in 1482 and went to work for the of Sforza dictators Milan, whose favor he courted by emphasizing his skills as a maker of bombs, heavy ordinance, and siege engines. He remained there until the French invasion of 1499; he then wandered about, finally accepting the patronage of the French king, under whose auspices he lived and worked until his death.

Paradoxically, considering his skill in fashioning deadly weapons, Leonardo was convinced of the essential divinity of all living things. He was a vegetarian—unusual at the time—and when he went to the marketplace to buy caged birds he released them to their native habitat when he had finished observing them. His approach to painting was that it should be the most accurate possible imitation of nature. He made careful studies: blades of grass, cloud formations, a waterfall. He obtained human corpses for dissection and reconstructed in drawing the minutest features of anatomy, carrying this knowledge over to his paintings. *The Virgin of the Rocks* typifies not only his technical skill but also his passion for science and his belief in the universe as a well-ordered place.

THE BIRTH OF VENUS. This painting was executed by Sandro Botticelli in Florence, and represents the artist's imaginative treatment of stories from ancient mythology. Here, he depicts the moment when Aphrodite, goddess of love, was spontaneously engendered from the foam of the sea by Chronos, the god of time.

THE VIRGIN OF THE ROCKS. This painting reveals Leonardo's interest in the variety of human faces and facial expressions and in natural settings.

The figures are arranged geometrically, with every stone and plant depicted in accurate detail. In *The Last Supper*, painted on the refectory walls of a monastery in Milan (and now in an advanced state of decay), he displayed his equally keen studies of human psychology. In this image, a serene Christ has just announced to his disciples that one of them will betray him. The artist succeeds in portraying the mingled emotions of surprise, horror, and guilt on the faces of the disciples as they gradually perceive the meaning of their master's statement. He also implicates the painting's viewers in this dramatic scene, since they too dine alongside Christ, in the very same room.

Renaissance Arts in Venice and Rome

The innovations of Florentine artists were widely imitated. By the end of the fifteenth century, they had influenced a group of painters active in the wealthy city of Venice, among them Tiziano Vecellio, better known as Titian (c. 1490–1576). Many of Titian's paintings evoke the luxurious, pleasure-loving life of this thriving commercial center; for although they copied Florentine techniques,

Analyzing Primary Sources

Leonardo da Vinci Applies for a Job

Few sources illuminate the tensions between Renaissance ideals and realities better than the résumé of accomplishments submitted by Leonardo da Vinci to a prospective employer, Ludovico Sforza of Milan. In the following letter, Leonardo explains why he deserves to be appointed chief architect and military engineer in the duke's household administration. He got the job and moved to Milan in 1481.

1. I have the kind of bridges that are extremely light and strong, made to be carried with great ease, and with them you may pursue, and, at any time, flee from the enemy; . . . and also methods of burning and destroying those of the enemy.

2. I know how, when a place is under attack, to eliminate the water from the trenches, and make endless variety of bridges . . . and other machines. . . .

3. . . . I have methods for destroying every rock or other fortress, even if it were built on rock, etc.

4. I also have other kinds of mortars [bombs] that are most convenient and easy to carry. . . .

5. And if it should be a sea battle, I have many kinds of machines that are most efficient for offense and defense. . . .

6. I also have means that are noiseless to reach a designated area by secret and tortuous mines. . . .

7. I will make covered chariots, safe and unattackable, which can penetrate the enemy with their artillery. . . .

8. In case of need I will make big guns, mortars, and light ordnance of fine and useful forms that are out of the ordinary.

9. If the operation of bombardment should fail, I would contrive catapults, mangonels, trabocchi [trebuchets], and other machines of marvelous efficacy and unusualness. In short, I can, according to each case in question, contrive various and endless means of offense and defense.

10. In time of peace I believe I can give perfect satisfaction that is equal to any other in the field of architecture and the construction of buildings. . . . I can execute sculpture in marble, bronze, or clay, and also in painting I do the best that can be done, and as well as any other, whoever he may be.

Having now, most illustrious Lord, sufficiently seen the specimens of all those who consider themselves master craftsmen of instruments of war, and that the invention and operation of such instruments are no different from those in common use, I shall now endeavor . . . to explain myself to your Excellency by revealing to your Lordship my secrets. . . .

Source: Excerpted from Leonardo da Vinci, *The Notebooks*, in *The Italian Renaissance Reader*, eds. Julia Conaway and Mark Mosa (Harmondsworth, UK: 1987), pp. 195–96.

Questions for Analysis

1. Based on the qualifications highlighted by Leonardo in this letter, what can you conclude about the political situation in Milan and the priorities of its duke? What can you conclude about the state of military technologies in this period and the conduct of warfare?

2. What do you make of the fact that Leonardo mentions his artistic endeavors only at the end of the letter? Does this fact alter your opinion or impression of him? Why or why not?

---

most Venetian painters showed little of that city's concerns for philosophical or religious allegory. Their aim was to appeal to the senses by painting idyllic landscapes and sumptuous portraits of the rich and powerful. In the subordination of form and meaning to color and elegance, they may have mirrored the tastes of the men for whom they worked.

Rome, too, became a major artistic center in this era and a place where the Florentine school exerted a more potent influence. Among its eminent painters was Raffaello Sanzio (1483–1520), or Raphael. Although influenced by Leonardo, Raphael cultivated a more spiritual and philosophical approach to his subjects. As we noted in Chapter 4, his fresco *The School of Athens* depicts both the harmony

THE LAST SUPPER. This fresco on the refectory wall of the monastery of Santa Maria delle Grazie in Milan is a testament to both the powers and limitations of Leonardo's artistry. It skillfully employs the techniques of one-point perspective to create the illusion that Jesus and his disciples are actually dining at the monastery's head table, but because Leonardo had not mastered the techniques of fresco painting, he applied tempera pigments to a dry wall that had been coated with a sealing agent. As a result, the painting's colors began to fade just years after its completion. By the middle of the sixteenth century, it had seriously deteriorated. Large portions of it are now invisible.

and the differences of Platonic and Aristotelian thought (see page 117). It also includes a number of Raphael's contemporaries as models. The image of Plato is actually a portrait of Leonardo, while the architect Donato Bramante (c. 1444–1514) stands in for the geometer Euclid, and Michelangelo for the philosopher Heraclitus.

Michelangelo Buonarroti (1475–1564), who spent many decades in Rome in the service of a papacy, was another native of Florence. Like Leonardo, he was a polymath: painter, sculptor, architect, poet—and he expressed himself in all these forms with a similar power. But if Leonardo was a naturalist, Michelangelo was an idealist—despite the harsh political and material realities of the conditions in which he worked. At the center of all of his work, as at the center of Renaissance humanism, is the male figure: the embodied masculine mind.

Michelangelo's greatest achievements in painting appear in a single location, the Sistine Chapel of the Vatican palace, yet they are products of two different periods in the artist's life and consequently exemplify two different artistic styles and outlooks on the human condition. More famous are the extraordinary frescoes painted on the ceiling from 1508 to 1512, depicting scenes from the book of Genesis. All the panels in this series, including *The Creation of Adam*, exemplify the young artist's commitment to classical artistic principles. Correspondingly, all affirm the sublimity of the Creation and the heroic qualities of humankind. But a quarter of a century later, when Michelangelo returned to work in the Sistine Chapel, both his style and mood had changed dramatically. In the enormous *Last Judgment*, a fresco completed on the chapel's altar wall in 1536, Michelangelo repudiated classical restraint and substituted a style that emphasized tension and distortion, a humanity wracked with fear, guilt, and frailty. He included himself in it—painting a grotesque self-portrait on the flayed skin of Saint Bartholomew, who was allegedly martyred by being skinned alive. One wonders whether Michelangelo intended this as a metaphor for the challenges of working in the service of the papal court.

SELF-PORTRAIT OF THE ARTIST AS A YOUNG MAN: DETAIL FROM *THE SCHOOL OF ATHENS*. We have already analyzed aspects of Raphael's famous group portrait of the Greek philosophers, with Plato and Aristotle at their center (see page 118). In addition to featuring his own contemporaries as models—including the artists Leonardo and Michelangelo and the architect Bramante—Raphael put himself in the picture, too. ▪ *What messages does this choice convey?*

Michelangelo and the Renaissance of Sculpture

Although sculpture was not a new medium for artists, as oil painting was, it became an important area of Renaissance innovation. For the first time since late antiquity, monumental

THE CREATION OF ADAM.
This is one of a series of frescoes painted on the ceiling of the Sistine Chapel of the Vatican palace in Rome, executed by Michelangelo over a period of many years and in circumstances of extreme physical hardship. It has since become an iconic image. ▪ *How might it be said to capture Renaissance ideals?*

statues became figures "in the round" rather than sculptural elements incorporated into buildings or featured as effigies on tombs. By freeing sculpture from its bondage to architecture, the Renaissance reestablished it as a separate art form.

The first great master of Renaissance sculpture was Donatello (c. 1386–1466). His bronze statue of David, triumphant over the head of the slain Goliath, is the first free-standing nude of the period. Yet this *David* is clearly an agile adolescent rather than a muscular Greek athlete like that of Michelangelo's *David*, executed in 1501, as a public expression of Florentine civic life: not merely graceful but heroic. Michelangelo regarded sculpture as the most exalted of the arts because it allowed the artist to imitate God most fully in re-creating human forms. Furthermore, in Michelangelo's view,

THE POWER AND VULNERABILITY OF THE MALE BODY. Donatello's *David* (left) was the first freestanding nude executed since antiquity. It shows the Hebrew leader as an adolescent youth and is a little over five feet tall. The *David* by Michelangelo (center) stands thirteen feet high and was placed prominently in front of Florence's city hall to proclaim the city's power and humanistic values. Michelangelo's *Descent from the Cross* (right), which shows Christ's broken body in the arms of the elderly Nicodemus, was made by the sculptor for his own tomb. (The Gospels describe Nicodemus as a Pharisee who became a follower of Jesus and who was present at his death.) ▪ *Why would Michelangelo choose this figure to represent himself?* ▪ *How does his representation of David—and the context in which this figure was displayed—compare to that of Donatello?*

the most God-like sculptor disdained slavish naturalism; anyone could make a plaster cast of a human figure, but only an inspired creative genius could endow his sculpted figures with a sense of life. Accordingly, Michelangelo's sculpture subordinated reality to the force of his imagination and sought to express his ideals in ever more astonishing forms. He also insisted on working in marble—the "noblest" sculptural material—and by creating figures twice as large as life. By sculpting a serenely confident young man at the peak of physical fitness, Michelangelo celebrated the Florentine republic's own determination in resisting tyrants and upholding ideals of civic justice.

Yet the serenity seen in *David* is no longer prominent in the works of Michelangelo's later life when, as in his painting, he began to explore the use of anatomical distortion to create effects of emotional intensity. While his statues remained awesome in scale, they also communicate rage, depression, and sorrow. The culmination of this trend is his unfinished but intensely moving *Descent from the Cross*, a depiction of an old man (the sculptor himself) grieving over the distorted, slumping body of the dead Christ.

Renaissance Architecture

To a much greater extent than either sculpture or painting, Renaissance architecture had its roots in the classical past. The Gothic style pioneered in northern France (see Chapter 9) had not found a welcome reception in Italy; most of the buildings constructed there were Romanesque in style, and the great architects influenced by the Renaissance movement generally adopted their building plans from these structures—some of which they believed (mistakenly) to be ancient. They also copied decorative devices from the authentic ruins of ancient Rome. But above all, they derived their influence from the writings of Vitruvius (fl. c. 60–15 B.C.E.), a Roman architect and engineer whose multivolume *On Architecture* was among the humanists' rediscovered ancient texts. The governing principles laid out by Vitruvius were popularized by Leon Battista Alberti in his own book, *On the Art of Building*, which began to circulate in manuscript around 1450.

In keeping with these classical models, Renaissance buildings emphasize geometrical proportion. These aesthetic values were also reinforced by the interest in Pla-

ST. PETER'S BASILICA, ROME. This eighteenth-century painting shows the massive interior of the Renaissance building. But were it not for the perspective provided by the tiny human figures, the human eye would be fooled into thinking this a much smaller space.

tonic philosophy, which taught that certain mathematical ratios reflect the harmony of the universe. For example, the proportions of the human body serve as the basis for the proportions of the quintessential Renaissance building: St. Peter's Basilica in Rome. Designed by some of the most celebrated architects of the time, including Bramante and Michelangelo, it is still one of the largest buildings in the world. Yet it seems smaller than a Gothic cathedral because it is built to human scale. The same artful proportions are evident in smaller-scale buildings too, as in the aristocratic country houses later designed by the northern Italian architect Andrea Palladio (1508–1580), who created secular miniatures of ancient temples (such as the Roman Pantheon) to glorify the aristocrats who dwelled within them.

THE RENAISSANCE NORTH OF THE ALPS

Despite Italian resentment of the political encroachment of foreign monarchs, contacts between Italy and northern Europe were close throughout this period. Italian merchants and financiers were familiar figures at northern courts; students from all over Europe studied at Italian universities such as Bologna or Padua; northern poets (including Geoffrey Chaucer; see Chapter 11) and their works traveled to and from Italy; and northern soldiers were frequent; combatants in Italian wars. Yet only at the very end of the fifteenth century did the innovative artistry and learning of Italy begin to be exported across the Alps into northern Europe and across the eastern Mediterranean into Spain.

A variety of explanations have been offered for this delay. Northern European intellectual life in the later Middle Ages was dominated by universities such as those of Paris, Oxford, and Prague, whose curricula focused on the study of philosophical logic, Christian theology, and (to a lesser extent) medicine. These rigorous courses of study left little room for the study of classical literature. In Italy, by contrast, universities were more often professional schools specializing in law and medicine and were more integrally tied to the nonacademic intellectual lives of the cities in which they were situated. As a result, a more secular, urban-oriented educational tradition took shape in Italy, as we saw in our previous discussion of humanism. In northern Europe, by contrast, those scholars who *were* influenced by Italian ideas usually worked outside the university system under the private patronage of kings and princes.

Before the turn of the sixteenth century, northern rulers were also less committed to patronizing artists and intellectuals than were the city-states and princes of Italy. In Italy, as we may have seen, such patronage was an important arena for competition between political rivals. In northern Europe, however, political units were larger and political rivals were fewer. It was therefore less necessary to use art for political purposes in a kingdom than it was in a city-state—a major exception being the independent duchy of Burgundy, which surpassed even the French court in its magnificence. A statue erected in a central square of Florence would be seen by all the city's residents. In Paris, such a statue would be seen by only a tiny minority of the French king's subjects. But as royal courts became more firmly established in royal capitals and so became showcases for royal power, kings needed to impress townspeople, courtiers, and visitors—and they consequently relied more and more on artists and intellectuals to advertise their wealth and taste.

Christian Humanism and the Career of Erasmus

In general, then, the Renaissance movement of northern Europe differed from that of Italy because it grafted certain Italian ideals onto preexisting traditions, rather than sweeping away older forms of knowledge. This can be seen very clearly in the case of the intellectual development known as Christian humanism. Although Christian humanists shared the Italian humanists' scorn for scholasticism's limitations, northern humanists were more committed to seeking ethical guidance from biblical and religious precepts, as well as from Cicero or Virgil. Like their Italian counterparts, they embraced the wisdom of antiquity, but the antiquity they favored was Christian as well as classical—the antiquity of the New Testament and the early Church. Similarly, northern artists were inspired by the accomplishments of Italian masters and copied their techniques, but they depicted classical subjects less frequently and almost never portrayed completely nude human figures.

Any discussion of Christian humanism must begin with the career of Desiderius Erasmus (c. 1469–1536). The illegitimate son of a priest, Erasmus was born near Rotterdam in the Netherlands. Later, as a result of his wide travels, he became a virtual citizen of all Europe. Forced into a monastery against his will when he was a teenager, the young Erasmus found little formal instruction there—but plenty of freedom to read what he liked. He devoured all the classics he could get his hands on, alongside the writings of the church fathers (see Chapter 6). When he

ERASMUS BY HANS HOLBEIN THE YOUNGER. This is generally regarded as the most evocative portrait of the preeminent Christian humanist.

Past and Present

The Reputation of Richard III

England's King Richard III (r. 1483–1485) has been a byword for villainy since the time of his death, when Sir Thomas More and other propagandists working for his successor, Henry VII, alleged that his physically deformed body was matched by the depravity of his actions. For centuries, historians have debated the truth of both claims. Was Richard really a hunchback—and a murderer, too? In 2012, the stunning discovery of Richard's body (under a parking lot near the medieval battlefield where he died) confirmed that he had indeed suffered from severe scoliosis. The other claim has yet to be proven.

 Watch related author interview on StudySpace
wwnorton.com/web/westernciv18

was about thirty years old, he obtained permission to leave the monastery and enroll in the University of Paris, where he completed the requirements for a bachelor's degree in divinity.

But Erasmus subsequently rebelled against what he considered the arid learning of Parisian academe. Nor did he ever serve actively as a priest. Instead, he made his living from teaching, writing, and the proceeds of various ecclesiastical offices that required no pastoral duties. Ever on the lookout for new patrons, he traveled often to England, stayed for three years in Italy, and resided in several different cities in Germany and the Low Countries before settling finally, toward the end of his life, in Basel (Switzerland). By means of a voluminous correspondence with learned friends, Erasmus became the leader of a humanist coterie. And through the popularity of his numerous publications, he also became the arbiter of northern European cultural tastes during his lifetime.

Erasmus's many-sided intellectual activity may be assessed from two different points of view: the literary and the doctrinal. As a Latin prose stylist, Erasmus was unequaled since the days of Cicero. Extraordinarily eloquent and witty, he reveled in tailoring his mode of discourse to fit his subject, creating dazzling verbal effects and coining puns that took on added meaning if the reader knew Greek as well as Latin. Above all, Erasmus excelled in the deft use of irony, poking fun at everything, including himself. For example, in his *Colloquies* (Discussions) he has a fictional character lament the evils of the times: "Kings make war, priests strive to line their pockets, theologians invent syllogisms, monks roam outside their cloisters, the commons riot, and Erasmus writes colloquies."

But although Erasmus's urbane Latin style and humor earned him a wide audience on those grounds alone, he intended everything he wrote to promote what he called the "philosophy of Christ." Erasmus believed that the society of his day had lost sight of the Gospels' teachings. Accordingly, he offered his contemporaries three different kinds of writings: clever satires in which people could recognize their own foibles, serious moral treatises meant to offer guidance toward proper Christian behavior, and scholarly editions of basic Christian texts.

In the first category belong the works of Erasmus that are still widely read today: *The Praise of Folly* (1509), in which he ridiculed pedantry and dogmatism, ignorance and gullibility—even within the Church; and the *Colloquies* (1518), in which he held up contemporary religious practices for examination, couching a serious message in the ironic tone we just noted. In these books, Erasmus let fictional characters do the talking so his own views on any given topic can only be determined by inference. But in his second mode, Erasmus spoke clearly in his own voice. In the *Handbook of the Christian Knight* (1503), he used the popular language of chivalry as a means to encourage a life of inward piety; in the *Complaint of Peace* (1517), he argued movingly for Christian pacifism. Erasmus's pacifism was one of his most deeply held values, and he returned to it again and again in his published works.

Despite the success of these writings, Erasmus considered textual scholarship his greatest achievement. Revering the authority of the earliest church fathers, he brought out reliable printed editions of works by Saints Augustine, Jerome, and Ambrose. He also used his extraordinary command of Latin and Greek to produce a more accurate edition of the New Testament. For after reading Lorenzo Valla's *Notes on the New Testament* in 1504, Erasmus became convinced that nothing was more imperative than divesting the Christian scriptures of myriad errors in transcription and translation that had piled up over the course of preceding centuries. He therefore spent ten years comparing all the early Greek biblical manuscripts he could find in order to establish an authoritative text. When it finally appeared in 1516, Erasmus's Greek New Testament, published together with explanatory notes and his own new Latin translation, became one of the most important scholarly landmarks of all time. In the hands of Martin Luther, it would play a critical role in the early stages of the Reformation (see Chapter 13).

The Influence of Erasmus

One of Erasmus's closest friends, and a close second to him in distinction among Christian humanists, was the Englishman Sir Thomas More (1478–1535). In later life, following a successful career as a lawyer and speaker of the House of Commons, More was appointed lord chancellor of England in 1529. He was not long in this position, however, before he opposed King Henry VIII's plan to establish a national church under royal control that would deny the supremacy of the pope (see Chapter 13). (He was eventually executed and is now revered as a Catholic martyr.) Much earlier, however, in 1516, More published his most famous book, *Utopia* (No Place).

Purporting to describe an ideal community on an imaginary island, the book is really an Erasmian critique of contemporary culture: disparities between poverty and wealth, drastic punishments, religious persecution, and the senseless slaughter of war. In contrast to Europeans, the inhabitants of the fictional Utopia hold all their goods in common, work only six hours a day (so that all may have leisure for intellectual pursuits), and practice the natural virtues of wisdom, moderation, fortitude, and justice. Although More advanced no explicit arguments here in favor of Christianity, he might have meant to imply that if the Utopians could manage their society so well without the benefit of Christian revelation, Europeans who knew the Gospels ought to be able to do even better.

Erasmus and More head a long list of energetic and eloquent northern humanists who made signal contributions to the collective enterprise of revolutionizing the

***SIR THOMAS MORE* BY HANS HOLBEIN THE YOUNGER.** Holbein's skill in rendering the gravity and interiority of his subject is matched by his masterful representation of the sumptuous chain of office, furred mantle, and velvet sleeves that indicate the political and professional status of Henry VIII's lord chancellor.

study of early Christianity, and their achievements had a direct influence on Protestant reformers—as we shall see in the next chapter. Yet very few of them were willing to join Luther and other Protestant leaders in rejecting the fundamental principles on which the power of the Roman Church was based. Most tried to remain within its fold while still espousing an ideal of inward piety and scholarly inquiry. But as the leaders of the Church grew less and less tolerant of dissent, even mild criticism came to seem like heresy. Erasmus himself died early enough to escape persecution, but several of his less fortunate followers did not.

The Literature of the Northern Renaissance

Although Christian humanism would be severely challenged by the Reformation, the artistic Renaissance in the North would flourish. Poets in France and England vied with one another to adapt the elegant lyric forms pioneered by Petrarch (Chapter 11) and popularized by many subsequent poets, including Michelangelo. The sonnet was particularly influential and would become one of the verse forms embraced by William Shakespeare (1554–1616; see chapter 14). Another English poet, Edmund Spenser (c. 1552–1599), drew on the literary innovation of Ariosto's *Orlando Furioso*: his *Faerie Queene* is a similarly long chivalric romance that revels in sensuous imagery. Meanwhile, the more satirical side of Renaissance humanism was embraced by the French writer François Rabelais (*RA-beh-lay*, c. 1494–1553).

Like Erasmus, whom he greatly admired, Rabelais began his career in the Church; but he soon left the cloister to study medicine. A practicing physician, Rabelais interspersed his professional activities with literary endeavors, the most enduring of these are the twin books *Gargantua* and *Pantagruel*, a series of "chronicles" describing the lives and times of giants whose fabulous size and gross appetites serve as vehicles for much lusty humor. Also like Erasmus, Rabelais also satirized religious hypocrisy, scholasticism, superstition, and bigotry. But unlike Erasmus, who wrote in a highly cultivated classical Latin style comprehensible only to learned readers, Rabelais chose to address a different audience by writing in extremely crude French and by glorifying every human appetite as natural and healthy.

Northern Architecture and Art

Although many architects in northern Europe continued to build in the flamboyant Gothic style of the later Middle Ages, the classical values of Italian architects can be seen in some of the splendid new castles constructed in France's Loire valley—châteaux too elegant to be defensible—and in the royal palace (now museum) of the Louvre in Paris, which replaced an old twelfth-century fortress. The influence of Renaissance ideals are also visible in the work of the German artist Albrecht Dürer (*DIRR-er*, 1471–1528). Dürer was the first northerner to master the techniques of proportion and perspective, and he shared with contemporary Italians a fascination with nature and the human body. He also took advantage of the printing press to circulate his work to a wide audience, making his delicate pencil drawings into engravings that could be mass produced.

But Dürer never really embraced classical subject, drawing inspiration instead from more traditional Christian legends and from the Christian humanism of Erasmus. For example, Dürer's serenely radiant engraving of Saint Jerome seems to express the scholarly absorption that Erasmus would have enjoyed while working quietly in his study. Indeed, Dürer aspired to immortalize Erasmus himself in a major portrait, but the paths of the two men crossed only once. Instead, the accomplishment of capturing Erasmus's pensive spirit in oils was left to another northern artist, the German Hans Holbein the Younger (1497–1543). Holbein also painted an acute portrait of Erasmus's friend and kindred spirit, Sir Thomas More. These two portraits, in themselves, exemplify a Renaissance emphasis on the making of naturalistic likenesses that express human individuality.

Tradition and Innovation in Music

Like the visual arts, the gorgeous music produced during this era was nourished by patrons' desire to surround themselves with beauty. Yet unlike painting and sculpture, musical practice did not reach back to classical antiquity but drew instead on well-established medieval conventions. Even before the Black Death, a musical movement called *ars nova* ("new art") was already flourishing in France, and it had spread to Italy during the lifetime of Petrarch. Its outstanding composers had been Guillaume de Machaut (c. 1300–1377) and Francesco Landini (c. 1325–1397).

The madrigals (part-songs) and ballads composed by these musicians and their successors expanded on earlier genres of secular music, but their greatest achievement was a highly complicated yet delicate contrapuntal style adapted for the liturgy of the Church. Machaut was the first-known composer to provide a polyphonic (harmonized) version of the major sections of the Mass. In the fifteenth century, the dissemination of this new musical aesthetic combined with a host of French, Flemish, and Italian elements in the multicultural courts of Europe, particularly that of Burgundy.

THE POLITICS OF CHRISTIAN EUROPE

We have already observed how the intellectual and artistic activity of the Renaissance movement was both fueled and hindered by the political developments of the later fifteenth century—within Italy, and throughout Europe. In 1453, France had emerged victorious in the Hundred Years' War, while England plunged into a further three decades of bloody civil conflict that touched every corner of that kingdom. The French monarchy was therefore able to rebuild its power and prestige while at the same time extending its control over regions that had long been controlled by the English crown and that were now part of an enlarged kingdom of France.

In 1494, the French king Charles VIII acted on a plan to expand his reach even further, into Italy. Leading an army of 30,000 well-trained troops across the Alps, he intended to press ancestral claims to the duchy of Milan and the kingdom of Naples. This effort yielded only a tenuous hold on Naples by the time Charles left a year later, and it solidified Italian opposition to French occupation, as we noted above; in our discussion of Machiavelli.

The rulers of Spain, whose territorial claims on Sicily also extended to Naples, were spurred by this to forge an uneasy alliance among the Papal States, some principalities of the Holy Roman Empire, Milan, and Venice. But the respite was brief. Charles's successor, Louis XII, launched a second invasion in 1499. For over a generation, until 1529, warfare in Italy was virtually uninterrupted. Alliances and counteralliances among city-states became further catalysts for violence and made Italy a magnet for mercenaries who could barely be kept in check by the generals who employed them.

Meanwhile, northern Italian city-states' virtual monopoly of trade with Asia, which had been one of the chief economic underpinnings of artistic and intellectual patronage, was being gradually eroded by the shifting of trade routes from the Mediterranean to the Atlantic (Chapters 10 and 11). It was also hampered by the increasing power of the Ottoman Empire, and even by the imperial pretensions of a new Russian ruler.

The Imperial Power of Ivan the Great

In previous chapters, we noted that the Russian duchy of Muscovy had become the champion of the Greek Orthodox Church and, as such, considered itself a true heir of Rome. After the fall of Constantinople to the Ottomans, the Muscovite grand duke even assumed the imperial title *tsar* (caesar)

***SAINT JEROME IN HIS STUDY* BY DÜRER.** Jerome, the biblical translator of the fourth century (see Chapter 6), was a hero to both Dürer and Erasmus: the paragon of inspired Christian scholarship. Note how the scene exudes contentment, even down to the sleeping lion, which seems more like an overgrown tabby cat than a symbol of Christ.

By the beginning of the sixteenth century, Franco-Flemish composers came to dominate many important courts and cathedrals, creating a variety of new forms and styles that bear a close affinity to Renaissance art and poetry.

Throughout Europe, the general level of musical proficiency in this era was very high. The singing of part-songs was a popular pastime in homes and at informal social gatherings, and the ability to read a part at sight was expected of the educated elite. Aristocratic women, in particular, were expected to display mastery of the new musical instruments that had been developed to add nuance and texture to existing musical forms, including the lute, the viol, the violin, and a variety of woodwind and keyboard instruments like the harpsichord.

Although most composers of this period were men trained in the service of the Church, they rarely made sharp distinctions between sacred and secular music. Like sculpture, music was coming into its own as a serious independent art. As such, it would become an important medium for the expression of both Catholic and Protestant ideals during the Reformation and also one of the few art forms equally acceptable to all.

THE EXPANSION OF MUSCOVITE RUSSIA TO 1505. The grand duchy of Moscow was the heart of what would soon become the Russian Empire. ■ *With what other empires and polities did the Muscovites have to compete during this period of expansion?* ■ *How did the relative isolation of Moscow, compared with early Kiev, allow for the growth of Muscovite power, on the one hand, and Moscow's distinctively non-Western culture, on the other?* ■ *How might the natural direction of the expansion of Muscovite power until 1505 help to encourage attitudes often at odds with those of western European civilization?*

and borrowed the Byzantine ideology of the ruler's divine election. These claims would eventually undergird the sacred position later ascribed to the tsars. But ideology alone could not have built the Russian Empire. Behind its growth lay the steadily growing power of its rulers, especially that of Grand Duke Ivan III (1462–1505), known as Ivan the Great, the first to lay down a distinctive imperial agenda.

Ivan launched a series of conquests that annexed all the independent principalities lying between Moscow and the border of Poland-Lithuania. After invading Lithuania in 1492 and 1501, Ivan even succeeded in bringing parts of that domain (portions of modern Belarus and Ukraine) under his control. Meanwhile, he married the niece of the last Byzantine emperor, giving real substance to the claim that Muscovy was New Rome. He also rebuilt his fortified Moscow residence, known as the Kremlin, in magnificent Italianate style. He would later adopt, as his imperial insignia, the double-headed eagle of Rome and its legions. By the

IVAN THE GREAT. This modern tribute to Ivan III prominently displays the two-headed eagle of imperial Rome. ■ *What is the significance of this symbolic choice?*

time of his death in 1505, Muscovy was firmly established as a dominant power. Indeed, the power of the tsar was more absolute in this period than that of any European monarch.

The Growth of National Churches

Meanwhile, as Muscovy laid claim to the mantle of Roman imperial power, the papacy was pouring resources into the glorification of the original Rome and the aggrandizement of the papal office. But neither the city nor its rulers could keep pace with their political and religious rivals. Following the Council of Constance (see Chapter 11), the papacy's victory over the conciliarists was a costly one. To win the support of Europe's kings and princes, various popes negotiated a series of religious treaties known as "concordats," which granted these rulers extensive authority over churches within their domains. The papacy thus secured its theoretical supremacy at the expense of its real power. Reigning popes also strengthened the national monarchies

that were emerging in this era. For under the terms of these concordats, kings now received many of the revenues that had previously gone to the papacy. They also acquired new powers to appoint candidates to church offices. It was, in many ways, a drastic reversal of the hard-won reforms of the eleventh and twelfth centuries that had created such a powerful papacy in the first place.

Having given away so many sources of revenue and authority, the popes of the late fifteenth century became even more dependent on their own territories in central Italy. But to tighten their hold on the Papal States, they had to rule like other Italian princes: leading armies, jockeying for alliances, and undermining their opponents by every possible means—including covert operations, murder, and assassination. Judged by the secular standards of the day, these efforts paid off: the Papal States became one of the better-governed and wealthier principalities in Italy. But such methods did nothing to increase the popes' reputation for piety, and disillusionment with the papacy as a force for the advancement of spirituality became even more widespread.

With both papal authority and Rome's spiritual prestige in decline, kings and princes became the primary figures to whom both clergy and laity looked for religious and moral guidance. Many secular rulers responded to such expectations aggressively, closing scandal-ridden monasteries, suppressing alleged heretics, regulating vice, and prohibiting the lower classes from dressing like the nobility. By these and other such measures, rulers could present themselves as champions of moral reform while also strengthening their political power. The result was an increasingly close link between national monarchies and national churches, a link that would become even stronger after the Reformation.

The Triumph of the "Reconquista"

The kingdoms of the Iberian Peninsula were also in constant conflict during this period. In Castile, civil war and incompetent governance allowed the Castilian nobility to gain greater control over the peasantry and greater independence from the monarchy. In Aragon, royal government benefited from the extended commercial influence of Catalonia, which was under Aragonese authority. But after 1458, Aragon too became enmeshed in a civil war, a war in which both France and Castile became involved.

A solution to the disputed succession that had caused the war in Aragon would ultimately lie in the blending of powerful royal families. In 1469, Prince Ferdinand of Aragon was recognized as the undisputed heir to that throne

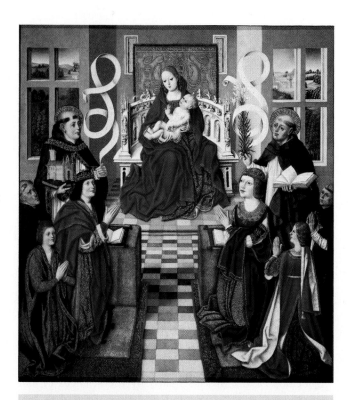

FERDINAND AND ISABELLA HONORING THE VIRGIN. In this contemporary Spanish painting, the royal couple are shown with two of their children and two household chaplains and in the company of the Blessed Virgin, the Christ Child, and saints from the Dominican order (the Dominicans were instrumental in conducting the affairs of the Spanish Inquisition). ▪ *How clear is the distinction between these holy figures and the royal family?* ▪ *What message is conveyed by their proximity?*

of their Christian subjects. Indeed, scholars often refer to this period of Spain's history as a time of *convivencia*, a word that means "living together" or "harmonious coexistence." While relations among various religious and ethnic groups were not always uniformly peaceful or positive, the policies of Muslim rulers in al-Andalus had enabled an extraordinary hybrid culture to flourish there.

The aims of the Spanish Reconquista were diametrically opposed to those of "living together." The crusading ideology of "reconquest" sought instead to forge a single, homogenous community, based on the fiction that Spain had once been entirely Christian and should be restored to its former purity. The year 1492 therefore marks not only the end of Muslim rule in medieval Spain but also the culmination of a process of Jewish exclusion that had accelerated in the late thirteenth century (see Chapter 9). Within this history, the Spanish expulsion of the Jews stands out for the staggering scope of the displacements and destruction it entailed: at least 100,000 and possibly as many as 200,000 men, women, and children were deprived of their homes and livelihoods.

The Christian monarchs' motives for ordering this expulsion are still debated. Tens of thousands of Spanish Jews had converted to Christianity between 1391 and 1420, many as a result of coercion but some from sincere religious conviction. And for a generation or so, it seemed possible that these converts, known as *conversos*, might successfully assimilate into Christian society. But the same civil wars that led to the union of Ferdinand and Isabella made the *conversos* targets of discriminatory legislation. Conflict may also have fueled popular suspicions that these converts remained Jews in secret. To make "proper" Christians out of the *conversos*, the "Most Catholic" monarchs—as they were now called—may have concluded that they needed to remove any potentially seditious influences that might stem from the continuing presence of a Jewish community in Spain.

What became of the Spanish Jews? Some traveled north, to the Rhineland towns of Germany or to eastern Europe, but most settled in Muslim regions of the Mediterranean and Middle East. Many found a haven in the Ottoman Empire. As we already noted, there were many opportunities for advancement in the Ottoman imperial bureaucracy, while the Ottoman economy benefited from the highly skilled labor of Jewish artisans and the vast trading networks of Jewish merchants. In time, new forms and expressions of Jewish culture would emerge, and new communities would form. And although the extraordinary opportunities afforded by the *Convivencia* could never be revived, the descendants of these Spanish Jews—known as

and, in the same year, secured this position by marrying Isabella, the heiress to Castile. Isabella became a queen in 1474, Ferdinand a king in 1479; and although Castile and Aragon continued to be ruled as separate kingdoms until 1714—there are tensions between the two former kingdoms even now—the marriage of Ferdinand and Isabella enabled the pursuit of several ambitious policies. In particular, their union allowed them to spend their combined resources on the creation of Europe's most powerful army, which was initially employed to conquer the last remaining principality of what had been al-Andalus: Muslim Spain. That principality, Granada, fell in 1492.

The End of the Convivencia and the Expulsion of the Jews

For more than seven relatively centuries, Spain's Jewish communities had enjoyed the many privileges extended by their Muslim rulers, who were also relatively tolerant

Sephardi Jews, or Sephardim—still treasure the traditions and customs formed in Spain over a thousand years ago.

The Extension of the Reconquista

Although the Christian kingdoms of Iberia had been devoted, for centuries, to the reconquest of territory, the victory over the Muslims of Granada and the expulsion of the Jews in 1492 were watershed events. They mark the beginning of a sweeping initiative to construct a new basis for the precariously united kingdoms of Aragon and Castile, one that could transcend rival regional identities. Like other contemporary monarchs, Ferdinand and Isabella sought to strengthen their emerging nation-state by constructing an exclusively Christian identity for its people and by attaching that new identity to the crown and promoting a single national language, Castilian Spanish. They also succeeded in capturing and redirecting another language: the rhetoric of crusade.

The problem with the crusading ethos, as we have seen, is that it always seeks new outlets. Having created a new exclusively Christian Spanish kingdom through the defeat of all external enemies and internal threats, where were the energies harnessed by the Reconquista to be directed? The answer came from an unexpected quarter and had very unexpected consequences. Just a few months after Ferdinand and Isabella marched victoriously into Granada, the queen granted three ships to a Genoese adventurer who promised to reach India by sailing westward across the Atlantic Ocean, claiming any new lands he found for Spain. Columbus never reached India, but he did help to extend the tradition of reconquest to the New World—with far-reaching consequences.

NEW TARGETS AND TECHNOLOGIES OF CONQUEST

The Spanish monarchs' decision to underwrite a voyage of exploration was spurred by their desire to counter the successful Portuguese ventures of the past half century. For it was becoming clear that a tiny kingdom on the northwestern tip of the Iberian Peninsula would soon dominate the sea-lanes if rival entrepreneurs did not attempt to find alternate routes and establish equally lucrative colonies. This competition with Portugal was another reason why Isabella turned to a Genoese sea captain when she sought

to expand Spain's wealth and global influence—not to a Portuguese one.

Prince Henry the Navigator and Portuguese Colonial Initiatives

Although Portugal had been an independent Christian kingdom since the twelfth century (see Chapter 9), it was never able to compete effectively with its more powerful neighbors (Muslim or Christian) on land. But when the focus of European economic expansion began to shift toward the Atlantic (see Chapter 10), Portuguese mariners were well placed to take advantage of the trend. A central figure in the history of Portuguese maritime imperialism is Prince Henry, later called "the Navigator" (1394–1460), a son of King João I of Portugal and his English queen, Philippa of Lancaster (sister of England's Henry IV).

Prince Henry was fascinated by the sciences of cartography and navigation, and he helped to ensure that Portuguese sailors had access to the latest charts and navigational instruments. He was also inspired by the stories told by John de Mandeville and Marco Polo—particularly the legend of Prester John, a mythical Christian king dwelling somewhere at the end of the earth, whom Europeans believed would be their ally against the Muslims if only they could locate him. More concretely, Prince Henry had ambitions to extend Portuguese control into the Atlantic, to tap into the burgeoning market for slaves in the Ottoman Empire and to establish direct links with the sources of African gold.

Prince Henry played an important part in organizing the Portuguese colonization of Madeira, the Canary Islands, and the Azores—and in the process he pioneered the Portuguese slave trade, which almost entirely eradicated the population of the Canaries before targeting Africa. By the 1440s, Portuguese explorers had reached the Cape Verde Islands. In 1444, they landed on the African mainland in the area that became known as the Gold Coast, where they began to collect cargoes of gold and slaves for export back to Portugal. Prince Henry personally directed eight of the thirty-five Portuguese voyages to Africa that occurred during his lifetime. And in order to outflank the cross-Saharan gold trade, largely controlled by the Muslims of North Africa and mediated by the Genoese, he decided to intercept this trade at its source by building a series of forts along the African coastline. This was also his main reason for colonizing the Canary

OVERSEAS EXPLORATION IN THE FIFTEENTH AND SIXTEENTH CENTURIES. ▪ *What were the major routes taken by European explorers of the fifteenth and sixteenth centuries?* ▪ *What appear to be the explorers' main goals?* ▪ *How might the establishment of outposts in Africa, America, and the East Indies have radically altered the balance of power in the Old World, and why?*

EXPLORERS
— Columbus: first voyage
— Columbus: next three voyages
— Bartholomeu Dias
— Vasco da Gama
— Amerigo Vespucci
— Magellan and Magellan's ship

CONQUISTADORES
····· Cortés
····· Pizarro

OUTPOSTS AND SETTLEMENTS
▪ Portuguese
▪ Spanish

Islands, which he saw as a staging ground for expeditions into the African interior.

From Africa to India and Beyond: An Empire of Spices

By the 1470s, Portuguese sailors had rounded the western coast of Africa and were exploring the Gulf of Guinea. In 1483, they reached the mouth of the Congo River. In 1488, the Portuguese captain Bartholomeu Dias was accidentally blown around the southern tip of Africa by a gale, after which he named the point "Cape of Storms." But King João II (r. 1481–95) took a more optimistic view of Dias's achievement: he renamed it the Cape of Good Hope and began planning a naval expedition to India. In 1497–98, accordingly, Vasco da Gama rounded the cape, and then, with the help of a Muslim navigator named Ibn Majid, crossed the Indian Ocean to Calicut, on the southwestern coast of India. For the first time, this opened a viable sea route between Europe and the Far Eastern spice trade. Although Gama lost half his fleet and one-third of his men on his two-year voyage, his cargo of spices was so valuable that his losses were deemed insignificant. His heroism became legendary, and his story became the basis for the Portuguese national epic, the *Lusiads*.

Now masters of the quickest route to riches in the world, the Portuguese swiftly capitalized on their decades of accomplishment. Not only did their trading fleets sail regularly to India, there were Portuguese efforts to monopolize the entire spice trade: in 1509, the Portuguese defeated an Ottoman fleet and then blockaded the mouth of the Red Sea, attempting to cut off one of the traditional routes by which spices had traveled to Alexandria and Beirut. By 1510, Portuguese military forces had established a series of forts along the western Indian coastline, including their headquarters at Goa. In 1511, Portuguese ships seized Malacca, a center of the spice trade on the Malay Peninsula. By 1515, they had reached the Spice Islands (East Indies) and the coast of China. So completely did the Portuguese now dominate the spice trade that by the 1520s even the Venetians were forced to buy their pepper in the Portuguese capital of Lisbon.

Naval Technology and Navigation

The Portuguese caravel—the workhorse ship of those first voyages to Africa—was based on ship and sail designs that had been in use among Portuguese fishermen since the thirteenth century. Starting in the 1440s, however, Portuguese shipwrights began building larger caravels of about 50 tons displacement equipped with two masts, each carrying a triangular (lateen) sail. Columbus's *Niña* was a ship of this design, although it was refitted with two square sails in the Portuguese-held Canary Islands to enable it to sail more efficiently before the wind during the Atlantic crossing. Such ships required much smaller crews than did the multi-oared galleys that were still commonly used in the Mediterranean. By the end of the fifteenth century, even larger caravels of around 200 tons were being constructed, with a third mast and a combination of square and lateen sails.

Europeans were also making significant advances in navigation during this era. Quadrants, which could calculate latitude in the Northern Hemisphere by the height of the North Star above the horizon, were in widespread use by the 1450s. As sailors approached the equator, however, the quadrant became less and less useful, and navigators instead made use of astrolabes, which reckoned latitude by the height of the sun. Like quadrants, astrolabes had been in use for centuries. But it was not until the 1480s that the astrolabe became a really practical instrument for seaborne navigation, thanks to the preparation of standard tables for the calculation of latitude whose preparation was sponsored by the Portuguese crown. Compasses, too, were coming into more widespread use during the fifteenth century. Longitude, however, remained impossible to calculate accurately until the eighteenth century, when the invention of the marine chronometer finally made it possible to keep accurate time at sea. In this prior age of discovery, Europeans sailing east or west across the oceans generally had to rely on their skill at dead reckoning to determine where they were.

European sailors also benefited from a new interest in maps and navigational charts. Especially important were books known as *rutters* or *routiers*. These contained detailed sailing instructions and descriptions of the coastal landmarks a pilot could expect to encounter en route to a variety of destinations. Mediterranean sailors had used similar portolan charts since the thirteenth century, mapping the ports along the coastlines, tracking prevailing winds and tides, and indicating dangerous reefs and shallow harbors (see Chapter 10). In the fifteenth century, these mapmaking techniques were extended to the Atlantic Ocean; by the end of the sixteenth century, the accumulated knowledge contained in rutters spanned the globe.

Artillery and Empire

Larger, more maneuverable ships and improved navigational aids made it possible for the Portuguese and other European mariners to reach Africa, Asia, and—eventually—

SPANISH GALLEON. The larger, full-bottomed ships that came into use during the fifteenth century would become engines of imperial conquest and the vessels that brought the riches of those conquests back to Europe. This wooden model was made for the Museo Storico Navale di Venezia (Naval History Museum) in Venice, Italy.

the Americas. But fundamentally, these European commercial empires were military achievements that capitalized on what Europeans had learned in their wars against each other. Perhaps the most critical military advance was the increasing sophistication of artillery, a development made possible not only by gunpowder but also by improved metallurgical techniques for casting cannon barrels. By the middle of the fifteenth century, as we observed in Chapter 11, the use of artillery pieces had rendered the stone walls of medieval castles and towns obsolete, a fact brought home in 1453 by the successful French siege of Bordeaux (which ended the Hundred Years' War), and by the Ottoman siege of Constantinople (which ended the Byzantine Empire).

Indeed, the new ship designs (first caravels, and then the heavier galleons) were important in part because their larger size made it possible to mount more effective artillery pieces on them. European vessels were now conceived as floating artillery platforms, with scores of guns mounted in fixed positions along their sides and swivel guns mounted fore and aft. These guns were vastly expensive, as were the ships that carried them, but for those rulers who could afford them, such ships made it possible to back mercantile ventures with military power. As we already noted, Vasco da Gama had been able to sail

into the Indian Ocean in 1498, but the Portuguese did not gain control of that ocean until 1509, when they defeated combined Ottoman and Indian naval forces. Portuguese trading outposts in Africa and Asia were essentially fortifications, built not so much to guard against the attacks of native peoples as to ward off assaults from other Europeans. Without this essential military component, the European maritime empires that were emerging in this period could not have existed.

Atlantic Colonization and a New Kind of Slavery

Although slavery had effectively disappeared in much of northwestern Europe by the early twelfth century, it continued in parts of the Mediterranean world and had been introduced into some regions of eastern Europe after the Black Death. But this slavery existed on a very small scale. There were no slave-powered factories or large-scale agricultural systems in this period. The only major slave markets and slave economies were in the Ottoman Empire, and there slaves ran the vast Ottoman bureaucracy and staffed the army. And in all these cases, as in antiquity, no aspect of slavery was racially based. In Italy and elsewhere in the medieval Mediterranean world, slaves were often captives from an array of locales. In eastern Europe, they were functionally serfs. Most Ottoman slaves were European Christians, predominantly Poles, Ukrainians, Greeks, and Bulgarians. In the early Middle Ages, Germanic and Celtic peoples had been widely enslaved. Under the Roman Empire, slaves had come from every part of the known (and unknown) world.

What was new about the slavery of the late fifteenth century was its increasing racialization—an aspect of modern slavery that has made an indelible impact on our own society. To Europeans, African slaves were visible in ways that other slaves were not, and it became convenient for those who dealt in them to justify the mass deportation of entire populations by claiming their racial inferiority and their "natural" fitness for a life of bondage. This nefarious practice, too, has had long-lasting and tragic consequences that still afflict the civilizations of our own world.

In Lisbon, which became a significant market for enslaved Africans during Prince Henry's lifetime, something on the order of 15,000 to 20,000 African captives were sold within a twenty-year period. In the following half century, by about 1505, the numbers amounted to 150,000. For the most part, the purchasers of these slaves regarded them as

The Ottomans' Army of Slaves

Although the growing African slave trade was creating a newly racialized idea of slavery in the Caribbean and the Americas, slavery in Europe was not tied to race. Indeed, slavery could be a path to upward mobility in the Ottoman Empire. The following account is from a memoir written by Konstantin Mihailovic, a Serbian Christian who was captured as a youth by the army of Sultan Mehmet II. For eight years, he served in the Ottoman janissary ("gate-keeper") corps. In 1463, the fortress he was defending for the sultan was captured by the Hungarians, after which he recorded his experiences for a Christian audience.

Whenever the Turks invade foreign lands and capture their people, an imperial scribe follows immediately behind them, and whatever boys there are, he takes them all into the janissaries and gives five gold pieces for each one and sends them across the sea [to Anatolia]. There are about two thousand of these boys. If, however, the number of them from enemy peoples does not suffice, then he takes from the Christians in every village in his land who have boys, having established what is the most every village can give so that the quota will always be full. And the boys whom he takes in his own land are called *cilik*. Each one of them can leave his property to whomever he wants after his death. And those whom he takes among the enemies are called *pendik*. These latter after their deaths can leave nothing; rather, it goes to the emperor, except that if someone comports himself well and is so deserving that he be freed, he may leave it to whomever he wants. And on the boys who are across the sea the emperor spends nothing; rather, those to whom they are entrusted must maintain them and send them where he orders. Then they take those who are suited for it on ships and there they study and train to skirmish in battle. There the emperor already provides for them and gives them a wage. From there he chooses for his own court those who are trained and then raises their wages.

Source: Konstantin Mihailovic, *Memoirs of a Janissary* (Michigan Slavic Translations 3), trans. Benjamin Stolz (Ann Arbor, MI: 1975), pp. 157–59.

Questions for Analysis

1. Why might the Ottoman emperor have established this system for "recruiting" and training janissaries? What are its strengths and weaknesses?

2. Based on your knowledge of Western civilizations, how unusual would you deem this method of raising troops? How does it compare to the strategies of other rulers we have studied?

---

status symbols; it became fashionable to have African footmen, page boys, and ladies' maids. In the Atlantic colonies—Madeira, the Canaries, and the Azores—land was still worked mainly by European settlers and sharecroppers. Slave labor, if it was employed at all, was generally used only in sugar mills. On Madeira and the Canaries, where sugar became the predominant cash crop during the last quarter of the fifteenth century, some slaves were introduced as agricultural laborers. But even sugar production did not lead to the widespread introduction of slavery on these islands.

However, a new kind of slave-based sugar plantation began to emerge in Portugal's eastern Atlantic colonies in the 1460s, starting on the Cape Verde Islands and then extending southward into the Gulf of Guinea. These islands were not populated when the Portuguese began to settle them, and their climate generally discouraged most Europeans from living there. They were ideally located, however, along the routes of slave traders venturing outward from the nearby West African coast. It was this plantation model that would be exported to Brazil by the Portuguese and to the Caribbean islands of the Americas by their Spanish conquerors, with incalculable consequences for the peoples of Africa, the Americas, and Europe (see Chapter 14).

EUROPEANS IN A NEW WORLD

Like his contemporaries, Christopher Columbus (1451–1506) understood that the world was a sphere. But like them, he also thought it was much smaller than it actually is. (As we saw in Chapter 4, the accurate calculation of the globe's circumference made in ancient Alexandria had been suppressed centuries later by Roman geographers.) Furthermore, it had long been accepted that there were only three continents, Europe, Asia, and Africa—hence Columbus's decision to reach Asia by sailing west, a plan that seemed even more plausible after the discovery and colonization of the Canary Islands and the Azores. The existence of these islands reinforced a new hypothesis that the Atlantic was dotted with similar lands all the way to Japan. This emboldened Columbus's royal patrons, who became convinced that the Genoese mariner could reach China in about a month, after a stop for provisions on the Canaries. This turned out to be a kind of self-fulfilling prophecy, for when Columbus reached the Bahamas and the island of Hispaniola after only a month's sailing, he reported that he had reached the outer islands of Asia.

The Shock of Discovery

Of course, Columbus was not the first European to set foot on the American continents. As we have already learned, Viking sailors briefly settled present-day Newfoundland, Labrador, and perhaps even portions of New England around the year 1000 (see Chapter 8). But knowledge of these Viking landings had been forgotten or ignored outside of Iceland for hundreds of years. It wasn't until the 1960s that the stories of these expeditions were corroborated by archaeological evidence. Moreover, the tiny Norwegian colony on Greenland—technically part of the North American landmass—had been abandoned in the fifteenth century, when the cooling of the climate (see Chapter 10) destroyed the fragile ecosystems that had barely sustained the lives of Norse settlers there.

Although Columbus brought back no spices to prove that he had found an alternate route to Asia, he did return with some small samples of gold and a few indigenous people—whose existence gave promise of entire tribes that might be "saved" by conversion to Christianity and whose lands could provide homes for Spanish settlers seeking new frontiers after the Reconquista. This provided sufficient incentive for the "Most Catholic" monarchs to finance three further expeditions by Columbus, and many more by other adventurers, missionaries, and colonists.

Meanwhile, the Portuguese, who had already obtained a papal bull granting them (hypothetical) ownership of all lands south of the Canaries, rushed to establish their own claims. After two years of wrangling and conflicting papal pronouncements, the Treaty of Tordesillas (1494) sought to demarcate Spanish and Portuguese possession of as-yet-undiscovered lands. The Spanish would ultimately emerge as the big winners in this gambling match. Within a decade, the coasts of two hitherto unknown continents were identified, as were clusters of new islands, most on the Spanish side of the (still disputed) meridian.

Gradually, Europeans reached the conclusion that the voyages of Columbus and his immediate successors had revealed an entirely "New World." And—shockingly—this world had not been foretold either by the teachings of Christianity or the wisdom of the ancients. Among the first to champion the fact of two new continents' existence was the Italian explorer and geographer Amerigo Vespucci (1454–1512), whose name was soon adopted as a descriptor for them. Eventually, those who came to accept this fact were forced to question the reliability of the key sources of knowledge on which Western civilizations had hitherto hinged (see Chapter 14).

At first, the realization that the Americas (as they were now called) were not an outpost of Asia came as a disappointment to the Spanish: two major land masses and two vast oceans disrupted their plans to beat the Portuguese to the Spice Islands. But new possibilities gradually became clear. In 1513, the Spanish explorer Vasco Núñez de Balboa first viewed the Pacific Ocean from the Isthmus of Panama, and news of the narrow divide between two vast oceans prompted Ferdinand and Isabella's grandson to renew their dream. This young monarch, Charles V (1500–1556), ruled not only Spain but the huge patchwork of territories encompassed by the Holy Roman Empire. In 1519, he accepted Ferdinand Magellan's proposal to see whether a route to Asia could be found by sailing around South America.

But Magellan's voyage demonstrated beyond question that the world was simply too large for any such plan to be feasible at that time. Of the five ships that left Spain under his command, only one returned, three years later, having been forced to circumnavigate the globe. Out of a crew of 265 sailors, only 18 survived. Most had died of scurvy or starvation; Magellan himself had been killed in a skirmish with native peoples in the Philippines.

This fiasco ended all hope of discovering an easy southwest passage to Asia—although the deadly dream

America as an Object of Desire

Under the influence of popular travel narratives that had circulated in Europe for centuries, Columbus and his fellow voyagers were prepared to find the New World full of cannibals. They also assumed that the indigenous peoples' custom of wearing little or no clothing—not to mention their "savagery"—would render their women sexually available. In a letter sent back home in 1495, one of Columbus's men recounted a notable encounter with a "cannibal girl" whom he had taken captive in his tent and whose naked body aroused his desire. He was surprised to find that she resisted his advances so fiercely that he had to tie her up—which of course made it easier for him to "subdue" her. In the end, he cheerfully reports, the girl's sexual performance was so satisfying that she might have been trained, as he put it, in a "school for whores."

The Flemish artist Jan van der Straet (1523–1605) would have heard many such reports of the encounters between (mostly male) Europeans and the peoples of the New World. This engraving, based on one of his drawings, is among the thousands of mass-produced images that circulated widely in Europe, thanks to the invention of printing. It imagines the first encounter between a male "Americus" (like Columbus or Amerigo Vespucci himself) and the New World, "America," depicted as a voluptuous, available woman. The Latin caption reads: "America rises to meet Americus; and whenever he calls her, she will always be aroused."

Questions for Analysis

1. Study the details of this image carefully. What does each symbolize, and how do they work together as an allegory of conquest and colonization?

2. On what stereotypes of indigenous peoples does this image draw? Notice, for example, the cannibalistic campfire of the group in the background or the posture of "America."

3. The New World itself—America—is imagined as female in this image. Why is this? What messages might this—and the suggestive caption—have conveyed to a European viewer?

Americen Americus retexit, & Semel vocauit inde semper excitam.

of a northwest passage survived and motivated many European explorers of North America into the twentieth century. It has been revived today: in our age of global warming, the retreat of Arctic pack ice has led to the opening of new shipping lanes, and in 2008 the first commercial voyage successfully traversed the Arctic Ocean.

The Dream of Gold and the Downfall of Empires

Although the unforeseen size of the globe made a westward passage to Asia untenable, given the technologies then available, Europeans were quick to capitalize on the sources of wealth that the New World itself could offer. What chiefly fired the imagination were those small samples of gold that Columbus had initially brought back to Spain. While rather paltry in themselves, they nurtured hopes that gold might lie piled in ingots somewhere in these vast new lands, ready to enrich any adventurer who discovered them. Rumor fed rumor, until a few freelance Spanish soldiers really did strike it rich beyond their most avaricious imaginings.

Their success, though, had little to do with their own efforts. Within a generation after the landing of the first ships under Columbus's command, European diseases had spread rapidly among the indigenous peoples of the Caribbean and the coastlines of the Americas. These diseases—especially measles and smallpox—were not fatal to those who carried them, because Europeans had developed immunities over many generations. But to the peoples of this New World, they were deadly in the extreme. For example, there were probably 250,000 people living on Hispaniola when Columbus arrived; within thirty years—a single generation—70 percent had perished from disease.

Moreover, the new waves of *conquistadores* (conquerors) were assisted by the complex political, economic, and military rivalries that already existed among the highly sophisticated societies they encountered. The Aztec Empire of Mexico rivaled any European state in its power, culture, and wealth—and like any successful empire it had subsumed many neighboring territories in the course of its own conquests. Its capital, Tenochtitlán (*ten-och-tit-LAN*, now Mexico City), amazed its European assailants, who had never seen anything like the height and grandeur of its buildings or the splendor of its public works. This splendor was itself evidence of the Aztecs' imperial might, which was resisted by many of the peoples from whom they demanded tribute.

The Aztecs' eventual conqueror, Hernán Cortés (1485–1547), had arrived in Hispaniola as a young man, in the wake of Columbus's initial landing. He had received a land grant from the Spanish crown and acted as magistrate of one of the first towns established there. In 1519, he headed an expedition to the mainland, which had been the target of some earlier exploratory missions that had not resulted in any permanent settlements—owing largely to the tight control of the Aztecs, whose imperial domain extended far beyond Tenochtitlán.

When Cortés arrived on the coast of the Aztec realm, he formed an intimate relationship with a native woman known as La Malinche. She became his consort and interpreter in the Nahua language, which was a lingua franca among the many different ethnic groups within the empire. With her help, he discovered that some peoples subjugated by the Aztecs were rebellious, and so he began to form stra-

THE AZTEC CITY OF TENOCHTITLÁN. The Spanish conquistador Bernal Díaz del Castillo (1492–1585) took part in the conquest of the Aztec Empire and later wrote a historical account of his adventures. His admiring description of the Aztec capital at Tenochtitlán records that the Spaniards were amazed to see such a huge city built in the midst of a vast lake, with gigantic buildings arranged in a meticulous urban plan around a central square and broad causeways linking the city to the mainland. This hand-colored woodcut was included in an early edition of Hernán Cortés's letters to Emperor Charles V, printed at Nuremberg (Germany) in 1524.

tegic alliances with their leaders. Cortés himself could only muster a force of a few hundred men, but his native allies numbered in the thousands.

These strategic alliances were crucial: although Cortés and his men had potentially superior weapons—guns and horses—these were more effective for their novelty than their utility. In fact, the rifles were of inferior quality, while gunpowder dampened by the humid climate had a tendency to misfire or fail to ignite altogether. So Cortés adopted the tactics and weaponry of his native allies in his dealings with the Aztec king, Montezuma II (r. 1502–1520), and in his final assaults upon the fortification of Tenochtitlán. In the end, though, it was European bacteria (not European technology or cunning) that led to his victory: the Aztecs were devastated by an outbreak of the plague virus that had arrived along with Cortés and his men. In 1521, their empire fell.

In 1533, another lucky conquistador, Francisco Pizarro, would manage to topple the highly centralized empire of the Incas, based in what is now Peru, by similar voluntary and involuntary means. In this case, he took advantage of an ongoing civil war that had weakened the reigning dynasty. He was also assisted by an epidemic of smallpox. Like Cortés, Pizarro promised his native allies liberation from an oppressive regime. Those formerly subject to the Aztecs and Incas would soon be able to judge how partial these promises were.

The Price of Conquest

The astonishing conquests of Mexico and Peru gave the conquistadors access to hoards of gold and silver that had been accumulated for centuries by Aztec and Inca rulers. Almost immediately, however, a search for the sources of these precious metals was launched by agents of the Spanish crown. The first gold deposits were discovered in Hispaniola, where surface mines were speedily established using native laborers, who were already dying in appalling numbers from disease and were now further decimated by brutality and overwork. The population dwindled further, to a mere 10 percent of its Pre-Columbian strength.

The loss of so many workers made the mines of Hispaniola uneconomical to operate, so European colonists turned instead to cattle raising and sugar production. Modeling their sugarcane plantations on those of the Cape Verde Islands and St. Thomas (São Tomé) in the Gulf of Guinea, colonists began to import thousands of African slaves to labor in the new industry. Sugar production was, by its nature, a capital-intensive undertaking. The need to import slave labor added further to its costs, guaranteeing that control over the new industry would fall into the hands of a few extremely wealthy planters and financiers.

Despite the establishment of sugar production in the Caribbean and cattle ranching on the Mexican mainland—whose devastating effects on the fragile ecosystem of Central America will be discussed in Chapter 14—it was mining that would shape the Spanish colonies most fundamentally in this period. If gold was the lure that had initially inspired the conquest, silver became its most lucrative export. Even before the discovery of vast silver deposits, the Spanish crown had taken steps to assume direct control over all colonial exports. It was therefore to the Spanish crown that the profits of empire were channeled. Europe's silver

SPANISH CONQUISTADORS IN MEXICO. This sixteenth-century drawing of conquistadors slaughtering the Aztec aristocracy emphasizes the advantages that plate armor and steel swords gave to the Spanish soldiers.

A Spanish Critique of New World Conquest

Not all Europeans approved of European imperialism or its "civilizing" effects on the peoples of the New World. One of the most influential contemporary critics was Bartolomé de las Casas (1484–1566). In 1502, when Bartolomé was eighteen years old, he and his father joined an expedition to Hispaniola. In 1510, he became the first ordained priest in the Americas and eventually became bishop of Chiapas (Mexico). Although he was a product of his times—he owned many slaves—he was also prescient in discerning the devastating effects of European settlement in the West Indies and Central America, and he particularly deplored the exploitation and extermination of indigenous populations. The following excerpt is from one of the many eloquent manifestos he published in an attempt to gain the sympathies of the Spanish crown and to reach a wide readership. It was printed in 1542 but draws on the impressions and opinions he had formed since his arrival in New Spain as a young man.

God made all the peoples of this area, many and varied as they are, as open and as innocent as can be imagined. The simplest people in the world—unassuming, long-suffering, unassertive, and submissive—they are without malice or guile, and are utterly faithful and obedient both to their own native lords and to the Spaniards in whose service they now find themselves. . . . They are innocent and pure in mind and have a lively intelligence, all of which makes them particularly receptive to learning and understanding the truths of our Catholic faith and to being instructed in virtue; indeed, God has invested them with fewer impediments in this regard than any other people on earth. . . .

It was upon these gentle lambs . . . that from the very first day they clapped eyes on them the Spanish fell like ravening wolves upon the fold, or like tigers and savage lions who have not eaten meat for days. The pattern established at the outset has remained unchanged to this day, and the Spaniards still do nothing save tear the natives to shreds, murder them and inflict upon them untold misery, suffering and distress, tormenting, harrying and persecuting them mercilessly. . . .

When the Spanish first journeyed there, the indigenous population of the island of Hispaniola stood at some three million; today only two hundred survive. The island of Cuba, which extends for a distance almost as great as that separating Valladolid from Rome, is now to all intents and purposes uninhabited; and two other large, beautiful and fertile islands, Puerto Rico and Jamaica, have been similarly devastated. Not a living soul remains today on any of the islands of the Bahamas . . . even though every single one of the sixty or so islands in the group . . . is more fertile and more beautiful than the Royal Gardens in Seville and the climate is as healthy as anywhere on earth. The native population, which once numbered some five hundred thousand, was wiped out by forcible expatriation to the island of Hispaniola, a policy adopted by the Spaniards in an endeavour to make up losses among the indigenous population of that island. . . .

At a conservative estimate, the despotic and diabolical behaviour of the Christians has, over the last forty years, led to the unjust and totally unwarranted deaths of more than twelve million souls, women and children among them. . . .

The reason the Christians have murdered on such a vast scale and killed anyone and everyone in their way is purely and simply greed. . . . The Spaniards have shown not the slightest consideration for these people, treating them (and I speak from first-hand experience, having been there from the outset) not as brute animals—indeed, I would to God they had done and had shown them the consideration they afford their animals—so much as piles of dung in the middle of the road. They have had as little concern for their souls as for their bodies, all the millions that have perished having gone to their deaths with no knowledge of God and without the benefit of the Sacraments. One fact in all this is widely known and beyond dispute, for even the tyrannical murderers themselves acknowledge the truth of it: the indigenous peoples never did the Europeans any harm whatever. . . .

Source: Bartolomé de las Casas, *A Short Account of the Destruction of the Indies*, trans. Nigel Griffin (Harmondsworth, UK: 1992), pp. 9–12.

Questions for Analysis

1. Given his perspective on the behavior of his countrymen, how might Bartolomé de las Casas have justified his own presence in New Spain (Mexico)? What do you think he may have hoped to achieve by publishing this account?

2. What comparisons does the author make between New Spain (Mexico) and the Old, and between indigenous peoples and Europeans? What is he trying to convey?

3. Compare this account with the contemporary engraving on page 000. What new light does this excerpt throw on that visual allegory? How might a reader-viewer of the time have reconciled these two very different pictures of European imperialism?

shortage, which had been acute for centuries, therefore came to an end.

Yet this massive infusion of silver into the European economy created more problems than it solved, because it accelerated an inflation that had already begun in the late fifteenth century. Initially, inflation had been driven by the renewed growth of the European population, an expanding colonial economy, and a relatively fixed supply of food. Thereafter, thanks to the influx of New World silver, inflation was driven by the hugely increased supply of coinage. As we shall see, this abundance of coinage led to the doubling and quadrupling of prices in the course of the sixteenth century and the collapse of this inflated economy—paradoxically driving a wave of impoverished Europeans to settle in the New World in ever greater numbers.

CONCLUSION

The expansion of the Mediterranean world into the Atlantic, which had been ongoing since the thirteenth century, was the essential preliminary to Columbus's voyages and to the rise of European empires in Africa, India, the Caribbean, and the Americas. Other events and innovations that we have surveyed in this chapter played a key role, too: the relatively rapid communications facilitated by the printing press; the tussle for power in Italy that led to the development of ever deadlier weapons; the navigational and colonial initiatives of the Portuguese; and the success of the Spanish Reconquista, which displaced Spain's venerable Jewish community and enabled Spanish rulers and adventurers to seek their fortunes overseas.

After You Read This Chapter

Visit StudySpace for quizzes, additional review materials, and multimedia documents. **wwnorton.com/web/westernciv18**

REVIEWING THE OBJECTIVES

- The artists of Italy were closely tied to those with political and military power. How did this relationship affect the kinds of work these artists produced?
- What aspects of Renaissance artistry and learning were adopted in northern Europe?
- What was the Reconquista, and how did it lead to a new way of thinking about Spanish identity?
- Europeans, especially the Portuguese, were developing new technologies and techniques that enabled exploration and colonial ventures in this period. What were they?
- The "discovery" of the New World had profound effects on the indigenous peoples and environment of the Americas. Describe some of these effects.

For the indigenous peoples and empires of the Americas, the results were cataclysmic. Within a century of Europeans' arrival, between 50 and 90 percent of some native populations had perished from disease, massacre, and enslavement. Moreover, Europeans' capacity to further their imperial ambitions wherever ships could sail and guns could penetrate profoundly destabilized Europe and its neighbors, sharpening the divisions among competing kingdoms and empires.

The ideals of the humanists and the artistry associated with the Renaissance often stand in sharp contrast to the harsh realities alongside which they coexisted and in which they were rooted. Artists could thrive in the atmosphere of competition and one-upmanship that characterized this period, but they could also find themselves reduced to the status of servants in the households of the wealthy and powerful—or forced to subordinate their artistry to the demands of warfare and espionage. Meanwhile, intellectuals and statesmen looked for inspiration to the precedents and glories of the past. But to which aspects of the past? Some humanists may have wanted to revive the principles of the Roman Republic, but many of them worked for ambitious despots who modeled themselves on Rome's dictators. The theories that undergirded European politics and colonial expansion were being used to legitimize many different kinds of power, including that of the papacy. All of these trends would be carried forward in the sixteenth century and would have a role to play in the upheaval that shattered Europe's fragile religious unity. It is to this upheaval, the Reformation, that we turn in Chapter 13.

PEOPLE, IDEAS, AND EVENTS IN CONTEXT

- Why was **GUTENBERG**'s invention of the **PRINTING PRESS** such a significant development?
- How did **NICCOLÒ MACHIAVELLI** respond to Italy's political situation within Europe? In what ways do artists like **LEONARDO DA VINCI** and **MICHELANGELO BUONARROTI** exemplify the ideals and realities of the Renaissance?
- How did northern European scholars like **DESIDERIUS ERASMUS** and **THOMAS MORE** apply humanist ideas to Christianity? How were these ideas expressed in art?
- What is significant about **IVAN THE GREAT**'s use of the title **TSAR**? In what other ways did the Russian emperor claim to be the heir of Rome?
- How did **ISABELLA OF CASTILE** and **FERDINAND OF ARAGON** succeed in creating a unified Spain through the **RECONQUISTA**?
- How does **PRINCE HENRY THE NAVIGATOR** exemplify the motives for pursuing overseas expansion? Why were the Portuguese so successful in establishing colonies in this period?
- What were the expectations that launched **COLUMBUS**'s voyage? What enabled the Spanish **CONQUISTADORS** to subjugate the peoples of the **AMERICAS**?

THINKING ABOUT CONNECTIONS

- Phrases like "Renaissance man" and "a Renaissance education" are still part of our common vocabulary. Given what you have learned in this chapter, how has your understanding of such phrases changed? How would you explain their true meaning to others?
- How do the patterns of conquest and colonization discussed in this chapter compare to those of earlier periods, for example the era of the Crusades or the empires of antiquity? How many of these developments were new?
- Although the growth of the African slave trade would result in a new racialization of slavery in the Atlantic world, the justifications for slavery had very old roots. How might Europeans have used Greek and Roman precedents in defense of these new ventures? (See Chapters 4 and 5.)

Before You Read This Chapter

The Age of Dissent and Division, 1500–1564

CORE OBJECTIVES

- **DEFINE** the main premises of Lutheranism.

- **EXPLAIN** why Switzerland emerged as an important Protestant center.

- **IDENTIFY** the ways in which family structures and values changed during the Reformation.

- **UNDERSTAND** the reasons behind England's unusual brand of Protestantism.

- **DESCRIBE** the Catholic Church's response to the challenge of Protestantism.

I n 1517, on the night before the Feast of All Saints—All Hallows' Eve, or Halloween—a professor of theology at a small university in northern Germany published a series of debating points on the door of Wittenberg's All Saints' Church, which served as the university's chapel. (It was also known as "Castle church," because it formed part of the princely palace recently built for the local ruler, the elector of Saxony.) This was not a prank; it was the usual method of announcing a scholarly disputation, and the door of the church had been used for this purpose since the university's founding in 1502. Yet there was something peculiarly appropriate in Martin Luther's choice of an evening traditionally associated with mischief-making. Although he cannot have anticipated the magnitude of mischief it would cause, the posting of ninety-five theses was a subversive act. For one thing, the sheer number of propositions that Dr. Luther offered to debate was unusual. But what really caught the attention of his fellow scholars was their unifying theme— the corruption of the Church and, in particular, the office of the pope—and the rational yet passionate manner in which that theme was expounded. It was a topic very much in vogue at the time, but it had seldom been dissected so clearly by a licensed theologian who was also a monk, an ordained priest, a charismatic teacher, and a man of strong convictions.

Thanks to Luther's well-placed correspondents, this document and the debate it stimulated soon found audiences well beyond Wittenberg. By the time the papacy formally retaliated, in 1520, dissent was widespread—and not only among academics. Many of Europe's kings and princes saw the political advantages of either defying or defending the pope, and they chose sides accordingly. Luther's own lord, Frederick III of Saxony, would spend the rest of his life shielding the man who had first expounded those theses in his own Castle church.

Luther had grown up in a largely peaceful Europe. After two centuries of economic, social, and political turmoil, its economy was expanding, its cities were growing, and its major monarchies were secure. Indeed, governments at every level were extending and deepening their control over people's lives, and the population itself was increasing. Europeans had also embarked on a new period of colonial expansion. Meanwhile, the Church had weathered the storms of the Avignon captivity and the Great Schism. Heresies had been suppressed or contained. In the struggle over conciliarism, the papacy had won the support of all major European rulers, which effectively relegated the conciliarists to academic isolation at the University of Paris. At the local level, the devotion of ordinary Christians was strong and the parish a crucial site of community identity. To be sure, there were some problems. The educational standards of parish clergy were higher than they had ever been, but reformers noted that too many priests were ignorant or neglectful of their spiritual duties. Monasticism, by and large, seemed to have lost its spiritual fire. Religious enthusiasm sometimes led to superstition. Yet, on the whole, these problems were manageable.

No one could have predicted that Europe's religious and political coherence would be irreparably shattered in the course of a generation, or that the next century would witness an appallingly destructive series of wars. Nor could anyone have foreseen that the catalyst for these extraordinary events would be a university professor. The debate ignited by Martin Luther (1483–1546) would set off the chain reaction we know as the Reformation. Initially intended as a call for another phase in the Church's long history of internal reforms, Luther's teachings instead launched a religious revolution that would splinter western Christendom into a variety of Protestant ("dissenting") faiths, while prompting the Roman Church to reaffirm its status as the only true Catholic ("universal") faith through a parallel revolution. At the same time, these movements deepened existing divisions among peoples, rulers, and states. The result was a profound transformation of the religious, social, and political landscape that affected the lives of everyone in Europe—and everyone in the new European colonies, then and now.

MARTIN LUTHER'S CHALLENGE

To explain the impact of Martin Luther's ideas, we must answer three central questions:

1. Why did Luther's theology lead him to break with Rome?
2. Why did large numbers of people rally to his cause?
3. Why did so many German princes and towns impose the new Protestant religion within their territories?

As we shall see, those who followed Luther found his message appealing for different reasons. Many peasants hoped that the new religion would free them from the exactions of their lords; towns and princes thought it would allow them to consolidate their political independence; national-

MARTIN LUTHER. This late portrait is by Lucas Cranach the Elder (1472–1553), court painter to the electors of Brandenburg and a friend of Luther.

ists thought it would liberate Germany from the demands of foreign popes bent on feathering their own nests in central Italy.

But what Luther's followers shared was a conviction that their new understanding of Christianity would lead to spiritual salvation, whereas the traditional religion of Rome would not. For this reason, *reformation* is a misleading term for the movement they initiated. Although Luther himself began as a reformer seeking to change the Church from within, he quickly developed into an uncompromising opponent of its principles and practices. Many of his followers were even more radical. The movement that began with Luther therefore went beyond "reformation." It was a frontal assault on religious, political, and social institutions that had been in place for a thousand years.

Luther's Quest for Justice

Although Martin Luther became an inspiration to millions, he was a terrible disappointment to his father. The elder Luther was a Thuringian peasant who had prospered through some in business ventures. Eager to see his clever son rise still further, he sent young Luther to the University of Erfurt to study law. In 1505, however, Martin shattered his hopes by becoming a monk of the Augustinian order. In some sense, though, Luther was a chip off the old block. Throughout his life, he lived simply and expressed himself in the vigorous, earthy vernacular of the German peasantry.

Luther arrived at his personal understanding of religious truth through a dramatic conversion experience. As a monk, he zealously pursued all the traditional means for achieving holiness. Not only did he fast and pray continuously, but also he reportedly confessed his sins so often that his exhausted confessor would sometimes jokingly suggest that he should do something really bad if he wanted to do penance. Yet, try as he might, Luther could find no spiritual peace; he feared that he could never perform enough good deeds to deserve so great a gift as salvation. But an insight then led to a new understanding of God's justice.

For years, Luther had worried that it seemed unfair for God to issue commandments that he knew humans could not observe—and then to punish them with eternal damnation. But after becoming a professor of theology at the University of Wittenberg, Luther's further study of the Bible suggested to him that God's justice lay not in his power to punish but rather in his mercy. As Luther later wrote, "I began to understand the justice of God as that by which God makes us just, in his mercy and through faith . . . and at this I felt as though I had been born again, and had gone through open gates into paradise." Since this realization came to Luther in the tower room of his monastery, it is often termed his "tower experience."

Lecturing at Wittenberg in the years immediately following this incident, which occurred around 1515, Luther pondered a passage in Saint Paul's Letter to the Romans—"[T]he just shall live by faith" (1:17)—until he reached his central doctrine of "justification by faith alone." Luther

LUTHER'S TRANSLATION OF THE BIBLE. The printing press was instrumental to the rapid dissemination of Luther's messages, as well as those of his supporters and challengers. Also essential was the fact that Luther addressed his audience in plain language, in their native German, and that pamphlets and vernacular Bibles like this one could be rapidly and cheaply mass produced.

concluded that God's justice does not demand endless good works and religious rituals for salvation, because humans can never be saved by their own weak efforts. Rather, humans are saved by God's grace alone, which God offers as an utterly undeserved gift to those whom he has predestined for salvation. Because this grace comes to humans through the gift of faith, men and women are "justified" (i.e., made worthy of salvation) by faith alone. Those whom God has justified through faith will manifest that fact by performing works of piety and charity; but such works are not what saves them. Piety and charity are merely visible signs of each believer's invisible spiritual state, which is known to God alone.

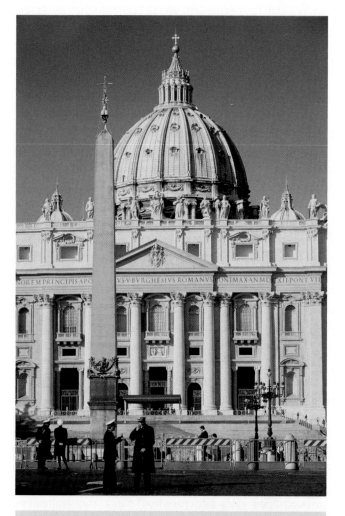

SAINT PETER'S BASILICA, ROME. The construction of a new papal palace and monumental church was begun in 1506. This enormous complex replaced a modest, dilapidated Romanesque basilica that had replaced an even older church built on the site of the apostle Peter's tomb. ▪ *How might this building project have been interpreted in different ways, depending on one's attitude toward the papacy?*

The essence of this doctrine was not original to Luther. It had been central to the thought of Augustine (see Chapter 6), the patron saint of Luther's own monastic order. During the twelfth and thirteenth centuries, however, theologians such as Peter Lombard and Thomas Aquinas (see Chapter 9) had developed a very different understanding of salvation. They emphasized the role that the Church itself (through its sacraments) and the individual believer (through acts of piety and charity) could play in the process of salvation. None of these theologians claimed that a human being could earn his or her way to heaven by good works alone, but the late medieval Church had encouraged this misunderstanding by presenting the process of salvation in increasingly quantitative terms—declaring, for example, that by performing a specific action (such as a pilgrimage or a pious donation), a believer could reduce the penance she or he owed to God by a specific number of days.

Since the fourteenth century, popes had claimed to dispense such special grace from the so-called Treasury of Merits, a storehouse of surplus good works piled up by Christ and the saints in heaven. By the late fifteenth century, when Luther was a child, the papacy began to claim that the dead could receive this grace, too, and so speed their way through purgatory. In both cases, grace was withdrawn from this "Treasury" through indulgences: special remissions of penitential obligations. When indulgences were first conceived in the eleventh and twelfth centuries, they could be earned only by demanding spiritual exercises, such as joining a crusade. By the end of the fifteenth century, however, indulgences were for sale.

To many, this looked like heresy, specifically simony: the sin of exchanging God's grace for cash. It had been a practice loudly condemned by Wyclif and his followers (see Chapter 11), and it was even more widely criticized by reformers like Erasmus (see Chapter 12). But Luther's objections to indulgences had much more radical consequences, because they rested on a set of theological premises that, taken to their logical conclusion, resulted in dismantling much of contemporary religious practice, not to mention the authority and sanctity of the Church. Luther himself does not appear to have realized this at first. But as the implications of his ideas became clear, he did not withdraw them. Instead, he pressed on.

The Scandal of Indulgences

Luther developed his ideas in an academic setting, but in 1517 he was provoked by a local abuse of spiritual power into attacking actual practice. The worldly bishop

POPE LEO X. Raphael's portrait shows the pope with his nephews: Giulio de' Medici (who would succeed him as pope in 1523) and Cardinal de Rossi.

Albert of Hohenzollern, youngest brother of the elector of Brandenburg, had sunk into debt and paid a large sum for papal permission to hold the lucrative bishoprics of Magdeburg and Halberstadt concurrently—even though, at twenty-three, he was not old enough to be a bishop at all. Moreover, when the prestigious archbishopric of Mainz fell vacant in the next year, Albert bought that, too. Obtaining the necessary funds by taking out loans from a German banking firm, he then struck a bargain with Pope Leo X (r. 1513–21): Leo would authorize the sale of indulgences in Albert's ecclesiastical territories—where Luther lived—with the understanding that half of the income would go to Rome for the building of St. Peter's Basilica, the other half to Albert.

Luther did not know the sordid details of Albert's bargain, but he did know that a Dominican friar named Tetzel was soon hawking indulgences throughout much of the region and that Tetzel was deliberately giving people the impression that an indulgence was an automatic ticket to heaven for oneself or one's loved ones in purgatory. For Luther, this was doubly offensive: not only was Tetzel violating Luther's conviction that people are saved by God's grace, not the purchase of papal favors; he was also misleading people into thinking that if they purchased an indulgence, they no longer needed to confess their sins to a priest. Tetzel was thus putting innocent souls at risk. So Luther's ninety-five theses were focused on dismantling the doctrine of indulgences.

Luther wrote up these points for debate in Latin, not German, but they were soon translated and published even more widely, and the hitherto obscure academic suddenly gained widespread notoriety. Tetzel and his allies demanded that Luther withdraw his theses. Rather than backing down, however, Luther became even bolder in his attacks. In 1519, at a public disputation held in Leipzig and attended by throngs of people, Luther defiantly maintained that the pope and all clerics were merely fallible men and that the highest authority for an individual's conscience was the truth of scripture.

Luther's year of greatest activity came in 1520, when he composed a series of pamphlets setting forth his three primary premises: justification by faith, the authority of scripture, and "the priesthood of all believers." We have already examined the meaning of the first premise. By the second, he meant that the reading of scripture took precedence over Church traditions—including the teachings of all theologians—and that beliefs (such as purgatory) or practices (such as prayers to the saints) not explicitly grounded in scripture should be rejected as human inventions. Luther also declared that Christian believers were spiritually equal before God, which meant denying that priests, monks, and nuns had any special qualities by virtue of their vocations: hence "the priesthood of all believers."

From these premises, a host of practical consequences logically followed. Because works could not lead to salvation, Luther declared fasts, pilgrimages, and the veneration of relics to be spiritually valueless. He also called for the dissolution of all monasteries and convents. He advocated a demystification of religious rites, proposing the substitution of German and other vernaculars for Latin and calling for a reduction in the number of sacraments from seven to two. In his view, the only true sacraments were baptism and the Eucharist, both of which had been instituted by Christ. (Later, he included penance.) Although Luther continued to believe that Christ was really present in the consecrated bread and wine of the Lord's Supper, he insisted that it was only through the faith of each individual believer that this sacrament could lead anyone to God; it was not a magical act performed by a priest.

To further emphasize that those who served the Church had no supernatural authority, Luther insisted on calling them "ministers" or "pastors" rather than priests. He also

Decoding Printed Propaganda

The printing press has been credited with helping to spread the teachings of Martin Luther, and so securing the success of the Protestant Reformation. But even before Luther's critiques were published, reformers were using the new technology to disseminate images that attacked the corruption of the Church.

After Luther rose to prominence, both his supporters and detractors vied with one another in disseminating propaganda that appealed, visually, to a lay audience and that could be understood even by those who were unable to read.

The first pair of images below is really a single printed artifact datable to around 1500: an early example of a "pop-up" card. It shows Pope Alexander VI (r. 1492–1503) as stately pontiff (image A) whose true identity is concealed by a flap. When the flap is raised (image B), he is revealed as a devil. The Latin texts read: "Alexander VI, *pontifex maximus*" (image A) and "I am the pope" (image B).

The other two examples represent two sides of the debate as it had developed by 1530, and both do so with reference to the same image: the seven-headed

A. Alexander as pontiff.

B. Alexander as a devil.

beast mentioned in the Bible's Book of Revelation. On the left (image C), a Lutheran engraving shows the papacy as the beast, with seven heads representing seven orders of Catholic clergy. The sign on the cross (referring to the sign hung over the head of the crucified Christ) reads, in German: "For money, a sack full of indulgences." The Latin words on either side say "Reign of the Devil." On the right (image D), a Catholic engraving produced in Germany shows Luther as Revelation's beast, with its seven heads labeled: "Doctor–Martin–Luther–Heretic–Hypocrite–Fanatic–Barabbas," the last alluding to the thief who should have been executed instead of Jesus, according to the Gospels.

Questions for Analysis

1. Given that this attack on Pope Alexander VI precedes Martin Luther's critique of the Church by nearly two decades, what can you conclude about its intended audience? To what extent can it be read as a barometer of popular disapproval? What might have been the reason(s) for the use of the concealing flap?

2. What do you make of the fact that both Catholic and Protestant propagandists were using the same imagery? What do you make of key differences: for example, the fact that the seven-headed beast representing the papacy sprouts out of an altar in which a Eucharistic chalice is displayed, while the seven-headed Martin Luther is reading a book?

3. All of these printed images also make use of words. Would the message of each image be clear without the use of texts? Why or why not?

C. The seven-headed papal beast.

D. The seven-headed Martin Luther.

proposed to abolish the entire ecclesiastical hierarchy from popes to bishops on down. Finally, on the principle that no spiritual distinction existed between clergy and laity, Luther argued that ministers could and should marry. In 1525, he himself took a wife, Katharina von Bora, one of a dozen nuns he had helped escape from a Cistercian convent.

The Break with Rome

Widely disseminated by means of the printing press, Luther's polemical pamphlets of 1520 electrified much of Germany, gaining him passionate popular support and touching off a national religious revolt against the papacy. In highly colloquial German, Luther declared that "if the pope's court were reduced ninety-nine percent it would still be large enough to give decisions on matters of faith"; that "the cardinals have sucked Italy dry and now turn to Germany"; and that, given Rome's corruption, "the reign of Antichrist could not be worse." As word of Luther's defiance spread, his pamphlets became a publishing sensation. Whereas the average press run of a printed book before 1520 had been 1,000 copies, the first run of *To the Christian Nobility* (1520) was 4,000—and it sold out in a few days. Many thousands of copies quickly followed. Even more popular were woodcut illustrations mocking the papacy and exalting Luther. These sold in the tens of thousands and could be readily understood even by those who could not read. (See **Interpreting Visual Evidence** on pages 428–29.)

Luther's denunciations reflected widespread public dissatisfaction with the conduct and corruption of the papacy. Pope Alexander VI (r. 1492–1503) had bribed cardinals to gain his office and had then used the money raised from the papal jubilee of 1500 to support the military campaigns of his illegitimate son. Julius II (r. 1503–13) devoted his reign to enlarging the Papal States in a series of wars; a contemporary remarked that he would have deserved the glory he won—if only he had been a secular prince. Leo X (r. 1513–21), Luther's opponent, was a member of the Medici family of Florence. Although an able administrator, he was also a self-indulgent aesthete. In *The Praise of Folly*, first published in 1511 and frequently reprinted (see Chapter 12), Erasmus had declared that if the popes of his day were ever forced to lead Christlike lives, as their office surely required, they would be incapable of it. In *Julius Excluded*, published anonymously in 1517, he went even further, imagining a conversation at the gates of heaven between Saint Peter and Julius II, in which Peter refuses to admit the pope because he cannot believe that this armored, vainglorious figure could possibly be his own earthly representative.

In Germany, resentment of the papacy ran especially high because there were no special agreements (concordats) limiting papal authority in its principalities, as there were in Spain, France, and England (see Chapter 12). As a result, German princes complained that papal taxes were so high that the country was drained of its wealth. And yet Germans had almost no influence over papal policy. Frenchmen, Spaniards, and Italians dominated the College of Cardinals and the papal bureaucracy, and the popes were almost invariably Italian—as they would continue to be until 1978 and the election of Pope John Paul II. As a result, graduates from the rapidly growing German universities almost never found employment in Rome. Instead, many joined the throngs of Luther's supporters to become leaders of the new religious movement.

Emperor Charles V and the Condemnation at Worms

In the year 1520, Pope Leo X issued a papal edict condemning Luther's publications as heretical and threatening him with excommunication if he did not recant. This edict was of the most solemn kind, known as a *bulla,* or "bull," from the lead seal it bore. Luther's reponse was flagrantly defiant: rather than acquiescing to the pope's demand, he staged a public burning of the document. Thereafter, his heresy confirmed, he was formally given over for punishment to his lay overlord, Frederick III "the Wise" of Saxony. Frederick, however, proved a supporter of Luther and a critic of the papacy. Rather than burning Luther at the stake for heresy, Frederick declared that Luther had not yet received a fair hearing. Early in 1521, he therefore brought him to the city of Worms to be examined by a select representative assembly known as a "diet."

At Worms, the diet's presiding officer was the newly elected Holy Roman Emperor, Charles V. As a member of the Habsburg family, he had been born and bred in his ancestral holding of Flanders, then part of the Netherlands. By 1521, however, through the unpredictable workings of dynastic inheritance, marriage, election, and luck, he had become not only the ruler of the Netherlands but also king of Germany and Holy Roman emperor, duke of Austria, duke of Milan, and ruler of the Franche-Comté. And as the grandson of Ferdinand and Isabella on his mother's side, he was also king of Spain; king of Naples, Sicily, and Sardinia; and ruler of all the Spanish possessions in the New World. Governing such an extraordinary combination

THE EUROPEAN EMPIRE OF CHARLES V, c. 1526. Charles V ruled a vast variety of widely dispersed territories in Europe and the New World, and as Holy Roman emperor he was also the titular ruler of Germany. ▪ *What were the main countries and kingdoms under his control?* ▪ *Which regions would have been most threatened by Charles's extraordinary power, and where might the rulers of these regions turn for allies?* ▪ *How might the expansion of the Ottoman Empire have complicated political and religious struggles within Christian Europe?*

of territories posed enormous challenges. Charles's empire had no capital and no centralized administrative institutions; it shared no common language, no common culture, and no geographically contiguous borders. It thus stood completely apart from the growing nationalism that was shaping late medieval states.

Charles recognized the diversity of his empire and tried wherever possible to rule it through local officials and institutions. But he could not tolerate threats to the two fundamental forces that held his empire together: himself as emperor and Catholicism—as the religion of Rome was coming to be called. Beyond such political calculations,

THE WARTBURG, EISENACH (GERMANY). This medieval stronghold became the refuge of Martin Luther after his condemnation at the Diet of Worms in 1520. His room in the castle has since been preserved.

THE EMPEROR CHARLES V. This portrait by the Venetian painter Titian depicts Europe's most powerful ruler sitting quietly in a chair, dressed in simple clothing of the kind worn by judges or bureaucrats. ▪ *Why might Charles have chosen to represent himself in this way—rather than in the regalia of his many royal, imperial, and princely offices?*

however, Charles was also a faithful and committed servant of the Church, and he was deeply disturbed by the prospect of heresy within his empire. There was therefore little doubt that the Diet of Worms would condemn Martin Luther for heresy. And when Luther refused to back down, thereby endangering his life, his lord Frederick the Wise once more intervened, this time arranging for Luther to be "kidnapped" and hidden for a year at the elector's castle of the Wartburg, where he was kept out of harm's way.

Thereafter, Luther was never again in mortal danger. Although the Diet of Worms proclaimed him an outlaw, this edict was never enforced. Instead, Charles V left Germany in order to conduct a war with France, and in 1522 Luther returned in triumph to Wittenberg, to find that the changes he had called for had already been put into practice by his university supporters. When several German princes formally converted to Lutheranism, they brought their territories with them. In a little over a decade, a new form of Christianity had been established.

The German Princes and the Lutheran Church

At this point, the last of our three major questions must be addressed: Why did some German princes, secure in their own powers, nonetheless establish Lutheran religious practices within their territories? This is a crucial development, because popular support for Luther would not have been enough to ensure the success of his teachings had they not been embraced by a number of powerful rulers and free cities. Indeed, it was only in those territories where Lutheranism was formally established that the new religion prevailed. Elsewhere in Germany, Luther's sympathizers were forced to flee, face death, or conform to Catholicism.

The power of individual rulers to control the practice of religion in their own territories reflects developments we have noted in previous chapters. Rulers had long sought to control appointments to Church offices in their own realms, to restrict the flow of money to Rome and to limit the independence of ecclesiastical courts. The monarchs of Europe—primarily the kings of France and Spain—had already taken advantage of the continuing struggles between the papacy and the conciliarists to extract many concessions from the embattled popes during the fifteenth century (see Chapters 11 and 12). But in Germany, as noted above, neither the emperor nor the princes were strong enough to secure special treatment.

This changed as a result of Luther's initiatives. As early as 1520, the papacy's fiery challenger had recognized

CONFESSIONAL DIFFERENCES, c. 1560. The religious affiliations (confessions) of Europe's territories had become very complicated by the year 1560, roughly a generation after the adoption of Lutheranism in some areas. ▪ *What major countries and kingdoms had embraced Protestantism by 1560?* ▪ *To what extent do these divisions conform to political boundaries, and to what extent would they have complicated the political situation?* ▪ *Why might Lutheranism have spread north into Scandinavia but not south into Bavaria or west across the Rhine?*

that he could never hope to institute new religious practices without the strong arms of princes, so he explicitly encouraged them to confiscate the wealth of the Church as an incentive. At first the princes bided their time, but when they realized that Luther had enormous public support and that Charles V could not act swiftly enough, several moved to introduce Lutheranism into their territories. Personal piety surely played a role in

individual cases, but political and economic considerations were generally more decisive. Protestant princes could consolidate authority by naming their own religious officials, cutting off fees to Rome, and curtailing the jurisdiction of Church courts. They could also guarantee that the political and religious boundaries of their territories would now coincide. No longer would a rival ecclesiastical prince (such as a bishop or archbishop) be able to use his spiritual position to undermine a neighboring secular prince's sovereignty.

Similar considerations also moved a number of free cities to adopt Lutheranism. Acting independently of any prince, town councils could establish themselves as the supreme governing authorities within their jurisdictions, cutting out local bishops or powerful monasteries. Given the added fact that under Lutheranism monasteries and convents could be shut down and their lands appropriated by the newly sovereign secular authorities, the practical advantages of the new faith were overwhelming.

Once safely ensconced in Wittenberg under princely protection, Luther began to express ever more vehemently his own political and social views, which tended toward the strong support of the new political order. In a treatise of 1523, *On Temporal Authority*, he insisted that "godly" (Protestant) rulers must be obeyed in all things and that even "ungodly" ones should never be targets of dissent because tyranny "is not to be resisted but endured." In 1525, when peasants throughout Germany rebelled against their landlords, Luther therefore responded with intense hostility. In his vituperative pamphlet of 1525, *Against the Thievish, Murderous Hordes of Peasants*, he urged readers to hunt the rebels down as though they were mad dogs: to "strike, strangle, stab secretly or in public, and remember that nothing can be more poisonous than a man in rebellion." After the ruthless suppression of this revolt, which may have cost as many as 100,000 lives, the firm alliance of Lutheranism with state power helped preserve and sanction the existing social order.

In his later years, Luther concentrated on debating with younger, more radical religious reformers who challenged his political conservatism, while offering spiritual counsel to all who sought it. Never tiring in his amazingly prolific literary activity, he wrote an average of one treatise every two weeks for twenty-five years.

THE SPREAD OF PROTESTANTISM

Originating as a term applied to Lutherans who "protested" the Catholic authority of Charles V, the word *Protestant* was soon applied to a much wider range of dissenting Christianities. Lutheranism itself struck lasting roots in northern Germany and Scandinavia, where it became the state religion of Denmark, Norway, and Sweden as soon as the 1520s. Other early Lutheran successes in southern Germany, Poland, and Hungary were eventually rolled back. Elsewhere in Europe, meanwhile, competing forms of Protestantism soon emerged from the seeds that Luther had sown. By the 1550s, Protestantism had become a truly international movement and also an increasingly diverse and divisive one.

Protestantism in Switzerland

In the early sixteenth century, Switzerland was ruled neither by kings nor by territorial princes; instead, prosperous Swiss cities were either independent or on the verge of becoming so. Hence, when the leading citizens of a Swiss municipality decided to adopt Protestant reforms, no one could stop them. Although religious arrangements varied from city to city, three main forms

THE ANABAPTISTS' CAGES, THEN AND NOW. After the three Anabaptist leaders of Münster were executed in 1535, their corpses were prominently displayed in cages hung from a tower of the marketplace church. As can be seen from the photo on the right, the bones are gone but the iron cages remain. ▪ *What would be the purpose of keeping these cages on display? What different meanings might this sight convey?*

of Protestantism emerged in Switzerland between 1520 to 1550: Zwinglianism, Anabaptism, and Calvinism.

Zwinglianism, founded by Ulrich Zwingli (*TSVING-lee*, 1484–1531) in Zürich, was the most theologically moderate form of the three. Zwingli had just begun his career as a Catholic priest when his humanist-inspired study of the Bible convinced him that Catholic theology and practice conflicted with the Gospels. His biblical studies eventually led him to condemn religious images and hierarchical authority within the Church. Yet he did not speak out publicly until Luther set a precedent. In 1522, accordingly, Zwingli began attacking the authority of the Catholic Church in Zürich. Soon much of northern Switzerland had accepted his religious leadership.

Although Zwingli's reforms closely resembled those of the Lutherans in Germany, Zwingli differed from Luther as to the theology of the Eucharist. Whereas Luther believed in the real presence of Christ's body in the sacrament, for Zwingli the Eucharist conferred no grace at all; it was simply a reminder and celebration of Christ's historical sacrifice on the cross. This fundamental disagreement prevented Lutherans and Zwinglians from uniting in a common Protestant front. When Zwingli died in battle against Catholic forces in 1531, his movement was absorbed by the more systematic Protestantism of John Calvin (see below).

Before Calvinism prevailed, however, an even more radical form of Protestantism arose in Switzerland and parts of Germany. The first Anabaptists were members of Zwingli's circle in Zürich, but they broke with him around 1525 on the issue of infant baptism. Because Anabaptists were convinced that the sacrament of baptism was only effective if administered to willing adults who understood its significance, they required followers who had been baptized as infants to be baptized again as adults (the term *Anabaptism* means "rebaptism"). This doctrine reflected the Anabaptists' fundamental belief that the true church was a small community of believers whose members had to make a deliberate, inspired decision to join it.

No other Protestant groups were prepared to go so far in rejecting the medieval Christian view of the Church as a single vast body to which all members of society belonged from birth. And in an age when almost everyone assumed that religious and secular authority were inextricably connected, Anabaptism was bound to be anathema to all established powers, both Protestant and Catholic. It was a movement that appealed to sincere religious piety in calling for pacifism, strict personal morality, and extreme simplicity of worship.

This changed when a group of Anabaptist extremists managed to gain control of the German city of Münster in 1534. These zealots were driven by millenarianism, the belief that God intends to institute a completely new order of justice and spirituality throughout the world before the end of time. Determined to help God bring about this goal, the extremists attempted to turn Münster into a new Jerusalem. A former tailor named John of Leyden assumed the title "king of the New Temple" and proclaimed himself the successor of the Hebrew king David. Under his leadership, Anabaptist religious practices were made obligatory, private property was abolished, and even polygamy was permitted on the grounds of Old Testament precedents. Such practices were deeply shocking to Protestants and Catholics alike. Accordingly, Münster was besieged and captured by Catholic forces little more than a year after the Anabaptist takeover. The new "David," together with two of his lieutenants, was put to death by torture, and the three bodies were displayed in iron cages in the town square.

Thereafter, Anabaptists throughout Europe were ruthlessly persecuted on all sides. The few who survived banded together in the Mennonite sect, named for its founder, the Dutchman Menno Simons (c. 1496–1561). This sect, dedicated to pacifism and the simple "religion of the heart" of original Anabaptism, is still particularly strong in the central United States.

John Calvin's Reformed Theology

A year after the events in Münster, a twenty-six-year-old Frenchman named John Calvin (1509–1564), published the first version of his *Institutes of the Christian Religion*, the most influential formulation of Protestant theology ever written. Born in Noyon, in northern France, Calvin had originally trained for the law; but by 1533, he was studying the Greek and Latin classics while living off the income from a priestly benefice. As he later wrote, he was "obstinately devoted to the superstitions of popery" until he experienced a miraculous conversion. He became a Protestant theologian and propagandist, eventually fleeing the Swiss city of Basel to escape persecution.

Although some aspects of Calvin's early career resemble those of Luther's, the two men were very different. Luther was an emotionally volatile personality and a lover of controversy. He responded to theological problems as they arose or as the impulse struck him; he never attempted to systematize his beliefs. Calvin, however, was a coolly analytical legalist, who resolved in his *Institutes* to set forth all the principles of Protestantism comprehensively, logically, and systematically. As a result, after several revisions and enlargements (the definitive edition appeared in 1559), Calvin's *Institutes* became the Protestant equivalent of Thomas Aquinas's *Summa Theologiae* (see Chapter 9).

JOHN CALVIN. This recently discovered portrait by an anonymous artist shows the young Protestant reformer as a serene and authoritative figure. It places the grotesque caricature of Calvin (right) in perspective.

CALVIN AS SEEN BY HIS ENEMIES. In this image, which circulated among Calvin's Catholic detractors, the reformer's facial features are a disturbing composite of fish, toad, and chicken.

Calvin's austere and stoical theology started with the omnipotence of God. For Calvin, the entire universe depends utterly on the will of the Almighty, who created all things for his greater glory and who knows all things present and to come. Because of man's original fall from grace, all human beings are sinners by nature, bound to an evil inheritance they cannot escape. Yet God (for reasons of his own) has predestined some for eternal salvation and damned all the rest to the torments of hell. Nothing that individual humans may do can alter fate; all souls are stamped with God's blessing or curse before they are born. Nevertheless, Christians cannot be indifferent to their conduct on earth. If they are among the elect, God will implant in them the desire to live according to his laws. Upright conduct is thus a sign, though not an infallible one, that an individual has been chosen to sit at the throne of glory. Membership in the Reformed Church (as Calvinist churches are more properly known) is another presumptive sign of election to salvation. But most of all, Calvin urged Christians to conceive of themselves as chosen instruments of God, charged to work actively to fulfill God's purposes on earth. Because sin offends God, Christians should do all they can to prevent it, not because their actions will lead to anyone's salvation (they will not), but simply because God's glory is diminished if sin is allowed to flourish unchecked by the efforts of those whom he has chosen for salvation.

Calvin always acknowledged a great theological debt to Luther, but his religious teachings diverged from those of the Wittenberg reformer in several essentials. First of all, Luther's attitude toward proper Christian conduct in the world was much more passive than Calvin's. For Luther, a Christian should endure the trials of this life through suffering, whereas for Calvin the world was to be mastered in unceasing labor for God's sake. Calvin's religion was also more controlling than Luther's. Luther, for example, insisted that his followers attend church on Sunday, but he did not demand that during the remainder of the day they refrain from all pleasure or work. Calvin, however, issued stern strictures against worldliness of any sort on the Sabbath and forbade all sorts of minor self-indulgences, even on non-Sabbath days.

The two men also differed on fundamental matters of church governance and worship. Although Luther broke with the Catholic system of hierarchical church government, Lutheran district superintendents exercised some of the same powers as bishops, including supervision of parish clergy. Luther also retained many features of traditional Christian worship, including altars, music, and ritual. Calvin, however, rejected everything that smacked to him of "popery." He argued for the elimination of all traces of hierarchy within any church. Instead, each congregation should elect its own ministers, and assemblies of ministers and "elders" (laymen responsible for maintaining proper religious conduct among the faithful) were to govern the Reformed Church as a whole. Calvin also insisted on the utmost simplicity in worship, prohibiting (among much else) vestments, processions, instrumental music, and religious images of any sort, including stained-glass windows. He also dispensed with all remaining vestiges of Catholic sacramental theology by making the sermon, rather than the Eucharist, the centerpiece of reformed worship.

Calvinism in Geneva

Consistent with his theological convictions, Calvin was intent on putting his religious teachings into practice. Sensing an opportunity in the French-speaking Swiss city of Geneva—then in the throes of political and religious upheaval—he moved there late in 1536 and immediately began preaching and organizing. In 1538, his activities caused him to be expelled by the city council, but in 1541 he returned and brought the city under his sway.

With Calvin's guidance, Geneva's government became a theocracy. Supreme authority was vested in a "consistory" composed of twelve lay elders and between ten and twenty pastors, whose weekly meetings Calvin dominated. In addition to passing legislation proposed by a congregation of ministers, the consistory's main function was to supervise morality, both public and private. To this end, Geneva was divided into districts, and a committee of the consistory visited every household, without prior warning, to check on the behavior of its members. Dancing, card playing, attending the theater, and working or playing on the Sabbath: all were outlawed as works of the devil. Innkeepers were forbidden to allow anyone to consume food or drink without first saying grace, or to permit any patron to stay up after nine o'clock. Adultery, witchcraft, blasphemy, and heresy all became capital crimes. Even penalties for lesser crimes were severe. During the first four years after Calvin gained control in Geneva, there were no fewer than fifty-eight executions in this city with a total population of only 16,000.

As rigid as such a regime may seem today, Calvin's Geneva was a beacon of light to thousands of Protestants throughout Europe in the mid-sixteenth century. Calvin's disciple John Knox (c. 1514–1572), who brought the reformed religion to Scotland, declared Geneva "the most perfect school of Christ that ever was on earth since the days of the Apostles." Converts such as Knox flocked to Geneva for refuge or instruction and then returned home to become ardent proselytizers for the new religion. Geneva thus became the center of an international movement dedicated to spreading reformed religion to France and the rest of Europe through organized missionary activity and propaganda.

These efforts were remarkably successful. By the end of the sixteenth century, Calvinists were a majority in Scotland (where they were known as Presbyterians) and Holland (where they founded the Dutch Reformed Church). They were also influential in England, although the Church of England adopted reformed theology but not reformed worship (Calvinists who sought further reforms in worship were known as Puritans). There were also substantial Calvinist minorities in France (where they were called Huguenots), Germany, Hungary, Lithuania, and Poland. By the end of the sixteenth century, Calvinism would spread to the New World.

The Beginnings of Religious Warfare

Less than a generation after Luther's challenge to the Church, wars between Catholic and Protestant rulers began. In Germany, Charles V attempted to establish Catholic unity by launching a military campaign against several German princes who had instituted Lutheran worship in their territories. But despite several notable victories, his efforts to defeat the Protestant princes failed. In part, this was because Charles was also involved in wars against France; but primarily, it was because the Catholic princes of Germany worked against him, fearing that any suppression of Protestant princes might also diminish their own independence. As a result, the Catholic princes' support for the foreign-born Charles was only lukewarm; at times, they even joined with Protestants in battle against him.

This regional warfare sputtered on and off until a compromise settlement was reached via the Peace of Augsburg in 1555. Its governing principle was *cuius regio, eius religio,* "as the ruler, so the religion." This meant that in those principalities where Lutherans ruled, Lutheranism would be the sole state religion; but where Catholic princes ruled, the people of their territories would also be Catholic. For better and for worse, the Peace of Augsburg was a historical milestone. For the first time since Luther had been excommunicated, Catholic rulers were forced to acknowledge the legality of Protestantism. Yet the peace also set a dangerous precedent because it established the principle that no sovereign state can tolerate religious diversity. Moreover, it excluded Calvinism entirely and thus spurred German Calvinists to become aggressive opponents of the status quo. As a result, Europe would be riven by religious warfare for another century and would export sectarian violence to the New World (see Chapter 14).

THE DOMESTICATION OF REFORM

Within two decades, Protestantism had become a diverse revolutionary movement whose radical claims for the spiritual equality of all Christians had the potential to undermine the political, social, and even gender hierarchies on which European society rested. Luther himself did not anticipate that his ideas might have such implications, and he was genuinely shocked when the rebellious German peasants and the radical Anabaptists at Münster interpreted his teachings in this way. And Luther was by no means the only staunchly conservative Protestant. None of the prominent early Protestants were social or political radicals; most depended on the support of existing elites: territorial princes, of course, but also the ruling elites of towns. As a result, the Reformation movement was speedily "domesticated" in two senses. Its revolutionary potential was muffled—Luther himself rarely spoke about "the priesthood of all believers" after 1525—and there was an increasing emphasis on the patriarchal family as the central institution of reformed life.

Reform and Discipline

As we have seen, injunctions to lead a more disciplined and godly life had been a frequent message of religious reform movements since the Black Death (see Chapter 11). Many of these efforts were actively promoted by princes and town councils, most famously perhaps in Florence, where the Dominican preacher Girolamo Savonarola led the city on an extraordinary but short-lived campaign of puritanism and moral reform between 1494 and 1498. And there are numerous other examples of rulers legislating against sin. When Desiderius Erasmus called on secular authorities to think of themselves as abbots and of their territories as giant monasteries, he was sounding an already-familiar theme.

Protestant rulers, however, took the need to enforce godly discipline with particular seriousness, because the depravity of human nature was a fundamental tenet of Protestant belief. Like Saint Augustine at the end of the fourth century (see Chapter 6), Protestants believed that people would inevitably turn out bad unless they were compelled to be good. It was therefore the responsibility of secular and religious leaders to control and punish the behavior of their people, because otherwise their evil deeds would anger God and destroy human society.

Protestant godliness began with the discipline of children. Luther himself wrote two catechisms (instructional tracts) designed to teach children the tenets of their faith and the obligations—toward parents, masters, and rulers—that God imposed on them. Luther also insisted that all children, boys and girls alike, be taught to read the Bible in their own languages. Schooling thus became a characteristically Protestant preoccupation and rallying cry. Even the Protestant family was designated a "school of godliness," in which fathers were expected to instruct and discipline their wives, their children, and their household servants.

But family life in the early sixteenth century still left much to be desired in the eyes of Protestant reformers. Drunkenness, domestic violence, illicit sexual relations, lewd dancing, and the blasphemous swearing of oaths were frequent topics of reforming discourse. Various methods of discipline were attempted, including private counseling, public confessions of wrongdoing, public penances and shamings, exclusion from church services, and even imprisonment. All these efforts met with varying, but generally modest, success. Creating godly Protestant families, and enforcing godly discipline on entire communities, was going to require the active cooperation of godly authorities.

Protestantism, Government, and the Family

The domestication of the Reformation in this sense took place principally in the free towns of Germany, Switzerland, and the Netherlands—and from there spread westward to North America. Protestant attacks on monasticism and clerical celibacy found a receptive audience among townsmen who resented the immunity of monastic houses from taxation and regarded clerical celibacy as a subterfuge for the seduction of their own wives and daughters. Protestant emphasis on the depravity of the human will and the consequent need for that will to be disciplined by authority also resonated powerfully with guilds and town governments, which were anxious to maintain and increase the control exercised by urban elites (mainly merchants and master craftsmen) over the apprentices and journeymen who made up the majority of the male population. By eliminating the competing jurisdictional authority of the Catholic Church, Protestantism allowed town governments to consolidate all authority within the city into their own hands.

Competing Viewpoints

Marriage and Celibacy: Two Views

These two selections illustrate the strongly contrasting views on the spiritual value of marriage versus celibacy that came to be embraced by Protestant and Catholic religious authorities. The first selection is part of Martin Luther's more general attack on monasticism, which emphasizes his contention that marriage is the natural and divinely intended state for all human beings. The second selection, from the decrees of the Council of Trent (1545–63), restates traditional Catholic teaching on the holiness of marriage but also emphasizes the spiritual superiority of virginity to marriage as well as the necessity of clerical celibacy.

Luther's Views on Celibacy (1535)

Listen! In all my days I have not heard the confession of a nun, but in the light of Scripture I shall hit upon how matters fare with her and know I shall not be lying. If a girl is not sustained by great and exceptional grace, she can live without a man as little as she can without eating, drinking, sleeping, and other natural necessities.

Nor, on the other hand, can a man dispense with a wife. The reason for this is that procreating children is an urge planted as deeply in human nature as eating and drinking. That is why God has given and put into the body the organs, arteries, fluxes, and everything that serves it. Therefore what is he doing who would check this process and keep nature from running its desired and intended course? He is attempting to keep nature from being nature, fire from burning, water from wetting, and a man from eating, drinking, and sleeping.

Source: E. M. Plass, ed., *What Luther Says,* vol. 2 (St. Louis, MO: 1959), pp. 888–89.

Canons on the Sacrament of Matrimony (1563)

Canon 1. If anyone says that matrimony is not truly and properly one of the seven sacraments . . . instituted by Christ the Lord, but has been devised by men in the Church and does not confer grace, let him be anathema [cursed].

Canon 9. If anyone says that clerics constituted in sacred orders or regulars [monks and nuns] who have made solemn profession of chastity can contract marriage . . . and that all who feel that they have not the gift of chastity, even though they have made such a vow, can contract marriage, let him be anathema, since God does not refuse that gift to those who ask for it rightly, neither does *he suffer us to be tempted above that which we are able.*

Canon 10: If anyone says that the married state excels the state of virginity or celibacy, and that it is better and happier to be united in matrimony than to remain in virginity or celibacy, let him be anathema.

Source: H. J. Schroeder, *Canons and Decrees of the Council of Trent* (St. Louis, MO: 1941), pp. 181–82.

Questions for Analysis

1. On what grounds does Luther attack the practice of celibacy? Do you agree with his basic premise?

2. How do the later canons of the Catholic Church respond to Protestant views like Luther's? What appears to be at stake in this defense of marriage and celibacy?

Meanwhile, Protestantism reinforced the control of individual men over their own households by emphasizing the family as the basic unit of religious education. In place of a priest, an all-powerful father figure was expected to assume responsibility for instructing and disciplining his household according to the precepts of reformed religion. At the same time, Protestantism introduced a new religious ideal for women. No longer was the original nun the exemplar of female holiness; in her place now stood the married and obedient Protestant "goodwife." As one Lutheran prince wrote in 1527: "Those who bear children please God better than all the monks and nuns singing and praying." To this extent, Protestantism resolved the tensions between piety and sexuality that had long characterized Christian teachings, by declaring the holiness of marital sex.

But this did not promote a new view of women's spiritual potential, nor did it elevate their social and political status. Quite the contrary: Luther regarded women as more sexually driven than men and less capable of controlling their sexual desires—reflecting the fact that Luther confessed himself incapable of celibacy. His opposition to convents allegedly rested on his belief that it was impossible for women to remain chaste, so sequestering them simply made illicit behavior inevitable. To prevent sin, it was necessary that all women should be married, preferably at a young age, and so placed under the governance of a godly husband.

For the most part, Protestant town governments were happy to cooperate in shutting down female monasteries. The convent's property went to the town, after all. But conflicts did arise between Protestant reformers and town fathers over marriage and sexuality, especially over the reformers' insistence that both men and women should marry young as a restraint on lust. In many towns, men were traditionally expected to delay marriage until they had achieved the status of master craftsman—a requirement that had become increasingly difficult to enforce as guilds sought to restrict the number of journeymen permitted to become masters. In theory, then, apprentices and journeymen were not supposed to marry. Instead, they were expected to frequent brothels and taverns, a legally sanctioned outlet for extramarital sexuality long viewed as necessary to men's physical well-being, but that Protestant reformers now deemed morally abhorrent.

Towns responded in a variety of ways to these opposing pressures. Some instituted special committees to police public morals, of the sort we have noted in Calvin's Geneva. Some abandoned Protestantism altogether. Others, like the German town of Augsburg, alternated between Protestantism and Catholicism for several decades. Yet regardless of a town's final choice of religious allegiance, by the end of the sixteenth century a revolution had taken place with respect to governments' attitudes toward public morality. In their competition with each other, neither Catholics nor Protestants wished to be seen as soft on sin. The result was the widespread abolition of publicly licensed brothels, the outlawing of prostitution, and far stricter governmental supervision of many other aspects of private life than had ever been the case in any Western civilization.

The Control of Marriage

Protestantism also increased parents' control over their children's choice of marital partners. The medieval Church had defined marriage as a sacrament that did not require the involvement of a priest. The mutual free consent of two individuals, even if given without witnesses or parental approval, was enough to constitute a legally valid marriage in the eyes of the Church. Opposition to this doctrine came from many quarters, especially from families who stood to lose from this liberal doctrine. Because marriage involved rights of inheritance to property, it was regarded as too important a matter to be left to the choice of adolescents. Instead, parents wanted the power to prevent unsuitable matches and, in some cases, to force their children to accept the marriage arrangements their families might negotiate on their behalf. Protestantism offered an opportunity to achieve such control. Luther had declared marriage to be a purely secular matter, not a sacrament at all, and one that could be regulated however the governing authorities thought best. Calvin largely followed suit, although Calvinist theocracy drew less of a distinction than did Lutheranism between the powers of church and state.

Even the Catholic Church was eventually forced to give way. Although it never abandoned its insistence that both members of a couple must freely consent to their marriage, by the end of the sixteenth century the Church's new doctrine required formal public notice of intent to marry and insisted on the presence of a priest at the actual wedding ceremony. Both were efforts to prevent elopements, allowing families time to intervene before an unsuitable marriage was concluded. Individual Catholic countries sometimes went even further in trying to assert parental control over their children's choice of marital partners. In France, for example, although couples might still marry without parental consent, those who did so now forfeited all of their rights to inherit their families' property. In somewhat different ways, both Protestantism and Catholicism thus moved to strengthen the control that parents could exercise over their children—and, in the case of Protestantism, that husbands could exercise over their wives.

THE REFORMATION OF ENGLAND

In England, the Reformation took a rather different course than it did in continental Europe. Although a long tradition of popular reform survived into the sixteenth century, the number of dissidents was too small and their influence too limited to play a significant role there. Nor was England particularly oppressed by the papal exactions and abuses that roiled Germany. When the sixteenth century began, English monarchs already exercised close control over Church appointments within the kingdom; they also received the lion's share of the papal taxation collected from England. Nor did ecclesiastical courts inspire any particular resentments. On the contrary, these courts would continue to function in Protestant England until the eighteenth century. Why, then, did sixteenth-century England become a Protestant country at all?

"The King's Great Matter"

In 1527, King Henry VIII of England had been married to Ferdinand and Isabella's daughter, Catherine of Aragon, for eighteen years. Yet all the offspring of this union had died

HENRY VIII OF ENGLAND. Hans Holbein the Younger executed several portraits of the English king. This one represents him in middle age, confident of his powers.

in infancy, with the exception of a daughter, Mary. Because Henry needed a male heir to preserve the peaceful succession to the throne and because Catherine was now past childbearing age, Henry had political reasons to propose a change of wife. He also had more personal motives, having become infatuated with a lady-in-waiting named Anne Boleyn.

Henry therefore appealed to Rome to annul his marriage to Catherine, arguing that because she had previously been married to his older brother Arthur (who had died in adolescence), Henry's marriage to Catherine had been invalid from the beginning. As Henry's representatives pointed out, the Bible pronounced it "an unclean thing" for a man to take his brother's wife and cursed such a marriage with childlessness (Leviticus 20:31). Even a papal dispensation, which Henry and Catherine had long before obtained for their marriage, could not exempt them from such a clear prohibition—as the marriage's childlessness proved.

Henry's petition put Pope Clement VII (r. 1523–34) in an awkward position. Both Henry and Clement knew that popes in the past had granted annulments to reigning monarchs on far weaker grounds than the ones Henry was alleging. If, however, the pope granted Henry's annulment, he would cast doubt on the validity of all papal dispensations. More seriously, he would provoke the wrath of the emperor Charles V, Catherine of Aragon's nephew, whose armies were in firm command of Rome and who at that moment held the pope himself in captivity. Clement was trapped; all he could do was procrastinate and hope that the matter would resolve itself. For two years, he allowed Henry's case to proceed in England without ever reaching a verdict. Then, suddenly, he transferred the case to Rome, where the legal process began all over again.

Exasperated by these delays, Henry began to increase the pressure on the pope. In 1531, he compelled an assembly of English clergy to declare him "protector and only supreme head" of the Church in England. In 1532, he encouraged Parliament to produce an inflammatory list of grievances against the English clergy and used this threat to force them to concede his right, as king, to approve or deny all Church legislation. In January 1533, Henry married Anne Boleyn (already pregnant) even though his marriage to Queen Catherine had still not been annulled. The new archbishop of Canterbury, Thomas Cranmer, later provided the required annulment in May, acting on his own authority.

In September, Princess Elizabeth was born; her father, disappointed again in his hopes for a son, refused to attend her christening. Nevertheless, Parliament settled the succession to the throne on the children of Henry and Anne,

Analyzing Primary Sources

The Six Articles of the English Church

Although Henry VIII withdrew the Church of England from obedience to the papacy, he continued to reject most Protestant theology. Some of his advisers, most notably Thomas Cromwell, were committed Protestants; and the king allowed his son and heir, Edward VI, to be raised as a Protestant. But even after several years of rapid (and mostly Protestant) change in the English Church, Henry reasserted a set of traditional Catholic doctrines in the Six Articles of 1539. These would remain binding on the Church of England until the king's death in 1547.

irst, that in the most blessed sacrament of the altar, by the strength and efficacy of Christ's mighty word, it being spoken by the priest, is present really, under the form of bread and wine, the natural body and blood of our Savior Jesus Christ, conceived of the Virgin Mary, and that after the consecration there remains no substance of bread or wine, nor any other substance but the substance of Christ, God and man;

Secondly, that communion in both kinds is not necessary for salvation, by the law of God, to all persons, and that it is to be believed and not doubted . . . that in the flesh, under the form of bread, is the very blood, and with the blood, under the form of wine, is the very flesh, as well apart as though they were both together;

Thirdly, that priests, after the order of priesthood received as afore, may not marry by the law of God;

Fourthly, that vows of chastity or widowhood by man or woman made to God advisedly ought to be observed by the law of God. . . .

Fifthly, that it is right and necessary that private masses be continued and admitted in this the king's English Church and congregation . . . whereby good Christian people . . . do receive both godly and goodly consolations and benefits; and it is agreeable also to God's law;

Sixthly, that oral, private confession is expedient and necessary to be retained and continued, used and frequented in the church of God.

Source: *Statutes of the Realm,* vol. 3 (London: 1810–28), p. 739 (modernized).

Questions for Analysis

1. Three of these six articles focus on the sacrament of the Eucharist (the Mass). Given what you have learned in this chapter, why would Henry have been so concerned about this sacrament? What does this reveal about his values and those of his contemporaries?

2. Given Henry's insistence on these articles, why might he have allowed his son to be raised a Protestant? What does this suggest about the political situation in England?

---

redirected all papal revenues from England into the king's hands, prohibited appeals to the papal court, and formally declared "the King's highness to be Supreme Head of the Church of England." In 1536, Henry executed his former tutor and chancellor Sir Thomas More (see Chapter 12) for his refusal to endorse this declaration of supremacy, and took the first steps toward dissolving England's many monasteries. By the end of 1539, the monasteries and convents were gone and their lands and wealth confiscated by the king, who distributed them to his supporters.

These measures, largely masterminded and engineered by Henry's Protestant adviser, Thomas Cromwell (c. 1485–1540), broke the bonds that linked the English Church to Rome. But they did not make England a Protestant country.

Although certain traditional practices (such as pilgrimages and the veneration of relics) were prohibited, the English Church remained overwhelmingly Catholic in organization, doctrine, ritual, and language. The Six Articles promulgated by Parliament in 1539 at Henry VIII's behest left no room for doubt as to official orthodoxy: oral confession to priests, masses for the dead, and clerical celibacy were all confirmed; the Latin Mass continued; and Catholic Eucharistic doctrine was not only confirmed but its denial made punishable by death. To most English people, only the disappearance of the monasteries and the king's own continuing matrimonial adventures (he married six wives in all) were evidence that their Church was no longer in communion with Rome.

The Reign of Edward VI

For truly committed Protestants, and especially those who had visited Calvin's Geneva, the changes Henry VIII enforced on the English Church did not go nearly far enough. In 1547, the accession of the nine-year-old king Edward VI (Henry's son by his third wife, Jane Seymour) gave them the opportunity to finish the task of reform. Encouraged by the apparent sympathies of the young king, Edward's government moved quickly to reform the doctrine and ceremonies of the English Church. Priests were permitted to marry; English services replaced Latin ones; the veneration of images was discouraged, and the images themselves were defaced or destroyed; prayers for the dead were declared useless, and endowments for such prayers were confiscated; and new articles of belief were drawn up, repudiating all sacraments except baptism and communion and affirming the Protestant creed of justification by faith alone. Most important, *The Book of Common Prayer*, authored by Archbishop Cranmer and considered one of the great landmarks of English literature, was published to define precisely how the new English-language services of the church were to be conducted. Much remained unsettled with respect to both doctrine and worship; but by 1553, when the youthful Edward died, the English Church appeared to have become a distinctly Protestant institution.

Mary Tudor and the Restoration of Catholicism

Edward's successor, however, was his pious and much older half sister Mary (r. 1553–58), granddaughter of "the most Catholic monarchs" of Spain, Ferdinand and Isabella (see Chapter 11). Mary speedily reversed her half brother's religious policies, restoring the Latin Mass and requiring married priests to give up their wives. She even prevailed on Parliament to vote a return to papal allegiance. Hundreds of Protestant leaders fled abroad, many to Geneva; others, including Archbishop Thomas Cranmer, were burned at the stake for refusing to abjure their Protestantism. News of the martyrdoms spread like wildfire through Protestant Europe. In England, however, Mary's policies sparked relatively little resistance. After two decades of religious upheaval, most English men and women were probably

QUEEN MARY AND QUEEN ELIZABETH. The two daughters of Henry VIII were the first two queens regnant of England: the first women to rule in their own right. Despite the similar challenges they faced, they had strikingly different fates and have been treated very differently in popular histories. ▪ *How do these two portraits suggest differences in their personalities and their self-representation as rulers?*

hoping that Mary's reign would bring some stability to their lives.

This, however, Mary could not do. The executions she ordered were insufficient to wipe out religious resistance—instead, Protestant propaganda about "Bloody Mary" caused widespread unease, even among those who welcomed the return of traditional religious forms. Nor could Mary do anything to restore monasticism: too many leading families had profited from Henry VIII's dissolution of the monasteries for this to be reversed. Mary's marriage to her cousin Philip, Charles V's son and heir to the Spanish throne, was another miscalculation. Although the marriage treaty stipulated that Philip could not succeed her in the event of her death, her English subjects never trusted him. When the queen allowed herself to be drawn by Philip into a war with France on Spain's behalf—in which England lost Calais, its last foothold on the European continent—many people became highly disaffected. Ultimately, however, what doomed Mary's policies was simply the accident of biology: Mary was unable to conceive an heir. When she died after only five years of rule, her throne passed to her Protestant sister, Elizabeth.

The Elizabethan Compromise

The daughter of Henry VIII and Anne Boleyn, Elizabeth (r. 1558–1603) was predisposed in favor of Protestantism by the circumstances of her parents' marriage as well as by her upbringing. But Elizabeth was no zealot and wisely recognized that supporting radical Protestantism in England might provoke bitter sectarian strife. Accordingly, she presided over what is often known as "the Elizabethan settlement." By a new Act of Supremacy (1559), Elizabeth repealed Mary's Catholic legislation, prohibiting foreign religious powers (i.e., the pope) from exercising any authority within England and declaring herself "supreme governor" of the English church—a more Protestant title than Henry VIII's "supreme head," since most Protestants believed that Christ alone was the head of the Church. She also adopted many of the Protestant liturgical reforms instituted by her half-brother, Edward, including Cranmer's revised version of *The Book of Common Prayer*. But she retained vestiges of Catholic practice, too, including bishops, church courts, and vestments for the clergy. On most doctrinal matters, including predestination and free will, Elizabeth's Thirty-nine Articles of Faith (approved in 1562) struck a decidedly Protestant, even Calvinist, tone. But the prayer book was more moderate and, on the critical issue of the Eucharist, deliberately ambiguous. By combining Catholic and Protestant interpretations ("This is my body. . . . Do this in remembrance of me") into a single declaration, the prayer book permitted an enormous latitude for competing interpretations of the service by priests and parishioners alike.

Yet religious tensions persisted in Elizabethan England, not only between Protestants and Catholics but also between moderate and more extreme Protestants. The queen's artful fudging of these competing Christianities was by no means a recipe for success. Rather, what preserved "the Elizabethan settlement" and ultimately made England a Protestant country was the extraordinary length of Queen Elizabeth's reign, combined with the fact that for much of that time Protestant England was at war with Catholic Spain. Under Elizabeth, Protestantism and English nationalism gradually fused together into a potent conviction that God himself had chosen England for greatness. After 1588, when English naval forces won an improbable victory over a Spanish Armada (see Chapter 14), Protestantism and Englishness became nearly indistinguishable to most of Queen Elizabeth's subjects. Laws against Catholic practices became increasingly severe, and although an English Catholic tradition did survive, its adherents were a persecuted minority. Significant, too, was the situation in Ireland, where the vast majority of the population remained Catholic despite the government's efforts to impose Protestantism on them. As a result, Irishness would be as firmly identified with Catholicism as was Englishness with Protestantism; but it was the Protestants who were in power in both countries.

THE REBIRTH OF THE CATHOLIC CHURCH

So far, our emphasis on the spread of Protestantism has cast the spotlight on dissident reformers such as Luther and Calvin. But there was also a powerful internal reform movement within the Church in these same decades, which resulted in the birth (or rebirth) of a Catholic ("universal") faith. For some, this movement is the "Catholic Reformation"; for others, it is the "Counter-Reformation." Those who prefer the former term emphasize that the Church was continuing significant reforming movements that can be traced back to the eleventh century (see Chapter 8) and which gained new momentum in the wake of the Great Schism (see Chapter 11). Others insist that most Catholic reformers of this period were reactionary, inspired primarily by the urgent need to resist Protestantism and to strengthen the power of the Roman Church in opposition to it.

Past and Present

Controlling Consumption

Although laws regulating the conspicuous consumption of expensive commodities—especially status-conscious clothing—were common during the later Middle Ages, it was not until after the Reformation that both Protestant and Catholic leaders began to criminalize formerly acceptable bodily practices and substances. New theories of sensory perception, the availability of new products like coffee and tobacco, and a new concern to internalize reform led some authorities to outlaw prostitution (hitherto legal) and to ban normal social practices like drinking and dancing. The image on the left shows the militant Catholic League founded in sixteenth-century France, which combatted Protestantism and promoted strict religious observance. The image on the right shows Czech protesters calling for the decriminalization of marijuana.

 Watch related author interview on StudySpace
wwnorton.com/web/westernciv18

Catholic Reforms

Even before Luther's challenge to the Church, as we have seen, there was a movement for moral and institutional reform within some religious orders. And while these efforts received strong support from several secular rulers, the papacy showed little interest in them. In Spain, for example, reforming activities directed by Cardinal Francisco Ximenes de Cisneros (1436–1517) led to the imposition of strict rules of behavior and the elimination of abuses prevalent among the clergy. Ximenes (*he-MEN-ez*) also helped to regenerate the spiritual life of the Spanish Church. In Italy, meanwhile, earnest clerics labored to make the Italian Church more worthy of its prominent position. Reforming existing monastic orders was a difficult task, not least because the papal court set such a poor example; but Italian reformers did manage to

establish several new orders dedicated to high ideals of piety and social service. In northern Europe, Christian humanists such as Erasmus and Thomas More also played a role in this Catholic reform movement, not only by criticizing abuses and editing sacred texts but also by encouraging the laity to lead lives of sincere religious piety (see Chapter 12).

As a response to the challenges posed by Protestantism, however, these internal reforms proved entirely inadequate. Starting in the 1530s, therefore, a more aggressive phase of reform began to gather momentum under a new style of vigorous papal leadership. The leading Counter-Reformation popes—Paul III (r. 1534–49), Paul IV (r. 1555–59), Pius V (r. 1566–72), and Sixtus V (r. 1585–90)—were the most zealous reformers of the Church since the eleventh century. All led upright lives; some, indeed, were so grimly ascetic that contemporaries longed for the bad old days. As a Spanish councilor wrote of Pius V in 1567, "We should like

THE COUNCIL OF TRENT. This fresco depicts the General Council of the Catholic Church, which met at intervals for nearly twenty years between 1545 and 1563 in the city of Trent (in modern-day Italy) in order to enact significant internal reforms.

THE INSPIRATION OF SAINT JEROME **BY GUIDO RENI (1635).** The Council of Trent declared Saint Jerome's Latin translation of the Bible, the Vulgate, to be the official version of the Catholic Church. Since biblical scholars had known since the early sixteenth century that Saint Jerome's translation contained numerous mistakes, Catholic defenders of the Vulgate insisted that even his mistakes had been divinely inspired. ▪ *How does Guido Reni's painting attempt to make this point?*

it even better if the present Holy Father were no longer with us, however great, inexpressible, unparalleled, and extraordinary His Holiness may be." In confronting Protestantism, however, an excessively holy pope was vastly preferable to a self-indulgent one. And these Counter-Reformation popes were not merely holy men. They were also accomplished administrators who reorganized papal finances and filled ecclesiastical offices with bishops and abbots no less renowned for austerity and holiness than were the popes themselves.

Papal reform efforts intensified at the Council of Trent, a general council of the entire Church convoked by Paul III in 1545, which met at intervals thereafter until 1563. The decisions taken at Trent (a provincial capital of the Holy Roman Empire, located in modern-day Italy) provided the foundations on which a new Catholic Church would be erected. Although the council began by debating some form of compromise with Protestantism, it ended by reaffirming all of the Catholic tenets challenged by Protestant critics. "Good works" were affirmed as necessary for salvation, and all seven sacraments were declared indispensable means of grace, without which salvation was impossible. Transubstantiation, purgatory, the invocation of saints, and the rule of celibacy

for the clergy were all confirmed as dogmas—essential elements—of the Catholic faith. The Bible, in its imperfect Vulgate form, and the traditions of apostolic teaching were held to be of equal authority as sources of Christian truth. Papal supremacy over every bishop and priest was expressly maintained, and the supremacy of the pope over any Church council was taken for granted outright, signaling a final defeat of the still-active conciliar movement. The Council of Trent even reaffirmed the doctrine of indulgences that had touched off the Lutheran revolt, although it condemned the worst abuses connected with their sale.

The legislation of Trent was not confined to matters of doctrine. To improve pastoral care of the laity, bishops and priests were forbidden to hold more than one spiritual office. To address the problem of an ignorant priesthood,

Analyzing Primary Sources

The Demands of Obedience

The necessity of obedience in the spiritual formation of monks and nuns can be traced back to the Rule *of Saint Benedict in the early sixth century, and beyond. In keeping with the mission of its founder, Ignatius of Loyola (1491–1556), the Society of Jesus brought a new militancy to this old ideal.*

Rules for Thinking with the Church

1. Always to be ready to obey with mind and heart, setting aside all judgment of one's own, the true spouse of Jesus Christ, our holy mother, our infallible and orthodox mistress, the Catholic Church, whose authority is exercised over us by the hierarchy.

2. To commend the confession of sins to a priest as it is practised in the Church; the reception of the Holy Eucharist once a year, or better still every week, or at least every month, with the necessary preparation. . . .

4. To have a great esteem for the religious orders, and to give the preference to celibacy or virginity over the married state. . . .

6. To praise relics, the veneration and invocation of Saints: also the stations, and pious pilgrimages, indulgences, jubilees, the custom of lighting candles in the churches, and other such aids to piety and devotion. . . .

9. To uphold especially all the precepts of the Church, and not censure them in any manner; but, on the contrary, to defend them promptly, with reasons drawn from all sources, against those who criticize them.

10. To be eager to commend the decrees, mandates, traditions, rites, and customs of the Fathers in the Faith or our superiors. . . .

11. That we may be altogether of the same mind and in conformity with the Church herself, if she shall have defined anything to be black which to our eyes appears to be white, we ought in like manner to pronounce it to be black. For we must undoubtingly believe, that the Spirit of our Lord Jesus Christ, and the Spirit of the Orthodox Church His Spouse, by which Spirit we are governed and directed to salvation, is the same. . . .

From the Constitutions of the Jesuit Order

Let us with the utmost pains strain every nerve of our strength to exhibit this virtue of obedience, firstly to the Highest Pontiff, then to the Superiors of the Society; so that in all things . . . we may be most ready to obey his voice, just as if it issued from Christ our Lord . . . leaving any work, even a letter, that we have begun and have not yet finished; by directing to this goal all our strength and intention in the Lord, that holy obedience may be made perfect in us in every respect, in performance, in will, in intellect; by submitting to whatever may be enjoined on us with great readiness, with spiritual joy and perseverance; by persuading ourselves that all things [commanded] are just; by rejecting with a kind of blind obedience all opposing opinion or judgment of our own. . . .

Source: Henry Bettenson, ed., *Documents of the Christian Church,* 2nd ed. (Oxford: 1967), pp. 259–61.

Questions for Analysis

1. How might Loyola's career as a soldier have inspired the language used in his "Rules for Thinking with the Church"?

2. In what ways do these Jesuit principles respond directly to the challenges of Protestant reformers?

---

a theological seminary was to be established in every diocese. The council also suppressed a variety of local religious practices and saints' cults, replacing them with new cults authorized and approved by Rome. To prevent heretical ideas from corrupting the faithful, the council further decided to censor or suppress dangerous books. In 1564, a specially appointed commission published the first *Index of Prohibited Books*, an official list of writings forbidden to faithful Catholics. Ironically, all of Erasmus's works were immediately placed on the *Index*, even though he had been a chosen champion of the Church against Martin Luther only forty years before. A permanent agency known as the

Congregation of the Index was later set up to revise the list, which was maintained until 1966, when it was abolished after the Second Vatican Council (1962–1965). For centuries, it was to become symbolic of the doctrinal intolerance that characterized sixteenth-century Christianity, both in its Catholic and Protestant varieties.

Ignatius Loyola and the Society of Jesus

In addition to the concerted activities of popes and the legislation of the Council of Trent, a third main force propelling the Counter-Reformation was the foundation of the Society of Jesus (commonly known as the Jesuits) by Ignatius Loyola (1491–1556). In the midst of a career as a mercenary, this young Spanish nobleman was wounded in battle in 1521, the same year in which Luther defied authority at the Diet of Worms. While recuperating, he turned from the reading of chivalric romances to a romantic vernacular retelling of the life of Jesus—and the impact of this experience convinced him to become a spiritual soldier of Christ.

For ten months, Ignatius lived as a hermit in a cave near the town of Manresa, where he experienced ecstatic visions and worked out the principles of his subsequent guidebook, the *Spiritual Exercises*. This manual, completed in 1535 and first published in 1541, offered practical advice on how to master one's will and serve God through a systematic program of meditations on sin and the life of Christ. It eventually became the basic handbook for all Jesuits and has been widely studied by Catholic laypeople as well. Indeed, Loyola's *Spiritual Exercises* ranks alongside Calvin's *Institutes* as the most influential religious text of the sixteenth century.

The Jesuit order originated as a small group of six disciples who gathered around Loyola during his belated career as a student in Paris. They vowed to serve God in poverty, chastity, and missionary work and were formally constituted by Pope Paul III in 1540. By the time of Loyola's death, the Society of Jesus already numbered some 1,500 members. It was by far the most militant of the religious orders fostered by the Catholic reform movements of the sixteenth century—not merely a monastic society but a company of soldiers sworn to defend the faith. Their weapons were not bullets and swords but eloquence, persuasion, and instruction in correct doctrines; yet the Society also became accomplished in more worldly methods of exerting influence. Its organization was patterned after that of a military unit, whose commander-in-chief enforced the iron discipline of all mem-

bers. Individuality was suppressed, and a stoical obedience was required from the rank and file. Indeed, the Jesuit general, sometimes known as the "black pope" (from the color of the order's habit), was elected for life and answered only to the pope in Rome, to whom all senior Jesuits took a special vow of strict obedience. As a result of this vow, all Jesuits were held to be at the pope's disposal at all times.

The activities of the Jesuits consisted primarily of proselytizing and establishing schools. This meant they were ideal missionaries. Accordingly, Jesuits were soon dispatched to preach to non-Christians in India, China, and Spanish America. One of Loyola's closest associates, Francis Xavier (ZAY-vyer, 1506–1552), baptized thousands of people and traveled thousands of miles in South and East Asia. Although Loyola had not at first conceived of his society as a batallion of "shock troops" in the fight against Protestantism, that is what it primarily became. Through preaching and diplomacy—sometimes at the risk of their lives—Jesuits in the second half of the sixteenth century helped to colonize the world. In many places, they were instrumental in keeping rulers and their subjects loyal to Catholicism; in others, they met martyrdom; and in some others, notably Poland and parts of Germany and France, they succeeded in regaining territory previously lost to followers of Luther and Calvin. Wherever they were allowed to settle, they set up schools and colleges, on the grounds that only a vigorous Catholicism nurtured by widespread literacy and education could combat Protestantism.

A New Catholic Christianity

The greatest achievement of these reform movements was the revitalization of the Church. Had it not been for such determined efforts, Catholicism would not have swept over the globe during the seventeenth and eighteenth centuries—or reemerged in Europe as a vigorous spiritual force. There were some other consequences as well. One was the rapid advancement of lay literacy in Catholic countries. Another was the growth of intense concern for acts of charity; because Catholicism continued to emphasize good works as well as faith, charitable activities took on an extremely important role.

There was also a renewed emphasis on the role of religious women. Reformed Catholicism did not exalt marriage as a route to holiness to the same degree as did Protestantism, but it did encourage the piety of a female religious elite. For example, it embraced the mysticism of Saint Teresa of Avila (1515–1582) and established new orders of nuns, such as the Ursulines and the Sisters of Charity. Both Protestants

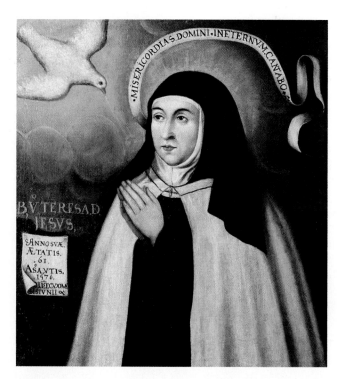

TERESA OF AVILA. Teresa of Avila (1515–1582) was one of many female religious figures who played an important role in the reformed Catholic Church. She was canonized in 1622. This image is dated 1576. The Latin wording on the scroll unfurled above Teresa's head reads: "I will sing forever of the mercy of the Holy Lord."

and Catholics continued to exclude women from the priesthood or ministry, but Catholic women could pursue religious lives with at least some degree of independence, and the convent continued to be a route toward spiritual and even political advancement in Catholic countries.

The reformed Catholic Church did not, however, perpetuate the tolerant Christianity of Erasmus. Instead, Christian humanists lost favor with the papacy, and even scientists such as Galileo were regarded with suspicion (see Chapter 16). Yet contemporary Protestantism was just as intolerant, and even more hostile to the cause of rational thought. Indeed, because Catholic theologians turned for guidance to the scholasticism of Thomas Aquinas, they tended to be much more committed to the dignity of human reason than were their Protestant counterparts, who emphasized the literal interpretation of the Bible and the importance of unquestioning faith. It is no coincidence that René Descartes, one of the pioneers of rational philosophy ("I think, therefore I am"), was educated by Jesuits.

It would be wrong, therefore, to claim that the Protestantism of this era was more forward-looking or progressive than Catholicism. Both were, in fact, products of the same troubled time. Each variety of Protestantism responded to specific historical conditions and the needs of specific peoples in specific places, while carrying forward certain aspects of the Christian tradition considered valuable by those communities. The Catholic Church also responded to new spiritual, political, and social realities—to such an extent that it must be regarded as distinct from either the early Church of the later Roman Empire or even the oft-reformed Church of the Middle Ages. That is why the phrase "Roman Catholic Church" has not been used in this book prior to this chapter, because the Roman Catholic Church as we know it emerged for the first time in the sixteenth century. Like Protestantism, it is a more modern phenomenon.

CONCLUSION

The Reformation grew out of complex historical processes that we have been tracing in the last few chapters. Foremost among these was the increasing power of Europe's sovereign states. As we have seen, those German princes who embraced Protestantism were moved to do so by the desire for sovereignty. The kings of Denmark, Sweden, and England followed suit for many of the same reasons. Since Protestant leaders preached absolute obedience to godly rulers, and since the state in Protestant countries assumed direct control of its churches, Protestantism bolstered state power. Yet the power of the state had been growing for a long time prior to this, especially in such countries as France and Spain, where Catholic kings already exercised most of the same rights that were seized by Lutheran authorities and by Henry VIII of England in the course of their own reformations. Those rulers who aligned themselves with Catholicism, then, had the same need to bolster their sovereignty and power.

Ideas of national identity, too, were already influential and thus available for manipulation by Protestants and Catholics alike. These religions, in turn, became new sources of both identity and disunity. Prior to the Reformation, peoples in the different regions of Germany spoke such different dialects that they had difficulty understanding each other. But Luther's Bible gained such currency that it eventually became the linguistic standard for all these disparate regions, which eventually began to conceive of themselves as part of a single nation. Yet religion alone could not achieve the political unification of Germany, which did not occur for another 300 years (see Chapter 21); indeed, it contributed to existing divisions by cementing the opposition of Catholic princes and peoples. Elsewhere in Europe—as in the Netherlands, where Protestants fought successfully against a foreign, Catholic overlord—religion created a shared identity where politics could not. In England, where it is arguable that a sense of nationalism had already been fostered before the Reformation, membership in the Church of England became a new, but not uncontested, attribute of "Englishness."

Ideals characteristic of the Renaissance also contributed something to the Reformation and the Catholic responses to it. The criticisms of Christian humanists helped to prepare Europe for the challenges of Lutheranism, and close textual study of the Bible led to the publication of the newer, more accurate editions used by Protestant reformers. For example, Erasmus's improved edition of the Latin New Testament enabled Luther to reach some crucial conclusions concerning the meaning of penance and became the foundation for Luther's own translation of the Bible. However, Erasmus was no supporter of Lutheran principles and most other Christian humanists followed suit, shunning Protestantism

After You Read This Chapter

Ⓢ Visit StudySpace for quizzes, additional review materials, and multimedia documents. **wwnorton.com/web/westernciv18**

REVIEWING THE OBJECTIVES

- The main premises of Luther's theology had religious, political, and social implications. What were they?
- Switzerland fostered a number of different Protestant movements. Why was this the case?
- The Reformation had a profound effect on the basic structures of family life and on attitudes toward marriage and morality. Describe these changes.
- The Church of England was established in response to a specific political situation. What was this?
- How did the Catholic Church respond to the challenge of Protestantism?

as soon as it became clear to them what Luther was actually teaching. Indeed, in certain basic respects, Protestant doctrine was completely at odds with the principles, politics, and beliefs of most humanists, who became staunch supporters of the Catholic Church.

In the New World and Asia, both Protestantism and Catholicism became forces of imperialism and new catalysts for competition. The race to secure colonies and resources now became a race for converts, too, as missionaries of both faiths fanned out over the globe. In the process, the confessional divisions of Europe were mapped onto these regions, often with violent results. Over the course of the ensuing century, newly sovereign nation-states would struggle for hegemony at home and abroad, setting off a series of religious wars that would cause as much destruction as any plague. Meanwhile, western civilizations' extension into the Atlantic would create new kinds of ecosystems, forms of wealth, and types of bondage.

PEOPLE, IDEAS, AND EVENTS IN CONTEXT

- How did **MARTIN LUTHER**'s attack on **INDULGENCES** tap into more widespread criticism of the papacy? What role did the printing press and the German vernacular play in the dissemination of his ideas?
- Why did many German principalities and cities rally to Luther's cause? Why did his condemnation at the **DIET OF WORMS** not lead to his execution on charges of heresy?
- How did the Protestant teachings of **ULRICH ZWINGLI**, **JOHN CALVIN**, and the **ANABAPTISTS** differ from one another and from those of Luther?
- What factors made some of Europe's territories more receptive to **PROTESTANTISM** than others? What was the meaning of the principle *CUIUS REGIO, EIUS REGIO*, established by the Peace of Augsburg?
- How did the **REFORMATION** alter the status and lives of women in Europe? Why did it strengthen male authority in the family?
- Why did **HENRY VIII** break with Rome? How did the **CHURCH OF ENGLAND** differ from other Protestant churches in Europe?
- What decisions were made at the **COUNCIL OF TRENT**? What were the founding principles of **IGNATIUS LOYOLA**'s **SOCIETY OF JESUS**, and what was its role in the **COUNTER-REFORMATION** of the **CATHOLIC CHURCH**?

THINKING ABOUT CONNECTIONS

- Our study of Western civilizations has shown that reforming movements are nothing new: Christianity has been continuously reformed throughout its long history. What made this Reformation so different?
- Was a Protestant break with the Catholic Church inevitable? Why or why not?
- The political, social, and religious structures put in place during this era continue to shape our lives in such profound ways that we scarcely notice them—or we assume them to be inevitable and natural. In your view, what is the most far-reaching consequence of this age of dissent and division, and why? In what ways has it formed your own values and assumptions?

Before You Read This Chapter

Europe in the Atlantic World, 1550–1660

CORE OBJECTIVES

- **TRACE** the new linkages between Western civilizations and the Atlantic world, and describe their consequences.

- **DESCRIBE** the different forms of unfree labor that developed in European colonies during this period.

- **IDENTIFY** the monarchies that dominated Europe and the Atlantic world and the newer powers whose influence was expanding.

- **EXPLAIN** the reasons for Europe's religious and political instability and its consequences for Europe's monarchies and the Atlantic world.

- **UNDERSTAND** how artists and intellectuals responded to the crises and uncertainties of this era.

The Atlantic Ocean thrashes the western shores of Europe and Africa with wind-driven waves that have traveled thousands of miles from the American coasts. Its immense area links continents shaped by a wide variety of climates, including the arid desert of the Sahara, the more temperate zones of Europe and North America, the tropical islands of the Gulf of Mexico and the Caribbean, and the rain forests of the Amazon basin in South America. This ecological diversity, and the hitherto infrequent and limited movement of peoples on opposite sides of the ocean, meant that each of these regions nurtured its own forms of plant and animal life, its own unique microbes and pathogens.

In the sixteenth century, the emergence of the Atlantic world as an arena of cultural and economic exchange broke down the isolation of these ecosystems. Transatlantic commerce and migration now eclipsed the importance of trade and movement in the Mediterranean, which had been the crucial connector of Western civilizations since the Bronze Age (see Chapter 2). Populations—humans, animals, and plants—on once-remote shores came into frequent and intense contact. On the one hand, Europeans brought diseases that devastated the peoples of the Americas, along with gunpowder and a hotly divided Christianity. On the other, the huge influx of silver from South America transformed (and eventually exploded) the cash-starved European economy while the arrival of American stimulants such as tobacco, sugar, and chocolate fostered new consumer appetites that could only be satisfied by new regimes of unfree labor.

Eventually, the need for slaves to power the plantations that supplied these consumer products fostered a vast industry of human trafficking, which led to the forcible removal of nearly 11 million people from Africa over the course of three centuries. Colonial settlement in North and South America also created new social hierarchies and new forms of inequality, which unsettled even long-established structures in Europe. The peoples of the Americas were forced to deal with the presence of newly

THE ISLAND OF BERMUDA. This map of "The Summer Isle" and the accompanying images of its major fortifications and sites, was drawn by Captain John Smith and published in *The Generall Historie of Virginia, New-England, and the Summer Isles* (1624). ▪ *Why would such features be of interest to readers of this pamphlet?*

arrived settlers, and settlers in turn confronted both indigenous peoples and the meddling interference of distant imperial bureaucracies.

Meanwhile, these European states were riven by internal dissent and engaged in deadly competitions among themselves—and these, too, were exported to the Atlantic world. Galvanized by the crisis of the Reformation (see Chapter 13), the Roman Catholic Church sought to redress the loss of religious dominance in Europe by spreading its influence to the Americas and Asia through the work of new missionary orders. The Spanish crown, which controlled the most developed colonial empire of the time, was also the most zealous defender of the Catholic faith—which meant that wars within Spain's Protestant Dutch provinces and with Protestant England affected colonial politics, too. Similar attempts by the Catholic Habsburg monarchy to enforce religious uniformity among the varied territories of central Europe led to the Thirty Years' War, one of the longest and bloodiest conflicts in history. In both direct and indirect ways, these deadly disputes stimulated the migration of persecuted minorities (Catholic and Protestant) across the Atlantic, replanting and propagating these rivalries.

But religion was not the only cause of conflict within Europe. Another was the growing tension between powerful monarchs and landowning elites, who disputed the right of the crown and its administrators to raise revenues through increased taxation. Supporting colonial expansion in the Atlantic world and fighting wars within Europe were expensive projects, and they placed strain on traditional alliances and ideas of kingship. Political and moral philosophers accordingly struggled to redefine the role of government in a world of religious pluralism and to articulate new political ideologies that did not necessitate violence among people of different faiths. Intellectuals and artists also strove to reassess Europeans' place in this expanding Atlantic world, to process the flood of new information and commodities, and to make sense of the profound changes in daily life.

THE EMERGENCE OF THE ATLANTIC WORLD

With the few exceptions that we have noted in previous chapters, even the most skilled of Europe's sailors were limited to coastal cruising along the Atlantic's eastern shores until the fifteenth century. But after the Portuguese and Spanish established settlements on the Canary Islands, this archipelago off the northwestern coast of Africa became a permanent base of operations for successive exploratory ventures. From here, generations of Portuguese sailors learned to navigate the West African coast, after which they successfully rounded the Cape of Good Hope and began to establish trading colonies in the Indian Ocean (see Chapter 12). During these years, Portuguese sailors also launched the first kidnapping raids for slaves along the Atlantic coast of Senegal. When they found that some African chieftains were willing to facilitate the capture of people from rival tribes, the Portuguese began to set up coastal outposts where they could trade livestock, foodstuffs, cotton, copper, and iron for ivory, gold, finished textiles, and human beings.

Competing Colonial Ventures

At the same time, Spanish successes in Mexico soon encouraged other European kingdoms to attempt imperial ventures of their own. Finding that Spanish and Portuguese holds on the Caribbean and South America were firm in practice as well as in theory—Protestant rulers were obviously not bound by the Treaty of Tordesillas (1494) and all subsequent papal pronouncements that favored Catholic colonial ventures—northern European explorers targeted the North American coast. Although the Englishman John Cabot had explored the mouth of the St. Lawrence River in 1497–98, it was nearly a century before Walter Raleigh's attempt to start an English colony just north of Spanish Florida in 1585. The settlement at Roanoke Island (present-day North Carolina) was intended to solidify English claims to the territory of Virginia, named for England's "Virgin Queen" Elizabeth and originally encompassing the North American seaboard from South Carolina to Maine, including Bermuda.

This ill-conceived experiment ended with the disappearance of the first colonists, but it was followed by Christopher Newport's expedition to the Chesapeake Bay in 1606, a voyage funded by a private London firm called the Virginia Company. Newport and his followers did not conceive of themselves as empire builders. They were not being sponsored by the English king, and they probably did not intend to settle permanently in the New World. They were "gentleman planters" whose goal was to provide agricultural goods for the European market and so to make their fortunes before returning home. Nevertheless, with the Spanish model much in mind, Newport's band reserved the right to "conquer" any peoples who proved uncooperative. So when Native Americans of the Powhatan tribe killed one-third of

the settlers during a raid in 1622, the colonists responded by crushing the Powhatans and seizing their lands.

For decades thereafter, the native populations of North America remained capable of both threatening and fostering the survival of fragile settlements that had gained a toehold on the continent. Bitter conflicts and occasional cooperation between newcomers and indigenous peoples are part of a larger history of intermittent struggle and coexistence that began the moment Columbus first landed on Hispaniola. Especially in the early years of colonization, when the number of European immigrants was small, some Native American peoples sought to take advantage of these new contacts, to trade for goods otherwise unavailable to them. European settlers, for their part, often exhibited a combination of paternalism and contempt for the peoples they encountered. Some hoped to convert Americans to Christianity, others sought to use them as labor for their economic enterprises. Ultimately, however, the balance was tipped by larger environmental, biological, and demographic factors that lay outside the control of individuals.

The Columbian Exchange

The accelerating rate of global connections in the sixteenth century precipitated an extraordinary movement of peoples, plants, animals, goods, cultures, and diseases. This is known as the "Columbian exchange," a term coined by the historian Alfred Crosby in 1972, with reference to Columbus's voyage. Yet this exchange soon came to encompass lands that still lay far beyond the purview of Columbus and his contemporaries: not just the African and Eurasian landmass and the vast terrain of the Americas but Australia and the Pacific Islands, too.

Because of its profound consequences for human populations and for the environment, the Columbian exchange is considered a fundamental turning point in both human history and the history of the earth's ecology. The exchange put new agricultural products into circulation, introduced new domesticated species of animals, and accidentally encouraged the spread of deadly diseases and the devastating takeovers of invasive plants and animals. Both natural ecosystems and human immune systems around the world were destroyed or transformed. For example, the introduction of pigs and dogs on islands in the Atlantic and Pacific resulted in the extinction of indigenous animals and birds. The landscapes of Central America and southwestern North America were denuded of vegetation after Spanish settlers turned to large-scale herding and ranching operations. Honeybees displaced native insect populations and encouraged the propagation of harmful plant species.

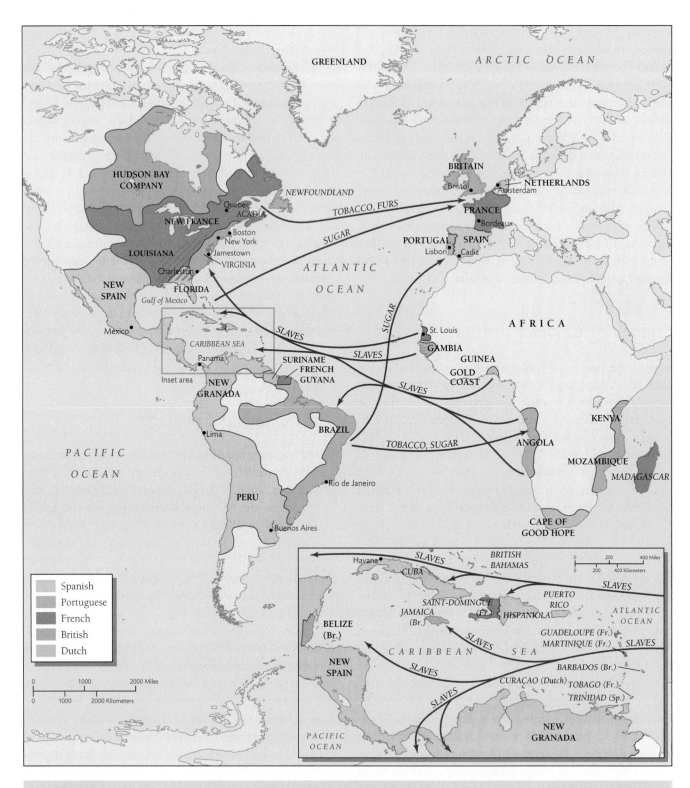

THE ATLANTIC WORLD. ▪ *Trace the routes of the triangular trade. What products did French and British colonies in North America provide to the European market?* ▪ *Which colonies were most dependent on slave labor?* ▪ *What products did they produce, and how did these enter into the triangle?*

Then there were the unintended exchanges: gray squirrels and raccoons from North America found their way to Britain and the European continent. Brown rats and even some species of earthworms were accidentally transported to the Americas. Insects from all over the world traveled to new environments and spread unfamiliar forms of bacteria and pollen.

Obviously, the transfer of human populations in the form of settlers, soldiers, merchants, sailors, indentured servants, and slaves accelerated the process of change. Some groups were wiped out through violence, forced resettlement, and bacteria. As much as 90 percent of the pre-Columbian population of the Americas died from communicable diseases such as smallpox, cholera, influenza, typhoid, measles, malaria, and bubonic plague—all brought from Europe. Syphilis, by contrast, appears to have been brought to Europe from the Americas; some scholars have even asserted that it was Columbus's own sailors who transmitted the disease across the Atlantic.

Meanwhile, the importation of foodstuffs from one part of the world to another, and their cultivation in new habitats, revolutionized the diets of local populations. The American potato (which could be grown in substandard soil and stored for long periods) eventually became the staple diet of the European poor. Tomatoes, although not widely consumed in Europe until the nineteenth century, are now an essential ingredient in many regional Italian dishes. Indeed, the foods and flavors that characterize today's iconic cuisines are, to an extraordinary degree, the result of the Columbian exchange—suggesting that many new, exotic foods quickly become fashionable and then habitual. Who can imagine an English meal without potatoes? Switzerland or Belgium without chocolate? Thai food without chili peppers? Or, on the other side of the Atlantic, Hawaii without pineapples? Florida without oranges? Colombia without coffee? Of the components that make up the quintessential American hamburger—ground-beef patties on a bun with lettuce, tomato, pickles, onion, and (if you like) cheese—only one of these ingredients is indigenous to America. Everything else is Old World: the beef, the wheat for the bun, the cucumber for the pickle, the onion, the lettuce. Even the name is European, a reference to the town of Hamburg in Germany.

THE COLUMBIAN EXCHANGE

The following list names just a few of the commodities and contagions that moved between the Old and New Worlds in this era.

Old World → New World	New World → Old World
• Wheat	• Corn
• Sugar	• Potatoes
• Bananas	• Beans
• Rice	• Squash
• Wine vines	• Pumpkins
• Horses	• Tomatoes
• Pigs	• Avocados
• Chickens	• Chili peppers
• Sheep	• Pineapples
• Cattle	• Cocoa
• *Smallpox*	• Tobacco
• *Measles*	• *Syphilis*
• *Typhus*	

Colonial Populations Compared

In contrast to the more than 7 million slaves who were taken from Africa to labor and die on plantations across the Atlantic, only about 1.5 million Europeans immigrated to the Americas in the two centuries after Columbus's first voyage. The total number who initially emigrated from Spain is estimated at 200,000 to 250,000; most of these were men. By 1570, given the high mortality of migrants and some returns to Europe, the population had been reduced to about 150,000. The Spanish crown did what it could to encourage a new wave of settlement, but even in a period of demographic growth the number of those who chose to seek their fortunes abroad remained relatively small. Transatlantic travel was expensive and uncertain, and the demand for a European labor force remained low as long as Native Americans could be conscripted and enslaved.

The population of the Spanish Americans thus remained largely urban during this period, with most colonists living in the military and administrative centers of the empire. Even the owners of large plantations lived in cities, corresponding from afar with the foremen who managed their estates. Only those who had been granted *encomiendas* tended to live on the lands entrusted to them by the Spanish crown (the Spanish verb *encomendar* means "to trust"). The *encomienda* system reminds us that Spanish conquests in the New World were an extension of the earlier Reconquista (see Chapter 12) of Spain itself. Originally set up to manage

Muslim populations in territories captured by Christian crusaders, this arrangement as carried forward in the new colonies of South America made *encomenderos* agents of the crown. Technically, the lands they oversaw were still owned by native peoples. But in practice, many *encomenderos* were able to exploit the land for their own profit, treating native workers like serfs. Some were descendants of the first conquistadors, others were drawn from Aztec and Inca elites. Many were women: the daughters of the Aztec emperor Montezuma had been given extensive lands to hold in trust after their father's capitulation to Cortés.

In North America, by contrast, English colonies in New England and the Chesapeake Bay were small and rural. But they also grew more quickly, with settlers numbering about 250,000 by 1700. Part of the reason for this was the greater impetus for emigration caused by overpopulation in the British Isles. The persecution of various Protestant groups also played an important role in driving immigration, especially to the New England colonies, where the relocation of entire families and even communities was common. The colonies in Virginia offered further incentives by granting 100 acres to each settler.

But these factors did not swell the numbers of migrants so much as the encouragement of indentured servitude, a practice that brought thousands of "free" European laborers across the Atlantic to work under terms that made them little different from slaves. Perhaps 75 to 80 percent of the people who arrived in the Chesapeake colony in the 1600s were indentured servants, and nearly a quarter of these were women. The successful use of indentured servants to grow tobacco in North America led some landowners to try the same system on plantations in the Caribbean islands. Ultimately, however, the plantation system rendered its greatest profits through the use of African slaves.

New Social Hierarchies in New Spain

After the conquests of the Aztec and Inca Empires (see Chapter 12), the Spanish established colonial governments in Peru and Mexico, controlled from a central bureaucracy in Madrid. This centralization was facilitated by the highly organized structure of Aztec society in Mexico and that of the Incas in Peru. Native peoples already lived, for the most part, in large, well-regulated villages and towns. The Spanish government could therefore work closely with local elites to maintain order. Indeed, the *encomienda* system was initially so effective because it was built on these existing structures and did not attempt to uproot or eliminate existing native cultures. Instead, it focused on controlling and exploiting native labor, especially in extracting mineral resources. Although farming

and ranching were encouraged in Central and South America, and later in Florida and California, the Spanish colonial economy was dominated by mining for a century and a half.

While the Spanish collected tribute from all the communities of their empire and worked assiduously to convert native peoples to Catholicism, they did not attempt to change basic patterns of life. The result was widespread cultural assimilation by the relatively small numbers of (usually male) settlers, which was also assisted by the normalcy of intermarriage between (male) colonizers and (female) colonial subjects. This pattern gave rise to a complex and distinctive caste system in New Spain, with a few "pure-blooded" Spanish immigrants at the top, a very large number of Creoles (peoples of mixed descent) in the middle, and Native Americans at the bottom.

In theory, these racial categories corresponded to class distinctions, but in practice race and class did not always coincide. Racial concepts and practices were extremely flexible, and prosperous individuals or families of mixed descent often found ways to establish their "pure" Spanish ancestry by adopting the social practices of the new Spanish colonial elites. The lingering effects of this complicated stratification are still evident in Latin America today.

Sugar, Slaves, and the Transatlantic Triangle

The Europeans who settled in the Americas faced a major problem: labor. Mining and plantation agriculture required many workers, and the indigenous labor supply of the Americas was limited; as we have seen, the introduction of new diseases resulted in the deaths of millions of Native Americans in the space of only a few decades. Meanwhile, the return of the bubonic plague to Europe in the seventeenth century, along with the slowing population growth that accompanied the wars of religion, meant that colonists could not look to Europe to satisfy their labor needs. Colonial agents thus began to import slaves from Africa to bolster the labor force and to produce the wealth they so avidly sought. And overwhelmingly, that wealth was derived not from gold or silver but from a new commodity for which there was an insatiable appetite in Europe: sugar.

Sugar was also at the center of the "Triangular Trade" that linked markets for goods in Africa, the Americas, and Europe—all of which were driven by slave labor. For example, slave ships that transported African slaves to the Caribbean might trade their human cargo for molasses made on the sugar plantations of the islands. These ships would then proceed to New England where the molasses

Enslaved Native Laborers at Potosí

Since the Spanish crown received one-fifth of all revenues from the mines of New Spain, as well as maintaining a monopoly over the mercury used to refine the silver ore into silver, it had an important stake in ensuring the mines' productivity. To this end, the crown granted colonial mine owners the right to conscript native peoples and gave them considerable freedom when it came to the treatment of the workers. This account, dated to about 1620, describes the conditions endured by these native laborers at Potosi (also discussed in Chapter 12).

According to His Majesty's warrant, the mine owners on this massive range [at Potosí] have a right to the conscripted labor of 13,300 Indians in the working and exploitation of the mines, both those [mines] which have been discovered, those now discovered, and those which shall be discovered. It is the duty of the *Corregidor* [municipal governor] of Potosí to have them rounded up and to see that they come in from all the provinces between Cuzco . . . and as far as the frontiers of Tarija and Tomina. . . .

The conscripted Indians go up every Monday morning to the . . . foot of the range; the *Corregidor* arrives with all the provincial captains or chiefs who have charge of the Indians assigned him for his miner or smelter; that keeps him busy till 1 P.M., by which time the Indians are already turned over to these mine and smelter owners.

After each has eaten his ration, they climb up the hill, each to his mine, and go in, staying there from that hour until Saturday evening without coming out of the mine; their wives bring them food, but they stay constantly underground, excavating and carrying out the ore from which they get the silver. They all have tallow candles, lighted day and night; that is the light they work with, for as they are underground, they have need for it all the time. . . .

These Indians have different functions in the handling of the silver ore; some break it up with bar or pick, and dig down in, following the vein in the mine; others bring it up; others up above keep separating the good and the poor in piles; others are occupied in taking it down from the range to the mills on herds of llamas; every day they bring up more than 8,000 of these native beasts of burden for this task. These teamsters who carry the metal are not conscripted, but are hired.

Source: Antonio Vázquez de Espinosa, *Compendium and Description of the West Indies*, trans. Charles Upson Clark (Washington, DC: 1968), p. 62.

Questions for Analysis

1. From the tone of this account, what do you think was the narrator's purpose in writing? Who is his intended audience?

2. Reconstruct the conditions in which these laborers worked. What would you estimate to be the human costs of this week's labor? Why, for example, would a fresh workforce be needed every Monday?

would be traded to distillers who used the sugary syrup to make rum. Loaded up with a consignment of rum, the slaver would return to the African coast to repeat the process. An alternative triangle might see cheap manufactured goods move from England to Africa, where they would be traded for slaves. Those slaves would then be shipped to Virginia and exchanged for tobacco, which would be shipped back to England to be processed and distributed.

Although the transatlantic slave trade was theoretically controlled by the governments of European colonial powers—Britain officially entered this trade in 1564, the year of William Shakespeare's birth—private entrepreneurs and working-class laborers were active at every stage of the supply chain: in the ports of West Africa, where captured slaves cast their eyes on their homelands for the last time; on the ships where these captives were imprisoned; and in the slave markets of the Americas, as agents for the landowners and merchants who bid against one another to purchase the human chattel that had survived the terrible voyage.

Many other branches of the economy in Europe and the Americas were also linked to the slave trade: from the investors in Amsterdam, London, Lisbon, and Bordeaux who financed the slave trader's journey, to the insurance brokers who negotiated complex formulas for protecting these investments, to the financial agents who offered a range of credit instruments, to those seeking to enter into the expensive and risky business of transatlantic trade. And this is to say nothing of the myriad ways in which the everyday lives of average people were bound to slavery. All those who bought the commodities produced by slave labor, or who manufactured the implements and weapons that enabled enslavement, were also implicated. The slave trade was not, as is sometimes assumed, a venture carried forward by a few unscrupulous men. It created wealth and prestige for every sector of European society, not merely for those who had direct contact with it. It was the engine that created the modern globalized economy.

Counting the Human Cost of the Slave Trade

The Portuguese were the first to bring African slaves to their sugarcane plantations in Brazil, in the 1540s. By this time, slavery was already crucial to the domestic economies of West African kingdoms. In the following decades, however, the ever-increasing demand for slaves would cause the permanent disintegration of political order in this region, by creating an incentive for war and raiding among rival tribes. Moreover, the increased traffic in human beings called for more highly systematized methods for corralling, sorting, and shipping them. At the end of the sixteenth century, accordingly, the Portuguese government established a fortified trading outpost on an island known as Luanda on the central African coast (near what is now Angola). Additional trading posts were then established at multiple places along the coast, to assist in processing the increasing number of captives.

On board ship, enslaved humans were shackled below decks in spaces barely wider than their own bodies, without sanitary facilities of any kind. It might seem surprising that the mortality rate on these voyages was relatively low: probably 10 or 11 percent. But this was only because the slaves chosen for transport were healthy to begin with, and slave traders were anxious to maintain their goods so as to sell at a profit. Those Africans who were actually transported, then, were already the hardy survivors of unimagi-

HOW SLAVES WERE STOWED ABOARD SHIP DURING THE MIDDLE PASSAGE. Men were "housed" on the right, women on the left, children in the middle. The human cargo was jammed onto platforms six feet wide without sufficient headroom to permit an adult to sit up. This diagram is from evidence gathered by English abolitionists and depicts conditions on the Liverpool slave ship *Brookes*.

nable hardships. For in order to place the above statistic in a larger context, we need to consider how many would have died before the ships were ready to transport them. One historian has estimated that 36 out of 100 people captured in the African interior would perish in the six-month-long forced march to the coast of Angola. Another dozen or so would die in the prisons there. Eventually, perhaps 57 of the original 100 captives would be taken on board a slave ship. Some 51 would survive the journey and be sold into slavery on arrival. If the destination was Brazil's sugar plantations, only 40 would still be alive after two years. In other words, the actual mortality rate of these new slaves was something more like 60 percent—and this doesn't begin to account for their life expectancy.

The people consigned to this fate struggled against it, and their initiatives helped to shape the emerging Atlantic world. When the opportunity presented itself, slaves banded together in revolt—a perpetual possibility that haunted slave owners and led to draconian regimes of violence and punishment (as in ancient Rome; see Chapter 5). When revolt was impossible, there were other forms of resistance, among them suicide and infanticide. Above all, slaves sought to escape. Almost as soon as the slave trade escalated, there were communities of escaped slaves throughout the Americas. Many of these independent settlements were large enough to assert and defend their autonomy. One such community, founded in 1603 in the hinterlands of Brazil's Pernambuco Province, persisted for over a century and had as many as 20,000 inhabitants. Most others were much smaller and more ephemeral, but their existence testifies to the limits of imperial authority at the fringes of the new American colonies.

CONFLICT AND COMPETITION IN EUROPE AND THE ATLANTIC WORLD

Most of Europe had enjoyed steady economic growth since the middle of the fifteenth century. The colonization of the Americas seemed to promise prosperity for the decades to come, while providing an outlet for European expansion and aggression. But in the second half of the sixteenth century, prolonged political, religious, and economic crises destabilized Europe. These crises were, in essential ways, the product of long-term developments within and between Europe's most powerful states, but they were exacerbated by these same states' imperial ambitions. Inevitably, then, European conflicts spread to European colonial holdings. Eventually,

the outcome of these conflicts would determine which European powers were best positioned to enlarge their presence in the Atlantic world—and beyond.

New World Silver and Old World Economies

In the latter half of the sixteenth century, an unprecedented inflation in prices profoundly destabilized the European economy. And because nothing on this scale had ever happened before, even during the Roman Empire's turbulent third century (see Chapter 6), it caused widespread panic. Although the twentieth century would see more dizzying inflations than this, skyrocketing prices were a terrifying novelty in this era, causing what some historians have termed a "price revolution."

Two developments in particular underlay this phenomenon. The first was demographic. After the plague-induced decline of the fourteenth century (see Chapter 11), Europe's population grew from roughly 50 million people

PEASANTS HARVESTING WHEAT, SIXTEENTH CENTURY.
The inflation that swept through Europe in the late sixteenth century affected poorer workers most acutely as the abundant labor supply dampened wages while at the same time the cost of food rose because of poor harvests.

POPULATION GROWTH c. 1600. ▪ *In what regions did the population grow more rapidly?* ▪ *Why were the largest gains in population on the coasts?* ▪ *How would urbanization affect patterns of life and trade?*

in 1450 to 90 million in 1600: that is, it increased by nearly 80 percent in a relatively short span of time. Yet Europe's food supply remained nearly constant, meaning that food prices were driven sharply higher by the greater demand for basic commodities. Meanwhile, the enormous influx of silver and gold from Spanish America flooded Europe's previously cash-poor economy (see Chapter 12). This sudden availability of ready coin drove prices higher still.

How? In just four years, from 1556 to 1560, about 10 million ducats' worth of silver passed through the Spanish port of Seville: that is roughly equivalent to 10 billion U.S. dollars in today's currency. (A single gold ducat, the standard unit of monetary exchange for long-distance trade, would be worth nearly a thousand dollars.) Consequently, the market was flooded with coins whose worth quickly became debased because there were so many of them. And still silver poured in, cheapening the coinage even more: between 1576 and 1580, the amount of imported silver had doubled, becoming 20 million ducats; and between 1591 and 1595 it more than quadrupled. Because most of this money was used by the Spanish crown to pay its armies and the many creditors who had financed its imperial ventures, a huge volume of coinage was put quickly into circulation through European banks, making the problem of inflation even more widespread. Since some people suddenly had more money to pay for goods and services, those who supplied these commodities could charge higher and higher prices. "I learned a proverb here," said a French traveler in Spain in 1603: "Everything costs a lot, except silver."

The New European Poor

In this climate, aggressive entrepreneurs profited from financial speculation, landholders from the rising prices of agricultural produce, and merchants from increasing demand for luxury goods. But laborers were caught in a vice. Prices were rising steeply, but wages were not keeping pace owing to the population boom that kept labor relatively cheap. As the cost of food staples rose, poor people had to spend an ever-greater percentage of their paltry incomes on necessities. In Flanders, for example, the cost of wheat tripled between 1550 and 1600; grain prices in Paris quadrupled; and the overall cost of living in England more than doubled in Shakespeare's lifetime. When disasters such as wars or bad harvests drove grain prices out of their reach, as they frequently did, the poor starved to death.

The price revolution also placed new pressures on the sovereign states of Europe. Inflation depressed the real value of money, so fixed incomes derived from taxes and rents yielded less and less actual wealth. Governments were therefore forced to raise taxes merely to keep their revenues constant. Yet most states needed even more revenue than before, because they were engaging in more wars and warfare was becoming increasingly expensive. The only recourse, then, was to raise taxes precipitously. Hence, governments faced continuous threats of defiance and even armed resistance from their citizens, who could not afford to foot these bills.

Although prices rose less rapidly after 1600, as both population growth and the flood of silver began to slow, the ensuing decades were a time of economic stagnation. A few areas—notably the Netherlands (see below)—bucked the trend, and the rich were usually able to hold their own, but the laboring poor made no advances. Wages continued to rise far more slowly than prices. Indeed, the lot of the poor in many places deteriorated further, as helpless civilians were plundered by rapacious tax collectors, looting soldiers, or sometimes both. In England, peasants who had been dispossessed of property or driven off once-common lands were branded as vagrants, and vagrancy itself became a criminal offense. It was this population of newly impoverished Europeans who became the indentured servants or deported criminals of the American colonies.

The Legacy of the Reformation: The French Wars of Religion

Compounding these economic problems were the wars that erupted within many European states. As we began to observe in Chapter 9, most medieval kingdoms were created through the colonization of smaller, traditionally autonomous territories—either by conquest or through marriage alliances with ruling families. Now these enlarged monarchies began to make ever-greater financial claims on their citizens while at the same time demanding religious uniformity among them. The result was regional and civil conflict, as local populations and even elites rebelled against the centralizing demands of monarchs who often embraced a different religion than that of their subjects. Although the Peace of Augsburg (1555) had established that each territory would follow the religion of its ruler, in an effort to end civil strife (see Chapter 13), it was based on the premise that no state can tolerate religious diversity. This was a dangerous precedent, considering the rapid spread of new religious ideas throughout Europe and their export to the New World.

France was the first of these monarchies to be enflamed by religious warfare. Calvinist missionaries from Geneva had made significant headway there (Calvin himself was French), assisted by the conversion of many aristocratic Frenchwomen, who in turn converted their husbands. By the 1560s, French Calvinists—known as Huguenots (HEW-guh-nohz)—made up between 10 and 20 percent of the population. But there was no open warfare until dynastic politics led factions within the government to break down along religious lines, pitting the (mostly southern) Huguenots against the (mostly northern) Catholic aristocracy. In some places, mobs incited by members of the clergy on both sides used this opportunity to settle local scores.

While the Huguenots were not strong enough to win any major scuffle, there were too many to be ignored, and in 1572 the two sides almost brokered a truce: the presumptive heir to the throne, Prince Henry of Navarre—who had become a Protestant—was to marry the Catholic sister of the reigning king, Charles IX. But the compromise was undone by the Queen Mother, Catherine de Medici, whose Catholic faction plotted to kill all the Huguenot leaders while they were assembled in Paris for her daughter's wedding. In the early morning of St. Bartholomew's Day (August 24), most of these Protestant aristocrats were

HENRY IV OF FRANCE. The rule of Henry of Navarre (r. 1589–1610) initiated the Bourbon dynasty that would rule France until 1792 and ended the bitter civil war between Catholic and Huguenot factions.

France had a regional component, the edict also reinforced a tradition of regional autonomy in southwestern France, in spite of the monarchy's centralized power. The success of this effort can be measured by the fact that peace was maintained in France even after Henry IV was assassinated by a Catholic in 1610.

The wars of religion may be one reason that France did not enter the competition for Atlantic wealth until the seventeenth century, despite their early involvement in North American explorations. It was not until 1608 that French colonial settlements received much royal support, after which Catholic (but not Huguenot) immigration to "New France" was encouraged. Meanwhile, there were three failed attempts to establish French outposts in Portuguese Brazil, the last of which (in 1612–15) resulted only in the export of six Amazonian villagers to France, where they aroused great curiosity in an organized tour of French towns. The Brazilians' Catholic hosts even arranged for them to be publicly baptized as part of an attempt to bolster support for the Catholic cause: an episode that further illustrates the strong connection between the expansion of European influence abroad and the politics of religion at home.

The Revolt of the Netherlands and the Dutch Trading Empire

Warfare between Catholics and Protestants also broke out in the Netherlands during this period. Controlled for almost a century by the same Habsburg family that ruled Spain and its overseas empire, the Netherlands had prospered through intense involvement with trade in the Atlantic world. Their inhabitants had the greatest per capita wealth in all Europe, and the metropolis of Antwerp was northern Europe's leading commercial and financial center. So when the Spanish king and emperor Philip II (r. 1556–98) attempted to tighten his hold there in the 1560s, the fiercely independent Dutch cities resented this imperial intrusion and were ready to fight it.

This conflict took on a religious dynamic because Calvinism had spread into the Netherlands from France. Philip, an ardent defender of the Catholic faith, could not tolerate this combination of political and religious disobedience. When crowds began ransacking and desecrating Catholic churches throughout the country, Philip dispatched an army of 10,000 Spanish soldiers to wipe out Protestantism in his Dutch territories. A reign of terror ensued: some 12,000 people were rounded up on charges of heresy or sedition, thousands of whom were convicted and executed for treason.

murdered in their beds, and thousands of humble Protestants were slaughtered in the streets or drowned in the Seine. When word of the Parisian massacre spread to the provinces, local massacres proliferated.

Henry of Navarre escaped, along with his bride, but the war continued for more than two decades. Finally, Catherine's death in 1589 was followed by that of her son, Henry III, who had produced no heir to supplant Henry of Navarre. He became Henry IV, renouncing his Protestant faith in order to placate France's Catholic majority. Then, in 1598, Henry made a landmark effort to end conflict by issuing the Edict of Nantes, which recognized Catholicism as the official religion of the realm but enabled Protestants to practice their religion in specified places. This was an important step toward a policy of religious tolerance: for the first time, French Protestants were allowed to hold public office and to enroll in universities and work in hospitals, and they were even allowed to fortify some towns for their own military defense. And because the religious divide in

PROTESTANTS RANSACKING A CATHOLIC CHURCH IN THE NETHERLANDS.
Protestant destruction of religious images provoked a stern response from Philip II.
- *Why would Protestants have smashed statuary and other devotional artifacts?*

These events catalyzed the Protestant opposition. A Dutch aristocrat, William of Orange, emerged as the anti-Spanish leader and sought help from religious allies in France, Germany, and England. Organized bands of Protestant privateers (that is, privately owned ships) began harassing the Spanish navy in the waters of the North Atlantic. In 1572, William's Protestant army seized control of the Netherlands' northern provinces. Although William was assassinated in 1584, his efforts were instrumental in forcing the Spanish crown to recognize the independence of a northern Dutch Republic in 1609. Once united, these seven northern provinces became wholly Calvinist; the southern region, still largely Catholic, remained under Spanish rule.

After gaining its independence, the new Dutch Republic emerged as the most prosperous European commercial empire of the seventeenth century. Indeed, its reach extended well beyond the Atlantic world, targeting the Indian Ocean and East Asia as well. In general, the Dutch colonial project owed more to the strategic "fort and factory" model of expansion favored by the Portuguese than to the Spanish technique of territorial conquest and settlement. For example, the Dutch established a colony on the Cape of Good Hope at the southern tip of Africa, which facilitated the eastward spread of their influence. Many of its early initiatives were spurred by the establishment of the Dutch East India Company, a private mercantile corporation that came to control Sumatra, Borneo, and the Moluccas (the so-called Spice Islands). This meant that the Dutch had a lucrative monopoly on the European trade in pepper, cinnamon, nutmeg, mace, and cloves. The company also secured an exclusive right to trade with Japan and maintained military and trading outposts in China and India, too.

In the Atlantic world itself, the Dutch did not have much of a significant presence. However, they did establish an outpost in North America, the colony known as New Amsterdam—until it was surrendered to the English in 1667, when it was renamed New York. Their remaining territorial holdings in the Atlantic were Dutch Guyana (present-day Surinam) on the coast of South America, and the islands of Curaçao and Tobago in the Caribbean. But if the Dutch did not match the Spanish or the English in their accumulation of land, the establishment of a second merchant enterprise, the Dutch West India Company, allowed them to dominate the Atlantic slave trade with Africa after 1621.

In constructing this new transoceanic trading empire in slaves and spices, the Dutch pioneered a new financial mechanism for investing in colonial enterprises: the joint-stock company. The Dutch East and West India Companies were early examples, raising cash by selling shares to individual investors whose liability was limited to the sum of their investment. These investors were not part of the company's management, but they were entitled to a share in the profits. Originally, the Dutch East India Company intended to pay off its investors within ten years, but when the period was up, they convinced investors who wanted to realize their profits immediately to sell their shares on the open market. The creation of a market in shares—we now call it a stock market—was an innovation that spread quickly. Arguably, stock markets now control the world's economy.

The Struggle of England and Spain

Religious strife could spark civil war, as in France, or political rebellion, as in the Netherlands. But it could also provoke warfare between sovereign states, as in the struggle between England and Spain. In this case, religious conflict was entangled with both dynastic claims and economic competition in the Atlantic world.

The dynastic competition came from the English royal family's division along confessional lines. The Catholic queen Mary (r. 1553–58), eldest daughter of Henry VIII and granddaughter of Ferdinand and Isabella of Spain (see Chapter 13), had married her cousin Philip II of Spain in 1554 and ruled at a time of great strife between Catholics and Protestants

THE NETHERLANDS AFTER 1609. ▪ *What were the two main divisions of the Netherlands?* ▪ *Which was Protestant, and which was Catholic?* ▪ *How could William of Orange and his allies use the geography of the northern Netherlands against the Spanish?*

on the high seas. In a particularly dramatic exploit lasting from 1577 to 1580, prevailing winds and a lust for booty propelled Drake all the way around the world, to return with stolen Spanish treasure worth twice as much as Queen Elizabeth's annual revenue.

After suffering numerous such attacks over a period of two decades, King Philip finally resolved to fight back after Elizabeth's government openly supported the Dutch rebellion against Spain in 1585. In 1588, he dispatched an enormous fleet, confidently called the "Invincible Armada," whose mission was to invade England. But the invasion never occurred. After an indecisive initial encounter between the two fleets, a fierce storm—hailed as a "Protestant wind" by the lucky English—drove the Spanish galleons off course, many of them wrecking off the coast of Ireland. The shattered flotilla eventually limped home after a disastrous circumnavigation of the British isles, with almost half its ships lost. Meanwhile, Elizabeth took credit for her country's miraculous escape. In subsequent years, continued threats from Spain and sporadic skirmishes nurtured a renewed sense of English nationalism and also fueled anti-Catholic sentiment in that realm.

England's Colonial Ambitions

In the early decades of the seventeenth century, the English challenge to Spanish supremacy in the Atlantic began to bear fruit. Unlike New Spain, England's North American colonies had no significant mineral wealth; instead, as we noted above, English colonists sought to profit from the establishment of large-scale agricultural settlements in North America and the Caribbean. The first permanent colony was founded at Jamestown, Virginia, in 1607. Although this settlement was not particularly successful, more than twenty autonomous settlements were planted over the next forty years by a total of about 80,000 English immigrants.

Many of these were motivated by a desire for religious freedom—hence the name we still give to the Pilgrims who landed at Plymouth, Massachusetts, in 1620. These radical Protestants were known as Puritans, and because they were also political dissidents they were almost as unwelcome as Catholics in an England whose church was, after all, an extension of the monarchy. Strikingly, however, English colonists showed little interest in trying to convert Native American peoples to Christianity. Missionizing played a much larger role in Spanish efforts to colonize Central and South America and in French efforts to penetrate the North American hinterlands.

Another difference between Spanish and English colonialism is the fact that these English colonies did not

in England. After Mary's death, her Protestant half sister Elizabeth (r. 1558–1603) came to the throne, and relations with Spain rapidly declined. They declined further when Catholic Ireland—an English colony—rose in rebellion in 1565, with Spain quietly supporting the Irish. Although it took almost thirty bloody years, English forces eventually suppressed the rebellion. Elizabeth then cemented the Irish defeat by encouraging intense colonial settlement in Ireland. Somewhat ironically, she did so in conscious imitation of Spanish policy in the Americas, sending thousands of Protestant English settlers to occupy land in Ireland in the hopes of creating a colonial state with a largely English identity. Instead, these measures created the deep ethnic and religious conflicts that still trouble the island.

England's conflict with Spain, meanwhile, was worsened by the fact that English economic interests were directly opposed to those of Spain. English traders were making steady inroads into Spanish commercial networks in the Atlantic, as English sea captains such as Sir Francis Drake and Sir John Hawkins plundered Spanish vessels

THE DUTCH EAST INDIA COMPANY WAREHOUSE AND TIMBER WHARF AT AMSTERDAM. The substantial warehouse, the stockpiles of lumber, and the company ship under construction in the foreground illustrate the degree to which overseas commerce could stimulate the economy of the mother country.

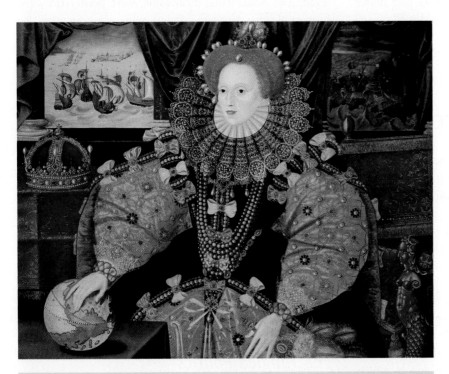

THE "ARMADA PORTRAIT" OF ELIZABETH. This is one of several portraits that commemorated the defeat of the Spanish Armada in 1588. Through the window on the left (the queen's right hand), an English flotilla sails serenely on sunny seas; on the right, Spanish ships are wrecked by a "Protestant wind." Elizabeth's right hand rests protectively—and commandingly—on the globe. ▪ *How would you interpret this image?*

begin as royal enterprises. They were private ventures, farmed either by individual landholders (as in Maryland and Pennsylvania) or managed by joint-stock companies (as in Virginia and the Massachusetts Bay Colony). Building on their experience in Ireland, where colonies had been called "plantations," many English settlers established plantations—planned communities—that attempted to replicate as many features of English life as possible. Geography largely dictated the foundation locations of these English settlements, which were located along the northeast Atlantic coast and on rivers and bays that provided good harbors. Aside from the Hudson, however, there were no great rivers to lead colonists very far inland, so the English colonies clung to the coastline and to each other. The densely populated corridor along the Atlantic seaboard is a direct result of these early settlement patterns.

Since most land in the Old World was owned by royal and aristocratic families, the accumulation of wealth through the control of land was a new and exciting prospect for small-and medium-scale landholders in the new English colonies. This helps to explain their rural, agricultural character—in contrast to the great cities of New Spain. But this focus on agricultural holdings also resulted from the demographic catastrophe that had decimated native populations in this region, as in so many others: by the early seventeenth century, a great deal of rich land had been abandoned simply because there were so few native farmers to till it. As a result, indigenous peoples who had not already succumbed to European diseases were now under threat from colonists who wanted complete and exclusive control over their lands.

To this end, the English soon set out to eliminate, through expulsion and massacre, the former inhabitants of the region. There were a few exceptions; in the Quaker colony of Pennsylvania, colonists and Native Americans maintained friendly relations for more than half a

PLYMOUTH PLANTATION. An English settlement was established at Plymouth in the Massachusetts Bay Colony in 1620. This image shows a reconstruction of the village as it might have looked in 1627. Although speculative, this reconstruction captures something of the plantation's diminutive fragility and isolation.

century. But in the Carolinas, by contrast, there was widespread enslavement of native peoples, either for sale to the West Indies or to work on the rice plantations along the coast. In another contrast to the Spanish and French colonies, intermarriage between English colonists and native populations was rare, creating a nearly unbridgeable racial divide in these North American colonies.

THE THIRTY YEARS' WAR AND THE RISE OF FRANCE

With the promulgation of the French Edict of Nantes in 1598, the end of open hostilities between England and Spain in 1604, and the truce between Spain and the Dutch Republic of 1609, religious warfare in Europe came briefly to an end. In 1618, however, a new series of wars broke out in Central Europe, in some of the German-speaking lands that had felt the first divisive effects of the Reformation and Counter-Reformation (see Chapter 13). Not only was this period of warfare one of the longest in history, it was one of the bloodiest and most widespread, engulfing most of the European continent before it ended thirty years later, in 1648. Although it began as a religious conflict, it quickly became an international struggle for dominance in which these initial provocations were all but forgotten. In the end, some 8 million people died and entire regions were devastated by the rapacity of criss-crossing of armies. The populations of several provinces never recovered and most of the great powers who had fought the war were impoverished

and weakened. The exception was France, which became a preeminent power in Europe for the first time.

The Beginnings of the Thirty Years' War

Like the number and variety of the combatants it involved, the causes of the Thirty Years' War are complicated. On one level, it was an outlet for deeper aggressions and tensions that had been building up since the Peace of Augsburg in 1555 (see above and Chapter 13). On another, it grew out of even longer-standing disputes among rulers and territories (Catholic and Protestant) in the patchwork of provinces that made up the Holy Roman Empire, disputes into which allied powers were drawn. On still another, it was an opportunity for players on the fringes of power to come into prominence.

The catalyst came in 1618, when the Austrian Habsburg (Catholic) prince, Ferdinand, who also ruled Hungary and Poland, was named as heir to the throne of Protestant Bohemia. This prompted a rebellion among the Bohemian aristocracy. A year later, the complex dynastic politics of Central Europe resulted in Ferdinand's election as Holy Roman Emperor. This gave him access to an imperial (Catholic) army, which he now sent in to crush the Protestant revolt. The Bohemians, meanwhile, were bolstered by the support of some Austrian nobility, many of whom were also Protestant and who saw a way to recover power from the Habsburg ruling family.

In 1620, the war escalated further when the Ottomans threw their support behind the Protestants and in so doing touched off a war with the staunchly Catholic kingdom of Poland, whose borders the Muslim army would need to cross in order to get to Prague. The Poles won and the Ottomans retreated. Meanwhile, Ferdinand's Habsburg cousin, the Spanish king and emperor Philip IV, had renewed the war against the Protestant Dutch Republic, which had won its independence from Catholic Spain in 1609; an alliance between the two Habsburg rulers made sense. It led to a major pitched battle between united Protestant forces and a Spanish-led Catholic army (including the young French philosopher, René Descartes) just outside of Prague. The Habsburgs were victorious, and Bohemia was forced to accept Ferdinand's Catholic rule.

The Tangled Politics and Terrible Price of War

The conflict, which had started in Bohemia, should have ended there. But it did not. It metastasized, like a terrible cancer. Unrest between Catholics and Protestants in other

Analyzing Primary Sources

The Devastation of the Thirty Years' War

The author of the following excerpt, Hans Jakob Christoph von Grimmelshausen (1621–1676), barely survived the horrors of the Thirty Years' War. His parents were killed, probably when he was thirteen years old, and he himself was kidnapped the following year and forced into the army. By age fifteen, he was a soldier. His darkly satiric masterpiece, Simplicissimus *("The Simpleton"), drew heavily on these experiences. Although technically a fictional memoir, it portrays with brutal accuracy the terrible realities of this era.*

 lthough it was not my intention to take the peaceloving reader with these troopers to my dad's house and farm, seeing that matters will go ill therein, yet the course of my history demands that I should leave to kind posterity an account of what manner of cruelties were now and again practised in this our German war: yes, and moreover testify by my own example that such evils must often have been sent to us by the goodness of Almighty God for our profit. For, gentle reader, who would ever have taught me that there was a God in Heaven if these soldiers had not destroyed my dad's house, and by such a deed driven me out among folk who gave me all fitting instruction thereupon? . . .

The first thing these troopers did was, that they stabled their horses: thereafter each fell to his appointed task: which task was neither more nor less than ruin and destruction. For though some began to slaughter and to boil and to roast so that it looked as if there should be a merry banquet forward, yet others there were who did but storm through the house above and below stairs. Others stowed together great parcels of cloth and apparel and all manner of household stuff, as if they would set up a frippery market. All that

they had no mind to take with them they cut in pieces. Some thrust their swords through the hay and straw as if they had not enough sheep and swine to slaughter: and some shook the feathers out of the beds and in their stead stuffed in bacon and other dried meat and provisions as if such were better and softer to sleep upon. Others broke the stove and the windows as if they had a never-ending summer to promise. Houseware of copper and tin they beat flat, and packed such vessels, all bent and spoiled, in with the rest. Bedsteads, tables, chairs, and benches they burned, though there lay many cords of dry wood in the yard. Pots and pipkins must all go to pieces, either because they would eat none but roast flesh, or because their purpose was to make there but a single meal.

Our maid was so handled in the stable that she could not come out, which is a shame to tell of. Our man they laid bound upon the ground, thrust a gag into his mouth, and poured a pailful of filthy water into his body: and by this, which they called a Swedish draught, they forced him to lead a party of them to another place where they captured men and beasts, and brought them back to our farm, in which company were my dad, my mother, and our Ursula.

And now they began: first to take the flints out of their pistols and in place of

them to jam the peasants' thumbs in and so to torture the poor rogues as if they had been about the burning of witches: for one of them they had taken they thrust into the baking oven and there lit a fire under him, although he had as yet confessed no crime: as for another, they put a cord round his head and so twisted it tight with a piece of wood that the blood gushed from his mouth and nose and ears. In a word each had his own device to torture the peasants, and each peasant his several tortures.

Source: Hans Jakob Christoph von Grimmelshausen, *Simplicissimus,* trans. S. Goodrich (New York: 1995), pp. 1–3, 8–10, 32–35.

Questions for Analysis

1. The first-person narrator here recounts the atrocities committed "in this our German war," in which both perpetrators and victims are German. How believable is this description? What lends it credibility?

2. Why might Grimmelshausen have chosen to publish his account as a satirical fiction rather than as a straightforward historical narrative or autobiography? How would this choice affect a reader's response to scenes such as this?

Legend:
- The church
- Spain
- Austria
- Brandenburg–Prussia
- Boundary of the Holy Roman Empire

EUROPE AT THE END OF THE THIRTY YEARS' WAR. This map shows the fragile political checkerboard that resulted from the Peace of Westphalia in 1648. ▪ *When you compare this map to the map on page 431, what are the most significant territorial changes between 1550 and 1648?* ▪ *Which regions would have been weakened or endangered by this arrangement?* ▪ *Which would be in a strong position to dominate Europe?*

THE BATTLE OF ROCROI, 1643. Spain's defeat by the French at Rocroi was the first time the Spanish army had lost a land battle since the reign of Ferdinand and Isabella (see Chapter 12) and was yet another contributing factor to the decline of Spanish power during the Thirty Years' War. This painting shows the victorious French general, Duke d'Enghien, surveying the battlefield from afar.

parts of Central Europe erupted into war. French Catholics and Protestants, who had enjoyed relatively peaceful relations since the Edict of Nantes in 1598, came into violent contact once again. Protestant Denmark, fearing that Catholic victories in neighboring parts of the Holy Roman Empire might threaten its sovereignty, was drawn in—losing valuable territories before it was forced to concede defeat.

In this new phase of the conflict, political expediency soon outweighed either religious or dynastic allegiances. When a confederation of Catholic princes seemed close to uprooting Protestantism throughout Germany in 1630, it found its way blocked by other German Catholic princes who were willing to ally with Protestants in order to preserve their own autonomy. Joining them was the (Protestant) king of Sweden, Gustavus Adolphus (r. 1611–32), who championed both the German Lutheran states and his own nation's sovereignty in the wake of Denmark's brush with disaster—but whose Protestant army was secretly subsidized by Catholic France, which would otherwise have been surrounded by a strong Habsburg alliance on its northern, eastern, and southern borders.

One of the great military commanders of all time, Gustavus had become king at age seventeen. Like another young general, Alexander the Great (see Chapter 4), he was not only an expert tactician but a splendid leader. His army became the best-trained and best-equipped fighting force of the era—what some have called the first modern army. When Gustavus died in battle in 1632, a month before his thirty-eighth birthday, Sweden had become one of Europe's great powers, rivaling Spain and Russia in size and prestige.

But in 1635, with Gustavus dead, France was compelled to join Sweden in declaring war on the Spanish and Austrian Habsburgs. In the middle lay the German-speaking lands of Central Europe, already weakened by seventeen years of war and now a helpless battleground. In the next thirteen years, Germany suffered more from warfare than at any time until the twentieth century. Several cities were besieged and sacked nine or ten times over, while soldiers from all nations, who had to sustain themselves by plunder, gave no quarter to defenseless civilians. With plague and disease adding to the toll of outright butchery, some towns and rural areas were nearly eradicated. Most horrifying was the loss of life in the final four years of the war, when the carnage continued even after peace negotiators arrived at broad areas of agreement.

The Peace of Westphalia and the Decline of Spain

The eventual adoption of the Peace of Westphalia in 1648 was a watershed in European history. It marked the emergence of France as the predominant power on the Continent, a position it would hold for the next two centuries. The greatest losers in the conflict (aside from the millions of German victims) were the Austrian Habsburgs, who were forced to surrender all the territory they had gained and to abandon their hopes of using the office of Holy Roman Emperor to dominate Central Europe.

The Spanish Habsburgs were also substantially weakened and were no longer able to fall back on the wealth of their Atlantic empire. Large portions of the Atlantic trade had been infiltrated by merchants from other countries, and the expansion of local economies in Spain's colonies had made them less dependent on trade with Spain itself. In 1600, the Spanish Empire had been the mightiest power in the world. A half century later, this empire had begun to fall apart.

As we've already noted, New Spain's great wealth had begun to turn into a liability when the infusion of silver spiked inflation and slowed economic development at home. Lacking both agricultural and mineral resources of its own, Spain might have developed its own industries and a balanced trading pattern, as some of its Atlantic rivals were doing. Instead, the Spanish used imperial silver to buy manufactured goods from other parts of Europe, offering no incentives to develop exports of their own. When the river of silver began to abate, Spain was plunged into debt.

Meanwhile, the Spanish crown's commitment to supporting the Catholic Church committed it to costly wars, as did attempts to maintain Spain's international dominance. Involvement in the Thirty Years' War was the last straw. The strains of warfare drove the kingdom, with its power base in Castile, to raise more money and soldiers from the other Iberian provinces. First Catalonia and then Portugal (incorporated into Spain in 1580) rose in revolt, followed by the southern Italians who rebelled against their Castilian viceroys in Naples and Sicily. It was only by chance that Spain's greatest external enemies, France and England, could not act in time to take advantage of its plight. This gave the Castilian-based government time to put down the Italian revolts; by 1652, it had also brought Catalonia to heel. But Portugal retained its independence while Spain remained isolated, weakened, and without European allies after the Peace of Westphalia.

The Emergence of French Power in Europe and North America

France emerged from the crisis of the Thirty Years' War with a stronger state, a more dynamic economy, and increased influence abroad. Like Spain, France had grown over the course of the previous centuries by absorbing formerly independent principalities whose inhabitants cherished traditions of local independence and were not always willing to cooperate with the royal government. The fact that France became more powerful as a result of this process, while Spain did not can be attributed in part to France's greater natural resources and the greater prestige of the French monarchy, which can be traced back to the rule of Louis IX (later canonized as Saint Louis; see Chapter 10). Most subjects of the French king, including the Protestants whose welfare had been cultivated by Henry IV, were loyal to the crown. Moreover, France had enormous economic resiliency, owing primarily to its rich and varied agricultural productivity. Unlike Spain, which had to import food, France was able to feed itself. Moreover, Henry IV's ministers had financed the construction of roads, bridges, and canals to facilitate the flow of goods. Royal factories manufactured luxury goods such as crystal, glass, and tapestries, and Henry also supported the production of silk, linen, and wool throughout the kingdom.

Henry's patronage had also allowed the explorer Samuel de Champlain to claim parts of Canada as France's first foothold in the New World. In 1608, Champlain founded the colony of Québec in the Saint Lawrence river valley. Whereas the English initially limited their colonial settlements to regions along the Atlantic coastline, the French set out to dominate the interior of the North American continent. French traders ranged far up and down the few Canadian rivers that led inland, exchanging furs and goods with the Native American groups they encountered, while French missionaries used the same arteries to spread Catholic Christianity from Québec to Louisiana. Eventually, French imperial ventures spread via the Great Lakes and the great river systems along the Mississippi to the prairies of America's Midwest.

These far-flung French colonies were established and administered as royal enterprises like those of Spain, a fact that distinguished them from the private commercial ventures put together by the English and the Dutch. Also like New Spain, the colonies of New France were overwhelmingly populated by men. The elite of French colonial society were military officers and administrators sent from Paris. Below their ranks were fishermen, fur traders, small farmers, and common soldiers who constituted the bulk of French settlers in North America. Because the

ILLINOIS INDIANS TRADING WITH FRENCH SETTLERS. This engraving from Nicholas de Fer's 1705 map of the Western Hemisphere illustrates the economic interdependence that developed between early French colonies and the native peoples of the surrounding region. ▪ *How did this differ from relations between Native Americans and English agricultural communities on the Atlantic coast?*

fishing and fur trades relied on cooperative relationships with native peoples, a mutual economic interdependence grew up between the French colonists and the peoples of surrounding regions. Intermarriage between French traders and native women was common.

Yet in contrast to both Spanish and English colonies, these French colonies remained dependent on the wages and supplies sent to them from the mother country. Only rarely did they become truly self-sustaining economic enterprises. Indeed, their financial rewards were modest. Furs, fish, and tobacco were exported to European markets, but it was not until the late seventeenth century that some French colonies began to realize large profits by building sugar plantations in the Caribbean islands of Hispaniola (the French portion of this large island, now Haiti, was known as Saint-Domingue), Guadeloupe, and Martinique. By 1750, 500,000 slaves on Saint-Domingue were laboring under extraordinarily harsh conditions to produce 40 percent of the world's sugar and 50 percent of its coffee (see Chapter 15).

The Policies of Cardinal Richelieu

This expansion of French power can be credited, in part, to Henry IV's de facto successor, Cardinal Richelieu (*REESH-eh-lyuh*). The real king of France, Henry's son Louis XIII (r. 1610–43), had come to the throne at the age of nine, so Richelieu, as his chief minister of state, dominated his reign. His chief aim was to centralize royal bureaucracy while exploiting opportunities to foster French influence abroad.

Within France, Richelieu amended the Edict of Nantes so that it no longer supported the military and political rights of the Huguenots. He also prohibited these French Protestants from settling in Québec. Yet considering that he owed his political power (in part) to his ecclesiastical

position in the Catholic Church, the fact that he allowed the edict to stand speaks to his larger interest in fostering a sense of French national identity that centered on monarchy. In keeping with this policy, he also imposed direct taxation on powerful provinces that had retained their financial autonomy up to that point. Later, to make sure taxes were efficiently collected, Richelieu instituted a new system of local government which empowered royal officials to put down provincial resistance.

These policies made the French royal government more powerful than any in Europe. It also doubled the crown's income, allowing France to engage in the Thirty Years' War that extended its power on the continent. Yet this increased centralization would provoke challenges to royal authority from aristocratic elites in the years after Richelieu's death. Eventually, the extreme centralization of royal authority in France would lead to the French Revolution (see Chapter 18).

The Challenge of the Fronde

One more immediate response to Richelieu's policies was a series of uncoordinated revolts known collectively as the *Fronde* (from the French word for a sling used to hurl stones). In 1643, just after the death of Richelieu, Louis XIII was succeeded by his five-year-old son, Louis XIV. The young king's regents were his mother, Anne of Austria, and her alleged lover, Cardinal Mazarin. Both were foreigners—Anne was a Habsburg and Mazarin was an Italian by birth—and many extremely powerful nobles hated them. They also hated the way that Richelieu's government had curtailed their own authority in their ancestral provinces. Popular resentments were aroused as well, because the costs of the ongoing Thirty Years' War were now combined with several consecutive years of bad harvests. So when cliques of nobles expressed their disgust for Mazarin, they found much popular support. In 1648, the levy of a new tax had protesters on the streets of Paris, armed with slings and projectiles.

However, neither the aristocratic leaders of the Fronde nor the commoners who joined them claimed to be resisting the young king; their targets were the corruption and mismanagement of Mazarin. Some of the rebels, it is true, insisted that part of Mazarin's fault lay in his pursuit of Richelieu's centralizing policy. But most aristocrats wanted to become part of this centralizing process. Years later, when Louis XIV began to rule in his own right in 1651, the memory of these early turbulent years haunted him. He resolved never to let the aristocracy or their provinces get out of hand. Pursuing this aim, he became the most effective absolute monarch in Europe (see Chapter 15).

THE CRISIS OF MONARCHY IN ENGLAND

Of all the crises that shook Europe in this era, the most radical in its consequences was the English Civil War. The causes of this conflict were similar to those that had sparked trouble in other countries: hostilities between the component parts of a composite kingdom; religious animosities between Catholics and Protestants; struggles for power among competing factions of aristocrats at court; and a fiscal system that could not keep pace with the increasing costs of government, much less those of war. But in England, these developments led to the unprecedented criminal trial and execution of a king, an event that sent shock waves throughout Europe and the Atlantic world.

The Origins of the Civil War

The chain of events leading to civil war in England can be traced to the last decades of Queen Elizabeth's reign. The expenses of England's defense against Spain, rebellion in Ireland, widespread crop failures, and the inadequacies of the antiquated English taxation system drove the queen's government deeply into debt. When Elizabeth was succeeded by her cousin, James Stuart—King James VI of Scotland, James I of England—bitter factional disputes at court were complicated by the financial crisis. When the English Parliament rejected James's demands for more taxes, he raised what revenues he could without parliamentary approval, imposing new tolls and selling trading monopolies to favored courtiers. These measures aroused resentment against the king and made voluntary grants of taxation from Parliament even less likely.

James also struggled with religious divisions among his subjects. His own kingdom of Scotland had been firmly Calvinist since the 1560s. England, too, was Protestant but of a very different kind, since the Church of England retained many of the rituals, hierarchies, and doctrines of the medieval Church (see Chapter 13). Indeed, a significant number of English Protestants, known as Puritans, wanted to bring their church more firmly into line with Calvinist principles; it was a group of Puritan refugees who founded the Massachusetts Bay Colony (above). Although James was largely successful in mediating these conflicts, he stirred up trouble in staunchly Catholic Ireland by encouraging thousands of Scottish Calvinists to settle in the northern Irish province of Ulster. In doing so, he exacerbated a situation that had already become violent under Elizabeth.

Parliament versus the King

English politics became more volatile in 1625, when James was succeeded by his surviving son, Charles. Charles alarmed his Protestant subjects by marrying the (Catholic) sister of France's Louis XIII, and he launched a new war with Spain, straining his already slender financial resources. When Parliament refused to grant him funds, he demanded forced loans from his subjects and punished those who refused by lodging soldiers in their homes. Others were imprisoned without trial. Parliament responded by imposing the Petition of Right in 1628, which declared that taxes not voted by Parliament were illegal, condemned arbitrary imprisonment, and prohibited quartering of soldiers in private houses. Thereafter, Charles tried to rule England without Parliament—something that had not been attempted since the establishment of that body 400 years earlier (see Chapter 9). He also ran into trouble with his Calvinist subjects in Scotland because he began to favor the most Catholic-leaning elements in the English Church. The Scots rebelled in 1640, and a Scottish army marched south into England to demand the withdrawal of Charles's "Catholicizing" measures.

To meet the Scottish threat, Charles was forced to summon Parliament, whose members were determined to impose radical reforms on the king's government before they would even consider granting him funds to raise an army. There was even support for the Scottish Calvinists among Puritans in Parliament. To avoid dealing with this difficult political situation, Charles tried to arrest

Cardinal Richelieu on the Common People of France

Armand Jean du Plessis, Duke of Richelieu and cardinal of the Roman Catholic Church, was the effective ruler of France from 1624 until his death in 1642. His Political Testament *was assembled after his death from historical sketches and memoranda of advice which he prepared for King Louis XIII, the ineffectual monarch whom he ostensibly served. This book was eventually published in 1688, during the reign of Louis XIV.*

All students of politics agree that when the common people are too well off it is impossible to keep them peaceable. The explanation for this is that they are less well informed than the members of the other orders in the state, who are much more cultivated and enlightened, and so if not preoccupied with the search for the necessities of existence, find it difficult to remain within the limits imposed by both common sense and the law.

It would not be sound to relieve them of all taxation and similar charges, since in such a case they would lose the mark of their subjection and consequently the awareness of their station. Thus being free from paying tribute, they would consider themselves exempted from obedience. One should compare them with mules, which being accustomed to work, suffer more when long idle than when kept busy. But just as this work should be reasonable, with the burdens placed upon these animals proportionate to their strength, so it is likewise with the burdens placed upon the people. If they are not moderate, even when put to good public use, they are certainly unjust. I realize that when a king undertakes a program of public works it is correct to say that what the people gain from it is returned by paying the *taille* [a heavy tax imposed on the peasantry]. In the same fashion it can be maintained that what a king takes from the people returns to them, and that they advance it to him only to draw upon it for the enjoyment of their leisure and their investments, which would be impossible if they did not contribute to the support of the state.

Source: *The Political Testament of Cardinal Richelieu,* trans. Henry Bertram Hill (Madison, WI: 1961), pp. 31–32.

Questions for Analysis

1. According to Cardinal Richelieu, why should the state work to subjugate the common people? What assumptions about the nature and status of "common people" underlie this argument?

2. What theory of the state emerges from this argument? What is the relationship between the king and the state and between the king and the people, according to Richelieu?

Parliament's leaders and force his own agenda. When he failed in this, he withdrew from London to raise his own army. Parliament responded by mustering a seperate military force and voting itself the taxation to pay for it. By the end of 1642, open warfare had erupted between the English king and the English government: something inconceivable in neighboring France, where the king and the government were inseparable.

Arrayed on the king's side were most of England's aristocrats and largest landowners, many of whom owned lands in the Atlantic colonies as well. The parliamentary forces were made up of smaller landholders, tradesmen, and artisans, many of whom were Puritan sympathizers. The king's royalist supporters were commonly known by the aristocratic name of Cavaliers. Their opponents, who cut their hair short in contempt for the fashionable custom of wearing curls, were derisively called Roundheads. After 1644, when the parliamentary army was effectively reorganized, the royalist forces were badly beaten, and in 1646 the king was compelled to surrender. Soon thereafter, the episcopal hierarchy of the Church of England was abolished and a Calvinist-style church was mandated throughout England and Wales.

The struggle might have ended here had not a quarrel developed within the parliamentary party. The majority of its members were ready to restore Charles to the throne as a limited monarch, under an arrangement whereby a uniformly Calvinist faith would be imposed on both Scotland seized control of the government. In order to ensure that the Puritan agenda would be carried out, he ejected all the moderates from Parliament by force. This "Rump" (remaining) Parliament then proceeded to put the king on trial and eventually to condemn him to death for treason against his own subjects. Charles Stuart was publicly beheaded on January 30, 1649: the first time in history that a reigning king had been legally deposed and executed. Europeans reacted to his death with horror, astonishment, or rejoicing, depending on their own political convictions (see *Interpreting Visual Evidence* on page 480).

After the king's execution, his son (the future King Charles II) joined with the remaining royalist forces in an attempt to restore the monarchy. But he was defeated by Cromwell's army and fled to France. With the heir to the English throne in exile, Cromwell and his supporters abolished Parliament's hereditary House of Lords and declared England a Commonwealth: an English translation of the Latin *res publica*. Technically, the Rump Parliament continued as the legislative body; but Cromwell, with the army at his command, possessed the real power and soon became exasperated by legislators' attempts to enrich themselves by confiscating their opponents' property. In 1653, he

CHARLES I. King Charles of England was a connoisseur of the arts and a patron of artists. He was adept at using portraiture to convey the magnificence of his tastes and the grandeur of his conception of kingship. ▪ *How does this portrait by Anthony van Dyck compare to the engravings of the "martyred" king on page 480 in* **Interpreting Visual Evidence?**

and England as the state religion. But a radical minority of Puritans, commonly known as Independents, insisted on religious freedom for themselves and all other Protestants. Their leader was Oliver Cromwell (1599–1658), who had risen to command the Roundhead army, which he had reconstituted as "the New Model Army." Ultimately, he became the new leader of Parliament, too.

The Fall of Charles Stuart and Oliver Cromwell's Commonwealth

Taking advantage of the dissension within the ranks of his opponents, Charles renewed the war in 1648. But he was forced to surrender after a brief campaign, and Cromwell

OLIVER CROMWELL AS PROTECTOR OF THE COMMONWEALTH. This coin, minted in 1658, shows the lord protector wreathed with laurel garlands like a classical hero or a Roman consul, but it also proclaims him to be "by the Grace of God Protector of the Commonwealth." ▪ *What mixed messages does this coin convey?*

marched a detachment of troops into the Rump Parliament and disbanded it.

The short-lived Commonwealth was thus replaced by the "Protectorate," a thinly disguised autocracy established under a constitution drafted by officers of the army. Called the *Instrument of Government*, this text is the nearest approximation to a written constitution England has ever had. Extensive powers were given to Cromwell as Lord Protector for life, and his office was made hereditary.

The Restoration of the Monarchy

Many intellectuals noted the similarities between these events and those that had given rise to the Principate of Augustus after the death of Julius Caesar (Chapter 5). And among the people, Cromwell's Puritan military dictatorship was growing unpopular, not least because it prohibited public recreation on Sundays and closed London's theatres. Many became nostalgic for the milder and more tolerant Church of England and began to hope for a restoration of the old royalist regime. The opportunity came with Cromwell's death in 1658. His son Richard had no sooner succeeded to the office of Lord Protector when a faction within the army removed him from power. As groups of royalists plotted an uprising, a new Parliament was organized, and, in April of 1660, it declared that King Charles II had been the ruler of England since his father's execution in 1649. Almost overnight, England became a monarchy again.

Charles II (r. 1660–85) revived the Church of England and was careful not to return to the provocative religious policies of his father. Quipping that he did not wish to "resume his travels," he agreed to respect Parliament and to observe the Petition of Right that had so enraged Charles I. He also accepted all the legislation passed by Parliament immediately before the outbreak of civil war in 1642, including the requirement that Parliament be summoned at least once every three years. England thus emerged from its civil war as a limited monarchy, in which power was exercised by "the king in Parliament." It remains a constitutional monarchy to this day.

The English Civil War and the Atlantic World

These tumultuous events had a significant influence on the development of a new political sensibility within England's Atlantic colonies. The English landed aristocracy had sided with the king during this conflict, but many in the colonies had sympathized with Parliament in its claims to protect the liberties of small landowners, who also bore a dispro-

portionate share of taxation. Even after the Restoration of the monarchy in 1660, many colonial leaders retained an antimonarchist and antiaristocratic bias.

The fact that the royal government had been almost entirely concerned with the business of putting down rebellion at home also meant that England's colonies became used, at an early stage, to a large degree of independence. As a result, once government was restored, all of Parliament's efforts to extend more control over the colonies would result in greater and greater friction (see Chapter 15). Slogans declaring the rights of "free-born Englishmen" would echo among farmers, while "free trade" became a rallying cry against royal interference in colonial commerce. The bitter religious conflicts that had divided the more radical Puritans from the Church of England also forced the colonies to come to grips with the problem of religious diversity. Some, like Massachusetts, took the opportunity to impose their own brand of Puritanism on settlers. Others experimented with forms of religious toleration that sometimes went beyond the forms of religious freedom that existed back in England.

Paradoxically, though, the spread of ideas about the protection of liberties and citizens' rights coincided with a rapid and considerable expansion of unfree labor in the colonies. Prior to the 1640s, the English colonies in North America and the Caribbean had been assured of a steady stream of immigrants, like the Puritan Pilgrims of Massachusetts in 1620. The outbreak of war in 1642 and the subsequent triumph of the Puritans under Cromwell caused a drop in this migration, since many who might have thought of emigrating decided to stay in England. In North America, the decline in the arrival of new settlers was so sudden that it caused a depression in local economies.

Meanwhile, the demand for labor was increasing rapidly owing to the expansion of tobacco plantations in Virginia and sugar plantations in Barbados and Jamaica, which the British captured from the Spanish in 1655. These plantations, with their punishing working conditions and high mortality rates from disease, were insatiable in their demand for workers. Plantation owners thus sought to meet this demand by investing ever more heavily in forms of unfree labor, including indentured servants and African slaves. The social and political crisis unleashed by the English Civil War also led to the forced migration of paupers and political prisoners, especially from Scotland, Wales, and Ireland; and this pattern continued during Cromwell's reign. These exiles, many without resources, swelled the ranks of the unfree and the very poor in England's Atlantic colonies, spurring the formation of new social hierarchies as earlier arrivals sought to distance themselves from newer immigrants they regarded

Debating the English Civil War

The English Civil War raised fundamental questions about political rights and responsibilities. Many of these are addressed in the two excerpts below. The first comes from a lengthy debate held within the General Council of Cromwell's army in October of 1647. The second is taken from the speech given by King Charles, moments before his execution in 1649.

The Army Debates, 1647

Colonel Rainsborough: Really, I think that the poorest man that is in England has a life to live as the greatest man, and therefore truly, sir, I think it's clear, that every man that is to live under a government ought first by his own consent to put himself under that government, and I do think that the poorest man in England is not at all bound in a strict sense to that government that he has not had a voice to put himself under . . . insomuch that I should doubt whether I was an Englishman or not, that should doubt of these things.

General Ireton: Give me leave to tell you, that if you make this the rule, I think you must fly for refuge to an absolute natural right, and you must deny all civil right, and I am sure it will come to that in the consequence. . . . For my part, I think it is no right at all. I think that no person has a right to an interest or share in the disposing of the affairs of the kingdom, and in determining or choosing those that shall determine what laws we shall be ruled by here, no person has a right to this that has not a permanent fixed interest in this kingdom, and those persons together are properly the represented of this kingdom who, taken together, and consequently are to make up the representers of this kingdom. . . .

We talk of birthright. Truly, birthright there is. . . . [M]en may justly have by birthright, by their very being born in England, that we should not seclude them out of England. That we should not refuse to give them air and place and ground, and the freedom of the highways and other things, to live amongst us, not any man that is born here, though he in birth or by his birth there come nothing at all that is part of the permanent interest of this kingdom to him. That I think is due to a man by birth. But that by a man's being born here he shall have a share in that power that shall dispose of the lands here, and of all things here, I do not think it is a sufficient ground.

Source: David Wootton, ed., *Divine Right and Democracy: An Anthology of Political Writing in Stuart England* (New York: 1986), pp. 286–87 (language modernized).

as inferiors. The crisis of kingship in England thus led to a substantial increase in the African slave trade and a sharpening of social and economic divisions in the English colonies. This is yet another indication of Europe's inseparable relationship with the Atlantic world.

THE PROBLEM OF DOUBT AND THE ART OF BEING HUMAN

On the first day of November in 1611, a new play by William Shakespeare premiered in London, at the royal court. *The Tempest* takes place on a remote island, where an exiled duke from the Italian city-state of Milan has used his magical arts to subjugate the island's inhabitants. This plot drew on widespread reports from the new European colonies of the Atlantic, especially the Caribbean, where slaves were called Caribans and where (it was rumored) cannibalism flourished—hence the name Shakespeare chose for the play's rebellious slave Caliban, who seeks to revenge himself on the magician Prospero, his oppressive master. When reminded that he owes his knowledge of the English language to the civilizing influence of Prospero's daughter, Miranda, Caliban retorts, "You taught me language, and my profit on't / Is, I know how to curse."

According to Caliban, the benefits of a European education could not outweigh the evils of colonization—and

Charles I on the Scaffold, 1649

think it is my duty, to God first, and to my country, for to clear myself both as an honest man, a good king, and a good Christian.

I shall begin first with my innocence. In truth I think it not very needful for me to insist long upon this, for all the world knows that I never did begin a war with the two Houses of Parliament, and I call God to witness, to whom I must shortly make an account, that I never did intend to incroach upon their privileges. . . .

As for the people—truly I desire their liberty and freedom as much as anybody whatsoever. But I must tell you that their liberty and freedom consists in having of government those laws by which their lives and goods may be most their own. It is not for having share in government. That is nothing pertaining to them. A subject and a sovereign are clean different things, and therefore, until they do

that—I mean that you do put the people in that liberty as I say—certainly they will never enjoy themselves.

Sirs, it was for this that now I am come here. If I would have given way to an arbitrary way, for to have all laws changed according to the power of the sword, I needed not to have come here. And therefore I tell you (and I pray God it be not laid to your charge) that I am the martyr of the people.

Source: Brian Tierney, Donald Kagan, and L. Pearce Williams, eds., *Great Issues in Western Civilization* (New York: 1967), pp. 46–47.

Questions for Analysis

1. What fundamental issues are at stake in both of these excerpts? How do the debaters within the parliamentary army (first excerpt) define "natural" and "civil" rights?

2. How does Charles defend his position? What is his theory of kingship, and how does it compare to that of Cardinal Richelieu's (page 475)? How does it conflict with the ideas expressed in the army's debate?

3. It is interesting that none of the participants in these debates seems to have recognized the implications their arguments might have for the political rights of women. Why would that have been the case?

could, in fact, be used to resist it. Shakespeare's audience was thus confronted with a spectacle of their own colonial ambitions gone awry, as well as with a number of other contemporary problems, including the perils of civil war, the struggle for political legitimacy, the fear of sorcery, and the availability of exotic commodities.

The doubt and uncertainty caused by Europe's extension into the Atlantic world were primary themes and motivators of this era's creative arts, which both documented and critiqued contemporary trends while emphasizing the redemptive qualities of human suffering and compassion. Another example of this artistic response is the novel *Don Quixote*, which its author, Miguel de Cervantes (*sehr-VAHN-tehs*, 1547–1616), composed largely in prison. It recounts the

adventures of an idealistic Spanish gentleman, Don Quixote of La Mancha, who becomes deranged by his constant reading of chivalric romances and sets out to have delusional adventures of his own. His sidekick, Sancho Panza, is his exact opposite: a plain, practical man content with modest bodily pleasures. Together, they represent different facets of human nature. On the one hand, *Don Quixote* is a devastating satire of Spain's decline. On the other, it is a sincere celebration of the human capacity for optimism and goodness.

Throughout the long century between 1550 and 1660, Europeans confronted a world in which all that they had once taken for granted was cast into confusion. Vast continents had been discovered, populated by millions of people whose very existence challenged Western civilizations'

Interpreting Visual Evidence

The Execution of a King

his allegorical engraving (image A) accompanied a pamphlet called *Eikon Basilike* ("The Kingly Image"), which began to circulate in Britain just weeks after the execution of King Charles I. It purported to be an autobiographical account of the king's last days and a justification of his royal policies. It was intended to arouse widespread sympathy for the king and his exiled heir, Charles II, and it succeeded admirably: the cult of Charles "King and Martyr" became increasingly popular. Here, the Latin inscription on the shaft of light suggests that Charles's piety will beam "brighter through the shadows," while the scrolls at the left proclaim that "virtue grows beneath weight" and "unmoved, triumphant." Charles's earthly crown (on the floor at his side) is "splendid and heavy," while the crown of thorns he grasps is "bitter and light" and the heavenly crown is "blessed and eternal." Even people who could not read these and other Latin mottoes would have known that Charles's last words were: "I shall go from a corruptible to an incorruptible Crown, where no disturbance can be."

At the same time, broadsides showing the moment of execution (image B) circulated in various European countries with explanatory captions. This one was printed in Germany, and there are almost identical versions surviving from the Netherlands. It shows members of the crowd fainting and turning away at the sight of blood spurting from the king's neck while the executioner holds up the severed head.

Questions for Analysis

1. How would you interpret the message of the first image? How might it have been read differently by Catholics and Protestants within Britain and Europe?

2. What would have been the political motives underlying the publication and display of these images? For example, would you expect the depiction of the king's execution to be intended as supportive of monarchy or as antiroyalist? Why?

3. Given what you have learned about political and religious divisions in Europe at the time of the king's execution, where do you think the first image would have found the most sympathetic audiences? Why might it be significant that the second circulated more in Germany and the Netherlands rather than in France or Spain?

A. King Charles I as a martyr.

B. The execution of King Charles I.

former parameters and Europeans' most basic assumptions. Not even religion could be seen as an adequate foundation on which to build new certainties, for European Christians now disagreed about the fundamental truths of their faith. Political allegiances were similarly under threat, as intellectuals and common people alike began to assert a right to resist princes with whom they disagreed. The very notions of morality and custom were beginning to seem arbitrary. Europeans responded to this pervasive climate of doubt in a variety of ways. What united their responses, however, was a sometimes desperate search for new bases on which to construct some measure of certainty in the face of such challenges.

Witchcraft and the Power of the State

Contributing to the anxiety of the age was the widespread conviction that witchcraft was a new and increasing threat to the world. Although the belief that certain individuals could heal or harm through the practice of magic had always been common, it was not until the late fifteenth century that authorities began to insist that such powers could derive only from some kind of satanic bargain. In 1484, Pope Innocent VIII had ordered papal inquisitors to use all means at their disposal to detect and eliminate witchcraft, including torture. Predictably, torture increased the number of accused witches who "confessed" to their alleged crimes. And as more accused witches "confessed," more witches were "discovered," tried, and executed—even in places like England and Scotland, where torture was not legal and where the Catholic Church had no influence. For both Luther and Calvin had also urged that accused witches be tried and sentenced with less leniency than ordinary criminals.

When religious authorities' efforts to detect witchcraft were backed by the coercive powers of secular governments, the fear of witches could escalate into persecution. It was therefore through this fundamental agreement between Catholics and Protestants, and with the complicity of modern secular states, that an early modern "witch craze" claimed tens of thousands of victims in this era. The final death toll will never be known, but the vast majority of the victims were women. In the 1620s, there were, on average, 100 burnings a year in the German cities of Würzburg and Bamberg; around the same time, it was said that the town square of Wolfenbüttel "looked like a little forest, so crowded were the stakes." And when accusations of witchcraft diminished in Europe, they became endemic in some European colonies, as at the English settlement of Salem in the Massachusetts Bay Colony.

This hunt for witches resulted in part from fears that traditional religious remedies (prayer, the sacraments) were no longer adequate to guard against the evils of the world. It also reflects Europeans' growing conviction that only the state had the power to protect them. Even in Catholic countries, where witchcraft prosecutions began in Church courts, these cases would be transferred to the state's courts for final judgment and punishment, because Church courts could not carry out capital penalties. In most Protestant countries, the entire process of detecting, prosecuting, and punishing suspected witches was carried out under state supervision.

The Search for a Source of Authority

The crisis of religious and political authority in Europe also led to more rational approaches to the problem of uncertainty. The French nobleman Michel de Montaigne (mohn-TEHN-yeh, 1533–1592), son of a Catholic father and a Huguenot mother of Jewish ancestry, applied a searching skepticism to all traditional ways of knowing the world and adopted instead a practice of profound introspection. His Essays, from the French word for "attempts" or "trials," were composed during the French wars of religion and proceed from the same basic question: Que sais-je? ("What do I know?").

The Essays' first premise is that every human perspective is limited. For example, in a famous essay "On Cannibals," Montaigne argued that what may seem indisputably true and moral to one group of people may seem absolutely false to another because "everyone gives the title of barbarism to everything that is not of his usage." From this follows Montaigne's second main premise: the need for moderation. Because all people think they follow the true religion or have the best form of government, Montaigne concluded that no religion or government is really perfect, and consequently no belief is worth fighting or dying for. Instead, people should accept the teachings of religion on faith and obey the governments constituted to rule over them but without resorting to fanaticism in either sphere.

Another French philosopher, Blaise Pascal (pahs-KAHL, 1623–1662), confronted the problem of doubt by embracing an extreme form of puritanical Catholicism known as Jansenism (after its Flemish founder, Cornelius Jansen). Until his death, he worked on a highly ambitious philosophical-religious project meant to establish the truth of Christianity by appealing simultaneously to intellect and emotion. In his posthumous work, Pensées (Thoughts), Pascal argued that only faith could resolve the contradictions of the world, because "the heart has its reasons, of which reason itself knows nothing."

Pascal's *Pensées* expressed the author's own anguish and awe in the face of evil and uncertainty but presented that awe as evidence for the existence of God. Pascal's hope was that, on this foundation, some measure of confidence in humanity and its capacity for self-knowledge could be rediscovered.

The Science of Politics

Montaigne's immediate contemporary, the French jurist Jean Bodin (*boh-DAN*, 1530–1596), took a more practical approach to the problem of uncertain authority and found a solution in the power of the state. Like Montaigne, Bodin was troubled by the upheavals of the religious wars. He had witnessed the St. Bartholomew's Day Massacre of 1572 and, in response, developed a theory of absolute sovereignty that would (he surmised) put an end to such catastrophes. His monumental *Six Books of the Commonwealth* (1576) argued that the state has its origins in the needs of family-oriented communities and that its paramount duty is to maintain order. He defined sovereignty as "the most high, absolute, and perpetual power over all subjects," which meant that a sovereign head of state could make and enforce laws without the consent of those governed: precisely what King Charles of England later argued when he tried to dispense with Parliament—and precisely what his subjects ultimately rejected. Even if the ruler proved a tyrant, Bodin insisted that the subject had no right to resist, for any resistance would open the door to anarchy, "which is worse than the harshest tyranny in the world."

In England, experience of the Civil War led Thomas Hobbes (1588–1679) to propose a different theory of state sovereignty in his treatise *Leviathan* (1651). Whereas Bodin assumed that sovereign power should be vested in a monarch, Hobbes argued that any form of government capable of protecting its subjects' lives and property might act as an all-powerful sovereign.

Hobbes' convictions about the need for a strong state arose from his pessimistic view of human nature. The "state of nature" that existed before government, he wrote, was "war of all against all." Because man naturally behaves as "a wolf" toward other men, human life without government is necessarily "solitary, poor, nasty, brutish, and short." To escape such consequences, people must surrender their liberties to a sovereign state, in exchange for the state's obligation to keep the peace. Bodin had seen the ultimate goal of the state as the protection of property; Hobbes saw it as the preservation of people's lives, even at the expense of their liberties.

Hobbes and Bodin developed such theories in response to their direct experience of political and social upheaval caused by the breakdown of traditional authorities. Their different political philosophies thus reflect a practical preoccupation with the observation and analysis of actual occurrences (empirical knowledge) rather than abstract or theological arguments. Because of this, they are seen as early examples of a new kind of discipline, what we now call "political science."

A similar preoccupation with observation and results was also emerging among those who sought to understand the physical universe. Historians have often referred to the rapid developments in the physical sciences in this era as the "scientific revolution," a phenomenon that had its beginnings in the later Middle Ages (see Chapters 12 and 13) and that will be treated at greater length in Chapter 16. This term remains a useful one, even though it belittles the slow accumulation of knowledge in these centuries and ignores the contributions of scientists in earlier eras (as in the Hellenistic world, discussed in Chapter 4).

The World of the Theater

In the late sixteenth century, the construction of public playhouses—enclosed theaters—made drama an especially effective mass medium for the formation of public opinion, the dissemination of ideas, and the articulation of national identities. This was especially so in England during the last two decades of Elizabeth's reign and that of her successor, James. Among the large number of playwrights at work in London during this era, the most noteworthy are Christopher Marlowe (1564–1593), Ben Jonson (c. 1572–1637), and William Shakespeare (1564–1616).

Marlowe, who may have been a spy for Elizabeth's government and who was mysteriously murdered in a tavern brawl, was extremely popular in his own day. In plays such as *Tamburlaine*—about the life of the Mongolian warlord Timur the Lame (see Chapter 12)—and *Doctor Faustus*, Marlowe created vibrant heroes who pursue larger-than-life ambitions only to be felled by their own human limitations. In contrast to the heroic tragedies of Marlowe, Ben Jonson wrote dark comedies that expose human vices and foibles. In the *Alchemist*, he balanced an attack on pseudo-scientific quackery with admiration for resourceful lower-class characters who cleverly take advantage of their supposed betters.

William Shakespeare, who died in the same year as Cervantes, was born into the family of a tradesman in the provincial town of Stratford-upon-Avon, where he attained a modest education before moving to London around the age of twenty. There, he composed or collaborated on an unknown number of plays, of which some forty survive in whole or in part. They owe their longevity to the author's

Montaigne on Skepticism and Faith

The Essays of Michel de Montaigne (1533–1592) reflect the sincerity of his own attempts to grapple with the contradictions of his time, even if he could not resolve those contradictions. Here, he discusses the relationship between human knowledge and the teachings of religious authorities.

Perhaps it is not without reason that we attribute facility in belief and conviction to simplicity and ignorance, for . . . the more a mind is empty and without counterpoise, the more easily it gives beneath the weight of the first persuasive argument. That is why children, common people, women, and sick people are most subject to being led by the ears. But then, on the other hand, it is foolish presumption to go around disdaining and condemning as false whatever does not seem likely to us; which is an ordinary vice in those who think they have more than common ability. I used to do so once. . . . But reason has taught me that to condemn a thing thus, dogmatically, as false and impossible, is to assume the advantage of knowing the bounds and limits of God's will and of the power of our mother Nature, and that there is no more notable folly in the world than to reduce these things to the measure of our capacity and competence. . . .

It is a dangerous and fateful presumption, besides the absurd temerity that it implies, to disdain what we do not comprehend. For after you have established, according to your fine understanding, the limits of truth and falsehood, and it turns out that you must necessarily believe things even stranger than those you deny, you are obliged from then on to abandon these limits. Now what seems to me to bring as much disorder into our consciences as anything, in these religious troubles that we are in, is this partial surrender of their beliefs by Catholics. It seems to them that they are being very moderate and understanding when they yield to their opponents some of the articles in dispute. But, besides the fact that they do not see what an advantage it is to a man charging you for you to begin to give ground and withdraw, and how much that encourages him to pursue his point, those articles which they select as the most trivial are sometimes very important. We must either submit completely to the authority of our ecclesiastical government, or do without it completely. It is not for us to decide what portion of obedience we owe it.

Source: *Montaigne: Selections from the Essays,* ed. and trans. Donald M. Frame (Arlington Heights, IL: 1971), pp. 34–38.

Questions for Analysis

1. Why does Montaigne say that human understanding is limited? How do his assumptions compare to those of Richelieu's (page 475)?

2. What does Montaigne mean by the "partial surrender" of belief? If a Catholic should place his faith in the Church, what then is the purpose of human intellect?

---

unrivaled gifts of verbal expression, humor, and psychological insight. Those written during the playwright's early years reflect the political, religious, and social upheavals of the late sixteenth century. These include many history plays that recount episodes from England's medieval past and the struggles that established the Tudor dynasty of Elizabeth's grandfather, Henry VII. They also include the lyrical tragedy *Romeo and Juliet* and a number of comedies that explore fundamental problems of identity, honor and ambition, love and friendship. The plays from Shakespeare's second period are, like other contemporary artworks, characterized by a troubled searching into the mysteries and meaning of human existence. They showcase the perils of indecisive idealism (*Hamlet*) and the abuse of power (*Macbeth, King Lear*). The plays composed toward the end of his career emphasize the possibilities of reconciliation and peace even after years of misunderstanding and violence: *The Tempest* is one of these.

Past and Present

Shakespeare's Popular Appeal

Although the plays of William Shakespeare are frequently described as elite entertainments, their enduring appeal can hardly be explained in those terms. In fact, Shakespeare wrote for a diverse audience—and a group of actors—who would have been more likely to see the inside of a prison than a royal court. His plays combine high politics, earthy comedy, and deeply human stories that still captivate and motivate audiences at the reconstructed Globe Theatre in London (left). They also lend themselves to inventive adaptations that comment on our own contemporary world, as in the recent film of *Coriolanus*.

 Watch related author interview on StudySpace
wwnorton.com/web/westernciv18

The Artists of Southern Europe

The ironies and tensions inherent in this age were also explored in the visual arts. In Italy and Spain, many painters cultivated a highly dramatic style sometimes known as "Mannerism." The most unusual of these artists was El Greco ("the Greek," c. 1541–1614), a pupil of the Venetian master Tintoretto (1518–1594). Born Domenikos Theotokopoulos on the Greek island of Crete, El Greco absorbed some of the stylized elongation characteristic of Byzantine icon painting (see Chapter 7) before traveling to Italy. He eventually settled in Spain. Many of his paintings were too strange to be greatly appreciated in his own day and even now appear so avant-garde as to be almost surreal. His *View of Toledo*, for example, is a transfigured landscape, mysteriously lit from within. Equally amazing are his swirling biblical scenes and the stunning portraits of gaunt, dignified saints who radiate austerity and spiritual insight.

In the seventeenth century, the dominant artistic style of southern Europe was that of the Baroque, a school whose name has become a synonym for elaborate, highly wrought sculpture and architectural details. This style originated in Rome during the Counter-Reformation and promoted a glorified Catholic worldview. Its most imaginative and influential figure was the architect and sculptor Gianlorenzo Bernini (1598–1680), a frequent employee of the papacy who created a magnificent celebration of papal grandeur in the sweeping colonnades leading up to St. Peter's Basilica. Breaking with the more serene classicism of Renaissance styles (see Chapter 12), Bernini's work drew inspiration from the restless motion and artistic bravado of Hellenistic statuary (see Chapter 4).

Characteristics of this Baroque style can also be found in paintings like those of the great Spanish master Diego Velázquez (*vay-LAH-skwez*, 1599–1660), who served the Spanish Habsburg court in Madrid. Although

VIEW OF TOLEDO BY EL GRECO. This is one of many landscape portraits representing the hilltop city that became the artist's home in later life. Its supple Mannerist style almost defies historical periodization.

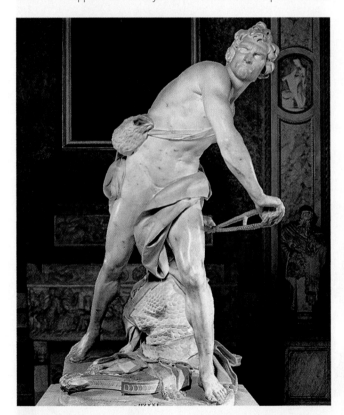

DAVID BY BERNINI (1598–1680). Whereas the earlier conceptions of David by the Renaissance sculptors Donatello and Michelangelo were serene and dignified (see page 000), the Baroque sculptor Bernini chose to portray his young hero at the peak of physical exertion. ▪ *Can you discern the influence of Hellenistic sculpture (see Chapter 4) in this work?* ▪ *What are some shared characteristics?*

many of his canvases display a Baroque attention to motion and drama, those most characteristic of his own style are more conceptually thoughtful and daring. An example is *The Maids of Honor*, completed around 1656 and a masterpiece of self-referentiality. It shows the artist himself at work on a double portrait of the Spanish king and queen, but the scene is dominated by the children and servants of the royal family.

Dutch Painting in the Golden Age

Southern Europe's main rival in the visual arts was the Netherlands, where many exemplary but dissimilar painters explored the theme of man's greatness and wretchedness to the full. Pieter Bruegel the Elder (*BROY-ghul*, c. 1525–1569) exulted in portraying the busy, elemental life of the peasantry. Most famous in this respect are his rollicking *Peasant Wedding* and *Peasant Wedding Dance* and his spacious *Harvesters*, in which field hands are taking a well-deserved break under the noonday sun. Such vistas celebrate the uninterrupted rhythms of life; but late in his career, Bruegel became appalled by the intolerance and bloodshed he witnessed during the Calvinist riots and the Spanish repression of the Netherlands, expressing his criticism in works like *The Massacre of the Innocents*. From a distance, this looks like a snug scene of village

THE MAIDS OF HONOR (LAS MEÑINAS) BY DIEGO VELÁZQUEZ. The artist himself (at left) is shown working at his easel and gazing out at the viewer—or at the subjects of his double portrait, the Spanish king and queen, depicted in a distant mirror. But the real focus of the painting is the delicate, impish princess in the center, flanked by two young ladies-in-waiting, a dwarf, and another royal child. Courtiers in the background look on.

life. In fact, however, soldiers are methodically breaking into homes and slaughtering helpless infants, as Herod's soldiers once did and as warring armies were doing in Bruegel's own day.

Another Dutch painter, Peter Paul Rubens (1577–1640), was inspired by very different politics. A native of Antwerp, still part of the Spanish Netherlands, Rubens was a staunch Catholic who glorified the Roman Church and the local aristocrats who supported the Habsburg regime. Even when his intent was not propagandistic, Rubens reveled in the sumptuous extravagance of the Baroque style; he is most famous today for the pink and rounded flesh of his well-nourished nudes. But Rubens was not lacking in subtlety or depth. Although he celebrated martial valor for most of his career, his late painting of *The Horrors of War* movingly captures what

he called "the grief of unfortunate Europe, which, for so many years now, has suffered plunder, outrage, and misery."

In some ways a blend of Bruegel and Rubens, Rembrandt van Rijn (*vahn-REEN*, 1606–1669) defies all attempts at easy characterization. Living across the border from the Spanish Netherlands in the staunchly Calvinist Dutch Republic, Rembrandt managed to put both realistic and Baroque traits to new uses. In his early career, he gained fame and fortune as a painter of biblical scenes and was also active as a portrait painter who knew how to flatter his subjects—to the great advantage of his purse. But as personal tragedies mounted in his middle and declining years, the painter's art gained in dignity, subtlety, and mystery. His later portraits, including several self-portraits, are highly introspective and suggest

THE MASSACRE OF THE INNOCENTS BY BRUEGEL (c. 1525–1569). This painting shows how effectively art can be used as a means of political and social commentary. Here, Bruegel depicts the suffering of the Netherlands at the hands of the Spanish in his own day, with reference to the biblical story of Herod's slaughter of Jewish children after the birth of Jesus—thereby collapsing these two historical incidents.

***THE HORRORS OF WAR* BY RUBENS (1577–1640).** In his old age, Rubens took a far more critical view of war than he had done for most of his earlier career. Here, the war-god Mars casts aside his mistress Venus, goddess of love, and threatens humanity with death and destruction.

SELF-PORTRAITS. Self-portraits became common during the sixteenth and seventeenth centuries, reflecting the intense introspection of the period. Left: Rembrandt painted more than sixty self-portraits; this one, dating from around 1660, captures the artist's creativity, theatricality (note the costume), and honesty of self-examination. Right: Judith Leyster was a contemporary of Rembrandt who pursued a successful career during her early twenties, before she married. Respected in her own day, she was all but forgotten for centuries thereafter but is once again the object of much attention.

that only part of the story is being told. Equally fearless is the frank gaze of Rembrandt's slightly younger contemporary, Judith Leyster (1609–1660), who looks out of her own self-portrait with a refreshingly optimistic and good-humored expression.

CONCLUSION

It would take centuries for Europeans to adapt themselves to the changes brought about by their integration into the Atlantic world and to process its implications. Finding new lands and cultures unknown to the ancients and unmentioned in the Bible had exposed the limitations of Western civilizations' accumulated knowledge and called for new ways of knowing and explaining the world. The Columbian exchange of people, plants, livestock, and pathogens that had previously been isolated from one another had a profound and lasting effect on populations and ecosystems throughout the Atlantic zone. The distribution of new agricultural products transformed the lives of the European poor and the rich alike. The transatlantic slave trade, which made all of this possible, brought Africans and their cultures into a world of growing global connections under

After You Read This Chapter

Ⓢ Visit StudySpace for quizzes, additional review materials, and multimedia documents. **wwnorton.com/web/westernciv18**

REVIEWING THE OBJECTIVES

- How were the peoples and ecosystems of the Americas, Africa, and Europe intertwined during this period? What were some consequences of these new linkages?
- Why did the colonies of the Spanish, the English, and the Dutch differ from one another? How did these differences affect the lives and labor of colonists, both free and unfree?
- Which European powers came to dominate the Atlantic world? What factors led to the decline of Spain and to the rise of France?
- What forms did religious and political conflict take in France, the Netherlands, and Germany? What were the causes of the English Civil War, and what impact did this event have on the English colonies?
- How do the arts and political philosophies of this period reflect the turmoil of Europe and the Atlantic world?

the worst possible circumstances for those who were enslaved—yet this did not prevent them from helping to shape this new world. Meanwhile, the influx of silver from New Spain precipitated the great price inflation of the sixteenth and seventeenth centuries, which bewildered contemporary observers and contributed to the atmosphere of crisis in post–Reformation Europe, already riven by religious and civil warfare. The response was a trend toward stronger centralized states, justified by theories of absolute government. Led by the French monarchy of Louis XIV, these absolutist regimes would reach their apogee in the coming century.

PEOPLE, IDEAS, AND EVENTS IN CONTEXT

- What was the **COLUMBIAN EXCHANGE**? How did it affect the relations among the peoples of the Americas, Africa, and Europe during this period?
- What circumstances led to the development of the **TRIANGULAR TRADE**?
- What were the main sources of instability in Europe during the sixteenth century? How did the **PRICE REVOLUTION** exacerbate these?
- How did **HENRY IV** of France and **PHILIP II** of Spain deal with the religious conflict that beset Europe during these years?
- What were the origins of the **THIRTY YEARS' WAR**? Was it primarily a religious conflict?
- How did the policies of **CARDINAL RICHELIEU** strengthen the power of the French monarchy?
- What policies of England's **CHARLES I** were most detested by his subjects? Why was his execution so momentous?
- In what ways did the **WITCH CRAZE** of early modern Europe reveal the religious and social tensions of the sixteenth and seventeenth centuries?
- What were the differences between **JEAN BODIN**'s theory of absolute sovereignty and that of **THOMAS HOBBES**?
- How did philosophers like **MONTAIGNE** and **PASCAL** respond to the uncertainties of the age? How were contemporary trends reflected in the works of **SHAKESPEARE** and in the visual arts?

THINKING ABOUT CONNECTIONS

- The emergence of the Atlantic world can be seen as a *cause* of new developments and as the *result* of historical processes. What long-term political, economic, and demographic circumstances drove the expansion of European influence into the Atlantic? What subsequent historical developments can we attribute to the creation of this interconnected world?
- The political crises of this era reveal the tensions produced by sectarian religious disputes and by a growing rift between powerful centralizing monarchies and landholding elites unwilling to surrender their authority and independence. What other periods in history display similar tensions? How do those periods compare to the one we have studied in this chapter?
- The intellectual currents of this era reveal that a new generation was challenging the assumptions of its predecessors. In what other historical eras do we find a similar phenomena? What social and political circumstances tend to produce consensus, and which tend to produce dissent, skepticism, and doubt?

STORY LINES

- After 1660, European rulers invoked an absolutist definition of sovereignty in order to expand the power of the monarchy. The most successful absolutist kings, such as Louis XIV of France or Peter the Great of Russia, limited the power of traditional aristocratic elites and the independence of religious institutions.

- Efforts by English monarchs to create an absolutist regime in England after the Civil War were resisted by political opponents in Parliament. Though they agreed with the king that a strong state was needed, they demanded a different definition of sovereignty, in which the king would rule alongside Parliament.

- Absolutism reinforced the imperial ambitions of European monarchies and led to frequent wars that were increasingly fought both in Europe and in colonial spaces in other parts of the world. The pressures of war favored dynasties capable of building strong centralized states with reliable sources of revenue from trade and taxation.

CHRONOLOGY

1643–1715	Reign of Louis XIV of France
1660	Restoration of the Stuart kings in England
1685	Revocation of the Edict of Nantes
1683	Ottoman siege of Vienna
1688	Glorious Revolution in England
1688–1697	War of the League of Augsburg
1690	Publication of John Locke's *Two Treatises of Government*
1689–1725	Peter the Great of Russia
1702–1713	War of the Spanish Succession
1713	Treaty of Utrecht

Before You Read This Chapter

European Monarchies and Absolutism, 1660–1725

I n the mountainous region of south-central France known as the Auvergne in the 1660s, the Marquis of Canillac had a notorious reputation. His noble title gave him the right to collect minor taxes on special occasions, but he insisted that these small privileges be converted into annual tributes. To collect these payments, he housed twelve accomplices in his castle that he called his apostles. Their other nicknames—one was known as Break Everything—gave a more accurate sense of their activities in the local villages. The marquis imprisoned those who resisted and forced their families to buy their freedom. In an earlier age, the marquis might have gotten away with this profitable arrangement. In 1662, however, he ran up against the authority of a king, Louis XIV, who was determined to demonstrate that the power of the central monarch was absolute. The marquis was brought up on charges before a special court of judges from Paris. He was found guilty and forced to pay a large fine. The king confiscated his property and had the marquis's castle destroyed.

Louis XIV's special court in the Auvergne heard nearly a thousand civil cases over four months in 1662. It convicted 692 people, and many of them, like the Marquis of Canillac, were noble. The verdicts were an extraordinary example of Louis XIV's

491

ability to project his authority into the remote corners of his realm and to do so in a way that diminished the power of other elites. During his long reign (1643–1715), Louis XIV systematically pursued such a policy on many fronts, asserting his power over the nobility, the clergy, and the provincial courts. Increasingly, these elites were forced to look to the crown to guarantee their interests, and their own power became more closely connected with the sacred aura of the monarchy itself. Louis XIV's model of kingship was so successful that it became known as absolute monarchy. In recognition of the success and influence of Louis XIV's political system, the period from around 1660 (when the English monarchy was restored and Louis XIV began his personal rule in France) to 1789 (when the French Revolution erupted) is traditionally known as the age of absolutism. This is a crucial period in the development of modern, centralized, bureaucratic states in Europe.

Absolutism was a political theory that encouraged rulers to claim complete sovereignty within their territories. An absolute monarch could make law, dispense justice, create and direct a bureaucracy, declare war, and levy taxation, without the approval of any other governing body. Assertions of absolute authority were buttressed by claims that rulers governed by divine right, just as fathers ruled over

their households. After the chaos and religious wars of the previous century, many Europeans came to believe that it was only by exalting the sovereignty of absolute rulers that order could be restored to European life.

European monarchs also continued to project their power abroad during this period. By 1660, as we have seen, the French, Spanish, Portuguese, English, and Dutch had all established important colonies in the Americas and in Asia. These colonies created trading networks that brought profitable new consumer goods such as sugar, tobacco, and coffee to a wide public in Europe. They also encouraged the colonies' reliance on slavery to produce these goods. Rivalry among colonial powers to control the trade in slaves and consumer goods was intense and often led to wars that were fought both in Europe and in contested colonies. These wars, in turn, increased the motivation of absolutist rulers to extract as much revenue as they could from their subjects and encouraged the development of institutions that enhanced their power: armies, navies, tax systems, tariffs and customs controls.

Absolutism was not universally successful during this period. The English monarchy, restored in 1660 after the turbulent years of the Civil War, attempted to impose absolutist rule but met with resistance from parliamentary leaders who insisted on more inclusive institutions of government. After 1688, England, Scotland, the Dutch Republic, Switzerland, Venice, Sweden, and Poland-Lithuania were all either limited monarchies or republics. In Russia, on the other hand, an extreme autocracy emerged that gave the tsar a degree of control over his subjects' lives and property far beyond anything imagined by western European absolutists. Even in Russia, however, absolutism was never unlimited in practice. Even the most absolute monarchs could rule effectively only with the consent of their subjects (particularly the nobility). When serious opposition erupted, even powerful kings were forced to back down. King George III of Britain discovered this when his North American colonies declared their independence in 1776, creating the United States of America. In 1789, an even more sweeping revolution began in France, and the entire structure of absolutism came crashing to the ground (see Chapter 18).

THE DEFENSE OF CADÍZ AGAINST THE ENGLISH **BY FRANCISCO ZURBARAN.** The rivalry between European powers that played out over the new colonial possessions further proved the decline of Spain, which lost the island of Jamaica and ships in the harbor of Cadíz to the English in the 1650s.

THE APPEAL AND JUSTIFICATION OF ABSOLUTISM

Absolutism's promise of stability and order was an appealing alternative to the disorder of the "iron century" that preceded it. The early theorists of absolutism such as Jean Bodin and Thomas Hobbes looked to strong royal governments as an answer to the violence of religious wars and the crisis of the sixteenth and seventeenth centuries (see Chapter 14). Louis XIV himself was profoundly disturbed by an aristocratic revolt that occurred while he was still a child. When marauding Parisians entered his bedchamber one night in 1651, Louis saw the intrusion as an affront not only to his own person but to the majesty of the French state. Such experiences convinced him that he needed to rule assertively and without limits to his power.

Absolutist monarchs sought control of the state's armed forces and its legal system, and they demanded the right to collect and spend the state's financial resources at will. To achieve these goals, they also needed to create an efficient, centralized bureaucracy that owed its allegiance directly to the monarch. Creating and sustaining such a bureaucracy was expensive but necessary in order to weaken the special interests that hindered the free exercise of royal power. The nobility and the clergy, with their traditional legal privileges; the political authority of semiautonomous regions; and representative assemblies such as parliaments, diets, or estates-general were all obstacles—in the eyes of absolutists—to strong, centralized monarchical government. The history of absolutism is the history of kings who attempted to bring such institutions to heel.

In most Protestant countries, the power of the church had already been subordinated to the state when the age of absolutism began. Even where Roman Catholicism remained the state religion, such as in France, Spain, and Austria, absolutist monarchs now devoted considerable attention to bringing the Church and its clergy under royal control. Louis XIV took an active role in religious matters, appointing his own bishops and encouraging the repression of religious dissidents. Unlike his predecessors, however, he rarely appointed members of the clergy to offices within his administration.

The most important potential opponents of royal absolutism were not churchmen, however, but nobles. Louis XIV deprived the French nobility of political power in the provinces but increased their social prestige by making them live at his lavish court at Versailles. Peter the Great of Russia (1689–1725) forced his nobles into lifelong government service, and successive monarchs in Brandenburg-Prussia managed to co-opt the powerful aristocracy by granting them immunity to taxation and giving them the right to enserf their peasants. In exchange, they ceded administrative control to the increasingly bureaucratized Prussian state. In most European monarchies, including Spain, France, Prussia, and England, the nobility retained their preponderant role within the military.

Struggles between monarchs and nobles frequently affected relations between local and central government. In France, the requirement that nobles live at the king's court undermined the provincial institutions that the nobility used to exercise their political power. In Spain, the monarchy, based in Castile, battled the independent-minded nobles of Aragon and Catalonia. Prussian rulers asserted control over formerly "free" cities by claiming the right to police and tax their inhabitants. The Habsburg emperors tried, unsuccessfully, to suppress the largely autonomous nobility of Hungary. Rarely, however, was the path of confrontation between crown and nobility successful in the long run. The most effective absolutist monarchies of the eighteenth century continued to trade privileges for allegiance, so that nobles came to see their own interests as tied to those of the crown. For this reason, wary cooperation between kings and nobles was more common than open conflict during the eighteenth century.

THE ABSOLUTISM OF LOUIS XIV

In Louis XIV's state portrait, it is almost impossible to discern the human being behind the facade of the absolute monarch dressed in his coronation robes and surrounded by the symbols of his authority. That facade was artfully constructed by Louis, who recognized, more fully than any other early modern ruler, the importance of theater to effective kingship. Louis and his successors deliberately staged spectacular demonstrations of their sovereignty to enhance their position as rulers endowed with godlike powers.

Performing Royalty at Versailles

Louis's most elaborate staging of his authority took place at his palace at Versailles (vuhr-SY), outside of Paris. The main facade of the palace was a third of a mile in length. Inside, tapestries and paintings celebrated French military victories and royal triumphs; mirrors reflected shimmering light throughout the building. In the vast gardens outside, statues of the Greek god Apollo, god of the sun, recalled Louis's claim to be the "Sun King" of France. Noblemen vied to attend him when he arose from bed, ate his meals

Interpreting Visual Evidence

The Performance and Display of Absolute Power at the Court of Louis XIV

istorians studying the history of absolutism and the court of Louis XIV in particular have emphasized the Sun King's brilliant use of symbols and display to demonstrate his personal embodiment of sovereignty. Royal portraits, such as that painted by Hyacinthe Rigaud in 1701, vividly illustrate the degree to which Louis's power was based on a studied performance. His pose, with his exposed and shapely calf, was an important indication of power and virility, necessary elements of legitimacy for a hereditary monarch. In the elaborate rituals of court life at Versailles, Louis often placed his own body at the center of attention, performing in one instance as the god Apollo in a ballet before his assembled courtiers. His movements through the countryside, accompanied by a retinue of soldiers, servants, and aristocrats, were another occasion for highly stylized ritual demonstrations of his quasi-divine status. Finally, of course, the construction of his palace at Versailles, with its symmetrical architecture and its sculpted gardens, was a demonstration that his power extended over the natural world as easily as it did over the lives of his subjects.

Questions for Analysis

1. Who was the intended audience for the king's performance of absolute sovereignty?

2. Who were Louis's primary competitors in this contest for eminence through the performance of power?

3. What possible political dangers might lie in wait for a regime that invested so heavily in the sumptuous display of semidivine authority?

A. Hyacinthe Rigaud's 1701 portrait of Louis XIV.

B. Louis XIV as the Sun King.

C. *The Royal Procession of Louis XIV*, 1664, by Adam Franz van der Meulen.

D. Louis XIV arrives at the Palace of Versailles.

Competing Viewpoints

Absolutism and Patriarchy

These selections show how two political theorists justified royal absolutism by deriving it from the absolute authority of a father over his household. Bishop Jacques-Bénigne Bossuet (1627–1704) was a famous French preacher who served as tutor to the son of King Louis XIV of France before becoming bishop of Meaux. Sir Robert Filmer (1588–1653) was an English political theorist. Filmer's works attracted particular attention in the 1680s, when John Locke directed the first of his Two Treatises of Government *to refuting Filmer's views on the patriarchal nature of royal authority.*

Bossuet on the Nature of Monarchical Authority

There are four characteristics or qualities essential to royal authority. First, royal authority is sacred; Secondly, it is paternal; Thirdly, it is absolute; Fourthly, it is subject to reason. . . . All power comes from God. . . . Thus princes act as ministers of God, and his lieutenants on earth. It is through them that he exercises his empire. . . . In this way . . . the royal throne is not the throne of a man, but the throne of God himself. . . .

We have seen that kings hold the place of God, who is the true Father of the human race. We have also seen that the first idea of power that there was among men, is that of paternal power; and that kings were fashioned on the model of fathers. Moreover, all the world agrees that obedience, which is due to public power, is only found . . . in the precept which obliges one to honor his parents. From all this it appears that the name "king" is a father's name, and that goodness is the most natural quality in kings. . . .

Royal authority is absolute. In order to make this term odious and insupportable, many pretend to confuse absolute government and arbitrary government. But nothing is more distinct, as we shall make clear when we speak of justice. . . . The prince need account to no one for what he ordains. . . . Without this absolute authority, he can neither do good nor suppress evil: his power must be such that no one can hope to escape him. . . . [T]he sole defense of individuals against the public power must be their innocence. . . .

One must, then, obey princes as if they were justice itself, without which there is neither order nor justice in affairs. They are gods, and share in some way in divine independence. . . . It follows from this that he who does not want to obey the prince . . . is condemned irremissibly to death as an enemy of public peace and of human society. . . . The prince can correct himself when he knows that he has done badly; but against his authority there can be no remedy. . . .

Source: Jacques-Bénigne Bossuet, *Politics Drawn from the Very Words of Holy Scripture*, trans. Patrick Riley (Cambridge: 1990), pp. 46–69 and 81–83.

(usually stone cold after having traveled the distance of several city blocks from kitchen to table), strolled in his gardens (even the way the king walked was choreographed by the royal dancing master), or rode to the hunt. France's leading nobles were required to reside with Louis at Versailles for a portion of the year; the splendor of Louis's court was deliberately calculated to blind them to the possibility of disobedience while raising their prestige by associating them with himself. At the same time, the almost impossibly detailed rules of etiquette at court left these privileged nobles in constant suspense, forever fearful of offending the king by committing some trivial violation of proper manners.

Of course, the nobility did not surrender social and political power entirely. The social order was still hierarchical, and noblemen retained enormous privileges and rights over local peasants within their jurisdiction. The absolutist system forced the nobility to depend on the crown, but it did not seek to undermine their superior place in society. In this sense, the relationship between

Filmer on the Patriarchal Origins of Royal Authority

The first government in the world was monarchical, in the father of all flesh, Adam being commanded to multiply, and people the earth, and to subdue it, and having dominion given him over all creatures, was thereby the monarch of the whole world; none of his posterity had any right to possess anything, but by his grant or permission, or by succession from him. . . . Adam was the father, king and lord over his family: a son, a subject, and a servant or a slave were one and the same thing at first. . . .

I cannot find any one place or text in the Bible where any power . . . is given to a people either to govern themselves, or to choose themselves governors, or to alter the manner of government at their pleasure. The power of government is settled and fixed by the commandment of "honour thy father"; if there were a higher power than the fatherly, then this commandment could not stand and be observed. . . .

All power on earth is either derived or usurped from the fatherly power, there being no other original to be found of any power whatsoever. For if there should be granted two sorts of power without any subordination of one to the other, they would be in perpetual strife which should be the supreme, for two supremes cannot agree. If the fatherly power be supreme, then the power of the people must be subordinate and depend on it. If the power of the people be supreme, then the fatherly power must submit to it, and cannot be exercised without the licence of the people, which must quite destroy the frame and course of nature. Even the power which God himself exercises over mankind is by right of fatherhood: he is both the king and father of us all. As God has exalted the dignity of earthly kings . . . by saying they are gods, so . . . he has been pleased . . . [t]o humble himself by assuming the title of a king to express his power, and not the title of any popular government.

Source: Robert Filmer, "Observations upon Aristotle's Politiques," in *Divine Right and Democracy: An Anthology of Political Writing in Stuart England*, ed. David Wootton (Harmondsworth, UK: 1986), pp. 110–118. First published 1652.

Questions for Analysis

1. Bossuet's definition of *absolutism* connected the sacred power of kings with the paternal authority of fathers within the household. What consequences does he draw from defining the relationship between king and subjects in this way?

2. What does Filmer mean when he says, "All power on earth is either derived or usurped from the fatherly power"? How many examples does he give of paternal or monarchical power?

3. Bossuet and Filmer make obedience the basis for order and justice in the world. What alternative political systems did they most fear?

Louis XIV and the nobility was more of a negotiated settlement than a complete victory of the king over other powerful elites. Louis XIV understood this, and in a memoir that he prepared for his son on the art of ruling he wrote, "The deference and the respect that we receive from our subjects are not a free gift from them but payment for the justice and the protection that they expect from us. Just as they must honor us, we must protect and defend them." In their own way, absolutists depended on the consent of those they ruled.

Administration and Centralization

Louis defined his responsibilities in absolutist terms: to concentrate royal power so as to produce domestic tranquillity. In addition to convincing the nobility to cede political authority, he also recruited the upper bourgeoisie as royal intendants, administrators responsible for running the thirty-six *generalités* into which France was divided. Intendants usually served outside the region where they were born and were thus unconnected with

Past and Present

The Persistence of Monarchies in a Democratic Age

In the past, monarchs such as Louis XIV (left) often ran roughshod over tradition as they sought ways to increase their power. Today, twelve European states still have reigning monarchs, such as Queen Elizabeth II (right), but their popularity would probably be called into question if they sought an active role in government.

 Watch related author interview on StudySpace
wwnorton.com/web/westernciv18

the local elites over whom they exercised authority. They held office at the king's pleasure and were clearly his men. Other administrators, often from families newly ennobled as a reward for their service, assisted in directing affairs of state from Versailles. These men were not actors in the theater of Louis the Sun King; rather, they were the hardworking assistants of Louis the royal custodian of his country's welfare.

Louis's administrators devoted much of their time and energy to collecting the taxes necessary to finance the large standing army on which his aggressive foreign policy depended. Absolutism was fundamentally an approach to government by which ambitious monarchs could increase their own power through conquest and display. As such, it was enormously expensive. In addition to the *taille*, or land tax, which increased throughout the seventeenth century, Louis's government introduced a *capitation* (a head tax) and pressed successfully for the collection of indirect taxes on salt (the *gabelle*), wine, tobacco, and other goods. Because the nobility was exempt from the taille, its burden fell most heavily on the peasantry, whose local revolts Louis easily crushed.

Regional opposition was curtailed but not eliminated during Louis's reign. By removing the provincial nobility to Versailles, Louis cut them off from their local sources of power and influence. To restrict the powers of regional parlements, Louis decreed that members of any parlement who refused to approve and enforce his laws would be summarily exiled. The Estates-General, the French representative assembly that met at the king's pleasure to act as a consultative body for the state, was last summoned in 1614. It did not meet at all during Louis's reign and, in fact, was not convened again until 1789.

Louis XIV's Religious Policies

Both for reasons of state and of personal conscience, Louis was determined to impose religious unity on France, regardless of the economic and social costs.

Although the vast majority of the French population was Roman Catholic, French Catholics were divided among Quietists, Jansenists, Jesuits, and Gallicans. Quietists preached retreat into personal mysticism, emphasizing a direct relationship between God and the individual human heart. Such doctrine, dispensing as it did with the intermediary services of the Church, was suspect in the eyes of absolutists wedded to the doctrine of *un roi, une loi, une foi* ("one king, one law, one faith"). Jansenism—a movement named for its founder Cornelius Jansen, a seventeenth-century bishop of Ypres—held to an Augustinian doctrine of predestination that could sound and look surprisingly like a kind of Catholic Calvinism. Louis vigorously persecuted Quietists and Jansenists, offering them a choice between recanting and prison or exile. At the same time, he supported the Jesuits in their efforts to create a Counter-Reformation Catholic Church in France. Louis's support for the Jesuits upset the traditional Gallican Catholics of France, however, who desired a French church independent of papal, Jesuit, and Spanish influence. As a result of this dissension among Catholics, the religious aura of Louis's kingship diminished during the course of his reign.

Against the Protestant Huguenots, Louis waged unrelenting war. Protestant churches and schools were destroyed, and Protestants were banned from many professions. In 1685, Louis revoked the Edict of Nantes, the legal foundation of the toleration Huguenots had enjoyed since 1598. Protestant clerics were exiled, laymen were sent to the galleys as slaves, and their children were forcibly baptized as Catholics. Many families converted, but 200,000 Protestant refugees fled to England, Holland, Germany, and America, bringing with them their professional and artisanal skills. Huguenots fleeing Louis XIV's persecution, for example, established the silk industries of Berlin and London. This migration was an enormous loss to France.

Colbert and Royal Finance

Louis's drive to unify France depended on a vast increase in royal revenues engineered by Jean-Baptiste Colbert, the king's finance minister from 1664 until his death in 1683. Colbert tightened the process of tax collection and eliminated wherever possible the practice of tax farming (which permitted collection agents to retain for themselves a percentage of the taxes they gathered for the king). When Colbert assumed office, only about 25 percent of the taxes collected throughout the kingdom reached the treasury. By the time he died, that figure had risen to 80 percent. Under Colbert's direction, the state sold public offices, including judgeships and mayoralties, and guilds purchased the right to enforce trade regulations. Colbert also tried to increase the nation's income by controlling and regulating foreign trade. As a confirmed mercantilist (see **Analyzing Primary Sources** on page 500), Colbert believed that France's wealth would increase if its imports were reduced and its exports increased. He therefore imposed tariffs on foreign goods imported into France while using state money to promote the domestic manufacture of formerly imported goods, such as silk, lace, tapestries, and glass. He was especially anxious to create domestic industries capable of producing the goods France would need for war. To encourage domestic trade, he improved France's roads, bridges, and waterways.

Despite Colbert's efforts to increase crown revenues, his policies ultimately foundered on the insatiable demands of Louis XIV's wars (see pages 505–506). Colbert himself foresaw this result when he lectured the king in 1680: "Trade is the source of public finance and public finance is the vital nerve of war. . . . I beg your Majesty to permit me only to say to him that in war as in peace he has never consulted the amount of money available in determining his expenditures." Louis, however, paid him no heed. By the end of Louis's reign, his aggressive foreign policy lay in ruins and his country's finances had been shattered by the unsustainable costs of war.

French Colonialism under Louis XIV

Finance minister Colbert regarded overseas expansion as an integral part of the French state's economic policy, and with his guidance, Louis IV's absolutist realm emerged as a major colonial power. Realizing the profits to be made in responding to Europe's growing demand for sugar, Colbert encouraged the development of sugar-producing colonies in the West Indies, the largest of which was Saint-Domingue (present-day Haiti). Sugar, virtually unknown in Christian Europe during the Middle Ages, became a popular luxury item in the late fifteenth century (see Chapter 14). It took the slave plantations of the Caribbean to turn sugar into a mass-market product. By 1750, slaves in Saint-Domingue produced 40 percent of the world's sugar and 50 percent of its coffee, exporting more sugar than Jamaica, Cuba, and Brazil combined. By 1700, France also dominated the interior of the North American continent, where French

Mercantilism and War

Jean-Baptiste Colbert (1619–1683) served as Louis XIV's finance minister from 1664 until his death. He worked assiduously to promote commerce, build up French industry, and increase exports. However much Colbert may have seen his economic policies as ends in themselves, to Louis they were always means to the end of waging war. Ultimately, Louis's wars undermined the prosperity that Colbert tried so hard to create. This memorandum, written to Louis in 1670, illustrates clearly the mercantilist presumptions of self-sufficiency on which Colbert operated: every item needed to build up the French navy must ultimately be produced in France, even if it could be acquired at less cost from elsewhere.

 nd since Your Majesty has wanted to work diligently at reestablishing his naval forces, and since afore that it has been necessary to make very great expenditures, since all merchandise, munitions and manufactured items formerly came from Holland and the countries of the North, it has been absolutely necessary to be especially concerned with finding within the realm, or with establishing in it, everything which might be necessary for this great plan.

To this end, the manufacture of tar was established in Médoc, Auvergne, Dauphiné, and Provence; iron cannons, in Burgundy, Nivernois, Saintonge and Périgord; large anchors in Dauphiné, Nivernois, Brittany, and Rochefort; sailcloth for the Levant, in Dauphiné; coarse muslin, in Auvergne; all the implements for pilots and others, at Dieppe and La Rochelle; the cutting of wood suitable for vessels, in Burgundy, Dauphiné, Brittany, Normandy, Poitou, Saintonge, Provence, Guyenne, and the Pyrenees; masts, of a sort once unknown in this realm, have been found in Provence, Languedoc, Auvergne, Dauphiné, and in the Pyrenees. Iron, which was obtained from Sweden and Biscay, is currently manufactured in the realm. Fine hemp for ropes, which came from Prussia and from Piedmont, is currently obtained in Burgundy, Mâconnais, Bresse, Dauphiné; and markets for it have since been established in Berry and in Auvergne, which always provides money in these provinces and keeps it within the realm.

In a word, everything serving for the construction of vessels is currently established in the realm, so that Your Majesty can get along without foreigners for the navy and will even, in a short time, be able to supply them and gain their money in this fashion. And it is with this same objective of having everything necessary to provide abundantly for his navy and that of his subjects that he is working at the general reform of all the forests in his realm, which, being as carefully preserved as they are at present, will abundantly produce all the wood necessary for this.

Source: Charles W. Cole, *Colbert and a Century of French Mercantilism*, 2 vols. (New York: 1939), p. 320.

Questions for Analysis

1. Why would Colbert want to manufacture materials for supplying the navy within France rather than buying them from abroad?

2. From this example, does Colbert see the economy as serving any other interest other than that of the state?

3. Was there a necessary connection between mercantilism and war?

---

traders brought furs to the American Indians and missionaries preached Christianity in a vast territory that stretched from Quebec to Louisiana. The financial returns from North America were never large, however. Furs, fish, and tobacco were exported to European markets but never matched the profits from the Caribbean sugar colonies or from the trading posts that the French maintained in India.

Like the earlier Spanish colonies (see Chapter 14), the French colonies were established and administered as direct crown enterprises. French colonial settlements in North America were conceived mainly as military outposts and trading centers, and they were overwhelmingly populated by men. The elite of French colonial society were military officers and administrators sent from Paris. Below their ranks were fishermen, fur traders, small farmers, and common soldiers who constituted the bulk of French settlers in North America. Because the fishing and the fur trades relied on cooperative relationships with native peoples, a mutual economic interdependence grew up between the French colonies and the peoples of the surrounding region. Intermarriage, especially between French traders and native women, was common. These North American colonies remained dependent on the wages and supplies sent to them from the mother country. Only rarely did they become truly self-sustaining economic enterprises.

The phenomenally successful sugar plantations of the Caribbean had their own social structure, with slaves at the bottom, people of mixed African and European descent forming a middle layer, and wealthy European plantation owners at the top, controlling the lucrative trade with the outside world. Well over half of the sugar and coffee sent to France was resold and sent elsewhere to markets throughout Europe. Because the monarchy controlled the prices that colonial plantation owners could charge French merchants for their goods, traders in Europe who bought the goods for resale abroad could also make vast fortunes. Historians estimate that as many as 1 million of the 25 million inhabitants of France in the eighteenth century lived off the money flowing through this colonial trade, making the slave colonies of the Caribbean a powerful force for economic change in France. The wealth generated from these colonies added to the prestige of France's absolutist system of government.

ALTERNATIVES TO ABSOLUTISM

Although absolutism was the dominant model for seventeenth- and eighteenth-century European monarchs, it was by no means the only system by which Europeans governed themselves. A republican oligarchy continued to rule in Venice. In the Polish-Lithuanian commonwealth, the monarch was elected by the nobility and governed alongside a parliament that met every two years. In the Netherlands, the territories that had won their independence from Spain during the early seventeenth century combined to form the United Provinces, the only truly new country to take shape in Europe during the early modern era. England, which had suffered through a violent civil war between 1642 and 1651, followed by the tumultuous years of Oliver Cromwell's Commonwealth and the Protectorate (see Chapter 14), also took a different path during these years, eventually arriving at a constitutional settlement that gave a larger role to Parliament and admitted a degree of participation by non-nobles in the affairs of state. Arriving at this settlement was not easy, however. The end of the civil wars and the collapse of Cromwell's Protectorate had made it clear that England would be a monarchy and not a republic, but the sort of monarchy England would be remained an open question. Two issues were paramount: the religious question and the relationship between Parliament and the king.

CHARLES II OF ENGLAND (r. 1660–85) IN HIS CORONATION ROBES. This full frontal portrait of the monarch, holding the symbols of his rule, seems to confront the viewer personally with the overwhelming authority of the sovereign's gaze. Compare this classic image of the absolutist monarch with the very different portraits of William and Mary, who ruled after the Glorious Revolution of 1688 (page 503). ■ *What had changed between 1660, when Charles II came to the throne, and 1688, when the more popular William and Mary became the rulers of England?*

The Restoration Monarchy in England

The king who took the throne following the Restoration of the Stuarts in 1660, Charles II (r. 1660–85), was initially welcomed by most English, despite being the son of the beheaded and much-despised Charles I (see Chapter 14). He restored bishops to the Church of England, but he did not initially return to the provocative religious policies of his father. He declared limited religious toleration for Protestant "dissenters" who were not members of the Church of England. He promised to observe the Magna Carta and the Petition of Right, which comforted members of Parliament. He also accepted the legislation passed by Parliament immediately before the outbreak of civil war in 1642, including the requirement that Parliament be summoned at least once every three years. England thus emerged from its civil war as a limited monarchy, in which power was exercised by the "king in Parliament." Meanwhile, the unbuttoned moral atmosphere of Charles II's court, with its risqué plays, dancing, and sexual licentiousness, may have reflected a public desire to forget the restraints of the Puritan past.

During the 1670s, however, Charles began openly to model his kingship on the absolutism of Louis XIV. As a result, the great men of England soon came to be publicly divided between Charles's supporters (known as "Tories," a popular nickname for Irish Catholic bandits) and his opponents (called "Whigs," a nickname for Scottish Presbyterian rebels). In fact, both sides feared absolutism, just as both sides feared a return to the bad old days of the 1640s, when resistance to the crown had led to civil war and ultimately to republicanism. What they could not agree on was which possibility frightened them more.

Charles's known sympathy for Roman Catholicism (he converted on his deathbed in 1685) also generated fodder for the opposition Whigs. During the 1670s, he briefly suspended civil penalties against Catholics and Protestant dissenters by asserting his right as king to ignore parliamentary legislation, and he retreated only in the face of public protest. The Whigs, meanwhile, rallied support by targeting Charles's Catholic brother James, the heir to the throne. The result was a series of Whig electoral victories between 1679 and 1681. A group of radical Whigs tried and failed to exclude James from succeeding his brother by law, and thereafter Charles found that his rising revenues from customs duties, combined with a secret subsidy from Louis XIV, enabled him to govern without relying on Parliament for money. Charles further alarmed Whig politicians by executing several of them on charges of treason and by remodeling local government to make it more amenable to royal control. Charles died in 1685 with his power enhanced, but he left behind a political and religious legacy that was to be the undoing of his less able and adroit successor.

James II was the very opposite of his worldly brother. A zealous Catholic convert, James admired the French monarchy's Gallican Catholicism that sought to further the work of the Church by harnessing it to the power of an absolutist bureaucratic state. His commitment to absolutism also led him to build up the English army and navy, which in turn led him to search for innovative solutions to the problems of taxation and the quartering of troops. To make the tax system more efficient he created new revenue agencies in many English towns. His quest for more accurate intelligence about political opponents led him to take control over the country's new post office, which made domestic surveillance routine, and his government also stepped up its efforts to prosecute seditious speech and writings. For the Whigs, James's policies were all that they had feared.

Meanwhile, James's Catholicism also alienated his Tory supporters, who were close to the established Church of England. Religion was not the only cause of his unpopularity, but resistance to his policies was often mixed with resentment against a perception that he favored Catholics. His decision to appoint Catholics as officers in the army was unpopular, but his decision to maintain a standing army in peacetime was even more so. Towns that were asked to quarter troops resented the expense and the disruptive presence of soldiers in their midst. When, in June 1688, he ordered all Church of England clergymen to read his decree of religious toleration from their pulpits, seven bishops refused and were promptly imprisoned. At their trial, however, they were declared not guilty of sedition, to the enormous satisfaction of the Protestant English populace.

The trial of the bishops was one event that galvanized the growing opposition to James. The other was the unexpected birth of a son in 1688 to James and his second wife, Mary of Modena. This child, who was to be raised a Catholic, replaced James's much older Protestant daughter Mary Stuart as heir to the thrones of Scotland and England. So unexpected was this birth that there were widespread rumors that the child was not in fact James's son at all but had been smuggled into the royal bedchamber in a warming pan.

With the birth of the "warming-pan baby," events moved swiftly toward a climax. A delegation of Whigs and Tories crossed the channel to Holland to invite Mary Stuart and her Protestant husband, William of Orange, to cross to England with an invading army to preserve English Protestantism and English liberties by summoning a new Parliament. As the leader of a continental coalition then at war with France, William also welcomed the opportunity to make England an ally against Louis XIV's expansionist foreign policy.

The Glorious Revolution

Following William and Mary's invasion, James fled the country for exile in France. Parliament declared the throne vacant, clearing the way for William and Mary to succeed him as joint sovereigns. The Bill of Rights, passed by Parliament and accepted by the new king and queen in 1689, reaffirmed English civil liberties, such as trial by jury, habeas corpus (a guarantee that no one could be imprisoned unless charged with a crime), and the right to petition the monarch through Parliament. The Bill of Rights also declared that the monarchy was subject to the law of the land. The Act of Toleration, also passed in 1689, granted Protestant dissenters the right to worship freely, though not to hold political office. And in 1701, the Act of Succession ordained

WILLIAM AND MARY. In 1688, William of Orange and his wife, Mary Stuart, became Protestant joint rulers of England, in a bloodless coup that took power from her father, the Catholic James II. Compare this contemporary print with the portraits of Louis XIV (page 494) and Charles II (page 501). ▪ *What relationship does it seem to depict between the royal couple and their subjects?* ▪ *What is the significance of the gathered crowd in the public square in the background?* ▪ *How is this different from the spectacle of divine authority projected by Louis XIV or the image of Charles II looking straight at the viewer?*

that every future English monarch must be a member of the Church of England. Queen Mary died childless, and the throne passed from William to Mary's Protestant sister Anne (r. 1702–14) and then to George, elector of the German principality of Hanover and the Protestant great-grandson of James I. In 1707, the formal Act of Union between Scotland and England ensured that the Catholic heirs of King James II would in future have no more right to the throne of Scotland than they did to the throne of England.

The English soon referred to the events of 1688 and 1689 as the "Glorious Revolution," because it firmly established England as a mixed monarchy governed by the "king in Parliament" according to the rule of law. Although William and Mary and their successors continued to exercise a large measure of executive power, after 1688 no English monarch attempted to govern without Parliament, which has met annually from that time on. Parliament, and especially the House of Commons, also strengthened its control over taxation and expenditure. Although Parliament never codified the legal provisions of this form of monarchy into one constitutional document, historians consider the settlement of 1688 as a founding moment in the development of a constitutional monarchy in Britain.

Yet 1688 was not all glory. Contrary to many historical accounts, the revolution of 1688 was not "bloodless." The accession of William and Mary was accompanied by violence in many parts of England, Scotland, and Ireland. There were attacks on royal troops by angry Whigs in York, Hull, Carlisle, Chester, and Portsmouth. James's revenue agencies were also attacked, as were his newly founded Catholic schools. Historians now see this violence as motivated as much by antiabsolutism as by religious bigotry—popular anger against James II focused not so much on his defense of tradition but his innovations, specifically his attempts to strengthen the power of the bureaucratic state. Furthermore, the revolution of 1688 consolidated the position of large property holders, whose control over local government had been threatened by the absolutist policies of Charles II and James II. It thus reinforced the power of a wealthy class of English elites in Parliament who would soon become even wealthier from government patronage and the profits of war. It also brought misery to the Catholic minority in Scotland and to the Catholic majority in Ireland. After 1690, when King William won a decisive victory over James II's forces at the Battle of the Boyne, power in Ireland would lie firmly in the hands of a "Protestant Ascendancy," whose dominance over Irish society would last until modern times.

At the same time, however, England's Glorious Revolution also established a climate that favored the growth and political power of the English commercial classes, especially the growing number of people concentrated in English cities whose livelihood depended on international commerce in the Atlantic world and beyond. In the decades to come, trade became a political issue, and merchant's associations began to lobby parliament for favorable legislation. Whigs in Parliament became the voice of this newly influential pressure group of commercial entrepreneurs, who sought to challenge the monopoly enjoyed by the East India Company (founded with a royal charter in 1600) and open up colonial trade to competitors. They also argued that royal charter companies discouraged English manufacture by importing cheaper goods from abroad. The Whigs also argued for revisions to the tax code that would benefit those engaged in manufacturing and trade, rather than the landed elites who benefited from the tax regime under the Stuarts. In 1694, the Whigs succeeded in establishing the Bank of England, with the explicit goal of facilitating the promotion of English power through the generation of wealth, inaugurating a financial revolution that would make London the center of a vast network of international banking and investment in the eighteenth century.

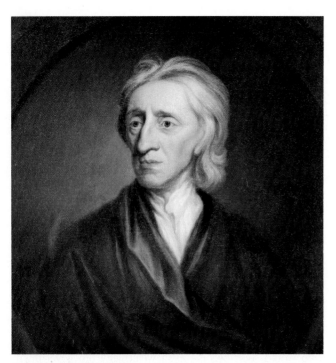

JOHN LOCKE (1632–1704). Locke was an important foundational thinker in the liberal political tradition, who had a profound influence on the Glorious Revolution of 1688 in England, as well as on the makers of the American Revolution, such as Thomas Jefferson, and French political theorists during the Enlightenment. His debate with Robert Filmer, a defender of absolutism, led him to elaborate a theory of government as a contract between the ruler and the ruled.

John Locke and the Contract Theory of Government

The Glorious Revolution was the product of unique circumstances, but it also reflected antiabsolutist theories of politics that were taking shape in the late seventeenth century in response to the ideas of writers such as Bodin, Hobbes, Robert Filmer, and Bishop Jacques-Bénigne Bossuet. Chief among these opponents of absolutism was the Englishman John Locke (1632–1704), whose *Two Treatises of Government* were written before the Glorious Revolution but published for the first time in 1690.

Locke maintained that humans had originally lived in a state of nature characterized by absolute freedom and equality, with no government of any kind. The only law was the law of nature (which Locke equated with the law of reason), by which individuals enforced for themselves their natural rights to life, liberty, and property. Soon, however, humans perceived that the inconveniences of the state of nature outweighed its advantages. Accordingly, they agreed first to establish a civil society based on absolute equality and then to set up a government to arbitrate the disputes that might arise within this civil society. But they did not make government's powers absolute. All powers not expressly surrendered to the government were reserved to the people themselves; as a result, governmental authority was both contractual and conditional. If a government exceeded or abused the authority granted to it, society had the right to dissolve it and create another.

Locke condemned absolutism in every form. He denounced absolute monarchy, but he was also critical of claims for the sovereignty of parliaments. Government, he argued, had been instituted to protect life, liberty, and property; no political authority could infringe these natural rights. The law of nature was therefore an automatic and absolute limitation on every branch of government.

In the late eighteenth century, Locke's ideas would resurface as part of the intellectual background of both the American and French Revolutions. Between 1690 and 1720, however, they served a far less radical purpose. The landed gentry who replaced James II with William and Mary read Locke as a defense of their conservative revolution. Rather than protecting their liberty and property, James II had threatened both; hence, the magnates were entitled to overthrow the tyranny he had established and replace it with a government that would defend their interests by preserving these natural rights. English government after 1689 would be dominated by Parliament; Parliament in turn was controlled by a landed aristocracy who were firm in the defense of their common interests, and who perpetuated their control by determining that only men possessed of substantial property could vote or run for office. During the beginning of the eighteenth century, then, both France and Britain had solved the problem of political dissent and social disorder in their own way. The emergence of a limited monarchy in England after 1688 contrasted vividly with the absolutist system developed by Louis XIV, but in fact both systems worked well enough to contain the threats to royal authority posed by powerful landed nobles and religious dissent.

The Dutch Republic

Another exception to absolutist rule in Europe was the Dutch Republic of the United Provinces, which had gained its independence from Spanish rule in 1648, after a long period of struggle (see Chapter 14). The seven provinces of the Dutch Republic (also known as the Netherlands) carefully preserved their autonomy with a federal legislature known as the States General, made up of delegations from each province. Through this flexible structure, the inhabitants of the republic worked hard to prevent the reestablishment of hereditary monarchy in the Dutch Republic. They were all the more jealous of their independence because several Catholic provinces of the southern Low Countries, including present-day Belgium and Luxembourg, remained under Spanish control.

The princes of the House of Orange served the Dutch Republic with a special title, *stadtholder*, or steward. The stadtholder did not technically rule and had no power to make laws, though he did exercise some influence over the appointments of officials and military officers. Instead, powerful merchant families in the United Provinces exercised real authority, through their dominance of the legislature. It was from the Dutch Republic that the stadtholder William of Orange launched his successful bid to become the king of England in the Glorious Revolution of 1688.

The Dutch United Provinces were not, perhaps, the first place that one would choose as a base for a commercial trading empire. Much of the territory of the Dutch Republic was below sea level, and the water was only kept out by an elaborate system of dikes that protected the land from floods. But the Dutch made good use of their proximity to the sea. By 1670, the prosperity of the Dutch Republic was strongly linked to trade: grains and fish from eastern Europe and the Baltic Sea; spices, silks, porcelains and tea from the Indian Ocean and Japan; slaves, silver, coffee, sugar, and tobacco from the Atlantic world. With a population of nearly 2 million and a capital, Amsterdam, that served as an international hub for goods and finance, the Dutch Republic's commercial network was global (see Chapter 14). Trade brought with it an extraordinary diversity of peoples and religions, as Spanish and Portuguese Jews, French Huguenots, English Quakers, and Protestant dissidents from central Europe all sought to take advantage of the relative spirit of toleration that existed in the Netherlands. This toleration did have limits. Jews were not required to live in segregated neighborhoods, as in many other European capitals, but they were prohibited from joining guilds or trade associations. Tensions between Calvinists and Catholics were a perennial issue, with Calvinists living in the western provinces and Catholics concentrated to the east and south.

The last quarter of the seventeenth century witnessed a decline in Dutch power, however, as the Low Countries were increasingly squeezed between the military strength and territorial ambitions of absolutist France to the south and competition from the maritime empire of the British in the Atlantic and Indian Oceans. The turning point came in 1672, when the French king, Louis XIV, put together a coalition that surrounded the United Provinces, threatening an invasion. The English took advantage of this moment of vulnerability to attack a major Dutch convoy returning from the eastern Mediterranean. Louis XIV invaded and quickly overran all but two of the Dutch provinces. Popular anger at the failures of Dutch leadership turned violent, and in response the panicked assemblies named William of Orange the new stadtholder of Holland, giving him the power to organize the defense of the republic and to quell internal dissent. William opened the dikes that held back the sea, and the French armies were forced to retreat in the face of rising waters. Soon after, the Spanish entered the war on the side of the Dutch, which caused Louis XIV to abandon his plans to conquer the United Provinces. After the Glorious Revolution of 1688 in England, which brought William of Orange to the English throne, the Dutch joined an alliance with the English against the French. This alliance protected the republic against further aggression from France, but it also forced the Dutch into heavy expenditures on fortifications and defense and involved them in a series of costly wars (see below). As a result, the dynamic and flexible political institutions that had been part of the strength of the Dutch Republic became more rigid and inflexible over time. Meanwhile, both the French and the British continued to pressure the Dutch commercial fleet at sea. In the eighteenth century, the Dutch no longer exercised the same influence abroad.

WAR AND THE BALANCE OF POWER, 1661–1715

By the beginning of the eighteenth century, then, Europe was being reshaped by wars whose effects were also felt far beyond Europe's borders. The initial causes of these wars lay in the French monarchy's efforts to challenge his main European rivals, the Habsburg powers in Spain, the Spanish Netherlands, and the Holy Roman Empire. Through his continued campaigns in the Low Countries, Louis XIV expanded his territory, eventually taking Strasbourg (1681), Luxembourg (1684), and Cologne (1688). In response, William of Orange organized the League of Augsburg, which over time included Holland, England, Spain, Sweden, Bavaria, Saxony, the Rhine Palatinate, and the Austrian Habsburgs. The resulting Nine Years' War between France and the League extended from Ireland to India to North America (where it was known as King William's War), demonstrating the broadening imperial reach of European dynastic regimes and the increasing significance of French and English competition in the Atlantic world.

These wars were a sign both of the heightening power of Europe's absolutist regimes and of a growing vulnerability. Financing the increasingly costly wars of the eighteenth century would prove to be one of the central challenges faced by all of Europe's absolutist regimes, and the pressure to raise revenues from royal subjects through taxation would eventually strain European society to a breaking point. By the end of the eighteenth century, popular unrest and political challenges to absolutist and imperial states were widespread, both on the European continent and in the colonies of the Atlantic world.

From the League of Augsburg to the War of the Spanish Succession

The League of Augsburg reflected the emergence of a new diplomatic goal in western and central Europe: the preservation of a balance of power. This goal would animate European diplomacy for the next 200 years, until the balance of power system collapsed with the outbreak of the First World War. The main proponents of balance of power diplomacy were England, the United Provinces (Holland), Prussia, and Austria. By 1697, the League forced Louis XIV to make peace, because France was exhausted by war and famine. Louis gave back much of his recent gains but kept Strasbourg and the surrounding territory of Alsace. In North America, the borders between French and English colonial territory remained the same for the time being (see below). Louis was nevertheless looking at the real prize: a French claim to succeed to the throne of Spain and so control the Spanish Empire in the Americas, Italy, the Netherlands, and the Philippines.

In the 1690s, it became clear that King Charles II of Spain (r. 1665–1700) would soon die without a clear heir, and both Louis XIV of France and Leopold I of Austria (r. 1658–1705) were interested in promoting their own relatives to succeed him. Either solution would have upset the balance of power in Europe, and several schemes to divide the Spanish realm between French and Austrian candidates were discussed. Meanwhile, King Charles II's advisers sought to avoid partition by passing the entire Spanish Empire to a single heir: Louis XIV's grandson, Philip of Anjou. Philip was to renounce any claim to the French throne in becoming king of Spain, but the terms of this were kept secret. When Charles II died, Philip V (r. 1700–46) was proclaimed king of Spain and Louis XIV rushed troops into the Spanish Netherlands while also sending French merchants into the Spanish Americas to break their monopoly on trade from the region. Immediately a war broke out, known as the War of the Spanish Succession, pitting England, the United Provinces, Austria, and Prussia against France, Bavaria, and Spain. Although the English king, William of Orange, died in 1702, just as the war was beginning, his generals led an extraordinary march deep into the European continent, inflicting a devastating defeat on the French and their Bavarian allies at Blenheim (1704). Soon after, the English captured Gibraltar, establishing a commercial foothold in the Mediterranean. The costs of the campaign nevertheless created a chorus of complaints from English and Dutch merchants, who feared the damage that was being done to trade and commerce. Queen Anne of England (Mary's sister and William's successor) gradually grew disillusioned with the war, and her government sent out peace feelers to France.

In 1713, the war finally came to an end with the Treaty of Utrecht. Its terms were reasonably fair to all sides. Philip V, Louis XIV's grandson, remained on the throne of Spain and retained Spain's colonial empire intact. In return, Louis agreed that France and Spain would never be united under the same ruler. Austria gained territories in the Spanish Netherlands and Italy, including Milan and Naples. The Dutch were guaranteed protection of their borders against future invasions by France, but the French retained both Lille and Strasbourg. The most significant consequences of the settlement, however, were played out in the Atlantic world, as the balance of powers among Europe's colonial empires underwent a profound shift.

Imperial Rivalries after the Treaty of Utrecht

The fortunes of Europe's colonial empires changed dramatically owing to the wars of the late seventeenth and early eighteenth centuries. Habsburg Spain proved unable to defend its early monopoly over colonial trade, and by 1700, although Spain still possessed a substantial empire, it lay at the mercy of its more dynamic rivals. Portugal, too, found it impossible to prevent foreign penetration of its colonial empire. In 1703, the English signed a treaty with Portugal allowing English merchants to export woolens duty free into Portugal and allowing Portugal to ship its wines duty free into England. Access to Portugal also led British merchants to trade with the Portuguese colony of Brazil, an important sugar producer and the largest of all the American markets for African slaves.

The 1713 Treaty of Utrecht opened a new era of colonial rivalries. The French retained Quebec and other territories in North America, as well as their small foothold in India. The biggest winner by far was Great Britain, as the combined kingdoms of England and Scotland were known after 1707. The British kept Gibraltar and Minorca in the

THE TREATY OF UTRECHT, 1713. This illustration from a French royal almanac depicts the treaty that ended the War of Spanish Succession and reshaped the balance of power in western Europe in favor of Britain and France.

Mediterranean and also acquired large chunks of French territory in the New World, including Newfoundland, mainland Nova Scotia, the Hudson Bay, and the Caribbean island of St. Kitts. Even more valuable, however, Britain also extracted from Spain the right to transport and sell African slaves in Spanish America. As a result, the British were now poised to become the principal slave merchants and the dominant colonial and commercial power of the eighteenth-century world.

The Treaty of Utrecht thus reshaped the balance of power in the Atlantic world in fundamental ways. Spain's collapse was already precipitous; by 1713, it was complete. Spain would remain the "sick man of Europe" for the next two centuries. The Dutch decline was more gradual, but by

1713 Dutch merchants' inability to compete with the British in the slave trade diminished their economic clout. In the Atlantic, Britain and France were now the dominant powers. Although they would duel for another half century for control of North America, the balance of colonial power tilted decisively in Britain's favor after Utrecht. Within Europe, the myth of French military supremacy had been shattered. Britain's navy, not France's army, would rule the new imperial and commercial world of the eighteenth century.

THE REMAKING OF CENTRAL AND EASTERN EUROPE

The decades between 1680 and 1720 were also decisive in reshaping the balance of power in central and eastern Europe. As Ottoman power waned, the Austro-Hungarian Empire of the Habsburgs emerged as the dominant power in central and southeastern Europe. To the north, Brandenburg-Prussia was also a rising power. The most dramatic changes, however, occurred in Russia, which emerged from a long war with Sweden as the dominant power in the Baltic Sea and would soon threaten the combined kingdom of Poland-Lithuania. Within these regimes, the main tension came from ambitious monarchs who sought to increase the power of the centralized state at the expense of other elites, especially aristocrats and the Church. In Brandenburg-Prussia and in Tsarist Russia, these efforts were largely successful, whereas in Habsburg Austria, regional nobilities retained much of their influence.

The Austrian Habsburg Empire

In the second half of the seventeenth century, as Louis XIV of France demonstrated the power of absolutism in western Europe, the Austrian Habsburg Empire, with its capital in Vienna, must have seemed increasingly like a holdover from a previous age. Habsburg Austria was the largest state within what remained of the medieval Holy Roman Empire, a complex federal association of nearly 300 nominally autonomous dynastic kingdoms, principalities, duchies, and archbishoprics that had been created to protect and defend the papacy. Some, such as the kingdom of Bavaria, were large and had their own standing armies. Each Holy Roman emperor was chosen by seven "electors" who were either of noble rank or archbishops—in practice, the emperor was always from the Habsburg family. Through strategic marriages with other royal lines, earlier generations of Habsburg rulers had consolidated their control over a substantial part of Europe, including Austria, Bohemia,

EUROPE AFTER THE TREATY OF UTRECHT (1713). ■ *What were the major Habsburg dominions?* ■ *What geographical disadvantage faced the kingdom of Poland as Brandenburg-Prussia grew in influence and ambition?* ■ *How did the balance of power change in Europe as a result of the Treaty of Utrecht?*

Moravia, and Hungary in central Europe; the Netherlands and Burgundy in the west; and, if one included the Spanish branch of the Habsburg family, Spain and its vast colonial empire as well. After 1648, when the Treaty of Westphalia granted individual member states within the Holy Roman Empire the right to conduct their own foreign policy, the influence of the Austrian Habsburgs waned, at precisely the moment that they faced challenges from France to the west and the Ottoman Empire to the east.

The complicated structure of the Holy Roman Empire limited the extent to which a ruler such as Leopold I of Austria could emulate the absolutist rule of Louis XIV in France. Every constituent state within the empire had its own local political institutions, its own entrenched nobilities, each with a strong interest in resisting any attempt to centralize crucial functions of government, such as taxation, or the raising of armies. Even if direct assertion of absolutist control was impossible, Habsburg rulers found ways of increasing their authority. In Bohemia and Moravia, the Habsburgs encouraged landlords to produce crops for export by forcing peasants to provide three days of unpaid work per week to their lords. In return, the landed elites of these territories permitted the emperors to reduce the political independence of their traditional legislative estates. In Hungary, however, the powerful and independent nobility resisted such compromises. When the Habsburgs began a campaign against Hungarian Protestants, in 1679 an insurrection broke out that forced Leopold to grant concessions to Hungarian nobles in exchange for their assistance in restoring order. When the Ottoman Empire sought to take advantage of this disorder to press an attack against Austria from the east, the Habsburgs survived only by enlisting the help of a Catholic coalition led by the Polish king John Sobieski (r. 1674–96).

In 1683, the Ottomans launched their last assault on Vienna but after their failure to capture the Habsburg capital, Ottoman power in southeastern Europe declined rapidly. By 1699, Austria had reconquered most of Hungary from the Ottomans; by 1718, it controlled all of Hungary and also Transylvania and Serbia. In 1722, Austria acquired the territory of Silesia from Poland. With Hungary now a buffer state between Austria and the Ottomans, Austria became one of the arbiters of the European balance of power. The same obstacles to the development of centralized absolutist rule persisted, however, and Austria was increasingly overshadowed in central Europe by the rise of another German-speaking state: Prussia.

The Rise of Brandenburg-Prussia

After the Ottoman collapse, the main threat to Austria came from the rising power of Brandenburg-Prussia. Like Austria, Prussia was a composite state made up of several geographically divided territories acquired through inheritance by a single royal family, the Hohenzollerns. Their two main holdings were Brandenburg, centered on its capital city, Berlin, and the duchy of East Prussia. Between these two territories lay Pomerania (claimed by Sweden) and an important part of the kingdom of Poland, including the port of Gdansk (Danzig). The Hohenzollerns' aim was to unite their state by acquiring these intervening territories. Over the course of more than a century of steady state building, they finally succeeded in doing so. In the process, Brandenburg-Prussia became a dominant military power and a key player in the balance-of-power diplomacy of the mid-eighteenth century.

The foundations for Prussian expansion were laid by Frederick William, the "Great Elector" (r. 1640–88). He obtained East Prussia from Poland in exchange for help in a war against Sweden. Behind the Elector's diplomatic triumphs lay his success in

building an army and mobilizing the resources to pay for it. He gave the powerful nobles of his territories (known as "Junkers" (*YUN-kurs*)) the right to enserf their peasants and guaranteed them immunity from taxation. In exchange, they staffed the officer corps of his army and supported his highly autocratic taxation system. Secure in their estates and made increasingly wealthy in the grain trade, the Junkers surrendered management of the Prussian state to the Elector's newly reformed bureaucracy, which set about its main task: increasing the size and strength of the Prussian army.

By supporting Austria in the War of the Spanish Succession, the Great Elector's son, Frederick I (r. 1688–1713) earned the right to call himself king of Prussia from the Austrian emperor. He too was a crafty diplomat, but his main attention was devoted to developing the cultural life of his new royal capital, Berlin. His son, Frederick William I (r. 1713–40) focused, like his grandfather, on building the army. During his reign, the Prussian army grew from 30,000 to 83,000 men, becoming the fourth largest army in Europe, after France, Austria, and Russia. To support his army, Frederick William I increased taxes and shunned the luxuries of court life. For him, the theater of absolutism was not the palace but the office, where he personally supervised his army and the growing bureaucracy that sustained it. Frederick William's son, known as Frederick the Great, would take this Prussian army and the bureaucracy that sustained it and transform the

PRUSSIANS SWEARING ALLEGIANCE TO THE GREAT ELECTOR AT KÖNIGSBERG, 1663.
The occasion on which the Prussian estates first acknowledged the overlordship of their ruler. This ceremony marked the beginning of the centralization of the Prussian state.

THE CITY OF STETTIN UNDER SIEGE BY THE GREAT ELECTOR FREDERICK WILLIAM IN THE WINTER OF 1677–78 (c. 1680). This painting depicts the growing sophistication and organization of military operations under the Prussian monarchy. Improvements in artillery and siege tactics forced cities to adopt new defensive strategies, especially the zone of battlements and protective walls that became ubiquitous in central Europe during this period. ▪ *How might these developments have shaped the layout of Europe's growing towns and cities?* ▪ *How might this emphasis on the military and its attendant bureaucracy have affected the relationship between the monarchy and the nobility or between the king and his subjects?*

Europe, however, this increase in state power often came at the expense of an intensification of feudal obligations that the peasantry owed to their local lords.

AUTOCRACY IN RUSSIA

An even more dramatic transformation took place in Russia under Tsar Peter I (r. 1672–1725). Peter's official title was "autocrat of all the Russias" but he was soon known as Peter the Great. His imposing height—he was six feet eight inches tall—and his mercurial personality—jesting one moment, raging the next—added to the outsize impression he made on his contemporaries. Peter was not the first tsar to bring his country into contact with western Europe, but his policies were decisive in making Russia a great European power.

The Early Years of Peter's Reign

Since 1613, Russia had been ruled by members of the Romanov dynasty, who had attempted to restore political stability after the chaotic "time

kingdom into a major power in central Europe after 1740 (see Chapter 17).

Thus, in both Prussia and Habsburg Austria, the divided nature of the respective realms and the entrenched strength of local nobilities forced the rulers in each case to grant significant concessions to noble landowners in exchange for incremental increases in the power of the centralized state. Whereas the nobility in France increasingly sought to maximize their power by participating in the system of absolutist rule at the court of Louis XIV, and wealthy landowners in England sought to exercise their influence through Parliament, the nobilities of Prussia and Habsburg Austria had more leverage to demand something in return for their cooperation. Often, what they demanded was the right to enserf or coerce labor from the peasantry in their domains. In both eastern and western Europe, therefore, the state became stronger. In eastern

of troubles" that followed the death of the bloodthirsty, half-mad tsar Ivan the Terrible in 1584. The Romanovs faced a severe threat to their rule between 1667 and 1671, when a Cossack leader (the Russian Cossacks were semiautonomous bands of peasant cavalrymen) named Stenka Razin led a rebellion in southeastern Russia. This uprising found widespread support, not only from oppressed serfs but also from non-Russian tribes in the lower Volga region who longed to cast off the domination of Moscow. Ultimately Tsar Alexis I (r. 1654–76) and the Russian nobility were able to defeat Razin's zealous but disorganized bands of rebels, slaughtering more than 100,000 of them in the process.

Like Louis XIV of France, Peter came to the throne as a young boy, and his minority was marked by political dissension and court intrigue. In 1689, however, at the age of seventeen, he overthrew the regency of his half sister Sophia and assumed personal control of the state. Determined to make Russia into a great military power, the young tsar traveled to Holland and England during the 1690s to study shipbuilding and to recruit skilled foreign workers to help him build a navy. While he was abroad, however, his elite palace guard (the *streltsy*) rebelled, attempting to restore Sophia to the throne. Peter quickly returned home from Vienna and crushed the rebellion with striking savagery. About 1,200 suspected conspirators were summarily executed, many of them gibbeted outside the walls of the Kremlin, where their bodies rotted for months as a graphic reminder of the fate awaiting those who dared challenge the tsar's authority.

The Transformation of the Tsarist State

Peter is most famous as the tsar who attempted to westernize Russia by imposing a series of social and cultural reforms on the traditional Russian nobility: ordering noblemen to cut off their long beards and flowing sleeves; publishing a book of manners that forbade spitting on the floor and eating with one's fingers; encouraging polite conversation between the sexes; and requiring noblewomen to appear, together with men, in Western garb at weddings, banquets, and other public occasions. The children of Russian nobles

EXECUTION OF THE *STRELTSY* (1698). A contemporary woodcut showing how Peter the Great ordered the public hanging of guard regiments who had rebelled against his authority. How does this display of autocratic power compare with the spectacle of power so carefully orchestrated by Peter's contemporary, Louis XIV of France?

Analyzing Primary Sources

The Revolt of the Streltsy and Peter the Great

The streltsy *were four regiments of Moscow guards that became involved in a conspiracy in support of Peter the Great's older sister, Sophia, who had earlier made claim to the throne while Peter was still a child. Approximately 4,000 of the rebels were defeated in June 1698 by troops loyal to Peter. Peter himself was abroad during the fighting, and although his officers had already tortured many of the streltsy to determine the involvement of other nobles, Peter ordered a more far-reaching investigation on his return. Over 1,000 of the streltsy were executed after being tortured again. Afterward, their bodies were placed on display in the capital. Johann Georg Korb, an Austrian diplomat in Moscow, recorded his observations of the power wielded by the Russian autocrat.*

How sharp was the pain, how great the indignation to which the Czar's Majesty was mightily moved, when he knew of the rebellion of the Strelitz [*streltsy*], betrayed openly a mind panting for vengeance. [SIC] . . . Going immediately to Lefort (the only person almost that he condescended to treat with intimate familiarity), he thus indignantly broke out: "Tell me, Francis, son of James, how I can reach Moscow, by the shortest way, in a brief space, so that I may wreak vengeance on this great perfidy of my people, with punishments worthy of their flagitious crime. Not one of them shall escape with impunity. Around my royal city, of which, with their impious efforts, they meditated the destruction, I will have gibbets and gallows set upon the walls and ramparts, and each and every of them will I put to a direful death." . . .

His first anxiety, after his arrival [in Moscow] was about the rebellion. In what it consisted? What the insurgents meant? Who had dared to instigate such a crime? And as nobody could answer accurately upon all points, and some pleaded their own ignorance, others the obstinacy of the Strelitz, he began to have suspicions of everybody's loyalty, and began to cogitate about a fresh investigation. The rebels that were kept in custody . . . were all brought in by four regiments of the guards, to a fresh investigation and fresh tortures. Prison, tribunal, and rack, for those that were brought in, was in Bebraschentsko. No day, holy, or profane, were the inquisitors idle; every day was deemed fit and lawful for torturing. As many as there were accused there were knouts, and every inquisitor was a butcher. Prince Feodor Jurowicz Romadonowski showed himself by so much more fitted for his inquiry, as he surpassed the rest in cruelty. He put the interrogatories, he examined the criminals, he urged those that were not confessing, he ordered such Strelitz as were more pertinaciously silent, to be subjected to more cruel tortures; those that had already confessed about many things were questioned about more; those who were bereft of strength and reason, and almost of their senses, by excess of torment, were handed over to the skill of the doctors, who were compelled to restore them to strength, in order that they might be broken down by fresh excruciations. The whole month of October was spent in butchering the backs of the culprits with knout and with flames: no day were those that were left alive exempt from scourging or scorching, or else they were broken upon the wheel, or driven to the gibbet, or slain with the axe—the penalties which were inflicted upon them as soon as their confessions had sufficiently revealed the heads of the rebellion.

Source: Johann Georg Korb, *Diary of an Austrian Secretary of Legation at the Court of Czar Peter the Great*, trans. Count MacDonnell (London: 1863), pp. 2:85–87.

Questions for Analysis

1. Why was it important for Korb to begin this description with the monarch's pain?

2. What does this episode reveal about Peter's conception of his own person and of the loyalty that his subjects owed him? Does it show that his power was fragile, immense, or both?

3. What does it mean to describe torture as an "investigation" even while it is also being described as "vengeance?"

PETER THE GREAT CUTS THE BEARD OF AN OLD BELIEVER. This woodcut depicts the Russian emperor's enthusiastic policy of westernization, as he pushed everybody in Russia who was not a peasant to adopt Western styles of clothes and grooming. The Old Believer (a member of a religious sect in Russia) protests that he has paid the beard tax and should therefore be exempt. ■ *Why would an individual's choices about personal appearance be so politically significant in Peter's Russia?* ■ *What customs were the target of Peter's reforms?*

were sent to western European courts for their education. Thousands of western European experts were brought to Russia to staff the new schools and academies Peter built; to design the new buildings he constructed; and to serve in the tsar's army, navy, and administration.

These measures were important, but the tsar was not primarily motivated by a desire to modernize or westernize Russia. Peter's policies transformed Russian life in fundamental ways, but his real goal was to make Russia a great military power, not to remake Russian society. His new taxation system (1724), for example, which assessed taxes on individuals rather than on households, rendered many of the traditional divisions of Russian peasant society obsolete. It was created, however, to raise more money for war. His Table of Ranks, imposed in 1722, had a similar impact on the nobility. By insisting that all nobles must work their way up from the (lower) landlord class

to the (higher) administrative class and to the (highest) military class, Peter reversed the traditional hierarchy of Russian noble society, which had valued landlords by birth above administrators and soldiers who had risen by merit. But he also created a powerful new incentive to lure his nobility into administrative and military service to the tsar.

As "autocrat of all the Russias," Peter the Great was the absolute master of his empire to a degree unmatched elsewhere in Europe. After 1649, Russian peasants were legally the property of their landlords; by 1750, half were serfs and the other half were state peasants who lived on lands owned by the tsar himself (by comparison, many peasants in western Europe owned their own land and very few were serfs). State peasants could be conscripted to serve as soldiers in the tsar's army, workers in his factories (whose productive capacity increased enormously during Peter's reign), or as forced laborers in his building projects. Serfs could also be taxed by the tsar and summoned for military service, as could their lords. All Russians, of whatever rank, were expected to serve the tsar, and all Russia was considered in some sense to belong to him. Russia's autocracy thus went even further than the absolutism of Louis XIV.

To further consolidate his power, Peter replaced the Duma—the nation's rudimentary national assembly—with a handpicked senate, a group of nine administrators who supervised military and civilian affairs. In religious matters, he took direct control over the Russian Orthodox Church by appointing an imperial official to manage its affairs. To cope with the demands of war, he also fashioned a new, larger, and more efficient administration, for which he recruited both nobles and non-nobles. But rank in the new bureaucracy did not depend on birth. One of his principal advisers, Alexander Menshikov, began his career as a cook and finished as a prince. This degree of social mobility would have been impossible in any contemporary western European country. In Russia, more so than in western Europe, noble status depended on governmental service, with all nobles expected to participate in Peter's army or administration. Peter was not entirely successful in enforcing this requirement, but the administrative machinery he devised furnished Russia with its ruling class for the next 200 years.

Russian Imperial Expansion

The goal of Peter's foreign policy was to secure year-round ports for Russia on the Black Sea and the Baltic Sea. In the

THE GROWTH OF THE RUSSIAN EMPIRE. ▪ *How did Peter the Great expand the territory controlled by Russia?* ▪ *What neighboring dynasties would have been the most affected by Russian expansion?* ▪ *How did the emergence of a bigger, more powerful Russia affect the European balance of power?*

Black Sea, his enemy was the Ottomans. Here, however, he had little success; although he captured the port of Azov in 1696, he was forced to return it in 1711. Russia would not secure its position in the Black Sea until the end of the eighteenth century. Nevertheless, Peter continued to push against the Ottoman Empire in the North Caucasus region throughout his reign. This mountainous area on Russia's southern flank became important sites for Russia's experiments in colonial expansion into central Asia, which began during the sixteenth century and would later mirror the process of colonial conquest undertaken by European powers and the United States in North and South America. Like France and Britain, the Russian state bureaucracy was built during a period of ambitious colonialism; and like Spain, the monarchy's identity was shaped by a long contest with Muslim power on its borders.

Since the late sixteenth century, successive Russian leaders had extended their control over bordering territories of central Asia to the south and east. Although merchants helped fund early expeditions into Siberia, this expansion was primarily motivated by geopolitical concerns; the tsar sought to gain access to the populations of Russia's border areas and bring them into the service of the expanding Russian state. In this sense, Russian colonialism during this period differed from western European expansion into the Atlantic world, which had primarily been motivated by hopes of commercial gain. Nevertheless, tsarist Russia's colonization of central Asia was similar to the process of European colonial expansion elsewhere in some respects. Like European colonizers in the Americas, Russian expansion brought Russian troops into contact with a variety of peoples with different religious beliefs and their own political structures. Some, such as the Muslim Kumyks of northern Dagestan had a highly centralized government. Others, such as the Kabardinians or the Chechens, were more fragmented politically.

In its early stages, as successive Russian emperors moved Russian troops into the region, they relied on a process of indirect rule, often seeking to co-opt local elites. Later in the eighteenth century, they had more success settling

Russians in border regions who ruled over local populations directly. Religion also provided a cover for expansion, and Peter and his successors funded missionary work by Georgian Christians among Muslims in the Caucasus. Efforts to convert Muslim populations to Orthodox Christianity had little effect, and in fact the opposite occurred: the region's commitment to Islam was continuously renewed through contact with different strains of Islamic practice coming from neighboring Ottoman lands and Persia.

Peter could point to more concrete success to the north. In 1700, he began what would become a twenty-one-year war with Sweden, then the dominant power in the Baltic Sea. By 1703, Peter had secured a foothold on the Gulf of Finland and immediately began to build a new capital city there, which he named St. Petersburg. After 1709, when Russian armies, supported by Prussia, decisively defeated the Swedes at the battle of Poltava, work on Peter's new capital city accelerated. An army of serfs was now conscripted to build the new city, whose centerpiece was a royal palace designed to imitate and rival Louis XIV's Versailles.

The Great Northern War with Sweden ended in 1721 with the Peace of Nystad. This treaty marks a realignment of power in eastern Europe comparable to that effected by the Treaty of Utrecht in the West. Sweden lost its North Sea territories to Hanover and its Baltic German territories to Prussia. Its eastern territories, including the entire Gulf of Finland, Livonia, and Estonia, passed to Russia. Sweden was now a second-rank power in the northern European world. Poland-Lithuania survived but it too was a declining power; by the end of the eighteenth century, the kingdom would disappear altogether, its territories swallowed up by its more powerful neighbors (see Chapter 17). The victors at Nystad were the Prussians and the Russians. These two powers secured their position along the Baltic coast, positioning themselves to take advantage of the lucrative eastern European grain trade with western Europe. Peter's accomplishments came at enormous cost. Direct taxation in Russia increased 500 percent during his reign, and his army in the 1720s numbered more than 300,000 men. Peter made Russia a force to be reckoned with on the European scene; but in so doing, he also aroused great resentment, especially among his nobility. Peter's only son and heir, Alexis, became the focus for conspiracies against the tsar, until finally Peter had him arrested and executed in 1718. As a result, when Peter died in 1725, he left no son to succeed him. A series of ineffective tsars followed, mostly creatures of the palace guard, under whom the resentful nobles reversed many of Peter the Great's reforms. In 1762, however, the crown passed to Catherine the Great, a ruler whose ambitions and determination were equal to those of her great predecessor (see Chapter 17).

CONCLUSION

By the time of Peter the Great's death in Russia in 1725, the power of Europe's absolutist realms to reinvigorate European political institutions was visible to all. Government had become more bureaucratic, state service had been more professionalized, administrators loyal to the king had become more numerous, more efficient, and more demanding. Despite the increasing scope of government, however, the structure and principles of government changed relatively little. Apart from Great Britain and the Dutch Republic, the great powers of eighteenth-century Europe were still governed by rulers who styled themselves as absolutist monarchs in the mold of Louis XIV, who claimed an authority that came directly from God and who ruled over a society where social hierarchies based on birth were taken for granted.

These absolutist regimes could not hide the fact, however, that their rule depended on a kind of negotiated settlement with other powerful elites within European society, in particular with landed aristocrats and with religious leaders. Louis XIV used his power to curb the worst excesses of nobles who abused their position, and he defended Catholic orthodoxy against dissident Catholics and Protestants. He could not hide the fact, however, that his power depended on a delicate exchange of favors—French aristocrats would surrender their political authority to the state in exchange for social and legal privileges and immunity from many (but not all) forms of taxation. The Church made a similar bargain. Peter the Great's autocratic rule in Russia worked out a slightly different balance of powers between his state and the Russian aristocracy, one that tied aristocrats more closely to an ideal of state service, a model that also worked well for the rulers of Brandenburg-Prussia. Even in England, the establishment of a limited constitutional monarchy and a king who ruled alongside parliament was not really a radical departure from the European absolutist model. It was merely a different institutional answer to the same problem—what relationship should the monarchical state have with other elites within society?

The demands of state building during this period required that kings raise enormous revenues—for the sumptuous displays of their sovereignty in royal residences like Louis XIV's palace at Versailles, for the sponsorship of royal academies and the patronage of artists, but most of all, for war. Territorial expansion within Europe and holding on to colonial empires in the Atlantic world was costly. Distributing the burden of taxation to pay for these endeavors became an intensely fought political issue for European monarchs during this period, and the financing of royal debt became an increasingly sophisticated art. Colbert's mercantilist policy was an attempt to harness the full power of the economy for the benefit of royal government, and the competition among Spain, Holland, England, and France to control the revenue flows coming from the Atlantic world forced Europe's monarchs to recognize that the "balance of powers" was increasingly being played out on a global stage.

These themes—the expansion of state powers; conflicts between the monarchy and the aristocracy or with religious dissidents; the intensification of the tax burden on the population; and the opening up of Europe to ever more frequent interactions with other peoples in the Atlantic world, the Indian Ocean, and eventually, the Pacific—prompted many in eighteenth-century Europe to reflect on the consequences of these developments. What were the limits to state power, and by what criteria were the actions of rulers to be judged? What was the proper measure of economic prosperity, and who was it for? Could

After You Read
This Chapter

Visit StudySpace for quizzes, additional review materials, and multimedia documents. **wwnorton.com/web/westernciv18**

REVIEWING THE OBJECTIVES

- Absolutist rulers claimed a monopoly of power and authority within their realms. Who were the most important absolutist rulers, how did they justify their innovations, and what did they do to achieve their goals?
- Mercantilism was an economic doctrine that guided the policies of absolutist rulers. What did mercantilists believe?
- Between 1660 and 1688, political leaders in England continued to debate the nature of the state, the role of Parliament, and religious divisions. What was the significance of these dates, and what was the outcome of these debates?
- What circumstances led to the decline of the Dutch Republic's power in this period?
- The wars begun by Louis XIV after 1680 drove his opponents to ally with one another to achieve a balance of power. What was the result of these conflicts in Europe and in the Atlantic world?

a well-ordered society tolerate religious diversity? Given Europe's growing awareness of cultures in other parts of the world with different religions, different political systems, and different ways of expressing their moral and ethical values, how might Europeans justify or take the measure of their own beliefs and customs? The intellectuals who looked for answers to these questions were similar to earlier generations of scientific researchers in their respect for reason and rational thought, but they turned their attention beyond problems of natural philosophy and science to the messy world of politics and culture. Their movement—known as the Enlightenment—reached its peak in the middle decades of the eighteenth century, and created the basis for a powerful critique of Europe's absolutist regimes. The Enlightenment itself emerged slowly from a revolution in scientific thinking that had begun earlier in the early modern period, and it is to this history that we now turn.

PEOPLE, IDEAS, AND EVENTS IN CONTEXT

- What did **LOUIS XIV** of France and **PETER THE GREAT** of Russia have in common? How did they deal with those who resisted their attempts to impose absolutist rule?

- Compare the religious policies of **LOUIS XIV** of France with the religious policies of the English Stuart kings **CHARLES II** and **JAMES II**. In what way did religious disagreements limit their ability to rule effectively?

- How did European monarchies use the economic theory known as **MERCANTILISM** to strengthen the power and wealth of their kingdoms, and how did this theory influence **FRENCH COLONIALISM**?

- What was the **CONTRACT THEORY OF GOVERNMENT** according to the English political thinker **JOHN LOCKE**?

- What limits to royal power were recognized in Great Britain as a result of the **GLORIOUS REVOLUTION**?

- What was significant about the new **BALANCE OF POWERS** that developed in Europe as a result of **LOUIS XIV**'s wars?

- What does the **TREATY OF UTRECHT** (1713) tell us about the diminished influence of Spain and the corresponding rise of Britain and France as European and colonial powers?

- What was different about the attempts by rulers in Habsburg Austria and Brandenburg-Prussia to impose **ABSOLUTISM** in central Europe?

- What innovations did **PETER THE GREAT** bring to Russia?

THINKING ABOUT CONNECTIONS

- What makes absolutism different from earlier models of kingship in earlier periods?

- Was the absolutist monarchs' emphasis on sumptuous displays of their authority something new? Is it different from the way that political power is represented today in democratic societies?

STORY LINES

- After c. 1550, new sciences in Europe questioned older beliefs about the physical universe. New methods of inquiry led to the development of astronomy, physics, biology, chemistry, and new institutions that supported scientific research and education.

- The scientific revolution entailed both theoretical breakthroughs in explaining the physical universe as well as advances in the practical knowledge of artisans who built mechanical devices such as telescopes. This combination of scientific inquisitiveness and craft techniques encouraged technological developments that would later be useful in industrialization.

- The new sciences did not mark a clean rupture with older traditions of religious thinking. Most scientists in the 1600s remained essentially religious in their worldview, and in any case, their work was only accessible to a small, literate minority who had access to books.

CHRONOLOGY

1543	Nicolaus Copernicus (1473–1543) publishes *On the Revolutions of the Heavenly Spheres*
1576	Tycho Brahe sets up Uraniborg observatory
1609	Johannes Kepler (1571–1643) publishes *Astronomia Nova*
1610	Galileo (1564–1642) publishes *Starry Messenger*
1620	Francis Bacon (1561–1626) publishes *Novum Organum*
1632	Galileo publishes *Dialogue Concerning the Two Chief World Systems*
1633	Galileo's trial
1637	René Descartes (1596–1650) publishes *Discourse on Method*
1660	Royal Society of London founded
1666	French Academy of Sciences founded
1687	Isaac Newton (1642–1727) publishes *Principia Mathematica*

Before You Read This Chapter

The New Science of the Seventeenth Century

CORE OBJECTIVES

- **DEFINE** *scientific revolution* and explain what is meant by *science* in this historical context.

- **UNDERSTAND** the older philosophical traditions that were important for the development of new methods of scientific investigation in the seventeenth century.

- **IDENTIFY** the sciences that made important advances during this period and understand what technological innovations encouraged a new spirit of investigation.

- **EXPLAIN** the differences between the Ptolemaic view of the universe and the new vision of the universe proposed by Nicolas Copernicus.

- **UNDERSTAND** the different definitions of *scientific method* that emerged from the work of Francis Bacon and René Descartes.

Doubt thou the stars are fire,
Doubt that the sun doth move,
Doubt truth to be a liar,
But never doubt I love.

SHAKESPEARE, *HAMLET*, II.2

Doubt thou the stars are fire" and "that the sun doth move." Was Shakespeare alluding to controversial ideas about the cosmos that contradicted the teachings of medieval scholars? *Hamlet* (c. 1600) was written more than fifty years after Copernicus had suggested, in his treatise *On the Revolutions of the Heavenly Spheres* (1543), that the sun did not move and that the earth did, revolving around the sun. Shakespeare probably knew of such theories, although they circulated only among small groups of learned Europeans. As Hamlet's love-torn speech to Ophelia makes clear, they were considered conjecture—or strange mathematical hypotheses. These theories were not exactly new—a heliocentric universe had been proposed as early as the second century B.C.E. by ancient Greek astronomers.

519

But they flatly contradicted the consensus that had set in after Ptolemy proposed an earth-centered universe in the second century C.E., and to Shakespeare's contemporaries, they defied common sense and observation. Learned philosophers, young lovers, shepherds, and sailors alike could watch the sun and the stars move from one horizon to the other each day and night, or so they thought.

Still, a small handful of thinkers did doubt. Shakespeare was born in 1564, the same year as Galileo. By the time the English playwright and the Italian natural philosopher were working, the long process of revising knowledge about the universe, and discovering a new set of rules that explained how the universe worked was under way. By the end of the seventeenth century a hundred years later, the building blocks of the new view had been put in place. This intellectual transformation brought sweeping changes to European philosophy and to Western views of the natural world and of humans' place in it.

Science entails at least three things: a body of knowledge, a method or system of inquiry, and a community of practitioners and the institutions that support them and their work. The *scientific revolution* of the seventeenth century (usually understood to have begun in the mid-sixteenth century and culminated in 1687 with Newton's *Principia*) involved each of these three realms. As far as the content of knowledge is concerned, the scientific revolution saw the emergence and confirmation of a heliocentric (sun-centered) view of the planetary system, which displaced the earth—and humans—from the center of the universe. Even more fundamental, it brought a new mathematical physics that described and confirmed such a view. Second, the scientific revolution established a method of inquiry for understanding the natural world: a method that emphasized the role of observation, experiment, and the testing of hypotheses. Third, *science* emerged as a distinctive branch of knowledge. During the period covered in this chapter, people referred to the study of matter, motion, optics, or the circulation of blood as natural philosophy (the more theoretical term), experimental philosophy, medicine, and—increasingly—science. The growth of societies and institutions dedicated to what we now commonly call scientific research was central to the changes at issue here. Science required not only brilliant thinkers but patrons, states, and communities of researchers; the scientific revolution was thus embedded in other social, religious, and cultural transformations.

The scientific revolution was not an organized effort. Brilliant theories sometimes led to dead ends, discoveries were often accidental, and artisans grinding lenses for telescopes played a role in the advance of knowledge just as surely as did great abstract thinkers. Educated women also claimed the right to participate in scientific debate, but their efforts were met with opposition or indifference. Old and new worldviews often overlapped as individual thinkers struggled to reconcile their discoveries with their faith or to make their theories (about the earth's movements, for instance) fit with received wisdom. Science was slow to work its way into popular understanding. It did not necessarily undermine religion, and it certainly did not intend to; figures like Isaac Newton thought their work confirmed and deepened their religious beliefs. In short, change came slowly and fitfully. But as the new scientific method began to produce radical new insights into the workings of nature, it eventually came to be accepted well beyond the small circles of experimenters, theologians, and philosophers with whom it began.

THE INTELLECTUAL ORIGINS OF THE SCIENTIFIC REVOLUTION

The scientific revolution marks one of the decisive breaks between the Middle Ages and the modern world. For all its novelty, however, it was rooted in earlier developments. Medieval artists and intellectuals had been observing and illustrating the natural world with great precision since at least the twelfth century. Medieval sculptors carved plants and vines with extraordinary accuracy, and fifteenth-century painters and sculptors devoted the same careful attention to the human face and form. Nor was the link among observation, experiment, and invention new to the sixteenth century. The magnetic compass had been known in Europe since the thirteenth century; gunpowder since the early fourteenth; printing, which permeated the intellectual life of the period and opened new possibilities—disseminating ideas quickly, collaborating more easily, buying books, and building libraries—since the middle of the fifteenth. "Printing, firearms, and the compass," wrote Francis Bacon, "no empire, sect or star appears to have exercised a greater power and influence on human affairs than these three mechanical discoveries." A fascination with light, which was a powerful symbol of divine illumination for medieval thinkers, encouraged the study of optics and, in turn, new techniques for grinding lenses. Lens grinders laid the groundwork for the seventeenth-century inventions of the telescope and microscope, creating reading glasses along the way. Astrologers were also active in the later Middle Ages, charting the heavens in the firm belief that the stars controlled the fates of human beings.

Behind these efforts to understand the natural world lay a nearly universal conviction that the natural world had been created by God. Religious belief spurred scientific study. One school of thinkers (the Neoplatonists) argued that nature was a book written by its creator to reveal the ways of God to humanity. Convinced that God's perfection must be reflected in nature, Neoplatonists searched for the ideal and perfect structures they believed must lie behind the "shadows" of the everyday world. Mathematics, particularly geometry, were important tools in this quest. The mathematician and astronomer Johannes Kepler, for example, was deeply influenced by Neoplatonism.

Renaissance humanism also helped prepare the grounds for the scientific revolution. The humanists' educational program placed a low value on natural philosophy, directing attention instead toward the recovery and study of classical antiquity. Humanists revered the authority of the ancients. Yet the energies the humanists poured into recovering, translating, and understanding classical texts (the source of conceptions of the natural world) made many of those important works available for the first time, and to a wider audience. Previously, Arabic sources had provided Europeans with the main route to ancient Greek learning; Greek classics were translated into Arabic and then picked up by late medieval scholars in Spain and Sicily. The humanists' return to the texts themselves—and the fact that the new texts could be more easily printed and circulated—encouraged new study and debate. Islamic scholars knew Ptolemy better than did Europeans until the humanist scholar and printer Johannes Regiomontanus recovered and prepared a new summary of Ptolemy's work. The humanist rediscovery of works by Archimedes—the great Greek mathematician who had proposed that the natural world operated on the basis of mechanical forces, like a great machine, and that these forces could be described mathematically—profoundly impressed important late-sixteenth- and seventeenth-century thinkers, including the Italian scientist Galileo, and shaped mechanical philosophy in the 1600s.

The Renaissance also encouraged collaboration between artisans and intellectuals. Twelfth- and thirteenth-century thinkers had observed the natural world, but they rarely tinkered with machines and they had little contact with the artisans who developed expertise in constructing machines for practical use. During the fifteenth century, however, these two worlds began to come together. Renaissance artists such as Leonardo da Vinci were accomplished craftsmen; they investigated the laws of perspective and optics, they worked out geometric methods for supporting the weight of enormous architectural domes, they studied the human body, and they devised new and more effective weapons for war. The Renaissance brought a vogue for alchemy and astrology; wealthy amateurs built observato-

ries and measured the courses of the stars. These social and intellectual developments laid the groundwork for the scientific revolution.

What of the voyages of discovery? Sixteenth-century observers often linked the exploration of the globe to new knowledge of the cosmos. An admirer wrote to Galileo that he had kept the spirit of exploration alive: "The memory of Columbus and Vespucci will be renewed through you, and with even greater nobility, as the sky is more worthy than the earth." The parallel does not work quite so neatly. Columbus had not been driven by an interest in science.

PTOLEMAIC ASTRONOMICAL INSTRUMENTS. Armillary sphere, 1560s, built to facilitate the observation of planetary positions relative to the earth, in support of Ptolemy's theory of an earth-centered universe. In the sphere, seven concentric rings rotated about different axes. When the outermost ring was set to align with a north–south meridian, and the next ring was set to align with the celestial pole (the North Star, or the point around which the stars seem to rotate), one could determine the latitude of the place where the instrument was placed. The inner rings were used to track the angular movements of the planets, key measurements in validating the Ptolemaic system. ■ *What forms of knowledge were necessary to construct such an instrument?* ■ *How do they relate to the breakthrough that is known as the scientific revolution?*

Past and Present

Has Science Replaced Religion?

Galileo recanted his claims about the movement of heavenly bodies when challenged by the Church (left); but physicists persisted in their research, leading eventually to the development of modern particle accelerators like the one located in this lab in Grenoble, France (right). Few would say, however, that science has replaced religion in the modern world.

 Watch related author interview on StudySpace
wwnorton.com/web/westernciv18

Moreover, it took centuries for European thinkers to process the New World's implications for different fields of study, and the links between the voyages of discovery and breakthroughs in science were largely indirect. The discoveries made the most immediate impact in the field of natural history, which was vastly enriched by travelers' detailed accounts of the flora and fauna of the Americas. Finding new lands and cultures in Africa and Asia and the revelation of the Americas, a world unknown to the ancients and unmentioned in the Bible, also laid bare gaps in Europeans' inherited body of knowledge. In this sense, the exploration of the New World dealt a blow to the authority of the ancients.

In sum, the late medieval recovery of ancient texts long thought to have been lost, the expansion of print culture and reading, the turmoil in the church and the fierce wars and political maneuvering that followed the Reformation,

and the discovery of a new world across the oceans to explore and exploit all shook the authority of older ways of thinking. What we call the scientific revolution was part of the intellectual excitement that surrounded these challenges, and, in retrospect, the scientific revolution enhanced and confirmed the importance of these other developments.

THE COPERNICAN REVOLUTION

Medieval cosmologists, like their ancient counterparts and their successors during the scientific revolution, wrestled with the contradictions between ancient texts and the evidence of their own observations. Their view of an earth-centered universe was particularly influenced by the teachings of Aristotle (384–322 B.C.E.), especially as they were systematized by Ptolemy of Alexandria (100–178 C.E.). In fact, Ptolemy's vision of an earth-centered universe contradicted an earlier proposal by Aristarchus of Samos (310–230 B.C.E.), who had deduced that the earth and other planets revolve around the sun. Like the ancient Greeks, Ptolemy's medieval followers used astronomical observations to support their theory, but the persuasiveness of the model for medieval scholars also derived from the ways that it fit with their Christian beliefs (see Chapter 4). According to Ptolemy, the heavens orbited the earth in a carefully organized hierarchy of spheres. Earth and the heavens were fundamentally different, made of different matter and subject to different laws of motion. The sun, moon, stars, and planets were formed of an unchanging (and perfect) quintessence or ether. The earth, by contrast, was composed of four elements (earth, water, fire, and air), and each of these elements had its natural place: the heavy elements (earth and water) toward the center and the lighter ones farther out. The heavens—first the planets, then the stars—traced perfect circular paths around the stationary earth. The motion of these celestial bodies was produced by a prime mover, whom Christians identified as God. The view fit Aristotelian physics, according to which objects could move only if acted on by an external force, and it fit with a belief that each fundamental element of the universe had a natural place. Moreover, the view both followed from and confirmed belief in the purposefulness of God's universe.

By the late Middle Ages astronomers knew that this cosmology, called the "Ptolemaic system," did not correspond exactly to what many had observed. Orbits did not conform to the Aristotelian ideal of perfect circles. Planets, Mars in particular, sometimes appeared to loop backward before continuing on their paths. Ptolemy had managed to account for these orbital irregularities, but with complicated mathematics. By the early fifteenth century, the efforts to make the observed motions of the planets fit into the model of perfect circles in a geocentric (earth-centered) cosmos had produced astronomical charts that were mazes of complexity. Finally, the Ptolemaic system proved unable to solve serious difficulties with the calendar. That practical crisis precipitated Nicolaus Copernicus's intellectual leap forward.

By the early sixteenth century, the old Roman calendar was significantly out of alignment with the movement of the heavenly bodies. The major saints' days, Easter, and the other holy days were sometimes weeks off where they should have been according to the stars. Catholic authorities tried to correct this problem, consulting mathematicians and astronomers all over Europe. One of these was a Polish church official and astronomer, Nicolaus Copernicus (1473–1543). Educated in Poland and northern Italy, he was a man of diverse talents. He was trained in astronomy, canon law, and medicine. He read Greek. He was well versed in ancient philosophy. He was also a careful mathematician and a devout Catholic, who did not believe that God's universe could be as messy as the one in Ptolemy's model. His proposed solution, based on mathematical calculations, was simple and radical: Ptolemy was mistaken; the earth was neither stationary nor at the center of the planetary system; the earth rotated on its axis and orbited with the other planets around the sun. Reordering the Ptolemaic system simplified the geometry of astronomy and made the orbits of the planets comprehensible.

Copernicus was in many ways a conservative thinker. He did not consider his work to be a break with either the Church or with the authority of ancient texts. He believed, rather, that he had restored a pure understanding

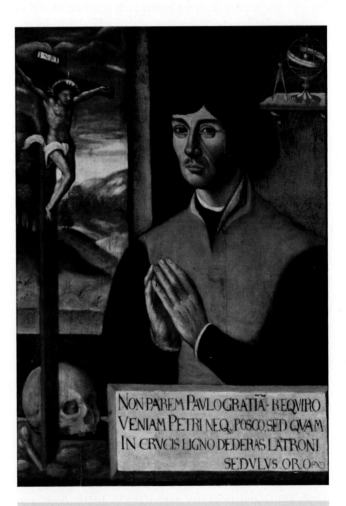

NICOLAUS COPERNICUS. This anonymous portrait of Copernicus characteristically blends his devotion and his scientific achievements. His scholarly work (behind him in the form of an early planetarium) is driven by his faith (as he turns toward the image of Christ triumphant over death). ■ *What relationship between science and religion is evoked by this image?*

of God's design, one that had been lost over the centuries. Still, the implications of his theory troubled him. His ideas contradicted centuries of astronomical thought, and they were hard to reconcile with the observed behavior of objects on earth. If the earth moved, why was that movement imperceptible? Copernicus calculated the distance from the Earth to the Sun to be at least 6 million miles. Even by Copernicus's very low estimate, the earth was hurtling around the sun at the dizzying rate of many thousands of miles an hour. How did people and objects remain standing? (The earth is actually about 93 million miles from the sun, moving through space at 67,000 miles an hour and spinning on its axis at about 1,000 miles an hour!)

Copernicus was not a physicist. He tried to refine, rather than overturn, traditional Aristotelian physics, but his effort to reconcile that physics with his new model of a sun-centered universe created new problems and inconsistencies that he could not resolve. These frustrations and complications dogged Copernicus's later years, and he hesitated to publish his findings. Just before his death, he consented to the release of his major treatise, *On the Revolutions of the Heavenly Spheres* (*De Revolutionibus*), in 1543. To fend off scandal, the Lutheran scholar who saw his manuscript through the press added an introduction to the book declaring that Copernicus's system should be understood as an abstraction, a set of mathematical tools for doing astronomy and not a dangerous claim about the nature of heaven and earth. For decades after 1543, Copernicus's ideas were taken in just that sense—as useful but not realistic mathematical hypotheses. In the long run, however, as one historian puts it, Copernicanism represented the first "serious and systematic" challenge to the Ptolemaic conception of the universe.

TYCHO'S OBSERVATIONS AND KEPLER'S LAWS

Within fifty years, Copernicus's cosmology was revived and modified by two astronomers also critical of the Ptolemaic model of the universe: Tycho Brahe (*TI-koh BRAH-hee*, 1546–1601) and Johannes Kepler (1571–1630). Each was considered the greatest astronomer of his day. Tycho was born into the Danish nobility, but he abandoned his family's military and political legacy to pursue his passion for astronomy. He was hotheaded as well as talented; at twenty, he lost part of his nose in a duel. Like Copernicus, he sought to correct the contradictions in traditional astronomy.

Unlike Copernicus, who was a theoretician, Tycho championed observation and believed careful study of the heavens would unlock the secrets of the universe. He first made a name for himself by observing a completely new star, a "nova," that flared into sight in 1572. The Danish king Friedrich II, impressed by Tycho's work, granted him the use of a small island, where he built a castle specially designed to house an observatory. For over twenty years, Tycho meticulously charted the movements of each significant object in the night sky, compiling the finest set of astronomical data in Europe.

Tycho was not a Copernican. He suggested that the planets orbited the sun and the whole system then orbited a stationary earth. This picture of cosmic order, though clumsy, seemed to fit the observed evidence better than the Ptolemaic system, and it avoided the upsetting physical and theological implications of the Copernican model. In the late 1590s, Tycho moved his work and his huge collection of data to Prague, where he became court astronomer to the Holy Roman emperor Rudolph II. In Prague, he was assisted by a young mathematician from a troubled family, Johannes Kepler. Kepler was more impressed with the Copernican model than was Tycho, and Kepler combined study of Copernicus's work with his own interest in mysticism, astrology, and the religious power of mathematics.

Kepler believed that everything in creation, from human souls to the orbits of the planets, had been created according to mathematical laws. Understanding those laws would thus allow humans to share God's wisdom and penetrate the inner secrets of the universe. Mathematics was God's language. Kepler's search for the pattern of mathematical perfection took him through musical harmonies, nested geometric shapes inside the planets' orbits, and numerical formulas. After Tycho's death, Kepler inherited Tycho's position in Prague, as well as his trove of observations and calculations. That data demonstrated to Kepler that two of Copernicus's assumptions about planetary motion simply did not match observations. Copernicus, in keeping with Aristotelian notions of perfection, had believed that planetary orbits were circular. Kepler calculated that the planets traveled in elliptical orbits around the sun; this finding became his First Law. Copernicus held that planetary motion was uniform; Kepler's Second Law stated that the speed of the planets varied with their distance from the sun. Kepler also argued that magnetic forces between the sun and the planets kept the planets in orbital motion, an insight that paved the way for Newton's law of universal gravitation formulated nearly eighty years later, at the end of the seventeenth century.

Each of Kepler's works, beginning with *Cosmographic Mystery* in 1596 and continuing with *Astronomia Nova* in 1609 and *The Harmonies of the World* in 1619, revised and augmented Copernicus's theory. His version of Copernicanism fit with remarkable accuracy the best observations of the time (which were Tycho's). Kepler's search for rules of motion that could account for the earth's movements in its new position was also significant. More than Copernicus, Kepler broke down the distinction between the heavens and the earth that had been at the heart of Aristotelian physics.

TYCHO BRAHE, 1662. This seventeenth-century tribute shows the master astronomer in his observatory. ▪ *How much scientific knowledge does one need to understand this image?* ▪ *Is this image, which celebrates science and its accomplishments, itself a scientific statement?* ▪ *What can one learn about seventeenth-century science from such imagery?*

NEW HEAVENS, NEW EARTH, AND WORLDLY POLITICS: GALILEO

Kepler had a friend deliver a copy of *Cosmographic Mystery* to the "mathematician named Galileus Galileus," then teaching mathematics and astronomy at Padua, near Venice. Galileo (1564–1642) thanked Kepler in a letter that nicely illustrates the Italian's views at the time (1597).

> So far I have only perused the preface of your work, but from this I gained some notion of its intent, and I indeed congratulate myself of having an associate in the study of Truth who is a friend of Truth. . . . I adopted the teaching of Copernicus many years ago, and his point of view enables me to explain many phenomena of nature which certainly remain inexplicable according to the more current hypotheses. I have written many arguments in support of him and in refutation of the opposite view—which, however, so far I have not dared to bring into the public light. . . . I would certainly dare to publish my reflections at once if more people like you existed; as they don't, I shall refrain from doing so.

Kepler replied, urging Galileo to "come forward!" Galileo did not answer.

At Padua, Galileo couldn't teach what he believed; Ptolemaic astronomy and Aristotelian cosmology were the established curriculum. By the end of his career, however, Galileo had provided powerful evidence in support of the Copernican model and laid the foundation for a new physics. What was more, he wrote in the vernacular (Italian) as well as in Latin. Kepler may have been a "friend of Truth," but his work was abstruse and bafflingly mathematical. (So was Copernicus's.) By contrast, Galileo's writings were widely translated and widely read, raising awareness of changes in natural philosophy across Europe.

Ultimately, Galileo made the case for a new relationship between religion and science, challenging in the process some of the most powerful churchmen of his day. His discoveries made him the most famous scientific figure of his time, but his work put him on a collision course with Aristotelian philosophy and the authority of the Catholic Church.

Galileo became famous by way of discoveries with the telescope. In 1609, he heard reports from Holland of a lens grinder who had made a spyglass that could magnify very distant objects. Excited, Galileo quickly devised his own telescope; trained it first on earthly objects to demonstrate that it worked; and then, momentously, pointed

Interpreting Visual Evidence

Astronomical Observations and the Mapping of the Heavens

One (often-repeated) narrative about the scientific revolution is that it marked a crucial break separating modern science from an earlier period permeated by an atmosphere of superstition and theological speculation. In fact, medieval scholars tried hard to come up with empirical evidence for beliefs that their faith told them must be true, and without these traditions of observation, scientists like Copernicus would never have been led to propose alternative cosmologies (see "Ptolemaic Astronomical Instruments" on page 521).

The assumption, therefore, that the "new" sciences of the seventeenth century marked an extraordinary rupture with a more ignorant or superstitious past is thus not entirely correct. It would be closer to the truth to suggest that works such as that of Copernicus or Galileo provided a new context for assessing the relationship between observations and knowledge that came from other sources. Printed materials provided opportunities for early modern scientists to learn as much from each other as from more ancient sources.

The illustrations here are from scientific works on astronomy both before and after the appearance of Coperni-

A. The Ptolemaic universe, as depicted in Peter Apian, *Cosmographia* (1540).

B. The Copernican universe (1543).

it at the night sky. Galileo studied the moon, finding on it mountains, plains, and other features of an earthlike landscape. His observations suggested that celestial bodies resembled the earth, a view at odds with the conception of the heavens as an unchanging sphere of heavenly perfection, inherently and necessarily different from the earth. He saw moons orbiting Jupiter, evidence that earth was not at the center of all orbits. He saw spots on the sun. Galileo published these results, first in *The Starry Messenger* (1610) and then in *Letters on Sunspots* in 1613. *The Starry Messenger*, with its amazing reports of Jupiter's moons, was short, aimed to be read by many, and bold. It only hinted at Galileo's Copernicanism, however. The *Letters on Sunspots* declared it openly.

cus's work. All of them were based on some form of observation and claimed to be descriptive of the existing universe. Compare the abstract illustrations of the Ptolemaic (image A) and Copernican (image B) universes with Tycho Brahe's (image C) attempt to reconcile heliocentric observations with geocentric assumptions or with Galileo's illustration of sunspots (image D) observed through a telescope.

Questions for Analysis

1. What do these illustrations tell us about the relationship between knowledge and observation in sixteenth- and seventeenth-century science? What kinds of knowledge were necessary to produce these images?

2. Are the illustrations A and B intended to be visually accurate, in the sense that they represent what the eye sees?

Can one say the same of D? What makes Galileo's illustration of the sunspots different from the others?

3. Are the assumptions about observation contained in Galileo's drawing of sunspots (D) applicable to other sciences such as biology or chemistry? How so?

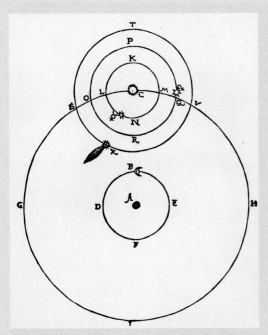

C. Brahe's universe (c. 1572, A, earth; B, moon; C, sun).

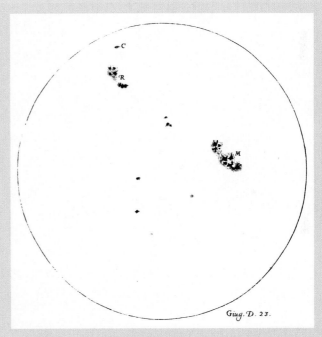

D. Galileo's sunspots, as observed through a telescope (1612).

A seventeenth-century scientist needed powerful and wealthy patrons. As a professor of mathematics, Galileo chafed at the power of university authorities who were subject to church control. Princely courts offered an inviting alternative. The Medici family of Tuscany, like others, burnished its reputation and bolstered its power by surrounding itself with intellectuals as well as artists. Per-

suaded he would be freer at its court than in Padua, Galileo took a position as tutor to the Medicis and flattered and successfully cultivated the family. He addressed *The Starry Messenger* to them. He named the newly discovered moons of Jupiter "the Medicean stars." He was rewarded with the title of chief mathematician and philosopher to Cosimo de' Medici, the grand duke of Tuscany. Now well positioned in Italy's networks of power and patronage, Galileo was able to pursue his goal of demonstrating that Copernicus's heliocentric (sun-centered) model of the planetary system was correct.

This pursuit, however, was a high-wire act, for he could not afford to antagonize the Catholic Church. In 1614, however, an ambitious and outspoken Dominican monk denounced Galileo's ideas as dangerous deviations from biblical teachings. Other philosophers and churchmen began to ask Galileo's patrons, the Medicis, whether their court mathematician was teaching heresy.

Disturbed by the murmurings against Copernicanism, Galileo penned a series of letters to defend himself, by addressing the relationship between natural philosophy and religion, and he argued that one could be a sincere Copernican and a sincere Catholic (see **Analyzing Primary Sources** on page 529). The Church, Galileo said, did

the sacred work of teaching scripture and saving souls. Accounting for the workings of the physical world was a task better left to natural philosophy, grounded in observation and mathematics. For the Church to take a side in controversies over natural science might compromise the Church's spiritual authority and credibility. Galileo envisioned natural philosophers and theologians as partners in a search for truth, but with very different roles. In a brilliant rhetorical moment, he quoted Cardinal Baronius in support of his own argument: the purpose of the Bible was to "teach us how to go to heaven, not how heaven goes."

Nevertheless, in 1616, the Church moved against Galileo. The Inquisition ruled that Copernicanism was "foolish and absurd in philosophy and formally heretical." Copernicus's *De Revolutionibus* was placed on the Index of Prohibited Books, and Galileo was warned not to teach Copernicanism.

GALILEO GALILEI BEFORE THE INQUISITION BY FRANÇOIS FLEURY-RICHARD. This nineteenth-century painting of Galileo before the Holy Office dramatizes the conflict between science and religion and depicts the Italian natural philosopher as defiant. In fact, Galileo submitted but continued his work under house arrest and published, secretly, in the Netherlands. ▪ *Would Galileo himself have subscribed to the message of this much later painting, that religion and science were opposed to one another?*

Galileo on Nature, Scripture, and Truth

One of the clearest statements of Galileo's convictions about religion and science comes from his 1615 letter to the grand duchess Christina, mother of Galileo's patron, Cosimo de' Medici, and a powerful figure in her own right. Galileo knew that others objected to his work. The church had warned him that Copernicanism was inaccurate and impious; it could be disproved scientifically, and it contradicted the authority of those who interpreted the Bible. Thoroughly dependent on the Medicis for support, he wrote to the grand duchess to explain his position. In this section of the letter, Galileo sets out his understanding of the parallel but distinct roles of the Church and natural philosophers. He walks a fine line between acknowledging the authority of the Church and standing firm in his convictions.

Possibly because they are disturbed by the known truth of other propositions of mine which differ from those commonly held, and therefore mistrusting their defense so long as they confine themselves to the field of philosophy, these men have resolved to fabricate a shield for their fallacies out of the mantle of pretended religion and the authority of the Bible. . . .

Copernicus never discusses matters of religion or faith, nor does he use arguments that depend in any way upon the authority of sacred writings which he might have interpreted erroneously. He stands always upon physical conclusions pertaining to the celestial motions, and deals with them by astronomical and geometrical demonstrations, founded primarily upon sense experiences and very exact observations. He did not ignore the Bible, but he knew very well that if his doctrine were proved, then it could not contradict the Scriptures when they were rightly understood. . . .

I think that in discussions of physical problems we ought to begin not from the authority of scriptural passages, but from sense-experiences and necessary demonstrations; for the holy Bible and the phenomena of nature proceed alike from the divine Word, the former as the dictate of the Holy Ghost and the latter as the observant executrix of God's commands. It is necessary for the Bible, in order to be accommodated to the understanding of every man, to speak many things which appear to differ from the absolute truth so far as the bare meaning of the words is concerned. But Nature, on the other hand, is inexorable and immutable; she never transgresses the laws imposed upon her, or cares a whit whether her abstruse reasons and methods of operation are understandable to men. For that reason it appears that nothing physical which sense-experience sets before our eyes, or which necessary demonstrations prove to us, ought to be called in question (much less condemned) upon the testimony of biblical passages which may have some different meaning beneath their words. For the Bible is not chained in every expression to conditions as strict as those which govern all physical effects; nor is God any less excellently revealed in Nature's actions than in the sacred statements of the Bible. . . .

Source: Galileo, "Letter to the Grand Duchess Christina," in *The Discoveries and Opinions of Galileo Galilei*, ed. Stillman Drake (Garden City, NY: 1957), pp. 177–83.

Questions for Analysis

1. How does Galileo deal with the contradictions between the evidence of his senses and biblical teachings?

2. For Galileo, what is the relationship between God, man, and nature?

3. Why did Galileo need to defend his views in a letter to Christina de' Medici?

For a while, he did as he was asked. But when his Florentine friend and admirer Maffeo Barberini was elected pope as Urban VIII in 1623, Galileo believed the door to Copernicanism was (at least half) open. He drafted one of his most famous works, *A Dialogue Concerning the Two Chief World Systems* published in 1632. The *Dialogue* was a hypothetical debate between supporters of the old Ptolemaic system, represented by a character he named Simplicio (simpleton), on the one hand, and proponents of the new astronomy, on the other. Throughout, Galileo gave the best lines to the Copernicans. At the very end, however, to satisfy the letter of the Inquisition's decree, he had them capitulate to Simplicio.

The Inquisition banned the *Dialogue* and ordered Galileo to stand trial in 1633. Pope Urban, provoked by Galileo's scorn and needing support from Church conservatives during a difficult stretch of the Thirty Years' War, refused to protect his former friend. The verdict of the secret trial shocked Europe. The Inquisition forced Galileo to repent his Copernican position, banned him from working on or even discussing Copernican ideas, and placed him under house arrest for life. According to a story that began to circulate shortly afterward, as he left the court for house arrest he stamped his foot and muttered defiantly, looking down at the earth: "Still, it moves."

The Inquisition could not put Galileo off his life's work. He refined the theories of motion he had begun to develop early in his career. He proposed an early version of the theory of inertia, which held that an object's motion stays the same until an outside force changed it. He calculated that objects of different weights fall at almost the same speed and with a uniform acceleration. He argued that the motion of objects follows regular mathematical laws. The same laws that govern the motions of objects on earth (which could be observed in experiments) could also be observed in the heavens—again a direct contradiction of Aristotelian principles and an important step toward a coherent physics based on a sun-centered model of the universe. Compiled under the title *Two New Sciences* (1638), this work was smuggled out of Italy and published in Protestant Holland.

Among Galileo's legacies, however, was exactly the rift between religion and science that he had hoped to avoid. Galileo believed that Copernicanism and natural philosophy in general need not subvert theological truths, religious belief, or the authority of the Church. But his trial seemed to show the contrary, that natural philosophy and Church authority could not coexist. Galileo's trial silenced Copernican voices in southern Europe, and the Church's leadership retreated into conservative reaction. It was therefore in northwest Europe that the new philosophy Galileo had championed would flourish.

METHODS FOR A NEW PHILOSOPHY: BACON AND DESCARTES

As the practice of the new sciences became concentrated in Protestant northwest Europe, new thinkers began to spell out standards of practice and evidence. Sir Francis Bacon and René Descartes (*deh-KAHRT*) loomed especially large

in this development, setting out methods or the rules that should govern modern science. Bacon (1561–1626) lived at roughly the same time as Kepler and Galileo—and Shakespeare; Descartes (1596–1650) was slightly younger. Both Bacon and Descartes came to believe that theirs was an age of profound change, open to the possibility of astonishing discovery. Both were persuaded that knowledge could take the European moderns beyond the ancient authorities. Both set out to formulate a philosophy to encompass the learning of their age.

FRONTISPIECE TO BACON'S *NOVUM ORGANUM* (1620). The illustration suggests that scientific work is like a voyage of discovery, similar to a ship setting out through uncharted waters. Is it a voyage of conquest? Compare this image with the fanciful image of Tycho Brahe at work in his observatory (page 525).

■ *What metaphors and allegorical imagery did scientists use during this period to characterize the significance of their work?*

"Knowledge is power." The phrase is Bacon's and captures the changing perspective of the seventeenth century and its new confidence in the potential of human thinking. Bacon trained as a lawyer, served in Parliament and, briefly, as lord chancellor to James I of England. His abiding concern was with the assumptions, methods, and practices that he believed should guide natural philosophers and the progress of knowledge. The authority of the ancients should not constrain the ambition of modern thinkers. Deferring to accepted doctrines could block innovation or obstruct understanding. "There is but one course left . . . to try the whole thing anew upon a better plan, and to commence a total reconstruction of sciences, arts, and all human knowledge, raised upon the proper foundations." To pursue knowledge did not mean to think abstractly and leap to conclusions; it meant observing, experimenting, confirming ideas, or demonstrating points. If thinkers will be "content to begin with doubts," Bacon wrote, "they shall end with certainties." We thus associate Bacon with the gradual separation of scientific investigation from philosophical argument.

Bacon advocated an *inductive* approach to knowledge: amassing evidence from specific observations to draw general conclusions. In Bacon's view, many philosophical errors arose from beginning with assumed first principles. The traditional view of the cosmos, for instance, rested on the principles of a prime mover and the perfection of circular motion for planets and stars. The inductive method required accumulating data (as Tycho had done, for example) and then, after careful review and experiment, drawing appropriate conclusions about the motions of heavenly bodies. Bacon argued that scientific knowledge was best tested through the cooperative efforts of researchers performing experiments that could be repeated and verified. The knowledge thus gained would be predictable and useful to philosophers and artisans alike, contributing to a wide range of endeavors from astronomy to shipbuilding.

Bacon's vision of science and progress is vividly illustrated by two images. The first, more familiar, is the title page of Bacon's *Novum Organum* (1620) with its bold ships sailing out beyond the Straits of Gibraltar, formerly the limits of the West, into the open sea, in pursuit of unknown but

FROM RENÉ DESCARTES, *L'HOMME* (1729; ORIGINALLY PUBLISHED AS *DE HOMINI*, 1662). Descartes's interest in the body as a mechanism led him to suppose that physics and mathematics could be used to understand all aspects of human physiology, and his work had an important influence on subsequent generations of medical researchers. In this illustration, Descartes depicts the optical properties of the human eye. ▪ *How might such a mechanistic approach to human perception have been received by proponents of Baconian science, who depended so much on the reliability of human observations?*

The New Science and The Foundations of Certainty

Francis Bacon (1561–1626) and René Descartes (1596–1650) were both enthusiastic supporters of science in the seventeenth century, but they differed in their opinions regarding the basis for certainty in scientific argumentation. Bacon's inductive method emphasized the gathering of particular observations about natural phenomena, which he believed could be used as evidence to support more general conclusions about causes, regularity, and order in the natural world. Descartes, on the other hand, defended a deductive method: he believed that certainty could be built only by reasoning from first principles that one knew to be true and was less certain of the value of evidence that came from the senses alone.

Aphorisms from *Novum Organum*

XXXI

It is idle to expect any advancement in science from the super-inducing and engrafting of new things upon old. We must begin anew from the very foundations, unless we would revolve forever in a circle with mean and contemptible progress....

XXXVI

One method of delivery alone remains to us which is simply this: we must lead men to the particulars themselves, and their series and order; while men on their side must force themselves for a while to lay their notions by and begin to familiarize themselves with facts....

XLV

The human understanding of its own nature is prone to suppose the existence of more order and regularity in the world than it finds. And though there be many things in nature which are singular and unmatched, yet it devises for them parallels and conjugates and relatives which do not exist. Hence the fiction that all celestial bodies move in perfect circles.... Hence too the element of fire with its orb is brought in, to make up the square with the other three which the sense perceives.... And so on of other dreams. And these fancies affect not dogmas only, but simple notions also....

XCV

Those who have handled sciences have been either men of experiment or men of dogmas. The men of experiment are like the ant, they only collect and use; the reasoners resemble spiders, who make cobwebs out of their own substance. But the bee takes a middle course: it gathers its material from the flowers of the garden and of the field, but transforms and digests it by a power of its own. Not unlike this is the true business of philosophy; for it neither relies solely or chiefly on the powers of the mind, nor does it take the matter which it gathers from natural history and mechanical experiments and lay it up in the memory whole ... but lays it up in the understanding altered and digested. Therefore, from a closer and purer league between these two faculties, the experimental and the rational (such as has never yet been made), much may be hoped....

Source: Michael R. Matthews, ed., *The Scientific Background to Modern Philosophy: Selected Readings* (Indianapolis, IN: 1989), pp. 47–48, 50–52.

From *A Discourse on Method*

Just as a great number of laws is often a pretext for wrong-doing, with the result that a state is much better governed when, having only a few, they are strictly observed; so also I came to believe that in the place of the great number of precepts that go to make up logic, the following four would be sufficient for my purposes, provided that I took a firm but unshakeable decision never once to depart from them.

The first was never to accept anything as true that I did not *incontrovertibly* know to be so; that is to say, carefully to avoid both *prejudice* and premature conclusions; and to include nothing in my judgments other than that which presented itself to my mind so *clearly* and *distinctly*, that I would have no occasion to doubt it.

The second was to divide all the difficulties under examination into as many parts as possible, and as many as were required to solve them in the best way.

The third was to conduct my thoughts in a given order, beginning with the *simplest* and most easily understood objects, and gradually ascending, as it were step by step, to the knowledge of the most *complex*; and *positing* an order even on those which do not have a natural order of precedence.

The last was to undertake such complete enumerations and such general surveys that I would be sure to have left nothing out.

The long chain of reasonings, every one simple and easy, which geometers habitually employ to reach their most difficult proofs had given me cause to suppose that all those things which fall within the domain of human understanding follow on from each other in the same way, and that as long as one stops oneself taking anything to be true that is not true and sticks to the right order so as to deduce one thing from another, there can be nothing so remote that one cannot eventually reach it, nor so hidden that one cannot discover it. . . .

[B]ecause I wished . . . to concentrate on the pursuit of truth, I came to think that I should . . . reject as completely false everything in which I could

detect the least doubt, in order to see if anything thereafter remained in my belief that was completely indubitable. And so, because our senses sometimes deceive us, I decided to suppose that nothing was such as they lead us to imagine it to be. And because there are men who make mistakes in reasoning, even about the simplest elements of geometry, and commit logical fallacies, I judged that I was as prone to error as anyone else, and I rejected as false all the reasoning I had hitherto accepted as valid proof. Finally, considering that all the same thoughts which we have while awake can come to us while asleep without any one of them then being true, I resolved to pretend that everything that had ever entered my head was no more true than the illusions of my dreams. But immediately afterwards I noted that, while I was trying to think of all things being false in this way, it was necessarily the case that I, who was thinking them, had to be something; and observing this truth: *I am thinking therefore I exist*, was so secure and certain that it could not be shaken by any of the most extravagant suppositions of the sceptics, I judged that I could accept it without scruple,

as the first principle of the philosophy I was seeking.

Source: René Descartes, *A Discourse on the Method,* trans. Ian Maclean (New York: 2006), pp. 17–18, 28.

Questions for Analysis

1. Descartes's idea of certainty depended on a "long chain of reasonings" that departed from certain axioms that could not be doubted and rejected evidence from the senses. What science provided him with the model for this idea of certainty? What was the first thing that he felt he could be certain about? Did he trust his senses?

2. Bacon's idea of certainty pragmatically sought to combine the benefits of sensory knowledge and experience (gathered by "ants") with the understandings arrived at through reason (cobwebs constructed by "spiders"). How would Descartes have responded to Bacon's claims? According to Bacon, was Descartes an ant or a spider?

3. What do these two thinkers have in common?

---

great things to come. The second is Bacon's description of an imagined factory of discovery, "Solomon's house," at end of his utopian *New Atlantis* (1626). Inside the factory, "sifters" would examine and conduct experiments, passing on findings to senior researchers who would draw conclusions and develop practical applications. The work of these scholars would be supplemented by accounts sent in by their emissaries abroad, traveling ambassadors of science who would gather data and information about the natural world and human societies in other places. Bacon's utopian image of

patient researchers and experimenters anticipated the modern university.

René Descartes was French, though he lived all over Europe. He was intellectually restless as well; he worked in geometry, cosmology, optics, and physiology—for a while dissecting cow carcasses daily. He was writing a (Copernican) book on physics when he heard of Galileo's condemnation in 1633, a judgment that impressed on him the dangers of "expressing judgements on this world." Descartes's *Discourse on Method* (1637), for which he is best known, began simply as a preface to three essays on optics, geometry, and meteorology. It is personal, recounting Descartes's dismay at the "strange and unbelievable" theories he encountered in his traditional education. His first response, as he described it, was to systematically doubt everything he had ever known or been taught. Better to clear the slate, he believed, than to build an edifice of knowledge on received assumptions. His first rule was "never to receive anything as a truth which [he] did not clearly know to be such." He took the human ability to think as his point of departure, summed up in his famous and enigmatic *Je pense, donc je suis,* later translated into Latin as *cogito ergo sum* and into English as "I think, therefore I am." As the phrase suggests, Descartes's doubting led (quickly, by our standards) to self-assurance and truth: the thinking individual existed, reason existed, God existed. For Descartes, then, doubt was a ploy, or a piece that he used in an intellectual chess game to defeat skepticism. Certainty, not doubt, was the centerpiece of the philosophy he bequeathed to his followers.

Descartes, like Bacon, sought a "fresh start for knowledge" or the rules for understanding of the world as it was. Unlike Bacon, Descartes emphasized *deductive* reasoning, proceeding logically from one certainty to another. "So long as we avoid accepting as true what is not so," he wrote in *Discourse on Method,* "and always preserve the right order of deduction of one thing from another, there can be nothing too remote to be reached in the end, or too well hidden to be discovered." For Descartes, mathematical thought expressed the highest standards of reason, and his work contributed greatly to the authority of mathematics as a model for scientific reasoning.

Descartes made a particularly forceful statement for *mechanism,* a view of the world shared by Bacon and Galileo and one that came to dominate seventeenth-century scientific thought. As the name suggested, mechanical philosophy proposed to consider nature as a machine. It rejected the traditional Aristotelian distinction between the works of humans and those of nature and the view that nature, as God's creation, necessarily belonged to a different—and higher—order. In the new picture of the universe that was emerging from the discoveries and writings of the early seventeenth century, it seemed that all matter was composed of the same material and all motion obeyed the same laws. Descartes sought to explain everything, including the human body, mechanically. As he put it firmly, "There is no difference between the machines built by artisans and the diverse bodies that nature alone composes." Nature operated according to regular and predictable laws and was thus accessible to human reason. The belief guided, indeed inspired, much of the scientific experiment and argument of the seventeenth century.

The Power of Method and the Force of Curiosity: Seventeenth-Century Experimenters

For nearly a century after Bacon and Descartes, most of England's natural philosophers were Baconian, and most of their colleagues in France, Holland, and elsewhere in northern Europe were Cartesians (followers of Descartes). The English Baconians concentrated on performing experiments in many different fields, producing results that could then be debated and discussed. The Cartesians turned instead toward mathematics and logic. Descartes himself pioneered analytical geometry. Blaise Pascal (1623–1662) worked on probability theory and invented a calculating machine before applying his intellectual skills to theology. The Cartesian thinker Christian Huygens (1629–1695) from Holland combined mathematics with experiments to understand problems of impact and orbital motion. The Dutch Cartesian Baruch Spinoza (1632–1677) applied geometry to ethics and believed he had gone beyond Descartes by proving that the universe was composed of a single substance that was both God and nature.

English experimenters pursued a different course. They began with practical research, putting the alchemist's tool, the laboratory, to new uses. They also sought a different kind of conclusion: empirical laws or provisional generalizations based on evidence rather than absolute statements of deductive truth. Among the many English laboratory scientists of the era were the physician William Harvey (1578–1657), the chemist Robert Boyle (1627–1691), and the inventor and experimenter Robert Hooke (1635–1703).

Harvey's contribution was enormous: he observed and explained that blood circulated through the arteries, heart, and veins. To do this, he was willing to dissect living animals (vivisection) and experiment on himself. Boyle performed experiments and established a law (known as Boyle's law) showing that at a constant temperature the volume of a gas decreases in proportion to the pressure placed on it. Hooke introduced the microscope to the experimenter's tool kit. The compound microscope had been invented in Holland early in the seventeenth century. But it was not until the 1660s that Hooke and others demonstrated its potential by using it to study the cellular structure of plants. Like the telescope before it, the microscope revealed an unexpected dimension of material phenomena. Examining even the most ordinary objects revealed detailed structures of perfectly connected smaller parts and persuaded many that

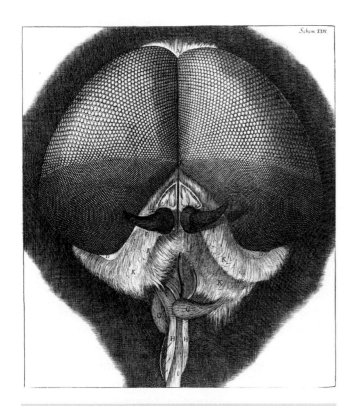

newly crowned King Charles II granted a group of natural philosophers and mathematicians a royal charter (1662) to establish the Royal Society of London, for the "improvement of natural knowledge" and committed to experimentation and collaborative work among natural philosophers. The founders of the Royal Society, in particular Boyle, believed it could serve a political as well as an intellectual purpose. The Royal Society would pursue Bacon's goal of collective research in which members would conduct formal experiments, record the results, and share them with other members. These members would in turn study the methods, reproduce the experiment, and assess the outcome. The enterprise would give England's natural philosophers a common sense of purpose and a system to reach reasoned, gentlemanly agreement on "matters of fact." By separating systematic scientific research from the dangerous language of politics and religion that had marked the civil war, the Royal Society could also help restore a sense of order and consensus to English intellectual life.

with improved instruments they would uncover even more of the world's intricacies.

The microscope also provided what many regarded as new evidence of God's existence. The way each minute structure of a living organism, when viewed under a microscope, corresponded to its purpose testified not only to God's existence but to God's wisdom as well. The mechanical philosophy did not exclude God but in fact could be used to confirm his presence. If the universe was a clock, after all, there must be a clock maker. Hooke himself declared that only imbeciles would believe that what they saw under the microscope was "the production of chance" rather than of God's creation.

The State, Scientific Academies, and Women Scientists

Seventeenth-century state building (see Chapter 14) helped secure the rise of science. In 1660, England's monarchy was restored after two decades of revolution and civil war. The

OBSERVING THE TRANSIT OF VENUS (1673). Elisabetha (1647–1693) and Johannes Hevelius (1611–1687) believed that precise observations about the timing of Venus's passage across the face of the sun when observed from different parts of the earth could be used to calculate the distance from the earth to the sun. This German-speaking husband and wife astronomy team from Gdansk in present-day Poland worked together on many of their projects. After Johannes's death, Elisabetha published their jointly written star catalog.

Analyzing Primary Sources

Gassendi on the Science of Observation and the Human Soul

Pierre Gassendi (1592–1655) was a seventeenth-century French Catholic priest and philosopher. A contemporary of Descartes's, Gassendi was part of a group of intellectuals in France who sought a new philosophy of nature that could replace the traditional teachings of Aristotle that had been so severely criticized by Copernicus and his followers. Gassendi had no doubt that his faith as a Christian was compatible with his enthusiasm for the new sciences of observation, but in order to demonstrate this to his contemporaries he had to show that the mechanical explanations of the universe and the natural world did not necessarily lead to a heretical materialism or atheism. In the following passage, taken from his posthumously published work Syntagma Philosophicum *(1658), Gassendi attempted to demonstrate that one might infer the existence of the human soul, even if it was not accessible to the senses.*

There are many such things for which with the passage of time helpful appliances are being found that will make them visible to the senses. For example, take the little animal the mite, which is born under the skin; the senses perceived it as a certain unitary little point without parts; but since, however, the senses saw that it moved by itself, reason had deduced from this motion as from a perceptible sign that this little body was an animal and because its forward motion was somewhat like a turtle's, reason added that it must get about by the use of certain tiny legs and feet. And although this truth would have been hidden to the senses, which never perceived these limbs, the microscope was recently invented by which sight could perceive that matters were actually as predicted. Likewise, the question had been raised what the galaxy in the sky with the name of the Milky Way was. Democritus, concerning whom it was said that even when he did not know something he was knowing, had deduced from the perceptible sign of its filmy whiteness that it was nothing more than an innumerable multitude of closely packed little stars which could not be seen separately, but produced that effect of spilt milk when many of them were joined together. This truth had become known to him, and yet had remained undisclosed to the senses until our day and age, until the moment that the telescope, recently discovered, made it clear that things were in fact what he had said. But there are many such things which, though they were hidden from the ancients, have now been made manifest for our eyes. And who knows but a great many of those which are concealed in our time, which we perceive only through the intelligence, will one day also be clearly perceived by the senses through the agency of some helpful appliance thought up by our descendants? . . .

Secondly, if someone wonders whether a certain body is endowed with a soul or not, the senses are not at all capable of determining that by taking a look as it were at the soul itself; yet there are operations which when they come to the senses' notice, lead the intellect to deduce as from a sign that there is some soul beneath them. You will say that this sign belongs to the empirical type, but it is not at all of that type, for it is not even one of the indicative signs since it does not inform us of something that the senses have ever perceived in conjunction with the sign, as they have seen fire with smoke, but informs us instead of something that has always been impenetrable to the senses themselves, like our skin's pores or the mite's feet before the microscope.

You will persist with the objection that we should not ask so much whether there is a soul in a body as what its nature is, if it is the cause of such operations, just as there is no question that there is a force attracting iron in a magnet or that there is a tide in the sea, but there are questions over what their nature is or what they are caused by. But let me omit these matters which are to be fully treated elsewhere, and let it be enough if we say that not every truth can be known by the mind, but at least some can concerning something otherwise hidden, or not obvious to the senses themselves. And we bring up the example of the soul both because vital action is proposed by Sextus Empiricus as an example of an indicative sign and because even though it pertains not so much to the nature of the soul as to its existence, still a truth of existence of such magnitude as this, which it is most valuable for us to know, is made indisputable. For when among other questions we hear it asked if God is or exists in the universe, that is a truth of existence which it would be a great service to establish firmly even if it is not proven at the same time what he is or what his nature is. Although God is such that he can no more come under the perusal of the senses than the soul can, still we infer that the soul exists in the body from the actions that occur before the senses and are so peculiarly appropriate to a soul that if one were not present, they would not be either. In the same way we deduce that God exists in the universe from his effects perceived by the senses, which could not be produced by anything but God and which therefore would not be observed unless God were present in the world, such as the great order of the universe, its great beauty, its grandeur, its harmony, which are so great that they can only result from a sovereignly wise, good, powerful, and inexhaustible cause. But these things will be treated elsewhere at greater length.

Source: Craig B. Brush, ed., *The Selected Works of Pierre Gassendi* (New York: 1972), pp. 334–36.

Questions for Analysis

1. What is the relationship between new knowledge and new scientific tools (the microscope and the telescope) in Gassendi's examples of the mite and the Milky Way? Is he a Baconian or a Cartesian?

2. What are the limitations of the senses when it comes to questions of the human soul, according to Gassendi?

3. Given these limitations, does Gassendi conclude that science will never be able to say anything about his religious faith?

The society's journal, *Philosophical Transactions,* reached out to professional scholars and experimenters throughout Europe. Similar societies began to appear elsewhere. The French Academy of Sciences was founded in 1666 and was also tied to seventeenth-century state building, in this case Bourbon absolutism (see Chapter 15). Royal societies, devoted to natural philosophy as a collective enterprise, provided a state (or princely) sponsored framework for science and an alternative to the important but uncertain patronage of smaller nobles or to the religious (and largely conservative, Aristotelian) universities. Scientific societies reached rough agreement about what constituted legitimate research. They established the modern scientific custom of crediting discoveries to those who were first to publish results. They enabled information and theories to be exchanged more easily across national boundaries, although philosophical differences among Cartesians, Baconians, and traditional Aristotelians remained very difficult to bridge. Science began to take shape as a discipline.

The early scientific academies did not have explicit rules barring women, but with few exceptions they contained only male members. This did not mean that women did not practice science, though their participation in scientific research and debate remained controversial. In some cases, the new science could itself become a justification for women's inclusion, as when the Cartesian philosopher François Poullain de la Barre used anatomy to declare in 1673 that "the mind has no sex." Since women possessed the same physical senses as men and the same nervous systems and brains, Poullain asked, why should they not equally occupy the same roles in society? In fact, historians have discovered more than a few women who taught at European universities in the sixteenth and seventeenth centuries, above all in Italy. Elena Cornaro Piscopia received her doctorate of philosophy in Padua in 1678, the first woman to do so. Laura Bassi became a professor of physics at the University of Bologna after receiving her doctorate there in 1733, and based on her exceptional contributions to mathematics she became a member of the Academy of Science in Bologna. Her papers—including titles such as "On the Compression of Air" (1746), "On the Bubbles Observed in Freely Flowing Fluid" (1747), "On Bubbles of Air That Escape from Fluids" (1748)—gained her a stipend from the academy.

Italy appears to have been an exception in allowing women to get formal recognition for their education and research in established institutions. Elsewhere, elite women could educate themselves by associating with learned men. The aristocratic Margaret Cavendish (1623–1673), a natural philosopher in England, gleaned the information necessary to start her career from her family and their friends, a network that included Thomas Hobbes and, while in exile in France in the 1640s, René Descartes. These connections were not enough to overcome the isolation she felt working in a world of letters that was still largely the preserve of men, but this did not prevent her from developing her own speculative natural philosophy and using it to critique those who would exclude her from scientific debate. The "tyrannical government" of men over women, she wrote, "hath so dejected our spirits, that we are become so stupid, that

FROM MARIA SYBILLA MERIAN, *METAMORPHOSIS OF THE INSECTS OF SURINAM* (1705). Merian, the daughter of a Frankfurt engraver, learned in her father's workshop the skills necessary to become an important early entymologist and scientific illustrator and conducted her research on two continents.

kept on in such capacity, mouths would gape even wider." In spite of this rejection, Winkelmann continued to work as an astronomer, training both her son and two daughters in the discipline.

Like Winkelmann, the entymologist Maria Sibylla Merian (1647–1717) also made a career based on observation. And like Winkelmann, Merian was able to carve out a space for her scientific work by exploiting the precedent of guild women who learned their trade in family workshops. Merian was the daughter of an engraver and illustrator in Frankfurt, and she served as an informal apprentice to her father before beginning her own career as a scientific illustrator, specializing in detailed engravings of insects and plants. Traveling to the Dutch colony of Surinam, Merian supported herself and her two daughters by selling exotic insects and animals she collected and brought back to Europe. She fought the colony's sweltering climate and malaria to publish her most important scientific work, *Metamorphosis of the Insects of Surinam*, which detailed the life cycles of Surinam's insects in sixty ornate illustrations. Merian's *Metamorphosis* was well received in her time; in fact, Peter I of Russia proudly displayed Merian's portrait and books in his study.

"AND ALL WAS LIGHT": ISAAC NEWTON

Sir Isaac Newton's work marks the culmination of the scientific revolution. Galileo, peering through his telescope in the early 1600s, had come to believe that the earth and the heavens were made of the same material. Galileo's experiments with pendulums aimed to discover the laws of motion, and he proposed theories of inertia. It was Newton who articulated those laws and presented a coherent, unified vision of how the universe worked. All bodies in the universe, Newton said, whether on earth or in the heavens, obeyed the same basic laws. One set of forces and one pattern, which could be expressed mathematically, explained why planets orbited in ellipses and why (and at what speed) apples fell from trees. An Italian mathematician later commented that Newton was the "greatest and most fortunate of mortals"—because there was only one universe, and he had discovered its laws.

Isaac Newton (1642–1727) was born on Christmas Day to a family of small landowners. His father died before his birth, and it fell to a succession of relatives, family friends, and schoolmasters to spot, then encourage, his genius. In

beasts being but a degree below us, men use us but a degree above beasts. Whereas in nature we have as clear an understanding as men, if we are bred in schools to mature our brains."

The construction of observatories in private residences enabled some women living in such homes to work their way into the growing field of astronomy. Between 1650 and 1710, 14 percent of German astronomers were women, the most famous of whom was Maria Winkelmann (1670–1720). Winkelmann had worked with her husband, Gottfried Kirch, in his observatory, and when he died she had already done significant work, discovering a comet and preparing calendars for the Berlin Academy of Sciences. When Kirch died, she petitioned the academy to take her husband's place in the prestigious body but was rejected. Gottfried Leibniz, the academy's president, explained, "Already during her husband's lifetime the society was burdened with ridicule because its calendar was prepared by a woman. If she were now to be

NEWTON'S EXPERIMENTS WITH LIGHT (1672). Newton's own sketch (left) elegantly displays the way he proved that white light was made up of differently colored light rays. Earlier scientists had explained the color spectrum produced by shining sunlight through a prism by insisting that the colors were a by-product of contaminating elements within the prism's glass. Newton disproved this theory by shining the sunlight through two consecutive prisms. The first produced the characteristic division of light into a color spectrum. When one of these colored beams passed through a second prism, however, it emerged on the other side unchanged, demonstrating that the glass itself was not the cause of the dispersal. He was not yet thirty when he published the results of this experiment.

1661, he entered Trinity College in Cambridge University, where he would remain for the next thirty-five years, first as a student, then as the Lucasian Professor of Mathematics. The man who came to represent the personification of modern science was reclusive, secretive about his findings, and obsessive. During his early work with optics, he experimented with his own eyes, pressing them to see how different shapes would change the effects of light and then, intrigued by what he found, inserting a very thick needle "betwixt my eye and the bone as neare to the backside of my eye as I could" to actually curve his eyeball. (Please do not try this at home.)

Newton's first great burst of creativity came at Cambridge in the years from 1664 to 1666, "the prime of my age for invention." During these years, Newton broke new ground in three areas. The first was optics. Descartes believed that color was a secondary quality produced by the speed of particulate rotation but that light itself was white. Newton, using prisms he had purchased at a local fair, showed that white light was composed of different-colored rays (see image on this page). The second area in which Newton produced innovative work during these years was in mathematics. In a series of brilliant insights, he invented both integral calculus and differential calculus, providing mathematical tools to model motion in space. The third area of his creative genius involved his early works on gravity. Newton later told different versions of the same story: the idea about gravity had come to him when he was in a "contemplative mood" and was "occasioned by the fall of an apple." Why did the apple "not go sideways or upwards, but constantly to the earth's center?...Assuredly the reason is, that the earth draws it. There must be a drawing power in matter." Voltaire, the eighteenth-century French essayist, retold the story to dramatize Newton's simple brilliance. But the theory of gravity rested on mathematical formulations, it was far from simple, and it would not be fully worked out until *Principia,* more than twenty years later.

Newton's work on the composite nature of white light led him to make a reflecting telescope, which used a curved mirror rather than lenses. The telescope earned him election to the Royal Society (in 1672) and drew him out of his sheltered obscurity at Cambridge. Encouraged by the Royal Society's support, he wrote a paper describing his theory of optics and allowed it to be published in *Philosophical Transactions.* Astronomers and scientists across Europe applauded the work. Robert Hooke, the Royal Society's curator of experiments, did not. Hooke was not persuaded by Newton's mode of argument; he found Newton's claims that science had to be mathematical both dogmatic and high-handed; and he objected—in a series of sharp exchanges with the reclusive genius—that Newton had not provided any physical explanation for his results. Stung by the conflict with Hooke and persuaded that few natural philosophers could understand his theories, Newton withdrew to Cambridge and long refused to share his work. Only the patient effort of friends and fellow scientists like the astronomer Edmond Halley (1656–1742), already well known for his astronomical observations in the Southern Hemisphere and the person for whom Halley's Comet is named, convinced Newton to publish again.

Newton's *Principia Mathematica* (Mathematical Principles of Natural Philosophy) was published in 1687. It was prompted by a visit from Halley, in which the astronomer asked Newton for his ideas on a question being discussed at the Royal Society: was there a mathematical basis for the elliptical orbits of the planets? Halley's question inspired Newton to expand calculations he had made earlier into an all-encompassing theory of celestial—and terrestrial—dynamics. Halley not only encouraged Newton's work but supervised and financed its publication (though he had less money than Newton); and on several occasions he had to persuade Newton, enraged again by reports of criticism from Hooke and others, to continue with the project and to commit his findings to print.

Principia was long and difficult—purposefully so, for Newton said he did not want to be "baited by little smatterers in mathematics." Its central proposition was that gravitation was a universal force and one that could be expressed mathematically. Newton built on Galileo's work on inertia, Kepler's findings concerning the elliptical orbits of planets, the work of Boyle and Descartes, and even his rival Hooke's work on gravity. He once said, "If

I have seen further, it is by standing on the shoulders of giants." But Newton's universal theory of gravity, although it drew on work of others before him, formulated something entirely new. His synthesis offered a single, descriptive account of mass and motion. "All bodies whatsoever are endowed with a principle of mutual gravitation." The law of gravitation was stated in a mathematical formula and supported by observation and experience; it was, literally, universal.

The scientific elite of Newton's time was not uniformly persuaded. Many mechanical philosophers, particularly Cartesians, objected to the prominence in Newton's theory of forces acting across empty space. Such attractions smacked of mysticism (or the occult); they seemed to lack any driving mechanism. Newton responded to these criticisms in a note added to the next edition of the *Principia (General Scholium,* 1713). He did not know what *caused* gravity, he said, and he did not "feign hypotheses." "For whatever is not deduced from the phenomena must be called hypothesis," he wrote, and has "no place in the experimental philosophy." For Newton, certainty

NEWTON AND SATIRE. The English artist and satirist William Hogarth mocking both philosophy and "Newton worship" in 1763. The philosophers' heads are being weighed on a scale that runs from "absolute gravity" to "absolute levity" or "stark fool."

Analyzing Primary Sources

Newton on the Purposes of Experimental Philosophy

When Newton added his General Scholium to the second edition of Principia *in 1713, he was seventy-one, president of the Royal Society, and widely revered. Responding to continental critics, he set out his general views on science and its methods, arguing against purely deductive reasoning and reliance on hypotheses about ultimate causes.*

itherto we have explained the phenomena of the heavens and of our sea by the power of gravity, but have not yet assigned the cause of this power. This is certain, that it must proceed from a cause that penetrates to the very centres of the sun and planets, without suffering the least diminution of its force; that operates not according to the quantity of the surfaces of the particles on which it acts (as mechanical causes used to do), but according to the quantity of the solid matter which they contain, and propagates its virtue on all sides to immense distances, decreasing always as the inverse square of the distances. . . . [H]itherto I have not been able to discover the cause of those properties of gravity from phenomena, and I frame no hypothesis; for whatever is not deduced from the phenomena is to be called an hypothesis and hypotheses, whether metaphysical or physical, whether of occult qualities or mechanical, have no place in experimental philosophy. In this philosophy particular propositions are inferred from the phenomena, and afterwards rendered general by induction. . . . And to us it is enough that gravity does really exist, and acts according to the laws which we have explained, and abundantly serves to account for all the motions of the celestial bodies, and of our sea.

Source: Michael R. Matthews, ed., *The Scientific Background to Modern Philosophy: Selected Readings* (Indianapolis, IN: 1989), p. 152.

Questions for Analysis

1. Why did Isaac Newton declare that "hypotheses, whether metaphysical or physical, whether of occult qualities or mechanical, have no place in experimental philosophy"?

2. Is Newton's thinking similar to Bacon's, or does he argue in ways similar to Descartes's?

and objectivity lay in the precise mathematical characterization of phenomena—"the mathematization of the universe," as one historian puts it. Science could not, and need not, always uncover causes. It did describe natural phenomena and accurately predict the behavior of objects as confirmed by experimentation.

Other natural philosophers immediately acclaimed Newton's work for solving long-standing puzzles. Thinkers persuaded that the Copernican version of the universe was right had been unable to piece together the physics of a revolving earth. Newton made it possible to do so. Halley provided a poem to accompany the first edition of *Principia.* "No closer to the gods can any mortal rise," he wrote, of the man with whom he had worked so patiently. Halley did have a financial as well as an intellectual interest in the book, and he also arranged for it to be publicized and reviewed in influential journals. John Locke (whose own *Essay Concerning Human Understanding* was written at virtually the same time, in 1690) read *Principia* twice and summarized it in French for readers across the Channel. By 1713, pirated editions of *Principia* were being published in Amsterdam for distribution throughout Europe. By the time Newton died, in 1727, he had become an English national hero and was given a funeral at Westminster Abbey. The poet Alexander Pope expressed the awe that Newton inspired in some of his contemporaries in a famous couplet:

> Nature and nature's law lay hid in night;
> God said, "Let Newton be!" and all was light.

Voltaire, the French champion of the Enlightenment (discussed in the next chapter), was largely responsible for Newton's reputation in France. In this, he was helped by a woman who was a brilliant mathematician in her own right, Emilie du Châtelet. Du Châtelet coauthored a book with

Voltaire introducing Newton to a French audience; and she translated *Principia*, a daunting scientific and mathematical task and one well beyond Voltaire's mathematical abilities. Newton's French admirers and publicists disseminated Newton's findings. In their eyes, Newton also represented a cultural transformation, a turning point in the history of knowledge.

Science and Cultural Change

From the seventeenth century on, science stood at the heart of what it meant to be "modern." It grew increasingly central to the self-understanding of Western culture, and scientific and technological power became one of the justifications for the expansion of Western empires and the subjugation of other peoples. For all these reasons, the scientific revolution was and often still is presented as a thorough-going break with the past, a moment when Western culture was recast. But, as one historian has written, "no house is ever built of entirely virgin materials, according to a plan bearing no resemblance to old patterns, and no body of culture is able to wholly reject its past. Historical change is not like that, and most 'revolutions' effect less sweeping changes than they advertise or than are advertised for them."

To begin with, the transformation we have canvassed in this chapter involved elite knowledge. Ordinary people inhabited a very different cultural world. Second, natural philosophers' discoveries—Tycho's mathematics and Galileo's observations, for instance—did not undo the authority of the ancients in one blow. They did not seek to do so. Third, science did not subvert religion. Even when traditional concepts collapsed in the face of new discoveries, natural philosophers seldom gave up on the project of restoring a picture of a divinely ordered universe. Mechanists argued that the intricate universe revealed by the discoveries of Copernicus, Kepler, Galileo, Newton, and others was evidence of God's guiding presence. Robert Boyle's will provided the funds for a lecture series on the "confutation of atheism" by scientific means. Isaac Newton was happy to have his work contribute to that project. "Nothing," he wrote to one of the lecturers in 1692, "can rejoice me more than to find [*Principia*] usefull for that purpose." The creation of "the Sun and Fixt stars," "the motion which the Planets now have could not spring from any naturall cause alone but were imprest with a divine Agent." Science was thoroughly compatible with belief in God's providential design, at least through the seventeenth century.

The greatest scientific minds were deeply committed to beliefs that do not fit present-day notions of science. Newton, again, is the most striking case in point. The great twentieth-century economist John Maynard Keynes was one of the first to read through Newton's private manuscripts. On the three hundredth anniversary of Newton's birth (the celebration of which was delayed because of the Second World War), Keynes offered the following reappraisal of the great scientist:

> I believe that Newton was different from the conventional picture of him. . . .
>
> In the eighteenth century and since, Newton came to be thought of as the first and greatest of the modern age of scientists, a rationalist, one who taught us to think on the lines of cold and untinctured reason.
>
> I do not see him in this light. I do not think that any one who has pored over the contents of that box which he packed up when he finally left Cambridge in 1696 and which, though partly dispersed, have come down to us, can see him like that. Newton was not the first of the age of reason. He was the last of the magicians, the last of the Babylonians and Sumerians, the last great mind which looked out on the visible and intellectual world with the same eyes as those who began to build our intellectual inheritance rather less than 10,000 years ago.

Like his predecessors, Newton saw the world as God's message to humanity, a text to be deciphered. Close reading and study would unlock its mysteries. This same impulse led Newton to read accounts of magic, investigate alchemist's claims that base metals could be turned into gold, and to immerse himself in the writings of the Church fathers and in the Bible, which he knew in intimate detail. If these activities sound unscientific from the perspective of the present, it is because the strict distinction between rational inquiry and belief in the occult or religious traditions simply did not exist in his time. Such a distinction is a product of the long history of scientific developments after the eighteenth century. Newton, then, was the last representative of an older tradition, and also, quite unintentionally, the first of a new one.

What, then, did the scientific revolution change? Seventeenth-century natural philosophers had produced new answers to fundamental questions about the physical world. Age-old questions about astronomy and physics had been recast and, to some extent (although it was not

ESTABLISHMENT OF THE ACADEMY OF SCIENCES AND FOUNDATION OF THE OBSERVATORY, 1667. The 1666 founding of the Academy of Sciences was a measure of the new prestige of science and the potential value of research. Louis XIV sits at the center, surrounded by the religious and scholarly figures who offer the fruits of their knowledge to the French state. ▪ *What was the value of science for absolutist rulers like Louis?*

yet clear to what extent), answered. In the process, there had developed a new approach to amassing and integrating information in a systematic way, an approach that helped yield more insights into the workings of nature as time went on. In this period, too, the most innovative scientific work moved out of the restrictive environment of the Church and the universities. Natural philosophers began talking to and working with each other in lay organizations that developed standards of research. England's Royal Society spawned imitators in Florence and Berlin and later in Russia. The French Royal Academy of Sciences had a particularly direct relationship with the monarchy and the French state. France's statesmen exerted control over the academy and sought to share in the rewards of any discoveries its members made.

New, too, were beliefs about the purpose and methods of science. The practice of breaking a complex problem down into parts made it possible to tackle more and different questions in the physical sciences. Mathematics assumed a more central role in the new science. Finally,

rather than simply confirming established truths, the new methods were designed to explore the unknown and provide means to discover new truths. As Kepler wrote to Galileo, "How great a difference there is between theoretical speculation and visual experience, between Ptolemy's discussion of the Antipodes and Columbus's discovery of the New World." Knowledge itself was reconceived. In the older model, to learn was to read: to reason logically, to argue, to compare classical texts, and to absorb a finite body of knowledge. In the newer one, to learn was to discover, and what could be discovered was boundless.

CONCLUSION

The pioneering natural philosophers remained circumspect about their abilities. Some sought to lay bare the workings of the universe; others believed humans could only catalog and describe the regularities observed in nature. By unspoken but seemingly mutual agreement, the question of first causes was left aside. The new science did not say *why*, but *how*. Newton, for one, worked toward explanations that would reveal the logic of creation laid out in mathematics. Yet, in the end, he settled for theories explaining motions and relationships that could be observed and tested.

The eighteenth-century heirs to Newton were much more daring. Laboratory science and the work of the

After You Read This Chapter

Visit StudySpace for quizzes, additional review materials, and multimedia documents. **wwnorton.com/web/westernciv18**

REVIEWING THE OBJECTIVES

- The scientific revolution marked a shift toward new forms of explanation in descriptions of the natural world. What made the work of scientists during this period different from earlier forms of knowledge or research?
- The scientific revolution nevertheless depended on earlier traditions of philosophical thought. What earlier traditions proved important in fostering a spirit of scientific investigation?
- Astronomical observations played a central role in the scientific revolution. What technological innovations made new astronomical work possible, and what conclusions did astronomers reach using these new technologies?
- Central to the scientific revolution was the rejection of the Ptolemaic view of the universe and its replacement by the Copernican model. What was this controversy about?
- Francis Bacon and René Descartes had contrasting ideas about scientific method. What approach to science did each of these natural philosophers defend?

scientific societies largely stayed true to the experimenters' rules and limitations. But as we will see in the next chapter, the natural philosophers who began investigating the human sciences cast aside some of their predecessors' caution. Society, technology, government, religion, even the individual human mind seemed to be mechanisms or parts of a larger nature waiting for study. The scientific revolution overturned the natural world as it had been understood for a millennium; it also inspired thinkers more interested in revolutions in society.

PEOPLE, IDEAS, AND EVENTS IN CONTEXT

- How did the traditions of **NEOPLATONISM**, **RENAISSANCE**, and **HUMANISM** contribute to a vision of the physical world that encouraged scientific investigation and explanation?

- In what way did the work of **NICOLAS COPERNICUS**, **TYCHO BRAHE**, **JOHANNES KEPLER**, and **GALILEO GALILEI** serve to undermine the intellectual foundations of the **PTOLEMAIC SYSTEM**? Why did their work largely take place outside of the traditional centers of learning in Europe, such as universities?

- What differences in scientific practice arose from **FRANCIS BACON**'s emphasis on observation and **RENÉ DESCARTES**'s insistence that knowledge could only be derived from unquestionable first principles?

- What were **ISAAC NEWTON**'s major contributions to the scientific revolution? Why have some suggested that Newton's interests and thinking were not all compatible with modern conceptions of scientific understanding?

- What was important about the establishment of institutions such as the British **ROYAL SOCIETY** or the French **ACADEMY OF SCIENCES** for the development of scientific methods and research?

- What prevented women from entering most of Europe's scientific academies? How did educated women such as **LAURA BASSI**, **MARGARET CAVENDISH**, **MARIA WINKELMANN**, and **MARIA SYBILLA MERIAN** gain the skills necessary to participate in scientific work?

THINKING ABOUT CONNECTIONS

- How did ideas about the value of ancient scholarship and philosophy change after the development of new sciences of observation in the seventeenth century?

- What possible connections might be made between the intellectual developments in scientific thinking during the seventeenth century and the Reformation of the sixteenth century? Was the new science incompatible with religious faith?

Before
You
Read
This
Chapter

Europe during the Enlightenment

CORE OBJECTIVES

- **DESCRIBE** the eighteenth-century consumer revolution in Europe and its relationship to the Enlightenment.

- **DEFINE** the term *Enlightenment* as eighteenth-century thinkers used it, and identify the figures most closely associated with this intellectual movement.

- **EXPLAIN** how the ideas associated with the Enlightenment spread and the consequences of this expanded world of public discussion.

- **EXPLORE** the ways that the Enlightenment was linked to imperial expansion as larger numbers of Europeans became more aware of the globe's diverse cultures and peoples.

- **UNDERSTAND** how Enlightenment thought challenged central tenets of eighteenth-century culture and politics.

I n 1762, the *Parlement* (law court) of Toulouse, in France, convicted Jean Calas of murdering his son. Calas was Protestant in a region where Catholic–Protestant tensions ran high. Witnesses claimed that the young Calas had wanted to convert to Catholicism, and the father had killed him to prevent this conversion. Following French law, Jean Calas was tortured twice: first to force a confession and, next, to identify his alleged accomplices. His arms and legs were slowly pulled apart, gallons of water were poured down his throat, and his body was publicly broken on the wheel, each of his limbs smashed with an iron bar. Then the executioner cut off his head. Throughout the trial, torture, and execution, Calas maintained his innocence. Two years later, the Parlement reversed its verdict, declared Calas not guilty, and offered the family a payment in compensation.

François Marie Arouet, also known as Voltaire, was appalled by the verdict and punishment. At the time of the case, Voltaire was the most famous personality in the European intellectual movement known as the Enlightenment. Prolific and well connected, Voltaire took up his pen to clear Calas's name. He hired

THE CRUEL DEATH OF CALAS. This print, reproduced in a pamphlet that circulated in Britain in the late eighteenth century, portrayed the French Protestant Jean Calas as a martyr to his beliefs and directly implicated the Roman Catholic Church in the cruelty of his execution by placing an enthusiastic priest prominently at the scene. The pamphlet may also have sought to reinforce anti-French sentiments among an increasingly nationalistic British population. ▪ *How might Enlightenment authors have used such a scene to promote their message of toleration?* ▪ *How might Church officials have responded to such attacks?*

and from the Italian writer Cesare Beccaria, whose *On Crimes and Punishments* appeared in 1764. Voltaire's reputation did not rest on his originality as a philosopher. It came from his effectiveness as a writer and advocate, his desire and ability to reach a wide audience in print.

The emergence of this wide audience for Voltaire's writings was just as significant as the arguments that he made. The growth of European cities, the spread of literacy and new forms of social interaction at all levels of society helped fuel the Enlightenment's atmosphere of critical reflection about religion, law, the power of the state, and the dignity of the individual. The fact that a writer such as Voltaire could become a celebrity showed that a new kind of literate reading public had developed in Europe. Enough people who read and had income to spare on printed material created a market for newspapers and novels, which in turn showed the emergence of a new kind of consumer society. The works of writers like Voltaire and his peers were discussed over sweetened caffeinated drinks in coffeehouses and cafes where ordinary people gathered to smoke and debate the issues of the day. (Coffee, sugar, and tobacco all came from the Atlantic colonial trade.) Similar scenes took place in the homes of aristocrats. The Enlightenment was thus not only an intellectual movement—it was a cultural phenomenon, which exposed an increasingly broad part of the population to new forms of consumption, of goods as well as ideas.

lawyers for the family and wrote briefs, letters, and essays to bring the case to the public eye. These essays circulated widely among an increasingly literate middle-class audience. For Voltaire, Calas's case exemplified nearly everything he found backward in European culture. Intolerance, ignorance, and religious "fanaticism" had made a travesty of justice. "Shout everywhere, I beg you, for Calas and against fanaticism, for it is this infamy that has caused their misery." Torture demonstrated the power of the courts but could not uncover the truth. Secret interrogations, trials behind closed doors, summary judgment (Calas was executed the day after being convicted, with no review by a higher court), and barbaric punishments defied reason, morality, and human dignity. Any criminal, however wretched, "is a man," wrote Voltaire, "and you are accountable for his blood."

Voltaire's writings on the Calas case illustrate the classic concerns of the Enlightenment: the dangers of arbitrary and unchecked authority, the value of religious toleration, and the overriding importance of law, reason, and human dignity in all affairs. He borrowed most of his arguments from others—from his predecessor the Baron de Montesquieu

PROSPERITY, COMMERCE, AND CONSUMPTION

The Enlightenment's audience consisted of urban readers and consumers who were receptive to new cultural forms: the essay, the political tract, the satirical engraving, the novel, the newspaper, theatrical spectacles, and even musical performances. Clearly, such developments could only occur in a society where significant numbers of people had achieved a level of wealth that freed them from the immediate cares of daily sustenance. By the beginning of the eighteenth century, this level of wealth had been achieved in the cities of northwestern Europe. The North Atlantic economies of France and

Britain, in particular, made these two countries the preponderant powers both in Europe and the wider world.

Economic Growth in Eighteenth-Century Europe

Rapid economic and demographic growth in northwestern Europe was made possible by cheaper food and declines in mortality from infectious disease. In Britain and Holland, new intensive agricultural systems produced more food per acre. Improved transportation and new farming methods resulted in fewer famines and a better-nourished population. New crops, especially maize and potatoes from the Americas, also increased the supply of food. Infectious disease continued to kill half of all Europeans before the age of twenty, but plague was ceasing to be a major killer, as a degree of immunity (perhaps the result of a genetic mutation) began to emerge within the European population. Better diet and improved sanitation may also have

POPULATION GROWTH C. 1600. ▪ *Where did the population grow more rapidly?* ▪ *Why were the largest gains in population on the coasts?* ▪ *How did urbanization affect patterns of life and trade?*

reduced infection rates from typhoid, cholera, smallpox, and measles.

Northwestern Europe was also increasingly urbanized. The total number of urban dwellers in Europe did not change much between 1600 and 1800. At both dates, approximately 200 cities in Europe had a population of over 10,000. These cities were increasingly concentrated in northern and western Europe, however, and the largest experienced extraordinary growth, especially those connected with Atlantic trade. Cities such as Hamburg in Germany, Liverpool in England, Toulon in France, and Cádiz in Spain grew by about 250 percent between 1600 and 1750. Amsterdam, the hub of early modern international commerce, increased in population from 30,000 in 1530 to 200,000 by 1800. Naples, the busy Mediterranean port, went from a population of 300,000 in 1600 to nearly 500,000 by the late eighteenth century. Spectacular population growth also occurred in the administrative capitals of Europe: London's population grew from 674,000 in 1700 to 860,000 a century later; Paris's went from 180,000 people in 1600 to more than 500,000 in 1800; and Berlin's grew from 6,500 in 1661 to 140,000 in 1783.

The rising prosperity of northwestern Europe also depended on developments in trade and manufacturing. Improvements in transportation led entrepreneurs to produce textiles in the countryside. They distributed, or "put out," wool and flax to rural workers who spun it and wove it into cloth on a piece-rate basis. The entrepreneur sold the finished cloth in a market that extended from local towns to international exporters. For country dwellers, this system (sometimes called "protoindustrialization") provided welcome employment during slack seasons of the agricultural year. The system also allowed merchants to avoid expensive guild restrictions in the towns and reduced their production costs. Urban cloth workers suffered, but the system led to increased employment and to higher levels of industrial production, not only for textiles but also for iron, metalworking, and even toy and clock making.

Some cities also became manufacturing centers during the eighteenth century. In northern France, many of the million or so men and women employed in the textile trade lived and worked in Amiens, Lille, and Rheims. The rulers of Prussia made it their policy to develop Berlin as a manufacturing center, taking advantage of an influx of French Protestants to establish a silk-weaving industry there. Most urban manufacturing took place in small shops employing from five to twenty journeymen working under a master. But the scale of such enterprise was growing and becoming more specialized, as workshops began to group together to form a single manufacturing district in which several thousand workers might be employed to produce the same product.

Techniques in some crafts remained much as they had been for centuries. In others, however, inventions changed the pattern of work as well as the nature of the product. Knitting frames, simple devices to speed the manufacture of textile goods, made their appearance in Britain and Holland. Wire-drawing machines and slitting mills, which allowed nail makers to convert iron bars into rods, spread from Germany into Britain. Techniques for printing colored designs directly on calico cloth were imported from Asia. New and more efficient printing presses appeared, first in Holland and then elsewhere.

Workers did not readily accept innovations of this kind. Labor-saving machines threw people out of work. Artisans, especially those organized into guilds, were by nature conservative, anxious to protect not only their rights but also the secrets of their trade. Governments would often intervene to block the use of machines if they threatened to increase unemployment or create unrest. States might also act to protect the interests of their powerful commercial and financial backers. Both Britain and France outlawed calico printing for a time, to protect local textile manufacturers and importers of Indian goods. Mercantilist doctrines could also impede innovation. In both Paris and Lyons, for example, the use of indigo dyes was banned because they were manufactured abroad. But the pressures for economic innovation were irresistible, because behind them lay an insatiable eighteenth-century appetite for goods.

A World of Goods

In the eighteenth century, a mass market for consumer goods emerged, concentrated at first in northwestern Europe. Houses became larger, particularly in towns; but even more strikingly, the houses of middling ranks were now stocked with hitherto uncommon luxuries such as sugar, tobacco, tea, coffee, chocolate, newspapers, books, pictures, clocks, toys, china, glassware, pewter, silver plate, soap, razors, furniture (including beds with mattresses, chairs, and chests of drawers), shoes, cotton cloth, and spare clothing. Demand for such products consistently outstripped the supply, causing prices for these items to rise faster than the price of foodstuffs throughout the century. But the demand for them continued unabated. Such goods were indulgences, of course, but they were also repositories of value in which families could invest their surplus cash, knowing that they could pawn them in hard times if cash was needed.

The exploding consumer economy of the eighteenth century also encouraged the provision of services. In eighteenth-century Britain, the service sector was the

***TOPSY-TURVY WORLD* BY JAN STEEN.** This Dutch painting depicts a household in the throes of the exploding consumer economy that hit Europe in the eighteenth century. Consumer goods ranging from silver and china to clothing and furniture cluttered the houses of ordinary people as never before.

fastest-growing part of the economy, outstripping both agriculture and manufacturing. Almost everywhere in urban Europe, the eighteenth century was the golden age of the small shopkeeper. People bought more prepared foods and more ready-made (as opposed to personally tailored) clothing. Advertising became an important part of doing business, helping create demand for new products and shaping popular taste for changing fashions. Even political allegiances could be expressed through consumption when people purchased plates and glasses commemorating favorite rulers or causes.

The result of all these developments was a European economy vastly more complex, more specialized, more integrated, more commercialized, and more productive than anything the world had seen before. These developments necessarily affected the way people thought of the world and their place in it—above all, people in the Enlightenment shared a sense of living in a time marked by change. Many Enlightenment thinkers defended such changes as "progress." Others were more critical, fearing that valued traditions were being lost. Such debates lay at the heart of Enlightenment thought.

The Foundations of the Enlightenment

Enlightenment thinkers did not agree on everything, but most shared a sense that they lived in an exciting moment in history in which human reason would prevail over the accumulated superstitions and traditions of the past. Enlightenment authors believed themselves to be the defenders of a new ideal, "the party of humanity."

The confidence that Enlightenment thinkers placed in the powers of human reason stemmed from the accomplishments of the scientific revolution. Even when the details of Newton's physics were poorly understood, his methods provided a model for scientific inquiry into other phenomena. Nature operated according to laws that could be grasped by study, observation, and thought. The work of the Scottish writer David Hume (*A Treatise of Human Nature,* 1739–40, and the *Enquiries Concerning Human Understanding,* 1748) provided the most direct bridge from science to the Enlightenment. Newton had refused speculation about ultimate causes, arguing instead for a precise description of natural phenomena (see Chapter 16). Hume took this same rigor and skepticism to the study of morality, the mind, and government, often drawing analogies to scientific laws. Hume criticized the "passion for hypotheses and systems" that dominated earlier philosophical thinking. Experience and careful observation, he argued, usually did not support the premises on which those systems rested.

Embracing human reason also required confronting the power of Europe's traditional monarchies and the religious institutions that supported them. "Dare to know!" the German philosopher Immanuel Kant challenged his contemporaries in his classic 1784 essay "What Is Enlightenment?" For Kant, the Enlightenment represented a declaration of intellectual independence. (He also called it an awakening and credited Hume with rousing him from his "dogmatic slumber.") Kant likened the intellectual history of humanity to the growth of a child. Enlightenment, in this view, was an escape from humanity's "self-imposed immaturity" and a long overdue break with humanity's self-imposed parental figure, the Catholic Church. Coming of age meant the "determination and courage to think without the guidance of someone else" as an individual. Reason required autonomy, and freedom from tradition.

Enlightenment thinkers nevertheless recognized a great debt to their predecessors, especially John Locke, Francis Bacon, and Isaac Newton. Enlightenment thinkers drew heavily on Locke's studies of human knowledge, especially his *Essay concerning Human Understanding* (1690).

DIVINE LIGHT. The frontispiece for Voltaire's book on the science of Isaac Newton portrays Newton as the source of a divine light that is reflected onto Voltaire's desk through a mirror held by Émilie du Châtelet, the French translator of Newton who also was Voltaire's lover. Newton's clouded throne and the adoring angels holding du Châtelet aloft were familiar motifs from earlier generations of religious paintings, but the significance of the carefully portrayed ray of light is recast by the books, inkwell, and precise scientific measuring tools surrounding Voltaire. ■ *What does this image say about the relationship between religious thought and Enlightenment science?*

Locke's theories of how humans acquire knowledge gave education and environment a critical role in shaping human character. All knowledge, he argued, originates from sense perception. The human mind at birth is a "blank tablet" (in Latin, *tabula rasa*). Only when an infant begins to perceive the external world with its senses, does anything register in its mind. Education, then, was essential to the creation of a good and moral individual. Locke's starting point,

which became a central premise for those who followed, was the goodness and perfectibility of humanity. Building on Locke, eighteenth-century thinkers made education central to their project, because education promised that social progress could be achieved through individual moral improvement. Locke's theories had potentially radical implications for eighteenth-century society: if all humans were capable of reason, education might also level hierarchies of status, sex, or race. As we will see, only a few Enlightenment thinkers made such egalitarian arguments. Still, optimism and a belief in universal human progress constituted a second defining feature of nearly all Enlightenment thinking.

Enlightenment thinkers sought nothing less than the organization of all knowledge. The *scientific method*, by which they meant the empirical observation of particular phenomena to arrive at general laws, offered a way to pursue research in all areas—to study human affairs as well as natural ones. Thus they collected evidence to learn the laws governing the rise and fall of nations, and they compared governmental constitutions to arrive at an ideal and universally applicable political system. As the English poet Alexander Pope stated in his *Essay on Man* (1733), "The science of human nature [may be] like all other sciences reduced to a few clear points," and Enlightenment thinkers became determined to learn exactly what those few clear points were. They took up a strikingly wide array of subjects in this systematic manner: knowledge and the mind, natural history, economics, government, religious beliefs, customs of indigenous peoples in the New World, human nature, and sexual (or what we would call gender) and racial differences.

As one can see from these examples, the culture of the *philosophes*, or Enlightenment thinkers, was international. French became the lingua franca of much Enlightenment discussion, but "French" books were often published in Switzerland, Germany, and Russia. Enlightenment thinkers admired British institutions and British scholarship, and Great Britain produced important Enlightenment thinkers: the historian Edward Gibbon and the Scottish philosophers David Hume and Adam Smith. The philosophes considered the Americans Thomas Jefferson and Benjamin Franklin to be a part of their group. Despite stiffer resistance from religious authorities, stricter state censors, and smaller networks of educated elites, the Enlightenment also flourished across central and southern Europe. Frederick II of Prussia housed Voltaire during one of his exiles from France, and he also patronized a small but unusually productive group of Enlightenment thinkers. Northern Italy was also an important center of Enlightenment thought.

THE WORLD OF THE PHILOSOPHES

Although Enlightenment thought was European in a broad sense, France provided the stage for some of the most widely followed Enlightenment projects. For this reason, Enlightenment thinkers, regardless of where they lived, are often called by the French word *philosophes*. Hardly any of the philosophes, with the exceptions of David Hume and Immanuel Kant, were true philosophers, in the sense of being highly original abstract thinkers. Most Enlightenment thinkers shunned forms of expression that might seem incomprehensible, priding themselves instead on their clarity. *Philosophe,* in French, simply meant "a free thinker," a person whose reflections were unhampered by the constraints of religion or dogma in any form.

Voltaire

The best known of the philosophes was Voltaire, born François Marie Arouet (1694–1778). As Erasmus two centuries earlier had embodied Christian humanism, Voltaire virtually personified the Enlightenment, commenting on an enormous range of subjects in a wide variety of literary forms. Educated by the Jesuits, he became a gifted and sharp-tongued writer. His gusto for provocation landed him in the Bastille (a notorious prison in Paris) for libel and soon afterward in temporary exile in England. In his three years there, Voltaire became an admirer of British political institutions, British culture, and British science; above all, he became an extremely persuasive convert to the ideas of Newton, Bacon, and Locke. His single greatest accomplishment may have been popularizing Newton's work in France and more generally championing the cause of British empiricism and the scientific method against the more Cartesian French.

Voltaire's *Philosophical Letters* ("*Letters on the English Nation*"), published after his return in 1734, made an immediate sensation. Voltaire's themes were religious and political liberty, and his weapons were comparisons. His admiration for British culture and politics became a stinging critique of France—and other absolutist countries on the Continent. He praised British open-mindedness and empiricism: the country's respect for scientists and its support for research. He considered the relative weakness of the British aristocracy a sign of Britain's political health. Unlike the French, the British respected commerce and people who engage in it, Voltaire wrote. The British tax system was rational, free of the complicated exemptions for the privileged that were ruining French finances. The British House of Commons represented

VOLTAIRE'S *CANDIDE*. Voltaire's best-selling novel gently mocked the optimism of some Enlightenment thinkers. The young Candide's tutor, Pangloss, insisted on repeating that "this is the best of all possible worlds," even as he, Candide, and Candide's love, the beautiful Cunegonde, suffered terrible accidents and misfortune. In the scene shown here Candide is thrown out of the castle by Cunegonde's father, with "great kicks in the rear" after they have been caught kissing behind a screen. This mix of serious message and humorous delivery was quite common in Enlightenment literature. ▪ *How might this combination of humor and philosophic meditation have been received by the educated middle-class audience that made up the readership of works such as* **Candide**?

the middle classes and, in contrast with French absolutism, brought balance to British government and checked arbitrary power. In one of the book's more incendiary passages, he argued that in Britain, violent revolution had actually produced political moderation and stability: "The idol of arbitrary power was drowned in seas of blood. . . . The English nation is the only nation in the world that has succeeded in moderating the power of its kings by resisting them."

Of all Britain's reputed virtues, religious toleration loomed largest of all. Britain, Voltaire argued, brought together citizens of different religions in a harmonious and productive culture. In this and other instances, Voltaire oversimplified: British Catholics, Dissenters, and Jews did not have equal civil rights. Yet the British policy of "toleration" did contrast with Louis XIV's intolerance of Protestants.

Revoking the Edict of Nantes (1685) had stripped French Protestants of civil rights and had helped create the atmosphere in which Jean Calas—and others—were persecuted.

Of all forms of intolerance, Voltaire opposed religious bigotry most, and with real passion he denounced religious fraud, faith in miracles, and superstition. His most famous battle cry was "*Écrasez l'infâme!*" ("Crush this infamous thing"), by which he meant all forms of repression, fanaticism, and bigotry. "The less superstition, the less fanaticism; and the less fanaticism, the less misery." He did not oppose religion per se; rather, he sought to rescue morality, which he believed to come from God, from dogma—elaborate ritual, dietary laws, formulaic prayers—and from a powerful Church bureaucracy. He argued for common sense and simplicity, persuaded that these would bring out the goodness in humanity and establish stable authority. "The simpler the laws are, the more the magistrates are respected; the simpler the religion will be, the more one will revere its ministers. Religion can be simple. When enlightened people will announce a single God, rewarder and avenger, no one will laugh, everyone will obey."

Voltaire relished his position as a critic, and he was regularly exiled from France and other countries, his books banned and burned. As long as his plays attracted large audiences, however, the French king felt he had to tolerate their author. Voltaire had an attentive international public, including Frederick of Prussia, who invited him to his court at Berlin, and Catherine of Russia, with whom he corresponded about reforms she might introduce in Russia. When he died in 1778, a few months after a triumphant return to Paris, he was possibly the best-known writer in Europe.

Montesquieu

The Baron de Montesquieu (*mahn-tuhs-KYOO,* 1689–1755) was a very different kind of Enlightenment figure. Montesquieu was born to a noble family. He inherited both an estate and, since state offices were property that passed from father to son, a position as magistrate in the Parlement of Bordeaux. He was not a stylist or a provocateur like Voltaire but a relatively cautious jurist, though he did write a satirical novel, *The Persian Letters* (1721), as a young man. The novel, which he published anonymously in Amsterdam, was composed as letters from two Persian visitors to France. The visitors detailed the odd religious superstitions they witnessed, compared manners at the French court with those in Turkish harems, and likened French absolutism to their own brands of *despotism,* or the abuse of government authority. *The Persian Letters* was an immediate best seller, which inspired many imitators,

MONTESQUIEU. The French baron's *Spirit of Laws* (1748) was probably the most influential single text of the Enlightenment. Montesquieu's suggestion that liberty could best be preserved in a government whose powers were divided among executive, legislative, and judicial functions had a notable influence on the authors of the U.S. Constitution.

as other authors used the formula of a foreign observer to criticize contemporary French society.

Montesquieu's treatise, *The Spirit of Laws* (1748), may have been the most influential work of the Enlightenment. It was a groundbreaking study in what we would call comparative historical sociology and very Newtonian in its careful, empirical approach. Montesquieu asked about the structures that shaped law. How had different environments, histories, and religious traditions combined to create such a variety of governmental institutions? What were the different forms of government: what spirit characterized each, and what were their respective virtues and shortcomings?

Montesquieu suggested that there were three forms of government: republics, monarchies, and despotisms. A republic was governed by many individuals—either an elite aristocracy of citizens or the people as a whole. The soul of a republic was virtue, which allowed individual citizens to transcend their particular interests and rule in accordance with the common good. In a monarchy, on the other hand, one person ruled in accordance with the law. The soul of a monarchy, wrote Montesquieu, was honor, which gave individuals an incentive to behave with loyalty toward their sovereign. The third form of government, despotism, was rule by a single person unchecked by law or other powers. The soul of despotism was fear, since no citizen could feel secure and punishment took the place of education. Lest this seem abstract, Montesquieu devoted two chapters to the French monarchy, in which he spelled out what he saw as a dangerous drift toward despotism in his own land. Like other Enlightenment thinkers, Montesquieu admired the British system and its separation of the executive, legislative, and judicial functions of government. Such a balance of powers preserved liberty by avoiding a concentration of authority in a single individual or group. His idealization of "checks and balances" had a formative influence on Enlightenment political theorists and helped to guide the authors of the U.S. Constitution in 1787.

Diderot and the Encyclopedia

The most remarkable and ambitious Enlightenment project was a collective one: the *Encyclopedia*. The *Encyclopedia* claimed to summarize all the most advanced contemporary philosophical, scientific, and technical knowledge, making it available to any reader. It demonstrated how scientific analysis could be applied in nearly all realms of thought, and it further aimed to encourage critical reflection of an enormous range of traditions and institutions. The guiding spirit behind the venture was Denis Diderot (1713–1784). Diderot was helped by the mathematician Jean Le Rond d'Alembert (1717–1783) and other leading men of letters, including Voltaire and Montesquieu. Published in installments between 1751 and 1772, the *Encyclopedia* ran to seventeen large volumes of text and eleven more of illustrations, with over 71,000 articles.

Diderot commissioned articles on science and technology, showing how machines worked and illustrating new industrial processes. The point was to demonstrate how science could promote progress and alleviate human misery. Diderot turned the same methods to politics and the social order, including articles on economics, taxes, and the slave trade. Censorship made it difficult to write openly antireligious articles. Diderot thumbed his nose at religion in oblique ways; at the entry on the Eucharist, the reader found a terse cross-reference: "See *cannibalism*." At one point, the French government revoked the publishing permit for the *Encyclopedia*, declaring in 1759 that the encyclopedists were trying to "propagate materialism" (by which they meant atheism) "to destroy Religion, to inspire a spirit of independence, and to nourish the corruption of morals." The volumes sold remarkably well despite such bans and their hefty price. Purchasers belonged to the elite: aristocrats, government officials, prosperous merchants, and a scattering of

TECHNOLOGY AND INDUSTRY. This engraving, from the mining section, is characteristic of Diderot's *Encyclopedia*. The project aimed to detail technological changes, manufacturing processes, and forms of labor—all in the name of advancing human knowledge.

members of the higher clergy. That elite stretched across Europe, including its overseas colonies.

Although the French philosophes sparred with the state and the church, they sought political stability and reform. Montesquieu hoped that an enlightened aristocracy would press for reforms and defend liberty against a despotic king. Voltaire, persuaded that aristocrats would represent only their particular narrow interests, looked to an enlightened monarch for leadership. Neither was a democrat, and neither conceived of reform from below. Still, their widely read critiques of arbitrary power stung. By the 1760s, the French critique of despotism provided the language in which many people across Europe articulated their opposition to existing regimes.

MAJOR THEMES OF ENLIGHTENMENT THOUGHT

Enlightenment thinkers across Europe raised similar themes: humanitarianism, or the dignity and worth of all individuals; religious toleration; and liberty. These ideals inspired important debates about three issues in particular: law and punishment, the place of religious minorities, and the state's relationship to society and the economy.

Law and Punishment

The Enlightenment beliefs about education and the perfectibility of human society led many thinkers to question the harsh treatment of criminals by European courts. An influential work by the Italian jurist Cesare Beccaria (1738–1794), *On Crimes and Punishments* (1764), provided Voltaire with most of his arguments in the Calas case. Beccaria criticized the use of arbitrary power and attacked the prevalent view that punishments should represent society's vengeance on the criminal. The only legitimate rationale for punishment was to maintain social order and to prevent other crimes. Beccaria argued for the greatest possible leniency compatible with deterrence; respect for individual dignity dictated that humans should punish other humans no more than is absolutely necessary.

Above all, Beccaria's book eloquently opposed torture and the death penalty. Public execution, he argued, was intended to dramatize the power of the state and the horrors of hell, but it dehumanized the victim, judge, and spectators. In 1766, a few years after the Calas case, another French trial provided an example of what horrified Beccaria and the philosophes. A nineteen-year-old French nobleman, convicted of blasphemy, had his tongue cut out and his hand cut off before he was burned at the stake. The court discovered the blasphemer had read Voltaire, and it ordered his *Philosophical Dictionary* burned along with the body. Sensational cases such as this helped publicize Beccaria's work. *On Crimes and Punishments* was quickly translated into a dozen languages. Owing primarily to its influence, most European countries by around 1800 abolished torture, branding, whipping, and mutilation and reserved the death penalty for capital crimes.

Humanitarianism and Religious Toleration

Humanitarianism and reason also counseled religious toleration. Enlightenment thinkers spoke almost as one on the need to end religious warfare and the persecution of heretics and religious minorities. Most Enlightenment authors distinguished between religious belief, which they accepted, and the Church as an institution and as dogma, which they rebelled against. It was in this sense that Voltaire opposed the Church's influence over society. Few Enlightenment authors were atheists—a notable exception was Paul-Henri d'Holbach (1723–1789)—and only a few more were agnostics. Many, including Voltaire, were deists, believing in a God that acted as a "divine watchmaker" who at the beginning of time constructed a perfect universe and left it to run with predictable regularity. Enlightenment inquiry proved compatible with very different stances on religion.

Nevertheless, Enlightenment support for toleration was sometimes limited. Most Christians saw Jews as heretics and Christ killers. Although Enlightenment thinkers deplored persecution, they commonly viewed Judaism and Islam as backward, superstitious religions. One of the few Enlightenment figures to treat Jews sympathetically was the German philosophe Gotthold Lessing (1729–1781). Lessing's play *Nathan the Wise* (1779) takes place in Jerusalem during the Fourth Crusade and begins with a pogrom—or violent,

INSTRUMENTS OF TORTURE. A man being stretched on the rack (left) and a thumbscrew (right), both from an official Austrian government handbook. By 1800, Beccaria's influence had helped phase out the use of such instruments.

orchestrated attack—in which the wife and children of Nathan, a Jewish merchant, are murdered. Nathan survives to become a sympathetic and wise father figure. He adopts a Christian-born daughter and raises her with three religions: Christianity, Islam, and Judaism. At several points, authorities ask him to choose the single true religion. Nathan shows none exists. The three great monotheistic religions are three versions of the truth. Religion is authentic, or true, only insofar as it makes the believer virtuous.

Lessing modeled his hero on his friend Moses Mendelssohn (1729–1786), a self-educated rabbi and bookkeeper (and the grandfather of the composer Felix Mendelssohn). Moses Mendelssohn moved—though with some difficulty—between the Enlightenment circles of Frederick II and the Jewish community of Berlin. Repeatedly attacked and invited to convert to Christianity, he defended Jewish communities against anti-Semitic policies and Judaism against Enlightenment criticism. At the same time, he also promoted reform within the Jewish community, arguing that his community had special reason to embrace the broad Enlightenment project: religious faith should be voluntary, states should promote tolerance, humanitarianism would bring progress to all.

Government, Administration, and the Economy

Enlightenment ideas had a very real influence over affairs of state. The philosophes defended reason and knowledge for humanitarian reasons. But they also promised to make nations stronger, more efficient, and more prosperous. Beccaria's proposed legal reforms were a good case in point; he sought to make laws not simply more just but also more effective. In other words, the Enlightenment spoke to individuals but also to states. The philosophes addressed issues of liberty and rights but also took up matters of administration, tax collection, and economic policy.

The rising fiscal demands of eighteenth-century states and empires made these issues newly urgent. Which economic resources were most valuable to states? In the seventeenth century, mercantilists had argued that regulation of trade was necessary to maximize government revenues (see Chapter 15). In the eighteenth century, Enlightenment economic thinkers known as the physiocrats argued that real wealth came from the land and agricultural production, which prospered with less government interference. They advocated simplifying the tax system and following a policy of laissez-faire, which comes from the French expression *laissez faire la nature* ("let nature take its course"), letting wealth and goods circulate without government interference.

LESSING AND MENDELSSOHN. This painting of a meeting between the philosophe Gotthold Lessing (standing) and his friend Moses Mendelssohn (seated right) emphasizes the personal nature of their intellectual relationship, which transcended their religious backgrounds (Christian and Jewish, respectively). The Enlightenment's atmosphere of earnest discussion is invoked both by the open book before them and the shelf of reading material behind Lessing. Compare this image of masculine discussion (note the role of the one woman in the painting) with the image of the aristocratic salon on page 570 and the coffeehouse on page 571. ▪ *What similarities and differences might one point to in these various illustrations of the Enlightenment public sphere?*

The classic expression of laissez-faire economics, however, came from the Scottish economist Adam Smith (1723–1790) and his landmark treatise, *Inquiry into the Nature and Causes of the Wealth of Nations* (1776). Smith disagreed with the physiocrats on the value of agriculture, but he shared their opposition to mercantilism. For Smith, the central issues were the productivity of labor and how labor was used in different sectors of the economy. Mercantile restrictions—such as high taxes on imported goods, one of the grievances of the colonists throughout the American empires—did not encourage the productive deployment of labor and thus did not create real economic health. For Smith, general prosperity could be obtained by allowing the famous "invisible hand" of competition to guide economic activity. Individuals, in other words, should pursue their own interests by buying and selling goods and labor freely on the open market without interference from state-chartered monopolies or legal restraints. As Smith wrote in his earlier *Theory of Moral Sentiments* (1759), self-interested individuals could be "led by an invisible hand . . . without knowing it, without intending it, [to] advance the interest of the society."

The Wealth of Nations spelled out, in more technical and historical detail, the different stages of economic development, how the invisible hand actually worked, and the beneficial aspects of competition. Its perspective owed much to Newton and to the Enlightenment's idealization of both nature and human nature. Smith thought of himself as the champion of liberty against state-sponsored economic privilege and monopolies. And he became the most influential of the new eighteenth-century economic thinkers. In the following century, his work and his followers became the target of reformers and critics who had less faith in the power of markets to generate wealth and prosperity for all.

EMPIRE AND ENLIGHTENMENT

The colonial world loomed large in Enlightenment thinking. Enlightenment thinkers saw the Americas as an uncorrupted territory where humanity's natural simplicity was expressed in the lives of native peoples. In comparison, Europe and Europeans appeared decadent or corrupt. European colonial activities—especially the slave trade—raised pressing issues about humanitarianism, individual rights, and natural law. The effects of colonialism on Europe were a central Enlightenment theme.

Smith wrote in *The Wealth of Nations* that the "discovery of America, and that of a passage to the East Indies by the cape of Good Hope are the two greatest and most important events recorded in the history of mankind. What benefits, or what misfortunes to mankind may hereafter result from those great events," he continued, "no human wisdom can foresee." Smith's language was nearly identical to that of a Frenchman, the abbé Guillaume Thomas François Raynal. Raynal's massive *Philosophical and Political History of European Settlements and Trade in the Two Indies* (1770), a coauthored work like the *Encyclopedia,* was one of the most widely read works of the Enlightenment, going through twenty printings and at least forty pirated editions. Raynal drew his inspiration from the *Encyclopedia* and aimed at nothing less than a total history of colonization: customs and civilizations of indigenous peoples, natural history, exploration, and commerce in the Atlantic world and India.

Raynal also asked whether colonization had made humanity happier, more peaceful, or better. The question was fully in the spirit of the Enlightenment. So was the answer: Raynal believed that industry and trade brought improvement and progress. Like other Enlightenment writers, however, he and his coauthors considered natural simplicity an antidote to the corruptions of their culture. They sought out and idealized what they considered examples of "natural" humanity, many of them in the New World. What Europeans considered savage life might be "a hundred times preferable to that of societies corrupted by despotism," and they lamented the loss of humanity's "natural liberty." They condemned the tactics of the Spanish in Mexico and Peru, of the Portuguese in Brazil, and of the British in North America. They echoed Montesquieu's theme that good government required checks and balances against arbitrary authority. In the New World, they argued, Europeans found themselves with virtually unlimited power, which encouraged them to be arrogant, cruel, and despotic. In a later edition, after the outbreak of the American Revolution, the book went even further, drawing parallels between exploitation in the colonial world and inequality at home: "We are mad in the way we act with our colonies, and inhuman and mad in our conduct toward our peasants," asserted one author. Eighteenth-century radicals repeatedly warned that overextended empires sowed seeds of decadence and corruption at home.

Such critiques did little, however, to check the growing importance of colonial commerce in the eighteenth century. The wealth generated by colonial trade tied the interests of governments and transoceanic merchants in an increasingly tight embrace. Merchants engaged in the colonial trade depended on their governments to protect and defend their overseas investments; but governments in turn depended on merchants and their financial backers to build the ships and sustain the trade on which national power depended. As this colonial trade grew in importance, no issue challenged Enlightenment thinkers as much as the institution of slavery, which was central to the Atlantic trade.

Slavery and the Atlantic World

The Atlantic slave trade (see Chapter 14) reached its peak in the eighteenth century. European slave traders sent at least 1 million Africans into New World slavery in the late seventeenth century, and at least 6 million in the eighteenth century. Control of the slave trade became fundamental to great power politics in Europe during this period, as the British used their dominance of the trade to their advantage in their long-running competition with France.

Analyzing Primary Sources

The Impact of the New World on Enlightenment Thinkers

The abbé Guillaume Thomas François Raynal (1713–1796) was a clergyman and intellectual who moved in the inner circles of the Enlightenment. As a senior cleric, he had access to the royal court; as a writer and intellectual, he worked with the encyclopedists and other authors who criticized France's institutions, including the Catholic Church of which Raynal himself was a part. Here, he tries to offer a perspective on the profound effects of discovering the Americas and ends by asking whether particular historical developments and institutions lead to the betterment of society.

 here has never been any event which has had more impact on the human race in general and for Europeans in particular, as that of the discovery of the New World, and the passage to the Indies around the Cape of Good Hope. It was then that a commercial revolution began, a revolution in the balance of power, and in the customs, the industries and the government of every nation. It was through this event that men in the most distant lands were linked by new relationships and new needs. The produce of equatorial regions were consumed in polar climes. The industrial products of the north were transported to the south; the textiles of the Orient became the luxuries of Westerners; and everywhere men mutually exchanged their opinions, their laws, their customs, their illnesses, and their medicines, their virtues and their vices. Everything changed, and will go on changing. But will the changes of the past and those that are to come be useful to humanity? Will they give man one day more peace, more happiness, or more pleasure? Will his condition be better, or will it be simply one of constant change?

Source: Abbé Guillaume Thomas François Raynal, *Philosophical and Political History of European Settlements and Trade in the Two Indies* (1770), as cited in Dorinda Outram, *The Enlightenment* (Cambridge: 1995), p. 73.

Questions for Analysis

1. Why does Raynal attribute such significance to the voyages of exploration that connected Europe to the Americas and to Africa and Asia? Which peoples were changed by these voyages?

2. Why is Raynal concerned with people's conduct and happiness rather than, say, the wealth of states?

3. Is Raynal clear about whether the changes he enumerates are a gain or a loss for humanity?

Even thinkers as radical as Raynal and Diderot hesitated to criticize the slave trade, however, and their hesitations are revealing about the tensions in Enlightenment thought. Enlightenment thinking began with the premise that individuals could reason for and govern themselves. Individual moral freedom lay at the heart of what the Enlightenment considered to be a just, stable, and harmonious society. Slavery defied natural law and natural freedom. Montesquieu, for instance, wrote that civil law created chains, but natural law would always break them. Nearly all Enlightenment thinkers condemned slavery in the metaphorical sense. That the "mind should break free of its chains" and that "despotism enslaved the king's subjects" were phrases that echoed through much eighteenth-century writing. It was common for the central characters of eighteenth-century fiction, such as Voltaire's hero Candide, to meet enslaved people, learning compassion as part of their moral education. Writers dealt more gingerly, however, with the actual enslavement and slave labor of Africans.

Some Enlightenment thinkers skirted the issue of slavery. Others reconciled principle and practice in different ways. Smith condemned slavery as uneconomical. Voltaire, quick to expose his contemporaries' hypocrisy, wondered whether Europeans would look away if Europeans—rather than Africans—were enslaved. Voltaire, however, did not question his belief that Africans were inferior peoples. Montesquieu (who came from Bordeaux, one of the central ports for the Atlantic trade) believed that slavery debased master and slave alike. But he also argued that all societies balanced their systems of labor in accordance with their different needs, and slave labor was one such system.

Slavery and the Enlightenment

The encyclopedists made an exhaustive and deliberate effort to comment on every institution, trade, and custom in Western culture. The project was conceived as an effort to catalog, analyze, and improve each facet of society. Writing in an age of burgeoning maritime trade and expanding overseas empires, they could not, and did not wish to, avoid the subject of slavery. These were their thoughts on plantation slavery, the African slaves who bore its brunt, and broader questions of law and liberty posed by the whole system.

Thus there is not a single one of these hapless souls—who, we maintain, are but slaves—who does not have the right to be declared free, since he has never lost his freedom; since it was impossible for him to lose it; and since neither his ruler nor his father nor anyone else had the right to dispose of his freedom; consequently, the sale of his person is null and void in and of itself: this Negro does not divest himself, indeed cannot under any condition divest himself of his natural rights; he carries them everywhere with him, and he has the right to demand that others allow him to enjoy those rights. Therefore, it is a clear case of inhumanity on the part of the judges in those free countries to which the slave is shipped, not to free the slave instantly by legal declaration, since he is their brother, having a soul like theirs.

Source: From *Encyclopédie*, vol. 16 (1765), as cited in David Brion Davis, *The Problem of Slavery in Western Culture* (Ithaca, NY: 1966), p. 416.

Questions for Analysis

1. What arguments against slavery does this *Encyclopedia* article present? What "natural rights" were violated by the practice, according to this view?

2. The enslavement of conquered peoples was historically an ancient and well-established custom, approved by civil and religious authorities. Even some Enlightenment figures, such as Thomas Jefferson, were slave owners. How did some Enlightenment philosophes use universal ideas of freedom to argue against custom in regard to slavery and other questions?

Finally, like many Enlightenment thinkers, Montesquieu defended property rights, including those of slaveholders.

The *Encyclopedia*'s article on the slave trade did condemn the slave trade in the clearest possible terms as a violation of self-government. Humanitarian antislavery movements, which emerged in the 1760s, advanced similar arguments. From deploring slavery to imagining freedom for slaves, however, proved a very long step, and one that few were willing to take. In the end, the Enlightenment's environmental determinism—the belief that environment shaped character—provided a common way of postponing the entire issue. Slavery corrupted its victims, destroyed their natural virtue, and crushed their natural love of liberty. Enslaved people, by this logic, were not ready for freedom. It was characteristic for Warville de Brissot's Society of the Friends of Blacks to call for abolition of the slave trade and to invite Thomas Jefferson, a slaveholder, to join the organization. Only a very few advocated abolishing slavery, and they insisted that emancipation be gradual. The debate about slavery demonstrated that different currents in Enlightenment thought could lead to very different conclusions.

Exploration and the Pacific World

The Pacific world also figured prominently in Enlightenment thinking. Systematically mapping new sections of the Pacific was among the crucial developments of the age and had tremendous impact on the public imagination. These explorations were also scientific missions, sponsored as part of the Enlightenment project of expanding scientific knowledge. In 1767, the French government sent Louis-Antoine de Bougainville (1729–1811) to the South Pacific in search of a new route to China, new lands suitable for colonization, and new spices for the ever lucrative trade. Bougainville found none of what he sought, but his travel accounts—above all his fabulously lush descriptions of the earthly paradise of Nouvelle-Cythère, or Tahiti—captured the imaginations of many at home. The British captain James Cook (1728–1779), who followed Bougainville, made two trips into the South Pacific (1768–1771 and 1772–1775), with impressive results. He charted the coasts of New Zealand and New Holland and added the New Hebrides and Hawaii to European maps. He explored the outer limits of the Antarctic continent, the shores of the Bering Sea, and the Arctic Ocean.

The artists and scientists who accompanied Cook and Bougainville vastly expanded the boundaries of European botany, zoology, and geology. Their drawings—such as Sydney Parkinson's extraordinary portraits of the Maori and William Hodge's portraits of Tahitians—appealed to a wide public. So did the accounts of dangers overcome and peoples encountered. A misguided attempt to communicate with South Pacific islanders, perhaps with the intention of conveying them to Europe, ended in the grisly deaths of Cook and four royal marines on Hawaii in late January 1779. Large numbers of people in Europe avidly read travel accounts of these voyages. When Cook and Bougainville brought Pacific islanders to the metropolis, they attracted large crowds.

The Impact of the Scientific Missions

Back in Europe, Enlightenment thinkers drew freely on reports of scientific missions. Since they were already committed to understanding human nature and the origins of society and to studying the effects of the environment on character and culture, stories of new peoples and cultures were immediately fascinating. In 1772, Diderot, one of many eager readers of Bougainville's accounts, published his own reflections on the cultural significance of those accounts, the *Supplément au Voyage de Bougainville*. For Diderot, the Tahitians were the original human beings and, unlike the inhabitants of the New World, were virtually free of European influence. They represented humanity in its natural state, Diderot believed, uninhibited about sexuality and free of religious dogma. Their simplicity exposed the hypocrisy and rigidity of overcivilized Europeans. Others considered the indigenous peoples of the Pacific akin to the classical civiliza-

tions of Greeks and Romans, associating Tahitian women, for instance, with Venus, the Roman goddess of love.

All these views said more about Europe and European utopias than about indigenous cultures in the Pacific. Enlightenment thinkers found it impossible to see other peoples as anything other than primitive versions of Europeans. Even these views, however, marked a change from former times. In earlier periods, Europeans had understood the world as divided between Christendom and heathen others. Now all peoples were seen to be part of a shared humanity, with cultures and beliefs that reflected their own experiences. In sum, during the eighteenth century a religious understanding of Western identity was giving way to more secular and historical explanations for human diversity.

One of the most important scientific explorers of the period was the German scientist Alexander von Humboldt. Humboldt spent five years in Spanish America, aiming to do nothing less than assess the civilization and natural resources of the continent. He went equipped with the most advanced scientific instruments Europe could provide. Humboldt, in good Enlightenment fashion, attempted to demonstrate that climate and physical environment determined which forms of life would survive in any given region. These investigations inspired nineteenth-century discussions of evolutionary change. Charles Darwin referred to Humboldt as "the greatest scientific traveler who ever lived,"

MAORIS IN A WAR CANOE NEAR LOOKOUT POINT. This copy of an illustration by Sydney Parkinson, who accompanied James Cook's explorations, is typical of the images of the South Pacific that may have circulated in Europe in the late eighteenth century.
- *What questions might have been prompted among Enlightenment thinkers by an increased awareness of different cultures throughout the globe?*

Interpreting Visual Evidence

The Europeans Encounter the Peoples of the Pacific in the Eighteenth Century

When European explorers set out to map the Pacific, they brought with them artists to paint the landscapes and peoples they encountered. Later, other artists produced engravings of the original paintings and these engravings were made available to a wider public. In this way, even people of modest means or only limited literacy could learn something about the different cultures and peoples that were now in more regular contact with European commerce elsewhere in the world.

These artists documented what they saw, but their vision was also shaped by the ideas that they brought with them and by the classical European styles of portraiture and landscape painting that they had been trained to produce. On the one hand, their images sometimes emphasized the exotic or essentially different quality of life in the Pacific. At the same time, the use of conventional poses in the portraiture or in the depiction of human forms suggested hints of a developing understanding of the extent to which Europeans and people elsewhere in the world shared essential human characteristics. This ambiguity was

A. *Portrait of Omai* by Joshua Reynolds (c. 1774).

B. "Omiah [*sic*] the Indian from Otaheite, presented to their Majesties at Kew," 1774.

and the German scientist's writing inspired Darwin's voyage to the Galápagos Islands off the coast of Ecuador.

Thus Europeans who looked outward did so for a variety of reasons and reached very different conclusions. For some Enlightenment thinkers and rulers, scientific reports from overseas fitted into a broad inquiry about civilization and human nature. That inquiry at times encouraged self-criticism and at others simply shored up Europeans' sense of their superiority. These themes reemerged during the nineteenth century, when new empires were built and the West's place in the world was reassessed.

THE RADICAL ENLIGHTENMENT

How revolutionary was the Enlightenment? Enlightenment thought did undermine central tenets of eighteenth-century culture and politics. It had wide resonance, well beyond a small group of intellectuals. Yet Enlightenment thinkers did not hold to any single political position. Even the most radical among them disagreed on the implications of their thought. Jean-Jacques Rousseau and Mary Wollstonecraft provide good examples of such radical thinkers.

C. *View of the Inside of a House in the Island of Ulietea, with the Representation of a Dance to the Music of the Country*, engraving after Sydney Parkinson, 1773.

The two artists had never visited the South Pacific, and their image is noteworthy for the way that the bodies of the islanders were rendered according to the classical styles of European art.

Questions for Analysis

1. Does the Reynolds portrait, in its choice of posture and expression, imply that Europeans and the peoples of the Pacific might share essential traits? What uses might Enlightenment thinkers have made of such a universalist implication?

2. How might a contemporary person in Britain have reacted to the portrait of Omai kneeling before the king?

3. Do you think image C is an accurate representation of life in the South Pacific? What purpose did such imaginary and idyllic scenes serve for their audience in Europe?

typical of Enlightenment political and social thought, which sought to uncover universal human truths, while at the same time remaining deeply interested and invested in exploring the differences they observed in peoples from various parts of the globe.

The first two images depict a Tahitian named Omai, who came to Britain as a crew member on a naval vessel in July 1774. Taken three days later to meet King George III and Queen Charlotte at Kew (image B), he became a celebrity in England and had his portrait drawn by Joshua Reynolds, a famous painter of the period (image A). The third image is an engraving by two Florentine artists after a drawing by Sydney Parkinson, who was with James Cook on his first voyage to the Pacific in 1768 (image C).

The World of Rousseau

Jean-Jacques Rousseau (*roo-SOH*, 1712–1778) was an "outsider" who quarreled with the other philosophes. He shared the philosophes' search for intellectual and political freedom, and he attacked inherited privilege, yet he introduced other strains into Enlightenment thought, especially what was then called "sensibility," or the cult of feeling. Rousseau's interest in emotions led him to develop a more complicated portrait of human psychology than that of Enlightenment writers, who emphasized reason as the most important attribute of human beings.

He was also considerably more radical than his counterparts, one of the first to talk about popular sovereignty and democracy.

Rousseau's milestone and difficult treatise on politics, *The Social Contract,* began with a now famous paradox: "Man was born free, and everywhere he is in chains." How had humans freely forged these chains? What were the origins of government? Was government's authority legitimate? If not, Rousseau asked, how could it become so?

Rousseau argued that in the state of nature all men had been equal. (On women, men, and nature, see **Competing Viewpoints** on pages 566–67) Social inequality, anchored

Analyzing Primary Sources

Rousseau's Social Contract (1762)

Jean-Jacques Rousseau (1712–1778) was one of the most radical Enlightenment thinkers. In his works, he suggested that humans needed not only a clearer understanding of natural laws but also a much closer relationship with nature itself and a thorough reorganization of society. He believed that a sovereign society, formed by free association of equal citizens without patrons or factions, was the clearest expression of natural law. This society would make laws and order itself by the genuinely collective wisdom of its citizens. Rousseau sets out the definition of his sovereign society and its authority in the passages reprinted here.

Book I, Chapter 6

"To find a form of association that defends and protects the person and possessions of each associate with all the common strength, and by means of which each person, joining forces with all, nevertheless obeys only himself, and remains as free as before." Such is the fundamental problem to which the social contract furnishes the solution.

Book II, Chapter 4

What in fact is an act of sovereignty? It is not an agreement between a superior and an inferior, but an agreement between the body and each of its members, a legitimate agreement, because it is based upon the social contract; equitable, because it is common to all; useful, because it can have no other purpose than the general good; and reliable, because it is guaranteed by the public force and the supreme power. As long as the subjects are only bound by agreements of this sort, they obey no one but their own will, and to ask how far the respective rights of the sovereign and citizens extend is to ask to what point the latter can commit themselves to each other, one towards all and all towards one.

Source: Jean-Jacques Rousseau, *Rousseau's Political Writings*, trans. Julia Conaway Bondanella, ed. Allan Ritter and Julia Conaway Bondanella (New York: 1988), pp. 92–103.

Questions for Analysis

1. What was the goal of political association, according to Rousseau?

2. How did Rousseau claim to overcome the tension between the need for some form of social constraint and the desire to preserve liberty?

3. What is more important for Rousseau: equality or liberty?

---

in private property, profoundly corrupted "the social contract," or the formation of government. Under conditions of inequality, governments and laws represented only the rich and privileged. They became instruments of repression and enslavement. Legitimate governments could be formed, Rousseau argued. "The problem is to find a form of association . . . in which each, while uniting himself with all, may still obey himself alone, and remain as free as before." Freedom did not mean the absence of restraint, it meant that equal citizens obeyed laws they had made themselves. Rousseau hardly imagined any social leveling, and by *equality* he meant only that no one would be "rich enough to buy another, nor poor enough to have to sell oneself."

Rousseau's argument about legitimate authority has three parts. First, sovereignty belonged to the people alone. This meant sovereignty should not be divided among different branches of government (as suggested by Montesquieu), and it could not be usurped by a king. Second, exercising sovereignty transformed the nation. Rousseau argued that when individual citizens formed a "body politic," that body became more than just the sum of its parts. He offered what was to many an appealing image of a regenerated and more powerful nation, in which citizens were bound by mutual obligation rather than coercive laws and united in equality rather than divided and weakened by privilege. Third, the national community would be united by what Rousseau called the "general will." This term is notoriously difficult. Rousseau proposed it as a way to understand the common interest, which rose above particular individual demands. The general will favored equality; that made it general, and in principle at least equality guaranteed that citizens' common interests would be represented in the whole.

Rousseau's lack of concern for balancing private interests against the general will leads some political theorists to

ENLIGHTENMENT EDUCATION AS ILLUSTRATED IN *EMILE*. These colored engravings from Rousseau's influential novel depict Emile's studies in the great outdoors as opposed to the classroom.

consider him authoritarian, coercive, or moralistic. Others interpret the general will as one expression of his utopianism. In the eighteenth century, *The Social Contract* was the least understood of Rousseau's works. Yet it provided influential radical arguments and, more important, extraordinarily powerful images and phrases, which were widely cited during the French Revolution.

Rousseau was also well known for his writing on education and moral virtue. His widely read novel *Emile* (1762) tells the story of a young man who learns virtue and moral autonomy in the school of nature rather than in the academy. Rousseau disagreed with other *philosophes'* emphasis on reason, insisting instead that "the first impulses of nature are always right." Children should not be forced to reason early in life. Books, which "teach us only to talk about things we do not know," should not be central to learning until adolescence. Emile's tutor thus walked him through the woods, studying nature and its simple precepts, cultivating his conscience, and above all, his sense of independence. "Nourished in the most absolute liberty, the greatest evil he can imagine is servitude."

Such an education aimed to give men moral autonomy and make them good citizens. Rousseau argued that women should have very different educations. "All education of women must be relative to men, pleasing them, being useful to them, raising them when they are young and caring for them when they are old, advising them, consoling them, making their lives pleasant and agreeable, these have been the duties of women since time began." Women were to be useful socially as mothers and wives. In *Emile,* Rousseau laid out just such an education for Emile's wife-to-be, Sophie. At times, Rousseau seemed convinced that women "naturally" sought out such a role: "Dependence is a natural state for women, girls feel themselves made to obey." At other moments he insisted that girls needed to be disciplined and weaned from their "natural" vices.

Rousseau's conflicting views on female nature provide a good example of the shifting meaning of nature, a concept central to Enlightenment thought. Enlightenment thinkers used nature as a yardstick against which to measure society's shortcomings. "Natural" was better, simpler, uncorrupted. What, though, was nature? It could refer to the physical world. It could refer to allegedly primitive societies. Often, it was a useful invention.

Rousseau's novels sold exceptionally well, especially among women. *Julie* (subtitled *La nouvelle Héloïse*), published just after *Emile*, went through seventy editions in three decades. *Julie* tells the story of a young woman who falls in love with one man but dutifully obeys her father's order to marry another. At the end, she dies of exposure after rescuing her children from a cold lake—a perfect example of domestic and maternal virtue. The tragic love story and Rousseau's conviction that the heart was as important as the mind and that passion was more important than reason appealed to his audience. Rousseau's novels became part of a larger cult of *sensibilité* ("feeling") in middle-class and aristocratic circles, an emphasis on spontaneous expressions of feeling, and a belief that sentiment was an expression of authentic humanity. Thematically, this aspect of Rousseau's work contradicted much of the Enlightenment's cult of reason. It is more closely related to the concerns of nineteenth-century romanticism.

The World of Wollstonecraft

Rousseau's sharpest critic was the British writer Mary Wollstonecraft (1759–1797). Wollstonecraft published her best known work, *A Vindication of the Rights of Woman,* in 1792, during the French Revolution. Her argument, however, was anchored in Enlightenment debates and needs to be

Competing Viewpoints

Rousseau and His Readers

Jean-Jacques Rousseau's writings provoked very different responses from eighteenth-century readers—women as well as men. Many women readers loved his fiction and found his views about women's character and prescriptions for their education inspiring. Other women disagreed vehemently with his conclusions. In the first excerpt here, from Rousseau's novel Emile (1762), the author sets out his views on a woman's education. He argues that her education should fit with what he considers her intellectual capacity and her social role. It should also complement the education and role of a man. The second selection is an admiring response to Emile from Anne-Louise-Germaine Necker, or Madame de Staël (1766–1817), a well-known French writer and literary critic. While she acknowledged that Rousseau sought to keep women from participating in political discussion, she also thought that he had granted women a new role in matters of emotion and domesticity. The third excerpt is from Mary Wollstonecraft, who shared many of Rousseau's philosophical principles but sharply disagreed with his assertion that women and men should have different virtues and values. She believed that women like Madame de Staël were misguided in embracing Rousseau's ideas.

Rousseau's Emile

Researches into abstract and speculative truths, the principles and axioms of sciences—in short, everything which tends to generalize our ideas—is not the proper province of women; their studies should be relative to points of practice; it belongs to them to apply those principles which men have discovered.... All the ideas of women, which have not the immediate tendency to points of duty, should be directed to the study of men, and to the attainment of those agreeable accomplishments which have taste for their object; for as to works of genius, they are beyond their capacity; neither have they sufficient precision or power of attention to succeed in sciences which require accuracy; and as to physical knowledge, it belongs to those only who are most active, most inquisitive, who comprehend the greatest variety of objects....

She must have the skill to incline us to do everything which her sex will not enable her to do herself, and which is necessary or agreeable to her; therefore she ought to study the mind of man thoroughly, not the mind of man in general, abstractedly, but the dispositions of those men to whom she is subject either by the laws of her country or by the force of opinion. She should learn to penetrate into the real sentiments from their conversation, their actions, their looks and gestures. She should also have the art, by her own conversation, actions, looks, and gestures, to communicate those sentiments which are agreeable to them without seeming to intend it. Men will argue more philosophically about the human heart; but women will read the heart of men better than they.... Women have most wit, men have most genius; women observe, men reason. From the concurrence of both we derive the clearest light and the most perfect knowledge which the human mind is of itself capable of attaining.

Source: Jean-Jacques Rousseau, Emile (1762), as cited in Mary Wollstonecraft, A Vindication of the Rights of Woman (New York: 1992), pp. 124–25.

understood here. Wollstonecraft shared Rousseau's political views and admired his writing and influence. Like Rousseau and her countryman Thomas Paine, a writer who supported the American and French Revolutions, Wollstonecraft was a republican. She called monarchy "the pestiferous purple which renders the progress of civilization a curse, and warps the understanding." She spoke even more forcefully than Rousseau against inequality and the artificial distinctions of rank, birth, or wealth. Believing that equality laid the basis for virtue, she contended, in classic Enlightenment language, that the society should seek "the perfection of our nature and capability of happiness." She argued more forcefully than any other Enlightenment thinker that (1) women had the same innate capacity for reason and self-government as men, (2) virtue should mean the same thing for men and women, and (3) relations between the sexes should be based on equality.

Madame De Staël

Though Rousseau has endeavoured to prevent women from interfering in public affairs, and acting a brilliant part in the theatre of politics; yet in speaking of them, how much has he done it to their satisfaction! If he wished to deprive them of some rights foreign to their sex, how has he for ever restored to them all those to which it has a claim! And in attempting to diminish their influence over the deliberations of men, how sacredly has he established the empire they have over their happiness! In aiding them to descend from an usurped throne, he has firmly seated them upon that to which they were destined by nature; and though he be full of indignation against them when they endeavour to resemble men, yet when they come before him with all the *charms, weaknesses, virtues,* and *errors* of their sex, his respect for their *persons* amounts almost to adoration.

Source: Cited in Mary Wollstonecraft, *A Vindication of the Rights of Woman* (New York: 1992), pp. 203–4.

Mary Wollstonecraft

Rousseau declares that a woman should never, for a moment, feel herself independent, that she should be governed by fear to exercise her *natural* cunning, and made a coquettish slave in order to render her a more alluring object of desire, a *sweeter* companion to man, whenever he chooses to relax himself. He carries the arguments, which he pretends to draw from the indications of nature, still further, and insinuates that truth and fortitude, the corner stones of all human virtue, should be cultivated with certain restrictions, because, with respect to the female character, obedience is the grand lesson which ought to be impressed with unrelenting rigour.

What nonsense! When will a great man arise with sufficient strength of mind to puff away the fumes which pride and sensuality have thus spread over the subject! If women are by nature inferior to men, their virtues must be the same in quality, if not in degree, or virtue is a relative idea; consequently, their conduct should be founded on the same principles, and have the same aim.

Source: Cited in Susan Bell and Karen Offen, eds., *Women, the Family, and Freedom: The Debate in Documents,* vol. 1, 1750–1880 (Stanford, CA: 1983), p. 58.

Questions for Analysis

1. Why did Rousseau seek to limit the sphere of activities open to women in society? What capacities did he feel they lacked? What areas of social life did he feel women were most suited for?

2. Did Madame de Staël agree with Rousseau that women's social roles were essentially different from men's roles in society?

3. What is the basis for Mary Wollstonecraft's disagreement with Rousseau?

4. Why did gender matter to Enlightenment figures such as Rousseau, De Staël, and Wollstonecraft?

Wollstonecraft did what few of her contemporaries even imagined. She applied the radical Enlightenment critique of monarchy and inequality to the family. The legal inequalities of marriage law, which among other things deprived married women of property rights, gave husbands "despotic" power over their wives. Just as kings cultivated their subjects' deference, so culture, she argued, cultivated women's weakness. "Civilized women are . . . so weakened by false refinement, that, respecting morals, their condition is much below what it would be were they left in a state nearer to nature." Middle-class girls learned manners, grace, and seductiveness to win a husband; they were trained to be dependent creatures. "My own sex, I hope, will excuse me, if I treat them like rational creatures instead of flattering their *fascinating* graces, and viewing them as if they were in a state of perpetual childhood, unable to stand

THE ENLIGHTENMENT AND EIGHTEENTH-CENTURY CULTURE

The Book Trade

MARY WOLLSTONECRAFT. The British writer and radical suggested that Enlightenment critiques of monarchy could also be applied to the power of fathers within the family.

alone. I earnestly wish to point out in what true dignity and human happiness consists—I wish to persuade women to endeavor to acquire strength, both of mind and body." A culture that encouraged feminine weakness produced women who were childish, cunning, cruel—and vulnerable. To Rousseau's specific prescriptions for female education, which included teaching women timidity, chasteness, and modesty, Wollstonecraft replied that Rousseau wanted women to use their reason to "burnish their chains rather than to snap them." Instead, education for women had to promote liberty and self-reliance. She was considered scandalously radical for merely hinting that women might have political rights.

The Enlightenment as a whole left a mixed legacy on gender, one that closely paralleled that on slavery. Enlightenment writers developed and popularized arguments about natural rights. They also elevated natural differences to a higher plane by suggesting that nature should dictate different, and quite possibly unequal, social roles. Mary Wollstonecraft and Jean-Jacques Rousseau shared a radical opposition to despotism and slavery, a moralist's vision of a corrupt society, and a concern with virtue and community. Their divergence on gender is characteristic of Enlightenment disagreements about nature and its imperatives and a good example of different directions in which the logic of Enlightenment thinking could lead.

What about the social structures that produced these debates and received these ideas? To begin with, the Enlightenment was bound up in a much larger expansion of printing and print culture. From the early eighteenth century on, book publishing and selling flourished, especially in Britain, France, the Netherlands, and Switzerland. National borders, though, mattered very little. Much of the book trade was both international and clandestine. Readers bought books from stores, by subscription, and by special mail order from book distributors abroad. Cheaper printing and better distribution also helped multiply the numbers of journals, some specializing in literary or scientific topics and others quite general. They helped bring daily newspapers, which first appeared in London in 1702, to Moscow, Rome, and cities and towns throughout Europe. By 1780, Britons could read 150 different magazines, and thirty-seven English towns had local newspapers. These changes have been called a "revolution in communication," and they form a crucial part of the larger picture of the Enlightenment.

Governments did little to check this revolutionary transformation. In Britain, the press encountered few restrictions, although the government did use a stamp tax on printed goods to raise the price of newspapers or books and discourage buyers. Elsewhere, laws required publishers to apply in advance for the license or privilege (in the sense of "private right") to print and sell any given work. In practice, publishers frequently printed books without advance permission, hoping that the regime would not notice. Russian, Prussian, and Austrian censors tolerated much less dissent, but those governments also sought to stimulate publishing and, to a certain degree, permitted public discussion. In the smaller states of Germany and Italy, governed by many local princes, it was easier to find progressive local patrons, and English and French works also circulated widely through those regions. That governments were patrons as well as censors of new scholarship illustrates the complex relationship between the age of absolutism and the Enlightenment.

As one historian puts it, censorship only made banned books expensive, keeping them out of the hands of the poor. Clandestine booksellers, most near the French border in Switzerland and the Rhineland, smuggled thousands of books across the border to bookstores, distributors, and private customers. What did readers want, and what does this tell us about the reception of the Enlightenment? Many clandestine dealers specialized in what they called "philosophical books," which meant subversive literature of all kinds: stories of languishing in prison, gossipy memoirs of life at the court, pornographic fantasies (often about religious and political figures), and tales of crime and criminals. Much of this flourishing eighteenth-century "literary underground" echoed the radical Enlightenment's themes, especially the corruption of the aristocracy and the monarchy's degeneration into despotism.

High Culture, New Elites, and the Public Sphere

The Enlightenment was not simply embodied in books; it was produced in networks of readers and new forms of sociability and discussion. These networks included people of diverse backgrounds. Eighteenth-century elite, or "high," culture was small in scale but cosmopolitan and very literate, and it took literary and scientific discussion seriously. Middle-class men and women also became consumers of literature. Meanwhile, popular discussions of Enlightenment themes developed in the coffeehouses and taverns of European cities, where printed material might be read aloud, allowing even illiterate people to have access to the news and debates of the day. Together, this permissive atmosphere of frequent discussion among people of different social position led to the development of a new idea: "public opinion."

Among the institutions that produced a new elite were learned societies: the American Philosophical Society of Philadelphia, British literary and philosophical societies, and the Select Society of Edinburgh. Such groups organized intellectual life outside of the universities, and they provided libraries, meeting places for discussion, and journals that published members' papers or organized debates on issues from literature and history to economics and ethics. Elites also met in "academies," financed by governments to advance knowledge, whether through research into the natural sciences (the Royal Society of London, and the French Academy of Science, both founded in 1660, and the Berlin Royal Academy in 1701), promoting the national language (the Académie Française, or French Academy of Literature), or safeguarding traditions in the arts (the various academies of painting). In smaller cities in the countryside, provincial academies played much the same role,

providing a way for Enlightenment discussions to spread beyond European capitals.

Salons provided an alternative venue for discussion but operated informally. Usually they were organized by well-connected and learned aristocratic women who invited local personalities to their homes to meet with authors and discuss their latest works. The prominent role of women distinguished the salons from the academies and universities. Salons brought together men and women of letters with members of the aristocracy for conversation, debate, drink, and food. Rousseau loathed this kind of ritual and viewed salons as a sign of superficiality and vacuity in a privileged and overcivilized world. Thomas Jefferson thought the influence of women in salons had put France in a "desperate state." Some of the salons reveled in parlor games. Others, such as the one organized in Paris by Madame Necker, wife of the future French reform minister, lay quite close to the halls of power and served as testing ground for new policy ideas. Madame Marie-Thérèse Geoffrin, another celebrated French *salonière*, became an important patron of the *Encyclopedia* and exercised influence in placing scholars in academies. Moses Mendelssohn held an open house for intellectuals in Berlin. Salons in London, Vienna, Rome, and Berlin worked the same way, and like academies, they promoted among their participants a sense of belonging to an active, learned elite.

Scores of similar societies emerged in the eighteenth century, eventually breaking the hold of elites over public debate and literate discussion. Masonic lodges, organizations with elaborate secret rituals whose members pledged themselves to the regeneration of society, attracted a remarkable array of aristocrats and middle-class men. The composer Wolfgang Amadeus Mozart, Emperor Frederick II, and Montesquieu were Masons. Behind their closed doors, the lodges were egalitarian. They pledged themselves to a common project of rational thought and benevolent action and to banishing religion and social distinction—at least from their ranks. Other networks of sociability were even less exclusive. Coffeehouses multiplied with the colonial trade in sugar, coffee, and tea, and they occupied a central spot in the circulation of ideas. A group of merchants gathering to discuss trade, for instance, could turn to politics; and the many newspapers lying about the cafe tables provided a ready-to-hand link between their smaller discussions and news and debates elsewhere.

Eighteenth-century cultural changes—the expanding networks of sociability, the flourishing book trade, the new genres of literature, and the circulation of Enlightenment ideas—widened the circles of reading and discussion, expanding what some historians and political theorists call the "public sphere." That, in turn, began to change politics. Informal deliberations, debates about how to regenerate

A READING IN THE SALON OF MADAME GEOFFRIN, 1755. Enlightenment salons encouraged a spirit of intellectual inquiry and civil debate, at least among educated elites. Such salon discussions were notable for the extent to which women helped organize and participate in the conversations. This fact led Rousseau to attack the salons for encouraging unseemly posturing and promiscuity between the sexes, which he believed were the antithesis of rational pursuits. In this painting, Madame Geoffrin, a famed hostess (at left in gray), presides over a discussion of a learned work. Note the bust of Voltaire in the background, the patron saint of rationalist discourse. ▪ *What developments were required for this notion of free public discussion among elites to become more general in society?* ▪ *Would Enlightenment thinkers favor such developments? (Compare with images on pages 557 and 571).*

the nation, discussions of civic virtue, and efforts to forge a consensus played a crucial role in moving politics beyond the confines of the court.

A French observer described the changes this way: "In the last thirty years alone, a great and important revolution has occurred in our ideas. Today, public opinion has a preponderant force in Europe that cannot be resisted." Few thought the "public" involved more than the elite. Yet, by the late eighteenth century, European governments recognized the existence of a civic-minded group that stretched from salons to coffeehouses, academies, and circles of government and to which they needed, in some measure, to respond.

Middle-Class Culture and Reading

Enlightenment fare constituted only part of the new cultural interests of the eighteenth-century middle classes. Lower on the social scale, shopkeepers, small merchants, lawyers, and professionals read more and more different kinds of books. Instead of owning one well-thumbed Bible to read aloud, a middle-class family would buy and borrow books to read casually, pass on, and discuss. This literature consisted of science, history, biography, travel literature, and fiction. A great deal of it was aimed at middle-class women, among the fastest-growing groups of readers in the eighteenth century. Etiquette books sold very well; so did how-to manuals for the household. Scores of books about the manners, morals, and education of daughters, popular versions of Enlightenment treatises on education and the mind, illustrate close parallels between the intellectual life of the high Enlightenment and everyday middle-class reading matter.

The rise of a middle-class reading public, much of it female, helps account for the soaring popularity and production of novels, especially in Britain. Novels were the single most popular new form of literature in the eighteenth century. A survey of library borrowing in late-eighteenth-century Britain, Germany, and North America showed that 70 percent of books taken out were novels. For centuries,

Europeans had read romances such as tales of the Knights of the Round Table. The setting of popular novels was closer to home. The novel's more recognizable, nonaristocratic characters seemed more relevant to common middle-class experience. Moreover, examining emotion and inner feeling also linked novel writing with a larger eighteenth-century concern with personhood and humanity. As we have seen, classic Enlightenment writers like Voltaire, Goethe, and Rousseau wrote very successful novels; and those should be understood alongside the *Pamela* or *Clarissa* of Samuel Richardson (1689–1761), the *Moll Flanders* or *Robinson Crusoe* of Daniel Defoe (1660–1731), and the *Tom Jones* of Henry Fielding (1707–1754).

Many historians have noted that women figured prominently among fiction writers. The works of Jane Austen (1775–1817), especially *Pride and Prejudice* and *Emma,* are to many readers the height of a novelist's craft. Women writers, however, were not the only ones to write novels, nor were they alone in paying close attention to the domestic or private sphere. Their work took up central eighteenth-century themes of human nature, morality, virtue, and reputation. Their novels, like much of the non-fiction of the period, explored those themes in domestic as in public settings.

Popular Culture: Urban and Rural

How much did books and print culture touch the lives of the common people? Literacy rates varied dramatically by gender, social class, and region, but were generally higher in northern than in southern and eastern Europe. It is not surprising that literacy ran highest in cities and towns—higher, in fact, than we might expect. In early eighteenth-century Paris, 85 percent of men and 60 percent of women could read. Well over half the residents of poorer Parisian neighborhoods, especially small shopkeepers, domestic servants and valets, and artisans, could read and sign their names. Even the illiterate lived in a culture of print, though they had few books on their own shelves. They saw one-page newspapers and broadsides or fly sheets posted on streets and tavern walls and regularly heard them read aloud. Moreover, visual material—inexpensive woodcuts, especially, but also prints, drawings, satirical cartoons—figured as prominently as text in much popular reading material. By many measures, then, the circles of reading and discussion were even larger than literacy rates might suggest, especially in cities.

Neither England nor France required any primary schooling, leaving education to haphazard local initiatives. In central Europe, some regimes made efforts to develop state-sponsored education. Catherine of Russia summoned an Austrian consultant to set up a system of primary schools, but by the end of the eighteenth century only 22,000 of a population of 40 million had attended any kind of school. In the absence of primary schooling, most Europeans were self-taught. The varied texts in the peddler's cart—whether religious, political propaganda, or entertainment—attest to a widespread and rapidly growing popular interest in books and reading.

Like its middle-class counterpart, popular culture rested on networks of sociability. Guild organizations offered discussion and companionship. Street theater and singers mocking local political figures offered culture to

A COFFEEHOUSE IN LONDON, 1798. Coffeehouses served as centers of social networks and hubs of opinion contributing to a public consciousness that was new to the Enlightenment. This coffeehouse scene illustrates a mixing of classes, lively debate, and a burgeoning culture of reading. Compare this image with that of the aristocratic salon on page 570 and the meeting of Lessing and Mendelssohn on page 557. ▪ *How were coffeehouses different from aristocratic salons or the middle-class drawing room discussion between the two German thinkers?* ▪ *Can they all be seen as expressions of a new kind of "public sphere" in eighteenth-century Europe?*

Past and Present

The Internet and the Enlightenment Public Sphere

In many ways, today's Internet is simply a technologically sophisticated version of the public sphere of literate readers that was created and celebrated by the philosophes of the Enlightenment. It contains the same confusing mix of the educational, the commercial, the pleasurable . . . and the perverse.

 Watch related author interview on StudySpace
wwnorton.com/web/westernciv18

people from different social classes. The difficulties of deciphering popular culture are considerable. Most testimony comes to us from outsiders who regarded the common people as hopelessly superstitious and ignorant. Still, historical research has begun to reveal new insights. It has shown, first, that popular culture did not exist in isolation. Particularly in the countryside, market days and village festivals brought social classes together, and popular entertainments reached a wide social audience. Folktales and traditional songs resist pigeonholing as elite, middle-class, or popular culture, for they passed from one cultural world to another, being revised and reinterpreted in the process. Second, oral and literate culture overlapped. In other words, even people who could not read often had a great deal of "book knowledge": they argued seriously about points from books and believed that books conferred authority. A group of villagers, for

instance, wrote this eulogy to a deceased friend: "He read his life long, and died without ever knowing how to read." The logic and worldview of popular culture needs to be understood on its own terms.

It remains true that the countryside, especially in less economically developed regions, was desperately poor. Life there was far more isolated than in towns. A yawning chasm separated peasants from the world of the high Enlightenment. The philosophes, well established in the summits of European society, looked at popular culture with distrust and ignorance. They saw the common people of Europe much as they did indigenous peoples of other continents. They were humanitarians, critical thinkers, and reformers; they were not democrats. The Enlightenment, while well entrenched in eighteenth-century elite culture, nonetheless involved changes that reached well beyond elite society.

WAR AND POLITICS IN ENLIGHTENMENT EUROPE

War and Empire in the Eighteenth-Century World

After 1713, western Europe remained largely at peace for a generation. In 1740, however, that peace was shattered when Frederick the Great of Prussia seized the Austrian province of Silesia (see below). In the resulting War of the Austrian Succession, France and Spain fought on the side of Prussia, hoping to reverse some of the losses they had suffered in the Treaty of Utrecht. As they had done since the 1690s, Britain and the Dutch Republic sided with Austria. Like those earlier wars, this war quickly spread beyond the frontiers of Europe. In India, the British East India Company lost control over the coastal area of Madras to its French rival; but in North America, British colonists from New England captured the important French fortress of Louisbourg on Cape Breton Island, hoping to put a stop to French interference with their fishing and shipping. When the war finally ended in 1748, Britain recovered Madras and returned Louisbourg to France.

Eight years later, these colonial conflicts reignited when Prussia once again attacked Austria. This time, however, Prussia allied itself with Great Britain. Austria found support from both France and Russia. In Europe, the Seven Years' War (1756–63) ended in stalemate. In India and North America, however, the war had decisive consequences. In India, mercenary troops employed by the British East India Company joined with native allies to eliminate their French competitors. In North America (where the conflict was known as the French and Indian War), British troops captured both Louisbourg and Québec and also drove French forces from the Ohio River Valley and the Great Lakes. By the Treaty of Paris in 1763, which brought the Seven Years' War to an end, France formally surrendered both Canada and India to the British. Six years later, the French East India Company was dissolved.

Enlightened Absolutism in Eastern Europe

The rulers of Prussia, Austria, and Russia who initiated these wars on the continent were among the pioneers of a new style of "enlightened absolutism" within their realms. They demonstrated their commitment to absolutist rule by centralizing their administrations, increasing taxation, creating a professional army, and tightening their control of the Church. They justified this expansion of powers, however, in the name of the enlightenment ideal of reason—as rational solutions to the problems of government.

Rulers influenced by the spirit of enlightened absolutism included Empress Maria Theresa (r. 1740–80) of Austria and her son Joseph II (r. 1765–90; from 1765 until 1780 the two were co-rulers). The two rulers created statewide systems of primary education, relaxed censorship, and instituted a more liberal criminal code for the Habsburg Empire. Joseph II was particularly energetic in challenging the power of the Church: he closed hundreds of monasteries, drastically limited the number of monks and nuns permitted to live in contemplative orders, and ordered that the education of priests be placed under government supervision (see Chapter 15).

The most emblematic enlightened absolutist, however, was Frederick II (1740-1786) of Prussia. As a young man, Frederick devoted himself to the flute and admired French culture, exasperating his military-minded father, Frederick William I. When Frederick rebelled by running away from court with a friend, his father had them apprehended and the friend was executed before Frederick's eyes. The grisly lesson took. Although Frederick never gave up his love of music and literature, he applied himself energetically to his royal duties, earning himself the title of Frederick the Great.

Frederick raised Prussia to the status of a major power. In 1740, as soon as he became king, he mobilized his army and occupied the Austrian province of Silesia, with French support. Empress Maria Theresa, also new to the throne, counterattacked; but, despite support of Britain and Hungary, she could not recover Silesia. Eventually Frederick consolidated his gains over all the Polish territories that lay between East Prussia and Brandenburg, transforming Prussia by 1786 into a powerful, contiguous kingdom. Frederick was careful to cultivate support from the Prussian nobility, known as the Junkers. His father had recruited civil servants according to merit rather than birth, but Frederick relied on the Junkers to staff the army and his expanding administration. Frederick's strategy worked. His nobility remained loyal, and he fashioned the most professional and efficient bureaucracy in Europe.

Frederick supervised a series of "enlightened" social reforms: he prohibited the judicial torture of accused criminals, abolished the bribing of judges, and established a system of elementary schools. Although strongly anti-Semitic,

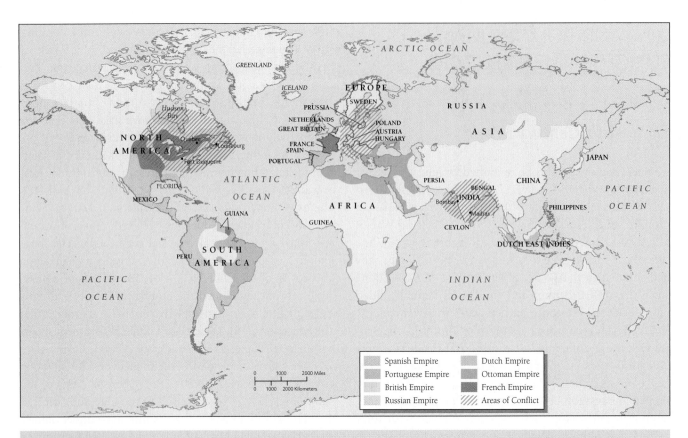

THE SEVEN YEARS' WAR, 1756–1763. ▪ *What continents were involved in the Seven Years' War?* ▪ *What was the impact of naval power on the outcome of the war?* ▪ *What were the consequences for the colonies involved in the conflict?*

he encouraged religious toleration toward Jews and declared that he would happily build a mosque in Berlin if he could find enough Muslims to fill it. On his own royal estates, he abolished capital punishment, curtailed the forced labor services of his peasantry, and granted these peasants long leases on the land they worked. He encouraged scientific forestry and the cultivation of new crops. He cleared new lands in Silesia and brought in thousands of immigrants to cultivate them. When wars ruined their farms, he supplied his peasants with new livestock and tools. But he never attempted to extend these reforms to the estates of the Prussian nobility. To have done so would have alienated the very group on whom Frederick's rule depended.

Like Frederick, Catherine the Great of Russia (r. 1762–96) thought of herself as an enlightened ruler and she corresponded with French philosophers. Also like Frederick, she could not afford to lose the support of the Russian nobility, who had placed her on the throne after executing her husband, the weak and possibly mad Peter III. Catherine's efforts at enlightened reform were limited: she founded hospitals and orphanages, created an elementary school system for the children of the provincial nobility, and called a commission to examine the possi-

bility of codifying Russian law. The commission's radical proposals—abolition of capital punishment and judicial torture, prohibitions on the selling of serfs—were set aside, however, after a massive peasant revolt in 1773–75 led by a Cossack named Emelyan Pugachev briefly threatened Moscow itself. Catherine's greatest achievements were gained through war and diplomacy. In 1774, she won control over the northern coast of the Black Sea after a war with the Ottoman Empire, and she also took several Ottoman provinces along the Danube River. Russia thus obtained a long-sought goal: a warm-water port for the Russian navy. In addition, Catherine succeeded in expanding Russian territory in the west, at the expense of the weaker kingdom of Poland.

The plan for Russia, Austria, and Prussia to divide Poland among them was originally proposed by Frederick the Great: Russia would abandon its Danubian provinces and receive in exchange the grain fields of eastern Poland (and between 1 and 2 million Poles); Austria would take Galicia (population 2.5 million) while Prussia would consolidate the divided lands of its kingdom by taking Poland's coastal regions on the Baltic coast. When the agreement was finalized in 1772, Poland had lost 30 percent of its

MARIA THERESA OF AUSTRIA AND HER FAMILY. A formidable and capable ruler who fought to maintain Austria's dominance in central Europe against the claims of Frederick the Great of Prussia, Maria Theresa had sixteen children, including Marie Antoinette, later queen of France as wife of Louis XVI. ■ *Why did she emphasize her role as mother in a royal portrait such as this one rather than her other undeniable political skills?* ■ *How does this compare to the portraits of Louis XIV or of William and Mary in Chapter 15, pages 494 and 503?*

CATHERINE THE GREAT. Rumored to have ordered the assassination of Peter III, Catherine oversaw an era of expansion in what was to become the longest female reign in Russian history.

territory and half of its population. After a second war between Russia and the Ottomans in 1788, Poland tried to reassert itself, but it was no match for the three major powers—Russia, Austria, and Prussia—and by 1795 Poland had disappeared from the map altogether.

As a political program, enlightened absolutism clearly had its limits. On the one hand, Catherine the Great, Frederick the Great, and Joseph II in Austria were clearly personally inspired by the literary culture of the philosophes, and their political programs reflected Enlightenment ideas about the rational organization of state institutions. On the other hand, they were ready to abandon the humanitarian impulse of Enlightenment thought and the ideal of self-government when it came to preserving their own power and the social hierarchies that sustained it.

The American Revolution

The American Revolution of 1776 provided a more fruitful opportunity for putting Enlightenment ideals into practice. Along the Atlantic seaboard, the rapidly growing Brit-

ish colonies chafed at rule from London. To recover some of the costs of the Seven Years' War and to pay for the continuing costs of protecting its colonial subjects, the British Parliament imposed a series of new taxes on its American colonies. These taxes were immediately unpopular. Colonists complained that because they had no representatives in Parliament, they were being taxed without their consent—a fundamental violation of their rights as British subjects. They also complained that British restrictions on colonial trade, particularly the requirement that certain goods pass first through British ports before being shipped to the Continent, were strangling American livelihoods and making it impossible to pay even the king's legitimate taxes.

The British government, led since 1760 by the young and inexperienced King George III, responded to these complaints with a badly calculated mixture of vacillation and force. Various taxes were imposed and then withdrawn in the face of colonial resistance. In 1773, however, when East India Company tea was dumped in Boston Harbor by rebellious colonials objecting to the customs duties that had been imposed on it, the British government closed the port of Boston and curtailed the colony's representative institutions. These "Coercive Acts" galvanized the support of the other American colonies for Massachusetts. In 1774, representatives from all the American colonies

The American Declaration of Independence

The Declaration of Independence, issued from Philadelphia on July 4, 1776, is perhaps the most famous single document of American history. But its familiarity does not lessen its interest as a piece of political philosophy. The indebtedness of the document's authors to the ideas of John Locke will be obvious from the selections here. But Locke, in turn, drew many of his ideas about the contractual and conditional nature of human government from the conciliarist thinkers of the fifteenth and early sixteenth centuries. The appeal of absolutism notwithstanding, the Declaration shows how vigorous the medieval tradition of contractual, limited government remained at the end of the eighteenth century.

When in the course of human events, it becomes necessary for one people to dissolve the political bonds which have connected them with another, and to assume among the powers of the earth the separate and equal station to which the Laws of Nature and of Nature's God entitle them, a decent respect to the opinions of mankind requires that they should declare the causes which impel them to the separation.... We hold these truths to be self-evident, that all men are created equal, that they are endowed by their Creator with certain unalienable rights, that among these are Life, Liberty and the pursuit of Happiness.... That to secure these rights, Governments are instituted among men, deriving their just powers from the consent of the governed.... That whenever any form of Government becomes destructive of these ends, it is the Right of the People to alter or to abolish it, and to institute new Government, laying its foundation upon such principles and organizing its power in such form, as to them shall seem most likely to effect their Safety and Happiness. Prudence, indeed, will dictate that Governments long established should not be changed for light and transient causes; and accordingly all experience has shown, that mankind are more disposed to suffer, while evils are sufferable, than to right themselves by abolishing the forms to which they are accustomed. But when a long train of abuses and usurpations, pursuing invariably the same Object, evinces a design to reduce them under absolute despotism, it is their right, it is their duty, to throw off such Government, and to provide new Guards for their future security.... Such has been the patient sufferance of these Colonies; and such is now the necessity which constrains them to alter their former Systems of Government....

Questions for Analysis

1. Who are "the people" mentioned in the first sentence of this selection? Are the rights of "the people" the same as individual rights? How did the authors of this document come to think of themselves as the representatives of such a body?

2. What is the purpose of government, according to this document? Who gets to decide if the government is doing its job?

3. How does this document's use of the term *political bonds* compare with Rousseau's "form of association" in the *Social Contract*? What is similar about these two texts? What is different?

---

met at Philadelphia to form the Continental Congress to negotiate with the Crown over their grievances. In April 1775, however, local militiamen at Lexington and Concord clashed with regular British troops sent to disarm them. Soon thereafter, the Continental Congress began raising an army, and an outright rebellion erupted against the British government.

On July 4, 1776, the thirteen colonies formally declared their independence from Great Britain, in language that showed their debt to Enlightenment writers (see *Analyzing Primary Sources* above). During the first two years of the war, it seemed unlikely that such independence would ever become a reality. In 1778, however, France, anxious to undermine the colonial hegemony Great Britain had established since 1713, joined the war on the side of the Americans. Spain entered the war in support of France, hoping to recover Gibraltar and Florida (the latter lost in 1763 to Britain). In 1780, Britain also declared war on the Dutch

DIVIDING THE ROYAL SPOILS. A contemporary cartoon showing the monarchs of Europe at work carving up a hapless Poland. Note there is little reference here to the people who lived in the Polish territories that were being divided up among Russia, Prussia, and the Habsburg Empire. All three of these realms already contained people who spoke different languages and practiced different religions. The result of such expansion was to increase the linguistic and cultural diversity of these kingdoms.
■ *How might this have complicated the internal politics of these monarchies?* ■ *What long-term consequences might one expect from such multiethnic or multireligious societies?*

gained its independence; its western border was fixed on the Mississippi River, and it secured valuable fishing rights off the eastern coast of Canada. France gained only the satisfaction of defeating its colonial rival, but even that satisfaction was short lived. Six years later, the massive debts France had incurred in supporting the American Revolution helped bring about another, very different kind of revolution in France that would permanently alter the history of Europe.

CONCLUSION

The Enlightenment arose from the scientific revolution, from the new sense of power and possibility that rational thinking made possible, and from the rush of enthusiasm for new forms of inquiry. Enlightenment thinkers scrutinized a remarkably wide range of topics: human nature, reason, understanding, religion, belief, law, the origins of government, economics, new forms of technology, and social practices—such as marriage, child rearing, and education. Enlightenment ideas about social improvement and progress could and did occasionally serve the interests of European rulers, who saw in them a means to both rationalize their administrations and to challenge social groups or institutions that resisted the centralization of authority. Maria Theresa in Austria, Frederick the Great in Prussia and Catherine the Great in Russia all found ways to harness aspects of Enlightenment thought to their strategies of government.

At the same time, however, the radical implications of the Enlightenment critique of tradition made many people uncomfortable. Ideas with subversive implications circulated in popular forms from pamphlets and journalism

Republic for continuing to trade with the rebellious colonies. Now facing a coalition of its colonial rivals, Great Britain saw the war turn against it. In 1781, combined land and sea operations by French and American troops forced the surrender of the main British army at Yorktown in Virginia. As the defeated British soldiers surrendered their weapons, their band played a song titled "The World Turned Upside Down."

Negotiations for peace began soon after the defeat at Yorktown but were not concluded until September 1783. The Treaty of Paris left Great Britain in control of Canada and Gibraltar. Spain retained its possessions west of the Mississippi River and recovered Florida. The United States

SEVENTEENTH- AND EIGHTEENTH-CENTURY WARS	
Glorious Revolution	1688–1689
War of the League of Augsburg	1689–1697
War of the Spanish Succession	1702–1713
Seven Years' War	1756–1763
American Revolution	1775–1783
The Russo-Turkish War	1787–1792

to plays and operas. The intellectual movement that lay behind the Enlightenment thus had broad consequences for the creation of a new kind of elite based not on birth but on the acquisition of knowledge and the encouragement of open expression and debate. A new sphere of public opinion had come into existence, one which was difficult for the state to monitor and to control, and one which would have profound consequences in the nineteenth and twentieth centuries.

The prosperity that had made the Enlightenment possible remained very unevenly distributed in late eighteenth-century Europe. In the cities, rich and poor lived separate lives in separate neighborhoods. In the countryside, regions bypassed by the developing commercial economy of the period continued to suffer from hunger and famine, just as they had done in the sixteenth and seventeenth centuries. In eastern Europe, the contrasts between rich and poor were even more extreme, as many peasants fell into a new style of serfdom that would last until the end of the nineteenth century. War, too, remained a fact of European life, bringing death and destruction to hundreds of thousands of people across the Continent and around the world—yet

After You Read This Chapter

Ⓢ Visit StudySpace for quizzes, additional review materials, and multimedia documents. **wwnorton.com/web/westernciv18**

REVIEWING THE OBJECTIVES

- Many eighteenth-century thinkers used the term *Enlightenment* to describe what their work offered to European society. Who were they, and what did they mean by the term?
- Enlightenment ideas spread rapidly throughout Europe and in European colonies. How did this expanded arena for public discussion shape the development of Enlightenment thought?
- Enlightenment debates were shaped by the availability of new information about peoples and cultures in different parts of the globe. How did Enlightenment thinkers incorporate this new information into their thought?
- Enlightenment thinkers were often critical of widely held cultural and political beliefs. What was radical about the Enlightenment?

another consequence of the worldwide reach of these European colonial empires.

Finally, the Atlantic revolutions (the American Revolution of 1776, the French Revolution of 1789, and the Latin American upheavals of the 1830s) were steeped in the language of the Enlightenment. The constitutions of the new nations formed by these revolutions made reference to the fundamental assumptions of Enlightenment liberalism: on the liberty of the individual conscience and the freedom from the constraints imposed by religious or government institutions. Government authority could not be arbitrary; equality and freedom were natural; and humans sought happiness, prosperity, and the expansion of their potential. These arguments had been made earlier, though tentatively, and even after the Atlantic revolutions, their aspirations were only partially realized. But when the North American colonists declared their independence from Britain in 1776, they called such ideas "self-evident truths." That bold declaration marked both the distance traveled since the late seventeenth century and the self-confidence that was the Enlightenment's hallmark.

PEOPLE, IDEAS, AND EVENTS IN CONTEXT

- How did the **COMMERCIAL REVOLUTION** change social life in Europe?
- Who were the **PHILOSOPHES**? What gave them such confidence in **REASON**?
- What did **DAVID HUME** owe to **ISAAC NEWTON**? What made his work different from that of the famous physicist?
- What did **VOLTAIRE** admire about the work of **FRANCIS BACON AND JOHN LOCKE**? What irritated Voltaire about French society?
- What was **MONTESQUIEU**'s contribution to theories of government?
- What made **DENIS DIDEROT'S** *ENCYCLOPEDIA* such a definitive statement of the Enlightenment's goals?
- What influence did **CESARE BECCARIA** have over legal practices in Europe?
- What contributions did **ADAM SMITH** make to economic theory?
- What was radical about **JEAN-JACQUES ROUSSEAU**'s views on education and politics?
- What does the expansion of the **PUBLIC SPHERE** in the eighteenth century tell us about the effects of the Enlightenment?

THINKING ABOUT CONNECTIONS

- Compare the Enlightenment as an intellectual movement to the Reformation of the sixteenth century. What is similar about the two movements? What is distinctive?
- Did increases in literacy; the rise of print culture; and the emergence of new forms of intellectual sociability such as salons, reading societies, and coffeehouses really make public opinion more rational? How has our understanding of public opinion changed since the eighteenth century?

STORY LINES

- The French Revolution of 1798–1799 overthrew Louis XVI and created a government committed in principle to the rule of law, the liberty of the individual, and an idea of the nation as a sovereign body of citizens. These political changes also opened the way for the expression of a wide variety of social grievances by peasants, laborers, women, and other social groups in Europe.

- The French Revolution encouraged the spread of democratic ideas, but it also led to an increase in the power of centralized nation-states in Europe. The pressures of the revolutionary wars led governments to develop larger national bureaucracies, modern professional armies, new legal codes, and new tax structures.

- The French Revolution was part of a broader set of changes that rocked the Atlantic world at the end of the eighteenth century. Along with the Haitian Revolution and the American Revolution, this wave of cataclysmic change reshaped the political order of Europe and the Americas.

CHRONOLOGY

May 1789	The Estates General meets
June 1789	The Tennis Court Oath
July 1789	The Fall of the Bastille
September 1792	First French Republic
January 1793	Execution of King Louis XIV
September 1793– July 1794	The Terror
1798–1799	Napoleon's invasion of Egypt
January 1804	Haitian independence
1804	Napoleon crowned emperor
1804	Civil code
1808	Invasion of Spain
1812	Invasion of Russia
1814–1815	Napoleon's abdication and defeat

Before
You
Read
This
Chapter

The French Revolution

CORE OBJECTIVES

- **UNDERSTAND** the origins of the French Revolution in 1789.

- **EXPLAIN** the goals of French revolutionaries and the reactions of people elsewhere in Europe and the Atlantic world.

- **DESCRIBE** the events that made the Revolution more radical in 1792–1794.

- **IDENTIFY** the connections between the Revolution and Napoleon's regime after 1799, and the effects of Napoleon's conquests on Europe.

- **CONSIDER** the links between the French Revolution and the Atlantic world, which also saw revolutions in the Americas and in the Caribbean during these decades.

When a crowd of Parisians attacked the antiquated and nearly empty royal prison known as the Bastille on July 14, 1789, they were doing several things all at once. On the one hand, the revolt was a popular expression of support for the newly created National Assembly. This representative body had only weeks earlier declared an intention to put an end to absolutism in France by writing a constitution that made the nation, rather than the king, the sovereign authority in the land. But the Parisians in the street on July 14 did not express themselves like members of the National Assembly, who spoke the language of the Enlightenment. The actions of the revolutionary crowd were an expression of violent anger at the king's soldiers, who they feared might turn their guns on the city in a royal attempt to restore order by force. When the governor of the Bastille prison opened fire on the attackers, killing as many as a hundred, they responded with redoubled fury. By the end of the day, the prison had fallen, and the governor's battered body was dragged to the square before the city hall, where he was beheaded. Among the first to meet such an end as a consequence of revolution in France, he would not be the last.

This tension between noble political aspirations and cruel violence lies at the heart of the French Revolution. The significance of this contradiction was not lost on the millions of people throughout Europe who watched in astonishment as France was engulfed in turmoil in the 1790s. In 1789, one European out of every five lived in France, a kingdom that many considered to be the center of European culture. Other kingdoms were not immune to the same social and political tensions that divided the French. Aristocrats across Europe and the colonies resented monarchical inroads on their ancient freedoms. Members of the middle classes chafed under a system of official privilege that they increasingly saw as unjust and outmoded. Peasants fiercely resented the endless demands of central government on their limited resources. Nor were resentments focused exclusively on absolutist monarchs. Bitter resentments and tensions existed between country and city dwellers, between rich and poor, overprivileged and underprivileged, slave and free. The French Revolution was the most dramatic and tumultuous expression of all of these conflicts.

This age of revolution opened on the other side of the Atlantic Ocean. The American Revolution of 1776 was a crisis of the British Empire, linked to a long series of conflicts between England and France over colonial control of North America. It led to a major crisis of the old regime in France. Among "enlightened" Europeans, the success with which citizens of the United States had thrown off British rule and formed a republic based on Enlightenment principles was a source of tremendous optimism. Change would come, many believed. Reform was possible. The costs would be modest.

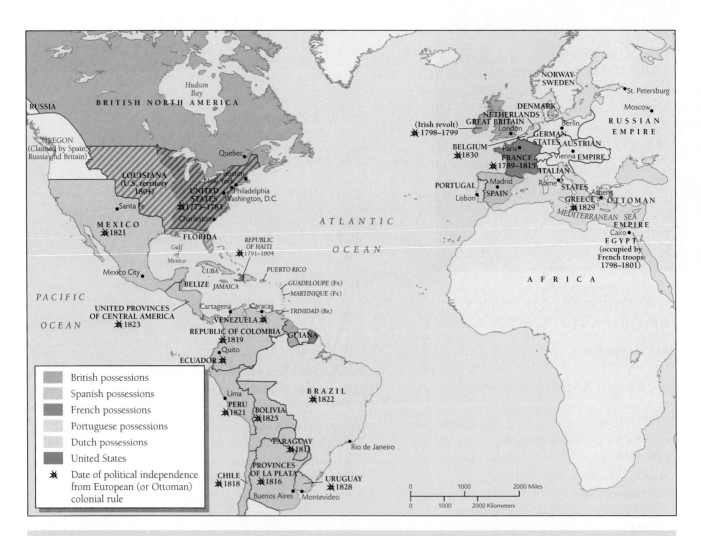

THE ATLANTIC REVOLUTIONS. The Atlantic revolutions shook nations and empires on both sides of the ocean, challenging the legitimacy of Europe's dynastic realms, lending further support to notions of popular sovereignty and forcing contemporaries to rethink the meanings of citizenship in a context of intense political and economic struggle. ▪ *How many of these struggles took place within Europe?* ▪ *How many appear to have taken place on the periphery of the Atlantic world?* ▪ *What circumstances may have made it more difficult for such revolutionary movements to develop within Europe itself?*

The French Revolution did not live up to these expectations, though change certainly did come. By any measure, the accomplishments of the revolutionary decade were extraordinary: it successfully proved that the residents of an old monarchy in the heart of Europe could come together to constitute themselves as citizens of a new political idea, the nation. Freed from the shackles of tradition, revolutionaries in France posed new questions about the role of women in public life, about the separation of church and state, about the rights of Jews and other minorities. A slave revolt in the French colonies convinced the revolutionaries that the new liberties they defended so ardently also belonged to African slaves, though few had suggested such a thing at the outset. Meanwhile, the European wars precipitated by the revolution marked the first time that entire populations were mobilized as part of a new kind of devastating international conflict, the first "total wars." In other words, in spite of the optimism of those who began the revolution in 1789, it quickly became something much more costly, complex, and violent. Its effects were to resonate throughout Europe for the next half century.

THE FRENCH REVOLUTION: AN OVERVIEW

The term *French Revolution* is a shorthand for a complex series of events between 1789 and 1799. (Napoleon ruled from 1799 to 1814–1815.) To simplify, those events can be divided into four stages. In the first stage, running from 1788 to 1792, the struggle was constitutional and relatively peaceful. An increasingly bold elite articulated its grievances against the king. Like the American revolutionaries, French elites refused taxation without representation; attacked despotism, or arbitrary authority; and offered an Enlightenment-inspired program to rejuvenate the nation. Reforms, many of them breathtakingly wide ranging, were instituted—some accepted or even offered by the king, and others passed over his objections. The peaceful, constitutional phase did not last. Unlike the American Revolution, the French Revolution did not stabilize around one constitution or one set of political leaders, for many reasons.

Reforms met with resistance, dividing the country. The threat of dramatic change within one of the most powerful countries in Europe created international tensions. In 1792, these tensions exploded into war, and the crises of war, in turn, spelled the end of the Bourbon monarchy and the beginning of the republic. This second stage of the revolution, which lasted from 1792 to 1794, was one of acute crisis, consolidation, and repression. A ruthlessly central-ized government mobilized all the country's resources to fight the foreign enemy as well as counterrevolutionaries at home, to destroy traitors and the vestiges of the Old Regime.

The Terror, as this policy was called, did save the republic, but it exhausted itself in factions and recriminations and collapsed in 1794. In the third phase, from 1794 to 1799, the government drifted. France remained a republic. It continued to fight with Europe. Undermined by corruption and division, the state fell prey to the ambitions of a military leader, Napoleon Bonaparte. Napoleon's rule, punctuated by astonishing victories and catastrophes, stretched from 1799 to 1815. It began as a republic, became an empire, and ended—after a last hurrah—in the muddy fields outside the Belgian village of Waterloo. After Napoleon's final defeat, the other European monarchs restored the Bourbons to the throne. That restoration, however, would be short lived, and the cycle of revolution and reaction continued into the nineteenth century.

THE COMING OF THE REVOLUTION

What were the long-term causes of the revolution in France? Historians long ago argued that the causes and outcomes should be understood in terms of class conflict. According to this interpretation, a rising bourgeoisie, or middle class, inspired by Enlightenment ideas and by its own self-interest, overthrew what was left of the aristocratic order. This interpretation drew on the writings of the nineteenth-century philosopher Karl Marx and on much twentieth-century sociology.

Historians have substantially modified this bold thesis. To be sure, the origins of the revolution lie in eighteenth-century French society. Yet that society was not simply divided between a bourgeois class and the aristocracy. Instead, it was increasingly dominated by a new elite or social group that brought together aristocrats, officeholders, professionals, and—to a lesser degree—merchants and businessmen. To understand the revolution, we need to understand this new social group and its conflicts with the government of Louis XVI.

French society was legally divided into Three Estates. (An individual's *estate* marked his standing, or status, and it determined legal rights, taxes, and so on.) The First Estate comprised all the clergy; the Second Estate, the nobility. The Third Estate, by far the largest, included everyone else, from wealthy lawyers and businessmen to urban laborers and poor peasants. Within the political and social elite of the country, a small but powerful group, these legal distinctions often seemed artificial. To begin with, in the upper reaches of society, the social boundaries between nobles and wealthy commoners were ill defined. Noble title was accessible to those who could afford to buy an ennobling office. For example, close to 50,000 new nobles were created between 1700 and 1789. The nobility depended on a constant infusion of talent and economic power from the wealthy social groups of the Third Estate.

To preserve their elite status, aristocrats spoke of a distinction between the nobility of the sword and of the robe, the former supposedly of a more ancient and distinguished lineage derived from military service, the latter aristocrats because they had purchased administrative or judicial office (hence the robe).

Nevertheless, wealth did not take predictable forms. Most noble wealth was proprietary—that is, tied to land, urban properties, purchased offices, and the like. Yet noble families did not disdain trade or commerce, as historians long thought. In fact, noblemen financed most industry, and they also invested heavily in banking and such enterprises as ship owning, the slave trade, mining, and metallurgy. Moreover, the very wealthy members of the Third Estate also preferred to invest in secure, proprietary holdings. Thus, throughout the century, much middle-class wealth was transformed into noble wealth, and a significant number of rich bourgeois became noblemen. Wealthy members of the bourgeoisie did not see themselves as a separate class. They thought of themselves as different from—and often opposed to—the common people, who worked with their hands, and they identified with the values of a nobility to which they frequently aspired.

There were, nonetheless, important social tensions. Less prosperous lawyers—and there were an increasing number of them—were jealous of the privileged position of a favored few in their profession. Over the course of the century, the price of offices rose, making it more difficult to buy one's way into the nobility, and creating tensions between middling members of the Third Estate and the very rich in trade and commerce who, by and large, were the only group able to afford to climb the social ladder. Less wealthy nobles resented the success of rich, upstart commoners whose income allowed them to live in luxury. In sum, several fault lines ran through the elite and the middle classes. All these social groups could nonetheless join in attacking a government and an economy that were not serving their interests.

The Enlightenment had changed public debate (see Chapter 17). Although ideas did not cause the revolution, they played a critical role in articulating grievances. The political theories of Locke, Voltaire, and Montesquieu could appeal to both discontented nobles and members of the

PREREVOLUTIONARY PROPAGANDA. Political cartoons in late-eighteenth-century France commonly portrayed the Third Estate as bearing the burden of taxation while performing the bulk of the nation's productive work. On the left, a peasant bears the burden of his tools and his harvest, as a cleric and a nobleman look on; on the right, the commoner is literally carrying his social superiors. ▪ *What visual cues indicate the status of individuals in these images?* ▪ *Would one expect the nobility or the clergy to defend their status on the basis of their usefulness to society?* ▪ *Can one detect the power of certain Enlightenment ideas behind these forms of social critique?* ▪ *Which ones?* ▪ *How might an opponent of Enlightenment thought have confronted such arguments?*

middle class. Voltaire was popular because of his attacks on noble privileges; Locke and Montesquieu gained widespread followings because of their defense of private property and limited sovereignty. Montesquieu's ideas appealed to the noble lawyers and officeholders who dominated France's powerful law courts, the *parlements*. They read his doctrine of checks and balances as support for their argument that parlements could provide a check to the despotism of the king's government. When conflicts arose, noble leaders presented themselves as defenders of the nation threatened by the king and his ministers.

The campaign for change was also fueled by economic reformers. The "physiocrats" urged the government to simplify the tax system and free the economy from mercantilist regulations. They advocated an end to price controls in the grain trade, which had been imposed to keep the cost of bread low. Such interventions, they argued, interfered with the market's ability to find an equilibrium between supply and demand.

In the countryside, peasants did not think in terms of markets. They were caught in a web of obligations to landlords, church, and state: a tithe, or levy, on farm produce owed to the church; fees for the use of a landlord's mill or wine press; fees to the landlord; and fees when land changed hands. In addition, peasants paid a disproportionate share of both direct and indirect taxes—the most onerous of which was the salt tax—levied by the government. (For some time, the production of salt had been a state monopoly; every individual was required to buy at least seven pounds a year from the government works. The result was a commodity whose cost was often as much as fifty or sixty times its actual value.) Further grievances stemmed from the requirement to maintain public roads (the corvée) and from the hunting privileges that nobles for centuries had regarded as the distinctive badge of their order.

Social and economic conditions deteriorated on the eve of the revolution. A general price increase during much of the eighteenth century, which permitted the French economy to expand by providing capital for investment, created hardship for the peasantry and for urban tradesmen and laborers. Their plight deteriorated further at the end of the 1780s, when poor harvests sent bread prices sharply higher. In 1788, families found themselves spending more than 50 percent of their income on bread, which made up the bulk of their diet. The following year the figure rose to as much as 80 percent. Poor harvests reduced demand for manufactured goods, and contracting markets in turn created unemployment. Many peasants left the countryside for the cities, hoping to find work there—only to discover that urban unemployment was far worse than that in rural areas. Evidence indicates that between 1787 and 1789 the unemployment rate in many parts of urban France was as high as 50 percent.

Failure and Reform

An inefficient tax system further weakened the country's financial position. Taxation differed according to social standings and varied from region to region—some areas were subject to a much higher rate than others. Special exemptions made the task of collectors more difficult. The financial system, already burdened by debts incurred under Louis XIV, all but broke down completely under the increased expenses brought on by French participation in the American Revolution. The cost of servicing the national debt in the 1780s consumed 50 percent of the nation's budget.

Problems with the economy reflected weaknesses in France's administrative structure, ultimately the responsibility of the country's absolutist monarch, Louis XVI (1774–1792).

LOUIS XVI. The last prerevolutionary French king, who was to lose his life in the Terror, combined in his person a strong attachment to the monarchy's absolutist doctrine with an inability to find workable solutions to the financial crisis facing his government. His royal portrait mimicked the forms of spectacular display that proved so useful to Louis XIV in shoring up the power of the monarchy. ▪ *What made this display so much less potent in the late eighteenth century?* ▪ *What caused the monarchy to lose its aura?*

Analyzing Primary Sources

What is the Third Estate? (1789)

The Abbé Emmanuel-Joseph Sieyès (1748–1836) was, by virtue of his office in the Church, a member of the First Estate of the Estates General. Nevertheless, his political savvy led him to be elected as a representative of the Third Estate from the district of Chartres. Sieyès was a formidable politician as well as a writer. His career during the revolution, which he ended by assisting Napoleon's seizure of power, began with one of the most important radical pamphlets of 1789. In What Is the Third Estate?, *Sieyès posed fundamental questions about the rights of the estate, which represented the great majority of the population and helped provoke its secession from the Estates General.*

he plan of this book is fairly simple. We must ask ourselves three questions.

1. What is the Third Estate? *Everything.*

2. What has it been until now in the political order? *Nothing.*

3. What does it want to be? *Something.*

It suffices to have made the point that the so-called usefulness of a privileged order to the public service is a fallacy; that without help from this order, all the arduous tasks in the service are performed by the Third Estate; that without this order the higher posts could be infinitely better filled; that they ought to be the natural prize and reward of recognized ability and service; and that if the privileged have succeeded in usurping all well-paid and honorific posts, this is both a hateful iniquity towards the generality of citizens and an act of treason to the commonwealth.

Who is bold enough to maintain that the Third Estate does not contain within itself everything needful to constitute a complete nation? It is like a strong and robust man with one arm still in chains. If the privileged order were removed, the nation would not be something less but something more. What then is the Third Estate? All; but an "all" that is fettered and oppressed. What would it be without the privileged order? It would be all; but free and flourishing. Nothing will go well without the Third Estate; everything would go considerably better without the two others.

Source: Emmanuel-Joseph Sieyès, *What Is the Third Estate?*, ed. S. E. Finer, trans. M. Blondel, (London: 1964), pp. 53–63.

Questions for Analysis

1. How might contemporaries have viewed Sieyès's argument that the Three Estates should be evaluated according to their usefulness to the "commonwealth"?

2. Was Sieyès's language—accusing the privileged orders of "treason" and arguing for their "removal"—an incitement to violence?

3. What did Sieyès mean by the term *nation*? Could one speak of France as a nation in these terms before 1789?

Louis wished to improve the lot of the poor, abolish torture, and shift the burden of taxation onto the richer classes, but he lacked the ability to accomplish these tasks. He appointed reformers like Anne-Robert-Jacques Turgot, a physiocrat, and Jacques Necker, a Swiss Protestant banker, as finance ministers, only to arouse the opposition of traditionalists at court. When he pressed for new taxes to be paid by the nobility, he was defeated by the provincial parlements, who defended the aristocracy's immunity from taxation. He allowed his wife, the young but strong-willed Marie Antoinette—daughter of Austria's Maria Theresa—a free hand to dispense patronage among her friends. The result was constant intrigue and frequently reshuffled alliances at Versailles. By 1788, a weak monarch, together with a chaotic financial situation and severe social tensions, brought absolutist France to the edge of political disaster.

THE DESTRUCTION OF THE OLD REGIME

The fiscal crisis precipitated the revolution. In 1787 and 1788, the king's principal ministers, Charles de Calonne and Loménie de Brienne, proposed new taxes to meet the growing deficit, notably a stamp duty and a direct tax on the annual produce of the land.

Hoping to persuade the nobility to agree to these reforms, the king summoned an Assembly of Notables from among the aristocracy. This group insisted that any new tax scheme must be approved by the Estates General, the representative body of the Three Estates of the realm, and that the king had no legal authority to arrest and imprison arbitrarily. These proposed constitutional changes echoed the English aristocrats of 1688 and the American revolutionaries of 1776.

Faced with economic crisis and financial chaos, Louis XVI summoned the Estates General (which had not met since 1614) to meet in 1789. His action appeared to many as the only solution to France's deepening problems. Long-term grievances and short-term hardships produced bread riots across the country in the spring of 1789. Fear that the forces of law and order were collapsing and that the common people might take matters into their own hands

spurred the Estates General. Each of the three orders elected its own deputies—the Third Estate indirectly through local assemblies. These assemblies were charged as well with the responsibility of drawing up lists of grievances (*cahiers des doléances*), further heightening expectations for fundamental reform.

The delegates of the Third Estate, though elected by assemblies chosen in turn by artisans and peasants, represented the outlook of an elite. Only 13 percent were men of business. About 25 percent were lawyers; 43 percent were government officeholders of some sort.

By tradition, each estate met and voted as a body. In the past, this had generally meant that the First Estate (the clergy) had combined with the Second (the nobility) to defeat the Third. Now the Third Estate made it clear it would not tolerate such an arrangement. The Third's interests were articulated most memorably by the Abbé Emmanuel Sieyès, a radical member of the clergy. "What is the Third Estate?" asked Sieyès, in his famous pamphlet

THE TENNIS COURT OATH BY JACQUES LOUIS DAVID (1748–1825). In June 1789, the members of the Third Estate, now calling themselves the National Assembly, swear an oath not to disband until France has a constitution. In the center stands Jean Bailly, president of the new assembly. The Abbé Sieyès is seated at the table. In the foreground, a clergyman, an aristocrat, and a member of the Third Estate embrace in a symbol of national unity. The single deputy who refused to take the oath sits at far right, his hands clasped against his chest. ▪ *What is the significance of this near unanimity expressed in defiance of the king?* ▪ *What options were available to those who did not support this move?*

of January 1789. Everything, he answered, and pointed to eighteenth-century social changes to bolster his point. In early 1789, Sieyès's views were still unusually radical. But the leaders of the Third Estate agreed that the three orders should sit together and vote as individuals. More important, they insisted that the Third Estate should have twice as many members as the First and Second.

The king first opposed "doubling the Third" and then changed his position. His unwillingness to take a strong stand on voting procedures cost him support he might otherwise have obtained from the Third Estate. Shortly after the Estates General opened at Versailles in May 1789, the Third Estate, angered by the king's attitude, took the revolutionary step of leaving the body and declaring itself the National Assembly. Locked out of the Estates General meeting hall on June 20, the Third Estate and a handful of sympathetic nobles and clergymen moved to a nearby indoor tennis court.

Here, under the leadership of the volatile, maverick aristocrat Mirabeau and the radical clergyman Sieyès, they bound themselves by a solemn oath not to separate until they had drafted a constitution for France. This Tennis Court Oath, sworn on June 20, 1789, can be seen as the beginning of the French Revolution. By claiming the authority to remake the government in the name of the people, the National Assembly was asserting its right to act as the highest sovereign power in the nation. On June 27, the king virtually conceded this right by ordering all the delegates to join the National Assembly.

First Stages of the French Revolution

The first stage of the French Revolution extended from June 1789 to August 1792. In the main, this stage was moderate, its actions dominated by the leadership of liberal nobles and men of the Third Estate. Yet three events in the summer and fall of 1789 furnished evidence that their leadership would be challenged.

POPULAR REVOLTS

From the beginning of the political crisis, public attention was high. It was roused not merely by interest in political reform but also by the economic crisis that, as we have seen, brought the price of bread to astronomical heights. Many believed that the aristocracy and the king were conspiring to punish the Third Estate by encouraging scarcity and high prices. Rumors circulated in Paris during the latter days of June 1789 that the king's troops were mobilizing to march on the city. The electors of Paris (those who had voted for the Third Estate—workshop masters, artisans, and shopkeepers) feared not only the king but also the Parisian poor, who had been parading through the streets and threatening violence. The common people would soon be referred to as sans-culottes (sahn koo-LAWTS). The term, which translates to "without breeches," was an antiaristocratic badge of pride: a man of the people wore full-length trousers rather than aristocratic breeches with stockings and gold-buckled shoes. Led by the electors, the people formed a provisional municipal government and organized a militia of volunteers to maintain order. Determined to obtain arms, they made their way on July 14 to the Bastille, an ancient fortress where guns and ammunition were stored. Built in the Middle Ages, the Bastille had served as a prison for many years but was no longer much used. Nevertheless, it symbolized hated royal authority. When crowds demanded arms from its governor, he procrastinated and then, fearing a frontal assault, opened fire, killing ninety-eight of the attackers. The crowd took revenge, capturing the fortress (which held only seven prisoners—five common criminals and two people confined for mental incapacity) and decapitating the governor. Similar groups took control in other cities across France. The fall of the Bastille was the first instance of the people's role in revolutionary change.

The second popular revolt occurred in the countryside. Peasants, too, expected and feared a monarchical and aristocratic counterrevolution. Rumors flew that the king's armies were on their way, that Austrians, Prussians, or "brigands" were invading. Frightened and uncertain, peasants and villagers organized militias; others attacked and burned manor houses, sometimes to look for grain but usually to find and destroy records of manorial dues. This "Great Fear," as historians have labeled it, compounded the confusion in rural areas. The news, when it reached Paris, convinced deputies at Versailles that the administration of rural France had simply collapsed.

The third instance of popular uprising, the "October Days of 1789," was brought on by economic crisis. This time, Parisian women from the market district, angered by the soaring price of bread and fired by rumors of the king's continuing unwillingness to cooperate with the assembly, marched to Versailles on October 5 and demanded to be heard. Not satisfied with its reception by the assembly, the crowd broke through the gates to the palace, calling for the king to return to Paris from Versailles. On the afternoon of the following day the king yielded and returned to Paris, accompanied by the crowd and the National Guard.

Each of these popular uprisings shaped the political events unfolding at Versailles. The storming of the Bastille persuaded the king and nobles to agree to the creation of the National Assembly. The Great Fear compelled the most

WOMEN OF PARIS LEAVING FOR VERSAILLES, OCTOBER 1789. A crowd of women, accompanied by Lafayette and the National Guard, marched to Versailles to confront the king about shortages and rising prices in Paris. ■ *Did the existence of the National Assembly change the meaning of such popular protests?*

sweeping changes of the entire revolutionary period. In an effort to quell rural disorder, on the night of August 4 the assembly took a giant step toward abolishing all forms of privilege. It eliminated the Church tithe (tax on the harvest), the labor requirement known as the corvée, the nobility's hunting privileges, and a wide variety of tax exemptions and monopolies. In effect, these reforms obliterated the remnants of feudalism. One week later, the assembly abolished the sale of offices, thereby sweeping away one of the fundamental institutions of the Old Regime. The king's return to Paris during the October Days of 1789 undercut his ability to resist further changes.

THE NATIONAL ASSEMBLY AND THE RIGHTS OF MAN

The assembly issued its charter of liberties, the Declaration of the Rights of Man and of the Citizen, in September 1789. It declared property to be a natural right, along with liberty, security, and "resistance to oppression." It declared freedom of speech, religious toleration, and liberty of the press inviolable. All citizens were to be treated equally before the law. No one was to be imprisoned or punished without due process of law. Sovereignty resided in the people,

who could depose officers of the government if they abused their powers. These were not new ideas; they represented the outcome of Enlightenment discussions and revolutionary debates and deliberations. The Declaration became the preamble to the new constitution, which the assembly finished in 1791.

Whom did the Declaration mean by "man and the citizen"? The constitution distinguished between "passive" citizens, guaranteed rights under law, and "active" citizens, who paid a certain amount in taxes and could thus vote and hold office. About half the adult males in France qualified as active citizens. Even their power was curtailed, because they could vote only for "electors," men whose property ownership qualified them to hold office. Later in the revolution, the more radical republic abolished the distinction between active and passive, and the conservative regimes reinstated it. Which men could be trusted to participate in politics and on what terms was a hotly contested issue.

Also controversial were the rights of religious minorities. The revolution gave full civil rights to Protestants, though in areas long divided by religious conflict those rights were challenged by Catholics. The revolution did, hesitantly, give civil rights to Jews, a measure that sparked protest in areas of eastern France. Religious toleration, a central theme of the Enlightenment, meant ending persecution; it did not mean that the regime was prepared to accommodate religious difference. The assembly abolished serfdom and banned slavery in continental France. It remained silent on colonial slavery, and although delegations pressed the assembly on political rights for free people of color, the assembly exempted the colonies from the constitution's provisions. Events in the Caribbean, as we will see, later forced the issue.

The rights and roles of women became the focus of sharp debate, as revolutionaries confronted demands that working women participate in guilds or trade organizations, and laws on marriage, divorce, poor relief, and education were reconsidered. The Englishwoman Mary Wollstonecraft's milestone book *A Vindication of the Rights of Woman* (see Chapter 17) was penned during the revolutionary debate over national education. Should girls be educated? To what end? Wollstonecraft, as we have seen, argued strongly that reforming education required forging a new concept of independent and equal womanhood. Even Wollstonecraft, however, only hinted at political representation, aware that such an idea would "excite laughter."

Only a handful of thinkers broached the subject of women in politics: the aristocratic Enlightenment thinker the Marquis de Condorcet and, from another shore, Marie Gouze, the self-educated daughter of a butcher. Gouze became an intellectual and playwright and renamed herself Olympe de Gouges. Like many "ordinary" people, she found in the explosion of revolutionary activity the opportunity to address the public by writing speeches, pamphlets, or newspapers. She composed her own manifesto, the *Declaration of the Rights of Woman and the Citizen* (1791). Beginning with the proposition that "social distinctions can only be based on the common utility," she declared that women had the same rights as men, including resistance to authority, participation in government, and naming the fathers of illegitimate children. This last demand offers a glimpse of the shame, isolation, and hardship faced by an unmarried woman.

De Gouges's demand for equal rights was unusual, but many women nevertheless participated in the everyday activities of the revolution, joining clubs, demonstrations, and debates and making their presence known, sometimes forcefully. Women artisans' organizations had a well-established role in municipal life, and they used the revolution as an opportunity to assert their rights to produce and sell goods. Market women were familiar public figures, often central to the circulation of news and spontaneous popular demonstrations (the October Days are a good example). Initially, the regime celebrated the support of women "citizens," and female figures were favorite symbols for liberty, prudence, and the bounty of nature in

DECLARATION OF THE RIGHTS OF MAN (1789). Presented as principles of natural law inscribed on stone, this print gives a good indication of how the authors of the Declaration wished it to be perceived by the French people. Over the tablets is a beneficent and all-seeing deity accompanied by two female allegorical figures representing strength and virtue on one side and the French nation on the other. Two armed soldiers wear the uniform of the newly created National Guard. The image's symbols refer to Masonic lore (the triangle or pyramid with an eye at the center, the snake grasping its tail), and a set of historical references from the Roman Republic: a Phrygian cap, used by Romans as a symbol of liberty, is mounted on a spear emerging from a bundle of sticks. This bundle was known as a *faisceau* and was carried in ancient Rome by magistrates as symbols of their authority. ■ *Given the absence of any monarchical symbolism or references to the Catholic Church, why was it important for the authors to come up with an alternative set of historical references?*

revolutionary iconography. When the revolution became more radical, however, some revolutionaries saw autonomous political activity by women's organizations as a threat to public order, and in 1793 the revolutionaries shut down the women's political clubs. Even so, many ordinary women were able to make use of the revolution's new legislation on marriage (divorce was legalized in 1792) and inheritance to support claims for relief from abusive husbands or absent

Declaration of the Rights of Man and of the Citizen

One of the first important pronouncements of the National Assembly after the Tennis Court Oath was the Declaration of the Rights of Man and of the Citizen. *The authors drew inspiration from the American Declaration of Independence, but the language is even more heavily influenced by the ideals of French Enlightenment philosophers, particularly Rousseau. Following are the* Declaration's *preamble and some of its most important principles.*

he representatives of the French people, constituted as the National Assembly, considering that ignorance, disregard, or contempt for the rights of man are the sole causes of public misfortunes and the corruption of governments, have resolved to set forth, in a solemn declaration, the natural, inalienable, and sacred rights of man, so that the constant presence of this declaration may ceaselessly remind all members of the social body of their rights and duties; so that the acts of legislative power and those of the executive power may be more respected . . . and so that the demands of the citizens, grounded henceforth on simple and incontestable principles, may always be directed to the maintenance of the constitution and to the welfare of all. . . .

Article 1. Men are born and remain free and equal in rights. Social distinctions can be based only on public utility.

Article 2. The aim of every political association is the preservation of the natural and imprescriptible rights of man. These rights are liberty, property, security, and resistance to oppression.

Article 3. The source of all sovereignty resides essentially in the nation. No body, no individual can exercise authority that does not explicitly proceed from it.

Article 4. Liberty consists in being able to do anything that does not injure another; thus the only limits upon each man's exercise of his natural laws are those that guarantee enjoyment of these same rights to the other members of society.

Article 5. The law has the right to forbid only actions harmful to society. No action may be prevented that is not forbidden by law, and no one may be constrained to do what the law does not order.

Article 6. The law is the expression of the general will. All citizens have the right to participate personally, or through representatives, in its formation. It must be the same for all, whether it protects or punishes. All citizens, being equal in its eyes, are equally admissable to all public dignities, positions, and employments, according to their ability, and on the basis of no other distinction than that of their virtues and talents. . . .

Article 16. A society in which the guarantee of rights is not secured, or the separation of powers is not clearly established, has no constitution.

Source: Declaration of the Rights of Man and of the Citizen, as cited in K. M. Baker, ed., *The Old Regime and the French Revolution* (Chicago: 1987), pp. 238–239.

Questions for Analysis

1. Who is the Declaration addressed to? Is it just about the rights of the French, or do these ideas apply to all people?

2. What gave a group of deputies elected to advise Louis XVI on constitutional reforms the right to proclaim themselves a National Assembly? What was revolutionary about this claim to represent the French nation?

3. Article 6, which states that "law is the expression of general will," is adapted from Rousseau's *Social Contract.* Does the Declaration give any indication of how the "general will" can be known?

---

fathers, claims that would have been impossible under the prerevolutionary legislation.

THE NATIONAL ASSEMBLY AND THE CHURCH

In November 1789 the National Assembly decided to confiscate all Church lands to use them as collateral for issuing interest-bearing notes known as *assignats*. The assembly hoped that this action would resolve the economy's inflationary crisis, and eventually these notes circulated widely as paper money. In July 1789, the assembly enacted the Civil Constitution of the Clergy, bringing the Church under state authority. The new law forced all bishops and priests to swear allegiance to the state, which henceforth paid their salaries. The aim was to make the Catholic Church of France a national institution, free from interference from Rome.

These reforms were bitterly divisive. Many people resented the privileged status of the Church, and its vast monastic land holdings. On the other hand, for centuries the parish church had been a central institution in small towns and villages, providing poor relief and other services, in addition to baptisms and marriages. The Civil Constitution of the Clergy sparked fierce resistance in some parts of rural France. When the pope threatened to excommunicate priests who signed the Civil Constitution, he raised the stakes: allegiance to the new French state meant damnation. Many people, especially peasants in the deeply Catholic areas of western France, were driven into open revolt.

The National Assembly made a series of economic and governmental changes with lasting effects. To raise money, it sold off Church lands, although few of the genuinely needy could afford to buy them. To encourage the growth of economic enterprise, it abolished guilds. To rid the country of local aristocratic power, it reorganized local governments, dividing France into eighty-three equal departments. These measures aimed to defend individual liberty and freedom from customary privilege. Their principal beneficiaries were, for the most part, members of the elite, people on their way up under the previous regime who were able to take advantage of the opportunities, such as buying land or being elected to office, that the new one offered. In this realm as elsewhere, the social changes of the revolution endorsed changes already under way in the eighteenth century.

A NEW STAGE: POPULAR REVOLUTION

In the summer of 1792, the revolution's moderate leaders were toppled and replaced by republicans, who repudiated the monarchy and claimed to rule on behalf of a sovereign people. Why this abrupt and drastic change? Was the revolution blown off course? These are among the most difficult questions about the French Revolution. Historians have focused on three factors to explain the revolution's radical turn: changes in popular politics, a crisis of leadership, and international polarization.

First, the revolution politicized the common people, especially in cities. Newspapers filled with political and social commentary multiplied, freed from censorship. From 1789 forward, a wide variety of political clubs became part of daily political life. Some were formal, almost like political parties, gathering members of the elite to debate issues facing the country and influence decisions in the assembly. Other clubs opened their doors to those excluded from formal politics, and they read aloud from newspapers and discussed the options facing the country, from the provisions of the constitution to the trustworthiness of the king and his ministers.

This political awareness was heightened by nearly constant shortages and fluctuating prices. Prices particularly exasperated the working people of Paris who had eagerly awaited change since their street demonstrations of 1789. Urban demonstrations, often led by women, demanded cheaper bread; political leaders in clubs and newspapers called for the government to control rising inflation. Club leaders spoke for men and women who felt cheated by the constitution.

A second major reason for the change of course was a lack of effective national leadership. Louis XVI remained a weak monarch. He was forced to support measures personally distasteful to him, in particular the Civil Constitution of the Clergy. He was sympathetic to the plottings of the queen, who was in contact with her brother Leopold II of Austria. Urged on by Marie Antoinette, Louis agreed to attempt an escape from France in June 1791, hoping to rally foreign support for counterrevolution. The members of the royal family managed to slip past their palace guards in Paris, but they were apprehended near the border at Varennes and brought back to the capital. The constitution of 1791 declared France a monarchy, but after the escape to Varennes, Louis was little more than a prisoner of the assembly.

The Counterrevolution

The third major reason for the dramatic turn of affairs was war. From the outset of the revolution, men and women across Europe had been compelled, by the very intensity of events in France, to take sides in the conflict. In the years immediately after 1789, the revolution in France won the enthusiastic support of a wide range of thinkers. The British poet William Wordsworth, who later became disillusioned, recalled his initial mood: "Bliss was it in that dawn to be alive." His sentiments were echoed across the Continent by poets and philosophers, including the German Johann Gottfried von Herder, who declared the revolution the most important historical moment since the Reformation. In Britain, the Low Countries, western Germany, and Italy, "patriots" proclaimed their allegiance to the new revolution.

Others opposed the revolution from the start. Exiled nobles, who fled France for sympathetic royal courts in Germany and elsewhere, did all they could to stir up counterrevolutionary sentiment. In Britain, the conservative cause was strengthened by the publication in 1790 of Edmund Burke's *Reflections on the Revolution in France*. A Whig politician who had sympathized with the American revolutionaries, Burke deemed the revolution in France a monstrous crime against the social order (see **Competing Viewpoints** on pages 594–95).

Social Grievances on the Eve of the Revolution (1789)

During the elections to the Estates General, communities drew up "notebooks of grievances" to be presented to the government. The following comes from a rural community, Lignère la Doucelle.

For a long time now, the inhabitants have been crushed beneath the excessive burden of the multiplicity of taxes that they have been obliged to pay. Their parish is large and spread out, but it is a hard land with many uncultivated areas, almost all of it divided into small parcels. There is not one single farm of appreciable size, and these small properties are occupied either by the poor or by people who are doing so poorly that they go without bread every other day. They buy bread or grain nine months of the year. No industries operate in this parish, and from the time they began complaining, no one has ever listened. The cry of anguish echoed all to the way to the ministry after having fruitlessly worn out their intendants. They have always seen their legitimate claims being continuously denied, so may the fortunate moment of equality revive them.

* * *

That all lords, country gentlemen, and others of the privileged class who, either directly or through their proxies, desire to make a profit on their wealth, regardless of the nature of that wealth, pay the same taxes as the common people.

* * *

That the seigneur's mills not be obligatory, allowing everyone to choose where he would like to mill his grain.

* * *

That the children of common people living on a par with nobles be admitted for military service, as the nobility is.

That the king not bestow noble titles upon someone and their family line, but that titles be bestowed only upon those deserving it.

That nobility not be available for purchase or by any fashion other than by the bearing of arms or other service rendered to the State.

* * *

That church members be only able to take advantage of one position. That those who are enjoying more than one be made to choose within a fixed time period.

That future abbeys all be placed into the hands of the king, that His Majesty benefit from their revenue as the head abbots have been able to.

That in towns where there are several convents belonging to the same order, there be only one, and the goods and revenue of those that are to be abolished go to the profit of the crown.

That the convents where there are not normally twelve residents be abolished.

That no tenth of black wheat be paid to parish priests, priors or other beneficiaries, since this grain is only used to prepare the soil for the sowing of rye.

That they also not be paid any tenths of hemp, wool, or lamb. That in the countryside they be required to conduct burials and funerals free of charge. That the ten sous for audit books, insinuations, and the 100 [sous] collected for the parish be abolished.

* * *

That grain be taxed in the realm at a fixed price, or rather that its exportation abroad be forbidden except in the case where it would be sold at a low price.

Source: Armand Bellée, ed., *Cahiers de plaintes & doléances des paroisses de la province du Maine pour les Etats-généraux de 1789*, vol. 2 (Le Mans: 1881–1892), pp. 578–582.

Questions for Analysis

1. Do these grievances reflect the interests of only one social group, or can one hear demands being made from different groups within this rural community?

2. What do you think were the main problems faced by this community?

3. How did the revolutionaries receive these grievances?

Debating the French Revolution: Edmund Burke and Thomas Paine

> The best-known debate on the French Revolution set the Irish-born conservative Edmund Burke against the British radical Thomas Paine. Burke opposed the French Revolution from the beginning. His Reflections on the Revolution in France was published early, in 1790, when the French king was still securely on the throne. Burke disagreed with the premises of the revolution. Rights, he argued, were not abstract and "natural" but the results of specific historical traditions. Remodeling the French government without reference to the past and failing to pay proper respect to tradition and custom had, in his eyes, destroyed the fabric of French civilization.
>
> Thomas Paine was one of many to respond to Burke. The Rights of Man (1791–1792) defended the revolution and, more generally, conceptions of human rights. In the polarized atmosphere of the revolutionary wars, simply possessing Paine's pamphlet was cause for imprisonment in Britain.

Edmund Burke

You will observe, that from the Magna Carta to the Declaration of Rights, it has been the uniform policy of our constitution to claim and assert our liberties, as an entailed inheritance derived to us from our forefathers.... We have an inheritable crown; an inheritable peerage; and a house of commons and a people inheriting privileges, franchises, and liberties, from a long line of ancestors....

You had all these advantages in your ancient states, but you chose to act as if you had never been moulded into civil society, and had every thing to begin anew. You began ill, because you began by despising every thing that belonged to you.... If the last generations of your country appeared without much luster in your eyes, you might have passed them by, and derived your claims from a more early race of ancestors.... Respecting your forefathers, you would have been taught to respect yourselves. You would not have chosen to consider the French as a people of yesterday, as a nation of low-born servile wretches until the emancipating year of 1789.... [Y]ou would not have been content to be represented as a gang of Maroon slaves, suddenly broke loose from the house of bondage, and therefore to be pardoned for your abuse of liberty to which you were not accustomed and ill fitted....

... The fresh ruins of France, which shock our feelings wherever we can turn our eyes, are not the devastation of civil war; they are the sad but instructive monuments of rash and ignorant council in time of profound peace. They are the display of inconsiderate and presumptuous, because unresisted and irresistible authority....

Nothing is more certain, than that of our manners, our civilization, and all the good things which are connected with manners, and with civilization, have, in this European world of ours, depended upon two principles; and were indeed the result of both combined; I mean the spirit of a gentleman, and the spirit of religion. The nobility and the clergy, the one by profession, the other by patronage, kept learning in existance, even

Burke's famous book aroused some sympathy for the counterrevolutionary cause, but active opposition came slowly. The first European states to express public concern about events in revolutionary France were Austria and Prussia, declaring in 1791 that order and the rights of the monarch of France were matters of "common interest to all sovereigns of Europe." The leaders of the French assembly pronounced the declaration an affront to national sovereignty. Nobles who had fled France played into their hands with plots and pronouncements against the government. Oddly, perhaps, both supporters and opponents of the revolution in France believed war would serve their cause. The National Assembly's leaders expected an aggressive policy to shore up the people's loyalty and bring freedom to the rest in the midst of arms and confusions. . . . Learning paid back what it received to nobility and priesthood. . . . Happy if they had all continued to know their indissoluble union, and their proper place.

Happy if learning, not debauched by ambition, had been satisfied to continue the instructor, and not aspired to be the master! Along with its natural protectors and guardians, learning will be cast into the mire, and trodden down under the hoofs of a swinish multitude.

Source: Edmund Burke, *Reflections on the Revolution in France (1790)* (New York: 1973), pp. 45, 48, 49, 52, 92.

Thomas Paine

Mr. Burke, with his usual outrage, abuses the *Declaration of the Rights of Man.* . . . Does Mr. Burke mean to deny that man has any rights? If he does, then he must mean that there are no such things as rights any where, and that he has none himself; for who is there in the world but man? But if Mr. Burke means to admit that man has rights, the question will then be, what are those rights, and how came man by them originally?

The error of those who reason by precedents drawn from antiquity, respecting the rights of man, is that they do not go far enough into antiquity. They stop in some of the intermediate stages of an hundred or a thousand years, and produce what was then a rule for the present day. This is no authority at all. . . .

To possess ourselves of a clear idea of what government is, or ought to be, we must trace its origin. In doing this, we shall easily discover that governments must have arisen either *out* of the people, or *over* the people. Mr. Burke has made no distinction. . . .

What were formerly called revolutions, were little more than a change of persons, or an alteration of local circumstances. They rose and fell like things of course, and had nothing in their existance or their fate that could influence beyond the spot that produced them. But what we now see in the world, from the revolutions of America and France, is a renovation of the natural order of things, a system of principles as universal as truth and the existence of man, and combining moral with political happiness and national prosperity.

Source: Thomas Paine, *The Rights of Man (1791)* (New York: 1973), pp. 302, 308, 383.

Questions for Analysis

1. How does Burke define *liberty*? Why does he criticize the revolutionaries for representing themselves as slaves freed from bondage?

2. What does Paine criticize about Burke's emphasis on history? According to Paine, what makes the French Revolution different from previous changes of regime in Europe?

3. How do these two authors' attitudes about the origins of human freedoms shape their understandings of the revolution?

of Europe. Counterrevolutionaries hoped the intervention of Austria and Prussia would undo all that had happened since 1789. Radicals, suspicious of aristocratic leaders and the king, believed that war would expose traitors with misgivings about the revolution and flush out those who sympathized with the king and European tyrants. On April 20, 1792, the assembly declared war against Austria and Prussia. Thus began the war that would keep the Continent in arms for a generation.

As the radicals expected, the French forces met serious reverses. By August 1792, the allied armies of Austria and Prussia had crossed the frontier and were threatening to capture Paris. Many, including soldiers, believed that the military disasters were evidence of the king's treason.

On August 10, Parisian crowds, organized by their radical leaders, attacked the royal palace. The king was imprisoned and a second and far more radical revolution began.

The French Republic

From this point, the country's leadership passed into the hands of the more egalitarian leaders of the Third Estate. These new leaders were known as Jacobins, the name of a political club to which many of them belonged. Although their headquarters were in Paris, their membership extended throughout France. Their members included large numbers of professionals, government officeholders, and lawyers; but they proclaimed themselves spokesmen for the people and the nation. An increasing number of artisans joined Jacobin clubs as the movement grew, and other, more democratic clubs expanded as well.

The National Convention, elected by free white men, became the effective governing body of the country for the next three years. It was elected in September 1792, at a time when enemy troops were advancing, spreading panic. Rumors flew that prisoners in Paris were plotting to aid the enemy. They were hauled from their cells, dragged before hastily convened tribunals, and killed. The "September Massacres" killed more than a thousand "enemies of the Revolution" in less than a week. Similar riots engulfed Lyons, Orléans, and other French cities.

The newly elected convention was far more radical than its predecessor, and its leadership was determined to end the monarchy. On September 21, the convention declared France a republic. In December, it placed the king on trial, and in January 1793 he was condemned to death by a narrow margin. The heir to the grand tradition of French absolutism met his end bravely as "citizen Louis Capet," beheaded by the guillotine. Introduced as a swifter

THE EXECUTION OF LOUIS XVI. The execution of Louis XVI shocked Europe. Even committed revolutionaries in France debated the necessity of such a dramatic act. The entire National Convention (over 700 members) acted as jury, and although the assembly was nearly unanimous in finding the king guilty of treason, a majority of only one approved the final death sentence. Those who voted for Louis XVI's execution were known forever after as "regicides." ▪ *What made this act necessary from the point of view of the most radical of revolutionaries?* ▪ *What made it repugnant from the point of view of the revolution's most heated enemies?*

and more humane form of execution, the frightful mechanical headsman came to symbolize revolutionary fervor.

The convention took other radical measures. It confiscated the property of enemies of the revolution, breaking up some large estates and selling them on easier terms to less-wealthy citizens. It abruptly canceled the policy of compensating nobles for their lost privileges. It repealed primogeniture, so that property would not be inherited exclusively by the oldest son but would be divided in substantially equal portions among all immediate heirs. It abolished slavery in French colonies (see below). It set maximum prices for grain and other necessities. In an astonishing effort to root out Christianity from everyday life, the convention adopted a new calendar. The calendar year began with the birth of the republic (September 22, 1792) and divided months in such a way as to eliminate the Catholic Sunday.

Most of this program was a hastily improvised response to crisis and political pressure from the common people in the cities and their leaders. In the three years after 1790, prices had risen staggeringly: wheat by 27 percent, beef by 136 percent, potatoes by 700 percent. While the government imposed its maximums in Paris, small vigilante militias, representing the sans-culottes, attacked those they considered hoarders and profiteers.

The convention also reorganized its armies, with astonishing success. By February 1793, Britain, Holland, Spain, and Austria were in the field against the French. Britain came into the war for strategic and economic reasons: it feared a French threat to Britain's growing global power. The allied coalition, though united only in its desire to contain France, was nevertheless a formidable force. To counter it, the revolutionary government mustered all men capable of bearing arms. The revolution flung fourteen hastily drafted armies into battle under the leadership of newly promoted, young, and inexperienced officers. What they lacked in training and discipline they made up for in organization, mobility, flexibility, courage, and morale. In 1793–1794, the French armies preserved their homeland. In 1794–1795, they occupied the Low Countries; the Rhineland; and parts of Spain, Switzerland, and Savoy. In 1796, they invaded and occupied key parts of Italy and broke the coalition that had arrayed itself against them.

The Reign of Terror

In 1793, however, those victories lay in a hard-to-imagine future. France was in crisis. In 1793, the convention drafted a new democratic constitution based on male suffrage. That constitution never took effect—suspended indefinitely by wartime emergency. Instead, the convention prolonged its own life year after year and increasingly delegated its responsibilities to a group of twelve leaders, the Committee of Public Safety. The committee's ruthlessness had two purposes: to seize control of the revolution and to prosecute all the revolution's enemies—"to make terror the order of the day." The Terror lasted less than two years but left a bloody and authoritarian legacy.

Perhaps the three best-known leaders of the radical revolution were Jean Paul Marat, Georges Jacques Danton, and Maximilien Robespierre, the latter two members of the Committee of Public Safety. Marat was educated as a physician and by 1789 had already earned enough distinction in that profession to be awarded an honorary degree by St. Andrews University in Scotland. Marat opposed nearly all of his moderate colleagues' assumptions, including their admiration for Great Britain, which Marat considered corrupt and despotic. Persecuted by powerful factions in the constituent assembly who feared his radicalism, he was forced to take refuge in unsanitary sewers and dungeons.

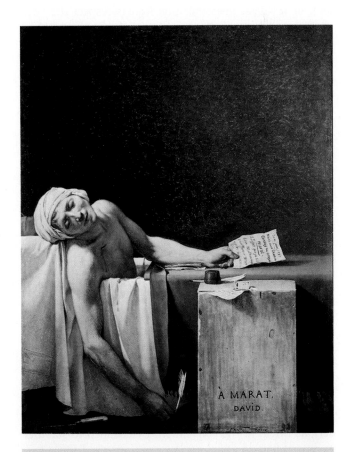

THE DEATH OF MARAT. This painting by the French artist Jacques-Louis David in 1793 immortalized Marat. The note in the slain leader's hand is from Charlotte Corday, his assassin. ▪ *Why was it important to represent Marat as a martyr?*

He persevered as the editor of the popular news sheet *The Friend of the People*. Exposure to infection left him with a chronic and painful skin disease, from which baths provided the only relief. In the summer of 1793, at the height of the crisis of the revolution, he was stabbed in his bath by Charlotte Corday, a young royalist, and thus became a revolutionary martyr.

Danton, like Marat, was a popular political leader, well known in the more plebian clubs of Paris. Elected a member of the Committee of Public Safety in 1793, he had much to do with organizing the Terror. As time went on, however, he wearied of ruthlessness and displayed a tendency to compromise, which gave his opponents in the convention their opportunity. In April 1794, Danton was sent to the guillotine. On mounting the scaffold, he is reported to have said, "Show my head to the people; they do not see the like every day."

The most famous of the radical leaders was Maximilien Robespierre. Born of a family reputed to be of Irish descent, Robespierre trained in law and quickly became a modestly successful lawyer. His eloquence and his consistent, or ruthless, insistence that leaders respect the "will of the people" eventually won him a following in the Jacobin club. Later, he became president of the National Convention and a member of the Committee of Public Safety. Though he had little to do with starting the Terror, he was nevertheless responsible for enlarging its scope. Known as "the Incorruptible," he came to represent ruthlessness justified as virtue and necessary to revolutionary progress.

The two years of the radical republic (August 1792–July 1794) brought dictatorship, centralization, suspension of any liberties, and war. The committee faced foreign enemies and opposition from both the political right and left at home. In June 1793, responding to an escalating crisis, leaders of the "Mountain," a party of radicals allied with Parisian artisans, purged moderates from the convention. Rebellions broke out in the provincial cities of Lyons, Bordeaux, and Marseilles, mercilessly repressed by the committee and its local representatives. The government also faced counterrevolution in the western region known as the Vendée, where movements enlisted peasants and artisans, who believed their local areas were being invaded and who fought for their local priest or against the summons from the revolutionaries' conscription boards. By the summer, the forces in the Vendée posed a serious threat to the convention. Determined to stabilize France, whatever the cost, the committee redeployed its forces, defeated the counterrevolutionaries, and launched murderous campaigns of pacification—torching villages, farms, and fields and killing all who dared oppose them and many who did not.

ROBESPIERRE GUILLOTINING THE EXECUTIONER. The original caption for this 1793 engraving read "Robespierre guillotines the executioner after having had all the French guillotined." In fact, Robespierre himself was guillotined after his fall from power in July 1794. ▪ *What made the struggle for power and authority among revolutionaries so merciless and uncompromising?*

During the period of the Terror, from September 1793 to July 1794, the most reliable estimates place the number of deaths at close to 40,000 to about 16,500 from actual death sentences, with the rest resulting from extra-judicial killings and deaths in prison. Approximately 300,000 were incarcerated between March 1793 and August 1794. These numbers, however, do not include the pacification of the Vendée and rebellious cities in the Rhone Valley, which took more than 100,000 lives. Few victims of the Terror were aristocrats. Many more were peasants or laborers accused of hoarding, treason, or counterrevolutionary activity. Anyone who appeared to threaten the republic, no matter what his or her social or economic position, was at risk. When some time later the Abbé Sieyès was asked what he had done to distinguish himself during the Terror, he responded dryly, "I lived."

The Legacy of the Second French Revolution

The "second" French Revolution affected the everyday life of French men, women, and children in a remarkably direct way. Workers' trousers replaced the breeches that had been a sartorial badge of the middle classes and the nobility. A red cap, said to symbolize freedom from slavery, became popular headgear, and wigs vanished. Men and women addressed each other as "citizen" or "citizeness." Public life was marked by ceremonies designed to dramatize the break with the Old Regime and celebrate new forms of fraternity. In the early stages of the revolution, these festivals seem to have captured genuine popular enthusiasm for new ways of living and thinking. Under the Committee of Public Safety, they became didactic and hollow.

The radical revolution of 1792–1793 also dramatically reversed the trend toward decentralization and democracy. The assembly replaced local officials, some of them still royalist in sympathy, with "deputies on mission," whose task was to conscript troops and generate patriotic fervor. When these deputies appeared too eager to act independently, they were replaced by "national agents," with instructions to report directly to the committee. In another effort to stabilize authority, the assembly closed down all the women's political clubs, decreeing them a political and social danger. Ironically, those who claimed to govern in the name of the people found the popular movement threatening.

Finally, the revolution eroded the strength of those traditional institutions—church, guild, parish—that had for centuries given people a common bond. In their place now stood patriotic organizations and a culture that insisted on loyalty to one national cause. Those organizations had first emerged with the election campaigns, meetings, and pamphlet wars of 1788 and the interest they heightened. They included the political clubs and local assemblies, which at the height of the revolution (1792–1793) met every day of the week and offered an apprenticeship in politics. The army of the republic became the premier national institution.

On the one hand, the revolution divided France, mobilizing counterrevolutionaries as well as revolutionaries. At the same time, the revolution, war, and culture of sacrifice forged new bonds. The sense that the rest of Europe, carrying what the verses of the "Marseillaise," the most famous anthem of the revolution, called the "blood-stained flag of tyranny," sought to crush the new nation and its citizens unquestionably strengthened French national identity.

FROM THE TERROR TO BONAPARTE: THE DIRECTORY

The Committee of Public Safety might have saved France from enemy armies, but it could not save itself. Inflation became catastrophic. The long string of military victories convinced growing numbers that the committee's demands for continuing self-sacrifice and Terror were no longer justified. By July 1794, the committee was virtually without allies. On July 27 (9 Thermidor, according to the new calendar), Robespierre was shouted down while attempting to speak on the floor of the convention. The following day, along with twenty-one other conspirators, he met his death by guillotine.

Ending the Terror did not immediately bring moderation. Vigilante groups of royalists hunted down Jacobins. The repeal of price controls, combined with the worst winter in a century, caused widespread misery. Other measures that had constituted the Terror were gradually repealed. In 1795, the National Convention adopted a new and more conservative constitution. It granted suffrage to all adult male citizens who could read and write. Yet it set up indirect elections: citizens voted for electors, who in turn chose the legislative body. Wealthy citizens thus held authority. Eager

PATRIOTIC WOMEN'S CLUB. The members of this patriotic club wear constitutional bonnets to show their support for the revolution and the reforms of the convention. ▪ *What can one conclude about the atmosphere in Paris during the revolution from the existence of such associations?*

to avoid personal dictatorship, it vested executive authority in a board of five men known as the Directory, chosen by the legislative body. The new constitution included not only a bill of rights but also a declaration of the duties of the citizen.

The Directory lasted longer than its revolutionary predecessors. It still faced discontent on both the radical left and the conservative right. On the left, the Directory repressed radical movements to abolish private property and parliamentary-style government, including one led by the radical "Gracchus Babeuf." Dispatching threats from the right proved more challenging. In 1797, the first free elections held in France as a republic returned a large number of

French Republic, 1792
Annexed to France, 1792–1795
Sister republics

0   100   200   300 Miles
0   100   200   300 Kilometers

FRANCE AND ITS SISTER REPUBLICS. ▪ *The French revolutionaries, fighting against the conservative monarchs of Europe, conquered and annexed large sections of what three countries?* ▪ *Who were potential supporters of the French Revolution in areas outside France during the Napoleonic era?* ▪ *Who was most likely to oppose it in these areas?*

monarchists to the councils of government, alarming politicians who had voted to execute Louis XVI. Backed by the army, the Directory annulled most of the election results. After two years of more uprisings and purges, and with the country still plagued by severe inflation, the Directors grew desperate. This time they called for help from a brilliant young general named Napoleon Bonaparte.

Bonaparte's first military victory had come in 1793, with the recapture of Toulon from royalist and British forces, and had earned him promotion from captain to brigadier general at the age of twenty-four. After the Terror, he was briefly arrested for his Jacobin associations. But he proved his usefulness to the Directory in October 1795 when he put down an uprising with "a whiff of grapeshot," saving the new regime from its opponents. Promoted, he won a string of victories in Italy, forcing Austria to withdraw (temporarily) from the war. He attempted to defeat Britain by attacking British forces in Egypt and the Near East, a campaign that went well on land but ran into trouble at sea, where the French fleet was defeated by Admiral Horatio Nelson (Abukir Bay, 1798). Bonaparte found himself trapped in Egypt by the British and unable to win a decisive victory.

It was at this point that the call came from the Directory. Bonaparte slipped away from Egypt and appeared in Paris, already having agreed to participate in a coup d'état with the leading Director, that former revolutionary champion of the Third Estate, the Abbé Sieyès. On November 9, 1799 (18 Brumaire), Bonaparte was declared a "temporary consul." He was the answer to the Directory's prayers: a strong, popular leader who was not a king. Sieyès declared that Bonaparte would provide "[c]onfidence from below, authority from above." With those words Sieyès pronounced the end of the revolutionary period.

NAPOLEON AND IMPERIAL FRANCE

Few figures in Western history have compelled the attention of the world as Napoleon Bonaparte did during the fifteen years of his rule in France. Few men lived on with such persistence as myth, not just in their own countries, but across the West. Why? For the great majority of ordinary Europeans, memories of the French Revolution were dominated by those of the Napoleonic Wars, which devastated Europe, convulsed its politics, and traumatized its peoples for a generation.

Yet Bonaparte's relationship to the revolution was not simple. His regime consolidated some of the revolution's political and social changes but sharply repudiated others. He presented himself as the son of the revolution, but he also borrowed freely from very different regimes, fashioning himself as the heir to Charlemagne or to the Roman Empire. His regime remade revolutionary politics and the French state; offered stunning examples of the new kinds of warfare; and left a legacy of conflict and legends of French glory that lingered in the dreams, or nightmares, of Europe's statesmen and citizens for more than a century.

Consolidating Authority: 1799–1804

Bonaparte's early career reinforced the claim that the revolution rewarded the efforts of able men. The son of a provincial Corsican nobleman, he attended the École Militaire in Paris. In prerevolutionary France he would have been unable to rise beyond the rank of major, which required buying a regimental command. The revolution, however, abolished the purchase of military office, and Bonaparte quickly became a general. Here, then, was a man who had risen from obscurity because of his own gifts, which he lent happily to the service of France's revolution.

Once in power, however, Bonaparte showed less respect for revolutionary principles. After the coup of 1799, he assumed the title of "first consul." A new constitution established universal white male suffrage and set up two legislative bodies. Elections, however, were indirect, and the power of the legislative bodies sharply curbed. "The government?" said one observer. "There is Bonaparte." Bonaparte instituted what has since become a common authoritarian device, the plebiscite, which put a question directly to popular vote. This allows the head of state to bypass politicians or legislative bodies who might disagree with him—as well as permitting local officials to tamper with ballot boxes. In 1802, flush with victory abroad, he asked the legislature to proclaim him consul for life. When the Senate refused to do so, Bonaparte's Council of State stepped in, offered him the title, and had it ratified by plebiscite. Throughout, his regime retained the appearance of consulting with the people, but its most important feature was the centralization of authority.

That authority came from reorganizing the state, and on this score Bonaparte's accomplishments were extraordinary and lasting. Bonaparte's regime confirmed the abolition of privilege, thereby promising "careers open to talent." Centralizing administrative departments, he accomplished what no recent French regime had yet achieved: an orderly and generally fair system of taxation. More efficient tax collection and fiscal management also helped halt the inflationary spiral that had crippled the revolutionary governments,

although Bonaparte's regime relied heavily on resources from areas he had conquered to fund his military ventures. As we have seen, earlier revolutionary regimes began to reorganize France's administration—abolishing the ancient fiefdoms with their separate governments, legal codes, privileges, and customs—setting up a uniform system of departments. Bonaparte continued that work, pressing it further and putting an accent on centralization. He replaced elected officials and local self-government with centrally appointed prefects and subprefects, who answered directly to the Council of State in Paris. The prefects wielded considerable power, much more than any elected representative: they were in charge of everything from collecting statistics and reporting on the economy and the population to education, roads, and public works. With more integrated administration, in which the different branches were coordinated (and supervised from above), a more professional bureaucracy, and more rational and efficient taxation (though the demands of war strained the system), Napoleon's state marked the transition from Bourbon absolutism to the modern state.

Law, Education, and a New Elite

Napoleon's most significant contribution to modern state building was the promulgation of a new legal code in 1804. Each revolutionary regime had taken up the daunting task of modernizing the laws; each had run out of time. Napoleon tolerated no delays, and threw himself into the project, pressing his own ideas and supervising half the meetings. The Napoleonic Code, as the civil code came to be called, pivoted on two principles that had remained significant through all the constitutional changes since 1789: uniformity and individualism. It cleared through the thicket of contradictory legal traditions that governed the ancient provinces of France, creating one uniform law. It confirmed the abolition of feudal privileges of all kinds: not only noble and clerical privileges but the special rights of craft guilds, municipalities, and so on. It set the conditions for exercising property rights: the drafting of contracts, leases, and stock companies. The code's provisions on the family, which Napoleon developed personally, insisted on the importance of paternal authority and the subordination of women and children. In 1793, during the most radical period of the revolution, men and women had been declared "equal in marriage"; now Napoleon's code affirmed the "natural supremacy" of the husband. Married women could not sell property, run a business, or have a profession without their husbands' permission. Fathers had the sole right to control their children's financial affairs, consent to their marriages, and (under the ancient right to correction) to imprison

Representing the People during the French Revolution

rom the moment the population of Paris came to the assistance of the beleaguered National Assembly in July 1789, representations of "the people" in the French Revolution took on an overwhelming significance. Building a new government that was committed to an idea of popular sovereignty meant that both the revolution's supporters and its opponents were deeply invested in shaping perceptions of the people. And of course, Article III of the Declaration of the Rights of Man ("The principle of sovereignty resides essentially in the

nation") meant that any individual, group, or institution that could successfully claim to represent the will of the people could wield tremendous power, as long as others accepted that claim.

Of course, revolutionary crowds did not always conform to the images of them that circulated so widely in prints and paintings during the period 1789–1799. Some were spontaneous, and others were organized; some were made up of recognizable social and professional groups with clear political goals, and others were a hodgepodge of conflicting and even inarticulate aspirations. Many were nonviolent; some were exceedingly

threatening and murderous. All politicians sought to use them to support their political programs, and many learned to fear their unpredictable behavior.

These four images give a sense of the competing visions of the people that appeared in the public realm during the French Revolution. The first (image A) shows the killing of Foulon, a royal official who was lynched and beheaded by an enthusiastic crowd barely a week after the fall of the Bastille because he was suspected of conspiring to starve the Parisian population as punishment for their rebellion against the king. The second (image B) shows a more care-

A. The punishment of Foulon (anonymous print, 1789).

B. *The Festival of Federation* by Charles Thévenin, 1790.

fully choreographed representation of the people during the Festival of Federation, organized in July 1790 by the revolutionary government to commemorate the first anniversary of the fall of the Bastille. Finally, the last two documents show contrasting images of the revolutionary sans-culottes, the working-class revolutionaries who supported the government during the Terror in 1792–1794. The first (image C), a sympathetic portrait of a sans-culottes as a virtuous and self-sacrificing working man, standing with an eye to the future, seems completely incongruous when paired with the British satirist James Gilray's portrait of a cannibalistic sans-culottes family (image D), drawn literally "without pants," feasting on the bodies of their victims after a hard day's work.

Questions for Analysis

1. Image A depicts an event from July 1789—that is, before the August publication of the Declaration of the Rights of Man. How does this image portray the crowd's vengeance on Foulon? What possible political messages are contained in this image?

2. Image B, on the other hand, chooses to display the people celebrating their own birth as a political body, by convening on the anniversary of the fall of the Bastille. What emotions is this painting designed to invoke, and how is it related to more disturbing images such as image A?

3. How are the positive and negative portrayals of sans-culottes as political actors (images C and D) constructed? Can one imagine a painting of a worker like image C being produced before 1789? What does image D tell us about how the revolution was viewed from Britain?

C. A typical sans-culotte, painting by Louis-Léopold Boilly, 1792.

D. A family of sans-culottes [sic] refreshing after the fatigues of the day. (British satirical cartoon by James Gilray, 1793).

them for up to six months without showing cause. Divorce remained legal, but under unequal conditions; a man could sue for divorce on the grounds of adultery, but a woman could do so only if her husband moved his "concubine" into the family's house. Most important to the common people, the code prohibited paternity suits for illegitimate children.

In all, Napoleon developed seven legal codes covering commercial law, civil law and procedures, crime, and punishment. Like the civil code, the new criminal code consolidated some of the gains of the revolution, treating citizens as equals before the law and outlawing arbitrary arrest and imprisonment. Yet it, too, reinstated brutal measures that the revolutionaries had abolished, such as branding and cutting off the hands of parricides. The Napoleonic legal regime was more egalitarian than law under the Old Regime but no less concerned with authority.

Napoleon also rationalized the educational system. He ordered the establishment of *lycées* (high schools) in every major town to train civil servants and army officers and a school in Paris to train teachers. To supplement these changes, Napoleon brought the military and technical schools under state control and founded a national university to supervise the entire system. It is not surprising that he built up a new military academy. He reorganized and established solid financing for the premier schools of higher education: the polytechnic (for engineers) and the normal (for teachers), to which students would be admitted based on examinations and from which would issue the technical, educational, and political elites of the country. Like almost all his reforms, this one reinforced reforms introduced during the revolution, and it intended to abolish privilege and create "careers open to talent." Napoleon also embraced the burgeoning social and physical sciences of the Enlightenment. He sponsored the Institute of France, divided into four sections, or academies: fine arts, sciences, humanities, and language (the famous Académie française). These academies dated back to the age of absolutism—now they were coordinated and put on a new footing. They acquired under Napoleon the character that they have preserved to this day: centralized, meritocratic, and geared to serving the state.

Who benefited from these changes? Like Bonaparte's other new institutions, the new schools helped confirm the power of a new elite. The new elite included businessmen, bankers, and merchants but was still composed primarily of powerful landowners. What was more, at least half of the fellowships to the high schools went to the sons of military officers and high civil servants. Finally, like most of Bonaparte's reforms, changes in education aimed to strengthen the empire: "My object in establishing a teaching corps is to have a means of directing political and moral opinion," Napoleon said bluntly.

Bonaparte's early measures were ambitious. To win support for them, he made allies without regard for their past political affiliations. He admitted back into the country exiles of all political stripes. His two fellow consuls were a regicide of the Terror and a bureaucrat of the Old Regime. His minister of police had been an extreme radical republican; his minister of foreign affairs was the aristocrat and opportunist Charles Talleyrand. The most remarkable act of political reconciliation came in 1801, with Bonaparte's concordat with the pope, an agreement that put an end to more than a decade of hostility between the French state and the Catholic Church. Although it shocked anticlerical revolutionaries, Napoleon, ever the pragmatist, believed that reconciliation would create domestic harmony and international solidarity. The agreement gave the pope the right to depose French bishops and to discipline the French clergy. In return, the Vatican agreed to forgo any claims to Church lands expropriated by the revolution. That property would remain in the hands of its new middle-class rural and urban proprietors. The concordat did not revoke the principle of religious freedom established by the revolution, but it did win Napoleon the support of conservatives who had feared for France's future as a godless state.

Such political balancing acts increased Bonaparte's general popularity. Combined with early military successes (peace with Austria in 1801 and with Britain in 1802), they muffled any opposition to his personal ambitions. He had married Josephine de Beauharnais, a Creole from Martinique and an influential mistress of the revolutionary period. Josephine had given the Corsican soldier-politician legitimacy and access among the revolutionary elite early in his career. Neither Bonaparte nor his ambitious wife were content to be first among equals, however; and in December of 1804, he finally cast aside any traces of republicanism. In a ceremony that evoked the splendor of medieval kingship and Bourbon absolutism, he crowned himself Emperor Napoleon I in the Cathedral of Notre Dame in Paris. Napoleon did much to create the modern state, but he did not hesitate to proclaim his links to the past.

In Europe as in France: Napoleon's Empire

The nations of Europe had looked on—some in admiration, others in horror, all in astonishment—at the phenomenon that was Napoleon. Austria, Prussia, and Britain led two coalitions against revolutionary France in 1792–1795 and in 1798, and both were defeated. After Napoleon came to power in 1799, the alliance split. Russia and Austria withdrew from the fray in 1801, and even the intransigent British were forced to make peace the following year.

By 1805, the Russians, Prussians, Austrians, and Swedes had joined the British in an attempt to contain France. Their efforts were to no avail. Napoleon's military superiority led to defeats, in turn, of all the continental allies. Napoleon was a master of well-timed, well-directed shock attacks on the battlefield: movement, regrouping, and pressing his advantage. He led an army that had transformed European warfare; first raised as a revolutionary militia, it was now a trained conscript army, loyal, well supplied by a nation whose economy was committed to serving the war effort, and led by generals promoted largely on the basis of talent. This new kind of army inflicted crushing defeats on his enemies. The battle of Austerlitz, in December 1805, was a triumph for the French against the combined forces of Austria and Russia and became a symbol of the emperor's apparent invincibility. His subsequent victory against the Russians at Friedland in 1807 only added to his reputation.

Out of these victories, Napoleon created his new empire and affiliated states. To the southeast, the empire included Rome and the pope's dominions, Tuscany, and the Dalmatian territories of Austria (now the coastline of Croatia). To the east, Napoleon's rule extended over a federation of German states known as the Confederation of the Rhine and a section of Poland. These new states were presented as France's gift of independence to patriots elsewhere in Europe, but in practice they served as a military buffer against renewed expansion by Austria. The empire itself was ringed by the allied kingdoms of Italy, Naples, Spain, and Holland, whose thrones were occupied by Napoleon's brothers, brothers-in-law, and trusted generals.

The empire brought the French Revolution's practical consequences—a powerful, centralizing state and an end to old systems of privilege—to Europe's doorstep, applying to the empire principles that had already transformed France. Administrative modernization, which meant overhauling the procedures, codes, and practices of the state, was the most powerful feature of changes introduced. The empire changed the terms of government service (careers open to talent), handing out new titles and recruiting new men for the civil service and the judiciary. It ended the nobility's monopoly on the officer corps. The new branches of government hired engineers, mapmakers, surveyors, and legal consultants. Public works and education were reorganized. Prefects in the outer reaches of the empire, as in France, built roads, bridges, dikes (in Holland), hospitals, and prisons; they reorganized universities and built observatories. In the empire and some of the satellite kingdoms, tariffs were eliminated, feudal dues abolished, new tax districts formed, and plentiful new taxes collected to support the new state.

In the realm of liberty and law, Napoleon's rule eliminated feudal and church courts and created a single legal system. The Napoleonic Code was often introduced, but not always or entirely. (In southern Italy measures against the Catholic Church were deemed too controversial.) Reforms eliminated many inequalities and legal privileges. The Duchy of Warsaw in Poland ended serfdom but offered no land reform, so former serfs became impoverished tenants. In most areas, the empire gave civil rights to Protestants and Jews. In Rome, the conquering French opened the gates of the Jewish ghetto—and made Jews subject to conscription. In some areas, Catholic monasteries, convents, and other landholdings were broken up and sold, almost always to wealthy buyers. In the empire as in France, and under Napoleon as during the revolution, many who benefited were the elite: people and groups already on their way up and with the resources to take advantage of opportunities.

In government, the regime sought a combination of legal equality (for men) and stronger state authority. The French and local authorities created new electoral districts, expanded the suffrage, and wrote constitutions, but newly elected representative bodies were dismissed if they failed to cooperate, few constitutions were ever fully applied, and political freedoms were often fleeting. Napoleon's regime referred to revolutionary principles to anchor its legitimacy, but authority remained its guiding light. All governmental direction emanated from Paris and therefore from Napoleon.

Finally, in the empire as in France, Napoleon displayed his signature passions. The first of these was an Enlightenment zeal for accumulating useful knowledge. The empire gathered statistics as never before, for it was important to know the resources—including population—that a state had at its disposal. That spirit had been evident already in Bonaparte's extraordinary 1798 excursion into Egypt. He took hundreds of scholars and artists along with the army, founded the Egyptian institute in Cairo, and sent researchers off to make a systematic inventory of the country (its geology, rivers, minerals, antiquities, animal life) and to conduct archaeological expeditions to Upper Egypt, where they sketched the pyramids and excavated what would turn out to be the Rosetta Stone (see Chapter 20). Napoleon's second passion was cultivating his relationship to imperial glories of the past. He poured time and energy into (literally) cementing his image for posterity. The Arc de Triomphe in Paris, designed to imitate the Arc of Constantine in Rome, is the best example; but Napoleon also ordered work to be undertaken to restore ruins in Rome, to make the Prado Palace in Madrid a museum, and to renovate and preserve the Alhambra in Granada.

Such were Napoleon's visions of his legacy and himself. How did others see him? Europe offered no single reaction. Some countries and social groups collaborated enthusiastically, some negotiated, some resisted. Napoleon's image as a military hero genuinely inspired young men from the elite, raised in a culture that prized military honor. By contrast, Catholic peasants in Spain fought him from the beginning. In many small principalities previously ruled by princes—the patchwork states of Germany, for example, and the repressive kingdom of Naples—reforms that provided for more efficient, less corrupt administration, a workable tax structure, and an end to customary privilege were welcomed by most of the local population. Yet the Napoleonic presence proved a mixed

blessing. Vassal states contributed heavily to the maintenance of the emperor's military power. The French levied taxes, drafted men, and required states to support occupying armies. In Italy, the policy was called "liberty and requisitions"; and the Italians, Germans, and Dutch paid an especially high price for reforms—in terms of economic cost and numbers of men recruited. From the point of view of the common people, the local lord and priest had been replaced by the French tax collector and army recruiting board.

It is telling that even Napoleon's enemies came to believe that the upstart emperor represented the wave of the future,

NAPOLEON'S EUROPEAN EMPIRE AT ITS HEIGHT. At the height of his power in 1812, Napoleon controlled most of Europe, ruling either directly or through dependent states and allies. ▪ *Compared to the map on page 600, by what means had Napoleon expanded French control on continental Europe?* ▪ *Which major countries remained outside of French control?* ▪ *Which areas felt the most long-lasting impact of Napoleon's reign?*

NAPOLEON ON HORSEBACK AT THE ST. BERNARD PASS BY JAÇQUES-LOUIS DAVID, 1801, AND *LITTLE BONEY GONE TO POT* BY GEORGE CRUIKSHANK, 1814. The depth of Napoleon's celebrity in Europe can be measured in the equal shares of adulation and hatred that he stirred up within Europe among his supporters and his enemies. David's portrait, painted before he became emperor of France, captures the ardent hopes that many attached to his person. The painting explicitly compared Napoleon to two previous European conquerors, Charlemagne and the ancient Roman emperor Hannibal, by evoking their names in the stones at the base of the painting. In George Cruikshanks's bitter caricature, published after Napoleon's exile to Elba, the devil offers him a pistol to commit suicide, and the former emperor, seated on a chamber pot, says he might, but only if the firing mechanism is disabled. Both images use assumptions about virility and masculine authority to make their point. ▪ *Who are the intended audiences for these images, and how do they convey their respective arguments?*

particularly in regard to the reorganization of the state. Though they fought Napoleon, Prussian and Austrian administrators set about instituting reforms that resembled his: changing rules of promotion and recruitment, remodeling bureaucracies, redrawing districts, eliminating some privileges, and so on. Many who came of age under Napoleon's empire believed that, for better or worse, his empire was modern.

THE RETURN TO WAR AND NAPOLEON'S DEFEAT: 1806–1815

Napoleon's boldest attempt at consolidation, a policy banning British goods from the Continent, was a dangerous failure. Britain had bitterly opposed each of France's revolutionary regimes since the death of Louis XVI; now it tried to rally Europe against Napoleon with promises of generous financial loans and trade. Napoleon's Continental System, established in 1806, sought to starve Britain's trade and force its surrender. The system failed for several reasons. Throughout the war, Britain retained control of the seas. The British naval blockade of the Continent, begun in 1807, effectively countered Napoleon's system. While the French Empire strained to transport goods and raw materials overland to avoid the British blockade, the British successfully developed a lively trade with South America. A second reason for the failure of the system was its internal tariffs. Europe divided into economic camps, at odds with each other as they tried to subsist on what the Continent alone could produce and manufacture. Finally, the system hurt the Continent more than Britain. Stagnant trade in Europe's ports and unemployment in its manufacturing centers eroded public faith in Napoleon's dream of a working European empire.

The Continental System was Napoleon's first serious mistake. His ambition to create a European empire, modeled on Rome and ruled from Paris, was to become a second cause of his decline. The symbols of his empire—reflected in painting, architecture, and the design of furniture and clothing—were deliberately Roman in origin. Where early revolutionaries referred to the Roman Republic for their imagery, Napoleon looked to the more ostentatious style of the Roman emperors. In 1809, he divorced the empress Josephine and ensured himself a successor of royal blood by marrying a Habsburg princess, Marie Louise—the great-niece of Marie Antoinette. Such actions lost Napoleon the support of revolutionaries, former Enlightenment thinkers, and liberals across the Continent.

Over time, the bitter tonic of defeat began to have an effect on Napoleon's enemies, who changed their own approach to waging war. After the Prussian army was humiliated at Jena in 1806 and forced out of the war, a whole generation of younger Prussian officers reformed their military and their state by demanding rigorous practical training for commanders and a genuinely national army made up of patriotic Prussian citizens rather than well-drilled mercenaries.

The myth of Napoleon's invincibility worked against him as well, as he took ever greater risks with France's military and national fortunes. Russian numbers and Austrian artillery inflicted horrendous losses on the French at Wagram in 1809, although these difficulties were forgotten in the glow of victory. Napoleon's allies and supporters shrugged off the British admiral Horatio Nelson's victory at Trafalgar in 1805 as no more than a temporary check to the emperor's ambitions. But Trafalgar broke French naval power in the Mediterranean and led to a rift with Spain, which had been France's equal partner in the battle and suffered equally in the defeat. In the Caribbean, too, Napoleon was forced to cut growing losses (see below).

A crucial moment in Napoleon's undoing came with his invasion of Spain in 1808. Napoleon overthrew the Spanish king, installed his own brother on the throne, and then imposed a series of reforms similar to those he had instituted elsewhere in Europe. Napoleon's blow against the Spanish monarchy weakened its hold on its colonies across the Atlantic, and the Spanish crown never fully regained its grip (see Chapter 20). But in Spain itself,

NAPOLEON ON THE BATTLEFIELD OF EYLAU. Amid bitter cold and snow, Napoleon engaged with the Russian army in February 1807. Although technically a victory for the French, it was only barely that, with the French losing at least 10,000 men and the Russians twice as many. This painting, characteristic of Bonaparte propaganda, emphasizes not the losses but the emperor's saintlike clemency—even enemy soldiers reach up toward him.

Napoleon reckoned without two factors that led to the ultimate failure of his mission: the presence of British forces and the determined resistance of the Spanish people, who detested Napoleon's interference in the affairs of the church. The Peninsular Wars, as the Spanish conflicts were called, were long and bitter. The smaller British force learned how to concentrate a devastating volume of gunfire on the French pinpoint attacks on the open battlefield and laid siege to French garrison towns. The Spanish quickly began to wear down the French invaders through guerrilla warfare. Terrible atrocities were committed by both sides; the French military's torture and execution of Spanish guerrillas and civilians was immortalized by the Spanish artist Francisco Goya (1746–1828) with sickening accuracy in his prints and paintings. Though at one point Napoleon himself took charge of his army, he could not achieve anything more than temporary victory. The Spanish campaign was the first indication that Napoleon could be beaten, and it encouraged resistance elsewhere.

The second, and most dramatic, stage in Napoleon's downfall began with the disruption of his alliance with Russia. As an agricultural country, Russia had suffered a severe economic crisis when it was no longer able to trade its surplus grain for British manufactures. The consequence was that Tsar Alexander I began to wink at trade with Britain and to ignore or evade the protests from Paris. By 1811, Napoleon decided that he could no longer endure this flouting of their agreement. He collected an army of 600,000 and set out for Russia in the spring of 1812. Only a third of the soldiers in this "Grande Armée" were French; nearly as many were Polish or German, joined by soldiers and adventurers from the rest of France's client states. It was the grandest of Napoleon's imperial expeditions, an army raised from across Europe and sent to punish the autocratic tsar. The invasion ended in disaster. The Russians refused to make a stand, drawing the French farther and farther into the heart of their country. Just before Napoleon reached the ancient Russian capital of Moscow, the Russian army drew the French forces into a bloody, seemingly pointless battle in the narrow streets of a town called Borodino, where both sides suffered terrible losses of men and supplies, harder on the French who were now so far from home. After the battle, the Russians permitted Napoleon to occupy Moscow. But on the night of his entry, Russian partisans put the city to the torch, leaving little but the blackened walls of the Kremlin palaces to shelter the French troops.

THE DISASTERS OF WAR BY FRANCISCO GOYA (1746–1828). Goya was a Spanish painter and political liberal who had initially supported the French revolution. After Napoleon invaded Spain in 1807, Spaniards rose up in revolt, leading to the Peninsular War of 1808–1814. Between 1810 and 1820, Goya documented the war's violence in a series of black-and-white prints containing stark images of atrocity, rape, and the aftermath of famine. Note the absence of political imagery and the pointed and bitter irony of Goya's caption: "A great heroic feat! With dead people!" ▪ *Who or what is the target of Goya's sarcasm here?*

Hoping that the tsar would eventually surrender, Napoleon lingered amid the ruins for more than a month. On October 19, he finally ordered the homeward march. The delay was a fatal blunder. Long before he had reached the border, the terrible Russian winter was on his troops. Frozen streams, mountainous drifts of snow, and bottomless mud slowed the retreat almost to a halt. To add to the miseries of frostbite, disease, and starvation, mounted Cossacks rode out of the blizzard to harry the exhausted army. Each morning the miserable remnant that pushed on left behind circles of corpses around the campfires of the night before. Temperatures dropped to −27°F. On December 13, a few thousand broken soldiers crossed the frontier into Germany—a fragment of the once proud Grande Armée. Nearly 300,000 of its soldiers and untold thousands of Russians lost their lives in Napoleon's Russian adventure.

After the retreat from Russia, the anti-Napoleonic forces took renewed hope. United by a belief that they might finally succeed in defeating the emperor, Prussia, Russia, Austria, Sweden, and Britain renewed their attack. Citizens of many German states in particular saw this as a war of liberation, and indeed most of the fighting took place in Germany. The climax of the campaign occurred in October 1813 when, at what was thereafter known as the Battle of the Nations, fought near Leipzig, the allies dealt the French a resounding defeat. Meanwhile, allied armies won significant victories in the Low Countries and Spain. By the beginning of 1814, they had crossed the Rhine into France. Left with an army of inexperienced youths, Napoleon retreated to Paris, urging the French people to resist despite constant setbacks at the hands of the larger invading armies. On March 31, Tsar Alexander I of Russia and King Frederick William III of Prussia made their triumphant entry into Paris. Napoleon was forced to abdicate unconditionally and was sent into exile on the island of Elba, off the Italian coast.

Napoleon was back on French soil in less than a year. In the interim, the allies had restored the Bourbon dynasty to the throne, in the person of Louis XVIII, brother of Louis XVI. Despite his administrative abilities, Louis could not fill the void left by Napoleon's abdication. It was no surprise that when the former emperor staged his escape from Elba, his fellow countrymen once more rallied to his

Analyzing Primary Sources

Napoleon the "Liberator"?

Did Napoleon continue the work of the French Revolution? These two documents, from early and late moments in Napoleon's career, allow one to judge the extent to which Napoleon's regime shared the goals of revolutionaries who preceded him.

The first document concerns Napoleon's decision to reestablish slavery in French colonies. The slaves of Saint-Domingue had freed themselves by insurrection in 1791, and the French revolutionary government made this freedom official by abolishing slavery on French territory in 1794. In 1802, Napoleon launched an expeditionary force to reimpose French control over the colony, and in the course of this conflict it became clear that his goal was reenslavement. The former slaves of Saint-Domingue defeated Napoleon's troops and established Haiti as an independent nation, but in the nearby French colonies of Tobago, Martinique, and Guadeloupe, as well as in French holdings in the Indian Ocean, Napoleon reinstituted slavery. The first excerpt below is from a preliminary draft for the law on reenslavement that Napoleon drew up himself.

The second selection is excerpted from a proclamation that Napoleon addressed to the sovereigns of Europe on his return to France in March 1815, after escaping from his exile on the island of Elba. It is an excellent illustration of Napoleon's self-image at the end of his career, his rhetoric, and his belief that he represented the force of history itself.

Letter to Consul Cambacérès, April 27, 1802

The consuls of the Republic and informed council of State decree:

Article One: According to the reports made to the captain-general of the colony of _____ by those individuals who will commit to this result, a list will be composed comprising first the names of black people who enjoyed freedom before 26 Pluviôse, Year II, and second, the names of blacks who have united to defend the territory of the Republic from its enemies, or who, in any other matter, have served the state.

Article Two: All the individuals named on this list will be declared free.

Article Three: Those among them who do not own property, and who have not trade or skill which can assure their subsistence, will be subjected to the regulations of the police who will assign them to property owners who will support them in agricultural work, determine their pay, and will stipulate above all arrangements for preventing vagabondage and insubordination.

Article Four: Insubordinates and outspoken vagabonds will be, in cases determined by the regulations, struck from the list and deprived of the advantages which result from it. One can substitute for this arrangement deportation to colonies where the emancipation laws have not been enacted.

Article Five: All blacks not included on the aforementioned list in article one will be subjected to the laws which in 1789 comprised the Black Code in the colonies [the Black Code was the law regulating the practice of slavery].

Article Six: It will be permitted to import blacks in the colony of _____ in accordance with the laws and regulations of the trade which were in place in 1789. The minister of the marine is charged with the execution of the present order.

Source: Laura Mason and Tracey Rizzo, *The French Revolution: A Document Collection* (Boston: 1999), pp. 349–50.

side. By the time Napoleon reached Paris, he had generated enough support to cause Louis to flee the country. The allies, meeting in Vienna to conclude peace treaties with the French, were stunned by the news of Napoleon's return. They dispatched a hastily organized army to meet the emperor's typically bold offensive push into the Low Countries. At the battle of Waterloo, fought over three bloody days from June 15 to 18, 1815, Napoleon was stopped by the forces of his two most persistent enemies, Britain and Prussia, and suffered his final defeat. This time, the allies took no chances and shipped their prisoner off to the bleak island of St. Helena in the South Atlantic. The once-mighty emperor, now the exile Bonaparte, lived out a dreary existence writing self-serving memoirs until his death in 1821.

Circular Letter to the Sovereigns of Europe, April 4, 1815

onsieur, My Brother, You will have learnt, during the course of last month, of my landing again in France, of my entry into Paris, and of the departure of the Bourbon family. Your Majesty must by now be aware of the real nature of these events. They are the work of an irresistible power, of the unanimous will of a great nation conscious of its duties and of its rights. A dynasty forcibly reimposed upon the French people was no longer suitable for it: the Bourbons refused to associate themselves with the natural feelings or the national customs; and France was forced to abandon them. The popular voice called for a liberator. The expectation which had decided me to make the supreme sacrifice was in vain. I returned; and from the place where my foot first touched the shore I was carried by the affection of my subjects into the bosom of my capital.

My first and heartfelt anxiety is to repay so much affection by the maintenance of an honourable peace. The re-establishment of the Imperial throne was necessary for the happiness of Frenchmen: my dearest hope is that it may also secure repose for the whole of Europe. Each national flag in turn has had its gleam of glory: often enough, by some turn of fortune, great victories have been followed by great defeats. . . . I have provided the world in the past with a programme of great contests; it will please me better in future to acknowledge no rivalry but that of the advocates of peace, and no combat but a crusade for the felicity of mankind. It is France's pleasure to make a frank avowal of this noble ideal. Jealous of her independence, she will always base her policy upon an unqualified respect for the independence of other peoples. . . .

Monsieur my Brother,
Your good Brother,
Napoleon

Source: K. M. Baker, ed., *The Old Regime and the French Revolution* (Chicago: 1987), pp. 419–420, 426–427.

Questions for Analysis

1. Who in the Caribbean colonies did Napoleon intend to send back into slavery in 1802? Who was to remain free? What did Napoleon hope to accomplish by returning to the prerevolutionary legislation that authorized slavery?

2. In his 1815 address to the monarchs of Europe, can one still detect certain aspects of revolutionary rhetoric in Napoleon's words, even as he harnessed this rhetoric to his project of reestablishing the empire after his 1814 defeat?

3. Looking back on his career of ambitious conquests, what can Napoleon have hoped to accomplish in 1815 by boasting that France's "jealous" protection of her own independence gave her an "unqualified respect for the independence of other peoples"? Do his statements reveal a contradiction between the French revolution's commitment to the "universal" rights of man and the pursuit of national self-interests?

Liberty, Politics, and Slavery: The Haitian Revolution

In the French colonies across the Atlantic, the revolution took a different course, with wide-ranging ramifications. The Caribbean islands of Guadeloupe, Martinique, and Saint-Domingue occupied a central role in the eighteenth-century French economy because of the sugar trade. Their planter elites had powerful influence in Paris.

The French National Assembly (like its American counterpart) declined to discuss the matter of slavery in the colonies, unwilling to encroach on the property rights of slave owners and fearful of losing the lucrative sugar islands to their British or Spanish rivals should discontented slave owners talk of independence from France. (Competition between the European powers for the islands of the Caribbean was intense; that islands would change hands was a real possibility.) French men in the National Assembly also had to consider the question of

Past and Present

The Atlantic Revolutions and Human Rights

The eighteenth-century revolutions in the Atlantic world, such as the slave revolt in Saint Domingue (left), were based on the idea that individual rights were universal—they applied to everybody. Since the world is divided into autonomous nation-states, however, it has been challenging for defenders of universal human rights, like the organization Amnesty International (right), to ensure their enforcement globally.

Watch related author interview on StudySpace
wwnorton.com/web/westernciv18

rights for free men of color, a group that included a significant number of wealthy owners of property (and slaves).

Saint-Domingue had about 40,000 whites of different social classes, 30,000 free people of color, and 500,000 slaves, most of them recently enslaved in West Africa. In 1790, free people of color from Saint-Domingue sent a delegation to Paris, asking to be seated by the assembly, underscoring that they were men of property and, in many cases, of European ancestry. The assembly refused. Their refusal sparked a rebellion among free people of color in Saint-Domingue. The French colonial authorities repressed the movement quickly—and brutally. They captured Vincent Ogé, a member of the delegation to Paris and one of the leaders of the rebellion, and publicly executed him and his allies by breaking on the wheel and decapitation. Radical deputies in Paris, including Robespierre, expressed outrage but could do little to change the assembly's policy.

In August 1791, the largest slave rebellion in history broke out in Saint-Domingue. How much that rebellion owed to revolutionary propaganda is unclear; like many rebellions during the period, it had its own roots. The British and the Spanish invaded, confident they could crush the rebellion and take the island. In the spring of 1792, the French government, on the verge of collapse and war with Europe, scrambled to win allies in Saint-Domingue by making free men of color citizens. A few months later (after the revolution of August 1792), the new French Republic dispatched commissioners to Saint-Domingue with troops and instructions to hold the island. There they faced a combination of different forces: Spanish and British troops, defiant Saint-Domingue planters, and slaves in rebellion. In this context, the local French commissioners reconsidered their commitment to slavery; in 1793, they promised freedom to slaves who would join the French. A year later, the assembly in Paris extended to slaves in all the colonies a liberty that had already been accomplished in Saint-Domingue, by the slave rebellion.

Emancipation and war brought new leaders to the fore, chief among them a former slave, Toussaint Bréda, later Toussaint L'Ouverture (*too-SAN LOO-vehr-tur*), meaning "the one who opened the way." Over the course of the next five years, Toussaint and his soldiers, now allied with the French army, emerged victorious over the French planters, the British (in 1798), and the Spanish (in 1801). Toussaint also broke the power of his rival generals in both the mulatto and former slave armies, becoming the statesman of the revolution. In 1801, Toussaint set up a constitution, swearing allegiance to France but denying France any right to interfere in Saint-Domingue affairs. The constitution abolished slavery, reorganized the military, established Christianity as the state religion (this entailed a rejection of vodoun, a blend of Christian and various West and Central African traditions), and made Toussaint governor for life. It was an extraordinary moment in the revolutionary period: the formation of an authoritarian society but also an utterly unexpected symbol of the universal potential of revolutionary ideas.

TOUSSAINT L'OUVERTURE. A portrait of L'Ouverture, leader of what would become the Haitian Revolution, as a general.

Toussaint's accomplishments, however, put him on a collision course with the other French general he admired and whose career was remarkably like his own: Napoleon Bonaparte. Saint-Domingue stood at the center of Bonaparte's vision of an expanded empire in the New World, an empire that would recoup North American territories France had lost under the Old Regime and pivot around the lucrative combination of the Mississippi, French Louisiana, and the sugar and slave colonies of the Caribbean. In January 1802, Bonaparte dispatched 20,000 troops to bring the island under control. Toussaint, captured when he arrived for discussions with the French, was shipped under heavy guard to a prison in the mountains of eastern France, where he died in 1803. Fighting continued in Saint-Domingue, however, with fires now fueled by Bonaparte's decree reestablishing slavery where the convention had abolished it. The war turned into a nightmare for the French. Yellow fever killed thousands of French troops, including one of Napoleon's best generals and brother-in-law. Armies on both sides committed atrocities. By December 1803, the French army had collapsed. Napoleon scaled back his vision of an American empire and sold the Louisiana territories to Thomas Jefferson. "I know the value of what I abandon . . . I renounce it with the greatest regret," he told an aide. In Saint-Domingue, a general in the army of former slaves, Jean-Jacques Dessalines, declared the independent state of Haiti in 1804.

The Haitian Revolution remained, in significant ways, an anomaly. It was the only successful slave revolution in history and by far the most radical of the revolutions that occurred in this age. It suggested that the emancipatory ideas of the revolution and Enlightenment might apply to non-Europeans and enslaved peoples—a suggestion that residents of Europe attempted to ignore but one that struck home with planter elites in North and South America. Combined with later rebellions in the British colonies, it contributed to the British decision to end slavery in 1838. And it cast a long shadow over nineteenth-century slave societies from the southern United States to Brazil. The Napoleonic episode, then, had wide-ranging effects across the Atlantic: in North America, the Louisiana purchase; in the Caribbean, the Haitian Revolution; in Latin America, the weakening of Spain and Portugal's colonial empires.

CONCLUSION

The tumultuous events in France formed part of a broad pattern of late-eighteenth-century democratic upheaval. The French Revolution was the most violent, protracted, and contentious of the revolutions of the era; but the dynamics of revolution were much the same everywhere. One of the most important developments of the French Revolution was the emergence of a popular movement, which included political clubs representing people previously excluded from politics, newspapers read by and to the common people, and political leaders who spoke for the sans-culottes. In the French Revolution, as in other revolutions, the popular movement challenged the early and moderate revolutionary leadership, pressing for more radical and democratic measures. And, as in other revolutions, the popular movement in France was defeated, and authority was reestablished by a quasi-military figure. Likewise, the revolutionary ideas of liberty, equality, and fraternity were not specifically French; their roots lay in the social structures of the eighteenth century and in the ideas and culture of the Enlightenment. Yet French armies brought them, literally, to the doorsteps of many Europeans.

What was the larger impact of the revolution and the Napoleonic era? Its legacy is partly summed up in three key concepts: liberty, equality, and nation. Liberty meant individual rights and responsibilities and, more

After You Read This Chapter

Visit StudySpace for quizzes, additional review materials, and multi-media documents. wwnorton.com/web/westernciv18

REVIEWING THE OBJECTIVES

- The French Revolution resulted both from an immediate political crisis and long-term social tensions. What was this crisis, and how did it lead to popular revolt against the monarchy?
- The revolutionaries in the National Assembly in 1789 set out to produce a constitution for France. What were their political goals, and what was the reaction of monarchs and peoples elsewhere in Europe?
- After 1792, a more radical group of revolutionaries seized control of the French state. How did they come to power, and how were their political goals different from their predecessors?
- Napoleon's career began during the revolution. What did he owe to the revolution, and what was different about his regime?
- Three major revolutions took place in the Atlantic world at the end of the eighteenth century: the American Revolution, the French Revolution, and the Haitian Revolution. What was similar about these revolutions? What was different?

specifically, freedom from arbitrary authority. By equality, as we have seen, the revolutionaries meant the abolition of legal distinctions of rank among European men. Though their concept of equality was limited, it became a powerful mobilizing force in the nineteenth century. The most important legacy of the revolution may have been the new term *nation*. Nationhood was a political concept. A nation was formed of citizens, not a king's subjects; it was ruled by law and treated citizens as equal before the law; sovereignty did not lie in dynasties or historic fiefdoms but in the nation of citizens. This new form of nation gained legitimacy when citizen armies repelled attacks against their newly won freedoms; the victories of "citizens in arms" lived on in myth and history and provided the most powerful images of the period. As the war continued, military nationhood began to overshadow its political cousin. By the Napoleonic period, this shift became decisive; a new political body of freely associated citizens was most powerfully embodied in a centralized state, its army and a kind of citizenship defined by individual commitment to the needs of the nation at war. This understanding of national identity spread throughout Europe in the coming decades.

PEOPLE, IDEAS, AND EVENTS IN CONTEXT

- Why was **LOUIS XVI** forced to convene the **ESTATES GENERAL** in 1789?
- What argument did **ABBÉ SIEYÈS** make about the role of the **THIRD ESTATE**?
- What made the **TENNIS COURT OATH** a revolutionary act?
- What was the role of popular revolt (the attack on the **BASTILLE**, the **GREAT FEAR**, the **OCTOBER DAYS**) in the revolutionary movements of 1789?
- What was the connection between the French Revolution with the **SLAVE REVOLT IN SAINT-DOMINGUE** that began in 1791?
- What was the **DECLARATION OF THE RIGHTS OF MAN AND OF THE CITIZEN**?
- What was the **CIVIL CONSTITUTION OF THE CLERGY**?
- What circumstances led to the abolition of the monarchy in 1792?
- Why did the **JACOBINS** in the **NATIONAL CONVENTION** support a policy of the **TERROR**?
- What were **NAPOLEON**'s most significant domestic accomplishments in France? What significance did Napoleon's military campaigns have for other parts of Europe and for the French Empire?
- What was the significance of the **HAITIAN REVOLUTION** of 1804?

THINKING ABOUT CONNECTIONS

- Popular movements in favor of democracy, social justice, or national self-determination in the more than two centuries since 1789 have often used the French Revolution as a point of reference or comparison. Obvious comparisons are those movements that saw themselves as "revolutionary," such as the Russian Revolution of 1917 or the Chinese Revolution of 1949. More recent comparisons might be the popular movements for democratic change in eastern Europe that resulted in the end of the Cold War in 1989 or the Arab Spring of 2011.
- Make a list of factors or circumstances that one might want to compare in considering the outcome of such movements. You might consider the degree to which elites support the current regime, the degree of consensus, and the goals of those who are protesting the status quo, economic circumstances, or international support for either the regime or for revolutionaries. What other factors might determine the outcome of revolutionary situations?

Before
You
Read
This
Chapter

The Industrial Revolution and Nineteenth-Century Society

J ames Watt, a Scottish mechanic and instrument maker, changed the course of human history when he took the primitive steam engine designed by Thomas Newcomen around 1712 and added a separate condenser, which allowed it to generate more power using less coal as fuel. Newcomen's engine used repeated heating and cooling of a steam container to generate a vacuum that could be used to pump water. Watt's engine, which he marketed after 1775 in a partnership with Matthew Boulton, was soon adapted to produce a rotary motion that could be used industrially in a multitude of ways, including grinding, milling, sawing, and weaving. The spread of Watt's steam technology throughout the north of England at the end of the eighteenth century transformed the manufacturing world, reshaped the landscape of the English countryside, and began a revolution in the way that people lived and worked.

The condensing steam engine also made Watt a very wealthy man—and he was well aware that wealth like his was different from that possessed by Britain's traditional elites. He distinguished this wealth from that of the landed aristocrat by linking it to his own efforts as an inventor and entrepreneur: "The Squire's land has not been so much of his own making as the condensing engine has been of mine. He has only passively inherited his property, while this invention has been the product of my own labour and of God knows how much anguish of mind and body."

Watt was correct in his claim that his wealth and status were different from the status claimed by the landed aristocracy, but this wealth was not the product of his labor alone. In addition to his engineering predecessors, like Newcomen, Watt's engine could only be profitable in a world in which foresters, cotton merchants, and landowners could see profits in the purchase of expensive industrial sawmills, mechanical looms, and steam-driven threshers. Watt's invention also depended on the labor of men and women who dug coal from the ground and who smelted the iron and copper that he used to produce his machines. The profits of industrial entrepreneurs, meanwhile, depended on their ability to find sawyers, weavers, and fieldworkers who were willing to accept a new way of working, where they no longer owned their own tools but rather worked as wage laborers for men of business seeking returns on their investment. Business owners also required customers for the larger amounts of finished timber, woven cloth, and grain that they were now bringing to market. Technology such as Watt's was an important part of the changes that historians call the "Industrial Revolution," but technology alone cannot explain the complicated social and economic transformation contained in the phrase.

The Industrial Revolution led to the proliferation of more capital-intensive enterprises, new ways of organizing human labor, and the rapid growth of cities. It was made possible by new sources of energy and power, which led to faster forms of mechanized transportation, higher productivity, and the emergence of large consumer markets for manufactured goods. In turn, these interrelated developments triggered social and cultural changes with revolutionary consequences for Europeans and their relationship to the rest of the world.

Of all the changes, perhaps the most revolutionary came at the very root of human endeavor: new forms of energy. Over the space of two or three generations, a society and an economy that had drawn on water, wind, and wood for most of its energy needs came to depend on machines driven by steam engines and coal. In 1800, the world produced 10 million tons of coal. In 1900, it produced 1 billion—a hundred times more. The Industrial Revolution brought the beginning of the fossil-fuel age, altering as it did so the balance of humanity and the environment.

Mechanization made possible enormous gains in productivity in some sectors of the economy, but the new machines were limited to a few sectors of the economy, especially at the outset, and did not always lead to a dramatic break with older techniques. Above all, technology did not dispense with human toil. Historians emphasize that the Industrial Revolution intensified human labor—carrying water on iron rails, digging trenches, harvesting cotton, sewing by hand, or pounding hides—much more often than it eased it. One historian has suggested that we would do better to speak of the "industrious revolution." This revolution did not lie solely in machines but in a new economic system based on mobilizing capital and labor on a much larger scale. The industrious economy redistributed wealth and power, creating new social classes and producing new social tensions.

It also prompted deep-seated cultural shifts. The English critic Raymond Williams has pointed out that in the eighteenth century, *industry* referred to a human quality: a hardworking woman was "industrious," an ambitious clerk showed "industry." By the middle of the nineteenth century, industry had come to mean an economic system, one that followed its own logic and worked on its own—seemingly independent of humans. This is our modern understanding of the term, and it was born in the early nineteenth century. As the Industrial Revolution altered the foundations of the economy, it also changed the very assumptions with which people approached economics and the ways in which they regarded the role of human beings in the economy. These new assumptions could foster a sense of power but also anxieties about powerlessness.

The dramatic changes of the late eighteenth and early nineteenth centuries emerged out of earlier developments. Overseas commercial exploration opened new territories to European trade. India, Africa, and the Americas had already been brought into the web of the European economy. Expanding trade networks created new markets for goods and sources for raw materials, and the need to organize commerce over long distances fostered financial innovations and sophisticated credit schemes for managing risk. These developments paved the way for industrialization. Within Europe, the commercialization of agriculture and the spread of handicraft manufacturing in rural areas also changed the economy in ways that anticipated later industrial developments. A final factor seems to have been population growth, which began to accelerate in the eighteenth century. Because these earlier developments did not affect all areas in Europe the same way, industrialization did not always follow the same pattern across the Continent. It happened first in Great Britain, and that is where we will begin.

THE INDUSTRIAL REVOLUTION IN BRITAIN, 1760–1850

Great Britain in the eighteenth century had a fortunate combination of natural, economic, and cultural resources. It was a small and secure island nation with a robust empire and control over crucial lanes across the oceans. It had ample supplies of coal, rivers, and a well-developed network of canals.

In addition, agriculture in Britain was already more thoroughly commercialized than elsewhere. British agriculture had been transformed by a combination of new techniques, new crops, and by the "enclosure" of fields and pastures, which turned small holdings, and in many cases commonly held lands, into large fenced tracts that were privately owned and individually managed by commercial landlords. The British Parliament encouraged enclosure with a series of bills in the second half of the eighteenth century. Commercialized agriculture was more productive and yielded more food for a growing and increasingly urban population. The concentration of property in fewer hands drove small farmers off the land, sending them to look for work in other sectors of the economy. Last, commercialized agriculture produced higher profits, wealth that would be invested in industry.

A key precondition for industrialization, therefore, was Britain's growing supply of available capital, in the forms of private wealth and well-developed banking and credit institutions. London had become the leading center for international trade, and the city was a headquarters for the transfer of raw material, capital, and manufactured products throughout the world. This capital was readily available to underwrite new economic enterprises and eased the transfer of money and goods—importing, for instance, silks from the East or Egyptian and North American cottons.

Social and cultural conditions also encouraged investment in enterprises. In Britain far more than on the Continent, the pursuit of wealth was perceived to be a worthy goal. European nobility cultivated the notion of gentlemanly conduct, in part to hold the line against those moving up from below. British aristocrats respected commoners with a talent for making money and did not hesitate to invest themselves. Their scramble to enclose their

ENCLOSED FIELDS IN CENTRAL BRITAIN. The large, uniform square fields in the background of this photograph are fields that were enclosed from smaller holdings and common lands in the 1830s. They contrast with the smaller and older strip fields in the foreground. The larger enclosed fields were more profitable for their owners, who benefited from legislation that encouraged enclosure, but the process created hardship for the village communities that depended on the use of these lands for their survival. ▪ *What circumstances made enclosure possible?* ▪ *What connection have historians made between enclosure and early industrialization?*

lands reflected a keen interest in commercialization and investment. Outside the aristocracy, an even lower barrier separated merchants from the rural gentry. Many of the entrepreneurs of the early Industrial Revolution came from the small gentry or independent farmer class. Eighteenth-century Britain was not by any means free of social snobbery: lords looked down on bankers and bankers looked down on craft workers. But a lord's disdain might well be tempered by the fact that his own grandfather had worked in the counting house.

Growing domestic and international markets made eighteenth-century Britain prosperous. The British were voracious consumers. The court elite followed and bought up yearly fashions, and so did most of Britain's landed and professional society. "Nature may be satisfied with little," one London entrepreneur declared. "But it is the wants of fashion and the desire of novelties that causes trade." The country's small size and the fact that it was an island encouraged the development of a well-integrated domestic market. Unlike continental Europe, Britain did not have a system of internal tolls and tariffs, so goods could be moved freely to wherever they might fetch the best price. A constantly improving transportation system boosted that freedom of movement. So did a favorable political climate. Some members of Parliament were businessmen themselves; others were investors. And both groups were eager to encourage by legislation the construction of canals, the establishment of banks, and the enclosure of common lands.

THE FIRST INDUSTRIAL NATION. Large-scale mechanization of industry developed first in Britain. ■ *The accumulation of large deposits of what two natural resources caused urban growth outside of London?* ■ *What new forms of transportation were critical for moving natural resources to market?* ■ *What else was necessary for industrialization to develop as it did?*

Foreign markets promised even greater returns than domestic ones, though with greater risks. British foreign policy responded to its commercial needs. At the end of every major eighteenth-century war, Britain wrested overseas territories from its enemies. At the same time, Britain penetrated hitherto unexploited territories, such as India and South America. In 1759, over one-third of all British exports went to the colonies; by 1784, if we include the former colonies in North America, that figure had increased to one-half. Production for export rose by 80 percent between 1750 and 1770; production for domestic consumption gained just 7 percent over the same period. The British possessed a merchant marine capable of transporting goods around the world and a navy practiced in the art of protecting its commercial fleets. By the 1780s, Britain's markets, together with its fleet and its established position at the center of world commerce, gave its entrepreneurs unrivaled opportunities for trade and profit.

Innovation in the Textile Industries

The Industrial Revolution began with dramatic technological leaps in a few industries, the first of which was cotton textiles. The industry was already long established. Tariffs prohibiting imports of East Indian cottons, which Parliament had imposed to protect British woolen goods, had spurred the manufacture of British cotton. British textile manufacturers imported raw materials from India and the American South and borrowed patterns from Indian spinners and weavers. What, then, were the revolutionary breakthroughs?

In 1733, John Kay's invention of the flying shuttle speeded the process of weaving. The task of spinning thread, however, had not kept up. A series of comparatively simple mechanical devices eliminated this spinning-to-weaving bottleneck. The most important device was the spinning jenny, invented by James Hargreaves, a hand-loom weaver, in 1764. The spinning jenny was a compound spinning wheel capable of producing sixteen threads at once—though the threads were not strong enough to be used for the longitudinal fibers, or warp, of cotton cloth. The invention of the water frame by Richard Arkwright, a barber, in 1769, made it possible to produce both warp and woof (latitudinal fibers) in great quantity. In 1799, Samuel Compton invented the spinning mule, which combined the features of both the jenny and the frame. All of these important technological changes were accomplished by the end of the eighteenth century.

COTTON SPINNING, 1861. An illustration from a series showing spinning at Walter Evans and Company, cotton manufacturers in Derby, England. ▪ *Why did textile factories prefer female employees?*

A jenny could spin from six to twenty-four times more yarn than a hand spinner. By the end of the eighteenth century, a mule could produce 200 to 300 times more. Just as important, the new machines made better-quality—stronger and finer—thread. These machines revolutionized production across the textile industry. Last, the cotton gin, invented by the American Eli Whitney in 1793, mechanized the process of separating cotton seeds from the fiber, thereby speeding up the production of cotton and reducing its price. The supply of cotton fibers could now expand to keep pace with rising demand from cotton cloth manufacturers. This cotton gin had many effects, including, paradoxically, making slavery more profitable in the United States. The cotton-producing slave plantations in the American South became enmeshed in the lucrative trade with manufacturers who produced cotton textiles in the northern United States and England.

The first textile machines were inexpensive enough to be used by spinners in their own cottages. But as machines

JAMES HARGREAVES'S SPINNING JENNY, 1764. Earlier innovations in textile looms allowed weavers to produce cloth more quickly, but the industry was stymied by the slowness of traditional spinning methods. Thread production simply could not keep up with the demand created by new weaving methods. Hargreaves found a solution in a spinning jenny, which allowed spinners to spin thread and yarns on multiple spindles simultaneously—this image from Germany shows a jenny with sixteen spindles. The spinning jenny was capable of producing thread so quickly that it flooded the market, driving down the price of cotton thread. Local spinners were so outraged at this affront to their livelihood that they broke into Hargreaves's workshop and destroyed his machines, forcing him to flee and set up a new manufacture elsewhere in secret. (See also "Ned Ludd and the Luddites" on page 623.)

grew in size and complexity, they were housed instead in workshops or mills located near water that could be used to power the machines. Eventually, the further development of steam-driven equipment allowed manufacturers to build mills wherever they could be used. Frequently, those mills went up in towns and cities in the north of England, away from the older commercial and seafaring centers but nearer to the coal fields that provided fuel for new machines. From 1780 on, British cotton textiles flooded the world market. In 1760, Britain imported 2.5 million pounds of raw cotton; in 1787, 22 million pounds; in 1837, 366 million pounds. By 1815, the export of cotton textiles amounted to 40 percent of the value of all domestic goods exported from Great Britain. Although the price of manufactured cotton goods fell dramatically, the market expanded so rapidly that profits continued to increase.

Behind these statistics lay a revolution in clothing and consumption. Cotton in the form of muslins and calicos was fine enough to appeal to wealthy consumers. Cotton was also light and washable. For the first time, ordinary people could have sheets, table linens, curtains, and underwear. (Wool was too scratchy.) As one writer commented in 1846, the revolution in textiles had ushered in a "brilliant trans-formation" in dress. "Every woman used to wear a blue or black dress that she kept ten years without washing it for fear that it would fall to pieces. Today her husband can cover her in flower-printed cotton for the price of a day's wages."

The explosive growth of textiles also prompted a debate about the benefits and tyranny of the new industries. The British Romantic poet William Blake famously wrote in biblical terms of the textile mills' blight on the English countryside:

> And did the Countenance Divine
> Shine forth upon our clouded hills?
> And was Jerusalem builded here
> Among these dark Satanic mills?

By the 1830s, the British House of Commons was holding hearings on employment and working conditions in factories, recording testimony about working days that stretched from 3:00 A.M. to 10:00 P.M., the employment of very young children, and workers who lost hair and fingers in the mills' machinery. Women and children counted for roughly two-thirds of the labor force in textiles. The principle of regulating any labor (and emphatically that of adult men), however, was controversial. Only gradually did a series of factory acts prohibit hiring children under age nine and limit the labor of workers under age eighteen to ten hours a day.

Coal and Iron

Meanwhile, decisive changes were transforming the production of iron. As in the textile industry, many important technological changes came during the eighteenth century. A series of innovations (coke smelting, rolling, and puddling) enabled the British to substitute coal (which they had in abundance) for wood (which was scarce and inefficient) to heat molten metal and make iron. The new "pig iron" was higher quality and could be used in building an enormous variety of iron products: machines, engines, railway tracks, agricultural implements, and hardware. Those iron products became, literally, the infrastructure of industrialization. Britain found itself able to export both coal and iron to rapidly expanding markets around the industrializing regions of the world. Between 1814 and 1852, exports of British iron doubled, rising to over 1 million tons of iron, more than half of the world's total production.

Rising demand for coal required mining deeper veins. In 1711, Thomas Newcomen's cumbersome but remarkably effective steam engine was immensely useful to the

Frame - Breaking.
£.200 Reward.

WHEREAS, on Thursday Night last, about Ten o'Clock, a great Number of Men, armed with Pistols, Hammers and Clubs, entered the Dwelling-house of *George Ball*, framework-knitter, of Lenton, near Nottingham, disguised with Masks and Handkerchiefs over their Faces, and in other ways,---and after striking and abusing the said *George Ball*, they *wantonly* and *feloniously* broke and destroyed five STOCKING FRAMES, standing in the Work-shop; four of which belonged to *George Ball*, and one Frame, 40 gage, belonging to Mr. *Francis Braithwaite*, hosier, Nottingham: *all of which were working at the FULL PRICE.*

NOTICE IS HEREBY GIVEN,

THAT if any Person will give Information of the Offender or Offenders, or any one of them who entered such Dwelling-house and were concerned in such Felony, he or she shall receive a Reward of

£. 200,

to be paid on Conviction, in the Proportions following, (viz.) £50 under the King's Proclamation, £25 from the Committee of the Corporation of Nottingham, and £125 from the said *Francis Braithwaite.*

WE, the under-signed Workmen of the above-named *George Ball*, do hereby certify that we were employed in working the under-mentioned Frames, on the Work and at the Prices hereinafter stated, when the Mob came to break them,---that we had never been abated in our Work, either by Mr. *Braithwaite*, the hosier, who employed the Frames, or by the said *George Ball*, our master; of whom we never complained, or had any Reason so to do.

QUALITY OF WORK.	PRICE.	WORKMEN.	OWNERS.
40 Gauge, Single Shape, Narrowed Two-plain,	Maid's, 29 Shillings per Dozen,	Thomas Rew,	Mr. Braithwaite.
36 Gauge, Single Shape, Narrowed Two-plain,	Men's, 29 Shillings per Dozen,	John Jackson,	George Ball.
38 Guage, Single Shape, Narrowed Two-plain,	Maid's, 26 Shillings per Dozen,	Thomas Naylor,	George Ball.

NB. Two other Frames were worked to another Hosier, but at the Full Price.

THOMAS REW,
JOHN JACKSON,
THOMAS NAYLOR.

Nottingham, 25th January, 1812.

NED LUDD AND THE LUDDITES. In 1811 and 1812, in northern England, bands of working men who resented the adoption of new mechanical devices in the weaving industries attacked several establishments and destroyed the frames used to weave cloth. The movement took the name Luddites from Ned Ludd, a man who had broken the frames belonging to his employer in 1779. His mythological presence in the movement is depicted in the illustration at the right. Although their anger was directed at the machines, the real target of their resentment may have been a new pricing scheme imposed on them by the merchants who bought finished work. The debate about prices is a central part of the poster on the left, which offers a reward for information leading to the conviction of frame breakers. The poster is signed by several workers of the establishment, who published the price they received for each piece of clothing and their lack of complaints about their employer. ▪ *How might the need to adjust to the price fluctuations of a market economy have been perceived by weavers accustomed to getting fixed prices for their goods?*

coal industry for pumping water from mines. After 1763, as we have seen, James Watt improved on Newcomen's machine, and by 1800 Watt and his partner, Matthew Boulton, had sold 289 engines for use in factories and mines. Watt and Boulton made their fortune from their invention's efficiency; they earned a regular percentage of the increased profits from each mine that operated an engine.

Steam power was still energy consuming and expensive and so only slowly replaced traditional water power. Even in its early form, however, the steam engine decisively transformed the nineteenth-century world with one application: the steam-driven locomotive. Railroads revolutionized industry, markets, public and private financing, and ordinary people's conceptions of space and time.

THE COMING OF RAILWAYS

Transportation had improved during the years before 1830, but moving heavy materials, particularly coal, remained a problem. It is significant that the first modern railway, built in England in 1825, ran from the Durham coal field of Stockton to Darlington, near the coast. Coal had traditionally been hauled short distances via tramways, or tracks along which horses pulled coal carts. The locomotives on the Stockton-Darlington line traveled at fifteen miles per hour, the fastest rate at which machines had yet moved goods overland. Soon they would move people as well, transforming transportation in the process.

Building railways became a massive enterprise and a risky but potentially profitable opportunity for investment. No sooner did the first combined passenger and goods service open in 1830, operating between Liverpool and Manchester, England, than plans were formulated and money pledged to extend rail systems throughout Europe, the Americas, and beyond. In 1830, there were no more than a few dozen miles of railway in the world. By 1840, there were over 4,500 miles; by 1850, over 23,000. British engineers, industrialists, and investors were quick to realize the global opportunities available in constructing railways overseas; a large part of Britain's industrial success in the later nineteenth century came through building other nations' infrastructures. The English contractor Thomas Brassey, for instance, built railways in Italy, Canada, Argentina, India, and Australia.

Throughout the world, a veritable army of construction workers built the railways. In Britain, they were called "navvies," derived from *navigator,* a term first used for the construction workers on Britain's eighteenth-century canals. Navvies were a rough lot, living with a few women in temporary encampments as they migrated across the countryside. Often they were immigrant workers and faced local hostility. A sign posted by local residents outside a mine in Scotland in 1845 warned the Irish navvies to get "off the ground and out of the country" in a week or else be driven out "by the strength of our armes and a good pick shaft." Later in the century railway building projects in Africa and the Americas were lined with camps of immigrant Indian and Chinese laborers, who also became targets of nativist (a term that means "opposed to foreigners") anger.

The magnitude of the navvies' accomplishment was extraordinary. In Britain and in much of the rest of the world, mid-nineteenth-century railways were constructed almost entirely without the aid of machinery. An assistant engineer on the London-to-Birmingham line calculated that the labor involved was the equivalent of lifting 25 billion cubic feet of earth and stone 1 foot high. He compared this feat with building the Great Pyramid, a task he estimated had involved the hoisting of some 16 billion tons. The building of the pyramid, however, had required over 200,000 men and had taken twenty years. The construction

CHILD LABOR IN THE MINES. This engraving of a young worker pulling a coal cart up through the narrow shaft of a mine accompanied a British Parliamentary report on child labor. ■ *What attitudes about government and the economy made it difficult for legislatures to regulate working conditions in the new industries?*

of the London-to-Birmingham railway was accomplished by 20,000 men in less than five years. If we translated this into individual terms, a navvy was expected to move an average of 20 tons of earth per day. Railways were produced by toil as much as by technology, by human labor as much as by engineering; they illustrate why some historians prefer to use the term *industrious revolution.*

Steam engines, textile machines, new ways of making iron, and railways—all these were interconnected. Changes in one area endorsed changes in another. Pumps run by steam engines made it possible to mine deeper veins of coal; steam-powered railways made it possible to trans-

MANCHESTER TO LIVERPOOL, LATE NINETEENTH CENTURY. Lower-class passengers, physically separated from their social superiors, are packed into the rear of the train.

BARRY DOCK AND ISLAND, WALES, 1895. The convergence of coal, steam power, railways, and maritime shipping were at the center of industrialization in Britain. ■ *In what way did the circular relationship between coal and iron production and the larger transportation revolution associated with the construction of railroads and, later, steamships help sustain the initial growth associated with industrial development?*

port coal. Mechanization fueled the production of iron for machines and the mining of coal to run steam engines. The railway boom multiplied the demand for iron products: rails, locomotives, carriages, signals, switches, and the iron to make all of these. Building railroads called for engineering expertise: scaling mountains, designing bridges and tunnels. Railway construction, which required capital investment beyond the capacity of any single individual, forged new kinds of public and private financing. The scale of production expanded and the tempo of economic activity quickened, spurring the search for more coal, the production of more iron, the mobilization of more capital, and the recruitment of more labor. Steam and speed were becoming the foundation of the economy and of a new way of life.

THE INDUSTRIAL REVOLUTION ON THE CONTINENT

Continental Europe followed a different path. Eighteenth-century France, Belgium, and Germany did have manufacturing districts in regions with raw materials, access to markets, and long-standing traditions of craft and skill.

Yet for a variety of reasons, changes along the lines seen in Britain did not occur until the 1830s. Britain's transportation system was highly developed; those of France and Germany were not. France was far larger than England: its rivers more difficult to navigate; its seaports, cities, and coal deposits farther apart. Much of central Europe was divided into small principalities, each with its own tolls and tariffs, which complicated the transportation of goods over any considerable distance. The Continent had fewer raw materials, coal in particular, than Britain. The abundance and cheapness of wood discouraged exploration that might have resulted in new discoveries of coal. It also meant that coal-run steam engines were less economical on the Continent. Capital, too, was less readily available. Early British industrialization was underwritten by private wealth; this was less feasible elsewhere. Different patterns of landholding formed obstacles to the commercialization of agriculture. In the East, serfdom was a powerful disincentive to labor-saving innovations. In the West, especially in France, the large number of small peasants, or farmers, stayed put on the land.

The wars of the French Revolution and Napoleon disrupted economies. During the eighteenth century, the population had grown and mechanization had begun in a few key industries. The ensuing political upheaval and the

The Factory System, Science, and Morality: Two Views

Reactions to the Industrial Revolution and the factory system it produced ranged from celebration to horror. Dr. Andrew Ure, a Scottish professor of chemistry, was fascinated with these nineteenth-century applications of Enlightenment science. He believed that the new machinery and its products would create a new society of wealth, abundance, and, ultimately, stability through the useful regimentation of production.

Friedrich Engels (1820–1895) was one of the many socialists to criticize Dr. Ure as shortsighted and complacent in his outlook. Engels was himself part of a factory-owning family and so was able to examine the new industrial cities at close range. He provides a classic nineteenth-century analysis of industrialization. The Condition of the Working Class in England *is compellingly written, angry, and revealing about middle-class concerns of the time, including female labor.*

Dr. Andrew Ure (1835)

This island [Britain] is preeminent among civilized nations for the prodigious development of its factory wealth, and has been therefore long viewed with a jealous admiration by foreign powers. This very pre-eminence, however, has been contemplated in a very different light by many influential members of our own community, and has even been denounced by them as the certain origin of innumerable evils to the people, and of revolutionary convulsions to the state. . . .

The blessings which physico-mechanical science has bestowed on society, and the means it has still in store for ameliorating the lot of mankind, has been too little dwelt upon; while, on the other hand, it has been accused of lending itself to the rich capitalists as an instrument for harassing the poor, and of exacting from the operative an accelerated rate of work. It has been said, for example, that the steam-engine now drives the power-looms with such velocity as to urge on their attendant weavers at the same rapid pace; but that the hand-weaver, not being subjected to this restless agent, can throw his shuttle and move his treddles at his convenience. There is, however, this difference in the two cases, that in the factory, every member of the loom is so adjusted, that the driving force leaves the attendant nearly nothing at all to do, certainly no muscular fatigue to sustain, while it produces for him good, unfailing wages, besides a healthy workshop *gratis*: whereas the non-factory weaver, having everything to execute by muscular exertion, finds the labour irksome, makes in consequence innumerable short pauses, separately of little account, but great when added together; earns therefore proportionally low wages, while he loses his health by poor diet and the dampness of his hovel.

Source: Andrew Ure, *The Philosophy of Manufacturers: Or, An Exposition of the Scientific, Moral, and Commercial Economy of the Factory System of Great Britain, 1835,* as cited in J. T. Ward, *The Factory System,* vol. 1 (New York: 1970), pp. 140–41.

---

financial strains of warfare did virtually nothing to help economic development. Napoleon's Continental System and British destruction of French merchant shipping hurt commerce badly. The ban on British-shipped cotton stalled the growth of cotton textiles for decades, though the armies' greater demand for woolen cloth kept that sector of textiles humming. Iron processing increased to satisfy the military's rising needs, but techniques for making iron remained largely unchanged. Probably the revolutionary change most beneficial to industrial advance in Europe was the removal of previous restraints on the movement of capital and labor—for example, the abolition of craft guilds and the reduction of tariff barriers across the Continent.

After 1815, a number of factors combined to change the economic climate. In those regions with a well-established commercial and industrial base—the northeast of France, Belgium, and swaths of territory across the Rhineland, Saxony, Silesia, and northern Bohemia (see map on page 000)—population growth further boosted economic development. Rising population did not by itself produce industrialization, however: in Ireland, where other necessary factors were absent, more people meant less food.

Friedrich Engels (1844)

Histories of the modern development of the cotton industry, such as those of Ure, Baines, and others, tell on every page of technical innovations. . . . In a well-ordered society such improvements would indeed be welcome, but social war rages unchecked and the benefits derived from these improvements are ruthlessly monopolized by a few persons. . . . Every improvement in machinery leads to unemployment, and the greater the technical improvement the greater the unemployment. Every improvement in machinery affects a number of workers in the same way as a commercial crisis and leads to want, distress, and crime. . . .

Let us examine a little more closely the process whereby machine-labour continually supersedes hand-labour. When spinning or weaving machinery is installed practically all that is left to be done by the hand is the piecing together of broken threads, and the machine does the rest. This task calls for nimble fingers rather than muscular strength. The labour of grown men is not merely unnecessary but actually unsuitable. . . . The greater the degree to which physical labour is displaced by the introduction of machines worked by water- or steam-power, the fewer grown men need be employed. In any case women and children will work for lower wages than men and, as has already been observed, they are more skillful at piecing than grown men. Consequently it is women and children who are employed to do this work. . . . When women work in factories, the most important result is the dissolution of family ties. If a woman works for twelve or thirteen hours a day in a factory and her husband is employed either in the same establishment or in some other works, what is the fate of the children? They lack parental care and control. . . . It is not difficult to imagine that they are left to run wild.

Source: Friedrich Engels, *The Condition of the Working Class in England in 1844,* ed. and trans. W. O. Henderson and W. H. Chaloner (New York: 1958), pp. 150–151, 158, 160.

Questions for Analysis

1. According to Andrew Ure, why was industrialization good for Britain? How can the blessings of "physico-mechanical science" lead to the improvement of humanity?

2. What criticism did Engels level at Ure and other optimists on industrialization? Why did Engels think conditions for workers were getting worse instead of better?

3. What consequences do these two writers see for society in the wake of technological change? What assumptions do they make about the relationship between economic development and the social order?

Transportation improved. The Austrian Empire added over 30,000 miles of roads between 1830 and 1847; Belgium almost doubled its road network in the same period; France built not only new roads but also 2,000 miles of canals. These improvements, combined with the construction of railroads in the 1830s and 1840s, opened up new markets and encouraged new methods of manufacturing. In many of the Continent's manufacturing regions, however, industrialists continued to tap large pools of skilled but inexpensive labor. Thus, older methods of putting out industry and handwork persisted alongside new-model factories longer than in Britain.

In what other ways was the continental model of industrialization different? Governments played a considerably more direct role in industrialization. France and Prussia granted subsidies to private companies that built railroads. After 1849, the Prussian state took on the task itself, as did Belgium and, later, Russia. In Prussia, the state also operated a large proportion of that country's mines. Governments on the Continent provided incentives for industrialization. Limited-liability laws, to take the most important example, allowed investors to own shares in a corporation or company without becoming liable for the company's debts—and they enabled enterprises to recruit investors to put together the capital for railroads, other forms of industry, and commerce.

Mobilizing capital for industry was one of the challenges of the century. In Great Britain, overseas trade had created well-organized financial markets; on the Continent, capital was dispersed and in short supply. New joint-stock investment banks, unlike private banks, could sell bonds to and take deposits from individuals and smaller companies. They could offer start-up capital in the form of long-term, low-interest commercial loans to aspiring entrepreneurs. The French Crédit Mobilier, for instance, founded in 1852 by the wealthy and well-connected Périere brothers, assembled enough capital to finance insurance companies; the Parisian bus system; six municipal gas companies; transatlantic shipping; enterprises in other European countries; and, with the patronage of the state, the massive railroad-building spree of the 1850s. The Crédit Mobilier collapsed in scandal, but the revolution in banking was well under way.

Finally, continental Europeans actively promoted invention and technological development. They were willing for the state to establish educational systems whose aim, among others, was to produce a well-trained elite capable of assisting in the development of industrial technology. In sum, what Britain had produced almost by chance, the Europeans began to reproduce by design.

Industrialization after 1850

Until 1850, Britain remained the pre-eminent industrial power. Between 1850 and 1870, however, France, Germany, Belgium, and the United States emerged as challengers to the power and place of British manufacturers. The British iron industry remained the largest in the world (in 1870 Britain still produced half the world's pig iron), but it grew more slowly than did its counterparts in France or Germany. Most of continental Europe's gains came as a result of continuing changes in those areas we recognize as important for sustained industrial growth: transport, commerce, and government policy.

The spread of railways encouraged the free movement of goods. International monetary unions were established and restrictions removed on international waterways such as the Danube. Free trade went hand in hand with removing guild barriers to entering trades and ending restrictions on practicing business. Guild control over artisanal production was abolished in Austria in 1859 and in most of Germany by the mid-1860s. Laws against usury, most of which had ceased to be enforced, were officially abandoned in Britain, Holland, Belgium, and in many parts of Germany. Governmental regulation of mining was surrendered by the Prussian state in the 1850s, freeing entrepreneurs to develop resources as they saw fit. Investment banks continued to form, encouraged by an increase in the money supply and an easing of credit after the California gold fields opened in 1849.

The first phase of the Industrial Revolution, one economic historian reminds us, was confined to a narrow set of industries and can be summed up rather simply: "cheaper and better clothes (mainly made of cotton), cheaper and better metals (pig iron, wrought iron, and steel) and faster travel (mainly by rail)." The second half of the century brought changes farther afield and in areas where Great Britain's early advantages were no longer decisive. Transatlantic cable

INTERIOR OF A CANUT HOUSEHOLD IN LYON C. 1830. The growth of the silk industry in Lyon in eighteenth-century France attracted many weavers and their families to the city's central neighborhoods: by the mid-1800s, there were 80,000 master artisans with their own shops in the trade and a further 40,000 *compagnons*, trained weavers who had not yet set up their own establishment and who worked as employees in the shops of others. The Canuts, as these weavers were called, worked as many as eighteen hours a day, and they were known for their militancy and their activism. They rose up in revolt in 1831, 1834, and 1848, and they were among the first examples of workers' insurrections in the nineteenth century. In the above image of a Canut household, the labor of nearly all the members of the family—weaving, spinning, and preparing the thread—can be identified.

(starting in 1865) and the telephone (invented in 1876) laid the ground for a revolution in communications. New chemical processes, dyestuffs, and pharmaceuticals emerged. So did new sources of energy: electricity, in which the United States and Germany led both invention and commercial development; and oil, which was being refined in the 1850s and widely used by 1900. Among the early exploiters of Russian oil discoveries were the Swedish Nobel brothers and the French Rothschilds. The developments that eventually converged to make the automobile came primarily from Germany and France. The internal combustion engine, important because it was small, efficient, and could be used in a very wide variety of situations, was developed by Carl Benz and Gottlieb Daimler in the 1880s. The removable pneumatic tire was patented in 1891 by Edouard Michelin, a painter who had joined with his engineer brother in running the family's small agricultural-equipment business. These developments are discussed fully in Chapter 23, but their pioneers' familiar names illustrate how industry and invention had diversified over the course of the century.

In eastern Europe, the nineteenth century brought different patterns of economic development. Spurred by the ever-growing demand for food and grain, large sections of eastern Europe developed into concentrated, commercialized agriculture regions that played the specific role of exporting food to the West. Many of those large agricultural enterprises were based on serfdom and remained so, in the face of increasing pressure for reform, until 1850. Peasant protest and liberal demands for reform only gradually chipped away at the nobility's determination to hold on to its privilege and system of labor. Serfdom was abolished in most parts of eastern and southern Europe by 1850 and in Poland and Russia in the 1860s.

Although industry continued to take a backseat to agriculture, eastern Europe had several important manufacturing regions. In the Czech region of Bohemia, textile industries, developed in the eighteenth century, continued to thrive. By the 1830s, there were machine-powered Czech cotton mills and iron works. In Russia, a factory industry producing coarse textiles—mostly linens—had grown up around Moscow. At mid-century, Russia was purchasing 24 percent of the total British machinery exports to mechanize its own mills. Many who labored in Russian industry actually remained serfs until the 1860s—about 40 percent of them employed in mines. Of the over 800,000 Russians engaged in manufacturing by 1860, however, most were employed in small workshops of about 40 persons.

By 1870, then, the core industrial nations of Europe included Great Britain, France, Germany, Italy, the Netherlands, and Switzerland. Austria stood at the margins. Russia, Spain, Bulgaria, Greece, Hungary, Romania, and Serbia formed the industrial periphery—and some regions of these nations seemed virtually untouched by the advance of industry. What was more, even in Great Britain, the most fully industrialized nation, agricultural laborers still constituted the single largest occupational category in 1860 (although they formed only 9 percent of the overall population). In Belgium, the Netherlands, Switzerland, Germany, France, Scandinavia, and Ireland, 25 to 50 percent of the population still worked on the land. In Russia, the number was 80 percent. *Industrial,* moreover, did not mean automation or machine production, which long remained confined to a few sectors of the economy. As machines were introduced in some sectors to do specific tasks, they usually intensified the tempo of handwork in other sectors. Thus even in the industrialized regions, much work was still accomplished in tiny workshops—or at home.

Industry and Empire

From an international perspective, nineteenth-century Europe was the most industrial region of the world. Europeans, particularly the British, jealously guarded their international advantages. They preferred to do so through financial leverage. Britain, France, and other European nations gained control of the national debts of China, the Ottoman Empire, Egypt, Brazil, Argentina, and other non-European powers. They also supplied large loans to other states, which bound those nations to their European investors. If the debtor nations expressed discontent, as Egypt did in the 1830s when it attempted to establish its own cotton textile industry, they confronted financial pressure and shows of force. Coercion, however, was not always necessary or even one-sided. Social change in other empires—China, Persia, and the Mughal Empire of India, for example—made those empires newly vulnerable and created new opportunities for the European powers and their local partners. Ambitious local elites often reached agreements with Western governments or groups such as the British East India Company. These trade agreements transformed regional economies on terms that sent the greatest profits to Europe after a substantial gratuity to the Europeans' local partners. Where agreements could not be made, force prevailed, and Europe took territory and trade by conquest (see Chapter 22).

Industrialization tightened global links between Europe and the rest of the world, creating new networks of trade and interdependence. To a certain extent, the world economy divided between the producers of manufactured goods—Europe itself—and suppliers of the necessary

THE INDUSTRIAL REVOLUTION. Rapid industrial growth depended on a circular network of relationships. ■ *According to the map key, what elements made up the circular networks of relationships?* ■ *How were these elements connected, and how might they have reinforced one another, contributing to rapid growth?* ■ *Why do you think the percentage of populations living in cities was so much greater in the United Kingdom?*

raw materials and buyers of finished goods—everyone else. Cotton growers in the southern United States, sugar growers in the Caribbean, and wheat growers in Ukraine accepted their arrangements with the industrialized West and typically profited by them. If there were disputes, however, those suppliers often found that Europe could look elsewhere for the same goods or dictate the terms of trade down the business end of a bank ledger or a cannon barrel.

In 1811, Britain imported 3 percent of the wheat it consumed. By 1891, that portion had risen to 79 percent. Why? In an increasingly urban society, fewer people lived off the land. The commercialization of agriculture, which began early in Britain, had taken even firmer hold elsewhere, turning new regions—Australia, Argentina, and North America (Canada and the United States)—into centers of grain and wheat production. New forms of transportation, finance, and communication made it easier to shuttle commodities and capital through international networks. Those simple percentages, in other words, dramatize the new interdependence of the nineteenth century; they illustrate as well as any statistics can how ordinary Britons' lives—like their counterparts' in other nations—were embedded in an increasingly global economy.

BRITISH CLIPPER SHIPS IN CALCUTTA HARBOR, 1860. Calcutta, a long-established city on the eastern coast of India, was one of the hubs of the British Empire—a center for trade in cotton, jute, opium, and tea. The dazzling new clipper ships, first built in the 1830s and 1840s, were very fast and central to the global economy of the nineteenth century. ▪ *What was the significance of this trade for the Indian economy?* ▪ *Could Indian merchants compete on equal terms with U.S. cotton producers in 1860?*

THE SOCIAL CONSEQUENCES OF INDUSTRIALIZATION

We have mentioned population growth as one factor in industrial development, but it deserves treatment on its own terms. By any measure, the nineteenth century constituted a turning point in European demographic history. In 1800, the population of Europe as a whole was estimated roughly at 205 million. By 1850, it had risen to 274 million; by 1900, 414 million; on the eve of the First World War, it was 480 million. (Over the same span of time, the world population went from about 900 million to 1.6 billion.) Britain, with its comparatively high standard of living, saw its population rise from 16 to 27 million. Increases, however, came in the largely rural regions as well. In Russia, the population rose from 39 million to 60 million during the same period.

Population

This population explosion did not occur because people were living longer—declines in mortality were not observable on a large scale until late in the nineteenth century, when improvements in hygiene and medicine had significant impact on the number of people who survived childhood to reach adulthood. Even in 1880, the average male life expectancy at birth in Berlin was no more than thirty years (in rural districts nearby, it was forty-three). Population growth in the nineteenth century resulted from increasing fertility—there were simply more babies being born. Men and women married earlier, which raised the average number of children born to each woman and increased the size of families. Peasants tended to set up households at a younger age. The spread of rural manufacturing allowed couples in the countryside to marry and set up households—even before they inherited any land. Not only did the age of marriage fall, but more people married. And because population growth increased the proportion of young and fertile people, the process reinforced itself in the next generation, setting the stage for a period of prolonged growth.

Interpreting Visual Evidence

Learning to Live in a Global Economy

The commercial networks of the Atlantic world were already well established before the Industrial Revolution, and Europeans were also trading widely with South and East Asia before the end of the eighteenth century. Nevertheless, the advent of an industrial economy in Europe at the beginning of the nineteenth century created such a demand for raw materials and such a need for new markets abroad that it became profitable for manufacturers and merchants to ship much larger amounts of goods over long distances than ever before. As different industrialized regions in Europe became more and more dependent on overseas markets, people in Europe came to be aware of the extent to which their own activities were linked to other parts of the world. Awareness of these linkages did not always mean that they possessed complete or accurate information about the people who produced the cotton that they wore, or who purchased the manufactured goods that they made, but the linkages stimulated their imagination and changed their consciousness of their place in the world.

This awareness is well illustrated in the cartoons shown here, which come from the British illustrated news in the 1850s and 1860s. The first (image A) depicts John Bull (representing British textile manufacturers) looking on as U.S. cotton suppliers fight one another during the Civil War in the United States. He states, "Oh! If you two like fighting better than business, I shall deal at the other shop." In the background, an Indian cotton merchant is happy to have him as a customer.

The second cartoon (image B) depicts the ways that the increasingly interconnected global economy might

A. John Bull and cotton merchants.

Life on the Land: The Peasantry

Even as the West grew more industrial, the majority of people continued to live on the land. Conditions in the countryside were harsh. Peasants—as farmers of humble origin were called in Europe—still did most of their sowing and harvesting by hand. Millions of tiny farms produced, at most, a bare subsistence living, and families wove, spun, made knives, and sold butter to make ends meet. The average daily diet for an entire family in a good year might amount to no more than two or three pounds of bread— a total of about 3,000 calories daily. By many measures, stimulate a new kind of political awareness. Emperor Napoleon III has placed a French worker in irons for participating in a revolutionary movement. The worker compares his situation to that of an African slave seated next to him, saying, "Courage, my friend! Am I not a man and a brother?" On the wall behind the two men a poster refers to the Portuguese slave trade—Napoleon III himself came to power by overthrowing the Second Republic in France, a government that had abolished the slave trade in French territories.

Questions for Analysis

1. What constellation of private and national interests were at play in the relationships portrayed in image A? What significance might contemporaries have attached to the possibility that the British may have chosen to buy their cotton from an Asian source "over the way" rather than from North America?

2. In image B, what is the message of the cartoon's suggestion that the slave and the worker might discover their equality only in the fact that they are both in chains? What was at stake in comparing a worker to a slave in mid-nineteenth-century Europe? Why does the caption read "Poor Consolation?"

3. How does the racial imagery of these images relate to their intended message?

POOR CONSOLATION.

Parisian. "COURAGE, MON AMI; 'AM I NOT A MAN AND A BROTHER?'"

B. Increasing global awareness in France.

living conditions for rural inhabitants of many areas in Europe grew worse in the first half of the nineteenth century, a fact of considerable political importance in the 1840s. Rising population put more pressure on the land. Small holdings and indebtedness were chronic problems in regions where peasants scraped by on their own lands.

Over the course of the century, some 37 million people—most of them peasants—left Europe, eloquent testimony to the bleakness of rural life. They settled in the United States, South America, northern Africa, New Zealand, Australia, and Siberia. In many cases, governments encouraged emigration to ease overcrowding.

Past and Present

Are there Limits to Economic Growth?

Even in its infancy, industrial society had its critics—those who regretted the changes that the new forms of manufacture brought to work, to the social order, and to the environment (left). The current concern about climate change caused by the burning of fossil fuels (right) is thus the latest chapter in a long history of debate and controversy over the consequences of industrialization.

 Watch related author interview on StudySpace
wwnorton.com/web/westernciv18

The most tragic combination of famine, poverty, and population in the nineteenth century came to Ireland in the Great Famine of 1845–1849. Potatoes, which had come to Europe from the New World, fundamentally transformed the diets of European peasants, providing much more nutrition for less money than corn and grain. They also grew more densely, an enormous advantage for peasants scraping a living from small plots of land. Nowhere did they become more important than in Ireland, where the climate and soil made growing grain difficult and both overpopulation and poverty were rising. When a fungus hit the potato crop—first in 1845 and again, fatally, in 1846 and 1847—no alternative foods were at hand. At least 1 million Irish died of starvation; of dysentery from spoiled foods; or of fever, which spread through villages and the overcrowded poorhouses. Before the famine, tens of thousands of Irish were already crossing the Atlantic to North

America; they accounted for one-third of all voluntary migration to the New World. In the ten years after 1845, 1.5 million people left Ireland for good. The potato blight also struck in Germany, Scotland, and the Netherlands but with less catastrophic results. Europe had known deadly famines for centuries. The tragic Irish famine came late, however, at a time when many thought that starvation was receding into the past, and it illustrated just how vulnerable the nineteenth-century countryside remained to bad harvests and shortages.

Changes in the land depended partly on particular governments. States sympathetic to commercial agriculture made it easier to transfer land, eliminate small farms, and create larger estates. In Britain, over half the total area of the country, excluding wasteland, was composed of estates of a thousand acres or more. In Spain, the fortunes of large-scale commercial agriculture fluctuated with changes in

Thomas Malthus on Population and Poverty

Thomas Malthus's enormously influential Essay on the Principle of Population *(1798) marked a shift away from Enlightenment optimism about the "perfectibility of society" and a break with a long tradition of considering a large population to be a sign of economic strength. The English cleric (1766–1834) argued that hopes for prosperity ran up against a simple and grim law of nature: population grew more rapidly than food supply. Famine, disease, poverty, infant malnutrition—Malthus considered all of these inevitable, indeed "positive," checks on population. Governments could do nothing to alleviate poverty, he argued; instead, the poor had to exercise "moral restraint," postpone marriage, and have fewer children.*

say that the power of population is indefinitely greater than the power in the earth to produce subsistence for man.

Population, when unchecked, increases in a geometrical ratio. Subsistence increases only in an arithmetical ratio. A slight acquaintance with numbers will shew the immensity of the first power in comparison of the second.

By that law of our nature which makes food necessary to the life of man, the effects of these two unequal powers must be kept equal.

This implies a strong and constantly operating check on population from the difficulty of subsistence. This difficulty must fall somewhere and must necessarily be severely felt by a large portion of mankind.

Through the animal and vegetable kingdoms, nature has scattered the seeds of life abroad with the most profuse and liberal hand. She has been comparatively sparing in the room and the nourishment necessary to rear them. The germs of existence contained in this spot of earth, with ample food, and ample room to expand in, would fill millions of worlds in the course of a few thousand years. Necessity, that imperious all pervading law of nature, restrains them within the prescribed bounds. The race of plants and the race of animals shrink under this great restrictive law. And the race of man cannot, by any efforts of reason, escape from it. Among plants and animals its effects are waste of seed, sickness, and premature death. Among mankind, misery and vice. The former, misery, is an absolutely necessary consequence of it. Vice is a highly probable consequence, and we therefore see it abundantly prevail, but it ought not, perhaps, to be called an absolutely necessary consequence. The ordeal of virtue is to resist all temptation to evil.

This natural inequality of the two powers of population and of production in the earth, and that great law of our nature which must constantly keep their effects equal, form the great difficulty that to me appears insurmountable in the way to the perfectibility of society. All other arguments are of slight and subordinate consideration in comparison of this. I see no way by which man can escape from the weight of this law which pervades all animated nature. No fancied equality, no agrarian regulations in their utmost extent, could remove the pressure of it even for a single century. And it appears, therefore, to be decisive against the possible existence of a society, all the members of which should live in ease, happiness, and comparative leisure; and feel no anxiety about providing the means of subsistence for themselves and families.

Consequently, if the premises are just, the argument is conclusive against the perfectibility of the mass of mankind.

Source: Thomas Malthus, *An Essay on the Principle of Population,* ed. Philip Appleman, *Norton Critical Edition,* 2nd ed. (New York: 2004), pp. 19–20.

Questions for Analysis

1. What assumptions about human behavior are contained in Malthus's argument that population will always increase more quickly than the available food supply? What are the possible checks on population growth that he considers? Why does he say that "misery" is "a necessary consequence" and "vice" only "highly probable"? Why does he conclude from this that society will never be "perfectible"?

2. The history of the Industrial Revolution and population growth in Europe in the nineteenth century seemed to prove that Malthus's belief in the ecological constraints on population growth were ill founded. What events that he could not have predicted changed the equilibrium between subsistence and population during this period?

3. Compare Malthus's views expressed here with the documents on pages 638–39 concerning the 1846 potato famine. Can one see the influence of his ideas in those documents?

IRISH POTATO FAMINE, 1845–1849. The Irish potato famine was widely held by many in Ireland to have human as well as natural causes. Historians have noted that food exports from Ireland continued and may have even increased for some products during the famine, as merchants sought higher prices abroad. The cartoon at left depicts armed soldiers keeping starving Irish Catholic families at bay as sacks of potatoes are loaded onto a ship owned by a prosperous Irish Protestant trader. At right, an 1848 engraving from the *Illustrated London News* depicts an impoverished tenant family being evicted from their cottage by their landlord for nonpayment of rent. Thousands of such evictions took place, adding to the misery of the tenant farmers, who were thus unable to plant new crops after losing the potato harvest to blight.

the political regime: in 1820, the liberal regime passed legislation encouraging the free transfer of land; when absolutism was restored in 1823, the law was repealed. In Russia some of the largest landowners possessed over half a million acres. Until the emancipation of the serfs in the 1860s, landowners claimed the labor of dependent peasant populations for as much as several days per week. But the system of serfdom gave neither landowners nor serfs much incentive to improve farming techniques.

European serfdom, which bound hundreds of thousands of men, women, and children to particular estates for generations, made it difficult to buy and sell land freely and created an obstacle to the commercialization of agriculture. Yet the opposite was also the case. In France, peasant landholders who had benefited from the French Revolution's sale of lands and laws on inheritance stayed in the countryside, continuing to work their small farms. Although French peasants were poor, they could sustain themselves on the land. This had important consequences. France suffered less agricultural distress, even in the 1840s, than did other European countries; migration from country to city was slower than in the other nations; far fewer peasants left France for other countries.

Industrialization came to the countryside in other forms. Improved communication networks not only afforded rural populations a keener sense of events and opportunities elsewhere but also made it possible for governments to intrude into the lives of these men and women to a degree previously impossible. Central bureaucracies now found it easier to collect taxes from the peasantry and

to conscript sons of peasant families into armies. Some rural cottage industries faced direct competition from factory-produced goods, which meant less work or lower piece rates and falling incomes for families, especially during winter months. In other sectors of the economy, industry spread out into the countryside, making whole regions producers of shoes, shirts, ribbons, cutlery, and so on in small shops and workers' homes. Changes in the market could usher in prosperity, or they could bring entire regions to the verge of starvation.

Vulnerability often led to political violence. Rural rebellions were common in the early nineteenth century. In southern England in the late 1820s, small farmers and day laborers joined forces to burn barns and haystacks, protesting the introduction of threshing machines, a symbol of the new agricultural capitalism. They masked and otherwise disguised themselves, riding out at night under the banner of their mythical leader, "Captain Swing." Their raids were preceded by anonymous threats, such as the one received by a large-scale farmer in the county of Kent: "Pull down your threshing machine or else [expect] fire without delay. We are five thousand men [a highly inflated figure] and will not be stopped." In the southwest of France, peasants, at night and in disguise, attacked local authorities who had barred them from collecting wood in the forests. Since forest wood was in demand for new furnaces, the peasants' traditional gleaning rights had come to an end. Similar rural disturbances broke out across Europe in the 1830s and 1840s: insurrections against landlords; against tithes, or taxes to the church; against laws curtailing customary rights; against unresponsive governments. In Russia, serf uprisings were a reaction to continued bad harvests and exploitation.

Many onlookers considered the nineteenth-century cities dangerous seedbeds of sedition. Yet conditions in the countryside and frequent flare-ups of rural protest remained the greatest source of trouble for governments, and rural politics exploded, as we will see, in the 1840s. Peasants were land poor, deep in debt, and precariously dependent on markets. More important, however, a government's inability to contend with rural misery made it look autocratic, indifferent, or inept—all political failings.

The Urban Landscape

The growth of cities was one of the most important facts of nineteenth-century social history, and one with significant cultural reverberations. Over the course of the nineteenth century, as we have seen, the overall population of Europe doubled. The percentage of that population living in cities tripled—that is, urban populations rose sixfold. In mining and manufacturing areas or along newly built railway lines, it sometimes seemed that cities (like Manchester,

Birmingham, and Essen) sprang up from nowhere. Sometimes the rates of growth were dizzying. Between 1750 and 1850, London (Europe's largest city) grew from 676,000 to 2.3 million. The population of Paris went from 560,000 to 1.3 million, adding 120,000 new residents between 1841 and 1846 alone! Berlin, which like Paris became the hub of a rapidly expanding railway system, nearly tripled in size during the first half of the century. Such rapid expansion was almost necessarily unplanned and brought in its wake new social problems.

Almost all nineteenth-century cities were overcrowded and unhealthy, their largely medieval infrastructures strained by the burden of new population and the demands of industry. Construction lagged far behind population growth, and working men and women who had left families behind in the country often lived in temporary lodging houses. The poorest workers dwelled in wretched basement or attic rooms, often without any light or drainage. A local committee appointed to investigate conditions in the British manufacturing town of Huddersfield—by no means the worst of that country's urban centers—reported that there were large areas without paving, sewers, or drains, "where garbage and filth of every description are left on the surface to ferment

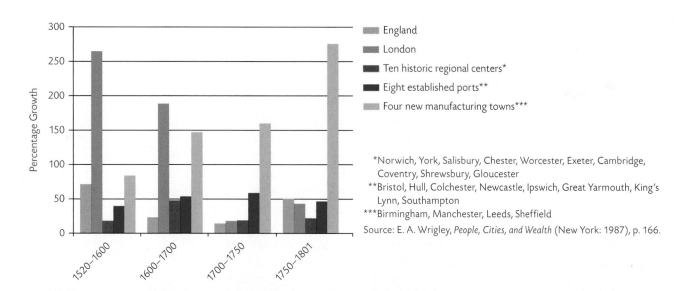

*Norwich, York, Salisbury, Chester, Worcester, Exeter, Cambridge, Coventry, Shrewsbury, Gloucester
**Bristol, Hull, Colchester, Newcastle, Ipswich, Great Yarmouth, King's Lynn, Southampton
***Birmingham, Manchester, Leeds, Sheffield
Source: E. A. Wrigley, *People, Cities, and Wealth* (New York: 1987), p. 166.

URBAN GROWTH IN EARLY MODERN ENGLAND. This figure shows the percentage increases in population in England as a whole, as well as in several distinct groups of population centers. London showed its greatest percentage increases in the periods 1520–1600 and 1600–1700, *before* the period of industrial expansion. The historic regional centers—cathedral and market towns—showed steady but unspectacular growth across these years, as did English port cities. The most remarkable growth, however, was observed in the new industrial areas of the north in the last half of the eighteenth century. *What can one conclude about the nature of population growth in England from this figure? What other sorts of information would allow you to draw more certain conclusions about the nature of these demographic shifts?*

Competing Viewpoints

The Irish Famine: Interpretations and Responses

When the potato blight appeared for the second year in a row in 1846, famine came to Ireland. The first letter excerpted here is from Father Theobald Mathew, a local priest, to Charles Edward Trevelyan, the English official in charge of Irish relief. While Father Mathew attributes the potato blight to "divine providence," he also worries that businessmen opposed to government intervention in a free market will let the Irish starve.

    The second and third excerpts are from letters that Trevelyan wrote to other British officials concerned with the crisis. Trevelyan makes clear that although he does not want the government to bear responsibility for starving its people, he believes that the famine will work to correct "social evils" in Ireland, by which he means everything from families having too many children to farmers failing to plant the right crops. In the nineteenth century, reactions to food crises were reshaped by the rise of new economic doctrines, changing social assumptions, and the shifting relationship between religion and government. These letters provide good examples of those changes and how they affected government officials.

The Reverend Theobald Mathew to Trevelyan

Cork, 7 August 1846.

Divine providence, in its inscrutable ways, has again poured out upon us the viol [sic] of its wrath. A blot more destructive than the simoom of the desert has passed over the land, and the hopes of the poor potato-cultivators are totally blighted, and the food of a whole nation has perished. On the 27th of last month I passed from Cork to Dublin, and this doomed plant bloomed in all the luxuriance of an abundant harvest. Returning on the 3rd instant, I beheld, with sorrow, one wide waste of putrefying vegetation. In many places the wretched people were seated on the fences of their decaying gardens, wringing their hands and wailing bitterly the destruction that had left them foodless.

It is not to harrow your benevolent feelings, dear Mr. Trevelyan, I tell this tale of woe. No, but to excite your sympathy in behalf of our miserable peasantry. It is rumoured that the capitalists in the corn and flour trade are endeavoring to induce government not to protect the people from famine, but to leave them at their mercy. I consider this a cruel and unjustifiable interference.

Trevelyan to Routh

Treasury, 3 February 1846.

That indirect permanent advantages will accrue to Ireland from the scarcity and the measures taken for its relief, I entertain no doubt; but if we were to pursue these incidental objects to the neglect of any of the precautions immediately required to save the people from actual starvation, our responsibility would be fearful indeed. Besides, the greatest improvement of all which could take place in Ireland would be to teach the people to depend upon themselves for developing the resources of their country, instead of having recourse to the assistance of the government on every occasion. Much has been done of late years to put this important matter on its proper footing; but if a firm stand is not made against the prevailing disposition to take advantage of this crisis to break down all barriers, the true permanent interest of the country will, I am convinced, suffer in a manner which will be irreparable in our time.

Trevelyan to Lord Monteagle

To the Right Hon. Lord Monteagle.

My Dear Lord,

I need not remind your lordship that the ability even of the most powerful government is extremely limited in dealing with a social evil of this description. It forms no part of the functions of government to provide supplies of food or to increase the productive powers of the land. In the great institution of the business of society, it falls to the share of government to protect the merchant and the agriculturist in the free exercise of their respective employments; but not itself to carry on those employments; and the condition of a community depends upon the result of the efforts which each member of it makes in his private and individual capacity. . . .

I must give expression to my feelings by saying that I think I see a bright light shining in the distance through the dark cloud which at present hangs over Ireland. A remedy has been already applied to that portion of the maladies of Ireland which was traceable to political causes, and the morbid habits which still to a certain extent survive are gradually giving way to a more healthy action. The deep and inveterate root of social evil remains, and I hope I am not guilty of irreverence in thinking that, this being altogether beyond the power of man, the cure has been applied by the direct stroke of an all-wise providence in a manner as unexpected and unthought of as it is likely to be effectual. God grant that we may rightly perform our part and not turn into a curse what was intended for a blessing. The ministers of religion and especially the pastors of the Roman Catholic Church, who possess the largest share of influence over the people of Ireland, have well performed their part; and although few indications appear from any proceedings which have yet come before the public that the landed proprietors have even taken the first step of preparing for the conversion of the land now laid down to potatoes to grain cultivation, I do not despair of seeing this class in society still taking the lead which their position requires of them, and preventing the social revolution from being so extensive as it otherwise must become.

Believe me, my dear lord,
yours very sincerely,
C. E. Trevelyan.
Treasury, 9 October 1846.

Source: Noel Kissane, *The Irish Famine: A Documentary History* (Dublin: 1995), pp. 17, 47, 50–51.

Questions for Analysis

1. Reverend Mathew's letter suggests that although the potato blight seems to be an act of God, the response to the crisis by those in government and in commerce plays a role in determining who has enough to eat. What relationship between hunger and the market does Mathew fear most?

2. What are the stakes in the crisis for Trevelyan, as the English official responsible for relief of the food shortage? What interests does he appear to serve and in what order of preference? What exactly is the responsibility of the government in the face of such an emergency, according to his view?

3. Do Mathew and Trevelyan agree on the relationship that should exist between the government and the economy? What accounts for their difference of opinion? Are the religious values of the reverend and the economic calculations of the official compatible with one another?

---

and rot; where pools of stagnant water are almost constant; where dwellings adjoining are thus necessarily caused to be of an inferior and even filthy description; thus where disease is engendered, and the health of the whole town perilled."

Governments gradually adopted measures in an attempt to cure the worst of these ills, if only to prevent the spread of catastrophic epidemics. Legislation was designed to rid cities of their worst slums by tearing them down and to improve sanitary conditions by supplying both water and drainage. Yet by 1850, these projects had only just begun. Paris, perhaps better supplied with water than any other European city, had enough for no more than two baths per person per year; in London, human waste remained uncollected in 250,000 domestic cesspools; in Manchester, fewer than one-third of the dwellings were equipped with toilets of any sort.

Industry and Environment in the Nineteenth Century

The Industrial Revolution began many of the environmental changes of the modern period. Nowhere were those changes more visible than in the burgeoning cities. Dickens's description of the choking air and polluted water of "Coketown," the fictional city in *Hard Times* (1854) is deservedly well known:

It was a town of red brick, or of brick that would have been red if the smoke and ashes had allowed it. . . . It was a town of machines and tall chimneys, out of which interminable serpents of smoke trailed themselves forever and ever, and never got uncoiled. It had a black canal in it, and a river that ran purple with ill-smelling dye, and vast piles of building full of windows where there was a rattling and a trembling all day long.

Wood-fired manufacturing and heating for homes had long spewed smoke across the skies, but the new concentration of industrial activity and the transition to coal made the air measurably worse. In London especially, where even homes switched to coal early, smoke from factories, railroads, and domestic chimneys hung heavily over the city; and the last third of the century brought the most intense pollution in its history. Over all of England, air pollution took an enormous toll on health, contributing to the bronchitis and tuberculosis that accounted for 25 percent of British deaths. The coal-rich and industrial regions of North America (especially Pittsburgh) and central Europe were other concentrations of pollution; the Ruhr, in particular, by the end of the century had the most polluted air in Europe.

Toxic water—produced by industrial pollution and human waste—posed the second critical environmental hazard in urban areas. London and Paris led the way in building municipal sewage systems, though those emptied into the Thames and the Seine. Cholera, typhus, and tuberculosis were natural predators in areas without adequate sewage facilities or fresh water. The Rhine River, which flowed through central Europe's industrial heartland and intersected with the Ruhr, was thick with detritus from coal mining, iron processing, and the chemical industry. Spurred by several epidemics of cholera, in the late nineteenth century the major cities began to purify their water supplies; but conditions in the air, rivers, and land continued to worsen until at least the mid-twentieth century.

The Social Question

Against the backdrop of the French Revolution of 1789 and subsequent revolutions in the nineteenth century (as we will see in the following chapters), the new "shock" cities of the nineteenth century and their swelling multitudes posed urgent questions. Political leaders, social scientists,

***VIEW OF LONDON WITH SAINT PAUL'S CATHEDRAL IN THE DISTANCE* BY WILLIAM HENRY CROME.** Despite the smog-filled skies and intense pollution, many entrepreneurs and politicians celebrated the new prosperity of the Industrial Revolution. As W. P. Rend, a Chicago businessman, wrote in 1892, "Smoke is the incense burning on the altars of industry. It is beautiful to me. It shows that men are changing the merely potential forces of nature into articles of comfort for humanity."

and public health officials across all of Europe issued thousands of reports—many of them several volumes long—on criminality, water supply, sewers, prostitution, tuberculosis and cholera, alcoholism, wet nursing, wages, and unemployment. Radicals and reformers grouped all these issues under a broad heading known as "the social question." Governments, pressed by reformers and by the omnipresent rumblings of unrest, felt they had to address these issues before complaints swelled into revolution. They did so, in the first social engineering: police forces, public health, sewers and new water supplies, inoculations, elementary schools, Factory Acts (regulating work hours), poor laws (outlining the conditions of receiving relief), and new urban regulation and city planning. Central Paris, for instance, would be almost entirely redesigned in the nineteenth century—the crowded, medieval, and revolutionary poor neighborhoods gutted; markets rebuilt; streets widened and lit (see Chapter 21). From the 1820s on, the social question hung over Europe like a cloud, and it formed part of the backdrop to the revolutions of 1848 (discussed in Chapter 21). Surveys and studies, early social science, provided direct inspiration for novelists such as Honoré de Balzac, Charles Dickens, and Victor Hugo. In his novel *Les Misérables* (1862), Hugo even used the sewers of Paris as a central metaphor for the general condition of urban existence. Both Hugo and Dickens wrote sympathetically of the poor, of juvenile delinquency, and of child labor; revolution was never far from their minds. The French writer

Balzac had little sympathy for the poor, but he shared his fellow writers' views on the corruption of modern life. His *Human Comedy* (1829–55) was a series of ninety-five novels and stories, including *Eugenie Grandet, Old Goriot, Lost Illusions,* and *A Harlot High and Low.* Balzac was biting in his observations about ruthless and self-promoting young men and about the cold calculations behind romantic liaisons. And he was but one of many writers to use prostitution as a metaphor for what he considered the deplorable materialism and desperation of his time.

Sex in the City

Prostitution flourished in nineteenth-century cities; in fact, it offers a microcosm of the nineteenth-century urban economy. At mid-century, the number of prostitutes in Vienna was estimated to be 15,600; in Paris, where prostitution was a licensed trade, 50,000; in London, 80,000. London newspaper reports of the 1850s cataloged the elaborate hierarchies of the vast underworld of prostitutes and their customers. Those included entrepreneurs with names like Swindling Sal who ran lodging houses; the pimps and "fancy men" who managed the trade of prostitutes on the street; and the relatively few "prima donnas" or courtesans who enjoyed the protection of rich, upper-middle-class lovers, who entertained lavishly and whose wealth allowed them to move on the fringes of more respectable high society. The heroines of Alexandre Dumas's novel *La Dame aux Camélias* ("The Lady of the Camellias") and of Giuseppe Verdi's opera *La Traviata* ("The Fallen Woman") were modeled on these women. Yet the vast majority of prostitutes were not courtesans but rather women (and some men) who worked long and dangerous hours in port districts of cities or at lodging houses in the overwhelmingly male working-class neighborhoods. Most prostitutes were young women who had just arrived in the city or working women trying to manage during a period of unemployment. Single women in the cities were very vulnerable to sexual exploitation. Many were abandoned by their partners if they became pregnant; others faced the danger of rape by their employers. Such experiences—abandonment and rape—could lead to prostitution since women in these circumstances were unlikely to secure "respectable" employment.

PROSTITUTION IN NINETEENTH-CENTURY EUROPEAN CITIES. This sketch by Constantin Guys (1802–1892) captures the moment when two *grisettes* (slang for flirtatious working-class women) entertain a proposition from two soldiers in the street. Guys's portrayal of the men's indistinct facial features and the saucy posture of the women captured the impersonal nature of the exchange as well as the mercenary intentions of all parties. ■ *How did the construction of new cities, with expanded streets designed to facilitate the efficient mixing and movement of peoples, change the way that individuals interacted with one another in modern cities?*

THE MIDDLE CLASSES

Nineteenth-century novelists such as Charles Dickens and William Thackeray in Britain, Victor Hugo and Honoré Balzac in France, and Theodor Fontane in Germany painted a sweeping portrait of middle-class society in the nineteenth century. Their novels are peopled with characters from all walks of life—journalists, courtesans, small-town mayors, mill owners, shopkeepers, aristocrats, farmers, laborers, and students. The plots of these stories explore the ways that older hierarchies of rank, status, and privilege were gradually giving way to a new set of gradations based on wealth and social class. In this new world, money trumped birth, and social mobility was an accepted fact rather than something to be hidden. One of Thackeray's characters observes caustically that "[o]urs is a ready-money society. We live among bankers and city big-wigs . . . and every man, as he talks to you, is jingling his guineas in his pocket." Works of literature need to be approached cautiously, for their characters express their authors' points of view. Still, literature and art offer an extraordinary source of social historical detail and insight. And we can safely say that the rising visibility of the middle classes and their new political and social power—lamented by some writers but hailed by others—were central facts of nineteenth-century society.

Who were the middle classes? (Another common term for this social group, the *bourgeoisie*, originally meant "city [*bourg*] dweller.") Its ranks included shopkeepers and their households, the families of lawyers, doctors, and other professionals, as well as well-off factory owners who might aspire to marry their daughters to titled aristocrats. At the lower end of the social scale the middle classes included the families of salaried clerks and office workers for whom white-collar employment offered hope of a rise in status.

Movement within middle-class ranks was often possible in the course of one or two generations. Very few, however, moved from the working class into the middle class. Most middle-class success stories began in the middle class itself, with the children of relatively well-off farmers, skilled artisans, or professionals. Upward mobility was almost impossible without education, and education was a rare, though not unattainable, luxury for working-class children. Careers open to talents, that goal achieved by the French Revolution, frequently meant opening jobs to middle-class young men who could pass exams. The examination system was an important path upward within government bureaucracies.

The journey from middle class to aristocratic, landed society was equally difficult. In Britain, mobility of this sort was easier to achieve than on the Continent. Sons from wealthy upper-middle-class families, if they were sent to elite schools and universities and if they left the commercial or industrial world for a career in politics, might actually move up. William Gladstone, son of a Liverpool merchant, attended the exclusive educational preserves of Eton (a private boarding school) and Oxford University, married into the aristocratic Grenville family, and became prime minister of England. Yet Gladstone was an exception to the rule, even in Britain, and most upward mobility was much less spectacular.

Nevertheless, the European middle class helped sustain itself with the belief that it was possible to get ahead by means of intelligence, pluck, and serious devotion to work. The Englishman Samuel Smiles, in his extraordinarily successful how-to-succeed book *Self-Help* (1859), preached a gospel dear to the middle class: "The spirit of self-help is the root of all genuine growth in the individual." As Smiles also suggested, those who succeeded were obliged to follow middle-class notions of respectability. The middle-class's

***THE LEGISLATIVE BELLY* BY HONORE DAUMIER, 1834.** Daumier's caricatures of bourgeois politicians mock the close link between politics and a prosperous elite made up of men of property.

claim to political power and cultural influence rested on arguments that they constituted a new and deserving social elite, superior to the common people yet sharply different from the older aristocracy, and the rightful custodians of the nation's future. Thus, middle-class respectability, like a code, stood for many values. It meant financial independence, providing responsibly for one's family, avoiding gambling and debt. It suggested merit and character as opposed to aristocratic privilege and hard work as opposed to living off noble estates. Respectable middle-class gentlemen might be wealthy, but they should live modestly and soberly, avoiding conspicuous consumption, lavish dress, womanizing, and other forms of dandyish behavior associated with the aristocracy. Of course, these were aspirations and codes, not social realities. They nonetheless remained key to the middle-class sense of self and understanding of the world.

Private Life and Middle-Class Identity

Family and home played a central role in forming middle-class identity. Few themes were more common in nineteenth-century fiction than men and women pursuing mobility and status by or through marriage. Families served intensely practical purposes: sons, nephews, and cousins were expected to assume responsibility in family firms when it came their turn; wives managed accounts; and parents-in-law provided business connections, credit, inheritance, and so on. The family's role in middle-class thought, however, did not arise only from these practical considerations; family was part of a larger worldview.

A well-governed household offered a counterpoint to the business and confusion of the world, and families offered continuity and tradition in a time of rapid change.

Gender and the Cult of Domesticity

There was no single type of middle-class family or home. Yet many people held powerful convictions about how a respectable home should be run. According to advice manuals, poetry, and middle-class journals, wives and mothers were supposed to occupy a "separate sphere" of life, in which they lived in subordination to their spouses. "Man for the field and woman for the hearth; man for the sword and for the needle she. . . . All else confusion," wrote the British poet Alfred, Lord Tennyson in 1847. These prescriptions were directly applied to young people. Boys were educated in secondary schools; girls at home. This nineteenth-century conception of separate spheres needs to be understood in relation to much longer-standing traditions of paternal authority, which were codified in law. Throughout Europe, laws subjected women to their husbands' authority. The Napoleonic Code, a model for other countries after 1815, classified women, children, and the mentally ill together as legally incompetent. In Britain, a woman transferred all her property rights to her husband on marriage. Although unmarried women did enjoy a degree of legal independence in France and Austria, laws generally assigned them to the "protection" of their fathers. Gender relations in the nineteenth century rested on this foundation of legal inequality. Yet the idea or doctrine of separate spheres was meant to underscore that men's and women's spheres complemented each other. Thus, for instance, middle-class writings were full of references to spiritual equality between men and women; and middle-class people wrote, proudly, of marriages in which the wife was a "companion" and "helpmate."

It is helpful to recall that members of the middle class articulated their values in opposition to aristocratic customs, on the one hand, and the lives of the common people, on the other. They argued, for instance, that middle-class marriages did not aim to found aristocratic dynasties and were not arranged to accumulate power and privilege; instead they were to be based on mutual respect and division of responsibilities. A respectable middle-class woman should be free from the unrelenting toil that was the lot of a woman of the people. Called in Victorian Britain the "angel in the house," the middle-class woman was responsible for the moral education of her children. It was understood that being a good wife and mother was a demanding task, requiring an elevated character. This belief, sometimes

called the "cult of domesticity," was central to middle-class Victorian thinking about women. Home life and, by extension, the woman's role in that life were infused with new meaning. As one young woman put it after reading a popular book on female education, "What an important sphere a woman fills! How thoroughly she ought to be qualified for it—I think hers the more honourable employment than a man's." In sum, the early nineteenth century brought a general reassessment of femininity. The roots of this reassessment lay in early-nineteenth-century religion and efforts to moralize society, largely to guard against the disorders of the French and Industrial Revolutions.

As a housewife, a middle-class woman had the task of keeping the household functioning smoothly and harmoniously. She maintained the accounts and directed the activities of the servants. Having at least one servant was a mark of middle-class status; and in wealthier families governesses and nannies cared for children, idealized views of motherhood notwithstanding. The middle classes, however, included many gradations of wealth, from a well-housed banker with a governess and five servants to a village preacher with one. Moreover, the work of running and maintaining a home was enormous. Linens and clothes had to be made and mended. Only the wealthy had the luxury of running water, and others had to carry and heat water for cooking, laundry, and cleaning. Heating with coal and lighting with kerosene involved hours of cleaning. If the "angel in the house" was a cultural ideal, it was partly because she had real economic value.

ILLUSTRATION FROM A VICTORIAN BOOK ON MANNERS.
Advice books such as this were very popular in the nineteenth century—a mark, perhaps, of preoccupation with status and the emergence of new social groups. ▪ *Why would people be concerned about "respectability" in an age of greater social mobility?*

Marriage, Sexuality, and the Facts of Life

In the nineteenth century, sexuality became the subject of much anxious debate, largely because it raised other issues: the roles of men and women, morality, and social respectability. Doctors threw themselves into the discussion, offering their expert opinions on the health (including the sexual lives) of the population. Yet doctors did not dictate people's private lives. Nineteenth-century men and women responded to what they experienced as the facts of life more than to expert advice. The first document provides an example of medical knowledge and opinion in 1870. The second offers a glimpse of the daily realities of family life in 1830.

A French Doctor Denounces Contraception (1870)

One of the most powerful instincts nature has placed in the heart of man is that which has for its object the perpetuation of the human race. But this instinct, this inclination, so active, which attracts one sex towards the other, is liable to be perverted, to deviate from the path nature has laid out. From this arises a number of fatal aberrations which exercise a deplorable influence upon the individual, upon the family and upon society. . . .

We hear constantly that marriages are less fruitful, that the increase of population does not follow its former ratio. I believe that this is mainly attributable to genesiac frauds. It might naturally be supposed that these odious calculations of egotism, these shameful refinements of debauchery, are met with almost entirely in large cities, and among the luxurious classes, and that small towns and country places yet preserve that simplicity of manners attributed to primitive society, when the *pater familias* was proud of exhibiting his numerous offspring. Such, however, is not the case, and I shall show that those who have an unlimited confidence in the patriarchal habits of our country people are deeply in error. At the present time frauds are practiced by all classes. . . .

The laboring classes are generally satisfied with the practice of Onan [withdrawal]. . . . They are seldom familiar with the sheath invented by Dr. Condom, and bearing his name.

Among the wealthy, on the other hand, the use of this preservative is generally known. It favors frauds by rendering them easier; but it does not afford complete security. . . .

Case X.—This couple belongs to two respectable families of vintners. They are both pale, emaciated, downcast, sickly. . . .

They have been married for ten years; they first had two children, one immediately after the other, but in order to avoid an increase of family, they have had recourse to conjugal frauds. Being both very amorous, they have found this practice very convenient to satisfy their inclinations. They have employed it to such an extent, that up to a few months ago, when their health began to fail, the husband had intercourse with his wife habitually two and three times in twenty-four hours.

The following is the condition of the woman: She complains of continual pains in the lower part of the abdomen and kidneys. These pains disturb the functions of the stomach and render her nervous. . . . By the touch we find a very intense heat, great sensibility to pressure, and all the signs of a chronic metritis. The patient attributes positively her present state to the too frequent approaches of her husband.

Outside the home, women had very few respectable options for earning a living. Unmarried women might act as companions or governesses—the British novelist Charlotte Brontë's heroine Jane Eyre did so and led a generally miserable life until "rescued" by marriage to her difficult employer. But nineteenth-century convictions about women's moral nature, combined as they were with middle-class aspirations to political leadership, encouraged middle-class wives to undertake voluntary charitable work or to campaign for social reform. In Britain and the United States, women played an important role in the struggle to abolish the slave trade and slavery in the British Empire. Many of these movements also drew on the energies of religious, especially Protestant, organizations, committed to the eradication of social evils

The husband does not attempt to exculpate himself, as he also is in a state of extreme suffering. It is not in the genital organs, however, that we find his dis-order, but in the whole general nervous system; his history will find its place in the part of this work relative to general disturbances. . . .

Source: Louis-François-Etienne Bergeret, *The Preventive Obstacle, or Conjugal Onanism*, trans. P. de Marmon (New York: 1870), pp. 3–4, 12, 20–22, 25, 56–57, 100–101, 111–113. Originally published in Paris in 1868.

Death in Childbirth (1830)

rs. Ann B. Pettigrew was taken in Labour after returning from a walk in the garden, at 7 o'clock in the evening of June 30, 1830. At 40 minutes after 11 o'clock, she was delivered of a daughter. A short time after, I was informed that the Placenta was not removed, and, at 10 minutes after 12 was asked into the room. I advanced to my dear wife, and kissing her, asked her how she was, to which she replied, I feel very badly. I went out of the room, and sent for Dr. Warren.

I then returned, and inquired if there was much hemorrhage, and was answered that there was. I then asked the midwife (Mrs. Brickhouse) if she ever used manual exertion to remove the placenta. She said she had more than fifty times. I then, fearing the consequences of hemorrhage, observed, Do, my dear sweet wife, permit Mrs. Brickhouse to remove it: To which she assented. . . .

After the second unsuccessful attempt, I desired the midwife to desist. In these two efforts, my dear Nancy suffered exceedingly and frequently exclaimed: "O Mrs. Brickhouse you will kill me," and to me, "O I shall die, send for the Doctor." To which I replied, "I have sent."

After this, my feelings were so agonizing that I had to retire from the room and lay down, or fall. Shortly after which, the midwife came to me and, falling upon her knees, prayed most fervently to God and to me to forgive her for saying that she could do what she could not. . . .

The placenta did not come away, and the hemorrhage continued with unabated violence until five o'clock in the morning, when the dear woman breathed her last 20 minutes before the Doctor arrived.

So agonizing a scene as that from one o'clock, I have no words to describe. O My God, My God! have mercy on me. I am undone forever. . . .

Source: Cited in Erna Olafson Hellerstein, Leslie Parker Hume, and Karen M. Offen, eds., *Victorian Women: A Documentary Account of Women's Lives in Nineteenth-Century England, France, and the United States.* (Stanford, CA: 1981) pp. 193–94, 219–20.

Questions for Analysis

1. The French doctor states that the impulse to have sexual relations is "one of the most powerful instincts" given to humans by nature, while simultaneously claiming that this natural instinct is "liable to be perverted." What does this reveal about his attitude toward "nature"?

2. What does he mean by "genesiac frauds"? Who is being deceived by this fraud? What consequences for individuals and for society as a whole does the doctor fear from this deception?

3. What does the story of Mrs. Pettigrew's death reveal about the dangers of childbirth and the state of obstetric medicine in the nineteenth century?

and moral improvement. Throughout Europe, a wide range of movements to improve conditions for the poor in schools and hospitals, for temperance, against prostitution, or for legislation on factory hours were often run by women. Florence Nightingale, who went to the Crimean Peninsula in Russia to nurse British soldiers fighting there in the 1850s, remains the most famous of those women, whose determination to right social wrongs compelled them to defy conventional notions of woman's "proper" sphere. Equally famous—or infamous, at the time—was the French female novelist George Sand (1804–1876), whose real name was Amandine Aurore Dupin Dudevant. Sand dressed like a man and smoked cigars, and her novels often told the tales of independent women thwarted by convention and unhappy marriage.

Queen Victoria, who came to the British throne in 1837, labored to make her solemn public image reflect contemporary feminine virtues of moral probity and dutiful domesticity. Her court was eminently proper, a marked contrast to that of her uncle George IV, whose cavalier ways had set the style for high life a generation before. Though possessing a bad temper, Victoria trained herself to curb it in deference to her ministers and her public-spirited, ultrarespectable husband, Prince Albert of Saxe-Coburg. She was a successful queen because she embodied the traits important to the middle class, whose triumph she seemed to epitomize and whose habits of mind we have come to call Victorian. Nineteenth-century ideas about gender had an impact on masculinity as well as femininity. Soon after the revolutionary and Napoleonic period, men began to dress in sober, practical clothing—and to see as effeminate or dandyish the wigs, ruffled collars, and tight breeches that had earlier been the pride of aristocratic masculinity.

"Passionlessness": Gender and Sexuality

Victorian ideas about sexuality are among the most remarked-on features of nineteenth-century culture. They have become virtually synonymous with anxiety, prudishness, and ignorance. An English mother counseling her daughter about her wedding night is said to have told her to "lie back and think of the empire." Etiquette apparently required that piano legs be covered. Many of these anxieties and prohibitions, however, have been caricatured. More recently, historians have tried to disentangle the teachings or prescriptions of etiquette books and marriage manuals from the actual beliefs of men and women. Equally important, they have sought to understand each on its own terms. Beliefs about sexuality followed from convictions, described earlier, concerning separate spheres. Indeed, one of the defining aspects of nineteenth-century ideas about men and women is the extent to which they rested on scientific arguments about nature. Codes of morality and methods of science combined to reinforce the certainty that specific characteristics were inherent to each sex. Men and women had different social roles, and those differences were rooted in their bodies. The French social thinker Auguste Comte provides a good example: "Biological philosophy teaches us that, through the whole animal scale, and while the specific type is preserved, radical differences, physical and moral, distinguish the sexes." Comte also spelled out the implications of biological difference: "[T]he equality of the sexes, of which so much is said, is incompatible with all social existence. . . . The economy of the human family could never be inverted without an entire change in our cerebral organism." Women were unsuited for higher education because their brains were smaller or because their bodies were fragile. "Fifteen or 20 days of 28 (we may say nearly always) a woman is not only an invalid, but a wounded one. She ceaselessly suffers from love's eternal wound," wrote the well-known French author Jules Michelet about menstruation.

Finally, scientists and doctors considered women's alleged moral superiority to be literally embodied in an absence of sexual feeling, or "passionlessness." Scientists and doctors considered male sexual desire natural, if not admirable—an unruly force that had to be channeled. Many governments legalized and regulated prostitution—which included the compulsory examination of women for venereal disease—precisely because it provided an outlet for male sexual desire. Doctors disagreed about female sexuality, but the British doctor William Acton stood among those who asserted that women functioned differently:

> I have taken pains to obtain and compare abundant evidence on this subject, and the result of my inquiries I may briefly epitomize as follows:— I should say that the majority of women (happily for society) are not very much troubled with sexual feeling of any kind. What men are habitually, women are only exceptionally.

Like other nineteenth-century men and women, Acton also believed that more open expressions of sexuality were disreputable and, also, that working-class women were less "feminine."

Convictions like these reveal a great deal about Victorian science and medicine, but they did not necessarily dictate people's intimate lives. As far as sexuality was concerned, the absence of any reliable contraception mattered more in people's experiences and feelings than sociologists' or doctors' opinions. Abstinence and withdrawal were the only common techniques for preventing pregnancy. Their effectiveness was limited, since until the 1880s doctors continued to believe that a woman was most fertile during and around her menstrual period. Midwives and prostitutes knew of other forms of contraception and abortifacients (all of them dangerous and most ineffective), and surely some middle-class women did as well, but such information was not respectable middle-class fare. Concretely, then, sexual intercourse was directly related to the very real dangers of frequent pregnancies. In England, 1 in 100 childbirths ended in the death of the mother; at a time when a woman might become pregnant eight or nine times in her life, this was a sobering prospect. Those dangers varied with social class, but even among wealthy and better-cared-for women, they took a real toll. It is not surprising that middle-class women's diaries and letters are full of their anticipations of childbirth, both joyful and anxious. Queen Victoria, who bore nine children, declared that childbirth was the "shadow side" of marriage—and she was a pioneer in using anesthesia!

Middle-Class Life in Public

The public life of middle-class families literally reshaped the nineteenth-century landscape. Houses and their furnishings were powerful symbols of material security. Solidly built, heavily decorated, they proclaimed the financial worth and social respectability of those who dwelt within. In provincial cities they were often freestanding villas. In London, Paris, Berlin, and Vienna, they might be in rows of five- or six-story townhouses or large apartments. Whatever particular shape they took, they were built to last a long time. The rooms were certain to be crowded with furniture, art objects, carpets, and wall hangings. The size of the rooms, the elegance of the furniture, the number of servants—all depended, of course, on the extent of one's income. A bank clerk did not live as elegantly as a bank director. Yet they shared many standards and aspirations, and those common values helped bind them to the same class, despite the differences in their material way of life.

As cities grew, they became increasingly segregated. Middle-class people lived far from the unpleasant sights and smells of industrialization. Their residential areas, usually built to the west of the cities, out of the path of the prevailing breeze and therefore of industrial pollution, were havens from congestion. The public buildings in the center, many constructed during the nineteenth century, were celebrated as signs of development and prosperity. The middle classes increasingly managed their cities' affairs, although members of the aristocracy retained considerable power, especially in central Europe. And it was these new middle-class civic leaders who provided new industrial cities with many of their architectural landmarks: city halls, stock exchanges, museums, opera houses, outdoor concert halls, and department stores. One historian has called these buildings the new cathedrals of the industrial age; projects intended to express the community's values and represent public culture, they were monuments to social change.

The suburbs changed as well. The advent of the railways made outings to concerts, parks, and bathing spots popular. They made it possible for families of relatively moderate means to take one- or two-week-long trips to the mountains or to the seashore. New resorts opened, offering racetracks, mineral springs baths, and cabanas on the beach. Mass

APARTMENT LIVING IN PARIS. This print shows that on the Continent, rich and poor often lived in the same buildings—the rich on the lower floors, the poor at the top. This sort of residential mixing was less common in Britain.

tourism would not come until the twentieth century. But the now-familiar impressionist paintings of the 1870s and 1880s testify to something that was dramatically new in the nineteenth century: a new range of middle-class leisures.

Working-Class Life

Like the middle class, the working class was divided into various subgroups and categories, determined in this case by skill, wages, gender, and workplace. Workers' experiences varied, depending on where they worked, where they lived, and, above all, how much they earned. A skilled textile worker lived a life far different from that of a ditch digger, the former able to afford the food, shelter, and clothing necessary for a decent existence, the latter barely able to scrape by.

Some movement from the ranks of the unskilled to the skilled was possible, if children were provided, or provided themselves, with at least a rudimentary education. Yet education was considered by many parents a luxury, especially since children could be put to work at an early age to supplement a family's meager earnings. Downward mobility from skilled to unskilled was also possible, as technological change—the introduction of the power loom, for example—drove highly paid workers into the ranks of the unskilled and destitute.

Working-class housing was unhealthy and unregulated. In older cities single-family dwellings were broken up into apartments, often of no more than one room per family. In new manufacturing centers, rows of tiny houses, located close by smoking factories, were built back to back, thereby eliminating any cross-ventilation or space for gardens. Crowding was commonplace. A newspaper account from the 1840s noted that in Leeds, a textile center in northern Britain, an ordinary worker's house contained no more than 150 square feet, and that in most cases those houses were "crammed almost to suffocation with human beings both day and night."

Household routines, demanding in the middle classes, were grinding for the poor. The family remained a survival network, in which everyone played a crucial role. In addition to working for wages, wives were expected to house, feed, and clothe the family on the very little money different members of the family earned. A good wife was able to make ends meet even in bad times. Working women's daily lives involved constant rounds of carrying and boiling water, cleaning, cooking, and doing laundry—in one- and two-room crowded, unventilated, poorly lit apartments. Families could not rely on their own gardens to help supply them with food. City markets catered to their needs for cheap goods, but these were regularly stale, nearly rotten, or dangerously adulterated. Formaldehyde was added to milk to prevent spoilage. Pounded rice was mixed into sugar. Fine brown earth was introduced into cocoa.

WORKING WOMEN IN THE INDUSTRIAL LANDSCAPE

Few figures raised more public anxiety and outcry in the nineteenth century than the working woman. Contemporaries worried out loud about the "promiscuous mixing of the sexes" in crowded and humid workshops. Nineteenth-century writers, starting in England and France, chronicled what they considered to be the economic and moral horrors of female labor: unattended children running in the streets, small children caught in accidents at the mills or the mines, pregnant women hauling coal, or women laboring alongside men in shops.

Women's work was not new, but industrialization made it more visible. Both before and after the Industrial Revolution labor was divided by gender, but as employers implemented new manufacturing processes, ideas about which jobs were appropriate for women shifted. In traditional textile production, for example, women spun and men operated the looms. In industrial textile factories, on the other hand, employers preferred women and children, both because they were considered more docile and less likely to make trouble and because it was believed that their smaller hands were better suited to the intricate job of tying threads on the power looms. Manufacturers sought to recruit women mill hands from neighboring villages, paying good wages by comparison with other jobs open to women. Most began to work at the age of ten or eleven, and when they had children they either put their children out to a wet nurse, brought them to the mills, or continued to work doing piecework at home. This transformation of the gendered structure of work caused intense anxiety in the first half of the nineteenth century and is one of the reasons that the emerging labor movement began to include calls for excluding women from the workplace in their programs.

Most women did not work in factories, however, and continued to labor at home or in small workshops—"sweatshops," as they came to be called—for notoriously low wages paid not by the hour but by the piece for each shirt stitched or each matchbox glued. The greatest number of unmarried working-class women worked less visibly in domestic service, a job that brought low wages and, to judge by the testimony of many women, coercive sexual relationships with male employers or their sons. Domestic service, however, provided room and board. In a time when a single woman simply could not survive on her own wages, a young woman who had just arrived in the city had few choices: marriage, which was unlikely to happen right away; renting a room in a boardinghouse, many of which were often centers of prostitution; domestic service; or living with someone. How women balanced the demands for money and the time for household work varied with the number and age of their children. Mothers were actually more likely to work when their children were very small, for there were more mouths to feed and the children were not yet old enough to earn wages.

Poverty, the absence of privacy, and the particular vulnerabilities of working-class women made working-class sexuality very different from its middle-class counterpart. Illegitimacy rose dramatically between 1750 and 1850. In Frankfurt, Germany, for example, where the illegitimacy rate had been a mere 2 percent in the early 1700s, it reached 25 percent in 1850. In Bordeaux, France, in 1840, one-third of the recorded births were illegitimate. Reasons for

CAPITAL AND LABOUR. In its earliest years, the British magazine *Punch*, though primarily a humorous weekly, manifested a strong social conscience. This 1843 cartoon shows the capitalists enjoying the rewards of their investments while the hungry workers shiver in cold. ▪ *How would a defender of the new industrial order respond to this cartoon?*

ality was a fact of life, midwives could help desperate pregnant girls, marriage was an avenue to respectability, and so on. The gulf that separated these expectations and codes from those of middle-class women was one of the most important factors in the development of nineteenth-century class identity.

A Life Apart: "Class Consciousness"

The new demands of life in an industrial economy created common experiences and difficulties. The factory system denied skilled workers the pride in craft they had previously enjoyed. Stripped of the protections of guilds and apprenticeships and prevented from organizing by legislation in France, Germany, and Britain in the first half of the nineteenth century, workers felt vulnerable in the face of their socially and politically powerful employers. Factory hours were long—usually twelve to fourteen hours. Textile mills were unventilated, and minute particles of lint lodged in workers' lungs. Machines were unfenced and posed dangers to child workers. British physicians cataloged the toll that long hours tending machines took on children, including spinal curvature and bone malformations. Children were also employed in large numbers in mines—over 50,000 worked in British mines in 1841.

Factories also imposed new routines and disciplines. Artisans in earlier times worked long hours for little pay, but they set their own schedules and controlled the pace of work, moving from their home workshops to their small garden plots as they wished. In a factory, all hands learned the discipline of the clock. To increase production, the factory system encouraged the breaking down of the manufacturing process into specialized steps, each with its own time. Workers began to see machinery itself as the tyrant that changed their lives and bound them to industrial slavery. A radical working-class song written in Britain in the 1840s expressed the feeling:

> There is a king and a ruthless king;
> Not a king of the poet's dream;
> But a tyrant fell, white slaves know well,
> And that ruthless king is steam.

this increase are difficult to establish. Greater mobility and urbanization meant weaker family ties, more opportunities for young men and women, and more vulnerabilities. Premarital sex was an accepted practice in preindustrial villages, but because of the social controls that dominated village life, it was almost always followed by marriage. These controls were weaker in the far more anonymous setting of a factory town or commercial city. The economic uncertainties of the early industrial age meant that a young working-man's promise of marriage based on his expectation of a job might frequently be difficult to fulfill. Economic vulnerability drove many single women into temporary relationships that produced children and a continuing cycle of poverty and abandonment. Historians have shown, however, that in the city as in the countryside, many of these temporary relationships became enduring ones: the parents of illegitimate children would marry later. Again, nineteenth-century writers dramatized what they considered the disreputable sexuality of the "dangerous classes" in the cities. Some of them attributed illegitimacy, prostitution, and so on to the moral weakness of working-class people, others to the systematic changes wrought by industrialization. Both sides, however, overstated the collapse of the family and the destruction of traditional morality. Working-class families transmitted expectations about gender roles and sexual behavior: girls should expect to work, daughters were responsible for caring for their younger siblings as well as for earning wages, sexu-

Yet the defining feature of working-class life was vulnerability—to unemployment, sickness, accidents in dangerous jobs, family problems, and spikes in the prices of food. Seasonal unemployment, high in almost all trades, made it impossible to collect regular wages. Markets for manufactured goods were small and unstable, producing cyclical economic depressions; when those came, thousands of workers found themselves laid off with no system of unemployment insurance to sustain them. The early decades of industrialization were also marked by several severe agricultural depressions and economic crises. During the crisis years of the 1840s, half the working population of Britain's industrial cities was unemployed. In Paris, 85,000 went on relief in 1840. Families survived by working several small jobs, pawning their possessions, and getting credit from local wineshops and grocery stores. The chronic insecurity of working-class life helped fuel the creation of workers' self-help societies, fraternal associations, and early socialist organizations. It also meant that economic crises could have explosive consequences (see Chapter 21).

By mid-century, various experiences were beginning to make working people conscious of themselves as different from and in opposition to the middle classes. Changes in the workplace—whether the introduction of machines and factory labor, speedups, subcontracting to cheap labor, or the loss of guild protections—were part of the picture. The social segregation of the rapidly expanding nineteenth-century cities also contributed to the sense that working people lived a life apart. Class differences seemed embedded in a very wide array of everyday experiences and beliefs: work, private life, expectations for children, the roles of men and women, and definitions of respectability. Over the course of the nineteenth century all of these different experiences gave concrete, specific meaning to the word *class*.

CONCLUSION

Why did the Industrial Revolution occur at this moment in human history? Why did it begin in Europe? Why did it not occur in other regions in the world with large populations and advanced technologies, such as China or India? These fundamental questions remain subject to serious debate among historians. One school of explanations focuses on the fact that the mechanization of industry occurred first in northern Europe and seeks to explain the Industrial Revolution's origins in terms of this region's vibrant towns,

After You Read This Chapter

Visit StudySpace for quizzes, additional review materials, and multimedia documents. **wwnorton.com/web/westernciv18**

REVIEWING THE OBJECTIVES

- The Industrial Revolution in Europe began in northern Great Britain. What circumstances made this process of economic development begin there?
- Certain industries were particularly suitable for the kinds of technological developments that encouraged industrialization. What were these industries, and where did they exist in Europe?
- Industrial development changed the nature of work and production in significant ways. What were these changes, and how did they change the relations between laborers and their employers, or local producers and wider markets?
- Industrialization had social effects far beyond the factories. What larger changes in European society were associated with the Industrial Revolution?
- A large and diverse group of middle-class people emerged in Europe as a result of the social changes brought on by industrialization. What kinds of people qualified as middle class during the nineteenth century, and how were they different from other social groups?

its well-developed commercial markets, and the presence of a prosperous land-owning elite that had few prejudices against entrepreneurial activity. These historians have suggested that industrialization is best understood as a process rooted in European culture and history.

More recently, however, historians with a more global approach have argued that it may be incorrect to assert that industrialization developed as it did because of the advantages enjoyed by a central, European, core. Instead, they have explored the possibility that the world's economies constituted a larger interlocking system that had no definitive center until *after* the takeoff of European industrialization. Before that period, when it came to agricultural practices, ecological constraints, population densities, urbanization, and technological development, *many* global regions were not so different from the western European model. In the end, suggest these historians, Europe was able to move more quickly to industrial production because its economies were better positioned to mobilize the resources available to them on the periphery of their trading sphere. The access enjoyed by European traders to agricultural products from slave-owning societies in the Americas helped them escape the ecological constraints imposed by their own intensely farmed lands and made the move to an industrial economy possible. Contingent factors—such as patterns of disease and epidemic or the location of coal fields—may have also played a role.

There is less debate about the consequences of the Industrial Revolution within Europe. New forms of industrial production created a new economy and changed the nature of work for both men and women. Industrialization changed the landscape of Europe and changed the structures of families and the private lives of people in both the cities and the countryside. Industrialization created new forms of wealth along with new kinds of poverty. It also fostered an acute awareness of the disparity between social groups. In the eighteenth century, that disparity would have been described in terms of birth, rank, or privilege. In the nineteenth century, it was increasingly seen in terms of class. Both champions and critics of the new industrial order spoke of a "class society." The identities associated with class were formed in the crowded working-class districts of the new cities, in experiences of work, and in the new conditions of respectability that determined life in middle-class homes. These new identities would be sharpened in the political events to which we now turn.

PEOPLE, IDEAS, AND EVENTS IN CONTEXT

- Why was **ENCLOSURE** an important factor in the Industrial Revolution?
- What was the **SPINNING JENNY**? What was the **COTTON GIN**? What effect did these machines have on industrial development?
- What was the significance of **EUROPEAN EMPIRE** and overseas expansion for industrialization?
- How did industrialization affect **POPULATION GROWTH** in Europe? What effects did it have on the **PEASANTRY**? On **URBAN POPULATIONS**?
- What environmental changes were associated with the use of new sources of fuel such as coal or the construction of large and concentrated centers of industrial manufacture?
- What was the **IRISH POTATO FAMINE**, and how was it related to the economic developments of nineteenth-century Europe? What might **THOMAS MALTHUS** have thought about the potato famine?

THINKING ABOUT CONNECTIONS

- What might the changes associated with the Industrial Revolution have done to people's conceptions of time and space? How might they have perceived their lives against what they knew of the experience of their parents' generation or what they anticipated for their children?
- Awareness that these changes made the present radically different from the recent past gave many people the sensation that time was hurtling ever faster into a future whose outlines could only dimly be perceived.
- In the early twenty-first century, innovations in information technology have created a similar sensation of accelerated change and diminishing distances in a more interconnected globe. What are the similarities between our own period and the period between the 1780s and 1830s, when large numbers of people first began to think of the power of technology to change the way that society was organized and to conceive of history as a headlong rush into the future? What are the differences?

STORY LINES

- The conservative regimes that defeated Napoleon in 1815 set out to reverse the changes in Europe caused by the French Revolution. They aimed for a balance of forces between European powers so that no single ruler could dominate Europe.

- Conservative rulers in Europe remained on the defensive. Liberalism, republicanism, and nationalism continued to fuel resistance to the conservative order. Socialism provided Europe's laborers with a new vocabulary to express their unhappiness with industrialization.

- The conservative political reaction after 1815 found its cultural counterpart in Romanticism. This movement rejected the Enlightenment's rationalism and emphasized instead the power of nature and human emotions.

CHRONOLOGY

1808	Slave trade prohibited by Britain and United States but not slavery itself
1810–1825	South American revolutions
1814–1815	Congress of Vienna
1821–1827	Greek war for independence
1823	France restores King Ferdinand of Spain
1825	Decembrist Revolt in Russia
1830	Revolutions in France and Belgium
1832	British Reform Bill
1833	British Empire abolishes slavery
1840s	Chartist movement in Britain
1846	Corn Laws repealed
1848	Karl Marx's *Communist Manifesto* published

Before
You
Read
This
Chapter

The Age of Ideologies: Europe in the Aftermath of Revolution, 1815–1848

CORE OBJECTIVES

- **UNDERSTAND** the political goals of the European leaders who met at the Congress of Vienna in 1815 and the challenges to the Concert of Europe in the decades between 1815 and 1848.

- **TRACE** the evolution of the debate about slavery after the French Revolution, and understand the reasons why an abolition movement developed even as slavery persisted in the United States, Latin America, and Cuba.

- **IDENTIFY** the core principles of conservatism, liberalism, republicanism, and socialism in Europe after 1815.

- **DEFINE** *nationalism* and understand how conservatives, liberals, republicans, and socialists were forced to grapple with this powerful political idea.

- **EXPLAIN** the ideas contained in the cultural movement known as Romanticism and its relationship to the Enlightenment.

When the defeated Napoleon left the field of battle at Waterloo on June 18, 1815, headed eventually to exile on the rocky island of St. Helena in the South Atlantic, his victorious opponents hoped the age of revolution had ended. The Austrian foreign minister, Klemens von Metternich, perhaps the most influential conservative diplomat of the early nineteenth century, called revolution a "sickness," "plague," and "cancer" and with his allies set out to inoculate Europe against any outbreak. In their view, revolution produced war and disorder. Peace depended on avoiding political turmoil and reinforcing the power of conservative monarchies in all corners of Europe. Bolstering the legitimacy of such monarchies was Metternich's primary goal in the post-Napoleonic decades.

The decades between 1815 and 1848 saw the legitimacy of these monarchies challenged on multiple fronts. Conservative efforts to restore the old order succeeded only in part. Why? To begin with, the developments of the eighteenth century proved impossible to reverse. The expansion of an informed public, begun in the Enlightenment, continued. The word *citizen* (and the liberal political ideas contained within it) was controversial in the aftermath of the French Revolution, but it was difficult to banish the term from political debates. Liberalism's fundamental principles—equality before the law, freedom of expression, and the consent of the governed—were still a potent threat to Europe's dynastic rulers, especially when coupled with the emotions stirred up by popular nationalism. Liberal nationalists believed that legitimate sovereignty could only be exercised by citizens acting collectively as a nation. Such a conception of sovereignty was diametrically opposed to conservative monarchs who believed their authority came not from the people but from God.

At the same time, the political opposition to the conservative order in Europe began to be infused with new and more radical political ideologies. Some liberals were comfortable living under a constitutional monarch—one who agreed to rule in accordance with the law. Others accepted the idea of representation but believed that voting was a privilege that should be extended only to wealthy property owners. Much more radical were republicans who called for universal (male) suffrage and an end to monarchy altogether. Socialists, disturbed by the inequalities produced in the new market economy of industrial society, went even further and argued that political reform was not enough to free the people from want and exploitation. To socialists, justice was possible only with a radical reordering of society that redistributed property equitably. Between 1815 and 1848, none of these more radical oppositional movements succeeded in carrying the day, but their ideas circulated widely and occupied the attention of conservative monarchs (and their police spies) throughout Europe.

In culture as well as in politics, imagination and a sense of possibility were among the defining characteristics of the first half of the century. Romanticism broke with what many artists considered the cold Classicism and formality of eighteenth-century art. The Enlightenment had championed reason; the Romantics prized subjectivity, feeling, and spontaneity. Their revolt against eighteenth-century conventions had ramifications far beyond literature and painting. The Romantics had no single political creed: some were fervent revolutionaries and others fervent traditionalists who looked to the past, to religion or history, for inspiration. Their sensibility, however, infused politics and culture. And to look ahead, their collective search for new means of expression sent nineteenth-century art off in a new direction.

THE SEARCH FOR ORDER IN EUROPE, 1815–1830

In 1814, the European powers—including the France of the restored king, Louis XVIII—met at the Congress of Vienna to settle pressing questions about the post-Napoleonic political order and to determine the territorial spoils of their victory over the French emperor. An observer of the lavish balls and celebrations that accompanied the Congress's diplomatic negotiations might well have assumed that the calendar had been turned back several decades, to a time when the European nobility had not yet been humiliated and terrorized by violent revolutionaries. But the celebrations of Louis XVIII's return to the throne and the glittering display of aristocratic men in wigs and fine clothes, accompanied by their bejeweled wives (and mistresses), could not hide the fact that twenty years of war, revolution, and political experimentation had changed Europe in fundamental ways. The task of the Congress of Vienna was to reinforce Europe's monarchical regimes against the powerful social and political forces that had been unleashed in the years since 1789.

The Congress of Vienna and the Restoration

The Russian tsar Alexander I (r. 1801–25) and the Austrian diplomat Klemens von Metternich (1773–1859) dominated the Congress of Vienna. After Napoleon's fall, Russia became the most powerful continental state. Alexander I presented himself during the Napoleonic Wars as the "liberator" of Europe, and many feared that he would substitute an all-powerful Russia for an all-powerful France. The French prince Charles Maurice de Talleyrand (1754–1838) had a surprisingly strong supporting role. Talleyrand had been a bishop and a revolutionary and survived the Terror in exile in the United States before becoming first Napoleon's foreign minister and then occupying the same post under Louis XVIII. That he was present at Vienna testified to his diplomatic skill—or opportunism.

Metternich, the architect of the peace, had witnessed the popular violence connected with the French Revolution while a student at the University of Strasbourg in 1789. It left him with a lifelong hatred of revolutionary movements. At the Congress of Vienna, his central concerns were checking Russian expansionism and preventing political

THE CONGRESS OF VIENNA. Note how the borders of European nations were established after the final defeat of Napoleon in 1815, and compare these boundaries to Europe in 1713 after the Peace of Utrecht (page 508). ▪ *What major changes had occurred in the intervening years in central Europe?* ▪ *Which territorial powers played an active role in determining the balance of power at the Congress of Vienna?* ▪ *What social or political developments might disrupt this balance?*

and social change. He favored treating the defeated French with moderation. Nevertheless, he remained an archconservative who readily resorted to harsh repressive tactics, including secret police and spying. But the peace he crafted was enormously significant and helped prevent a major European war until 1914.

The Congress sought to restore order by insisting that Europe's dynastic rulers were the only legitimate political authority. It recognized Louis XVIII as the legitimate sovereign of France and confirmed the restoration of Bourbon

rulers in Spain and the Two Sicilies. Other European monarchs had no interest in undermining the French restoration: Louis XVIII was a bulwark against revolution. But after Napoleon's Hundred Days, the allies imposed an indemnity of 700 million francs and an occupying army for five years. France's borders remained the same as in 1789—less than the revolution's "greater France" but not as punitive as they might have been.

The guiding principle of the peace was the balance of power, according to which no country should be powerful enough to destabilize international relations. Metternich's immediate goal, therefore, was to build a barrier against renewed French expansion. The Dutch Republic, conquered by the French in 1795, was restored as the kingdom of the Netherlands, securing France's northern border. The Congress also ceded the left bank of the Rhine to Prussia, and Austria expanded into northern Italy.

In central Europe, the allied powers reorganized the German states, reducing them from over 300 in number to 39. Prussia and Habsburg Austria joined these German states in a loosely structured German Confederation, with Austria careful to reserve for itself the presidency of this new body, as a check against attempts by the Prussians to increase their regional influence. Eventually, this confederation became the basis for German unification, but this was not the intention in Vienna in 1815. Bavaria, Württemburg, and Saxony remained independent kingdoms. Poland became a particular bone of contention, and the final compromise saw a nominally independent kingdom of Poland placed under the control of Tsar Alexander, with large slices of formerly Polish territory being handed over to Austria and Prussia. Meanwhile, Britain demanded compensation for its long war with Napoleon and received formerly French territories in South Africa and South America, as well as the island of Ceylon.

The Congress of Vienna also called for a Concert of Europe to secure the peace. Britain, Austria, Prussia, and Russia pledged to cooperate in the suppression of any disturbances—and France officially joined this conservative alliance in 1818. Alexander I pushed for what he called a Holy Alliance, dedicated to justice, Christian charity, and peace. The British foreign minister remained skeptical—calling the Holy Alliance "a piece of sublime mysticism and nonsense"—but agreed that the European powers should defend their conception of authority, centered on legitimacy. A ruler was legitimate if his power was guaranteed not only by claims of divine right but also by international treaties and support by his recognized peers. The Concert of Europe's opposition to liberal notions of political representation and national self-determination could not have been clearer. King Leopold of Belgium, himself placed on the throne by the allied powers in 1831, observed that war now threatened to become "a conflict of principles," sparked by revolutionary ideas, setting "peoples" against emperors. "From what I know of Europe," he continued, "such a conflict would change her form and overthrow her whole structure." Metternich and his fellow diplomats at Vienna dedicated their lives to seeing that such a conflict would never take place.

Revolt against Restoration

Much of the resistance to the Restoration was clandestine. On the Italian peninsula, the Carbonari (the name came from the charcoal they used to blacken their faces) vowed to oppose the government in Vienna and its conservative allies. Their political views varied: some called for constitutions and representative government and others praised Bonaparte. The Carbonari's influence spread through southern Europe and France in the 1820s, with members meeting in secret and identifying one another with closely guarded rituals. Veterans of Napoleon's armies and military officers were prominent in their ranks.

In Naples and Piedmont, and especially in Spain and the Spanish Empire, opposition to Metternich's Concert of Europe turned to revolt when monarchs restored by the Congress of Vienna betrayed their promises of reform. Metternich responded by spurring Austria, Prussia, and Russia to take a strong stand against revolution. In the Troppau Memorandum (1820), the conservative regimes pledged to assist one another in suppressing revolt. Austria dealt firmly with the Italian revolts, and France sent 200,000 troops to the Iberian Peninsula in 1823, crushing the Spanish revolutionaries and restoring King Ferdinand's authority.

Revolution in Latin America

King Ferdinand's empire in Latin America, however, would not be restored. Napoleon's conquest of Spain (1807) had shaken Spain's once vast empire. Local elites in the colonies who resented Spanish imperial control took advantage of the crown's weakness to push for independence. Rio de la Plata (now Argentina) was the first to succeed, declaring independence in 1816. Soon after, a monarchist general from Rio de la Plata, José de San Martin (1778–1850), led an expedition to liberate Chile and Peru. At the same time, Simón Bolívar (1783–1830), a republican leader, sparked a series of uprisings from Venezuela to Bolivia. Bolívar and Martin joined forces, though Bolívar's plans were more radical—he envisioned mobilizing free people of color and slaves (who made up roughly a quarter of those fighting the Spanish) as well as Indians to fight against Spanish rule. Bolívar's goal was to create a pan-American republic on the continent, along the lines of the United States. These political revolts unleashed violent social conflicts and, in some cases, civil

SECRET MEETING OF THE CARBONARI. Not all resistance took the form of open protest. The Carbonari, an Italian organization named for the charcoal that obscured the faces of its members, was an underground expression of opposition to the Restoration.

era of Portuguese colonialism in South America. Together, these revolutions demonstrated the circular relationships that bound the Atlantic world together. Encouraged by political movements associated with the French Revolution and Napoleon, the Latin American revolutionaries would in turn inspire nationalists in Europe who sought to overthrow Metternich's conservative Concert of Europe.

Russia: The Decembrists

Revolt also broke out in conservative Russia. In 1825, Tsar Alexander died, and a group of army officers known as the Decembrists led an uprising to push the pace of reform. Many were veterans of the Napoleonic Wars, and they feared that Russia could not live up to its promise to be the "liberator of Europe" without change in its social and political order. Serfdom contradicted the promise of liberation. So did the tsar's monopoly on power. Not only were Russian peasants enslaved, argued the Decembrists, the nobles were "slaves to the tsar."

The officers failed to gain support from the rank-and-file soldiers, and without that support they could not succeed. The new tsar, Nicholas I (r. 1825–55), interrogated hundreds of mutinous soldiers, sentencing many to hard labor and exile. The five leaders—all young and leading members of the aristocratic elite—were sentenced to death. Fearing they would be seen as martyrs, the tsar had them hung at dawn behind the walls of a fortress in St. Petersburg and buried in secret graves.

Nicholas went on to rule in the manner of his predecessor, becoming Europe's most uncompromising conservative. He created a powerful political police force, the Third Section, to prevent further domestic disorder. Still, Russia was not immune to change. Bureaucracy became more centralized, more efficient, and less dependent on the nobility. Accomplishing this task required making Russia's complex legal system more systematic and uniform. To accomplish this task Nicholas oversaw the publication of a new Code of Law, which recategorized every law passed since 1648 and published them in forty-eight volumes, a measure comparable to Napoleon's Civil Code of 1804. Meanwhile, landowners responded to increased demand for Russian grain by reorganizing their estates to increase productivity, and the state began to build railroads to transport the grain to Western markets. At the same time, opponents of the regime, such as the writer Alexander Herzen, carried on the Decembrists' unresolved political legacy.

war. Elite landowners who wanted only to free themselves from Spain opposed groups who wanted land reform and an end to slavery. In the end, the radical movements were suppressed, and the newly independent Latin American nations were dominated by an alliance of conservative landowners and military officers.

Britain and the newly ambitious United States prevented the European powers from intervening in the Latin American revolutions. In 1823, U.S. president James Monroe issued the Monroe Doctrine, declaring that European meddling in the Americas would be seen as a hostile act, a declaration that signaled a new willingness on the part of the United States to play a role on the world stage. Without British support, however, the Monroe Doctrine was unenforceable. Britain saw the new South American republics as potential trading partners and used its navy to prevent Spain from intervening. By the 1820s, the Spanish Empire had vanished, ending an age that had begun in 1492. Brazil's independence in 1823 similarly ended the

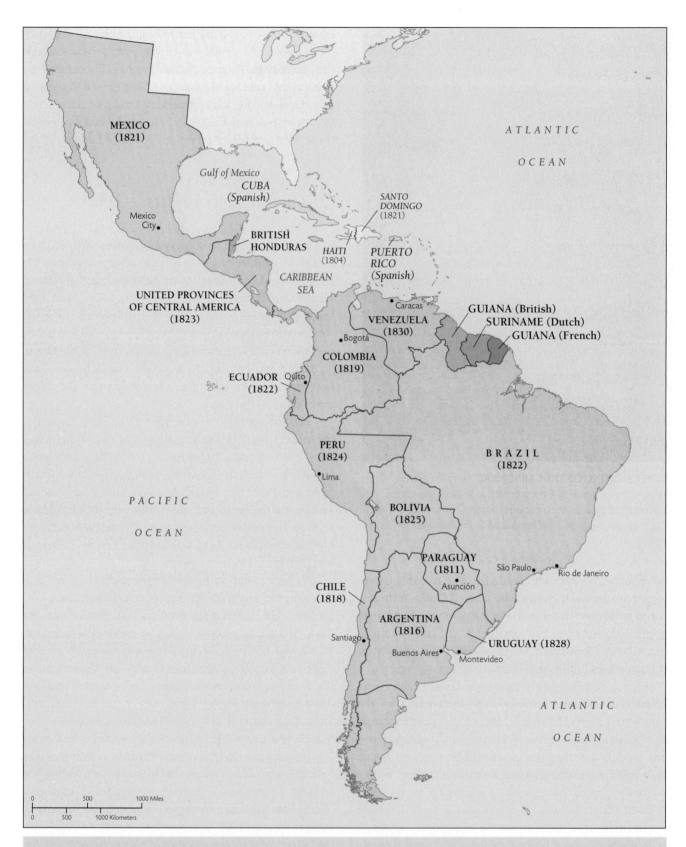

MEXICO
(1821)

Gulf of Mexico

CUBA
(Spanish)

Mexico
City.

SANTO
DOMINGO
(1821)

BRITISH
HONDURAS

HAITI
(1804)

PUERTO
RICO
(Spanish)

CARIBBEAN
SEA

UNITED PROVINCES
OF CENTRAL AMERICA
(1823)

ATLANTIC

OCEAN

Caracas•

GUIANA (British)
SURINAME (Dutch)
GUIANA (French)

VENEZUELA
(1830)

Bogotá•

COLOMBIA
(1819)

ECUADOR   Quito•
(1822)

PACIFIC

OCEAN

PERU
(1824)

Lima•

B R A Z I L
(1822)

BOLIVIA
(1825)

PARAGUAY
(1811)

São Paulo•   •Rio de Janeiro

Asunción•

CHILE
(1818)

ARGENTINA
(1816)

Santiago•

URUGUAY (1828)

Buenos Aires• •Montevideo

ATLANTIC

OCEAN

0   500   1000 Miles

0   500   1000 Kilometers

NEW NATIONS OF LATIN AMERICA. After Haiti became the Western Hemisphere's second independent nation, many areas of Central and South America also broke away from colonial rule. ▪ *When did the nations of Latin America gain their independence?* ▪ *What major events in Europe contributed to this move to independence?* ▪ *What is their relation to the Atlantic revolutions established in the late eighteenth century?*

Southeastern Europe: Greece and Serbia

When the Greeks and Serbians revolted against the once powerful Ottoman Empire, the conservative European powers showed themselves to be more tolerant of rebellion. Although the Ottoman Empire had defeated Napoleon Bonaparte's attempt to invade Egypt in 1798 (with British help), the episode strained the Ottoman hold on the eastern Mediterranean. Serbs in the Balkans rebelled against the Ottomans as early as 1804 and, with the help of the Russians, succeeded in establishing hereditary rule by a Serbian prince in 1817. This Serbian quasi-state persisted as an Orthodox Christian principality with a significant minority Muslim population until finally achieving formal independence from the Ottoman Empire in 1878.

The Serb revolt and the subsequent Greek war for independence (1821–27), were part of a new pattern in Ottoman history beginning in the early nineteenth century in which groups within the empire's border regions began to seek independence from Ottoman rule. Eighteenth-century revolts against Ottoman control in these regions had usually not sought outright separation and had generally been resolved within the imperial system, by redistributing tax burdens or instituting legal reforms. After 1800, European powers were more likely to get involved and the result was the establishment of new independent states and a weakening of Ottoman power. The French and the British viewed the eastern Mediterranean as an important arena of commercial competition while Russians viewed their frontiers with the Ottoman Empire's Balkan holdings as a natural place to exert foreign influence.

The Greek revolt immediately gained support from the British government, and sympathy for the Greeks was widespread in Europe. Christians in Europe cast the rebellion as part of an ongoing struggle between Christianity and Islam, whereas secular observers sought to interpret the struggle as one between an ancient pre-Christian European heritage and the Ottoman Empire. "We are all Greeks," wrote Percy Shelley, the Romantic poet. "Our laws, our literature, our religion, our arts have their roots in Greece." George Gordon, better known as Lord Byron (1788–1824), another Romantic poet, fought in Greece along with other volunteers, before dying there from fever. Celebrating the Greeks went hand in hand with demonizing the Ottomans, in spite of the fact that the Ottoman Empire's adaptable imperial system had frequently done better than Europeans in preserving the peace between diverse peoples and different religions over the many centuries of their rule.

THE MASSACRE AT CHIOS BY EUGÈNE DELACROIX (1789–1863). Delacroix was a Romantic painter of dramatic and emotional scenes. Here, he put his brush to work for the cause of Greek nationalism, eulogizing the victims of killings on the island of Chios during the Greek war for independence against the Ottoman Empire. ▪ *How did the choices that Delacroix made in his depiction of the massacre's victims shape the vision of the conflict for his European audience?*

On the ground in Greece, the struggle was brutal and massacres of civilians occurred on both sides. In March 1822, the Greeks invaded the island of Chios and proclaimed its independence. When Ottoman troops arrived to retake the island, the Greek invaders killed their prisoners and fled. The Ottoman armies took revenge by slaughtering thousands of Greeks and selling 40,000 more into slavery. The French Romantic painter Eugène Delacroix memorialized the event in a painting that characteristically depicted only Ottoman brutality (see above).

In the end, Greek independence depended on great-power politics, as it did in Serbia. In 1827, British, French, and Russian troops sided with the Greeks against the Ottomans, who were forced to concede and grant Greek independence. The new nations of Serbia and Greece were small and fragile. Only 800,000 Greeks actually lived in the new Greek state. Serbia, meanwhile, could not survive without Russian protection. Moreover, neither of the new nations broke their close links with the Ottomans, and

Greek and Serbian merchants, bankers, and administrators were still very present in the Ottoman Empire. The region remained a borderland of Europe, a region where peoples alternated between tolerant coexistence and bitter conflict.

As Ottoman control in southeastern Europe waned, the European powers often played a double game. On the one hand, they recognized that regional stability depended on the continued existence of the Ottoman Empire and that its collapse would constitute a serious threat to European peace. By continuing to pursue their own self-interests, however, and by meddling in the affairs of the Ottoman Empire's rebellious subjects, they contributed to the weakening of Ottoman authority.

Leaders of independence movements were likely to succeed when they could take advantage of conflict between great powers, as in Latin America, or when those movements aligned with Europe's competition with the Ottoman Empire, as in Greece and Serbia. Meanwhile, Metternich's ability to prevent the spread of nationalism and liberalism—both ideologies associated with the French Revolution—increasingly depended on repressive political regimes that could not tolerate open expressions of dissent. Containing these movements for political and social change would eventually become impossible.

CITIZENSHIP AND SOVEREIGNTY, 1830–1848

In the aftermath of the French Revolution, then, debates about citizenship, sovereignty, and social inequality remained divisive in many parts of Europe, even in those kingdoms with conservative monarchies that supported the Concert of Europe. In France, Belgium, and Poland, political movements challenging the post-Napoleonic settlement led to open revolt in the years 1830–32. A similar threat developed in the 1840s. During these same decades, many in Britain feared that conflicts over voting rights and the treatment of the poor might lead to a similar crisis. In the end, political leaders in Britain succeeded in negotiating reforms that prevented open rebellion during these years, whereas the revolutionary movements of the 1830s and 1840s on the Continent proved to be a prelude to a wave of revolutions in 1848 that swept across Europe (see Chapter 21).

The 1830 Revolution in France

The first decisive blow against the Concert of Europe came in 1830 in France. In 1815, the Congress of Vienna returned a Bourbon monarch to the throne. Louis XVIII was the oldest of the former king's surviving brothers. Louis claimed absolute power, but in the name of reconciliation he granted a "charter" and conceded some important rights: legal equality, careers open to talent, and a two-chamber parliamentary government. Voting rights excluded most citizens from government. Louis XVIII's narrow base of support, combined with the sting of military defeat, nostalgia for a glorious Napoleonic past, and memories of the revolution undermined the Restoration in France.

In 1824, Louis XVIII succeeded his far more conservative brother, Charles X (r. 1824–30). Charles pleased the ultra-royalists by pushing the assembly to compensate nobles whose land had been confiscated and sold during the revolution, but the measure antagonized property holders. He restored the Catholic Church to its traditional place in French schools, provoking discontent among French liberals, who began to organize an oppositional movement in Parliament. Economic troubles encouraged the opposition, and in Paris and the provinces worried police reports documented widespread unemployment, hunger, and anger. Confronted with alarming evidence of the regime's unpopularity, Charles called for new elections; when they went against him, he tried to overthrow the parliament with his so-called July Ordinances of 1830: he dissolved the new assembly before it had met, restricted suffrage even further, and announced strict press censorship.

In return, Charles got revolution. Parisian workers, artisans, and students took to the streets in three days of intense street battles. Crucial to the spread of the movement was the press, which defied the censors and quickly spread the news of the initial confrontations between protesters and the forces of order. In the end, the army was unwilling to fire into the crowd, and Charles was forced to abdicate, his support evaporating. Although many revolutionaries who had fought in the streets wanted another republic, the leaders of the movement opted for stability by crowning the former king's cousin, the Duke of Orléans, Louis-Philippe (r. 1830–48), as a constitutional monarch. The July Monarchy, as it was called, doubled the number of voters, though voting was still based on steep property requirements. The propertied classes benefited most from the revolution of 1830, but it also brought the common people back into politics, revived memories of 1789, and spurred movements elsewhere in Europe. For opponents of the Restoration, the year 1830 suggested that history was moving in a new direction and that the political landscape had changed since the Congress of Vienna.

LIBERTY LEADING THE PEOPLE BY EUGÈNE DELACROIX. This painting is among the best-known images of the revolutions of 1830. Delacroix is the same artist who had mourned the extinction of liberty in his painting of the *Massacre at Chios* in Greece (see page 659). The allegorical female figure of liberty leads representatives of the united people: a middle-class man (identified by his top hat), a worker, and a boy of the streets wielding a pistol. Neither middle-class people nor children fought on the barricades, and the image of revolutionary unity was romanticized. ▪ *What made this mix of social classes important for Delacroix's image of the French people in revolt?* ▪ *And why this particular image of liberty, carrying a rifle, with exposed breasts?*

Belgium and Poland in 1830

In 1815, the Congress of Vienna joined Belgium (then called the Austrian Netherlands) to Holland to form a buffer against France known as the United Provinces. The Belgians had never accepted this arrangement, and the 1830 revolution in France energized the Belgian opposition. The city of Brussels rebelled and forced Dutch troops to withdraw. Unwilling to intervene, the great powers agreed to guarantee Belgian independence and neutrality—a provision that remained in force until 1914. Although the economy of Belgian cities suffered by being separated from the Atlantic trade of the Dutch ports, religious divisions between the largely Catholic provinces of Belgium and Protestant Holland reinforced the division. French-speaking elites in Belgium also supported independence, though Flemish-speaking Belgians continue to cultivate a sense of cultural distinctiveness even today.

The years 1830–32 thus became full-fledged crisis for the Concert of Europe. After France and Belgium, revolt also spread to Poland, governed by the Russian tsar's brother, Constantine. Poland had its own parliament (or *diet*), a relatively broad electorate, a constitution, and basic liberties of speech and the press. The Russian head of state increasingly ignored these liberties, however, and news of the French Revolution of 1830 tipped Poland into revolt. The revolutionaries—including

aristocrats, students, military officers, and middle-class people—drove out Constantine. Within less than a year, Russian forces retook Warsaw, and the conservative tsar Nicholas crushed the revolt and put Poland under military rule.

Reform in Great Britain

Why was there no revolution in England between 1815 and 1848? One answer is that there almost was. After an era of political conservatism comparable to that of the Continent's, however, Britain became one of the most liberal nations in Europe.

The end of the Napoleonic Wars brought a major agricultural depression to Britain. Low wages, unemployment, and bad harvests provoked regular social unrest. In the new industrial towns of the north, radical members of the middle class joined with workers to demand increased representation in Parliament. When 60,000 people gathered in 1819 to demonstrate for political reform at St. Peter's Field in Manchester, the militia and soldiers on horseback charged the crowd, killing 11 and injuring 400. Radicals condemned "Peterloo," a domestic Waterloo, and criticized the nation's army for turning against its own citizens. Parliament quickly passed the Six Acts (1819), outlawing "seditious" literature, increasing the stamp tax on newspapers, allowing house searches, and restricting rights of assembly.

British political leaders reversed their opposition to reform in response to pressure from below. The reforms actually began under the conservative Tory Party, when Catholics and non-Anglican Protestants were allowed to participate in public life. The Tories nevertheless refused to reform representation in the House of Commons. About two-thirds of the members of the House of Commons owed their seats to the patronage of the richest titled landowners in the country. In districts known as "rotten" or "pocket" boroughs, landowners used their power to return members of Parliament who would serve their interests. Defenders of this system argued that the interests of landed property coincided with the nation at large.

Liberals in the Whig Party, the new industrial middle class, and radical artisans argued passionately for reform. They were not necessarily democrats—liberals in particular wanted only to enfranchise responsible citizens—but they made common cause with organized middle-class and working-class radicals to push for reform. A Birmingham banker named Thomas Atwood, for example, organized the Political Union of the Lower and Middle Classes of the People. By July 1830, similar organizations arose in several cities, and some clashed with the army and police. Middle-class shopkeepers announced they would withhold taxes and form a national guard. The country appeared to be on the verge of serious general disorder, if not outright revolution. Lord Grey, head of the Whig Party, seized the opportunity to push through reform.

The Reform Bill of 1832 eliminated the rotten boroughs and reallocated 143 parliamentary seats, mostly from the rural south, to the industrial north. The bill expanded the franchise, but only one in six men could vote. Landed aristocrats had their influence reduced but not destroyed. This modest reform nevertheless brought British liberals and members of the middle class into a junior partnership with a landed elite that had ruled Britain for centuries.

What changes did this more liberal parliament produce? It abolished slavery in the British colonies in 1838 (see Chapter 21). The most significant example of middle-class power came in the repeal of the Corn Laws in 1846. The Corn Laws (the British term for grain is *corn*) protected British landowners and farmers from foreign competition by establishing tariffs for imports, and they kept bread prices high. The middle class increasingly saw this as an unfair protection of the aristocracy and pushed for their repeal in the name of free trade. The Anti-Corn Law League held meetings throughout the north of England and lobbied Parliament, eventually resulting in a repeal of the law and a free-trade policy that lasted until the 1920s.

British Radicalism and the Chartist Movement

Reformers disappointed with the narrow gains of 1832 pushed for expanded political reforms. Their attention focused on a petition known as the "People's Charter," which contained six demands: universal white male suffrage, a secret ballot, an end to property qualifications as a condition of public office, annual parliamentary elections, salaries for members of the House of Commons, and equal electoral districts. The Chartists organized committees across the country, and the charter was eventually signed by millions.

Chartism spread in a climate of economic hardship during the 1840s. The movement tapped into local traditions of worker self-help, but the Chartists often disagreed about tactics and goals. Should Irish Catholics be included in the movement or excluded as dangerous competitors? Should women be included in the franchise?

THE GREAT CHARTIST RALLY OF APRIL 10, 1848. The year 1848 brought revolution to continental Europe and militant protest to England. This photo shows the April rally in support of the Chartists' six points, which included expanding the franchise, abolishing property qualifications for representatives, and instituting a secret ballot.

Analyzing Primary Sources

Women in the Anti-Corn Law League, 1842

Members of the Anti-Corn Law League sought to repeal the protectionist laws that prohibited foreign grain from entering the British market. The laws were seen as an interference with trade that kept bread prices artificially high, benefiting British landowners and grain producers at the expense of the working population. The campaign to repeal the Corn Laws enlisted many middle-class women in its ranks, and some later campaigned for woman suffrage. This article, hostile to the reform, deplored women's participation in the reform movement.

 e find that the council of the Manchester Anti-Corn Law Association had invited the inhabitants to "an *anti-Corn-law tea-party*, to be held on the 20th of May, 1841—gentlemen's tickets, 2s.; ladies 1s. 6d." . . . [L]adies were advertised as *stewardesses* of this assembly. So now the names of about 300 Ladies were pompously advertised as the *Patroness* and *Committee* of the *National Bazaar.* We exceedingly wonder and regret that the members of the Association . . . and still more that anybody else, should have chosen to exhibit their wives and daughters in the character of political agitators; and we most regret that so many ladies—modest, excellent, and amiable persons we have no doubt in their domestic circles—should have been persuaded to allow their names to be *placarded* on such occasions—for be it remembered, this Bazaar and these *Tea-parties* did not even pretend to be for any *charitable* object, but entirely for the purposes of *political agitation.* . . .

We have before us a letter from Mrs. Secretary Woolley to one body of workmen. . . . She "appeals to them to stand forth and denounce as *unholy*, unjust, and cruel all restrictions on the food of the people." She acquaints them that "the ladies are resolved to perform *their* arduous part in the attempt to *destroy a monopoly* which, for *selfishness* and its *deadly* effects, has no parallel in the history of the world." "We therefore," she adds, "ask you for contributions. . . ." Now surely . . . not only should the *poorer classes* have been exempt from such unreasonable solicitations, but whatever subscriptions might be obtainable from the wealthier orders should have been applied, not to *political agitation* throughout England, but to charitable relief at home.

Source: J. Croker, "Anti-Corn Law Legislation," *Quarterly Review* (December 1842), as cited in Patricia Hollis, ed., *Women in Public: The Women's Movement 1850–1900* (London: 1979), p. 287.

Questions for Analysis

1. Why does the article highlight the participation of women in the Anti-Corn Law Association? What does this argument tell us about attitudes toward women's political activity?

2. Does the article actually mention any of the arguments in favor of repealing the Corn Laws? What alternative to repeal does the article appear to support?

The Chartist William Lovett, a cabinetmaker, was a fervent believer in self-improvement and advocated a union of educated workers that could claim its fair share of the nation's increasing industrial wealth. The Chartist Feargus O'Connor appealed to the more impoverished and desperate class of workers by attacking industrialization and the resettlement of the poor on agricultural allotments. Chartist James Bronterre O'Brien shocked the crowds by openly expressing his admiration for Robespierre and attacking "the big-bellied, little-brained, numbskull aristocracy." Chartism had many faces, but the movement's common goal was social justice through political democracy.

In spite of the Chartists' efforts to present massive petitions to the Parliament in 1839 and 1842, the Parliament rejected them both times. Members of the movement resorted to strikes, trade union demonstrations, and attacks on factories and manufacturers who imposed low wages and long hours or who harassed unionists. The movement peaked in April 1848. Inspired by revolutions in continental Europe (see Chapter 21), the Chartists' leaders planned a major demonstration in London. Twenty-five thousand workers carried to Parliament a petition with 6 million signatures. Confronted with the specter of class conflict, special constables and regular army units were marshaled by the aged Duke of Wellington to resist any threat to public order. In the end, only a small delegation presented the petition, and rain and an unwillingness to do battle with the constabulary put an end to the Chartist movement. A relieved liberal observer, Harriet Martineau, observed, "From that day it was a settled matter that England was safe from revolution."

THE POLITICS OF SLAVERY AFTER 1815

These political conflicts within nations about citizenship, sovereignty, and equality were also linked to a transnational debate about slavery and its legitimacy, which was taking place at the same time. When the age of revolution opened in the 1770s, slavery was legal everywhere in the Atlantic world. By 1848, slavery remained legal only in the southern United States, Brazil, and Cuba. (It endured, too, in most of Africa and parts of India and the Islamic world.) Given the importance of slavery to the Atlantic economy, this was a remarkable shift. The debate about slavery was fundamental, because it challenged the defenders of citizenship rights to live up to the claims of universality that had been a central part of Enlightenment political thought. If "all men" were "created equal," how could some be enslaved?

Slavery, Enlightenment, and Revolution

In fact, the revolutions of the eighteenth century by no means brought emancipation in their wake. Eighteenth-century Enlightenment thinkers had persuaded many Europeans that slavery contradicted natural law and natural freedom (see Chapter 17). As one historian trenchantly puts it, however, "Slavery became a metaphor for everything that was bad—except the institution of slavery itself." Thus, Virginia planters who helped lead the American Revolution angrily refused to be "slaves" to the English king while at the same time defending plantation slavery. The planters' success in throwing off the British king expanded their power and strengthened slavery.

Likewise, the French revolutionaries denounced the tyranny of a king who would "enslave" them but refused to admit free people of color to the revolutionary assembly for fear of alienating the planters in the lucrative colonies of Martinique, Guadeloupe, and Saint-Domingue. Only a slave rebellion in Saint-Domingue in 1791 forced the French revolutionaries, eventually, to contend with the contradictions of revolutionary policy. Napoleon's failure to repress that rebellion allowed for the emergence of Haiti in 1804 (see Chapter 18). The Haitian Revolution sent shock waves through the Americas, alarming slave owners and offering hope to slaves and former slaves. In the words of a free black sailmaker in Philadelphia, the Haitian nation signaled that black people "could not always be detained in their present bondage."

Yet the revolution in Haiti had other, contradictory consequences. The "loss" of slave-based sugar production in the former Saint-Domingue created an opportunity for its expansion elsewhere, in Brazil, where slavery expanded in the production of sugar, gold, and coffee, and in the American South. Slavery remained intact in the French, British, and Spanish colonial islands in the Caribbean, backed by the Congress of Vienna in 1815.

The Slow Path to Abolition

An abolitionist movement did emerge, in England. The country that ruled the seas was "the world's leading purchaser and transporter of African slaves," and the movement aimed to abolish that trade. From the 1780s on, pamphlets and books (the best known is *The Interesting Narrative of the Life of Olaudah Equiano,* 1789) detailed the horrors of the slave ships to an increasingly sympathetic audience. Abolitionist leaders like William Wilberforce believed that the slave trade was immoral and hoped that banning it would improve conditions for the enslaved, though like most abolitionists Wilberforce did not want to foment revolt. In 1807, the reform movement compelled Parliament to pass a bill declaring the "African Slave Trade to be contrary to the principles of justice, humanity and sound policy" and prohibiting British ships from participating in it, effective 1808. The United States joined in the agreement; ten years later the Portuguese agreed to a limited ban on traffic north of the equator. More treaties followed, which slowed but did not stop the trade.

What roots did abolitionism tap? Some historians argue that slavery was becoming less profitable and that its decline made humanitarian concern easier to accept. Others argue that slavery was expanding: among other things, ships carried 2.5 million slaves to markets in the Americas in the four decades *after* the abolition of the slave trade.

Some historians believe economic factors undermined slavery. Adam Smith and his followers argued that free labor, like free trade, was more efficient. This was not necessarily the case, but such arguments still had an effect. Critics claimed slavery was wasteful as well as cruel. Economic calculations, however, did less to activate abolitionism than did a belief that the slave trade and slavery itself represented the arrogance and callousness of wealthy British traders, their planter allies, and the British elite in general. In a culture with high literacy and political traditions of activism, calls for "British liberty" mobilized many.

In England, and especially in the United States, religious revivals supplied much of the energy for the abolitionist movement. The hymn "Amazing Grace" was written by a former slave trader turned minister, John Newton, to describe his conversion experience and salvation. The moral and religious dimensions of the struggle made it acceptable for women, who would move from antislavery to the Anti-Corn Law League and, later, to woman suffrage. Finally, the issue spoke to laborers whose sometimes brutal working conditions and sharply limited political rights we have discussed in the previous chapters. To oppose slavery and to insist that labor should be dignified, honorable, and minimally free resonated broadly in the social classes accustomed to being treated as "servile." The issue, then, cut across material interests and class politics, and antislavery petitions were signed by millions in the 1820s and 1830s.

Slave rebellions and conspiracies to rebel also shook opinion, especially after the success of the Haitian Revolution (see Chapter 19). In 1800, slaves rebelled in Virginia; in 1811, there was an uprising in Louisiana; and in 1822, an alleged conspiracy took hold in South Carolina. The British colonies saw significant rebellions in the Barbados (1816); Demerara, just east of Venezuela (1823); and, most important, the monthlong insurrection in Jamaica (1831). All of these were ferociously repressed. Slave rebellions had virtually no chance of succeeding and usually erupted only when some crack in the system opened up: divisions within the white elite or the (perceived) presence of a sympathetic outsider. Still, these rebellions had important

consequences. They increased slaveholders' sense of vulnerability and isolation. They polarized debate. Outsiders (in England or New England) often recoiled at the brutality of repression. Slave owners responded to antislavery sentiment much as Russian serf owners had responded to their critics, by insisting that slavery was vital to their survival, that emancipation of inferior peoples would sow chaos, and that abolitionists were dangerously playing with fire.

In Great Britain, the force of abolitionism wore down the defense of slavery. In the aftermath of the Great Reform Bill of 1832, Great Britain emancipated 800,000 slaves in its colonies—effective in 1838, after four years of "apprenticeship." In France, republicans took the strongest antislavery stance, and emancipation came to the French colonies when the revolution of 1848 brought republicans, however briefly, to power (see Chapter 21).

In Latin America, slavery's fate was determined by demographics, economics, and the politics of breaking away from the Spanish and Portuguese empires. In most of mainland Spanish America (in other words, not Cuba or Brazil), slavery had been of secondary importance, owing to the relative ease of escape and the presence of other sources of labor. As the struggles for independence escalated, nationalist leaders recruited slaves and free people of

FEAR OF SLAVE VIOLENCE. This cartoon, published in Britain in 1789 in opposition to the movement to end slavery, played on public fears of the consequences of abolition. The former slaves, dressed in the fashionable attire of the landed gentry, dine at their former master's table, and beat the master in retaliation for what they have suffered. In the background, other former slave owners are stooped in labor in the cane fields. By the logic of this cartoon, such a reversal was intolerable, and given the choice between "Abolition" and "Regulation" (the two heads at the bottom) the cartoonist chose "Regulation" as the wiser course.

color to fight against the Spanish, promising emancipation in return. Simón Bolívar's 1817 campaign to liberate Venezuela was fought in part by slaves, ex-slaves, and 6,000 troops from Haiti. The new nations in Spanish America passed emancipation measures in stages but had eliminated slavery by the middle of the century.

Cuba was starkly different: with 40 percent of its population enslaved, the Spanish island colony had almost as many slaves as all of mainland Spanish America together. A Cuban independence movement would have detonated a slave revolution, a fact that provided a powerful incentive for Cuba to remain under the Spanish crown. Spain, for its part, needed the immensely profitable sugar industry and could not afford to alienate Cuban planters pushing for an end to slavery. Only a combination of slave rebellion in Cuba and liberal revolution in Spain brought abolition, beginning in the 1870s. Brazil too was 40 percent enslaved and, like Cuba, had a large population of free people of color. Unlike Cuba, Brazil won national independence, breaking away from Portugal with relative ease (1822). Like the American South, Brazil came through the revolution for independence with slavery not only intact but expanding, and slavery endured in Brazil until 1888.

TAKING SIDES: NEW IDEOLOGIES IN POLITICS

Debates about citizenship, sovereignty, and slavery made it clear that issues raised by the French Revolution were very much alive in Europe after 1815. The Congress of Vienna was able to place the Bourbon family back on the throne in France, but it could not make debates about popular sovereignty, national independence, or the authority of conservative dynastic regimes go away. Throughout Europe, political actors increasingly understood themselves to be facing a choice. If the debate about political change after the French Revolution was one between groups holding incompatible worldviews, then winning meant imposing your vision of the world on your opponents by any means necessary. Such assumptions naturally encouraged extremists on all sides of the debate. On the other hand, if disputing groups could come to some kind of mutual understanding about the goals of political association, then some compromise or middle way might be possible. It was within this context that modern political ideologies of conservatism, liberalism, socialism, and nationalism began to come into clearer focus.

Early nineteenth-century politics did not have parties as we know them today. But more clearly defined groups and competing doctrines, or ideologies, took shape during this time. An ideology may be defined as a coherent system of thought that claims to represent the workings and structure of the social order and its relationship to political powers and institutions. Ideologies consciously compete with other views of how the world is or should be, and their defenders seek to establish their views as dominant. The roots of conservatism, liberalism, and nationalism lay in earlier times, but ongoing political battles about the legacy of the French Revolution brought them to the fore. The Industrial Revolution (see Chapter 19) and the social changes that accompanied it proved a tremendous spur to political and social thought and led to the development of socialism as a political and social project. Would the advance of industry yield progress or misery? What were the "rights of man," and who would enjoy them? Did equality necessarily go hand in hand with liberty? A brief survey of the political horizon will show how different groups formulated their responses to these questions and will dramatize how the ground had shifted since the eighteenth century.

Principles of Conservatism

At the Congress of Vienna and in the Restoration generally, the most important guiding concept was legitimacy. Legitimacy had broad appeal as a general antirevolutionary policy. It might be best understood as a code word for a new political order that the Congress sought to impose. Conservatives aimed to make legitimate—and thus to solidify—both the monarchy's authority and the hierarchical social order undermined by the French Revolution. The most thoughtful conservatives of the period did not believe that the old order would survive completely intact or that time could be reversed, especially after the events of the 1820s made it clear that the Restoration would be challenged. They did believe, however, that the monarchy guaranteed political stability, that the nobility were the rightful leaders of the nation, and that both needed to play active and effective roles in public life. They insisted that, as a matter of strategy, the nobility and the crown shared a common interest, despite their disagreements in the past. Conservatives believed that change had to be slow, incremental, and managed so as to strengthen rather than weaken the structures of authority. Conserving the past and cultivating tradition would ensure an orderly future.

Edmund Burke's writings became a point of reference for nineteenth-century conservatives. His *Reflections on the*

Edmund Burke, *Reflections on the Revolution in France*

Edmund Burke's Reflections on the Revolution in France *was first published in 1790, while the French Revolution was still under way. Burke's opposition to revolutionary change had a profound influence on conservatives in the decades after the Congress of Vienna in 1815. The following passages contain Burke's defense of hereditary elites, his insistence on the power of tradition—here referred to as "convention"—and his criticism of the doctrine of natural rights.*

he power of perpetuating our property in our families is one of the most valuable and interesting circumstances belonging to it, and that which tends the most to the perpetuation of society itself. It makes our weakness subservient to our virtue; it grafts benevolence even upon avarice. The possessors of family wealth, and of the distinction which attends hereditary possession . . . are the natural securities for this transmission. With us, the house of peers is formed upon this principle. It is wholly composed of hereditary property and hereditary distinction; and made therefore the third of the legislature; and in the last event, the sole judge of all property in all its subdivisions. The house of commons too, though not necessarily, yet in fact, is always so composed in the far greater part. Let those large proprietors be what they will, and they have their chance of being amongst the best, they are at the very worst, the ballast in the vessel of the commonwealth. [. . .]

If civil society be the offspring of convention, that convention must be its law. That convention must limit and modify the descriptions of constitution which are formed under it. Every sort of legislative, judicial, or executor power are its creatures. They can have no being in any other state of things; and how can any man claim, under the conventions of civil society, rights which do not so much as suppose its existence? Rights which are absolutely repugnant to it? One of the first motives to civil society, and which becomes one of its fundamental rules, is *that no man should be judge in his own cause.* By this each person has at once divested himself of the first fundamental right of uncovenanted man, that is, to judge for himself, and to assert his own cause. He abdicates all right to be his own governor. He inclusively, in a great measure, abandons the right of self-defense, the first law of nature. Men cannot enjoy the rights of an uncivil and of a civil state together. That he may obtain justice he gives up his right of determining what it is in points the most essential to him. That he may secure some liberty, he makes a surrender in trust of the whole of it. [. . .]

Government is not made in virtue of natural rights, which may and do exist in total independence of it; and in a much greater degree of abstract perfection; but their abstract perfection is their practical defect. . . . The moment you abate anything from the full rights of men, each to govern himself, and suffer any artificial positive limitation upon those rights, from that moment the whole organization of government becomes a consideration of convenience. That is which makes the constitution of a state, and the due distribution of its powers, a matter of the most delicate and complicated skill. It requires a deep knowledge of human nature and human necessities, and of the things which facilitate or obstruct the various ends which are to be pursued by the mechanism of civil institutions. The state is to have recruits to its strength and remedies to its distempers. What is the use of discussing a man's abstract right to food or to medicine? The question is upon the method of procuring and administering them. In that deliberation I shall always advise to call in the aid of the farmer and the physician, rather than the professor of metaphysics.

Source: Edmund Burke, *Reflections on the Revolution in France* (London: J. Dodsley, 1791, 9th edition), pp. 75–76, 86–88, 89–90.

Questions for Analysis

1. Note that Burke does not defend hereditary elites with reference to God or a divinely inspired order. How does he justify the authority of the hereditary aristocracy?

2. What power does Burke grant to "convention" in the construction of the state and its laws?

3. What is Burke's principal complaint about revolutionaries who base their programs on "natural rights"?

Revolution in France was more influential in this new context than it had been during the 1790s, when it was first published. Burke did not oppose all change; he had argued, for instance, that the British should let the North American colonies go. But he opposed talk of natural rights, which he considered dangerous abstractions. He believed enthusiasm for constitutions to be misguided and the Enlightenment's emphasis on what he called the "conquering power of reason" to be dangerous. Instead, Burke counseled deference to experience, tradition, and history. Other conservatives, such as the French writers Joseph de Maistre (1753–1821) and Louis-Gabriel-Ambroise Bonald (1754–1840), penned carefully elaborated defenses of absolute monarchy and its main pillar of support, the Catholic Church. De Maistre, for instance, blamed the Enlightenment's critique of the Catholic Church for the French Revolution, and he assailed Enlightenment individualism for ignoring the bonds and collective institutions (the Church, for instance, or family) that he believed held society together. As conservatives saw it, monarchy, aristocracy, and the Church were the mainstays of the social and political order. Those institutions needed to stand together in face of the challenges of the new century.

Conservatism was not simply the province of intellectuals. A more broadly based revival of religion in the early nineteenth century also expressed a popular reaction against revolution and an emphasis on order, discipline, and tradition. What was more, conservative thinkers also exercised influence well beyond their immediate circle. Their emphasis on history, on the untidy and unpredictable ways in which history unfolded, and their awareness of the past became increasingly central to social thought and artistic visions of the first half of the century.

Liberalism

Liberalism's core was a commitment to individual liberties, or rights. Liberals believed that the most important function of government was to protect liberties and that doing so would benefit all, promoting justice, knowledge, progress, and prosperity. Liberalism had three components. First, liberalism called for equality before the law, which meant ending traditional privileges and the restrictive power of rank and hereditary authority. Second, liberalism held that government needed to be based on political rights and the consent of the governed. Third, with respect to economics, liberals believed that individuals should be free to engage in economic activities without interference from the state or their community.

The roots of legal and political liberalism lay in the late seventeenth century, in the work of John Locke, who had defended the English Parliament's rebellion against absolutism and the "inalienable" rights of the British people (see Chapter 15). Liberalism had been developed by the Enlightenment writers of the eighteenth century and was especially influenced by the founding texts of the American and French Revolutions (the Declaration of Independence and the Declaration of the Rights of Man). Freedom from arbitrary authority, imprisonment, and censorship; freedom of the press; the right to assemble and deliberate—these principles were the starting points for nineteenth-century liberalism. Liberals believed in individual rights, that those rights were inalienable, and that they should be guaranteed in written constitutions. (Conservatives, as we saw earlier, considered constitutions abstract and dangerous.) Most liberals called for constitutional as opposed to hereditary monarchy; all agreed that a monarch who abused power could legitimately be overthrown.

Liberals advocated direct representation in government—at least for those who had the property and public standing to be trusted with the responsibilities of power. Liberalism by no means required democracy. In the July Monarchy in France, established after the 1830 revolution, the property qualifications were so high that only 2 percent of the population could vote. Even after the Reform Bill of 1832 in England, only 18 percent of the population could vote for parliamentary representatives. Nineteenth-century liberals, with fresh memories of the French Revolution of 1789, were torn between their belief in rights and their fears of political turmoil. They considered property and education essential prerequisites for participation in politics. Wealthy liberals opposed extending the vote to the common people. To demand universal male suffrage was too radical, and to speak of enfranchising women or people of color even more so. As far as slavery was concerned, nineteenth-century liberalism inherited the contradictions of the Enlightenment. Belief in individual liberty collided with vested economic interests, determination to preserve order and property, and increasingly "scientific" theories of racial inequality (see Chapter 23).

Economic liberalism was newer. Its founding text was Adam Smith's *Wealth of Nations* (1776), which attacked mercantilism (the government practice of regulating manufacturing and trade to raise revenues) in the name of free markets. Smith's argument that the economy should be based on a "system of natural liberty" was reinforced by a second generation of economists and popularized in journals such as the *Economist*, founded in 1838. The economists (or political economists, as they were called) sought to identify basic economic laws: the law of supply and demand, the balance of trade, the law of diminishing returns, and so on. They argued that economic policy had to begin by recognizing these laws. David Ricardo (1772–1823) of Britain, for example, set out laws of wages and of rents, trying to determine the long-run outcomes of fluctuations in each.

Liberal political economists such as Smith and Ricardo believed that economic activity should be unregulated. Labor should be contracted freely, unhampered by guilds or unions, or state interference. Property should be unencumbered by feudal restrictions. Goods should circulate freely, which meant, concretely, an end to government-granted monopolies, trade barriers, import tariffs, and traditional practices of regulating markets, especially in valuable commodities such as grain, flour, or corn. At the time of the Irish famine, for instance, their writings played a role in hardening opposition to government intervention or relief

ADAM SMITH POINTING TO HIS BOOK *THE WEALTH OF NATIONS* (1776). Smith was an Enlightenment thinker whose work was popularized in the nineteenth century, and he helped to establish "political economy," or economics.

(see Chapter 19). Liberal economists believed that the functions of the state should be kept to a minimum, though they also argued that markets could not function without states to preserve the rule of law and government's role was to preserve order and protect property but not to interfere with the natural play of economic forces, a doctrine known as *laissez-faire,* which translates, roughly, as "leave things to go on their own." This strict opposition to government intervention makes nineteenth-century liberalism different from common understandings of "liberalism" in the United States today.

Liberty and freedom meant different things in different countries. In lands occupied by other powers, liberal parties demanded freedom from foreign rule. The colonies of Latin America demanded liberty from Spain, and similar struggles set Greece and Serbia against the Ottoman Empire, northern Italy against the Austrians, Poland against Russian rule, and so on. In central and southeastern Europe, liberty meant eliminating feudal privilege and allowing at least the educated elite access to political power, more rights for local parliaments, and creating representative national political institutions. Some cited the British system of government as a model; others pointed to the French Declaration of the Rights of Man. Most shied away from the radicalism of the French Revolution. The issue was constitutional, representative government. In such countries as Russia, Prussia, and France under the restored Bourbon monarchy, liberty meant political freedoms, such as the right to vote, assemble, and print political opinions without censorship.

In Great Britain, where political freedoms were relatively well established, liberals focused on expanding the franchise, on laissez-faire economics and free trade, and on reforms aimed at creating limited and efficient government. In this respect, one of the most influential British liberals was Jeremy Bentham (1748–1832). Bentham's major work, *The Principles of Morals and Legislation* (1789), illustrates how nineteenth-century liberalism continued the Enlightenment legacy and also transformed it. Unlike, for instance, Smith, Bentham did not believe that human interests were naturally harmonious or that a stable social order could emerge naturally from a body of self-interested individuals. Instead he proposed that society adopt the organizing principle of utilitarianism. Social institutions and laws (an electoral system, for instance, or a tariff) should be measured according to their social usefulness—according to whether they produced the "greatest happiness of the greatest number." If a law passed this test, it could remain on the books; if it failed, it should be jettisoned. Utilitarians acknowledged the importance of the individual. Each individual best understood his or her own interests and was, therefore, best left free, whenever possible, to pursue those interests as he or she saw fit. Only when an individual's interests conflicted with the interests—the happiness—of the greatest number was individual freedom to be curtailed. The intensely practical spirit of utilitarianism enhanced its influence as a creed for reform. In his personal political views, Bentham went further than many liberals—he befriended Jacobins and believed in granting equal rights for women. Nevertheless, his rationalist approach to measuring the "utility" of laws and reforms nevertheless was an essential contribution to the liberal tradition.

Radicalism, Republicanism, and Early Socialism

The liberals were flanked on their left by two radical groups: republicans and socialists. Whereas liberals advocated a constitutional monarchy (in the name of stability and keeping power in the hands of men of property), republicans, as their name implies, pressed further, demanding a government by the people, an expanded franchise, and democratic participation in politics. The crucial distinction between the more moderate liberals and radical republicans, therefore, depended on the criteria they used for defining citizenship. Both groups believed that government

should have the consent of citizens, but liberals were more likely to support restricted qualifications for citizenship, such as property ownership or the amount of taxes paid. Republicans were more committed to political equality and advocated more open definitions of citizenship, regardless of wealth or social standing. In thinking about the legacy of the French Revolution, therefore, liberals were likely to look favorably on the attempts by the National Assembly to create a constitution between 1789 and 1791. Republicans sympathized more openly with the Jacobins of the French Republic after 1792. Likewise, liberals remained suspicious of direct democracy and "mob rule" and sought constitutional measures that would allow propertied elites to exert their control over the political process and maintain social order. Radical republicans, on the other hand, were more likely to support civil militias, free public education, and civic liberties such as a free press and the right to assemble. In the debates between liberals and republicans, however, a general consensus about gender remained uncontroversial: only a very few liberals or republicans supported allowing women to vote. The virtues necessary for citizenship—rationality, sobriety, and independence of mind—were assumed by nearly all political thinkers of the period to be essentially masculine traits.

Where liberals called for individualism and laissez-faire, and republicans emphasized direct democracy and political equality, socialists pointed out that giving men the

QUADRILLE DANCING AT NEW LANARK, ROBERT OWEN'S MODEL COMMUNITY. Owen's Scottish experiment with cooperative production and community building, including schooling for infants, was only one of many utopian ventures in early-nineteenth-century Europe and North America.

Past and Present

Revolts against Reason

After the French Revolution, confidence in the power of reason and social progress was diminished in some quarters: many conservatives were skeptical about human improvement and some radicals, including the Saint-Simonians in France (left), sought a different kind of community and a different future than one solely based on rationality. Some of these cultural movements proved enduring and persist today in novel but recognizable forms, such as the "back-to-nature" movement of the 1960s (right).

 Watch related author interview on StudySpace
wwnorton.com/web/westernciv18

vote would not necessarily eradicate other persistent forms of injustice and inequality. To put it in the terms that were used at the time, socialists raised the "social question." How could the growing economic inequalities produced by industrialization and the miseries of working people be remedied? This "social" question, socialists insisted, was an urgent political matter. Socialists offered varied responses to this question and different ways of redistributing economic and social power. These solutions ranged from cooperation and new ways of organizing everyday life to collective ownership of the means of production; some were speculative, others very concrete.

Socialism was a nineteenth-century system of thought and a response in large measure to the visible problems ushered in by industrialization: the intensification of labor, the poverty of working-class neighborhoods in industrial cities, and the widespread perception that a hierarchy based on rank and privilege had been replaced by one based on

social class. For the socialists, the problems of industrial society were not incidental; they arose from the core principles of competition, individualism, and private property. The socialists did not oppose industry and economic development. On the contrary, what they took from the Enlightenment was a commitment to reason and human progress. They believed society could be both industrial and humane.

These radical thinkers were often explicitly utopian. Robert Owen, a wealthy industrialist turned reformer, bought a large cotton factory at New Lanark in Scotland and proceeded to organize the mill and the surrounding town according to the principles of cooperation rather than those of profitability. New Lanark organized decent housing and sanitation, good working conditions, child care, free schooling, and a system of social security for the factory's workers. Owen advocated a general reorganization of society on the basis of cooperation and mutual respect, and he tried to persuade other manufacturers of the rightness of his cause. The Frenchman Charles Fourier, too, tried to organize utopian communities based on the abolition of the wage system, the division of work according to people's natural inclinations, the complete equality of the sexes, and collectively organized child care and household labor. The charismatic socialist Flora Tristan (1803–1844) toured France speaking to workers about the principles of cooperation and the equality of men and women. Numerous men and women followed like-minded leaders into experimental communities. That so many took utopian visions seriously is a measure of people's unhappiness with early industrialization and of their conviction that society could be organized along radically different lines.

Other socialists proposed simpler, practical reforms. Louis Blanc, a French politician and journalist, campaigned for universal male suffrage with an eye to giving working-class men control of the state. Instead of protecting private property and the manufacturing class, the transformed state would become "banker of the poor," extending credit to those who needed it and establishing "associations of production," a series of workshops governed by laborers that would guarantee jobs and security for all. Such workshops were established, fleetingly, during the French Revolution of 1848. So were clubs promoting women's rights. Pierre-Joseph Proudhon (1809–1865) also proposed establishing producers' cooperatives, which would sell goods at a price workers could afford; working-class credit unions; and so on. Proudhon's "What Is Property?"—to which the famous answer was "Property is theft"—became one of the most widely read socialist pamphlets, familiar to artisans, laborers, and middle-class intellectuals, including Karl Marx. As we will see, a period of economic depression and widespread impoverishment in the 1840s brought the socialists many more working-class followers.

Karl Marx's Socialism

The father of modern socialism, Karl Marx (1818–1883), was barely known in the early nineteenth century. His reputation rose later, after 1848, when a wave of revolutions and violent confrontation seemed to confirm his distinctive theory of history and make earlier socialists' emphasis on cooperation, setting up experimental communities, and peaceful reorganization of industrial society seem naive.

Marx grew up in Trier, a city in the Rhineland close to the French border, in a region and a family keenly interested in the political debates and movements of the revolutionary era. His family was Jewish, but his father had converted to

KARL MARX, 1882. Despite the unusual smile in this portrait, Marx was near the end of his life, attempting to recuperate in Algeria from sickness and the deaths of his wife and daughter.

Protestantism to be able to work as a lawyer. Marx studied law briefly at the University of Berlin before turning instead to philosophy and particularly the ideas of Georg Wilhelm Friedrich Hegel. With the so-called Young Hegelians, a group of rebellious students who chafed under the narrow thinking of a deeply conservative Prussian university system, Marx appropriated some of Hegel's concepts for his radical politics. His radicalism (and atheism, for he repudiated all his family's religious affiliations) made it impossible for him to get a post in the university. He became a journalist, writing now-famous articles on, for instance, peasants "stealing" wood from forests that used to be common land. From 1842 to 1843 he edited the liberal *Rhineland Gazette* ("*Rheinische Zeitung*"). The paper's criticism of legal privilege and political repression put it on a collision course with the Prussian government, which closed it down and sent Marx into exile—first in Paris, then Brussels, and eventually London.

While in Paris, Marx studied early socialist theory, economics, and the history of the French Revolution. He also began a lifelong intellectual and political partnership with Friedrich Engels (1820–1895). Engels was the son of a textile manufacturer from the German Rhineland and had been sent to learn business with a merchant firm in Manchester, one of the heartlands of England's Industrial Revolution (see Chapter 19). Engels worked in the family business until 1870, but this did not prevent him from taking up his pen to denounce the miserable working and living conditions in Manchester and what he saw as the systematic inequalities of capitalism (*The Condition of the Working Classes in England,* 1844). Marx and Engels joined a small international group of radical artisans called the League of the Just, in 1847 renamed the Communist League. The league asked Marx to draft a statement of its principles, published in 1848 as *The Communist Manifesto,* with Engels listed as a coauthor.

The Communist Manifesto laid out Marx's theory of history in short form. From Hegel, Marx imported the view of history as a dynamic process, with an inner logic, moving toward human freedom. (This is a good example of the larger influence of conservative historical thinking.) In Hegel's view, the historical process did not unfold in any simple and predictable way. Instead history proceeded "dialectically," or through conflict. Hegel saw the conflict as one between ideas: a "thesis" produced an "antithesis," and the clash between the two created a distinctive and new "synthesis." In a classic example, Hegel posited that the natural but limited freedom of the savage (thesis) encountered its opposite (antithesis) in the constraints imposed on the individual by the family and by the developing institutions of civil society. The result of this clash was a new and superior freedom (synthesis), the freedom of individuals in society, protected by moral customs, law and the state.

Marx applied Hegel's dialectic, or theory of conflict, to history in a different way. He did not begin with ideas, as Hegel had, but rather with the material social and economic forces. According to this materialist vision, world history had passed through three major stages, each characterized by conflict between social groups or "classes" whose divisions were linked to the underlying economic order: master versus slave in ancient slavery, lord versus serf in feudalism, and bourgeois capitalist versus proletariat (industrial laborer) in capitalism. For Marx, this "class struggle" was the motor of human history. He believed that the feudal stage of history, where an aristocratic class dominated the enserfed peasantry, had ended in 1789, with the French Revolution. What followed was a new order, dominated by an entrepreneurial middle class—he called them "bourgeois"—who built the world of industrial capitalism.

In *The Communist Manifesto,* Marx and Engels admired the revolutionary accomplishments of capitalism, saying that the bourgeoisie had "created more impressive and more colossal productive forces than had all preceding generations together." But, they argued, the revolutionary character of capitalism would also undermine the bourgeois economic order. As capital became more concentrated in the hands of the few, a growing army of wageworkers would become increasingly aware of its economic and political disenfranchisement. This struggle between competing classes was central to industrial capitalism itself. Eventually, *The Communist Manifesto* predicted, recurring economic crises, caused by capitalism's unending need for new markets and the cyclical instability of overproduction, would bring capitalism to collapse. Workers would seize the state, reorganize the means of production, abolish private property, and eventually create a communist society based on egalitarian principles. In other words, this ultimate revolution would abolish the division of labor altogether, ending the class conflict that had been the motor of history and ushering in a future whose outlines Marx could only hesitantly describe.

What was distinctive about Marx's version of socialism? It took up the disparity between public proclamations of progress and workers' daily experiences in a systematic, scholarly manner. Marx was an inexhaustible reader and thinker, with an extraordinarily broad range. He took insights where he found them: in British economics, French history, and German philosophy. He wove others' ideas that labor was the source of value and that property was expropriation into a new theory of history that was also a thoroughgoing critique of nineteenth-century liberalism. Most important, he differed from his utopian socialist predecessors by identifying industrial laborers as a revolutionary class and by linking revolution to a vision of human history as a whole. Because the Marxist view of history began with assumptions about the economic or material base of society, and because he borrowed the idea of the dialectic from Hegel, his theory of history is sometimes referred to as *dialectical materialism.*

Citizenship and Community: Nationalism

Of all the political ideologies of the early nineteenth century, nationalism is most difficult to grasp. What, exactly, counted as a nation? Who demanded a nation, and what did their demand mean? In the early nineteenth century, nationalism was usually aligned with liberalism against the conservative states that dominated Europe after Napoleon's fall. As the century progressed, however, it became increasingly clear that nationalism could be molded to fit any doctrine.

The meaning of *nation* has changed over time. The term comes from the Latin verb *nasci,* "to be born," and suggests "common birth." In sixteenth-century England,

Karl Marx and Pierre-Joseph Proudhon, *Correspondence*

> *Karl Marx was both a prolific political and economic theorist and a political militant who corresponded with socialists and other political radicals throughout Europe. Along with Friedrich Engels, Marx was the author of* The Communist Manifesto *(1848), a widely circulated polemical critique of the capitalist economic system, which predicted the emergence of a revolutionary movement led by Europe's industrial working classes. This exchange of letters with a prominent French socialist thinker, Pierre-Joseph Proudhon, reveals disagreements among socialists in Europe about the desirability of revolution, as well as Marx's ideas about how intellectuals such as himself might participate in the revolutionary movement.*

Brussels, 5 May 1846

My dear Proudhon,

. . . I have made arrangements with the German communists and socialists for a constant interchange of letters which will be devoted to discussing scientific questions, and to keeping an eye on popular writings, and the socialist propaganda that can be carried on in Germany by this means. The chief aim of our correspondence, however, will be to put the German socialists in touch with the French and English socialists; to keep foreigners constantly informed of the socialist movements that occur in Germany and to inform the Germans in Germany of the progress of socialism in France and England. In this way differences of opinion can be brought to light and an exchange of ideas and impartial criticism can take place. It will be a step made by the social movement in its *literary* manifestation to rid itself of the barriers of *nationality*. And when the moment for action comes, it will clearly be much to everyone's advantage to be acquainted with the state of affairs abroad as well as at home.

Our correspondence will embrace not only the communists in Germany, but also the German socialists in Paris and London. Our relations with England have already been established. So far as France is concerned, we all of us believe that we could find no better correspondent than yourself. As you know, the English and Germans have hitherto estimated you more highly than have your own compatriots.

So it is, you see, simply a question of establishing a regular correspondence and ensuring that it has the means to keep abreast of the social movement in the different countries, and to acquire a rich and varied interest, such as could never be achieved by the work of one single person. . . .

Yours most sincerely
Karl Marx

---

the nation designated the aristocracy, or those who shared noble birthright. The French nobility also referred to itself as a nation. Those earlier and unfamiliar usages are important. They highlight the most significant development of the late eighteenth and early nineteenth centuries: the French Revolution redefined *nation* to mean "the sovereign people." The revolutionaries of 1789 boldly claimed that the nation, and no longer the king, was the sovereign power. *Vive la nation,* or "long live the nation"— a phrase found everywhere, from government decrees to revolutionary festivals, engravings, and memorabilia— celebrated a new political community, not a territory or

Lyon, 17 May 1846

My dear Monsieur Marx,

I am happy to become a recipient of your correspondence, whose goal and organization seem to me to be very useful. I cannot promise to write you at length or often, however, as my many occupations and my natural laziness will not permit such epistolary efforts. I would also like to take the liberty of expressing several reservations about a few of the passages in your letter.

First, [. . .] I believe that it is my duty, and the duty of all socialists, to maintain for the time being a skeptical or critical perspective, in a word, I claim [in matters of economics] an almost absolute antidogmatism.

Let us search together, if you wish, the laws of society, and the ways that these laws make themselves felt, and the process of development that allows us to discover them; but by God, after having demolished all the *a priori* dogmatisms, let us not dream of then indoctrinating the people ourselves, do not fall into the same contradiction faced by your compatriot Martin Luther, who after having overthrown Catholic theology, set about at once excommunicating others, in order to found a Protestant theology. [. . .] I applaud with all my heart your idea of bringing forth all possible opinions; let us therefore pursue a good and loyal argument; let us offer the world an example of a wise and perceptive toleration, but we should not, simply because we are the leaders of a movement, seek to pose as the apostles of a new religion, even if this religion is that of logic, of reason. Under these terms, I am happy to join your association, but if not–then No!

I would also like to comment on these words in your letter: *At the moment of action.* You may still think that no reform is possible at present without a bold stroke, without what was formerly called a revolution [. . .] Having myself held this opinion for a long time, I confess now that my more recent works have made me revisit this idea completely. I believe that we do not need [a revolution] to succeed, because this alleged solution would simply be an appeal to force, to something arbitrary, in short, a contradiction. I see the problem like this: *to find a form of economic combination that would restore to society the wealth that has been taken from it by another form of economic combination.* In other words, [. . .] to turn Property against Property, in such a way as to establish what you German socialists call *community,* and which I limit myself to calling *liberty, equality.* [. . .] I prefer to burn Property with a slow fuse, rather than to give it new energy by massacring the property owners.

Your very devoted
Pierre-Joseph Proudhon

Source: Karl Marx, Frederick Engels, *Collected Works,* vol. 38 (New York: International Publishers, 1982), pp. 38–40. P.-J. Proudhon, Amédée Jérôme, *Correspondance de P.-J. Proudhon* (Paris: A. Lacroix, 1875), pp. 198–200.

Questions for Analysis

1. What is the purpose of the network of correspondents that Marx was inviting Proudhon to join, and why did he believe it necessary to overcome "the barriers of nationality"?

2. Why does Proudhon compare Marx's analysis of "scientific questions" or "the laws of society" to religious dogmas?

3. Why does Proudhon reject Marx's assumption that a revolution is necessary, and what alternative does he propose?

---

an ethnicity. Philosophically, the French revolutionaries and the others who developed their views took from Jean-Jacques Rousseau the argument that a regenerated nation, based on the equality of its members (or on the limits of that equality; see Chapter 18), was not only more just but also more powerful. On a more concrete level, the revolutionaries built a national state, a national army, and a national legal system whose jurisdiction trumped the older regional powers of the nobility and local courts. In the aftermath of the French Revolution of 1789, the nation became what one historian calls "the collective image of modern citizenry."

MAJOR EUROPEAN LANGUAGE GROUPS, c. 1850. Compare the distribution of language groups in Europe with the political boundaries of European nations in 1848. ■ *Do they line up?* ■ *Which political units were forced to deal with a multitude of languages within their borders?* ■ *How might this distribution of language groups be related to the history of European nationalisms?*

In the early nineteenth century, then, *nation* symbolized legal equality, constitutional government, and unity, or an end to feudal privileges and divisions. Conservatives disliked the term. National unity and the creation of national political institutions threatened to erode the local power of aristocratic elites. New nations rested on constitutions, which, as we have seen, conservatives considered dangerous abstractions. Nationalism became an important rallying cry for liberals across Europe in the early nineteenth century precisely because it was associated with political transformation. It celebrated the achievements and political awakening of the common people.

Nationalism also went hand in hand with liberal demands for economic modernity. Economists, such as the influential German Friedrich List (1789–1846), sought to develop national economies and national infrastructures:

larger, stronger, better integrated, and more effective systems of banking, trade, transportation, production, and distribution. List linked ending the territorial fragmentation of the German states and the development of manufacturing to "culture, prosperity, and liberty."

Nationalism, however, could easily undermine other liberal values. When liberals insisted on the value and importance of individual liberties, those committed to building nations replied that their vital task might require the sacrifice of some measure of each citizen's freedom. The Napoleonic army, a particularly powerful symbol of nationhood, appealed to conservative proponents of military strength and authority as well as to liberals who wanted an army of citizens.

Nineteenth-century nationalists wrote as if national feeling were natural, inscribed in the movement of history. They waxed poetic about the sudden awakening of feelings slumbering within the collective consciousness of a "German," an "Italian," a "French," or a "British" people. This is misleading. National identity (like religious, gender, or ethnic identities) developed and changed historically. It rested on specific nineteenth-century political and economic developments; on rising literacy; on the creation of national institutions such as schools or the military; and on the new importance of national rituals, from voting to holidays, village festivals, and the singing of anthems. Nineteenth-century governments sought to develop national feeling, to link their peoples more closely to their states. State-supported educational systems taught a "national" language, fighting the centrifugal forces of traditional dialects. Italian became the official language of the Italian nation, despite the fact that only 2.5 percent of the population spoke it. In other words, even a minority could define a national culture. Textbooks and self-consciously nationalist theater, poetry, and painting helped elaborate and sometimes "invent" a national heritage.

Political leaders associated the nation with specific causes. But ordinary activities, such as reading a daily newspaper in the morning, helped people imagine and identify with their fellow citizens. As one influential historian puts it, "All communities larger than primordial villages of face-to-face contact (and perhaps even these) are imagined." The nation is imagined as "limited," "sovereign," and "finally, it is imagined as a community, because regardless of the actual inequality and exploitation that may prevail . . . , the nation is always conceived as a deep, horizontal comradeship." The different meanings of *nationhood,* the various political beliefs it evoked, and the powerful emotions it tapped made nationalism exceptionally unpredictable.

Eventually, conservatives, liberals, and republicans all implicitly recognized the power of nationalism by attempting to describe a vision of the nation that was compatible with their core principles. Conservatives linked dynastic ruling families and aristocratic elites to "national" traditions embodied in the history of territorially rooted peasant cultures and their traditional rulers. Liberals and republicans praised the nation as a body of free citizens. Marxist socialists, on the other hand, rejected the claims of nationalists, saying that the interest of social classes trumped national identity. The resolutely internationalist message of *The Communist Manifesto* was embodied in its concluding motto: "Workers of the world unite!"

Conservatism, liberalism, republicanism, socialism, and nationalism were the principal political ideologies of the early nineteenth century. They were rooted in the eighteenth century but brought to the forefront by the political turmoil of the early nineteenth century. Some nineteenth-century ideologies were continuations of the French revolutionary trio: liberty (from arbitrary authority), equality (or the end of legal privilege), and fraternity (the creation of new communities of citizens). Others, like conservatism, were reactions against the French Revolution. All could be reinterpreted. All became increasingly common points of reference as the century unfolded.

CULTURAL REVOLT: ROMANTICISM

Romanticism, the most significant cultural movement in the early nineteenth century, touched all the arts and permeated politics as well. It marked a reaction against the Classicism of the eighteenth century and the Enlightenment. Whereas Classicism aspired to reason, discipline, and harmony, Romanticism stressed emotion, freedom, and imagination. Romantic artists prized intense individual experiences and considered intuition and emotion to be better guides to truth and human happiness than reason and logic.

British Romantic Poetry

Romanticism developed first in England and Germany as a reaction against the Enlightenment. Early Romantics developed ideas originating from some of the Enlightenment's dissenters, such as Jean-Jacques Rousseau (see Chapter 17). The poet William Wordsworth (1770–1834) took up Rousseau's central themes—nature, simplicity, and feeling—in his *Lyrical Ballads* (1798). For Wordsworth, poetry was "the spontaneous overflow of powerful feelings," and like Rousseau, he also emphasized the ties of compassion that bind all humankind, regardless of social class. "We have all of us one human heart," he wrote, "men who do not wear fine cloths can feel deeply." Wordsworth considered nature to be humanity's most trustworthy teacher and the source of true feeling. His poems were inspired by the wild hills and tumbledown cottages of England's Lake District. In "The Ruined Cottage," he quoted from the Scottish Romantic poet Robert Burns:

> Give me a spark of Nature's fire,
> 'Tis the best learning I desire . . .
> My muse, though homely in attire,
> May touch the heart.

Wordsworth's poetry, along with that of his colleague Samuel Taylor Coleridge (1772–1834), offered a key theme of nineteenth-century Romanticism: a view of nature that rejected the abstract mechanism of eighteenth-century Enlightenment thought. Nature was not a system to be dissected by science but the source of a sublime power that nourished the human soul.

The poet William Blake (1757–1827) sounded similar themes in his fierce critique of industrial society and the factories (which he called "dark satanic mills") that blighted the English landscape. Blake championed the individual imagination and poetic vision, seeing both as transcending the limits of the material world. Imagination could awaken human sensibilities and sustain belief in different values, breaking humanity's "mind-forged manacles." Blake's poetry paralleled early socialist efforts to imagine a better world. And like many Romantics, Blake looked back to a past in which he thought society had been more organic and humane.

English Romanticism peaked with the next generation of poets—Lord Byron (1788–1824); Percy Bysshe Shelley (1792–1822); and John Keats (1795–1821). Their lives and loves often appealed to readers as much as their writings. Byron was an aristocrat, rich, handsome, and defiant of convention. Poetry, he wrote, was the "lava of the imagination, whose eruption prevents an earthquake." His love affairs helped give Romantics their reputation as rebels against conformity, but they were hardly carefree. Byron treated his wife cruelly and drove her away after a year. Byron also rebelled against Britain's political leaders, labeling them corrupt and repressive. A Romantic hero, he defended working-class movements and fought in the war for Greek independence, during which he died of tuberculosis. Byron's friend Percy Shelley emphasized similar themes of individual audacity in his poem, *Prometheus*

***NEWTON* BY WILLIAM BLAKE, 1795.** Blake was also a brilliant graphic artist. Here, he depicts Sir Isaac Newton shrouded in darkness, distracted by his scientific calculations from the higher sphere of the imagination. Blake's image is a Romantic critique of Enlightenment science, for which Newton had become a hero.

Unbound (1820). Prometheus defied an all-powerful god, Zeus, by stealing fire for humanity and was punished by being chained to a rock while an eagle tore out his heart. The poem celebrated the title character as a selfless mythic hero, comparable to Christ in his willingness to sacrifice himself for others. Shelley himself in his correspondence described the play as a parable about revolutionary change, and the need to overthrow tyranny in the name of a new political ideal of struggle and hope, a sentiment captured in the play's closing lines:

> To suffer woes which Hope thinks infinite;
> To forgive wrongs darker than Death or Night;
> To defy Power, which seems omnipotent;
> To love, and bear; to hope till Hope creates
> From its own wreck the thing it contemplates;
> Neither to change nor falter nor repent
> This, like thy glory, Titan! is to be
> Good, great, and joyous, beautiful and free;
> This is alone Life, Joy, Empire, and Victory.

Women Writers, Gender, and Romanticism

No romantic work was more popular than Mary Shelley's *Frankenstein* (1818). Shelley was the daughter of radical celebrities—the philosopher William Godwin and the feminist Mary Wollstonecraft (see Chapter 17), who died as her daughter was born. Mary Godwin met Percy Shelley when she was sixteen, had three children by him before they were married, and published *Frankenstein* at twenty. The novel captured the Romantic critique of science and Enlightenment reason and tells the story of an eccentric doctor determined to find the secret of human life. Conducting his research on corpses and body parts retrieved from charnel houses, Dr. Frankenstein produced life in the form of a monster. The monster had human feelings but was overwhelmed by loneliness and self-hatred when his creator cast him out. Shelley told the story as a twisted creation myth, a study of individual genius gone wrong. The novel remains one of the most memorable characterizations in literature of the limits of reason and the impossibility of controlling nature.

The Romantic's belief in individuality and creativity led in several directions. It became a cult of artistic genius—of the "inexplicably and uniquely creative individual" who could see things others could not. It also led people to seek out experiences that would elicit intense emotions and spark their imagination and creativity, ranging from foreign travel to using opium. The Romantic style encouraged the daring to defy convention as did Lord Byron, the Shelleys, and the French writer George Sand (1804–1876). Sand, like Byron, cultivated a persona—in her case, by living as a woman writer, taking lovers at her pleasure, and wearing men's clothing.

Women played an important role in Romantic writing, and Romanticism stimulated new thinking about gender and creativity. It was common at the time to assert that men were rational and women emotional or intuitive. Many Romantics, like their contemporaries, accepted such gender differences as natural, and some exalted the superior moral virtues of women. Since Romanticism placed such value on the emotions as an essential part of artistic creation, however, some female writers or painters were able to use these ideas to claim a place for themselves in the world of letters

MARY SHELLEY'S *FRANKENSTEIN*. Perhaps the best-known work of Romantic fiction, *Frankenstein* joined the Romantic critique of Enlightenment reason with early-nineteenth-century ambivalence about science to create a striking horror story. Shelley (pictured at left, around the time she published *Frankenstein*) was the daughter of the philosopher William Godwin and the feminist Mary Wollstonecraft; she married the poet Percy Shelley. On the right is an engraving from the first illustrated edition (1831) by Theodore von Holst.

MARY SHELLEY AT NINETEEN

and the arts. Germaine de Staël (1766–1817), for example, emigrated from revolutionary France to Germany and played a key part in popularizing German Romanticism in France. The language of Romanticism allowed Madame de Staël to describe herself as a genius, by way of explaining her own subversion of social norms. Romantics such as Madame de Staël suggested that men too could be emotional and that feelings were a part of a common human nature shared by both sexes. For many literate middle-class people, the language of Romanticism gave them a way to express their own search for individual expression and feeling in writing—and in thinking—about love. In this way, Romanticism reached well beyond small circles of artists and writers into the everyday writing and thoughts of European men and women.

Romantic Painting

Painters carried the Romantic themes of nature and imagination onto their canvases (see **Interpreting Visual Evidence** on pages 682–83). In Great Britain, John Constable (1776–1837) and J. M. W. Turner (1775–1851) developed more emotional and poetic approaches to depicting nature. "It is the soul that sees," wrote Constable, echoing Wordsworth. Constable studied Isaac Newton and the properties of light but aimed to capture the "poetry" of a rainbow. Turner's intensely subjective paintings were even more unconventional. His experiments with brushstroke and color produced remarkable images. Critics assailed the paintings, calling them incomprehensible, but Turner merely responded, "I did not paint it to be understood." In France, Théodore Géricault (1791–1824) and Eugène Delacroix (1799–1863) produced very different paintings from Turner's, but like the English painter they too were preoccupied by subjectivity and the creative process. The poet Charles Baudelaire credited Delacroix with showing him new ways to see: "The whole visible universe is but a storehouse of images and signs. . . . All the faculties of the human soul must be subordinated to the imagination." These Romantic experiments prepared the way for the later development of modernism in the arts.

Romantic Politics: Liberty, History, and Nation

Victor Hugo (1802–1885) wrote that "Romanticism is only . . . liberalism in literature." Hugo's plays, poetry, and historical novels focused sympathetically on the experience of common people, especially *Notre Dame de Paris* (1831)

and *Les Misérables* (1862). Delacroix's painting *Liberty Leading the People* gave a revolutionary face to Romanticism, as did Shelley's and Byron's poetry. In works such as these, political life was no longer the preserve of social elites, and the commoners in the street could embrace new freedoms with a violent passion that would have surprised the *philosophes,* with their emphasis on reasoned debate.

Yet Romantics could also be ardently conservative. French conservative François Chateaubriand's *Genius of Christianity* (1802) emphasized the primacy of religious emotions and feeling in his claim that religion was woven into the national past and could not be ignored without threatening the culture as a whole. The period, in fact, witnessed a broad and popular religious revival and a renewed interest in medieval literature, art, and architecture, all of which drew heavily on religious themes.

Early nineteenth-century nationalism took the Romantic emphasis on individuality and turned it into a faith in the uniqueness of individual cultures. Johann von Herder, among the most influential of nationalist thinkers, argued that civilization sprang from the culture of the common people, not from a learned or cultivated elite, as the *philosophes* had argued in the Enlightenment. Herder extolled the special creative genius of the German people, the *Volk,* and insisted that each nation must be true to its own particular heritage and history.

The Romantic's keen interest in history and the lives of ordinary people led to new kinds of literary and historical works. The brothers Grimm, editors of the famous collection of fairy tales (1812–1815), traveled across Germany to study native dialects and folktales. The poet Friedrich Schiller retold the story of William Tell (1804) to promote German national consciousness, but the Italian composer Gioacchino Rossini turned Schiller's poem into an opera that promoted Italian nationalism. In Britain, Sir Walter Scott retold the popular history of Scotland and the Pole Adam Mickiewicz wrote a national epic *Pan Tadeusz* ("Lord Thaddeus") as a vision of a Polish past that had been lost. After 1848, these nationalist enthusiasms would overwhelm the political debates that divided conservatives from liberals and socialists in the first half of the nineteenth century (see Chapter 21).

Orientalism

This passion for theories and histories of distinctive cultures also created broad interest in what contemporary Europeans called the "Orient"—a catch-all term used rather indiscriminately and confusedly to refer to the non-European cultures of North Africa, the eastern Mediterranean, the

Arabian Peninsula, and eventually to the vast and densely populated lands of southern and eastern Asia. Napoleon wrote, "This Europe of ours is a molehill. Only in the East, where 600 million human beings live, is it possible to found great empires and realize great revolutions." The dozens of scholars who accompanied Napoleon on his invasion of Egypt in 1798 collected information on Egyptian history and culture. Among the artifacts the French took from Egypt was the Rosetta Stone, with versions of the same text in three different languages: hieroglyphic writing (pictorial script), demotic (an early alphabetic writing), and Greek, which scholars used to decode and translate the first two. The twenty-three volume, lavishly illustrated *Description of Egypt*, published in French between 1809 and 1828, was a major event, heightening the soaring interest in Eastern languages and history. "We are now all orientalists," wrote Victor Hugo in 1829. The political echoes to this cultural fascination with the East could be seen in great power rivalries that surfaced in the British incursion into India, in the Greek war for independence, and in the French invasion of Algeria in 1830.

Nineteenth-century Europeans cast the "Orient" as a contrasting mirror for their own civilization, a process that did more to create a sense of their own identity as Europeans than it did to promote an accurate understanding of the diversity of cultures that lay beyond Europe's uncertain eastern and southern frontiers. During the Greek war for independence, Europeans identified with Greek heritage against Oriental despotism. Romantic painters such as Delacroix depicted the landscapes of the East in bold and sensuous colors and emphasized the sensuality, mystery, and irrationality of Eastern peoples. The fascination with medieval history and religion shared by many Romantic writers also bred interest in the medieval crusades in the Holy Lands of the Middle East—important subjects for Romantics such as Scott and Chateaubriand. These habits of mind, encouraged by Romantic literature and art, helped to crystallize a sense of what were felt to be essential differences between the East and the West.

Goethe and Beethoven

Two important artists of the period are especially difficult to classify. Johann Wolfgang von Goethe (1749–1832) had an enormous influence on the Romantic movement with his early novel *The Passions of Young Werther* (1774), which told the story of a young man's failure in love and eventual suicide. The novel brought international fame to its young author, though many who sympathized with the main character perhaps missed the point about the self-destructiveness of

***WOMEN OF ALGIERS* BY EUGÈNE DELACROIX.** This is one of many paintings done during Delacroix's trips through North Africa and a good example of the Romantics' Orientalism.

the "cult of feeling." Rumors spread that some in his audience identified so strongly with Werther's alienation that they killed themselves in imitation. Though scholars now doubt that such suicides occurred, the rumor itself indicates the fascination that Goethe's emotionally complex character exerted over the reading public. The significance of the novel lay in Goethe's ability to capture in prose the longing that many middle-class readers felt for something more meaningful than a life lived in strict conformity with social expectations. It also revealed that a new sense of self and aspirations for self-fulfillment might be emerging in Europe alongside the narrower definitions of individualism that one might find in liberal political or economic theory. In his masterpiece, *Faust*, published in part in 1790 and finished just before his death in 1832, Goethe retold the German story of a man who sold his soul to the devil for eternal youth and universal knowledge. *Faust*, written in dramatic verse, was more Classical in its tone, though it still expressed a Romantic concern with spiritual freedom and humanity's daring in probing life's divine mysteries.

The composer Ludwig van Beethoven (1770–1827) was steeped in the principles of Classical music composition, but his insistence that instrumental music without vocal

Romantic Painting

Romantic painters shared with Romantic poets a fascination with the power of nature. To convey this vision of nature as both an overwhelming power and source of creative energy, Romantic painters created new and poetic visions of the natural world, where human beings and their activities were reduced in significance, sometimes nearly disappearing altogether. At times, these visions also were linked to a backward-looking perspective, as if the dramatic changes associated with industrialization provoked a longing for a premodern past, where Europeans sought and found their sense of place in the world from an awareness of a quasi-divine natural setting invested with powerful mysteries. John Martin's *The Bard* (image A) shows a highly romanticized vision of a medieval subject: a single Welsh bard strides across rocky peaks above a mountain river, after escaping a massacre ordered by the English king Edward I. Across the river, Edward's troops can barely be seen leaving the scene of the crime, which still glows with destructive fires. The emotional qualities of this early expression of Romantic nationalism are reinforced by the forbidding and dynamic sky above, where the clouds merge into the Welsh mountaintops as if they were stirred by the hand of God himself.

Other Romantic painters minimized the significance of human activity in their landscapes, though without reference to history. John Constable's *Weymouth Bay* (image B) contains a tiny, almost imperceptible human figure in the middle ground, a man walking on the beach, near a thin stone wall that snakes up a hill in the background. These passing references to human lives are completely dominated, however, by Constable's sky and the movement of the clouds in particular, which seem to be the real subject of the painting.

Of all the Romantic painters, J. M. W. Turner (image C) may have tackled the tricky subject of the new industrialized landscape in the most novel way. His painting *Rain, Steam, Speed—The Great Western Railway* (1844) boldly places the most modern technology of the period,

A. John Martin, *The Bard*, 1817.

B. John Constable, *Weymouth Bay*, 1816.

C. J. M. W. Turner, *Rain, Steam, Speed—The Great Western Railway*, 1844.

the steam train on an arched bridge, into a glowing and radiant painting where both nature's forces and the tremendous new power unleashed by human activity seem to merge into one continuous burst of energy. To the left of the train, on the river's edge, a fire of indeterminate but evidently industrial origin burns, illuminating several small but ecstatic figures with its light. Most enigmatic of all, a tiny rabbit sprints ahead of the train between the rails (unfortunately invisible in this reproduction), highlighting the painting's complex message about nature and human creation. Are they heading in the same direction? Will one overtake the other and destroy it in the process?

Questions for Analysis

1. In Martin's *Bard*, what vision of the individual emerges from this painting, and how is it different from the rational, rights-bearing individual that political liberalism sought to protect?

2. Is Constable's painting concerned with nature as a source of nourishment for humans, or is it presented as a value in itself?

3. How is one to interpret Turner's explicit connection between the power of nature and the new force of industrial societies? Is he suggesting that contemplating the industrial landscape can be just as moving to a human observer as is the sight of nature's magnificence?

accompaniment could be more expressive of emotion made him a key figure for later Romantic composers. The glorification of nature and Romantic individuality rang clearly throughout his work. Like many of his contemporaries, Beethoven was enthusiastic about the French Revolution in 1789, but he became disillusioned with Napoleon. At the age of thirty-two he began to lose his hearing, and by 1819 he was completely deaf—the intensely personal crisis that this catastrophe produced in the young musician drove him to retreat into the interior of his own musical imagination, and the compositions of his later life expressed both his powerfully felt alienation as well as his extraordinary and heroic creativity in the face of enormous hardship.

Beethoven and Goethe marked the transition between eighteenth-century artistic movements that prized order and harmony to the turbulent and disruptive emotions of the nineteenth-century artists and writers. Their work embraced the cult of individual heroism, sympathized with the Romantic's quasi-mystical view of nature, and represented different aspects of a shared search for new ways of seeing and hearing. The many shapes of Romanticism make a simple definition of the movement elusive, but at the core, the Romantics sought to find a new way of expressing emotion, and in doing so, they sent nineteenth-century art in a new direction.

CONCLUSION

With the fizzling of the Chartist movement, the British monarchy avoided an outbreak of revolution in 1848. Monarchs on the Continent were not so lucky. As we will see in the next chapter, a wave of revolutionary activity unprecedented since the 1790s spread to nearly every capital in Europe in 1848. This resurgence of rebellion and revolt pointed to the powerful ways that the French Revolution of 1789 polarized Europe in the first half of the nineteenth century. In its aftermath, the Congress of Vienna aimed to establish a new conservative, international system and to prevent further revolutions. It succeeded in the first aim but only partially in the second. A combination of new political movements and economic hardship undermined the conservative order. Social grievances and political disappointments created powerful movements for change, first in Latin America and the Balkans and then in western Europe and Great Britain.

All of the contesting ideologies of these postrevolutionary decades could point to a longer history: conservatives could point to traditional religious justifications for royal authority and the absolutist's conception of indivisible monarchical power; liberals could point to the debates

After You Read This Chapter

Visit StudySpace for quizzes, additional review materials, and multimedia documents. **wwnorton.com/web/westernciv18**

REVIEWING THE OBJECTIVES

- The European leaders who met at the Congress of Vienna possessed a conservative vision for post–Napoleonic Europe. What were their goals and what challenges did their political system face between 1815 and 1848?
- Slavery persisted long after the French Revolution. What accounts for the development of an abolition movement, and why did it persist in the United States, Latin America, and Cuba?
- Conservatives, liberals, and republicans differed from one another about the lessons to be learned from the French Revolution, while socialists sought to address the inequalities produced by the Industrial Revolution. What were the core principles of conservatism, liberalism, republicanism, and socialism?
- Nationalism reshaped the political landscape in Europe between 1815 and 1848. How did conservatives, liberals, republicans, and socialists view the claims of nationalists?
- Romanticism was a cultural movement defined in opposition to the Enlightenment. Who were the Romantics and what did they believe?

about the rule of law in the English revolution of the seventeenth century; even socialists could point to age-old collective traditions among rural communities as precedents for their defense of communal property and egalitarianism. Nevertheless, all of these ideologies were shaped and brought into clearer focus during these decades by the combined effects of the French Revolution and industrialization. Conservatives may have differed among themselves as to why they preferred a government of monarchs and landed aristocrats, but they were united by their horror of revolutionary violence and dismayed by the social disruptions that attended industrialization. Liberals may have disagreed with each other about who qualified for citizenship, but they defended the revolutionary's insistence that the only legitimate government was one whose institutions and laws reflected the consent of at least some, if not all, of the governed. Many socialists, Marx included, celebrated the insurrectionary tradition of the French revolutionaries, even as they demanded a reordering of society that went far beyond the granting of new political rights to include a redistribution of society's wealth. Meanwhile, nationalists throughout Europe remained inspired by the collective achievements of the French nation that was forged in revolution in the 1790s.

The reemergence of social and political conflict in 1848 pit the defenders of these ideologies against one another under the most dramatic of circumstances, making the revolutions of 1848 the opening act of a much larger drama. In France, as in 1792 and 1830, revolutionaries rallied around an expanded notion of representative government and the question of suffrage, though they were divided on how much responsibility their new government had for remedying social problems. In southern and central Europe, as we will see in the next chapter, the issues were framed differently, around new struggles for national identity. The eventual failure of these revolutions set a pattern that was also observed elsewhere: exhilarating revolutionary successes were followed by a breakdown of revolutionary unity and the emergence of new forms of conservative government. The crisis of 1848 became a turning point for all of Europe. The broad revolutionary alliances that had pushed for revolutionary change since 1789 were broken apart by class politics, and earlier forms of utopian socialism gave way to Marxism. In culture as in politics, Romanticism lost its appeal, its expansive sense of possibility replaced by the more biting viewpoint of realism. No nationalist, conservative, liberal, or socialist was exempt from this bitter truth after the violent conflicts of 1848.

PEOPLE, IDEAS, AND EVENTS IN CONTEXT

- Who was **KLEMENS VON METTERNICH** and what was the **CONCERT OF EUROPE**?

- How did the **CARBONARI** in Italy, the **DECEMBRISTS** in Russia, and **GREEK NATIONALISTS** in the Balkans in the 1820s disturb the conservative order in Europe after Napoleon's defeat?

- Where did revolutions occur in 1830–1832, and what was their outcome?

- What political changes did movements such as the **CHARTISTS** or the **ANTI-CORN LAW LEAGUE** accomplish in Britain? Why was there no revolution in Britain?

- What beliefs made **EDMUND BURKE** a conservative?

- What beliefs made **ADAM SMITH** and **JEREMY BENTHAM** liberals? What was **UTILITARIANISM**?

- What beliefs did **UTOPIAN SOCIALISTS** such as **ROBERT OWEN** and **CHARLES FOURIER** share? What made **KARL MARX**'s brand of socialism different from his predecessors'?

- How did the values of **ROMANTICISM** challenge Europeans to reconsider their assumptions about the differences between men and women?

- What beliefs led romantic writers such as **WILLIAM WORDSWORTH**, **WILLIAM BLAKE**, and **LORD BYRON** to reject the rationalism of the Enlightenment and embrace emotion and imagination as the most essential and vital aspects of human experience?

THINKING ABOUT CONNECTIONS

- What new ideas about historical change made it possible to think in terms of a political conflict between "conservatives" and "revolutionaries" during the decades immediately before and after 1800? Would such an opposition have been conceivable in earlier periods of history?

- Terms such as *conservative*, *liberal*, and *socialist* are still used today in contemporary political debates. Do they still mean the same thing as they did between 1815 and 1848?

Before
You
Read
This
Chapter

Revolutions and Nation Building, 1848–1871

CORE OBJECTIVES

- **EXPLAIN** why so many revolutions occurred nearly simultaneously in Europe in 1848.

- **UNDERSTAND** the causes and failure of the revolutions of 1848 in France.

- **DESCRIBE** the goals of revolutionaries in the German-speaking lands of central Europe and their relationship to the monarchies of Prussia and Austria.

- **IDENTIFY** the social groups that supported a process of national unification from below, by the people, in Italy and Germany and those that favored a process of national unification directed from the top, by the state.

- **DESCRIBE** the process of nation building in Russia and the United States in the nineteenth century and the ensuing debates about slavery.

- **IDENTIFY** the powers involved in the Crimean War, the Austro-Prussian War, and the Franco-Prussian War, and understand how these wars changed the balance of power in Europe.

The year 1848 was a tumultuous one. From Paris to Berlin, and Budapest to Rome, insurgents rushed to hastily built barricades, forcing kings and princes to beat an equally hasty—though only temporary—retreat. Perhaps the most highly symbolic moment came on March 13, 1848, when Klemens von Metternich, the primary architect of the Concert of Europe, was forced to resign as minister of state in the Austrian capital of Vienna while a revolutionary crowd outside celebrated his departure. Metternich's balanced system of international relations, where stability was guaranteed by reinforcing the legitimacy of traditional dynastic rulers against movements for reform, was swept aside in a wave of enthusiasm for liberal political ideals and popular anger. Metternich himself was forced to flee to England, which less than one month earlier had also welcomed King Louis-Philippe of France, after another revolution in France.

Metternich's downfall and the collapse of the French monarchy made clear that the 1848 revolutions were strongly linked to powerful forces for change unleashed earlier by the French Revolution. At the same time, however, this was also the year that Karl Marx and Friedrich Engels published *The Communist Manifesto*, which announced as its goal an even more sweeping remaking of society than that imagined by the French revolutionaries of 1789. If 1848 was the last wave of the revolutionary movements that began in Europe and the Atlantic world at the end of the eighteenth century, it was also the first chapter in a new revolutionary movement that would have enormous consequences in the twentieth century.

Revolutionary regime change, territorial expansion, economic development, and debates about who deserved citizenship: all of these were issues in 1848, and all were related to the spread of nationalism and nation building in Europe and the Americas. As we saw in the last chapter, the term *nation* had taken on a new meaning at the end of the eighteenth century and had come to mean "a sovereign people." *Nationalism* was a related political ideal, based on the assumption that governments could be legitimate only if they reflected the character, history, and customs of the nation—that is, the common people. This idea undermined the assumptions of Europe's dynastic rulers, as hereditary monarchs had emphasized the differences between themselves and the people they ruled. Kings and aristocrats often did not even speak the same language as their subjects. Nobody would have thought this odd before 1789, since peasants often spoke regional dialects that were different from the language spoken in cities. But once the notion of national sovereignty emanating from the people became widespread, such discrepancies between the language and culture of elites and of the common people loomed larger as political questions that needed to be solved. Intellectuals, revolutionaries, and governments all propagated the radical new idea that nations of like peoples and the states that ruled over them should be congruent with one another. This simple idea lay at the heart of all forms of nationalism, but there was often bitter debate about who best represented the nation and what the goals of a unified nationalist government should be.

Between 1789 and 1848, Europeans commonly associated nationalism with liberalism. Liberals saw constitutions, the rule of law, and elected assemblies as necessary expressions of the people's will, and they sought to use popular enthusiasm for liberal forms of nationalism against the conservative monarchs of Europe. The upheavals of 1848 marked the high point of this period of liberal revolution, and their failure marked the end of that age. By the end of the nineteenth century, conservative governments also found ways to mobilize popular support by invoking nationalist themes. The only political movement to swim against the tide of nationalism was that of the socialists, who stressed the importance of class unity across national boundaries: Marx and his followers believed that German, French, and British workers had more in common with each other than with their middle-class employers. Even so, however, socialist movements in Europe developed in distinctly different nationalist political contexts, making traditions of French socialism different from German socialism, or from Italian socialism, for example.

The years following the 1848 revolutions witnessed a shift in the connections between liberalism, nationalism, and nation building. In the United States, territorial changes such as the treaty of Guadalupe Hidalgo transformed the boundaries of nations; equally significant was the American Civil War, which resulted in wrenching political change. The unification of Germany and Italy in the years after 1848 also involved the conquest of territory, but the process could not have been completed without political reforms and new state structures that changed how governments worked and how they related to their citizens. The governments of France, Britain, Russia, and Austria undertook vast projects of administrative reform during this period: they overhauled their bureaucracies, expanded their electorates, and reorganized relations among ethnic groups. The Russian tsar abolished serfdom, and Abraham Lincoln, an American president, abolished slavery, decades after the French and British had prohibited slavery in their territories.

As the process of nation building continued, the balance of power in Europe shifted toward the states that were the earliest to industrialize and most successful in building strong, centralized states. Older imperial powers such as the Habsburg Empire in Austria-Hungary or the Ottoman Empire found their influence waning, in spite of their long history of successful rule over vast territories with diverse populations. At the heart of this nineteenth-century period of nation building lay changing relations between states and those they governed, and these changes were hastened by reactions to the revolutionary upheavals of 1848.

THE REVOLUTIONS OF 1848

Throughout Europe, the spring of 1848 brought a dizzying sequence of revolution and repression. The roots of revolution lay in economic crisis, social antagonisms, and political grievances. But these revolutions were also shaped decisively by nationalism, especially in southern, central, and eastern Europe. To be sure, reformers and revolutionaries had liberal goals: representative government, an end to privilege, economic development, and so on. They also sought some form of national unity. Indeed, reformers in Germany, Italy, Poland, and the Austrian Empire believed that their liberal goals might be realized only in a vigorous, "modern" nation-state. The fate of the 1848 revolutions in these regions demonstrated nationalism's power to mobilize opponents of the regime and also its potential to splinter revolutionary alliances and to override other allegiances and values entirely.

The Hungry Forties

A deteriorating economic climate in Europe was an important contributing factor to the outbreak of revolution in 1848, one that helps to explain why revolutions occurred in so many places nearly simultaneously. Poor harvests in the early 1840s were followed by two years in 1845–46 when the grain harvest failed completely. A potato blight brought starvation in Ireland and hunger in Germany (see **Competing Viewpoints** on pages 690–91). Food prices doubled in 1846–47, and bread riots broke out across Europe. Villagers attacked carts carrying grain, refusing to let merchants take it to other markets. At times, hungry people seized the grain and forced the merchants to sell it at what they thought was a "just" price. Compounding the problem was a cyclical industrial slowdown that spread across Europe, throwing thousands into unemployment. Starving peasants and unemployed laborers swamped public-relief organizations in many European cities. The years 1846 and 1847 were "probably the worst of the entire century in terms of want and human suffering," and the decade has earned the name the "Hungry Forties."

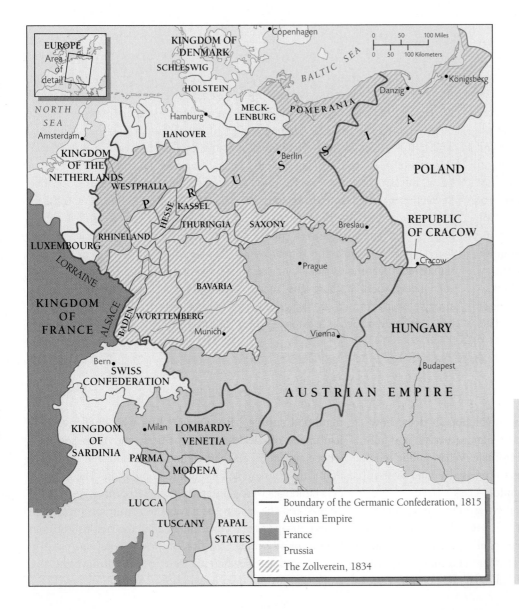

GERMAN CONFEDERATION, 1815. Compare this map with the one on page 714. ▪ *What major areas were left out of the German Confederation?* ▪ *Why do you think they were left out?* ▪ *What obstacles made it difficult to establish a unified German nation during this period?*

Competing Viewpoints

Two Views of the June Days, France, 1848

> These two passages make for an interesting comparison. The socialist Karl Marx reported on the events of
> 1848 in France as a journalist for a German newspaper. For Marx, the bloodshed of the June Days shattered
> the "fraternal illusions" of February 1848, when the king had been overthrown and the provisional government
> established. That bloodshed also symbolized a new stage in history: one of acute class conflict.
>
> The French liberal politician Alexis de Tocqueville also wrote about his impressions of the revolution.
> (Tocqueville's account, however, is retrospective, for he wrote his memoirs well after 1848.) For Marx, a socialist
> observer, the June Days represented a turning point: "The working class was knocking on the gates of history."
> For Tocqueville, a member of the government, the actions of the crowd sparked fear and conservative reaction.

Karl Marx's Journalism

The last official remnant of the February Revolution, the Executive Commission, has melted away, like an apparition, before the seriousness of events. The fireworks of Lamartine [French Romantic poet and member of the provisional government] have turned into the war rockets of Cavaignac [French general, in charge of putting down the workers' insurrection]. *Fraternité,* the fraternity of antagonistic classes of which one exploits the other, this *fraternité,* proclaimed in February, on every prison, on every barracks— its true, unadulterated, its prosaic expression is civil war, civil war in its most fearful form, the war of labor and capital. This fraternity flamed in front of all the windows of Paris on the evening of June 25, when the Paris of the bourgeoisie was illuminated, whilst the Paris of the proletariat [Marxist term for the working people] burnt, bled, moaned. . . . The February Revolution was the beautiful revolution, the revolution of universal sympathy, because the antagonisms, which had flared up in it against the monarchy, slumbered peacefully side by side, still undeveloped, because the social struggle which formed its background had won only a joyous existence, an existence of phrases, of words. The June revolution is the ugly revolution, the repulsive revolution, because things have taken the place of phrases, because the republic uncovered the head of the monster itself, by striking off the crown that shielded and concealed it.—Order! was the battle cry of Guizot . . . Order! shouts Cavaignac, the brutal echo of the French National Assembly and of the republican bourgeoisie. Order! thundered his grape-shot, as it ripped up the body of the proletariat. None of the numerous revolutions of the French bourgeoisie since 1789 was an attack on order; for they allowed the rule of

Hunger itself cannot cause revolution. It does, however, test governments' abilities to manage a crisis, and failure can make a ruler seem illegitimate. When public relief foundered in France and troops repressed potato riots in Berlin, when regimes armed middle-class citizens to protect themselves against the poor, governments looked both authoritarian and inept. In the 1840s, European states already faced a host of political challenges: from liberals who sought constitutional government and limits on royal power, from republicans who campaigned for universal manhood suffrage, from nationalists who challenged the legitimacy of their hereditary rulers, and from socialists whose appeal lay in their claim to speak for the most economically vulnerable among the population. These political challenges were reinforced by the economic crisis of the 1840s, and the result was a wave of revolution that swept across Europe as one government after another lost the confidence of its people. The first of these revolutions came in France, and as elsewhere in 1848, it did not have the outcome that revolutionaries had hoped for.

the class, they allowed the slavery of the workers, they allowed the bourgeois order to endure, however often the political form of this rule and of this slavery changed. June has attacked this order. Woe to June!"

Source: *Neue Rheinische Zeitung* (New Rhineland Gazette), June 29, 1848, as cited in Karl Marx, *The Class Struggles in France* (New York: 1964), pp. 57–58.

Alexis de Tocqueville Remembers the June Days (1893)

Now at last I have come to that insurrection in June which was the greatest and the strangest that had ever taken place in our history, or perhaps in that of any other nation: the greatest because for four days more than a hundred thousand men took part in it, and there were five generals killed; the strangest, because the insurgents were fighting without a battle cry, leaders, or flag, and yet they showed wonderful powers of coordination and a military expertise that astonished the most experienced officers.

Another point that distinguished it from all other events of the same type during the last sixty years was that its object was not to change the form of government, but to alter the organization of society. In truth it was not a political struggle (in the sense in which we have used the word "political" up to now), but a class struggle, a sort of "Servile War." . . . One should not see it only as a brutal and a blind, but as a powerful effort of the workers to escape from the necessities of their condition, which had been depicted to them as an illegitimate depression, and by the sword to open up a road towards that imaginary well-being that had been shown to them in the distance as a right. It was this mixture of greedy desires and false theories that engendered the insurrection and made it so formidable. These poor people had been assured that the goods of the wealthy were in some way the result of a theft committed against themselves. They had been assured that inequalities of fortune were as much opposed to morality and the interests of society as to nature. This obscure and mistaken conception of right, combined with brute force, imparted to it an energy, tenacity and strength it would never have had on its own.

Source: From Alexis de Tocqueville, *Recollections: The French Revolution of 1848,* ed. J. P. Mayer and A. P. Kerr, trans. George Lawrence (New Brunswick, NJ: 1987), pp. 436–37.

Questions for Analysis

1. Was Tocqueville sympathetic to the revolutionaries of June?

2. Did Tocqueville think the events were historically significant?

3. Where did Tocqueville agree and disagree with Marx?

The French Revolution of 1848: A Republican Experiment

The French monarchy after the revolution of 1830 (see Chapter 20) seemed little different from its predecessor. King Louis Philippe gathered around him members of the banking and industrial elite. Confronted with demands to enlarge the franchise, the prime minister quipped that everyone was free to acquire enough property to qualify for the vote: "Enrich yourselves!" Building projects, especially the railway, presented ample opportunities for graft, and the reputation of the government suffered. Protest movements, in the form of republican societies, proliferated in French cities. In 1834, the government declared these organizations illegal. Rebellions broke out in Paris and Lyon, bringing a harsh repression that resulted in deaths and arrests. The government's refusal to compromise drove even moderates into opposition. In 1847, the opposition organized a campaign for electoral reform around repeated political "banquets"—an attempt to get around the laws against assembly. When they called for a giant banquet on February 22, 1848, the king responded by banning the meeting. A sudden and surprising popular revolution in the streets caused Louis Philippe to abdicate his throne only days later. A hastily assembled group of French political figures declared France a republic, for the first time since 1792.

The provisional government of the new republic consisted of liberals, republicans, and—for the first time— socialists. They produced a new constitution, with elections based on universal male suffrage. Among their first acts was the abolition of slavery in France and French colonies (slavery had been abolished in 1794 during the revolution but reestablished by Napoleon in 1802). In spite of these accomplishments, tensions between propertied republicans and socialists shattered the unity of the coalition that toppled Louis Philippe. Suffering because of the economic crisis, working men and women demanded the "right to work," the right to earn a living wage. The provisional government responded by creating the National Workshops, a program of public works, to give jobs to the unemployed, headed by the socialist Louis Blanc. Initial plans were made to employ 10,000–12,000 workers, but unemployment was so high that 120,000 job-seekers had gathered in the city by June 1848. Meanwhile, voters in rural areas resented the increase in taxation that was required to pay for the public works program.

Popular politics flourished in Paris in 1848. The provisional government lifted restrictions on speech and assembly. One hundred seventy new journals and more than 200 clubs formed within weeks. Delegations claiming to represent the oppressed of Europe—Chartists, Hungarians, Poles—moved freely about the city. Women's clubs and newspapers appeared, demanding universal suffrage and living wages. Many middle-class Parisians were alarmed, and more conservative rural populations also looked for stern measures to restore order. When elections for parliament were held—the first elections ever in France under a regime of universal male suffrage—the conservative voices won out, and a majority of moderate republicans and monarchists were elected.

A majority in the new assembly believed the National Workshops were a financial drain and a threat to order. In May, they closed the workshops to new enrollment, excluded

***THE BURNING OF THE THRONE* (1848).** A contemporary print shows revolutionaries burning the king's throne. Note the man with a top hat standing next to a man in a worker's smock. Delacroix used similar images to depict cooperation between workers and middle-class revolutionaries (see page 661).

recent arrivals to Paris, and sent members between the ages of eighteen and twenty-five into the army. On June 21, they abolished the workshops altogether. In defense of this social program, the workers of Paris—laborers, journeymen, the unemployed—rose in revolt, building barricades across Paris. For four days, June 23–26, they fought a hopeless battle against armed forces recruited from the provinces. The repression of the June Days shocked many observers. About 3,000 were killed and 12,000 arrested. Many of the prisoners were deported to Algerian labor camps. After this repression, support for the republic among the workers in Paris declined rapidly.

In the aftermath, the government moved quickly to restore order. The parliament hoped for a strong leader in the presidential election. Four candidates ran: Alphonse de Lamartine, the moderate republican and poet; General Louis Eugène de Cavaignac, who had perfected the art of urban warfare in the conquest of Algeria and who used these skills in repressing the workers' revolt in Paris; Alexandre Ledru-Rollin, a socialist; and Louis Napoleon Bonaparte, the nephew of the former emperor, who had spent his life in exile. Buoyed by enthusiastic support from rural voters, the upstart Louis Napoleon polled more than twice as many votes as the other three candidates combined.

"All facts and personages of great importance in world history occur twice . . . the first time as tragedy, the second as farce." Karl Marx's judgment on Louis Napoleon's relationship to his famous uncle was shared by many, but his name gave him wide appeal. Conservatives believed

BARRICADE IN THE RUE DE LA MORTELLERIE, JUNE, 1848 BY ERNEST MEISSONIER (1815–1891). A very different view of 1848, a depiction of the June Days.

class joined the opposition, allying with radicals who could not topple the regime alone. Yet demands for reform soon led to fears of disorder and the desire for a strong state. This dynamic led to the collapse of the republic and to the rule of Napoleon III. The abandonment of the revolution's social goals—most visibly evident in the National Workshops—led to a stark polarization along class lines, with middle-class and working-class people demanding different things from the state. This political conflict would grow even more intense as socialism came into its own as an independent political force.

Nationalism, Revolution, and the German Question in 1848

The revolutions of 1848 in the German-speaking lands of Europe shared some similarities with the revolutions in France. Like liberals in France, liberal Germans wanted a ruler who would abide by a constitution, allow for greater press freedoms, and accept some form of representative government, though not necessarily universal suffrage. As in France, artisans and urban laborers in German cities gravitated toward more radical ideologies of republicanism and socialism, and protested against new methods of industrial production. More so than in France, German peasants still faced the burden of feudal obligations owed to an entrenched and powerful aristocracy. The great difference between France and Germany in 1848, however, was that France already had a centralized state and a unified territory. In central Europe, a unified Germany did not exist in 1848. In 1815, the Congress of Vienna had created the German Confederation, a loose organization of thirty-nine states, including Habsburg Austria with its Catholic monarchy, and Prussia, ruled by a Protestant king. The German Confederation did not include Prussian and Austrian territories in Poland and Hungary with large non-German populations. This confederation was intended to provide only common defense. It had no real executive power. As a practical matter, Prussia and Austria competed with one another to occupy the dominant position in German politics, and as a result revolutionaries in the German states were forced to reckon with these two powers as they struggled to achieve the national unity that they hoped would allow them to achieve their political goals.

In 1806, Prussia had been defeated by the French under Napoleon. Many Prussians considered the defeat an indictment of the country's inertia since the reign of Frederick the Great (r. 1740–86). Aiming to revive "patriotism and a national honor and independence," they passed a series of aggressive reforms, imposed from above. Prussian

he would protect property and order. Some on the left had read his book *The Extinction of Pauperism* and noted his correspondence with important socialists. One old peasant put it succinctly, "How could I help voting for this gentleman—I whose nose was frozen at Moscow?"

Louis Napoleon used his position to consolidate his power. He rallied the Catholics by restoring the Church to its former role in education and by sending an expedition to Rome to rescue the pope from revolutionaries (see Chapter 4). He banned radical activities, workers' associations, and suspended press freedoms. In 1851, he called for a plebiscite to give him the authority to change the constitution, and one year later another plebiscite allowed him to establish the Second Empire, ending the Republican experiment. He assumed the title of Napoleon III (r. 1852–70), emperor of the French.

The dynamics of the French Revolution of 1848—initial success, followed by divisions among the supporters of revolution, followed by a reassertion of authoritarian control—would be repeated elsewhere, especially evidenced in the pivotal role of the propertied middle classes. Louis Philippe's reign had been proudly bourgeois but alienated many of its supporters. Key groups in the middle reformers reconstituted the army, following the Napoleonic example. Officers were recruited and promoted on the basis of merit rather than birth, although the large majority continued to come from the Junker class. Other reforms modernized training at the royal cadet school in Berlin and encouraged the middle class to take a more active role in the civil service. In 1807, serfdom and the estate system were abolished. A year later, in a conscious attempt to increase middle-class Germans' sense of themselves as citizens, cities and towns were allowed to elect their councilmen and handle their own finances. (Justice and security continued to be administered by the central government in Berlin.) The Prussian reformers expanded facilities for both primary and secondary education and founded the University of Berlin, which numbered among its faculty several ardent nationalists.

Prussia aimed to establish itself as the leading German state and a counter to Austrian power in the region. Prussia's most significant victory in this respect came with the *Zollverein*, or customs union, in 1834, which established free trade among the German states and a uniform tariff against the rest of the world—an openly protectionist policy advocated by the economist Friedrich List. By the 1840s, the union included almost all of the German states except German Austria and offered manufacturers a market of almost 34 million people. The spread of the railways after 1835 accelerated exchange within this expanded internal market.

During the 1840s, in both Prussia and the smaller German states, political clubs of students and other radicals joined with middle-class groups of lawyers, doctors, and businessmen to press new demands for representative government and reform. Newspapers multiplied, defying censorship. Liberal reformers resented both Prussian domination of the German Confederation and the conservatism of the Habsburgs, who ruled the Austrian Empire. They attacked the combination of autocracy and bureaucratic authority that stifled political life in Prussia and Austria. German nationhood, they reasoned, would break Austrian or Prussian domination and end the sectional fragmentation that made reform so difficult.

When Frederick William IV (r. 1840–61) succeeded to the Prussian throne in 1840, hopes ran high. The new king did gesture toward liberalizing reforms. When economic troubles hit in the 1840s, however, Frederick William asserted firmly that his authority could not be questioned by his subjects. He sent the army to crush a revolt among the textile weavers of Silesia, who were protesting British imports and, more generally, unemployment, falling wages, and hunger. The brutality of the regime's response shocked

many. The king also opposed constitutionalism and any representative participation in issues of legislation and budgets—like the "enlightened" absolutists who preceded him, the Prussian king firmly believed that his leadership did not need assistance from elected legislatures or from civil society as a whole.

As in France, liberals and radicals in Prussia and the German states continued their reform campaigns. And when revolution came to France in the spring of 1848, unrest spread across the Rhine. In the Catholic south German state of Bavaria, a student protest forced King Ludwig I to grant greater press freedoms, and when revolutionary movements appeared elsewhere in the smaller German states, kings and princes yielded surprisingly quickly. The governments promised elections, expanded suffrage, jury

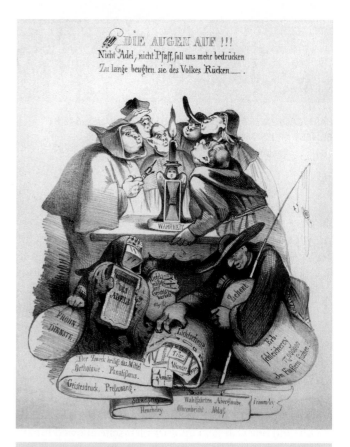

"EYES OPEN!" (c. 1845). This German cartoon from just before the 1848 revolution warns that aristocrats and clergy are conspiring to deny the German people their rights. The caption reads "Eyes Open! Neither the nobility nor the clergy shall oppress us any longer. For too long they have broken the backs of the people." ▪ *Did supporters of the revolution consider the aristocracy or the clergy to be legitimate members of the nation? Compare the cartoon with the pamphlet of Abbé Sieyès in the French Revolution (see page 586).*

Past and Present

Germany's Place in Europe

The unification of Germany under Prussian leadership in 1870 (left) destabilized the balance of power in Europe. World War I and World War II confirmed for many people the dangers of a strong German state. The history of European integration after 1945 nevertheless depended on rebuilding Germany and binding it more closely to its European neighbors. In spite of recent troubles in the European Union, including a financial crisis that threatened the euro currency (right), this history remains one of the great success stories of late-twentieth-century Europe.

 Watch related author interview on StudySpace
wwnorton.com/web/westernciv18

trials, and other liberal reforms. In Prussia, Frederick William, shaken by unrest in the countryside and stunned by a showdown in Berlin between the army and revolutionaries in which 250 were killed, promised to grant a constitution and met with representatives of the protest movement.

The Frankfurt Assembly and German Nationhood

The second and most idealistic stage of the revolution began with the election of 800 delegates to an all-German assembly in Frankfurt, where representatives from Prussia, Austria, and the small German states met to discuss creating a unified German nation. Most of the delegates came from the professional classes—lawyers, professors, administrators—and most were moderate liberals. Their views were not as

radical as those of the workers and artisans who had led the street protests against the king. The delegates assumed that the Frankfurt Assembly would draft a constitution for a liberal, unified Germany, much as an assembly of Frenchmen had done for their country in 1789. The comparison was mistaken. In 1789, a French nation-state and a centralized sovereign power already existed, to be reformed and redirected by the assembled French delegates. By contrast, the Frankfurt Assembly had no resources, no sovereign power to take, no single legal code, and, of course, no army.

On the assembly floor, questions of nationality proved contentious and destructive. Which Germans would be in the new state? A majority of the assembly's delegates argued that Germans were all those who, by language, culture, or geography, felt themselves bound to the enterprise of unification. They believed the German nation should include as many Germans as possible—a position encouraged by the

Analyzing Primary Sources

Frederick William IV Refuses the Throne

In March 1849, after months of deliberation and constitution making, the Frankfurt Assembly offered the throne of its proposed German state to the Prussian monarch Frederick William IV, who quickly turned it down. He had already reflected on the matter. In an earlier (December 1848) letter to one of his advisers, the diplomat Christian von Bunsen, he had set out his reasoning as follows.

want the princes' approval of neither *this* election nor *this* crown. Do you understand the words emphasized here? For you I want to shed light on this as briefly and brightly as possible. First, *this* crown is no crown. The crown which a Hohenzoller [the Prussian royal house] could accept, *if* circumstances *permitted,* is not one *made* by an assembly sprung from a revolutionary seed in the genre of the crown of cobble stones of Louis Philippe—even if this assembly was established with the sanction of princes . . . but one which bears the stamp of God, one which makes [the individual] on whom it [the crown] is placed, after his anointment, a "divine right" monarch—just as it has elevated more than 34 princes to Kings of the Germans by divine right and just as it bonds the last of these to his predecessors. The crown worn by Ottonians, Staufens [earlier German royal houses], Habsburgs can of course also be worn by a Hohenzoller; it honors him overwhelmingly with the luster of a thousand years. But *this* one, to which you regrettably refer, overwhelmingly dishonors [its bearer] with its smell of the gunpowder of the 1848 revolution—the silliest, dumbest, worst, though—thank God!—not the most evil of this century. Such an imaginary headband, baked out of dirt and the letters of the alphabet, is supposed to be welcome to a legitimate divine right king: to put it more precisely, to the King of Prussia who is blessed with a crown which may not be the oldest but, of all those which have never been stolen, is the most noble? . . . I will tell you outright: if the thousand-year-old crown of the German nation . . . should be bestowed again, it will be *I* and my equals who will bestow it. And woe to those who assume [powers] to which they have no title.

Source: Ralph Menning, *The Art of the Possible: Documents on Great Power Diplomacy, 1814–1914* (New York: 1996), p. 82.

Questions for Analysis

1. For Frederick William IV, what was the only legitimate source of a monarch's authority?

2. Why did he call the crown offered to him by the Frankfurt Assembly a "crown of cobble stones . . . with its smell of gunpowder of the 1848 revolution"?

3. Frederick William referred to himself by his family name, Hohenzollern, and to his title, king of Prussia, but he also used the expression "German nation" once in his letter. What relationship did he see among his family, the kingdom of Prussia, and the possibility of a unified German nation?

---

spectacle of disintegration in the Habsburg Empire. This was the "Great German" position. It was countered by a minority who called for a "Small Germany," one that left out all lands of the Habsburg Empire, including German Austria. Great Germans had a majority but were stymied by other nationalities unwilling to be included in their fold. Many Czechs in Bohemia, for instance, wanted no part of Great Germany, believing that they needed the protection of the Habsburg monarchy to avoid being swallowed up by a new German state on one side and the Russian monarchy on the other. After a long and difficult debate, the Austrian emperor withdrew his support, and the assembly retreated to the Small German solution. In April 1849, the Frankfurt Assembly offered the crown of a new German nation to the Prussian king, Frederick William IV.

By this time, however, Frederick William was negotiating from a position of greater strength. Already in the fall of 1848, he had used the military to repress the radical revolutionaries in Berlin while the delegates debated the constitutional question in Frankfurt. He was also encouraged by a backlash against revolutionary movements in Europe after the bloody repression during the June Days

THE FRANKFURT PREPARLIAMENT MEETS AT ST. PAUL'S CHURCH, 1848. This assembly brought together 500 delegates from the various German states to establish a constitution for a new German nation. An armed militia lined the square, and lines of student gymnasts (dressed in white with wide-brimmed hats) escorted the delegates. Their presence was a sign that the organizers of the preparliament feared violence. The black, red, and gold banners were also associated with republicanism. ■ *What image did the organizers mean to convey with this pageantry, the disciplined lines of students and delegates, their forms of dress, and their use of republican symbols?*

als began to have second thoughts about the pace of change. Peasants ransacked tax offices and burned castles; workers smashed machines in protests against industrialization. In towns and cities, citizen militias formed, threatening the power of established elites. New daily newspapers multiplied. So did political clubs. For the first time, many of these clubs admitted women (although they denied them the right to speak), and newly founded women's clubs demanded political rights. This torrent of popular unrest made moderate reformers uneasy; they considered universal manhood suffrage too radical. While peasant and worker protests had forced the king to make concessions in the early spring of 1848, moderate reformers now found those protests threatening. Throughout the German states, rulers took advantage of this shift in middle-class opinion to undo the concessions that they had granted in 1848 and to push through counterrevolutionary measures in the name of order.

For German liberals, national unification was now seen as necessary to maintain political stability. "In order to realize our ideas of freedom and equality, we want above all a strong and powerful government," claimed one candidate during the election campaigns for the Frankfurt Assembly. Popular sovereignty, he continued, "strengthened by the authority of a hereditary monarchy, will be able to repress with an iron hand any disorder and any violation of the law." In this context, nationhood stood for a new constitution and political community but also for a sternly enforced rule of law. After the failure of the Frankfurt Assembly, therefore, German liberals increasingly looked to a strong Prussian state as the only possible route toward national unification.

in Paris. He therefore refused to become a constitutional monarch on the terms offered by the Frankfurt Assembly. The proposed constitution, he said, was too liberal and receiving his crown from a parliament would be demeaning. The Prussian monarch wanted both the crown and a larger German state, but on his own terms, and he therefore dissolved the assembly before they could approve it with an official vote. After brief protests, summarily suppressed by the military, the Frankfurt delegates went home, disillusioned by their experience and convinced that their liberal and nationalist goals were incompatible. Some fled repression by immigrating to the United States. Others convinced themselves to sacrifice their liberal views for the seemingly realistic goal of nationhood. In Prussia itself, the army dispatched what remained of the revolutionary forces.

Elsewhere in the German-speaking states as popular revolution was taking its own course, many moderate liber-

Peoples against Empire: The Habsburg Lands

In the sprawling Habsburg (Austrian) Empire, nationalism played a different role. On the one hand, the Habsburg emperors could point to a remarkable record of political success: as

"NO PIECE OF PAPER WILL COME BETWEEN MYSELF AND MY PEOPLE" (1848). In this cartoon, Frederick William IV and a military officer refuse to accept the constitution for a new Germany offered to him by the Frankfurt Assembly. Note that the caption refers to a conservative definition of the relationship between a monarch and "his people." Compare this autocratic vision of the nation-state with the liberal nationalist's demand for a government that reflects the people's will. ▪ *What contrasting visions of the nation and its relation to the state are contained in this cartoon?*

HUNGARIAN REVOLUTIONARY LAJOS KOSSUTH, 1851.
A leader of the Hungarian nationalist movement who combined aristocratic style with rabble-rousing politics, Kossuth almost succeeded in an attempt to separate Hungary from Austria in 1849.

heir to the medieval Holy Roman Empire, Habsburg kings had ruled for centuries over a diverse array of ethnicities and language groups in central Europe that included Germans, Czechs, Magyars, Poles, Slovaks, Serbs, and Italians, to name only the most prominent. In the sixteenth century, under Charles V, the empire had included Spain, parts of Burgundy, and the Netherlands. In the nineteenth century, however, the Habsburgs found it increasingly difficult to hold their empire together as the national demands of the different peoples in the realm escalated after 1815. Whereas the greater ethnic and linguistic homogeneity of the German-speaking lands allowed for a convergence between liberal ideas of popular sovereignty and national unification, no such program was possible in the Habsburg Empire. Popular sovereignty for peoples defined in terms of their ethnic identity implied a breakup of the Habsburg lands.

At the same time, however, the existence of nationalist movements did not imply unity, even within territories that spoke the same language. In the Polish territories of the empire, nationalist sentiment was strongest among aristocrats, who were especially conscious of their historic role as leaders of the Polish nation. Here, the Habsburg Empire successfully set Polish serfs against Polish lords, ensuring

that social grievances dampened ethnic nationalism. In the Hungarian region, national claims were likewise advanced by the relatively small Magyar aristocracy. (*Hungarian* is a political term; *Magyar*, which was often used, refers to the Hungarians' non-Slavic language.) Yet they gained an audience under the gifted and influential leadership of Lajos (Louis) Kossuth (*KAW-shut*). A member of the lower nobility, Kossuth was by turns a lawyer, publicist, newspaper editor, and political leader. To protest the closed-door policy of the empire's barely representative Diet (parliament), Kossuth published transcripts of parliamentary debates and distributed them to a broader public. He campaigned for independence and a separate Hungarian parliament, but he also (and more influentially) brought politics to the people. Kossuth staged political "banquets" like those in France, at which local and national personalities made speeches in the form of toasts and interested citizens could eat, drink, and participate in politics. The Hungarian political leader combined aristocratic style with rabble-rousing politics: a delicate balancing act but one that, when it worked, catapulted him to the center of Habsburg politics. He was as well known in the Habsburg capital of Vienna as he was in Pressburg and Budapest.

The other major nationalist movement that troubled the Habsburg Empire was pan-Slavism. Slavs included Russians, Poles, Ukrainians, Czechs, Slovaks, Slovenes, Croats, Serbs, Macedonians, and Bulgarians. Before 1848, pan-Slavism was primarily a cultural movement united by a general pro-Slavic sentiment. It was internally divided, however, by the competing claims of different Slavic languages and traditions. Pan-Slavism inspired the works of the Czech historian and political leader, František Palacký, author of the *History of the Bohemian People*, and the Slovak Jan Kollár, whose book *Salvy Dcera* ("Slava's Daughter") mourned the loss of identity among Slavs in the Germanic world. The movement also influenced the Polish Romantic poet Adam Mickiewicz (*mihtz-KYAY-vihch*), who sought to rekindle Polish nationhood against foreign oppression.

The fact that Russia and Austria were rivals in eastern Europe made pan-Slavism a volatile and unpredictable political force in the regions of eastern Europe where the two nations vied for power and influence. Tsar Nicholas of Russia sought to use pan-Slavism to his advantage, making arguments about "Slavic" uniqueness part of his "autocracy, orthodoxy, nationality" ideology after 1825. Yet the tsar's Russian-sponsored pan-Slavism alienated Western-oriented Slavs who resented Russia's ambitions. Here, as elsewhere, nationalism created a tangled web of alliances and antagonisms.

Austria and Hungary in 1848: Springtime of Peoples and the Autumn of Empire

The empire's combination of political, social, and ethnic tensions came to the point of explosion in 1848. The opening salvo came from the Hungarians. Emboldened by uprisings in France and Germany, Kossuth stepped up his reform campaigns, pillorying the "Metternich system" of Habsburg autocracy and control, demanding representative institutions throughout the empire and autonomy for the Hungarian Magyar nation. The Hungarian Diet prepared to draft its own constitution. In Vienna, the seat of Habsburg power, a popular movement of students and artisans demanding political and social reforms built barricades and attacked the imperial palace. A Central Committee of Citizens took shape, as did a middle-class militia, or national guard, determined at once to maintain order and to press demands for reform. The Habsburg regime tried to shut the movement down by closing the university, but that only unleashed more popular anger. The regime found itself forced to retreat almost entirely. Metternich, whose political system had weathered so many storms, fled to Britain in disguise—a good indication of the political turmoil—leaving the emperor Ferdinand I in Vienna. The government conceded to radical demands for male suffrage and a single house of representatives. It agreed to withdraw troops from Vienna and to put forced labor and serfdom on a path to abolition. The government also yielded to Czech demands in Bohemia, granting that kingdom its own constitution. To the south, Italian liberals and nationalists attacked the empire's territories in Naples and Venice. In Milan, the forces of King Charles Albert of Piedmont routed the Austrians, raising hopes of victory. As what would be called "the springtime of peoples" unfolded, Habsburg control of its various provinces seemed to be coming apart.

Yet the explosion of national sentiment that shook the empire later allowed it to recoup its fortunes. The paradox of nationalism in central Europe was that no cultural or ethnic majority could declare independence in a given region without prompting rebellion from other minority groups that inhabited the same area. In Bohemia, for instance, Czechs and Germans who lived side by side had worked together to pass reforms scuttling feudalism. Within a month, however, nationalism began to fracture their alliance. German Bohemians set off to attend the all-important Frankfurt Assembly, but the Czech majority refused to send representatives and countered by convening a confederation of Slavs in Prague. What did the delegates at the Slav confederation want? Some were hostile to what the Russian anarchist Mikhail Bakunin called the "monstrous Austrian Empire." But the majority of delegates preferred to be ruled by the Habsburgs (though with some autonomy) than to be dominated by either the Germans or the Russians.

This bundle of animosities allowed the Austrians to divide and conquer. In May 1848, during the Slav Congress, a student- and worker-led insurrection broke out in Prague. On the orders of the newly installed liberal government, Austrian troops entered the city to restore order, sent the Slav Congress packing, and reasserted control in Bohemia. For economic as well as political reasons, the new government was determined to keep the empire intact. The regime also sent troops to regain control in the Italian provinces of Lombardy and Venetia, and quarrels among the Italians helped the Austrians succeed.

Nationalism and counternationalism in Hungary set the stage for the final act of the drama. The Hungarian parliament had passed a series of laws including new provisions for the union of Hungary and Austria. In the heat of 1848, Ferdinand I had little choice but to accept them. The Hungarian parliament abolished serfdom and ended noble privilege to prevent a peasant insurrection. It also established freedom

THE FIRST UNCENSORED NEWSPAPER AFTER THE REVOLUTION IN VIENNA, JANUARY 1848. This watercolor illustrates the power of public information during the 1848 revolution in the Austrian capital. An uncensored newspaper, wall posters, caps with political insignia and slogans, and an armed citizenry all are evidence of a vibrant and impassioned public discussion on the events of the day. Note, too, the modest dress of the woman selling the papers, the top hat and fashionable dress of the middle-class man smoking a pipe, and the presence of military uniforms, all of which illustrate support for the revolution among a broad portion of the population. ▪ *How does this vision of the public sphere in action compare with previous depictions of public debate in the Enlightenment (see page 571) or in the French Revolution (see page 599, or elsewhere in Europe in 1848 (see page 704)?*

dent organizations, and put twenty-five revolutionary leaders to death in front of a firing squad. Kossuth went into hiding and lived the rest of his life in exile.

Paradoxically, then, the Habsburg Empire of Austria was in part saved during the revolutions of 1848 by the very nationalist movements that threatened to tear it apart. Although nationalists in Habsburg lands, especially in Hungary, gained the support of significant numbers of people, the fact that different nationalist movements found it impossible to cooperate with one another allowed the new emperor, Franz Josef, to defeat the most significant challenges to his authority one by one and consolidate his rule (with Russian help), ultimately gaining popular support from many quarters, especially from middle-class populations that came to express a certain civic pride in the spirit of toleration that allowed so many peoples to live together within such a patchwork of peoples and tongues. Franz Josef would survive these crises, and many others, until his death in 1916 during World War I, a much larger conflict that would finally overwhelm and destroy the Habsburg Empire for good.

of the press and of religion and changed the suffrage requirements, enfranchising small property holders. Many of these measures (called the March laws) were hailed by Hungarian peasants, Jewish communities, and liberals. But other provisions—particularly the extension of Magyar control—provoked opposition from the Croats, Serbs, and Romanians within Hungary. On April 14, 1848, Kossuth upped the ante, severing all ties between Hungary and Austria. The new Austrian emperor, Franz Josef, now played his last card: he asked for military support from Nicholas I of Russia. The Habsburgs were unable to win their "holy struggle against anarchy," but the Russian army of over 300,000 found it an easier task. By mid-August 1849, the Hungarian revolt was crushed.

In the city of Vienna itself, the revolutionary movement had lost ground. When economic crisis and unemployment helped spark a second popular uprising, the emperor's forces, with Russian support, descended on the capital. On October 31, the liberal government capitulated. The regime reestablished censorship, disbanded the national guard and stu-

The Early Stages of Italian Unification in 1848

The Italian peninsula had not been united since the Roman Empire. At the beginning of the nineteenth century, like the German-speaking lands of central Europe, the area that is now Italy was a patchwork of small states (see map on page 655). Austria occupied the northernmost states of Lombardy and Venetia, which were also the most urban and industrial. Habsburg dependents also ruled Tuscany, Parma, and Modena, extending Austria's influence over the north of the peninsula. The independent Italian states included the southern kingdom of the Two Sicilies, governed by members of the Bourbon family; the Papal States, ruled by Pope Gregory XVI (1831–46); and most important, Piedmont-Sardinia, ruled by the reform-minded monarch Charles Albert (r. 1831–49) of the House of Savoy. Charles Albert had no particular commitment to creating an Italian

LANGUAGES OF CENTRAL AND EASTERN EUROPE. In Habsburg Austria-Hungary, ethnic/linguistic boundaries did not conform to political boundaries between states.
- *How many different language groups can you count in the Austrian Empire?* ▪ *Why was it ultimately easier for the German states to unify when looking at this map?* ▪ *How did the diversity of peoples in the Habsburg Empire make a convergence between liberal revolution and nationalism more difficult to achieve?*

national state, but by virtue of Piedmont-Sardinia's economic power, geographical location, and long tradition of opposition to the Habsburgs, Charles Albert's state played a central role in nationalist and anti-Austrian politics.

The leading Italian nationalist in this period—one whose republican politics Charles Albert disliked—was Giuseppe Mazzini (1805–1872) from the city of Genoa, in Piedmont. Mazzini began his political career as a member of the Carbonari (see Chapter 20), an underground society pledged to resisting Austrian control of the region and establishing constitutional rule. In 1831, Mazzini founded his own society, Young Italy, which was anti-Austrian and in favor of constitutional reforms but also dedicated to Italian unification. Charismatic and persuasive, Mazzini was one of the best-known nationalists of his time. He spoke in characteristically Romantic tones of the awakening of the Italian people and of the common people's mission to bring republicanism to the world. Under his leadership, Young Italy clubs multiplied. Yet the organization's favored tactics, plotting mutinies and armed rebellions, proved ineffective. In 1834, Mazzini launched an

invasion of the kingdom of Sardinia. Without sufficient support, it fizzled, driving Mazzini into exile in England.

Mazzini's republican vision of a united Italy clashed with the goals of his potential allies. Many liberals shared his commitment to creating a single Italian state but not his enthusiasm for the people and popular movements. They hoped instead to merge existing governments into some form of constitutional monarchy or, in a few cases, for a government under the pope. Mazzini's insistence on a democratic republic committed to social and political transformation struck pragmatic liberals as utopian and well-to-do members of the middle classes as dangerous.

The turmoil that swept across Europe in 1848 raised hopes for political and social change and put Italian unification on the agenda. As in Germany, those who hoped for change were divided in their goals, but they shared a common hope that national unification might allow them to achieve the reforms they sought, whether it was a constitution, civil liberties, universal suffrage, or revolutionary social change that would benefit the working poor. In March

Competing Viewpoints

Building the Italian Nation: Three Views

> The charismatic revolutionary Giuseppe Mazzini left more than fifty volumes of memoirs and writings. In the first excerpt, he sets out his vision of the "regeneration" of the Italian nation and the three Romes: ancient Rome, the Rome of the popes, and (in the future) the Rome of the people, which would emancipate the peoples of Europe. Mazzini's conception of Italian nationalism was Romantic in its interpretation of Italy's distinctive history and destiny and revolutionary in its emphasis on the Italian people rather than on statesmen.
>
> The National Society was formed in 1857 to support Italian unification. By the 1860s, the society had over 5,000 members. It was especially strong in the Piedmont, where it was formed, and in central Italy. Giuseppe la Farina was a tenacious organizer; he drafted the society's political creed and had it printed and sold throughout Italy.
>
> The unification of Italy owed as much to Cavour's hard-nosed diplomacy as it did to middle-class movements for unification. In 1862, one of Cavour's contemporaries offered an assessment of the count and how he had found "an opening in the complicated fabric of European politics," reprinted in the third piece here.

Mazzini and Romantic Nationalism

I saw regenerate Italy becoming at one bound the missionary of a religion of progress and fraternity. . . .

The worship of Rome was a part of my being. The great Unity, the One Life of the world, had twice been elaborated within her walls. Other peoples—their brief mission fulfilled—disappeared for ever. To none save to her had it been given twice to guide and direct the world. . . . There, upon the vestiges of an epoch of civilization anterior to the Grecian, which had had its seat in Italy . . . the Rome of the Republic, concluded by the Caesars, had arisen to consign the former world to oblivion, and borne her eagles over the known world, carrying with them the idea of right, the source of liberty.

In later days . . . she had again arisen, greater than before, and at once constituted herself, through her Popes—the accepted center of a new Unity. . . .

Why should not a new Rome, the Rome of the Italian people . . . arise to create a third and still vaster Unity; to link together and harmonize earth and heaven, right [law] and duty; and utter, not to individuals but to peoples, the great word Association—to make known to free men and equal their mission here below?

Source: Giuseppe Mazzini, *The Life and Writings of Joseph Mazzini* (London: 1964), as cited in Denis Mack Smith, *The Making of Italy, 1796–1870* (New York: 1968), pp. 48–49.

The Political Creed of the National Society, February 1858

Italian independence should be the aim of every man of spirit and intelligence. Neither our educational system in Italy, nor our commerce and industry, can ever be flourishing or properly modernized while Austria keeps one foot on our neck. . . . What good is it to be born in the most fertile and beautiful country in the world, to lie midway between East and West with magnificent ports in both the Adriatic and Mediterranean, to be descended from the Genoese, the Pisans, the men of Amalfi, Sicily and Venice? What use is it to have invented the compass, to have discovered the New World and been the progenitor of two civilizations? . . .

To obtain political liberty we must expel the Austrians who keep us enslaved. To win freedom of conscience we must expel the Austrians who keep us slaves of the Pope. To create a national literature we must chase away the Austrians who keep us uneducated. . . .

Italy must become not only independent but politically united. Political unity alone can reconcile various interests and laws, can mobilize credit and put out collective energies to speeding up communications. Only thus will we find sufficient capital for large-scale industry. Only thus will we create new markets, suppress internal obstacles to the free flow of commerce, and find the strength and reputation needed for traffic in distant lands. . . .

Everything points irresistibly to political unification. Science, industry, commerce, and the arts all need it. No great enterprise is possible any longer if we do not first put together the skill, knowledge, capital and labor of the whole of our great nation. The spirit of the age is moving toward concentration, and woe betide any nation that holds back!

Source: A. Franchi, ed., *Scritti politici di Giuseppe La Farina,* vol. 2 (Milan: 1870), as cited in Denis Mack Smith, *The Making of Italy, 1796–1870* (New York: 1968), pp. 224–25.

Count Cavour as a Leader

Count Cavour undeniably ranks as third among European statesmen after Lord Palmerston [British prime minister 1855–1858, 1859–1865] and the Emperor Napoleon. . . . Count Cavour's strength does not lie in his principles; for he has none that are altogether inflexible. But he has a clear, precise aim, one whose greatness would—ten years ago—have made any other man reel: that of creating a unified and independent Italy. Men, means, circumstances were and still are matters of indifference to him. He walks straight ahead, always firm, often alone, sacrificing his friends, his sympathies, sometimes his heart, and often his conscience. Nothing is too difficult for him. . . .

Count Cavour . . . always has the talent to assess a situation and the possibilities of exploiting it. And it is this wonderful faculty that has contributed to form the Italy of today. As minister of a fourth-rate power, he could not create situations like Napoleon III, nor has he possessed the support of a great nation like Palmerston.

Count Cavour had to seek out an opening in the complicated fabric of European politics; he had to wriggle his way in, conceal himself, lay a mine, and cause an explosion. And it was by these means that he defeated Austria and won the help of France and England. Where other statesmen would have drawn back, Cavour plunged in headlong—as soon as he had sounded the precipice and calculated the possible profit and loss. The Crimean expeditionary force . . . the cession of Nice, the invasion of the Papal States last autumn [i.e., in 1860], were all the outcome of his vigorous stamina of mind.

There in brief you have the man of foreign affairs. He is strong; he is a match for the situation, for the politicians of his time or indeed of any time.

Source: F. Petruccelli della Gattina, *I moribundi del Palazzo Carignano* (Milan: 1862), as cited in Denis Mack Smith, *The Making of Italy, 1796–1870* (New York: 1968), pp. 181–82.

Questions for Analysis

1. Compare Mazzini's romantic vision of Italian history with the more pragmatic arguments for political unity coming from the liberal supporters of the National Society. Are there any points of overlap?

2. How would a supporter of Mazzini or a member of the National Society react to the third document's claim that an individual, Cavour, deserved primary credit for Italian unification?

3. Why should history and claims about "the spirit of the age" be so important to Italian nationalists?

SIEGE OF VENICE, 1848. This image, designed to provoke an anti-Austrian and nationalist sentiment among Italians, shows Venetian women and children donating their jewels to support their city while it was besieged by the Austrian army in 1848. ▪ *What makes the image of women and children sacrificing their possessions for the larger good so powerful?* ▪ *What does it say about the connections between nationalism and social obligations associated with gender?* ▪ *Did nationalism depend on a vision of the family as well as a vision of the nation?*

1848, only a few weeks after revolution had toppled the French monarchy, popular revolts broke out in the northern provinces of Venetia and Lombardy, fueled by anger at the Austrian occupation. In Milan, the capital of Lombardy, thousands of people marched on the palace of the Austrian governor general calling for reforms, leading to pitched battles in the streets. In Venice, the revolutionaries forced the Austrian troops out of the city and declared a republic. Charles Albert of Piedmont-Sardinia provided the rebels with military support and took up the banner of Italian nationalism, although many charged that he was primarily interested in expanding his own power. At the same time, Charles Albert pleased Italian liberals by creating an elected legislature and relaxing press censorship in his kingdom.

In August 1848, an insurrection of laborers broke out in Bologna, challenging the authority of the pope in the Papal States. Soon after, a popular uprising in Rome confronted the pope directly, and by February 1849 a new government in Rome had declared itself a republic. The next month, Mazzini arrived from exile to join the revolutionary movement in Rome.. These movements were neither coordinated nor ultimately successful. Charles Albert hesitated to confront the Austrians directly, and over the next few months the Austrians regained the upper hand in the north. French forces under Louis Napoleon intervened in Rome and the Papal States; and although they met fierce resistance from the Roman republicans joined by Giuseppe Garibaldi (see below), they nonetheless restored the pope's power and defeated the Roman Republic. The Venetian Republic was the last of the Italian revolutions to fall after a blockade and

GIUSEPPE MAZZINI (1805–1872). Born in Genoa when it was ruled by Napoleon's France, Mazzini devoted his life to the cause of Italian unification and independence. As a young man, Mazzini was a member of the underground revolutionary organization known as the Carbonari, and in 1831 he founded a new group, Young Italy, which soon attracted many adherents. Early attempts at insurrection resulted in political exile, but he returned during the 1848 revolutions to help lead the Roman Republic. Although his hopes for a Republican Italy were blocked by Cavour's plans for unification under the leadership of Piedmont-Sardinia, Mazzini remained a hero to many Italians, and his description of a "United States of Europe" anticipated the European Union.

an artillery bombardment from the Austrian army in August 1849. Like most of the radical movements of 1848, these Italian uprisings all failed. Still, they raised the hopes of nationalists who spoke of a *risorgimento*, or Italian resurgence, that would restore the nation to the position of leadership it had held in Roman times and during the Renaissance.

BUILDING THE NATION-STATE

In the wake of the revolutions of 1848, new nation-states were built or consolidated—often by former critics of nationalism. Since the French Revolution of 1789, conservative politicians had associated nationhood with liberalism: constitutions, reforms, new political communities. During the second half of the century, however, the political ground shifted dramatically. States and governments took the national initiative. Alarmed by revolutionary ferment, they promoted economic development, pressed social and political reforms, and sought to shore up their base of support. Rather than allow popular nationalist movements to emerge from below, statesmen consolidated their governments' powers and built nations from above.

France under Napoleon III

Napoleon III, like his uncle, believed in personal rule and a centralized state. As emperor, he controlled the nation's finances, the army, and foreign affairs. The assembly, elected by universal male suffrage, could approve only legislation drafted at the emperor's direction. Napoleon's regime aimed to undermine France's traditional elites by expanding the bureaucracy and cultivating a new relationship with the people. "The confidence of our rough peasants can be won by an energetic authority," asserted one of the emperor's representatives.

Napoleon III also took steps to develop the economy. He harbored a near-utopian faith in the power of industrial expansion to bring prosperity, political support, and national glory. An adviser to the emperor put it this way: "I see in industry, machinery, and credit the indispensable auxiliaries of humanity's moral and material progress." His government encouraged credit and new forms of financing, passed new limited-liability laws, and signed a free-trade treaty with Britain in 1860. The government also supported the creation of the Crédit Mobilier, an investment banking institution that sold shares and financed railroads, insurance and gas companies, coal and construction companies, and the building of the Suez Canal (see Chapter 22).

Napoleon also reluctantly permitted the existence of trade unions and legalized strikes. By appealing to both workers and the middle class, he sought to gain support for his goal of reestablishing France as a leading world power.

Most emblematic of the emperor's ambition was his transformation of the nation's capital. Paris's medieval infrastructure was buckling under the weight of population growth and industrial development. Cholera epidemics in 1832 and 1849 killed tens of thousands. In 1850, only one house in five had running water. Official concerns about public health were reinforced by political fears of crime and revolutionary militancy in working-class neighborhoods. A massive rebuilding project razed much of the medieval center of the city and erected 34,000 new buildings, including elegant hotels with the first elevators. The construction installed new water pipes and sewer lines, laid out 200 kilometers of new streets, and rationalized the traffic flow. Wide new boulevards, many named for Napoleon I's most famous generals, radiated from the Arc de Triomphe. The renovation did not benefit everyone. Although the regime built model worker residences, rising rents drove working people from the city's center into increasingly segregated suburbs. Baron Haussmann, the prefect of Paris who presided over the project, considered the city a monument to "cleanliness and order." Others called Haussmann an "artist of demolition."

Victorian Britain and the Second Reform Bill (1867)

Less affected by the revolutionary wave of 1848, Great Britain was able to chart a course of significant social and political reform, continuing a process that had begun in 1832 with the First Reform Bill. The government faced mounting demands to extend the franchise beyond the middle classes. Industrial expansion sustained a growing stratum of highly skilled and relatively well-paid workers (almost exclusively male). These workers, concentrated for the most part within the building, engineering, and textile industries, turned away from the tradition of militant radicalism that had characterized the Hungry Forties. Instead, they favored collective self-help through cooperative societies or trade unions, whose major role was to accumulate funds for insurance against old age and unemployment. They saw education as a tool for advancement and patronized the mechanics' institutes and similar institutions founded by them or on their behalf. These prosperous workers created real pressure for electoral reform.

Some argued for the vote in the name of democracy. Others borrowed arguments from earlier middle-class campaigns for electoral reform: they were responsible workers, respectable and upstanding members of society, with strong religious convictions and patriotic feelings. Unquestionably loyal to the state, they deserved the vote and direct representation just as much as the middle class. These workers were joined in their campaign by many middle-class dissenting reformers in the Liberal party, whose religious beliefs (as dissenters from the Church of England) linked them to the workers' campaigns for reform. Dissenters had long faced discrimination. They were denied posts in the civil service and the military, which liberals felt should be open to talent, and for centuries had been excluded from the nation's premier universities, Oxford and Cambridge, unless they renounced their faith and subscribed to the articles of the Anglican church. Moreover, they resented paying taxes to support the Church of England, which was largely staffed by sons of the gentry and run in the interests of landed society. The fact that the community of dissent crossed class lines was vital to Liberal party politics and the campaign for reforming the vote.

PARIS REBUILT. Baron Haussmann, prefect of Paris under Napoleon III, presided over the wholesale rebuilding of the city, with effects we still see today. The Arc de Triomphe, seen here in a photograph from the 1960s, became the center of an *étoile* (star) pattern, with the wide boulevards named after Napoleon I's famous generals.

Working-class leaders and middle-class dissidents joined in a countrywide campaign for a new reform bill and a House of Commons responsive to their interests. They were backed by some shrewd Conservatives, such as Benjamin Disraeli (1804–1881), who argued that political life would be improved, not disrupted, by including the "aristocrats of labor." In actuality, Disraeli was betting that the newly enfranchised demographic would vote Conservative; and in 1867, he steered through Parliament a bill that reached further than anything proposed by his political opponents. The 1867 Reform Bill doubled the franchise by extending the vote to any men who paid poor rates or rent of £10 or more a year in urban areas (this meant, in general, skilled workers) and to rural tenants paying rent of £12 or more. As in 1832, the bill redistributed seats, with large northern cities gaining representation at the expense of the rural south. The success of the 1867 Reform Bill also points to the lingering influence of the Chartist movement of the 1840s (see Chapter 20). Although the Chartists' goal of universal manhood suffrage remained unfulfilled, the 1867 law allowed the responsible working class to participate in the affairs of state.

The reform bill was silent on women, but an important minority insisted that liberalism should include women's enfranchisement. These advocates mobilized a woman suffrage movement, building on women's remarkable participation in earlier reform campaigns, especially the Anti-Corn Law League and the movement to abolish slavery. Their cause found a passionate supporter in John Stuart Mill, perhaps the century's most brilliant, committed, and influential defender of personal liberty. Mill's father had worked closely with the utilitarian philosopher Jeremy Bentham, and the young Mill had been a convinced utilitarian himself (see Chapter 20). He went on, however, to develop much more expansive notions of human freedom. In 1859, Mill wrote *On Liberty,* which many consider the classic defense of individual freedom in the face of the state and the "tyranny of the majority." During the same period he coauthored—with his lover and eventual wife, Harriet Taylor—essays on women's political rights, the law of marriage, and divorce. At the time, Taylor was trapped in an unhappy marriage and divorce required an act of Parliament. Taylor's relationship with Mill thus added a measure of personal scandal to their political views, which contemporaries considered scandalous enough. His *Subjection of Women* (1869), published after Harriet died, argued what few could even contemplate: that women had to be considered individuals on the same plane as men and that women's freedom was a measure of social progress. *Subjection* was an international success and with *On Liberty* became one of the defining texts of Western liberalism. Mill's arguments, however, did not carry the day. Only militant suffrage movements and the crisis of the First World War brought women the vote.

The decade or so following the passage of the Reform Bill of 1867 marked the high point of British liberalism. By opening the doors to political participation, liberalism had accomplished a peaceful restructuring of political institutions and social life. It did so under considerable pressure from below, however, and in Britain, as elsewhere, liberal leaders made it clear that these doors were unquestionably not open to everyone. Their opposition to woman's suffrage is interesting for what it reveals about their views on male and female nature. They insisted that female individuality (expressed in voting, education, or wage earning) would destabilize family life. Yet their opposition to woman's suffrage also reflected conception of the vote: casting a ballot was a privilege granted only to specific social groups in return for their contributions to and vested interest in society. Men of property might champion the rule of law and representative government, but they balked at the prospect of a truly democratic politics and did not shy from heavy-handed law-and-order politics. Expanding the franchise created new constituencies with new ambitions and paved the way for socialist and labor politics in the last quarter of the century. Tensions within liberalism remained and forecast conflicts in the future.

Italian Unification: Cavour and Garibaldi

After the failure of Italian unification in 1848, nationalists in Italy faced a choice between two strategies for achieving statehood. One group, supported by Mazzini and his follower Giuseppe Garibaldi, envisioned a republican Italy built from below by a popular uprising. A second group of more moderate nationalists sought to unify Italy as a constitutional monarchy under the leadership of the kingdom of Piedmont-Sardinia. Giuseppe Garibaldi was a guerrilla fighter who had been exiled twice: first in Latin America, where he fought along with independence movements, and again in the United States. Like Mazzini, Garibaldi was committed to achieving national unification through a popular movement.

The more conservative supporters of Piedmont-Sardinia, on the other hand, sought to steer clear of democracy and the destabilizing forces that it might unleash. The king of Piedmont-Sardinia, Charles Albert, had drawn the attention of Italian nationalists in 1848 when he took up the anti-Austrian cause. Though he later died in exile, his son Victor Emmanuel II (r. 1849–1861) brought a man into his government who would embody the conservative vision of nationhood: the shrewd Sardinian nobleman Count Camillo Benso di Cavour (1810–1861). "In Italy a democratic movement has almost no chance of success," Cavour declared. He instead pursued ambitious but pragmatic reforms guided by the state. As prime minister, he promoted economic expansion, encouraged the construction of a modern transportation infrastructure, reformed the currency, and sought to raise Piedmont-Sardinia's profile in international relations. Garibaldi and Cavour thus represented two different routes to Italian unification: Garibaldi stood for unification from below, Cavour for unification guided from above.

MILL'S LOGIC, OR FRANCHISE FOR FEMALES
"Pray clear the way, there, for these—ah—persons."

JOHN STUART MILL AND SUFFRAGETTES. By 1860, when this cartoon was published, Mill had established a reputation as a liberal political philosopher and a supporter of women's right to vote. Mill argued that women's enfranchisement was essential both from the standpoint of individual liberty and for the good of society as a whole. ▪ *What was amusing about Mill's assertion that women be considered persons in their own right?*

GIUSEPPE GARIBALDI. Note the simple uniform Garibaldi wears in this commemorative portrait, with its iconic symbols of his nationalist movement: the red shirt and the flag of Italy in the background. Compare this with the official portraits of absolutist rulers in previous chapters. ▪ *What was significant about the absence of finery and precious materials in this painting?* ▪ *What does it say about images of masculine leadership in mid-nineteenth-century nationalist imagination? (Compare this with the drawing of Garibaldi and Victor Emmanuel on page 710.)*

Cavour's plan depended on diplomacy. Since Piedmont-Sardinia did not have the military capacity to counter the Austrians in northern Italy, Cavour skillfully cultivated an alliance with one of Austria's traditional rivals: Napoleonic France. In 1858, Cavour held a secret meeting with Napoleon III, who agreed to cooperate in driving the Austrians from Italy if Piedmont would cede Savoy and Nice to France. A war with Austria was duly provoked in 1859, and for a time all went well for the Franco-Italian allies. After the conquest of Lombardy, however, Napoleon III suddenly withdrew, concerned that he might either lose the battle or antagonize French Catholics, who were alienated by Cavour's hostility to the pope. Deserted by the French,

Piedmont could not expel the Austrians from Venetia. Yet the campaign made extensive gains. Piedmont-Sardinia annexed Lombardy. The duchies of Tuscany, Parma, and Modena agreed by plebiscite to join the new state. By the end of this process in 1860, Piedmont-Sardinia had grown to more than twice its original size and was by far the most powerful state in Italy.

As Cavour consolidated the northern and central states, events in the southern states seemed to put those areas up for grabs as well. The unpopular Bourbon king of the Two Sicilies, Francis II (r. 1859–60), faced a fast-spreading peasant revolt that rekindled the hopes of earlier insurrections of the 1820s and 1840s. That revolt, in turn, got a much needed boost from Garibaldi, who landed in Sicily in May of 1860. "The Thousand," as Garibaldi's volunteer fighters called themselves, embodied the widespread support for Italian unification: they came from the north as well as from the south and counted among them members of the middle class as well as workers and artisans. Garibaldi's troops took Sicily and continued on to the mainland. By November 1860, Garibaldi's forces, alongside local insurgents, had taken Naples and toppled the kingdom of Francis II. Emboldened by success, Garibaldi looked to Rome, where French troops guarded the pope.

Garibaldi's rising popularity put him on a collision course with Cavour. Cavour worried that Garibaldi's forces would bring French or Austrian intervention, with unknown consequences. He feared Garibaldi's "irresistible" prestige. Above all, Cavour preferred that Italian unification happen quickly, under Piedmont-Sardinia's stewardship, without domestic turmoil or messy, unpredictable negotiations with other Italian states. "As long as he [Garibaldi] is faithful to his flag, one has to march along with him," Cavour wrote. "This does not alter the fact that it would be eminently desirable for the revolution . . . to be accomplished without him." Determined to recoup the initiative, Cavour dispatched Victor Emmanuel and his army to Rome. Flush with success, the king ordered Garibaldi to cede him military authority, and Garibaldi obeyed. Most of the peninsula was united under a single rule, and Victor Emmanuel assumed the title of king of Italy (r. 1861–78). Cavour's vision of Italian nationhood had won the day.

The final steps of Italy's territorial nation building came indirectly. Venetia remained in the hands of the Austrians until 1866, when Austria was defeated by Prussia and forced to relinquish their last Italian stronghold. Rome had resisted conquest largely because of the military protection that Napoleon III accorded the pope. But in 1870, the

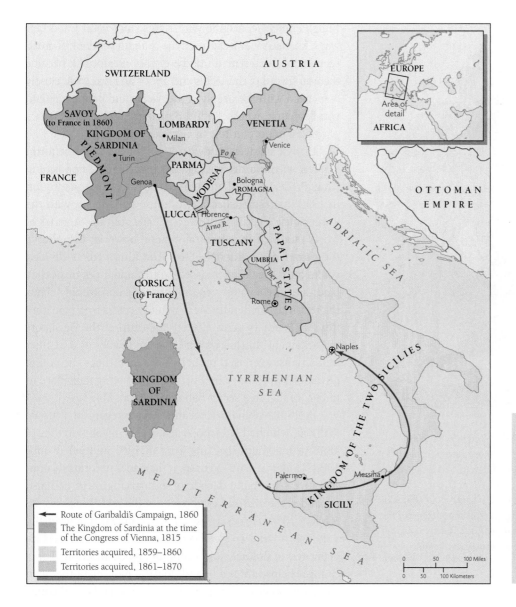

Route of Garibaldi's Campaign, 1860
The Kingdom of Sardinia at the time of the Congress of Vienna, 1815
Territories acquired, 1859–1860
Territories acquired, 1861–1870

0   50   100 Miles
0   50   100 Kilometers

THE UNIFICATION OF ITALY.
▪ *How many phases were involved in Italian unification, according to the map key?*
▪ *Why did it take an extra decade to incorporate Rome and Venetia into the Italian state?*
▪ *Why was Italian unification incomplete until the early twentieth century?*

outbreak of the Franco-Prussian War compelled Napoleon to withdraw his troops. That September, Italian soldiers occupied Rome, and in July 1871 Rome became capital of the united Italian kingdom.

What of the pope's authority? The Italian parliament passed the Law of Papal Guarantees to define and limit the pope's status—an act promptly defied by the reigning pontiff, Pius IX, who refused to have anything to do with a disrespectful secular government. His successors continued to close themselves off in the Vatican until 1929, when a series of agreements between the Italian government and Pius XI settled the dispute.

In 1871, Italy was a state, but nation building was hardly over. A minority of the "Italian" population spoke Italian; the rest used local and regional dialects so diverse

that schoolteachers sent from Rome to Sicily were mistaken for foreigners. As one politician remarked, "We have made Italy; now we must make Italians." The task did not prove easy. The gap between an increasingly industrialized north and a poor and rural south remained wide. Cavour and those who succeeded him as prime minister had to contend with those economic and social inequalities, with rising tensions beween landlords and agricultural workers in rural regions and with lingering resentments of the centralized northern-oriented state. Banditry in the territory of the former kingdom of the Two Sicilies compelled the central administration to dispatch troops to quell serious uprisings, killing more people than in the war of unification. Regional differences and social tensions, then, made building the Italian nation an ongoing process.

"RIGHT LEG IN THE BOOT AT LAST." This image shows Garibaldi helping Victor Emmanuel, former king of Piedmont-Sardinia and the newly crowned king of Italy, get his foot in the Italian boot. What is the significance of their different forms of dress and postures? (Compare this with the portrait of Garibaldi on page 708.) ▪ *How does this image portray the outcome of the contest between the conservative nationalism of Cavour and the more romantic and democratic nationalism of Garibaldi?*

The Unification of Germany: Realpolitik

In 1853, the former revolutionary August Ludwig von Rochau wrote a short book with a long title: *The Principles of Realpolitik Applied to the Conditions of Germany.* Rochau banished the idealism and revolutionary fervor of his youth. "The question of who ought to rule . . . belongs in the realm of philosophical speculation," he wrote. "Practical politics has to do with the simple fact that it is power alone that can rule." Rochau's vision of *Realpolitik*—practical, realistic politics—held that finding ways to achieve and maintain power were more important than moral or ideological goals such as justice or freedom. This view rejected the aspirations of earlier generations of liberal reformers in Germany who believed that progress depended on constitutions and

Enlightenment conceptions of rights. In several important ways, Rochau's views captured the changing outlook of broad sections of the German middle classes. Realpolitik became the watchword of the 1850s and 1860s and was most closely associated with the deeply conservative and pragmatic Otto von Bismarck, whose skillful diplomacy and power politics played an important role in German unification.

Despite its decisive defeat in 1848, German liberalism revived within a decade, against considerable opposition. King Frederick William granted a Prussian constitution in 1850 that established a two-house parliament, with the lower house elected by universal male suffrage. A series of edicts modified the electoral system, however, to preserve the power of traditional elites. The king's edicts divided voters into three classes based on the amount of taxes they paid, and their votes were apportioned accordingly. Thus the relatively small number of wealthy voters who paid one-third of Prussia's taxes elected one-third of the legislators in Parliament. In this way, a large landowner or a wealthy industrialist exercised perhaps seventeen times the voting power of a working man. Furthermore, voting took place in public, orally, so a secret ballot was impossible.

In 1858, William I became prince regent of Prussia. William, who had led troops against the revolutionaries of 1848 in his youth, became king in 1861 and ruled until 1888. Under his rule, Prussia remained a notoriously conservative state, but a decade of industrial growth had also expanded the size and confidence of the middle classes. By the late 1850s, Prussia had an active liberal intelligentsia, a thoughtful and engaged press, and a liberal civil service dedicated to political and economic modernization. These changes helped forge a liberal political movement that won a majority in elections to the lower house and could confidently confront the king.

Liberals in Prussia were especially opposed to the king's high levels of military spending. William wanted to expand the standing army, reduce the role of reserve forces (a more middle-class group), and ensure that military matters were not subject to parliamentary control. Opponents in Parliament suspected the king of making the military his own private force or a state within a state. Between 1859 and 1862, relations deteriorated; and when liberals' protests went unanswered, they refused to approve the regular budget. Faced with a crisis, in 1862 William named Otto von Bismarck minister-president of Prussia. (A prime minister answers to Parliament; Bismarck did not.) This crucial moment in Prussian domestic politics became a decisive turning point in the history of German nationhood.

Born into the Junker class of conservative, land-owning aristocrats, Bismarck had fiercely opposed the liberal movement of 1848–49. He was not a nationalist. He was before all else a Prussian. He did not institute domestic reforms because he favored the rights of a particular group but because he thought that these policies would unify and strengthen Prussia. When he maneuvered to bring other German states under Prussian domination, he did so not in pursuit of a grand German design but because he believed that union in some form was inevitable and that Prussia had to seize the initiative. Bismarck happily acknowledged that he admired power and that he considered himself destined for greatness. He had a reputation for cynicism, arrogance, and uninhibited frankness in expressing his views. Yet a Latin phrase he frequently quoted distilled a more careful assessment of the relationship between individuals and history: "Man cannot create or control the tide of time, he can only move in the same direction and try to direct it."

In Prussia, Bismarck defied parliamentary opposition. When the liberal majority refused to pass a budget because of disagreements about spending for the army, he dissolved Parliament, claiming that the constitution, whatever its purposes, had not been designed to subvert the state. His most decisive actions, however, were in foreign policy. Once opposed to nationalism, Bismarck skillfully played the national card to preempt his liberal opponents at home and to make German nation building an accomplishment—and an extension—of Prussian authority.

The other "German" power was Austria, which wielded considerable influence within the German Confederation and especially over the largely Catholic regions in the south. Bismarck saw a stark contrast between Austrian and Prussian interests and skillfully exploited Austria's economic disadvantages and the Habsburgs' internal ethnic struggles. He inflamed a long-smoldering dispute with Denmark over Schleswig (SHLAYS-vihg) and Holstein, two provinces peopled by Germans and Danes and claimed by both the German Confederation and Denmark. In 1864, the Danish king attempted to annex the provinces, prompting a German nationalist outcry. Bismarck cast the conflict as a Prussian matter and persuaded Austria to join Prussia in a war against Denmark. The war was short, and it forced the Danish ruler to cede the two provinces to Austria and Prussia. As Bismarck hoped, the victorious alliance promptly fell apart. In 1866, casting Prussia as the defender of larger German interests, he declared war on Austria. The conflict, known as the Seven Weeks' War, ended in Prussian victory. Austria gave up all claims to Schleswig and Holstein, surrendered Venetia to the Italians, and agreed to dissolve the German Confederation. In its place, Bismarck created the North German Confederation, a union of all the German states north of the Main River.

Bismarck "played power politics with an eye to public opinion." Both wars had strong public support, and Prussian victories weakened liberal opposition to the king and his president-minister. In the aftermath of the Austrian defeat, Prussian liberals gave up their battle over budgets, the military, and constitutional provisions. Bismarck also sought support among the masses. He understood that Germans did not necessarily support business elites, the bureaucracies of their own small states, or the Austrian Habsburgs. The constitution of the North German Confederation gave the appearance of a more liberal political body, with a bicameral legislature, freedom of the press, and universal male suffrage in the lower house. Its structure, however, gave Prussia and the conservative emperor a decisive advantage in the North German Confederation—and in the soon to be expanded empire.

The final step in the completion of German unity was the Franco-Prussian War of 1870–71. Bismarck hoped that a conflict with France would arouse German nationalism in Bavaria, Württemberg, and other southern states still outside the confederation and overcome their historic wariness of Prussia. A diplomatic tempest concerning the right of the Hohenzollerns (Prussia's ruling family) to occupy the Spanish throne created an opportunity to foment a Franco-German misunderstanding. King William agreed to meet with the French ambassador at the resort spa of Ems in Prussia to discuss the Spanish succession. William initially acquiesced to French demands, but when the French blundered by asking for "perpetual exclusion" of the Hohenzollern family from the Spanish throne, Bismarck seized his opportunity. He edited a telegraph from King William so as to make it appear that the Prussian king had rebuffed the French ambassador. Once the redacted report reached France, the nation reacted with calls for war. Prussia echoed the call, and Bismarck published evidence that he claimed proved French designs on the Rhineland.

As soon as war was declared, the south German states rallied to Prussia's side. The conflict was quickly over. No European powers came to France's aid. Austria, the most likely candidate, remained weakened by its recent war with Prussia. The Hungarians welcomed a strengthened Prussia, for the weaker Austria was as a German power, the stronger would be the Magyar claims to power sharing in the empire. On the battlefield, France could not match Prussia's professionally trained and superbly equipped forces. The war began in July and ended in September with the defeat of the French and the capture of Napoleon III at Sedan in France. Insurrectionary forces in Paris continued to hold out against the Germans through the winter of 1870–71, but the French imperial government collapsed. On January 18, 1871, in the Hall of Mirrors at Versailles, symbol of the powerful past of French absolutism, the German Empire was proclaimed. All the German

The New German Nation

In order to silence their critics at home and abroad, nationalists in Germany sought to create a vision of German history that made unification the natural outcome of a deep historical process that had begun hundreds of years before. In image A, the family of a cavalry officer prepares to hang a portrait of King William on the wall, next to portraits of Martin Luther, Frederick the Great, and Field Marshal von Blücher, who commanded the Prussian forces at Waterloo. In the lower left corner, two boys roll up a portrait of the defeated French emperor, Napoleon III. The implication, of course, was that the unification of Germany was the inevitable culmination of generations of German heroes who all worked toward the same goal.

This unity was itself controversial among German people. Image B, a pro-Bismarck cartoon, shows the German minister-president dragging the unwilling liberal members of the Prussian par-liament along with him as he pulls a triumphal chariot toward his military confrontation with Austria in 1866. The caption reads: "And in this sense, too, we are in agreement with Count Bismarck, and we have pulled the same rope as him." Image C, on the other hand, expresses reservations about Prussian dominance in the new empire. The title "Germany's Future" and the caption:

A. *Homage to Kaiser Wilhelm I* by Paul Bürde, 1871.

states that had not already been absorbed into the Prussian fold, except Austria, declared their allegiance to William I, henceforth emperor or kaiser. Four months later, at Frankfurt, a treaty between the French and the Germans ceded the border region of Alsace to the new German Empire and forced the French to pay an indemnity of 5 billion francs. Prussia accounted for 60 percent of the new state's territory and population. The Prussian kaiser, prime minister, army, and most of the bureaucracy remained intact, now reconfigured as the German nation-state. This was not the new nation for which Prussian liberals had hoped. It marked a "revolution from above" rather than from below. Still, the more optimistic believed that the German Empire would evolve in a different political direction and that they could eventually "extend freedom through unity."

The State and Nationality: Centrifugal Forces in the Austrian Empire

Germany emerged from the 1860s a stronger, unified nation. The Habsburg Empire faced a very different situation, with different resources, and emerged a weakened,

"Will it fit under one hat? I think it will only fit under a [Prussian] Pickelhaube." The *Pickelhaube*—the characteristic pointed helmet of the Prussian army—had already become a much-feared symbol of Prussian military force. Such an image may well have struck a chord with residents of the non-Prussian German states who now paid taxes to the Prussian monarchy and served in an army dominated by Prussian officers.

Questions for Analysis

1. What is the significance of the familial setting in image A? Why was it important for nationalists to emphasize a multigenerational family as the repository of German national spirit?

2. How do images B and C treat the question of Prussia's role within the new German nation? Was German national identity seen as something

built from below or defined from above by a strong monarchy?

3. What is the place of the individual citizen in these representations of the German nation?

C. "Germany's Future" (1870).

B. Prussian liberals and Bismarck after Königgrätz (1866).

precariously balanced, multiethnic dual monarchy, also called Austria-Hungary.

As we have seen, ethnic nationalism was a powerful force in the Habsburg monarchy in 1848. Yet the Habsburg state, with a combination of military repression and tactics that divided its enemies, had proved more powerful. It abolished serfdom but made few other concessions to its opponents. The Hungarians, who had nearly won independence in the spring of 1848, were essentially reconquered. Administrative reforms created a new and more uniform legal system, rationalized taxation, and imposed a single-language policy that favored German. The issue of man-

aging ethnic relations, however, only grew more difficult. Through the 1850s and 1860s, the subject nationalities, as they were often called, bitterly protested the powerlessness of their local diets, military repression, and cultural disenfranchisement. The Czechs in Bohemia, for instance, grew increasingly alienated by policies that favored the German minority of the province. In response, they became more insistent on their Slavic identity—a movement welcomed by Russia, which became the sponsor of a broad pan-Slavism. The Hungarians, or Magyars, the most powerful of the subject nationalities, sought to reclaim the autonomy they had glimpsed in 1848.

NORTH SEA
SWEDEN
DENMARK
Copenhagen
BALTIC SEA
Memel
Königsberg
EAST PRUSSIA
SCHLESWIG
Kiel
HOLSTEIN
Lübeck
POMERANIA
Danzig
WEST PRUSSIA
MECKLENBURG-SCHWERIN
Stettin
POSEN
POLAND
Hamburg
OLDENBURG
Bremen
HANOVER
Hanover
Berlin
BRANDENBURG
Posen
Warsaw
RUSSIAN
Amsterdam
NETHERLANDS
Lodz
EMPIRE
WESTPHALIA
Breslau
SILESIA
Antwerp
Rhine R.
Leipzig
Weimar
Dresden
BELGIUM
Bonn
Cologne
THURINGIAN STATES
SAXONY
Lemberg
RHINE PROVINCE
Sadowa (1866)
Cracow
LUXEMBOURG
Mainz
Frankfurt
BOHEMIA
Prague
MORAVIA
Sedan (1870)
HESSE
Olmütz
Verdun
Metz
PALATINATE
Karlsruhe
Nuremberg
BAVARIA
AUSTRIAN
LORRAINE
Toul
Strasbourg
Stuttgart
Danube R.
Vienna
ALSACE
Munich
AUSTRIA
BADEN
HUNGARY
FRANCE
Zurich
Berne
EMPIRE
SWITZERLAND
Milan
Venice
Trieste
EUROPE
Area of detail
ADRIATIC SEA
AFRICA
ITALY

— German Confederation boundary (1815)
  Prussian acquisitions
  From Austria in 1763   Prussia
  From partitions of Poland   (1815)
  in 1772, 1793, 1795
  States annexed by Prussia in 1866
  States joining Prussia in Confederation of 1867
— North German Confederation boundary
  States added to form German Empire (1871)
  Territories ceded by France (1871)
✳ Battle
■ Fortifications

TOWARD THE UNIFICATION OF GERMANY. Note the many elements that made up a unified Germany and the stages that brought them together. ▪ *Did this new nation have any resemblance to the unified Germany envisioned by the liberal revolutionaries of the Frankfurt Preparliament in 1848? (See page 697.)* ▪ *How many stages were involved in the unification of Germany, and how many years did it take?* ▪ *What region filled with German-speaking peoples was not included in the new unified Germany and why?*

In this context, Austria's defeats at the hands of Piedmont-Sardinia in 1859 and Prussia in 1866 became especially significant. The 1866 war forced the emperor Franz Josef to renegotiate the very structure of the empire. To stave off a revolution by the Hungarians, Francis Joseph agreed to a new federal structure in the form of the Dual Monarchy. Austria-Hungary had a common system of taxa-

tion, a common army, and made foreign and military policy together. Francis Joseph was emperor of Austria and king of Hungary. But internal and constitutional affairs were separated. The Ausgleich, or Settlement, allowed the Hungarians to establish their own constitution; their own legislature; and their own capital, combining the cities of Buda and Pest.

What of the other nationalities? The official policy of the Dual Monarchy stated that they were not to be discriminated against and that they could use their own languages. Official policy was only loosely enforced. More important, elevating the Hungarians and conferring on them alone the benefits of political nationhood could only worsen relations with other groups. On the Austrian side of the Dual Monarchy, minority nationalities such as the Poles, Czechs, and Slovenes resented their second-class status. On the Hungarian side, the regime embarked on a project of Magyarization, attempting to make the state, the civil service, and the schools more thoroughly Hungarian—an effort that did not sit well with Serbs and Croats.

In spite of these divisions, however, the Austro-Hungarian Empire succeeded for a time in creating a different kind of political and culture space within a Europe that was increasingly given over to nation-states who perceived their interests to be irrevocably opposed. The Austrian capital of Vienna developed a reputation for intellectual and cultural refinement that was in part a product of the many different peoples who made up the Habsburg lands, including Germans, Jews, Hungarians, Italians, Czechs, Poles, Serbs, Croats, and Balkan Muslims from lands that formerly belonged to the Ottoman Empire. This polyglot culture produced Béla Bartók (1881–1945), the great Hungarian composer and admirer of folk musical traditions; Gustav Mahler (1860–1911), a German-Austrian composer whose romantic symphonies and conducting prowess made him a global celebrity by the time of his death. From the same intellectual milieu came Sigmund Freud (1856–1939), a German-speaking Jewish doctor from Vienna whose writings helped shape modern psychology; and Gustav Klimt (1862–1918), a painter and founding member of the Viennese Secession movement, which rejected the reigning classicism of the Austrian art world and made the Austrian capital an important center for the birth of modern art.

The Austrian emperor's deep opposition to nationalism was not just geopolitical, therefore, but also a defense of a different relationship between the nation-state and culture. Unlike the governments of France, England, Italy, or Germany, the Habsburgs did not seek to build a nation-state based on a common cultural identity. It tried instead to build a state and administrative structure strong enough to keep the pieces from spinning off, at times playing different minorities off against each other, but also conceding greater autonomy to different groups when it seemed necessary. As the nineteenth century unfolded, however, discontented subject nationalities would appeal to other powers—Serbia, Russia, the Ottomans—and this balancing act would become more difficult.

NATION AND STATE BUILDING IN RUSSIA AND THE UNITED STATES

The challenges of nationalism and nation building also occupied Russia, the United States, and Canada. In all three countries, nation building entailed territorial and economic expansion, the incorporation of new peoples, and—in Russia and the United States—contending with the enormous problems of slavery and serfdom.

Territory, the State, and Serfdom: Russia

Serfdom in Russia, which had been legally formalized in 1649, had begun to draw significant protest from the intelligentsia under the reign of Catherine the Great (r. 1762–96). After 1789, and especially after 1848, the abolition of serfdom elsewhere in Europe made the issue more urgent. Abolishing serfdom became part of the larger project of building Russia as a modern nation. How that should happen was the subject of much debate. Two schools of thought emerged. The "Slavophiles," or Romantic nationalists, sought to preserve Russia's distinctive features. They idealized traditional Russian culture and the peasant commune, rejecting Western secularism, urban commercialism, and bourgeois culture. In contrast, the "westernizers" wished to see Russia adopt European developments in science, technology, and education, which they believed to be the foundation for Western liberalism and the protection of individual rights. Both groups agreed that serfdom must be abolished. The Russian nobility, however, tenaciously opposed emancipation. Tangled debates about how lords would be compensated for the loss of "their" serfs, and how emancipated serfs would survive without full-scale land redistribution, also checked progress on the issue. The Crimean War (see below) broke the impasse. In its aftermath, Alexander II (r. 1855–81) forced the issue. Worried that the persistence of serfdom had sapped Russian strength and contributed to its defeat in the war, and persuaded that serfdom would only continue to prompt violent conflict, he ended serfdom by decree in 1861.

The emancipation decree of 1861 was a reform of massive scope, but paradoxically it produced limited change. It granted legal rights to some 22 million serfs and authorized their title to a portion of the land they had worked. It also required the state to compensate landowners for the properties they relinquished. Large-scale landowners vastly inflated their compensation claims, however, and

Competing Viewpoints

The Abolition of Serfdom in Russia

> The abolition of serfdom was central to Tsar Alexander II's program of modernization and reform after the Crimean War. Emancipated serfs were now allowed to own their land, ending centuries of bondage. The decree, however, emphasized the tsar's benevolence and the nobility's generosity—not peasant rights. The government did not want emancipation to bring revolution to the countryside; it sought to reinforce the state's authority, the landowners' power, and the peasants' obligations. After spelling out the detailed provisions for emancipation, the decree added the paragraphs reprinted here.
>
> Emancipation did not solve problems in the Russian countryside. On the contrary, it unleashed a torrent of protest, including complaints from peasants that nobles were undermining attempts to reform. These petitions in the second section detail the struggles that came in the wake of emancipation in two villages.

Tsar Alexander II's Decree Emancipating the Serfs, 1861

And We place Our hope in the good sense of Our people.

When word of the Government's plan to abolish the law of bondage [serfdom] reached peasants unprepared for it, there arose a partial misunderstanding. Some [peasants] thought about freedom and forgot about obligations. But the general good sense [of the people] was not disturbed in the conviction that anyone freely enjoying the goods of society correspondingly owes it to the common good to fulfill certain obligations, [a conviction held] both by natural reason and by Christian law, according to which "every soul must be subject to the governing authorities." . . . Rights legally acquired by the landlords cannot be taken from them without a decent return or [their] voluntary concession; and that it would be contrary to all justice to make use of the lords' land without bearing the corresponding obligation.

And now We hopefully expect that the bonded people, as a new future opens before them, will understand and accept with gratitude the important sacrifice made by the Well-born Nobility for the improvement of their lives.

Source: James Cracraft, ed., *Major Problems in the History of Imperial Russia* (Lexington, MA: 1994), pp. 340–44.

Emancipation: The View from Below

Petition from Peasants in Podosinovka (Voronezh Province) to Alexander II, May 1863

The most merciful manifesto of Your Imperial Majesty from 19 February 1861, with the published rules, put a limit to the enslavement of the people in blessed Russia. But some former serfowners—who desire not to improve the peasants' life, but to oppress and ruin them—apportion land contrary to the laws, choose the best land from all the fields for themselves, and give the poor peasants . . . the worst and least usable lands.

To this group of squires must be counted our own, Anna Mikhailovna Raevskaia. . . . Of our fields and resources, she chose the best places from amidst our strips, and, like a cooking ring in a hearth, carved off 300 dessiatines [measures of land] for herself. . . .

But our community refused to accept so ruinous an allotment and requested that we be given an allotment in accordance with the local Statute. . . . The peace arbitrator . . . and the police chief . . . slandered us before the governor, alleging that we were rioting and that it is impossible for them to enter our village.

The provincial governor believed this lie and sent 1,200 soldiers of the penal command to our village.... Without any cause, our village priest Father Peter—rather than give an uplifting pastoral exhortation to stop the spilling of innocent blood—joined these reptiles, with the unanimous incitement of the authorities.... They summoned nine township heads and their aides from other townships.... In their presence, the provincial governor—without making any investigation and without interrogating a single person—ordered that the birch rods be brought and that the punishment commence, which was carried out with cruelty and mercilessness. They punished up to 200 men and women; 80 people were at four levels (with 500, 400, 300 and 200 blows); some received lesser punishment... and when the inhuman punishment of these innocent people had ended, the provincial governor said: "If you find the land unsuitable, I do not forbid you to file petitions wherever you please," and then left....

We dare to implore you, Orthodox emperor and our merciful father, not to reject the petition of a community with 600 souls, including wives and children. Order with your tsarist word that our community be allotted land... as the law dictates without selecting the best sections of fields and meadows, but in straight lines.... [Order that] the meadows and haylands along the river Elan be left to our community without any restriction; these will enable us to feed our cattle and smaller livestock, which are necessary for our existence.

Petition from Peasants in Balashov District to Grand Duke Constantin Nikolaevich, January 25, 1862

Your Imperial Excellency! Most gracious sire! Grand Duke Konstantin Nikolaevich! ...

After being informed of the Imperial manifesto on the emancipation of peasants from serfdom on 1861 ... we received this [news] with jubilation.... But from this moment, our squire ordered that the land be cut off from the entire township. But this is absolutely intolerable for us: it not only denies us profit, but threatens us with a catastrophic future. He began to hold repeated meetings and [tried to] force us to sign that we agreed to accept the above land allotment. But, upon seeing so unexpected a change, and bearing in mind the gracious manifesto, we refused.... After assembling the entire township, they tried to force us into making illegal signatures accepting the land cut-offs. But when they saw that this did not succeed, they had a company of soldiers sent in.... Then [Colonel] Globbe came from their midst, threatened us with exile to Siberia, and ordered the soldiers to strip the peasants and to punish seven people by flogging in the most inhuman manner. They still have not regained consciousness.

Source: Gregory L. Freeze, ed., *From Supplication to Revolution: A Documentary Social History of Imperial Russia* (New York: 1988), pp. 170–73.

Questions for Analysis

1. What did Tsar Alexander II fear most in liberating the serfs from bondage? What provisions did he make to ensure that the emancipation would not destabilize his regime?

2. What issues mattered most to the peasantry? What is their attitude toward the tsar?

3. Given the immediate danger to social peace, why did the tsar feel that emancipating the serfs was necessary?

managed to retain much of the most profitable acreage for themselves. As a result, the land granted to peasants was often of poor quality and insufficient to sustain themselves and their families. Moreover, the newly liberated serfs had to pay in installments for their land, which was not granted to them individually but rather to a village commune, which collected their payments. As a result, the pattern of rural life in Russia did not change drastically. The system of payment kept peasants in the villages—not as freestanding farmers but as agricultural laborers for their former masters.

While the Russian state undertook reforms, it also expanded its territory. After midcentury, the Russians pressed east and south. They invaded and conquered several independent Islamic kingdoms along the former Silk Road and expanded into Siberia in search of natural resources. Russian diplomacy wrung various commercial concessions from the Chinese that led to the founding of the Siberian city of Vladivostok in 1860. Racial, ethnic, and religious differences made governing a daunting task. In most cases, the Russian state did not try to assimilate the populations of the new territories: an acceptance of ethnic particularity was a pragmatic response to the difficulties of governing such a heterogeneous population. When the state did attempt to impose Russian culture, the results were disastrous. Whether power was wielded by the nineteenth-century tsars or, later, by the Soviet Union, powerful centrifugal forces pulled against genuine unification. Expansion helped Russia create a vast empire that was geographically of one piece but by no means one nation.

Territory and the Nation: The United States

The American Revolution had bequeathed to the United States a loose union of slave and free states, tied together in part by a commitment to territorial expansion. The so-called Jeffersonian Revolution combined democratic aspirations with a drive to expand the nation's boundaries. Leaders of the movement, under the Democratic-Republican president Thomas Jefferson (1801–1809), campaigned to add the Bill of Rights to the Constitution and were almost exclusively responsible for its success. Though they supported, in principle, the separation of powers, they believed in the supremacy of the people's representatives and viewed with alarm attempts of the executive and judicial branches to increase their power. They supported a political system based on an aristocracy of "virtue and talent," in which respect for personal liberty would be the guiding principle. They opposed the establishment of a national religion and special privilege, whether of birth or of wealth. Yet the Jeffersonian vision of the republic rested on the independence of yeoman farmers, and the independence and prosperity of those farmers depended on the availability of new lands. This made territorial expansion, as exemplified by the Louisiana Purchase in 1803, central to Jeffersonian America. Expansion brought complications. While it did provide land for many yeoman farmers in the north and south, it also added millions of acres of prime cotton land, thus extending the empire of slavery. The purchase of the port of New Orleans made lands in the south well worth developing but led the American republic forcibly to remove Native Americans from the Old South west of the Mississippi River. This process of expansion and expropriation stretched from Jefferson's administration through the age of Jackson, or the 1840s.

Under Andrew Jackson (1829–1837), the Democrats (as some of the Democratic-Republicans were now called) transformed the circumscribed liberalism of the Jeffersonians. They campaigned to extend the suffrage to all white males; they argued that all officeholders

THE EMANCIPATION OF THE SERFS. This engraving depicts officials delivering the formal decree liberating serfs. A massive reform granting legal rights to millions of people, emancipation was undermined by the payments serfs owed to their former owners.

AMERICAN EXPANSION IN THE EARLY NINETEENTH CENTURY. ▪ *What three European powers had a substantial role to play in American expansion?* ▪ *What events enabled the United States to acquire all lands west of the Mississippi River?* ▪ *How did the loss of these lands affect European powers?*

should be elected rather than appointed; and they sought the frequent rotation of men in positions of political power—a doctrine that permitted politicians to use patronage to build national political parties. Moreover, the Jacksonian vision of democracy and nationhood carried over into a crusade to incorporate more territories into the republic. It was the United States' "Manifest Destiny," wrote a New York editor, "to overspread the continent allotted by Providence for the free development of our yearly multiplying millions." That "overspreading" brought Oregon and Washington into the Union through a compromise with the British and brought Arizona, Texas, New Mexico, Utah, Nevada, and California through war with Mexico—all of which led to the wholesale expropriation of Native American lands. Territorial expansion was key to nation building, but it was built on increasingly impossible conflict over slavery.

The American Civil War, 1861–1865

The politics of slavery had already led to its abolition in France and Britain (see Chapter 20), but in the United States the combination of a growing abolitionist movement, a slave-owning class that feared the economic power of the north, and territorial expansion created deadlock and crisis. As the country expanded west, the North and South engaged in a protracted tug of war about whether new states were to be "free" or "slave." In the North, territorial expansion heightened calls for free labor; in the South, it deepened whites' commitment to an economy and society based on plantation slavery. Ultimately, the changes pushed southern political leaders toward secession. The failure of a series of elaborate compromises led to the outbreak of the Civil War in 1861.

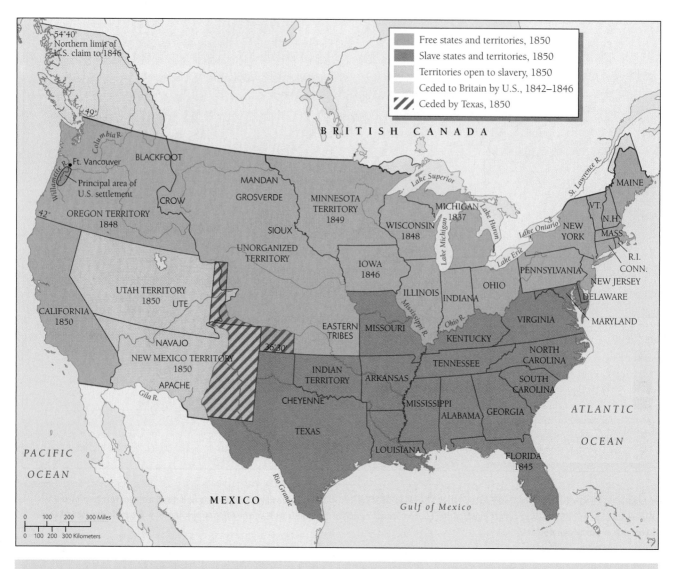

AMERICAN EXPANSION IN THE LATE NINETEENTH CENTURY. Note the stages of American settlement across the North American continent and the dates for the extension of slavery into new territories. ▪ *How did the question of slavery shape the way that new territories were absorbed into the republic?* ▪ *Compare American expansion with European colonialism?*

The protracted and costly struggle proved a first experience of the horrors of modern war and prefigured the First World War. It also decisively transformed the nation. First, it abolished slavery. Second, it established the preeminence of the national government over states' rights. The Fourteenth Amendment to the Constitution stated specifically that all Americans were citizens of the United States and not of an individual state or territory. In declaring that no citizen was to be deprived of life, liberty, or property without due process of law, it established that "due process" was to be defined by the national, not the state or territorial, government. Third, in the aftermath of the Civil War, the U.S. economy expanded with stunning rapidity. In 1865, there were 35,000 miles of railroad track in the United States; by 1900, there were almost 200,000. Industrial and agricultural production rose, putting the United States in a position to compete with Great Britain. As we will see later on, American industrialists, bankers, and retailers introduced innovations in assembly-line manufacturing, corporate organization, and advertising that startled their European counterparts and gave the United States new power in world politics. These developments were all part of the process of nation building. They did not overcome deep racial, regional, or class divides. Though the war brought the South back into the Union, the rise of northern capitalism magnified the backwardness of the South as an underdeveloped agricultural region whose wealth was extracted by northern industrialists. The railroad corporations, which pieced together the national infrastructure, became the classic foe of labor and agrarian reformers. In

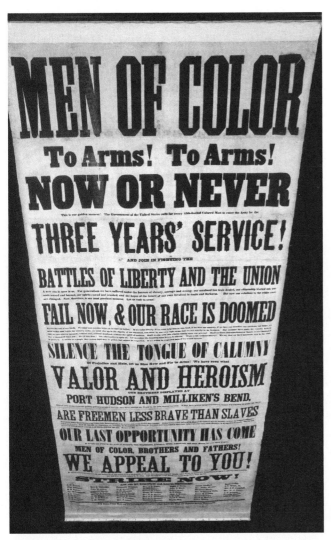

CIVIL WAR RECRUITING POSTER. This poster, created by northern African American abolitionists, exhorts fellow blacks to fight in the American Civil War.

these ways, the Civil War laid the foundations for the modern American nation-state.

"EASTERN QUESTIONS": INTERNATIONAL RELATIONS AND THE DECLINE OF OTTOMAN POWER

During the nineteenth century, questions of national identity and international power were inextricable from contests over territory. War and diplomacy drew and redrew boundaries as European nations groped toward a sustainable balance of power. The rise of new powers, principally the German Empire, posed one set of challenges to continental order. The waning power of older regimes posed another. The Crimean War, which lasted from 1853 to 1856, was a particularly gruesome attempt to cope with the most serious such collapse. As the Ottoman Empire lost its grip on its provinces in southeastern Europe, the "Eastern Question" of who would benefit from Ottoman weakness drew Europe into war. At stake were not only territorial gains but also strategic interests, alliances, and the balance of power in Europe. And though the war occurred before the unification of the German and Italian states, it structured the system of Great Power politics that guided Europe until (and indeed toward) the First World War.

The Crimean War, 1853–1856

The root causes of the war lay in the Eastern Question and the decline of the Ottoman Empire. The crisis that provoked it, however, involved religion—namely French and Russian claims to protect religious minorities and the holy places of Jerusalem within the Muslim Ottoman Empire. In 1853, a three-way quarrel among France (on behalf of Roman Catholics), Russia (representing Eastern Orthodox Christians), and Turkey devolved into a Russian confrontation with the Turkish sultan. Confident that Turkey would be unable to resist, concerned that other powers might take advantage of Turkish weakness, and persuaded (mistakenly) that they had British support, the Russians moved troops into the Ottoman-governed territories of Moldavia and Walachia (see the map on page 722). In October 1853, Turkey, also persuaded they would be supported by the British, declared war on Russia. The war became a disaster for the Turks, who lost their fleet at the battle of Sinope in November. But Russia's success alarmed the British and the French, who considered Russian expansion a threat to their interests in the Balkans, the eastern Mediterranean, and, for the British, the route to India. Determined to check that expansion, France and Britain each declared war on Russia in March 1854. In September, they landed on the Russian peninsula of Crimea and headed for the Russian naval base at Sevastopol, to which they laid siege. France, Britain, and the Ottomans were joined in 1855 by the small but ambitious Italian state of Piedmont-Sardinia, all fighting against the Russians. This was the closest Europe had come to a general war since 1815.

The war was relatively short, but its conduct was devastating. Conditions on the Crimean peninsula were dire, and the disastrous mismanagement of supplies and hygiene by the British and French led to epidemics among the troops.

THE CRIMEAN WAR. Note the theater of operations and the major assaults of the Crimean War. ▪ *Which empires and nations were in a position to take advantage of Ottoman weakness?* ▪ *Who benefited from the outcome, and who was most harmed?* ▪ *In what ways was the Crimean War the first modern war?*

At least as many soldiers died from typhus or cholera as in combat. The fighting was bitter, marked by such notoriously inept strategies as the British "charge of the Light Brigade," in which a British cavalry unit was slaughtered by massed Russian artillery. Vast battles pitted tens of thousands of British and French troops against Russian formations, combat that was often settled with bayonets. Despite the disciplined toughness of the British and French troops, and despite their nations' dominance of the seas around Crimea, the Russians denied them a clear victory. Sevastopol, under siege for nearly a year, did not fall until September 1855. The bitter, unsatisfying conflict was ended by treaty in 1856.

For the French and Sardinians, the bravery of their soldiers bolstered positive national sentiments at home; for the British and Russians, however, the poorly managed war provoked waves of intense criticism. As far as international relations were concerned, the peace settlement dealt a blow to Russia, whose influence in the Balkans was

drastically curbed. The provinces of Moldavia and Walachia were united as Romania and became an independent nation. Austria's refusal to come to the aid of Russia cost Russia the support of its powerful former ally. The Crimean War embarrassed France and left Russia and Austria considerably weaker, opening an advantage for Bismarck in the 1860s, as we saw earlier.

The Crimean War was important in other ways as well. Though fought largely with the same methods and mentalities employed in the Napoleonic Wars forty years earlier, the war brought innovations that forecast the direction of modern warfare. It saw the first significant use of rifled muskets, underwater mines, and trench warfare as well as the first tactical use of railroads and telegraphs.

In addition, the war was covered by the first modern war correspondents and photojournalists, making it the most public war to date. Reports from the theater of war were sent "live" by telegraph to Britain and France with

CAPTAIN DAMES OF THE ROYAL ARTILLERY, 1855. Roger Fenton studied painting in London and then Paris, where he learned about and started to experiment with photography. He developed a mobile darkroom and ventured into the English countryside. In 1855, he went to the Crimea, subsidized by the British government. Photographs of movement and troops in battle were still impossible, and political restraint kept him from photographing the horrors of the increasingly unpopular Crimean War. Still, his were the first war photographs.

objective and sobering detail; the (London) *Times* reporter William Howard Russell, for instance, heaped criticism on the government for the deplorable conditions British soldiers endured. The care and supply of the troops became national scandals in the popular press, prompting dramatic changes in the military's administrative and logistical systems and making heroes of individual doctors and nurses such as Florence Nightingale. The British government and commercial publishers both sent photographers to document the war's progress and perhaps also to counter charges that troops were undersupplied and malnourished. Roger Fenton, the most prominent and prolific of these war photographers, employed the new medium to capture the grim realities of camp life. Technological limitations and political considerations kept him from photographing the more gruesome carnage of the battlefield, but Fenton's photographs introduced a new level of realism and immediacy to the public's conception of war.

CONCLUSION

The decades between 1848 and 1870 brought intense nation building in the Western world. The unification of Germany and Italy changed the map of Europe, with important consequences for the balance of power. The emergence of the United States as a major power also had international ramifications. For old as well as new nation-states, economic development and political transformation—often on a very large scale—were important means of increasing and securing the state's power. Even though the liberal revolutionaries of 1848 had not achieved the goals

***THE STONE BREAKERS* BY GUSTAVE COURBET, 1849.** Courbet was a French realist painter who depicted everyday men and women in an honest and unromantic manner. Considered one of his most important works, this painting of two ordinary peasants building a road was destroyed in Dresden during the Second World War.

AUTHOR LEO TOLSTOY. Although a wealthy landowner, Tolstoy often dressed as a peasant. He became increasingly ascetic, casting off the corruptions of the world, and pacifist. In this picture, he is leaving his home for a hermitage.

they sought, their demands for more representative government, the abolition of privilege, and land reform still had to be reckoned with, as did the systems of slavery and serfdom. Trailing the banner of nationhood was an explosive set of questions about how to balance the power and interests of minorities and majorities, of the wealthy and poor, of the powerful and the dispossessed. Nation building not only changed states, it transformed relations between states and their citizens.

These transformations were anything but predictable. Nationalism showed itself to be a volatile, erratic, and malleable force during the mid-nineteenth century. It provided

After You Read This Chapter

Ⓢ Visit StudySpace for quizzes, additional review materials, and multimedia documents. **wwnorton.com/web/westernciv18**

REVIEWING THE OBJECTIVES

- Revolutions broke out in 1848 in almost every capital of Europe except for London and St. Petersburg. What accounts for this wave of simultaneous revolutionary movements?

- Liberal revolutionaries in France in 1848 did not have the same goals as their socialist allies. What were their goals and why did they fail to achieve them?

- Liberal revolutionaries in the German-speaking lands of central Europe in 1848 were forced to reckon with Austrian and Prussian states in their bid for national unification. What did they want, and why did they fail?

- Nationalists in both Germany and Italy were divided between those who supported the creation of a new nation from below, through popular movements, and those who preferred nation building from above. How did these divisions work themselves out in the process of national unification?

- Creating a modern nation in Russia entailed the end of serfdom, whereas in the United States, political leaders from the North and South debated the place of slavery in the modern nation-state. In what ways were national debates about citizenship in these countries shaped by the widespread practices of bondage?

- The three major European wars of this period were of relatively short duration, but they had profound effects on the international balance of power in Europe. Which countries emerged stronger from these conflicts, and which found their interests most damaged?

much of the fuel for revolutionary movements in 1848, but it also helped tear their movements apart, undermining revolutionary gains. Those who had linked their democratic goals to the rise of new nation-states were sorely disappointed. In the aftermath of the defeated revolutions, most nation building took a conservative tack. Nationalism came to serve the needs of statesmen and bureaucrats who did not seek an "awakening of peoples" and who had serious reservations about popular sovereignty. For them, nations simply represented modern, organized, and stronger states.

The result of these many tensions was an age that seemed a contradictory mix of the old and the new, of monarchies beset with debates about nationality and citizenship, of land-owning aristocratic elites rubbing elbows with newly wealthy industrialists, and of artisan handworkers meeting up with factory laborers in worker's associations that debated the proper path toward realizing their socialist goals. Remarkably, the result of this period of intense nation building was a period of unusual stability on the Continent, which ushered in an era of unprecedented capitalist and imperial expansion. The antagonisms unleashed by German unification and the crumbling of the Ottoman Empire would reemerge, however, in the Great Power politics that precipitated the First World War.

PEOPLE, IDEAS, AND EVENTS IN CONTEXT

- What circumstances led to the downfall of **LOUIS PHILIPPE**'s government in France? What divisions between supporters of the revolution led to the **JUNE DAYS** in Paris in 1848?
- What role did the **ZOLLVEREIN** and the **FRANKFURT PARLIAMENT** play in the creation of a unified Germany?
- How and why did **OTTO VON BISMARCK** aim for a policy of German national unification during his time in office?
- How did **GIUSEPPE GARIBALDI** and **CAMILLO BENSO DI CAVOUR** initially see the process of Italian unification? Whose vision came closest to reality?
- Who was **NAPOLEON III**, and how did his policies contribute to nation building in France?
- What was the contribution of **JOHN STUART MILL** to debates about citizenship in Britain?
- Why were nationalist movements such as **PAN-SLAVISM** or **MAGYAR NATIONALISM** such a danger to the Austro-Hungarian Empire?
- Why did **TSAR ALEXANDER II** decide to **EMANCIPATE THE SERFS**?
- What made the **CRIMEAN WAR** different from previous conflicts and more like the wars of the twentieth century?

THINKING ABOUT CONNECTIONS

- Revolutionaries in 1848, whether they were in Paris, Rome, Berlin, or Vienna, must have been aware of connections between their own struggles and the historical example of the French Revolution of 1789–99. Did revolutionaries in 1848 have goals that were similar to the goals of French revolutionaries at the end of the eighteenth century?
- How might the failure of the 1848 revolutions have shaped the beliefs of European conservatives and liberals or the beliefs of supporters of more radical ideologies such as republicanism and socialism?

STORY LINES

- Industrialization, rapid technological development, and the concentration of economic wealth gave western European nations great power during this period, along with the confidence to use this power to extend their control to other parts of the world.

- Colonial expansion occurred simultaneously with the development of mass politics and the spread of consumer culture in Europe, a combination that made colonies and the power to control them an important part of national identity for many people in Europe, especially in Britain, France, and Germany.

- The new imperialism ushered in a new era of conflict: between European powers and newly colonized peoples in Africa and Asia, and between the colonizing nations themselves, as they competed with one another for global influence and resources.

CHRONOLOGY

1788	British establish colony in New South Wales, Australia
1797–1818	British expand foothold in India
1830	France invades Algeria
1839–1842	Opium Wars in China
1840	British establish colony in New Zealand
1857	Sepoy Mutiny in India
1870–1900	European scramble for Africa
1875	Britain gains control of Suez Canal
1882	British occupation of Egypt begins
1883–1893	France moves into Vietnam, Laos, and Cambodia
1884–1885	Berlin West Africa Conference
1896	Italian forces defeated by Ethiopians
1898	Fashoda Crisis
1898	Spanish-American War
1898–1901	Boer War
1900	London Pan-African Conference
1904–1905	Russo-Japanese War

Before
You
Read
This
Chapter

Imperialism and Colonialism, 1870–1914

CORE OBJECTIVES

- **DEFINE** *imperialism* and locate the major colonies established by European powers in Africa and Asia in the nineteenth century.

- **UNDERSTAND** the major reasons for European colonial expansion in the nineteenth century.

- **DESCRIBE** the choices faced by colonized peoples in the face of European power.

- **EXPLAIN** how imperialism shaped the culture of European nations at home.

- **UNDERSTAND** the nature of the crisis faced by European imperial powers at the end of the nineteenth century.

I n 1869, the Suez Canal opened with a grand celebration. The imperial yacht *Eagle,* with Empress Eugénie of France on board, entered the canal on November 17, followed by sixty-eight steamships carrying the emperor of Austria, the crown prince of Prussia, the grand duke of Russia, and scores of other dignitaries. Flowery speeches flowed freely, as did the champagne. The ceremony cost a staggering £1.3 million (about $121 million today). Even so, the size of the celebration paled in comparison to the canal itself. The largest project of its kind, the canal sliced through a hundred miles of Egyptian desert to link the Mediterranean and Red seas, cutting the trip from London to Bombay in half. The canal dramatically showcased the abilities of Western power and technology to transform the globe, but the human cost was high: 30,000 Egyptians worked on the canal as forced laborers, and thousands died during cholera epidemics in the work camps.

The building of the canal was the result of decades of European involvement in Egypt. French troops under Napoleon led the way, but Britain's bankers soon followed. European financial interests developed a close relationship with those who governed Egypt as a semi-independent state inside the Ottoman Empire. By 1875, the British controlled the canal, after purchasing 44 percent of the canal's shares from the Egyptian khedive (viceroy) when he was threatened with bankruptcy. By the late 1870s, these economic and political relationships had produced debt and instability in Egypt. In a bid for national independence, a group of Egyptian army officers led by 'Urabi Pasha took control of Egypt's government in 1882.

The British government, determined to protect its investments, decided to intervene. The Royal Navy shelled Egyptian forts along the canal into rubble, and a British task force landed near 'Urabi Pasha's central base, overwhelming the Egyptian lines. This striking success rallied popular support at home, and the political consequences lasted for seventy years. Britain took effective control of Egypt. A British lord, Evelyn Baring, assumed the role of proconsul in a power-sharing relationship with Egyptian authorities, but real power rested with Britain. Britain demanded the repayment of loans and regulated the trade in Egyptian cotton that helped supply Britain's textile mills. Most important, the intervention secured the route to India and the markets of the East.

The Suez Canal and the conquest of Egypt was made possible by the convergence of technology, money, politics, and a global strategy of imperial control. A similar interplay between economics and colonialism produced the stunning expansion of European empires in the late nineteenth century. The years 1870 to 1914 brought both rapid industrialization throughout the West and an intense

THE INAUGURATION OF THE SUEZ CANAL. This allegory illustrates the union of the Mediterranean and Red Seas attended by Ismail Pasha, the khedive of Egypt, Abdul Aziz, sultan of the Ottoman Empire, Ferdinand de Lesseps, president of the Suez Canal Company, Empress Eugénie of France, and several mermaids. It also represents the nineteenth-century vision of imperialism as a bearer of global progress, promoting technological advance and breaking down barriers between the Orient and the West. ▪ *Who was the audience for this image?*

push to expand the power and influence of Western power abroad. The "new imperialism" of the late nineteenth century was distinguished by its scope, intensity, and long-range consequences. It transformed cultures and states in Europe, Africa, and Asia. Projects such as the Suez Canal changed—literally—the landscape and map of the world. They also represented an ideology: the belief in technology and Western superiority. In the minds of imperialists, the elimination of geographic barriers had opened the entire world, its lands and its peoples, to the administrative power of the West.

The new imperialism, however, was not a one-way street. Europeans could not simply conquer vast territories and dictate their terms to the rest of the world. The new political and economic relationships between colonies and dependent states, on the one hand, and the "metropole" (the colonizing power), on the other, ran both ways, bringing changes to both parties. Fierce competition among nations upset the balance of power. The new imperialism was an expression of European strength, but it was also profoundly destabilizing.

IMPERIALISM

Imperialism is the process of extending one state's control over another—a process that takes many forms. Sometimes this control was exercised by *direct rule*, by which the colonizing nation annexed territories outright and subjugated the peoples who lived there. At times, colonialism worked through *indirect rule*, by which conquering European nations reached agreements with local leaders and governed through them. Finally, *informal imperialism* could be a less visible exercise of state power, where stronger states allowed weaker states to maintain their independence while reducing their sovereignty. Informal imperialism took the form of carving out zones of European sovereignty and privilege, such as treaty ports, within other states. There was no single technique of colonial control; as we will see, resistance forced colonial powers to shift strategies frequently.

Both formal and informal imperialism expanded dramatically in the nineteenth century. The "scramble for Africa" was the most startling case of formal imperialism: from 1875 to 1902, Europeans seized up to 90 percent of the continent. The overall picture is no less remarkable: between 1870 and 1900, a small group of states (France, Britain, Germany, the Netherlands, Russia, and the United States) colonized about one quarter of the world's land surface. In addition, these same states extended informal empire in China and Turkey, across South and East Asia, and into Central and South America. So striking was this expansion of European power that contemporaries spoke of the "new imperialism." Nevertheless, imperialism was not new. It is more helpful to think of these nineteenth-century developments as a new stage of European empire building, after the collapse of Europe's early modern empires in North and South America at the end of the eighteenth century.

The nineteenth-century empires rose against the backdrop of industrialization, liberal revolution, and the rise of nation-states. Industrialization produced greater demand for raw materials from distant locations. At the same time, many Europeans became convinced in the nineteenth century that their economic development, science, and technology would inevitably bring progress to the rest of the world. Finally, especially in Britain and France, nineteenth-century imperial powers were in principle democratic nations, where government authority relied on consent and on notions of civic equality. This made conquest difficult to justify and raised thorny questions about the status of colonized peoples. Earlier European conquerors had claimed a missionary zeal to convert people to Christianity as a justification for their actions. Nineteenth-century imperialists justified their projects by saying that their investment in infrastructure—railroads, harbors, and roads—and their social reforms would fulfill Europe's secular mission to bring civilization to the rest of the world. This vision of the "white man's burden"—the phrase is Rudyard Kipling's—became a powerful argument in favor of imperial expansion throughout Europe (see **Competing Viewpoints** on pages 756–57).

In spite of these ambitious goals, the resistance of colonized peoples did as much to shape the history of colonialism as did the ambitious plans of the colonizers. The Haitian revolution of 1804 compelled the British and the French to end the slave trade and slavery in their colonies in the 1830s and the 1840s, though new systems of forced labor cropped up to take their places. The American Revolution encouraged the British to grant self-government to white settler states in Canada (1867), Australia (1901), and New Zealand (1912). Rebellion in India in 1857 caused the British to place the colony under the direct control of the crown, rather than the East India Company. In general, nineteenth-century imperialism involved less independent entrepreneurial activity by merchants and traders and more "settlement and discipline." This required legal distinctions made on racial or religious grounds in order to organize relationships between Europeans and different indigenous groups and an administration to enforce such distinctions. (Apartheid in South Africa is but one example.) Defending such empires thus became a vast project, involving legions of government officials, schoolteachers, and engineers. Nineteenth-century imperialism produced new forms of government and management in the colonies, and as it did so, it forged new interactions between Europeans and indigenous peoples.

The New Imperialism and Its Causes

As early as 1902, British author J. A. Hobson charged that the interests of a small group of wealthy financiers had driven the "scramble for Africa." British taxpayers subsidized armies of conquest and occupation, and journalists whipped up the public's enthusiasm for imperialism. Hobson, a reformer and a social critic, argued that international finance and business had distorted conceptions of England's real national interests. He hoped that a genuine democracy would curb the country's imperial policies.

Hobson's analysis inspired an influential Marxist critique of imperialism made by Vladimir Ilyich Lenin. Like Hobson, Lenin believed that imperialism was best understood on economic grounds. Unlike Hobson, however, Lenin believed that imperialism was an integral part of late-nineteenth-century capitalism. With domestic markets saturated and growth limited by competition at home, capitalists were forced to invest and search for new markets overseas, producing an ever more intensive pressure for the expansion of European imperialism. Lenin published *Imperialism: The Highest Stage of Capitalism* (1917) at the height of the First World War, and he used this argument to assert that hopes for a democratic reform of capitalism were misplaced and that the only solution was the replacement of capitalism with a revolutionary new economic order.

Historians now agree that economic pressures were only one of the causes of imperialism. Only half of Britain's £4 billion in foreign investments was at work within its empire, and in France the proportion was even smaller: one fifth of French capital was invested overseas. The French had more capital invested in their ally Russia than in all their colonial possessions. Nevertheless, Europeans expected the colonies to produce profits. French newspapers, for instance, reported that the Congo was "rich, vigorous, and fertile virgin territory" with "fabulous quantities" of gold, copper, ivory, and rubber. Such hopes contributed to expansionism, even if the profits did not meet expectations.

A second interpretation of imperialism emphasized strategic and nationalist motives. International rivalries made European powers more determined to control less-developed nations and territories. French politicians hoped that imperialism would restore the honor France had lost in their defeat by the Prussians in 1870. The British looked with alarm at Germany's industrialization and feared losing their share of world markets. The Germans, recently unified into a modern nation-state, saw overseas empire as the only way to become a great power.

This interpretation suggests a link between imperialism and nineteenth-century state and nation building. Colonies demonstrated military power; they showed the vigor of a nation's economy; the strength of its citizens, the force of its law, the power of its culture. A strong national community could assimilate others, bringing progress to new lands and new peoples. One German proponent of expansion called colonialism the "national continuation of the German desire for unity." Lobby groups such as the German Colonial Society, the French Colonial Party, and the Royal Colonial Institute in Britain argued for empire in similar terms, as did newspapers, which recognized the profits to be made in selling sensational stories of overseas conquest.

Finally, imperialism had important cultural dimensions. A French diplomat once described the British imperial adventurer Cecil Rhodes as a "force cast in an idea"; the same might be said of imperialism itself. Scottish missionary David Livingston believed that the British conquest of Africa would end the East African slave trade and "introduce the Negro family into the body of corporate nations." Taking arms against the slave trade, famine, disorder, and illiteracy seemed to many Europeans not only a reason to invade Africa but also a duty and proof of a somehow superior civilization. These convictions did not cause imperialism, but they illustrate how central empire building became to the West's self-image.

In short, it is difficult to disentangle the economic, political, and strategic causes of imperialism. It is more important to understand how the motives overlapped. Economic interests often helped convince policy makers that strategic interests were at stake. Different constituencies—the military, international financiers, missionaries, colonial lobby groups at home—held different and often clashing visions of the purpose and benefits of imperialism. Imperial policy, therefore, was less a matter of long-range planning than a series of quick responses, often improvised, to particular situations. And of course, Europeans were not the only players on the stage. Their goals and intentions were shaped by social changes in the countries in which they became involved; by the independent interests of local peoples; and by resistance, which, as often as not, Europeans found themselves unable to understand and powerless to stop.

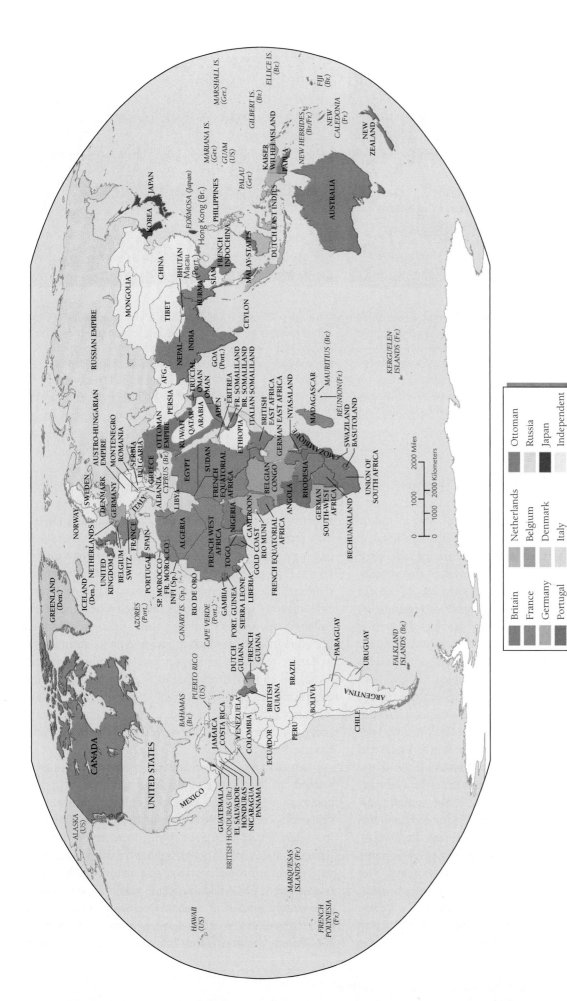

EUROPEAN EMPIRES IN 1900. ■ *Where were Britain's major imperial interests, and what trade routes did they have most incentive to protect?* ■ *Where were France's most important imperial holdings and who was their major competitor?* ■ *How substantial were German, Dutch, Portuguese, or U.S. colonies in comparison to British and French holdings?*

Legend:
- Britain
- France
- Germany
- Portugal
- Spain
- Netherlands
- Belgium
- Denmark
- Italy
- United States
- Ottoman
- Russia
- Japan
- Independent

IMAGES OF WOMEN IN THE COLONIES. Photographs and engravings of women in Africa and Asia circulated widely in Europe during the nineteenth century, and these images shaped attitudes toward colonization. Many images—some openly pornographic—portrayed African or Asian women as attractive, exotic, and in postures that invited European fantasies of domination. "Reclining Jewess" (left) is a typical example of such imagery, from French Algeria. Other images portrayed colonial women as victims of barbaric customs, such as sati, a social funeral practice in which a new widow would burn herself during the cremation of her deceased husband (right). This image, which first appeared in a work by a missionary who had been to Calcutta, was widely reproduced later as an illustration of the need for the British to bring "civilization" to India. ▪ *Could these images have the same impact without the emphasis on the gender of the subject?*

IMPERIALISM IN SOUTH ASIA

India was the center of the British Empire, the jewel of the British crown, secured well before the period of the new imperialism. The conquest of most of the subcontinent began in the 1750s and quickened during the age of revolution. Conquering India helped compensate for "losing" North America. General Cornwallis, defeated at Yorktown, went on to a brilliant career in India. By the mid-nineteenth century, India was the focal point of Britain's newly expanded global power, which reached from southern Africa across South Asia and to Australia. Keeping this region involved changing tactics and forms of rule.

Until the mid-nineteenth century, British territories in India were under the control of the British East India Company. The company had its own military, divided into European and (far larger) Indian divisions. The company held the right to collect taxes on land from Indian peasants. Until the early nineteenth century, the company had legal monopolies over trade in all goods, including indigo, textiles, salt, minerals, and—most lucrative of all—opium. The British government had granted trade monopolies in its northern American colonies. Unlike North America, however, India never became a settler state. In the 1830s, Europeans were a tiny minority, numbering 45,000 in an Indian population of 150 million. The company's rule was

repressive and enforced by the military. Soldiers collected taxes; civil servants wore military uniforms; British troops brashly commandeered peasants' oxen and carts for their own purposes. Typically, though, the company could not enforce its rule uniformly. It governed some areas directly, others through making alliances with local leaders, and others still by simply controlling goods and money. Indirect rule, here as in other empires, meant finding indigenous collaborators and maintaining their goodwill. Thus, the British cultivated groups that had provided administrators in earlier regimes: the Rajputs and Bhumihars of North India, whom they considered especially effective soldiers, and merchants of big cities such as Calcutta. They offered economic privileges, state offices, or military posts to either groups or entire nations that agreed to ally with the British against others.

British policy shifted between two poles: one group wanted to "Westernize" India; another believed it safer, and more practical, to defer to local culture. Christian missionaries, whose numbers rose as occupation expanded, were determined to replace "blind superstition" with the "genial influence of Christian light and truth." Indignant at such practices as child marriage and *sati* (in which a widow immolated herself on her husband's funeral pyre), missionaries sought support in England for a wide-ranging assault on Hindu culture. Secular reformers, many of them liberal, considered "Hindoos" and "Mahommedans" susceptible to forms of despotism—both in the family and in the state. They turned their reforming zeal to legal and political change. But other British administrators warned their countrymen not to meddle with Indian institutions. "Englishmen are as great fanatics in politics as Mahommedans in religion. They suppose that no country can be saved without English institutions," said one British administrator. Indirect rule, they argued, would work only with the cooperation of local powers. Conflicts such as these meant that the British never agreed on any single cultural policy.

From Mutiny to Rebellion

The East India Company's rule often met resistance and protest. In 1857–58, it was badly shaken by a revolt of Indian soldiers in the British army, now known in India as the Great Mutiny of 1857. The uprising began near Delhi, when the military disciplined a regiment of *sepoys* (the traditional term for Indian soldiers employed by the British) for refusing to use rifle cartridges greased with pork fat—unacceptable to either Hindus or Muslims. Yet, as the British prime minister Disraeli later observed, "The decline and fall of empires are not affairs of greased cartridges." The causes of the mutiny were deeper and involved social, economic, and political grievances. Indian peasants attacked law courts and burned tax rolls, protesting debt and

corruption. In areas that had recently been annexed, rebels defended their traditional leaders, who had been ousted by the British. Army officers from privileged castes resented arbitrary treatment at the hands of the British; they were first promoted as loyal allies and then forced to serve without what they considered titles and honors. The mutiny spread through large areas of northwest India. European troops, which counted for fewer than one-fifth of those in arms, found themselves losing control. Religious leaders, both Hindu and Muslim, seized the occasion to denounce Christian missionaries sent in by the British and their assault on local traditions.

At first, the British were faced with a desperate situation, with areas under British control cut off from one another and pro-British cities under siege. Loyal Indian troops were brought south from the frontiers, and British troops, fresh from the Crimean War, were shipped directly from Britain to suppress the rebellion. The fighting lasted more than a year, and the British matched the rebels' early massacres with a systematic campaign of repression. Whole rebel units were killed rather than being allowed to surrender or tried on the spot and executed. Towns and villages that supported the rebels were burned, just as the rebels had burned European homes and outposts. Yet the defeat of the rebellion caught the British public's imagination. After the bloody, inconclusive mess of Crimea, the terrifying threat to British India and the heroic rescue of European

THE EXECUTION OF INDIANS WHO PARTICIPATED IN THE REBELLION OF 1857. The British were determined to make an example of rebel Indian soldiers after the Great Mutiny. The engraving on the left shows executions in which the condemned were blown apart by cannons. The cartoon on the right, "The Execution of 'John Company,'" shows the same cannons destroying the British East India Company, which was abolished by the British government as a result of the rebellion. ■ *What do these images tell us about public awareness of the rebellion's violence and its suppression?*

Lord Curzon on the Importance of India and Indians to the British Empire

Lord George Nathaniel Curzon (1859–1925) served as viceroy of India from 1898 to 1905 and as foreign secretary from 1919 to 1924. He made his reputation in India, and as a prominent Tory politician he became among the most vocal proponents of the new imperialism. In this speech, Curzon spells out the benefits of empire and underscores British dependence on India.

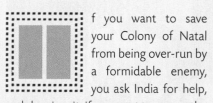

If you want to save your Colony of Natal from being over-run by a formidable enemy, you ask India for help, and she gives it; if you want to rescue the white men's legations from massacres at Peking, and the need is urgent, you request the Government of India to despatch an expedition, and they despatch it; if you are fighting the Mad Mullah in Somaliland, you soon discover that Indian troops and an Indian general are best qualified for the task, and you ask the Government of India to send them; if you desire to defend any of your extreme out-posts or coaling stations of the Empire, Aden, Mauritius, Singapore, Hong-Kong, even Tien-tsin or Shan-hai-kwan, it is to the Indian Army that you turn; if you want to build a railway to Uganda or in the Soudan, you apply for Indian labour. When the late Mr. Rhodes was engaged in developing your recent acquisition of Rhodesia, he came to me for assistance. It is with Indian coolie labor that you exploit the plantations equally of Demerara and Natal; with Indian trained officers that you irrigate and dam the Nile; with Indian forest officers that you tap the resources of Central Africa and Siam; with Indian surveyors that you explore all the hidden places of the earth. . . . [Moreover,] India is a country where there will be much larger openings for the investment of capital in the future than has hitherto been the case, and where a great work of industrial and commercial exploitation lies before us.

Source: Andrew Porter, ed., *The Oxford History of the British Empire*, vol. 3, *The Nineteenth Century* (Oxford: 1999), p. 403.

Questions for Analysis

1. Curzon not only served as viceroy of India and foreign minister but also had extensive knowledge of Afghanistan and Persia. Drawing on his expertise, what did he think was the greatest value of India to the British Empire?

2. Was there any risk involved in the British Empire's reliance on colonial troops? What compensation might Indian soldiers have come to expect for their participation in the defense of empire?

hostages and British territory by British troops were electrifying news. Pictures of the Scottish highland regiments (wearing wool kilts in the sweltering heat of India) liberating besieged white women and children went up in homes across the United Kingdom. At a political level, British leaders were stunned by how close the revolt had brought them to disaster and were determined never to repeat the same mistakes.

After the mutiny, the British were compelled to reorganize their Indian empire, developing new strategies of rule. The East India Company was abolished, replaced by the British crown. The British *raj* (or rule) was governed directly, though the British also sought out collaborators and cooperative interest groups. Princely India was left to the local princes, who were subject to British advisers. The British also reorganized the military and tried to change relations among soldiers. Indigenous troops were separated from each other to avoid the kind of fraternization that proved subversive. As one British officer put it, "If one regiment mutinies I should like to have the next so alien that it would fire into it." Even more than before, the British sought to rule through the Indian upper classes rather than in opposition to them. Queen Victoria, now empress of India, set out the principles of indirect rule: "We shall respect the rights, dignity and honour of native princes as our own, and we desire that they, as well as our own subjects, should enjoy that prosperity and that social advancement which can only be secured by internal peace and good government."

Past and Present

The Legacy of Colonialism

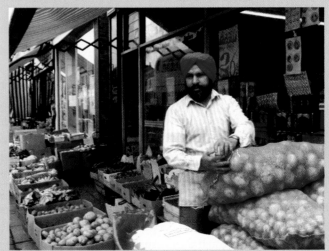

Decolonization in the 1950s and 1960s brought an end to the era of European imperialism (left), but the colonial past continues to shape the relations among European nations and former colonies elsewhere in the world. These links are reinforced by the large number of people from former colonies that now live in Europe, including the diverse neighborhood of Southall, London (right).

 Watch related author interview on StudySpace
wwnorton.com/web/westernciv18

Civil-service reform opened new positions to members of the Indian upper classes. The British had to reconsider their relationship to Indian cultures. Missionary activity was no longer encouraged, and the British channeled their reforming impulses into the more secular projects of economic development, railways, roads, irrigation, and so on. Still, consensus on effective colonial strategies was lacking. Some administrators counseled more reform; others sought to support the princes. The British tried both policies, in fits and starts, until the end of British rule in 1947.

In India, the most prominent representative of the new imperialism was Lord Curzon, the viceroy of India from 1898 to 1905. Curzon deepened British commitments to the region. Concerned about the British position in the world, he warned of the need to fortify India's borders against Russia. He urged continued economic investment. Curzon worried that the British would be worn down by resistance to the raj and that, confronted with their apparent inability to

transform Indian culture, they would become cynical, get "lethargic and think only of home." In the same way that Rudyard Kipling urged the British and the Americans to "take up the white man's burden" (see **Competing Viewpoints** on pages 756–57), Curzon pleaded with his countrymen to see how central India was to the greatness of Britain.

What did India do for Great Britain? By the eve of the First World War, India was Britain's largest export market. One tenth of all the British Empire's trade passed through India's port cities of Madras, Bombay, and Calcutta. India mattered enormously to Britain's balance of payments; surpluses earned there compensated for deficits with Europe and the United States. Equally important to Great Britain were the human resources of India. Indian laborers worked on tea plantations in Assam, near Burma, and they built railways and dams in southern Africa and Egypt. Over a million indentured Indian servants left their country in the second half of the century to work elsewhere in the empire.

India also provided the British Empire with highly trained engineers, land surveyors, clerks, bureaucrats, schoolteachers, and merchants. The nationalist leader Mohandas Gandhi, for instance, first came into the public eye as a young lawyer in Pretoria, South Africa, where he worked for an Indian law firm. The British deployed Indian troops across the empire. (They would later call up roughly 1.2 million troops in the First World War.) For all these reasons, men such as Curzon found it impossible to imagine their empire, or even their nation, without India.

How did the British raj shape Indian society? The British practice of indirect rule sought to create an Indian elite that would serve British interests, a group "who may be the interpreters between us and the millions whom we govern—a class of persons Indian in colour and blood, but English in tastes, in opinion, in morals, and in intellect," as one British writer put it. Eventually, this practice created a class of British-educated Indian civil servants and businessmen, well trained for government and skeptical about British claims that they brought progress to the subcontinent. This group provided the leadership for the nationalist movement that challenged British rule in India. At the same time, this group became increasingly distant from the rest of the nation. The overwhelming majority of Indians remained desperately poor peasants struggling to subsist on diminishing plots of land and, in many cases, in debt to British landlords. Meanwhile, villagers working in the textile trade were beaten down by imports of cheap manufactured goods from England.

IMPERIALISM IN CHINA

In China, too, European imperialism began early, well before the period of the new imperialism. Yet there it took a different form. Europeans did not conquer and annex whole regions. Instead, they forced favorable trade agreements at gunpoint, set up treaty ports where Europeans lived and worked under their own jurisdiction, and established outposts of European missionary activity. The Chinese spoke of their country as being "carved up like a melon."

Since the seventeenth century, European trade with China focused on coveted luxuries such as silk, porcelain, art objects, and tea. The Chinese government, however, was determined to keep foreign traders, and foreign influence in general, at bay. By the early nineteenth century, Britain's global ambitions and rising power were setting the stage for a confrontation. Freed from the task of fighting Napoleon, the British set their sights on improving the terms of the China trade, demanding the rights to come into open harbors and to have special trading privileges. The other source of constant friction involved the harsh treatment of British subjects by Chinese law courts—including the summary execution of several Britons convicted of crimes. By the 1830s, these diplomatic conflicts had been intensified by the opium trade.

The Opium Trade

Opium provided a direct link among Britain, British India, and China. Since the sixteenth century, the drug had been produced in India and carried by Dutch and, later, British traders. In fact, opium (derived from the poppy plant) was one of the very few commodities that Europeans could sell in China. For this reason, it became crucial to the balance of East–West trade. When the British conquered northeast India, they also annexed one of the world's richest opium-growing areas and became deeply involved in the trade—so much so that historians have called the East India Company's rule a "narco-military empire." British agencies designated specific poppy-growing regions and gave cash advances to Indian peasants who cultivated the crop. Producing opium was a labor-intensive process: peasant cultivators collected sap from the poppy seeds, and others cleaned the sap and formed it into opium balls that were dried before being weighed and shipped out. In the opium-producing areas northwest of Calcutta, "factories" employed as many as a thousand Indian workers, who formed and cured the opium, as well as young boys, whose job it was to turn the opium balls every four days.

From India, the East India Company sold the opium to "country traders"—small fleets of British, Dutch, and Chinese shippers who carried the drug to Southeast Asia and China. The East India Company used the silver it earned from the sale of opium to buy Chinese goods for the European market. The trade, therefore, was not only profitable, but it was also key to a triangular European-Indian-Chinese economic relationship. Production and export rose dramatically in the early nineteenth century, in spite of the Chinese emperor's attempts to discourage the trade. By the 1830s, when the British-Chinese confrontation was taking shape, opium provided British India with more revenues than any other source except taxes on land.

People all over the world consumed opium, for medicinal reasons as well as for pleasure. The Chinese market was especially lucrative. Eighteenth-century China witnessed a craze for tobacco smoking that taught users how to smoke opium. A large, wealthy Chinese elite of merchants and government officials provided much of the market, but opium smoking also became popular among

AN OPIUM FACTORY IN PATNA, INDIA, c. 1851. Balls of opium dry in a huge warehouse before being shipped to Calcutta for export to China and elsewhere.

soldiers, students, and Chinese laborers. In the nineteenth century, opium imports followed Chinese labor all over the world—to Southeast Asia and San Francisco. In 1799, in an effort to control the problem, the Chinese government banned opium imports, prohibited domestic production, criminalized smoking, and in the 1830s began a full-scale campaign to purge the drug from China. That campaign set the Chinese emperor on a collision course with British opium traders. In one confrontation, the Chinese drug commissioner Lin confiscated 3 million pounds of raw opium from the British and washed it out to sea. In another, the Chinese authorities blockaded British ships in port, and local citizens demonstrated angrily in front of British residences.

THE OPIUM WARS

In 1839, these simmering conflicts broke into what was called the first Opium War. Drugs were not the core of the matter. The dispute over the drug trade highlighted larger issues of sovereignty and economic status. The Europeans claimed the right to trade with whomever they pleased, bypassing Chinese monopolies. They wished to set up zones of European residence in defiance of Chinese

sovereignty and to proselytize and open schools. The Chinese government could not accept these challenges to its authority, and war flared up several times over the course of the century. After the first war of 1839–42, in which British steam vessels and guns overpowered the Chinese fleet, the Treaty of Nanking (1842) compelled the Chinese to give the British trading privileges, the right to reside in five cities, and the port of Hong Kong "in perpetuity." After a second war, the British secured yet more treaty ports and privileges, including the right to send in missionaries. In the aftermath of those agreements between the Chinese and the British, other countries demanded similar rights and economic opportunities. By the end of the nineteenth century, the French, Germans, and Russians had claimed mining rights and permission to build railroads, to begin manufacturing with cheap Chinese labor, and to arm and police European communities in Chinese cities. In Shanghai, for instance, 17,000 foreigners lived with their own courts, schools, churches, and utilities. The United States, not wanting to be shouldered aside, demanded its own Open Door Policy. Japan was an equally active imperialist power in the Pacific, and the Sino-Japanese War of 1894–95 was a decisive moment in the history of the region. The Japanese victory forced China to concede trading privileges, the independence of Korea, and the Liaotung Peninsula in Manchuria. It opened a scramble for spheres of influence and for mining and railway concessions. The demand for reparations forced the Chinese government to levy greater taxes. All these measures heightened resentment and destabilized the regime.

Surrendering privileges to Europeans and the Japanese seriously undermined the authority of the Chinese Qing (Ching) emperor at home and heightened popular hostility to foreign intruders. Authority at the imperial center had been eroding for more than a century by 1900, hastened by the Opium Wars and by the vast Taiping Rebellion (1852–64), an enormous, bitter, and deadly conflict in which radical Christian rebels in south-central China challenged the authority of the emperors. On the defensive against the rebels, the dynasty hired foreign generals, including the British commander Charles Gordon, to lead its forces. The war devastated China's agricultural heartland; and the death toll, never confirmed, may have reached 20 million.

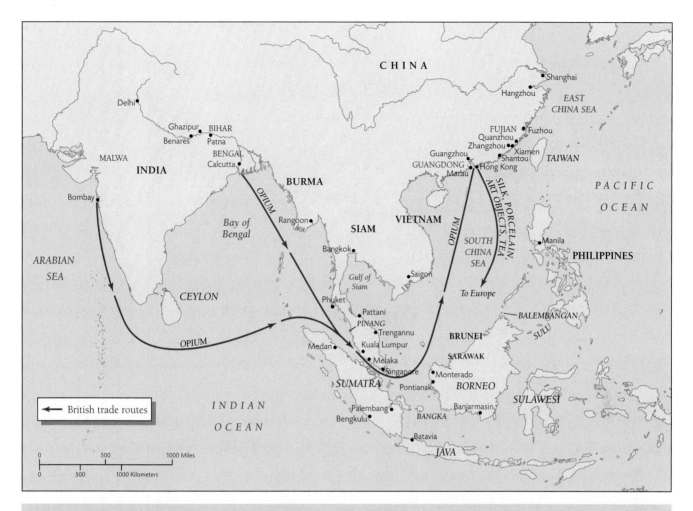

BRITISH OPIUM TRADE. Note the way that the British trade in opium linked the economies of India, China, and Europe. ▪ *What were the major products involved in trade between East Asia, South Asia, and Europe during this period?* ▪ *In what ways did the opium trade destabilize East Asia?* ▪ *What efforts did the Chinese government make to restrict the sale of opium?* ▪ *What was the response of European nations involved in this trade?*

This ruinous disorder and the increasing inability of the emperor to keep order and collect the taxes necessary to repay foreign loans, led European countries to take more and more direct control of the China trade.

The Boxer Rebellion

From a Western perspective, the most important of the nineteenth-century rebellions against the corruptions of foreign rule was the Boxer Rebellion of 1900. The Boxers were a secret society of young men trained in Chinese martial arts and believed to have spiritual powers. Anti-foreign and antimissionary, they provided the spark for a loosely organized but widespread uprising in northern China. Bands of Boxers attacked foreign engineers, tore up railway lines, and in the spring of 1900 marched on Beijing. They laid siege to the foreign legations in the city, home to several thousand Western diplomats and merchants and their families. The legations' small garrison defended their walled compound with little more than rifles, bayonets, and improvised artillery; but they withstood the siege for fifty-five days until a large relief column arrived. The rebellion, particularly the siege at Beijing, mobilized a global response. Europe's Great Powers, rivals everywhere else in the world, drew together in response to this crisis to tear China apart. An expedition numbering 20,000 troops—combining the forces of Britain, France, the United States, Germany, Italy, Japan, and Russia—ferociously repressed the Boxer movement. The outside powers then demanded indemnities, new trading concessions, and reassurances from the Chinese government.

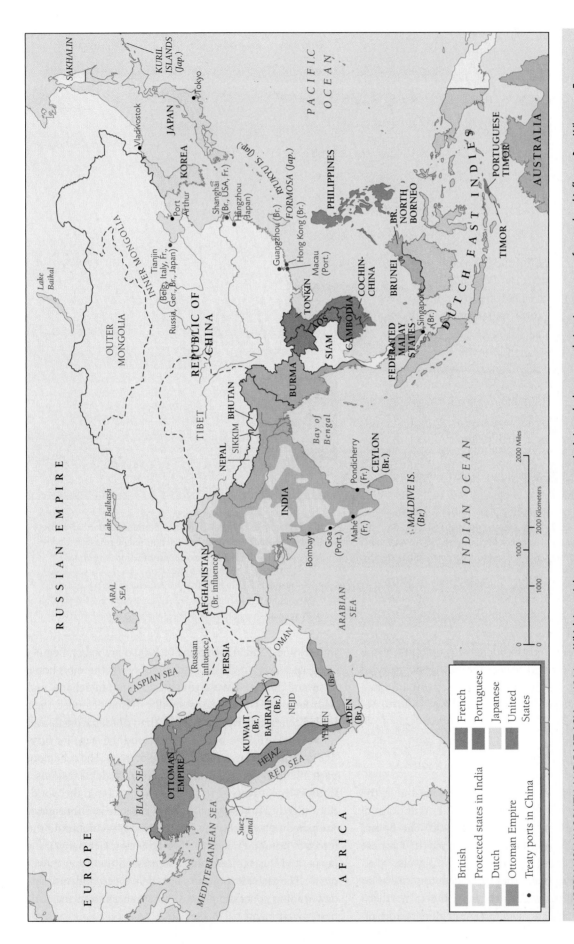

IMPERIALISM IN SOUTH AND EAST ASIA, c. 1914. ■ *Which imperial powers were most present in Asia and where were their primary zones of control and influence?* ■ *Why were European nations and the United States interested in establishing treaty ports in China?* ■ *How were the Chinese treaty ports different from the territorial conquest pursued by the British, French, and Dutch in their respective Asian colonies?*

THE OPIUM TRADE, 1880s. A European merchant examines opium. At first, European traders were forced to carry silver to China to pay for the luxury goods they wanted. The discovery that they could sell this highly addictive narcotic in China allowed them to correct this trade imbalance and increase their profits.

maintaining their far-flung influence. In the process of repression, the Europeans became committed to propping up corrupt and fragile governments to protect their agreements and interests, and they were drawn into putting down popular uprisings against local inequalities and foreign rule.

In China, the age of the new imperialism capped a century of conflict and expansion. By 1900, virtually all of Asia had been divided up among the European powers. Japan, an active imperial power in its own right, maintained its independence. British rule extended from India across Burma, Malaya, Australia, and New Zealand. The Dutch, Britain's longstanding trade rivals, secured Indonesia. Thailand remained independent. During the 1880s, the French moved into Indochina. Imperial rivalries (among Britain, France, and Russia, China and Japan, Russia and Japan) drove European powers to press for influence and economic advantage in Asia; that struggle, in turn, encouraged the development of nationalist feeling among local populations. Imperial expansion was showing its destabilizing effects.

The Boxer Rebellion was one of several anti-imperialist movements at the end of the nineteenth century. The rebellion testified to the vulnerability of Europeans' imperial power. It dramatized the resources Europeans would have to devote to

AN AMERICAN CARICATURE OF THE BOXER REBELLION. Uncle Sam (to the obstreperous Boxer), "I occasionally do a little boxing myself."

Russian Imperialism

Russia championed a policy of annexation—by conquest, treaty, or both—of lands bordering on the existing Russian state throughout the nineteenth century. Beginning in 1801, with the acquisition of Georgia after a war with Persia, the tsars continued to pursue their expansionist dream. Bessarabia and Turkestan (taken from the Turks) and Armenia (from the Persians) vastly increased the empire's size. This southward colonization brought large Muslim populations in central Asia into the Russian Empire. It also brought the Russians close to war with the British twice: first in 1881, when Russian troops occupied territories in the trans-Caspian region, and again in 1884–87, when the tsar's forces advanced to the frontier of Afghanistan. In both cases, the British feared incursions into areas they deemed within their sphere of influence in the Middle East. They were concerned, as well, about a possible threat to India. The maneuvering, spying, and support of friendly puppet governments by Russia and Britain became known

BUILDING THE RUSSIAN EMPIRE. ▪ *In what directions did the Russian Empire primarily expand after 1795?* ▪ *What drove Russian expansion?* ▪ *Which areas were most contentious and why?*

as the "Great Game" and foreshadowed Western countries' jockeying for the region's oil resources in the twentieth century.

Russian expansion also moved east. In 1875, the Japanese traded the southern half of Sakhalin Island for the previously Russian Kurile Islands. The tsars' eastward advance was finally halted in 1904, when Russian expansion in Mongolia and Manchuria came up against Japanese expansion. In the Russo-Japanese War of 1904, Russia's huge imperial army more than met its match. Russia's navy was sent halfway around the world to reinforce the beleaguered Russian troops but was ambushed and sunk by the better-trained and -equipped Japanese fleet. This national humiliation helped provoke a revolt in Russia and led to an American-brokered peace treaty in 1905 (see Chapter 23). The defeat shook the already unsteady regime of the tsar and proved that European nations were not the only ones who could play the imperial game successfully.

THE FRENCH EMPIRE AND THE CIVILIZING MISSION

Like British expansion into India, French colonialism in northern Africa began before the new imperialism of the late nineteenth century. By the 1830s, the French had created a general government of their possessions in Algeria, the most important of which were cities along the Mediterranean coast. From the outset, the Algerian conquest was different from most other colonial ventures: Algeria became a settler state, one of the few apart from South Africa. Some of the early settlers were utopian socialists, out to create ideal communities; some were workers the French government deported after the revolution of 1848 to be "resettled" safely as farmers; some were winegrowers whose vines at home had been destroyed by an insect infestation. The settlers were by no means all French; they included Italian, Spanish, and Maltese merchants and shopkeepers of modest means, laborers, and

THE ENTRY OF THE CRUSADERS INTO CONSTANTINOPLE BY EUGÉNE DELACROIX, 1840. The invasion of Algeria in 1830 became an occasion for thinking about Europe's long historical relationship with Muslim civilizations in Africa and the Middle East. Delacroix's work, painted while the conquest of Algeria was going on, portrays these civilizations as exotic and subservient, even as it glorifies the figures of conquering Christian armies. ▪ *How might this long historical view have shaped European attitudes toward conquest in the nineteenth century?*

peasants. By the 1870s, in several of the coastal cities, this new creole community outnumbered indigenous Algerians, and within it, other Europeans outnumbered the French. With the French military's help, the settlers appropriated land, and French business concerns took cork forests and established mining in copper, lead, and iron. Economic activity was for European benefit. The first railroads, for instance, did not even carry passengers; they took iron ore to the coast for export to France, where it would be smelted and sold.

The settlers and the French government did not necessarily pursue common goals. In the 1870s, the new and still-fragile Third Republic (founded after Napoleon III was defeated in 1870; see Chapter 21), in an effort to ensure the settlers' loyalty, made the colony a department of France. This gave the French settlers the full rights of republican citizenship. It also gave them the power to pass laws in Algeria that consolidated their privileges and community (naturalizing all

Europeans, for instance) and further disenfranchised indigenous Muslim populations, who had no voting rights at all. French politicians in Paris occasionally objected to the settlers' contemptuous treatment of indigenous peoples, arguing that it subverted the project of "lifting up" the natives. The French settlers in Algeria had little interest in such a project; although they paid lip service to republican ideals, they wanted the advantages of Frenchness for themselves. Colonial administrators and social scientists differentiated the "good" mountain-dwelling Berbers, who they believed could be brought into French society, from the "bad" Arabs, whose religion made them supposedly unassimilable. France's divide and rule strategy, which treated European settlers, Arabs, Berbers, and Jews very differently, illustrates the contradictions of "the civilizing mission" in action.

Before the 1870s, colonial activities aroused relatively little interest among the French at home. But after the

SLAVES IN CHAINS, 1896. In Africa, native labor was exploited by Europeans and by other Africans.

Coast. Even with reforms and centralization in 1902, French control remained uneven. Despite military campaigns of pacification, resistance remained. The French dealt gingerly with tribal leaders, at times deferring to their authority and at others trying to break their power. They established French courts and law only in cities, leaving Islamic or tribal courts to run other areas. The federation aimed to rationalize the economic exploitation of the area and to replace "booty capitalism" with a more careful management and development of resources. The French called this "enhancing the value" of the region, which was part of the civilizing mission of the modern republic. The federation embarked on an ambitious program of public works. Engineers rebuilt the huge harbor at Dakar, the most important on the coast, to accommodate rising exports. With utopian zeal they redesigned older cities, tried to improve sanitation and health, improved water systems, and built roads and railways. The French republic was justifiably proud of the Pasteur Institute for bacteriological research, which opened in France in 1888; overseas institutes became part of the colonial enterprise. One plan called for a large-scale West African railroad network to lace through the region. A public-school program built free schools in villages not controlled by missionaries. Education, though, was not compulsory and was usually for boys.

Such programs plainly served French interests. "Officially this process is called civilizing, and after all, the term is apt, since the undertaking serves to increase the degree of prosperity of our civilization," remarked one Frenchman who opposed the colonial enterprise. None of these measures aimed to give indigenous peoples political rights. As one historian puts it, "the French Government General was in the business not of making citizens, but of civilizing its subjects." More telling, however, the French project was not often successful. The French government did not have the resources to carry out its plans, which proved much more expensive and complicated than anyone imagined. Transportation costs ran very high. Labor posed the largest problems. Here as elsewhere, Europeans faced massive resistance from the African peasants, whom they wanted to do everything from building railroads to working mines and carrying rubber. The Europeans resorted to forced labor, signing agreements with local tribal leaders to deliver workers, and they turned a blind eye to the continuing use of slave labor in the interior. For all of these reasons, the colonial project did not produce the profits some expected. In important respects, however, the French investment in colonialism was cultural.

humiliating defeat in the Franco-Prussian War (1870–71) and the establishment of the Third Republic, colonial lobby groups and politicians became increasingly adamant about the benefits of colonialism. These benefits were not simply economic. Taking on the "civilizing mission" would reinforce the international influence of the French republic and the prestige of the French people. It was France's duty "to contribute to this work of civilization." Jules Ferry, a republican leader, successfully argued for expanding the French presence in Indochina, saying, "We must believe that if Providence deigned to confer upon us a mission by making us masters of the earth, this mission consists not of attempting an impossible fusion of the races but of simply spreading or awakening among the other races the superior notions of which we are the guardians." Those "superior notions" included a commitment to economic and technological progress and to liberation from slavery, political oppression, poverty, and disease. Ferry argued that "the superior races have a right vis-à-vis the inferior races . . . they have a right to civilize them."

Under Ferry, the French acquired Tunisia (1881), northern and central Vietnam (Tonkin and Annam; 1883), and Laos and Cambodia (1893). They also carried this civilizing mission into their colonies in West Africa. European and Atlantic trade with the west coast of Africa—in slaves, gold, and ivory—had been well established for centuries. In the late nineteenth century, trade gave way to formal administration. The year 1895 saw the establishment of a Federation of French West Africa, a loosely organized administration to govern an area nine times the size of France, including Guinea, Senegal, and the Ivory

Railroads, schools, and projects such as the Dakar harbor were, like the Eiffel Tower (1889), symbols of the French nation's modernity, power, and world leadership.

THE "SCRAMBLE FOR AFRICA" AND THE CONGO

French expansion into West Africa was only one instance of Europe's voracity on the African continent. The scope and speed with which the major European powers conquered and asserted formal control was astonishing. The effects were profound. In 1875, 11 percent of the continent was in European hands. By 1902, the figure was 90 percent. European powers mastered logistical problems of transport and communication; they learned how to keep diseases at bay. They also had new weapons. The Maxim gun, adopted by the British army in 1889 and first used by British colonial troops, pelted out as many as 500 rounds a minute; it turned encounters with indigenous forces into bloodbaths and made armed resistance virtually impossible.

The Congo Free State

In the 1870s, the British had formed new imperial relationships in the north and west of Africa and along the southern and eastern coasts. A new phase of European involvement struck right at the heart of the continent. Until the latter part of the nineteenth century, this territory had been out of bounds for Europeans. The rapids downstream on such strategic rivers as the Congo and the Zambezi made it difficult to move inland, and tropical diseases were lethal to most European explorers. But during the 1870s, a new drive into central Africa produced results. The target was the fertile valleys around the river Congo, and the European colonizers were a privately financed group of Belgians paid by their king, Leopold II (1865–1909). They followed in the footsteps of Henry Morton Stanley, an American newspaperman and explorer who later became a British subject and a knight of the realm. Stanley hacked his way through thick canopy jungle into territory where no European had previously set foot. His "scientific" journeys inspired the creation of a society of researchers and students of African culture in Brussels, in reality a front organization for the commercial company set up by Leopold. The ambitiously named International Association for the Exploration and Civilization of the Congo was set up in 1876 and soon set about signing treaties with local elites, which opened the whole Congo River basin to commercial exploitation. The vast resources of palm oil and natural rubber and the promise of minerals (including diamonds) were now within Europeans' reach.

The strongest resistance that Leopold's company faced came from other colonial powers, particularly Portugal, which objected to this new drive for occupation. In 1884, a conference was called in Berlin to settle the matter of control over the Congo River basin. It was chaired by the master of European power politics, Otto von Bismarck, and attended by all the leading colonial nations as well as by the United States. The conference established ground rules for a new phase of European economic and political expansion. Europe's two great overseas empires, Britain and France, and the strongest emerging power inside Europe, Germany, joined forces in a settlement that seemed to be perfectly in line with nineteenth-century liberalism. The Congo valleys would be open to free trade and commerce; a slave trade still run by some of the Islamic kingdoms in the region would be suppressed in favor of free labor; and a Congo Free State would be set up, denying the region to the formal control of any single European country.

In reality, the Congo Free State was run by Leopold's private company, and the region was opened up to unrestricted exploitation by a series of large European corporations. The older slave trade was suppressed, but the European companies took the "free" African labor guaranteed in Berlin and placed workers in equally bad conditions. Huge tracts of land, larger than whole European countries, became diamond mines or plantations for the extraction of palm oil, rubber, or cocoa. African workers labored in appalling conditions, with no real medicine or sanitation, too little food, and according to production schedules that made European factory labor look mild by comparison. Hundreds of thousands of African workers died from disease and overwork. Because European managers did not respect the different cycle of seasons in central Africa, whole crop years were lost, leading to famines. Laborers working in the heat of the dry season often carried individual loads on their backs that would have been handled by heavy machinery in a European factory. Thousands of Africans were pressed into work harvesting goods Europe wanted. They did so for little or no pay, under the threat of beatings and mutilation for dozens of petty offenses against the plantation companies, who made the laws of the Free State. Eventually the scandal of the Congo became too great to go on unquestioned. A whole generation of authors and journalists, most famously Joseph Conrad in his *Heart of Darkness*, publicized the arbitrary brutality and the vast scale of suffering. In 1908, Belgium was forced to take direct control of the Congo, turning it into a Belgian colony. A few restrictions at least were imposed on the activities of the great plantation companies that had brought a vast new store of raw materials to European industry by using slavery in all but name.

The Partition of Africa

The occupation of Congo, and its promise of great material wealth, pressured other colonial powers into expanding their holdings. By the 1880s, the "scramble for Africa" was well under way, hastened by stories of rubber forests or diamond mines in other parts of central and southern Africa. The guarantees made at the 1884 Berlin conference allowed the Europeans to take further steps. The French and Portuguese increased their holdings. Italy moved into territories along the Red Sea, beside British-held land and the independent kingdom of Ethiopia.

Germany came relatively late to empire overseas. Bismarck was reluctant to engage in an enterprise that he believed would yield few economic or political advantages. Yet he did not want either Britain or France to dominate Africa, and Germany seized colonies in strategic locations. The German colonies in Cameroon and most of modern Tanzania separated the territories of older, more established powers. Though the Germans were not the most enthusiastic colonialists, they were fascinated by the imperial adventure and jealous of their territories. When the Herero people of German Southwest Africa (now Namibia) rebelled in the early 1900s, the Germans responded with a vicious campaign of village burning and ethnic killing that nearly annihilated the Herero.

Great Britain and France had their own ambitions. The French aimed to move west to east across the continent, an important reason for the French expedition to Fashoda (in the Sudan) in 1898 (discussed later). Britain's part in the scramble took place largely in southern and eastern Africa and was encapsulated in the dreams and career of one man: the diamond tycoon, colonial politician, and imperial visionary Cecil Rhodes. Rhodes, who made a fortune from the South African diamond mines in the 1870s and 1880s and founded the diamond-mining company DeBeers, became prime minister of Britain's Cape Colony in 1890. (He left part of this fortune for the creation of the Rhodes scholarships to educate future leaders of the empire at Oxford.) In an uneasy alliance with the Boer settlers in their independent republics and with varying levels of support from London, Rhodes pursued two great personal and imperial goals. The personal goal was to build a southern African empire that was founded on diamonds. "Rhodesia" would fly the Union Jack out of pride but send its profits into Rhodes's own companies. Through bribery, double dealing, careful coalition politics with the British and Boer settlers, warfare, and outright theft, Rhodes helped carve out territories occupying the modern nations of Zambia, Zimbabwe, Malawi, and Botswana—most of the savannah of southern Africa. Rhodes had a broader imperial vision, one that he shared with the new British colonial secretary in the late 1890s, Joseph Chamberlain. The first part of that vision was a British presence along the whole of eastern Africa, symbolized by the goal of a Cape-to-Cairo railway. The second was that the empire should make Britain self-sufficient, with British

"THE RHODES COLOSSUS" (left). This cartoon, which appeared in *Punch* magazine, satirized the ambitions of Cecil Rhodes, the driving force behind British imperialism in South Africa. **"NOW WE SHANT BE LONG TO CAIRO" (right).** So read the banner across Engine No. 1, taking the first train from Umtali to Salisbury, Rhodesia. In Cecil Rhodes's vision, the Capetown-to-Cairo railway symbolized British domination of the African continent.

industry able to run on the goods and raw materials shipped in from its colonies, then exporting many finished products back to those lands. Once the territories of Zambeziland and Rhodesia were taken, Rhodes found himself turning against the European settlers in the region, a conflict that led to the Boer war in 1899 (discussed later in this chapter).

This battle over strategic advantage, diamonds, and European pride was typical of the scramble. As each European power sought its "place in the sun," in the famous phrase of the German kaiser William II, they brought more and more of Africa under direct colonial control. It created a whole new scale of plunder as companies were designed and managed to strip the continent of its resources. African peoples thus faced a combination of direct European control and indirect rule, which allowed local elites friendly to European interests to lord over those who resisted. The partition of Africa was the most striking instance of the new imperialism, with broad consequences for the subject peoples of European colonies and for the international order as a whole.

IMPERIAL CULTURE

Imperialism was thoroughly anchored in the culture of late-nineteenth-century Europe and the United States. Images of empire were everywhere, not just in the propagandist literature of colonialism's supporters but on tins of tea and boxes of cocoa and as background themes in posters advertising everything from dance halls to sewing machines. Museums and world's fairs displayed the products of empire and introduced spectators to "exotic peoples." Music halls rang to the sound of imperialist songs. Empire was present in novels of the period, sometimes appearing as a faraway setting for fantasy, adventure, or stories of self-discovery. Even the tales of Sherlock Holmes, set in London and not overtly imperialist, often used references to empire—tiger carpets, hookahs and opium dens, Malaysian servants—to add mystery and fascination to their plots. The popular literature of empire showed a particular fascination with sexual practices in faraway places—photos and postcards of North African harems and unveiled Arab women were common in European pornography, as were colonial memoirs that chronicled the sexual adventures of their authors.

Empire thus played an important part in establishing European identity during these years. In France, the "civilizing mission" demonstrated to French citizens the grandeur of their nation. Building railroads and "bringing progress to other lands" illustrated the vigor of the French republic. Many British writers spoke in similar tones. One author wrote, "The British race may safely be called a missionary race. The command to go and teach all nations is

THINKING ABOUT EMPIRE AT HOME. By the end of the nineteenth century, advertisers had begun to use images of empire to sell their products to consumers. The advertisement for Pears' Soap appeared in the American magazine *McClure's* in 1899. The image of the white-uniformed officer washing his hands connects the theme of cleanliness and personal hygiene to notions of racial superiority and the necessity of bringing civilization to "the dark corners of the earth." The packaging of Huntley & Palmers Biscuits, on the other hand, transported the familiar domestic scene of teatime to an exotic imperial location with a supporting cast of elephants. The image, which adorned biscuit boxes in many English parlors during the late Victorian period, seemed to reinforce the idea that essential aspects of British culture could be maintained even as they traveled to distant parts of the globe.

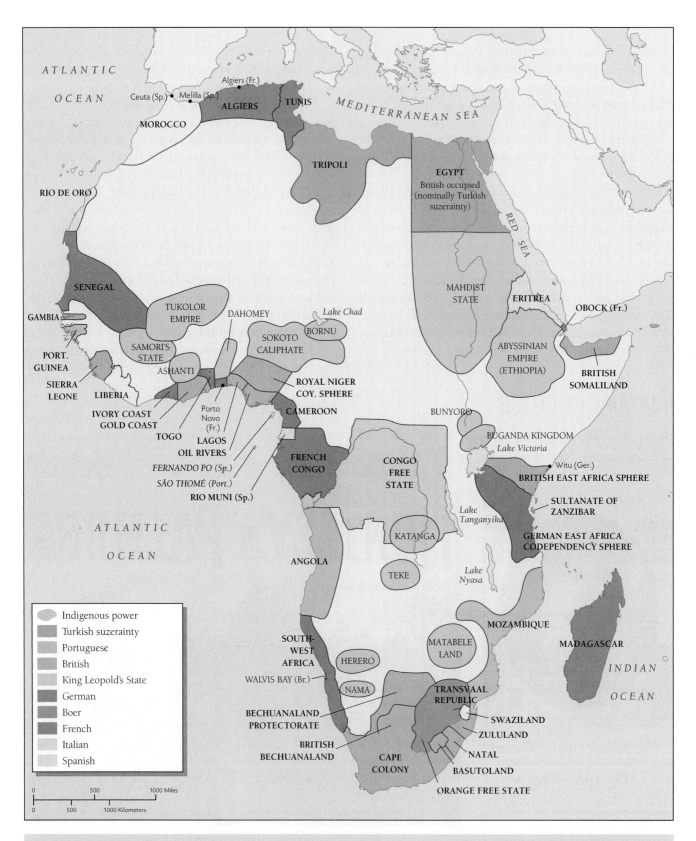

ATLANTIC
OCEAN

MEDITERRANEAN SEA

Algiers (Fr.)
Ceuta (Sp.) • Melilla (Sp.)
ALGIERS   TUNIS
MOROCCO

RIO DE ORO

TRIPOLI

EGYPT
British occupied
(nominally Turkish
suzerainty)

RED SEA

SENEGAL

GAMBIA

TUKOLOR
EMPIRE

DAHOMEY

Lake Chad

BORNU

MAHDIST
STATE

ERITREA

OBOCK (Fr.)

PORT.
GUINEA

SAMORI'S
STATE

SOKOTO
CALIPHATE

ABYSSINIAN
EMPIRE
(ETHIOPIA)

SIERRA
LEONE

ASHANTI

ROYAL NIGER
COY. SPHERE

BRITISH
SOMALILAND

LIBERIA

IVORY COAST
GOLD COAST

Porto
Novo
(Fr.)

CAMEROON

BUNYORO

TOGO

LAGOS
OIL RIVERS

FERNANDO PO (Sp.)

FRENCH
CONGO

BUGANDA KINGDOM
Lake Victoria

Witu (Ger.)

SÃO THOMÉ (Port.)

RIO MUNI (Sp.)

CONGO
FREE
STATE

BRITISH EAST AFRICA SPHERE

SULTANATE OF
ZANZIBAR

ATLANTIC

OCEAN

Lake
Tanganyika

GERMAN EAST AFRICA
CODEPENDENCY SPHERE

KATANGA

ANGOLA

TEKE

Lake
Nyasa

MOZAMBIQUE

MADAGASCAR

INDIAN

OCEAN

	Indigenous power
	Turkish suzerainty
	Portuguese
	British
	King Leopold's State
	German
	Boer
	French
	Italian
	Spanish

SOUTH-
WEST
AFRICA

HERERO

MATABELE
LAND

WALVIS BAY (Br.)

NAMA

TRANSVAAL
REPUBLIC

SWAZILAND

BECHUANALAND
PROTECTORATE

ZULULAND

BRITISH
BECHUANALAND

NATAL

CAPE
COLONY

BASUTOLAND

ORANGE FREE STATE

0   500   1000 Miles
0   500   1000 Kilometers

AFRICA, c. 1886. ▪ *What is the single biggest difference in terms of rulership between the two maps?* ▪ *Who were the winners and losers in the scramble for Africa before the First World War?* ▪ *What does the result of the scramble for Africa suggest about how European powers regarded each other?*

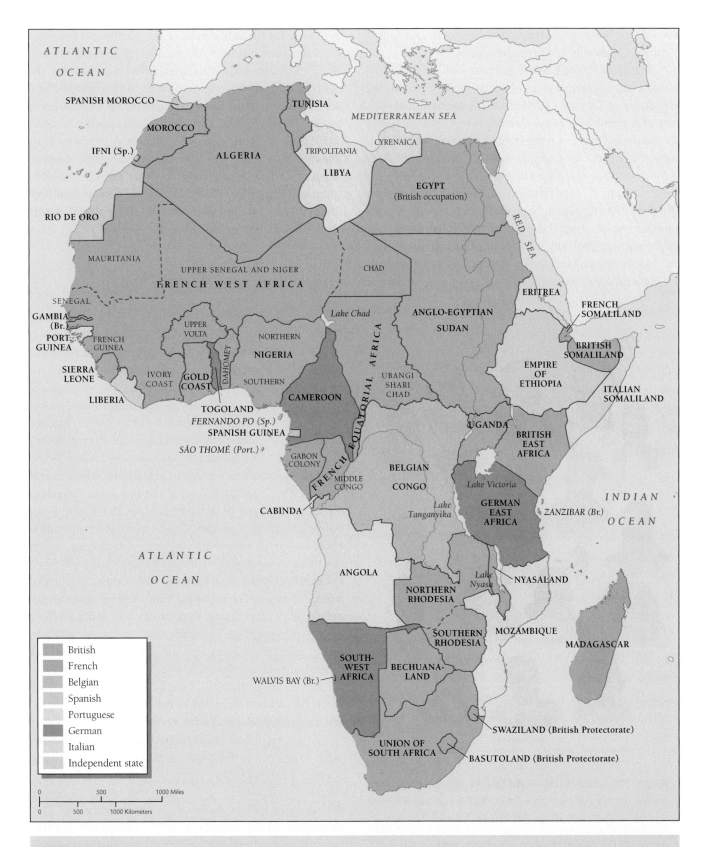

ATLANTIC
OCEAN

SPANISH MOROCCO
MOROCCO
IFNI (Sp.)
RIO DE ORO
MAURITANIA

TUNISIA
MEDITERRANEAN SEA
ALGERIA
TRIPOLITANIA
CYRENAICA
LIBYA

EGYPT
(British occupation)

RED SEA

UPPER SENEGAL AND NIGER
FRENCH WEST AFRICA

CHAD

ANGLO-EGYPTIAN
SUDAN

ERITREA
FRENCH
SOMALILAND

SENEGAL
GAMBIA
(Br.)
PORT.
GUINEA
FRENCH
GUINEA
SIERRA
LEONE
LIBERIA

Lake Chad

UPPER
VOLTA
NORTHERN

IVORY
COAST
GOLD
COAST
DAHOMEY
NIGERIA
SOUTHERN

TOGOLAND
FERNANDO PO (Sp.)
SPANISH GUINEA
SÃO THOMÉ (Port.)

CAMEROON

FRENCH EQUATORIAL AFRICA

UBANGI
SHARI
CHAD

BRITISH
SOMALILAND

EMPIRE
OF
ETHIOPIA

ITALIAN
SOMALILAND

UGANDA
BRITISH
EAST
AFRICA

GABON
COLONY
MIDDLE
CONGO

BELGIAN
CONGO

Lake Victoria

GERMAN
EAST
AFRICA

ZANZIBAR (Br.)

INDIAN
OCEAN

CABINDA

Lake
Tanganyika

ATLANTIC
OCEAN

ANGOLA

Lake
Nyasa
NYASALAND

NORTHERN
RHODESIA

MOZAMBIQUE

MADAGASCAR

SOUTHERN
RHODESIA

WALVIS BAY (Br.)

SOUTH-
WEST
AFRICA

BECHUANA-
LAND

British
French
Belgian
Spanish
Portuguese
German
Italian
Independent state

SWAZILAND (British Protectorate)

UNION OF
SOUTH AFRICA

BASUTOLAND (British Protectorate)

0   500   1000 Miles
0   500   1000 Kilometers

AFRICA, c. 1914.

one that the British people have, whether rightly or wrongly, regarded as specially laid upon themselves."

This sense of high moral purpose was not restricted to male writers or to figures of authority. In England, the United States, Germany, and France, the speeches and projects of women's reform movements were full of references to empire and the civilizing mission. Britain's woman suffrage movement, for example, was fiercely critical of the government but was also nationalist and imperialist. For these militants, women's participation in politics also meant the right to participate in imperial projects. British women reformers wrote about the oppression of Indian women by child marriage and sati and saw themselves shouldering the "white women's burden" of reform. In France, suffragist Hubertine Auclert criticized the colonial government in Algeria for its indifference to the condition of Muslim women in their domains. She used an image of women suffering in polygamous marriages abroad to dramatize the need for reform. Arguments such as these enabled European women in their home countries to see themselves as bearers of progress, as participants in a superior civilization. Similarly, John Stuart Mill often used Hindu or Muslim culture as a foil when he wanted to make a point of freedom of speech and religion. This contrast between colonial backwardness and European civility and cultural superiority shaped Western culture and political debate about liberal ideas in particular.

Imperialism and Racial Thought

Imperial culture gave new prominence to racial thinking. Count Arthur de Gobineau (*GOH-bih-noh*, 1816–1882) wrote a massive work, *The Inequality of the Races*, in the 1850s, but it sparked little interest until the period of the new imperialism, when it was translated into English and widely discussed. For Gobineau, race offered the "master key" for understanding human societies in the modern world. "The racial question overshadows all other problems of history . . . the inequality of the races from whose fusion a people is formed is enough to explain the whole course of its destiny." Gobineau's work followed from Enlightenment investigations of different cultures in the world, but unlike Enlightenment authors who attributed these differences largely to environmental factors, Gobineau argued that "blood" was the determining factor in human history. Gobineau claimed that humans were originally divided into three races, "black," "white," and "yellow," and that the peoples of the present day were variously mixed from these original components. The white race, he argued, had preserved purer bloodlines and was therefore superior. The others suffered "adulteration" and were therefore degenerate and no longer capable of civilization. Gobineau's readers included some defenders of the confederacy during the American Civil War and Adolf Hitler.

Followers of Gobineau's racial thinking looked increasingly to science to legitimate their theories. The natural scientist Charles Darwin, no racist himself, attracted wide attention with a theory of evolution that sought to explain the variety of species observable in the natural world. Darwin suggested that only the most "fit" individuals in a species survived to bear viable offspring, and that this process of "natural selection" explained how species diverged from one another: variations that made individuals better able to find food and mates were likely to be passed on to future generations. Social scientists such as Herbert Spencer

RACIAL THINKING IN THE AGE OF EMPIRE. This plate was published in 1906 in England and the United States in a geography book that was aimed at a mass audience. It is a good example of the ways that racial categories were given scientific legitimacy and disseminated in a way that lent them credibility in the popular imagination of the reading public. ▪ *How does this print convey the notion of racial hierarchy, the idea that some "races" were superior to others? Is the idea of "race" contained in this print purely biological? Does it also contain implications about human history?*

sought to use a similar logic of competition among individuals for scarce resources to explain the evolution of social groups, suggesting that inequalities of wealth or ability could also be explained as the result of a process of "natural selection." Racial theorists and followers of Gobineau such as Houston Stewart Chamberlain (1855–1927) wasted little time in harnessing such scientific arguments to the claim that human "races" evolved over time. Chamberlain's books sold tens of thousands of copies in England and Germany.

Francis Galton (1822–1911), a half cousin of Charles Darwin and a scientist who studied evolution, went so far as to advocate improving the population's racial characteristics by selective breeding of "superior types." Galton and others feared that improvements in health care and hygiene might allow individuals with inferior traits to survive to reproductive age, and his system of racial management, which he called *eugenics*, would save European populations from a decline in their vitality and biological fitness. Theories such as Galton's or Gobineau's did not cause imperialism, and they were closely linked with other developments in European culture, in particular renewed anxieties about social class and a fresh wave of European anti-Semitism. Yet the increasingly scientific racism of late-nineteenth-century Europe made it easier for many to reconcile the rhetoric of progress, individual freedom, and the civilizing mission with contempt for other peoples.

Opposition to Imperialism

Support for imperialism was not unanimous. Hobson and Lenin condemned the entire enterprise as an act of greed and arrogance. Polish-born Joseph Conrad, a British novelist, shared much of the racism of his contemporaries, but he nevertheless believed that imperialism was an expression of deeply rooted pathologies in European culture. Other anti-imperialists were men and women from the colonies themselves who brought their case to the metropole. The British Committee of the Indian National Congress gathered together many members of London's Indian community to educate British public opinion about the exploitation of Indian peoples and resources.

Perhaps the most defiant anti-imperialist action was the London Pan-African Conference of 1900, staged at the height of the scramble for Africa and during the Boer War (discussed on page 000). The conference grew out of an international tradition of African American, British, and American antislavery movements and brought the rhetoric used earlier to abolish slavery to bear on the tactics of European imperialism. They protested forced labor in the mining compounds of South Africa as akin to slavery and asked in very moderate tones for some autonomy and representation

for African peoples. The Pan-African Conference of 1900 was small, but it drew delegates from the Caribbean, West Africa, and North America, including the thirty-two-year-old Harvard Ph.D. and leading African American intellectual, W. E. B. Du Bois (1868–1963). The conference issued a proclamation "To the Nations of the World," with a famous introduction written by Du Bois. "In the metropolis of the modern world, in this closing year of the nineteenth century," the proclamation read, "there has been assembled a congress of men and women of African blood, to deliberate solemnly upon the present situation and outlook of the darker races of mankind. The problem of the twentieth century is the problem of the colour-line." The British government ignored the conference, but pan-Africanism, like Indian nationalism, grew rapidly after the First World War.

Colonial Cultures

Imperialism also created new colonial cultures in other parts of the world. Cities such as Bombay, Calcutta, and Shanghai boomed, more than tripling in size. Treaty ports like Hong Kong were transformed as Europeans built banks, shipping enterprises, schools, and religious missions. As Europeans and indigenous peoples encountered and transformed one another, new hybrid cultures emerged. Elsewhere, new social instabilities were produced as European demands for labor brought men out of their villages, away from their families, and crowded them into shantytowns bordering sprawling new cities. Hopes that European rule would create a well-disciplined labor force were quickly dashed.

People on both sides of the colonial divide worried about preserving national traditions and identity in the face of these hybrid and changing colonial cultures. In Africa and the Middle East, Islamic scholars debated the proper response to European control. In China and India, suggestions that local populations adopt European models of education set off fierce controversies. Chinese elites, already divided over such customs as foot-binding and concubinage (the legal practice of maintaining formal sexual partners for men outside their marriage), found their dilemmas heightened as imperialism became a more powerful force. Should they defend such practices as integral to their culture? Should they argue for a Chinese path to reform? Proponents of change in China or India thus had to sort through their stance toward Western culture and traditional popular culture.

For their part, British, French, and Dutch authorities fretted that too much familiarity between colonized and colonizer would weaken European prestige and authority. In Phnom Penh, Cambodia (part of French Indochina),

Address to the Nations of the World by the Pan-African Conference in London, 1900

The Pan-African Conference that met in 1900 in London brought together a group of people of African heritage from many parts of the world who were determined to add their voices to those who were discussing and debating the consequences of European imperialism in the last decades of the nineteenth century. The declaration that they produced gives a clear picture of their vision of history, their sense of the injustices associated with colonial conquest, and their hopes for the future. The chair of the committee who wrote the address was W. E. B. Du Bois (1868–1963), an African American professor of history, sociology, and economics who had studied at Harvard and the University of Berlin and who in 1909 became a founding member of the National Association for the Advancement of Colored People.

n the metropolis of the modern world, in this the closing year of the nineteenth century, there has been assembled a congress of men and women of African blood, to deliberate solemnly upon the present situation and outlook of the darker races of mankind. The problem of the twentieth century is the problem of the colour-line, the question as to how far differences of race—which show themselves chiefly in the colour of the skin and the texture of the hair—will hereafter be made the basis of denying to over half the world the right of sharing to their utmost ability the opportunities and privileges of modern civilization.

To be sure, the darker races are today the least advanced in culture according to European standards. This has not, however, always been the case in the past, and certainly the world's history, both ancient and modern, has given many instances of no despicable ability and capacity among the blackest races of men.

In any case, the modern world must remember that in this age when the ends of the world are being brought so near together the millions of black men in Africa, America, and the Islands of the Sea, not to speak of the brown and yellow myriads elsewhere, are bound to have a great influence upon the world in the future, by reason of sheer numbers and physical contact. If now the world of culture bends itself towards giving Negroes and other dark men the largest and broadest opportunity for education and self-development, then this contact and influence is bound to have a beneficial effect upon the world and hasten human progress. But if, by reason of carelessness, prejudice, greed and injustice, the black world is to be exploited and ravished and degraded, the results must be deplorable, if not fatal—not simply to them, but to the high ideals of justice, freedom and culture which a thousand years of Christian civilization have held before Europe.

And now, therefore, to these ideals of civilization, to the broader humanity of the followers of the Prince of Peace, we, the men and women of Africa in world congress assembled, do now solemnly appeal:

Let the world take no backward step in that slow but sure progress which has successively refused to let the spirit of class, of caste, of privilege, or of birth, debar from life, liberty and the pursuit of happiness a striving human soul.

Let not color or race be a feature of distinction between white and black men, regardless of worth or ability.

Let not the natives of Africa be sacrificed to the greed of gold, their liberties

---

French citizens lived separated from the rest of the city by a moat, and authorities required "dressing appropriately and keeping a distance from the natives." Sexual relations provoked the most anxiety and the most contradictory responses. "In this hot climate, passions run higher," wrote a French administrator in Algeria. "French soldiers seek out Arab women due to their strangeness and newness." "It was common practice for unmarried Englishmen resident in China to keep a Chinese girl, and I did as the others did," reported a British man stationed in Shanghai. He married an Englishwoman, however, and sent his Chinese mistress and their three children to England to avoid awkwardness. European administrators fitfully tried to prohibit liaisons between European men and local women, labeling such affairs as "corrupting." Such prohibitions only drove these relations underground, increasing the gap between the public facade of colonial rule and the private reality of colonial lives.

taken away, their family life debauched, their just aspirations repressed, and avenues of advancement and culture taken from them.

Let not the cloak of Christian missionary enterprise be allowed in the future, as so often in the past, to hide the ruthless economic exploitation and political downfall of less developed nations, whose chief fault has been reliance on the plighted faith of the Christian Church.

Let the British nation, the first modern champion of Negro Freedom, hasten to crown the work of Wilberforce, and Clarkson, and Buxton, and Sharpe, Bishop Colenso, and Livingstone, and give, as soon as practicable, the rights of responsible government to the black colonies of Africa and the West Indies.

Let not the spirit of Garrison, Phillips, and Douglass wholly die out in America; may the conscience of a great nation rise and rebuke all dishonesty and unrighteous oppression toward the American Negro, and grant to him the right of franchise, security of person and property, and generous recognition of the great work he has accomplished in a generation toward raising nine millions of human beings from slavery to manhood.

Let the German Empire, and the French Republic, true to their great past, remember that the true worth of colonies lies in their prosperity and progress, and that justice, impartial alike to black and white, is the first element of prosperity.

Let the Congo Free State become a great central Negro State of the world, and let its prosperity be counted not simply in cash and commerce, but in the happiness and true advancement of its black people.

Let the nations of the World respect the integrity and independence of the first Negro States of Abyssinia, Liberia, Haiti, and the rest, and let the inhabitants of these States, the independent tribes of Africa, the Negroes of the West Indies and America, and the black subjects of all nations take courage, strive ceaselessly, and fight bravely, that they may prove to the world their incontestible right to be counted among the great brotherhood of mankind.

Thus we appeal with boldness and confidence to the Great Powers of the civilized world, trusting in the wide spirit of humanity, and the deep sense of justice of our age, for a generous recognition of the righteousness of our cause.

ALEXANDER WALTERS (Bishop)
President Pan-African Association
HENRY B. BROWN
Vice-President
H. SYLVESTER-WILLIAMS
General Secretary
W. E. BURGHARDT DU BOIS
Chairman Committee on Address

Source: Ayodele Langley, *Ideologies of Liberation in Black Africa* (London: 1979), pp. 738–39.

Questions for Analysis

1. What value do the authors ascribe to "race" as a description of human difference?

2. According to the authors, what choices do European powers have to make as they exercise their power in Africa? What are their hopes for Africans in a world shaped by European expansion?

3. What are the specific "ideals of civilization" that the authors of this declaration invoke? Do they share these ideals with people from elsewhere?

4. Are there echoes of European liberalism or nationalism in the address's pan-Africanism?

CRISES OF EMPIRE AT THE TURN OF THE TWENTIETH CENTURY

The turn of the twentieth century brought a series of crises to the Western empires. Those crises did not end European rule. They did, however, create sharp tensions among Western nations. The crises also drove imperial nations to expand their economic and military commitments in territories overseas. They shook Western confidence. In all of these ways, they became central to Western culture in the years before the First World War.

Fashoda

In the fall of 1898, British and French armies nearly went to war at Fashoda, in the Egyptian Sudan. The crisis had

Displays of Imperial Culture: The Paris Exposition of 1889

The French colonies were very visible during the celebration of the centenary of the French Revolution in 1889. In that year, the French government organized a "Universal Exposition" in the capital that attracted over 6 million visitors to a broad esplanade covered with exhibitions of French industry and culture, including the newly constructed Eiffel Tower, a symbol of modern French engineering.

At the base of the Eiffel Tower (image A), a colonial pavilion placed objects from France's overseas empire on display, and a collection of temporary architectural exhibits placed reproductions of buildings from French colonies in Asia and Africa as well as samples of architecture from other parts of the world. The photographs here show a reproduction of a Cairo Street (image B); the Pagoda of Angkor, modeled after

A. The Eiffel Tower in 1889.

the Khmer temples of Angkor Wat in Cambodia, a French protectorate (image C); and examples of West African dwellings (image D). The Cairo Street was the second most popular tourist destination at the fair, after the Eiffel Tower. It con-

tained twenty-five shops and restaurants, and employed dozens of Egyptian servers, shopkeepers, and artisans who had been brought to Paris to add authenticity to the exhibit. Other people on display in the colonial pavilion included Senegalese villagers and a Vietnamese theater troupe.

Questions for Analysis

1. What vision of history and social progress is celebrated in this linkage between France's colonial holdings and the industrial power on display in the Eiffel Tower?

2. What might account for the popularity of the Cairo Street exhibit among the public?

3. Why was it so important for the exposition to place people from European colonies on display for a French audience?

B. Reproduction of a Cairo Street at the Paris World's Fair, 1889.

C. Pagoda of Angkor at the Paris World's Fair, 1889.

D. West African houses at the Paris World's Fair, 1889.

complex causes: in the early 1880s, the British had used a local uprising in the Sudan as an excuse to move southward from Egypt in an attempt to control the headwaters of the Nile River. This project began with grandiose dreams of connecting Cairo to the Cape of Good Hope, but it ran into catastrophe when an army led by Britain's most flamboyant general, Charles Gordon, was massacred in Khartoum in 1885 by the forces of the Mahdi, a Sufi religious leader who claimed to be the successor to the prophet Muhammad. Avenging Gordon's death preoccupied the British for more than a decade, and in 1898 a second large-scale rebellion gave them the opportunity. An Anglo-Egyptian army commanded by General Horatio Kitchener attacked Khartoum and defeated the Mahdi's army using modern machine guns and artillery.

The victory brought complications, however. France, which held territories in central Africa adjacent to the Sudan, saw the British victory as a threat. A French expedition was sent to the Sudanese town of Fashoda (now Kodok) to challenge British claims in the area. The French faced off with troops from Kitchener's army, and for a few weeks in September 1898 the situation teetered on the brink of war. The matter was resolved diplomatically, however, and France ceded the southern Sudan to Britain in exchange for a stop to further expansion. The incident was a sobering reminder of the extent to which imperial competition could lead to international tensions between European powers.

EMPEROR MENELIK II. Ethiopia was the last major independent African kingdom, its prosperity a counter to the European opinion of African cultures. Menelik soundly defeated the Italian attempt to conquer his kingdom in 1896.

Ethiopia

During the 1880s and 1890s, Italy had been developing a small empire on the shores of the Red Sea. Italy annexed Eritrea and parts of Somalia, and shortly after the death of Gordon at Khartoum, the Italians defeated an invasion of their territories by the Mahdi's forces. Bolstered by this success, the Italians set out to conquer Ethiopia in 1896. Ethiopia was the last major independent African kingdom, ruled by a shrewd and capable emperor, Menelik II. His largely Christian subjects engaged in profitable trade on the East African coast, and revenues from this trade allowed Menelik to invest in the latest European artillery. When the Italian army—mostly Somali conscripts and a few thousand Italian troops—arrived, Menelik allowed them to penetrate into the mountain passes of Ethiopia. To keep to the roads, the Italians were forced to divide their forces into separate columns. Meanwhile, the Ethiopians moved over the mountains themselves, and at Adowa in March 1896 Menelik's army attacked, destroyed the Italian armies completely, and killed

6,000. Adowa was a national humiliation for Italy and an important symbol for African political radicals during the early twentieth century.

South Africa: The Boer War

In the late 1800s, competition between Dutch settlers in South Africa—known as Afrikaners or Boers—and the British led to a shooting war between Europeans. The Boers (an appropriation of the Dutch word for farmer) arrived in South Africa in the early nineteenth century and had long had a troubled relationship with their British neighbors in the colony. In the 1830s, the Boers trekked inland from the cape, setting up two republics away from British influence: the Transvaal and the Orange Free State. Gold reserves were found in the Transvaal in the 1880s, and Cecil Rhodes, the diamond magnate, tried to provoke war between Britain and the Boers to gain control of the Afrikaners' diamond mines. The war finally

Rudyard Kipling and His Critics

> Rudyard Kipling (1865–1936) remains one of the most famous propagandists of empire. His novels, short stories, and poetry about the British imperial experience in India were defining texts for the cause in which he believed. Kipling's poem was—and continues to be—widely read, analyzed, attacked, and praised. His immediate goal was to influence American public opinion during the Spanish–American War, but he also wanted to celebrate the moral and religious values of European imperialism in general.

The White Man's Burden

Take up the White Man's burden—
   Send forth the best ye breed—
Go, bind your sons to exile
   To serve your captives' need;
To wait, in heavy harness,
   On fluttered folk and wild—
Your new-caught sullen peoples,
   Half devil and half child.

Take up the White Man's burden—
   In patience to abide,
To veil the threat of terror
   And check the show of pride;
By open speech and simple,
   An hundred times made plain,
To seek another's profit
   And work another's gain.

Take up the White Man's burden—
   The savage wars of peace—
Fill full the mouth of Famine,
   And bid the sickness cease;

And when your goal is nearest
   (The end for others sought)
Watch sloth and heathen folly
   Bring all your hope to nought.

Take up the White Man's burden—
   No iron rule of kings,
But toil of serf and sweeper—
   The tale of common things.
The ports ye shall not enter,
   The roads ye shall not tread,
Go, make them with your living
   And mark them with your dead.

Take up the White Man's burden,
   And reap his old reward—
The blame of those ye better
   The hate of those ye guard—
The cry of hosts ye humour
   (Ah, slowly!) toward the light:—
"Why brought ye us from bondage,
   Our loved Egyptian night?"

Take up the White Man's burden—
   Ye dare not stoop to less—
Nor call too loud on Freedom
   To cloak your weariness.
By all ye will or whisper,
   By all ye leave or do,
The silent sullen peoples
   Shall weigh your God and you.

Take up the White Man's burden!
   Have done with childish days—
The lightly-proffered laurel,
   The easy ungrudged praise:
Comes now, to search your manhood
   Through all the thankless years,
Cold, edged with dear-bought wisdom,
   The judgment of your peers.

Source: Rudyard Kipling, "The White Man's Burden," *McClure's Magazine* 12 (Feb. 1899).

To the Editor of *The Nation*

Sir: The cable informs us that "Kipling's stirring verses, the 'Call to America,' have created a . . . profound impression" on your side. What that impression may be, we can only conjecture. There is something almost sickening in this "imperial" talk of assuming and bearing burdens for the good of others. They are never assumed or held where they are not found to be of material advantage or ministering to honor or glory. Wherever empire (I speak of the United Kingdom) is extended, and the climate suits the white man, the aborigines are, for the benefit of the white man, cleared off or held in degradation for his benefit. . . .

Taking India as a test, no one moves a foot in her government that is not well paid and pensioned at her cost. No appointments are more eagerly contended for than those in the Indian service. A young man is made for life when he secures one. The tone of that service is by no means one "bound to exile," "to serve . . . captives' need," "to wait in heavy harness," or in any degree as expressed in Mr. Kipling's highfalutin lines. It is entirely the contrary: "You are requested not to beat the servants" is a not uncommon notice in Indian hotels. . . . So anxious are we, where good pay is concerned, to save Indians the heavy burden of enjoying them, that, while our sons can study and pass at home for Indian appointments, her sons must study and pass in England; and even in India itself whites are afforded chances closed to natives. . . .

There never was a fostered trade and revenue in more disastrous consequences to humanity than the opium trade and revenue. There never was a more grinding and debilitating tax than that on salt. . . .

Source: Alfred Webb, "Mr. Kipling's Call to America," *The Nation* 68 (Feb. 23, 1899).

Questions for Analysis

1. What benefits did Kipling think imperialism brought, and to whom?

2. What, exactly, was the "burden"?

3. What were Webb's arguments against Kipling? Why did he think that imperial talk was "almost sickening"? Did Europeans really suffer in their colonial outposts? In British India, with its well-established civil service, Webb thought not. Why did he mention the opium trade and the salt tax?

broke out in 1899, but the British were unprepared for the ferocity of Boer resistance. British columns were shot to pieces by Afrikaner forces who knew the territory, and the British towns of Ladysmith and Mafeking were besieged. Angered by these early failures, the British replaced their commanders and began to fight in earnest, using the railroads built to service the diamond mines to bring in modern military hardware.

The Afrikaners responded by taking to the hills, fighting a costly guerilla war that lasted another three years. The British tactics became more brutal as the campaign went on, setting up concentration camps—the first use of the term—where Afrikaner civilians were rounded up and forced to live in appalling conditions so that they would not be able to help the guerillas. Nearly 20,000 civilians died in the camps owing to disease and poor sanitation over the course of two years. Black Africans, despised by both sides, also suffered the effects of famine and disease as the war destroyed valuable farmland.

Meanwhile, the concentration camps aroused opposition in Britain and internationally, and protesters campaigned against these violations of "European" rights, without saying anything about the fate of Africans in the conflict. In the end, the Afrikaners ceded control of their republics to a new British Union of South Africa that gave them a share of political power. In the aftermath of the

LA GUERRE AU TRANSVAAL
Les camps de reconcentration

AN ENGLISH CONCENTRATION CAMP DURING THE BOER WAR. In an attempt to block support to guerilla fighters, the English restricted Afrikaner civilians to camps where appalling conditions led to the death of nearly 20,000 people over two years. This illustration appeared in a French newspaper, *Le Petit Journal*, in 1901.

Crises of Empire at the Turn of the Twentieth Century | 757

war, both British and Afrikaners preserved their high standards of living by relying on cheap African labor and, eventually, a system of racial segregation known as apartheid.

U.S. Imperialism: The Spanish-American War of 1898

Imperialism also brought Spain and the United States to war in 1898. American imperialism in the nineteenth century was closely bound up with nation building, the conquest of new territories, and the defeat of the North American Indians (see Chapter 21). In the 1840s, the United States provoked Mexico into war over Texas and California after unsuccessfully trying to purchase the territories. Mexico's defeat, and the treaty of Guadalupe Hidalgo that followed in 1848, gave the American Southwest to the United States, an enormous territorial gain that made the question of slavery more acute in the years before the American Civil War.

The conflict with Spain followed a similar pattern. In the 1880s and 1890s, Spain's imperial powers were considerably weakened, and they faced rebellion in their colonies in the Caribbean and the Pacific. American economic interests had considerable investments in Cuba, and when an American battleship accidentally exploded at port in Havana, advocates of empire and the press in general

IMPERIALISM IN THE BALANCE. This cartoon, titled "A Study—Imperialism" appeared in the United States in 1899 during the beginning of the Philippine-American War. The image shows the scales of justice weighing imperialism against the many victims of U.S. military action, and demonstrates that the populations of colonial powers were far from unanimous about the virtues of imperial expansion and the "civilizing mission."

After You Read This Chapter

Visit StudySpace for quizzes, additional review materials, and multimedia documents. **wwnorton.com/web/westernciv18**

REVIEWING THE OBJECTIVES

- European imperialism in the nineteenth century differed from earlier phases of colonial expansion. How was it different, and which parts of the globe were singled out for special attention by European imperial powers?

- European nations justified the cost and effort of their colonial policies in many ways. What were the major reasons for colonial expansion in the nineteenth century?

- The subjugated peoples of European colonies faced a choice between resistance and accommodation, though these choices were rarely exclusive of one another. What examples of resistance to colonialism can you identify? Of accommodation?

- Imperialism also shaped cultural developments within Europe in the nineteenth century. How did imperialism change the lives of Europeans and their sense of their place in the world?

- Imperialism unleashed destabilizing competitive forces that drove European colonial powers into conflict with one another by the end of the nineteenth century. Where were the flashpoints of these conflicts?

clamored for revenge. President William McKinley gave in to political necessity, in spite of his misgivings, and the United States declared war on Spain in 1898, determined to protect its economic interests in the Americas and the Pacific. The United States swiftly won.

In Spain, the Spanish-American War provoked an entire generation of writers, politicians, and intellectuals to national soul searching. The defeat undermined the Spanish monarchy, which fell in 1912. The ensuing political tensions resurfaced in the Spanish Civil War of the 1930s, an important episode in the origins of the Second World War.

In the United States, this "splendid little war" was followed by the annexation of Puerto Rico, the establishment of a protectorate over Cuba, and a short but brutal war against Philippine rebels who liked American colonialism no better than the Spanish variety. In the Americas, the United States intervened in a rebellion in Panama in 1903, quickly backing the rebels and helping establish a republic while building the Panama Canal on land leased from the new government. The Panama Canal opened in 1914, and like Britain's canal at Suez, it cemented U.S. dominance of the seas in the Western Hemisphere and the eastern Pacific. Later interventions in Hawaii and Santo Domingo gave further evidence of U.S. imperial power and committed the former colony to a broad role in its new and greater sphere of influence.

CONCLUSION

In the last quarter of the nineteenth century, the long-standing relationship between Western nations and the rest of the world entered a new stage. That stage was distinguished by the stunningly rapid extension of formal Western control, by new forms of economic exploitation, and by new patterns of social discipline and settlement. It was driven by the rising economic needs of the industrial West; by territorial conflict; and by nationalism, which by the late nineteenth century linked nationhood to empire. Among its immediate results was the creation of a self-consciously imperial culture in the West. At the same time, however, it plainly created unease and contributed powerfully to the sense of crisis that swept through the late-nineteenth-century West.

For all its force, this Western expansion was never unchallenged. Imperialism provoked resistance and required constantly changing strategies of rule. During the First World War, mobilizing the resources of empire would become crucial to victory. In the aftermath, reimposing the conditions of the late nineteenth century would become nearly impossible. And over the longer term, the political structures, economic developments, and racial ideologies established in this period would be contested throughout the twentieth century.

PEOPLE, IDEAS, AND EVENTS IN CONTEXT

- What was the **EAST INDIA COMPANY**? How did the British reorganize their rule in India after the **SEPOY MUTINY**?
- What did the French mean when they justified colonial expansion in the name of the **CIVILIZING MISSION**?
- How did the **OPIUM WARS** change the economic and political relationships between Europe and China?
- How did the **BERLIN CONFERENCE** of 1884 shape the subsequent colonization of Africa?
- What limits to the exercise of colonial power were revealed by the **BOXER REBELLION**, the failed **ITALIAN INVASION OF ETHIOPIA**, or the **RUSSO-JAPANESE WAR**?
- What expressions of anti-imperialism emerged from the London **PAN-AFRICAN CONFERENCE**?
- How did the **BOER WAR** and the **FASHODA INCIDENT** contribute to a sense of crisis among European colonial powers?
- What effects did the **SPANISH-AMERICAN WAR** have on attitudes toward imperialism in the United States, itself a former European colony?

THINKING ABOUT CONNECTIONS

- Compare the consequences of late-nineteenth-century European colonial conquest with earlier episodes of imperial expansion such as the Roman Empire or early modern colonization in the Atlantic world. What was similar? What was different?
- What challenges were faced by colonial regimes such as France and Britain, which expanded their institutions of representative and elected government at home even as they subjugated the conquered peoples in their new colonies during the nineteenth century?
- The histories of colonial conquest in the nineteenth century helped to establish a network of political and cultural connections that shaped the history of the world in the twentieth century. What was the legacy of these connections during the period of decolonization?
- How was the history of industrialization connected to the history of colonialism?

Before
You
Read
This
Chapter

Modern Industry and Mass Politics, 1870–1914

CORE OBJECTIVES

- **UNDERSTAND** the origins and consequences of the second industrial revolution.

- **DEFINE** *mass politics* and explain how the expansion of voting rights in European nations led to the development of organized political parties that sought the support of the working classes.

- **UNDERSTAND** the arguments both for and against woman suffrage during this period.

- **IDENTIFY** the ways that European liberalism and conservatism evolved as new social and political tensions emerged with the advent of mass politics and intensified industrial development.

- **EXPLAIN** the contributions of scientists and other cultural figures who came to prominence in the final decades of the nineteenth century and their contributions to debates about human nature, modern society, and the natural world.

"We are on the extreme promontory of ages!" decreed the Italian poet and literary editor F. T. Marinetti in 1909. In a bombastic manifesto—a self-described "inflammatory declaration" printed on the front page of a Paris newspaper—Marinetti introduced Europe to an aggressive art movement called futurism. Revolting against what he considered the tired and impotent conservatism of Italian culture, Marinetti called for a radical renewal of civilization through "courage, audacity, and revolt." Enamored with the raw power of modern machinery, with the dynamic bustle of urban life, he trumpeted "a new form of beauty, the beauty of speed." Most notable, Marinetti celebrated the heroic violence of warfare and disparaged the moral and cultural traditions that formed the bedrock of nineteenth-century liberalism.

Few Europeans embraced the modern era with the unflinching abandon of the futurists, but many would have agreed with Marinetti in his claim that modern life was above all characterized by flux, movement, and an accelerating rate of change. In the last decades of the nineteenth century, a second industrial revolution produced new techniques for manufacturing and new sources of power, including electricity and petroleum-based fuels. These developments transformed the infrastructure of European towns and cities, and people felt the immediate effects of these changes in their daily lives.

At the same time, European nation-states faced new political realities as their electorates expanded and new blocs of voters began participating directly in shaping parliamentary bodies and their legislative agendas. New mass-based political parties brought new demands to the political arena, and national governments struggled to maintain order and legitimacy in the face of these challenges. Socialists mobilized growing numbers of industrial workers, while suffragists demanded the franchise for women. The ability of traditional elites to control the political life of nations was sorely tested, even in nations that continued to be governed by hereditary monarchs.

In the arts and sciences new theories challenged older notions of nature, society, truth, and beauty. Since the eighteenth century at least, science had been a frequent ally of political liberalism, as both liberals and scientists shared a common faith in human reason and an openness to rational inquiry into the laws of society and nature. In the late nineteenth century, however, this common agenda was strained by scientific investigations in new fields such as biology and psychology that challenged liberal assumptions about human nature. Meanwhile, in the arts, a new generation of artists and writers embraced innovation and rejected the established conventions in painting, sculpture, poetry, and literature. A period of intense experimentation in the arts followed, leading artists and writers to develop radically new forms of expression.

The nineteenth century, then, ended in a burst of energy as many Europeans embraced a vision of their society racing headlong into what they hoped was a more promising and better future. Behind this self-confidence, however, lay significant uncertainty about the eventual destination. What aspects of the European past would continue to be relevant in the modern age? In politics and social life and in the culture as a whole, such questions produced more conflict than consensus.

NEW TECHNOLOGIES AND GLOBAL TRANSFORMATIONS

In the last third of the nineteenth century, new technologies transformed the face of manufacturing in Europe, leading to new levels of economic growth and complex realignments among industry, labor, and national governments. Like Europe's first industrial revolution, which began in the late eighteenth century and centered on coal, steam, and iron, this second industrial revolution relied on innovation in three key areas: steel, electricity, and chemicals.

Harder, stronger, and more malleable than iron, steel had long been prized as a construction material. But until the mid-nineteenth century, producing steel cheaply and in large quantities was impossible. That changed between the 1850s and 1870s, as different processes for refining and mass-producing alloy steel revolutionized the metallurgical industry. Britain's shipbuilders made a quick and profitable switch to steel construction and thus kept their lead in the industry. Germany and America dominated the

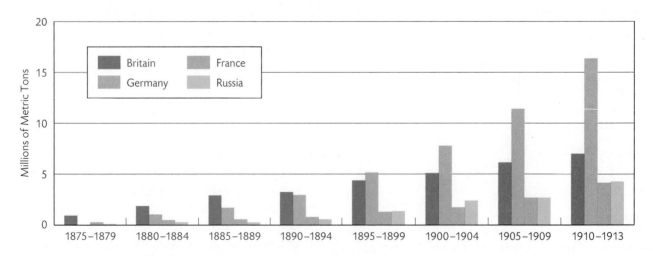

ANNUAL OUTPUT OF STEEL (IN MILLIONS OF METRIC TONS).
Source: Carlo Cipolla, *The Fontana Economic History of Europe*, vol. 3, pt. 2 (London: 1976), p. 775.

rest of the steel industry. By 1901, Germany was producing almost half again as much steel as Britain, allowing Germany to build a massive national and industrial infrastructure.

Like steel, electricity had been discovered earlier, and its advantages were similarly well known. Easily transmitted over long distances to be converted into heat, light, and other types of energy, electricity was made available for commercial and domestic use in the 1880s, after the development of alternators and transformers capable of producing high-voltage alternating current. By century's end, large power stations, which often used cheap water power, could send electric current over vast distances. In 1879, Thomas Edison and his associates invented the incandescent-filament lamp and changed electricity into light. The demand for electricity skyrocketed, and soon entire metropolitan areas were electrified. As a leading sector in the new economy, electrification powered subways, tramways, and, eventually, long-distance railroads; it made possible new techniques in the chemical and metallurgical industries, and gradually, it dramatically altered living habits in ordinary households.

The chemical industry was a third sector of important new technologies. The efficient production of alkali and sulfuric acid transformed the manufacture of such consumer goods as paper, soaps, textiles, and fertilizer. Britain and particularly Germany became leaders in the field. Heightened concerns for household hygiene and new techniques in mass marketing enabled the British entrepreneur Harold Lever to market his soaps and cleansers around the world. German production, on the other hand, focused on industrial use, such as developing synthetic dyes and methods for refining petroleum, and came to control roughly 90 percent of the world's chemical market.

Other innovations contributed to the second industrial revolution. The growing demand for efficient power spurred the invention of the liquid-fuel internal combustion engine. By 1914, most navies had converted from coal to oil, as had domestic steamship companies. The new engines' dependence on crude petroleum and distilled gasoline at first threatened their general application, but the discovery of oil fields in Russia, Borneo, Persia, and Texas around 1900 allayed fears. Protecting these oil reserves thus became a vital state prerogative. The adoption of oil-powered machinery had another important consequence:

THE SECOND INDUSTRIAL REVOLUTION. A German electrical engineering factory illustrates the scale of production during the second industrial revolution. ▪ *What changes in business practices and labor management made factories of this size possible?*

industrialists who had previously depended on nearby rivers or coal mines for power were free to take their enterprises to regions bereft of natural resources. The potential for worldwide industrialization was in place. Of course, the internal combustible engine would bring even more radical changes to twentieth-century transportation in the future, but the automobile and the airplane were both still in their infancies before 1914.

Changes in Scope and Scale

These technological changes were part of a much larger process—impressive increases in the scope and scale of industry. Technologies were both causes and consequences of the race toward a bigger, faster, cheaper, and more efficient world. At the end of the nineteenth century, size mattered. The rise of heavy industry and mass marketing had factories and cities growing hand in hand, while advances in media and mobility spurred the creation of national mass cultures. For the first time, ordinary people followed the news on national and global levels. They watched as European powers divided the globe, enlarging their empires with prodigious feats of engineering mastery; railroads, dams, canals, and harbors grew to monumental proportions. Such projects embodied the ideals of modern European industry. They also generated enormous income for builders, investors, bankers, entrepreneurs, and,

THE INDUSTRIAL REGIONS OF EUROPE. This map shows the distribution of mineral resources, rail lines, and industrial activity. ▪ *What nations enjoyed advantages in the development of industry and why?* ▪ *What resources were most important for industrial growth in the second half of the nineteenth century?* ▪ *What resources in England became dominant as a result of industrialization?*

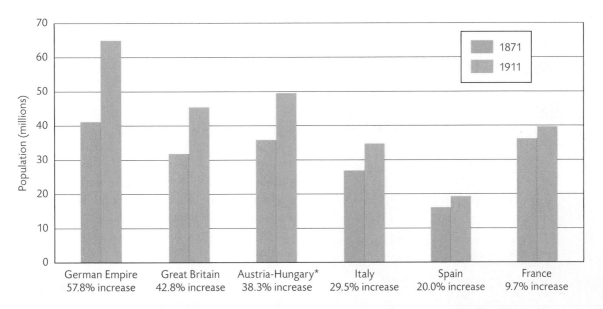

POPULATION GROWTH IN MAJOR STATES BETWEEN 1871 AND 1911 (POPULATION IN MILLIONS).
*Not including Bosnia-Herzegovina.
Source: Colin Dyer, *Population and Society in Twentieth-Century France* (New York: 1978), p. 5.

of course, makers of steel and concrete. Canals in central Europe, railroads in the Andes, and telegraph cables spanning the ocean floors: these "tentacles of empire," as one historian dubs them, stretched across the globe.

Yet industrialization also brought profound, if less spectacular, changes in Europe. The population grew constantly, particularly in central and eastern Europe. Russia's population increased by nearly a quarter and Germany's by half in the space of a generation. Britain's population, too, grew by nearly one-third between 1881 and 1911. Thanks to improvements in both crop yields and shipping, food shortages declined, which rendered entire populations less susceptible to illness and high infant mortality. Advances in medicine, nutrition, and personal hygiene diminished the prevalence of dangerous diseases such as cholera and typhus, and improved conditions in housing and public sanitation transformed the urban environment.

Credit and Consumerism

Changes in scope and scale not only transformed production but also altered consumption. Indeed it was during this period that consumption began to shift, slowly, to the center of economic activity and theory. The era in which economists would worry about consumer confidence and experts could systematically track the public's buying habits did not begin until the middle of the twentieth century, but developments pointed toward that horizon. Department stores offering both practical and luxury goods to the

middle class were one mark of the times—of urbanization, economic expansion, and the new importance attached to merchandising. Advertising took off as well. The lavishly illustrated posters of the late nineteenth century that advertised concert halls, soaps, bicycles, and sewing machines were only one sign of underlying economic changes. Even more significant, by the 1880s new stores sought to attract working-class people by introducing the all-important innovation of credit payment. In earlier times, working-class families pawned watches, mattresses, or furniture to borrow money; now they began to buy on credit, a change that would eventually have seismic effects on both households and national economies.

These new late-nineteenth-century patterns of consumption, however, were largely urban. In the countryside, peasants continued to save money under mattresses; pass down a few pieces of furniture for generations; make, launder, and mend their own clothes and linens; and offer a kilo of sugar as a generous household gift. Only slowly did retailers whittle away at these traditional habits. Mass consumption remained difficult to imagine in what was still a deeply stratified society.

The Rise of the Corporation

Economic growth and the demands of mass consumption spurred reorganization, consolidation, and regulation of capitalist institutions. Although capitalist enterprises had been financed by individual investors through the joint-stock

POSTER FOR *MOTOCYCLES COMIOT*, 1899. The rise of consumer spending in the middle class created a new industry and a new art: advertising. This advertisement, like many from the period, contrasted new with old, leisure with toil, and speed, or freedom, with inertia.

from company founders and local directors to distant bankers and financiers. Because financial institutions represented the interests of investors whose primary concern was the bottom line, bankers' control over industrial growth encouraged an ethos of impersonal finance capital.

Equally important, the second industrial revolution created a strong demand for technical expertise, which undercut traditional forms of family management. University degrees in engineering and chemistry became more valuable than on-the-job apprenticeships. The emergence of a white-collar class (middle-level salaried managers who were neither owners nor laborers) marked a significant change in work life and for society's evolving class structure.

The drive toward larger business enterprises was spurred by a desire for increased profits. It was also encouraged by a belief that consolidation protected society against the hazards of boom-and-bust economic fluctuations and against the wasteful inefficiencies of unbridled, "ruinous" competition. Some industries combined vertically, attempting to control every step of production from the acquisition of raw materials to the distribution of finished products. Andrew Carnegie's steel company in Pittsburgh controlled costs by owning the iron and coal mines necessary for steel production as well as by acquiring its own fleet of steamships and railways to transport ore to the mills. A second form of corporate self-protection was horizontal alignment. Organizing into cartels, companies in the same industry would band together to fix prices and control competition, if not eliminate it outright. Coal, oil, and steel companies were especially suited to the organization of cartels, since only a few major players could afford the huge expense of building, equipping, and running mines, refineries, and foundries. In 1894, for example, the Rhenish-Westphalian Coal Syndicate captured 98 percent of Germany's coal market by using ruthless tactics against small competitors, who could join the syndicate or face ruin. Through similar tactics, both legal and illegal, John D. Rockefeller's Standard Oil Company came to control the refined petroleum market in the United States, producing over 90 percent of the country's oil by the 1880s. The monopoly was sustained through the Standard Oil Trust, a legal innovation that enabled Rockefeller to control and manage assets of allied companies through the government. Cartels were particularly strong in Germany and America but less so in Britain, where dedication to free-trade policies made price fixing difficult, and in France, where family firms and laborers both opposed cartels and where there was also less heavy industry.

Though governments sometimes tried to stem the burgeoning power of cartels, the dominant trend of this period was increased cooperation between governments

principle at least since the sixteenth century, it was during the late nineteenth century that the modern corporation came into its own. To mobilize the enormous funds needed for large-scale enterprises, entrepreneurs needed to offer better guarantees on investors' money. To provide such protection, most European countries enacted or improved their limited-liability laws, which ensured that stockholders could lose only the value of their shares in the event of bankruptcy. Insured in this way, many thousands of middle-class men and women now considered corporate investment a promising venture. After 1870, stock markets ceased to be primarily a clearinghouse for state paper and railroad bonds and instead attracted new commercial and industrial ventures.

Limited liability was one part of a larger trend of incorporation. Whereas most firms had been small or middle size, companies now incorporated to attain the necessary size for survival. In doing so, they tended to shift control

The Dangers of Consumer Culture

By 1880 the Bon Marché in Paris, the world's first department store, was turning over the astronomical sum of 80 million francs annually and came to embody the new rhythm and tempo of mass consumer culture. The vast scale of selling sparked debate about the decline of the family store, the recreation of browsing and window shopping, and, above all, the "moral disaster" of women's limitless desire for goods. In writing the novel The Ladies' Paradise (1883), *Émile Zola noted he wanted to "write the poem of modern activity." The passage here captures the fascination for Denise, a clerk in her uncle's fabric shop, of the fictitious department store the Ladies' Paradise.*

But what fascinated Denise was the Ladies' Paradise on the other side of the street, for she could see the shop-windows through the open door. The sky was still overcast, but the mildness brought by rain was warming the air in spite of the season; and in the clear light, dusted with sunshine, the great shop was coming to life, and business was in full swing.

Denise felt that she was watching a machine working at high pressure; its dynamism seemed to reach to the display windows themselves. They were no longer the cold windows she had seen in the morning; now they seemed to be warm and vibrating with the activity within. A crowd was looking at them, groups of women were crushing each other in front of them, a real mob, made brutal by covetousness. And these passions in the street were giving life to the materials: the laces shivered, then drooped again, concealing the depths of the shop with an exciting air of mystery; even the lengths of cloth, thick and square, were breathing, exuding a tempting odour, while the overcoats were throwing back their shoulders still more on the dummies, which were acquiring souls, and the huge velvet coat was billowing out, supple and warm, as if on shoulders of flesh and blood, with heaving breast and quivering hips. But the furnace-like heat with which the shop was ablaze came above all from the selling, from the bustle at the counters, which could be felt behind the walls. There was the continuous roar of the machine at work, of customers crowding into the departments, dazzled by the merchandise, then propelled towards the cash-desk. And it was all regulated and organized with the remorselessness of a machine: the vast horde of women were as if caught in the wheels of an inevitable force. . . .

Source: Émile Zola, *The Ladies' Paradise,* trans. Brian Nelson (New York: 1995), pp. 15–16.

Questions for Analysis

1. Why did Zola choose to represent the new department store as a giant machine?

2. The first industrial revolution faced the challenge of production. In what ways was consumption the challenge of the late nineteenth century? What obstacles did merchants confront when encouraging people to consume?

and industry. Contrary to the laissez-faire mentality of early capitalism, corporations developed close relationships with the states in the West—most noticeably in colonial industrial projects, such as the construction of railroads, harbors, and seafaring steamships. These efforts were so costly, or so unprofitable, that private enterprise would not have undertaken them alone. But because they served larger political and strategic interests, governments funded them willingly. Such interdependence was underscored by the appearance of businessmen and financiers as officers of state. The German banker Bernhard Dernburg was the German secretary of state for colonies. Joseph Chamberlain, the British manufacturer and mayoral boss of industrial Birmingham, also served as the colonial secretary. And in France, Charles Jonnart, president of the Suez Canal Company and the Saint-Étienne steelwork, was later governor general of Algeria. Tied to imperial interests, the rise of modern corporations had an impact around the globe.

Global Economics

From the 1870s on, the rapid spread of industrialization heightened competition among nations. The search for markets, goods, and influence fueled much of the imperial expansion and, consequently, often put countries at odds with each other. Trade barriers arose again to protect home markets. All nations except Britain raised tariffs, arguing that the needs of the nation-state trumped laissez-faire doctrine. Yet changes in international economics fueled the continuing growth of an interlocking, worldwide system of manufacturing, trade, and finance. For example, the near universal adoption of the gold standard in currency exchange greatly facilitated world trade. Pegging the value of currencies, particularly Britain's powerful pound sterling, against the value of gold meant that currencies could be readily exchanged. The common standard also allowed nations to use a third country to mediate trade and exchange to mitigate trade imbalances—a common problem for the industrializing West. Almost all European countries, dependent on vast supplies of raw materials to sustain their rate of industrial production, imported more than they exported. To avoid the mounting deficits that this practice would otherwise incur, European economies relied on "invisible" exports: shipping, insurance, and banking services. The extent of Britain's exports in these areas was far greater than that of any other country. London was the money market of the world, to which would-be borrowers looked for assistance before turning elsewhere. By 1914, Britain had $20 billion invested overseas, compared with $8.7 billion for France and $6 billion for Germany. Britain also used its invisible trade to secure relationships with food-producing nations, becoming the major overseas buyer for the wheat of the United States and Canada, the beef of Argentina, and the mutton (lamb) of Australia. These goods, shipped cheaply aboard refrigerated vessels, kept down food prices for working-class families and eased the demand for increased wages.

During this period, the relationship between European manufacturing nations and the overseas sources of their materials—whether colonies or not—was transformed, as detailed in the last chapter. Those changes, in turn, reshaped economies and cultures on both sides of the imperial divide. Europeans came to expect certain foods on their tables; whole regions of Africa, Latin America, and Asia geared toward producing for the European market. This international push toward mass manufacturing and commodity production necessarily involved changes in deep-seated patterns in consumption and in production. It altered the landscape and habits of India as well as those of Britain. It brought new rhythms of life to women working in clothing factories in Germany, to porters carrying supplies to build railways in Senegal, to workers dredging the harbor of Dakar.

LABOR POLITICS, MASS MOVEMENTS

The rapid expansion of late-nineteenth-century industry brought a parallel growth in the size, cohesion, and activism of Europe's working classes. The men and women who worked as wage laborers resented corporate power—resentment fostered not only by the exploitation and inequalities they experienced on the job but also by living "a life apart" in Europe's expanding cities (see Chapter 19). Corporations had devised new methods of protecting and promoting their interests, and workers did the same. Labor unions, which were traditionally limited to skilled male workers in small-scale enterprises, grew during the late nineteenth century into mass, centralized, nationwide organizations. This "new unionism" emphasized organization across entire industries and, for the first time, brought unskilled workers into the ranks, increasing power to negotiate wages and job conditions. More important, though, the creation of national unions provided a framework for a new type of political movement: the socialist mass party.

Why did socialism develop in Europe after 1870? Changing national political structures provide part of the answer. Parliamentary constitutional governments opened the political process to new participants, including socialists. Now part of the legislative process, socialists in Parliament led efforts to expand voting rights in the 1860s and 1870s. Their success created new constituencies of working-class men. At the same time, traditional struggles between labor and management moved up to the national level; governments aligned with business interests, and legislators countered working-class agitation with antilabor and antisocialist laws. To radical leaders, the organization of national mass political movements seemed the only effective way to counter industrialists' political strength. Thus, during this period, socialist movements abandoned their earlier revolutionary traditions (exemplified by the romantic image of barricaded streets) in favor of legal, public competition within Europe's parliamentary systems.

The Spread of Socialist Parties— and Alternatives

The emergence of labor movements in Europe owed as much to ideas as to social changes. The most influential radical thinker was Karl Marx, whose early career was discussed

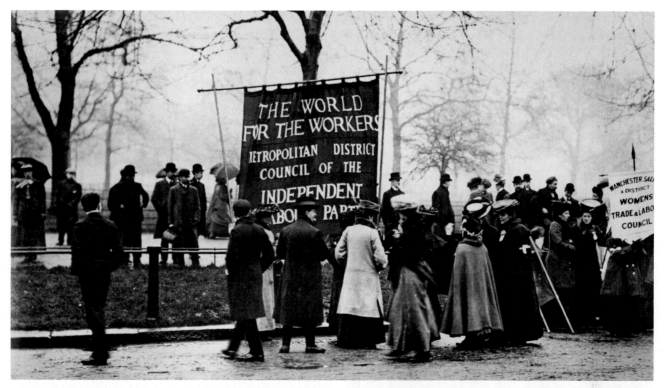

INDEPENDENT LABOR PARTY DEMONSTRATION IN ENGLAND, c. 1893. Activism among workers swelled in the late nineteenth century. Increasingly powerful labor unions had a profound impact on politics because male workers without property could now vote in local and national elections.

in Chapter 20. Since the 1840s, Marx and his collaborator Friedrich Engels had been intellectuals and activists, participating in the organization of fledgling socialist movements. In 1867, Marx published the first of three volumes of *Capital*, a work he believed was his greatest contribution to human emancipation. *Capital* attacked capitalism using the tools of economic analysis, allowing Marx to claim a scientific validity for his work, and he was contemptuous of other socialists whose opposition to industrial economies were couched only in moral terms. Marx's work claimed to offer a systematic analysis of how capitalism forced workers to exchange their labor for subsistence wages while enabling their employers to amass both wealth and power. Followers of Marx called for workers everywhere to ally with one another to create an independent political force, and few other groups pushed so strongly to secure civil liberties, expand conceptions of citizenship, or build a welfare state. Marxists also made powerful claims for gender equality, though in practice woman suffrage took a backseat to class politics.

Not all working-class movements were Marxist, however. Differences among various left-wing groups remained strong, and the most divisive issues were the role of violence and whether socialists should cooperate with liberal governments—and if so, to what end. Some "gradualists" were willing to work with liberals for piecemeal reform, while anarchists and syndicalists rejected parliamentary politics altogether. When European labor leaders met in 1864 at the first meeting of the International Working Men's Association, Marx argued strongly in favor of political mass movements, which would prepare the working classes for revolution. He was strongly opposed by the anarchist Mikhail Bakunin, who rejected any form of state or party organization and called instead for terror and violence to destabilize society.

Between 1875 and 1905, Marxist socialists founded political parties in Germany, Belgium, France, Austria, and Russia. These parties were disciplined workers' organizations that aimed to seize control of the state to make revolutionary changes in the social order. The most successful was the German Social Democratic party (SPD). Initially intending to work for political change within the parliamentary political system, the SPD became more radical in the face of Bismarck's oppressive antisocialist laws. By the outbreak of the First World War, the German Social Democrats were the largest, best-organized workers' party in the world. Rapid and extensive industrialization, a large urban working class, and a national government hostile to organized labor, made German workers particularly receptive to the goals and ideals of social democracy.

In Britain—the world's first and most industrialized economy—the socialist presence was much smaller and more moderate. Why? The answer lies in the fact that much of the socialist agenda was advanced by radical Liberals in Britain, which forestalled the growth of an independent socialist party. Even when a separate Labour party was formed in 1901, it remained moderate, committed to reforming capitalism with measures such as support for public housing or welfare benefits, rather than a complete overhaul of the economy. For the Labour party, and for Britain's many trade unions, Parliament remained a legitimate vehicle for achieving social change, limiting the appeal of revolutionary Marxism.

Militant workers seeking to organize themselves for political action found alternatives to Marxism in the ideas of anarchists and syndicalists. Anarchists shared many values with Marxist socialists, but they were opposed to centrally organized economies and to the very existence of the state. Rather than participating in parliamentary politics, therefore, the anarchists aimed to establish small-scale, localized, and self-sufficient democratic communities that could guarantee a maximum of individual sovereignty. Renouncing parties, unions, and any form of modern mass organization, the anarchists fell back on the tradition of conspiratorial violence, which Marx had denounced. Anarchists assassinated Tsar Alexander II in 1881 and five other heads of state in the following years, believing that such "exemplary terror" would spark a popular revolt. Syndicalists, on the other hand, did not call for terror but embraced a strategy of strikes and sabotage by workers. Their hope was that a general strike of all workers would bring down the capitalist state and replace it with workers' syndicates or trade associations. Anarchism's opposition to any form of organization kept it from making substantial gains as a movement. Likewise, the syndicalists' refusal to participate in politics limited their ability to command wide influence, but the tradition was kept alive, especially in France, through participation in trade unions.

By 1895, popular socialist movements had made impressive gains in Europe: seven socialist parties had captured between a quarter and third of the votes in their countries. But just as socialists gained a permanent foothold in national politics, they were also straining under limitations and internal conflicts. Working-class movements, in fact, had never gained full worker support. Some workers remained loyal to older liberal traditions or to religious parties, and many others were excluded from socialist politics by its narrow definition of who constituted the working class—male industrial workers.

Furthermore, some committed socialists began to question Marx's core assumptions about the inevitability of workers' impoverishment and the collapse of the capitalist order. A German group of so-called revisionists, led by Eduard Bernstein, challenged Marxist doctrine and called for a shift to moderate and gradual reform, accomplished through electoral politics. Radical supporters of direct action were incensed at Bernstein's betrayal of Marxist theory of revolution, because they feared that the official reforms that favored workers might make the working class more accepting of the status quo. The radicals within the labor movement were inspired by the unexpected (and unsuccessful) revolution in Russia in 1905. German Marxists such as Rosa Luxembourg called for mass strikes, hoping to ignite a widespread proletarian revolution.

Conflicts over strategy peaked just before the First World War, but these divisions did not diminish the strength and appeal of socialism among workers. On the eve of the

SOCIALIST PARTY PAMPHLET, c. 1895. Socialism emerged as a powerful political force throughout Europe in the late nineteenth century, although appearing in different forms depending on the region. This German pamphlet quotes from Marx's *Communist Manifesto* of 1848, calling for workers of Asia, Africa, America, and Australia to unite under the banners of equality and brotherhood. ▪ *What was the significance of this claim for equality, given the image's apparent references to racial difference?*

DEMANDING EQUALITY: SUFFRAGE AND THE WOMEN'S MOVEMENT

Le Petit Journal

Le Petit Journal   5 Centimes   SUPPLÉMENT ILLUSTRÉ   5 Centimes   ABONNEMENTS

DIMANCHE 30 AVRIL 1905   Numéro 754

SANGLANTES ÉMEUTES A LIMOGES
Les manifestants essayent d'enfoncer les portes de la prison

"BLOODY RIOTS IN LIMOGES." Labor unions used strikes to draw attention to low wages and dangerous working conditions and to extract concessions from their employers. Some militant groups, known as syndicalists, hoped that a general strike of all workers would lead to a revolutionary change. Fear of labor militancy was a common theme in the popular press, as in this newspaper illustration from Limoges in France, where soldiers are depicted defending the gates of a prison from laborers brandishing the revolutionary red flag of socialism. ▪ *What connection might this newspaper's readers have made with earlier revolutionary movements in Europe?*

war, governments discreetly consulted with labor leaders about workers' willingness to enlist and fight. Having built impressive organizational and political strength since the 1870s, working-class parties now affected the ability of nation-states to wage war. In short, they had come of age. Much to the disappointment of socialist leaders, however, European laborers—many of whom had voted for socialist candidates in previous elections—nevertheless donned the uniforms of their respective nations and marched off to war in 1914, proving that national identities and class identities were not necessarily incompatible with one another.

Since the 1860s, the combination of working-class activism and liberal constitutionalism had expanded male suffrage rights across Europe: by 1884, Germany, France, and Britain had enfranchised most men. But nowhere did women have the right to vote. Nineteenth-century political ideology relegated women to the status of second-class citizens, and even egalitarian-minded socialists seldom challenged this entrenched hierarchy. Excluded from the workings of parliamentary and mass party politics, women pressed their interests through independent organizations and through forms of direct action. The new women's movement won some crucial legal reforms during this period; and after the turn of the century, its militant campaign for suffrage fed the growing sense of political crisis, most notably in Britain.

Women's organizations, such as the General German Women's Association, pressed first for educational and legal reforms. In Britain, women's colleges were established at the same time that women won the right to control their own property. (Previously, women surrendered their property, including wages, to their husbands.) Laws in 1884 and 1910 gave Frenchwomen the same right and the ability to divorce their husbands. German women, too, won more favorable divorce laws by 1870, and in 1900 they were granted full legal rights.

After these important changes in women's status, suffrage crystallized as the next logical goal. Indeed, votes became *the* symbol for women's ability to attain full personhood. As the suffragists saw it, enfranchisement meant not merely political progress but economic, spiritual, and moral advancement as well. By the last third of the century, middle-class women throughout western Europe had founded clubs, published journals, organized petitions, sponsored assemblies, and initiated other public activities to press for the vote. The number of middle-class women's societies rapidly multiplied; some, such as the German League of Women's Voting Rights, established in 1902, were founded solely to advocate votes. To the left of middle-class movements were organizations of feminist socialists, women such as Clara Zetkin and Lily Braun who believed that only a socialist revolution would free women from economic as well as political exploitation. Meanwhile, the French celebrity journalist and novelist Gyp (the pseudonym of Sibylle de Riguetti de Mirabeau) carved out a name for herself on the nationalist and anti-Semitic right, with her acerbic commentary on current events.

In Britain, woman suffrage campaigns exploded in violence. Millicent Fawcett, a distinguished middle-class woman with connections to the political establishment, brought together sixteen different organizations into the National Union of Women's Suffrage Societies (1897), committed to peaceful, constitutional reform. But the movement lacked the political or economic clout to sway a male legislature. They became increasingly exasperated by their inability to win over either the Liberal or Conservative party, each of which feared that female suffrage would benefit the other. For this reason Emmeline Pankhurst founded the Women's Social and Political Union (WSPU) in 1903, which adopted tactics of militancy and civil disobedience. WSPU women chained themselves to the visitors' gallery in the House of Commons, slashed paintings in museums, inscribed "Votes for Women" in acid on the greens of golf courses, disrupted political meetings, burned politicians' houses, and smashed department-store windows. The government countered violence with repression. When arrested women went on hunger strikes in prisons, wardens fed them by force—tying them down, holding their mouths open with wooden and metal clamps, and running tubes down their throats. In 1910, the suffragists' attempt to enter the House of Commons set off a six-hour riot with policemen and bystanders, shocking and outraging a nation unaccustomed to such kinds of violence from women. The intensity of suffragists' moral claims was dramatically embodied by the 1913 martyrdom of Emily Wilding Davison who, wearing a "Votes for Women" sash, threw herself in front of the king's horse on Derby Day and was trampled to death.

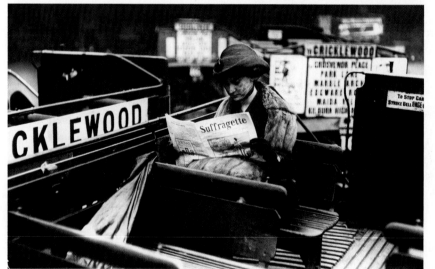

FEMINIST PROTEST IN THE AGE OF MASS POLITICS. These two images demonstrate the variety of ways that supporters of the vote for women in Britain sought to use the public realm to their political advantage. Emily Davison, shown in the top image being fatally struck by the king's horse at a racetrack, sought to draw attention to the injustice of women's exclusion from political citizenship by disrupting the Epsom Derby, the richest race in Britain and an annual society event. Her death, widely seen as a martyrdom in the cause of women's rights by her supporters, became the occasion for a public funeral procession through London. The image on the bottom shows a woman reading a feminist paper, *Suffragette*, on a British tram. By the end of the nineteenth century, the penny press and growing literacy rates vastly increased the ability of organized political groups to get their message out.

Redefining Womanhood

The campaign for woman suffrage was perhaps the most visible and inflammatory aspect of a larger cultural shift, in which traditional Victorian gender roles were redefined. In the last third of the nineteenth century, economic, political, and social changes were undermining the view that men and women should occupy distinctly different spheres. Women became increasingly visible in the workforce as growing numbers of them took up a greater variety of jobs. Some working-class women joined the new factories and workshops in an effort to stave off their families' poverty, in spite of some working-class men's insistence that stable families required women at home. In addition, the expansion of government and corporate bureaucracies, coupled with a scarcity of male labor owing to industrial growth, brought middle-class women to the workforce as social workers and clerks. The increase in hospital services and the advent of national compulsory education required more nurses and teachers. Again, a shortage of male workers and a need to fill so many new jobs as cheaply as possible made women a logical choice. Thus women, who had campaigned vigorously for access to education, began to see doors opening to them. Swiss universities and medical schools began to admit women in the 1860s. In the 1870s and 1880s, British women established their own colleges at Cambridge and Oxford. Parts of the professional world began to look dramatically different: in Prussia, for instance, 14,600 full-time women teachers were staffing schools by 1896. These changes in women's employment began to deflate the myth of female domesticity.

Women became more active in politics—an area previously termed off limits. This is not to say that female political activity was unprecedented; in important ways, the groundwork for women's new political participation had been laid earlier in the century. Reform movements of the early nineteenth century depended on women and raised women's standing in public. First with charity work in religious associations and later with hundreds of secular associations, women throughout Europe directed their energies toward poor relief, prison reform, Sunday school, temperance, ending slavery and prostitution, and expanding educational opportunities for women. Reform groups brought women together outside the home, encouraging them to speak their minds as freethinking equals and to pursue political goals—a right denied them as individual females. And while some women in reform groups supported political emancipation, many others were drawn into reform politics by appeals to the belief that they had a special moral mission: they saw their public activities as merely an extension of feminine domestic duties. Nonetheless, nineteenth-century reform movements had opened up the world beyond the home, particularly for the middle classes, and widened the scope of possibilities for later generations.

These changes in women's roles were paralleled by the emergence of a new social type, dubbed the "new woman." A new woman demanded education and a job; she refused to be escorted by chaperones when she went out; she rejected the restrictive corsets of mid-century fashion. In other words, she claimed the right to a physically and intellectually active life and refused to conform to the norms that defined nineteenth-century womanhood. The new woman was an image—in part the creation of artists

CHANGES IN WHITE-COLLAR WORK. Clerical work was primarily male until the end of the nineteenth century, when cadres of women workers and the emergence of new industries and bureaucracies transformed employment. ▪ *How might these changing patterns of employment have affected family life or attitudes toward marriage and child-rearing?*

and journalists, who filled newspapers, magazines, and advertising billboards with pictures of women riding bicycles in bloomers (voluminous trousers with a short skirt); smoking cigarettes; and enjoying the cafés, dance halls, tonic waters, soaps, and other emblems of consumption. Very few women actually fit this image: among other things, most were too poor. Still, middle- and working-class women demanded more social freedom and redefined gender norms in the process. For some onlookers, women's newfound independence amounted to shirking domestic responsibilities, and they attacked women who defied convention as ugly "half-men," unfit and unable to marry. For supporters, though, these new women symbolized a welcome era of social emancipation.

Opposition to these changes was intense, sometimes violent, and not exclusively male. Men scorned the women who threatened their elite preserves in universities, clubs, and public offices; but a wide array of female antisuffragists also denounced the movement. Conservatives such as Mrs. Humphrey Ward maintained that bringing women into the political arena would sap the virility of the British Empire. Octavia Hill, a noted social worker, stated that women should refrain from politics and, in so doing, "temper this wild struggle for place and power." Christian commentators criticized suffragists for bringing moral decay through selfish individualism. Still others believed feminism would dissolve the family, a theme that fed into a larger discussion on the decline of the West amid a growing sense of cultural crisis. Indeed, the struggle for women's rights provided a flashpoint for an array of European anxieties over labor, politics, gender, and biology—all of which suggested that an orderly political consensus, so ardently desired by middle-class society, was slipping from reach.

LIBERALISM AND ITS DISCONTENTS: NATIONAL POLITICS AT THE TURN OF THE CENTURY

Having championed doctrines of individual rights throughout the nineteenth century, middle-class liberals found themselves on the defensive after 1870. Previously, political power had rested on a balance between middle-class interests and traditional elites. The landed aristocracy shared power with industrial magnates; monarchical rule coexisted with constitutional freedoms. During the late nineteenth century, the rise of mass politics upset this balance. An expanding franchise and rising expectations brought newcomers to the political stage. As we have seen, trade unions, socialists, and feminists all challenged Europe's governing classes by demanding that political participation be open to all. Governments responded in turn, with a mix of conciliatory and repressive measures. As the twentieth century approached, political struggles became increasingly fierce, and by the First World War the foundation of traditional parliamentary politics was crumbling. For both the left and the right, for both insiders and outsiders, negotiating this unfamiliar terrain required the creation of new and distinctly modern forms of mass politics.

ORGANIZED ANTIFEMINISM. Male students demonstrate against admitting women to Cambridge University in England, 1881. A female figure is hung in effigy to the right of center, and the suspended banner reads (in part): "There's No Place for You Maids."

France: The Third Republic and the Paris Commune

The Franco-Prussian War of 1870, which completed the unification of the victorious Germany, was a bruising defeat for France. The government of the Second Empire folded. In its wake, the French proclaimed a republic whose legitimacy was contested from the start. Crafting a durable republican system proved difficult. The new constitution of the Third Republic, which was finally instituted in 1875, signaled a triumph of democratic and parliamentary principles. Establishing democracy, however, was a volatile process, and the Third Republic faced class conflicts, scandals and the rise of new forms of right-wing politics that would poison politics for decades to come.

No sooner had the government surrendered than it faced a crisis that pitted the nation's representatives against the radical city of Paris. During the war, the city had appointed its own municipal government, the Commune. Paris not only refused to surrender to the Germans but proclaimed itself the true government of France. The city had been besieged by the Germans for four months; most people who could afford to flee had done so; and the rest, hungry and radicalized, defied the French government sitting in Versailles and negotiating the terms of an armistice with the Germans. The armistice signed, the French government turned its attention to the city. After long and fruitless negotiations, in March 1871 the government sent troops to disarm the capital. Since the Commune's strongest support came from the workers of Paris, the conflict became a class war. For a week, the "communards" battled against the government's troops, building barricades to stop the invaders, taking and shooting hostages, and retreating very slowly into the northern working-class neighborhoods of the city. The French government's repression was brutal. At least 25,000 Parisians were executed, killed in fighting, or consumed in the fires that raged through the city; thousands more were deported to the penal colony of New Caledonia in the South Pacific. The Paris Commune was a brief episode, but it cast a long shadow and reopened old political wounds. For Marx, who wrote about the Commune, and for other socialists, it illustrated the futility of an older insurrectionary tradition on the left and the need for more mass-based democratic politics.

The Dreyfus Affair and Anti-Semitism as Politics

On the other side of the French political spectrum, new forms of radical right-wing politics emerged that would foreshadow developments elsewhere. As the age-old foundations of conservative politics, the Catholic Church and the landed nobility, slipped, more radical right-wing politics took shape. Stung by the defeat of 1870 and critical of the republic and its premises, the new right was nationalist, antiparliamentary, and antiliberal (in the sense of commitment to individual liberties). Maurice Barrès, for instance, elected deputy in 1889, declared that parliamentary government had sown "impotence and corruption" and was too weak to defend the nation. During the first half of the nineteenth century, nationalism had been associated with the left (see Chapter 20). Now it was more often invoked by the right and linked to xenophobia (fear of foreigners) in general and anti-Semitism in particular.

The power of popular anti-Semitism in France was made clear by a public controversy that erupted in the 1890s known as the Dreyfus Affair. In 1894, a group of monarchist officers in the army accused Alfred Dreyfus, a Jewish captain on the general staff, of selling military secrets to Germany. Dreyfus was convicted and deported for life to Devil's Island, a ghastly South American prison colony in French Guiana. Two years later, an intelligence officer named Georges Picquart discovered that the documents used to convict Dreyfus were forgeries. The War Department refused to grant Dreyfus a new trial, and the case became an enormous public scandal, fanned on both sides by the involvement of prominent intellectual figures. Republicans, some socialists, liberals, and intellectuals such as the writer Émile Zola backed Dreyfus, claiming that the case was about individual rights and the legitimacy of the republic and its laws. Nationalists, prominent Catholics, and other socialists who believed that the case was a distraction from economic issues, opposed Dreyfus and refused to question the military's judgment. One Catholic newspaper insisted that the question was not whether Dreyfus was guilty or innocent but whether Jews and unbelievers were not the "secret masters of France."

The anti-Semitism of the anti-Dreyfus camp was a combination of three strands of anti-Jewish thinking in Europe: (1) long-standing currents of anti-Semitism within Christianity, which damned the Jewish people as Christ killers; (2) economic anti-Semitism, which insisted that the wealthy banking family of Rothschild was representative of all Jews; and (3) late-nineteenth-century racial thinking, which opposed a so-called Aryan (Indo-European) race to an inferior Semitic race. Anti-Dreyfus propagandists whipped these ideas into a potent form of propaganda in anti-Semitic newspapers such as Edouard Drumont's *La Libre Parole* ("*Free Speech*"), a French daily that claimed a circulation of 200,000 during the height of the Dreyfus Affair.

In 1899, Dreyfus was pardoned and freed by executive order. In 1906, the French Supreme Court declared him free of all guilt, and he was reinstated in the army as a major. A major consequence of the controversy was passage of laws between 1901 and 1905 that separated church and state in France. Convinced that the church and the army were

Liberalism and the State

In the second half of the nineteenth century, some British liberals responded to calls from an expanding electorate by moving away from a laissez-faire position that called for minimal state interference in society and the economy. This laissez-faire position still had its adherents among liberals, most notably the libertarian social philosopher Herbert Spencer. In the face of a more organized labor movement and what was perceived to be a very real threat of revolution, however, other liberals began to argue that some forms of government action to alleviate social distress were not only compatible with individual liberty in the economic realm but were in fact also necessary to preserve it. Compare Herbert Spencer's arguments against assistance to the poor from 1851 with L. T. Hobhouse's defense of state pension plans in 1911.

Herbert Spencer, *Social Statics* (1851)

In common with its other assumptions of secondary offices, the assumption by a government of the office of Reliever-general to the poor, is necessarily forbidden by the principle that a government cannot rightly do anything more than protect. In demanding from a citizen contributions for the mitigation of distress—contributions not needed for the due administration of men's rights—the state is, as we have seen, reversing its function, and diminishing that liberty to exercise the faculties which it was instituted to maintain. Possibly, unmindful of the explanations already given, some will assert

that by satisfying the wants of the pauper, a government is in reality extending *his* liberty to exercise his faculties, inasmuch as it is giving him something without which the exercise of them is impossible; and that hence, though it decreases the ratepayer's sphere of action, it compensates by increasing that of the rate-receiver. But this statement of the case implies a confounding of two widely-different things. To enforce the fundamental law—to take care that every man has freedom to do all that he wills, provided he infringes not the equal freedom of any other man—this is the special purpose for which the civil power exists. Now insuring to each the

right to pursue within the specified limits the objects of his desires without let or hindrance, is quite a separate thing from insuring him satisfaction. Of two individuals, one may use his liberty of action successfully—may achieve the gratifications he seeks after, or accumulate what is equivalent to many of them—property; whilst the other, having like privileges, may fail to do so. But with these results the state has no concern. All that lies within its commission is to see that each man is allowed to use such powers and opportunities as he possesses; and if it takes from him who has prospered to give to him who has not, it violates its duty

hostile to the republic, the Republican legislature passed new laws that prohibited any religious orders in France that were not authorized by the state and forbade clerics to teach in public schools.

The French Republic withstood the attacks of radical anti-Semites in the first decade of the twentieth century, but the same right-wing and nationalist forces made their voices known elsewhere in Europe. The mayor of Vienna in 1897 was elected on an anti-Semitic platform. The Russian secret police forged and published a book called *The Protocols of the Learned Elders of Zion* (1903 and 1905), which imagined a Jewish plot to dominate the world and held

Jews responsible for the French Revolution and the dislocating effects of industrialization. Political anti-Semitism remained popular among a substantial number of Europeans who accepted its insistence that social and political problems could be understood in racial terms.

Zionism

Among the many people to watch with alarm as the Dreyfus Affair unfolded was Theodor Herzl (1860–1904), a Hungarian-born journalist working in Paris. The rise of towards the one to do more than its duty towards the other. Or, repeating the idea elsewhere expressed, it breaks down the vital law of society, that it may effect what social vitality does not call for.

Source: Herbert Spencer, *Social Statics: or, The Conditions essential to Happiness specified, and the First of them Developed* (London: John Chapman, 1851), p. 311–12.

L. T. Hobhouse, *Liberalism* (1911)

For the mass of the people, therefore, to be assured of the means of a decent livelihood must mean to be assured of continuous employment at a living wage, or, as an alternative, of public assistance. Now, as has been remarked, experience goes to show that the wage of the average worker, as fixed by competition, is not and is not likely to become sufficient to cover all the fortunes and misfortunes of life, to provide for sickness, accident, unemployment and old age, in addition to the regular needs of an average family. In the case of accident the State has put the burden of making provision on the employer. In the case of old age it has, acting, as I think, upon a sounder principle, taken the burden upon itself. It is very important to realize precisely what the new departure involved in the Old Age Pensions Act amounted to in point of principle. The Poor Law already guaranteed the aged person and the poor in general against actual starvation. But the Poor Law came into operation only at the point of sheer destitution. It failed to help those who had helped themselves. Indeed, to many it held out little inducement to help themselves if they could not hope to lay by so much as would enable them to live more comfortably on their means than they would live in the workhouse. The pension system throws over the test of destitution. It provides a certain minimum, a basis to go upon, a foundation upon which independent thrift may hope to build up a sufficiency. It is not a narcotic but a stimulus to self help and to friendly aid or filial support, and it is, up to a limit, available for all alike. It is precisely one of the conditions of independence of which voluntary effort can make use, but requiring voluntary effort to make it fully available.

Source: L. T. Hobhouse, *Liberalism* (New York: Henry Holt & Co., 1911), pp. 177–78.

Questions for Analysis

1. According to Spencer, what is the primary function of government? Why does he deem assistance to the poor to be a violation of that duty?

2. According to Hobhouse, what circumstances make assistance to the poor, such as of state-sponsored pension plans, necessary?

3. What assumptions lie behind their disagreement about the state's responsibility to remedy social inequalities? What values do they share?

---

virulent anti-Semitism in the land of the French Revolution troubled Herzl deeply. He considered the Dreyfus Affair "only the dramatic expression of a much more fundamental malaise." Despite Jewish emancipation, or the granting of civil rights, Herzl came to believe Jewish people might never be assimilated into Western culture and that staking the Jewish community's hopes on acceptance and tolerance was dangerous folly. Herzl endorsed the different strategy of Zionism, the building of a separate Jewish homeland outside of Europe (though not necessarily in Palestine). A small movement of Jewish settlers, mainly refugees from Russia, had already begun to establish settlements outside of Europe. Herzl was not the first to voice these goals, but he was the most effective advocate of political Zionism. He argued that Zionism should be recognized as a modern nationalist movement, capable of negotiating with other states. In 1896, Herzl published *The State of the Jews*; a year later he convened the first Zionist Congress in Switzerland. Throughout, he was involved in high politics, meeting with British and Ottoman heads of state. Herzl's vision of a Jewish homeland had strong utopian elements, for he believed that building a new state had to be based on a new and transformed society, eliminating inequality and

JEWISH MIGRATION IN THE LATE NINETEENTH CENTURY. ▪ *Where did Jews primarily flee from in the late nineteenth century?* ▪ *What drove Jewish people to flee from eastern Europe in the late nineteenth century?* ▪ *To what areas did Jewish people migrate and why?*

establishing rights. Although Herzl's writings met with much skepticism, they received an enthusiastic reception among Jews who lived in areas of eastern Europe where anti-Semitism was especially violent. During the turmoil of the First World War, specific wartime needs prompted the British to become involved in the issue, embroiling Zionism in international diplomacy (see Chapter 24).

Germany's Search for Imperial Unity

Through deft foreign policy, three short wars, and a groundswell of national sentiment, Otto von Bismarck united Germany under the banner of Prussian conservatism during the years 1864 to 1871. In constructing a federal political system, Bismarck sought to create the centralizing institutions of a modern nation-state while safeguarding

Interpreting Visual Evidence

Anti-Semitism and the Popular Press in France

The Dreyfus Affair lasted twelve years, from 1894, when Captain Alfred Dreyfus was first arrested and convicted of treason by a military court, to 1906, when he was finally absolved of all guilt and reinstated in the army. During the affair, most people in France followed the events of the case through the popular press, which had undergone rapid expansion as public schooling became more general and literacy spread through the population. The newspapers milked every episode of the case for all of its sensational drama, and editors openly took sides in order to increase their circulation and profits. The illustrated press was particularly popular, and the images associated with expressions of anti-Semitism became ubiquitous in both the respectable and the more popular press. Image A shows Jakob Rothschild, a French Jewish banker, stretching his demonic hands around the globe. Edouard Drumont, the anti-Semitic editor of *La Libre Parole* used the scandal to launch his own political career. His celebrity status is evident in a caricature of himself that appeared in a competing paper, *Le Rire* (image B). Even illustrations that did not aim at caricature could carry a powerful message about the intensity of popular anti-Semitism in France during the affair, as in image C, which depicts young people burning Alfred Dreyfus's brother Mathieu in effigy during a demonstration. Mathieu Dreyfus played a key role in the effort to establish his brother's innocence.

Questions for Analysis

1. What fears about the economy are exploited in image A? (Compare this with the image on page 770 of socialists circling the globe, hand in hand.)

2. Is *Le Rire*'s portrait of Edouard Drumont (image B) an anti-Semitic image, or is it critical of Drumont's anti-Semitism?

3. Taken together, what do these images tell us about the connections among anti-Semitism, the popular press, and the definitions of national identity that were current in France during the affair?

A. Anti-Semitic French cartoon with caricature of Jakob Rothschild, 1898.

B. "The Ogre's Meal," caricature of Edouard Drumont, editor of *La Libre Parole*, from *Le Rire*, 1896.

C. "Anti-Semitic Agitation in Paris: Mathieu Dreyfus burned in effigy in Montmartre (Paris)."

OTTO VON BISMARCK LEAVES OFFICE, 1890. This political cartoon shows Bismarck resigning as Kaiser Wilhelm II childishly plays with "Socialism," a doll made of dynamite. Germany anxiously watches the scene from the background.

trade and economic growth. To strengthen ties with these liberal coalitions, Bismarck unleashed an anti-Catholic campaign in Prussia. In what is known as the *Kulturkampf*, or "cultural struggle," Bismarck passed laws that imprisoned priests for political sermons, banned Jesuits from Prussia, and curbed the church's control over education and marriage. The campaign backfired, however, and public sympathy for the persecuted clergy helped the Catholic Center party win fully one-quarter of the seats in the Reichstag in 1874.

Bismarck responded by fashioning a new coalition that included agricultural and industrial interests as well as socially conservative Catholics. This new alliance passed protectionist legislation (grain tariffs, duties on iron and steel) that riled both laissez-faire liberals and the German working class, which was represented by the SPD. Just as Bismarck had used anti-Catholic sentiments to solidify his previous alliance, he now turned against a new enemy of the empire—Social Democrats—and couched his protectionist and antisocial legislation in terms of defending a "Christian moral order."

In 1878, after two separate attempts on the life of the emperor, Bismarck declared a national crisis to push through a series of antisocialist laws that forbade Social Democrats to assemble or distribute their literature. Additional legislation further expelled socialists from major cities. In effect, these laws obliged the Social Democratic party to become a clandestine organization, fostering a subculture of workers who increasingly viewed socialism as the sole answer to their political needs.

Having made the stick to beat down organized-labor politics, Bismarck now offered a carrot to German workers with an array of social reforms. Workers were guaranteed sickness and accident insurance, rigorous factory inspection, limited working hours for women and children, a maximum workday for men, public employment agencies, and old-age pensions. By 1890, Germany had put together a raft of social legislation, with the exception of unemployment insurance, that became a prototype for the majority of Western nations in the decades to come. The laws nevertheless failed to achieve Bismarck's short-term political goal of winning workers' loyalty: votes for the SPD more than quadrupled between 1881 and 1890, the year that Bismarck resigned.

The embittered atmosphere created by Bismarck's domestic policies prompted the new kaiser, Wilhelm II, to

the privileges of Germany's traditional elites, including a dominant role for Prussia. Bismarck's constitution assigned administrative, educational, and juridical roles to local state governments and established a bicameral parliament to oversee Germany's national interests. The appointed delegates of the upper house (the Bundesrat) served as a conservative counterbalance to the more democratic lower house (the Reichstag), which was elected through universal male suffrage. In the executive branch, power rested solely with Wilhelm I, the Prussian king and German kaiser (emperor), who wielded full control of foreign and military affairs. Unlike in France or Britain, Germany's cabinet ministers had no responsibility to the Parliament but answered only to the kaiser.

Under a government that was neither genuinely federal nor democratic, building a nation with a sense of common purpose was no easy task. Three fault lines in Germany's political landscape especially threatened to crack the national framework: the divide between Catholics and Protestants; the growing Social Democratic party; and the potentially divisive economic interests of agriculture and industry.

Between 1871 and 1878, Bismarck governed principally with liberal factions interested in promoting free legalize the SPD. By 1912, the Social Democrats were the largest single bloc in the Reichstag, yet the kaiser refused to allow any meaningful political participation beyond a tight-knit circle of elites. Any conclusion to this volatile standoff was preempted by the outbreak of the First World War.

Britain: From Moderation to Militance

During the half century before 1914, the British prided themselves on what they believed to be an orderly and workable system of government. After the passage of the Second Reform Bill in 1867, which extended suffrage to more than a third of the nation's adult males, the two major political parties, Liberal and Conservative, vied with each other to win the support of this growing voting bloc. Parliament responded to new voters' concerns with laws that recognized the legality of trade unions, commissioned the rebuilding of large urban areas, provided elementary education for all children, and permitted male religious dissenters to attend the elite universities of Oxford and Cambridge. In 1884, suffrage expanded to include more than three-fourths of adult males.

Two central figures, the Conservative Benjamin Disraeli and the Liberal William Gladstone, dominated the new parliamentary politics. Disraeli, a converted Jew and bestselling novelist, was eminently pragmatic, whereas Gladstone, a devout Anglican, was committed to political and social reform out of a sense of moral obligation. Despite their opposing sensibilities and bitter parliamentary clashes, the two men led parties that, in retrospect, seem to share largely similar outlooks. Leaders of both parties were drawn from the upper middle class and the landed gentry, and both Liberals and Conservatives offered moderate programs that appealed to the widening electorate. Steered by men whose similar education and outlooks promised middling solutions, the British political system was stable and "reasonable."

Even Britain's working-class movements were notably moderate until the turn of the century, when at last new trade unions and middle-class socialist societies combined to create the independent Labour party in 1901. Pressed from the left, the Liberal ministry that took office in 1906 passed sickness, accident, old-age, and unemployment insurance acts, along with other concessions to trade unions. To pay for the new welfare programs—and for a larger navy to counter the German buildup—the chancellor of the exchequer (finance minister), David Lloyd George, proposed an explosively controversial budget in 1909, which included progressive income and inheritance taxes, designed to make the wealthy pay at higher rates. The bill provoked a rancorous showdown with the House of Lords, which was forced not only to pass the budget but also to surrender permanently its power to veto legislation passed by the Commons. The acrimony of this debate pointed to an increasingly militant tenor in British politics, which to many seemed headed for chaos.

Indeed, after 1900, Britain's liberal parliamentary framework, which had so successfully channeled the rising demands of mass society since the 1860s, began to buckle, as an array of groups rejected legislative activity in favor of radical action. Industrial militants launched enormous labor protests, including nationwide strikes of coal and rail workers and citywide transportation strikes in London and Dublin. Woman suffragists adopted violent forms of direct action (discussed earlier). Meanwhile, in Ireland, disagreements over Irish home rule, or self-government, threatened to produce armed confrontations between increasingly radical Irish nationalists and Protestants opposed to home rule.

Ireland had been put under the direct government of the British Parliament in 1800, and various political and military efforts to regain Irish sovereignty over the course of the nineteenth century had failed. By the 1880s, a modern nationalist party (the Irish Parliamentary party) had begun to make substantial political gains through the legislative process, but as with other reform-minded groups (such as woman suffrage), its agenda was increasingly eclipsed toward the turn of the century by more radical organizers. These proponents of "new nationalism" disdained the party's representatives as ineffectual and out of touch. New groups revived interest in Irish history and culture and provided organizational support to the radical movement, as did such militant political organizations as Sinn Féin and the Irish Republican Brotherhood. Firmly opposed to the nationalists was the Protestant Ulster Volunteer force, led by military officers who were determined to resist the imposition of home rule by force, if necessary. In 1913, as a Liberal plan to grant home rule was once again on the table, Britain now seemed on the verge of a civil war—a prospect delayed only by the outbreak of the First World War in Europe.

Russia: The Road to Revolution

The industrial and social changes that swept Europe proved especially unsettling in Russia. An autocratic political system was ill equipped to handle conflict and the pressures of modern society. Western industrialization challenged Russia's military might. Western political doctrines—liberalism, democracy, socialism—threatened its internal political stability. Like other nations, tsarist Russia negotiated these challenges with a combination of repression and reform.

In the 1880s and 1890s, Russia launched a program of industrialization that made it the world's fifth largest economy by the early twentieth century. The state largely directed this industrial development, for despite the creation of a mobile workforce after the emancipation of the serfs in 1861, no independent middle class capable of raising capital and stewarding industrial enterprises emerged. In fact, the Russian state financed more domestic industrial development than any other major European government during the nineteenth century.

Rapid industrialization heightened social tensions. The transition from country to city life was sudden and harsh. Men and women left agriculture for factory work, straining the fabric of village life and rural culture. In the industrial areas, workers lived in large barracks and were marched, military-style, to and from the factories, where working conditions were among the worst in Europe. They coped by leaving their villages only temporarily and returning to their farms for planting or the harvest. Social change strained Russia's legal system, which did not recognize trade unions or employers' associations. Laws still distinguished among nobles, peasants, clergy, and town dwellers, categories that did not correspond to an industrializing society. Outdated banking and financial laws failed to serve the needs of a modern economy.

Real legal reform, however, would threaten the regime's stability. When Alexander II (r. 1855–81), the liberator of the serfs, was killed by a radical assassin in 1881, his successor, Alexander III (r. 1881–94), steered the country sharply to the right. Russia had nothing in common with western Europe, Alexander III claimed; his people had been nurtured on mystical piety for centuries and would be utterly lost without a strong autocratic system. This principle guided stern repression. The regime curtailed all powers of local assemblies, increased the authority of the secret police, and subjected villages to the governmental authority of nobles appointed by the state. The press and schools remained under strict censorship.

Nicholas II (r. 1894–1917) continued these repressive policies. Like his father, he ardently advocated Russification, or government programs to extend the language, religion, and culture of greater Russia over the empire's non-Russian subjects. Russification amounted to coercion, expropriation, and physical oppression: Finns lost their constitution, Poles studied their own literature in Russian translation, and Jews perished in pogroms. (*Pogrom* is a Russian term for violent attacks on civilians, which in the late nineteenth century were usually aimed at Jewish communities.) The Russian government did not organize pogroms, but it was openly anti-Semitic and made a point of looking the other way when villagers massacred Jews and destroyed their homes, businesses, and synagogues. Other groups whose repression by the state led to long-lasting undercurrents of anti-Russian nationalism included the Georgians, Armenians, and Azerbaijanis of the Caucasus Mountains.

The most important radical political group in late-nineteenth-century Russia was a large, loosely knit group of men and women who called themselves populists. Populists believed that Russia needed to modernize on its own terms, not the West's. They envisioned an egalitarian Russia based on the ancient institution of the village commune (*mir*). Advocates of populism sprang primarily from the middle class; many of its adherents were young students, and women made up about 15 percent—a significantly large proportion for the period. They formed secret bands, plotting the overthrow of tsarism through anarchy and insurrection. They dedicated their lives to "the people," attempting wherever possible to live among common laborers so as to understand and express the popular will. Populism's emphasis on peasant socialism influenced the Social Revolutionary party, formed in 1901, which also concentrated on increasing the political power of the peasant and building a socialist society based on the agrarian communalism of the mir.

The emergence of industrial capitalism and a new, desperately poor working class created Russian Marxism. Organized as the Social Democratic party, Russian Marxists concentrated their efforts on behalf of urban workers and saw themselves as part of the international working-class movement. They made little headway in a peasant-dominated Russia before the First World War, but they provided disaffected urban factory workers and intellectuals alike with a powerful ideology that stressed the necessity of overthrowing the tsarist regime and the inevitability of a better future. Autocracy would give way to capitalism and capitalism to an egalitarian, classless society. Russian Marxism blended radical, activist opposition with a rational, scientific approach to history, furnishing revolutionaries with a set of concepts with which to understand the upheavals of the young twentieth century.

In 1903, the leadership of the Social Democratic party split over an important disagreement on revolutionary strategy. One group, temporarily in the majority and quick

Past and Present

The Age of Mass Politics

Granting the vote to all adult men ushered in an age of mass politics. Political groups competed with one another to gain the support of this new constituency, and to prevent opponents from gaining power (left, in this 1878 cartoon, Otto von Bismarck tries to put socialism back in the box). Then, as now, political groups sought simple messages that would give them an edge, leading to more sharply defined ideological competition, as well as populist demagoguery and scapegoating of minorities (right, Marine Le Pen at rally for the extreme-right party in France, the National Front).

 Watch related author interview on StudySpace
wwnorton.com/web/westernciv18

to name itself the Bolsheviks (majority group), believed that the Russian situation called for a strongly centralized party of active revolutionaries. The Bolsheviks also insisted that the rapid industrialization of Russia meant that they did not have to follow Marx's model for the West. Instead of working for liberal capitalist reforms, Russian revolutionaries could skip a stage and immediately begin to build a socialist state. The Mensheviks (which means minority) were more cautious or "gradualist," seeking slow changes and reluctant to depart from Marxist orthodoxy. When the Mensheviks regained control of the Social Democratic party, the Bolsheviks formed a splinter party under the leadership of the young, dedicated revolutionary Vladimir Ilyich Ulyanov, who lived in political exile in western Europe between 1900 and 1917. He wrote under the pseudonym of Lenin, from the Lena River in Siberia, where he had been exiled earlier.

Lenin's theoretical abilities and organizational energy commanded respect, enabling him to remain the leader of the Bolsheviks even while living abroad. From exile, Lenin preached unrelenting class struggle; the need for a coordinated revolutionary socialist movement throughout Europe; and, most important, the belief that Russia was passing into an economic stage that made it ripe for revolution. It was the Bolsheviks' responsibility to organize a revolutionary party on behalf of workers, for without the party's discipline, workers could not effect change. Lenin's treatise *What Is to Be Done?* (1902) set out his vision of Russia's special destiny, and it denounced gradualists who had urged collaboration with moderate parties. Lenin considered revolution the only answer to Russia's problems, and he argued that organizing for revolution needed to be done, soon, by vanguard agents of the party acting in the name of the working class.

AUTOCRACY AND REPRESENTATIVE GOVERNMENT. In response to the revolution of 1905 in Russia, Tsar Nicholas II allowed for the creation of a new legislative body for Russia in 1905, a form of parliament called the Duma. Although he later succeeded in limiting the powers of this body, its very existence indicated that even the autocratic and conservative Russian state was forced to pay lip service to the principle of representative government. In the image above, note the extent to which the opening ceremony evoked the traditional hierarchies of Russian society, exemplified in the presence of the tsar, the military, the aristocracy, and the clergy.

THE FIRST RUSSIAN REVOLUTION

The revolution that came in 1905, however, took all of these radical movements by surprise. Its unexpected occurrence resulted from Russia's resounding defeat in the Russo-Japanese War of 1904–5. But the revolution had deeper roots. Rapid industrialization had transformed Russia unevenly; certain regions were heavily industrial, whereas others were less integrated into the market economy. The economic boom of the 1880s and 1890s turned to bust in the early 1900s, as demand for goods tapered off, prices plummeted, and the nascent working class suffered high levels of unemployment. At the same time, low grain prices resulted in a series of peasant uprisings, which, combined with students' energetic radical organizing, became overtly political.

As dispatches reported the defeats of the tsar's army and navy, the Russian people grasped the full extent of the regime's inefficiency. Hitherto apolitical middle-class subjects clamored for change, and radical workers organized strikes and held demonstrations in every important city. Trust in the benevolence of the tsar was severely shaken on January 22, 1905—"Bloody Sunday"—when a group

of 200,000 workers and their families, led by a priest, Father Gapon, went to demonstrate their grievances at the tsar's winter palace in St. Petersburg. When guard troops killed 130 demonstrators and wounded several hundred, the government seemed not only ineffective but arbitrary and brutal.

Over the course of 1905, general protest grew. Merchants closed their stores, factory owners shut down their plants, lawyers refused to plead cases in court. The autocracy lost control of entire rural towns and regions as local authorities were ejected and often killed by enraged peasants. Forced to yield, Tsar Nicholas II issued the October Manifesto, pledging guarantees of individual liberties, a moderately liberal franchise for the election of a Duma, and genuine legislative veto powers for the Duma. Although the 1905 revolution brought the tsarist system perilously close to collapse, it failed to convince the tsar that fundamental political change was necessary. Between 1905 and 1907, Nicholas revoked most of the promises made in the October Manifesto. Above all, he deprived the Duma of its principal powers and decreed that it be elected indirectly on a class basis, which ensured a legislative body of obedient followers.

Nonetheless, the revolt of 1905 persuaded the tsar's more perceptive advisers that reform was urgent. The agrarian programs sponsored by the government's leading minister, Peter Stolypin, were especially significant. Between 1906 and 1911 the Stolypin reforms provided for the sale of 5 million acres of royal land to peasants, granted permission to peasants to withdraw from the mir and form independent farms, and canceled peasant property debts. Further decrees legalized labor unions, reduced the working day (to ten hours in most cases), and established sickness and accident insurance. Liberals could reasonably hope that Russia was on the way to becoming a progressive nation on the Western model, yet the tsar remained stubbornly autocratic. Russian agriculture remained suspended between an emerging capitalist system and the traditional peasant commune; Russian industry, though powerful enough to allow Russia to maintain its status as a world power, had hardly created a modern, industrial society capable of withstanding the enormous strains that Russia would face during the First World War.

Analyzing Primary Sources

Lenin's View of a Revolutionary Party

At the turn of the century, Russian revolutionaries debated political strategy. How could Russian autocracy be defeated? Should revolutionaries follow the programs of their counterparts in the West? Or did the Russian situation require different tactics? In What Is to Be Done? *(1902) Lenin (Vladimir Ilyich Ulyanov, 1870–1924) argued that Russian socialists needed to revise the traditional Marxist view, according to which a large and politically conscious working class would make revolution. In Russia, Lenin argued, revolution required a small but dedicated group of revolutionaries to lead the working class. Lenin's vision was important, for it shaped the tactics and strategies of the Bolsheviks in 1917 and beyond.*

he national tasks of Russian Social-Democracy are such as have never confronted any other socialist party in the world. We shall have occasion further on to deal with the political and organisational duties which the task of emancipating the whole people from the yoke of autocracy imposes upon us. At this point, we wish to state only that the *role of vanguard fighter can be fulfilled only by a party that is guided by the most advanced theory*. . . .

I assert: (1) that no revolutionary movement can endure without a stable organisation of leaders maintaining continuity; (2) that the broader the popular mass drawn spontaneously into the struggle, which forms the basis of the movement and participates in it, the more urgent the need for such an organisation, and the more solid this organisation must be (for it is much easier for all sorts of demagogues to side-track the more backward sections of the masses); (3) that such an organisation must consist chiefly of people professionally engaged in revolutionary activity; (4) that in an autocratic state, the more we *confine* the membership of such an organisation to people who are professionally engaged in revolutionary activity and who have been professionally trained in the art of combating the political police, the more difficult will it be to unearth the organisation; and (5) the *greater* will be the number of people from the working class and from the other social classes who will be able to join the movement and perform active work in it. . . .

Social-Democracy leads the struggle of the working class, not only for better terms for the sale of labour-power, but for the abolition of the social system that compels the propertyless to sell themselves to the rich. Social-Democracy represents the working class, not in its relation to a given group of employers alone, but in its relation to all classes of modern society and to the state as an organised political force. Hence, it follows that not only must Social-Democrats not confine themselves exclusively to the economic struggle. . . . We must take up actively the political education of the working class and the development of its political consciousness.

Source: Vladimir Lenin, *What Is to Be Done?* in *Collected Works of V. I. Lenin,* vol. 5 (Moscow: 1964), pp. 369–70, 373, 375.

Questions for Analysis

1. What were the key features of Lenin's thought?

2. Here Lenin more or less set down the rules for the revolutionary vanguard. What historical experiences and political theories shaped his thinking? In what ways was the Russian experience unique?

Nationalism and Imperial Politics: The Balkans

In southeastern Europe in the last decades of the nineteenth century, nationalism continued to divide the disintegrating Ottoman Empire. When the sultan's government repressed uprisings in Bosnia, Herzegovina, and Bulgaria in 1875–76, the Russians saw an opportunity to intercede following reports of atrocities committed against Christians in the region. In the ensuing Russo-Turkish War (1877–78), the tsar's armies won a smashing victory. The Treaty of San Stefano forced the sultan to surrender nearly all of his European territory, except for a remnant around Constantinople.

BLOODY SUNDAY. Demonstrating workers who sought to bring their grievances to the attention of the tsar were met and gunned down by government troops, January 1905.

under centralized Turkish control. That effort, intended to compensate for the loss of territories in Europe, undercut the popularity of the new reformist regime.

THE SCIENCE AND SOUL OF THE MODERN AGE

Nineteenth-century liberals believed in individualism, progress, and science. Not only did science deliver technological and material rewards but it also confirmed liberals' faith in the power of human reason to uncover and command the laws of nature. Toward the end of the century, however, scientific developments defied these expectations. Darwin's theory of evolution, psychology, and social science all introduced visions of humanity that were sharply at odds with conventional wisdom. At the same time, artists and intellectuals mounted their own revolt against nineteenth-century conventions. Morals, manners, institutions, traditions—all established values and assumptions were under question, as a generation of self-consciously avant-garde artists called for a radical break with the past. These upheavals in the world of ideas unsettled older conceptions of individuality, culture, and consciousness. The modern individual no longer seemed the free and rational agent of Enlightenment thought but rather the product of irrational inner drives and uncontrollable external circumstances. As Georg Simmel, one of the founders of modern sociology, wrote in 1902: "The deepest problems of modern life derive from the claim of the individual to preserve the autonomy and individuality of his existence in the face of overwhelming social forces, of historical heritage, of external culture, and of the technique of life."

Darwin's Revolutionary Theory

If Marx changed conceptions of society, Charles Darwin did him one better, perhaps, for his theory of organic evolution by natural selection transformed conceptions of nature itself. As both a scientific explanation and an imaginative metaphor for political and social change, Darwin's theory of evolution introduced an unsettling new picture of human biology, behavior, and society. As with Marxism, its core concepts were embraced by some and abhorred by others,

Britain and Austria took action to ensure that Russia would not be the only beneficiary of the Ottoman withdrawal, and in 1878 a congress of great powers in Berlin divided the spoils: Bessarabia went to Russia, Thessaly to Greece, and Bosnia and Herzegovina fell under the control of the Austrian Empire. Montenegro, Serbia, and Romania became independent states, launching the modern era of Balkan nationalism. This trend continued in 1908, when the Bulgars succeeded in wresting independence for Bulgaria from the Ottomans—a move that drove the Austrians to annex Bosnia and Herzegovina outright. The power vacuum in the Orient significantly strained Europe's imperial balance of power.

A nationalist movement also emerged in the Ottoman Empire itself. Educated Turks had grown impatient with the sultan's weakness, and some began to call for national rejuvenation through the introduction of Western science and democratic reforms. These reformers called themselves "Young Turks," and in 1908 they successfully forced the sultan to establish a constitutional government. In the following year, they deposed Sultan Abdul Hamid II (1876–1909) and placed his brother, Mohammed V (1909–1918), on the throne. The powers of government were entrusted to a grand vizier and ministers responsible to an elected parliament. Non-Turkish inhabitants of the empire were not given the vote, however; and the Young Turks launched a vigorous effort to "Ottomanize" all their imperial subjects, trying to bring both Christian and Muslim communities

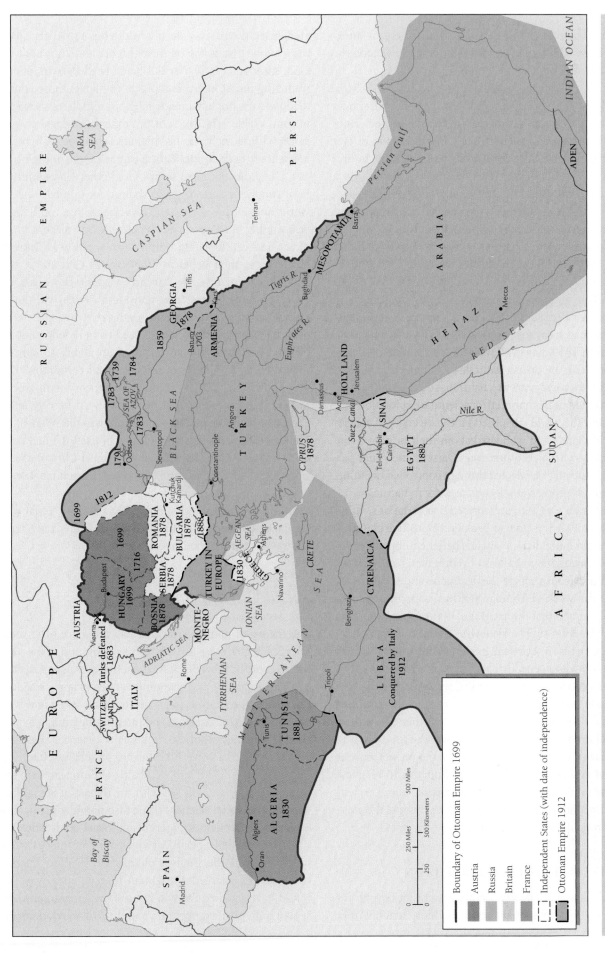

THE DECLINE OF THE OTTOMAN EMPIRE, 1699–1912. ■ *What were the farthest points that the Ottoman Empire reached into Europe and Africa?* ■ *How do you explain the slow decline of Ottoman power in relationship to Europe and the emerging global economy?* ■ *The decline of Ottoman power had enormous significance for relations among European nations themselves. Why?*

Map labels:

RUSSIAN EMPIRE
ARAL SEA
CASPIAN SEA
PERSIA
Tehran
Tiflis
GEORGIA 1878
1859
ARMENIA
Kars
1703
Batum
MESOPOTAMIA
Basra
Persian Gulf
ARABIA
HEJAZ
Mecca
Baghdad
Tigris R.
Euphrates R.
TURKEY
Angora
BLACK SEA
Sevastopol
Odessa
1791
1783–1739
1784
1783
SEA OF AZOV
Constantinople
Kutchuk Kainardji
ROMANIA 1878
BULGARIA 1878
1888
1812
1699
AUSTRIA
Vienna
Turks defeated 1683
Budapest
HUNGARY 1699
1716
BOSNIA 1878
SERBIA 1878
MONTE-NEGRO
TURKEY IN EUROPE
AEGEAN SEA
GREECE 1830
Athens
Navarino
IONIAN SEA
ADRIATIC SEA
SWITZER-LAND
ITALY
Rome
TYRRHENIAN SEA
FRANCE
EUROPE
SPAIN
Madrid
Bay of Biscay
MEDITERRANEAN SEA
CRETE
CYPRUS 1878
Damascus
Acre
HOLY LAND
Jerusalem
Suez Canal
SINAI
Tel-el-Kebir
Cairo
EGYPT 1882
Nile R.
SUDAN
AFRICA
CYRENAICA
Benghazi
LIBYA Conquered by Italy 1912
Tripoli
TUNISIA 1881
Tunis
ALGERIA 1830
Algiers
Oran
RED SEA
ADEN
INDIAN OCEAN

Scale:
500 Miles
500 Kilometers
250 Miles
250
0

Legend:
Boundary of Ottoman Empire 1699
Austria
Russia
Britain
France
Independent States (with date of independence)
Ottoman Empire 1912

The Science and Soul of the Modern Age | 787

and were interpreted and deployed in a variety of unexpected, often conflicting, ways that profoundly shaped the late nineteenth and early twentieth centuries.

Theories of evolution did not originate with Darwin, but none of the earlier theories had gained widespread scientific or popular currency. Geologists in the nineteenth century had challenged the biblical account of creation with evidence that the world was formed by natural processes over millions of years, but no one had found a satisfactory explanation for the existence of different species. One important attempt at an answer was proposed in the early nineteenth century by the French biologist Jean Lamarck, who argued that behavioral changes could alter an animal's physical characteristics within a single generation and that these new traits would be passed on to offspring. Over time, Lamarck suggested, the inheritance of acquired characteristics produced new species of animals.

A more convincing hypothesis of organic evolution appeared in 1859, however, with the publication of *On the Origin of Species* by British naturalist Charles Darwin. Darwin traveled for five years as a naturalist on the HMS *Beagle,* a ship that had been chartered for scientific exploration on a trip around the world. He observed the diversity of species in different lands and wondered about their origins. From a familiarity with pigeon breeding, Darwin knew that particular traits could be selected through controlled breeding. Was a similar process of selection at work in nature?

His answer was yes. He theorized that variations within a population (such as longer beaks or protective coloring) made certain individual organisms better equipped for survival, increasing their chances of reproducing and passing their advantageous traits to the next generation. His theory drew on the work of Thomas Malthus, a political economist who argued that human populations grow faster than the available food supply, leading to a fatal competition for scarce resources. In Darwin's explanation, this Malthusian competition was a general rule of nature, where the strong survived and the weak perished. Competition with other individuals and struggle with the environment produced a "natural selection" of some traits over others, leading to a gradual evolution of different species over time. Eventually, Darwin applied this theory of evolution not only to plant and animal species but also to humans. In his view, the human race had evolved from an apelike ancestor, long since extinct but probably a common precursor of the existing anthropoid apes and humans.

DARWINIAN THEORY AND RELIGION

The implications of Darwin's writings went far beyond the domain of the evolutionary sciences. Most notably, they challenged the basis of deeply held religious beliefs, sparking a public discussion on the existence and knowability of God. Although popular critics denounced Darwin for contradicting literal interpretations of the Bible, those contradictions were not what made religious middle-class readers uncomfortable. The work of prominent theologians, such as David Friedrich Strauss, had already helped Christians adapt their faith to biblical inaccuracies and inconsistencies. They did not need to abandon either Christianity or faith simply because Darwin showed (or argued) that the world and its life forms had developed over millions of years rather than six days. What religious readers in the nineteenth century found difficult to accept was Darwin's challenge to their belief in a benevolent God and a morally guided universe. By Darwin's account, the world was governed not by order, harmony, and divine will but by random chance and constant, undirected struggle. Moreover, the Darwinian worldview seemed to redefine notions of good and bad only in terms of an ability to survive, thus robbing humanity of critical moral certainties. Darwin himself was able to reconcile his theory with a belief in God, but others latched on his work to fiercely attack Christian orthodoxy. One such figure was the philosopher Thomas Henry Huxley, who earned himself the nickname of "Darwin's bulldog" by inveighing against Christians who were appalled by the implications of Darwinian theory. Opposed to all forms of dogma, Huxley argued that the thinking person should simply follow reason "as far as it can take you" and recognize that the ultimate character of the universe lay beyond his or her grasp.

Social Darwinism

The theory of natural selection also influenced the social sciences, which were just developing at the end of the nineteenth century. New disciplines such as sociology, psychology, anthropology, and economics aimed to apply scientific methods to the analysis of society and introduced new ways of quantifying, measuring, and interpreting human experience. Under the authoritative banner of "science," these disciplines exerted a powerful influence on society, oftentimes to improve the health and well-being of European men and women. But, as we will see with the impact of Social Darwinism, the social sciences could also provide justification for forms of economic, imperial, and racial dominance.

The so-called Social Darwinists, whose most famous proponent was the English philosopher Herbert Spencer (1820–1903), adapted Darwinian thought in a way that would have shocked Darwin himself, by applying his concept of individual competition and survival to relationships among classes, races, and nations. Spencer, who coined the phrase *survival of the fittest,* used evolutionary theory to expound the virtues of free competition and attack state welfare programs. As a champion of individualism, Spencer condemned all forms of collectivism as primitive and counterproductive, relics of an earlier stage of social evolution. Government attempts to relieve economic and social hardships—or to place constraints on big business—were, in Spencer's view, hindrances to the vigorous advancement of civilization, which could occur only through individual adaptation and competition. Particularly in America, such claims earned Spencer high praise from some wealthy industrialists, who were no doubt glad to be counted among the fittest.

Unlike the science of biological evolution, a popularized Social Darwinism was easy to comprehend, and its concepts (centering on a struggle for survival) were soon integrated into the political vocabulary of the day. Proponents of laissez-faire capitalism and opponents of socialism used Darwinist rhetoric to justify marketplace competition and the "natural order" of rich and poor. Nationalists embraced Social Darwinism to rationalize imperialist expansion and warfare. Spencer's doctrine also became closely tied to theories of racial hierarchy and white superiority, which claimed that the white race had reached the height of evolutionary development and had thus earned the right to dominate and rule other races (see Chapter 25). Ironically, some progressive middle-class reformers relied on a similar set of racial assumptions: their campaigns to improve the health and welfare of society played to fears that Europe, though dominant, could move down the evolutionary ladder. Despite its unsettling potential, Darwinism was used to advance a range of political objectives and to shore up an array of ingrained prejudices.

Challenges to Rationality: Pavlov, Freud, and Nietzsche

Although the new social scientists self-consciously relied on the use of rational, scientific principles, their findings often stressed the opposite: the irrational, even animalistic nature of human experience. Darwin had already called into question the notion that humanity was fundamentally superior to the rest of the animal kingdom, and similarly discomfiting conclusions came from the new field of psychology. The Russian physician Ivan Pavlov (1849–1936) asserted that animal behavior could be understood as a series of trained responses to physical stimuli. Pavlov's famous experiment showed that if dogs were fed after they heard the ringing of a bell, the animals would eventually salivate at the sound of the bell alone, exactly as if they had smelled and saw food. Moreover, Pavlov insisted that such conditioning constituted a significant part of human behavior as well. Known as "behaviorism," this type of physiological psychology avoided vague concepts such as mind and consciousness, concentrating instead on the reaction of muscles, nerves, glands, and visceral organs. Rather than being governed by reason, human activity was recast by behaviorists as a bundle of physiological responses to stimuli in the environment.

Like behaviorism, a second major school of psychology also suggested that human behavior was largely motivated by unconscious and irrational forces. Founded by the Austrian physician Sigmund Freud (1856–1939), the discipline of psychoanalysis posited a new, dynamic, and unsettling theory of the mind, in which a variety of unconscious drives and desires conflict with a rational and moral conscience.

CEPHALOGRAPH. This illustration from Herbert Spencer's autobiography shows a device designed to measure skulls. He believed that the size of one's skull determined brain capacity and applied the idea of "survival of the fittest" to justify theories of white racial superiority.

Darwin and His Readers

> *Charles Darwin's* On the Origin of Species *(1859) and his theory of natural selection transformed Western knowledge of natural history. The impact of Darwin's work, however, extended well beyond scientific circles. It assumed a cultural importance that exceeded even Darwin's scholarly contribution. How Darwinism was popularized is a complex question, for writers and readers could mold Darwin's ideas to fit a variety of political and cultural purposes. The first excerpt comes from the conclusion to* On the Origin of Species *itself, and it sets out the different laws that Darwin thought governed the natural world. The second excerpt comes from the autobiography of Nicholas Osterroth (1875–1933), a clay miner from western Germany. Osterroth was ambitious and self-educated. The passage recounts his reaction to hearing about Darwin and conveys his enthusiasm for late-nineteenth-century science.*

On the Origin of Species

The natural system is a genealogical arrangement, in which we have to discover the lines of descent by the most permanent characters, however slight their vital importance may be.

The framework of bones being the same in the hand of a man, wing of a bat, fin of the porpoise, and leg of the horse,—the same number of vertebrae forming the neck of the giraffe and of the elephant,—and innumerable other such facts, at once explain themselves on the theory of descent with slow and slight successive modifications. The similarity of pattern in the wing and leg of a bat, though used for such different purposes,—in the jaws and legs of a crab,—in the petals, stamens, and pistils of a flower, is likewise intelligible on the view of the gradual modification of parts or organs, which were alike in the early progenitor of each class. . . .

It is interesting to contemplate an entangled bank, clothed with many plants of many kinds, with birds singing on the bushes, with various insects flitting about, and with worms crawling through the damp earth, and to reflect that these elaborately constructed forms, so different from each other, and dependent on each other in so complex a manner, have all been produced by laws acting around us. These laws, taken in the largest sense, being Growth with Reproduction; Inheritance which is almost implied by reproduction; Variability from the indirect and direct action of the external conditions of life, and from use and disuse; a Ratio of Increase so high as to lead to a Struggle for Life, and as a consequence to Natural Selection, entailing Divergence of Character and the Extinction of less-improved forms. Thus, from the war of nature, from famine and death, the most exalted object which we are capable of conceiving, namely, the production of the higher animals, directly follows. There is grandeur in this view of life, with its several powers, having been originally breathed into a few forms or into one; and that, whilst this planet has gone cycling on according to the fixed law of gravity, from so simple a beginning endless forms most beautiful and most wonderful have been, and are being, evolved.

Source: Charles Darwin, *On the Origin of Species* (Harmondsworth, UK: 1968), pp. 450–51, 458–60.

Developed over many years of treating patients with nervous ailments, Freud's model of the psyche contained three elements: (1) the id, or undisciplined desires for pleasure, sexual gratification, aggression, and so on; (2) the superego, or conscience, which registers the prohibitions of morality and culture; and (3) the ego, the arena in which the conflict between id and superego works itself out. Freud believed that most cases of mental disorder result from an irreconcilable tension between natural drives and the restraints placed on individuals. Freud believed that by studying

Nicholas Osterroth: A Miner's Reaction

The book was called *Moses or Darwin?* ... Written in a very popular style, it compared the Mosaic story of creation with the natural evolutionary history, illuminated the contradictions of the biblical story, and gave a concise description of the evolution of organic and inorganic nature, interwoven with plenty of striking proofs.

What particularly impressed me was a fact that now became clear to me: that evolutionary natural history was monopolized by the institutions of higher learning; that Newton, Laplace, Kant, Darwin, and Haeckel brought enlightenment only to the students of the upper social classes; and that for the common people in the grammar school the old Moses with his six-day creation of the world still was the authoritative world view. For the upper classes there was evolution, for us creation; for them productive liberating knowledge, for us rigid faith; bread for those favored by fate, stones for those who hungered for truth!

Why do the people need science? Why do they need a so-called Weltanschauung [worldview]? The people must keep Moses, must keep religion; religion is the poor man's philosophy. Where would we end up if every miner and every farmhand had the opportunity to stick his nose into astronomy, geology, biology, and anatomy? Does it serve any purpose for the divine world order of the possessing and privileged classes to tell the worker that the Ptolemaic heavens have long since collapsed; that out there in the universe there is an eternal process of creation and destruction; that in the universe at large, as on our tiny earth, everything is in the grip of eternal evolution; that this evolution takes place according to inalterable natural laws that defy even the omnipotence of the old Mosaic Jehovah.... Why tell the dumb people that Copernicus and his followers have overturned the old Mosaic creator, and that Darwin and modern science have dug the very ground out from under his feet of clay?

That would be suicide! Yes, the old religion is so convenient for the divine world order of the ruling class! As long as the worker hopes faithfully for the beyond, he won't think of plucking the blooming roses in this world....

The possessing classes of all civilized nations need servants to make possible their godlike existence. So they cannot allow the servant to eat from the tree of knowledge.

Source: Alfred Kelly, ed., *The German Worker: Working-Class Autobiographies from the Age of Industrialization* (Berkeley, CA: 1987), pp. 185–86.

Questions for Analysis

1. Was the theory of evolution revolutionary? If so, how? Would it be fair to say that Darwin did for the nineteenth century what Newton did for the seventeenth and eighteenth centuries?

2. Why did people think the natural world was governed by laws? Was this a religious belief or a scientific fact?

3. What aspects of Darwin appealed to Osterroth and why?

such disorders, as well as dreams and slips of the tongue, scientists could glimpse the submerged areas of consciousness and thus understand seemingly irrational behavior. Freud's seach for an all-encompassing theory of the mind was deeply grounded in the tenets of nineteenth-century science. By stressing the irrational, however, Freud's theories fed a growing anxiety about the value and limits of human reason. Likewise, they brought to fore a powerful critique of the constraints imposed by the moral and social codes of Western civilization.

individual, or "superman," was one who abandoned the burdens of cultural conformity and created an independent set of values based on artistic vision and strength of character. Only through individual struggle against the chaotic universe did Nietzsche forecast salvation for Western civilization.

Religion and Its Critics

Faced with these various scientific and philosophical challenges, the institutions responsible for the maintenance of traditional faith found themselves on the defensive. The Roman Catholic Church responded to the encroachments of secular society by appealing to its dogma and venerated traditions. In 1864, Pope Pius IX issued a Syllabus of Errors, condemning what he regarded as the principal religious and philosophical errors of the time. Among them were materialism, free thought, and indifferentism (the idea that one religion is as good as another). The pope also convoked the first Church council since the Catholic Reformation, which in 1871 pronounced the dogma of papal infallibility. This meant that in his capacity "as pastor and doctor of all Christians," the pope was infallible in regard to all matters of faith and morals. Though generally accepted by pious Catholics, the claim of papal infallibility provoked a storm of protest and was denounced by the governments of several Catholic countries, including France, Spain, and Italy. The death of Pius IX in 1878 and the accession of Pope Leo XIII, however, brought a more accommodating climate to the Church. The new pope acknowledged that there was good as well as evil in modern civilization. He added a scientific staff to the Vatican and opened archives and observatories but made no further concessions to liberalism in the political sphere.

Protestants were also compelled to respond to a modernizing world. Since they were taught to understand God with the aid of little more than the Bible and a willing conscience, Protestants, unlike Catholics, had little in the way of doctrine to help them defend their faith. Some fundamentalists chose to ignore the implications of scientific and philosophical inquiry altogether and continued to believe in the literal truth of the Bible. Others were willing to agree with the school of American philosophers known as pragmatists (principally Charles S. Peirce and William James), who taught that "truth" was whatever produced useful, practical results; by their logic, if belief in God provided mental peace or spiritual satisfaction, then the belief was true. Other Protestants sought solace from religious doubt in founding missions, laboring among the poor,

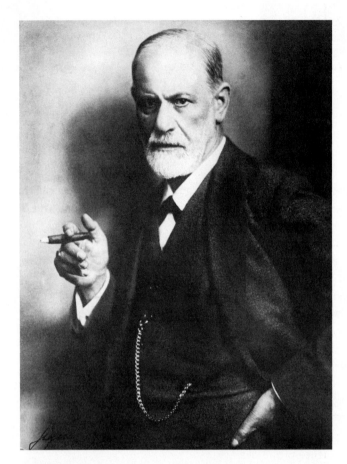

SIGMUND FREUD. Freud's theory of the mind and the unconscious broke with many of the basic assumptions about human nature during his time. He remained, however, a committed nineteenth-century scientist and believed he had uncovered new laws that governed culture as well as individuals.

No one provided a more sweeping or more influential assault on Western values of rationality than the German philosopher Friedrich Nietzsche (*NEE-chuh*, 1844–1900). Like Freud, Nietzsche had observed a middle-class culture that he believed to be dominated by illusions and self-deceptions, and he sought to unmask them. In a series of works that rejected rational argumentation in favor of an elliptical, suggestive prose style, Nietzsche argued that bourgeois faith in such concepts as science, progress, democracy, and religion represented a futile, and reprehensible, search for security and truth. Nietzsche categorically denied the possibility of knowing truth or reality, since all knowledge comes filtered through linguistic, scientific, or artistic systems of representation. He famously ridiculed Judeo-Christian morality for instilling a repressive conformity that drained civilization of its vitality. Nietzsche's philosophy resounded with themes of personal liberation, especially freedom from the stranglehold of history and tradition. Indeed, Nietzsche's ideal

POPULAR RELIGION IN THE MODERN AGE. The political and social changes that accompanied the second industrial revolution and the advent of mass politics transformed European society in fundamental ways, but this did not lead to a waning of traditional religious faith. Instead, the practices of religious devotion changed with the society as a whole. A good example of this is the emergence of new popular destinations for Catholic pilgrimage, such as the Grotto of Lourdes, where a young girl had a series of visions of the Virgin Mary in 1858. After the vision was verified by a local bishop in 1860, the site became a pilgrimage site for the faithful. In 2012, it was estimated that 200 million people had visited the site since 1860. ▪ *What developments during the second industrial revolution helped to make this pilgrimage a global phenomenon?*

other places, from political speeches to novels and crime reports.

The diffusion of these new ideas was facilitated by rising literacy rates and by new forms of printed mass culture. Between 1750 and 1870, readership had expanded from the aristocracy to include middle-class circles and, thereafter, to an increasingly literate general population. In 1850, approximately half the population of Europe was literate. In subsequent decades, country after country introduced state-financed elementary and secondary education to provide opportunities for social advancement, to diffuse technical and scientific knowledge, and to inculcate civic and national pride. By 1900, approximately 85 percent of the population in Britain, France, Belgium, the Netherlands, Scandinavia, and Germany could read.

In those countries where literacy rates were highest, commercial publishers such as Alfred Harmsworth in Britain and William Randolph Hearst in the United States hastened to serve the new reading public. New newspapers appealed to the newly literate by means of sensational journalism and spicy, easy-to-read serials. Advertisements drastically lowered the costs of the mass-market newspapers, enabling even workers to purchase one or two newspapers a day. The yellow journalism of the penny presses merged entertainment and sensationalism with the news, aiming to increase circulation and thus secure more lucrative advertising sales. The era of mass readership had arrived, and artists, activists—and above all—governments would increasingly focus their message on this mass audience.

and other good works. Many adherents to this social gospel were also modernists who accepted the ethical teachings of Christianity but discarded beliefs in miracles and original sin.

New Readers and the Popular Press

The effect of various scientific and philosophical challenges on the men and women who lived at the end of the nineteenth century cannot be measured precisely. Millions undoubtedly went about the business of life untroubled by the implications of evolutionary theory, content to believe as they had believed before. Yet the changes we have been discussing eventually had a profound impact. Darwin's theory was not too complicated to be popularized. If educated men and women had neither the time nor inclination to read *On the Origin of Species,* they read magazines and newspapers that summarized (not always correctly) its implications. They encountered some of its central concepts in

The First Moderns: Innovations in Art

In the crucible of late-nineteenth-century Europe— bubbling with scientific, technological, and social transformations—artists across the Continent began critically and systematically to question the moral and cultural values of liberal, middle-class society. Some did so with grave hesitation, others with heedless abandon. In a dizzying array of experiments, innovations, ephemeral art movements, and bombastic manifestos, the pioneers of what would later be termed "modernism" developed the artistic forms and aesthetic values that came to dominate much of the twentieth century.

***BLACK LINES* BY WASSILY KANDINSKY, 1913.** Kandinsky broke from the traditional representational approach of nineteenth-century painting with his abstractions and was one of a generation of turn-of-the-century artists who reexamined and experimented with their art forms.

Modernism encompassed a diverse and often contradictory set of theories and practices that spanned the entire range of cultural production—from painting, sculpture, literature, and architecture to theater, dance, and musical composition. Despite such diversity, however, modernist movements did share certain key characteristics: first, a sense that the world had radically changed and that change should be embraced (hence the modernists' interest in science and technology); second, a belief that traditional values and assumptions were outdated; and third, a new conception of what art could do, one that stressed expression over representation and insisted on experiment and freedom.

Early modernism was also distinguished by a new understanding of the relationship between art and society. Some artists remained interested in purely aesthetic questions but many others embraced the notion that art could effect profound social and spiritual change. The abstract painter Wassily Kandinsky (1866–1944) believed that the materialism of the nineteenth century was a source of social and moral corruption, and he looked toward a future in which artists would nourish a human spirit that was threatened by the onset of industrial society. Other artists believed they had a duty to document unflinchingly what they saw as the pathological aspects of life in modern cities or the inward chaos of the human mind. In the political arena, modernist hostility toward conventional values sometimes translated into support for antiliberal or revolutionary movements of the extreme right or left.

THE REVOLT ON CANVAS

Like most artistic movements, modernism defined itself in opposition to a set of earlier principles. For painters in particular, this meant a rejection both of mainstream academic art, which affirmed the chaste and moral outlook of museumgoers, and of the socially conscious realist tradition, which strove for rigorous, even scientific exactitude in representing material reality. The rebellion of modern artists went even further, however, by discarding altogether the centuries-old tradition of realist representation. Since the Renaissance, Western art had sought to accurately depict three-dimensional visual reality; paintings were considered to be mirrors or windows on the world. But during the late nineteenth century, artists turned their backs to the visual world, focusing instead on subjective, psychologically oriented, intensely emotional forms of self-expression. As the Norwegian painter Edvard Munch claimed: "Art is the opposite of nature. A work of art can come only from the interior of man."

The first significant breaks with traditional representational art emerged with the French impressionists, who came to prominence as young artists in the 1870s. Strictly speaking, the impressionists were realists. Steeped in scientific theories about sensory perception, they attempted to record natural phenomena objectively. Instead of painting objects themselves, they captured the transitory play of light on surfaces, giving their works a sketchy, ephemeral quality that differed sharply from realist art. And though subsequent artists revolted against what they deemed the cold objectivity of this scientific approach, the impressionist painters, most famously Claude Monet (*moh-NAY*, 1840–1926) and Pierre-Auguste Renoir (1841–1919), left two important legacies to the European avant-garde. First, by developing new techniques without reference to past styles, the impressionists paved

SELF-PORTRAIT, BY EGON SCHIELE, 1912. The Viennese artist Schiele represents another side of early modernism that, instead of moving toward abstraction, sought to portray raw psychological expression.

***PORTRAIT OF AMBROISE VOLLARD* BY PABLO PICASSO, 1909.** In the early twentieth century, Picasso and George Braque radically transformed painting with their cubist constructions, breaking the depiction of reality into fragmented planes. Vollard, an important art dealer of the period, loses recognizable form as his figure descends. ▪ *Compare this portrait with Schiele's self-portrait, at left. What do these paintings say about the task of the artist?* ▪ *What makes them "modern"?*

the way for younger artists to experiment more freely. Second, because the official salons rejected their work, the impressionists organized their own independent exhibitions from 1874 to 1886. These shows effectively undermined the French Academy's centuries-old monopoly on artistic display and aesthetic standards, and they established a tradition of autonomous outsider exhibits, which figures prominently in the history of modernism.

In the wake of impressionism, a handful of innovative artists working at the end of the nineteenth century laid the groundwork for an explosion of creative experimentation after 1900. Chief among them was the Frenchman Paul Cézanne (1839–1906). Perhaps more so than anyone, Cézanne shattered the window of representational art. Instead of a reflection of the world, painting became a vehicle for an artist's self-expression. The Dutchman Vincent van Gogh also explored art's expressive potential, with greater emotion and subjectivity. For Van Gogh, painting was a labor of faith, a way to channel his violent passions. For Paul Gauguin, who fled to the Pacific islands in 1891, art promised a utopian refuge from the corruption of Europe.

After the turn of the century, a diverse crop of avant-garde movements flowered across Europe. In Germany and Scandinavia, expressionists such as Emil Nolde (1867–1956), and Edvard Munch (1863–1944) turned to acid colors and violent figural distortions to express the interior consciousness of the human mind. The Austrian Egon Schiele (1890–1918) explored sexuality and the body with disturbingly raw, graphic imagery. In bohemian Paris, the Frenchman Henri Matisse (1869–1954) and Pablo Picasso (1881–1973), a Catalan Spaniard, pursued their groundbreaking aesthetic experiments in relative quiet. Clamoring for attention, on the other hand, were groups of artists who reveled in the energetic dynamism of modern life.

The cubists in Paris, vorticists in Britain, and futurists in Italy all embraced a hard, angular aesthetic of the machine age. While other modernists sought an antidote to end-of-the-century malaise by looking backward to so-called primitive cultures, these new movements embraced the future in all its uncertainty—often with the kind of aggressive, hypermasculine language that later emerged as a hallmark of fascism. In the futurist *Manifesto,* for instance, F. T. Marinetti proclaimed: "We will glorify war—the only true hygiene of the world—militarism, patriotism, the destructive gesture of anarchist, the beautiful Ideas which kill." In Russia and Holland, meanwhile, a few intensely idealistic painters made perhaps the most revolutionary aesthetic leap of early modernism, into totally abstract, or "object-less" painting.

The breadth and diversity of modern art defy simple categories and explanations. Though they remained the province of a small group of artists and intellectuals before 1914, these radical revisions of artistic values entered the cultural mainstream soon after the First World War (see Chapter 25).

CONCLUSION

Many Europeans who had grown up in the period from 1870 to 1914, but lived through the hardships of the First World War, looked back on the prewar period as a golden age of

After You Read This Chapter

 Visit StudySpace for quizzes, additional review materials, and multimedia documents. **wwnorton.com/web/westernciv18**

REVIEWING THE OBJECTIVES

- The second industrial revolution was made possible by technological innovations that stimulated the production of steel and new energy sources. What were the consequences of this era of rapid growth for the economy and for European society?

- Expanded electorates meant that more people were participating in politics, especially among the working classes. What parties and movements emerged to represent European workers, and what were their goals?

- At the end of the nineteenth century, militant agitation in favor of women's suffrage increased. What obstacles faced women who demanded the vote?

- Liberalism and nationalism were changed by the advent of mass politics. How did the expansion of the electorate change political life across Europe?

- Technological innovations and scientific ideas about human nature and modern society changed the way that people thought about their place in the world, stimulating artists and writers to new and revolutionary forms of creative expression. What were these scientific ideas and why were they so controversial at the end of the nineteenth century?

European civilization. In one sense, this retrospective view is apt. After all, the continental powers had successfully avoided major wars, enabling a second phase of industrialization to provide better living standards for the growing populations of mass society. An overall spirit of confidence and purpose fueled Europe's perceived mission to exercise political, economic, and cultural dominion in the far reaches of the world. Yet European politics and culture also registered the presence of powerful—and destabilizing—forces of change. Industrial expansion, relative abundance, and rising literacy produced a political climate of rising expectations. As the age of mass politics arrived, democrats, socialists, and feminists clamored for access to political life, threatening violence, strikes, and revolution. Marxist socialism especially changed radical politics, redefining the terms of debate for the next century. Western science, literature, and the arts explored new perspectives on the individual, undermining some of the cherished beliefs of nineteenth-century liberals. The competition and violence central to Darwin's theory of evolution, the subconscious urges that Freud found in human behavior, and the rebellion against representation in the arts all pointed in new and baffling directions. These experiments, hypotheses, and nagging questions accompanied Europe into the Great War of 1914. They would help shape Europeans' responses to the devastation of that war. After the war, the political changes and cultural unease of the period from 1870 to 1914 would reemerge in the form of mass movements and artistic developments that would define the twentieth century.

PEOPLE, IDEAS, AND EVENTS IN CONTEXT

- Why was the British **LABOUR PARTY** more moderate in its goals than the German **SOCIAL DEMOCRATIC PARTY**?
- What disagreements about political strategy divided **ANARCHISTS** and **SYNDICALISTS** from **MARXISTS** in European labor movements?
- What legal reforms were successfully achieved by **WOMEN'S ASSOCIATIONS** in late-nineteenth-century western European nations?
- What was the **DREYFUS AFFAIR**, and how was it related to the spread of popular **ANTI-SEMITISM** and the emergence of **ZIONISM** in European Jewish communities?
- What were the goals of the **BOLSHEVIKS** and the **MENSHEVIKS** in the **RUSSIAN REVOLUTION OF 1905**?
- Who were the **YOUNG TURKS**?
- What was **CHARLES DARWIN**'s **THEORY OF EVOLUTION**, and why did it stimulate so much debate between religious and secular thinkers?
- Why was the psychology of **SIGMUND FREUD** so troubling for liberals in Europe?
- What common ideas did the artists and writers who came to be known as **MODERNISTS** share?

THINKING ABOUT CONNECTIONS

- How did the expansion of the electorate and the spread of representative political institutions in Europe at the end of the nineteenth century change the nature of debates about the power of public opinion and the responsibility of government for the people?
- Compare the age of mass politics at the end of the nineteenth century in Europe with earlier periods of rapid change, such as the Reformation of the sixteenth century or the period of the French Revolution. What was similar? What was different?
- Compare the age of mass politics in Europe circa 1900 with the political life of Europe or the United States today. What has changed? What remains the same?

STORY LINES

- In 1914, the balance of power in Europe collapsed in a total war that mobilized the full resources of modern industrialized nations, their global empires, and their populations.

- The war transformed the relationship between state and society. Governments conscripted an entire generation of young men, encouraged women to work in industry, and took control of the economy to produce goods and material for the military.

- The war provoked the first successful socialist revolution in modern history when the Russian Empire collapsed and the Bolsheviks seized power in October 1917. The Russian Revolution set the stage for the major ideological confrontations of the twentieth century.

CHRONOLOGY

1879	The Dual Alliance (Germany and Austria-Hungary)
1904	The Triple Entente (France, Russia, and Britain)
June 1914	Assassination of Franz Ferdinand in Sarajevo
September 1914	Battle of the Marne
April 1915	Gallipoli campaign begins
May 1915	Italy enters the war against Austria-Hungary
February 1916	Battle of Verdun begins
July 1916	British offensive on the Somme begins
January 1917	Germany begins unrestricted submarine warfare
April 1917	United States enters the war
November 1917	Bolshevik Revolution
March 1918	Treaty of Brest-Litovsk
November 1918	Armistice
June 1919	Treaty of Versailles signed

Before
You
Read
This
Chapter

The First World War

The battle of the Somme began on June 24, 1916, with a fearsome British artillery barrage against German trenches along a twenty-five-mile front. Hour after hour, day and night, the British guns swept across the barbed wire and fortifications that faced their own lines, firing 1.5 million rounds over seven days. Mixing gas with explosive rounds, the gunners pulverized the landscape and poisoned the atmosphere. Deep in underground bunkers on the other side, the German defenders huddled in their masks. When the big guns went silent, tens of thousands of British soldiers rose up out of their trenches, each bearing sixty pounds of equipment, and made their way into the cratered No Man's Land that separated the two armies. They had been told that wire-cutting explosives would destroy the labyrinth of barbed wire between the trenches during the barrage, leaving them free to charge across and occupy the front trench before the stunned Germans could recover. To their horror, they found the barbed wire intact. Instead of taking the German trench, they found themselves caught in the open when the German machine-gunners manned the defensive parapets. The result proved all too eloquently the efficiency of the First World

799

War's mechanized methods of killing. Twenty-one thousand British soldiers were killed on the first day of the battle of the Somme. A further 30,000 were wounded. Because some British units allowed volunteers to serve with their friends—the "Pals Battalions"—there were neighborhoods and villages in Britain in which every married woman became a widow in the space of a few minutes. The British commanders pressed the offensive for nearly five more months, and the combined casualties climbed over a million. The German line never broke.

This contest between artillery and machine gun was a war that was possible only in an industrialized world. Before beginning the assault, the British had stockpiled 2.9 million artillery shells—Napoleon had only 20,000 at Waterloo. Although European armies marched off to war in 1914 with a confidence and ambition bred by their imperial conquests, they soon confronted the ugly face of industrial warfare and the grim capacities of the modern world. In a catastrophic combination of old mentalities and new technologies, the war left 9 million dead soldiers in its wake.

Soldiers were not the only casualties. Four years of fighting destroyed many of the institutions and assumptions of the previous century, from monarchies and empires to European economic dominance. It disillusioned many, even the citizens of the victorious nations. As the British writer Virginia Woolf put it, "It was a shock—to see the faces of our rulers in the light of shell-fire." The war led European states to take over their national economies, as they set quotas for production and consumption and took responsibility for sustaining the civilian population during the crisis. By toppling the Prussian and Austrian monarchies, the war banished older forms of authoritarianism, and by provoking the Russian Revolution of 1917, the war ushered in new ones that bore the distinctive mark of the twentieth century. Finally, the war proved nearly impossible to settle; antagonisms bred in battle only intensified in the war's aftermath and would eventually lead to the Second World War. Postwar Europe faced more problems than peace could manage.

THE JULY CRISIS

In the decades before 1914, Europe had built a seemingly stable peace. Through the complex negotiations of Great Power geopolitics, Europe had settled into two systems of alliance: the Triple Entente (later the Allied Powers) of Britain, France, and Russia rivaled the Triple Alliance (later the Central Powers) of Germany, Austria-Hungary, and Italy. Within this balance of power, the nations of Europe challenged one another for economic, military, and imperial advantage. The scramble for colonies abroad accompanied a fierce arms race at home, where military leaders assumed that superior technology and larger armies would result in a quick victory in a European war. Yet none of the diplomats, spies, military planners, or cabinet ministers of Europe—or any of their critics—predicted the war they eventually got. Nor did many expect that the Balkan crisis of July 1914 would touch off that conflict, engulfing all of Europe in just over a month's time.

The Balkan Peninsula had long been a satellite of the Ottoman Empire. During the nineteenth century, however, Ottoman power became severely weakened, and both the Austro-Hungarian Empire and the Russian monarchy competed with one another to replace the Ottomans as the dominant force in the region. The region was also home to ambitious national movements of Serbs and Bulgarians who took advantage of Ottoman decline to declare their independence in the decades before the First World War. Russia, as the most powerful Slavic monarchy, was the traditional sponsor of these Slavic nationalist movements and had a particularly close relationship with Serbia. Austria-Hungary, on the other hand, sought to minimize the influence of Slavic nationalisms because they constituted a threat to its own multi-ethnic empire. In 1912 and 1913, the region was destabilized by two wars involving the Ottoman Empire and the independent Balkan states of Serbia, Greece, Bulgaria, and Montenegro. The Great Powers steered clear of entanglement and these wars remained localized. The alliance system could only ensure stability, however, if the Great Powers could maintain this posture of nonintervention. Once one of them became embroiled in a local conflict, the system of alliances would lead directly to a wider war.

The spark came from the Balkan province of Bosnia, a multi-ethnic region of Serbs, Croats, and Bosnian Muslims that had been under Austrian rule since 1878. In Bosnia, members of the local Serb population longed to secede from Austrian rule altogether and join the independent state of Serbia. When Bosnian Serbs found their way blocked by the Austrians, some began to conspire with Serbia, and on June 28, 1914, a group of Bosnian Serbs assassinated the heir to the Austro-Hungarian throne, Franz Ferdinand (1889–1914) as he paraded through Sarajevo, the capital of Bosnia.

Shocked by Ferdinand's death, the Austrians treated the assassination as a direct attack by the Serbian government. Three weeks later, the Austrians announced an ultimatum to Serbia, demanding that they denounce the activities of Bosnian Serbs, abstain from propaganda that served their cause, and allow Austro-Hungarian officials to prosecute members of the Serbian government who they believed were involved in the assassination. The demands were deliberately unreasonable—the Austrians wanted war, to crush Serbia and restore order in Bosnia. The Serbs mobilized their army before agreeing to all but the most important demands, and Austria responded with its own mobilization order on July 28, 1914. Shaken from their summer distractions, Europeans began to realize that the treaty system they relied on for stability was actually leading to a much larger confrontation: Austria and its ally Germany were facing a war with Serbia, Serbia's ally Russia, and by extension, Russia's ally France.

Diplomats tried and failed to prevent the outbreak of wider war. When Russia announced a "partial mobilization" to defend Serbia against Austria, the German ministers telegraphed the French to find out if they intended to honor France's defensive treaty with Russia. The French responded that France would "act in accordance with her interests"—meaning that they would immediately mobilize against Germany. Facing the dual threat from both sides that they had long feared, Germany mobilized on August 1 and declared war on Russia—and two days later, on France. The next day, the German army invaded Belgium on its way to take Paris.

EUROPEAN ALLIANCES ON THE EVE OF THE FIRST WORLD WAR. ▪ *What major countries were part of the Triple Alliance?* ▪ *Of the Triple Entente?* ▪ *From the map, why would Germany have declared war on France so quickly once Russia began to mobilize?* ▪ *According to the map, why were the Balkan countries such a volatile region?*

THE BALKAN CRISIS, 1878–1914. ▪ *What major empires were involved in the Balkans during this period?* ▪ *According to the maps, what was the major change in the Balkans between 1878 and 1914?* ▪ *What problems did nationalism, ethnicity, and race create in this region?*

The invasion of neutral Belgium provided a rallying cry for British generals and diplomats who wanted Britain to honor their secret obligations to France and join the war against Germany. This was not a foregone conclusion—the Liberal government was opposed to war and acquiesced partly to avoid being voted out of office. Proponents of war insisted that to maintain the balance of power—a central tenet of British foreign policy—no single nation should be allowed to dominate the continent. On August 4, Britain entered the war against Germany.

Other nations were quickly drawn into the struggle. On August 7, the Montenegrins joined the Serbs against Austria. Two weeks later, the Japanese declared war on Germany, mainly to attack German possessions in the Far East. On August 1, Turkey allied with Germany and in October began the bombardment of Russian ports on the Black Sea. Italy had been allied with Germany and Austria before the war, but at the outbreak of hostilities, the Italians declared neutrality, insisting that since Germany had invaded neutral Belgium, they owed Germany no protection.

The diplomatic maneuvers during the five weeks that followed the assassination at Sarajevo have been called a "tragedy of miscalculation." Austria's determination to punish Serbia, Germany's unwillingness to restrain their

FRANZ FERDINAND AND HIS WIFE, SOPHIE. The Austrian archduke and archduchess, in Sarajevo on June 28, 1914, approaching their car before they were assassinated.
▪ *What made their deaths the spark that unleashed a general war in Europe?*

decades of progress and prosperity at risk. Bankers and financiers, who might have hoped to profit from increased wartime production or from captured colonial markets, were among those most opposed to the war. They correctly predicted that a major war would create financial chaos. Many young men, however, enlisted with excitement. On the Continent, volunteer soldiers added to the strength of conscript armies, while in Britain (where conscription wasn't introduced until 1916) over 700,000 men joined the army in the first eight weeks alone. Like many a war enthusiast, these men expected the war to be over by Christmas.

If less idealistic, the expectations of the politicians and generals in charge were also soon to be disproved. Military planners foresaw a short, limited, and decisive war—a tool to be used where diplomacy failed. They thought that a modern economy simply could not function amid a sustained war effort and that modern weaponry made protracted war impossible. They placed their bets on size and speed: bigger armies, more powerful weapons, and faster offensives would win the war. But for all of their planning, they were unable to respond to the uncertainty and confusion of the battlefield.

The Germans based their offensive on what is often called the Schlieffen Plan, named for Count Alfred von Schlieffen (*SHLEE-fen*), chief of the German General Staff from 1890 to 1905. Schlieffen called for attacking France first to secure a quick victory that would neutralize the Western Front and free the German army to fight Russia in the east. With France expecting an attack through Alsace-Lorraine, the Germans would instead invade through Belgium and sweep down through northwestern France to fight a decisive battle near Paris. For over a month, the German army advanced swiftly, but the plan overestimated the army's physical and logistical capabilities. The speed of the operation—advancing twenty to twenty-five miles a day—was simply too much for soldiers and supply lines to keep up with. They were also slowed by the resistance of Belgian forces and by the intervention of Britain's small but highly professional field army. Fearing the Russians would move faster than expected, German commanders altered the offensive plan by dispatching some troops to the east instead of committing them all to the assault on France.

Austrian allies, and Russia's desire to use Serbia as an excuse to extend their influence in the Balkans all played a part in making the war more likely. Diplomats were further constrained by the strategic thinking and rigid timetables set by military leaders, and all sides clearly felt that it was important to make a show of force during the period of negotiation that preceded the outbreak of war. It is clear, however, that powerful German officials were arguing that war was inevitable. They insisted that Germany should fight before Russia recovered from their 1905 loss to Japan and before the French army could benefit from its new three-year conscription law, which would put more men in uniform. This sense of urgency characterized the strategies of all combatant countries. The lure of a bold, successful strike against one's enemies, and the fear that too much was at stake to risk losing the advantage created a rolling tide of military mobilization that carried Europe into battle.

THE MARNE AND ITS CONSEQUENCES

Declarations of war were met with a mix of public fanfare and private concern. Though saber-rattling romantics envisioned a war of national glory and spiritual renewal, plenty of Europeans recognized that a continental war put

Toward the First World War: Diplomacy in the Summer of 1914

The assassination of Franz Ferdinand in Sarajevo on June 28, 1914, set off an increasingly desperate round of diplomatic negotiations. As the following exchanges show, diplomats and political leaders on both sides swung from trying to provoke war to attempting to avert or, at least, contain it. A week after his nephew, the heir to the throne, was shot, Franz Joseph set out his interpretation of the long-standing conflict with Serbia and its larger implications—reprinted here.

The second selection comes from an account of a meeting of the Council of Ministers of the Austro-Hungarian Empire on July 7, 1914. The ministers disagreed sharply about diplomatic strategies and about how crucial decisions should be made.

The British foreign secretary Sir Edward Grey, for one, was shocked by Austria's demands, especially its insistence that Austrian officials would participate in Serbian judicial proceedings. The Serbian government's response was more conciliatory than most diplomats expected, but diplomatic efforts to avert war still failed. The Austrians' ultimatum to Serbia included the following demands given in the final extract here.

Emperor Franz Joseph of Austria-Hungary to Kaiser Wilhelm II of Germany, July 5, 1914

The plot against my poor nephew was the direct result of an agitation carried on by the Russian and Serb Pan-Slavs, an agitation whose sole object is the weakening of the Triple Alliance and the destruction of my realm.

So far, all investigations have shown that the Sarajevo murder was not perpetrated by one individual, but grew out of a well-organized conspiracy, the threads of which can be traced to Belgrade. Even though it will probably be impossible to prove the complicity of the Serb government, there can be no doubt that its policy, aiming as it does at the unification of all Southern Slavs under the Serb banner, encourages such crimes, and that the continuation of such conditions constitutes a permanent threat to my dynasty and my lands. . . .

This will only be possible if Serbia, which is at present the pivot of Pan-Slav policies, is put out of action as a factor of political power in the Balkans.

You too are [surely] convinced after the recent frightful occurrence in Bosnia that it is no longer possible to contemplate a reconciliation of the antagonism between us and Serbia and that the [efforts] of all European monarchs to pursue policies that preserve the peace will be threatened if the nest of criminal activity in Belgrade remains unpunished.

Austro-Hungarian Disagreements over Strategy

[Count Leopold Berchtold, foreign minister of Austria-Hungary] . . . both Emperor Wilhelm and [chancellor] Bethmann Hollweg had assured us emphatically of Germany's unconditional support in the event of military complications with Serbia. . . . It was clear to him that a military conflict with Serbia might bring about war with Russia. . . .

[Count Istvan Tisza, prime minister of Hungary] . . . We should decide what our demands on Serbia will be [but] should only present an ultimatum if Serbia rejected them. These demands must be hard but not so that they cannot be complied with. If Serbia accepted them, we could register a noteworthy diplomatic success and our prestige in the Balkans would be enhanced. If Serbia rejected our demands, then he too would favor military action. But he would already now go on record that we could aim at the down sizing but not the complete annihilation of Serbia because, first, this would provoke Russia to fight to the death and, second, he—as Hungarian premier—could never consent to the monarchy's annexation of a part of Serbia. Whether or not we ought to go to war with Serbia was not a matter for Germany to decide. . . .

[Count Berchtold] remarked that the history of the past years showed that diplomatic successes against Serbia might enhance the prestige of the monarchy temporarily, but that in reality the tension in our relations with Serbia had only increased.

[Count Karl Stürgkh, prime minister of Austria] . . . agreed with the Royal Hungarian Prime Minister that we and not the German government had to determine whether a war was necessary or not . . . [but] Count Tisza should take into account that in pursuing a hesitant and weak policy, we run the risk of not being so sure of Germany's unconditional support. . . .

[Leo von Bilinsky, Austro-Hungarian finance minister] . . . The Serb understands only force, a diplomatic success would make no impression at all in Bosnia and would be harmful rather than beneficial. . . .

Austro-Hungary's Ultimatum to Serbia

The Royal Serb Government will publish the following declaration on the first page of its official *journal* of 26/13 July:

"The Royal Serb Government condemns the propaganda directed against Austria-Hungary, and regrets sincerely the horrible consequences of these criminal ambitions.

"The Royal Serb Government regrets that Serb officers and officials have taken part in the propaganda above-mentioned and thereby imperiled friendly and neighbourly relations.

"The Royal Government . . . considers it a duty to warn officers, officials and indeed all the inhabitants of the kingdom [of Serbia], that it will in future use great severity against such persons who may be guilty of similar doings.

The Royal Serb Government will moreover pledge itself to the following.

1. to suppress every publication likely to inspire hatred and contempt against the Monarchy;

2. to begin immediately dissolving the society called *Narodna Odbrana,** to seize all its means of propaganda and to act in the same way against all the societies and associations in Serbia, which are busy with the propaganda against Austria-Hungary;

3. to eliminate without delay from public instruction everything that serves or might serve the propaganda against Austria-Hungary, both where teachers or books are concerned;

4. to remove from military service and from the administration all officers and officials who are guilty of having taken part in the propaganda against Austria-Hungary, whose names and proof of whose guilt the I. and R. Government [Imperial and Royal, that is, the Austro-Hungarian empire] will communicate to the Royal Government;

5. to consent to the cooperation of I. and R. officials in Serbia in suppressing the subversive movement directed against the territorial integrity of the Monarchy;

6. to open a judicial inquest [*enquête judiciaire*] against all those who took part in the plot of 28 June, if they are to be found on Serbian territory; the I. and R. Government will delegate officials who will take an active part in these and associated inquiries;

The I. and R. Government expects the answer of the Royal government to reach it not later than Saturday, the 25th, at six in the afternoon. . . .

*Narodna Odbrana, or National Defense, was pro-Serbian and anti-Austrian but nonviolent. The Society of the Black Hand, to which Franz Ferdinand's assassin belonged, considered Narodna Odbrana too moderate.

Source (for all three excerpts): Ralph Menning, *The Art of the Possible: Documents on Great Power Diplomacy, 1814–1914* (New York: 1996), pp. 400, 402–03, and 414–15.

Questions for Analysis

1. Emperor Franz Joseph's letter to Kaiser Wilhelm II tells of the Austrian investigation into the assassination of Archduke Franz Ferdinand. What did Franz seek from his German ally? What did the emperors understand by the phrase "if Serbia . . . is put out of action as a factor of political power in the Balkans"? Why might the Germans support a war against Serb-sponsored terrorism?

2. Could the Serbians have accepted the Austrian ultimatum without total loss of face and sacrifice of their independence? British and Russian foreign ministers were shocked by the demands on Serbia. Others thought the Austrians were justified and that Britain would act similarly if threatened by terrorism. If, as Leo von Bilinsky said, "The Serb understands only force," why didn't Austria declare war without an ultimatum?

THE SCHLIEFFEN PLAN AND THE GERMAN OFFENSIVE. The map on the left details the offensive strategy developed (and modified several times) by Alfred von Schlieffen, chief of the German General Staff, and Helmuth von Moltke, his successor in the decade after 1890.
▪ *What strategy did they propose, and why?* ▪ *The map on the right shows the German offensive. How was the plan modified, and why?*
▪ *With what consequences?* ▪ *Why did the German offensive fail to achieve its ultimate goal?*

At first, French counterattacks into Alsace-Lorraine failed, and casualties mounted as the French lines retreated toward Paris. The French commander, Jules Joffre, nevertheless reorganized his armies and slowly drew the Germans into a trap. In September, with the Germans just thirty miles outside of the capital, Britain and France launched a successful counteroffensive at the battle of the Marne. The German line retreated to the Aisne River, and what remained of the Schlieffen Plan was dead.

After the Marne, unable to advance, the armies tried to outflank one another to the north, racing to the sea. After four months of swift charges across open ground, Germany set up a fortified, defensive position that the Allies could not break. Along an immovable front, stretching over 400 miles from the northern border of Switzerland to the English Channel, the Great Powers literally dug in for a protracted battle. By Christmas, trench warfare was born, and the war had just begun.

The Marne proved to be the most strategically important battle of the entire war. This single battle upended Europe's expectations of war and dashed hopes that it would quickly finish. The war of movement had stopped dead in its tracks, where it would remain for four years. Politicians and generals began a continual search for

ways to break the stalemate and to bring the war out of trenches, seeking new allies, new theaters, and new weapons. But they also remained committed to offensive tactics on the Western Front. Whether through ignorance, stubbornness, callousness, or desperation, military leaders continued to order their men to go "over the top."

Allied success at the Marne resulted in part from an unexpectedly strong Russian assault in eastern Prussia, which pulled some German units away from the attack on the west. But Russia's initial gains were obliterated at the battle of Tannenberg, August 26–30. Plagued with an array of problems, the Russian army was tired and half-starved; the Germans devastated it, taking 92,000 prisoners and virtually destroying the Russian Second Army. The Russian general killed himself on the battlefield. Two weeks later, the Germans won another decisive victory at the battle of the Masurian Lakes, forcing the Russians to retreat from German territory. Despite this, Russian forces were able to defeat Austrian attacks to their south, inflicting terrible losses and thereby forcing the Germans to commit more troops to Russia. Through 1915 and 1916, the Eastern Front remained bloody and indecisive, with neither side able to capitalize on its gains.

RUSSIAN PRISONERS IN LATE AUGUST 1914, AFTER THE BATTLE OF TANNENBERG. The German army, under Paul von Hindenburg and Erich Ludendorff, crushed the Russians and took 92,000 prisoners. The Russians continued to fight, but the photograph highlights the weakness of even a massive army and the scale of the combat.

STALEMATE, 1915

In the search for new points of attack, both the Allies and the Central Powers added new partners. The Ottoman Empire (Turkey) joined Germany and Austria at the end of 1914. In May 1915, Italy joined the Allies, persuaded by the popular support of its citizens and lured by promises of financial reparations, parts of Austrian territory, and pieces of Germany's African colonies when (and if) the Allies won the war. Bulgaria also hoped to gain territory in the Balkans and joined the war on the side of the Central Powers a few months later. The entry of these new belligerents expanded the geography of the war and introduced the possibility of breaking the stalemate in the west by waging offensives on other fronts.

Gallipoli and Naval Warfare

Turkey's involvement, in particular, altered the dynamics of the war, for it threatened Russia's supply lines and endangered Britain's control of the Suez Canal. To defeat Turkey quickly—and in hopes of bypassing the Western Front—the British first lord of the admiralty, Winston Churchill (1911–15), argued for a naval offensive in the Dardanelles, the narrow strait separating Europe and Asia Minor. Under particularly incompetent leadership, however, the Royal Navy lacked adequate planning, supply lines, and maps to mount a successful campaign, and quickly lost six ships. The Allies then attempted a land invasion of the Gallipoli Peninsula, in April 1915, with a combined force of French, British, Australian, and New Zealand troops. The Turks defended the narrow coast from positions high on fortified cliffs, and the shores were covered with nearly impenetrable barbed wire. During the disastrous landing, a British officer recalled, "the sea behind was absolutely crimson, and you could hear the groans through the rattle of musketry." The battle became entrenched on the beaches at Gallipoli, and the casualties mounted for seven months before the Allied commanders admitted defeat and ordered a withdrawal in December. The Gallipoli campaign—the first large-scale amphibious attack in history—brought death into London's neighborhoods and the cities of Britain's industrial north. Casualties were particularly devastating in the "white dominions"—practically every town and hamlet in Australia, New Zealand, and Canada lost young men, sometimes all the sons of a single family. The defeat cost the Allies 200,000 soldiers and did little to shift the war's focus away from the deadlocked Western Front.

By 1915, both sides realized that fighting this prolonged and costly "modern" war would require countries to mobilize all of their resources. As one captain put it in a letter home, "It is absolutely certainly a war of 'attrition,' as somebody said here the other day, and we have got to stick it out longer than the other side and go on producing men, money, and material until they cry quits, and that's about it, as far as I can see."

The Allies started to wage war on the economic front. Germany was vulnerable, dependent as it was on imports for at least one-third of its food supply. The Allies' naval blockade against all of central Europe aimed to slowly drain their opponents of food and raw materials. Germany responded with a submarine blockade, threatening to attack any vessel in the seas around Great Britain. On May 7, 1915, the German submarine *U-20*, without warning, torpedoed the passenger liner *Lusitania*, which was secretly carrying war supplies. The attack killed 1,198 people, including 128 Americans. The attack provoked the animosity of the United States, and Germany was forced to promise that it would no longer fire without warning. (This promise proved only temporary: in 1917, Germany

War Propaganda

oster art was a leading form of propaganda used by all belligerents in the First World War to enlist men, sell war bonds, and sustain morale on the home front. Posters also demonized the enemy and glorified the sacrifices of soldiers to better rationalize the unprecedented loss of life and national wealth. The posters shown here, from a wide range of combatant nations during the war, share a common desire to link the war effort to a set of assumptions about the different roles assigned to men and women in the national struggle.

A. British Poster: "Women of Britain say 'Go!'"

B. Russian Poster: "Women Workers! Take up the Rifle!"

Questions for Analysis

1. Why would nationalists resort to such gendered images in a time of crisis?

2. What do these images tell us about the way that feelings of national belonging are created and sustained in times of urgency?

3. How might the changes that the war brought about—an increase in the number of women working in industry or outside the home, increased autonomy for women in regard to their wages or management of their household affairs—have affected the way that individuals responded to such images?

C. German Poster: "Collect women's hair that has been combed out. Our industry needs it for drive belts."

D. American Poster: "Destroy This Mad Brute. Enlist." The mad beast, meant to represent Germany, with *militarism* on his helmet, threatens American civilization with a club of *Kultur* (culture).

THE NEW TECHNOLOGIES OF WAR IN THE AIR AND AT SEA. The use of airplanes and submarines, both produced in large numbers during World War I, changed the nature of warfare. Air war helped dissolve the boundaries between the front line and the home front as civilian populations were brought within range of the enemy's destructive power. Germany's decision to use submarines against merchant ships trading with Britain and France led to the sinking of the *Lusitania* in 1915, which turned public opinion in the United States. The same issue led President Wilson to commit U.S. troops to the Allied side in 1917. The image on the left shows the German submarine base in Kiel, on the Baltic coast. On the right is a German plane attacking an English tank.

would again declare unrestricted submarine warfare, drawing America into the war.) Although the German blockade against Britain destroyed more tonnage, the blockade against Germany was more devastating in the long run, as the continued war effort placed increasing demands on the national economy.

Trench Warfare

While the war escalated economically and politically, life in the trenches—the "lousy scratch holes," as a soldier called them—remained largely the same: a cramped and miserable existence of daily routines and continual killing. Indeed, some 25,000 miles of trenches snaked along the Western Front, normally in three lines on each side of "No Man's Land." The front line was the attack trench, lying anywhere from fifty yards to a mile away from the enemy. Behind the front lay a maze of connecting trenches and lines, leading to a complex of ammunition dumps, telephone exchanges, water points, field hospitals, and command posts. These logistical centers were supposed to allow an army to project its power forward, but just as often, they acted as a tether, making it difficult to advance.

The common assertion that railroads, the central symbol of an industrial age, made war more mobile, is misleading. Trains might take men to the front, but mobility ended there. Machine guns and barbed wire gave well-supplied and entrenched defenders an enormous advantage

even against a larger attacking force, but logistics stymied generals' efforts to regain a war of movement.

The British and French trenches were wet, cold, and filthy. Rain turned the dusty corridors into squalid mud pits and flooded the floors up to waist level. "Hell is not fire," was the grim observation of a French soldiers' paper. "The real hell is the mud." Soldiers lived with lice and large black rats, which fed on the dead soldiers and horses that cast their stench over everything. Cadavers could go unburied for months and were often just embedded in the trench walls. It was little wonder that soldiers were rotated out of the front lines frequently—after only three to seven days—to be relieved from what one soldier called "this present, ever-present, eternally present misery, this stinking world of sticky, trickling earth ceilinged by a strip of threatening sky." Indeed, the threat of enemy fire was constant: 7,000 British men were killed or wounded daily. This "wastage," as it was called, was part of the routine, along with the inspections, rotations, and mundane duties of life on the Western Front. Despite this danger, the trenches were a relatively reliable means of protection, especially compared to the casualty rates of going on the offensive.

As the war progressed, new weapons added to the frightening dimensions of daily warfare. Besides artillery, machine guns, and barbed wire, the instruments of war now included exploding bullets, liquid fire, and poison gas. Gas, in particular, brought visible change to the battlefront. First used effectively by the Germans in April 1915 at the second battle of Ypres, poison gas was not only physically devastating—especially in its later forms—but also

POISON GAS. Poison gases (mustard gas, chlorine gas, and phosgene were the most commonly used) caused thousands of casualties in World War I and were greatly feared by the troops. Such weapons led to offensive breakthroughs when first used, but gas was difficult to control and did not change the balance of forces in the war. Both sides developed gas masks to protect their troops. The environmental damage was severe—concentrations of gas residue were intense enough to cause injury to farmers decades after the war ended, and unexploded gas shells are still occasionally found in former battlefields.

psychologically disturbing. The deadly cloud frequently hung over the trenches, although the quick appearance of gas masks limited its effectiveness. Like other new weapons, poison gas solidified the lines and took more lives but could not end the stalemate. The war dragged through its second year, bloody and stagnant. Soldiers grew accustomed to the stalemate, while their leaders plotted ways to end it.

SLAUGHTER IN THE TRENCHES: THE GREAT BATTLES, 1916–1917

The bloodiest battles of all—those that epitomize the First World War—occurred in 1916–17, when first the Germans and later the British and French launched major offensives in attempts to end the stalemate. Massive campaigns in the war of attrition, these assaults produced hundreds of thousands of casualties and only minor territorial gains. These battles encapsulated the military tragedy of the war: a strategy of soldiers in cloth uniforms marching against machine guns. The result, of course, was carnage. The common response to these staggering losses was to replace the generals in charge. But though commanders changed, commands did not. Military planners continued to believe that their original strategies were the right ones and that their plans had simply been frustrated by bad luck and German determination. The "cult of the offensive" insisted that a breakthrough was possible with enough troops and enough weapons.

But the manpower needed could not be moved efficiently or protected adequately. Unprotected soldiers armed with rifles, grenades, and bayonets were simply no match for machine guns and deep trenches. Another major problem of military strategy—and another explanation for the continued slaughter—was the lack of effective communication between the front lines and general headquarters. If something went wrong at the front (which happened frequently) it was impossible for the leaders to know in time to make meaningful corrections. As the battles of the Great War illustrate, firepower had outpaced mobility, and the Allied generals simply did not know how to respond.

Verdun

The first of these major battles began with a German attack on the French stronghold of Verdun, near France's eastern border, in February 1916. Verdun had little strategic importance, but it quickly became a symbol of France's strength and was defended at all costs. Germany's goal was not necessarily to take the city but rather to break French morale—France's "remarkable devotion"—at a moment of critical weakness. As the German general Erich von Falkenhayn (1914–16) said, the offensive would "compel the French to throw in every man they have. If they do so the forces of France will bleed to death." One million shells were fired on the first day of battle, inaugurating a ten-month struggle of back-and-forth fighting offensives and counteroffensives of intense ferocity at enormous cost and zero gain. Led by General Henri Pétain (1914–18), the French pounded the Germans with artillery and received heavy bombardment in return. The Germans relied on large teams of horses, 7,000 of which were killed in a single day, to drag their guns through the muddy, cratered terrain. The French moved supplies and troops into Verdun continually. Approximately 12,000 delivery trucks were employed for service. So were 259 out of the 330 regiments of the French army. Neither side could gain a real advantage—one small village on the front changed hands thirteen times in one month alone—but both sides incurred devastating losses of life. By the end of June, over 400,000 French and German soldiers were dead. "Verdun," writes one historian, "had become a place of terror and death that could not yield victory." In the end, the advantage fell to the French, who survived and who bled the Germans as badly as they suffered themselves.

The Somme

Meanwhile, the British opened their own offensive against Germany farther west, beginning the battle of the Somme on June 24, 1916. The Allied attack began with a fierce bombardment, blasting the German lines with 1,400 guns. The blasts could be heard all the way across the English Channel. The British assumed that this preliminary attack would break the mesh of German wire, destroy Germany's trenches, and clear the way for Allied troops to advance forward. They were tragically wrong. The shells the British used were designed for surface combat, not to penetrate the deep, reinforced trenches dug by the Germans. The wire and trenches withstood the bombardment. When the British soldiers were ordered over the top toward enemy lines, they found themselves snared in wire and facing fully operational German machine guns. Each man carried sixty pounds of supplies that were to be used during the expected fighting in the German trenches. A few British commanders who had disobeyed orders and brought their men forward before the shelling ended were able to break through German lines. Elsewhere it was hardly a battle; whole British divisions were simply mowed down. Those who made it to the enemy trenches faced bitter hand-to-hand combat with pistols, grenades, knives, bayonets, and bare hands. On the first day of battle alone, a stunning 21,000 British soldiers died, and another 30,000 were wounded. The carnage continued from July until mid-November, resulting in massive casualties on both sides: 500,000 German, 400,000 British, and 200,000 French. The losses were unimaginable, and the outcome was equally hard to fathom: for all their

THE LINES OF BATTLE ON THE WESTERN FRONT. A British reconnaissance photo showing three lines of German trenches (right), No Man's Land (the black strip in the center), and the British trenches (partially visible to the left). The upper right-hand quadrant of the photo shows communications trenches linking the front to the safe area. ▪ *What technologies gave these defenses such decisive advantages?*

sacrifices, neither side made any real gains. The first lesson of the Somme was offered later, by a war veteran: "Neither side had won, nor could win, the War. The War had won, and would go on winning." The futility of offensive war was not lost on the soldiers, yet morale remained surprisingly strong. Although mutinies and desertions occurred on both sides, they were rare before 1917; and surrenders became an important factor only in the final months of the war.

With willing armies and fresh recruits, military commanders maintained their strategy and pushed for victories on the Western Front again in 1917. The French general Robert Nivelle (1914–17) promised to break through the German lines with overwhelming manpower, but the "Nivelle Offensive" (April–May 1917) failed immediately, with first-day casualties like those at the Somme. The British also reprised the Somme at the third battle of Ypres (July–October 1917), in which a half-million casualties earned Great Britain only insignificant gains—and no breakthrough. The one weapon with the potential to break the stalemate, the tank, was finally introduced into

YPRES. Entrenched in craters, the Sixteenth Canadian Machine Gun Company endures the mud after the third battle of Ypres, usually called the Battle of Passchendaele (July–November 1917). ("Passiondale" in the British pronunciation.) Ypres, along the Yperlee River near the Belgian coast, was the object of three major battles during the war. The third, an Allied offensive, aimed to attack German submarine bases and to strengthen the Allied position if Russia withdrew from the war.

battle in 1916, but with such reluctance by tradition-bound commanders that its halfhearted employment made almost no difference. Other innovations were equally indecisive. Airplanes were used almost exclusively for reconnaissance, though occasional "dogfights" did occur between German and Allied pilots. And though the Germans sent zeppelins to raid London, they did little significant damage.

Off the Western Front, fighting produced further stalemate. The Austrians continued to fend off attacks in Italy and Macedonia, while the Russians mounted a successful offensive against them on the Eastern Front. The initial Russian success brought Romania into the war on Russia's side, but the Central Powers quickly retaliated and knocked the Romanians out of the war within a few months.

The war at sea was equally indecisive, with neither side willing to risk the loss of enormously expensive battleships. The British and German navies fought only one major naval battle early in 1916, which ended in stalemate. Afterward, they used their fleets primarily in the economic war of blockades.

As a year of great bloodshed and growing disillusionment, 1916 showed that not even the superbly organized Germans had the mobility or fast-paced communications to win the western ground war. Increasingly, warfare would be turned against entire nations, including civilian populations on the home front and in the far reaches of the European empires.

WAR OF EMPIRES

Coming as it did at the height of European imperialism, the Great War quickly became a war of empires, with far-reaching repercussions. As the demands of warfare rose, Europe's colonies provided soldiers and material support. Britain, in particular, benefited from its vast network of colonial dominions and dependencies, bringing in soldiers from Canada, Australia, New Zealand, India, and South Africa. Nearly 1.5 million Indian troops served as British forces, some on the Western Front and many more in the Middle East, fighting in Mesopotamia and Persia against the Turks. The French Empire, especially North and West Africa, sent 607,000 soldiers to fight with the Allies; 31,000 of them died in Europe. Colonial recruits were also employed in industry. In France, where even some French conscripts were put to work in factories, the international labor force numbered over 250,000, including workers from China, Vietnam, Egypt, India, the West Indies, and South Africa.

As the war stalled in Europe, colonial areas also became strategically important theaters for armed engagement. Although the campaign against Turkey began poorly for Britain with the debacle at Gallipoli, beginning in 1916 Allied forces won a series of battles, pushing the Turks out of Egypt and eventually capturing Baghdad, Jerusalem, Beirut, and other cities throughout the Middle East. The British commander in Egypt and Palestine was Edmund Allenby (1919–25), who led a multinational army against the Turks. In his campaigns, the support of different Arab peoples seeking independence from the Turks proved crucial. Allenby allied himself to the successful Bedouin (nomadic peoples speaking Arabic) revolts that split the Ottoman Empire; the British officer T. E. Lawrence (1914–18) popularized the Arabs' guerrilla actions. When one of the senior Bedouin aristocrats, the emir Abdullah, captured the strategic port of Aqaba in July 1917, Lawrence took credit and entered popular mythology as "Lawrence of Arabia."

Britain encouraged Arab nationalism for its own strategic purposes, offering a qualified acknowledgment of Arab political aspirations. At the same time, for similar but conflicting strategic reasons, the British declared their support of "the establishment in Palestine of a national home for the Jewish people." Britain's foreign secretary, Arthur Balfour,

1914–1915
— Fronts, end of 1914
--- Fronts, end of 1915

GREAT BRITAIN (Aug. 4, 1914)

British Blockade, Nov. 1914

NORWAY

SWEDEN

DENMARK

NORTH SEA

BALTIC SEA

KURLAND

• Moscow

• Riga

EUROPE

Area of detail

AFRICA

JAPAN (Aug. 23, 1914)

Kiel

Hamburg

• London

The Hague

NETH.

BEL. (Aug. 4, 1914)

LUX.

GERMANY (Aug. 1, 1914)

Berlin •

Invasion, Aug. 1914

Limit of German Advance, 1915

Battle of the Marne Sept. 1914

Paris •

Allied Offensive Sept.–Nov. 1915

ATLANTIC OCEAN

Bordeaux •

FRANCE (Aug. 3, 1914)

SWITZER-LAND

Munich •

Milan •

Marseilles •

SAN MARINO (June 3, 1915)

ITALY (May 23, 1915)

Rome •

Tannenberg Aug. 27–30, 1914

× Masurian Lakes Sept. 1914

POLAND

Warsaw •

Brest-Litovsk •

Prague •

GALICIA

Vienna •

AUSTRIA-HUNGARY (July 28, 1914)

Budapest •

Belgrade •

Sarajevo •

SERBIA (July 28, 1914)

ADRIATIC SEA

MONTE-NEGRO (Aug. 5, 1914)

ALBANIA

GREECE

• Kiev

RUSSIA (Aug. 1, 1914)

ROMANIA

Bucharest •

BLACK SEA

BULGARIA (Oct. 14, 1914)

Sofia •

Constantinople •

Gallipoli •

Salonika •

OTTOMAN EMPIRE (Nov. 2, 1914)

Dardanelles

Allied Offensive Feb. 1915–Jan. 1916

PORTUGAL

SPAIN

THE FIRST WORLD WAR
■ Allied Powers   ■ Central Powers
■ Neutral nations

Dates of entry into the war: (Aug. 1, 1914)

0   125   250 Miles
0   125   250 Kilometers

Jutland May–June 1916 ×

NORWAY

SWEDEN

DENMARK

NORTH SEA

BALTIC SEA

KURLAND

• Moscow

• Riga

RUSSIA

GREAT BRITAIN

Kiel •

Hamburg •

The Hague •

NETH.

• London

BEL.

LUX.

GERMANY

Berlin •

POLAND Independent, Nov. 5, 1916

Warsaw •

Brest-Litovsk •

Russian Offensive June–Dec. 1916

ATLANTIC OCEAN

Somme, June–Nov. 1916 ×

Paris •

Verdun, July–Dec. 1916

FRANCE

SWITZER-LAND

Prague •

Munich •

Milan •

Marseilles •

GALICIA

CARPATHIAN MTS.

Vienna •

AUSTRIA-HUNGARY

Budapest •

Belgrade •

MONTENEGRO Surrender, Jan. 1916

SERBIA

ADRIATIC SEA

ROMANIA (Aug. 27, 1916)

BLACK SEA

Bucharest •

BULGARIA

Sofia •

Constantinople •

OTTOMAN EMPIRE

PORTUGAL (Mar. 9, 1916)

SPAIN

ITALY

Rome •

ALBANIA

Salonika •

GREECE (Oct. 18, 1916)

MEDITERRANEAN   **SEA**

1916
— Fronts, Aug. 31, 1916
--- Fronts, Dec. 31, 1916

0   125   250 Miles
0   125   250 Kilometers

A. THE GREAT WAR, 1914–1916. ■ *What were the farthest points of German expansion on both fronts?* ■ *Why did the British blockade have a large impact on the war?* ■ *Why did the war become stalemated?*

1917

— Fronts, Jan. 31, 1917
---- Fronts, Dec. 31, 1917

United States
(Apr. 6, 1917)

FINLAND
Indep. July 1917

RUSSIA
Revolution, Mar. 1917
Socialist Revolution, Nov. 1917
Armistice, Dec. 1917

Second Russian Offensive,
July 1917

ROMANIA
Armistice, Dec. 1917

OTTOMAN EMPIRE

Caporetto,
Oct. 1917

Ypres, May–
Dec. 1917

EUROPE   Area of
detail

AFRICA

1918

— Fronts, June, 1918
---- Fronts at end of war

FINLAND

ESTONIA
Indep. Feb. 1918

LATVIA
Indep. May
1918

RUSSIA
Treaty of Brest-Litovsk,
Mar. 1918

GERMANY
Revolution–Armistice,
Nov. 1918

Spring
Offensive

UKRAINE
Indep. Jan. 1918

To Romania
1918

German
Advance

TRANSCAUCASIA
Indep. May 1918

Compiegne
Château-Thierry
Counter-Offensive

Armistice Line,
Nov. 11, 1918

**AUSTRIA-
HUNGARY**
Armistice,
Nov. 1918

ROM.

BULGARIA
Armistice,
Nov. 1918

PERSIA

SERBIA

OTTOMAN EMPIRE
Armistice, Nov. 1918

Damascus

Jerusalem

British
Advance

Cairo

B. THE GREAT WAR, 1917–1918. ▪ *What were the key events of 1917, and how did they change the course of the war?*
▪ *Consider the map of 1918. Why might many German people have believed they nearly won the war?* ▪ *Why were developments in the Middle East significant in the war's aftermath?*

made the pledge. European Zionists, who were seeking a Jewish homeland, took the Balfour Declaration very seriously. The conflicting pledges to Bedouin leaders and Zionists sowed the seeds of the future Arab-Israeli conflict. First the war and then the promise of oil drew Europe more deeply into the Middle East, where conflicting dependencies and commitments created numerous postwar problems.

Irish Revolt

The Ottoman Empire was vulnerable; so was the British. The demands of war strained precarious bonds to the breaking point. Before the war, long-standing tensions between Irish Catholics and the Protestant British government had reached fever pitch, and some feared civil war. The Sinn Féin (We Ourselves) party had formed in 1900 to fight for Irish independence, and a home rule bill had passed Parliament in 1912. But with the outbreak of war in 1914, national interests took precedence over domestic politics: the "Irish question" was tabled, and 200,000 Irishmen volunteered for the British army. The problem festered, however, and on Easter Sunday 1916 a group of nationalists

revolted in Dublin. The insurgents' plan to smuggle in arms from Germany failed, and they had few delusions of achieving victory. The British army arrived with artillery and machine guns; they shelled parts of Dublin and crushed the uprising within a week.

The revolt was a military disaster but a striking political success. Britain shocked the Irish public by executing the rebel leaders. Even the British prime minister David Lloyd George (1916–22) thought the military governor in Dublin exceeded his authority with these executions. The martyrdom of the "Easter Rebels" seriously damaged Britain's relationship with its Irish Catholic subjects. The deaths galvanized the cause of Irish nationalism and touched off guerrilla violence that kept Ireland in turmoil for years. Finally, a new home rule bill was enacted in 1920, establishing separate parliaments for the Catholic south of Ireland and for Ulster, the northeastern counties where the majority population was Protestant. The leaders of the so-called Dáil Éireann (Irish Assembly), which had proclaimed an Irish Republic in 1918 and therefore been outlawed by Britain, rejected the bill but accepted a treaty that granted dominion status to Catholic Ireland in 1921. Dominion was followed almost immediately by civil war between those who abided by the treaty and those who wanted to

BRITISH REPRESSION OF EASTER REBELLION, DUBLIN, 1916. British troops line up behind a moveable barricade made up of household furniture during their repression of the Irish revolt. The military action did not prevent further conflict.

absorb Ulster, but the conflict ended in an uneasy compromise. The Irish Free State was established, and British sovereignty was partially abolished in 1937. Full status as a republic came, with some American pressure and Britain's exhausted indifference, in 1945.

THE HOME FRONT

When the war of attrition began in 1915, the belligerent governments were unprepared for the strains of sustained warfare. The costs of war—in both money and manpower—were staggering. In 1914, the war cost Germany 36 million marks per day (five times the cost of the war of 1870), and by 1918 the cost had skyrocketed to 146 million marks per day. Great Britain had estimated it would need 100,000 soldiers but ended up mobilizing 3 million. The enormous task of feeding, clothing, and equipping the army became as much of a challenge as breaking through enemy lines; civilian populations were increasingly asked—or forced—to support these efforts. Bureaucrats and industrialists led

the effort to mobilize the home front, focusing all parts of society on the single goal of military victory. The term *total war* was introduced to describe this intense mobilization of society. Government propagandists insisted that civilians were as important to the war effort as soldiers, and in many ways they were. As workers, taxpayers, and consumers, civilians were vital parts of the war economy. They produced munitions; purchased war bonds; and shouldered the burden of tax hikes, inflation, and material privations.

The demands of industrial warfare led first to a transition from general industrial manufacturing to munitions production and then to increased state control of all aspects of production and distribution. The governments of Britain and France managed to direct the economy without serious detriment to the standard of living in their countries. Germany, meanwhile, put its economy in the hands of army and industry; under the Hindenburg Plan, named for Paul von Hindenburg (1916–19), the chief of the imperial staff of the German army, pricing and profit margins were set by individual industrialists.

Largely because of the immediate postwar collapse of the German economy, historians have characterized Germany's wartime economy as a chaotic, ultimately disastrous system governed by personal interest. New research, however, suggests that this was not the case: Germany's systems of war finance and commodity distribution, however flawed, were not decisively worse than those of Britain or France.

Women in the War

As Europe's adult men left farms and factories to become soldiers, the composition of the workforce changed: thousands of women were recruited into fields that had previously excluded them. Young people, foreigners, and unskilled workers were also pressed into newly important tasks; in the case of colonial workers, their experiences had equally critical repercussions. But because they were more visible, it was women who became symbolic of many of the changes brought by the Great War. In Germany, one-third of the labor force in heavy industry was female by the end of the war, and in France 684,000 women worked in the munitions industry alone. In England, the "munitionettes," as they were dubbed, numbered nearly 1 million. Women also entered the clerical and service sectors. In the villages of France, England, and Germany, women became mayors, school principals, and mail carriers. Hundreds of thousands of women worked with the army as nurses and ambulance drivers, jobs that brought them very close to the front lines. With minimal supplies and under squalid conditions, they worked to save lives or patch bodies together.

In some cases, war offered new opportunities. Middle-class women often said that the war broke down the restrictions on their lives; those in nursing learned to drive and acquired rudimentary medical knowledge. At home, they could now ride the train, walk the street, or go out to dinner without an older woman present to chaperone them. In terms of gender roles, an enormous gulf sometimes seemed to separate the wartime world from nineteenth-century Victorian society. In one of the most famous autobiographies of the war, *Testament of Youth,* author Vera Brittain (1896–1970) recorded the dramatic new social norms that she and others forged during the rapid changes of wartime. "As a generation of women we were now sophisticated to an extent which was revolutionary when compared with the romantic ignorance of 1914. Where we had once spoken with polite evasion of 'a certain condition,' or 'a certain profession,' we now unblushingly used the words 'pregnancy' and 'prostitution.'" For every Vera Brittain who celebrated the changes, however, journalists, novelists, and other observers grumbled that women were now smoking, refusing to wear the corsets that gave Victorian dresses their hourglass shape, or cutting their hair into the new fashionable bobs. The "new woman" became a symbol of profound and disconcerting cultural transformation.

How long lasting were these changes? In the aftermath of the war, governments and employers scurried to send women workers home, in part to give jobs to veterans, in part to deal with male workers' complaints that women were undercutting their wages. Efforts to demobilize women faced real barriers. Many women wage earners—widowed, charged with caring for relatives, or faced with inflation and soaring costs—needed their earnings more than ever. It was also difficult to persuade women workers who had grown accustomed to the relatively higher wages in heavy industry to return to their poorly paid traditional sectors of employment: the textile and garment industries and domestic service. The demobilization of women after the war, in other words, created as many dilemmas as had their mobilization. Governments passed "natalist" policies to encourage women to go home, marry, and—most important—have children. These policies did make maternity benefits—time off, medical care, and some allowances for the poor—available to women for the first time. Nonetheless, birth rates had been falling across Europe by the early twentieth century, and they continued to do so after the war. One upshot of the war was the increased availability of birth control—Marie Stopes (1880–1958) opened a birth-control clinic in London in 1921—and a combination of economic hardship, increased knowledge, and the demand for freedom made men and women more likely to use it. Universal suffrage, and the vote for all adult men and women, and for women in particular, had been one of the most controversial issues in European politics before the war. At the end of the fighting it came in a legislative rush. Britain was first off the mark, granting the vote to all men and women over thirty with the Representation of the People Act in 1918; the United States gave women the vote with the Nineteenth Amendment the following year. Germany's new republic and the Soviet Union did likewise. France was much slower to offer woman suffrage (1945) but did provide rewards and incentives for the national effort.

Mobilizing Resources

Along with mobilizing the labor front, the wartime governments had to mobilize men and money. All the belligerent countries had conscription laws before the war, except for Great Britain. Military service was seen as a duty,

WOMEN AT WORK. The all-out war effort combined with a manpower shortage at home brought women into factories across Europe in unparalleled numbers. Men and women work side by side in a British shell factory (left); German women assemble military equipment (right). • *How might the participation of women in the industrial workforce have changed attitudes toward women's labor?* • *What tensions might this have created within families or between male and female workers?*

not an option. Bolstered by widespread public support for the war, this belief brought millions of young Europeans into recruitment offices in 1914. The French began the war with about 4.5 million trained soldiers, but by the end of 1914—just four months into the war—300,000 were dead and 600,000 injured. Conscripting citizens and mustering colonial troops became increasingly important. Eventually, France called up 8 million citizens: almost two-thirds of Frenchmen aged eighteen to forty. In 1916, the British finally introduced conscription, dealing a serious blow to civilian morale; by the summer of 1918, half its army was under the age of nineteen.

Government propaganda, while part of a larger effort to sustain both soldier and civilian morale, was also important to the recruitment effort. From the outset, the war had been sold to the people on both sides of the conflict as a moral and righteous crusade. In 1914, the French president Raymond Poincaré (1913–20) assured his fellow citizens that France had no other purpose than to stand "before the universe for Liberty, Justice and Reason." Germans were presented with the task of defending their superior *Kultur* (culture) against the wicked encirclement policy of the Allied nations: "May God punish England!" was practically a greeting in 1914. By the middle of the war, massive propaganda campaigns were under way. Film, posters, postcards, newspapers—all forms

of media proclaimed the strength of the cause, the evil of the enemy, and the absolute necessity of total victory. The success of these campaigns is difficult to determine, but it is clear that they had at least one painful effect—they made it more difficult for any country to accept a fair, nonpunitive peace settlement.

Financing the war was another heavy obstacle. Military spending accounted for 3 to 5 percent of government expenditure in the combatant countries before 1914 but soared to perhaps half of each nation's budget during the war. Governments had to borrow money or print more of it. The Allied nations borrowed heavily from the British, who borrowed even more from the United States. American capital flowed across the Atlantic long before the United States entered the war. And though economic aid from the United States was a decisive factor in the Allies' victory, it left Britain with a $4.2 billion debt and hobbled the United Kingdom as a financial power after the war. The situation was far worse for Germany, which faced a total blockade of money and goods. In an effort to get around this predicament, and lacking an outside source of cash, the German government funded its war effort largely by increasing the money supply. The amount of paper money in circulation increased by over 1,000 percent during the war, triggering a dramatic rise in inflation. During the war, prices in Germany rose about

Woman's Work in Wartime

Although women in Europe had worked in some industries—such as textiles—long before World War I, the mobilization of women during the war years brought an unprecedented number of them into the industrial workforce. Inevitably, such profound changes in conceptions of gender and work generated controversy. These two documents provide a window into this debate both from the point of view of the highest government authorities and from women who took advantage of the new opportunities available to them in war work. The first document is a letter from the German chief of the General Staff, General Paul von Hindenburg to Chancellor Bethmann Hollweg, written in October 1916. The second is the testimony taken in 1918 from Helen Ross, an African American woman who had worked in domestic service before taking a wartime job in Topeka, Kansas.

General Paul von Hindenburg to Chancellor Bethmann Hollweg, October 1916

 t is also my opinion that women's work should not be overestimated. Almost all intellectual work, heavy physical labour, as well as all real manufacturing work will still fall on men—in addition to the entire waging of the war. It would be good if clear, official expression were given to these facts and if a stop were put to women's agitation for parity in all professions, and thereby, of course, for political emancipation. I completely agree with your Excellency that compulsory labour for women would be an inappropriate measure. After the war, we will need the woman as spouse and mother. . . .

If I *nevertheless* urge that the requirement to work be extended to all women who are either unemployed or working in trivial positions, now and for the duration of the war, I do so because, in my opinion, women can be employed in many areas to a still greater degree than previously and men can thereby be freed for other *work*. But first industry and agriculture must be urged even more to employ women. Further, the choice of occupation must not be left up to the women alone, but rather, it must [be] regulated according to ability, previous experience and social status. In particular, I want to stress again that I consider it especially wrong to keep secondary schools and universities, which have been almost completely emptied of men by conscription, open only for women. It is valueless, because the scholarly gain is minimal; furthermore, because precisely that rivalry with the family that needs to be combated would be promoted; and *finally*, because it would represent the coarsest injustice if the young man, who is giving everything for his Fatherland, is forced behind the woman.

Source: Letter of Chief of the General Staff General Paul von Hindenburg to Chancellor Bethmann Hollweg, October 1916. Quoted in Ute Daniel, *The War from Within: German Working-Class Women in the First World War*, trans. Margaret Ries (Oxford: 1997), pp. 68–69, emphasis in the original.

---

400 percent, double the inflation in Britain and France. For middle-class people living on pensions or fixed incomes, these price hikes were a push into poverty.

The Strains of War, 1917

The demands of total war worsened as the conflict dragged into 1917. On the front lines, morale fell as war-weary soldiers began to see the futility of their commanders' strategies.

After the debacle of the Nivelle Offensive, the French army recorded acts of mutiny in two-thirds of its divisions; similar resistance arose in nearly all major armies in 1917. Military leaders portrayed the mutineers as part of a dangerous pacifist movement, but most were nonpolitical. As one soldier put it: "All we wanted was to call the government's attention to us, make it see that we are men, and not beasts for the slaughterhouse." Resistance within the German army was never organized or widespread but existed in subtler forms. Self-mutilation rescued some soldiers

Helen Ross, Employee of the Santa Fe Railroad, Topeka, Kansas, October 1918

All the colored women like this work and want to keep it. We are making more money at this than any work we can get, and we do not have to work as hard as at housework which requires us to be on duty from six o'clock in the morning until nine or ten at night, with might little time off and at very poor wages.... What the colored women need is an opportunity to make money. As it is, they have to take what employment they can get, live in old tumbled down houses or resort to street walking, and I think a woman ought to think more of her blood than to do that. What occupation is open to us where we can make really good wages? We are not employed as clerks, we cannot all be school teachers, and so we cannot see any use in working our parents to death to get educated. Of course we should like easier work than this if it were opened to us. With three dollars a day, we can buy bonds . . . , we can dress decently, and not be tempted to find our living on the streets.

Source: Helen Ross, Freight House, Santa Fe RR, Topeka, Kansas, 28 October 1918, File 55, Women's Service Section, Record Group 14 [Records of the United States Railroad Administration], National Archives, Washington, D.C. Also quoted in M. W. Greenwald, *Women, War and Work: The Impact of World War I on Women Workers in the United States* (Ithaca, NY: 1980, reprinted, 1990), p. 27.

Questions for Analysis

1. What reservations does Hindenburg express about demands made by women for political emancipation, and how does he connect this to the question of women's wartime employment? Why does he nevertheless support women's wartime labor in Germany?

2. How did Helen Ross perceive the opportunity to earn wages in her railroad job compared to her previous work as a domestic servant? How had her life changed?

3. What long-lasting effects might the experience of wartime labor have had for women who worked in such jobs?

---

from the horror of the trenches; many more were released because of various emotional disorders. Over 6,000 cases of "war neuroses" were reported among German troops—an indication, if not of intentional disobedience, then of the severe physical and psychological trauma that caused the mutinies.

The war's toll also mounted for civilians, who often suffered from the same shortages of basic supplies that afflicted the men at the front. In 1916–17, the lack of clothing, food, and fuel was aggravated in central Europe by abnormally cold, wet weather. These strains provoked rising discontent on the home front. Although governments attempted to solve the problem with tighter controls on the economy, their policies often provoked further hostilities from civilians. "The population has lost all confidence in promises from the authorities," a German official reported in 1917, "particularly in view of earlier experiences with promises made in the administration of food."

In urban areas, where undernourishment was worst, people stood in lines for hours to get food and fuel rations that scarcely met their most basic needs. The price of bread and potatoes—still the central staples of working-class meals—soared. Prices were even higher in the thriving black market that emerged in cities. Consumers worried aloud that speculators were hoarding supplies and creating artificial shortages, selling tainted goods, and profiting from others' miseries. They decried the government's "reckless inattention" to families. Governments, however, were concentrated on the war effort and faced difficult decisions about who needed supplies the most—soldiers at the front, workers in the munitions industry, or hungry and cold families.

Like other nations, Germany moved from encouraging citizens to restrain themselves—"those who stuff themselves full, those who push out their paunches in all directions, are traitors to the Fatherland"—to direct control, issuing ration cards in 1915. Britain was the last to institute control, rationing bread only in 1917 when Germany's submarines sank an average of 630,000 tons per month and brought British food reserves within two the overthrow of the tsar and the rise of Bolshevism, was only the most dramatic response to widespread social problems.

DESPERATION ON THE GERMAN HOME FRONT, 1918. A German photograph of women digging through garbage in search of food. The last year of the war brought starvation to cities in Germany and Austria-Hungary, sending many people into the countryside to forage for provisions. Such foraging was often illegal, a violation of rationing rules. ▪ *How might the need to break the law in this way have affected support for the war effort and the state?*

THE RUSSIAN REVOLUTIONS OF 1917

The first country to break under the strain of total war was tsarist Russia. The outbreak of war temporarily united Russian society against a common enemy, but Russia's military effort quickly turned sour. All levels of Russian society became disillusioned with Tsar Nicholas II who was unable to provide leadership but was nonetheless unwilling to open government to those who could. The political and social strains of war brought two revolutions in 1917. The first, in February, overthrew the tsar and established a transitional government. The second, in October, was a communist revolution that marked the emergence of the Soviet Union.

The First World War and the February Revolution

Like the other participants in the First World War, Russia entered the war with the assumption that it would be over quickly. Autocratic Russia, plagued by internal difficulties before 1914 (see Chapter 23), could not sustain the political strains of extended warfare. In all the warring countries success depended on leaders' ability not only to command but also to maintain social and political cooperation. Tsar Nicholas II's political authority had been shaky for many years, undermined by his unpopular actions following the October Revolution of 1905 and his efforts to erode the minimal political power he had grudgingly granted to the Duma, Russia's parliament. Corruption in the royal court further tarnished the tsar's image. The best Nicholas's supporters could say about him was that he was morally upright and devoted to his family. Once war broke out, the tsar insisted on personally commanding Russian troops, leaving the government in the hands of his court,

weeks of starvation level. But rations indicated only what was allowed, not what was available. Hunger continued despite mass bureaucratic control. Governments regulated not only food but also working hours and wages; and unhappy workers directed their anger at the state, adding a political dimension to labor disputes and household needs. The bread lines, filled mainly by women, were flash points of political dissent, petty violence, even large-scale riots. Likewise, the class conflicts of prewar Europe had been briefly muffled by the outbreak of war and mobilization along patriotic lines, but as the war ground on, political tensions reemerged with new intensity. Thousands of strikes erupted throughout Europe, involving millions of frustrated workers. In April 1917, 300,000 in Berlin went on strike to protest ration cuts. In May, a strike of Parisian seamstresses touched off a massive work stoppage that included even white-collar employees and munitions workers. Shipbuilders and steelworkers in Glasgow went on strike as well, and the British government replied by sending armored cars to "Red Glasgow." Stagnation had given way to crisis on both sides. The strains of total war and the resulting social upheavals threatened political regimes throughout Europe. Governments were pushed to their limits. The Russian Revolution, which resulted in

GRIGORII RASPUTIN. Rasputin won the trust of the tsar's family by presenting himself as a faith healer and one who could help the tsar's son, Alexei, who suffered from hemophilia. The rising influence of the "holy man" heightened perceptions that the tsar was mired in the past and unable to lead Russia to the future.

especially his wife, Alexandra, and her eccentric spiritual mentor and faith healer, Grigorii Rasputin (1869–1916). Rasputin won the tsarina's sympathy by treating her hemophiliac son, and he used his influence to operate corrupt and self-aggrandizing schemes. His presence only added to the image of a court mired in decadence, incompetent to face the modern world.

In 1914 and 1915, Russia suffered terrible defeats. All of Poland and substantial territory in the Baltics fell to the Germans at the cost of a million Russian casualties. Although the Russian army was the largest in Europe, it was poorly trained and, at the beginning of the war, undersupplied and inadequately equipped. In the first battles of 1914, generals sent soldiers to the front without rifles or shoes, instructing them to scavenge supplies from fallen comrades. By 1915, to the surprise of many, Russia was producing enough food, clothing, and ammunition, but political problems blocked the supply effort. The tsarist government distrusted public initiatives and tried to direct all provisioning itself. Tsarist officials insisted on making crucial decisions about the allocation of supplies without

any consultation. Another major offensive in the summer of 1916 brought hope for success but turned into a humiliating retreat. When word came that the government was requisitioning grain from the countryside to feed the cities, peasants began to desert en masse, returning to their farms to guard their families' holdings. By the end of 1916, a combination of political ineptitude and military defeat brought the Russian state to the verge of collapse.

The same problems that hampered the Russian war effort also crippled the tsar's ability to override domestic discontent and resistance. As the war dragged on, the government faced not only liberal opposition in the Duma, soldiers unwilling to fight, and an increasingly militant labor movement but also a rebellious urban population. City dwellers were impatient with inflation and shortages of food and fuel. In February 1917, these forces came together in Petrograd (now St. Petersburg). The revolt began on International Women's Day, February 23, an occasion for a loosely organized march of women—workers, mothers, wives, and consumers—demanding food, fuel, and political reform. The march was the latest in a wave of demonstrations and strikes that had swept through the country during the winter months. This time, within a few days the unrest spiraled into a mass strike of 300,000 people. Nicholas II sent in police and military forces to quell the disorder. When nearly 60,000 troops in Petrograd mutinied and joined the revolt, what was left of the tsar's power evaporated. Nicholas II abdicated the throne on March 2. This abrupt decision brought a century-long struggle over Russian autocracy to a sudden end.

After the collapse of the monarchy, two parallel centers of power emerged. Each had its own objectives and policies. The first was the provisional government, organized by leaders in the Duma and composed mainly of middle-class liberals. The new government hoped to establish a democratic system under constitutional rule. Its main task was to set up a national election for a constituent assembly, and it also acted to grant and secure civil liberties, release political prisoners, and redirect power into the hands of local officials. The other center of power lay with the *soviets,* a Russian term for local councils elected by workers and soldiers. Since 1905, socialists had been active in organizing these councils, which claimed to be the true democratic representatives of the people. A soviet, organized during the 1905 revolution and led by the well-known socialist Leon Trotsky, reemerged after February 1917 and asserted claim to be the legitimate political power in Russia. The increasingly powerful soviets pressed for social reform, the redistribution of land, and a negotiated settlement with Germany and Austria. Yet the provisional government refused to concede military defeat. Continuing the war effort made domestic reform impossible and cost valuable popular support. More fighting during 1917 was just as disastrous as before, and this time the provisional government paid the price. By autumn, desertion in the army was rampant, administering the country was nearly impossible, and Russian politics teetered on the edge of chaos.

The Bolsheviks and the October Revolution

The Bolsheviks, a branch of the Russian socialist movement, had little to do with the events of February 1917. Over the course of the next seven months, however, they became enough of a force to overthrow the provisional government. The chain of events leading to the October revolution surprised most contemporary observers, including the Bolsheviks themselves. Marxism had been quite weak in late-nineteenth-century Russia, although it made small but rapid inroads during the 1880s and 1890s. In 1903, the leadership of the Russian Social Democrats split over revolutionary strategy and the steps to socialism. One group, which won a temporary majority (and chose to call itself the Bolsheviks, or "members of the majority"), favored a centralized party of active revolutionaries. They believed that revolution alone would lead directly to a socialist regime. The Mensheviks (members of the minority), like most European socialists, wanted to move toward socialism gradually, supporting bourgeois or liberal revolution in the short term. Because peasants constituted 80 to 85 percent of the population, the Mensheviks also reasoned that a proletarian revolution was premature and that Russia needed to complete its capitalist development first. The Mensheviks regained control of the party, but the Bolshevik splinter party survived under the leadership of the young, dedicated revolutionary Vladimir Ilyich Ulyanov, who adopted the pseudonym Lenin.

Lenin was a member of the middle class; his father had been an inspector of schools and a minor political functionary. Lenin himself had been expelled from university for engaging in radical activity after his elder brother was executed for involvement in a plot to assassinate Tsar Alexander III. Lenin spent three years as a political prisoner in Siberia. After that, from 1900 until 1917, he lived and wrote as an exile in western Europe.

Lenin believed that the development of Russian capitalism made socialist revolution possible. To bring revolution, he argued, the Bolsheviks needed to organize on behalf of the new class of industrial workers. Without the party's disciplined leadership, Russia's factory workers could not accomplish change on the necessary scale. Lenin's Bolsheviks remained a minority among Social Democrats well into 1917 and industrial workers, a small part of the population. But the Bolsheviks' dedication to the singular goal of revolution and their tight, almost conspiratorial organization gave them tactical advantages over larger and more loosely organized opposition parties. The Bolsheviks merged a peculiarly Russian tradition of revolutionary zeal with Western Marxism, creating a party capable of seizing the moment when the tsar left the scene.

Throughout 1917, the Bolsheviks consistently demanded an end to the war, improvement in working and living conditions for workers, and redistribution of aristocratic land to the peasantry. While the provisional government struggled to hold together the Russian war effort, Lenin led the Bolsheviks on a bolder course, shunning any collaboration with the "bourgeois" government and condemning its imperialist war policies. Even most Bolsheviks considered Lenin's approach too radical. Yet as conditions in Russia deteriorated, his uncompromising calls for "Peace, Land, and Bread, Now" and "All Power to the Soviets" won the Bolsheviks support from workers, soldiers, and peasants. As many ordinary people saw it, the other parties could not govern, win the war, or achieve an honorable peace. While unemployment continued to climb and starvation and chaos reigned in the cities, the Bolsheviks' power and credibility were rising fast.

RUSSIAN REVOLUTION. Russian demonstrators scatter as tsarist troops shoot into the crowd during the February revolution, 1917.

Toward the October Revolution: Lenin to the Bolsheviks

In the fall of 1917, Lenin was virtually the only Bolshevik leader who believed that an insurrection should be launched immediately. As the provisional government faltered, he attempted to convince his fellow Bolsheviks that the time for revolution had arrived.

Having obtained a majority in the Soviets of Workers' and Soldiers' Deputies of both capitals, the Bolsheviks can and *must* take power into their hands.

They can do so because the active majority of the revolutionary elements of the people of both capitals is sufficient to attract the masses, to overcome the resistance of the adversary, to vanquish him, to conquer power and to retain it. For, in offering immediately a democratic peace, in giving the land immediately to the peasants, in re-establishing the democratic institutions and liberties which have been mangled and crushed by Kerensky [leader of the provisional government], the Bolsheviks will form a government which *nobody* will overthrow. . . .

The majority of the people is *with us*. . . . [T]he majority in the Soviets of the capitals is the *result* of the people's progress *to our side*. The vacillation of the Socialist-Revolutionaries and Mensheviks . . . is proof of the same thing . . .

To "wait" for the Constituent Assembly would be wrong. . . . Only our party, having assumed power, can secure the convocation of the Constituent Assembly, and, after assuming power, it could blame the other parties for delaying it and could substantiate its accusations. . . .

It would be naive to wait for a "formal" majority on the side of the Bolsheviks, no revolution ever waits for *this*. . . . History will not forgive us if we do not assume power now.

No apparatus? There is an apparatus: the Soviets and democratic organisations. The international situation *just now*, on the *eve* of a separate peace between the English and the Germans, is *in our favour*. It is precisely now that to offer peace to the peoples means to *win*.

Assume power *at once* in Moscow and in Petrograd . . . ; we will win *absolutely and unquestionably*.

Source: Vladimir Ilyich Lenin, *Bol'sheviki dolzhny vzyat'vlast'* (*The Bolsheviks Must Seize Power*), cited in Richard Sakwa, *The Rise and Fall of the Soviet Union, 1917–1991* (New York and London: 1999), p. 45.

Questions for Analysis

1. Lenin was surprised by the sudden collapse of the tsarist regime in the February revolution of 1917. Why did he think the Bolsheviks could seize power? What were the key elements of his strategy for winning the necessary popular support?

2. Convinced he was right, Lenin returned to Petrograd in disguise and personally presented his arguments for an armed takeover to the Bolshevik Central Committee. What did he mean by saying that "it would be naive to wait for a 'formal' majority on the side of the Bolsheviks, no revolution ever waits for *this*"?

In October 1917, Lenin convinced his party to act. He goaded Leon Trotsky, who was better known among workers, into organizing a Bolshevik attack on the provisional government on October 24–25, 1917. On October 25, Lenin appeared from hiding to announce to a stunned meeting of soviet representatives that "all power had passed to the Soviets." The head of the provisional government fled to rally support at the front lines, and the Bolsheviks took over the Winter Palace, the seat of the provisional government. The initial stage of the revolution was quick and

relatively bloodless. In fact, many observers believed they had seen nothing more than a coup d'état, one that might quickly be reversed. Life in Petrograd went on as normal.

The Bolsheviks took the opportunity to rapidly consolidate their position. First, they moved against all political competition, beginning with the soviets. They immediately expelled parties that disagreed with their actions, creating a new government in the soviets composed entirely of Bolsheviks. Trotsky, sneering at moderate socialists who walked out to protest what they saw as an illegal seizure

VLADIMIR ILYICH LENIN. Lenin speaking in Moscow in 1918, at the first anniversary of the October revolution. A forceful speaker and personality, Lenin was the single most powerful politician in Russia between October 1917 and his death in 1924.

of power, scoffed: "You are a mere handful, miserable, bankrupt; your role is finished, and you may go where you belong—to the garbage heap of history." The Bolsheviks did follow through on the provisional government's promise to elect a Constituent Assembly. But when they did not win a majority in the elections, they refused to let the assembly reconvene. From that point on, Lenin's Bolsheviks ruled socialist Russia, and later the Soviet Union, as a one-party dictatorship.

In the countryside, the new Bolshevik regime did little more than ratify a revolution that had been going on since the summer of 1917. When peasant soldiers at the front heard that a revolution had occurred, they streamed home to take land they had worked for generations and believed was rightfully theirs. The provisional government had set up commissions to deal methodically with the legal issues surrounding the redistribution of land, a process that threatened to become as complex as the emancipation of the serfs in 1861. The Bolsheviks simply approved the spontaneous redistribution of the nobles' land to peasants without compensation to former owners. They nationalized banks and gave workers control of factories.

Most important, the new government sought to take Russia out of the war. It eventually negotiated a separate treaty with Germany, signed at Brest-Litovsk in March 1918. The Bolsheviks surrendered vast Russian territories: the rich agricultural region of Ukraine, Georgia, Finland,

Russia's Polish territories, the Baltic states, and more. However humiliating, the treaty ended Russia's role in the fighting and saved the fledgling communist regime from almost certain military defeat at the hands of the Germans. The treaty enraged Lenin's political enemies, both moderates and reactionaries, who were still a force to be reckoned with—and who were prepared to wage a civil war rather than accept the revolution. Withdrawing from Europe's war only plunged the country into a vicious civil conflict (see Chapter 25).

Russian autocracy had fended off opposition for the better part of a century. After a long struggle, the regime, weakened by the war, had collapsed with little resistance. By the middle of 1917, Russia was not suffering a crisis of government but rather an absence of government. In June, at the First All-Russian Congress of Soviets, a prominent Menshevik declared, "At the present moment, there is not a political party in Russia that would say: Hand the power over to us, resign, and we will take your place. Such a party does not exist in Russia." Lenin shouted back from the audience, "It does exist!" Indeed, seizing power had been easy for the Bolsheviks, but building the new state proved vastly more difficult.

John Reed, an American journalist covering the Russian Revolution, called the events of October "ten days that shook the world." What had been shaken? First, the Allies, for the revolution allowed the Germans to win the war on the Eastern Front. Second, conservative governments, which in the aftermath of the war worried about a wave of revolution sweeping away other regimes. Third, the expectations of many socialists, startled to see a socialist regime gain and hold power in what many considered a backward country. Over the long run, 1917 was to the twentieth century what the French Revolution had been to the nineteenth century. It was a political transformation, it set the agenda for future revolutionary struggles, and it created the frames of mind on the right and the left for the century that followed.

THE ROAD TO GERMAN DEFEAT, 1918

Russia's withdrawal dealt an immediate strategic and psychological blow to the Allies. Germany could soothe domestic discontent by claiming victory on the Eastern Front, and it could now concentrate its entire army in the west. The Allies feared that Germany would win the war before the United States, which entered the conflict in April 1917, could make a difference. It almost happened. With striking results, Germany shifted its offensive strategy to infiltration by small groups under flexible command. On March 21, Germany initiated a major assault on the west and quickly broke through the Allied lines. The British were hit hardest. Some units, surrounded, fought to the death with bayonets and grenades, but most recognized their plight and surrendered, putting tens of thousands of prisoners in German hands. The British were in retreat everywhere and their commander, Sir Douglas Haig, issued a famous order warning that British troops "now fight with our backs to the wall." The Germans advanced to within fifty miles of Paris by early April. Yet the British—and especially troops from the overseas empire—did just as they were asked and stemmed the tide. As German forces turned southeast instead, the French, who had refused to participate in the foolish attacks over the top, showed stubborn courage on the defensive, where they bogged down in heat, mud, and casualties. It had been a last great try by the well-organized German army; exhausted, it now waited for the Allies to mount their own attack.

When it came in July and August, the Allied counterattack was devastating and quickly gathered steam. New offensive techniques had finally materialized. The Allies improved their use of tanks and the "creeping barrage," in which infantry marched close behind a rolling wall of shells to overwhelm their targets. In another of the war's ironies these new tactics were pioneered by the conservative British, who launched a crushing counterattack in July, relying on the survivors of the armies of the Somme reinforced by troops from Australia, Canada, and India. The French made use of American troops, whose generals attacked the Germans with the same harrowing indifference to casualties shown in 1914. Despite their lack of experience, the American troops were tough and resilient. When combined with more experienced French and Australian forces, they punched several large holes through German lines, crossing into the "lost provinces" of Alsace and Lorraine by October. At the beginning of November, the sweeping British offensive had joined up with the small Belgian army and was pressing toward Brussels.

The Allies finally brought their material advantage to bear on the Germans, who were suffering acutely by the spring of 1918. This was not only because of the continued effectiveness of the Allied blockade but also because of growing domestic conflict over war aims. On the front lines, German soldiers were exhausted. Following the lead of their distraught generals, the troops let morale sink, and many surrendered. Facing one shattering blow after another, the German army was pushed deep into Belgium. Popular discontent mounted, and the government, which was now largely in the hands of the military, seemed unable either to win the war or to meet basic household needs.

Germany's network of allies was also coming undone. By the end of September, the Central Powers were headed for defeat. In the Middle East, Allenby's army, which combined Bedouin guerrillas, Indian sepoys, Scottish highlanders, and Australian light cavalry, decisively defeated Ottoman forces in Syria and Iraq. In the Balkans, France's capable battlefield commander, Louis Franchet d'Espèrey (1914–21), transformed the Allied expedition in Greece and drew that country into the war. The results were remarkable. In September, a three-week offensive by the Greek and Allied forces knocked Bulgaria out of the war. Meanwhile Austria-Hungary faced disaster on all sides, collapsing in Italy as well as the Balkans. Czech and Polish representatives in the Austrian government began pressing for self-government. Croat and Serb politicians proposed a "kingdom of Southern Slavs" (soon known as Yugoslavia). When Hungary joined the chorus for independence the emperor, Karl I, accepted reality and sued for peace. The empire that had started the conflict surrendered on November 3, 1918, and disintegrated soon after.

Germany was now left with the impossible task of carrying on the struggle alone. By the fall of 1918, the country was starving and on the verge of civil war. A plan to use the German surface fleet to attack the combined British and American navies only produced a mutiny among German sailors at the start of November. Revolutionary tremors swelled into an earthquake. On November 8, a republic was proclaimed in Bavaria, and the next day nearly all of Germany was in the throes of revolution. The kaiser's abdication was announced in Berlin on November 9; he fled to

CASUALTY OF WAR. A German soldier killed during the Allies' October 1917 offensive.

Holland early the next morning. Control of the German government fell to a provisional council headed by Friedrich Ebert (1912–23), the socialist leader in the Reichstag. Ebert and his colleagues immediately took steps to negotiate an armistice. The Germans could do nothing but accept the Allies' terms, so at five o'clock in the morning of November 11, 1918, two German delegates met with the Allied army commander in the Compiègne Forest and signed papers officially ending the war. Six hours later the order for cease fire was given across the Western Front. That night, thousands of people danced through the streets of London, Paris, and Rome, engulfed in a different delirium from that four years before, a joyous burst of exhausted relief.

The United States as a World Power

The final turning point of the war had been the entry of the United States in April 1917. Although America had supported the Allies financially throughout the war, its official intervention undeniably tipped the scales. The United States created a fast and efficient wartime bureaucracy, instituting conscription in May 1917. About 10 million men were registered, and by the next year, 300,000 soldiers a month were being shipped "over there." Large amounts of food and supplies also crossed the Atlantic, under the armed protection of the U.S. Navy. This system of convoys effectively neutralized the threat of German submarines to Allied merchant ships: the number of ships sunk fell from 25 to 4 percent. America's entry—though not immediately decisive—gave a quick, colossal boost to British and French morale, while severely undermining Germany's.

The direct cause of America's entry into the war was the German U-boat. Germany had gambled that unrestricted submarine warfare would cripple Britain's supply lines and win the war. But by attacking neutral and unarmed American ships, Germany only provoked an opponent it could not afford to fight. Germany correctly suspected that the British were clandestinely receiving war supplies from U.S. passenger ships; and on February 1, 1917, the kaiser's ministers announced that they would sink all ships on sight, without warning. The American public was further outraged by an intercepted telegram from Germany's foreign minister, Arthur Zimmerman (1916–17), stating that Germany would support a Mexican attempt to capture American territory if the United States entered the war. The United States cut off diplomatic relations with Berlin, and on April 6, President Woodrow Wilson (1913–21) requested and received a declaration of war by Congress.

Wilson vowed that America would fight to "make the world safe for democracy," to banish autocracy and militarism, and to establish a league or society of nations in place of the old diplomatic maneuvering. The Americans' primary interest was maintaining the international balance of power. For years, U.S. diplomats and military leaders believed that American security depended on the equilibrium of strength in Europe. As long as Britain could prevent any one nation from achieving supremacy on the Continent, the United States was safe. But now Germany threatened not only the British navy—which had come to be seen as the shield of American security—but also the international balance of power. American involvement stemmed those threats in 1918, but the monumental task of establishing peace still lay ahead.

Total War

The search for peace was spurred by shock at the murderousness of the war. As early as 1915, contemporaries were speaking of "the Great War"; the transformations were there for all to see. The changing technologies of warfare altered strategic calculations. New artillery was heavier, with a longer range and more deadly results: German mobile

U.S. TROOPS AT THE FRONT. Soldiers in the American Expedition Forces wearing gas masks.

howitzers, such as "Big Bertha," could fire shells of over a thousand pounds at targets nine miles and even farther away. (One shelled Paris from seventy-five miles out.) This was modern, industrialized warfare, first glimpsed in the American Civil War but now more advanced and on a much larger scale. It still deployed cloth-uniformed men, heartbreakingly unprotected against the newly destructive weapons. And it still required human intelligence, speed, brute force—or courage—on a massive scale. The statistics and what they imply still strain the imagination: 74 million soldiers were mobilized on both sides; 6,000 people were killed each day for more than 1,500 days.

The warring nations, Europe's new industrial power-houses, were also empires, and this "world" war consumed resources and soldiers from all over the globe. Mobilization also reached more deeply into civilian society. Economies bent to military priorities. Propaganda escalated to sustain the effort, fanning old hatreds and creating new ones. Atrocities against civilians came in its wake. Europe had known brutal wars against civilians before, and guerilla war during the time of Napoleon, but the First World War vastly magnified the violence and multiplied the streams of refugees. Minorities who lived in the crumbling Russian, Austro-Hungarian, or Ottoman Empires were especially vulnerable. Jewish populations in Russia had lived in fear of pogroms before 1914; now they were attacked by Russian soldiers who accused them of encouraging the enemy. Austria-Hungary, likewise, summarily executed minorities suspected of Russian sympathies. The worst atrocities came against the Armenian community in Turkey. Attacked by the Allies at Gallipoli and at war with the Russians to the north, the Turkish government turned on its Armenian subjects, labeling them a security risk. Orders came down for "relocation," and relocation became genocide. Armenian leaders were arrested; Armenian men were shot; and entire Armenian villages were force marched to the south, robbed and beaten to death along the way. Over the course of the war, a million Armenians died.

All of these developments—military, economic, and psychological mobilization; a war that tested the powers of a state and its economy; violence against civilians—were the component parts of total war and foreshadowed the conflict to be unleashed in 1939.

The Peace Settlement

The Paris Peace Conference, which opened in January 1919, was an extraordinary moment, one that dramatized just how much the world had been transformed by the war and the decades that preceded it. Gone were the Russian, Austro-Hungarian, and German Empires. That the American president Woodrow Wilson played such a prominent role marked the rise of the United States as a world power. The United States' new status was rooted in the economic development of the second industrial revolution during the nineteenth century. In mass production and technological innovation, it had rivaled the largest European powers (England and Germany) before the war. During the war, American intervention (although it came late) had decisively broken the military-economic deadlock. And in the war's aftermath, American industrial culture, engineering, and financial networks loomed very large on the European continent. Wilson and his entourage spent several months in Paris at the conference—a first for an American president while in office and European leaders' first extended encounter with an American head of state.

American prominence was far from the only sign of global change. Some thirty nations sent delegates to the peace conference, a reflection of three factors: the scope of the war, heightened national sentiment and aspiration, and the tightening of international communication and economic ties in the latter part of the nineteenth century. The world in 1900 was vastly more globalized than it had been fifty years earlier. Many more countries had political, economic, and human investments in the war and its settlement. A belief that peace would secure and be secured by free peoples in sovereign nations represented the full flowering of nineteenth-century liberal nationalism. Delegates came to work for Irish home rule, for a Jewish state in Palestine and for nations in Poland, Ukraine, and Yugoslavia. Europe's colonies, which had been key to the war effort and were increasingly impatient with their status, sent delegates to negotiate for self-determination. They discovered, however, that the western European leaders' commitment to the principle of national self-determination was hedged by their imperial assumptions. Non-state actors—in other words international groups asking for woman suffrage, civil rights, minimum wages, or maximum hours—came to the Paris Peace Conference as well, for these were now seen as international issues. Last, reporters from all over the world wired news home from Paris, a sign of vastly improved communications, transatlantic cables, and the mushrooming of the mass press.

Although many attended, the conference was largely controlled by the so-called Big Four: the U.S. president Woodrow Wilson, the British prime minister David Lloyd George (1916–22), the French premier Georges Clemenceau (1917–20), and the Italian premier Vittorio Orlando (1917–19). The debates among these four personalities were fierce, as they all had conflicting ambitions and interests. In total, five separate treaties were signed, one with each of the

The Legacy of World War I

World War I had severe consequences for civilian populations, resulting not only from military conflict but also from economic dislocation, food shortages, and disease (see photo of a feeding station in Vienna for hungry families in 1918, on left). Recognizing the contribution of civilians to the war effort, states involved in World War I intervened massively in the economy, paying separation allowances to the families of soldiers, unemployment benefits to those thrown out of work, and regulating the sale and production of consumer goods. This example of the ways a government could play a role in the economy set a precedent for later in the twentieth century, and is part of the history of current debates about the role the state can play in remedying inequality (see photo of protesters demonstrating against cuts in social security, on right).

 Watch related author interview on StudySpace
wwnorton.com/web/westernciv18

defeated nations: Germany, Austria, Hungary, Turkey, and Bulgaria. The settlement with Germany was called the Treaty of Versailles, after the town in which it was signed.

Wilson's widely publicized Fourteen Points represented the spirit of idealism. Wilson had proposed the Fourteen Points before the war ended, as the foundation of a permanent peace. Based on the principle of "open covenants of peace, openly arrived at," they called for an end to secret diplomacy, freedom of the seas, removal of international tariffs, and reduction of national armaments "to the lowest point consistent with safety." They also called for the "self-determination of peoples" and for the establishment of a League of Nations to settle international conflicts. Thousands of copies of the Fourteen Points had been scattered by Allied planes over the German trenches and behind the lines in an attempt to convince both soldiers and civilians that the Allied nations were striving for a just and durable peace. They shaped the expectations that

Germans brought to the peace talks. "The day of conquest and aggrandizement is gone by; so is also the day of secret covenants entered into in the interest of particular governments," Wilson had said. "It is this happy fact . . . which makes it possible for every nation whose purposes are consistent with justice and the peace of the world to avow now or at any other time the objects it has in view."

Idealism, however, was undermined by other imperatives. Throughout the war, Allied propaganda led soldiers and civilians to believe that their sacrifices to the war effort would be compensated by payments extracted from the enemy. Total war demanded total victory. Lloyd George had campaigned during the British election of 1918 on the slogan "Hang the Kaiser!" Clemenceau had twice in his long lifetime seen France invaded and its existence imperiled. With the tables turned, he believed that the French should take full advantage of their opportunity to place Germany under strict control. The devastation of the war and the

"LONG LIVE WILSON!" Paris crowds greet President Wilson after the war. Despite public demonstrations of this sort, Wilson's attempt to shape the peace was a failure.

was left to a Reparations Commission, which set the total at $33 billion in 1921. The Germans deeply resented these harsh demands, but others outside of Germany also warned of the dangers of punitive reparations. In *The Economic Consequences of the Peace,* the noted British economist John Maynard Keynes (1883–1946) argued that reparations would undermine Europe's most important task: repairing the world economy.

The other treaties at the Paris Peace Conference were based partly on the Allies' strategic interests, and partly on the principle of national self-determination. The experience of the prewar years convinced leaders that they should draw nations' boundaries to conform to the ethnic, linguistic, and historical traditions of the people they were to contain. Wilson's idealism about freedom and equal representation confirmed these aims. Thus, representatives of Yugoslavia were granted a state. Czechoslovakia was created, Poland reestablished, Hungary separated from Austria, and the Baltic states made independent (see the map on page 000). These national boundaries did not, indeed in most cases could not, follow ethnic divisions; they were created according to facts on the ground, hasty compromises, and political dictates—such as insulating western Europe from the communist threat of the Soviet Union. The peacemakers carved new nations from older, multiethnic empires, especially the Austro-Hungarian Empire, whose fragility had helped spark the war and whose structure had collapsed with the conflict. Creating nations, however, almost invariably created new minorities within those nations. The architects of the new Europe wrestled, briefly, with the problem of minorities, but did not resolve it. The issue would return and undermine European stability in the 1930s.

The Ottoman Empire ended as well, with two results: the creation of the modern Turkish state and a new structure for British and French colonial rule. As territories were taken from the Ottomans, Greece chose to seize some by force. The effort was successful at first, but the Turks counterattacked, driving out Greek forces by 1923 and creating the modern state of Turkey under the charismatic leadership of General Mustafa Kemal Attaturk (1923–38). Ottoman territories placed under French and British control became part of the colonial "mandate system," which

fiction that Germany could be made to pay for it made compromise impossible. The settlement with Germany was shaped more by this desire for punishment than by Wilson's idealism.

The Versailles treaty required Germany to surrender the "lost provinces" of Alsace and Lorraine to France and to give up other territories to Denmark and the new state of Poland. The treaty gave Germany's coal mines in the Saar basin to France for fifteen years, at which point the German government could buy them back. Germany's province of East Prussia was cut off from the rest of its territory. The port of Danzig, where the majority of the population was German, was put under the administrative control of the League of Nations and the economic domination of Poland. The treaty disarmed Germany, forbid a German air force, and reduced its navy to a token force to match an army capped at 100,000 volunteers. To protect France and Belgium, all German soldiers and fortifications were to be removed from the Rhine Valley.

The most important part of the Versailles treaty, and one of the parts at odds with Wilson's original plan, was the "war-guilt" provision in Article 231. Versailles held Germany and its allies responsible for the loss and damage suffered by the Allied governments and their citizens "as a consequence of the war imposed upon them by the aggression of Germany and her allies." Germany would be forced to pay massive reparations. The exact amount legitimized Europe's dominance over territories in the Middle East, Africa, and the Pacific. Territories were divided into groups on the basis of their location and their "level of development," or how far, in European eyes, they would have to travel to earn self-government. Choice pieces of land became mandates held, in principle, by the League of Nations but administered by Britain (Transjordan, Iraq, and Palestine) and France (Lebanon and Syria). The British and French Empires, then, expanded after the war, although those territories held trouble ahead—the British faced revolt in Iraq and escalating tensions in Palestine, where they tried to juggle promises made to Zionist settlers and claims of indigenous Arab communities. Arab leaders, accompanied by their advocate T. E. Lawrence, attended the Versailles conference and listened as their hopes for independence were strictly circumscribed.

The peoples of the Allies' existing colonies were also disappointed. Ho Chi Minh, a young student from Indochina attending a Parisian university, was one of many colonial activists who attended the conference to protest conditions in the colonies and to ask that the rights of nations be extended to their homelands. Well-organized delegations from French West Africa and from the Congress Party of India, which favored dominion status in return for the wartime efforts of millions of Indian soldiers who had fought for the British Empire, were also snubbed. The peacemakers' belief in democracy and self-determination collided with their baseline assumptions—inherited from the nineteenth century—about Western superiority; those assumptions justified imperial rule. Although the European powers spoke about reforming colonialism, little was done. Many nationalists in the colonies who had favored moderate legislative change decided that active struggle might be the only answer to the injustices of colonialism.

Each of the five peace treaties incorporated the Covenant of the League of Nations, an organization envisioned as the arbiter of world peace, but it never achieved the idealistic aims of its founders. The League was handicapped from the start by a number of changes to its original design. The arms-reduction requirement was watered down, and the League's power to enforce it was rendered almost nonexistent. Japan would not join unless it was allowed to keep former German concessions in China. France demanded that both Germany and Russia be excluded from the League. This contradicted Wilson's goals but had already been legitimized in Paris, where neither Soviet Russia nor the defeated Central Powers were allowed at the talks. The League received an even more debilitating blow when the U.S. Congress, citing the long-standing national preference for isolation, refused to approve U.S. membership in the League. Hobbled from the start, the international organization had little potential to avert conflicts.

The League began as a utopian response to global conflict and registered the urgency of reorganizing world governance. Its history, however, reflected the larger problems of power politics that emerged after the war.

CONCLUSION

Europe fought the First World War on every front possible—military, political, social, and economic. Consequently, the war's effects extended far beyond the devastated landscapes of the Western Front. Statistics can only hint at the enormous loss of human life: of the 70 million men who were mobilized, nearly 9 million were killed. Russia, Germany, France, and Hungary recorded the highest number of deaths, but the smaller countries of southeast Europe had the highest percentages of soldiers killed. Almost 40 percent of Serbia's soldiers died in battle. With the addition of war-related deaths caused by privation and disease, Serbia lost 15 percent of its population. In comparison, Britain, France, and Germany lost only 2 to 3 percent of their populations. But the percentages are much more telling if we focus on the young men of the war generation. Germany lost one-third of men aged nineteen to twenty-two in 1914. France and Britain sustained similar losses, with mortality among young men reaching eight to ten times the normal rate. This was the "lost generation."

The breakdown of the prewar treaty system and the scale of the diplomatic failure that produced the war discredited the political classes in many countries. Meanwhile, the war itself planted seeds of political and social discontent around the globe. Relations between Russia and western Europe grew sour and suspicious. The Allies had attempted to overthrow the Bolsheviks during the war and had excluded them from the negotiations afterward; these actions instilled in the Soviets a mistrust of the West that lasted for generations. The Allied nations feared that Russia would dominate the new states of eastern Europe, building a "Red Bridge" across the continent. Elsewhere, the conflicting demands of colonialism and nationalism struck only a temporary balance, while the redrawn maps left ethnic and linguistic minorities in every country. The fires of discontent raged most fiercely in Germany, where the Treaty of Versailles was decried as outrageously unjust. Nearly all national governments agreed that it

TERRITORIAL CHANGES IN EUROPE AND THE NEAR EAST AFTER THE FIRST WORLD WAR. Note the changes in geography as a result of the First World War. ■ What areas were most affected by the changes within Europe, and why? ■ Can you see any obvious difficulties created by the redrawing of the map of Europe? ■ What historical circumstances and/or new threats guided the victors to create such geopolitical anomalies?

Legend:
- 1914 boundaries
- New boundaries as a result of postwar treaties
- To United Kingdom
- To France
- To Italy
- To Romania
- To Denmark
- To Yugoslavia (Serbia and Montenegro)
- To Belgium
- To Greece
- Became independent

Scale: 0 — 250 — 500 Miles / 0 — 250 — 500 Kilometers

would eventually have to be revised. Neither war nor peace had ended the rivalries that caused the Great War.

The war also had powerful and permanent economic consequences. Beset by inflation, debt, and the difficult task of industrial rebuilding, Europe found itself displaced from the center of the world economy. The war had accelerated the decentralization of money and markets. Many Asian, African, and South American nations benefited financially as their economies became less dependent on Europe, and they were better able to profit from Europe's need for their natural resources. The United States and Japan reaped the biggest gains and emerged as leaders in the new world economy.

The war's most powerful cultural legacy was disillusionment. A generation of men had been sacrificed to no apparent end. Surviving soldiers—many of them permanently injured, both physically and psychologically—were sickened by their participation in such useless slaughter. Women and other civilians had also made extraordinary sacrifices on the home front, for little apparent gain. Both veterans and civilians were disgusted by the greedy abandonment of principles by the politicians at Versailles. In the postwar period, many younger men and women mistrusted the "old men" who had dragged the world into the war. These feelings of loss and alienation were voiced in the vastly popular genre of war literature—memoirs and

After You Read This Chapter

 Visit StudySpace for quizzes, additional review materials, and multimedia documents. **wwnorton.com/web/westernciv18**

REVIEWING THE OBJECTIVES

- The First World War broke out as a result of conflicts in the Balkans. Why?
- The Western Front was seen by all sides as a crucial theater of the conflict. What measures did the French, British, and Germans take to break the stalemate, and why did they fail?
- European governments intervened in extraordinary ways in the economy to ensure the production of material for the war effort and to remedy the social crisis caused by mobilization. How did governments intervene in the economy?
- The war led European nations to mobilize people and resources from their colonies. How did colonial subjects participate in the war effort, and what did many of them expect in return?
- Russia was devastated by the war, and the population lost confidence in the tsar's government. What circumstances allowed the Bolsheviks to seize power in 1917, and what were their goals?
- The Versailles Peace Treaty blamed the Germans for the war. Who were the most important participants in the peace conference, and who shaped the terms of the treaty the most?

fiction that commemorated the experience of soldiers on the front lines. The German writer and ex-soldier Erich Maria Remarque captured the disillusion of a generation in his novel *All Quiet on the Western Front:* "Through the years our business has been killing;—it was our first calling in life. Our knowledge of life is limited to death. What will happen afterwards? And what shall come out of us?"

That was the main question facing postwar Europe. The German novelist Thomas Mann recognized that 1918 had brought "an end of an epoch, revolution and the dawn of a new age" and that he and his fellow Germans were "living in a new and unfamiliar world." The struggle to define this new world would increasingly be conceived in terms of rival ideologies—democracy, communism, and fascism—competing for the future of Europe. The eastern autocracies had fallen with the war, but liberal democracy was soon on the decline as well. While militarism and nationalism remained strong, calls for major social reforms gained force during worldwide depression. Entire populations had been mobilized during the war, and they would remain so afterward—active participants in the age of mass politics. Europe was about to embark on two turbulent decades of rejecting and reinventing its social and political institutions. As Tomáš Masaryk, the first president of newly formed Czechoslovakia, described it, postwar Europe was "a laboratory atop a graveyard."

PEOPLE, IDEAS, AND EVENTS IN CONTEXT

- Why was **FRANZ FERDINAND** assassinated, and how did his death contribute to the outbreak of the war?
- What was the **SCHLIEFFEN PLAN**, and how was it related to the outbreak of the war?
- What was the significance of the first **BATTLE OF THE MARNE** in 1914?
- Why did the British attempt to attack the Ottoman Empire at **GALLIPOLI**?
- What was the goal of the attacking forces at **VERDUN** and the **SOMME** in 1916? What was accomplished?
- Why did many people in Russia, and especially soldiers in the Russian army, lose faith in **TSAR NICHOLAS II** of Russia?
- Who were the **BOLSHEVIKS** and the **MENSHEVIKS**, and what were their disagreements?
- How did **LENIN** make use of the **SOVIETS** in challenging the **PROVISIONAL GOVERNMENT** in Russia after the fall of the tsar?
- What policies did the **BOLSHEVIKS** follow after seizing power in Russia?
- What were **WOODROW WILSON**'s **FOURTEEN POINTS**?
- What treatment did Germany receive under the terms of the **TREATY OF VERSAILLES**?

THINKING ABOUT CONNECTIONS

- What made World War I different from previous military conflicts in Europe that had involved large numbers of states, such as the Napoleonic Wars of the early nineteenth century (see Chapter 18), or the Thirty Years' War of the seventeenth century (see Chapter 15)?
- In what way might the effects and consequences of World War I have shaped the lives of Europeans in the decades to come? How did it change the lives of various peoples from other parts of the world who were drawn into the conflict?

Before
You
Read
This
Chapter

Turmoil between the Wars

CORE OBJECTIVES

- **UNDERSTAND** the direction taken by the Russian Revolution after 1917 and the consequences of Stalin's revolution from above in the 1930s.

- **DEFINE** fascism and explain Mussolini's rise to power in Italy in the 1920s.

- **DESCRIBE** the challenges faced by the Weimar Republic and other democracies in Britain, France, and the United States after the First World War.

- **EXPLAIN** Hitler's rise to power in Germany in 1933 and the reasons for the broad support the Nazis enjoyed among many Germans.

- **UNDERSTAND** the ways that the interwar atmosphere of social and political crisis was reflected in the world of the arts, literature, and popular culture.

Käthe Kollwitz, a Berlin painter and sculptor, understood as well as anybody in Europe the terrible costs and futility of the First World War. Her youngest son, Peter, was killed on October 22, 1914, in Germany's failed attack on France. Her diary recorded the last moments she spent with him, an evening walk from the barracks on October 12, the day before his departure for the front: "It was dark, and we went arm in arm through the wood. He pointed out constellations to me, as he had done so often before." Her entry for October 30 was more succinct, a quotation from the postcard she had received from his commanding officer: "Your son has fallen." Kollwitz's pain at this loss found expression in her later work, which explored in naked terms the grief and powerlessness that she and her family had felt during the war years. Her suffering found expression, too, in a commitment to socialism, a political ideology that provided her with an antidote to the nationalism that pervaded German society during the war years and after. Kollwitz's socialism drew her to the attention of the Gestapo after the Nazis came to power in 1933, and she was fired from her position at the Academy of Art. She put up

837

with house searches and harassment but refused invitations from friends abroad to go into exile. She died in Germany in 1945, having survived long enough to see her cherished grandson, also named Peter, killed in a second war while fighting as a German soldier on the Eastern Front in Russia in 1942.

The story of Käthe Kollwitz and her family between 1914 and 1945 is only unusual for the fact that she was a well-known artist. The suffering was all too familiar to others, as was the search for new political ideologies that might save Europeans from their past. The Great War left 9 million dead in its wake and shattered the confidence that had been such a characteristic of nineteenth-century European culture. It led tragically to another world war, even more horrific than the first. Many in the interwar years shared Kollwitz's hope for a socialist or communist future, and many others turned to extremisms of the right. The result in the 1920s was a near collapse of democracy. By the late 1930s, few Western democracies remained. Even in those that did, most notably Britain, France, and the United States, regimes were frayed by the same pressures and strains that wrecked democratic governments elsewhere.

The foremost cause of democracy's decline in this period was a series of continuing disruptions in the world economy, caused first by the First World War and later, by the Great Depression of 1929–33. A second source of crisis lay in increased social conflict, exacerbated by the war. Although many hoped that these conflicts would be resolved by the peace and a renewed commitment to democratic institutions, the opposite occurred. Broad swathes of the electorate rallied to extremist political parties that promised radical transformations of nations and their cultures. Nationalism, sharpened by the war, proved a key source of discontent in its aftermath, and in Italy and Germany frustrated nationalist sentiment turned against their governments.

The most dramatic instance of democracy's decline came with the rise of new authoritarian dictatorships, especially in the Soviet Union, Italy, and Germany. The experiences of these three nations differed significantly as a result of varying historical circumstances and personalities. In each case, however, many citizens allowed themselves to be persuaded that only drastic measures could bring order

***WIDOWS AND ORPHANS* BY KÄTHE KOLLWITZ, 1919.** Kollwitz (1867–1945), a German artist and socialist activist in Berlin, lost a son in the First World War and a grandson in the Second World War. Her work poignantly displayed the effects of poverty and war on the lives of ordinary people.

from chaos. Those measures, including the elimination of parliamentary government, strict restrictions on political freedom, and increasingly virulent repression of "enemies" of the state were implemented with a combination of violence, intimidation, and propaganda. That so many citizens seemed willing to sacrifice their freedoms—or those of others—was a measure of their alienation, impatience, or desperation.

THE SOVIET UNION UNDER LENIN AND STALIN

The Russian Civil War

The Bolsheviks seized power in October 1917. They signed a separate peace with Germany in March 1918 (the Treaty of Brest-Litovsk) and then turned to consolidating their own position. The October Revolution and withdrawing from the war, however, had divided Russian society, igniting a war that turned out to be far more costly than conflict with Germany. Fury at the terms of Brest-Litovsk mobilized the Bolsheviks' enemies. Known collectively as "Whites," the Bolsheviks' opponents were only loosely bound by their common goal of removing the "Reds" from power. Their military force came mainly from supporters of the old regime, including tsarist military officers, reactionary monarchists, the former nobility, and disaffected liberal supporters of the monarchy. The Whites were joined by groups as diverse as liberal supporters of the provisional government, Mensheviks, Social Revolutionaries, and anarchist peasant bands known as "Greens" who opposed all central state power. The Bolsheviks also faced insurrections from strong nationalist movements in some parts of the former Russian Empire: Ukraine, Georgia, and the north Caucasus regions. Finally, several foreign powers, including the United States, Great Britain, and Japan, launched small but threatening interventions on the periphery of the old empire. Outside support for the Whites proved to be an insignificant threat to the Bolsheviks, but it heightened Bolshevik mistrust of the capitalist world which, in the Marxists' view, would naturally oppose the existence of the world's first "socialist" state.

The Bolsheviks eventually won the civil war because they gained greater support—or at least tacit acceptance—from the majority of the population and because they were better organized for the war effort itself. Leon Trotsky, the revolutionary hero of 1905 and 1917, became the new commissar of war and created a hierarchical, disciplined military machine that grew to some 5 million men by 1920. Trotsky's Red Army triumphed over the White armies by the end of 1920, although fighting continued into 1922. The Bolsheviks also invaded Poland and nearly reached Warsaw before being thrown back.

When the civil war was over, the country had suffered some 1 million combat casualties, several million deaths from hunger and disease caused by the war, and 100,000–300,000 executions of noncombatants as part of Red and White terror. The barbarism of the war engendered lasting hatreds within the emerging Soviet nation, especially among ethnic minorities, and it brutalized the fledgling society that came into existence under the new Bolshevik regime.

The civil war also shaped the Bolsheviks' approach to the economy. On taking power in 1917, Lenin expected to create, for the short term at least, a state-capitalist system that resembled the successful European wartime economies. The new government took control of large-scale industry, banking, and all other major capitalist concerns while allowing small-scale private economic activity, including agriculture, to continue. The civil war pushed the new government toward a more radical economic stance known as "war communism." The Bolsheviks began to req-

uisition grain from the peasantry, and they outlawed private trade in consumer goods as "speculation," militarized production facilities, and abolished money. Many believed that war communism would replace the capitalist system that had collapsed in 1917.

Such hopes were largely unfounded. War communism sustained the Bolshevik military effort but further disrupted the already war-ravaged economy. The civil war devastated Russian industry and emptied major cities. The population of Moscow fell by 50 percent between 1917 and 1920. The masses of urban workers, who had strongly supported the Bolshevik revolution, melted back into the countryside; and industrial output in 1920–21 fell to only 20 percent of prewar levels. Most devastating were the effects of war communism on agriculture. The peasants had initially benefited from the revolution when they spontaneously seized and redistributed noble lands. Nonetheless, the agricultural system was severely disrupted by the civil war, by the grain requisitioning of war communism, and by the outlawing of all private trade in grain. Large-scale famine resulted in 1921 and claimed some 5 million lives.

LENIN AND STALIN. Under Stalin, this picture was used to show his close relationship with Lenin. In fact, the photograph has been doctored. ▪ *What opportunities for propaganda and manipulation were offered by new technologies of photography and film?*

Lenin's Theses on the National and Colonial Question, 1920

The success of the Russian Revolution forced the new Soviet leadership to declare what its relationship would be with other movements for revolutionary change, including the movements for national independence that were developing in European colonies in Africa and Asia. These nationalist movements posed a dilemma, however, because many of them were led by middle-class activists, that is, by representatives of the "bourgeois" order that socialists hoped to overthrow. Lenin's Theses on the National and Colonial Question *was the outcome of a debate he had with a young Indian communist, Manabendra Nath Roy (1887–1954), and he argues here that communists might consider temporary alliances with these nationalist movements but that they should never allow them to merge with or subsume the communist movement.*

1. An abstract or formal conception of the question of equality in general and of national equality in particular is in the very nature of bourgeois democracy. Under the guise of the equality of individuals in general, bourgeois democracy proclaims the formal, legal equality of the property owner and the proletarian, the exploiter and the exploited, thereby grossly deceiving the oppressed classes. . . . The real meaning of the demand for equality consists in its being a demand for the abolition of classes.

2. As the conscious expression of the proletarian class struggle to shake off the yoke of the bourgeoisie, the Communist Party, in line with its basic task of struggling against bourgeois democracy and exposing its lies and duplicity, should not base its policy on the national question on abstract and formal principles. Instead, it should first be based on an exact appraisal of specific historical and above all economic conditions. Second, it should clearly differentiate between the interests of the oppressed classes, the toilers, the exploited, and the general concept of the so-called interests of the people, which means the interests of the ruling class. Third, it should with equal precision distinguish between the oppressed, dependent nations that do not have equal rights and the oppressor, exploiting nations that do. . . .

3. The imperialist war of 1914 . . . was justified by both sides with platitudes about national liberation and self-determination. Nonetheless, both the treaties of Brest-Litovsk and Bucharest and those of Versailles and St. Germain showed that the victorious bourgeoisie ruthlessly sets even "national" borders according to its economic interests. For the bourgeoisie even "national" borders are objects of trade . . . [T]he proletariat can achieve genuine national liberation and unity only through revolutionary struggle and by overpowering the bourgeoisie. . . .

4. It follows from these principles that the entire policy of the Communist International on the national and colonial questions must be based primarily upon uniting the proletarians and toiling masses of all nations and countries in common revolutionary struggle to overthrow the landowners and the bourgeoisie. . . .

5. The international political situation has now put the dictatorship of the proletariat on the order of the day. All events in world politics necessarily focus on one single central issue: the struggle of the world bourgeoisie against the Russian Soviet Republic, which rallies around itself both the soviet movement of the advanced workers of all countries and all national liberation movements of the colonies and oppressed peoples. . . .

6. Consequently, we cannot limit ourselves at this time merely to recognizing or proclaiming the friendship of the toilers of various nations. Rather we must pursue a policy of implementing the closest possible alliance of all national and colonial liberation movements with Soviet Russia. The forms of this alliance will be determined by the level of development of the Communist movement within the proletariat of each country or of the revolutionary liberation movement in the backward countries and among the backward nationalities.

7. Federation is a transitional form toward full unity of the toilers of all nations. Federation has already shown its usefulness in practice—in the Russian Soviet Federated Socialist Republic's relations to the other soviet republics . . . and also within the Russian Soviet Federated Socialist Republic itself toward the nationalities that formerly had neither a state nor self-government. . . .

8. . . . [W]e must strive for an ever closer federal association. We must take into consideration first, that the soviet republics, surrounded by imperialist states of the whole world that are considerably stronger militarily, cannot

possibly exist without close association with each other. Second, a close economic alliance of the soviet republics is necessary, without which it is impossible to restore the productive forces destroyed by imperialism and ensure the well-being of the toilers. Third, that there is a tendency to create a world economy unified according to a common plan, controlled by proletarians of all countries. . . .

9. . . . Communist parties must incessantly expose in their entire propaganda and agitation the continually repeated violations of the equality of nations and guaranteed rights of national minorities in all capitalist countries despite their "democratic" constitutions. In addition, it must be explained persistently that only the soviet order can ensure true national equality by uniting first the proletariat and then the whole mass of the toilers in struggle against the bourgeoisie. Moreover, all Communist parties must directly support the revolutionary movement among the nations that are dependent and do not have equal rights (for example Ireland, the Negroes in America, and so forth), and in the colonies. . . .

10. . . . The fight against . . . the most deeply rooted petty-bourgeois, nationalist prejudices (which are expressed in all possible forms, such as racism, national chauvinism, and anti-Semitism) must be given all the more priority as the question becomes more pressing of transforming the dictatorship of the proletariat from a national framework (that is, a dictatorship that exists only in one country and is incapa-

ble of carrying out an independent international policy) into an international one (that is, a dictatorship of the proletariat in at least several advanced countries, capable of exercising a decisive influence on all of world politics).

Petty-bourgeois nationalism declares that internationalism consists of the mere recognition of the equality of nations (although this recognition is strictly verbal) and considers national egoism to be sacrosanct. Proletarian internationalism, on the contrary, requires subordinating the interests of the proletarian struggle in one country to the interests of this struggle on a world scale. It also requires that the nation that has overthrown its bourgeoisie has the ability and willingness to make the greatest national sacrifices in order to overthrow international capitalism. . . .

11. With respect to the states and nations that have a more backward, predominantly feudal, patriarchal, or patriarchal-peasant character, the following points in particular must be kept in mind:

a. All Communist parties must support with deeds the revolutionary liberation movement in these countries. . . .

b. A struggle absolutely must be waged against the reactionary and medieval influence of the clergy, the Christian missions, and similar elements.

c. It is necessary to struggle against the Pan-Islamic and Pan-Asian movements and similar currents that try to link the liberation struggle against European and American imperialism with strengthening the power of Turkish and Japanese imperialism and of the

nobles, large landowners, clergy, and so forth.

d. It is especially necessary to support the peasant movement in the backward countries against the landowners and all forms and vestiges of feudalism. . . .

Questions for Analysis

1. Why does Lenin begin these theses with a critique of "bourgeois democracy" and "national liberation and self-determination"? What alternative goals does he announce?

2. Why does he say that an alliance between the communist movement and movements for anticolonial liberation is worth pursuing?

3. What possible dangers does he nevertheless identify in some of the anticolonial movements that he mentions?

Source: John Riddell, ed., *Workers of the World and Oppressed Peoples, Unite!: Proceedings and Documents of the Second Congress, 1920,* Vol. 1 (New York: Pathfinder Press, 1991), pp. 283–88.

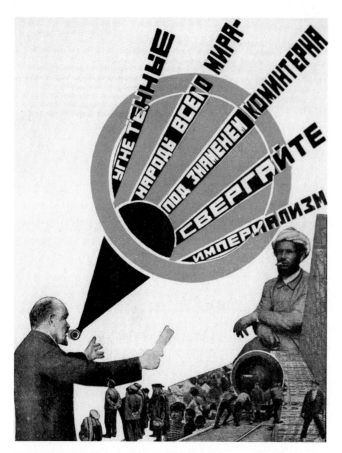

THE YOUNG GUARD. In the years following 1917, many within the Russian avant-garde wished to aid the revolution with their work. This literary magazine, which here has a constructivist-style cover, promoted Bolshevik values.

As the civil war came to a close, urban workers and soldiers became increasingly impatient with the Bolshevik regime, which had promised socialism and workers' control but had delivered something more akin to a military dictatorship. Large-scale strikes and protests broke out in late 1920, but the Bolsheviks moved swiftly and effectively to subdue the "popular revolts." In crushing dissent, the Bolshevik regime that emerged from the civil war made a clear statement that public opposition would not be tolerated.

The NEP Period

In response to these political and economic difficulties, the Bolsheviks abandoned war communism and in March 1921 embarked on a radically different course known as the New Economic Policy (NEP). The NEP reverted to the state capitalism that had been tried immediately after the revolution. The state continued to own all major industry and financial concerns, while individuals were allowed to own private property, trade freely within limits, and—most important—farm their land for their own benefit. Fixed taxes on the peasantry replaced grain requisitioning; what peasants grew beyond the tax requirements was theirs to do with as they saw fit. The Bolshevik most identified with the NEP was Nikolai Bukharin (1888–1938), a young and brilliant Marxist theoretician who argued that the Bolsheviks could best industrialize the Soviet Union by taxing private peasant economic activity. Lenin himself described the NEP as "one step backward in order to take two steps forward."

The NEP was undeniably successful in allowing Soviet agriculture to recover from the civil war; by 1924, agricultural harvests had returned to prewar levels. Peasants were largely left alone to do as they pleased, and they responded by redividing noble lands among themselves to level wealth discrepancies between rich and poor, by reinforcing traditional social structures in the countryside (especially the peasant commune), and by producing enough grain to feed the country, though they continued to use very primitive farming methods to do so. The NEP was less successful, however, in encouraging peasants to participate in markets to benefit urban areas. The result was a series of shortages in grain deliveries to cities, a situation that prompted many Bolsheviks to call for revival of the radical economic practices of war communism. The fate of these radical proposals, however, was tied to the fate of the man who would, contrary to all expectations, replace Lenin as the leader of the USSR and become one of the most notorious dictators of all time: Joseph Stalin.

Stalin and the "Revolution from Above"

Stalin's rise was swift and unpredicted. His political success was rooted in intraparty conflicts in the 1920s, but it was also closely tied to the abrupt end of the NEP period in the late 1920s and to the beginning of a massive program of social and economic modernization. This "revolution from above," as many call it, was the most rapid social and economic transformation any nation has seen in modern history. It was carried out, however, at unprecedented human cost.

Stalin (1879–1953), the son of a poor shoemaker, was a Bolshevik from the Caucasus nation of Georgia. His real name was Iosep Jughashvili. Receiving his early education in an Orthodox seminary, he participated in revolutionary activity in the Caucasus and spent many years in Siberian exile before the revolution. He was an important member of the Bolshevik party during the Russian Revolution, but

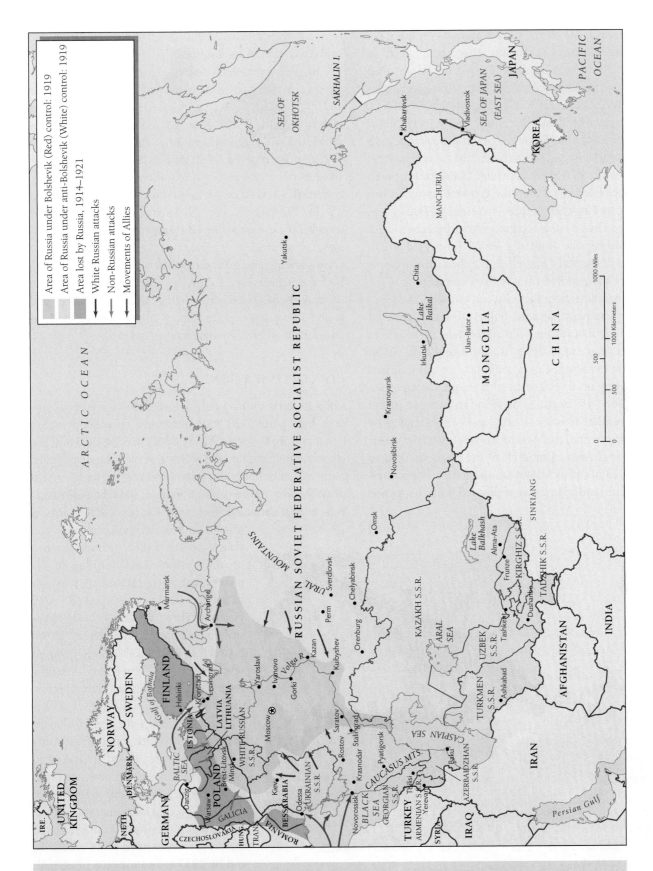

THE SOVIET UNION, 1918–1945. ■ *What were the areas lost by Russia in the Treaty of Brest-Litovsk?* ■ *How did the possession of Moscow and Leningrad (St. Petersburg) aid the Bolsheviks in their victory over the Whites?* ■ *How did the civil war of 1917–20 affect the new Soviet state?*

he was not one of the central figures and was certainly not a front runner for party leadership. After Lenin's death in 1924, the civil war hero Leon Trotsky was widely assumed to be the best candidate to succeed him. Other top Bolsheviks, however, also aspired to a leading role.

Though not a brilliant orator like Trotsky or a respected Marxist theoretician like Bukharin, Stalin was nonetheless a master political strategist, and he played the game of internal party politics almost without fault after Lenin's death. Stalin sidelined his opponents within the Bolshevik party by isolating and expelling each of them successively. Trotsky was the first to go, driven out of top party circles by a coalition of Stalin and others who, ironically, feared Trotsky's desire to take control of the party himself. Stalin then turned on his former allies and removed them in turn, culminating in the removal of Bukharin from the Politburo in 1928–29.

Stalin's campaign against Bukharin was connected to his desire to discard the NEP system and to launch an all-out industrialization drive. By the late 1920s, Stalin believed that the Soviet Union could not hope to industrialize by relying on taxes generated from small-scale peasant agriculture. He began to push for an increase in the tempo of industrialization as early as 1927, prompted by fears of falling behind the West and by the perceived threat of another world war. Almost all of the Bolshevik leaders supported Stalin's plan to step up the tempo of industrialization. But hardly anybody supported what happened next: an abrupt turn toward forced industrialization and collectivization of agriculture.

In 1927, a poor harvest caused yet another crisis in the grain-collection system. Low prices for agricultural goods and high prices for scarce industrial goods led peasants to hoard grain, resulting in food shortages in cities and difficulties in collecting taxes from the peasantry. In early 1928, Stalin ordered local officials in the distant Urals and Siberian areas to begin requisitioning grain. He soon applied this revival of war communism to the entire country. In 1929, the upper echelons of the party abruptly reversed the course set by NEP and embarked on the complete collectivization of agriculture, beginning in the major grain-growing areas. Peasants there were to be convinced, by force if necessary, to give up private farmlands. They would either join collective farms, pooling resources and giving a set portion of the harvest to the state, or work on state farms, where they were paid as laborers.

COLLECTIVIZATION

Collectivization was initially expected to be a gradual process, but in late 1929 Stalin embarked on collectivization of agriculture by force. Within a few months, the Politburo (short for political bureau, which governed the Communist party and state) began to issue orders to use force against peasants who resisted collectivization, though those orders were at first shrouded in secrecy. The process that ensued was brutal and chaotic. Local party and police officials forced peasants to give up their private land, farming implements, and livestock and to join collective farms. Peasants resisted, often violently. There were some 1,600 large-scale rebellions in the Soviet Union between 1929 and 1933; some involved several thousand people, and quelling them required military intervention, including the use of artillery. Peasants also resisted collectivization by slaughtering their livestock instead of turning it over to the farms, a loss that hampered agricultural production for years to follow. Sensing a possible crisis, Stalin called the process to a temporary halt in early 1930 but soon thereafter ordered the process to proceed more gradually, and by 1935 collectivization of agriculture was complete in most areas of the Soviet Union.

WINTER DEPORTATIONS, 1929–1930. Ukrainian families charged with being kulaks were deported from their homes because of their refusal to join Stalin's collective farming plan. Many of the evicted families were shipped north by train to the Arctic, where they perished owing to the lack of adequate food and shelter.

To facilitate collectivization, Stalin also launched an all-out attack on peasants designated as *kulaks* (a derogatory term for well-to-do farmers, literally meaning "tight-fisted ones"). Most kulaks, though, were not any better off than their neighbors, and the word became one of many terms for peasants hostile to collectivization. Between 1929 and 1933, some one and a half million peasants were uprooted, dispossessed of their property, and resettled from their farmlands to either inhospitable reaches of the Soviet east and north or to poor farmland closer to their original homes. The land and possessions of these unfortunate peasants were distributed to collective farms or, just as often, to the local officials and peasants participating in the liquidation process. The liquidation of kulaks as a class magnified the disruptive effects of agricultural collectivization, and the two together produced one of the most devastating famines in modern European history. Peasants who were forced into collective farms had little incentive to produce extra food, and exiling many of the most productive peasants not surprisingly weakened the agricultural system. In 1932–33, famine spread across the southern

region of the Soviet Union. This was the most productive agricultural area in the country, and the famine that struck there was thus particularly senseless. The 1933 famine cost some 3 million to 5 million lives. During the famine, the Bolsheviks maintained substantial grain reserves in other parts of the country, enough to save many hundreds of thousands of lives at a minimum, but they refused to send this grain to the affected areas, preferring instead to seal off famine-stricken regions and allow people to starve. Grain reserves were instead sold overseas for hard currency and stockpiled in case of war. After 1935, there would never again be any large-scale resistance to Soviet power in the countryside.

The Five-Year Plans

In Stalin's view, collectivization provided the resources for the other major aspect of his revolution from above: a rapid campaign of forced industrialization. The road map for this industrialization process was the first Five-Year Plan (1928–1932), an ambitious set of goals that Stalin and his cohorts drew up in 1927 and continued to revise upward. The plan called for truly herculean industrialization efforts, and its results rank as one of the most stunning periods of economic growth the modern world has ever seen. Soviet statistics boasted of annual growth rates of 20 percent a year. Even the more cautious Western estimates of 14 percent annual growth were remarkable, given the worldwide depression elsewhere. The Bolsheviks built entirely new industries in entirely new cities. The factory town of Magnitogorsk, for example, emerged from absolutely barren, uninhabited steppes in 1929 to become a steel-producing factory town of some 250,000 residents in 1932; at least in scale, it rivaled anything that the West had built. The industrialization drive transformed the nation's landscape and population as well. Cities such as Moscow and Leningrad doubled in size in the early 1930s, while new cities sprang up across the country. In 1926, only one-fifth of the population lived in towns. Fifteen years later, in 1939, roughly a third did. The urban population had grown from 26 million to 56 million in under fifteen years. The Soviet Union was well on its way to becoming an urban, industrial society.

This rapid industrialization came, however, at enormous human cost. Many large-scale projects were carried out with prison labor, especially in the timber and mining industries. The labor camp system, known as the *gulag*, became a central part of the Stalinist economic system. People were arrested and sent to camps on a bewildering

"WE SMITE THE LAZY WORKERS!" This Russian propaganda poster was used to mobilize workers to the "Five-Year Plan."

Stalin's Industrialization of the Soviet Union

How did the Soviet people experience Stalin's industrialization drive? New archives have helped historians glimpse what the common people lived through and how they responded. The first excerpt is a speech Stalin gave at a Conference of Managers of Socialist Industry in 1931. In his usual style, he invoked fears of Soviet backwardness and Russian nationalism while summoning all to take up the task of industrial production.

The letters in the second selection come from several hundred that workers and peasants sent to Soviet newspapers and authorities recounting their experiences and offering their opinions. Both of the ones printed here were sent to the Soviet paper Pravda.

"The Tasks of Business Executives"

It is sometimes asked whether it is not possible to slow down the tempo somewhat, to put a check on the movement. No, comrades, it is not possible! The tempo must not be reduced! On the contrary, we must increase it as much as is within our powers and possibilities. This is dictated to us by our obligations to the workers and peasants of the USSR. This is dictated to us by our obligations to the working class of the whole world.

To slacken the tempo would mean falling behind. And those who fall behind get beaten. But we do not want to be beaten. No, we refuse to be beaten. One feature of the history of old Russia was the continual beatings she suffered because of her backwardness. She was beaten by the Mongol khans. She was beaten by the Turkish beys.... She was beaten by the British and French capitalists. She was beaten by the Japanese barons. All beat her—for her backwardness: for military backwardness, for cultural backwardness, for political backwardness, for industrial backwardness, for agricultural backwardness....

We are fifty or a hundred years behind the advanced countries. We must make good this distance in ten years. Either we do it, or we shall be crushed....

In ten years at most we must make good the distance which separates us from the advanced capitalist countries. We have all the 'objective' possibilities for this. The only thing lacking is the ability to take proper advantage of these possibilities. And that depends on us. *Only* on us!... It is time to put an end to the rotten policy of non-interference in production. It is time to adopt a new policy, a policy adapted to the present times—the policy of interfering in everything. If you are a factory manager, then interfere in all the affairs of the factory, look into everything, let nothing escape you, learn and learn again. Bolsheviks must master technique. It is time Bolsheviks themselves became experts....

array of charges, ranging from petty criminal infractions to contact with foreigners to having the ill fortune to be born of bourgeois or kulak parents. The camp system spread throughout the USSR in the 1930s: by the end of the decade, roughly 3.6 million people were incarcerated by the regime. This army of prisoners was used to complete the most arduous and dangerous industrialization tasks, such as the construction of the Moscow–White Sea canal. To save money, the canal connecting Moscow to the seaports of the north was constructed without the use of any machinery. It was literally dug by hand, with human labor used to power everything from conveyor belts to pile drivers. Tens of thousands of individuals lost their lives during construction. One of Stalin's pet projects, it never functioned properly, was too shallow, and froze over in winter. It was bombed early in the Second World War.

The economic system created during this revolution from above was also fraught with structural problems that would plague the Soviet Union for its entire history. The command economy, with each year's production levels entirely planned in advance in Moscow, never functioned in a rational way. Heavy industry was always favored over

There are no fortresses which Bolsheviks cannot capture. We have assumed power. We have built up a huge socialist industry. We have swung the middle peasants to the path of socialism. . . . What remains to be done is not so much: to study technique, to master science. And when we have done that we will develop a tempo of which we dare not even dream at present.

Source: Joseph Stalin, "The Tasks of Business Executives" (speech given at the First All-Union Conference of Managers of Socialist Industry, February 4, 1931), as cited in Richard Sakwa, *The Rise and Fall of the Soviet Union, 1917–1991* (New York: 1999), pp. 187–88.

Stalin's Industrial Development: The View from Below

It should not be forgotten that many millions of workers are participating in the building of socialism. A horse with its own strength can drag seventy-five poods,* but its owner has loaded it with a hundred poods, and in addition he's fed it poorly. No matter how much he uses the whip, it still won't be able to move the cart.

This is also true for the working class. They've loaded it with socialist competition, shock work, over-fulfilling the industrial and financial plan, and so forth. A worker toils seven hours, not ever leaving his post, and this is not all he does. Afterward he sits in meetings or else attends classes for an hour and a half or two in order to increase his skill level, and if he doesn't do these things, then he's doing things at home. And

what does he live on? One hundred fifty grams of salted mutton, he will make soup without any of the usual additives, neither carrots, beets, flour, nor salt pork. What kind of soup do you get from this? Mere "dishwater."

—B. N. Kniazev, Tula, Sept. 1930.

Comrade Editor, Please give me an answer. Do the local authorities have the right to forcibly take away the only cow of industrial and office workers? What is more, they demand a receipt showing that the cow was handed over voluntarily and they threaten you by saying if you don't do this, they will put you in prison for failure to fulfill the meat procurement. How can you live when the cooperative distributes only black bread, and at the market goods have the prices

of 1919 and 1920? Lice have eaten us to death, and soap is given only to railroad workers. From hunger and filth we have a massive outbreak of spotted fever.

—Anonymous, from Aktybinsk, Kazakhstan

*A pood is a Russian unit of weight, equal to 36.11 pounds.

Source: Lewis Siegelbaum and Andrei Sokolov, *Stalinism as a Way of Life: A Narrative in Documents* (New Haven, CT: 2000), pp. 39–41.

Questions for Analysis

1. What are Stalin's priorities?

2. What images does Stalin use to capture his audience's attention?

3. How did the Soviet people experience Stalin's industrialization drive?

light industry, and the emphasis on quantity made quality practically meaningless. A factory that was charged with producing a certain number of pairs of shoes, for example, could cut costs by producing all one style and size. The consumer would be left with useless goods, but the producer would fulfill the plan. Stalin's industrialization drive did transform the country from an agrarian nation to a world industrial power in the space of a few short years, but in the longer run, the system would become an economic disaster.

The Stalin revolution also produced fundamental cultural and economic changes. The revolution from

above altered the face of Soviet cities and the working class populating them. New cities were largely made up of first-generation peasants who brought their rural traditions to the cities with them, changing the fragile urban culture that had existed during the 1920s. Women, too, entered the urban workforce in increasing numbers in the 1930s—women went from 20 percent to almost 40 percent of the workforce in one decade, and in light industry they made up two-thirds of the labor force by 1940.

At the same time, Stalin promoted a sharply conservative shift in all areas of culture and society. In art, the radical

"IMPERIALISTS CANNOT STOP THE SUCCESS OF THE FIVE-YEAR PLAN!" ■ *Did propaganda like this also appeal to Russian nationalist pride?*

the double burden of familial and wage labor to support Stalin's version of Soviet society. All areas of Soviet cultural and social policy experienced similar reversals.

The Great Terror

The apogee of Stalinist repression came with the "Great Terror" of 1937–38, which left nearly a million people dead and as many as one and a half million more in labor camps. As Stalin consolidated his personal dictatorship over the country, he eliminated enemies—real and imagined—along with individuals and groups he considered superfluous to the new Soviet society. As we have seen, repression was central to the Stalinist system from the early 1930s, yet the years 1937–38 brought a qualitative and quantitative change—a whirlwind of mass repression unprecedented in scale.

The Terror was aimed at various categories of internal "enemies," from the top to the very bottom of Soviet society. Former and current political elites were perhaps the most visible victims. The top level of the Bolshevik party itself was purged almost completely; some 100,000 party members were removed, most facing prison sentences or execution. Many top party officials, including Bukharin, were condemned at carefully staged show trials and then shot. The purge also struck—with particular ferocity—nonparty elites, industrial managers, and intellectuals. Between 1937 and 1938, Stalin purged the military of people he deemed potential threats, arresting some 40,000 officers and shooting at least 10,000. These purges disrupted the government and the economy but allowed Stalin to promote a new, young cadre of officials who had no experience in the pre-Stalinist era and who owed their careers, if not their lives, to Stalin personally. Whole ethnic groups were viewed with suspicion, including Poles, Ukrainians, Lithuanians, Latvians, Koreans, and others with supposed cross-border ties that, in Stalin's mind, represented a national security threat. From the bottom, some 200,000–300,000 "dekulakized" peasants, petty criminals, and other social misfits were arrested, and many shot.

The Great Terror remains one of the most puzzling aspects of Stalin's path to dictatorial power. The Terror succeeded, with a certain paranoid logic, in solidifying Stalin's personal control over all aspects of social and political life in the Soviet Union, but it did so by destroying the most talented elements in Soviet society.

The results of the Stalin revolution were profound. No other regime in the history of Europe had ever attempted to reorder completely the politics, economy, and society of a major nation. The Soviets had done so in a mere ten

modernism of the 1920s was crushed by socialist realism, a deadening aesthetic that celebrated the drive toward socialism and left no room for experimentation. Family policy and gender roles underwent a similar reversal. Early Bolshevik activists had promoted a utopian attempt to rebuild one of the basic structures of prerevolutionary society—the family—and to create a genuinely new proletarian social structure. The Bolsheviks in the 1920s legalized divorce, expelled the Orthodox Church from marriage ceremonies, and legalized abortion. Stalin abandoned these ideas of communist familial relations in favor of efforts to strengthen traditional family ties: divorce became more difficult, abortion was outlawed in 1936 except in cases that threatened the life of the mother, and homosexuality was declared a criminal offense. State subsidies and support for mothers, which were progressive for the time, could not change the reality that Soviet women were increasingly forced to carry years. By 1939, private manufacturing and trade had been almost entirely abolished. Factories, mines, railroads, and public utilities were exclusively owned by the state. Stores were either government enterprises or cooperatives in which consumers owned shares. Agriculture had been almost completely socialized. The decade was not entirely grim, however. There were advances, especially in the area of social reform. Illiteracy was reduced from nearly 50 percent to about 20 percent, and higher education was made available to increasingly large numbers. Government assistance for working mothers and free hospitalization did a great deal to raise the national standard of health. The society that emerged from this terrible decade was industrial, more urban than rural, and more modern than traditional. But it was a society badly brutalized in the process, one in which many of the most productive peasants, gifted intellectuals, and experienced economic and social elites were purged from society in the name of total dictatorial power. The USSR that emerged from this tumultuous period would barely be able to withstand the immense strains placed on it when the Germans struck less than three years after the end of the Terror.

THE EMERGENCE OF FASCISM IN ITALY

Like many European nations, Italy emerged from the First World War as a democracy in distress. Italy was on the winning side, but the war had cost nearly 700,000 Italian lives and over $15 billion. Moreover, Italy had received secret promises of specific territorial gains during the war, only to find those promises withdrawn when they conflicted with principles of self-determination. Italian claims to the west coast of the Adriatic, for instance, were denied by Yugoslavia. Italy received most of the Austrian territories it demanded, but many maintained that these were inadequate rewards for their sacrifices. Groups of militant nationalists seized Fiume, a port city on the Adriatic, and held it for a year before being disbanded by the Italian army. At first, the nationalists blamed the "mutilated victory" on President Wilson, but after a short time they turned on their own rulers and what they considered the weaknesses of parliamentary democracy.

Italy had long-standing problems that were made worse by the war. Since unification, the Italian nation had been rent by an unhealthy economic split—divided into a prosperous industrialized north and a poor agrarian south. Social conflict over land, wages, and local power caused friction in the countryside as well as in urban centers. Governments were often seen as corrupt, indecisive, and

defeatist. This was the background for the more immediate problems that Italy faced after the war.

Inflation and unemployment were perhaps the most destructive effects of the war. Inflation produced high prices, speculation, and profiteering. And though normally wages would have risen also, the postwar labor market was glutted by returning soldiers. Furthermore, business elites were shaken by strikes, which became increasingly large and frequent, and by the closing of foreign markets. The parliamentary government that was set up after the war failed to ease these dire conditions, and Italians wanted radical reforms. For the working class, this meant socialism. In 1919, the socialists won about a third of the seats in the Chamber of Deputies. The movement grew increasingly radical: in 1920, the socialist and anarchist workers seized scores of factories, most in the metallurgy sector, and tried to run them for the benefit of the workers themselves. In the countryside, many peasants had no land at all, and worked for wages as rural laborers on large estates. Demands for land reform grew more militant. In some rural areas, so-called Red Leagues tried to break up large estates and force landlords to reduce their rents. In all these actions, the model of the Russian Revolution, although it was only vaguely understood, encouraged the development of local radicalism. In large numbers, voters abandoned the poorly organized parties of the center and the moderate left. They supported two more radical groups: the Socialists and the Catholic People's party (newly formed with the pope's blessing), which appealed to the common people, especially in the countryside. Neither party preached revolution, yet both urged wide-ranging social and economic reforms.

The rising radical tide, especially seen against the backdrop of the Bolshevik revolution, worried other social groups. Industrialists and landowners feared for their property. Small shopkeepers and white-collar workers—social groups that did not think the working-class movement supported their interests—found themselves alienated by business elites on the one hand and by apparently revolutionary radicals on the other. The threat from the left provoked a strong surge to the right. Fascism appeared in the form of vigilante groups breaking up strikes, fighting with workers in the streets, or ousting the Red Leagues from lands occupied in the countryside.

The Rise of Mussolini

"I am fascism," said Benito Mussolini, and indeed, the success of the Italian fascist movement depended heavily on his leadership. Mussolini (1883–1945) was the son of a socialist blacksmith. His mother was a schoolteacher, and he deferentially followed in her footsteps. But he was restless and dissatisfied, soon leaving Italy for further study in Switzerland. There he gave part of his time to his books and the rest to writing articles for socialist newspapers. Expelled from the country for fomenting strikes, he returned to Italy, where he became a journalist and eventually the editor of *Avanti,* the leading socialist daily.

Mussolini did not hold to any particular doctrine, and he reversed himself at several points. When war broke out in August 1914, Mussolini insisted that Italy should remain neutral. He had scarcely adopted this position when he began urging participation on the Allied side. Deprived of his position as the editor of *Avanti,* he founded a new paper, *Il Popolo d'Italia,* and dedicated its columns to arousing enthusiasm for war.

As early as October 1914, Mussolini had organized groups, called fasci, to help drum up support for the war. Members of the fasci were young idealists, fanatical nationalists. After the war, these groups formed the base of Mus-

EUROPE IN 1923. ▪ *Which countries and empires lost territories after the First World War, and with what consequences? ▪ How did the Russian Revolution change European politics? ▪ What problems arose in the central and eastern European nations created after the First World War?*

solini's fascist movement. (The word *fascism* derives from the Latin *fasces*: an ax surrounded by a bundle of sticks that represented the authority of the Roman state. The Italian *fascio* means "group" or "band.") In 1919, Mussolini drafted the original platform of the Fascist party. It had several surprising elements, such as universal suffrage (including woman), an eight-hour workday, and a tax on inheritances. A new platform, adopted in 1920, abandoned all references to economic reforms. Neither platform earned the fascists much political success.

What the fascists lacked in political support, they made up for in aggressive determination. They gained the respect of the middle class and landowners and intimidated many others by force-fully repressing radical movements of industrial workers and peasants. They attacked socialists, often physically, and succeeded in taking over some local governments. As the national regime weakened, Mussolini's coercive politics made him look like a solution to the absence of leadership. In September 1922, he began to negotiate with other parties and the king for fascist participation in government. On October 28, an army of about 50,000 fascist militia, in black-shirted uniforms, marched into Rome and occupied the capital. The premier resigned, and the following day the king, Victor Emmanuel III, reluctantly invited Mussolini to form a cabinet. Without firing a shot the Black Shirts had gained control of the Italian government. The explanation of their success is to be found less in the strength of the fascist movement itself than in the Italian disappointments after the war and the weakness of the older governing classes.

The parliamentary system had folded under pressure. And though Mussolini had "legally" been granted his power, he immediately began to establish a one-party dictatorship. The doctrines of Italian fascism had three components. The first was statism. The state was declared to incorporate every interest and every loyalty of its members. There was to be "nothing above the state, nothing outside the state, nothing against the state." The second was nationalism. Nationhood was the highest form of society, with a life and a soul of its own, transcending the individuals who composed it. The third was militarism. Nations that did not expand would eventually wither and die. Fascists believed that war ennobled man and regenerated sluggish and decadent peoples.

MUSSOLINI REVIEWS A FASCIST YOUTH PARADE. Mobilizing youth was central to fascism and Nazism; it demonstrated the vigor of the movements.

Mussolini began to rebuild Italy in accordance with these principles. The first step was to change electoral laws so they granted his party solid parliamentary majorities and to intimidate the opposition. He then moved to close down parliamentary government and other parties entirely. He abolished the cabinet system and all but extinguished the powers of the Parliament. He made the Fascist party an integral part of the Italian constitution. Mussolini assumed the dual position of prime minister and party leader (*duce*), and he used the party's militia to eliminate his enemies by intimidation and violence. Mussolini's government also controlled the police, muzzled the press, and censored academic activity.

Meanwhile, Mussolini preached the end of class conflict and its replacement by national unity. He began to reorganize the economy and labor, taking away the power of the country's labor movement. The Italian economy was placed under the management of twenty-two corporations, each responsible for a major industrial enterprise. In each corporation were representatives of trade unions, whose members were organized by the Fascist party, the employers, and the government. Together, the members of these corporations were given the task of determining working conditions, wages, and prices. It is not surprising, however, that the decisions of these bodies were closely supervised by the government and favored the position of management. Indeed, the government quickly aligned with big business, creating more of a corrupt bureaucracy than a revolutionary economy.

Mussolini secured some working-class assent with state-sponsored programs, including massive public-works projects, library building, paid vacations for workers, and social security. In 1929, he settled Italy's sixty-year-old conflict with the Roman Catholic Church. He signed a treaty that granted independence to the papal residence in the Vatican City and established Roman Catholicism as the official religion of the state. The treaty also guaranteed religious education in the nation's schools and made religious marriage ceremonies mandatory.

In fact, Mussolini's regime did much to maintain the status quo. Party officers exercised some political supervision over bureaucrats yet did not infiltrate the bureaucracy in significant numbers. Moreover, Mussolini remained on friendly terms with the elites who had assisted his rise to power. Whatever he might proclaim about the distinctions between fascism and capitalism, the economy of Italy remained dependent on private enterprise.

The Italian dictator boasted that fascism had pulled the country back from economic chaos. Like other European economies, the Italian economy did improve in the late 1920s. The regime created the appearance of efficiency, and Mussolini's admirers famously claimed that he had at last "made the trains run on time." Fascism, however, did little to lessen Italy's plight during the worldwide depression of the 1930s.

GERMAN WOMEN SMOKING CIGARS DURING THE WEIMAR REPUBLIC, 1927. The Weimar years were marked by a new atmosphere of cultural experimentation, especially in German cities. The traumatic experience of World War 1, which destroyed so many families and overturned the social and political order, also made prewar social conventions about sex, marriage, and gender seem quaint and outdated. This scene, in which women are smoking and drinking in public, while wearing masculine hairstyles and casually demonstrating their affection for one another was almost unimaginable in 1910. In the 1920s, however, such scenes were common enough to provoke controversy and scandal, becoming fodder for the media, and providing material for best-selling novels. Similar debates over the "New Woman" of the 1920s took place in other European countries, and Hitler and the Nazi party used such images in their campaign to discredit Weimar society as "degenerate."

Like Nazism later, fascism had contradictory elements. It sought to restore traditional authority and, at the same time, mobilize all of Italian society for economic and nationalist purposes—a process that inevitably undercut older authorities. It created new authoritarian organizations and activities that comported with these goals: exercise programs to make the young fit and mobilized, youth camps, awards to mothers of large families, political rallies, and parades in small towns in the countryside. Activities like these offered people a feeling of political involvement though they no longer enjoyed political rights. This mobilized but essentially passive citizenship was a hallmark of fascism.

WEIMAR GERMANY

On November 9, 1918—two days before the armistice ending the First World War—a massive and largely unexpected uprising in Berlin resulted in the kaiser's abdication and the

birth of a new German republic. The leader of the new government was Friedrich Ebert, a member of the Social Democratic party (SPD) in the Reichstag. The revolution spread quickly. By the end of the month, councils of workers and soldiers controlled hundreds of German cities. The "November Revolution" was fast and far reaching, though not as revolutionary as many middle- and upper-class conservatives feared. The majority of socialists steered a cautious, democratic course: they wanted reforms but were willing to leave much of the existing imperial bureaucracy intact. Above all, they wanted a popularly elected national assembly to draft a constitution for the new republic.

Two months passed, however, before elections could be held—a period of crisis that verged on civil war. The revolutionary movement that had brought the SPD to power now threatened it. Independent socialists and a nascent Communist party wanted radical reforms, and in December 1918 and January 1919, they staged armed uprisings in the streets of Berlin. Fearful of a Bolshevik-style revolution, the Social Democratic government turned against its former allies and sent militant bands of workers and volunteers to crush the uprisings. During the conflict, the government's fighters murdered Rosa Luxemburg and Karl Liebknecht—two German communist leaders who became instant martyrs. Violence continued into 1920, creating a lasting bitterness among groups on the left.

More important, the revolutionary aftermath of the war gave rise to bands of militant counterrevolutionaries. Veterans and other young nationalists joined so-called *Freikorps* (free corps). Such groups developed throughout the country, drawing as many as several hundred thousand members. Former army officers who led these militias continued their war experience by fighting against Bolsheviks, Poles, and communists. The politics of the Freikorps were fiercely right wing. Anti-Marxist, anti-Semitic, and antiliberal, they openly opposed the new German republic and its parliamentary democracy. Many of the early Nazi leaders had fought in the First World War and participated in Freikorps units.

Germany's new government—known as the Weimar Republic (*VY-mahr*) for the city in which its constitution was drafted—rested on a coalition of socialists, Catholic centrists, and liberal democrats, a necessary compromise since no single party won a majority of the votes in the January 1919 election. The Weimar constitution was based on the values of parliamentary liberalism and set up an open, pluralistic framework for German democracy. Through a series of compromises, the constitution established universal suffrage (for both women and men) and a bill of rights that guaranteed not only civil liberties but also a range of social entitlements. On paper, at least, the revolutionary movement had succeeded.

Yet the Weimar government lasted just over a decade. By 1930, it was in crisis, and in 1933 it collapsed. What happened? Many of Weimar's problems were born from Germany's defeat in the First World War, which was not only devastating but also humiliating. Many Germans soon latched onto rumors that the army hadn't actually been defeated in battle but instead had been stabbed in the back by socialists and Jewish leaders in the German government. Army officers cultivated this story even before the war was over; and though untrue, it helped salve the wounded pride of German patriots. In the next decade, those in search of a scapegoat also blamed the republican regime, which had signed the Versailles treaty. What was needed, many critics argued, was authoritative leadership to guide the nation and regain the world's respect.

The Treaty of Versailles magnified Germany's sense of dishonor. Germany was forced to cede a tenth of its territory, accept responsibility for the war, and slash the size of its army to a mere hundred thousand men—a punishment

HYPERINFLATION. German children use stacks of money as toys. In July 1922, the American dollar was worth 670 German marks; in November 1923 it was worth 4,210,500,000,000.
■ *How might hyperinflation have affected attitudes in Germany toward the Weimar Republic's government?*

that riled the politically powerful corps of officers. Most important, the treaty saddled Germany with punitive reparations. Negotiating the $33 billion debt created problems for all the governments involved; it provoked anger from the German public and, in a global economy, had unintended effects on the recipients as well as the debtors. Some opponents of the reparations settlement urged the government not to pay, arguing that the enormous sum would doom Germany's economy. In 1924, Germany accepted a new schedule of reparations designed by an international committee headed by the American financier Charles G. Dawes. At the same time, the German chancellor Gustav Stresemann moved Germany toward a foreign policy of cooperation and rapprochement that lasted throughout the 1920s. Many German people, however, continued to resent reparations, Versailles, and the government that refused to repudiate the treaty.

Major economic crises also played a central role in Weimar's collapse. The first period of emergency occurred in the early 1920s. Still reeling from wartime inflation, the government was hard-pressed for revenues. Funding postwar demobilization programs, social welfare, and reparations forced the government to continue to print money. Inflation became nearly unstoppable. By 1923, as one historian writes, the economic situation had "acquired an almost surrealistic quality." A pound of potatoes cost about 9 marks in January, 40 million marks by October. Beef went for almost 2 trillion marks per pound. The government finally took drastic measures to stabilize the currency in 1924, but millions of Germans had already been ruined. For those on fixed incomes, such as pensioners and stockholders, savings and security had vanished. Middle-class employees, farmers, and workers were all hard hit by the economic crisis, and many of them abandoned the traditional political parties in protest. In their eyes, the parties that claimed to represent the middle classes had created the problems and proved incapable of fixing them.

Beginning in 1925, however, Germany's economy and government seemed to be recovering. By borrowing money, the country was able to make its scaled-down reparations payments and to earn money by selling cheap exports. In large cities, socialist municipal governments sponsored building projects that included schools, hospitals, and low-cost worker housing. But such economic and political stability was misleading. The economy remained dependent on large infusions of capital from the United States set up by the Dawes Plan as part of the effort to settle reparations. That dependence made the German economy especially vulnerable to American economic developments. When the U.S. stock market crashed in 1929, beginning the Great Depression (see below), capital flow to Germany virtually stopped.

The Great Depression pushed Weimar's political system to the breaking point. In 1929, there were 2 million unemployed; in 1932, 6 million. In those three years production dropped by 44 percent. Artisans and small shopkeepers lost both status and income. Farmers fared even worse, having never recovered from the crisis of the early 1920s. Peasants staged mass demonstrations against the government's agricultural policies even before the depression hit. For white-collar and civil service employees, the depression meant lower salaries, poor working conditions, and a constant threat of unemployment. Burdened with plummeting tax revenues and spiraling numbers of Germans in need of relief, the government repeatedly cut welfare benefits, which further demoralized the electorate. Finally, the crisis created an opportunity for Weimar's opponents. Many leading industrialists supported a return to authoritarian government, and they were allied with equally conservative landowners, united by a desire for protective economic policies to stimulate the sale of domestic goods and foodstuffs. Those conservative forces wielded considerable power in

Germany, beyond the control of the government. So too did the army and the civil service, which were staffed with opponents of the republic—men who rejected the principles of parliamentary democracy and international cooperation that Weimar represented.

HITLER AND THE NATIONAL SOCIALISTS

National Socialism in Germany emerged out of the bitterness of the defeat in the First World War, but Adolf Hitler's political party did not gain mass support until the economic crisis caused by the Depression in 1929 led many Germans to give up on the traditional political parties. At each stage in the movement's development, Hitler found a way to capitalize on the mistakes of his opponents and draw more support to his cause.

Adolf Hitler was born in 1889 in Austria, not Germany. The son of a petty customs official in the Austrian civil service, Hitler dropped out of school and went to Vienna in 1909 to become an artist. That failed. He was rejected by the academy and forced to eke out a dismal existence doing manual labor and painting cheap watercolors in Vienna. Meanwhile, he developed the violent political prejudices that would become the guiding principles of the Nazi regime. He ardently admired the Austrian politicians preaching anti-Semitism, anti-Marxism, and pan-Germanism. When war broke out in 1914, Hitler was among the jubilant crowds in the streets of Munich; and though he was an Austrian citizen, he enlisted in the German army, where he claimed to have finally found meaning in his life. After the war, he joined the newly formed German Workers' party, whose name changed in 1920 to the National Socialist Workers' party (abbreviated in popular usage to Nazi). The Nazis were but one among many small, militant groups of disaffected Germans devoted to racial nationalism and to the overthrow of the Weimar Republic. They grew out of the political milieu that refused to accept the defeat or the November Revolution and that blamed both on socialists and Jews.

Ambitious and outspoken, Hitler quickly moved up the rather short ladder of party leadership as a talented stump orator. By 1921, he was the *Führer*—the leader—to his followers in Bavaria. The wider public saw him as a "vulgar demagogue"—if they noticed him at all. In November 1923, during the worst days of the inflation crisis, the Nazis made a failed attempt (the Beer Hall Putsch in Munich) at overthrowing the state government of Bavaria. Hitler spent the next seven months in prison, where he wrote his autobiography and political manifesto *Mein Kampf* (*myn KAHMPF;*

Past and Present

The Great Depression and Today's Economy

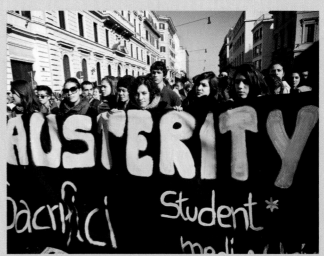

What parallels can one see between the history of the Great Depression in the 1930s and the situation in the world's economy today, after the crisis of 2008? In both cases, the debate has focused on whether or not financial markets can operate without significant government oversight, and what responsibilities the government has to alleviate the pain of those whose jobs or wages are cut as a result of economic collapse. Left, in 1930s France, laborers battle police over wage cuts; right, in 2011, protesters demonstrate in Italy against the government's "austerity" policy, which saw reductions in pension benefits and job cuts.

 Watch related author interview on StudySpace
wwnorton.com/web/westernciv18

"*My Struggle*") in 1924. Combining anti-Semitism with anti-communism, the book set out at great length the popular theory that Germany had been betrayed by its enemies and that the country needed strong leadership to regain international prominence. The failed 1923 putsch proved an eye-opening experience for Hitler; he recognized that the Nazis would have to play politics if they wanted to gain power. Released from prison in 1924, Hitler resumed leadership of the party. In the next five years, he consolidated his power over a growing membership of ardent supporters. Actively cultivating the image of the Nazi movement as a crusade against Marxism, capitalism, and Jews, he portrayed himself as the heroic savior of the German people.

An equally important factor in Hitler's rise to power was the Nazis' ambitious and unprecedented campaign program. In the "inflation election" of 1924, the Nazis polled 6.6 percent of the vote as a protest party at the radical

fringe. With the economic stabilization of the mid-1920s, their meager share dropped to below 3 percent. But during this time of seeming decline, the Nazis were building an extensive organization of party activists that helped lay the foundation for the party's electoral gains later.

After 1928, political polarization between the right and left worked to Hitler's advantage and made it impossible for the Weimar government to put together a coalition that could support the continuation of democracy in Germany. Alienated voters, especially in rural areas, deserted the traditional political parties. The Nazis quickly learned how to benefit from this splintering of the electorate. Having failed to win over the German working class from the left, the Nazis stepped up their efforts to attract members of the rural and urban middle classes. Guided by their chief propagandist, Joseph Goebbels, the party hammered home its critique of Weimar society: its parliamentary system, the power of the left and the labor movement, liberal moral codes, women wearing "decadent" flapper fashions, and "cosmopolitan" (Jewish or insufficiently nationalist) movies such as *All Quiet on the Western Front*. Presenting itself as young and dynamic, the Nazis built a national profile as an alternative to the parties of middle-class conservatives. By 1930, they were better funded and better organized than ever, winning 18.3 percent of the vote.

Who voted for the Nazis? The Nazis polled highly with small property holders and the rural middle class long before the depression. Other segments of the middle class—notably pensioners, the elderly, and war widows—came to support the Nazis during the economic crisis, when they feared reduction of insurance or pension benefits and when the older conservative parties failed to meet their needs. The Nazis also courted the traditionally elitist civil service. And though they failed to win votes from industrial workers, the Nazis found some of their strongest support among workers in handicrafts and small-scale manufacturing.

In 1930, the Nazi party won 107 of 577 seats in the Reichstag, second only to the Social Democrats, who controlled 143. No party could gain a majority. No governing

NAZISM AND THE RURAL MYTH. To stress the rural roots of Aryan Germany, Hitler appeared in lederhosen in the 1920s.
- *Which social groups in Germany were explicitly excluded by this myth?*

coalition was possible without Nazi support. And the Nazis refused to join any cabinet that was not headed by Hitler. The chancellor, Heinrich Brüning of the Catholic Center party, continued to govern by emergency decrees, but his deflationary economic policies were disastrous. Industrial production continued to crash and unemployment continued to climb. In 1932, Hitler ran for president and narrowly lost, although he staged an unprecedented campaign by airplane, visiting twenty-one cities in six days. When another parliamentary election was called in July 1932, the Nazis won 37.4 percent of the vote, which, though not a majority, was a significant plurality. The Nazis could claim that they were the party able to draw support across class, geographic, and generational lines. They benefited from their position as outsiders, untainted by involvement in unpopular parliamentary coalitions. Indeed, the failure of the traditional parties was key to the success of the Nazis.

Despite its electoral success in 1932, the Nazi party had not won a majority; Hitler was not in power. Instead, Hitler was appointed chancellor in January 1933 by President Hindenburg, who hoped to create a conservative coalition government by bringing the Nazis into line with the less radical parties. Hindenburg and others in the government had underestimated the Nazis' power and popularity. Legally installed in office, Hitler immediately made the most of it. When a Dutch anarchist with links to the Communist party set fire to the Reichstag on the night of February 27, Hitler seized the opportunity to suspend civil rights "as a defensive measure against communist acts of violence." He convinced Hindenburg to dissolve the Reichstag and to order a new election on March 5, 1933. Under Hitler's sway, the new parliament legally granted him unlimited powers for the next four years. Hitler proclaimed his new government the Third Reich. (The first Reich was the German empire of the Middle Ages; the second was that of the kaisers.)

Nazi Germany

By the fall of 1933, Germany had become a one-party state. The socialist and communist left was crushed by the new regime. Almost all non-Nazi organizations had been either abolished or forced to become part of the Nazi system. Nazi party leaders took over various government departments; party *Gauleiters,* or regional directors, assumed administrative responsibility throughout the country. Party propaganda sought to impress citizens with the regime's "monolithic efficiency." But in fact, the Nazi government was a tangled bureaucratic maze, with both agencies and individuals vying fiercely for Hitler's favor.

Ironically, at the end of the party's first year in power, the most serious challenges to Hitler came from within the party. Hitler's paramilitary Nazi storm troopers (the SA) had been formed to maintain discipline within the party and impose order in society. SA membership soared after 1933, and many in the SA hailed Hitler's appointment as the beginning of a genuinely Nazi revolution. Such radicalism was alarming to the more traditional conservative groups that had helped make Hitler chancellor. If Hitler was to maintain power, then, he needed to tame the SA. On the night of June 30, 1934, more than a thousand high-ranking SA officials, including several of Hitler's oldest associates, were executed in a bloody purge known as the Night of Long Knives. The purge was accomplished by a second paramilitary organization, the *Schutzstaffel* ("bodyguard"), or SS. Headed by the fanatical Heinrich Himmler, the SS became the most dreaded arm of Nazi terror. As Himmler saw it, the mission of the SS was to fight political and racial enemies of the regime, which included building the system of concentration camps. The first camp, at Dachau, opened in March 1933. The secret state police, known as the Gestapo, were responsible for the arrest, incarceration in camps, and murder of thousands of Germans. But the police force was generally understaffed and deluged with paperwork—as one historian has shown, the Gestapo was not "omniscient, omnipotent, and omnipresent." In fact, the majority of arrests was based on voluntary denunciations made by ordinary citizens against each other, often as petty personal attacks. It was not lost on the Gestapo leadership that these denunciations created a level of control that the Gestapo itself could never achieve.

Hitler and the Nazis enjoyed a sizable amount of popular support. Many Germans approved of Hitler's use of violence against the left. The Nazis could play on deep-seated fears of communism, and they spoke a language of intense national pride and unity that had broad appeal. Many Germans saw Hitler as a symbol of a strong, revitalized Germany. Propagandists fostered a Führer cult, depicting Hitler as a charismatic leader with the magnetic energy to bring people to their knees. Hitler's appeal also rested on his ability to give the German people what they wanted: jobs for workers, a productive economy for industrialists, a bulwark against communism for those who feared the wave of revolution. His appeal lay not so much in the programs he championed, many of which were ill-conceived or contradictory, but in his revolt against politics as they had been practiced in Germany. Finally, he promised to lead Germany back to national greatness and to "overthrow" the Versailles settlement.

Hitler's plans for national recovery called for full-scale rearmament and economic self-sufficiency. With policies similar to those of other Western nations, the Nazis made massive public investments, set strict market controls to stop inflation and stabilize the currency, and sealed Germany off from the world economy. The regime launched state-financed construction projects—highways, public housing, reforestation. Late in the decade, as the Nazis rebuilt the entire German military complex, unemployment dropped from over 6 million to under 200,000. The German economy looked better than any other in Europe. Hitler claimed this as his "economic miracle." Such improvements were significant, especially in the eyes of Germans who had lived through the continual turmoil of war, inflation, political instability, and economic crisis.

Like Mussolini, Hitler moved to abolish class conflict by stripping working-class institutions of their power. He outlawed trade unions and strikes, froze wages, and organized workers and employers into a National Labor Front. At the same time, the Nazis increased workers' welfare benefits, generally in line with the other Western nations. Class distinctions were somewhat blurred by the regime's attempts to infuse a new national "spirit" into the entire society. Popular organizations cut across class lines, especially among the youth. The Hitler Youth, a club modeled on the Boy Scouts, was highly successful at teaching children the values of Hitler's Reich; the National Labor Service drafted students for a term to work on state-sponsored building and reclamation projects. Government policy encouraged women to withdraw from the labor force, both to ease unemployment and to conform to Nazi notions of a woman's proper role. "Can woman," one propagandist asked, "conceive of anything more beautiful than to sit with her husband in her cozy home and listen inwardly to the loom of time weaving the weft and warp of motherhood?"

NAZI RACISM

At the core of Nazi ideology lay a particularly virulent racism. Much of this racism was not new. Hitler and the Nazis drew on a revived and especially violent form of nineteenth-century Social Darwinism, according to which nations and people struggled for survival, with the superior peoples strengthening themselves in the process. By the early twentieth century, the rise of the social sciences had taken nineteenth-century prejudices and racial thinking into new terrain. Just as medical science had cured bodily ills, doctors, criminologists, and social workers sought ways to cure social ills. Across the West, scientists and intellectuals worked to purify the body politic, improve the human race, and eliminate the "unfit." Even progressive-minded individuals sometimes subscribed to eugenics, a program of racial engineering to improve either personal or public fitness. Eugenic policies

Nazi Propaganda

The Nazis promised many things to many people. As the document by Goebbels shows, anti-Semitism allowed them to blend their racial nationalism, vaguely defined (and anti-Marxist) socialism, and disgust with the state of German culture and politics. Joseph Goebbels, one of the early members of the party, became director of propaganda for the party in 1928. Later, Hitler appointed him head of the National Ministry for Public Enlightenment and Propaganda. The Nazis worked hard to win the rural vote, as evidenced by the Nazi campaign pamphlet reprinted in the second excerpt. The Nazis tried to appeal to farmers' economic grievances; their fears of socialism, on the one hand, and big business, on the other; and their more general hostility to urban life and culture.

Joseph Goebbels, "Why Are We Enemies of the Jews?"

We are NATIONALISTS because we see in the NATION the only possibility for the protection and the furtherance of our existence.

The NATION is the organic bond of a people for the protection and defense of their lives. He is nationally minded who understands this IN WORD AND IN DEED. . . .

Young nationalism has its unconditional demands, BELIEF IN THE NATION is a matter of all the people, not for individuals of rank, a class, or an industrial clique. The eternal must be separated from the contemporary. The maintenance of a rotten industrial system has nothing to do with nationalism. I can love Germany and hate capitalism; not only CAN I do it, I also MUST do it. The germ of the rebirth of our people LIES ONLY IN THE DESTRUCTION OF THE SYSTEM OF PLUNDERING THE HEALTHY POWER OF THE PEOPLE.

WE ARE NATIONALISTS BECAUSE WE, AS GERMANS, LOVE GERMANY. And because we love Germany, we demand the protection of its national spirit and we battle against its destroyers.

WHY ARE WE SOCIALISTS?

We are SOCIALISTS because we see in SOCIALISM the only possibility for maintaining our racial existence and through it the reconquest of our political freedom and the rebirth of the German state. SOCIALISM has its peculiar form first of all through its comradeship in arms with the forward-driving energy of a newly awakened nationalism. Without nationalism it is nothing, a phantom, a theory, a vision of air, a book. With it, it is everything, THE FUTURE, FREEDOM, FATHERLAND! . . .

WHY DO WE OPPOSE THE JEWS?

We are ENEMIES OF THE JEWS, because we are fighters for the freedom of the German people. THE JEW IS THE CAUSE AND THE BENEFICIARY OF OUR MISERY. He has used the social difficulties of the broad masses of our people to deepen the unholy split between Right and Left among our people. He has made two halves of Germany. He is the real cause for our loss of the Great War.

The Jew has no interest in the solution of Germany's fateful problems. He CANNOT have any. FOR HE LIVES ON THE FACT THAT THERE HAS BEEN NO SOLUTION. If we would make the German people a unified community and give them freedom before the world, then the Jew can have no place among us. He has the best trumps in his hands when a people lives in inner and outer slavery. THE JEW IS RESPONSIBLE FOR OUR MISERY AND HE LIVES ON IT.

That is the reason why we, AS NATIONALISTS and AS SOCIALISTS, oppose the Jew. HE HAS CORRUPTED OUR RACE, FOULED OUR MORALS, UNDERMINED OUR CUSTOMS, AND BROKEN OUR POWER.

in the Third Reich began with a 1933 law for the compulsory sterilization of "innumerable inferior and hereditarily tainted" people. This "social-hygienic racism" later became the systematic murder of mentally and physically ill patients. Social policy was governed by a basic division between those who possessed "value" and those who did not, with the aim of creating a racial utopia.

The centerpiece of Nazi racism was anti-Semitism. This centuries-old phenomenon was part of Christian society from the Middle Ages on. By the nineteenth century, traditional Christian anti-Semitism was joined by a current of nationalist anti-Jewish theory. A great many of the theorists of European nationalism saw the Jewish people as permanent outsiders who could only be assimilated and

National Socialist Campaign Pamphlet, 1932

GERMAN FARMER YOU BELONG TO HITLER! WHY?

The German farmer stands between two great dangers today:

The one danger is the American economic system—Big capitalism!

it means "world economic crisis"

it means "eternal interest slavery" . . .

it means that the world is nothing more than a bag of booty for Jewish finance in Wall Street, New York, and Paris

it enslaves man under the slogans of progress, technology, rationalization, standardization, etc.

it knows only profit and dividends

it wants to make the world into a giant trust

it puts the machine over man

it annihilates the independent, earth-rooted farmer, and its final aim is the world dictatorship of Jewry [. . .]

it achieves this in the political sphere through parliament and the swindle of democracy. In the economic sphere, through the control of credit, the mortgaging of land, the stock exchange and the market principle [. . .]

The farmer's leagues, the Landvolk and the Bavarian Farmers' League all pay homage to this system.

The other danger is the Marxist economic system of bolshevism:

it knows only the state economy

it knows only one class, the proletariat

it brings in the controlled economy

it doesn't just annihilate the self-sufficient farmer economically—it roots him out [. . .]

it brings the rule of the tractor

it nationalizes the land and creates mammoth factory-farms

it uproots and destroys man's soul, making him the powerless tool of the communist idea—or kills him

it destroys the family, belief, and customs [. . .]

it is anti-Christ, it desecrates the churches [. . .]

its final aim is the world dictatorship of the proletariat, that means ultimately the world dictatorship of Jewry, for the Jew controls this powerless proletariat and uses it for his dark plans

Big capitalism and bolshevism work hand in hand; they are born of Jewish thought and serve the master plan of world Jewry.

Who alone can rescue the farmer from these dangers?

NATIONAL SOCIALISM!

Source (for both documents): Anton Kaes, Matin Jay, and Edward Dimendberg, *The Weimar Republic Sourcebook* (Los Angeles: 1994), pp. 137–38, 142.

Questions for Analysis

1. How did Goebbels use metaphors of illness and health, growth and decay? Do the metaphors suggest what the Nazis would try to do to cure the ills of Germany if they took power?

2. How does Goebbels's anti-Semitism differ from the nineteenth-century French anti-Semitism documented on page 779?

3. The Nazi campaign pamphlet of 1932 targeted German farmers. How did the pamphlet play on their fears of market manipulation by American big business and Bolshevik demands for collectivization and seizure of private land? How did the Nazis identify themselves with Christianity and traditional values, sincerely or not?

4. How, specifically, does the party propose to deal with the "two great dangers of today"?

become citizens if they denied their Jewish identity. At the end of the nineteenth century, during the Dreyfus Affair in France (see Chapter 23), French and European anti-Semites launched a barrage of propaganda against Jews—scores of books, pamphlets, and magazines blamed Jews for all the troubles of modernity, from socialism to international banks and mass culture. The late nineteenth century also brought a wave of pogroms—violent assaults on Jewish communities—especially in Russia. Racial anti-Semitism drew the line between Jews and non-Jews on the basis of erroneous biology. Religious conversion, which traditional Christian anti-Semites encouraged, would not change biology. Nor would assimilation, which was counseled by more secular nationalist thinkers.

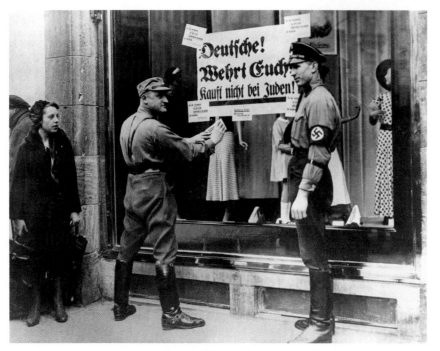

NAZI BOYCOTT OF JEWISH SHOPS IN BERLIN, 1933. Nazis stand in front of a Jewish-owned clothing store. "Germans! Buy nothing from the Jews!"

Jews faced discrimination, exclusion from rights as citizens, and violence. Racial laws excluded Jews from public office as early as April 1933. The Nazis encouraged a boycott of Jewish merchants, while the SA created a constant threat of random violence. In 1935, the Nuremberg Decrees deprived Jews (defined by bloodline) of their German citizenship and prohibited marriage between Jews and other Germans. Violence escalated. In November 1938, the SA attacked some 7,500 Jewish stores, burned nearly 200 synagogues, killed ninety-one Jews, and beat up thousands more in a campaign of terror known as *Kristallnacht,* the Night of Broken Glass. Violence like this did raise some opposition from ordinary Germans. Legal persecution, however, met only silent acquiescence. And from the perspective of Jewish people, *Kristallnacht* made it plain that there was no safe place for them in Germany. Unfortunately, only one year remained before the outbreak of war made it impossible for Jews to escape.

What did national socialism and fascism have in common? Both arose in the interwar period as responses to the First World War and the Russian Revolution. Both were violently antisocialist and anticommunist, determined to "rescue" their nations from the threat of Bolshevism. Both were intensely nationalistic; they believed that national solidarity came before all other allegiances and superseded all other rights. Both opposed parliamentary government and democracy as cumbersome and divisive. Both found their power in mass-based authoritarian politics. Similar movements existed in all the countries of the West, but only in a few cases did they actually form regimes. Nazism, however, distinguished itself by making a racially pure state central to its vision, a vision that would lead to global struggle and mass murder.

It is important not to generalize, but anti-Semitism in these different forms was a well-established and open political force in most of the West. By attacking Jews, anti-Semites attacked modern institutions—from socialist parties and the mass press to international banking—as part of an "international Jewish conspiracy" to undermine traditional authority and nationality. Conservative party leaders told shopkeepers and workers that "Jewish capitalists" were responsible for the demise of small businesses, for the rise of giant department stores, and for precarious economic swings that threatened their livelihoods. In Vienna, middle-class voters supported the openly anti-Semitic Christian Democrats. In Germany, in 1893, sixteen avowed anti-Semites were elected to the Reichstag, and the Conservative party made anti-Semitism part of its official program. Hitler gave this anti-Semitism an especially murderous twist by tying it to doctrines of war and social-hygienic racism.

To what extent was the Nazis' virulent anti-Semitism shared? Although the "Jewish Question" was clearly Hitler's primary obsession during the early 1920s, he made the theme less central in campaign appearances as the Nazi movement entered mainstream politics, shifting instead to attacks on Marxism and the Weimar democracy. Moreover, anti-Semitic beliefs would not have distinguished the Nazi from any other party on the political right; it was likely of only secondary importance to people's opinions of the Nazis. Soon after Hitler came to power, though, German

THE GREAT DEPRESSION IN THE DEMOCRACIES

The histories of the three major Western democracies—Great Britain, France, and the United States—run roughly parallel during the years after the First World War. In all three countries, governments put their trust in prewar policies and assumptions until the Great Depression forced them to make major social and economic reforms, reforms that would lay the foundations of the modern welfare state. These nations weathered the upheavals of the interwar years, but they did not do so easily.

Both France and Britain sought to keep the price of manufactured goods low in the 1920s, to stimulate demand in the world markets. This policy of deflation kept businessmen happy but placed a great burden on French and British workers, whose wages and living standards remained low. In both countries, class conflict boiled just below the surface, as successive governments refused to raise taxes to pay for social reforms. Workers' resentment in Britain helped elect the first Labour party government in 1924 and again in 1929. A general strike in Britain in 1926 succeeded only in increasing middle-class antipathy toward workers. In France, a period of strikes immediately after the war subsided and was followed by a period in which employers refused to bargain with labor unions. When the French government passed a modified social insurance program in 1930—insuring against sickness, old age, and death— French workers remained unsatisfied.

Among the democracies, the United States was a bastion of conservatism. Presidents Warren G. Harding, Calvin Coolidge, and Herbert Hoover held a social philosophy formulated by the barons of big business in the nineteenth century. The Supreme Court used its power of judicial review to nullify progressive legislation enacted by state governments and occasionally by Congress.

The conservative economic and social policies of the prewar period were dealt their deathblow by the Great Depression of 1929. This worldwide depression peaked during the years 1929–33, but its effects lasted a decade. For those who went through it, the depression was perhaps the formative experience of their lives and the decisive crisis of the interwar period. It was an important factor in the rise of Nazism; but in fact, it forced every country to forge new economic policies and to deal with unprecedented economic turmoil.

The Origins of the Great Depression

What caused the Great Depression? Its deepest roots lay in the instability of national currencies and in the interdependence of national economies. Throughout the 1920s, Europeans had seen a sluggish growth rate. A major drop in world agricultural prices hurt the countries of southern and eastern Europe, where agriculture was small in scale and high in cost. Unable to make a profit on the international market, these agricultural countries bought fewer manufactured goods from the more industrial sectors of

northern Europe, causing a widespread drop in industrial productivity. Restrictions on free trade crippled the economy even more. Although debtor nations needed open markets to sell their goods, most nations were raising high trade barriers to protect domestic manufacturers from foreign competition.

Then in October of 1929, prices on the New York Stock Exchange collapsed. On October 24, "Black Thursday," 12 million shares were traded amid unprecedented chaos. Even more surprising, the market kept falling. Black Thursday was followed by Black Monday and then Black Tuesday: falling prices, combined with an enormously high number of trades, made for the worst day in the history of the stock exchange to that point. The rise of the United States as an international creditor during the Great War meant that the crash had immediate, disastrous consequences in Europe. When the value of stocks dropped, banks found themselves short of capital and then, when not rescued by the government, forced to close. International investors called in their debts. A series of banking houses shut their doors, among them Credit Anstalt, the biggest bank in Austria and one with significant interests in two-thirds of Austrian industry. Workers lost their jobs; indeed, manufacturers laid off virtually entire workforces. In 1930, 4 million Americans were unemployed; in 1933, 13 million—nearly a third of the workforce. By then, per capita income in the United States had fallen 48 percent. In Germany, too, the drop was brutal. In 1929, 2 million were unemployed; in 1932, 6 million. Production dropped 44 percent in Germany, 47 percent in the United States. The stock-market collapse led to widespread bank failure and brought the economy virtually to a standstill.

The governments of the West initially responded to the depression with monetary measures. In 1931, Great Britain abandoned the gold standard; the United States followed suit in 1933. By no longer pegging their currencies to the price of gold, these countries hoped to make money cheaper and thus more available for economic recovery programs. This action was the forerunner of a broad program of currency management, which became an important element in a general policy of economic nationalism. In another important move, Great Britain abandoned its time-honored policy of free trade in 1932, raising protective tariffs as high as 100 percent. But monetary policy alone could not end the hardships of ordinary families. Governments were increasingly forced to address their concerns with a wide range of social reforms.

Britain was the most cautious in its relief efforts. A national government composed of Conservative, Liberal, and Labour party members came to power in 1931. To underwrite effective programs of public assistance, however, the government would have to spend beyond its income—something it was reluctant to do. France, on the other hand, adopted the most advanced set of policies to combat the effects of the depression. In 1936, responding to a threat from ultraconservatives to overthrow the republic, a Popular Front government under the leadership of the socialist Léon Blum was formed by the Radical, Radical Socialist, and Communist parties, and lasted for two years. The Popular Front nationalized the munitions industry and reorganized the Bank of France to break the largest stockholders' monopolistic control over credit. The government also decreed a forty-hour week for all urban workers and initiated a program of public works. For the benefit of the farmers, it established a wheat office to fix the price and regulate the distribution of grain. Although the Popular Front temporarily quelled the threat from the political right, conservatives were generally uncooperative and unimpressed by the attempts to aid the French working class. Both a socialist and Jewish, Blum faced fierce anti-Semitism in France. Fearing that Blum was the forerunner of a French Lenin, conservatives declared, "Better Hitler than Blum." They got their wish before the decade was out.

The most dramatic response to the depression came in the United States for two reasons. First, the United States had clung longest to nineteenth-century economic philosophy. Before the depression, the business classes adhered firmly to the creed of freedom of contract. Industrialists insisted on their right to form monopolies, and they used the government as a tool to frustrate the demands of both workers and consumers. Second, the depression was more severe in the United States than in the European democracies. America had survived the First World War unscathed—and, indeed, had benefited enormously—but now its economy was ravaged even more than Europe's. In 1933, Franklin D. Roosevelt succeeded Herbert Hoover as president and announced the New Deal, a program of reform and reconstruction to rescue the country.

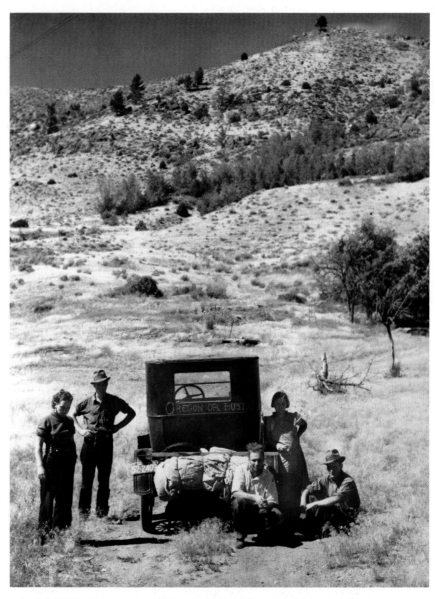

U.S. FARMERS ON THEIR WAY WEST IN THE 1930s. Forced from their land by depression, debts, and drought, thousands of farmers and their families headed to California, Oregon, and Washington in search of employment.

The New Deal aimed to get the country back on its feet without destroying the capitalist system. The government would manage the economy, sponsor relief programs, and fund public-works projects to increase mass purchasing power. These policies were shaped by the theories of the British economist John Maynard Keynes, who had already proved influential during the 1919 treaty meetings at Paris. Keynes argued that capitalism could create a just and efficient society if governments played a part in its management. First, Keynes abandoned the sacred cow of balanced budgets. Without advocating continuous deficit financing, he would have the government deliberately operate in the red whenever private investments weren't enough. Keynes also favored the creation of large amounts of venture capital—money for high-risk, high-reward investments—which he saw as the only socially productive form of capital. Finally, he recommended monetary control to promote prosperity and full employment.

Along with Social Security and other programs, the United States adopted a Keynesian program of "currency management," regulating the value of the dollar according to the needs of the economy. The New Deal helped both individuals and the country recover, but it left the crucial problem of unemployment unsolved. In 1939, after six years of the New Deal, the United States still had more than 9 million jobless workers—a figure that exceeded the combined unemployment of the rest of the world. Only with the outbreak of a new world war—which required millions of soldiers and armament workers—did the United States reach the full recovery that the New Deal had failed to deliver.

INTERWAR CULTURE: ARTISTS AND INTELLECTUALS

The interwar period also brought dramatic upheavals in the arts and sciences. Artists, writers, architects, and composers brought the revolutionary artistic forms of the turn of the century into the mainstream as they rejected traditional aesthetic values and experimented with new forms of expression. Scientists and psychologists challenged deeply held beliefs about the universe and human nature. Finally, radio, movies, and advertising created a new kind of mass culture that fed off the atmosphere of crisis in politics and the arts, and contributed to the anxieties of the age.

Interwar Intellectuals

Novelists, poets, and dramatists were disillusioned by the world war. Much literature in the interwar period reflected the themes of frustration, cynicism, and disenchantment that emerged from the failure of victory to fulfill its promises. The mood of the era is captured in the early work of the American Ernest Hemingway, whose novel *The Sun Also Rises* (1926) described a "lost generation." The poetry of the Anglo-American T. S. Eliot explored a peculiarly modern form of despair: life as a living death, to be endured as boredom and frustration. The German author Bertolt Brecht depicted the cynical corruption of elite members of society in plays written for a working-class audience in cabarets.

Other writers focused their attention on consciousness and inner life, often experimenting with new forms of prose. The Irish writer James Joyce perfected a style that became known as "stream of consciousness" in *Ulysses* (1922), a technique also associated with French author Marcel Proust. In the same vein, British author Virginia Woolf offered an eloquent and biting critique of Britain's elite institutions, from the universities that isolated women in separate, underfunded colleges to the suffocating decorum of middle-class families and relationships.

The depression of the 1930s fostered a second wave of more politicized literature, as a new generation felt called on to indict injustice and point the way to a better society. In *The Grapes of Wrath* (1939), the American writer John Steinbeck depicted the plight of impoverished farmers fleeing from the Dust Bowl to California only to find the land monopolized by companies that exploited their workers. Younger British authors such as W. H. Auden, Stephen Spender, and Christopher Isherwood were communist sympathizers who believed that their duty as artists was to support the revolution.

Interwar Artists

The innovations of the prewar avant-garde thrived in the postwar period. Visual art responded to the rapid transformations of twentieth-century society: new technologies, scientific discoveries, the abandonment of traditional beliefs, and the influence of non-Western cultures. Like the writers of the period, visual artists pushed the boundaries,

MARCEL DUCHAMP. In these photos, Duchamp used shaving cream to transform his appearance. Much of Duchamp's artwork showed his questioning of the role of the artist.

ARCHITECTURAL STYLE IN GERMANY BETWEEN THE WARS. The Bauhaus, by Walter Gropius (1883–1969). This school in Dessau, Germany, is a starkly functional prototype of the interwar "international style."

moving far beyond the conventional tastes of average men and women.

Pablo Picasso pursued his experiments in cubist variations and inventions. The "expressionists" argued that color and line expressed inherent psychological qualities by themselves, so paintings did not need a representational subject at all. The Russian Wassily Kandinsky followed this position to its logical conclusion, creating abstract and colorful paintings that he called "improvisations." A second group of expressionists rejected such experiments and claimed that their goal was "objectivity," by which they meant a candid appraisal of the state of humanity. Chief among this group was the German George Grosz (*Grohz*) whose cruel, satiric line has been likened to a "razor lancing a carbuncle." His scathing cartoonlike images became the most popular portraits of the despised Weimar government.

The dadaists went further, rebelling against the very idea of aesthetic principle. Principles were based on reason, and the world had proved that reason did not exist. Pulling their name at random from a dictionary, the dadaists rejected formal artistic conventions, preferring random juxtapositions from cutouts and collage, bizarre assemblages from wood, glass, and metal. The artists—the Frenchman Marcel Duchamp, the German Max Ernst, and the Alsation Jean (Hans Arp)—claimed their works were meaningless and playful, but critics saw them as expressions of the subconscious. In Germany, dadaism took on political undertones as their anarchistic social critique challenged the very basis of national culture.

Other artists found inspiration for their work in social and political conflict. Mexican muralists Diego Rivera and José Clemente Orozco and the Americans Thomas Hart Benton and Reginald Marsh sought to depict the social conditions of the modern world, presenting in graphic detail the lives of ordinary working people. These artists avoided the experimentalism of the dadaists or the expressionists and aimed instead for an intelligible art, available to all.

Architects, too, rejected tradition, seeking a style that was more in harmony with the needs of modern civilization. Otto Wagner in Austria, Charles Édouard Jeanneret (known as Le Corbusier) in France, and Louis Sullivan and Frank Lloyd Wright in the United States pioneered a style known as "functionalism." Functionalists believed that the appearance of a building should proclaim its use and purpose. Ornament was designed to reflect an age of science and machines. The German functionalist Walter Gropius established a school in 1919—the Bauhaus—to serve as a center for the development of modern architecture. Their style of design, the so-called international style, explored the use of new materials—chromium, glass, steel, and concrete.

Interwar Scientific Developments

One powerful influence on the artists and intellectuals of the day was neither social nor political but scientific. The pioneering work of the German physicist Albert Einstein revolutionized not only the entire structure of physical science but also challenged ordinary people's most basic beliefs about the universe. Quickly recognized as one of the greatest intellects of all time, Einstein began to question the very foundations of traditional physics early in the twentieth century. By 1915, he had proposed entirely new ways of thinking about space, matter, time, and gravity.

Einstein's theories paved the way for another revolutionary development in physics—the splitting of the atom. As early as 1905, Einstein became convinced of the equivalence of mass and energy and worked out a formula for the conversion of one into the other: $E = mc^2$.

The formula had no practical application for years. Then in 1932, when the Englishman Sir James Chadwick discovered the neutron, scientists had an ideal weapon for bombarding the atom—that is, a way to split it. In 1939, two German physicists, Otto Hahn and Fritz Strassman, successfully split atoms of uranium by bombarding them with neutrons. The initial reaction produced a chain of reactions: each atom that was split shot off more neutrons, which split even more atoms. Scientists in Germany, Great Britain, and the United States were spurred on by governments anxious to turn these discoveries into weapons during the Second World War. American scientists soon prepared an atomic bomb, the most destructive weapon ever created. The legacy was ironic for Einstein, a man who devoted much of his life to promoting pacifism, liberalism, and social justice.

Another important contribution to physics that quickly entered popular culture was the "uncertainty principle" posited by the German physicist Werner Heisenberg in 1927. Heisenberg, who was strongly influenced by Einstein, showed that it is impossible—even in theory—to measure both the position and the speed of an object at the same time. The theory was of consequence only when dealing with atoms or subatomic particles. Though the public had little to no understanding of these groundbreaking scientific concepts, metaphorical invocations of relativity and the uncertainty principle fitted the ambiguities of the modern world. For many people, nothing was definite, everything was changing—and science seemed to be proving it.

Mass Culture and Its Possibilities

Cultural change, however, extended far beyond circles of artistic and intellectual elites. The explosive rise of mass media in the interwar years transformed popular culture and the lives of ordinary people. New mass media—especially radio and films—reached audiences of unprecedented size. Political life incorporated many of these new media, setting off worries that the common people, increasingly referred to as the "masses," could be manipulated by demagogues and propaganda. In 1918, mass politics was rapidly becoming a fact of life: that meant nearly universal suffrage (varying by country), well-organized political parties reaching out to voters, and, in general, more participation in political life. Mass politics was accompanied by the rise of mass culture: books, newspapers, films, and fashions were produced in large numbers and standardized formats, which were less expensive and more accessible, appealing not only to more but to more kinds of people. Older forms of popular culture were often local and class specific; mass culture, at least in principle, cut across lines of class and ethnicity, and even nationality. The term, however, can easily become misleading. The world of culture did not suddenly become homogenous. No more than half the population read newspapers regularly. Not everyone listened to the radio, and those who did certainly did not believe everything they heard. The pace of cultural change, however, did quicken perceptibly. And in the interwar years, mass culture showed that it held both democratic and authoritarian potential.

The expansion of mass culture rested on widespread applications of existing technologies. Wireless communication, for instance, was invented before the turn of the twentieth century and saw limited use in the First World War. With major financial investment in the 1920s, though, the radio industry boomed. Three out of four British families had a radio by the end of the 1930s; and in Germany, the ratio was even higher. In every European country, broadcasting rights were controlled by the government; in the United States, radio was managed by corporations. The radio broadcast soon became the national soapbox for politicians, and it played no small role in creating new kinds of political language. President Franklin Roosevelt's reassuring "fireside chats" took advantage of the way that radio bridged the public world of politics with the private world of the home. Hitler cultivated a different kind of radio personality, barking his fierce invectives; he made some fifty addresses in 1933 alone. In Germany, Nazi propagandists beamed their messages into homes or blared them through loudspeakers in town squares, constant and repetitive. Broadcasting created new rituals of political life—and new means of communication and persuasion.

So did advertising. Advertising was not new, but it was newly prominent. Businesses spent vastly more on advertising than they had before. Hard-hitting visual images replaced older ads that simply announced products, prices, and brand names. Many observers considered advertising the most "modern" of art forms. Why? It was efficient communication, streamlined and standardized, producing images that would appeal to all. It was scientific, drawing on modern psychology; advertising agencies claimed to have a science of selling to people. In a world remade by mass politics, and at a moment when the purchasing power of the common people was beginning to rise, however slowly, the high stakes in advertising (as in much of mass culture) were apparent to many.

The most dramatic changes came on movie screens. The technology of moving pictures came earlier; the

The Fascist Spectacle of Mass Participation

Like other revolutionary movements, fascism in Italy and national social ism in Germany needed to project an image of popular support for their political programs. As far back as the French Revolution of 1789, representations of "the people" as political actors took on special significance in revolutionary propaganda (see **Interpreting Visual Evidence**, pages 602–03), and both Hitler and Mussolini understood how to use such images to create the impression of an organic and seamless connection between the party's leadership and the rank and file who made up the movement.

A. Benito Mussolini visits a youth camp where recruits to his Black Shirts were in training, 1935.

B. Still image from Leni Riefenstahl, *Triumph of the Will* (1935), a film about a Nazi party rally in Nuremberg, Germany, 1934.

1890s were the era of nickelodeons and short action pictures. And in that period, France and Italy had strong film industries. Further popularized by news shorts during the war, film boomed in the war's aftermath. When sound was added to movies in 1927, costs soared, competition intensified, and audiences grew rapidly. By the 1930s, an estimated 40 percent of British adults went to the movies once a week, a strikingly high figure. Many went more often than that. The U.S. film industry gained a competitive edge in Europe, buoyed by the size of its home market, by huge investments in equipment and distribution, by aggressive marketing, and by Hollywood's star system of long-term contracts with well-known actors who, in a sense, standardized the product and guaranteed a film's success.

Germany, too, was home to a particularly talented group of directors, writers, and actors, and to a major production company, UFA (Universum Film AG), which ran the largest and best-equipped studios in Europe. The UFA's history paralleled the country's: it was run by the government during the First World War, devastated by the economic crisis of the early 1920s, rescued by wealthy German nationalists in the late 1920s, and finally taken over by the Nazis. During the Weimar years, UFA produced some of the most

C. I. M. Swire (right), a leading figure in the women's section of the British Union of Fascists wearing the organization's female black-shirted uniform (1933).

Representations of the people in nineteenth-century liberal revolutionary movements emphasized an activist definition of political participation, as citizens came together to constitute a national body that reflected their will. Both Italian fascism and German national socialism defined themselves in opposition to democratic or parliamentary regimes, and they explicitly rejected the individualism that was the basis for liberal citizenship. In their orchestration of public celebrations for their program, both fascists and national socialists emphasized images of obedience and subordination to the leader (image A), or to the national movement (image B). Though the pageantry of fascism and national socialism typically emphasized an aggressively masculine image of enthusiastic devotion, most fascist movements also organized special female sections within their movements. In these groups, women could clothe themselves in uniforms like their male counterparts and express their own allegiance to the spirit of self-sacrifice that was at the heart of such collective movements (image C).

Questions for Analysis

1. Each of these images was carefully staged and orchestrated to project a specific message. What are the messages contained in each of these images? What details are important?

2. What do these images tell us about the place of the individual in fascist society?

3. What sense of belonging do you think these images are designed to produce? What made such images so attractive to so many people?

remarkable films of the period, including *Der letzte mann* ("The Last Man"; released as "The Last Laugh" in English), a universally acclaimed film directed by F. W. Murnau, one of the two great masters of German expressionism. Fritz Lang was the other, directing such masterpieces as the science-fiction film *Metropolis* (1926) and his most famous German film, *M* (1931). After Hitler's rise to power, the Nazis took control of UFA, placing it under the control of Joseph Goebbels and the Ministry of Propaganda. Though production continued unabated during the Third Reich, many of the industry's most talented members fled from the oppressive regime, ending the golden age of German cinema.

Many found the new mass culture disturbing. As they perceived it, the threat came straight from the United States, which deluged Europe with cultural exports after the war. Hollywood westerns, cheap dime novels, and jazz music—which became increasingly popular in the 1920s—introduced Europe to new ways of life. Advertising, comedies, and romances disseminated new and often disconcerting images of femininity. With bobbed haircuts and short dresses, "new women" seemed assertive, flirtatious, capricious, and materialistic. The Wild West genre was popular with teenage boys, much to the dismay of their parents and teachers, who saw westerns as an inappropriate,

VOICE OF THE PEOPLE, VOICE OF GOD BY GEORGE GROSZ (1920). Industrialization, the First World War, and political change combined to make early-twentieth-century Berlin a center of mass culture and communication. In this drawing, the radical artist and social critic George Grosz deplores the newspapers' power over public opinion. That public opinion could be manipulated was a common theme for many who wrote about early-twentieth-century democracy. ■ *How does this cynicism about the public sphere compare with earlier defenders of free speech, such as John Stuart Mill?*

FRITZ LANG'S *M.* In this film, Peter Lorre, a Jewish actor, played the role of a child murderer, who maintains that he should not be punished for his crimes. Lorre's speech at the end of the film was used in the Nazi propaganda film *The Eternal Jew* as proof that Jews were innate criminals who showed no remorse for their actions.

lower-class form of entertainment. In Europe, the cross-class appeal of American popular culture grated against long-standing social hierarchies. Conservative critics abhorred the fact that "the parson's wife sat nearby his maid at Sunday matinees, equally rapt in the gaze of Hollywood stars." American critics expressed many of the same concerns. Yet the United States enjoyed more social and political stability than Europe. War and revolution had shaken Europe's economies and cultures, and in that context "Americanization" seemed a handy shorthand for economic as well as cultural change. One critic expressed a common concern: "America is the source of that terrible wave of uniformity that gives everyone the same [*sic*]: the same overalls on the skin, the same book in the hand, the same pen between the fingers, the same conversation on the lips, and the same automobile instead of feet."

Authoritarian governments, in particular, decried these developments as decadent threats to national culture. Fascist, communist, and Nazi governments alike tried to control not only popular culture but also high culture and modernism, which were typically out of line with the designs of the dictators. Stalin much preferred socialist realism to the new Soviet avant-garde. Mussolini had a penchant for classical kitsch, though he was far more accepting of modern art than Hitler, who despised its decadence. Nazism had its own cultural aesthetic, promoting "Aryan" art and architecture and rejecting the modern, international style they associated with the "international Jewish conspiracy." Modernism, functionalism, and atonality were banned: the hallmarks of Weimar Germany's cultural preeminence were replaced by a state-sponsored revival of an alleged mystical and heroic past. Walter Gropius's acclaimed experiments in modernist architecture, for example, stood as monuments to everything the Nazis hated. The Bauhaus school was closed in 1933, and Hitler hired Albert Speer as his personal architect, commissioning him to design grandiose neoclassical buildings, including an extravagant plan to rebuild the entire city of Berlin.

The Nazis, like other authoritarian governments, used mass media as efficient means of indoctrination and control. Movies became part of the Nazis' pioneering use of "spectacular politics." Media campaigns, mass rallies, parades

Cinema: Fritz Lang on the Future of the Feature Film in Germany, 1926

Fritz Lang (1890–1976) came from Austria to Berlin after the First World War and became one of the German Weimar Republic's most brilliant movie directors, best known for Metropolis *(1926) and* M *(1931). In this essay, Lang reflects on the technological, artistic, and human potential of film. Like many European filmmakers he was fascinated by American movies. In 1932, Joseph Goebbels, dazzled by Lang's work, asked him to work on movies for the Nazis. Lang immediately left Germany for Paris and, from there, for the United States where he continued to make films in Hollywood.*

here has perhaps never before been a time so determined as ours in its search for new forms of expression. Fundamental revolutions in painting, sculpture, architecture, and music speak eloquently of the fact that people of today are seeking and finding their own means of lending artistic form to their sentiments. . . .

The speed with which film has developed in the last five years makes all predictions about it appear dangerous, for it will probably exceed each one by leaps and bounds. Film knows no rest. What was invented yesterday is already obsolete today. This uninterrupted drive for new modes of expression, this intellectual experimentation, along with the joy Germans characteristically take in overexertion, appear to me to fortify my contention that film as art will first find its form in Germany. . . .

Germany has never had, and never will have, the gigantic human and financial reserves of the American film industry at its disposal. To its good fortune. For that is exactly what forces us to compensate a purely material imbalance through an intellectual superiority. . . .

The first important gift for which we have film to thank was in a certain sense *the rediscovery of the human face.* Film has revealed to us the human face with unexampled clarity in its tragic as well as grotesque, threatening as well as blessed expression.

The second gift is that of visual empathy: in the purest sense the expressionistic representation of thought processes. No longer will we take part purely externally in the workings of the soul of the characters in film. We will no longer limit ourselves to seeing the effects of feelings, but will experience them in our own souls, from the instant of their inception on, from the first flash of a thought through to the logical last conclusion of the idea. . . .

The internationalism of filmic language will become the strongest instrument available for the mutual understanding of peoples, who otherwise have such difficulty understanding each other in all too many languages. To bestow upon film the double gift of ideas and soul is the task that lies before us. . . .

Source: Anton Kaes, Matin Jay, and Edward Dimendberg, *The Weimar Republic Sourcebook* (Los Angeles: 1994), pp. 622–23.

Questions for Analysis

1. Why does Lang suggest that his own time is in search of "new forms of expression"? Do artists always search for new forms, or might this be a specifically twentieth-century phenomenon?

2. What did Lang mean by calling "the rediscovery of the human face" and "visual empathy" gifts of film? Did television, video, and electronic media have comparable effects on how we see the world and other beings in it?

3. How does Lang see the technological, artistic, and human potential of film?

and ceremonies: all were designed to display the strength and glory of the Reich and to impress and intimidate spectators. In 1934, Hitler commissioned the filmmaker Leni Riefenstahl to record a political rally staged by herself and Albert Speer in Nuremberg. The film, titled *Triumph of the Will,* was a visual hymn to the Nordic race and the Nazi regime. Everything in the film was on a huge scale: masses of bodies stood in parade formation, and flags rose and fell in unison; the film invited viewers to surrender to the power of grand ritual and symbolism. The comedian Charlie Chaplin riposted in his celebrated lampoon *The Great Dictator* (1940), an enormously successful parody of Nazi pomposities.

The Nazis also tried to eliminate the influences of American popular culture, which even before 1933 had been decried as an example of biological and cultural degeneracy. For instance, critics associated American dances and jazz (which were increasingly popular in German cities) with what the Nazis deemed "racially inferior" blacks and Jews. With culture, however, the Nazis were forced to strike a balance between party propaganda and popular entertainment. The regime allowed many cultural imports, including Hollywood films, to continue while consciously cultivating German alternatives to American cinema, music, fashions, and even dances. Joseph Goebbels, the minister of propaganda who controlled most film production, placed a high value on economic viability. During the Third Reich, the German film industry turned out comedies, escapist fantasies, and sentimental romances. It developed its own star system and tried to keep audiences happy; meanwhile, it became a major competitor internationally. For domestic consumption, the industry also produced vicious anti-Semitic films, such as *The Eternal Jew* (1940) and *Jew Suss* (1940), a fictional tale of a Jewish moneylender who brings the city of Württemberg to ruin in the eighteenth century. In the final scene of the film, the town expels the entire Jewish community from its midst, asking that "posterity honor this law." Goebbels reported that the entire Reich cabinet had viewed the film and considered it "an incredible success."

After You Read This Chapter

Visit StudySpace for quizzes, additional review materials, and multimedia documents. **wwnorton.com/web/westernciv18**

REVIEWING THE OBJECTIVES

- After 1917, the Bolsheviks in Russia debated how fast they should move to reorganize society along the lines demanded by their revolutionary ideology. What circumstances determined the outcome of this debate and what were the consequences of Stalin's revolution from above in the 1930s?

- Mussolini's Fascist party offered an alternative to Italian voters disappointed with their government in the aftermath of the First World War. What was fascism, and how did Mussolini come to power?

- The Weimar Republic failed in its attempt to establish a stable democracy in Germany while other democracies in France, Britain, and the United States underwent severe strain. What challenges did democratic regimes face during the interwar period?

- Hitler came to power legally in 1933 through the German electoral system. What did he stand for, and why did so many Germans support his cause?

- Artists, writers, and other intellectuals in the interwar period could not help but reflect the atmosphere of social and political crisis in their work. How did artists and writers react to the crisis of the interwar period?

CONCLUSION

The strains of the First World War created a world that few recognized—transformed by revolution, mass mobilization, and loss. In retrospect, it is hard not to see the period that followed as a succession of failures. Capitalism foundered in the Great Depression, democracies collapsed in the face of authoritarianism, and the Treaty of Versailles proved hollow. Stalin's Soviet Union paid a terrible price for the creation of a modern industrial economy in the years of famine, political repression, and state terror. Hitler's Germany and Mussolini's Italy offered a vision of the future that held no comfort for those committed to basic human freedoms and equality under the law. Yet we better understand the experiences and outlooks of ordinary people if we do not treat the failures of the interwar period as inevitable. By the late 1920s, many were cautiously optimistic that the Great War's legacy could be overcome and that problems were being solved. The Great Depression wrecked these hopes, bringing economic chaos and political paralysis. Paralysis and chaos, in turn, created new audiences for political leaders offering authoritarian solutions and brought more voters to their political parties. Finally, economic troubles and political turmoil made contending with rising international tensions, to which we now turn, vastly more difficult. By the 1930s, even cautious optimism about international relations had given way to apprehension and dread.

PEOPLE, IDEAS, AND EVENTS IN CONTEXT

- What is the difference between the Bolshevik policies of **WAR COMMUNISM** and the **NEW ECONOMIC POLICY (NEP)**?
- What were **JOSEPH STALIN**'s goals in implementing his catastrophic plan for **COLLECTIVIZATION** of agriculture, and what did he hope to accomplish with his purging of an entire generation of Bolshevik leaders, along with millions of other Soviet citizens, in the **GREAT TERROR**?
- What was the basis of **BENITO MUSSOLINI**'s rejection of liberal democracy? What kinds of changes in Italian society followed from the adoption of **FASCISM** as the official state ideology?
- How important was **ANTI-SEMITISM** to **ADOLF HITLER**'s political career? What do events like **KRISTALLNACHT** tell us about the depth of German anti-Semitism?
- What effects did the **GREAT DEPRESSION** have on the European economy, and how did this economic crisis affect the political developments of the 1930s?
- How did the **NEW DEAL** attempt to deal with the economic crisis in the United States?

THINKING ABOUT CONNECTIONS

- What did Soviet communism, national socialism in Germany, and Italian fascism have in common during the years 1919–39? What made them different from one another?
- How much of the crisis of the interwar period can be attributed to the effects of World War I? To the economic upheaval of the Great Depression? Is it possible to see the ideological conflicts of these years as the result of a much longer history?

STORY LINES

- In the 1930s, Hitler's Germany and Mussolini's Italy allied with imperial Japan to form the Axis. The Axis eventually provoked a Second World War, against a group of Allied powers that included Britain, the United States, Canada, Australia, and the Soviet Union.

- The Nazi regime's military successes in 1939 brought almost all of Europe under German control. The Russian victory at Stalingrad in 1942 proved to be a turning point, and from 1942 to 1945 the Allies progressively rolled back the German and Japanese armies, leading to Allied victory in 1945.

- The Nazi state embarked on a genocidal project of mass murder to exterminate its racial and ideological enemies—Europe's Jews, homosexuals, and the Roma (Gypsies).

- Attacks on civilian populations and the plundering of resources by occupying armies made the Second World War a "total war" in which the distinction between military and home front meant little for many Europeans.

CHRONOLOGY

1931	Japanese invasion of Manchuria
1936–1939	Spanish Civil War
September 1938	Sudeten Crisis and Munich Conference
August 1939	Nazi-Soviet Pact
September 1939	German invasion of Poland
May 1940	German invasion of the Low Countries and France
June 1941	German invasion of the Soviet Union
December 1941	Japanese attack on Pearl Harbor
September 1942–January 1943	Battle of Stalingrad
June 1944	D-Day Invasion
May 1945	German surrender
August 1945	The United States drops atomic bombs on Hiroshima and Nagasaki
August 1945	Japanese surrender

Before
You
Read
This
Chapter

The Second World War

n 1939, Adolf Hitler wanted war. By the spring of that year, he had already revealed to the world the weakness of France and Britain, which had stood by while he dismantled Czechoslovakia, a democratic nation created at the end of World War I. He turned his eyes next to Poland, confident that Britain and France could do little to prevent him from fulfilling his pledge to unleash the full power of a rearmed Germany to conquer *Lebensraum*—"living space"—for the German people in the east. Before he could invade Poland, however, he needed to come to an understanding with another long-standing enemy—the Soviet Union of Josef Stalin. Since 1934, Stalin had participated in a broad-based anti-fascist coalition in Europe, the Popular Front, an alliance that had brought the Soviets to side with the "bourgeois democracies" that were their sworn enemies. The Popular Front had led to Soviet support for the Republican side in the Spanish Civil War, though the Republicans had lost to the Nationalists who were backed by Hitler's Germany and Mussolini's Italian fascists. Hitler's propaganda campaign against the Soviets was relentless. He portrayed the Soviet regime as a cabal

873

run by Jewish communists and referred continuously to Stalin's commissar for foreign affairs, Maxim Litvinov, as "Finkelstein" (his brother was a rabbi). Given this history of conflict, what possible understanding could Hitler hope to achieve with Stalin?

In fact, by 1939, Stalin himself had been forced to recalculate his alliances in Europe. The loss in the Spanish Civil War, and the failure of France and Britain to uphold their obligations to preserve the international order guaranteed by the Versailles peace treaty led the Soviet leader to believe that his regime had no choice but to come to an agreement with Hitler, in an attempt to gain time and preserve the Soviet Union from an immediate war. The hope was that the other European powers—France, Britain, Italy, and Germany—would weaken themselves in a general war, thus benefiting the cause of the Soviet Union. To show his willingness to talk, he fired Litvinov on May 3 and replaced him with his closest adviser, Vyacheslav Molotov (1890–1986), an ethnic Russian. In August, Hitler responded by sending his own foreign minister, Joachim von Ribbentrop (1893–1946), to Moscow to meet with Stalin. When the German envoy arrived, the Moscow airport was decorated with swastikas. The two sides cynically agreed to carve Poland up between them, and when the agreement was announced on August 23, 1939, the world was shocked to discover that these two powers, sworn ideological enemies, had made common cause to destroy Poland. On September 1, 1939, Hitler invaded Poland. Stalin, looking to what was to become a global conflict, had already attacked Japanese forces along the Mongolian border in Central Asia on August 20. The Second World War had begun.

Like the First World War, the Second World War was triggered by threats to the European balance of power. Yet even more than the Great War, the Second World War was a conflict among nations, whole peoples, and fiercely opposing ideals. Adolf Hitler and his supporters in Germany and abroad cast the conflict as a racial war against the twin enemies of national socialism: the democracies in western Europe and the United States, on the one hand, and the communist order of the Soviet Union, on the other. Hitler's opponents in the West and the East believed just as fervently that they were defending a way of life and a vision of justice that was bigger than narrow definitions of national interest.

Belief that the world was now characterized by ideologies and worldviews that were necessarily in mortal combat with one another meant that the scale of the killing overtook even that of the First World War. In 1914, military firepower outmatched mobility, resulting in four years of static, mud-sodden slaughter. In 1939, mobility was joined to firepower on a massive scale, with terrifying results. On the battlefield, the tactics of high-speed armored warfare (*Blitzkrieg*), aircraft carriers sinking ships far below the horizon, and submarines used in vast numbers to dominate shipping lanes changed the scope and the pace of fighting. This was not a war of trenches and barbed wire but a war of motion, dramatic conquests, and terrible destructive power. The devastation of 1914–18 paled in comparison to this new, global conflict.

The other great change involved not tactics but targets. Much of the unprecedented killing power now available was aimed directly at civilians. Cities were laid waste by artillery and aerial bombing. Whole regions were put to the torch, and towns and villages were systematically cordoned off and leveled. Whole populations were targeted as well, in ways that continue to appall. The Nazi regime's systematic murder of gypsies, homosexuals, and other "deviants," along with the effort to exterminate the Jewish people completely, made the Second World War a horrifyingly unique event. So did the United States' use of a weapon whose existence would dominate politics and society for the next fifty years: the atomic bomb. The naive enthusiasm that had marked the outbreak of the Great War was absent from the start. Terrible memories of the first conflict lingered. Yet those who fought against the Axis Powers (and many of those who fought for them) found that their determination to fight and win grew as the war went on. Unlike the seemingly meaningless killing of the Great War, the Second World War was cast as a war of absolutes, of good and evil, of national and global survival. Nevertheless, the scale of destruction brought with it a profound weariness. It also provoked deep-seated questions about the value of Western "civilization" and the terms on which it, and the rest of the world, might live peaceably in the future.

THE CAUSES OF THE WAR: UNSETTLED QUARRELS, ECONOMIC FALLOUT, AND NATIONALISM

Historians have isolated four main causes for the Second World War: the punishing terms of the Versailles peace settlement, the failure to create international guarantees for peace and security after 1918, the successive economic crises of the interwar years, and the violent forms of nationalism that emerged in Europe in the 1930s.

The peace settlement of 1919–20 created as many problems as it solved. The senior Allied heads of state annexed German territory and created satellite states out of the eastern European empires. In doing so, the peacemakers created fresh bitterness and conflict. The Versailles treaty and its champions, such as President Woodrow Wilson, proclaimed the principle of self-determination for the peoples of eastern and southern Europe. Yet the new states created by the treaty crossed ethnic boundaries, created new minorities without protecting them, and frustrated many of the expectations they had raised. The unsteady new boundaries would be redrawn by force in the 1930s. The Allied powers also kept up the naval blockade against Germany after the end of the fighting. This forced the new German government to accept harsh terms that deprived Germany of its political power in Europe and saddled the German economy with the bill for the conflict in a "war guilt" clause. The blockade and its consequences created grievances that many angry, humiliated Germans considered legitimate.

Power politics persisted after the peace conference. Although Woodrow Wilson and other sponsors of the League of Nations acclaimed the League as a means to eliminate power struggles, it did nothing of the sort. The signatures on the peace treaties were hardly dry when the victors began carving out new alliances to maintain their supremacy, interfering in the new central European states and the mandate territories added to the British and French empires in the Middle East. Even the League itself was fundamentally an alliance of the victors against the vanquished. It is not surprising that politicians feared international relations would be undermined by this imbalance of power.

Another cause of the Second World War was the failure to create lasting, binding standards for peace and security. Diplomats spent the ten years after Versailles trying to restore such standards. Some put their faith in the legal and moral authority of the League. Others saw disarmament as the most promising means of guaranteeing peace. In 1925, an effort was made to secure the frontiers on the Rhine established at Versailles in order to reassure the French against any resurgence of German expansionism. In 1928, the Kellogg-Briand Pact attempted to make war an international crime. None of these pacts carried any real weight. Each nation tried to include special provisions and exceptions for "vital interests," and these efforts compromised the treaties from the start. Had the League of Nations been better organized, it might have relieved some of the tensions or at least prevented clashes between nations. But the League was never a league of all nations. Essential members were absent, since Germany and the Soviet Union were excluded for most of the interwar period and the United States never joined.

Economic conditions were a third important cause of renewed conflict. The huge reparations imposed on the Germans and France's occupation of much of Germany's industrial heartland helped slow Germany's recovery. German and French stubbornness about the pace of repayments combined disastrously to bring on the German inflation of the early 1920s. The spiraling inflation made German money nearly worthless, damaging the stability and credibility of Germany's young republic almost beyond repair.

The depression of the 1930s contributed to the coming of the war in several ways. It intensified economic nationalism. Baffled by problems of unemployment and business stagnation, governments imposed high tariffs in an effort to preserve the home market for their own producers. The collapse of investment and terrible domestic unemployment caused the United States to withdraw even further from world affairs. Although France suffered less than some other countries, the depression still inflamed tensions between management and labor. This conflict exacerbated political battles between left and right, making it difficult for either side to govern France. Britain turned to its empire, raising tariffs for the first time and guarding its financial investments jealously.

In Germany, the Great Depression was the last blow to the Weimar Republic. In 1933, power passed to the Nazis, who promised a total program of national renewal. In the fascist states (and, exceptionally, the United States), public works projects of one kind or another were prescribed as an answer to mass unemployment. This produced highways, bridges, and railroads; it also produced a new arms race.

Despite the misgivings of many inside the governments of Britain and France, Germany was allowed to ignore the terms of the peace treaties and rearm. Armaments expansion on a large scale first began in Germany in 1935, with the result that unemployment was reduced and the effects of the depression eased. Other nations followed the German example, not simply as a way to boost their economies but in response to growing Nazi military power. In the Pacific, the decline of Japanese exports meant that the nation did not have enough foreign currency to pay for vital raw materials from overseas. This played into the hands of Japan's military regime. Japanese national ambitions and Japanese leaders' perception of the political and cultural inferiority of the Chinese led Japan to fresh imperial adventures in the name of establishing economic stability in East Asia. They began in 1931 with the invasion of Manchuria and moved from there to create a "Greater Pacific Co-Prosperity Sphere," which involved seizing other territories as Japanese colonies. Raw materials could then be bought with Japanese money and more of Asia would serve the needs of Japan's empire.

Imperial success could serve as consolation when economic methods failed. As the depression dragged on in fascist Italy, Mussolini tried to distract his public with national conquests overseas, culminating in the invasion of Ethiopia in 1935.

In sum, the tremendous economic hardship of the depression, a contested peace treaty, and political weakness undermined international stability. But the decisive factor in the crises of the 1930s and the trigger for another world war lay in a blend of violent nationalism and modern ideologies that glorified the nation and national destiny. This blend, particularly in the forms of fascism and militarism, appeared around the world in many countries. By the middle of the 1930s, recognizing common interests, fascist Italy and Nazi Germany formed an Axis, an alliance binding their goals of national glory and international power. They were later joined by Japan's military regime. In Spain, the ultranationalist forces that tried to overthrow the Spanish Republic, setting off the Spanish Civil War (discussed below), believed they were reviving the stability, authority, and morality of the nation. Fascist, semifascist, or authoritarian regimes spread in eastern Europe, in Yugoslavia, Hungary, and Romania. One exception to this sobering trend toward authoritarianism was Czechoslovakia. Czechoslovakia boasted no ethnic majority. Although the Czechs practiced an enlightened policy of minority self-government, and though their government was remarkably stable, questions of nationality remained a potential source of friction. Those questions became a key factor as international tensions mounted in the late 1930s.

THE 1930s: CHALLENGES TO THE PEACE, APPEASEMENT, AND THE "DISHONEST DECADE"

The 1930s brought the tensions and failures caused by the treaties of 1919–20 to a head, creating a global crisis. Fascist and nationalist governments flouted the League of Nations by launching new conquests and efforts at national expansion. With the memories of 1914–18 still fresh, these new crises created an atmosphere of deepening fear and apprehension. Each new conflict seemed to warn that another, much wider war would follow unless it could somehow be averted. Ordinary people, particularly in Britain, France, and the United States, were divided. Some saw the actions of the aggressors as a direct challenge to civilization, one that had to be met with force if necessary. Others hoped to avoid premature

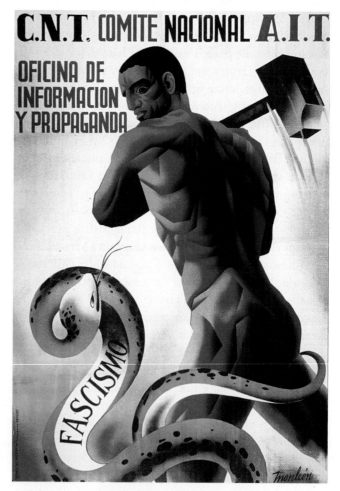

ANTIFASCIST PROPAGANDA, SPANISH CIVIL WAR. This poster, produced by a left-wing labor organization affiliated with the international anarchist movement, shows a worker delivering a killing blow to a fascist snake.

GIANT PORTRAIT OF MUSSOLINI IN ETHIOPIA, 1935. Central to Mussolini's popularity in Italy was his ability to connect a vision of his personal leadership with a militant and expansionist nationalism. This portrait stood over an Italian military camp in Ethiopia in November 1935 during the invasion of this East African nation.

or unnecessary conflict. Their governments tried instead at several points to negotiate with the fascists and keep a tenuous peace. Writers, intellectuals, and politicians on the left vilified these efforts. Many saw the period as a series of missed opportunities to prevent renewed warfare. In 1939, on the first day of the Second World War, the British poet and leftist W. H. Auden condemned the behavior of Western governments, calling the 1930s "a low, dishonest decade."

The object of Auden's venom was the policy of "appeasement" pursued by Western governments in the face of German, Italian, and Japanese aggression. Appeasement was neither simple power politics nor pure cowardice. It was grounded in three deeply held assumptions. The first assumption was that doing anything to provoke another war was unthinkable. The 1914–18 slaughter and its aftermath left many in the West embracing pacifism and not wanting to deal with the uncompromising aggression of the fascist governments, especially Nazi Germany. Second, many in Britain and the United States argued that Germany had been mistreated by the Versailles treaty and harbored legitimate grievances that should be acknowledged and resolved. Finally, many appeasers were staunch anticommunists. They believed that the fascist states in Germany and Italy were an essential bulwark against the advance

of Soviet communism and that division among the major European states only played into the hands of the USSR. One group, however, believed that the Soviets posed the greater threat and that accommodating Hitler might create a common interest against a common enemy. The other faction believed that Nazi Germany presented the true threat to European stability. Nevertheless, they believed, Hitler would have to be placated until Britain and France finished rearming. At that point, they hoped, their greater military power would deter Hitler or Mussolini from risking a general European war. It took most of the 1930s for the debate among appeasers to come to a head. Meanwhile, the League of Nations faced more immediate and pressing challenges.

The 1930s brought three crucial tests for the League: crises in China, Ethiopia, and Spain. In China, the Japanese invasion of Manchuria in 1931 turned into an invasion of the whole country. Chinese forces were driven before the Japanese advance, and the Japanese deliberately targeted civilians to break the Chinese will to fight. In 1937, the Japanese laid siege to the strategic city of Nanjing. Their orders on taking the city were simple: "kill all, burn all, destroy all." More than 200,000 Chinese citizens were slaughtered in what came to be known as the "Rape of Nanjing." The League voiced shock and disapproval but did nothing. In

GUERNICA BY PABLO PICASSO (1937). One of Picasso's most influential paintings, *Guernica* was painted as a mural for the Spanish republican government as it fought for survival in the Spanish Civil War. The Basque town of Guernica had been bombed by German fighters just a few months earlier, in April 1937. Near the center a horse writhes in agony; to the left a distraught woman holds her dead child. Compare Picasso's image to the antifascist propaganda poster on page 876. ▪ *What is different about the way that the two images deliver their political messages?* ▪ *Does Picasso's rejection of realism diminish the power of his political message?* ▪ *Does the antifascist poster seek any outcome other than the annihilation of the enemy?*

1935, Mussolini began his efforts to make the Mediterranean an Italian empire by returning to Ethiopia to avenge the defeat of 1896. This time the Italians came with tanks, bombers, and poison gas. The Ethiopians fought bravely but hopelessly, and this imperial massacre aroused world opinion. The League attempted to impose sanctions on Italy and condemned Japan. But for two reasons, no enforcement followed. The first was British and French fear of communism and their hope that Italy and Japan would act as counterweights to the Soviets. The second reason was practical. Enforcing sanctions would involve challenging Japan's powerful fleet or Mussolini's newly built battleships. Britain and France were unwilling, and dangerously close to unable, to use their navies to those ends.

The Spanish Civil War

The third challenge came closer to home. In 1936, civil war broke out in Spain. A series of weak republican governments, committed to large-scale social reforms, could not overcome opposition to those measures and political polarization. War broke out as extreme right-wing military officers rebelled. Although Hitler and Mussolini had signed a pact of nonintervention with the other Western powers, both leaders sent troops and equipment to assist the rebel commander, Francisco Franco (1939–75). The Soviet Union countered with aid to communist troops serving under the banner of the Spanish Republic. Again Britain and France failed to act decisively. Thousands of volunteers from England, France, and the United States— including many working-class socialists and writers, such as George Orwell and Ernest Hemingway—took up arms as private soldiers for the Republican government. They saw the war as a test of the West's determination to resist fascism and military dictatorships. Their governments were much more hesitant. For the British, Franco was anticommunist at least, just like Mussolini and the Japanese. The French prime minister Léon Blum, a committed antifascist, stood at the head of a Popular Front government—an alliance of socialists, communists, and republicans. The Popular Front had been elected on a program of social reform and opposition to Hitler abroad and fascism in France. Yet Blum's margin of support was limited. He feared that intervening in Spain would further polarize his country, bring down his government, and make it impossible to follow through on any commitment to the conflict. In Spain, despite some heroic fighting, the Republican camp degenerated into a hornet's nest of competing factions: republican, socialist, communist, and anarchist.

THE SPANISH CIVIL WAR. ▪ *Why did thousands of foreign fighters join the war?* ▪ *How did the strategies and weapons used in the war anticipate those used in the Second World War?* ▪ *What were the consequences of Franco's victory?*

The Spanish Civil War was brutal. Both the German and the Soviet "advisers" saw Spain as a "dress rehearsal" for a later war between the two powers. They each brought in their newest weapons and practiced their skills in destroying civilian targets from the air. In April 1937, a raid by German dive bombers utterly destroyed the town of Guernica in northern Spain in an effort to cut off Republican supply lines and terrorize civilians. It shocked public opinion and was commemorated by Pablo Picasso in one of the most famous paintings of the twentieth century. Both sides committed atrocities. The Spanish Civil War lasted three years, ending with a complete victory for Franco in 1939. In the aftermath, Britain and France proved reluctant to admit Spanish Republicans as refugees, even though Republicans faced recriminations from Franco's regime. Franco sent 1 million of his Republican enemies to prison or concentration camps.

Hitler drew two lessons from Spain. The first was that if Britain, France, and the Soviet Union ever tried to contain fascism, they would have a hard time coordinating their efforts. The second was that Britain and France were deeply averse to fighting another European war. This meant that the Nazis could use every means short of war to achieve their goals.

German Rearmament and the Politics of Appeasement

Hitler took advantage of this combination of international tolerance and war weariness to advance his ambitions. As Germany rearmed, Hitler played on Germans' sense of shame and betrayal, proclaiming their right to regain their former power in the world. In 1933, he removed Germany from the League of Nations, to which it had finally been admitted in 1926. In 1935, he defied the disarmament provisions of the Treaty of Versailles and revived conscription and universal military training. Hitler's stated goals were the restoration of Germany's power and dignity inside Europe and the unification of all ethnic Germans inside his Third German Reich. As the first step in this process, Germany reoccupied the Rhineland in 1936. It was a risky move, chancing war with the much more powerful French army. But France and Britain did not mount a military response. In retrospect, this was an important turning point; the balance of power tipped in Germany's favor. While the Rhineland remained demilitarized and German industry in the Ruhr valley was unprotected, France held the upper hand. After 1936, it no longer did so.

In March 1938, Hitler annexed Austria, reaffirming his intention to bring all Germans into his Reich. Once more, no official reaction came from the West. The Nazis' next target was the Sudetenland in Czechoslovakia, a region with a large ethnic German population. With Austria now a part of Germany, Czechoslovakia was almost entirely surrounded by its hostile neighbor. Hitler declared that the Sudetenland was a natural part of the Reich and that he intended to occupy it. The Czechs did not want to give way. Hitler's generals were wary of this gamble. Czechoslovakia had a strong, well-equipped army and a line of fortifications along the border. Many in the French and Polish governments were willing to come to the Czechs' aid. According to plans already being laid for a wider European war, Germany would not be ready for another three to four years. But Hitler gambled, and the British prime minister, Neville Chamberlain, obliged him. Chamberlain decided to take charge of international talks about the Sudetenland and agreed to Hitler's terms. Chamberlain's logic was that this dispute was about the balance of power in Europe. If Hitler were allowed to unify all Germans in one state, he reasoned, then German ambitions would be satisfied. Chamberlain also believed that his country could not commit to a sustained war. Finally, defending eastern European boundaries against Germany ranked low on Great Britain's list of priorities, at least in comparison to ensuring free trade in western Europe and protecting the strategic centers of the British Empire.

On September 29, 1938, Hitler met with Chamberlain, Premier Édouard Daladier (1938–40) of France, and Mussolini in a four-power conference in Munich. The result was another capitulation by France and Britain. The four negotiators bargained away a major slice of Czechoslovakia while Czech representatives were left to await their fate outside the conference room. Chamberlain returned to London proclaiming "peace in our time." Hitler soon proved

GERMAN SOLDIERS ENTER RHINELAND IN COLOGNE, 1936. Hitler's reoccupation of the Rhineland—an area bordering France, Belgium, and the Netherlands—was a direct violation of the Treaty of Versailles, but it was difficult for the French and British governments to respond effectively, because voters in these nations were reluctant to go to war over Hitler's decision to move troops into what was, after all, German territory.

Map Legend

Germany

German advances
- Reoccupied Rhineland, March 1936
- Annexed Austria, March 1938
- Annexed Sudetenland, October 1938
- Annexed Bohemia and Moravia, March 1939
- Annexed Memel, March 1939

Italy
- Annexed Albania, April 1939

Poland and Hungary
- Annexed Czech territory, 1938 and 1939

( ) Former independent nations: Albania, Austria, and Czechoslovakia

Area of detail

EUROPE

AFRICA

NORWAY

Stockholm

ESTONIA

SWEDEN

LATVIA

NORTH SEA

Moscow

DENMARK
Copenhagen

BALTIC SEA

MEMEL

LITHUANIA

DANZIG

GERMANY

SOVIET UNION

Amsterdam

NETHERLANDS

Berlin

Warsaw

GERMANY

POLAND

Bern

BELGIUM

SUDETENLAND

RHINELAND

Prague

(CZECH.)

LUXEMBOURG

Rhine R.

Nuremberg

BOHEMIA & MORAVIA

SLOVAKIA

Annexed Czech Territory

UKRAINE

FRANCE

Vienna

Bern

SWITZERLAND

(AUSTRIA)

Budapest

HUNGARY

ROMANIA

ITALY

ADRIATIC SEA

Belgrade

Bucharest

Danube R.

BLACK SEA

CORSICA

Rome

YUGOSLAVIA

Sofia

BULGARIA

SARDINIA

(ALBANIA)

Istanbul

MEDITERRANEAN SEA

SICILY

GREECE

Athens

TURKEY

0   100   200   300 Miles
0 100 200 300 Kilometers

GERMAN AND ITALIAN EXPANSION, 1936–1939. ▪ *What were Hitler's first steps to unify all the ethnic Germans in Europe?* ▪ *How did he use these initial gains to annex territory from the Czechs?* ▪ *After winning Czechoslovakia, why did Hitler choose to invade Poland?*

that he should look elsewhere for security. Tempted by the traditional Soviet desire for territory in Poland, Stalin was promised a share of Poland, Finland, the Baltic states, and Bessarabia by Hitler's representatives. In a cynical reversal of their anti-Nazi proclamations that stunned many, the Soviets signed a nonaggression pact with the Nazis in August 1939. By going to Munich, Britain and France had put their interests first; the Soviet Union would now look after its own.

THE OUTBREAK OF HOSTILITIES AND THE FALL OF FRANCE

After his success in Czechoslovakia, Hitler demanded the abolition of the Polish Corridor. This was a narrow strip of land connecting Poland with the Baltic Sea. The corridor also divided East Prussia from the rest of Germany, separating yet another large German population from union with the Reich. Judging Britain and France by past performance, Hitler believed their pledges to Poland were worthless. With the Soviets now in his camp, he expected that Poland would consent and the Western allies would back down again. When Poland stood firm instead, Hitler attacked. On September 1, 1939, German troops crossed the Polish border. Britain and France sent a joint warning to Germany to withdraw. There was no reply. On September 3, Britain and France declared war.

The conquest of Poland was shockingly quick. It demanded great resources—Germany committed nearly all of its combat troops and planes to the invasion—but the results were remarkable. Well-coordinated attacks by German *panzers* (tanks) and armored vehicles, supported by devastating air power, cut the large but slow-moving Polish army to pieces. German infantry still moved on foot or via horse-drawn transport, but their disciplined advance followed the devastating work of the panzers. The Poles fought doggedly but were so stunned and disorganized that they had little hope of mounting an effective defense. The "lightning war" (*Blitzkrieg*, blitz-KREEG) for which the German officer corps had trained so long was a complete success. Within three weeks German troops were laying siege to Warsaw. German terror bombing, designed to destroy the heart of Warsaw from the air and frighten the population into surrender, was successful. Poland, a large country with a large army, was dismembered in four weeks.

In accordance with its agreement with Nazi Germany, the Soviet Union also invaded Poland from the east, taking its share of Polish territory and using Stalin's signature

JOHN HEARTFIELD, *HAVE NO FEAR—HE'S A VEGETARIAN.*
Heartfield (born Helmut Herzfeld) was a German radical associated with the Dada movement and communism. This photomontage appeared in a French magazine in 1936 as Hitler's warlike intentions became clear. Pierre Laval, then prime minister of France and later architect of French collaboration with the Nazis, whispers reassuringly to a rooster, a symbol for France, as Hitler sharpens his knife.

that boast hollow. In March 1939, Germany invaded what was left of Czechoslovakia, annexed Bohemia and Moravia, and established a puppet regime in Slovakia. This was Germany's first conquest of non-German territory, and it sent shock waves across Europe. It convinced public and political opinion outside Germany of the futility of appeasement. Chamberlain was forced to shift his policies completely. British and French rearmament sped up dramatically. Together with France, Britain guaranteed the sovereignty of the two states now directly in Hitler's path, Poland and Romania.

Meanwhile, the politics of appeasement had fueled Stalin's fears that the Western democracies might strike a deal with Germany at Soviet expense, thus diverting Nazi expansion eastward. The Soviet Union had not been invited to the Munich conference, and suspicious that Britain and France were unreliable allies, Stalin became convinced methods to deal with the enemy: rounding up millions to be deported, imprisoned, or executed. Wary that German aggression would turn on them, the Soviets also hastened to shore up their position to the north, on the Russo-Finnish border. Since at least 1938, the Soviets had demanded from Finland various arrangements to protect Leningrad, from access to strategic locations and permission to build fortifications in Finland to the outright ceding of territory—all of which the Finns had refused. Shortly after the invasion of Poland, then, the Soviets attacked Finland. Despite the Soviets' overwhelming superiority in numbers and material, the Finns fought back tenaciously. The Soviets faced a very difficult campaign—an alarming demonstration of the damaging effects of Stalin's terror on the Soviet military. Although the Soviet Union concluded the undeclared four-month Winter War with a precarious victory in March 1940, Hitler and the rest of the world had made note of Stalin's weaknesses.

After the fall of Poland, the conflict became an ominous "phony war," or *Sitzkrieg*, as it was sometimes called. The fighting in Poland was followed by a winter of anxious nonactivity with occasional headlines about naval skirmishes. In the spring of 1940, that calm was broken by a terrible storm. The Germans struck first in Scandinavia, taking Denmark in a day and invading Norway. Britain

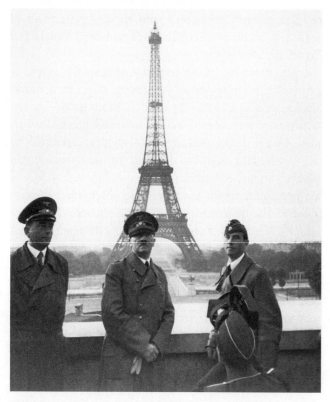

JUNE 23, 1940. Hitler and Nazi architect Albert Speer pose across the river from the Eiffel Tower after capturing Paris.

and France tried to aid the Norwegian defense and sank a large number of German ships, but the Allied expedition failed. Then the real blow was struck. On May 10, German forces swarmed through Belgium and the Netherlands on their way to France. The two nations were conquered in short order. When the Dutch succeeded in flooding canals that protected their major cities and defended that line with hard-fighting marines, Hitler ordered his air force to bomb the city of Rotterdam. More than 800 Dutch civilians died, and the Netherlands surrendered the next day. The Belgians' stubborn and effective defense of their nation was cut short when King Albert suddenly surrendered after two weeks of fighting, fearing similar destruction. In turn, Albert stayed on as a figurehead for the Nazis, reviled by Belgians who found other ways to carry on the fight against Germany.

The large French army was carved up by the *Blitzkrieg*. Its divisions were isolated, outflanked, and overwhelmed by German aircraft and armored columns working according to an exacting plan. French units either fought fierce battles until they were hopelessly surrounded or simply collapsed. The French army and French artillery, much of it better built than its German equivalent, were poorly organized and rendered useless in the face of rapid German maneuvers. The defeat turned quickly into a rout. Hundreds of thousands of civilians, each carrying a few precious possessions loaded on carts, fled south. They were joined by thousands of Allied soldiers without weapons, and these columns of refugees were attacked constantly by German dive bombers. The disorganized British made a desperate retreat to the port of Dunkirk on the English Channel, where many of Britain's best troops were sacrificed holding off the panzers. At the beginning of June 1940, despite heavy German air attacks, Britain's Royal Navy evacuated more than 300,000 British and French troops, with the help of commercial and pleasure boats that had been pressed into emergency service.

After Dunkirk, the conflict was bitter but the outcome inevitable. French reservists fought, as their commanders asked, "to the last cartridge," killing thousands of Germans. Without proper organization and more firepower, however, this bravery was useless. The Germans swept through the northwest and the heart of the country, reaching Paris in mid-June 1940. The political will of France's government collapsed along with its armies. Rather than withdrawing to Britain or French colonies in North Africa, the French surrendered on June 22. The armistice cut the country in two. The Germans occupied all of northern France, including Paris and the Channel ports. The south, and French territories in North Africa, lay under the jurisdiction of a deeply conservative government formed at the spa town of Vichy (*VIH-shee*) under the leadership of an elderly First World War hero, Marshal Philippe Pétain. France had fallen. One of Germany's historic enemies, the victor of the previous war, an imperial power and nation of almost 60 million citizens, was reduced to chaos and enemy occupation in forty days.

The penalties exacted on France did not end with defeat. Many liberals within France, and most of the Free French movement quickly established in London, soon felt they had two enemies to fight: Germany and Pétain's regime. The Vichy government proposed to collaborate with the Germans in return for retaining a small measure of sovereignty, or so it believed. The regime also instituted its own National Revolution, which came very close to fascism. Vichy repudiated the republic, accusing it of sapping France's strength. The state proceeded to reorganize French life and political institutions, strengthening the authority of the Catholic Church and the family and helping the Germans crush any resistance. "Work, Family, and Country"—this was Vichy's call to order.

NOT ALONE: THE BATTLE OF BRITAIN AND THE BEGINNINGS OF A GLOBAL WAR

Before launching an invasion across the Channel, the Nazis attempted to establish superiority in the air. From July 1940 to June 1941, in the Battle of Britain, thousands of planes dropped millions of tons of bombs on British targets: first aircraft and airfields and then, as the focus shifted to breaking Britain's will, civilian targets such as London. More than 40,000 British civilians died. Yet the British stood firm. This was possible in part because of a German mistake. After a daring British bombing raid on Berlin, Hitler angrily told his generals to concentrate on civilian targets. This spared the Royal Air Force, whose bases had been steadily devastated up to that point. Given the chance to keep fighting, the R.A.F. forced a costly stalemate in the air. Hitler scrapped the invasion plans, turning his attention east toward Russia.

Another important reason for the determined British resistance was a change of political leadership. In May 1940, Chamberlain's catalog of failures finished his career. He was toppled by a coalition government that brought together Conservative, Liberal, and Labour politicians for the sake of national unity. It was led by the most unlikely of the choices offered to replace him: Winston Churchill (1940–45, 1951–55). Churchill was a political maverick who had changed parties more than once. He was extremely talented but also arrogant. He had a sharp temper and sometimes seemed unstable, and before 1939 his political career was judged to be over. As prime minister, he was not much of an administrator, constantly proposing wild schemes, but he had two genuine gifts. The first was language. Churchill spoke extraordinary words of courage and defiance just when the British public wanted and needed to hear them. He was utterly committed to winning the war.

"You ask what is our policy," Churchill said in his first speech as prime minister in May of 1940, before the Battle of Britain began. "I will say, it is to wage war with all our might, with all the strength that God can give us, to wage war against a monstrous tyranny never surpassed in the dark, lamentable catalogue of human crime."

The second was personal diplomacy. He convinced the American president Franklin Roosevelt (1933–45), who supported the Allies, to break with American neutrality and send massive amounts of aid and weapons to Britain free of charge, under a program called Lend-Lease. Churchill

LONDON DURING THE BATTLE OF BRITAIN. German air raids that lasted from August 1940 to June 1941 wrought destruction but did not achieve Hitler's goal of breaking the British. The Holland House Library in London lost its roof but managed to engage in business as usual.

THE SECOND WORLD WAR IN EUROPE. ▪ *What parts of the European theater were controlled by the Allies?* ▪ *The Axis?* ▪ *Which countries were neutral in 1941?* ▪ *In what parts of the European theater did the major Axis and Allied campaigns occur?* ▪ *What was Germany's greatest geographical challenge during the Second World War?*

also allowed the new government coalition to work to best effect. The ablest Conservative ministers stayed, but Labour politicians were also allowed to take positions of genuine power. Most of the Labour representatives turned out to be excellent administrators and were directly in touch with Britain's huge working class, which now felt fully included in the war effort.

With Britain's survival, the war moved into different theatres: the Atlantic (a battle over sea lanes and supplies), North Africa (strategically important for the Suez Canal and access to oil), the Pacific (the war with Japan), and the Soviet Union (where Hitler's determination to annihilate Stalin merged with his murderous campaign against the Jewish populations of Europe).

The Atlantic and North Africa

The Battle of the Atlantic, launched as a submarine campaign to starve out the British, was a dire threat to the Allies. Learning from the First World War, the Germans sent hundreds of submarines (U-boats) out in "wolf packs" to stalk the major sea lanes to Britain. German submarines sank millions of tons of merchant shipping, as far away as the coasts of Brazil and Florida. Britain's supplies of weapons, raw materials, and food hung in the balance. The British devoted a huge naval effort and great technical resourcefulness to saving their convoys. They developed modern sonar and new systems of aerial reconnaissance and cracked the Germans' codes for communicating with the wolf packs. These efforts kept supplies coming. When the United States entered the war in December 1941 (see below), the British supplied the experience and technology and the Americans the numbers and firepower to sink many more U-boats. By late 1942, the threat receded.

The war in North Africa began because Britain had to protect the Suez Canal, but Britain was soon drawn into a larger conflict. Indian, South African, and West African troops fighting for the British drove the Italians from Ethiopia in May 1941. The Soviets and the British invaded Iran to keep its shah (ruler) from making a deal with Germany over Iranian oil and held the country until 1946. A small, well-led British army in Egypt humiliated a much larger Italian invasion force. The British nearly captured Italy's colony of Libya, and this forced Germany to intervene. An elite armored force called the Afrika Korps, led by Germany's most daring tank commander, Erwin Rommel, drove the British back in the spring of 1941 and started a grudging two-year war in the desert. The British fielded an international army, which included as many Australians, Indians, and New Zealanders as it did Britons, pitted against the Germans and Italians. The fighting swung back and forth for eighteen months, with the British taking the worst of it. Then the momentum shifted. Despite heavy losses from German planes and submarines, the British defeated the Italian navy and took control of the Mediterranean. They also established domination in the air over the desert. When Rommel tried to invade Egypt, his forces were stopped and badly defeated near the town of El Alamein in July, then driven back toward Tunisia later that fall. "This is not the end," said Winston Churchill in his inimitable style, after the British victory at El Alamein. "It is not even the beginning of the end. But it is, perhaps, the end of the beginning."

The United States intervened in November 1942, landing in the French territories of Algeria and Morocco. A conference was held at Casablanca, Morocco, among the Allied powers to discuss the future course of the war and the fate of French territories in North Africa. French administrators in Algeria and Morocco, who had supported Vichy, at least in public, surrendered peacefully or joined the Allied side. Rommel still defended Tunisia against the Allies for four months, but a joint offensive broke the German lines in March 1943, ending the fighting.

The Allies and Japan in the Pacific

The war became truly global when Japan struck the American naval base at Pearl Harbor, Hawaii, on the morning of December 7, 1941. The Japanese had been involved in a costly war in China since the 1930s. To win and to establish a Japanese empire throughout Asia, they would have to destroy America's Pacific fleet and seize the colonies of the British, Dutch, and French Empires. Like Germany, Japan began with lightning blows. The attack on Pearl Harbor

"A DATE WHICH WILL LIVE IN INFAMY," DECEMBER 7, 1941. The U.S.S. *West Virginia* was one of eight battleships sunk during the Japanese surprise attack targeting Battleship Row at the American naval base at Pearl Harbor. More than 2,000 people were killed, but most of the American fleet, en route to or from other locations in the Pacific, was spared.

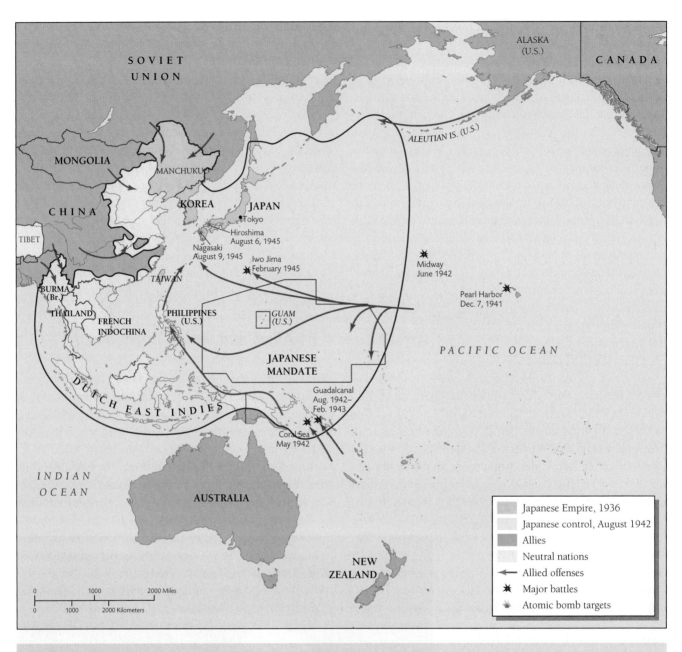

WORLD WAR II IN THE PACIFIC. ▪ *What areas did the Japanese and Allies each control in the Pacific theater during the Second World War?* ▪ *Based on tracing the route of the Allied offense of the map, what did the main Allied strategy appear to be?* ▪ *What factors led the Americans to decide that the dropping of atomic bombs on Hiroshima and Nagasaki was the most expeditious way to end the war rather than invading Japan?*

was a brilliant act of surprise that devastated the American fleet and shocked the American public. It was not, however, the success that the Japanese wanted. Eight U.S. battleships were sunk and more than 2,000 lives lost; but much of the American fleet—including its aircraft carriers, submarines, and many smaller ships—were safely at sea on the day of the strike. The unprovoked attack galvanized American public opinion in a way the war in Europe had not. When Germany rashly declared war on the United States as well,

America declared itself ready to take on all comers and joined the Allies.

Despite the mixed results at Pearl Harbor the Japanese enjoyed other, stunning successes. For the European colonial powers, Japan's entry into the war was a catastrophe. Japanese troops swept through the British protectorate of Malaya in weeks, sinking the Pacific squadrons of both the British and Dutch navies in the swift attacks. Britain's fortified island port at Singapore, the keystone of British defenses in the Pacific, fell at the end of December 1941. The shock of the loss nearly took Churchill's government with it. Thousands of British and Australian troops were captured and sent off to four years of torture, forced labor, and starvation in Japanese prison camps. The Japanese also invaded the Philippines in December; and while American soldiers and marines held out on the island of Corregidor for some time, they too were forced to surrender. Some took to the hills to fight as guerrillas; the rest were forced on a death march to Japanese labor camps. The Dutch East Indies fell next, and it seemed there would be no stopping Japanese ships and soldiers before they reached Australia.

Reeling from Japan's blows, the Allies finally reorganized during 1942. After taking Singapore, Japanese troops pressed on into Burma. Several famous British generals tried and failed to defend Burma, with disastrous losses of men and matériel. After these failures, command fell to an obscure Indian army officer, William Slim. For a British officer, Slim had quite humble origins. He was a career soldier, a minor hero in the First World War, and perhaps the best strategist in the British army. Even more important, the millions of nonwhite imperial troops from India and Africa who were under his command liked and respected him as an honest, unprejudiced man. He reorganized imperial defenses, and a joint force of British and Indian troops defeated an attempted Japanese invasion of India at the border near the end of 1942. After that, with an army drawn from around the world, Slim began to push the Japanese back. In New Guinea, Australian troops fresh from North Africa were first to defeat the Japanese on land in bitter hand-to-hand fighting and staged a counterattack through the high mountain jungles. At sea, America's navy benefited from a rapidly increased production schedule that turned out new ships and planes to outnumber the Japanese, and two gifted admirals, Chester Nimitz and William Halsey, who outfought them. In 1942, the United States won crucial victories in the Coral Sea and at Midway, a battle fought at sea and in the air by aircraft flown from each side's carriers. American marines landed on the island of Guadalcanal in early 1942 and captured this strategic Japanese base after months of bitter fighting. Their success began a campaign of island hopping as the marines destroyed Japan's network of island bases throughout the Pacific. This was brutal warfare, often settled with grenades and bayonets. Each side considered the other racially inferior. The Japanese often refused to surrender; the Americans and Australians also took few prisoners. By 1943, the Japanese victories had been halted, the Japanese navy had lost most of its capital ships, and the Allies began a slow march to Singapore and the Philippines.

THE RISE AND RUIN OF NATIONS: GERMANY'S WAR IN THE EAST AND THE OCCUPATION OF EUROPE

While battles ebbed and flowed in the Atlantic and the North African desert, Germany moved southeast into the Balkans. In 1941, Germany took over Yugoslavia almost without a fight. The Germans split Yugoslavia's ethnic patchwork by establishing a Croatian puppet state, pitting Croats against their Serb neighbors who were ruled directly by the Nazis. Romania, Hungary, and Bulgaria joined the Nazis' cause as allies. The Greeks, who had dealt a crushing defeat to an Italian invasion, were suddenly confronted with a massive German force that overran the country. The Greeks stubbornly refused to surrender. An unexpected combination of Greek, British, and New Zealand troops nearly defeated the German paratroopers sent to capture the island of Crete in June of 1941. Many Greeks also took to the mountains as guerrillas, but in the end the country fell. By the summer of 1941, with the exceptions of Spain, Portugal, Sweden, and Switzerland, the whole European continent was either allied with the Nazis or subject to their rule. These victories, and the economy of plunder that enriched Germany with forced labor and other nations' money, won Hitler considerable popularity at home. But these were only the first steps in a larger plan.

Hitler's ultimate goals, and his conception of Germany's national destiny, lay to the east. Hitler had always seen the nonaggression pact with the Soviet Union as an act of convenience, to last only until Germany was ready for this final conflict. By the summer of 1941, it seemed Germany was ready. On June 22, 1941, Hitler began Operation Barbarossa, the invasion of the Soviet Union. The elite of the German army led the way, defeating all the forces the Russians could put in front of them. Stalin's purges of the 1930s had exiled or executed many of his most capable army officers, and the effects showed in Russian disorganization and disaffection in the face of the panzers. Hundreds of thousands of prisoners were taken as German forces pressed deep into Byelorussia (modern Belarus), the Baltic states, and Ukraine. Like Napoleon, the Germans led a multinational army; it included Italians, Hungarians, most of the Romanian army, and freelance soldiers from the Baltics and Ukraine who bore grudges against Stalin's authoritarian regime. During the fall of 1941, the Nazis destroyed much of the Red Army's fighting strength and vigorously pursued their two goals: the destruction of communism and racial purification.

The war against the Soviets was a war of ideologies and of racial hatred. The advancing Nazi forces left burning fields and towns in their wake and methodically wiped the occupied territories clean of "undesirable elements." When Russian guerrillas counterattacked with sniping and sabotage, German forces shot or hanged hundreds of innocent hostages at a time in reprisal, often torturing their victims first. The Russian guerrillas quickly chose to deliver the same punishment to any captured Germans. By the end of 1941, it was clear that the war in the East was a war of destruction and that both sides believed that only one side would be allowed to survive. In 1941, it seemed the victors would be German. Their forces were on the march toward the capital at Moscow. On orders from Berlin, however, some of the German forces pushing toward Moscow were diverted south to attack Russia's industrial heartland in an effort to destroy the Soviets' ability to resist before the Russian winter set in. Moscow was never taken, and the Russian population, its leaders, and its armies began to organize a much more determined resistance.

Hitler nonetheless managed to piece together an empire that stretched across the entire continent of Europe. "We come as the heralds of a New Order and a new justice," his regime announced. Hitler specifically compared his rule to a "new Indian empire," and claimed to have studied British imperial techniques. Much of the New Order was improvised and rested on a patchwork of provisional regimes: military government in Poland and Ukraine, collaborators in France, allied fascists in Hungary, and so on. The clearest principle was German supremacy. "The emphatic German decision to organize Europe hierarchically, like a pyramid with Germany at the top, is known to all," said an Italian diplomat at the time. The empire was meant to feed German citizens and maintain their morale and support for the war, which would prevent the "stab in the back" that Hitler believed had thwarted a German victory in 1914–18. Occupied countries paid inflated "occupation costs" in taxes, food, industrial production, and manpower. More than 2 million foreign workers were brought into Germany in 1942–43 from France, Belgium, Holland, and the Soviet Union. As they conscripted workers, the Nazis spoke of uniting Europe to save it from the "Red Menace" of communism. This propaganda seems to have had little effect. To the contrary, deporting citizens to labor in Germany did more than any other policy to drive individuals into the resistance, especially in France and Greece.

The demands of enemy occupation and the political and moral questions of collaboration and resistance, were issues across occupied Europe. The Nazis set up puppet regimes in a number of occupied territories. Both Norway and the Netherlands were deeply divided by the occupa-

"CULTURAL TERROR," 1944. Produced in Nazi-occupied Holland, this cultural Frankenstein's monster warns of the looming destruction of European identity with the advance of American troops who will bring American culture with them. The terror of this culture is embodied in a long list of references: aerial bombardment, the violence of lynching and the Ku Klux Klan, African American jazz, Jewish racial threats, sexual license, and common criminality and financial manipulation. ▪ *What image of European culture was this image designed to defend?*

tion. In both countries, a relatively small but dedicated party of Nazis governed in the name of the Germans while at the same time well-organized and determined resistance movements gathered information for the Allies and carried out acts of sabotage. In Denmark, the population was much more united against their German occupiers, engaging in regular acts of passive resistance that infuriated German administrators. They also banded together as private citizens to smuggle most of the country's Jewish population out to safety in neutral Sweden.

Elsewhere, the relationship among collaboration, resistance, and self-interested indifference was more complex. In France, collaboration ranged from simple survival tactics under occupation to active support for Nazi ideals and goals. The worst example of this was the Vichy regime's active anti-Semitism and the aid given by French authori-

NORTH
SEA

NORWAY

SWEDEN

FINLAND

•Leningrad

IRELAND

UNITED
KINGDOM

DENMARK

ESTONIA

LATVIA

•Moscow

BALTIC SEA

LITHUANIA

SOVIET
UNION

MEMELAND
Danzig

Vilna•

NETHLERANDS

London•

EAST
PRUSSIA

BIALYSTOK

GREATER
GERMANY

•Berlin

POSEN

•Warsaw

EASTERN
POLAND

ATLANTIC
OCEAN

BELGIUM

EUREN

•Paris

LUX.

•Kiev

Occupied

GOVERNMENT
GENERAL
OF
POLAND

NORTHERN
BUKOVINA

FRANCE

LORRAINE
ALSACE

SUDETEN-
LAND

BOHEMIA

MORAVIA

•Lemberg

SLOVAKIA

•Vichy

SWITZ.

AUSTRIA

•Budapest

BESSARABIA

VICHY
FRANCE
Unoccupied until
November 1942

•Milan

HUNGARY

CROATIA

ROMANIA

PORTUGAL

•Toulon

ADRIATIC SEA

YUGOSLAVIA
Partitioned
April, 1941

Belgrade•

•Bucharest

BLACK SEA

SPAIN

ITALY

CORSICA
(Vichy)

SERBIA

•Sofia

BULGARIA

•Rome

BALEARIC
ISLANDS

SARDINIA
(It.)

CATTARO
(It.)

ALBANIA
(It.)

•Istanbul

T U R K E Y

•Ankara

GREECE

MOROCCO

ALGERIA
(Fr.)

SICILY

Athens•

CRETE

CYPRUS

M E D I T E R R A N E A N

S E A

LEBANON

TUNISIA
(Fr.)

LIBYA
(It.)

EGYPT

PALESTINE

0   250   500 Miles

0   250   500 Kilometers

EUROPE

Area of
detail

AFRICA

Axis states and annexed areas

Axis allies

Axis occupied

Sudetenland

AXIS EUROPE, 1941. ▪ *How had Hitler and Mussolini come to dominate the bulk of mainland Europe by the eve of the German invasion of the Soviet Union?* ▪ *Why did Hitler choose to annex certain territories to Germany but settle for occupation in others?* ▪ *Looking at this map, doesn't a German victory look inevitable? Why or why not?*

ties in isolating, criminalizing, and deporting Jews in France to the concentration camps. Living with the German conquerors forced citizens in France (and elsewhere) to make choices. Many chose to protect their own interests by sacrificing those of others, particularly such "undesirables" as Jews and communists. At the same time, communist activists, some members of the military, and ordinary citizens—such as the people of France's central mountains, who had a long tradition of smuggling and resisting government—became active guerrillas and saboteurs. They established links with the Free French movement in London, led by the charismatic, stiff-necked general Charles de Gaulle, and supplied important intelligence to the Allies. In eastern Europe, resistance movements provoked both open warfare against the fascists and civil war within their own countries. The Germans' system of occupation in Yugoslavia pitted a fascist Croat regime against most Serbs; the Croatian fascist guard, the Ustasha, massacred hundreds of thousands of Orthodox Christian Serbs. Josip Broz (Tito), born in Croatia to a Croatian father and a Slovene mother, emerged as the leader of the most powerful Yugoslavian resistance movement—militarily the most significant resistance in the war. Tito's troops were communists and strong enough to form a guerrilla army. They fought Germans, Italians, and Croat fascists, and they gained support and supplies from the Allies.

Perhaps the most important moral issue facing citizens of occupied Europe was not their national allegiance but rather their personal attitude to the fate of the Nazis'

sworn enemies: Jews, communists, gypsies, homosexuals, and political "undesirables." Some French Jews along the Riviera found the Italian Catholic army officers who occupied the area more willing to save them from deportation than their fellow Frenchmen. This deeply personal dilemma—whether to risk family, friends, and careers to aid the deportees or simply to look the other way and allow mass murder—was one of the most powerful of the war.

RACIAL WAR, ETHNIC CLEANSING, AND THE HOLOCAUST

From the beginning, the Nazis had seen the conflict as a racial war. In *Mein Kampf*, Hitler had already outlined his view that war against the *Untermenschen*, or "subhuman" Jews, Gypsies, and Slavs, was natural and necessary. Not only would it purify the German people, but it would also conquer territory for their expansion. Thus, as soon as the war broke out, the Nazis began to implement ambitious plans for redrawing the racial map of the Reich, or what is now called ethnic cleansing. In the fall of 1939, with Poland conquered, Heinrich Himmler directed the SS to begin massive population transfers. Ethnic Germans were moved from elsewhere into the borders of the Reich, while Poles and Jews were deported to specially designated areas in the east. Over 200,000 ethnic Germans from the Baltic states were resettled in western Prussia. Welcoming these ethnic Germans went hand in hand with a brutal campaign of terror against the Poles, especially Polish Jews. The Nazis sought to root out all sources of potential resistance. Professors at the University of Cracow, considered dangerous intellectuals, were deported to concentration camps, where they died. The SS shot "undesirables," such as the inmates of Polish mental asylums, partly to allow SS troops to occupy the asylums' barracks. Poles were deported to forced labor camps. The Nazis began to transport Jews by the thousands to the region of Lublin, south of Warsaw. Special death squads also began to shoot Jews in the streets and in front of synagogues. These Polish campaigns took 100,000 Jewish lives in 1940.

The elimination of European Jewry stood at the center of the Nazis' *Rassenkampf*, or "racial struggle." We have seen the role of anti-Semitism in Hitler's rise to

POLISH JEWS, EVICTED FROM THE WARSAW GHETTO, BEING DEPORTED.
Most of the trains led to death camps.

Legend:
- ■ Main concentration camp
- • Subcamps
- — Present-day boundary

WHERE WERE THE CAMPS? In 2013, historians compiled a list of more than 42,000 separate extermination camps, detention centers, ghettos, and slave labor sites in German-controlled Europe during the war years. Their conclusion, that virtually every population center was close to such a site, has caused historians to revise upward their estimates of who in Europe had knowledge of the extermination policy.

power and the escalating campaign of terror against the Jewish community inside Germany in the 1930s, including the Night of the Broken Glass (see Chapter 25). Most historians now agree that although Hitler and other Nazis verbally announced "war" against the Jews early on, such a policy was not possible until the conquest of territory in the east after 1941 suddenly brought millions of Jews under Nazi control. Until the organized pogroms of 1938, the Nazis' anti-Jewish policy aimed not at extermination but at emigration, and until 1941 the Nazi leadership continued to consider plans to deport Europe's Jews to Madagascar, a French colony off the coast of Africa. These schemes took

shape against the background of daily terror and frequent massacres, especially in Poland. The invasion of the Soviet Union turned these atrocities into something much more deadly. Operation Barbarossa was animated by the Nazis' intense ideological and racial hatreds, directed against Slavs, Jews, and Marxists. Goebbels, for example, called the Russians, "not a people but an agglomeration of animals." The invasion of the Soviet Union was thus openly a "war of extermination." The campaign's initial success also created pressing practical problems for the German army in the newly conquered territories, as they debated how to control the millions of people, including military prisoners, eastern

The Nazis and "The Gypsy Question"

Historians do not know the exact numbers of Roma people (commonly known as "gypsies" among non-Roma speakers) killed by the Nazis as part of their quest for a racially pure society. The U.S. Holocaust Museum estimates that 220,000 of the slightly fewer than 1 million Roma living in Europe were killed, either by the Germans themselves or by their allies. The Ustasha militia of Croatia, for example, was responsible for killing between 15,000 and 20,000 Roma. At Auschwitz, where 19,000 of the 23,000 Roma inmates died, Josef Mengele conducted pseudoscientific medical experiments on many Roma individuals. The documents reproduced here show the evolution of German policy toward the Roma people from 1938 to 1943 and provide a clear example of the way that German racial laws were applied to an entire population.

ircular Directive of December 8, 1938, by the Reichsführer-SS and Chief of German Police, pertaining to the "Settlement of the Gypsy Question"

A. General Directives

I. Domestic Gypsies

1. (1) The experiences collected so far in combating the Gypsy plague, and the knowledge gained from racial-biological research would make it seem advisable to tackle the settlement of the Gypsy Question with the nature of this race in mind. According to experience, individuals of mixed race contribute the largest share to Gypsy criminality. Conversely, it has been shown that all attempts to settle Gypsies in a permanent place of residence failed in particular with pure-blooded Gypsies because of their strong urge to roam. Thus, it will be necessary to deal separately with the pure-blooded Gypsies and those of mixed blood when it comes to the final solution of the Gypsy Question.

(3) I therefore direct that all Gypsies, whether sedentary or not, as well as all persons roaming in Gypsy fashion must be rounded up [*erfaßt*] by the Reich Criminal Police Office—Central Reich Administration for Combating Gypsy Malefaction.

3. (1) The ultimate determination as to whether one deals with a Gypsy, a Gypsy of mixed blood, or some person roaming in Gypsy fashion will be made by the Reich Criminal Police Office based on the testimony of an expert.

(2) I therefore direct . . . that all Gypsies, Gypsies of mixed blood, and persons roaming in Gypsy fashion be compelled to submit to a racial-biological examination required for the presentation of a testimony by an expert, and to provide the necessary information about their descent. The implementation of this directive is to be ensured by means of forceful police measures.

. . .

II. Foreign Gypsies

1. Foreign gypsies must be prevented from entering German territory. Refusal to grant entry permits and to move them back is required procedure even if foreign Gypsies are in possession of passports entitling them to immigrate, of substitute documents in lieu of passports, or of visa.

. . .

Express Letter of August 17, 1939 from the Reich Security Main Office, pertaining to the "rounding up" ["Erfassung"] of Gypsies

Berlin, October 10, 1939
Reich Security Main Office
Tgb. No. RKPA. 149/1939-g
Express Letter

European Jews, and other civilians, who had now fallen into Nazi hands. Although Hitler had certainly prepared the way for what followed in his long-nurtured campaigns against Jews, historians now believe that a significant part of the driving force for the Holocaust came from rivalries within the Nazi bureaucracy, which led to a radicalization of persecution and murder on a scale few could have imagined.

As the Nazi army swept into the Soviet Union in 1941, captured communist officials, political agitators, and any hostile civilians were imprisoned, tortured, or shot. About 5.5 million military prisoners were taken and marched to camps. Over half of them died of starvation or were executed. Poles from regions that had been under Soviet rule, Jews, and Russians were deported to Germany to work as slave labor in German factories. On the heels of the army came special battalions of *Einsatzgruppen,* or "death squads." Joined by 11,000 extra SS troops, they stormed through Jewish villages and towns with Russian or Polish populations

To the State Criminal Police—Regional and Local Commands of the Criminal Police . . .

Subject: Rounding Up of Gypsies

By order of the *Reichsführer-SS* and Chief of German Police the Gypsy Question will be fundamentally settled before long within the entire German territory by a uniform standard applied throughout the Reich. I therefore ask you to initiate the following measures at once:

1. The local police stations and the Rural Police must be instructed immediately to notify all Gypsies and Gypsies of mixed blood within their respective districts that effective immediately they may not leave their residence or their present whereabouts until further notice. Anybody in violation of this injunction will be threatened with dispatch to a concentration camp.

. . .

Express letter of January 29, 1943 from the Reich Security Main Office, pertaining to the confinement of "Gypsies of Mixed Blood," "Romany Gypsies" and "Balkan Gypsies" to a concentration camp

Berlin, January 29, 1943
Reich Security Main Office
VA No. 59/43 g
Express Letter

. . .

Subject: Confinement of Gypsies of mixed blood, Romany Gypsies and Balkan Gypsies in a concentration camp

. . .

I. By order of the *Reichsführer-SS* dated December 16, 1942 . . . , Gypsies of mixed blood, Romany Gypsies and members of Gypsy clans of non-German blood and of Balkan origins are to be selected according to fixed guidelines, and in the course of an operation lasting only a few weeks are to be confined in a concentration camp. People affected [*Personenkreis*] will henceforth briefly be referred to as "Persons of Gypsy origin."

Confinement will take place by families, regardless of the degree of mixed blood, in Concentration Camp (Gypsy Camp) Auschwitz.

. . .

(III) 1. Attempts should be made to obtain consent for sterilization from persons of Gypsy origin above 12 years of age and not yet sterilized;

. . .

4. In case of refusal, the Reich Criminal Police Office, after having ascertained the reasons, will decide what steps are to be taken.

Source: Reinhard Rürup, ed., *Topography of Terror: Gestapo, SS, and Reichssicherheitshauptamt on the "Prinz-Albrecht-Terrain"*, translated by Werner T. Augress (Berlin: Arenhövel, 1989).

Questions for Analysis

1. How was the language of racial science used to justify discriminatory practices against the Roma in the 1938 text? Why was it necessary to differentiate among "Gypsies, Gypsies of mixed blood, and persons roaming in Gypsy fashion"?

2. What was the significance of the 1939 document's statement that "the Gypsy Question will be fundamentally settled before long within the entire German territory by a uniform standard applied throughout the Reich"? If the goal was extermination, why use such bureaucratic language? If the goal was other than extermination, why was it necessary to "round up" the Gypsies?

3. By 1943, the extermination policy was already under way—why, then, was it necessary to continue to speak in vague terms of "Gypsies of mixed blood, Romany Gypsies and members of Gypsy clans of non-German blood and of Balkan origins"?

identified as "difficult." The men of the villages were shot; the women and children either deported to labor camps or massacred along with the men. By September 1941, the *Einsatzgruppen* reported that in their efforts at pacification they had killed 85,000 people, most of them Jews. By April 1942, the number was 500,000. This killing began before the gas chambers had gone into operation and continued through the campaigns on the Eastern Front. As of 1943, the death squads had killed roughly 2.2 million Jews.

As Operation Barbarossa progressed, German administrations of occupied areas herded local Jewish populations even more tightly into the ghettos some Jewish communities had occupied for centuries; Warsaw and Lodz in Poland were the largest. There, Nazi administrators, accusing Jewish people in the ghettos of hoarding supplies, refused to allow food to go in. The ghettos became centers of starvation and disease. Those who left the ghetto were shot rather than returned. A German doctor summarized the regime's

THE LIBERATION OF THE CONCENTRATION CAMPS. Many allied soldiers documented the liberation of the concentration camps at the end of the war, taking photographs and films of the appalling scenes they encountered. In many cases, German civilians were brought into the camps and compelled to witness the countless bodies of camp prisoners that remained unburied, before being conscripted to help with the disposal of the corpses to prevent the spread of disease. In this photograph, local residents view the victims of Nazi crimes at the Landesburg camp near Dachau, Germany in 1945. ▪ *What complications faced the Allies in the task of assigning responsibility for these crimes?*

logic about killing this way: "One must, I can say it quite openly in this circle, be clear about it. There are only two ways. We sentence the Jews in the ghetto to death by hunger or we shoot them. Even if the end result is the same, the latter is more intimidating." In other words, the point was not simply death but terror.

Through the late summer and fall of 1941, Nazi officials discussed and put together plans for mass killings in death camps. The ghettos had already been sealed; now orders came down that no Jews were to leave any occupied areas. That summer, the Nazis had experimented with vans equipped with poison gas, which could kill thirty to fifty people at a time. Those experiments and the gas chambers were designed with the help of scientists from the T-4 euthanasia program, which had already killed 80,000 racially, mentally, or physically "unfit" individuals in Germany. By October 1941, the SS was building camps with gas chambers and deporting people to them. Auschwitz-Birkenau (*OWSH-vihts BIHR-kuh-now*), which had been built to hold Polish prisoners, was built up to be the largest of the camps. Auschwitz eventually held many different types of prisoners—"undesirables" like Jehovah's Witnesses and homosexuals, Poles, Russians, and even some British POWs—but Jews and gypsies were the ones systematically annihilated there. Between the spring of 1942 and the fall of 1944, over 1 million people were killed at Auschwitz-Birkenau alone. The opening of the death camps set off the greatest wave of slaughter from 1942 to 1943. Freight cars hauled Jewish people to the camps, first from the ghettos of Poland, then from France, Holland, Belgium, Austria, the

Balkans, and later from Hungary and Greece. Bodies were buried in pits dug by prisoners or burned in crematoria.

The death camps have come to symbolize the horrors of Nazism as a system of modern mass murder. Yet it is worth emphasizing that much of the slaughter was not anonymous, industrialized, or routine and that it took place in

"JEWISH COUPLE IN BUDAPEST," EVGENY KHALDEI (1945). Khaldei, a Soviet photographer and journalist who traveled with the Red Army, left a remarkable and moving account of his encounter with this woman and man. "There was a Jewish couple wearing Stars of David. They were afraid of me. There was still fighting going on in the city, and they thought I might be an SS soldier. So I said *Sholem Aleichem* [hello] to them, and the woman began to cry. After I'd taken the picture, I pulled their stars off and said, 'The fascists are beaten. It's terrible to be marked like that.'"

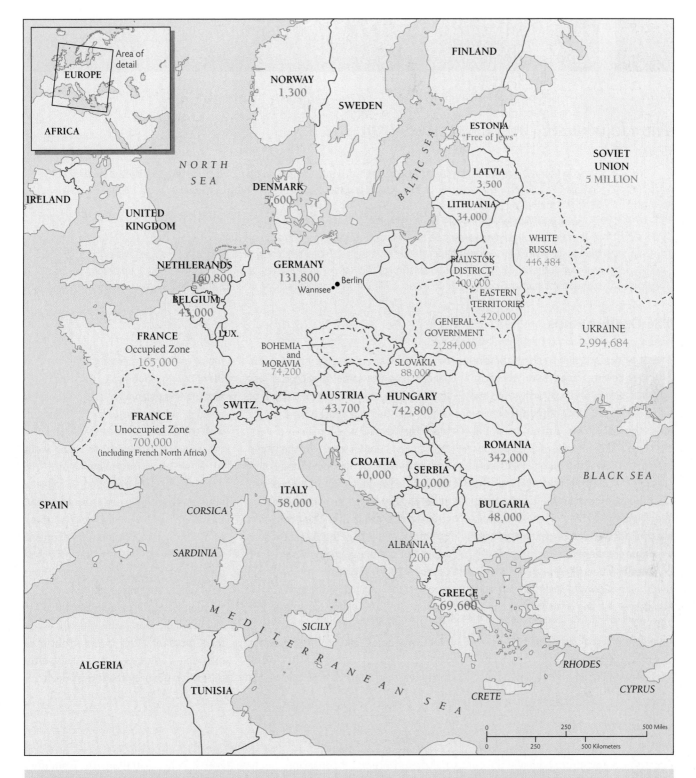

Area of detail

EUROPE

AFRICA

NORTH
SEA

NORWAY
1,300

SWEDEN

FINLAND

ESTONIA
"Free of Jews"

LATVIA
3,500

SOVIET
UNION
5 MILLION

IRELAND

UNITED
KINGDOM

DENMARK
5,600

LITHUANIA
34,000

BALTIC SEA

NETHLERANDS
160,800

GERMANY
131,800   ● Berlin
Wannsee ●

BIALYSTOK
DISTRICT
400,000

WHITE
RUSSIA
446,484

BELGIUM
43,000

LUX.

FRANCE
Occupied Zone
165,000

BOHEMIA
and
MORAVIA
74,200

EASTERN
TERRITORIES
420,000

GENERAL
GOVERNMENT
2,284,000

UKRAINE
2,994,684

SLOVAKIA
88,000

SWITZ.

AUSTRIA
43,700

HUNGARY
742,800

FRANCE
Unoccupied Zone
700,000
(including French North Africa)

CROATIA
40,000

SERBIA
10,000

ROMANIA
342,000

BLACK SEA

SPAIN

CORSICA

ITALY
58,000

BULGARIA
48,000

SARDINIA

ALBANIA
200

ALGERIA

MEDITERRANEAN SEA

SICILY

GREECE
69,600

RHODES

CYPRUS

TUNISIA

CRETE

0   250   500 Miles
0   250   500 Kilometers

HITLER'S "FINAL SOLUTION": JEWS MARKED FOR DEATH. On January 20, 1942, German officials met at Wannsee (just outside Berlin) to discuss the "Final Solution" to the "Jewish problem." They also discussed what they believed to be the remaining number of Jewish people in territories they controlled or soon hoped to control. Examine these figures closely. ▪ *How many millions of innocent people did the Nazis propose to slaughter?* ▪ *Based on your reading, what percentage of the Jews did they actually kill?* ▪ *What two countries were scheduled for the most executions?*

Competing Viewpoints

The Holocaust: Two Perspectives from the SS

An SS officer charged with inspecting the death camps wrote the first account here of his visit to Belzec, a camp in occupied Poland, near the former Russian border. He opposed the regime. Shortly after leaving this description, in 1945, he committed suicide.

Heinrich Himmler (1900–1945), one of the founding members of the Nazi Party and head of the SS, became one of the most powerful members of the Nazi government. He directed the purge of the rebellious SA in 1934, expanded the SS, supervised the network of death camps, and by 1943—when the speech reprinted here was given—had become minister of the interior for the administration of the Reich. Few represent better the combination of ambition, ideology, and ruthlessness that characterized Nazi leaders. Himmler committed suicide when captured by Allied troops in 1945.

The Death Camps

Next morning, shortly before seven, I was told: 'the first transport will arrive in ten minutes'. And, in fact, after a few minutes, the first train arrived from the direction of Lemberg (Lvov). 45 wagons with 6,700 people, of whom 1,450 were already dead on arrival. Behind the barred hatches stared the horribly pale and frightened faces of children, their eyes full of the fear of death. Men and women were there too. . . .

The chambers fill up. 'Pack them in'— that is what Captain Wirth has ordered. People are treading on each others' toes. 700–800 in an area of twenty-five square metres, in forty-five cubic metres! The SS push them in as far as possible. The doors shut; in the meantime, the others are waiting outside in the open, naked. 'It is the same in winter', I was told. 'But they could catch their death of cold', I say. 'But that's just what they are there for', replied an SS man in dialect. Now at last I understood why the whole apparatus is called the Heckenholt Foundation. Heckenholt is the driver of the diesel engine, a little technician who constructed the installation. The people are going to be killed by the diesel exhaust gases. But the diesel engine won't start! Captain Wirth arrives. He is clearly embarrassed that this should happen just on the day when I am here. Yes indeed, I can see the whole thing. And I wait. My stop watch faithfully records it all. Fifty minutes, 70 seconds [sic!]. Still the diesel won't start. The people wait in their gas chambers. In vain. One can hear them crying, sobbing. . . . Captain Wirth hits the Ukrainian who is responsible for helping *Unterscharführer* Heckenholt with the diesel engine twelve or thirteen times in the face with his riding whip. After two hours forty-nine minutes—the stop watch has recorded it all—the engine starts. Up to this moment, the people have been living in these four chambers, four times 750 people in four times forty-five cubic metres. A further twenty-five minutes pass. That's right, many are now dead. One can see through the little peepholes when the electric light illuminates the chambers for a moment. After twenty-eight minutes, only a few are still alive. At last, after thirty-two minutes, they are all dead. . . .

face-to-face encounters outside the camps. Jews and other victims were not simply killed. They were tortured, beaten, and executed publicly while soldiers and other onlookers recorded the executions with cameras—and sent photos home to their families. During the last phases of the war, inmates still in the concentration camps were taken on death marches whose sole purpose was suffering and death. Nor was the killing done by the specially indoctrinated SS and *Einsatzgruppen*. The Nazi regime called up groups of conscripts, such as Reserve Police Battalion 101, from duty in its home city of Hamburg and sent it into occupied territories. Once there, the unit of middle-aged policemen received and obeyed orders to kill, in one day, 1,500 Jewish men, women, and children in one village. The commander offered to excuse men who did not feel they could carry out this assignment; only a few asked for a different task. In one Polish town, occupied first by the Soviets and then retaken by the Nazis, the Polish villagers themselves, with minimal

Himmler's Instructions to the SS

I also want to talk to you quite frankly about a very grave matter. We can talk about it quite frankly among ourselves and yet we will never speak of it publicly. Just as we did not hesitate on 30 June 1934 to do our duty as we were bidden, and to stand comrades who had lapsed up against the wall and shoot them, so we have never spoken about it and will never speak of it. It appalled everyone, and yet everyone was certain that he would do it the next time if such orders should be issued and it should be necessary.

I am referring to the Jewish evacuation programme, the extermination of the Jewish people. It is one of those things which are easy to talk about. "The Jewish people will be exterminated," says every party comrade, "It's clear, it's in our programme. Elimination of the Jews, extermination and we'll do it." And then they come along, the worthy eighty million Germans, and each one of them produces his decent Jew. It's clear the others are swine, but this one is a fine

Jew. Not one of those who talk like that has watched it happening, not one of them has been through it. Most of you will know what it means when a hundred corpses are lying side by side, or five hundred or a thousand are lying there. To have stuck it out and—apart from a few exceptions due to human weakness—to have remained decent, that is what has made us tough. This is a glorious page in our history and one that has never been written and can never be written. For we know how difficult we would have made it for ourselves if, on top of the bombing raids, the burdens and the deprivations of war, we still had Jews today in every town as secret saboteurs, agitators and troublemakers. We would now probably have reached the 1916–17 stage when the Jews were still part of the body of the German nation.

We have taken from them what wealth they had. I have issued a strict order, which SS *Obergruppenführer* Pohl has carried out, that this wealth should, as a matter of course, be handed over to

the Reich without reserve. We have taken none of it for ourselves. . . . All in all, we can say that we have fulfilled this most difficult duty for the love of our people. And our spirit, our soul, our character has not suffered injury from it. . . .

Source (for both documents): J. Noakes and G. Pridham, *Nazism: A History in Document and Eye-witness Accounts, 1919–1945*, Vol. 2 (New York: 1988), pp. 1151–52, 1199–1200.

Questions for Analysis

1. "This is a glorious page in our history," says Himmler, but one that "can never be written." How does he reconcile that contradiction? What was glorious? To what extent did the Nazis try to conceal what they were doing?

2. What does Himmler's speech suggest about the psychology of Nazism or about the ways in which members of the SS were persuaded to become murderers?

---

guidance or help from German soldiers, turned on their Jewish neighbors and killed hundreds in a day.

How many people knew of the extent of the Holocaust? No operation of this scale could be carried out without the cooperation or knowledge of many: the Nazi hierarchy; architects who helped build the camps; engineers who designed the gas chambers and crematoria; municipal officials of cities from which people were deported; train drivers; residents of villages near the camps, who reported the

smell of bodies burning; and so on. Recent research has shown that the number of extermination camps, ghettos, slave-labor sites, and detention centers in Nazi-controlled Europe was greater than 42,000. Given the difficulty of hiding sites that required guards, logistical support, and access to transportation networks, it is now clear that many more people must have been aware of what was happening. It is not surprising that most who suspected the worst were terrified and powerless. It is also not surprising that

The Architecture of Mass Murder

The camp at Auschwitz-Birkenau was the largest of the German concentration camps whose central purpose was the murder of Europe's Jews. Almost 1.1 million people, of whom 1 million were Jews, were murdered in Auschwitz.

Auschwitz-Birkenau was in fact a complex of three camps: an extermination center, a prisoner-of-war camp, and a labor camp built with the cooperation of German industrial firms such as IG Farben. Forty other smaller installations and work camps in the surrounding area were also run by the camp's administration. The

construction of the Auschwitz-Birkenau complex occupied thousands of workers and continued throughout the war. When the Soviet army arrived in January 1945, they found that the Germans had burned the camp archives before fleeing, but they had not burned the construction archive, which was kept separately. Hundreds of

A. Blueprint for Crematorium II, Birkenau, dated November 1941. The five shaded squares in the lower drawing are the gas ovens in the structure's underground level, and the area to the right is labeled "Corpses Room."

many people did not want to know and did their best to ignore evidence and carry on with their lives. Many who continued to support the Nazis did so for other reasons, out of personal opportunism or because they opposed communism and wanted order restored. Yet mere popular indifference does not provide a satisfactory explanation for the Nazis' ability to accomplish the murder of so many people. Many Europeans—German, French, Dutch, Polish, Swiss, and Russian—had come to believe that there was a "Jewish problem" that had to be "solved." The Nazis tried to conceal

the death camps. Yet they knew they could count on vocal support for requiring Jews to be specially identified, for restrictions on marriage and property ownership, and for other kinds of discrimination. For reasons that had to do with both traditional Christian anti-Semitism and modern, racialized nationalism, many Europeans had come to see Jewish Europeans as "foreign," no longer members of their national communities.

What of other governments? Their level of cooperation with the Nazis' plans varied. The French Vichy regime, on its technical drawings were found in this archive, and after the collapse of the Soviet Union in 1991, these drawings became accessible to historians. A further cache of such documents was discovered in an abandoned building in Berlin in 2008. They are now held by Yad Vashem, the Holocaust archive in Jerusalem, Israel.

The discovery of these drawings did not add substantially to what was already known about the murder of Jews and other prisoners at Auschwitz, but they provide an arresting example of the bureaucratic apparatus—and the chilling coldness of the planning—that went into the Nazi extermination policy.

Questions for Analysis

1. Who would have seen these plans and been made aware of their purpose?

2. What do these images tell us about the nature of the effort that went into the Nazi extermination policy?

3. Is there a way to understand the relationship between the careful renderings, the precise measurements, and the rectilinear lines, and the ultimate purpose of the buildings depicted?

B. Blueprint for the "Delousing Facility" at Auschwitz-Birkenau, showing a room of 11.6 meters by 11.2 meters marked *"Gaskammer"* (gas chamber).

own initiative, passed laws that required Jews to wear identifying stars and strictly limited their movements and activities. When the German government demanded roundups and deportations of Jews, Vichy cooperated. On the other hand, Italy, though a fascist country, participated less actively. Not until the Germans occupied the north of Italy in 1943 were drastic anti-Semitic measures implemented. The Hungarian government, also fascist and allied with the Nazis, persecuted Jews but dragged its heels about deportations. Thus, the Hungarian Jewish community survived—until March

1944, when Germans, disgusted with their Hungarian collaborators, took direct control and immediately began mass deportations. So determined were the Nazis to carry out their "final solution" that they killed up to 12,000 Hungarian Jews a day at Auschwitz in May 1944, contributing to a total death toll of 600,000 Jews from Hungary.

In the face of this Nazi determination, little resistance was possible. The concentration camps were designed to numb and incapacitate their inmates, making them acquiesce in their own slow deaths even if they were not

DEPORTATION RAILWAYS. Between March 1942 and November 1944, Jews are known to have been deported from every location on this map—as well as from numerous other locales. Note the effort made by the Nazis to transport Jews from the very frontiers of the empire at the height of a two-front war. ▪ *According to the map, to which site were most Jews deported?* ▪ *Looking back at Hitler's "Final Solution" map on page 895, why was Auschwitz in Poland chosen as the main deportation site?* ▪ *What does this say about the Nazi regime in particular and about other states willing to collaborate with the Nazis?*

Past and Present

European Integration Then and Now

Hitler's conquest of Europe was a plan for European integration, based on a theory of racial domination, whereby "pure" Aryan settlements (see photo from "model" Nazi village of Adolf Hitler-Koog) would take over territory from "racially inferior" people who would eventually be eliminated. The great success of European integration after the Second World War (see photo of German Chancellor Konrad Adenauer shaking hands with Jean Monnet, a key figure in European integration) was to create a structure for international cooperation based on democratic institutions and mutual economic interest.

 Watch related author interview on StudySpace
wwnorton.com/web/westernciv18

killed right away. In his famous account, the survivor Primo Levi writes: "Our language lacks words to express this offence, the demolition of a man. . . . It is not possible to sink lower than this; no human condition is more miserable than this, nor could it conceivably be so. Nothing belongs to us any more; they have taken away our clothes, our shoes, even our hair; if we speak, they will not listen to us, and if they listen, they will not understand." A few rebellions in Auschwitz and Treblinka were repressed with savage efficiency. In the villages of Poland, Ukraine, and elsewhere, people rounded up to be deported or shot had to make split-second decisions to escape. Saving oneself nearly always meant abandoning one's children or parents, which very few could—or would—do. The countryside offered no shelter; local populations were usually either hostile or too terrified to help. Reprisals horrified all. Families of Jews and gypsies were ordinary people whose lives could not have prepared them for the kind of violence that rolled over them.

The largest Jewish resistance came in the Warsaw ghetto, in the spring of 1943. The previous summer, the Nazis had deported 80 percent of the ghetto's residents to the camps, making it clear that those left behind had little hope of survival. Those in the ghetto had virtually no resources, yet when deportations started again, a small Jewish underground movement—a thousand fighters, perhaps, in a community of 70,000—took on the Nazis with a tiny arsenal of gasoline bombs, pistols, and ten rifles. The Nazis responded by burning the ghetto to the ground and executing and deporting to the camps nearly everyone who was left. Some 56,000 Jews died. "The Warsaw Ghetto is no more," reported the SS commander at the end. Word of the rising did spread, but the repression made it clear that the targets of Nazi extermination could choose only between death in the streets or death in the camps. Sustained resistance, as one person remarked, would have required "the prospect of victory."

Racial War, Ethnic Cleansing, and the Holocaust | 901

The Holocaust claimed between 4.1 and 5.7 million Jewish lives. Even those numbers do not register the nearly total destruction of some cultures. In the Baltic states (Latvia and Lithuania), Germany, Czechoslovakia, Yugoslavia, and Poland, well over 80 percent of the long-established Jewish communities were annihilated. Elsewhere, the figures were closer to 50 percent. The Holocaust was part of a racial war and of an even longer period of ethnically motivated mass murder. Through both world wars and afterward ethnic and religious groups—Jews, Armenians, Poles, Serbian Orthodox, ethnic Germans—were hunted, massacred, and legally deported en masse. Hitler's government had planned to build a "new Europe," safe for ethnic Germans and their allies and secure against communism, on the graveyards of whole cultures.

TOTAL WAR: HOME FRONTS, THE WAR OF PRODUCTION, BOMBING, AND THE BOMB

The Second World War was a "total war." Even more than the First World War, it involved the combined efforts of whole populations, massive resources, and a mobilization of entire economies within combatant nations. Standards of living changed around the world. In the neutral nations of Latin America, which supplied vast amounts of raw materials to the Allies, wartime profits led to a wave of prosperity known as the "dance of the millions." In the lands occupied by Germany or Japan, economies of forced extraction robbed local areas of resources, workers, and even food. In East Asia, deprivations caused rising resentment of the Japanese, who had been seen initially as liberators ending the rule of the old colonial powers. In the United States, Detroit produced no new models of car or truck between 1940 and 1945. Work schedules were grueling. Women and the elderly, pressed back into wage work or working for the first time, put in long shifts (in Britain and Russia, these sometimes ran over twelve hours) before returning home to cook, clean, and care for families and neighbors also affected by enemy bombing and wartime shortages. Diets changed. Though Germany lived comfortably off the farmlands of Europe for several years and the United States could lean on its huge agricultural base, food, gasoline, and basic household goods were still rationed. In occupied Europe and the Soviet Union, rations were just above starvation level and sometimes fell below in areas near the fighting. Britain, dependent on its empire and other overseas sources for food and raw materials, ran a comprehensive

rationing system that kept up production and ensured a drab but consistent diet on the table.

Production—the industrial ability to churn out more tanks, tents, planes, bombs, and uniforms than the other side—was essential to winning the war. Britain, the Soviet Union, and America each launched comprehensive, well-designed propaganda campaigns that encouraged the production of war equipment on an unmatched scale. Appeals to patriotism, to communal interests, and to a common stake in winning the war struck a chord. The Allied societies proved willing to regulate themselves and commit to the effort. Despite strikes and disputes with government officials, the Allied powers devoted more of their economies to war production, more efficiently, than any nations in history. They built tanks, ships, and planes capable of competing with advanced German and Japanese designs by the tens of thousands, swamping the enemy with constant reinforcements and superior firepower. Japan nearly reached comparable levels of production but then slowly declined, as Allied advances on land and American subma-

"JUST A GOOD AFTERNOON'S WORK!" A British poster mobilizing women for part-time factory work.

rines cut off overseas sources of vital supplies. Germany, despite its reputation for efficiency and its access to vast supplies of slave labor, was less efficient in its use of workers and materials than the Allied nations. The Germans' ability to produce devastatingly successful weapons led to a damaging side effect—vast amounts of money and time spent developing the pet projects of high-ranking Nazi officials or trying to make unsuccessful designs work. Rather than losing time and resources pursuing perfection, the Allies developed working, standard designs and produced them in overwhelming numbers.

Because industry was essential to winning the war, centers of industry became vital military targets. The Allies began bombing German ports and factories almost as soon as the Germans started their own campaigns. Over time, American and British planners became equally ruthless on an even larger scale. Both of these Allied nations made a major commitment to strategic bombing, developing new planes and technology that allowed them to put thousands of bombers in the air both night and day over occupied Europe. As the war wore on and Germany kept fighting, the Allies expanded their campaign. They moved from pinpoint bombing of the military and industry in Germany to striking such targets across all of occupied Europe and bombing Germany's civilian population in earnest. For the British, despite a public debate about the morality of bombing, it was a war of retribution; for the Americans, it was an effort to grind the Germans down without sacrificing too many Allied lives. The Allies killed tens of thousands of German civilians as they struck Berlin, ports such as Hamburg, and the industrial cities of the Ruhr, but German war production persisted. At the same time, German fighter planes shot down hundreds of Allied bombers, causing heavy losses. After the Allied invasion of Europe, bombing expanded well beyond targets of military value. The German city of Dresden, a center of culture and education that lacked heavy industry, was firebombed with a horrifying death toll. This gave Allied generals and politicians pause, but strategic bombing continued. German industry was slowly degraded, but the German will to keep fighting, like Britain's or the Soviet Union's, remained intact.

The Race to Build the Bomb

Allied scientists in the United States also developed the world's first nuclear weapon during the war years, a bomb that worked by splitting the atom, creating a chain reaction that could release tremendous energy in an explosion. Physicists in Britain and Germany first suggested that such a weapon might be possible, but only the United States had the resources to build such a bomb before the end of the war. A group of physicists at the University of Chicago, under the leadership of Enrico Fermi and including many refugees from fascist regimes in Europe, built the world's first nuclear reactor. In December 1942, Fermi and his group staged the first controlled chain reaction at the site. Fearful that the Germans would develop a bomb of their own, the U.S. government built a laboratory at Los Alamos, New Mexico, and charged the physicists to build an atomic bomb. Physicist J. Robert Oppenheimer directed the top-secret plan, known to the researchers as the Manhattan Project. The idea was to perfect a bomb that could be dropped by plane and detonated above the target. The physicists successfully tested a device on July 16, 1945, in New Mexico, vaporizing the test tower in a wave of heat and fire that rose in a mushroom shape overhead. The United States now possessed the most destructive weapon ever devised.

THE ALLIED COUNTERATTACK AND THE DROPPING OF THE ATOMIC BOMB

Hitler had invaded the Soviet Union in June 1941. Within two years, the war in the East had become his undoing; within four years, it brought about his destruction.

The early successes of the German-led invasion were crippling. Nearly 90 percent of the Soviets' tanks, most of their aircraft, and huge stores of supplies were destroyed or captured. Nazi forces penetrated deep into European Russia. The Soviets fought regardless. By late 1941, German and Finnish forces had cut off and besieged Leningrad (St. Petersburg). Yet the city held out for 844 days—through three winters, massive destruction by artillery and aircraft, and periods of starvation—until a large relief force broke the siege. Russian partisans stepped up their campaigns of ambush and terrorism, and many of the Germans' former allies in Ukraine and elsewhere turned against them in reaction to Nazi pacification efforts.

The Eastern Front

In the East, the character of the war changed as Russians rallied to defend the *rodina*, the Russian motherland. Stalin's efforts were aided by the weather—successive winters took a heavy toll in German lives. At the same time, Soviet industry made an astonishing recovery during the war years. Whole industries were rebuilt behind the safety of the Ural mountains and entire urban populations were sent to work in them, turning out tanks, fighter planes, machine guns, and ammunition. Finally, the Germans were the victims of their own success with their *Blitzkrieg* tactics, as their lines extended deep into Russian territory, spreading their forces more thinly, and opening them up to attack from unexpected angles.

The turning point came in 1942–43, when the Germans attempted to take Stalingrad, in an effort to break the back of Soviet industry. The Russians drew the invading army into the city where they were bogged down in house-to-house fighting that neutralized the German tanks and gave the outnumbered Soviet forces greater chances of success, despite their lack of equipment. The Germans found their supplies running low as winter set in, and in November 1942 large Russian armies encircled the city and besieged the invaders in a battle that continued through a cruel winter. At the end of January 1943, the German commander defied his orders and surrendered. More than a half million German, Italian, and Romanian soldiers had been killed; Russian casualties were over a million, including a hundred thousand civilians.

After Stalingrad, a series of Soviet attacks drove the Germans back toward the frontier and beyond. In what may have been the largest battle ever fought, Soviet armies destroyed a German force at Kursk in the summer of 1943—the battle involved over 6,000 tanks and 2 million men. Following this victory, the Russians launched a major offensive into Ukraine, and by the spring of 1944 Ukraine was back in Soviet hands. Meanwhile, Leningrad was liberated and Romania forced to capitulate. Soviet armies

PRISONERS OF WAR. Over 90,000 captured German troops were forced to march through the streets of Stalingrad after a defeat by the Soviet forces. The combination of the battle and the Russian winter resulted in the German loss of over 300,000 men.

entered the Balkans where they met with Tito's partisans in Yugoslavia. In Poland, successive German armies collapsed, and the Soviets, joined by communist partisans from eastern Europe, retook large parts of Czechoslovakia. Hitler's ambitious goal of conquest in the East had brought the downfall of the Nazi regime and death to another generation of German soldiers.

The Western Front

When the Nazis invaded Russia, Stalin called on the Allies to open a second front in the West. In response, the Americans led an attack on Italy in 1943, beginning with an invasion of Sicily in July. Italy's government deposed Mussolini and surrendered in the summer of 1943 while the nation collapsed into civil war. Italian partisans, especially the communists, sided with the Americans, while dedicated fascists fought on. The Germans occupied Italy with more than a dozen elite divisions, and the hard-fought and bitter campaign with American and British forces lasted eighteen months.

The most important second front was opened on June 6, 1944, with the massive Allied landings in Normandy. Casualties were high, but careful planning and deception allowed the Allied invasion to gain a foothold in northern Europe, eventually leading to breakthrough of the German lines. A second landing in southern France also succeeded, aided by the resistance. By August, these Allied armies had liberated Paris and pushed into Belgium. In

STORMING "FORTRESS EUROPE." American troops landing on Omaha Beach June 6, 1944. In the three months that followed, the Allies poured more than 2 million men, almost a half million vehicles, and 4 million tons of supplies onto the Continent—a measure of how firmly the Germans were established.

the fall, the Germans managed to defeat a British airborne invasion in the Netherlands and an American thrust into the Rhineland forests before mounting a devastating attack in December 1944, in the Battle of the Bulge. The Allied lines nearly broke, but the American forces held long enough for a crushing counterattack. In April 1945, the Allies crossed the Rhine into Germany, and the last defenders of the German Reich were swiftly overwhelmed. This military success was helped by the fact that most Germans preferred to surrender to Americans or Britons than face the Russians to the east.

Those Soviet troops were approaching fast. The Russian army took Prague and Vienna, and by late April they reached the suburbs of Berlin. In the savage ten-day battle to take the German capital more than 100,000 Russians and Germans died. Adolf Hitler killed himself in a bunker beneath the Chancellery on April 30. On May 2, the heart of the city was captured, and the Soviets' red banner flew from the Brandenburg Gate. On May 7, the German high command signed a document of unconditional surrender. The war in Europe was over.

The War in the Pacific

The war in the Pacific ended four months later. The British pushed the Japanese out of Burma while the Germans were surrendering in the West, and soon after, Australian forces recaptured the Dutch East Indies. In the fall of 1944, the U.S. Navy had destroyed most of Japan's surface ships in the gulfs of the Philippine Islands, and American troops took Manila house by house in bloody fighting. The remaining battles—amphibious assaults on a series of islands running toward the Japanese mainland—were just as brutal. Japanese pilots mounted suicide attacks on American ships while American marines and Japanese soldiers fought over

THE ATOM BOMB. A mushroom cloud hovers over Nagasaki after the city was bombed. Hiroshima was bombed three days earlier.

The Atomic Bomb and Its Implications

In July 1945, scientists associated with the Manhattan Project became involved in debates about how the atomic bomb could be deployed. Members of the Scientific Panel of the secretary of war's Interim Advisory Committee agreed that a bomb could be used militarily but disagreed about whether it could be used without prior warning and demonstration. Other groups of scientists secretly began to circulate petitions, such as the one reprinted here, in which they set out their views. The petitions never reached the president, but they raised issues that did emerge in the postwar period.

In the section of his memoirs reprinted here, President Harry S Truman sets out the views of other scientists on the secretary of war's advisory committee. He explains the logic of his decision to use the atomic bomb against Hiroshima (August 6, 1945) and Nagasaki (August 9, 1945) and the events as they unfolded.

A Petition to the President of the United States

July 17, 1945

A PETITION TO THE PRESIDENT OF THE UNITED STATES

We, the undersigned scientists, have been working in the field of atomic power. Until recently we have had to fear that the United States might be attacked by atomic bombs during this war and that her only defense might lie in a counterattack by the same means. Today, with the defeat of Germany, this danger is averted and we feel impelled to say what follows:

The war has to be brought speedily to a successful conclusion and attacks by atomic bombs may very well be an effective method of warfare. We feel, however, that such attacks on Japan could not be justified, at least not unless the terms which will be imposed after the war on Japan were made public in detail and Japan were given an opportunity to surrender. . . .

[I]f Japan still refused to surrender our nation might then, in certain circumstances, find itself forced to resort to the use of atomic bombs. Such a step, however, ought not to be made at any time without seriously considering the moral responsibilities which are involved.

The development of atomic power will provide the nations with new means of destruction. The atomic bombs at our disposal represent only the first step in this direction, and there is almost no limit to the destructive power which will become available in the course of their future development. Thus a nation which sets the precedent of using these newly liberated forces of nature for purposes of destruction may have to bear the responsibility of opening the door to an era of devastation on an unimaginable scale.

If after this war a situation is allowed to develop in the world which permits rival powers to be in uncontrolled possession of these new means of destruction, the cities of the United States as well as the cities of other nations will be in continuous danger of sudden annihilation. . . .

The added material strength which this lead [in the field of atomic power] gives to the United States brings with it the obligation of restraint and if we were to violate this obligation our moral position would be weakened in the eyes of the world and in our own eyes. It would then be more difficult for us to

live up to our responsibility of bringing the unloosened forces of destruction under control.

In view of the foregoing, we, the undersigned, respectfully petition: first, that you exercise your power as Commander-in-Chief, to rule that the United States shall not resort to the use of atomic bombs in this war unless the terms which will be imposed upon Japan have been made public in detail and Japan knowing these terms has refused to surrender; second, that in such an event the question of whether or not to use atomic bombs be decided by you in the light of the considerations presented in this petition as well as all the other moral responsibilities which are involved.

Source: Michael B. Stoff, Jonathan F. Fanton, and R. Hal Williams, eds., *The Manhattan Project: A Documentary Introduction to the Atomic Age* (New York: 2000), p. 173.

President Truman's Memoirs

I had realized, of course, that an atomic bomb explosion would inflict damage and casualties beyond imagination. On the other hand, the scientific advisers of the committee reported, "We can propose no technical demonstration likely to bring an end to the war; we see no acceptable alternative to direct military use." It was their conclusion that no technical demonstration they might propose, such as over a deserted island, would be likely to bring the war to an end. It had to be used against an enemy target.

The final decision of where and when to use the atomic bomb was up to me. Let there be no mistake about it. I regarded the bomb as a military weapon and never had any doubt that it should be used. The top military advisers to the President recommended its use, and when I talked to Churchill he unhesitatingly told me that he favored the use of the atomic bomb if it might aid to end the war.

In deciding to use this bomb I wanted to make sure that it would be used as a weapon of war in the manner prescribed by the laws of war. That meant that I wanted it dropped on a military target. I had told Stimson that the bomb should be dropped as nearly as possibly upon a war production center of prime military importance.

Stimson's staff had prepared a list of cities in Japan that might serve as targets. Kyoto, though favored by General Arnold as a center of military activity, was eliminated when Secretary Stimson pointed out that it was a cultural and religious shrine of the Japanese.

Four cities were finally recommended as targets: Hiroshima, Kokura, Niigata, and Nagasaki. They were listed in that order as targets for the first attack. The order of selection was in accordance with the military importance of these cities, but allowance would be given for weather conditions at the time of the bombing. Before the selected targets were approved as proper for military purposes, I personally went over them in detail with Stimson, Marshall, and Arnold, and we discussed the matter of timing and the final choice of the first target. . . .

On August 6, the fourth day of the journey home from Potsdam, came the historic news that shook the world. I was eating lunch with members of the *Augusta's* crew when Captain Frank Graham, White House Map Room watch officer, handed me the following message:

To the President from the Secretary of War

Big bomb dropped on Hiroshima August 5 at 7:15 P.M. Washington time. First reports indicate complete success which was even more conspicuous than earlier test.

I was greatly moved. I telephoned Byrnes aboard ship to give him the news and then said to the group of sailors around me, "This is the greatest thing in history. It's time for us to get home."

Source: Harry S. Truman, *Memoirs*, vol. 1, *Year of Decisions* (Garden City, NY: 1955), pp. 419–21.

Questions for Analysis

1. To express their fears about how the atomic bomb would be used, scientists circulated petitions. Look at the outcomes the scientists proposed. Which came closest to subsequent events? Which was the most prudent? The most honest?

2. Is it appropriate for scientists to propose how new weapons should be used? Are they overreaching in trying to give advice in foreign affairs and military strategy? Or are they obligated to voice moral qualms?

every inch of the shell-blasted rocks in the Pacific. Okinawa fell to the Americans after eighty-two days of desperate fighting, giving the United States a foothold less than 500 miles from the Japanese home islands. The government in Tokyo called on its citizens to defend the nation against an invasion.

On July 26, the U.S., British, and Chinese governments jointly called on Japan to surrender or be destroyed. The United States had already been using long-range B-29 bombers in systematic attacks on Japanese cities, killing hundreds of thousands of Japanese civilians in firestorms produced by incendiary bombs. When the Japanese government refused to surrender, the United States decided to use its atomic bomb.

Many senior military and naval officers argued that the use of the bomb was not necessary, on the assumption that Japan was already beaten. Some of the scientists involved, who had done their part to defeat the Nazis, believed that using the bomb for political ends would set a deadly precedent. Harry Truman, who became president when Roosevelt died in April 1945, decided otherwise. On August 6, a single American plane dropped an atomic bomb on Hiroshima, obliterating 60 percent of the city. Three days later, the United States dropped a second bomb on Nagasaki. On August 14, Japan surrendered unconditionally.

The decision to use the bomb was extraordinary. It did not greatly alter the American plans for the destruction of Japan—in fact many more Japanese died in the earlier fire bombings than in the two atomic blasts. Yet the bomb was an entirely new kind of weapon, revealing a new and terrifying relationship between science and political power. The instant, total devastation of the blasts, and the lingering effects of cancerous radiation that could claim victims decades later was something terribly new. The world now had a weapon that could destroy not just cities and peoples, but humanity itself.

CONCLUSION

After the First World War, many Europeans awoke to find a world they no longer recognized. In 1945, many Europeans came out from shelters or began the long trips back to their homes, faced with a world that hardly existed at all. The products of industry—tanks, submarines, strategic bombing—had destroyed the structures of industrial society—factories, ports, and railroads. The tools of mass culture—fascist and communist appeals, patriotism proclaimed via radios and movie screens, mobilization of mass armies and industry—had been put to full use. In the after-

After You Read This Chapter

Visit StudySpace for quizzes, additional review materials, and multimedia documents. **wwnorton.com/web/westernciv18**

REVIEWING THE OBJECTIVES

- The Second World War stemmed from the political and economic crises of the 1930s. What caused the war?
- British and French leaders in the 1930s hoped to avoid another war in Europe through diplomatic negotiation with Hitler. What were the consequences of these negotiations?
- The populations of nations occupied by the Germans faced a difficult set of choices. What were the consequences of occupation for European nations, and what possibilities existed for resistance?
- The mass murder of European Jews, homosexuals, and Gypsies reached a climax during the invasion of the Soviet Union, though the victims came from every corner of Europe. What efforts did this enormous project entail, and how did it come about?
- The Nazi regime and their allies eventually collapsed after costly defeats in both eastern and western Europe. Where and when did the major defeats take place, and what was their human cost?
- The Japanese government surrendered in August 1945 after the United States dropped two atomic bombs, on Hiroshima and Nagasaki. What events led to the decision to drop these bombs, and what were their consequences?

math, much of Europe lay destroyed and, as we will see, vulnerable to the rivalry of the postwar superpowers: the United States and the Soviet Union.

The two world wars profoundly affected Western empires. Nineteenth-century imperialism had made twentieth-century war a global matter. In both conflicts the warring nations had used the resources of empire to their fullest. Key campaigns, in North Africa, Burma, Ethiopia, and the Pacific, were fought in and over colonial territories. Hundreds of thousands of colonial troops—sepoys and Gurkhas from India and Nepal, Britain's King's African Rifles, French from Algeria and West Africa—served in armies on both sides of the conflict. After two massive mobilizations, many anticolonial leaders found renewed confidence in their own peoples' courage and resourcefulness, and they seized the opportunity of European weakness to press for independence. In many areas that had been under European or Japanese imperial control, from sections of China to Korea, Indochina, Indonesia, and Palestine—the end of the Second World War only paved the way for a new round of conflict. This time, the issue was when imperial control would be ended, and by whom.

The Second World War also carried on the Great War's legacy of massive killing. Historians estimate that nearly 50 million people died. The killing fields of the east took the highest tolls: 25 million Soviet lives. Of those, 8.5 million were in the military, and the rest civilians; 20 percent of the Polish population and nearly 90 percent of the Polish Jewish community; 1 million Yugoslavs, including militias of all sides; 4 million German soldiers and 500,000 German civilians, not including the hundreds of thousands of ethnic Germans who died while being deported west at the end of the war, in one of the many acts of ethnic cleansing that ran through the period. Even the United States, shielded from the full horrors of total war by two vast oceans, lost 292,000 soldiers in battle and more to accidents or disease.

Why was the war so murderous? The advanced technology of modern industrial war and the openly genocidal ambitions of the Nazis offer part of the answer. The global reach of the conflict offers another. Finally, the Second World War overlapped with, and eventually devolved into, a series of smaller, no less bitter conflicts: a civil war in Greece; conflicts among Orthodox, Catholics, and Muslims in Yugoslavia; and political battles for control of the French resistance. Even when those struggles claimed fewer lives, they left deep political scars. So did memories of the war. Hitler's empire could not have lasted as long as it did without active collaboration or passive acquiescence from many, a fact that produced bitterness and recrimination for years.

PEOPLE, IDEAS, AND EVENTS IN CONTEXT

- What was Hitler asking for at the **MUNICH CONFERENCE** of 1938, and what made many people in Europe think that **APPEASEMENT** was their best option?
- What was the **HITLER-STALIN PACT** of 1939?
- What was *BLITZKRIEG*, and what effect did it have on those who faced Hitler's invasions?
- What were Hitler's goals in **OPERATION BARBAROSSA**, the invasion of the Soviet Union in 1941? What were the consequences of the German defeat at **STALINGRAD**?
- What made the **SECOND WORLD WAR** a global war? Where were the main consequences of the war felt most keenly outside of Europe?
- What was the **MANHATTAN PROJECT**, and how did it affect the outcome of the Second World War?

THINKING ABOUT CONNECTIONS

- What long-term causes going back to the history of Europe in the nineteenth century might one point to in order to understand the outbreak of the Second World War? Can one link the story of this war with the history of European imperialism in the nineteenth century? With the successes and failures of movements for German national unification?
- What circumstances made the Second World War a global conflict?

STORY LINES

- Postwar Europeans looked to rebuild their shattered continent in the shadow of a cold war between the United States and the Soviet Union. The new international order sharply curtailed the ability of European nations to act independently.

- After 1945, European imperial powers faced a challenge from movements for national independence in Africa, the Middle East, and Asia. By the early 1960s, almost all of Britain's and France's colonies had gained their independence.

- Western European nations increasingly turned toward political and economic cooperation, leading to unprecedented economic growth in the 1950s and 1960s. In Eastern Europe the socialist regimes of the Eastern bloc sought to chart a different path under Soviet sponsorship, achieving more modest growth in economies that emphasized heavy industries more than the manufacture of consumer goods.

CHRONOLOGY

1946–1964	Twenty French colonies, eleven British colonies, Belgian Congo, and Dutch Indonesia become independent nations
1947	Truman Doctrine
1948	Soviets create the Eastern bloc
1948	Marshall Plan
1949	Chinese Revolution
1949	Formation of NATO
1950–1953	Korean War
1953–1956	Revolts in East Germany, Poland, and Hungary
1955	Formation of Warsaw Pact
1957	Treaty of Rome creates the European Economic Community (EEC, the Common Market)
1961	Building of the Berlin Wall
1964–1975	U.S. Vietnam War

Before
You
Read
This
Chapter

The Cold War World: Global Politics, Economic Recovery, and Cultural Change

CORE OBJECTIVES

- **UNDERSTAND** the origins of the Cold War and the ways that the United States and the Soviet Union sought to influence the political and economic restructuring of Europe in the postwar period.

- **IDENTIFY** the policies that led to the economic integration of Western European nations in the postwar decades and the reasons for the rapid economic growth that accompanied this integration.

- **DESCRIBE** the process of decolonization that brought the colonial era in Africa and Asia to an end.

- **EXPLAIN** developments in European postwar culture, as intellectuals, writers, and artists reacted to the loss of European influence in the world and the ideological conflicts of the Cold War.

"The war ended the way a passage through a tunnel ends," wrote Heda Kovály, a Czech woman who survived the concentration camps. "From far away you could see the light ahead, a gleam that kept growing, and its brilliance seemed ever more dazzling to you huddled there in the dark the longer it took to reach it. But when at last the train burst out into the glorious sunshine, all you saw was a wasteland." The war left Europe a land of wreckage and confusion. Millions of refugees trekked hundreds or thousands of miles on foot to return to their homes while others were forcibly displaced from their lands. In some areas, housing was practically nonexistent, with no available means to build anew. Food remained in dangerously short supply; a year after the war, roughly 100 million people in Europe still lived on fewer than 1,500 calories per day. Families scraped vegetables from their gardens or traded smuggled goods on the black market. Governments continued to ration food, and without rationing, a large portion of the Continent's population would have starved. During the winter of 1945–46, many regions had little or no fuel for heat. What coal there was—less than half

911

the prewar supply—could not be transported to the areas that needed it most. The brutality of international war, civil war, and occupation had divided countries against themselves, shredding relations among ethnic groups and fellow citizens. Ordinary people's intense relief at liberation often went hand in hand with recriminations over their neighbors' wartime betrayal, collaboration, or simple opportunism.

How does a nation, a region, or a civilization recover from a catastrophe on the scale of the Second World War? Nations had to do much more than deliver food and rebuild economic infrastructures. They had to restore—or create—government authority, functioning bureaucracies, and legitimate legal systems. They had to rebuild bonds of trust and civility between citizens, steering a course between demands for justice, on the one hand, and the overwhelming desire to bury memories of the past, on the other. On the contrary, rebuilding entailed a commitment to renewing democracy—to creating democratic institutions that could withstand threats such as those the West had experienced in the 1930s. Some aspects of this process were extraordinarily successful, more so than even the most optimistic forecaster might have thought possible in 1945. Others failed or were deferred until later in the century.

The war's devastating effects brought two dramatic changes in the international balance of power. The first change was the emergence of the so-called superpowers,

the United States and the Soviet Union, and the swift development of a "cold war" between them. The Cold War divided Europe, with Eastern Europe occupied by Soviet troops, and Western Europe dominated by the military and economic presence of the United States. In both Western and Eastern Europe, the Cold War led to increased political and economic integration, resulting in the emergence of the European Common Market in the West and a socialist bloc dominated by the Soviet Union in the East. The second great change came with the dismantling of the European empires that had once stretched worldwide. The collapse of empires and the creation of newly emancipated nations raised the stakes in the Cold War and brought superpower rivalry to far-flung sections of the globe. Those events, which shaped the postwar recovery and necessarily created a new understanding of what "the West" meant, are the subject of this chapter.

THE COLD WAR AND A DIVIDED CONTINENT

No peace treaty ended the Second World War. Instead, as the war drew to a close, relations between the Allied powers began to fray over issues of power and influence in Central and Eastern Europe. After the war, they descended from mistrust to open conflict. The United States and Soviet Union rapidly formed the centers of two imperial blocs. Their rivalry, which came to be known as the Cold War, pitted against each other two military powers, two sets of state interests, and two ideologies: capitalism and communism. The Cold War's repercussions reached well beyond Europe, for anticolonial movements, sensing the weakness of European colonial powers, turned to the Soviets for help in their struggles for independence. The Cold War thus structured the peace, shaped international relations for four decades, and affected governments and peoples across the globe who depended on either of the superpowers.

THE REMAINS OF DRESDEN, 1947. Dresden was devastated by a controversial Allied bombing in February 1945. Kurt Vonnegut dramatically portrayed its destruction and the aftermath in his novel *Slaughterhouse-Five*. ■ *How did the war's new strategies of aerial bombardment—culminating in the use of atomic weapons—change the customary division between combatants and noncombatant civilians?*

The Iron Curtain

The Soviet Union had insisted during the wartime negotiations at Tehran (1943) and Yalta (1945) that it had a legitimate claim to control Eastern Europe, a claim that some Western

Legend:

- Allied occupation of Germany and Austria, 1945–1955
- Territory lost by Germany
- Territory gained by Soviet Union
- Postwar national boundaries, to 1989
- "Iron Curtain" to 1989
- **1945** Year Communist control of government was gained

NORWAY

Oslo

SWEDEN

Stockholm

FINLAND

From Finland, 1940–1956

Helsinki

Leningrad

NORTH SEA

DENMARK

Copenhagen

BALTIC SEA

ESTONIA
To U.S.S.R., 1940

LATVIA
To U.S.S.R., 1940

LITHUANIA
To U.S.S.R., 1940

Incorporated into U.S.S.R., 1945

Gdansk (Danzig)

Incorporated into Poland, 1945

WHITE RUSSIA

NETHERLANDS

U.S. Zone

Bremen

British Zone

Amsterdam

Soviet Zone

Berlin

EAST GERMANY (1949)

Warsaw

POLAND (1947)

Brest

From Poland, 1940–1947

UKRAINE

Brussels

BELGIUM

Bonn

French Zone

WEST GERMANY

U.S. Zone

LUXEMBOURG

Prague

CZECHOSLOVAKIA (1948)

From Czechoslovakia, 1945–1947

From Romania, 1940–1947

SOVIET UNION (1917)

SWITZERLAND

Bern

Munich

French Zone

U.S. Zone

Vienna

Soviet Zone

AUSTRIA

British Zone

Budapest

HUNGARY (1949)

ROMANIA (1947)

BESSARABIA

CRIMEA

Yalta

Milan

From Italy, 1945

Bucharest

BLACK SEA

Danube R.

From Romania, 1940–1947

CORSICA (Fr.)

ITALY

Rome

YUGOSLAVIA (1945)

ADRIATIC SEA

BULGARIA (1946)

Sofia

SARDINIA (It.)

Tirane

ALBANIA (1944)

GREECE

Istanbul

TURKEY

SICILY (It.)

Athens

CRETE

CYPRUS

MEDITERRANEAN SEA

East Germany inset:

EAST GERMANY

French Sector

WEST BERLIN

British Sector

U.S. Sector

Potsdam

EAST

Soviet Sector

BERLIN

Berlin Wall (1961–1989)

0   10 Miles
0   10 Kilometers

EUROPE

Area of detail

AFRICA

0   200   400 Miles
0   200   400 Kilometers

TERRITORIAL CHANGES IN EUROPE AFTER THE SECOND WORLD WAR. At the end of the Second World War, the Soviet Union annexed territory in Eastern Europe to create a buffer between it and Western Europe. At the same time, the United States established a series of military alliances in Western Europe to stifle the spread of communism in Europe. ▪ *What Eastern European countries fell under Russian control?* ▪ *Where is Berlin located, and why did its location and control cause so much tension?* ▪ *How did these new territorial boundaries aggravate the tensions between the Soviet Union and the United States?*

The End of the Second World War and the Onset of the Cold War

The need to defeat Nazi Germany brought the United States and the Soviet Union together in a common struggle, in spite of their contrasting political systems. Both nations emerged from the Second World War with a renewed sense of purpose, and both tried to use the victory against fascism to promote their claims for legitimacy and leadership in Europe. These circumstances placed a special burden on European nations and their postwar governments, as they were forced to take sides in this global confrontation at a moment of weakness and uncertainty.

The images here, all from May 1945 in Czechoslovakia, display several different possibilities for representing the German defeat in this Eastern European country. Image A shows a Czech civilian rending the Nazi flag, with the Prague skyline in the background and the flags of the major Allied powers and Czechoslovakia overhead. Image B depicts a triumphant Czech laborer wielding a rifle and socialist red flag standing over the body of a dead German soldier. Image C depicts portraits of Stalin and the Czech

A. Czech propaganda poster celebrating German defeat, May 1945.

B. Another Czech propaganda poster, May 1945.

leaders accepted as the price of defeating Hitler and others ignored so as to avoid a dangerous confrontation. When visiting Moscow in 1944, Churchill and Stalin quietly bargained over their respective spheres of influence, offering each other "percentages" of the countries that were being liberated. The Declaration of Principles of Liberated Europe issued at Yalta in 1945 guaranteed free elections, but Stalin believed that the framework of Allied cooperation gave him a free hand in Eastern Europe. Stalin's siege mentality pervaded his authoritarian regime and cast nearly everyone at home or abroad as a potential threat or enemy of the state. Yet Soviet policy did not rest on personal paranoia alone. The country's catastrophic wartime losses made the Soviets determined to maintain political, economic, and military control of the lands they had liberated from Nazi rule. For

the Soviets, Eastern Europe served as both "a sphere and a shield." When their former allies resisted their demands, the Soviets became suspicious, defensive, and aggressive.

In Eastern Europe, the Soviet Union used a combination of diplomatic pressure, political infiltration, and military power to create "people's republics" sympathetic to Moscow. In country after country, the same process unfolded: first, states set up coalition governments that excluded former Nazi sympathizers; next came coalitions dominated by communists; finally, one party took hold of all the key positions of power. This was the process that prompted Winston Churchill, speaking at a college graduation in Fulton, Missouri, in 1946, to say that "an Iron Curtain" had "descended across Europe." In 1948, the Soviets crushed a Czechoslovakian coalition government—a break president Edvard Benes above two columns of Soviet and Czech soldiers marching together under their respective flags. Benes, who had been president of Czechoslovakia before the war, was returned to office in October 1945, only to be forced to resign in 1948 after a successful coup by the Soviet-backed Communist party.

Questions for Analysis

1. How do these three images portray the victory over the Germans?

2. How do these images deal with the question of Czechoslovakian nationalism?

3. Which of the three images most coincides with the Soviet view of the Czech situation?

C. Czech propaganda card, May 1945.

with Yalta's guarantee of democratic elections that shocked many. By that year, governments dependent on Moscow had also been established in Poland, Hungary, Romania, and Bulgaria. Together, these states were referred to as the Eastern bloc.

The Soviet campaign to control Eastern Europe did not go unchallenged. The Yugoslavian communist and resistance leader Marshal Tito (Josip Broz, 1892–1980) fought to keep his government independent of Moscow. Unlike most Eastern European communist leaders, Tito came to power on his own during the war. He drew on support from Serbs, Croats, and Muslims in Yugoslavia—thanks to his wartime record, which gave him political authority rooted in his own country. Moscow charged that Yugoslavia had "taken the road to nationalism," or become a "colony of the impe-

rialist nations," and expelled the country from the communist countries' economic and military pacts. Determined to reassert control elsewhere, the Soviets demanded purges in the parties and administrations of various satellite governments. These began in the Balkans and extended through Czechoslovakia, East Germany, and Poland. The fact that democratic institutions had been shattered before the war made it easier to establish dictatorships in its aftermath. The purges succeeded by playing on fears and festering hatreds; in several areas, those purging the governments attacked their opponents as Jewish. Anti-Semitism, far from being crushed, remained a potent political force—it became common to blame Jews for bringing the horrors of war.

The end of war did not mean peace. In Greece, as in Yugoslavia and through much of the Balkans, war's end brought a local communist-led resistance to the verge of seizing power. The British and the Americans, however, were determined to keep Greece in their sphere of influence, as per informal agreements with the Soviets. Only large infusions of aid to the anticommunist monarchy allowed them to do so. The bloody civil war that lasted until 1949 took a higher toll than the wartime occupation. Greece's bloodletting became one of the first crises of the Cold War and a touchstone for the United States' escalating fear of communist expansion. "Like apples in a barrel infected by the corruption of one rotten one, the corruption of Greece would infect Iran and all to the East . . . Africa . . . Italy and France," warned Dean Acheson in 1947, then deputy head of America's State Department. "[N]ot since Rome and Carthage had there been such a polarization of power on this earth."

Defeated Germany lay at the heart of these two polarizing power blocs and soon became the front line of their conflict. The Allies had divided Germany into four zones of occupation. Although the city of Berlin was deep in Soviet territory, it too was divided. The occupation zones were intended to be temporary, pending an official peace settlement. But the Soviets and the French, British, and Americans quarreled over reparations and policies for the economic development of Germany. Administrative

conflicts among the Western powers were almost as intense as their disagreements with the Soviets; Britain and the United States nearly had a serious falling out over food supply and trade in their zones. Yet the quickening Cold War put those arguments on hold, and in 1948 the three Western allies began to create a single government for their territories. They passed reforms to ease the economic crisis and introduced a new currency—a powerful symbol of economic unity. The Soviets retaliated by cutting all road, train, and river access from the western zone to West Berlin, but the Western allies refused to cede control over the capital. For eleven months, they airlifted supplies over Soviet territory to the besieged western zone of Berlin, a total of 12,000 tons of supplies carried by hundreds of flights every day. The Berlin blockade lasted nearly a year, from June 1948 to May 1949. It ended with the creation of two Germanies: the Federal Republic in the west and the German Democratic Republic in the former Soviet zone. Within a few short years both countries looked strikingly like armed camps.

The Marshall Plan

The United States countered the expansion of Soviet power and locally based communist movements with massive programs of economic and military aid to Western Europe. In a 1947 speech to Congress arguing for military assistance to anticommunists in Greece, President Harry Truman set out what would come to be called the Truman Doctrine, a pledge to support the resistance of "free peoples" to communism. The Truman Doctrine, however, also tied the contest for political power to economics. The American president declared the Soviet–American conflict to be a choice between "two ways of life." A few months later, Secretary of State George Marshall outlined an ambitious plan of economic aid to Europe, including, initially, the Eastern European states: the European Recovery Program. The Marshall Plan provided $13 billion of aid over four years (beginning in 1948), targeted to industrial redevelopment. The plan supplied American tractors, locomotive engines, food, technical equipment, and capital to participating states. Unlike a relief plan, however, the Marshall Plan encouraged the participating states to diagnose their own economic problems and to develop their own solutions. The Marshall Plan also encouraged coordination between European countries, partly out of idealism (some spoke of a "United States of Europe") and partly to dissuade France from asking for reparations and trying to dismantle the German economy. With a series of other economic agreements, the Marshall Plan became one of the building blocks of European economic unity. The American program, however, required

GERMAN COMMUNISTS PROTEST IN BERLIN AGAINST THE MARSHALL PLAN, 1952. Cold War tensions between the United States and the Soviet Union divided Europeans against one another. The signs in this protest read "Strength and Labor through Trade with the East!" and "Against the Marshall Plan [which] brings unemployment and poverty." ■ *What made the question of U.S. economic assistance so controversial for Germans?*

GERMANY DIVIDED AND THE BERLIN AIRLIFT. In the summer of 1948, the Soviet Union blocked routes through the German Democratic Republic to the Western Allies zone of Berlin. The blockade exacerbated tensions between the Soviet Union and the United States and forced the Allies to airlift supplies to West Berlin. At one point, planes landed in Berlin every three minutes. ■ *Looking at the map, why were the Western Allies able to airlift so much food with so much frequency?* ■ *How did this event lead to the eventual division of Germany into two nations?* ■ *What were the consequences of this division for the German people?*

measures such as decontrol of prices, restraints on wages, and balanced budgets. The Americans encouraged opposition to left-leaning politicians and movements that might be sympathetic to communism.

The United States also hastened to shore up military defenses. In April 1949, Canada, the United States, and representatives of Western European states signed an agreement establishing the North Atlantic Treaty Organization (NATO). Greece, Turkey, and West Germany were

later added as members. An armed attack against any one of the NATO members would now be regarded as an attack against all and bring a united military response. NATO established a joint military command in 1950, with Dwight Eisenhower, the wartime commander of Allied forces in the West, as its senior military officer. NATO's ground forces began with thirty divisions in 1950, and by 1953 had nearly sixty—including, perhaps most surprising, a dozen divisions from the young state of West Germany. West German rearmament had been the subject of agonizing debate, particularly in Britain and France, but American pressure and a sense of strategic necessity led to its acceptance within Western Europe. Among the most striking aspects of the Second World War's aftermath was how rapidly Germany was reintegrated into Europe. In the new Cold War world, *the West* quickly came to mean anticommunism. Potentially reliable allies, whatever their past, were not to be punished or excluded.

NATO's preparations for another European war depended heavily on air power, a new generation of jet bombers that would field the ultimate weapon of the age, the atomic bomb. Thus any conflict that broke out along the new German frontier threatened to dwarf the slaughter that had so recently passed.

Two Worlds and the Race for the Bomb

The Soviets viewed NATO, the Marshall Plan, and especially the United States' surprising involvement in Europe's affairs with mounting alarm. Rejecting an original offer of Marshall Plan aid, they established an Eastern European version of the plan, the Council for Mutual Economic Assistance, or Comecon. In 1947, the Soviets organized an international political arm, the Cominform (Communist Information Bureau), responsible for coordinating worldwide communist policy and programs. They responded to NATO with the establishment of their own military alliances, confirmed by the Warsaw Pact of 1955. This agreement set up a joint command among the states of Albania, Bulgaria, Czechoslovakia, Hungary, Poland, Romania, and East Germany and guaranteed the continued presence of Soviet troops in all those countries.

All these conflicts were darkened by the shadow of the nuclear arms race. In 1949, the Soviet Union surprised American intelligence by testing its first atom bomb (modeled on the plutonium bomb that Americans had tested in 1945). In 1953, both superpowers demonstrated a new weapon, the hydrogen or "super" bomb, which was a thousand times more powerful than the bomb dropped on Hiroshima. Within a few years, both countries developed smaller bombs and systems of delivery that made them usable. Intercontinental missiles were built that could field first one and then several nuclear warheads, fired from land or from a new generation of atomic-powered submarines that roamed the seas at all times ready to act. J. Robert Oppenheimer warned that the H-bomb so dramatically raised the ability to make war against civilians that it could become a "weapon of genocide." Beyond the grim warnings that nuclear war would wipe out human civilization, the bomb had more specific strategic consequences. The nuclearization of warfare fed into the polarizing effect of the Cold War, for countries without nuclear arms found it difficult to avoid joining either the Soviet or American pact.

Over the long term, it encouraged a disparity between two groups of nations: on the one hand, the superpowers, with their enormous military budgets and, on the other, nations that came to rely on agreements and international law. It changed the nature of face-to-face warfare as well, encouraging "proxy wars" between clients of the superpowers and raising fears that local conflicts might trigger general war.

The hydrogen bomb quickly took on enormous cultural significance as the single most compelling symbol of the age. It seemed to confirm both humanity's power and its vulnerability. The leaps in knowledge that it represented boosted contemporaries' confidence in science and progress. At the same time, weapons of mass destruction and

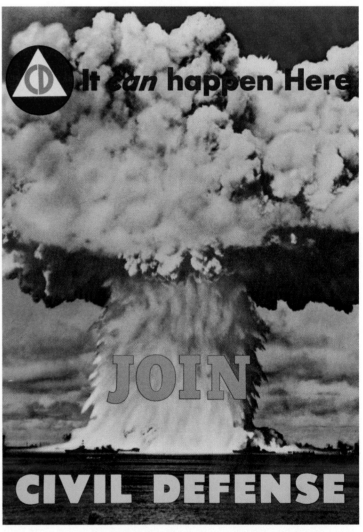

U.S. AND SOVIET VIEWS OF THE ARMS RACE. From 1946 to 1958, the United States exploded multiple nuclear weapons in tests at the Bikini Atoll in the Pacific Ocean. The Soviet Union's first successful nuclear test came in 1949. These posters, both apparently depicting the Pacific site of U.S. nuclear testing, demonstrate the attempts by both governments to use images of nuclear warfare in communicating with their populations. The U.S. civil defense poster (right) seeks to convince the American population that "it *can* happen here" while the Soviet poster (left) states simply *"het!"* ("no!") ▪ *Coming so soon after the destruction of World War II, how might such images have been received by the populations of the United States and the Soviet Union?*

humanity's emerging power to obliterate itself raised gnawing questions about whether that confidence was misplaced.

Was the Cold War inevitable? Could the Americans and the Soviets have negotiated their disagreements? On the Soviet side, Stalin's personal suspiciousness, ruthlessness, and autocratic ambitions combined with genuine security concerns to fuel the Cold War mentality. U.S. leaders, for their part, believed that the devastation of the Continent gave the Soviets an opportunity to establish communist regimes in Western as well as Eastern Europe. Western Europeans alone could not respond effectively to multiplying postwar crises in Germany, Greece, and elsewhere. The United States, too, was unwilling to give up the military, economic, and political power it had acquired during the war. As it turned away from its traditional isolationism, the U.S. thus articulated new strategic interests with global consequences, including access to European industry and far-flung military bases. These interests played into Soviet fears. In this context, trust became all but impossible.

A new international balance of power quickly produced new international policies. In 1946, George Kennan argued that the United States needed to make containing the Soviet threat a priority. The Soviets had not embarked on world revolution, Kennan said. Thus the United States needed to respond not with "histrionics: with threats or blustering or superfluous gestures of outward toughness" but rather "by the adroit and vigilant application of counterforce at a series of constantly shifting geographical and political points." Containment became the point of reference for U.S. foreign policy for the next forty years.

At its height, the Cold War had a chilling effect on domestic politics in both countries. In the Soviet Union, writers and artists were attacked for deviation from the party line. The party disciplined economists for suggesting that Western European industry might recover from the damage it had sustained. The radio blared news that Czech or Hungarian leaders had been exposed as traitors. In the United States, congressional committees launched campaigns to root out "communists" everywhere. On both sides of the Iron Curtain, the Cold War intensified everyday anxiety, bringing air-raid drills, spy trials, warnings that a way of life was at stake, and appeals to defend family and home against the menacing "other."

Khrushchev and the Thaw

Stalin died in 1953. Nikita Khrushchev's slow accession to power, not secure until 1956, signaled a change of direction. Khrushchev possessed a kind of earthy directness that, despite his hostility to the West, helped for a time to ease tensions. Stalin had secluded himself in the Kremlin; Khrushchev traveled throughout the world. On a visit to the United States in 1959, he traded quips with Iowa farmers and was entertained at Disneyland. Khrushchev was a shrewd politician, switching quickly between angry anti-American rhetoric and diplomatic reconciliation. Showing his desire to reduce international conflict, Khrushchev soon agreed to a summit meeting with the leaders of Britain, France, and the United States. This summit led to a series of understandings that eased the frictions in heavily armed Europe and produced a ban on testing nuclear weapons above ground in the early 1960s.

Khrushchev's other change of direction came with his famous "secret speech" of 1956, in which he acknowledged (behind the closed doors of the Twentieth Party Congress) the excesses of Stalin's era. Though the speech was secret, Krushchev's accusations were widely discussed. The harshness of Stalin's regime had generated popular discontent and demands for a shift from the production of heavy machinery and armaments to the manufacture of consumer goods, for a measure of freedom in the arts, for an end to police repression. How, under these circumstances, could the regime keep de-Stalinization within safe limits? The thaw did unleash forces that proved difficult to

NIKITA KHRUSHCHEV. Premier (1958–64) and first secretary of the Communist party (1953–64) of the Soviet Union, Khrushchev visited the United States in 1959. Here he is shown joking with an Iowa farmer. ▪ *Why was it important for Khrushchev to engage a foreign audience in this way?*

Competing Viewpoints

The Cold War: Soviet and American Views

The first excerpt is from a speech titled "The Sinews of Peace" that was delivered by Winston Churchill at Westminster College in Fulton, Missouri, in early 1946. In it, he coined the phrase Iron Curtain, warning of the rising power of the Soviet Union in Eastern Europe.

The next excerpt is from an address by Nikita Khrushchev, who became first secretary of the Communist party in 1953. Three years later, his power secure, he began publicly to repudiate the crimes of Joseph Stalin. Khrushchev presided over a short-lived thaw in Soviet–American relations. Yet, as can be seen in his address, Khrushchev shared Churchill's conception of the world divided into two mutually antagonistic camps.

Winston Churchill's "Iron Curtain" Speech

A shadow has fallen upon the scenes so lately lighted by the Allied victory. Nobody knows what Soviet Russia and its Communist international organization intend to do in the immediate future, or what are the limits, if any, to their expansive and proselytizing tendencies. I have a strong admiration and regard for the valiant Russian people and for my wartime comrade, Marshal Stalin. There is deep sympathy and goodwill in Britain . . . towards the people of all the Russias and a resolve to persevere through many differences and rebuffs in establishing lasting friendships. We understand the Russian need to be secure on her western frontiers by the removal of all possibility of German aggression. We welcome Russia to her rightful place among the leading nations of the world. We welcome her flag upon the seas. Above all, we welcome constant, frequent and growing contacts between the Russian people and our own people on both sides of the Atlantic. It is my duty however . . . to place before you certain facts about the present position in Europe.

From Stettin in the Baltic to Trieste in the Adriatic, an iron curtain has descended across the Continent. Behind that line lie all the capitals of the ancient states of Central and Eastern Europe. Warsaw, Berlin, Prague, Vienna, Budapest, Belgrade, Bucharest and Sofia, all these famous cities and the populations around them lie in what I must call the Soviet sphere, and all are subject in one form or another, not only to Soviet influence but to a very high and, in many cases, increasing measure of control from Moscow. . . .

From what I have seen of our Russian friends and Allies during the war, I am convinced that there is nothing they admire so much as strength, and there is nothing for which they have less respect than for weakness, especially military weakness. For that reason the old doctrine of a balance of power is unsound. We cannot afford, if we can help it, to work on narrow margins, offering temptations to a triad of strength. If the Western Democracies stand together in strict adherence to the principles of the United Nations Charter, their influences for furthering those principles will be

control. Between 1956 and 1958, the Soviet prison camps released thousands of prisoners. Soviet citizens besieged the regime with requests to rehabilitate relatives who had been executed or imprisoned under Stalin, partly to make themselves again eligible for certain privileges of citizenship, such as housing. In the new cultural climate, private life—family issues, the shortage of men after the war, and the problem of orphans—became a legitimate subject of concern and discussion.

The thaw provided a brief window of opportunity for some of the Soviet Union's most important writers. In 1957, Boris Pasternak's novel *Doctor Zhivago* could not be published in the Soviet Union, and Pasternak was barred from receiving his Nobel Prize. That Aleksandr Solzhenitsyn's (*suhl-zhih-NYEE-tsihn*) first novel, *One Day in the Life of Ivan Denisovich*, could be published in 1962 marked the relative cultural freedom of the thaw. *Ivan Denisovich* was based on Solzhenitsyn's own experiences in the camps, where he had immense and no one is likely to molest them. If however they become divided or falter in their duty and if these all-important years are allowed to slip away then indeed catastrophe may overwhelm us all.

Source: Winston Churchill, *Winston S. Churchill: His Complete Speeches, 1897–1963*, vol. 7, 1943–1949, ed. Robert Rhodes James (New York: 1983), pp. 7290–91.

Nikita Khrushchev, "Report to the Communist Party Congress" (1961)

Comrades! The competition of the two world social systems, the socialist and the capitalist, has been the chief content of the period since the 20th party Congress. It has become the pivot, the foundation of world development at the present historical stage. Two lines, two historical trends, have manifested themselves more and more clearly in social development. One is the line of social progress, peace and constructive activity. The other is the line of reaction, oppression and war.

In the course of the peaceful competition of the two systems capitalism has suffered a profound moral defeat in the eyes of all peoples. The common people are daily convinced that capitalism is incapable of solving a single one of the urgent problems confronting mankind. It becomes more and more obvious that only on the paths to socialism can a solution to these problems be found. Faith in the capitalist system and the capitalist path of development is dwindling. Monopoly capital, losing its influence, resorts more and more to intimidating and suppressing the masses of the people, to methods of open dictatorship in carrying out its domestic policy and to aggressive acts against other countries. But the masses of the people offer increasing resistance to reaction's acts.

It is no secret to anyone that the methods of intimidation and threat are not a sign of strength but evidence of the weakening of capitalism, the deepening of its general crisis. As the saying goes, if you can't hang on by the mane, you won't hang on by the tail! Reaction is still capable of dissolving parliaments in some countries in violation of their constitutions, of casting the best representatives of the people into prison, of sending cruisers and marines to subdue the "unruly." All this can put off for a time the approach of the fatal hour for the rule of capitalism. The imperialists are sawing away at the branch on which they sit. There is no force in the world capable of stopping man's advance along the road of progress.

Source: *Current Soviet Policies IV*, ed. Charlotte Saikowski and Leo Gruliow, from the translations of *Current Digest of the Soviet Press*, Joint Committee on Slavic Studies (Columbia University Press: 1962) pp. 42–45.

Questions for Analysis

1. Whom did Churchill blame for building the Iron Curtain between the Soviet sphere and the Western sphere?

2. Was the Soviet Union actively trying to create international communism? Was the United States trying to spread the Western way of life on a global scale?

spent eight years for criticizing Stalin in a letter, and was a powerful literary testimony to the repression Khrushchev had acknowledged. By 1964, however, Khrushchev had fallen and the thaw ended, driving criticism and writers such as Solzhenitsyn underground. *The First Circle* (1968), also autobiographical, told the story of a group of imprisoned scientists doing research for the secret police. Solzhenitsyn kept working on what would become *The Gulag Archipelago*, the first massive historical and literary study of the Stalinist camps (gulags). He secretly collected memoirs and personal testimony from prisoners, kept notes on cigarette rolling papers, and buried drafts of chapters behind his house. The Soviet secret police found a copy of the manuscript in a taxicab just when Solzhenitsyn had finished it. *The Gulag Archipelago* was published nonetheless in 1973 in Paris, but one year later the regime arrested Solzhenitsyn on charges of treason and sent him into exile. The most celebrated Soviet dissident was neither a democrat nor pro-Western. He was an idealist and a moralist, with roots among nineteenth-century Russian authors and philosophers. From exile

Solzhenitsyn attacked the corruptions of American commercialism as well as Soviet repressiveness.

Repression in Eastern Europe

The year of Stalin's death, tensions had exploded in Eastern Europe. The East German government, burdened by reparations payments to the Soviet Union, faced an economic crisis. The government's awareness of West German economic success made matters worse. The illegal exodus of East German citizens to the West rose sharply: 58,000 left in March 1953 alone. In June, when the government demanded hefty increases in industrial productivity, strikes broke out in East Berlin. Unrest spread throughout the country. The Soviet army put down the uprising, and hundreds were executed in the subsequent purge. In the aftermath, the East German government, under the leadership of Walter Ulbricht, used fears of disorder to solidify one-party rule.

In 1956, emboldened by Khrushchev's de-Stalinization, Poland and Hungary rebelled, demanding more independence in the management of their domestic affairs. Striking workers led the opposition in Poland. The government wavered, responding first with military repression and then with a promise of liberalization. Eventually the anti-Stalinist Polish leader Władysław Gomułka won Soviet permission for his country to pursue its own "ways of Socialist development" by pledging Poland's loyalty to the terms of the Warsaw Pact.

Events in Hungary turned out very differently. The charismatic leader of Hungary's communist government, Imre Nagy, was as much a Hungarian nationalist as a communist. Under his government, protests against Moscow's policies developed into a much broader anticommunist struggle and, even more important, attempted secession from the Warsaw Pact. Khrushchev might contemplate looser ties between Eastern Europe and Moscow, but he would not tolerate an end to the pact. On November 4, 1956, Soviet troops occupied Budapest, arresting and executing leaders of the Hungarian rebellion. The Hungarians took up arms, and street fighting continued for several weeks. The Hungarians had hoped for Western aid, but Dwight Eisenhower, newly elected to a second term as president, steered clear of giving support. Soviet forces installed a new government under the staunchly communist Janos Kadar, the repression continued, and tens of thousands of Hungarian refugees fled for the West. Khrushchev's efforts at presenting a gentler, more conciliatory Soviet Union to the West had been shattered by revolt and repression.

Khrushchev's policy of "peaceful coexistence" with the West did not reduce his determination to stave off any military threat to Eastern Europe. By the mid-1950s, NATO's policy of putting battlefield nuclear weapons in

THE BERLIN WALL, 1961 AND 1989. By 1960, the East German economy was in severe trouble, and many people, especially educated professionals, were fleeing to the West—200,000 in 1960 and 103,000 in the first six months of 1961. On August 13, 1961, the East German government placed armed guards and barbed wire around West Berlin to stop the flow. This bold move allowed the East German nation to survive, but it also created a powerful symbol of the regime's repressive character. In 1989, the breach in the wall was the final sign of the East German government's collapse, and the freedom to enter West Berlin marked a turning point after nearly three decades of enforced isolation. In the photo at right, Chancellor Helmut Kohl of West Germany shakes the hand of an East German in December 1989.

West Germany seemed evidence of just such a threat. What was more, East Germans continued to flee the country via West Berlin. Between 1949 and 1961, 2.7 million East Germans left, blunt evidence of the unpopularity of the regime. Attempting to stem the tide, Khrushchev demanded that the West recognize the permanent division of Germany with a free city in Berlin. When that demand was refused, in 1961 the East German government built a ten-foot wall separating the two sectors of the city. The wall brought a dangerous show of force on both sides, as the Soviets and Americans mobilized reservists for war. The newly elected American president, John F. Kennedy, marked Berlin's contested status with a visit when he proclaimed that "all free men" were fellow citizens of noncommunist West Berlin. For almost thirty years, until 1989, the Berlin Wall remained a monument to how the hot war had gone cold, and mirrored, darkly, the division of Germany and Europe as a whole.

ECONOMIC RENAISSANCE

Despite the ongoing tensions of a global superpower rivalry, the postwar period brought a remarkable recovery in Western Europe: the economic "miracle." Economists still debate its causes. Some factors resulted directly from the war, which encouraged a variety of technological innovations that could be applied in peacetime: improved communications (the invention of radar, for example), the development of synthetic materials, the increasing use of aluminum and alloy steels, and advances in the techniques of prefabrication. Wartime manufacturing had added significantly to nations' productive capacity. The Marshall Plan seems to have been less central than many claimed at the time, but it solved immediate problems having to do with the balance of payments and a shortage of American dollars to buy American goods. This boom was fueled by a third set of factors: high consumer demand and, consequently, very high levels of employment throughout the 1950s and 1960s. Brisk domestic and foreign consumption encouraged expansion, continued capital investment, and technological innovation. Rising demand for Europe's goods hastened agreements that encouraged the free flow of international trade and currencies (discussed below).

It was now assumed that states would do much more economic management—directing investment, making decisions about what to modernize, coordinating policies between industries and countries—than before. This, too, was a legacy of wartime. As one British official observed, "We are all planners now." Government tactics for steering the economy varied. West Germany provided tax breaks to encourage business investment; Britain and Italy offered investment allowances to their steel and petroleum industries. France, Britain, Italy, and Austria led the way in experiments with nationalizing industry and services in an effort to raise productivity. The result was a series of "mixed" economies combining public and private ownership. In France, where public ownership was already well advanced in the 1930s, railways, electricity and gas, banking, radio and television, and a large segment of the automobile industry were brought under state management. In Britain, the list was equally long: coal and utilities; road, railroad, and air transport; and banking. Though nationalization was less common in West Germany, the railway system (state owned since the late nineteenth century); some electrical, chemical, and metallurgical concerns; and the Volkswagen company—the remnant of Hitler's attempt to produce a "people's car"—were all in state hands, though the latter was largely returned to the private sector in 1963.

These government policies and programs contributed to astonishing growth rates. Between 1945 and 1963, the average yearly growth of West Germany's gross domestic product (gross national product [GNP] minus income received from abroad) was 7.6 percent; in Austria, 5.8 percent; in Italy, 6 percent; in the Netherlands, 4.7 percent; and so on. Not only did the economies recover from the war but they reversed prewar economic patterns of slack demand, overproduction, and insufficient investment. Production facilities were hard pressed to keep up with soaring demand.

West Germany's recovery was particularly spectacular, and particularly important to the rest of Europe. Production increased sixfold between 1948 and 1964. Unemployment fell to record lows, reaching 0.4 percent in 1965, when there were six jobs for every unemployed person. The contrast with the catastrophic unemployment of the Great Depression heightened the impression of a miracle. Prices rose but then leveled off, and many citizens could plunge into a domestic buying spree that caused production to soar. In the 1950s, the state and private industry built a half million new housing units each year, to accommodate citizens whose homes had been destroyed; new resident refugees from East Germany and Eastern Europe; and transient workers from Italy, Spain, Greece, and elsewhere drawn by West Germany's high demand for labor. German cars, specialized mechanical goods, optics, and chemicals returned to their former role leading world markets. West German women were included in the process: during the 1950s, German politicians encouraged women to take up a role as "citizen consumers," as active but prudent buyers of goods that would keep the German economy humming.

Under the direction of a minister for planning, Jean Monnet, the French government played a direct role in industrial reform, contributing not only capital but expert advice, and facilitating shifts in the national labor pool to place workers where they were most needed. The plan gave priority to basic industries; the production of electricity doubled, the steel industry was thoroughly modernized, and the French railway system became the fastest and most efficient on the Continent. Italy's industrial "miracle" came later but was even more impressive. Stimulated by infusions of capital from the government and from the Marshall Plan, Italian companies soon began to compete with other European international giants. The products of Olivetti, Fiat, and Pirelli became familiar in households around the world to an extent that no Italian goods had in the past. Electric power production doubled between 1938 and 1953. By 1954, real wages were 50 percent higher than they had been in 1938.

European nations with little in common in terms of political traditions or industrial patterns all shared in the general prosperity. Rising GNPs, however, did not level the differences among and within states. In southern Italy, illiteracy remained high, and land continued to be held by a few rich families; the per capita GNP in Sweden was almost ten times that of Turkey. Britain remained a special case. The Conservative prime minister, Harold Macmillan, campaigned successfully for reelection in 1959 with the slogan "You've never had it so good"—an accurate enough boast. British growth was respectable when compared with past performance. Yet the British economy remained sluggish. The country was burdened with obsolete factories and methods, the legacy of its early industrialization, and by an unwillingness to adopt new techniques in old industries or invest in more successful new ones. It was plagued as well by a series of balance-of-payments crises precipitated by an inability to sell more goods abroad than it imported.

European Economic Integration

The Western European renaissance was a collective effort. From the Marshall Plan on, a series of international economic organizations began to bind the Western European countries together. The first of these was the European Coal and Steel Community (ECSC), founded in 1951 to coordinate trade in, and the management of, Europe's most crucial resources. Coal was still king in mid-twentieth-century Europe; it fueled everything from steel manufacturing and trains to household heating, and counted for 82 percent of Europe's primary energy consumption. It was also key to relations between West Germany, with abundant coal

mines, and France, with its coal-hungry steel mills. The ECSC joint High Authority, which consisted of experts from each of the participating countries, had power to regulate prices, to increase or limit production, and to impose administrative fees. In 1957, the Treaty of Rome transformed France, West Germany, Italy, Belgium, Holland, and Luxembourg—into the European Economic Community (EEC), or Common Market. The EEC aimed to abolish trade barriers among its members. Moreover, the organization pledged itself to common external tariffs, to the free movement of labor and capital among the member nations, and to building uniform wage structures and social security systems to create similar working conditions throughout the Common Market. A commission headquartered in Brussels administered the program; by 1962, Brussels had more than 3,000 "Eurocrats."

Integration did not proceed smoothly. Great Britain stayed away, fearing the effects of the ECSC on its declining coal industry and on its longtime trading relationship with Australia, New Zealand, and Canada. Britain did not share France's need for raw materials and the others' need for markets; it continued to rely on its economic relations with the Empire and Commonwealth. One of the few victors in the Second World War, Britain assumed that it could hold its global economic position in the postwar world. In the other countries, domestic opposition to EEC provisions on wages or agricultural prices often threatened to scuttle agreements. The French and other countries insisted on protecting agriculture, sensitive to the importance of the peasantry to political stability and invested in the countryside's place in national identity.

The seismic shifts that began to make oil and atomic power more important than coal (see Chapter 28) made the ECSC less effective. Still, the EEC was a remarkable success. By 1963, it had become the world's largest importer. Its steel production was second only to that of the United States, and total industrial production was over 70 percent higher than it had been in 1950. Last, it established a new long-term political trend: individual countries sought to Europeanize solutions to their problems.

Likewise, crucial agreements reached in Bretton Woods, New Hampshire, in July 1944 aimed to coordinate the movements of the global economy and to internationalize solutions to economic crises, avoiding catastrophes such as those that plagued the 1930s. Bretton Woods created the International Monetary Fund and the World Bank, both designed to establish predictable and stable exchange rates, prevent speculation, and enable currencies—and consequently trade—to move freely. All other currencies were pegged to the dollar, which both reflected and enhanced the United States' role as the foremost financial power. The new international system was formed with the American–European sphere in mind, but these organizations soon began to play a role in economic development in what came to be known as the Third World. The postwar period, then, quickened global economic integration, largely on American terms.

Economic Development in the East

Although economic development in Eastern Europe was not nearly so dramatic as that in the West, significant advances occurred there as well. National incomes rose and output increased. Poland and Hungary, in particular, strengthened their economic connections with the West, primarily with France and West Germany. By the late 1970s, about 30 percent of Eastern Europe's trade was conducted outside the Soviet bloc. Nevertheless, the Soviet Union required its satellites to design their economic policies to serve more than their own national interests. Regulations governing Comecon, the Eastern European equivalent of the Common Market, ensured that the Soviet Union could sell its exports at prices well above the world level and compelled other members to trade with the Soviet Union to their disadvantage. Emphasis initially was on heavy industry and collectivized agriculture, though political tension in countries such as Hungary and Poland forced the Soviets eventually to moderate their policies so as to permit the manufacture of more consumer goods and the development of a modest trade with the West.

The Welfare State

Economic growth became one of the watchwords of the postwar era. Social welfare was another. The roots of the new legislation extended back to the insurance plans for old age, sickness, and disability introduced by Bismarck in Germany in the late 1880s. But economic expansion allowed postwar European states to fund more comprehensive social programs, and commitments to putting democracy on a stronger footing provided the political motivation. Clement Atlee, a socialist and the leader of the British Labour party, coined the term *welfare state*; his government, in power until 1951, led the way in enacting legislation that provided free medical care to all through the National Health Service, assistance to families, and guaranteed secondary education of some kind. The welfare state also rested on the assumption that governments could and should try to support popular purchasing power, gen-

erate demand, and provide either employment or unemployment insurance, assumptions spelled out earlier by John Maynard Keynes (*General Theory,* 1936) or William Beveridge's important 1943 report on full employment. Although the British Labour party and continental socialist parties pressed these measures, welfare was a consensus issue, backed by the moderate coalitions that governed most postwar Western European states. Understood in this way, welfare was not poor relief but an entitlement. Thus it marked a break with centuries-old ways of thinking about poverty and citizenship.

European Politics

Postwar political leaders were overwhelmingly pragmatic. Konrad Adenauer, the West German chancellor from 1949 to 1963, despised German militarism and blamed that tradition for Hitler's rise to power. Still, he was apprehensive about German parliamentary democracy and governed in a paternalistic, sometimes authoritarian, manner. His determination to end the centuries-old hostility between France and Germany contributed significantly to the movement toward economic union. Alcide De Gasperi, the Italian premier from 1948 to 1953, was also centrist. Among postwar French leaders, the most colorful was the Resistance hero General Charles de Gaulle. De Gaulle had retired from politics in 1946 when French voters refused to accept his proposals for strengthening the executive branch of the government. In 1958, faced with civil turmoil caused by the Algerian war and an abortive coup attempt by a group of right-wing army officers, France's government collapsed and de Gaulle was invited to return. De Gaulle accepted but insisted on a new constitution. That constitution, which created the Fifth Republic in 1958, strengthened the executive branch of the government in an effort to avoid the parliamentary deadlocks that had weakened the country earlier. De Gaulle used his new authority to restore France's power and prestige. "France is not really herself unless in the front rank," he wrote in his memoirs. "France cannot be France without greatness." Greatness, for de Gaulle, involved reorienting foreign policy, which included an end to France's grip on Algeria. Resisting U.S. influence in Europe, he pulled French forces out of NATO in 1966. He cultivated better relations with the Soviet Union and with West Germany. Finally, he accelerated French economic and industrial expansion by building a modern military establishment, complete with atomic weapons. Like his counterparts, de Gaulle was not, by nature, a democrat. He steered a centrist course, working hard to produce practical

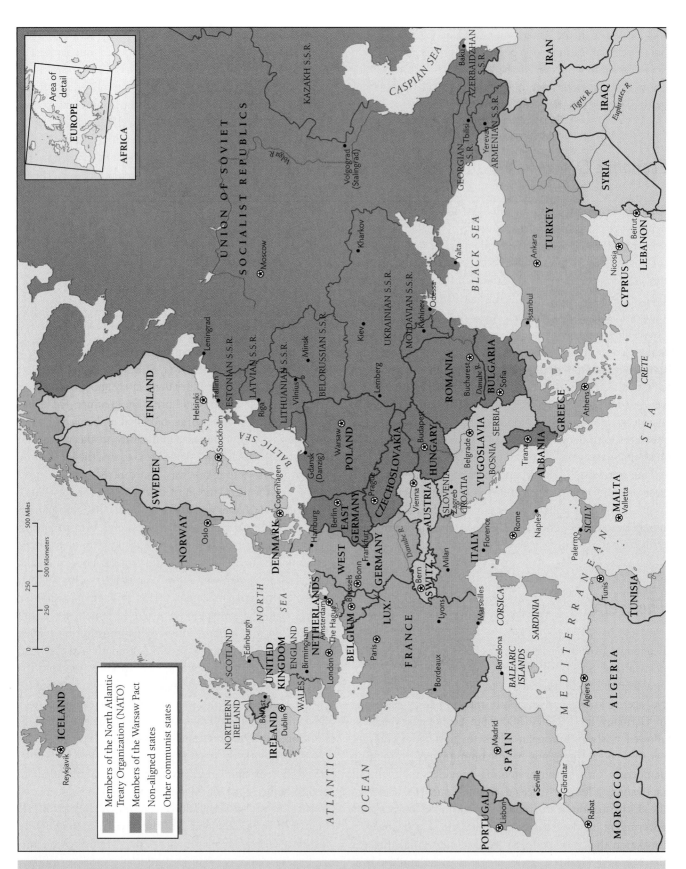

EUROPE DURING THE COLD WAR. Examine the membership of NATO and the Warsaw Pact, respectively. ■ *What were the member states in NATO?* ■ *Why do you think some countries did not join NATO?* ■ *Why did the membership of each alliance stay relatively stable for nearly a half century?*

CHARLES DE GAULLE PRESENTING HIS PLAN TO STRENGTHEN THE EXECUTIVE BRANCH OF THE GOVERNMENT IN 1946. When voters rejected his ideas, he retired, only to return in 1958 to outline a new constitution.

solutions to political problems and thereby undermine radicalism in any form. Most other Western European nations did the same.

REVOLUTION, ANTICOLONIALISM, AND THE COLD WAR

In the colonial world as in Europe, the end of war unleashed new conflicts. Those conflicts became closely bound up with Europe's political and economic recovery, they had an enormous if delayed effect on Western culture, and they complicated the Cold War. The Cold War, as we have seen, created two powerful centers of gravity for world politics. But the wave of anticolonial independence movements that swept through postwar Asia and Africa created a new group of nations that would attempt to avoid aligning with one or the other bloc, and would call itself the "Third World."

The Chinese Revolution

The Chinese Revolution was the single most radical change in the developing world after the Second World War. A civil war had raged in China since 1926, with Mao Zedong's (*mow zeh-DOONG*, 1893–1976) communist insurgents in the north in revolt against the Nationalist forces of Jiang Jeishi (Chiang Kai-shek, 1887–1975). Though they agreed on a truce to face the Japanese during the war years, the civil war resumed after the Japanese defeat, and in 1949, Mao's insurgents took control of the Chinese government and drove the Nationalists into exile.

The Chinese Revolution was above all a peasant revolution, even more so than the Russian Revolution. Mao adapted Marxism to conditions very different from those imaged by Marx himself, emphasizing radical reform in the countryside (reducing rents, providing healthcare and education, and reforming marriage) and autonomy from Western colonial powers. The leaders of the revolution set about turning China into a modern industrial nation within a generation, at huge human cost and with very mixed results.

To anticolonial activists in many parts of the world, the Chinese Revolution stood as a model. To colonial powers, it represented the dangers inherent in decolonization. The "loss of China" provoked fear and consternation in the West, particularly in the United States. Although Mao and Stalin distrusted each other and relations between the two regimes were extremely difficult, the United States considered both nations a communist bloc until the early 1970s, and the Chinese Revolution intensified Western military and diplomatic anxiety about governments in Asia.

The Korean War

Anxiety about China turned Korea into a hot spot in the Cold War. Korea, effectively a Japanese colony since the 1890s, had been brutally exploited by the occupiers. The Soviet Union forced the Japanese out at the end of the Second World War, and the peninsula was divided into two states, similar to Germany: communist North Korea, run by the Soviet client Kim Il Sung, and South Korea, led by the anticommunist autocrat Syngman Rhee, who was backed by the United States. In June 1950, communist North Korean troops attacked, crushing resistance and forcing a small American garrison to retreat to the far end of the peninsula. The United States took advantage of a temporary Russian boycott of the United Nations to bring the invasion before the Security Council, which gave its permission for an American-led "police action" to defend South Korea.

A RED GUARD DEMONSTRATION. Middle-school students display their solidarity with Mao Zedong's revolution by waving copies of a book of his quotations. The slogan proclaims, "Not only are we able to destroy the old world, we are able to build a new world instead—Mao Zedong." ■ *What made the Chinese Revolution different from the Bolshevik Revolution in 1917?*

U.S. General Douglas MacArthur, a Second World War hero, mounted an amphibious attack behind North Korean lines and drove the Korean communists to the Chinese border. He pressed for the authority to attack them as they retreated into China, clearly hoping to help reverse the Chinese Revolution. President Harry Truman (1945–53) denied this rash request and relieved MacArthur of command. The price had already been paid, however; more than a million Chinese troops flooded across the border in support of the North Koreans, forcing the international troops into a bloody retreat. General Matthew Ridgeway, replacing MacArthur, stemmed the retreat, but the war became a stalemate, pitting Chinese and North Korean troops against UN forces—largely American and South Korean forces but also containing contingents from Britain, Australia, Ethiopia, the Netherlands, Turkey and elsewhere. Two years later, the war ended inconclusively, with Korea divided roughly along the original line. South Korea had not been "lost," but with over 53,000 Americans and over 1 million Koreans and Chinese dead, neither side could claim a decisive

victory. As in Germany, the inability of major powers to achieve their goals resulted in a divided nation.

Decolonization

The Chinese Revolution proved the start of a larger wave. Between 1947 and 1960, the sprawling European empires built during the nineteenth century disintegrated. Opposition to colonial rule had stiffened after the First World War, forcing war-weakened European states to renegotiate the terms of empire. After the Second World War, older forms of empire quickly became untenable. In some regions, European states simply sought to cut their losses and withdraw. In others, well-organized and tenacious nationalist movements successfully demanded new constitutional arrangements and independence. In a third set of cases, European powers were drawn into complicated, multifaceted, and extremely violent struggles between different movements of indigenous peoples and European settler communities—conflicts the European states had helped create.

The British Empire Unravels

India was the first and largest of the colonies to win self-government after the war. As we have seen, rebellions such as the Sepoy Mutiny challenged the representatives of Britain in India throughout the nineteenth century (see Chapter 25). During the early stages of the Second World War, the Indian National Congress (founded 1885), the umbrella party for the independence movement, called on Britain to "quit India." The extraordinary Indian nationalist Mohandas K. (Mahatma) Gandhi (1869–1948) had been at work in India since the 1920s and had pioneered anticolonial ideas and tactics that echoed the world over. In the face of colonial domination, Gandhi advocated not violence but *swaraj*, or self-rule, urging Indians individually and collectively to develop their own resources and to withdraw from the imperial economy—by going on strike, refusing to pay taxes, or boycotting imported textiles and wearing homespun. By 1947, Gandhi and his fellow nationalist Jawaharlal Nehru (1889–1964, prime minister 1947–1964), the leader of the proindependence Congress party, had gained such widespread support that the British found it impossible to continue in power. The Labour party government elected in Britain in 1945 had always favored Indian independence. Now that independence became a British political necessity.

While talks established the procedures for independence, however, India was torn by ethnic and religious conflict. A Muslim League, led by Mohammed Ali Jinnah (1876–1948), wanted autonomy in largely Muslim areas and feared the predominantly Hindu Congress party's authority in a single united state. Cycles of rioting broke out between the two religious communities. In June 1947, British India was partitioned into the nations of India (majority Hindu) and Pakistan (majority Muslim). The process of partition brought brutal religious and ethnic warfare. More than 1 million Hindus and Muslims died, and an estimated 12 million became refugees, evicted from their lands or fleeing the fighting. Throughout the chaos, Gandhi, now eighty, continued to protest violence and to focus attention on overcoming the legacy of colonialism. He argued that "real freedom will come when we free ourselves of the dominance of western education, western culture, and western way of living which have been ingrained in us." In January 1948, he was assassinated by a Hindu zealot. Conflict continued between the independent states of India and Pakistan. Nehru, who became first prime minister of India, embarked on a program of industrialization and modernization—not at all what Gandhi would have counseled. Nehru proved particularly adept at maneuvering in

DECOLONIZATION IN THE MIDDLE EAST. ▪ *What were the colonial possessions of the British and French in the Middle East?* ▪ *What were the three stages of decolonization in the Middle East?* ▪ *Why did the British hold on to the small states bordering the Persian Gulf and Arabian Sea until 1971?*

the Cold War world, steering a course of nonalignment with either of the blocs, getting aid for industry from the Soviet Union and food imports from the United States.

PALESTINE

The year 1948 brought more crises for the British Empire, including an end to the British mandate in Palestine. During the First World War, British diplomats had encouraged Arab nationalist revolts against the Ottoman Empire. With the 1917 Balfour Declaration, they had also promised a "Jewish homeland" in Palestine for European Zionists. Contradictory promises and the flight of European Jews from Nazi Germany contributed to rising conflict between Jewish settlers and Arabs in Palestine during the 1930s and provoked an Arab revolt bloodily suppressed by the British. At the same time, the newly important oil

Mohandas Gandhi and Nonviolent Anticolonialism

After leading a campaign for Indian rights in South Africa between 1894 and 1914, Mohandas K. Gandhi (1869–1948), known as Mahatma ("great-souled") Gandhi, became a leader in the long battle for home rule in India. This battle was finally won in 1947 and brought with it the partition of India and the creation of Pakistan. Gandhi's insistence on the power of nonviolent noncooperation brought him to the forefront of Indian politics and provided a model for many later liberation struggles, including the American Civil Rights Movement. Gandhi argued that only nonviolent resistance, which dramatized the injustice of colonial rule and colonial law, had the spiritual force to unite a community and end colonialism.

assive resistance is a method of securing rights by personal suffering; it is the reverse of resistance by arms. When I refuse to do a thing that is repugnant to my conscience, I use soul-force. For instance, the Government of the day has passed a law which is applicable to me. I do not like it. If by using violence I force the Government to repeal the law, I am employing what may be termed body-force. If I do not obey the law and accept the penalty for its breach, I use soul-force. It involves sacrifice of self.

Everybody admits that sacrifice of self is infinitely superior to sacrifice of others. Moreover, if this kind of force is used in a cause that is unjust, only the person using it suffers. He does not make others suffer for his mistakes. Men have before now done many things which were subsequently found to have been wrong. . . . It is therefore meet that he should not do that which he knows to be wrong, and suffer the consequence whatever it may be. This is the key to the use of soul-force. . . .

It is contrary to our manhood if we obey laws repugnant to our conscience. Such teaching is opposed to religion and means slavery. If the Government were to ask us to go about without any clothing, should we do so? If I were a passive resister, I would say to them that I would have nothing to do with their law. But we have so forgotten ourselves and become so compliant that we do not mind any degrading law.

A man who has realized his manhood, who fears only God, will fear no one else. Man-made laws are not necessarily binding on him. Even the Government does not expect any such thing from us. They do not say: "You must do such and such a thing." But they say: "If you do not do it, we will punish you." We are sunk so low that we fancy that it is our duty and our religion to do what the law lays down. If man will only realize that it is unmanly to obey laws that are unjust, no man's tyranny will enslave him. This is the key to self-rule or home-rule.

Source: M. K. Gandhi, "Indian Home Rule (1909)," in *The Gandhi Reader: A Source Book of His Life and Writings*, ed. Homer A. Jack (Bloomington, IN: 1956), pp. 104–21.

Questions for Analysis

1. Why did Gandhi believe that "sacrifice of self" was superior to "sacrifice of others"?

2. What did Gandhi mean when he said that "it is contrary to our manhood if we obey laws repugnant to our conscience"?

concessions in the Middle East were multiplying Britain's strategic interests in the Suez Canal, Egypt, and the Arab nations generally. Mediating local conflicts and balancing their own interests proved an impossible task. In 1939, in the name of regional stability, the British strictly limited further Jewish immigration. They tried to maintain that limit after the war, but now they faced pressure from tens of thousands of Jewish refugees from Europe. The conflict quickly became a three-way war: among Palestinian Arabs fighting for what they considered their land and their independence, Jewish settlers and Zionist militants determined to defy British restrictions, and British administrators with divided sympathies, embarrassed and shocked by the plight of Jewish refugees and committed to maintaining good Anglo-Arab relations. The British responded militarily. By 1947, there was one British soldier for every eighteen inhabitants of the Mandate. The years of fighting, however, with terrorist tactics on all sides, persuaded the British to leave. The United Nations voted (by a narrow margin) to partition the territory into two states. Neither

DECOLONIZATION IN ASIA. ▪ *Among colonial powers, who were the biggest losers post–World War II?* ▪ *What was the single most important geopolitical change in Asia during this period?* ▪ *What role did the Soviet Union and the United States play in Asia?*

Jewish settlers nor Palestinian Arabs found the partition satisfactory and both began to fight for territory even before British troops withdrew. No sooner did Israel declare its independence in May 1948 than five neighboring states invaded. The new but well-organized Israeli nation survived the war and extended its boundaries. On the losing side, a million Palestinian Arabs who fled or were expelled found themselves clustered in refugee camps in the Gaza Strip and on the West Bank of the Jordan River, which the armistice granted to an enlarged state of Jordan. It is remarkable that the conflict did not become a Cold War confrontation at the start. For their own reasons, both Soviets and Americans recognized Israel. The new nation, however, marked a permanent change to the culture and balance of power in the region.

AFRICA

A number of West African colonies established assertive independence movements before and during the 1950s, and the British government moved hesitantly to meet their demands. By the middle of the 1950s, Britain agreed to a variety of terms for independence in these territories, leaving them with written constitutions and a British legal system but little else in terms of modern infrastructure or economic support. Defenders of British colonialism claimed that these formal institutions would give advantages to the independent states, but without other resources, even the most promising foundered. Ghana, known formerly as the Gold Coast and the first of these colonies to gain independence, was seen in the early 1960s as a model for free African nations. Its politics soon degenerated, however, and

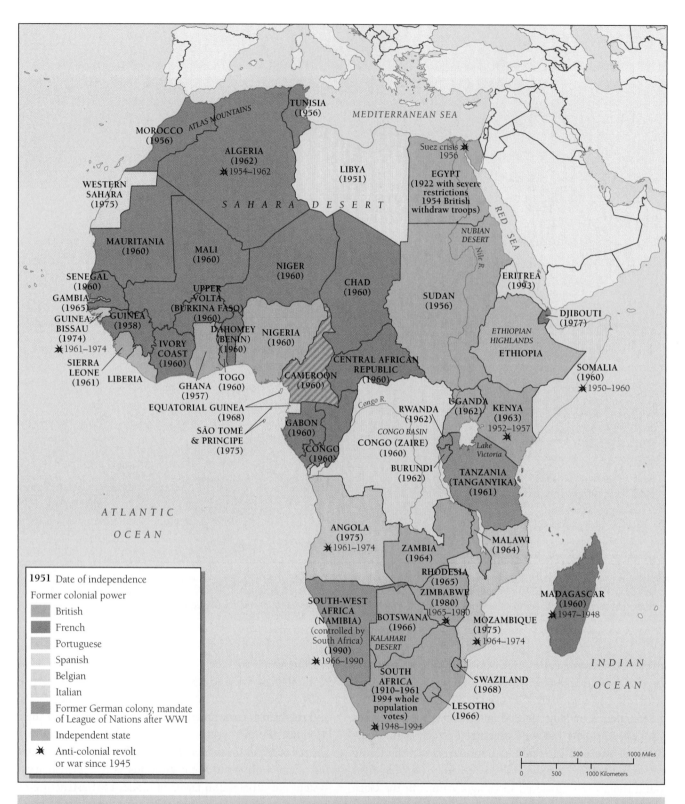

MEDITERRANEAN SEA

MOROCCO (1956)

ATLAS MOUNTAINS

TUNISIA (1956)

ALGERIA (1962)
✳ 1954–1962

LIBYA (1951)

Suez crisis ✳ 1956

EGYPT (1922 with severe restrictions 1954 British withdraw troops)

WESTERN SAHARA (1975)

S A H A R A   D E S E R T

NUBIAN DESERT

Nile R.

RED SEA

MAURITANIA (1960)

MALI (1960)

NIGER (1960)

CHAD (1960)

SUDAN (1956)

ERITREA (1993)

SENEGAL (1960)

GAMBIA (1965)

GUINEA BISSAU (1974)
✳ 1961–1974

GUINEA (1958)

UPPER VOLTA (BURKINA FASO) (1960)

DAHOMEY (BENIN) (1960)

NIGERIA (1960)

CENTRAL AFRICAN REPUBLIC (1960)

DJIBOUTI (1977)

ETHIOPIAN HIGHLANDS

ETHIOPIA

SOMALIA (1960)
✳ 1950–1960

IVORY COAST (1960)

SIERRA LEONE (1961)

LIBERIA

GHANA (1957)

TOGO (1960)

CAMEROON (1960)

Congo R.

RWANDA (1962)

UGANDA (1962)

KENYA (1963)
✳ 1952–1957

EQUATORIAL GUINEA (1968)

SÃO TOMÉ & PRINCIPE (1975)

GABON (1960)

CONGO (1960)

CONGO BASIN

CONGO (ZAIRE) (1960)

BURUNDI (1962)

Lake Victoria

TANZANIA (TANGANYIKA) (1961)

ATLANTIC OCEAN

ANGOLA (1975)
✳ 1961–1974

ZAMBIA (1964)

MALAWI (1964)

RHODESIA (1965)

ZIMBABWE (1980)
✳ 1965–1980

MADAGASCAR (1960)
✳ 1947–1948

SOUTH-WEST AFRICA (NAMIBIA) (controlled by South Africa) (1990)
✳ 1966–1990

BOTSWANA (1966)

KALAHARI DESERT

MOZAMBIQUE (1975)
✳ 1964–1974

INDIAN OCEAN

SWAZILAND (1968)

SOUTH AFRICA (1910–1961 1994 whole population votes)
✳ 1948–1994

LESOTHO (1966)

1951 Date of independence

Former colonial power

British

French

Portuguese

Spanish

Belgian

Italian

Former German colony, mandate of League of Nations after WWI

Independent state

✳ Anti-colonial revolt or war since 1945

0   500   1000 Miles

0   500   1000 Kilometers

DECOLONIZATION OF AFRICA. ▪ *Who were the biggest imperial losers in the decolonization of Africa?* ▪ *By what decade had most African countries achieved their independence?* ▪ *What were the forces behind decolonization in Africa?*

its president, Kwame Nkrumah, became the first of several African leaders driven from office for corruption and autocratic behavior.

Belgium and France also withdrew from their holdings. By 1965, virtually all of the former African colonies had become independent, and virtually none of them possessed the means to redress losses from colonialism to make that independence work. As Belgian authorities raced out of the Congo in 1960, they left crumbling railways and fewer than two dozen indigenous people with college educations.

The process of decolonization was relatively peaceful—except where large populations of European settlers complicated European withdrawal. In the north, settler resistance made the French exit from Algeria wrenching and complex (discussed below). In the east, in Kenya, the majority Kikuyu population revolted against British rule and against a small group of settlers. The uprising, which came to be known as the Mau Mau rebellion, soon turned bloody. British troops fired freely at targets in rebel-occupied areas, sometimes killing civilians. Internment camps set up by colonial security forces became sites of atrocities that drew public investigations and condemnation by even the most conservative British politicians and army officers. In 1963, a decade after the rebellion began, the British conceded Kenyan independence.

In the late 1950s, the British prime minister Harold Macmillan endorsed independence for a number of Britain's African colonies as a response to powerful winds of change. In southern Africa, the exceptionally large and wealthy population of European settlers set their sails against those winds, a resistance that continued on for decades. These settlers, a mixture of English migrants and the Franco-Dutch Afrikaners who traced their arrival to the eighteenth century, controlled huge tracts of fertile farmland along with some of the most lucrative gold and diamond mines on earth. This was especially true in South Africa. There, during the late 1940s, Britain's Labour government set aside its deep dislike of Afrikaner racism in a fateful political bargain. In return for guarantees that South African gold would be used carefully to support Britain's global financial power, Britain tolerated the introduction of apartheid in South Africa. Even by other standards of segregation, apartheid was especially harsh. Under its terms, Africans, Indians, and colored persons of mixed descent lost all political rights. All the institutions of social life, including marriage and schools, were segregated. What was more, the government tried to block the dramatic social consequences of the expansion of mining and industrialization in general, especially African migration to cities and a new wave of labor militancy in the mines. Apartheid required Africans to live in designated "homelands," forbade them to travel without specific permits, and created elaborate government bureaus to manage the labor essential to the economy. The government also banned any political protest. These measures made Western powers uncomfortable with the segregationist regime, but white South Africans held on to American support by presenting themselves as a bulwark against communism.

To the north, in the territories of Rhodesia, the British government encouraged a large federation, controlled by white settlers but with the opportunity for majority rule in the future. By the early 1960s, however, the federation was on the verge of collapse; the majority-rule state of Malawi was allowed to exit the federation in 1964, and Rhodesia split on northern and southern lines. In the north, the premier relented and accepted majority government under the black populist Kenneth Kaunda. In the south, angry Afrikaners backed by 200,000 right-wing English migrants who had arrived since 1945 refused to accept majority rule. When the British government attempted to force their hand, the settlers unilaterally declared independence in 1965 and began a bloody civil war against southern Rhodesia's black population that lasted a half generation.

CRISIS IN SUEZ AND THE END OF AN ERA

For postwar Britain, empire was not only politically complicated but cost too much. Britain began to withdraw from naval and air bases around the world because they had become too expensive to maintain. The Labour government did try to maintain British power and prestige in the postwar world. In Malaya, British forces repressed a revolt by ethnic Chinese communists and then helped support the independent states of Singapore and Malaysia, maintaining British companies' and banks' ties with Malaysia's lucrative rubber and oil reserves. Labour also launched carefully targeted efforts at "colonial development" to tap local natural resources Britain hoped to sell on world markets. "Development," however, was underfunded and largely disregarded in favor of fulfilling Cold War commitments elsewhere. In the Middle East, the British government protected several oil-rich states with its military and helped overthrow a nationalist government in Iran to ensure that the oil states invested their money in British financial markets.

In Egypt, however, the British refused to yield a traditional point of imperial pride. In 1951, nationalists compelled the British to agree to withdraw their troops from Egyptian territory within three years. In 1952, a group of nationalist army officers deposed Egypt's King Farouk, who had close ties to Britain, and proclaimed a republic. Shortly after the final British withdrawal an Egyptian colonel, Gamal Abdel Nasser (1918–1970), became president of the country (1956–70). His first major public act as president was to nationalize the Suez Canal Company. So doing would help finance the construction of the Aswan Dam on the Nile, and both the dam and nationalizing the canal represented economic independence and Egyptian national pride. Nasser also helped develop the anticolonial ideology of pan-Arabism, proposing that Arab nationalists throughout the Islamic world should create an alliance of modern nations, no longer beholden to the West. Finally, Nasser was also willing to take aid and support from the Soviets to achieve that goal, which made the canal a Cold War issue.

Three nations found Nasser and his pan-Arab ideals threatening. Israel, surrounded on all sides by unfriendly neighbors, was looking for an opportunity to seize the strategic Sinai Peninsula and create a buffer against Egypt. France, already fighting a war against Algerian nationalists, hoped to destroy what it considered the Egyptian source of Arab nationalism. Britain depended on the canal as a route to its strategic bases and was stung by this blow to imperial dignity. Though the British were reluctant to intervene, they were urged on by their prime minister, Sir Anthony Eden; Eden had developed a deep personal hatred of Nasser. In the autumn of 1956, the three nations colluded in an attack on Egypt. Israel occupied the Sinai while British and French jets destroyed Egypt's air force on the ground. The former colonial powers landed troops at the mouth of the canal but lacked the resources to push on in strength toward Cairo. As a result the war left Nasser in power and made him a hero to the Egyptian public for holding the imperialists at bay. The attack was condemned around the world. The United States angrily called its allies' bluff, inflicting severe financial penalties on Britain and France. Both countries were forced to withdraw their expeditions. For policy makers in Great Britain and France, the failure at Suez marked the end of an era.

French Decolonization

In two particular cases, France's experience of decolonization was bloodier, more difficult, and more damaging to French prestige and domestic politics than any in Britain's experience, with the possible exception of Northern Ireland. The first was Indochina, where French efforts to restore imperial authority after losing it in the Second World War only resulted in military defeat and further humiliation. The second case, Algeria, became not only a violent colonial war but also a struggle with serious political ramifications at home.

THE FIRST VIETNAM WAR, 1946–1954

Indochina was one of France's last major imperial acquisitions in the nineteenth century. Here, as elsewhere, the two world wars had helped galvanize first nationalist and then, also, communist independence movements. In Indonesia, nationalist forces rebelled against Dutch efforts to restore colonialism, and the country became independent in 1949. In Indochina, the communist resistance became particularly effective under the leadership of Ho Chi Minh. Ho was French educated and, his expectations raised by the Wilsonian principles of self-determination, had hoped his country might win independence at Versailles in 1919 (see Chapter 24). He read Marx and Lenin and absorbed the Chinese communists' lessons about organizing peasants around social and agrarian as well as national issues. During the Second World War, Ho's movement fought first the Vichy government of the colony and later Japanese occupiers and provided intelligence reports for the Allies. In 1945, however, the United States and Britain repudiated their relationship with Ho's independence movement and allowed the French to reclaim their colonies throughout Southeast Asia. The Vietnamese communists, who were fierce nationalists as well as Marxists, renewed their guerrilla war against the French.

The fighting was protracted and bloody; France saw in it a chance to redeem its national pride. After one of France's most capable generals, Jean de Lattre de Tassigny, finally achieved a military advantage against the rebels in 1951, the French government might have decolonized on favorable terms. Instead, it decided to press on for total victory, sending troops deep into Vietnamese territory to root out the rebels. One major base was established in a valley bordering modern Laos, at a hamlet called Dien Bien Phu. Ringed by high mountains, this vulnerable spot became a base for thousands of elite French paratroopers and colonial soldiers from Algeria and West Africa—the best of France's troops. The rebels besieged the base. Tens of thousands of Vietnamese nationalist fighters hauled heavy artillery by hand up the mountainsides and bombarded the network of forts set up by the French. The siege lasted for months, becoming a protracted national crisis in France.

When Dien Bien Phu fell in May 1954, the French government began peace talks in Geneva. The Geneva Accords, drawn up by the French, Vietnamese politicians including the communists, the British, and the Americans, divided Indochina into three countries: Laos, Cambodia, and Vietnam, which was partitioned into two states. North Vietnam was taken over by Ho Chi Minh's party; South Vietnam by a succession of Western-supported politicians. Corruption, repression, and instability in the south, coupled with Ho

The Vietnam War: American Analysis of the French Situation

At the end of the Second World War, the French government sought to recoup its prestige and empire by reasserting control of the former colony of Indochina. The French faced fierce resistance from nationalist forces under the French-educated leader Ho Chi Minh. Within a few years, American advisers were beginning to shore up the faltering French army. Cold War ideology, anxiety about China and Korea, and a conviction that they could do what the French could not combined to draw the Americans more deeply into the war. In 1950, the Central Intelligence Agency drew up this analysis of the strategic situation.

 or more than three years, an intense conflict has been in progress in Indochina in which nationalistic Vietnamese forces under the leadership of the Moscow-trained revolutionist, Ho Chi Minh, have opposed the reimposition of French authority. Within Vietnam ... a precarious military balance exists between the French and their Vietnamese followers on the one hand and Ho's resistance forces on the other. Thus far, French progress toward both political and military objectives has been substantially less than is necessary to eliminate the threat to French tenure posed by the resistance.

The French position and Bao Dai's [emperor of Vietnam since 1926] prospects have recently been further weakened: politically by Chinese Communist and Soviet recognition of Ho Chi Minh, and militarily by the ability of the Chinese Communist forces to make military supplies available to Ho's forces. Unless the French and Bao Dai receive substantial outside assistance, this combined political and military pressure may accelerate a French withdrawal from all or most of Indochina which, previous to the Chinese Communist and Soviet recognition of Ho, had been estimated as probably occurring within two years. . . .

The fighting in Indochina constitutes a progressive drain on French military resources which is weakening France as a partner in the Western alliance. If France is driven from Indochina, the resulting emergence of an indigenous Communist-oriented regime in Vietnam, in combination with the pressures which will be exerted by the new government of China and the Soviet Union, can be expected to cause adjacent Thailand and Burma to yield to this Communist advance. Under these conditions Malaya and Indonesia would also become highly vulnerable.

The French are trying to halt the present unfavorable trend by according certain aspects of sovereignty to Emperor Bao Dai. . . . The French political aim is to attract non-Communist nationalists from the leadership of Ho Chi Minh to that of Bao Dai.

Meanwhile, Soviet and Chinese Communist recognition of Ho's regime has made it clear that the Kremlin is now prepared to exert greater pressure to achieve its objective of installing a Communist regime in Indochina. France alone is incapable of preventing such a development and can turn only to the US for assistance in thwarting this Communist strategy. Having already publicly proclaimed support of Bao Dai, the US is now faced with the choice of bolstering his weak and vulnerable position or of abandoning him and accepting the far-reaching consequences of Communist control of Indochina.

Source: National Archives, College Park, MD. Record Group 263 (Records of the Central Intelligence Agency), *Estimates of the Office of Research Evaluation, 1946–1950,* box 4.

Questions for Analysis

1. Explain how the author of this CIA report has used George Kennan's policy of containment. What would happen if the French military forces withdrew? Why was Southeast Asia such a hot spot in the decade following the Second World War?

2. Did the French or American military, just coming off a European theater of war, have any idea what it would be like to wage war in a place like Southeast Asia?

"DIEN-BIEN-PHU . . . THEY SACRIFICED THEMSELVES FOR LIBERTY." The sentiments expressed in this poster, which was intended to commemorate the French soldiers who died at Dien Bien Phu in May 1954, helped to deepen French commitments to colonial control in Algeria.

Chi Minh's nationalist desire to unite Vietnam, guaranteed that the war would continue. The U.S. government, which had provided military and financial aid to the French, began to send aid to the South Vietnamese regime. The Americans saw the conflict through the prism of the Cold War: their project was not to restore colonialism but to contain communism and prevent it from spreading through Southeast Asia. The limits of this policy would not become clear until the mid-1960s.

ALGERIA

Still reeling from the humiliation of Dien Bien Phu, France faced a complex colonial problem closer to home, in Algeria. Since the 1830s, the colony had evolved into a settler society of three social groups. First, in addition to a small class of French soldiers and administrators, there were also 1 million European settlers. They typically owned farms and vineyards near the major cities or formed the working-class and merchant communities inside those cities. All of them were citizens of the three administrative districts of Algeria, which were legally part of France. The community produced some of France's best-known writers and intellectuals: Albert Camus, Jacques Derrida, and Pierre Bourdieu, among others. In the small towns and villages of Algeria lived a second group of (largely Muslim) Berbers, whose long history of service in the French army entitled them to certain formal and informal privileges within the colony. Finally, there were millions of Muslim Arabs, some living in the desert south but most crowded into impoverished neighborhoods in the cities. The Arabs were the largest and most deprived group in Algerian society. Between the world wars the French government had offered small reforms to increase their rights and representation, and it had hoped to meld the three groups into a common Algerian society. Reforms came too late and were also undercut by European settlers anxious to maintain their privileges.

At the end of the Second World War, Algerian nationalists called on the Allies to recognize Algeria's independence in return for good service during the war. Public demonstrations became frequent and in several cases turned into attacks on settler-landowners. In one rural town, Setif, celebrations of the defeat of Germany flared into violence against settlers. French repression was harsh and immediate: security forces killed several thousand Arabs. After the war, the French government approved a provincial assembly for all of Algeria, elected by two pools of voters, one made up of settlers and mostly Berber Muslims, the other of Arabs. This very limited enfranchisement gave Arab Algerians no political power. The more important changes were economic. All of Algeria suffered in the difficulties after the war. Many Arab Algerians felt they had to emigrate; several hundred thousand went to work in France. While

COUNTERINSURGENCY IN ALGERIA. An Algerian POW imprisoned by the French in a cellar for animals during the Algerian War of Independence, 1961.

citizens of mainland France read their papers and frowned over the war in Indochina, the situation in Algeria grew more serious. By the middle of the 1950s, a younger generation of Arab activists, unhappy with the leadership of the moderates, had taken charge of a movement dedicated to independence by force. The National Liberation Front (FLN) was organized, which leaned toward socialism and demanded equal citizenship for all.

The war in Algeria became a war on three fronts. The first was a guerrilla war between the regular French Army and the FLN, fought in the mountains and deserts of the country. This war continued for years, a clear military defeat for the FLN but never a clear-cut victory for the French. The second war, fought out in Algeria's cities, began with an FLN campaign of bombing and terrorism. European civilians were killed, and the French administration retaliated with its own campaign. French paratroopers hunted down and destroyed the networks of FLN bombers. The information that allowed the French to break the FLN network was extracted through systematic torture conducted by French security forces. The torture became an international scandal, bringing waves of protest in France. This third front of the Algerian war divided France, brought down the government, and ushered de Gaulle back into power.

De Gaulle visited Algiers to wild cheering from settlers and declared that Algeria would always be French. After another year of violence, he and his advisers had changed their minds. By 1962, talks had produced a formula for independence: a referendum would be held, voted on by the whole population of Algeria. On July 1, 1962, the referendum passed by a landslide vote. Arab political groups and guerrillas from the FLN entered Algiers in triumph. Settlers and Berbers who had fought for the French army fled Algeria for France by the hundreds of thousands. Later, these refugees were joined in France by another influx of Arab economic migrants.

Algeria illustrated the dramatic domestic impact of decolonization. The war cut deep divides through French society, largely because the very identity of France seemed at stake. Withdrawing from Algeria meant reorienting French views of what it meant to be a modern power. De Gaulle summed up the trade-off in his memoirs: to stay in Algeria would "keep France politically, financially, and militarily bogged down in a bottomless quagmire when, in fact, she needed her hands free to bring about the domestic transformation necessitated by the twentieth century and to exercise her influence abroad unencumbered." In France and other imperial powers, the conclusions seemed clear. Traditional forms of colonial rule could not withstand the demands of postwar politics and culture; the leading European nations, once distinguished by their empires, would

THE STRUGGLE FOR NATIONAL INDEPENDENCE IN ALGERIA. Ben Cherif, a commander in the FLN, handcuffed in 1961. ■ *How might this struggle for independence against the French have shaped the generation of political leaders who took power after decolonization?*

have to look for new forms of influence. The domestic transformation of which de Gaulle spoke—recovery from the war, economic restructuring, and political renewal—had to take place on a radically changed global stage.

POSTWAR CULTURE AND THOUGHT

The postwar period brought a remarkable burst of cultural production. Writers and artists did not hesitate to take up big issues: freedom, civilization, and the human condition itself. The search for democratic renewal gave this literature urgency; the moral dilemmas of war, occupation, and resistance gave it resonance and popular appeal. The process of decolonization, too, forced the issues of race, culture, and colonialism to center stage in Western debates.

The Black Presence

The journal *Présence Africaine* ("*African Presence*"), founded in Paris in 1947, was only one in a chorus of new cultural voices. *Présence Africaine* published such writers as Aimé

Analyzing Primary Sources

Anticolonialism and Violence

Born in the French Caribbean colony of Martinique, Frantz Fanon (1925–1961) studied psychiatry in France before moving on to work in Algeria in the early 1950s. Fanon became a member of the Algerian revolutionary National Liberation Front (FLN) and an ardent advocate of decolonization. Black Skin, White Masks, published in 1952 with a preface by Jean-Paul Sartre, was a study of the psychological effects of colonialism and racism on black culture and individuals. The Wretched of the Earth (1961) was a revolutionary manifesto, one of the most influential of the period. Fanon attacked nationalist leaders for their ambition and corruption. He believed that revolutionary change could come only from poor peasants, those who "have found no bone to gnaw in the colonial system." Diagnosed with leukemia, Fanon sought treatment in the Soviet Union and then in Washington, DC, where he died.

n decolonization, there is therefore the need of a complete calling in question of the colonial situation. If we wish to describe it precisely, we might find it in the well-known words: "The last shall be first and the first last." Decolonization is the putting into practice of this sentence. . . .

The naked truth of decolonization evokes for us the searing bullets and bloodstained knives which emanate from it. For if the last shall be first, this will only come to pass after a murderous and decisive struggle between the two protagonists. That affirmed intention to

place the last at the head of things, and to make them climb at a pace (too quickly, some say) the well-known steps which characterize an organized society, can only triumph if we use all means to turn the scale, including, of course, that of violence.

You do not turn any society, however primitive it may be, upside down with such a program if you have not decided from the very beginning, that is to say from the actual formation of that program, to overcome all the obstacles that you will come across in so doing. The native who decides to put the program into practice, and to become its moving force, is ready for violence at all time.

From birth it is clear to him that this narrow world, strewn with prohibitions, can only be called in question by absolute violence.

Source: Frantz Fanon, *The Wretched of the Earth,* trans. Constance Farrington (New York: 1963), pp. 35–37.

Questions for Analysis

1. Why did Fanon believe that violence lay at the heart of both the colonial relationship and anticolonial movements?

2. What arguments would he offer to counter Gandhi?

Césaire (1913–2008), the surrealist poet from Martinique, and Léopold Senghor of Senegal (1906–2001). Césaire and Senghor were brilliant students, educated in the most elite French universities, and elected to the French National Assembly. Césaire became an important political figure in Martinique, a French Caribbean colony that became a department of France in 1946. In 1960, Senghor was elected the first president of Senegal. Both men, in important respects models of Frenchness, became the most influential exponents of *Négritude,* which could be translated as "black consciousness" or "black pride." Senghor wrote:

Assimilation was a failure. We could assimilate mathematics of the French language, but we could

never strip off our black skins or root out black souls. And so we set out on a fervent quest for . . . our collective soul. Negritude is the whole complex of civilized values—cultural, economic, social and political—which characterize the black people.

Césaire's early work took its lead from surrealism and the exploration of consciousness. Later, his work became more political. *Discourse on Colonialism* (1950) was a powerful indictment of the material and spiritual squalor of colonialism, which, he argued, not only dehumanized colonial subjects but degraded the colonizers themselves.

Césaire's student Frantz Fanon (1925–1961), also from Martinique, went further. He argued that withdrawing into an insular black culture (as he interpreted Negritude) was not an effective response to racism. People of color, he believed, needed a theory of radical social change. Fanon trained in psychiatry and worked in Algeria, where he became a member of the National Liberation Front. In *Black Skin, White Masks* (1952), he examined the effects of colonialism and racism from the point of view of a radical psychiatrist. *The Wretched of the Earth* (1961) became one of the most influential revolutionary manifestos of the period. More than Césaire, and bluntly rejecting Gandhi's theories and practice, Fanon argued that violence was rooted in colonialism and, therefore, in anticolonial movements. But he also believed that many anticolonial leaders would be corrupted by their ambition and by collaboration with former colonial powers. Revolutionary change, he believed, could come only from poor peasants, or those who "have found no bone to gnaw in the colonial system."

How did these writers fit into postwar culture? Western intellectuals sought to revive humanism and democratic values after the atrocities of the Second World War. Fanon and others pointed out that the struggles over colonialism made that project more difficult; the violent repression of anticolonial movements in places such as Algeria seemed to be a relapse into brutality. They pointed to the ironies of Europe's "civilizing mission" and demanded a reevaluation of blackness as a central concept in Western culture. The

SIMONE DE BEAUVOIR (1908–1986). A philosopher, novelist, memoirist, and path-breaking theorist of sex and gender, Beauvoir's work challenged widespread beliefs about femininity and womanhood.

West's postwar recovery would entail eventually facing this challenge to the universal claims of its culture.

Existentialism

The French existentialist writers, most prominently Jean-Paul Sartre (*SAHR-truh*, 1905–1980) and Albert Camus (*KAM-oo*, 1913–1960), put the themes of individuality, commitment, and choice at center stage. The existentialists took themes from Nietzsche, Heidegger, and Kierkegaard, reworking them in the new context of war-torn Europe. Their starting point was that "existence precedes essence." In other words, meaning in life is not given but created. Thus, individuals were "condemned to be free" and to give their lives meaning by making choices and accepting responsibility. To deny one's freedom or responsibility was to act in "bad faith." War, collaboration and resistance, genocide, and the development of weapons of mass destruction all provided specific points of reference and gave these abstractions new meaning. The existentialists' writing was also clear and accessible, which contributed to their enormous popularity. Although Sartre wrote philosophical treatises, he also published plays and short stories. Camus's own experience in the resistance gave him tremendous moral authority—he became the symbol of a new generation. His novels—including *The Stranger* (1942), *The Plague* (1947), and *The Fall* (1956)—often revolved around metaphors for the war, showing that people were responsible for their own dilemmas and, through a series of antiheroes, exploring the limited ability of men and women to help each other.

Existentialist insights opened other doors. The existentialist approach to race, for instance, emphasized that no meaning inhered in skin color; instead, race derived meaning from a lived experience or situation. As Frantz Fanon wrote, white and black exist "only insofar as they create one another." The same approach could be applied to gender. In her famous introduction to *The Second Sex* (1949), Simone de Beauvoir (*duh bohv-WAHR*, 1908–1986) argued, "One is not born a woman, one becomes one." Women, like men, were condemned to be free. Beauvoir went on to ask why women seemed to accept their secondary status or why, in her words, they "dreamed the dreams of men." The scope and ambition of *The Second Sex* helped make it enormously influential; it was virtually encyclopedic, analyzing history, myth, biology, and psychology, bringing the insights of Marx and Freud to bear on the "woman question." Beauvoir's life also contributed to the book's high profile. A brilliant student from a strict middle-class background, she had a lifelong affair with Sartre but did not marry him, leading many to romanticize her as a liberated and accomplished woman intellectual. She had little to do with feminism, however, until the late 1960s. When *The Second Sex* was published, it was associated with existentialism; only later would it become a key text of the women's movement (see Chapter 28).

Memory and Amnesia: The Aftermath of War

The theme of individual helplessness in the face of state power ran through countless works of the period, beginning, most famously, with George Orwell's *Animal Farm* (1946) and *1984* (1949). The American Joseph Heller's wildly popular *Catch-22* (1961) represented a form of popular existentialism, concerned with the absurdity of war and offering a biting commentary on regimentation and its toll on individual freedom. The Czech author Milan Kundera, who fled the repressive Czech government to live in Paris, eloquently captured the bittersweet efforts to resist senseless bureaucracy. Some writers expressed their despair by escaping into the absurd and fantastic. In Samuel Beckett's deeply pessimistic *Waiting for Godot* (1953, by an Irishman in French) and in the Briton Harold Pinter's *Caretaker*

THE COLD WAR IN EVERYDAY LIFE. A Soviet matchbook label, 1960, depicts a Soviet fist destroying a U.S. plane. Soviet nationalism had been a potent force since the Second World War. ■ *Could the Soviet leadership sustain this nationalist sentiment without an external threat?*

(1960) and *Homecoming* (1965), nothing happens. Characters speak in banalities, paralyzed by the absurdity of modern times.

Other authors ventured into the realms of hallucination, science fiction, and fantasy. The novels of the Americans William Burroughs and Kurt Vonnegut carry readers from interior fantasies to outer space. One of the most popular books of the period was *The Lord of the Rings* (1954–1955), written before and during the Second World War by the Briton J. R. R. Tolkien. Set in the fantasy world of Middle Earth, Professor Tolkien's tribute to the ancient Celtic and Scandinavian languages he studied and the power of human myths was seized on by a generation of young romantics who rebelled against postwar Western culture for their own reasons.

Questions of terror and dictatorship haunted social and political thought of the postwar era, and especially the work of émigrés from Europe. Representatives of the "Frankfurt school" of German Marxism, by wartime refugees in the United States, sought to understand how fascism and Nazism had taken root in Western culture and politics. Theodor Adorno joined Max Horkheimer in a series of essays, *Dialectic of Enlightenment* (1947), the best known of which indicted the "culture industry" for depoliticizing the masses and crippling democracy. Adorno also coauthored *The Authoritarian Personality* (1950), which used social surveys in an effort to discover how people become receptive to racism, prejudice, and dictatorship. Whatever the specific roots of German Nazism, the Frankfurt school suggested, there were also more general tendencies in modern societies that should give cause for concern.

Hannah Arendt (1906–1975), a Jewish refugee from Germany, was the first to propose that both Nazism and Stalinism should be understood as forms of a novel, twentieth-century form of government: totalitarianism (*The Origins of Totalitarianism,* 1951). Unlike earlier forms of tyranny or despotism, totalitarianism worked by mobilizing mass support. It used terror to crush resistance, break down political and social institutions, and atomize the public. Totalitarianism, Arendt argued, also forged new ideologies. Totalitarian regimes did not concern themselves with whether killing was justified by law; they justified camps and extermination by pointing to the objective laws of history or racial struggle. By unleashing destruction and eliminating entire populations, totalitarian politics made collective resistance virtually impossible. Arendt returned to the same theme in a provocative and disturbing essay on the trial of a Nazi leader, *Eichmann in Jerusalem* (1963). To many readers' distress, she pointedly refused to demonize Nazism. Instead, she explored what she termed "the banality of evil": how the rise of new forms of state power and

Analyzing Primary Sources

The War That Refuses to Be Forgotten

Heda Margolis Kovály was born in Prague and returned to her city after surviving the concentration camps. Like many refugees and survivors, she received an uncertain welcome home. In Czechoslovakia and elsewhere, the Nazi occupation left a legacy of bitterness and division that persisted for decades. Survivors reminded other Europeans of the war and made them defensive. Paradoxically, as Kovály shows, it was common to blame the victims for the war's troubles.

 nd so ended that horrible long war that refuses to be forgotten. Life went on. It went on despite both the dead and the living, because this was a war that no one had quite survived. Something very important and precious had been killed by it or, perhaps, it had just died of horror, of starvation, or simply of disgust—who knows? We tried to bury it quickly, the earth settled over it, and we turned our backs on it impatiently. After all, our real life was now beginning and what to make of it was up to us.

People came crawling out of their hide-outs. They came back from the forests, from the prisons, and from the concentration camps, and all they could think was, "It's over; it's all over." . . . Some people came back silent, and some talked incessantly as though talking about a thing would make it vanish. . . . While some voices spoke of death and flames, of blood and gallows, in the background, a chorus of thousands repeated tirelessly, "You know, we also suffered. . . . [N]othing but skimmed milk. . . . No butter on our bread. . . ."

Sometimes a bedraggled and barefoot concentration camp survivor plucked up his courage and knocked on the door of prewar friends to ask, "Excuse me, do you by any chance still have some of the stuff we left with you for safekeeping?" And the friends would say, "You must be mistaken, you didn't leave anything with us, but come in anyway!" And they would seat him in their parlor where his carpet lay on the floor and pour herb tea into antique cups that had belonged to his grandmother. . . . He would say to himself, "What does it matter? As long as we're alive? What does it matter?" . . .

It would also happen that a survivor might need a lawyer to retrieve lost documents and he would remember the name of one who had once represented large Jewish companies. He would go to see him and sit in an empire chair in a corner of an elegant waiting room, enjoying all that good taste and luxury, watching pretty secretaries rushing about. Until one of the pretty girls forgot to close a door behind her, and the lawyer's sonorous voice would boom through the crack, "You would have thought we'd be rid of them finally, but no, they're impossible to kill off—not even Hitler could manage it. Every day there're more of them crawling back, like rats. . . ." And the survivor would quietly get up from his chair and slip out of the waiting room, this time not laughing. On his way down the stairs his eyes would mist over as if with the smoke of the furnaces at Auschwitz.

Source: Heda Margolis Kovály, *Under a Cruel Star: A Life in Prague 1941–1968*, trans. Franci Epstein and Helen Epstein with the author (Cambridge, MA: 1986), pp. 45–46.

Questions for Analysis

1. What did Kovály mean when she remarked that the Second World War was "a war that no one had quite survived"? Can such an argument be made about all wars? In what ways was the Second World War distinctive?

2. Kovály describes individual encounters. Do her stories illuminate larger social and cultural developments?

---

terror had created a world in which Nazis such as Adolf Eichmann could implement genocide as simply one more policy. The crisis of totalitarianism, Arendt argued, was the moral collapse of society, for it destroyed human feeling and the power of resistance in executioners and victims— "tormentors and the tormented"—alike.

Discussions of the war and its legacy, however, were limited. Some memoirs and novels dealing directly with the war and its brutal aftermath did reach a large international public: Jerzy Kosinski's novel about a boy in wartime Poland, *The Painted Bird*; Czesław Miłosz's memoir of intellectual collaboration in Eastern Europe, *The Captive*

Mind (1951); the German Günter Grass's *Tin Drum* (1959), which portrayed the Nazi and war experience in a semi-autobiographical genre and earned Grass recognition as "the conscience of his generation." Of all the memoirs, *The Diary of a Young Girl* by Anne Frank, published in 1947, was undoubtedly the most widely read. Yet the main current in postwar culture ran in a different direction, toward repressing painful issues and bad memories. Postwar governments could not or would not purge all those implicated in war crimes. In France, the courts sentenced 2,640 to death and executed 791; in Austria, 13,000 were convicted of war crimes and 30 executed. Those who called for justice grew demoralized and cynical. Others responded by mythologizing the Resistance and exaggerating participation in it and by avoiding discussion of collaboration. For ten years, French television considered *The Sorrow and the Pity* (1969), Marcel Ophüls's brilliant and unsparing documentary on a French town under Vichy, too controversial for broadcast. Most Jewish survivors, wherever they lived, found that few editors were interested in publishing their stories. In 1947, only a small publishing house would take on the Italian survivor Primo Levi's *Survival in Auschwitz;* the book and Levi's other writings did not find a wide audience until later.

The Cold War was an important factor in burying and distorting memories. West of the Iron Curtain, the eagerness to embrace West Germany as an ally, the single-minded emphasis on economic development, and ardent anticommunism blurred views of the past. One example involved Klaus Barbie, an agent for the Gestapo in occupied France who, among other things, arrested and personally tor-

tured members of the Resistance and deported thousands, including Jewish children, to concentration camps. After the war, American intelligence services recruited Barbie for his anticommunist skills and paid to smuggle him out of Europe, beyond the reach of those who wanted to prosecute him for war crimes. He was finally extradited from Bolivia in 1983, tried in France for crimes against humanity, and convicted. In the Eastern bloc, regimes declared fascism to be a thing of the past and did not scrutinize that past or seek out the many who collaborated with the Nazis. Thus, reckoning with history was postponed until the fall of the Soviet Union. On both sides of the Iron Curtain, the vast majority of people turned inward, cherishing their domestic lives, relieved to have privacy.

THE CUBAN MISSILE CRISIS

One of the last serious and most dramatic confrontations of the Cold War came in 1962, in Cuba. A revolution in 1958 had brought the charismatic communist Fidel Castro to power. Immediately after, the United States began to work with exiled Cubans, supporting, among other ventures, a bungled attempt to invade via the Bay of Pigs in 1961. Castro not only aligned himself with the Soviets but invited them to base nuclear missiles on Cuban soil, only a few minutes' flying time from Florida. When American spy planes identified the missiles and related military equipment in 1962, Kennedy confronted Khrushchev. After deliberating about the repercussions of an air strike, Kennedy ordered a naval blockade of Cuba. On October 22, he appeared on television, visibly tired and without makeup, announced the grave situation to the public, and challenged Khrushchev to withdraw the weapons and "move the world back from the abyss of destruction." Terrified of the looming threat of nuclear war, Americans fled urban areas, prepared for a cramped and uncomfortable existence in fallout shelters, and bought firearms. After three nerve-wracking weeks, the Soviets agreed to withdraw and to remove the bombers and missiles already on Cuban soil. But citizens of both countries spent many anxious hours in their bomb shelters, and onlookers the world over wrestled with their rising fears that a nuclear Armageddon was upon them.

BAY OF PIGS, 1961. American president John F. Kennedy brandishes the combat flag of the Cuban landing brigade.

Past and Present

The Divisions of the Cold War

The Cold War conflict between the United States and the Soviet Union (captured in the image of the Berlin Wall, left) was largely seen as a split between the East and the West, though global competition between the two powers also had profound effects on other regions of the world. The movement of the "Non-Aligned Nations" (represented here by Prime Minister Jawaharlal Nehru of India, President Kwame Nkrumah of Ghana, President Gamal Abdel Nasser of Egypt, President Sukarno of Indonesia, and President Tito of Yugoslavia) was an attempt to provide an alternative to this division.

 Watch related author interview on StudySpace
wwnorton.com/web/westernciv18

The Cuban missile crisis provided one inspiration for Stanley Kubrick's classic *Dr. Strangelove* (1964), a devastating and dark comedy with many Cold War themes. The story concerns an "accidental" nuclear attack and the demented characters responsible for it. It also concerns the repression of memory and the sudden reversals of alliances brought about by the Cold War. The wildly eccentric German scientist Dr. Strangelove shuttles between his present life working for the Americans and his barely repressed past as an enthusiastic follower of Hitler. The screenplay was based on the British writer Peter Bryant's *Two Hours to Doom* (1958), one of many 1950s novels with an apocalyptic scenario. The Cuban missile crisis brought the plot so close to home that when the film came out Columbia Pictures felt compelled to issue a disclaimer: "It is the stated position of the United States Air Force that their safeguards would prevent the occurrence of such events as are depicted in this film." Black humor

seemed to be a common cultural mechanism for dealing with the terrible possibility of world annihilation. The protagonist of Bob Dylan's 1963 "Talkin' World War III Blues" playfully narrates an apocalyptic dream in which he drives an abandoned Cadillac ("a good car to drive after a war"), approaches the inhabitants of a bunker for a TV dinner, and lights a cigarette on a radioactive parking meter.

CONCLUSION

The Cold War reached deep into postwar culture and it dominated postwar politics. It decisively shaped the development of both the Soviet and American states. Fearful of losing control of territory they had conquered at such cost in the Second World War, the Soviets intervened repeatedly in the politics of their Eastern European allies in the 1940s and 1950s, ensuring the creation of hard-line governments in East Germany, Czechoslovakia, Poland, Hungary, and elsewhere in the Eastern bloc. In the United States, anti-communism became a powerful political force, shaping foreign policy and preparations for military confrontation with the Soviet Union to such an extent that President Eisenhower warned in his farewell address that a "military-industrial complex" had taken shape in the United States and that its "total influence—economic, political, even spiritual—is felt in every city, every statehouse, every office of the federal government."

In Western Europe, rebuilding the economy and creating a new political order in the aftermath of the Second World War meant accepting the new power and influence of the United States, but Europeans also searched for ways to create and express a European identity that would retain some independence and freedom of action. Led by the efforts of France and Germany, Western Europeans eventually found elements of this freedom in increasing integration and economic cooperation. In Eastern Europe, on the other hand, the political leadership found fewer opportunities for independent action and the threat of military intervention by the Soviet

After You Read This Chapter

Visit StudySpace for quizzes, additional review materials, and multimedia documents. **wwnorton.com/web/westernciv18**

REVIEWING THE OBJECTIVES

- The Cold War between the United States and the Soviet Union began as the Second World War ended. How did these two nations seek to influence the postwar political order in Europe?
- Postwar economic growth was accompanied by greater economic integration among Western European nations. What were the goals of those who sought to create the unified European market and which nations played key roles in its development?
- Between the late 1940s and the mid-1960s, almost all the European colonies in Asia and Africa demanded and received their independence, either peacefully or through armed conflict. What combination of events made Europeans less able to defend their colonial empires against the claims of nationalists who sought independence from Europe?
- Decolonization and the Cold War reinforced a sense that Europe's place in the world needed to be rethought. How did intellectuals, writers, and artists react to the loss of European influence in the world?

Union made any innovations or experimentation difficult or impossible.

The sense that Europeans were no longer in a position to act independently or exert their influence in other parts of the world was compounded by the loss of colonies abroad. Former European colonies in Africa and Asia became independent nations, and this loss of influence may have further encouraged the former European imperial powers in their attempts to lay the groundwork for a more integrated Europe. The consensus in the West about the new role that the state should take in economic planning, education, and ensuring social welfare helped lay the groundwork for a Europe that was dedicated to ensuring equal opportunities to its citizens. These commitments were driven by the search for stable forms of democratic government—the memories of the violent ideological conflicts of the 1920s and 1930s were still fresh, and the achievement of an integrated Western Europe (under U.S. sponsorship) on the hinge of Franco-German cooperation must be seen as one of the major victories of the postwar decades. The hard-won stability of this period was to be temporary, however, and beginning in the 1960s a new series of political conflicts and economic crises would test the limits of consensus in Cold War Europe.

PEOPLE, IDEAS, AND EVENTS IN CONTEXT

- When Allied leaders met to discuss the postwar order at **YALTA** and **POTSDAM** in 1945, what were the major issues they discussed?
- What were the goals of the U.S. **MARSHALL PLAN**? How did **JOSEPH STALIN** react to its implementation?
- What was the **TRUMAN DOCTRINE** and how was it related to the creation of **NATO**?
- How did the Soviet Union's successful explosion of an **ATOMIC BOMB** in 1949 change the dynamic of the **COLD WAR**?
- How did the political climate in the Soviet Union and Eastern Europe change under **NIKITA KHRUSHCHEV** during the Thaw that followed Stalin's death?
- What nations were key to the plans for the **EUROPEAN UNION**?
- Why was the decolonization of settler colonies in Africa such as Algeria, Kenya, and Rhodesia more violent than in other colonies on the continent?
- What was apartheid, and why was it adopted by the settler government in South Africa?

THINKING ABOUT CONNECTIONS

- Insofar as one can determine them from today's perspective, what were the long-term consequences of the Cold War for people in both Western and Eastern Europe?
- What challenges did the process of decolonization pose to those who believed that European traditions of democratic rule and individual rights—ideas associated with the Enlightenment and the French Revolution—were universal?

STORY LINES

- The postwar economy in Western Europe saw record growth that lasted until the 1970s. Labor shortages led many nations to recruit workers from abroad, causing tensions when unemployment rates went up as the boom came to an end.

- Radio, television, and film combined to create a new kind of global mass culture that contributed to a spirit of novelty and rebellion among young people. More open discussion of sexual matters and an end to restrictions on contraception led some to speak of a "sexual revolution."

- Movements for national independence in the colonial world found an echo in the Civil Rights Movement in the United States and in student protests in Europe and the Americas in the 1960s. These protest movements peaked in 1968, provoking a conservative backlash in the 1970s and 1980s.

- Support for the Soviet Union waned in the 1980s as its economy stagnated and its political system failed to adapt. The Eastern bloc collapsed suddenly in 1989, ending the Cold War.

CHRONOLOGY

1957	Treaty of Rome forms European Common Market
1961	Berlin Wall built
1963	Betty Friedan, *The Feminine Mystique*
1964–1975	Vietnam War
mid-1960s	Birth control pill becomes available
1968	Czech revolt, Prague spring
1968	Student protests in Europe and the Americas
1970s	Détente between Soviet Union and Western powers
1973–1980s	Rising oil prices and worldwide recession
1980	Polish Solidarity workers movement
1989	Berlin Wall falls
1990	Reunification of Germany
1991–1995	Yugoslavian civil wars
1992	Soviet Union dissolved
1993	European Union

Before You Read This Chapter

Red Flags and Velvet Revolutions: The End of the Cold War, 1960–1990

CORE OBJECTIVES

- **DESCRIBE** postwar changes in employment and consumption and their effects on daily life and mass culture in Europe.

- **UNDERSTAND** the shift in attitudes toward sexuality, reproduction, and conceptions of male and female social roles that took place in the postwar decades and the consequences of this shift for women in Europe.

- **IDENTIFY** the motives and goals of the social and political movements that climaxed in 1968 in both Western and Eastern Europe.

- **EXPLAIN** the reasons for the economic downturn that began in the 1970s and its consequences for governments and populations in Europe.

- **UNDERSTAND** the events that led to the collapse of the Soviet bloc in 1989.

- **EXPLAIN** the reasons for the uncertainty and violence that followed the conclusion of the Cold War in Europe in the 1990s.

In 1964, a photograph of a Portuguese laborer named Armando Rodriguez appeared on the cover of the German news magazine *Der Spiegel*. Rodriguez had been met at the border by an official delegation and celebrated as the one millionth "guest worker" to arrive in Germany. As a prize, he received the gift of a motorcycle. The moment reflected the confidence of the West German government that their postwar economic recovery would continue, and that material prosperity would bring a new stability to Europe. In fact, the early 1960s seemed golden and full of promise for many in Western Europe. Despite nearly constant international tension, everyday life seemed to be improving. Full employment drove increases in living standards, the mass availability of consumer items and modern appliances transformed daily life, and a life of relative prosperity and ample leisure now seemed accessible to many. Television, radio, and film promoted images of American middle-class life, and Europeans looked across the Atlantic and saw their own aspirations reflected back at them. Even amid the uncertainties of the Cold War, a new spirit of cooperation animated European governments, party divisions had given way to a broad consensus in favor of an expanded welfare state, and the future looked good.

By the 1990s, however, most of that confidence was gone, and the European landscape had been dramatically transformed. Western Europeans could no longer be so certain of their prosperity or of their leaders' ability to provide the sort of life they took for granted. Already in the late 1960s, the economic boom had come to an end, and movements of social protest, especially among young people, shattered the postwar consensus. The material comforts of a consumer society proved less satisfying than they had once seemed, and environmentalists, feminists, and other cultural critics criticized the assumptions of the older generation. These problems were compounded after 1975 by a continuing economic crisis that threatened the security that the postwar generation had labored so hard to achieve. European societies began to fragment in unexpected ways, well before the epochal transformations that accompanied the end of the Cold War.

The challenges of these decades proved even more fundamental in the Soviet sphere. Economic decay combined with political and social stagnation to produce another wave of revolt. The year 1989 marked the beginning of an extraordinarily rapid and surprising series of events. Communist rule collapsed in Eastern Europe. Hopes for peace were soon replaced by fears of conflict from unexpected quarters. Immigrants were no longer celebrated in Germany and elsewhere—instead they became targets of suspicion or even violence. Shortly after the reunification of Germany in 1991, a wave of attacks against immigrants and refugees in Eastern Germany by right-wing extremists took the lives of seventeen foreigners in Germany, including two Turkish women and a Turkish girl who died in an arson attack by neo-Nazi skinheads in Schleswig-Holstein. Similar attacks took place in France, Britain, Italy, and elsewhere. When postsocialist Yugoslavia collapsed into a brutal civil war in the early 1990s, Europeans faced once again the spectacle of mass political movements motivated by hatred and fear, leading to ethnic violence and mass murder in a European land.

The startlingly sudden dissolution of the Soviet bloc brought an end to the postwar era of superpower confrontation, and observers of European society were forced to confront the uncomfortable fact that the Cold War had provided its own form of stability. Seen from the early 1990s, the future looked much less certain. Could the emerging institutions of an integrated Europe absorb *all* the peoples of the former Soviet sphere? What would such a Europe look like, and who would determine its larger boundaries? What these changes meant for the future of democracy, the stability of the European economy, and definitions of European identity, remained an open question.

SOCIAL CHANGE AND CULTURAL DYNAMISM, 1945–1968

The "boom" of the 1950s, made especially striking by contrast with the bleak years immediately after the Second World War, had profound and far-reaching effects on social life. To begin with, the population expanded, though unevenly. It shifted across the Continent. Both West Germany and France found it necessary to import workers to sustain their production booms. By the mid-1960s, there were 1.3 million foreign workers in West Germany and 1.8 million in France as wages rose and unemployment fell. Most came from the south, particularly from the agrarian areas of southern Italy, where unemployment remained high. Workers from former colonies emigrated to Britain, often to take low-paid, menial jobs and encounter pervasive discrimination at work and in the community. Migrations of this sort, in addition to the vast movement of political and ethnic refugees that occurred during and immediately after the war, contributed to the breakdown of national barriers that was accelerated by the creation of the Common Market.

The most dramatic changes were encapsulated in the transformation of the land and agriculture. Agricultural productivity had barely changed over the first half of the century. After mid-century it soared. To take one example, West German farm land (and labor) sufficient to feed five people in 1900 would feed six in 1950 and thirty-five in 1980. In West Germany and France, Common Market policy; state-sponsored programs of modernization; new agricultural machinery; and new kinds of fertilizer, seed, and animal feed helped produce the transformation. In Poland and the Eastern bloc, socialist regimes replaced small peasant holdings with large-scale agriculture. The effects reached across the economic and social landscape. Abundance meant lower food prices. Families spent a smaller proportion of their budgets on food, freeing up money for other forms of consumption and fueling economic growth. The percentage of the labor force employed in agriculture fell, fueling an expansion in industry and, especially, the service sector. Peasants with large holdings or valuable specialized crops (dairy products or wine), who could withstand debt, adjusted. Others lost ground. The French spoke of an "end of the peasantry"; in the 1960s, a hundred thousand moved from the countryside each year. These changes sparked continuous protest as farmers tried to protect their standard of living. The Common Market agreed to policies of shoring up agricultural prices, but the dynamics remained the same.

Change came in the workplace, eroding traditional social distinctions. Many commentators noted the striking growth in the number of middle-class, white-collar employees—the result, in part, of the dramatic bureaucratic expansion of the state. By 1964, the total number of men and women employed in government service in most European states exceeded 40 percent of the labor force, significantly higher than the number in the 1920s and 1930s. In business and industry, the number of middle-management employees grew as well. In industry, even within the factory workforce, salaried employees—supervisors, inspectors, technicians, and drafters—multiplied. In West Germany, for example, the number of such workers increased by 95 percent between 1950 and 1961. Industrial labor meant something far different from what it had meant in the nineteenth century. Skills were more specialized, based on technological expertise rather than custom and routine. *Skill* meant the ability to monitor automatic controls; to interpret abstract signals; and to make precise, mathematically calculated adjustments. More women entered the workforce, meeting less resistance than they had in the past, and their jobs were less starkly differentiated from men's.

Nineteenth-century society had been marked by clearly defined class cultures. The working class lived "a life apart," with easily identifiable patterns of consumption, dress, leisure, notions of respectability, gender relations, and so on. In 1900, no one would have mistaken a peasant for a worker, and middle-class people had their own schools, recreations, and stores. But economic changes after 1950 chipped away at those distinctive cultures. Trade unions remained powerful institutions: the largest of the French general unions had a membership of 1.5 million; of the Italian, 3.5 million; of the German, 6.5 million. Britain's Trades Union Congress, an affiliation of separate unions, boasted close to 8 million members—including many more women than in the past. Communist parties had powerful electoral clout. But new social movements also grew. Workers still identified themselves as such, but class had a less rigidly defined meaning.

The expansion of education helped shift social hierarchies. All Western nations passed laws providing for the extension of compulsory secondary education—up to the age of sixteen in France, West Germany, and Britain. New legislation combined with rising birthrates to boost school populations dramatically. Between 1950 and 1960, secondary school enrollment in France, Holland, and Belgium doubled. In Britain and West Germany it grew by more than 50 percent. Education did not automatically produce social mobility, but when combined with economic prosperity, new structures of labor, and the consumerist boom, it began to lay the foundation for what would be called "postindustrial" society.

How did patterns differ in the Eastern bloc? Soviet workers were not noted for their specialized skills—in fact, a major factor in the slowdown of the Soviet economy was its failure to innovate. Workers in the "workers' state" commonly enjoyed higher wages than people in middle-class positions (with the exception of managers), but they had far less status. Their relatively high wages owed little to independent trade unions, which had been effectively abolished under Stalin; they were the product of persistent labor shortages and the accompanying fear of labor unrest. As far as the middle classes were concerned, two wars and state socialism devastated traditional, insular bourgeois culture throughout Eastern Europe, though the regimes also created new ways of gaining privilege and status and commentators spoke of a new class of bureaucrats and party members. Educational reforms instituted by Nikita Khrushchev in 1958 encouraged bright children to

MORNING CALISTHENICS AT RUSSIAN FACTORY, 1961. The growing number of industrial workers and women in the workforce in the latter half of the twentieth century was reflected in this Soviet factory. The workers' state still bestowed little status on its workers—a factor that contributed to the weakened Russian economy.

pursue a course of study leading eventually to managerial positions. Soviet education also aimed to unify a nation that remained culturally heterogeneous. Turkish Muslims, for instance, constituted a sizable minority in the Soviet Union. Afraid that the pull of ethnic nationality might tear at the none-too-solid fabric of the Soviet "union" increased the government's desire to impose one unifying culture by means of education, not always with success.

Mass Consumption

Rising employment, higher earnings, and lower agricultural prices combined to give households and individuals more purchasing power. They had more to spend on newspapers, cigarettes, tickets to sporting events, movies, and health and hygiene (which registered the largest increase). Families put money into their homes. Household appliances and cars were the most striking emblems of what was virtually a new world of everyday objects. In 1956, 8 percent of British households had refrigerators. By 1979, that figure had skyrocketed to 69 percent. Vacuum cleaners, washing machines, and telephones all became common features of everyday life. They did not simply save labor or create free time, for household appliances came packaged with more demanding standards of housekeeping and new investments in domesticity—"more work for mother," in the words of one historian. We should not exaggerate the transformation. In 1962, only 40 percent of French households had a refrigerator; in 1975, only 35 percent had a telephone; but even this was still vastly more than the poorer nations of Europe or elsewhere in the world.

In 1948, 5 million Western Europeans had cars; in 1965, 40 million did. In 1950, Italian workers rode bicycles to work; ten years later the factories were building parking lots for their employees' automobiles. Cars captured imaginations throughout the world; in magazines, advertisements, and countless films, the car was central to new images of romance, movement, freedom, and vacation. Of course automobiles alone did not allow workers to take inexpensive holidays; reducing the workweek from forty-eight hours to about forty-two was more important, as was the institution of annual vacations—in most countries workers received over thirty days of paid vacation per year.

These changes marked a new culture of mass consumption. They were boosted by new industries devoted to marketing, advertising, and credit payment. They also entailed shifts in values. In the nineteenth century, a responsible middle-class family did not go into debt; discipline and thrift were hallmarks of respectability. By the second half of the twentieth century, banks and retailers, in the name of

mass consumption and economic growth, were persuading middle- and working-class people alike not to be ashamed of debt. Abundance, credit, consumer spending, and standards of living—all these terms became part of the vocabulary of everyday economic life. Most important, the new vocabulary gradually came to reshape how citizens thought about their needs, desires, and entitlements. Standards of living, for instance, created a yardstick for measuring—and protesting—glaring social inequalities. Politicians, economists, and marketing experts paid much closer attention to the spending habits of ordinary people.

In Eastern Europe and the Soviet Union, consumption was organized differently. Governments rather than markets determined how consumer goods would be distributed. Economic policy channeled resources into heavy industry at the expense of consumer durables. This resulted in general scarcity, erratic shortages of even basic necessities, and often poor-quality goods. Women in particular often waited for hours in store lines after finishing a full day of wage work. Though numbers of household appliances

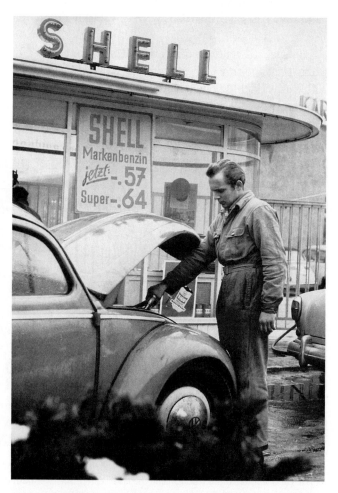

A CAR FOR THE PEOPLE. Originally designed in Hitler's Germany as a car for the people (*das Volk*), the Volkswagen Beetle was produced in large numbers after 1945 and sold in many countries.

called a cultural revolution: a transformation of culture, of its role in the lives of ordinary men and women, and of the power wielded by the media.

MUSIC AND YOUTH CULTURE

Much of the new mass culture of the 1960s depended on the spending habits and desires of the new generation. That new generation stayed in school longer, prolonging the adolescent years. Young people had more distance from their parents and the workforce and more time to be with each other. In the countryside especially, schooling began to break down the barriers that had separated the activities of boys and girls, creating one factor in the "sexual revolution" (discussed later). From the late 1950s on, music became *the* cultural expression of this new generation. The transistor radio came out at the time of the Berlin airlift; by the mid-1950s, these portable radios began to sell in the United States and Europe. Radio sets gave birth to new radio programs and, later, to magazines reporting on popular singers and movie stars. All of these helped create new communities of interest. As one historian puts it, these radio programs were the "capillaries of youth culture." Social changes also affected the content of music: its themes and lyrics aimed to reach the young. Technological changes made records more than twice as long as the old 78s and less expensive. The price of record players fell, multiplying the number of potential buyers. Combined, these developments changed how music was produced, distributed, and consumed. It was no longer confined to the concert hall or cafe but instead reverberated through people's homes or cars and teenagers' rooms—providing a sound track for everyday life.

Postwar youth culture owed much to the hybrid musical style known as rock and roll. During the 1930s and 1940s, the synthesis of music produced by whites and

increased dramatically in the Soviet Union and in Eastern Europe, the inefficiencies of Soviet consumption made women's double burden of work and housework especially heavy. Citizens' growing unhappiness with scarcities and seemingly irrational policies posed serious problems. As one historian puts it, the failure of policies on consumption was "one of the major dead ends of communism," and it contributed to the downfall of communist regimes.

Mass Culture

New patterns of consumption spurred wide-ranging changes in mass culture. The origins of "mass" culture lay in the 1890s, in the expansion of the popular press, music halls, organized sports, and "Nickelodeons," all of which started the long process of displacing traditional, class-based forms of entertainment: village dances, boulevard theater, middle-class concerts, and so on. Mass culture quickened in the 1920s, its importance heightened by mass politics (see Chapter 25). The social transformations of the 1950s, which we have traced above, meant that families had both more spending money and more leisure time. The combination created a golden opportunity for the growing culture industry. The postwar desire to break with the past created further impetus for change. The result can fairly be

MUSIC MEETS TELEVISION. Paul McCartney instructs popular variety show host Ed Sullivan on the electric bass, 1964.

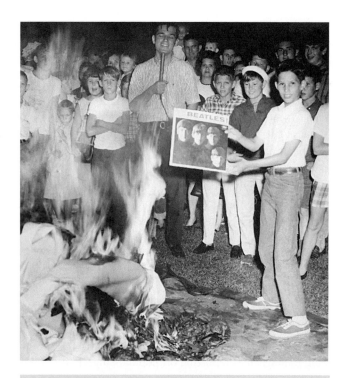

MASS CULTURE IN A MEDIA AGE. When John Lennon declared the Beatles were "more popular than Jesus," he raised a storm of protest. Here an American teenager tosses *Meet the Beatles* in a bonfire. ▪ *What was different about this kind of celebrity when compared with earlier generations of popular entertainers?*

BOB DYLAN POSING FOR THE COVER OF *BLONDE ON BLONDE,* **1966.** Dylan's mid-1960s departure from his acoustic folk style into a blues-based rock and roll shocked his original following.

African Americans in the American South found its way into northern cities. After the Second World War, black rhythm and blues musicians and white Southern rockabilly performers found much wider audiences through the use of new technology—electric guitars, better equipment for studio recording, and wide-band radio stations in large cities. The blend of styles and sounds and the cultural daring of white teenagers who listened to what recording studios at the time called "race music" came together to create rock and roll. The music was exciting, sometimes aggressive, and full of energy—all qualities that galvanized young listeners, eager to buy the latest records by their favorite performers.

In Europe, rock and roll found its way into working-class neighborhoods, particularly in Britain and Ireland. There, local youths took American sounds, echoed the inflections of poverty and defiance, and added touches of music-hall showmanship to produce successful artists and bands, collectively referred to as the "British invasion." During the 1960s, British sounds and stars had blended with their American counterparts. As the music's popularity spread, music culture came loose from its national moorings. In France before the 1960s, trendy American songs had been covered by the performer Johnny Hallyday, who sang French popular music as well. The Beatles, though,

managed to get their own music on the hit lists in France, Germany, and the United States. By the time of Woodstock (1969), youth music culture was international. Rock became the sound of worldwide youth culture, absorbing Eastern influences such as the Indian sitar and the rebellious energy of a folk-music revival. It provided a bridge across the Cold War divide: despite Eastern bloc limits on importing "capitalist" music, pirated songs circulated—sometimes on X-ray plates salvaged from hospitals. Recording studios latched onto the earning potential of the music and became corporations as powerful as car manufacturers or steel companies.

Art and Painting

The cultural revolution we have been tracing changed high as well as popular art. Record companies' influence reached well beyond rock. New recording techniques made it possible to reissue favorites in classical music, and companies marketed them more aggressively. Record companies buoyed the careers of internationally acclaimed stars, such as the soprano Maria Callas and (much later) the tenor Luciano Pavarotti, staging concerts, using their influence on orchestras, and offering new recordings of their art.

Painting and art, too, were changed by the rise of mass and consumer culture. The art market boomed. The power of the dollar was one factor in the rise of New York as a center of modern art, one of the most striking developments of the period. Immigration was another: a slow stream of immigrants from Europe nourished American art as well as social and political thought (see Chapter 27) and New York proved hospitable to European artists. The creative work of the school of abstract expressionism sealed New York's postwar reputation. The abstract expressionists—William de Kooning (from the Netherlands), Mark Rothko (from Russia), Franz Kline, Jackson Pollock, Helen Frankenthaler, and Robert Motherwell—followed trends established by the cubists and surrealists, experimenting with color, texture, and technique to find new forms of expression. Many of them emphasized the physical aspects of paint and the act of painting. Pollock is a good example. He poured and even threw paint on the canvas, creating powerful images of personal and physical expressiveness. Some dubbed the process "action painting." His huge-scale canvases, which defied conventional artistic structures, gained immediate attention. Critics called the drip paintings "unpredictable, undisciplined, and explosive" and saw in them the youthful exuberance of postwar American culture. Mark Rothko created a series of remote yet extraordinarily compelling abstractions with glowing or somber rectangles of color imposed on other rectangles, saying they represented "no associations, only sensation." The enormous influence of abstract expressionism moved one critic to declare in grandiose fashion that "the main premises of Western art" had moved to the United States, along with "industrial production and political power."

But abstract expressionism also produced its opposite, sometimes called pop art. Pop artists distanced themselves from the moody and elusive meditations of abstract expressionism. They refused to distinguish between avant garde and popular art, or between the artistic and the commercial. They lavished attention on commonplace, instantly recognizable, often commercial images; they borrowed techniques from graphic design; they were interested in the immediacy of everyday art and ordinary people's visual experience. Jasper Johns's paintings of the American flag formed part of this trend. So did the work of Andy Warhol and Roy Lichtenstein, who took objects such as soup cans and images of comic-strip heroes as their subjects. Warhol

ACTION PAINTING. Photographer Martha Holmes reveals the dynamic technique of abstract expressionist Jackson Pollock as he paints, 1950.

did not see his work as a protest against the banality of commercial culture. Instead, he argued that he was continuing to experiment with abstractions. Treating popular culture with this tongue-in-cheek seriousness became one of the central themes of 1960s art.

Film

Mass culture made its most powerful impact in the visual world, especially through film. Film flourished after the Second World War, developing along several different lines. The Italian neorealists of the late 1940s and 1950s, antifascists and socialists, set out to capture authenticity, or "life as it was lived," by which they usually meant working-class existence. They dealt with the same themes that marked the literature of the period: loneliness, war, and corruption. They shot on location, using natural light and little-known actors, deliberately steering away from the artifice and high production values they associated with the tainted cinema of fascist and wartime Europe. Not strictly realists, they played with nonlinear plots, unpredictable characters and motivations. Roberto Rossellini's *Rome: Open City* (1945) was a loving portrait of Rome under Nazi occupation. Vittorio de Sica's *Bicycle Thief* (1948) tells a story of a man struggling against unemployment and poverty, who desperately needs his bicycle to keep his job as a poster hanger.

The film highlighted the contrast between rich and poor—the man's son enviously watches another's family enjoying huge plates of pasta—and between American glamour, represented by movie stars on the posters, and Italy's war-scarred poverty. Federico Fellini came out of the neorealist school and began his career writing for Rossellini. Fellini's break-out film *La Dolce Vita* (1959, starring Marcello Mastroianni) took Italian film to screens throughout Europe and the United States, and it also marked Fellini's transition to his signature surrealist and carnivalesque style, developed in *8½* (1963).

The French directors of the new wave continued to develop this unsentimental, naturalistic, and enigmatic social vision. New wave directors worked closely with each other, casting each other (and their wives and lovers) in their films, encouraged improvisation, and experimented with disjointed narrative. François Truffaut (1932–1984), *400 Blows* (1959) and *The Wild Child* (1969), and Jean-Luc Godard (1930–), *Breathless* (1959) and *Contempt* (1963, with Brigitte Bardot), are leading examples. *Closely Watched Trains* (1966) was the Czech director Jiří Menzel's (1938–) contribution to the new wave. The new wave raised the status of the director, insisting that the film's camera work and vision (rather than the writing) constituted the real art—part, again, of the new value accorded to the visual. France made other contributions to international film by sponsoring the Cannes Film Festival. The first Cannes Festival was held before the Second World War, but the city opened its gates again in 1946 under the banner of artistic internationalism. As one

commentator put it, "There are many ways to advance the cause of peace. But the power . . . of cinema is greater than other forms of expression, for it directly and simultaneously touches the masses of the world." Placing itself at the center of an international film industry became part of France's ongoing recovery from the war, and Cannes became one of the world's largest markets for film.

HOLLYWOOD AND THE AMERICANIZATION OF CULTURE

The American film industry, however, had considerable advantages, and the devastating aftereffects of the Second World War in Europe allowed Hollywood to consolidate its earlier gains (see Chapter 27). The United States' huge domestic market gave Hollywood its biggest advantage. In 1946 an estimated hundred million Americans went to the movies every week. By the 1950s, Hollywood was making 500 films a year and counted for between 40 and 75 percent of films shown in Europe. The same period brought important innovations in filmmaking: the conversion to color and new optical formats, including widescreen. As far as their themes were concerned, some American directors moved in the same direction as the European neorealists. As one critic put it, they tried to "base fictional pictures on fact and, more importantly, to shoot them not in painted studio sets but in actual places."

The domestic politics of the Cold War weighed heavily on filmmaking in the United States. Between 1947 and 1951, the infamous House Un-American Activities Committee called before it hundreds of persons, investigating alleged sympathies with communism or association with any left-wing organization. Hundreds of actors, directors, and writers were blacklisted by the studios. At the same time, paradoxically, American censorship was breaking down, with dramatic consequences on screen. Since the early 1930s, the Motion Picture Production Code had refused to approve "scenes of passion" (including married couples sharing a bed), immorality and profanity (the code banned the words *virgin* and *cripes*), depictions of guns, details of crimes, suicide, or murder. Foreign films, however, came into the United States without the code's seal of approval. The state of New York tried to ban a film (*The Miracle*, directed by Rossellini and written by Fellini) as "sacrilegious," but in 1952 the Supreme Court ruled that film was protected by the First Amendment. A 1955 Otto Preminger movie in which Frank Sinatra played a heroin addict (*The Man with the Golden Arm*) was released despite the disapproval of the Production Code and went on to become a box-office success—a sign of changing mores. *Rebel without a Cause* (1955) made juvenile delinquency a

FEDERICO FELLINI ON THE SET OF *LA STRADA*, 1954. Fellini was an Italian neorealist filmmaker who sought to depict life as it was lived.

legitimate subject for film. By the 1960s, the Production Code had been scuttled. The extremely graphic violence at the end of Arthur Penn's *Bonnie and Clyde* (1967) marked the scope of the transformation.

Hollywood's expanding influence was but one instance of the "Americanization" of Western culture. Europeans had worried about the United States as a model since at least the 1920s; the United States seemed to be the center for the "production and organization of mass civilization." American films in the 1950s multiplied these worries. So did television, which by 1965 had found its way into 62 million homes in the United States, 13 million in Britain, 10 million in West Germany, and 5 million each in France and Italy and had an even more important impact on everyday life and sociability. The issues were not simply cultural; they included the power of American corporations, American business techniques, aggressive marketing, and American domination of global trade networks. Many concerns were raised, and sometimes they contradicted each other. Some observers believed that the United States and its cultural exports were materialistic, conformist, and complacent. Others considered Americans to be rebellious, lonely, and sexually unhappy. *Rebel without a Cause*, for instance, with James Dean as an alienated teenager in a dysfunctional family and with its scenes of knife fights and car races, provoked cries of outrage from German critics who deplored the permissiveness of American parents and expressed shock that middle-class children behaved like "hoodlums."

Is it helpful, though, to speak of the *Americanization* of culture? First, the term refers to many different processes.

JAMES DEAN IN *REBEL WITHOUT A CAUSE*. Films from the 1950s and 1960s contributed to the romanticization of automobiles, sexuality, and youthful rebellion.

U.S. industrialists openly sought greater economic influence and economic integration: opening markets to American goods, industry to American production techniques, and so on. The U.S. government also aimed to export American political values, above all anticommunism, via organizations such as Radio Free Europe. Yet the farthest-reaching American influences were conveyed, unintentionally, by music and film: images of rebellious teenagers, a society of abundance, cars and the romance of the road, tangled race relations, flirting working girls (who seemed less identifiably working-class than their European counterparts), or bantering couples. These images could not be completely controlled, and they had no single effect. Movies about young Americans might represent the romance of American power, they might represent a rebellion against that power. Second, *American* goods were put to different use in local cultures. Third, journalists, critics, and ordinary men and women tended to use *American* as an all-purpose label for various modern or mass culture developments that were more properly global, such as inexpensive electronics from Asia. As one historian puts it, America was less of a reality than an idea—and a contradictory one at that.

Gender Roles and Sexual Revolution

What some called the sexual revolution of the 1960s had several aspects. The first was less censorship, which we have already seen in film, and fewer taboos regarding discussion of sexuality in public. In the United States, the notorious Kinsey reports on male and female sexuality (in 1948 and 1953, respectively) made morality and sexual behavior front-page news. Alfred Kinsey was a zoologist turned social scientist, and the way in which he applied science and statistics to sex attracted considerable attention. An enthusiastic journalist in Europe reported that the massive numbers Kinsey compiled would, finally, reveal the "truth of sex." The truth, though, was elusive. At the very least Kinsey showed that moral codes and private behaviors did not line up neatly. For instance, 80 to 90 percent of the women he interviewed disapproved of premarital sex, but 50 percent of the women he interviewed had had it. *Time* magazine warned that publicizing disparities between beliefs and behavior might prove subversive—that women and men would decide there was "morality in numbers."

Across Europe and North America, however, young men and women seemed to be reaching rebellious conclusions on their own. As one Italian teenager said, defending her moral codes, "It is our elders who behave scandalously. . . . [W]omen were kept under lock and key, girls married to men who were twice their age. . . . [B]oys, even the very youngest, had total freedom and so queued up at the brothels." Teenage girls in Italy and France told researchers and reporters that taboos were not just old fashioned but damaging, that their mothers had kept them in the dark about matters as rudimentary as menstruation, leaving them unprepared for life.

Was the family crumbling? Transformations in agriculture and life in the countryside did mean that the peasant family was no longer the institution that governed birth, work, courtship, marriage, and death. Yet the family became newly important as the center of consumption, spending, and leisure time, for television took people (usually men) out of bars, cafes, and music halls. It became the focus of government attention in the form of family allowances, health care, and Cold War appeals to family values. People brought higher expectations to marriage, which raised rates of divorce, and they paid more attention to children, which brought smaller families. Despite a postwar spike in the birth rate that produced the "baby boom," over the long term, fertility declined, even in countries that outlawed contraception. The family assumed new meanings as its traditional structures of authority—namely paternal control over wives and children—eroded under the pressure of social change.

A second aspect of the revolution was the centrality of sex and eroticism to mass consumer culture. Magazines, which flourished in this period, offered advice on how to succeed in love and be attractive. Cultivating one's looks, including sexiness, fit with the new accent on consumption; indeed health and personal hygiene was the fastest rising category of family spending. Advertising, advice columns, TV, and film blurred boundaries between buying consumer goods, seeking personal fulfillment, and sexual desire. There was nothing new about appeals to eroticism. But the fact that sexuality was now widely considered a form of self-expression—perhaps even the core of oneself—was new to the twentieth century. These developments helped propel change, and they also made the sexual revolution prominent in the politics of the time.

The third aspect of the revolution came with legal and medical or scientific changes in contraception. Oral contraceptives, first approved for development in 1959, became mainstream in the next decade. The Pill did not have revolutionary effects on the birth rate, which was already falling. It marked dramatic change, however, because it was simple (though expensive) and could be used by women themselves. By 1975, two-thirds of British women between fifteen and forty-four said they were taking the Pill. Numbers like these marked a long, drawn-out end to centuries-old views that to discuss birth control was pornographic, an affront to religion, and an invitation to indulgence and promiscuity. By and large, Western countries legalized contraception in

the 1960s and abortion in the 1970s. In 1965, for instance, the U.S. Supreme Court struck down laws banning the use of contraception, though selling contraceptives remained illegal in Massachusetts until 1972. The Soviet Union legalized abortion in 1950, after banning it during most of Stalin's regime. Throughout Eastern Europe, abortion rates were extremely high. Why? Contraceptives proved as difficult to obtain as other consumer goods; men often refused to use them; and women—doubly burdened with long hours of work and housework and facing, in addition, chronic housing shortages—had little choice but to resort to abortion.

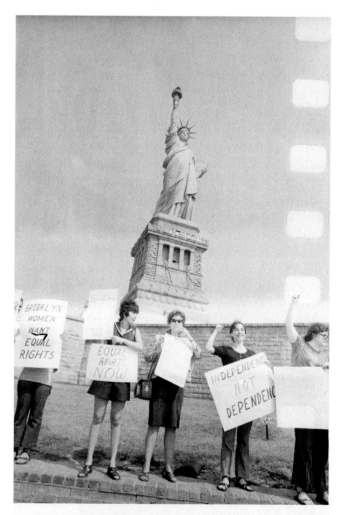

SECOND-WAVE FEMINISM. U.S. women celebrating the passage of the Equal Rights Amendment by the House of Representatives in 1970 beneath the Statue of Liberty. The bill did not pass the Senate and never became law. "Second wave" feminists distinguished themselves from the "first wave" of feminism in Europe and the Americas, which had focused on gaining voting rights in the nineteenth and early twentieth centuries. Second-wave feminists argued that votes for women had not ended pervasive gender discrimination. They demanded equal pay for equal work and challenged widespread expectations about the roles that women were expected to play in families and in the workplace.

Legal changes would not have occurred without the women's movements of the time. For nineteenth-century feminists, winning the right to vote was the most difficult practical and symbolic struggle (see Chapter 23). For the revived feminism of the 1960s and 1970s, the family, work, and sexuality—all put on the agenda by the social changes of the period—were central. Since the Second World War, the assumption that middle-class women belonged in the home had been challenged by the steadily rising demand for workers, especially in education and the service sector. Thus, many more married women and many more mothers were part of the labor force. Moreover, across the West young middle-class women, like men, were part of the rising number of university students. But in the United States, to take just one example, only 37 percent of women who enrolled in college in the 1950s finished their degrees, believing they should marry instead. As one of them explained, "We married what we wanted to be": doctor, professor, manager, and so on. Women found it difficult to get nonsecretarial jobs; received less pay for the same work; and, even when employed, had to rely on their husbands to establish credit.

The tension between rising expectations that stemmed from abundance, growth, and the emphasis on self-expression on the one hand and the reality of narrow horizons on the other created quiet waves of discontent. Betty Friedan's *The Feminine Mystique* (1963) brought much of this discontent into the open, contrasting the cultural myths of the fulfilled and happy housewife with the realities of economic inequality, hard work, and narrowed horizons. In 1949, Simone de Beauvoir had asked how Western culture (myth, literature, and psychology) had created an image of woman as the second, and lesser sex; Friedan, using a more journalistic style and writing at a time when social change had made readers more receptive to her ideas, showed how the media, the social sciences, and advertising at once exalted femininity and lowered women's expectations and possibilities. Friedan cofounded NOW (National Organization for Women) in 1966; smaller and often more radical women's movements multiplied across Europe in the following decades. For this generation of feminists, reproductive freedom was both a private matter and a basic right—a key to women's control over their lives. Outlawing contraception and abortion made women alone bear responsibility for the consequences of sweeping changes in Western sexual life. Such measures were ineffective as well as unjust, they argued. French feminists dramatized the point by publishing the names of 343 well-known women, including Beauvoir, who admitted to having had illegal abortions. A similar petition came out in Germany the following year and was followed by petitions from doctors and tens of thousands of supporters. In sum, the legal changes followed from political demands, and those in turn reflected a quiet or subterranean rebellion of many women (and men)—one with longer-term causes. Mass consumption, mass culture, and startlingly rapid transformations in public and private life were all intimately related.

SOCIAL MOVEMENTS DURING THE 1960s

The social unrest of the 1960s was international. Its roots lay in the political struggles and social transformations of the postwar period. Of these, the most important were anticolonial and civil rights movements. The successful anticolonial movements (see Chapter 27) reflected a growing racial consciousness and also helped encourage that consciousness. Newly independent African and Caribbean nations remained wary about revivals of colonialism and the continuing economic hegemony of Western Europe and America. Black and Asian immigration into those nations produced tension and frequent violence. In the West, particularly in the United States, people of color identified with these social and economic grievances.

The Civil Rights Movement

The emergence of new black nations in Africa and the Caribbean was paralleled by growing African American insurgency. The Second World War increased African American migration from the American South to northern cities, intensifying a drive for rights, dignity, and independence that began in the prewar era with organizations such as the National Association for the Advancement of Colored People and the National Urban League. By 1960, various civil rights groups, led by the Congress of Racial Equality (CORE), had started to organize boycotts and demonstrations directed at private businesses and public services that discriminated against blacks in the South. The preeminent figure in the Civil Rights Movement in the United States during the 1960s was Martin Luther King, Jr. (1929–1968). A Baptist minister, King embraced the philosophy of nonviolence promoted by the Indian social and political activist Mohandas K. Gandhi. King's personal participation in countless demonstrations, his willingness to go to jail for a cause that he believed to be just, and his ability as an orator to arouse both blacks and whites with his message led to

The "Woman Question" on Both Sides of the Atlantic

How did Western culture define femininity, and did women internalize those definitions? These questions were central to postwar feminist thought, and they were sharply posed in two classic texts: Simone de Beauvoir's The Second Sex *(1949) and Betty Friedan's* The Feminine Mystique *(1963). Beauvoir (1908–1986) started from the existentialist premise that humans were "condemned to be free" and to give their own lives meaning. Why, then, did women accept the limitations imposed on them and, in Beauvoir's words, "dream the dreams of men"? Although dense and philosophical,* The Second Sex *was read throughout the world. Betty Friedan's equally influential bestseller drew heavily on Beauvoir. Friedan sought the origins of the "feminine mystique," her term for the model of femininity promoted by experts, advertised in women's magazines, and seemingly accepted by middle-class housewives in the postwar United States. As Friedan points out in the excerpt here, the new postwar mystique was in many ways more conservative than prewar ideals had been, despite continuing social change, a greater range of careers opening up to women, the expansion of women's education, and so on. Friedan (1921–2006) cofounded the National Organization for Women in 1966 and served as its president until 1970.*

Simone de Beauvoir, *The Second Sex* (1949)

But first, what is a woman? . . . Everyone agrees there are females in the human species; today, as in the past, they make up about half of humanity; and yet we are told that "femininity is in jeopardy;" we are urged, "Be women, stay women, become women." . . . Although some women zealously strive to embody it, the model has never been patented. It is typically described in vague and shimmering terms borrowed from a clairvoyant's vocabulary. . . .

If the female function is not enough to define woman, and if we also reject the explanation of the "eternal feminine," but if we accept, even temporarily, that there are women on the earth, we then have to ask: what is a woman?

Merely stating the problem suggests an immediate answer to me. It is significant that I pose it. It would never occur to a man to write a book on the singular situation of males in humanity. If I want to define myself, I first have to say, "I am a woman;" all other assertions will arise from this basic truth. A man never begins by positing himself as an individual of a certain sex: that he is a man is obvious. The categories "masculine" and "feminine" appear as symmetrical in a formal way on town hall records or identification papers. The relation of the two sexes is not that of two electrical poles: the man represents both the positive and the neuter. . . . Woman is the negative, to such a point that any determination is imputed to her as a limitation, without reciprocity. . . . [A] man is in his right by virtue of being man; it is the woman who is in the wrong. . . . Woman has ovaries and a uterus; such are the particular conditions that lock her in her subjectivity; some even say she thinks with her hormones. Man vainly forgets that his anatomy also includes hormones and testicles. He grasps his body as a direct and normal link with the world that he believes he apprehends in all objectivity whereas he considers woman's body an obstacle, a prison, burdened by everything that particularises it. "The female is female by virtue of a certain *lack* of qualities," Aristotle said. "We should regard women's nature as suffering from natural defectiveness." And St. Thomas in his turn decreed that woman was an "incomplete man," an "incidental" being. This is what the Genesis story symbolises, where Eve appears as if drawn from Adam's "supernumerary" bone, in Bossuet's words. Humanity is male, and man defines woman, not in herself, but in relation to himself; she is not considered an autonomous being. . . . And she is nothing other than what man decides; she is thus called "the sex," meaning that the male sees her essentially as a sexed being; for him she is sex, so she is it in the absolute. She determines and differentiates herself in relation to man, and he does not in relation to her; she is the inessential in front of the essential. He is the Subject, he is the Absolute. She is the Other.

Source: Simone de Beauvoir, *The Second Sex*, trans. Constance Borde and Sheila Malovany-Chevallier (London: 2009), pp. 3–6.

Betty Friedan, *The Feminine Mystique* (1963)

In 1939, the heroines of women's magazine stories were not always young, but in a certain sense they were younger than their fictional counterparts today. They were young in the same way that the American hero has always been young: they were New Women, creating with a gay determined spirit a new identity for women—a life of their own. There was an aura about them of becoming, of moving into a future that was going to be different from the past. . . .

These stories may not have been great literature. But the identity of their heroines seemed to say something about the housewives who, then as now, read the women's magazines. These magazines were not written for career women. The New Woman heroines were the ideal of yesterday's housewives; they reflected the dreams, mirrored the yearning for identity and the sense of possibility that existed for women then. . . .

In 1949 . . . the feminine mystique began to spread through the land. . . .

The feminine mystique says that the highest value and the only commitment for women is the fulfillment of their own femininity. It says that the great mistake of Western culture, through most of its history, has been the undervaluation of this femininity. . . . The mistake, says the mystique, the root of women's troubles in the past, is that women envied men, women tried to be like men, instead of accepting their own nature, which can find fulfillment only in sexual passivity, male domination, and nurturing maternal love.

But the new image this mystique gives to American women is the old image: "Occupation: housewife." The new mystique makes the housewife-mothers, who never had a chance to be anything else, the model for all women; it presupposes that history has reached a final and glorious end in the here and now, as far as women are concerned. . . .

It is more than a strange paradox that as all professions are finally open to women in America, "career woman" has become a dirty word; that as higher education becomes available to any woman with the capacity for it, education for women has become so suspect that more and more drop out of high school and college to marry and have babies; that as so many roles in modern society become theirs for the taking, women so insistently confine themselves to one role. Why . . . should she accept this new image which insists she is not a person but a "woman," by definition barred from the freedom of human existence and a voice in human destiny?

Source: Betty Friedan, *The Feminine Mystique* (New York: 2001), pp. 38, 40, 42–43, 67–68.

Questions for Analysis

1. Why does Beauvoir ask, "What is a woman?"

2. Why does Friedan think that a "feminine mystique" emerged after the Second World War?

---

his position as the most highly regarded—and most widely feared—defender of black rights. His inspiring career was tragically ended by assassination in 1968.

King and organizations such as CORE aspired to a fully integrated nation. Other charismatic and important black leaders sought complete independence from white society, fearing that integration would leave African Americans without the spiritual or material resources necessary for a community's pride, dignity, and autonomy. The most influential of the black nationalists was Malcolm X (1925–1965),

who assumed the "X" after having discarded his "white" surname (Little). For most of his adult life, Malcolm X, a spokesman for the Black Muslim movement, urged blacks to renew their commitment to their own heritage; to establish black businesses for economic autonomy; and to fortify economic, political, and psychological defenses against white domination. Like King, he was assassinated, in 1965 while addressing a rally in Harlem.

Civil rights laws passed under President Lyndon B. Johnson (1963–1969) in the 1960s did bring African

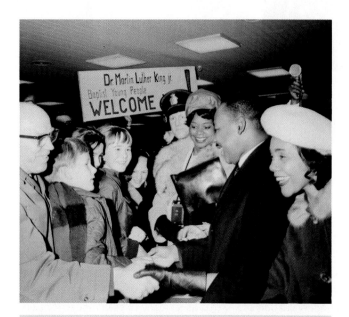

MARTIN LUTHER KING, JR., 1964. The African American civil rights leader is welcomed in Oslo, Norway, on a trip to accept the Nobel Peace Prize. He would be assassinated four years later. ■ *How might Europeans have viewed King's campaign?* ■ *Would it affect their vision of the United States?*

The Antiwar Movement

The United States' escalating war in Vietnam became a lightning rod for discontent. In 1961, President John F. Kennedy (1917–1963) promised to "bear any burden" necessary to fight communism and to ensure the victory of American models of representative government and free-market economics in the developing nations. Kennedy's plan entailed massive increases in foreign aid, much of it in weapons. It provided the impetus for humanitarian institutions such as the Peace Corps, intended to improve local conditions and show Americans' benevolence and good intentions. Bearing burdens, however, also meant fighting guerrillas who turned to the Soviets for aid. This involved covert interventions in Latin America, the Congo, and, most important, Vietnam.

By the time of Kennedy's death in 1963, nearly 15,000 American "advisers" were on the ground alongside South Vietnamese troops. Kennedy's successor, Lyndon Johnson, began the strategic bombing of North Vietnam and rapidly drew hundreds of thousands of American troops into combat in South Vietnam. The rebels in the south, known as the Viet Cong, were solidly entrenched, highly experienced guerrilla fighters, and were backed by the professional, well-equipped North Vietnamese army under Ho Chi Minh, who also received support from the Soviet Union. The South Vietnamese government resisted efforts at reform, losing popular support. Massive efforts by the United States produced only stalemate, mounting American casualties, and rising discontent.

Vietnam did much to cause the political turmoil of the 1960s in the United States. As Martin Luther King, Jr., pointed out, the war—which relied on a disproportionate number of black soldiers to conduct a war against a small nation of color—echoed and magnified racial inequality at home. Exasperated by troubles in the field, American planners continued to escalate military commitments, with no effect. Peace talks in Paris stalled while the death toll on all sides increased. The involuntary draft of young American men expanded and polarized the public. In 1968, criticism forced President Johnson to abandon his plans to run for a second term. Johnson's successor, Richard M. Nixon, who won a narrow victory on the basis of promises to end the war, expanded it instead. Student protests against the war frequently ended in violence. The government brought criminal conspiracy charges against Benjamin Spock, the nation's leading pediatrician, and William Sloane Coffin, the chaplain of Yale University, for encouraging young people to resist the draft. Avoiding the draft became so widespread that the system was changed in 1970. And from

Americans some measure of equality with regard to voting rights—and, to a much lesser degree, school desegregation. In other areas, such as housing and job opportunities, white racism continued. Economic development passed by many African American communities, and subsequent administrations pulled back from the innovative programs of the Johnson era.

These problems were not confined to the United States. West Indian, Indian, and Pakistani immigrants in Britain met with discrimination in jobs, housing, and everyday interaction with the authorities—producing frequent racial disturbances in major British cities. France witnessed hostility toward Algerian immigration, Germany toward the importation of Turkish labor. In Western Europe, as in the United States, struggles for racial and ethnic integration became central to the postcolonial world.

The Civil Rights Movement had enormous significance for the twentieth century, and it galvanized other movements as well. It dramatized as perhaps no other movement could the chasm between the egalitarian promises of American democracy and the real inequalities at the core of the American social and political life—a chasm that could be found in other Western nations as well. African American claims were morally and politically compelling, and the Civil Rights Movement sharpened others' criticisms of what they saw as a complacent, narrowly individualistic, materialist culture.

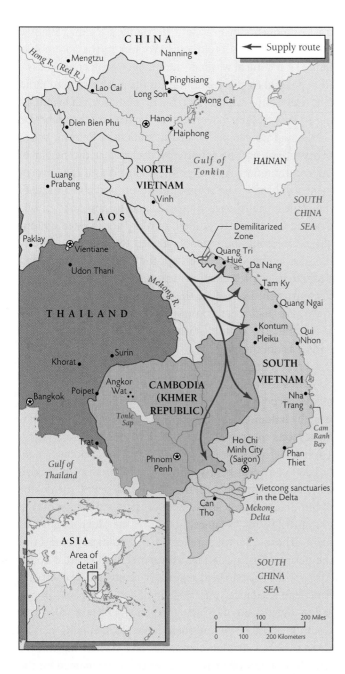

CHINA
Mengtzu
Nanning
Hong R. (Red R.)
Pinghsiang
Lao Cai
Long Son
Mong Cai
Dien Bien Phu
Hanoi
Haiphong
Gulf of Tonkin
HAINAN
Luang Prabang
NORTH VIETNAM
Vinh
SOUTH CHINA SEA
LAOS
Paklay
Vientiane
Demilitarized Zone
Udon Thani
Quang Tri
Hué
Da Nang
Mekong R.
Tam Ky
THAILAND
Quang Ngai
Kontum
Pleiku
Qui Nhon
Khorat
Surin
SOUTH VIETNAM
Bangkok
Poipet
Angkor Wat
CAMBODIA (KHMER REPUBLIC)
Nha Trang
Tonle Sap
Cam Ranh Bay
Trat
Ho Chi Minh City (Saigon)
Phan Thiet
Gulf of Thailand
Phnom Penh
Can Tho
Vietcong sanctuaries in the Delta
Mekong Delta
SOUTH CHINA SEA
ASIA
Area of detail
Supply route
0   100   200 Miles
0   100   200 Kilometers

THE WAR IN VIETNAM AND SOUTHEAST ASIA. The 1954 Geneva Accords divided Vietnam at the seventeenth parallel. The north went to Ho Chi Minh, the communist leader, and the south was controlled by Ngo Dinh Diem, an ally of the United States. In 1956, South Vietnam refused to hold the elections mandated in the Geneva Accords. Ho Chi Minh mobilized a guerrilla army, the Viet Cong, and the Vietnam War began. ▪ *What other countries in this region were drawn into the war?* ▪ *How did the Viet Cong use the proximity of Cambodia and Laos to their strategic advantage?* ▪ *Why did the United States choose to get involved?*

other countries' points of view, the Vietnam War became a spectacle: one in which the most powerful, wealthiest nation of the world seemed intent on destroying a land of poor peasants in the name of anticommunism, democracy, and freedom. The tarnished image of Western values stood at the center of 1960s protest movements in the United States and Western Europe.

The Student Movement

The student movement itself can be seen as a consequence of postwar developments: a growing cohort of young people with more time and wealth than in the past;

generational consciousness heightened, in part, by the marketing of mass youth culture; and educational institutions unable to deal with rising numbers and expectations. In France, the number of students in high school rose from 400,000 in 1949 to 2 million in 1969; in universities, over the same period, enrollments skyrocketed, from 100,000 to 600,000. The same was true in Italy, Britain, and West Germany. Universities, which had been created to educate a small elite, found both their teaching staffs and their facilities overwhelmed. Lecture halls were packed, university bureaucracies did not respond to requests, and thousands of students took exams at the same time. More philosophically, students raised questions about the role and meaning of elite education in a democratic society and about the relationships among the university as a "knowledge factory," consumer culture, and neocolonial ventures such as the Vietnam War and—for the French—the Algerian wars. Conservative traditions made intellectual reform difficult. In addition, student demands for fewer restrictions on personal life—for instance, permission to have a member of the opposite sex in a dormitory room—provoked authoritarian reactions from university representatives. Waves of student protest were not confined to the United States and Western Europe. They swept across Poland and Czechoslovakia where students protested one-party bureaucratic rule, stifling intellectual life, and authoritarianism, and helped sustain networks of dissidents. By the mid-1960s, simmering anger in Eastern Europe had once again reached a dangerous point.

1968

The year 1968 was an extraordinary one, quite similar to 1848 with its wave of revolution (see Chapter 20). It was even more intensely international, a reflection of tightening global ties. International youth culture fostered a sense of collective identity. The new media relayed images of civil rights protests in the United States to Europe, and broadcast news footage of the Vietnam War on television screens from West Virginia to West Germany. The wave of unrest shook both the Eastern and Western blocs. Protest movements assailed bureaucracy and the human costs of the Cold War: on the Soviet side, bureaucracy, authoritarianism, and indifference to civilians; on the Western side, bias and monopolies in the news media, the military-industrial complex, and American imperialism. The Soviet regime, as we have seen, responded with repression. In the United States and Western Europe, traditional political parties had little idea what to make of these new movements and those who participated in them. In both cases, events rapidly overwhelmed political systems.

PARIS

The most serious outbreak of student unrest in Europe came in Paris in the spring of 1968. The French Republic had been shaken by conflicts over the Algerian war in the early 1960s. Even more important, the economic boom had undermined the foundations of the regime and de Gaulle's traditional style of rule. French students at the University of Paris demanded reforms that would modernize their university. Protest first peaked at Nanterre, a new branch of the university built on a former air force depot. Nanterre was in a poor and poorly served neighborhood, starved for funds, and overcrowded with students. Petitions, demonstrations, and confrontations with university authorities traveled quickly from Nanterre to the Sorbonne, in central Paris. In the face of growing disorder, the University of Paris shut down—sending students into the streets and into uglier confrontations with the police. The police reacted with repression and violence, which startled onlookers and television audiences and backfired on the regime. Sympathy with the students' cause expanded rapidly, bringing in

THE PRESS IS POISON. Criticizing the official media was central to the politics of May 1968.

other opponents of President de Gaulle's regime. Massive trade-union strikes broke out. Workers in the automobile industry, technical workers, and public-sector employees—from gas and electricity utilities to the mail system to radio and television—went on strike. By mid-May, an astonishing 10 million French workers had walked off their jobs. De Gaulle had no sympathy for the students: "Reform, yes—bed wetting, no," he reportedly declared at the height of the confrontation. At one point, it looked as if the government would fall. The regime, however, was able to satisfy the strikers with wage increases and to appeal to public demand for order. The student movements, isolated, gradually petered out and students agreed to resume university life. The regime did recover, but the events of 1968 helped weaken de Gaulle's position as president and contributed to his retirement from office the following year.

There had been protest and rebelliousness in the 1950s, but the scale of events in 1968 was astonishing. Paris was not the only city to explode in 1968. Student protest broke out in West Berlin, targeting the government's close ties to the autocratic shah of Iran and the power of media corporations. Clashes with the police turned violent. In Italian cities, undergraduates staged several demonstrations to draw attention to university overcrowding. Twenty-six universities were closed. The London School of Economics was nearly shut down by protest. In Mexico City, a confrontation with the police ended with the deaths of hundreds of protesters, most of them students—on the eve of the 1968 Olympics, hosted by the Mexican government. Those Olympics reflected the political contests of the period: African nations threatened to boycott if South Africa, with its apartheid regime, participated. Two African American medalists raised their hands in a black power salute during an awards ceremony—and the Olympic Committee promptly sent them home. In Vietnam, the Viet Cong defied American claims to have turned the tide by launching a new offensive. The Tet offensive, named for the Vietnamese new year, brought the highest casualty rates to date in the Vietnam War and an explosion of protest. Antiwar demonstrations and student rebellions spread across the country. President Johnson, battered by the effects of Tet and already worn down by the war, chose not to run for reelection. The year 1968 also saw damage and trauma for the country's political future, because of the assassinations of Martin Luther King, Jr. (April 4, 1968) and presidential candidate Robert F. Kennedy (June 5, 1968). King's assassination was followed by a wave of rioting in more than fifty cities across the United States, followed in late summer by street battles between police and student protesters at the Democratic National Convention in Chicago. Some saw

1960s Politics: The Situationists

In 1957, a small group of European artists and writers formed a group called the Situationist International. The movement combined the artistic traditions of dada and surrealism with anarchism and Marxism. Unlike traditional Marxists, the situationists did not focus on the workplace. Instead, they developed a broad critique of everyday life, protesting the stifling of art, creativity, and imagination in contemporary society. They denounced the "tyranny" of consumer culture, which constantly invented new needs and desires to fuel consumption. Capitalism, they said, had "colonized" everyday life. The situationists' ideas and especially their unorthodox, surrealist style, became influential during the events of May 1968 in France. All around Paris students painted situationist slogans such as those printed here.

The social movements of 1968 cut across Cold War boundaries, attacking Western consumerism as well as Soviet authoritarianism. A group of students and situationists sent a telegram (second excerpt) to the Politburo of the Communist Party of the Soviet Union in May 1968.

Situationist Anticapitalism, 1968

OCCUPY THE FACTORIES

POWER TO THE
WORKERS COUNCILS

ABOLISH CLASS SOCIETY

DOWN WITH THE
SPECTACLE-COMMODITY SOCIETY

ABOLISH ALIENATION

ABOLISH THE UNIVERSITY

HUMANITY WON'T BE HAPPY
TILL THE LAST BUREAUCRAT
IS HUNG WITH THE GUTS
OF THE LAST CAPITALIST

DEATH TO THE COPS

FREE ALSO THE 4 GUYS
CONVICTED FOR LOOTING
DURING THE 6 MAY RIOT

—Occupation committee of the Autonomous
and Popular Sorbonne University

Situationist Anticommunist Slogans, 1968

17 MAY 1968 / To the Politburo of the Communist party of the USSR the Kremlin Moscow / Shake in your shoes bureaucrats. The international power of the workers councils will soon wipe you out. Humanity won't be happy till the last bureaucrat is hung with the guts of the last capitalist. Long live the struggle of the Kronstadt sailors and of the Makhnovshchina against Trotsky and Lenin. Long live the 1956 Councilist insurrection of Budapest • Down with the state • Long live revolutionary Marxism. Occupation committee of the Autonomous and Popular Sorbonne

Sources: "Slogans to Be Spread Now by Every Means," in *Situationist International Anthology*, ed. and trans. Ken Knabb (Berkeley, CA: 1981), pp. 334–45.

Questions for Analysis

1. Are there any common themes in these sets of slogans?

2. Why has 1968 often been called "the year of the barricades"?

the flowering of protest as another "springtime of peoples." Others saw it as a long nightmare.

PRAGUE

The student movement in the United States and Western Europe also took inspiration from one of the most significant challenges to Soviet authority since the Hungarian revolt of 1956 (see Chapter 27): the "Prague spring" of 1968. The events began with the emergence of a liberal communist government in Czechoslovakia, led by the Slovak Alexander Dubček (*DOOB-chehk*). Dubček had outmaneuvered the more traditional, authoritarian party leaders. He advocated "socialism with a human face"; he encouraged debate within the party, academic and artistic freedom, and less censorship. As was often the case, party members were

ANTIGOVERNMENT PROTESTS IN MEXICO CITY, 1968. On October 2, 1968, ten days before the opening of the Summer Olympics in Mexico City, police opened fire on student protesters and arrested over one thousand people.

divided between proponents of reform and those fearful that reform would unleash revolution. The reformers, however, also gained support from outside the party, from student organizations, the press, and networks of dissidents. As in Western Europe and the United States, the protest movement overflowed into traditional party politics.

In the Soviet Union, Khrushchev had fallen in 1964, and the reins of Soviet power passed to Leonid Brezhnev as secretary of the Communist party. Brezhnev was more conservative than Khrushchev, less inclined to bargain with the West, and prone to defensive actions to safeguard the Soviet sphere of influence. Initially, the Soviets tolerated Dubček as a political eccentric. The events of 1968 raised their fears. Most Eastern European communist leaders denounced Czech reformism, but student demonstrations of support broke out in Poland and Yugoslavia, calling for an end to one-party rule, less censorship, and reform of the judicial system. In addition, Josip Broz Tito of Yugoslavia and Nicolae Ceaușescu (*chow-SHEHS-koo*) of Romania—two of the more stubbornly independent communists in Eastern Europe—visited Dubček. To Soviet eyes, these activities looked as if they were directed against the Warsaw Pact and Soviet security; they also saw American intervention in Vietnam as evidence of heightened anticommunist activities around the world. When Dubček attempted to democratize the Communist party and did not attend a meeting of members of the Warsaw Pact, the Soviets sent tanks and troops into Prague in August 1968. Again, the world watched as streams of Czech refugees left the country and a repressive government, picked by Soviet security

forces, took charge. Dubček and his allies were subjected to imprisonment or "internal exile." Twenty percent of the members of the Czech Communist party were expelled in a series of purges. After the destruction of the Prague spring, Soviet diplomats consolidated their position according to the new Brezhnev Doctrine. The doctrine stated that no socialist state could adopt policies endangering the interests of international socialism and that the Soviet Union could intervene in the domestic affairs of any Soviet bloc nation if communist rule was threatened. In other words, the repressive rules applied to Hungary in 1956 would not change.

What were the effects of 1968? De Gaulle's government recovered. The Republican Richard M. Nixon won the U.S. election of 1968. From 1972 to 1975, the United States withdrew from Vietnam; in the wake of that war came a refugee crisis and a new series of horrific regional conflicts. In Prague, Warsaw Pact tanks put down the uprising, and in the Brezhnev Doctrine the Soviet regime reasserted its right to control its satellites. Serious Cold War confrontations rippled along Czechoslovakia's western border as refugees fled west, and in the Korean peninsula after North Korea's seizure of an eavesdropping ship from the U.S. Navy. Over the long term, however, the protesters' and dissidents' demands proved more difficult to contain. In Eastern Europe and the Soviet Union, dissent was defeated but not eliminated. The crushing of the Czech rebellion proved thoroughly disillusioning, and in important respects the events of 1968 prefigured the collapse of Soviet control in 1989. In Western Europe and the United States, the student movement subsided but its issues and the kinds of politics that it pioneered proved more enduring. Feminism (or, more accurately, "second wave" feminism) really came into its own after 1968, its numbers expanded by women a generation younger than Simone de Beauvoir and Betty Friedan. They had been in student political organizations in the 1960s and their impatience with traditional political parties and, often, their male student allies, sent them into separate groups, where they championed equality in sexual relationships and in the family. In a phrase that captured some of the changes of the 1950s and 1960s, they insisted that "the personal is political." As one English woman said, "We wanted to redefine the meaning of politics to include an analysis of our daily lives," which meant sexuality, health, child care, cultural

A RUSSIAN TANK ATTACKED DURING THE PRAGUE SPRING, 1968. The Soviet-led invasion of Czechoslovakia on August 20–21, 1968 put an end to Alexander Dubček's experiment in creating "Socialism with a human face."

images of women, and so on. The antiwar movement took up the issue of nuclear weapons—a particularly volatile issue in Europe. Finally, the environmental movement took hold—concerned not only with pollution and the world's dwindling resources but also with mushrooming urbanization and the kind of unrestrained economic growth that had given rise to the 1960s. Over the long term, in both Europe and the United States, voters' loyalties to traditional political parties became less reliable and smaller parties multiplied; in this way, new social movements eventually became part of a very different political landscape.

ECONOMIC STAGNATION: THE PRICE OF SUCCESS

Economic as well as social problems plagued Europe during the 1970s and 1980s, but these problems had begun earlier. By the middle of the 1960s, for example, the West German growth rate had slowed. Demand for manufactured goods fell, and in 1966 the country suffered its first postwar recession. Volkswagen, the symbol of the German miracle, introduced a shortened workweek; almost 700,000 West Germans were thrown out of work altogether. In France, a persistent housing shortage increased the cost of living. Though new industries continued to prosper, the basic industries—coal, steel, and railways—began to run up deficits. Unemployment was rising in tandem with prices. Prime Minister Harold Wilson's pledge to revive Britain's economy by introducing new technology foundered on crises in the foreign-exchange value of the pound, which were compounded by continued low levels of growth. The Common Market—expanded in 1973 to include Britain, Ireland, and Denmark, and again in the early 1980s to admit Greece, Spain, and Portugal—struggled to overcome problems stemming from the conflict between the domestic economic regulations characteristic of many European states and the free-market policies that prevailed within what would become the European Economic Community (EEC) countries.

Oil prices spiked for the first time in the early 1970s, compounding these difficulties. In 1973, the Arab-dominated

Ludvík Vaculík, "Two Thousand Words" (1968)

During the Prague spring of 1968, a group of Czech intellectuals published a document titled "Two Thousand Words That Belong to Workers, Farmers, Officials, Scientists, Artists, and Everybody" that has become known simply as the "Two Thousand Words." This manifesto called for further reform, including increased freedom of the press. Seen as a direct affront by Moscow, the manifesto heightened Soviet-Czech tensions. In August 1968, Warsaw Pact tanks rolled into Prague, overthrowing the reformist government of Alexander Dubček.

Most of the nation welcomed the socialist program with high hopes. But it fell into the hands of the wrong people. It would not have mattered so much that they lacked adequate experience in affairs of state, factual knowledge, or philosophical education, if only they had enough common prudence and decency to listen to the opinion of others and agree to being gradually replaced by more able people. . . .

The chief sin and deception of these rulers was to have explained their own whims as the "will of the workers." Were we to accept this pretense, we would have to blame the workers today for the decline of our economy, for crimes committed against the innocent, and for the introduction of censorship to prevent anyone writing about these things. The workers would be to blame for misconceived investments, for losses suffered in foreign trade, and for the housing shortage. Obviously no sensible person will hold the working class responsible for such things. We all know, and every worker knows especially, that they had virtually no say in deciding anything. . . .

Since the beginning of this year we have been experiencing a regenerative process of democratization. . . .

Let us demand the departure of people who abused their power, damaged public property, and acted dishonorably or brutally. Ways must be found to compel them to resign. To mention a few: public criticism, resolutions, demonstrations, demonstrative work brigades, collections to buy presents for them on their retirement, strikes, and picketing at their front doors. But we should reject any illegal, indecent, or boorish methods. . . . Let us convert the district and local newspapers, which have mostly degenerated to the level of official mouthpieces, into a platform for all the forward-looking elements in politics; let us demand that editorial boards be formed of National Front representatives, or else let us start new papers. Let us form committees for the defense of free speech. . . .

There has been great alarm recently over the possibility that foreign forces will intervene in our development. Whatever superior forces may face us, all we can do is stick to our own positions, behave decently, and initiate nothing ourselves. We can show our government that we will stand by it, with weapons if need be, if it will do what we give it a mandate to do. . . .

The spring is over and will never return. By winter we will know all.

Source: Jaromir Navratil, *The Prague Spring 1968*, trans. Mark Kramer, Joy Moss, and Ruth Tosek (Budapest: 1998), pp. 177–81.

Questions for Analysis

1. Where, according to the authors of this document, did socialism go wrong?

2. What specific reforms do they demand?

Organization of the Petroleum Exporting Countries (OPEC) instituted an oil embargo against the Western powers. In 1973, a barrel of oil cost $1.73; in 1975, it cost $10.46; by the early 1980s, the price had risen to over $30. This increase produced an inflationary spiral; interest rates rose and with them the price of almost everything else Western consumers were used to buying. Rising costs produced wage demands and strikes. The calm industrial relations of the 1950s and early 1960s were a thing of the past. At the same time, European manufacturers encountered serious competition not only from such highly developed countries as Japan but also from the increasingly active economies of Asia and Africa, in which the West had invested capital eagerly in the previous decades. By 1980, Japan had captured 10 percent of the automobile market in West Germany and 25 percent in Belgium. In 1984, unemployment in Western Europe reached about 19 million. The lean years had arrived.

UNEMPLOYMENT DEMONSTRATION, 1974. A crowd of workers in Rome, Italy, gathered to protest inflation and unemployment, in a strike that lasted twenty-four hours.

Europe, and goods and services, even in prosperous times, were scarce.

Western governments struggled for effective reactions to the abrupt change in their economic circumstances. The new leader of the British Conservative Party, Margaret Thatcher, was elected prime minister in 1979—and reelected in 1983 and 1987—on a program of curbing trade-union power, cutting taxes to stimulate the economy, and privatizing publicly owned enterprises. The economy remained weak, with close to 15 percent of the workforce unemployed by 1986. In West Germany, a series of Social Democratic governments attempted to combat economic recession with job-training programs and tax incentives, both financed by higher taxes. These programs did little to assist economic recovery, and the country shifted to the right.

The fact that governments of right and left were unable to re-create Europe's unprecedented postwar prosperity suggests the degree to which economic forces remain outside the control of individual states. The continuing economic malaise renewed efforts to Europeanize common problems. By the end of the 1980s, the EEC embarked on an ambitious program of integration. Long-term goals, agreed on when the EU (European Union) was formed in 1991, included a monetary union—with a central European bank and a single currency—and unified social policies to reduce poverty and unemployment. As the twenty-first century opened, the European member states had begun to institute several of these steps. It remained unclear whether that new European "federal" state would overcome its members' claims of national sovereignty or whether it would develop the economic and political strength to counter the global domination of the United States.

Solidarity in Poland

In 1980, unrest again peaked in Eastern Europe, this time with the Polish labor movement Solidarity. Polish workers organized strikes that brought the government of the country to a standstill. The workers formulated several key demands. First, they objected to working conditions imposed by the government to combat a severe economic crisis. Second, they protested high prices and especially shortages, both of which had roots in government policy

Economies in the Soviet bloc also stalled. The expansion of heavy industry had helped recovery in the postwar period, but by the 1970s, those sectors no longer provided growth or innovation. The Soviet Communist party proclaimed in 1961 that by 1970 the USSR would exceed the United States in per capita production. By the end of the 1970s, however, Soviet per capita production was not much higher than in the less industrialized countries of southern Europe. The Soviets were also overcommitted to military defense industries that had become inefficient, though lucrative for the party members who ran them. The Soviet economy did get a boost from the OPEC oil price hikes of 1973 and 1979. (OPEC was founded in 1961; the Soviet Union did not belong, but as the world's largest producer of oil, it benefited from rising prices.) Without this boost, the situation would have been far grimmer.

Following an impressive economic performance during the early 1970s, the Eastern European nations encountered serious financial difficulties. Their success had rested in part on capital borrowed from the West. By 1980, those debts weighed heavily on their national economies. Poland's hard-currency indebtedness to Western countries, for example, was almost four times greater than its annual exports. The solution to this problem, attempted in Poland and elsewhere, was to cut back on production for domestic consumption in order to increase exports. Yet this policy encountered strong popular opposition. Although there was virtually no unemployment in Eastern Europe, men and women were by no means happy with their economic situation. Working hours were longer than in Western and priorities. Above all, though, the Polish workers in Solidarity demanded truly independent labor unions instead of labor organizations sponsored by the government. Their belief that society had the right to organize itself and, by implication, create its own government, stood at the core of the movement. The strikers were led by an electrician from the Gdansk shipyards, Lech Wałęsa. Wałęsa's charismatic personality appealed not only to the Polish citizenry but to sympathizers in the West. Again, however, the Soviets assisted a military regime in reimposing authoritarian rule. The Polish president, General Wojciech Jaruzelski, had learned from Hungary and Czechoslovakia and played a delicate game of diplomacy to maintain the Polish government's freedom of action while repressing Solidarity itself. But the implied Soviet threat remained.

EUROPE RECAST: THE COLLAPSE OF COMMUNISM AND THE END OF THE SOVIET UNION

One of history's fascinations is its unpredictability. There has been no more telling example of this in recent times than the sudden collapse of the Eastern European communist regimes in 1989, the dramatic end to the Cold War, and the subsequent disintegration of the once-powerful Soviet Union.

Gorbachev and Soviet Reform

This sudden collapse flowed, unintended, from a new wave of reform begun in the mid-1980s. In 1985, a new generation of officials began taking charge of the Soviet Communist party, a change heralded by Mikhail Gorbachev's appointment to the party leadership. In his mid-fifties, Gorbachev was significantly younger than his immediate predecessors and less prey to the habits of mind that had shaped Soviet domestic and foreign affairs. He was frankly critical of the repressive aspects of communist society as well as its sluggish economy, and he did not hesitate to voice those criticisms openly. His twin policies of *glasnost* (intellectual openness) and *perestroika* (economic restructuring) held out hope for a freer, more prosperous Soviet Union. Under Gorbachev, a number of imprisoned dissidents were freed, among them Andrei Sakharov, the scientist known as the "father of the Soviet hydrogen bomb" and later a fierce critic of the Cold War arms race.

The policies of glasnost took aim at the privileges of the political elite and the immobility of the state bureaucracy by allowing greater freedom of speech, instituting competitive elections to official positions, and limiting terms of office. Gorbachev's program of perestroika called for a shift from the centrally planned economy instituted by Stalin to a mixed economy combining planning with the operation of market forces. In agriculture, perestroika accelerated the move away from cooperative production and instituted incentives for the achievement of production targets. Gorbachev planned to integrate the Soviet Union into the international economy by participating in organizations such as the International Monetary Fund.

Even these dramatic reforms, however, were too little too late. Ethnic unrest, a legacy of Russia's nineteenth-century imperialism, threatened to split the Soviet Union apart, while secession movements gathered steam in the Baltic republics and elsewhere. From 1988 onward, fighting between Armenians and Azerbaijanis over an ethnically Azerbaijani region located inside Armenia threatened to escalate into a border dispute with Iran. Only Soviet troops patrolling the border and Gorbachev's willingness to suppress a separatist revolt in Azerbaijan by force temporarily quelled the conflict.

Spurred on by these events in the Soviet Union, the countries of Eastern Europe began to agitate for independence from Moscow. Gorbachev encouraged open discussion—glasnost—not only in his own country but also in the satellite nations. He revoked the Brezhnev Doctrine's insistence on single-party socialist governments and made frequent and inspiring trips to the capitals of neighboring satellites.

Glasnost rekindled the flame of opposition in Poland, where Solidarity had been defeated but not destroyed by the government in 1981. In 1988, the union launched a new series of strikes. These disturbances culminated in an agreement between the government and Solidarity that legalized the union and promised open elections. The results, in June 1989, astonished the world: virtually all of the government's candidates lost; the Citizen's Committee, affiliated with Solidarity, won a sizable majority in the Polish parliament.

In Hungary and Czechoslovakia, events followed a similar course during 1988 and 1989. Janos Kadar, the Hungarian leader since the Soviet crackdown of 1956, resigned in the face of continuing demonstrations in May 1988 and was replaced by the reformist government of the Hungarian Socialist Workers' party. By the spring of 1989, the Hungarian regime had been purged of Communist party supporters. The government also began to dismantle its security fences along the Austrian border. A year later,

GORBACHEV IN POLAND AT THE HEIGHT OF HIS POWER IN 1986. Perestroika aimed at the privileges of the political elite and would eventually lead to his fall from power.

the Hungarian Democratic Forum, pledging it would reinstate full civil rights and restructure the economy, secured a plurality of seats in the National Assembly.

The Czechs, too, staged demonstrations against Soviet domination in late 1988. Brutal beatings of student demonstrators by the police in 1989 radicalized the nations' workers and provoked mass demonstrations. Civic Forum, an opposition coalition, called for the installation of a coalition government to include noncommunists, for free elections, and for the resignation of the country's communist leadership. It reinforced its demands with continuing mass demonstrations and threats of a general strike that resulted in the toppling of the old regime and the election of the playwright and Civic Forum leader Václav Havel as president.

Fall of the Berlin Wall

The most significant political change in Eastern Europe during the late 1980s was the collapse of communism in East Germany and the unification of East and West Germany. Although long considered the most prosperous of the Soviet satellite countries, East Germany suffered from severe economic stagnation and environmental degradation. Waves of East Germans registered their discontent with worsening conditions by massive illegal immigration to the West. This exodus combined with evidence

of widespread official corruption to force the resignation of East Germany's longtime, hard-line premier, Erich Honecker. His successor, Egon Krenz, promised reforms, but he was nevertheless faced with continuing protests and continuing mass emigration.

On November 4, 1989, the government, in a move that acknowledged its powerlessness to hold its citizens captive, opened its border with Czechoslovakia. This move effectively freed East Germans to travel to the West. In a matter of days, the Berlin Wall—the embodiment of the Cold War, the Iron Curtain, and the division of East from West—was demolished, first by groups of ordinary citizens and later by the East German government. Jubilant throngs from both sides walked through the gaping holes that now permitted men, women, and children to take the few steps that symbolized the return to freedom and a chance for national unity. Free elections were held throughout Germany in March 1990, resulting in a victory for the Alliance for Germany, a coalition allied with the West German chancellor Helmut Kohl's Christian Democratic Union. With heavy emigration continuing, reunification talks quickly culminated in the formal proclamation of a united Germany on October 3, 1990.

The public mood, in Eastern Europe and perhaps worldwide, was swept up with the jubilation of these peaceful "velvet revolutions" during the autumn of 1989. Yet the end of one-party rule in Eastern Europe was not accomplished without violence. The single most repressive government in the old Eastern bloc, Nicolae Ceauşescu's outright dictatorship in Romania, came apart with much more bloodshed. By December, faced with the wave of popular revolts in surrounding countries and riots by the ethnic Hungarian minority in Transylvania, a number of party officials and army officers in Romania tried to hold

REAGAN AT THE BERLIN WALL. On June 12, 1987, President Reagan challenged Mikhail Gorbachev to tear down the Berlin Wall in a speech given before the Brandenburg Gate in Berlin.

Analyzing Primary Sources

The Reunification of Germany, 1989–1990

On November 28, 1989, two weeks after the fall of the Berlin Wall, the chancellor of West Germany, Helmut Kohl, proposed a ten-point program of cooperation between the two Germanies, with an eye toward the eventual unification of the two separate nations into one nation-state. Events moved quickly after the ruling party in East Germany lost the first free elections held in March 1990. A coalition government in East Germany led by Lothar de Maizière, the head of the East German wing of Helmut Kohl's political party, the Christian Democratic Union, negotiated the terms of the merger with the West Germans, which included complex economic and political measures. The legislative bodies of both Germanies approved the unification treaty in September 1990, and unification officially took place at midnight on October 3, 1990. Kohl's speech reveals the delicate nature of the negotiations, which necessitated balancing complex domestic pressures with geopolitical considerations.

1. Immediate measures are called for as a result of events of recent weeks, particularly the flow of resettlers and the huge increase in the number of travellers. The Federal Government will provide immediate aid where it is needed. We will assist in the humanitarian sector and provide medical aid if it is wanted and considered helpful. . . .

The GDR must itself provide travellers with the necessary foreign exchange. We are, however, prepared to contribute to a currency fund for a transitional period, provided that persons entering the GDR no longer have to exchange a minimum amount of currency, that entry into the GDR is made considerably easier, and that the GDR itself contributes substantially to the fund.

Our aim is to facilitate traffic as much as possible in both directions.

2. The Federal Government will continue its cooperation with the GDR in all areas where it is of direct benefit to the people or both sides, especially in the economic, scientific, technological and cultural fields. It is particularly important to intensify cooperation in the field of environmental protection. . . .

We also want to extensively increase telephone links with the GDR and help expand the GDR's telephone network. . . .

[W]e need to take a thorough look at transport and rail systems in the GDR and the Federal Republic in the light of the new situation. Forty years of separation also mean that traffic routes have in some cases developed quite differently. This applies not only to border crossing-points but to the traditional East–West lines of communication in central Europe. . . .

3. I have offered comprehensive aid and cooperation should the GDR bindingly undertake to carry out a fundamental change in the political and economic system and put the necessary measures irreversibly into effect. . . .

We support the demand for free, equal and secret elections in the GDR, in which, of course, independent, that is to say, non-socialist, parties would also participate. The SED's monopoly on power must be removed. The introduction of a democratic system means, above all, the abolition of laws on political crimes and the immediate release of all political prisoners.

Economic aid can only be effective if the economic system is radically reformed. This is obvious from the situation in all Comecon states and is not a question of our preaching to them. The centrally-planned economy must be dismantled.

We do not want to stabilize conditions that have become indefensible. Economic improvement can only occur if the GDR opens its doors to Western investment, if conditions of free enterprise are created, and if private initiative becomes possible. I don't understand those who accuse us of tutelage in this respect. There are daily examples of this in Hungary and Poland which can surely be followed by the GDR, likewise a member of Comecon. . . .

4. Prime Minister Modrow spoke in his government policy statement of a 'contractual community'. We are prepared to adopt this idea. The proximity of our two states in Germany and the special nature of their relationship demand an increasingly close network of agreements in all sectors and at all levels.

5. We are also prepared to take a further decisive step, namely, to develop confederative structures between the two states in Germany with a view to creating a federation. But this presupposes the election of a democratic government in the GDR. . . .

Previous policy towards the GDR had to be limited mainly to small steps by which we sought above all to alleviate the consequences of division and to keep alive and strengthen the people's awareness of the unity of the nation. If, in the future, a democratically legitimized, that is, a freely elected government, becomes our partner, that will open up completely new perspectives.

Gradually, new forms of institutional cooperation can be created and further developed. Such coalescence is inherent in the continuity of German history. State organization in Germany has nearly always taken the form of a confederation or federation. We can fall back on this past experience. Nobody knows at the present time what a reunited Germany will look like. I am, however, sure that unity will come, if it is wanted by the German people.

6. The development of intra-German relations remains embedded in the pan-European process, that is to say in the framework of East–West relations. The future architecture of Germany must fit into the future architecture of Europe as a whole. Here the West has shown itself to be the pacemaker with its concept of a lasting and equitable peaceful order in Europe.

In our joint declaration of June this year, which I have already quoted, General Secretary Gorbachev and I spoke of the structural elements of a "common European home." They are, for example:

—Unqualified respect for the integrity and security of each state. Each state has the right freely to choose its own political and social system.

—Unqualified respect for the principles and rules of international law, especially respect for the people's right of self-determination.

—The realization of human rights.

—Respect for and maintenance of the traditional cultures of the nations of Europe.

With all of these points, as Mr Gorbachev and I laid down, we aim to follow Europe's long traditions and help overcome the division of Europe.

7. The attraction and aura of the European Community are and remain a constant feature of pan-European development. We want to and must strengthen them further still.

9. Overcoming the division of Europe and Germany presupposes far-reaching and rapid steps in the field of disarmament and arms control. Disarmament and arms control must keep pace with political developments and thus be accelerated where necessary. . . .

10. With this comprehensive policy we are working for a state of peace in Europe in which the German nation can recover its unity in free self-determination. Reunification—that is regaining national unity—remains the political goal of the Federal government. . . .

The linking of the German question to pan-European developments and East–West relations, as explained in these ten points, will allow a natural development which takes account of the interests of all concerned and paves the way for peaceful development in freedom, which is our objective.

Questions for Analysis

1. What priorities are evident in Kohl's speech? How did he seek to balance the practical questions of concern to ordinary citizens with the larger political context?

2. What traditions in German history did Kohl refer to in making his case for cooperation, and how did he define the possibility of unity?

3. What references did Kohl make to the larger Cold War context of the division of the two Germanies?

on to their own positions by deposing Ceaușescu. His extensive secret police, however, organized resistance to the coup; the result was nearly two weeks of bloody street fighting in the capital Bucharest. Individual snipers loyal to Ceaușescu were still killing passing civilians from rooftops, forcing dangerous efforts to root them out, while the rest of Eastern Europe celebrated Christmas and the new year with new political systems. Ceaușescu himself and his wife were seized by populist army units and executed; images of their bloodstained bodies flashed worldwide by satellite television.

Throughout the rest of Eastern Europe, single-party governments in the countries behind what was left of the tattered Iron Curtain—Albania, Bulgaria, and Yugoslavia—collapsed in the face of democratic pressure for change. Meanwhile, in the Soviet Union itself, inspired by events in Eastern Europe, the Baltic republics of Lithuania and Latvia strained to free themselves from Soviet rule. In 1990, they unilaterally proclaimed their independence from the Soviet Union, throwing into sharp relief the tension between "union" and "republics." Gorbachev reacted with an uncertain mixture of armed intervention and promises of greater local autonomy. In the fall of 1991, Lithuania and Latvia, along with the third Baltic state of Estonia, won international recognition as independent republics.

The Collapse of the Soviet Union

While Soviet influence eroded in Eastern Europe, at home the unproductive Soviet economy continued to fuel widespread ire. With the failure of perestroika—largely the result of a lack of resources and an inability to increase production—came the rise of a powerful political rival to Gorbachev, his erstwhile ally Boris Yeltsin. The reforming mayor of Moscow, Yeltsin was elected president of the Russian Federation—the largest Soviet republic—on an anti-Gorbachev platform in 1990. Pressure from the Yeltsin camp weakened Gorbachev's ability to maneuver independent of reactionary factions in the Politburo and the military, undermining his reform program and his ability to remain in power.

The Soviet Union's increasingly severe domestic problems led to mounting protests in 1991, when Gorbachev's policies failed to improve—indeed diminished—the living standard of the Soviet people. Demands increased that the bloated government bureaucracy respond with a dramatic cure for the country's continuing economic stagnation. Gorbachev appeared to lose his political nerve, having first ordered and then canceled a radical 500-day economic reform plan, at the same time agreeing to

negotiations with the increasingly disaffected republics within the union, now clamoring for independence. Sensing their political lives to be in jeopardy, a group of highly placed hard-line Communist party officials staged an abortive coup in August 1991. They made Gorbachev and his wife prisoners in their summer villa, then declared a return to party-line orthodoxy in an effort to salvage what remained of the Soviet Union's global leverage and the Communist party's domestic power. The Soviet citizenry, especially in large cities like Moscow and Leningrad, defied their self-proclaimed saviors. Led by Boris Yeltsin, who at one point mounted a tank in a Moscow street to rally the people, they gathered support among the Soviet republics and the military and successfully called the plotters' bluff. Within two weeks, Gorbachev was back in power and the coup leaders were in prison.

Ironically, this people's counterrevolution returned Gorbachev to office while destroying the power of the Soviet state he led. Throughout the fall of 1991, as Gorbachev struggled to hold the union together, Yeltsin joined the presidents of the other large republics to capitalize on the discontent. On December 8, 1991, the presidents of the republics of Russia, Ukraine, and Byelorussia (now called Belarus) declared that the Soviet Union was no more: "The USSR as a subject of international law and geopolitical reality is ceasing to exist." Though the prose was flat, the message was momentous. The once-mighty Soviet Union, founded seventy-five years before in a burst of revolutionary fervor and violence, had evaporated nearly overnight, leaving in its wake a collection of eleven far from powerful nations loosely joined together as the Commonwealth of Independent States. On December 25, 1991, Gorbachev resigned and left political life, not pushed from office in the usual way but made irrelevant as other actors dismantled

RUSSIAN TANKS IN RED SQUARE NEAR THE KREMLIN. Boris Yeltsin convinced many in the military not to support the coup of August 1991, ensuring the failure of the plotters, and hastening the collapse of the Soviet Union.

Past and Present

Shock Therapy in Post-Soviet Russia

The transition from a command economy to open markets in Russia after 1991 (on left, the banner reads "Privatization Yes") proved destabilizing in Russia, and for many ordinary people the first experience of the new order was profoundly unsettling. When Vladimir Putin came to power after 2000, he moved against the independence of this new business class, imprisoning some (including Mikhail Khodorkovsky, right, who awaits the verdict in his 2005 trial for fraud) and forcing others into exile.

 Watch related author interview on StudySpace
wwnorton.com/web/westernciv18

the state. The Soviet flag—the hammer and sickle symbolizing the nation that for fifty years had kept half of Europe in thrall—was lowered for the last time over the Kremlin.

The mighty fall left mighty problems in its wake. Food shortages worsened during the winter of 1992. The value of the ruble plummeted. The republics could not agree on common military policies or resolve difficult and dangerous questions concerning the control of nuclear warheads. Yeltsin's pleas for economic assistance from the West resulted in massive infusions of private and public capital, which nevertheless failed to prevent serious economic hardship and dislocation. Free enterprise brought with it unemployment and encouraged profiteering through crime. Yeltsin's determination to press ahead with his economic program met with stiff resistance from a parliament and citizenry alarmed by the ruthlessness and rapidity of the change they were experiencing. When the parliament balked at Yeltsin's proposals in September 1993, he dissolved it. This helped provoke

an attempted coup two months later, staged by conservative politicians and army officers. Officials loyal to Yeltsin put the revolt down with far more force than the 1991 coup attempt—television viewers worldwide watched artillery shells slam into the rebel-occupied parliament building in Moscow during a bloody shootout. When the parliament was restored, elections in 1995 served as a benchmark of discontent: the resurgent communists claimed roughly one-third of the seats, while xenophobic nationalists led by Vladimir Zhirinovsky also took a notable bloc of the vote, thanks to the steady blame he heaped on the West for Russia's troubles.

Meanwhile, ethnic and religious conflict plagued the republics. In the first years after the dissolution of the Soviet Union, warfare flared in Georgia, Armenia, and Azerbaijan. The most serious conflict arose in the predominantly Muslim area of Chechnya, bordering Georgia in the Caucasus, which had declared its independence from Russia in late 1991. The Chechen rebels were heirs to a tradition of banditry and separatism against Russian authority that stretched into the nineteenth century. In 1994, the Russian government, weary of this continuing challenge to its authority, launched a concerted effort to quash resistance. As Russian forces moved into the Chechen capital, Grozny, they were ambushed with firepower largely stolen from disused Russian armories. The result was a massacre of the invading Russians, followed by a long and bloody siege to take the city. This in turn fueled a long and particularly bloody guerrilla war between Russian and Chechen forces, marked by repeated atrocities on both sides. After brief pauses in 1995 and 1997, this Chechen war dragged on into the new century, echoing Russia's conflict in Afghanistan on a scale that was both bloodier and closer to home.

The Iron Curtain had established one of the most rigid borders in European history. The collapse of the Soviet Union opened up both Russia and its former imperial dominions. That transformation brought the Cold War to an end. It also created a host of unforeseen problems throughout Eastern Europe and the advanced industrial world: ethnic conflict, diplomatic uncertainty about the new Russian government, and single superpower domination, sometimes called American unilateralism. Within the Russian and several of the former Soviet republics there emerged a new era that some called the Russian "Wild West." Capitalist market relations began to develop without clearly defined property relations or a stable legal framework. Former government officials profited from their positions of power to take over whole sectors of the economy. Corruption ran rampant. Organized crime controlled industries, stock exchanges, a thriving trade in illegal drugs, and even some local governments. Even the most energetic central governments in the large republics such as Russia, Ukraine, and Kazakhstan found themselves faced with enormous problems. Post-Soviet openness could lay the groundwork for a new democratic Russia; it could also set in motion the resurgence of older forms of tyranny.

Postrevolutionary Troubles: Eastern Europe after 1989

The velvet revolutions of Central and Eastern Europe raised high hopes: local hopes that an end to authoritarian government would produce economic prosperity and cultural pluralism and Western hopes that these countries would join them as capitalist partners in an enlarged European Community. The reality was slower and harder than the optimists of 1989 foresaw. The largest struggle, one with continuing implications for the European continent,

has been the reunification of Germany. The euphoria of reunification masked uncertainty even among Germans themselves. The foundering East German economy has remained a problem. Piled onto other economic difficulties in the former West Germany during the 1990s, it has produced much resentment of the need to "rescue" the East. What the writer Günter Grass described as the "wall in the mind" still divided the countries. Though there has been great progress in integrating elections and the bureaucracies of the two German states, economic and cultural unity has been much harder to come by.

Adapting to change has been difficult throughout Eastern Europe. Attempts to create free-market economies have brought inflation, unemployment, and—in their wake—anticapitalist demonstrations. Inefficient industries, a workforce resistant to change, energy shortages, lack of venture capital, and a severely polluted environment have combined to hinder progress and dash hopes. Uprisings in Bulgaria and Albania in early 1997 were fueled by the inability of those governments to resolve basic economic and social problems. In addition, racial and ethnic conflicts have continued to divide newly liberated democracies, recalling the divisions that led to the First World War and that have plagued Eastern Europe throughout its history. Minorities waged campaigns for autonomous rights or outright secession that often descended into violence.

Czechoslovakia's velvet revolution collapsed into a "velvet divorce," as Slovakia declared itself independent from the Czechs, forcing Havel's resignation and slowing down the promising cultural and economic reforms begun in 1989. Poland enjoyed an upswing in its economy during the 1990s, after many years of hardship, but most of the rest of Eastern Europe continues to find transformation rough going. These difficulties have been accompanied by revived ethnic tensions formerly suppressed by centralized communist governments. There has been violence against non-European immigrants throughout Eastern Europe, against gypsies (Romani) in the Czech Republic and Hungary, and against ethnic Hungarians in Romania.

The most extreme example of these conflicts came with the implosion of the state of Yugoslavia. After the death of Tito in 1980, the government that had held Yugoslavia's federalist ethnic patchwork together came undone. The 1960s and 1970s brought uneven economic growth, benefiting the capital, Belgrade, and the provinces of Croatia and Slovenia the most; but heavy industrial areas in Serbia, Bosnia-Hercegovina, and the tiny district of Kosovo began to lag far behind. A number of Serb politicians, most notably Slobodan Milosevic, began to redirect Serbs' frustration with economic hardship toward subjects of national pride and sovereignty.

Soviet Union
Eastern Bloc countries
✴ Sites of popular demonstrations
⊛ Capital cities

EASTERN EUROPE IN 1989. ▪ *What political changes in the Soviet Union allowed for the spread of demonstrations throughout Eastern Europe?* ▪ *Why did the first political upheavals of 1989 occur in Poland and East Germany?* ▪ *In what countries were demonstrations the most widespread and why?*

of his times. More important for Milosevic, it catapulted him into crucial positions of authority. In these posts, he alienated representatives from the non-Serb republics. Inspired by the peaceful transformations of 1989, representatives of the small province of Slovenia declared they had been denied adequate representation and economic support inside the republic. In 1991, on a tide of nationalism and reform, the Slovenes seceded from Yugoslavia. After a brief attempt to hold the union together by force, the Yugoslav government relented and let Slovenia claim its independence. Ethnic nationalists in the other republics followed suit. A much deeper, bloodier process of disintegration had begun.

The large republic of Croatia, once part of the Habsburg Empire and briefly an independent state allied with the Nazis during the Second World War, cited injustices by Serb officials in the Yugoslav government and declared independence as a free, capitalist state. War broke out between federal Yugoslav forces and the well-armed militias of independent Croatia, a conflict that ended in arbitration by the United Nations. The religious nature of the conflict—between Catholic Croats and Orthodox Serbs—and the legacies of fighting in the Second World War produced violence on both sides. Towns and villages where Serbs and Croats had lived together since the 1940s were torn apart as each ethnic group rounded up and massacred members of the other.

Nationalism, particularly Serb and Croat nationalism, had long dogged Yugoslavia's firmly federal political system. Feelings ran especially deep among Serbs. Serbian national myths reach back to the Middle Ages, and the country also has more recent traditions of political separatism on ethnic grounds. Milosevic and the Serb nationalists who gathered around him ignited those political flashpoints in ways that caught the fears and frustrations

The next conflict came in the same place that in 1914 had sparked a much larger war: the province of Bosnia-Hercegovina. Bosnia was the most ethnically diverse republic in Yugoslavia. Its capital, Sarajevo, was home to several major ethnic groups and had often been praised as an example of peaceful coexistence. When Bosnia

Representing the People in Eastern Europe, 1989

The enthusiasm of the mass demonstrations that preceded the revolutionary changes in Eastern Europe in 1989 gave the events a sense of immediate drama, and images of Eastern Europeans massed together in protest, crossing boundaries that had been closed to them, and celebrating the downfall of their repressive governments spread quickly around the world. The symbolism of these images was stark and resonated with a triumphant story about the progress of democratic ideals in an increasingly unified and integrated Europe. In the East, the people's desire to join with the West, long denied, had finally been realized.

The unity of these early days nevertheless obscured a basic uncertainty about the aspirations of the populations of the newly independent nations in Eastern Europe. Many East Germans expressed reservations about the rapid pace of German reunification, and people from the West and the East continued to talk about "the wall in the head" long after the Berlin wall had been torn down. The unity of Czechoslovakia's peaceful velvet revolution in 1989 led quickly to the "velvet divorce" that produced the dissolution of Czechoslovakia into the Czech Republic and Slovakia in 1993. Throughout the region, many commentators continued to speak of a persistent *Ostalgia*—a nostalgia for an alternative Eastern European past that had been lost in the abrupt transition.

We have seen in earlier chapters how representations of the people served to give meaning to moments of rapid social and political change in the French Revolution or in the unification of Germany. The images here, from media coverage of the events of 1989, also serve to frame the interpretations that contemporaries gave to the unfolding events. Image A shows a crowd in Prague waving the Czechoslovakian flag in November 1989. Image B shows a line of East Berliners forming in front of a West Berlin grocery store in the days after the fall of the Berlin Wall. Image C shows the last of the Leipzig Monday demonstrations on March 12, 1990—the caption reads, "Also after the last demonstration: We are the People. We are *one* people."

A. Crowd during Czechoslovakia's Velvet Revolution.

seceded from Yugoslavia in 1992, ethnic coexistence came apart. Bosnia began the war with no formal army: armed bands equipped by the governments of Serbian Yugoslavia, Croatia, and Bosnia battled each other throughout the new country. The Serbs and Croats, both of whom disliked the Muslim Bosnians, were especially well equipped and organized. They rained shells and bullets on towns and villages, burned houses with families inside, imprisoned Muslim men in detention camps and starved them to death, and raped thousands of Bosnian women. All sides committed atrocities. The Serbs, however, orchestrated and carried out the worst crimes. These included what came to

B. East Berliners line up to shop in West Berlin, November 12, 1989.

C. "We Are the People. We Are One People."

"We are the people" was the slogan of the weekly demonstrations in Leipzig in 1989 that did so much to discredit the government in the months before the wall fell. "We are *one* people" became the slogan of Helmut Kohl's government as it pushed for rapid reunification of the two Germanies.

Questions for Analysis

1. In image A, how should one interpret the wave of nationalist enthusiasm that engulfed Czechoslovakia in 1989, in light of what we know of the subsequent failure to keep Czechoslovakia together as a unified nation?

2. Photographs such as image B were extremely common in the media in 1989, showing East Berliners shopping in Western stores. What do such images suggest about how the East's previous isolation was interpreted in the West, and what does it say about how both sides may have viewed the consequences of their newfound freedom?

3. What is the difference between "We are the people" and "We are *one* people" as political slogans?

be called ethnic cleansing. This involved sending irregular troops on campaigns of murder and terror through Muslim and Croat territories to encourage much larger populations to flee the area. During the first eighteen months of the fighting as many as 100,000 people were killed, including 80,000 civilians, mostly Bosnian Muslims. Although the campaigns appalled Western governments, those countries worried that intervention would result only in another Vietnam or Afghanistan with no clear resolution of the horrific ethnic slaughter itself. The outside forces, mostly European troops in United Nations blue helmets, concentrated on humanitarian relief, separating combatants, and creating safe areas for persecuted ethnic populations from all parties.

The crisis came to a head in the autumn of 1995. Sarajevo had been under siege for three years, but a series of mortar attacks on public marketplaces in Sarajevo produced fresh Western outrage and moved the United States to act. Already Croat forces and the Bosnian army had turned the war on the ground against the Serb militias, and now they were supported by a rolling wave of American air strikes. The American bombing, combined with a Croat-Bosnian offensive, forced the Bosnian Serbs to negotiate. Elite French troops supported by British artillery broke the siege of Sarajevo. Peace talks were held at Dayton, Ohio. The agreement divided Bosnia, with the majority of land in the hands of Muslims and Croats and a small, autonomous "Serb Republic" in areas that included land ethnically cleansed in 1992. Stability was restored, but three years of war had killed over 200,000 people.

The legacy of Bosnia flared into conflict again over Kosovo, the medieval homeland of the Orthodox Christian Serbs, now occupied by a largely Albanian, Muslim population. Milosevic accused the Albanians of plotting secession and of challenging the Serb presence in Kosovo. In the name of a "greater Serbia," Serb soldiers fought Albanian separatists rallying under the banner of "greater Albania." Both sides used terrorist tactics. Western nations were anx-

ious lest the conflict might spread to the strategic, ethnically divided country of Macedonia and touch off a general Balkan conflict. Western political opinion was outraged, however, as Serbian forces used many of the same murderous tactics in Kosovo that they had employed earlier in Bosnia. Talks between Milosevic's government and the Albanian rebels were sponsored by the NATO powers but fell apart in early 1999. That failure was followed by a fresh wave of American-led bombing against Serbia itself, as well as against Serbian forces in Kosovo. A new round of ethnic cleansing drove hundreds of thousands of Albanians from their homes. Unwilling to fight a war on the ground in the mountainous, unforgiving terrain of the southern Balkans, the United States and its European allies concentrated on strategic attacks on bridges, power plants, factories, and Serbian military bases. The Russian government, bothered by this unilateral attack on fellow Slavs, nonetheless played an important part in brokering a cease-fire. Milosevic was forced to withdraw from Kosovo, leaving it in the hands of another force of armed NATO peacekeepers.

Finally, Serb-dominated Yugoslavia, worn by ten years of war and economic sanctions, turned against Milosevic's regime. Wars and corruption had destroyed Milosevic's credentials as a nationalist and populist. After he attempted to reject the results of a democratic election in 2000, his government fell to popular protests. He died in 2006, while being tried by a UN tribunal for war crimes.

As we gain perspective on the twentieth century, it is clear that the Yugoslavian wars of the 1990s were not an isolated instance of Balkan violence. The issues are thoroughly Western. The Balkans form one of the West's borderlands, where cultures influenced by Roman Catholicism, Eastern Orthodoxy, and Islam meet, overlap, and contend for political domination and influence. Since the nineteenth century, this region of enormous religious, cultural, and ethnic diversity has struggled with the implications of nationalism. We have seen how conflicts over the creation of new national states drawn

MASS FUNERAL IN KOSOVO, 1999. Ethnic Albanians bury victims of a Serbian massacre toward the end of Yugoslavia's ten years of fighting. ▪ *Although the nature of war has changed radically in the last hundred years, "ethnic cleansing" has remained remarkably constant and frequent in the modern period. What prevents states from taking effective action to prevent it?*

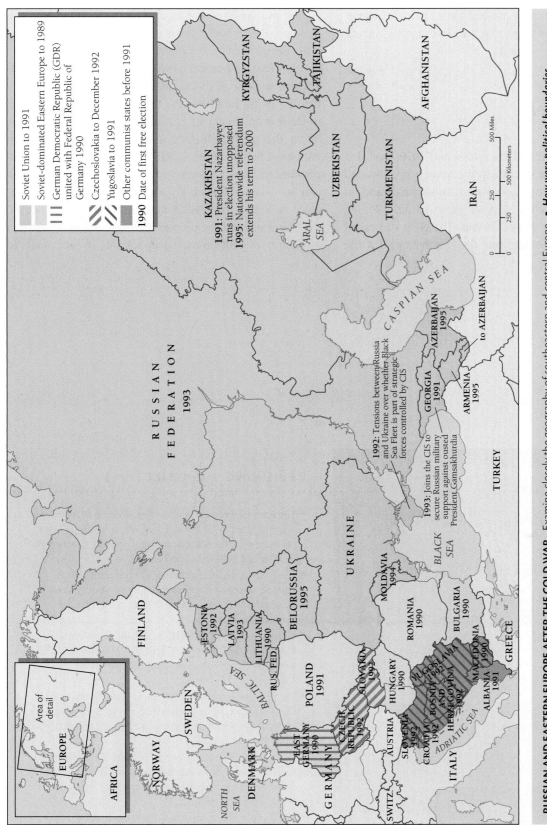

KAZAKHSTAN
1991: President Nazarbayev
runs in election unopposed
1995: Nationwide referendum
extends his term to 2000

1992: Tensions between Russia
and Ukraine over whether Black
Sea Fleet is part of strategic
forces controlled by CIS

1993: Joins the CIS to
secure Russian military
support against ousted
President Gamsakhurdia

RUSSIAN AND EASTERN EUROPE AFTER THE COLD WAR. Examine closely the geography of southeastern and central Europe. ■ *How were political boundaries reorganized?* ■ *How did the collapse of the Soviet Union and the end of the Cold War allow for the reemergence of certain forces in the political landscape of Europe?* ■ *How were the boundaries of the Soviet Union reorganized after 1991?*

mostly on ethnic lines were worked out in Central Europe, with many instances of tragic violence. The Yugoslav wars fit into some of the same patterns.

CONCLUSION

The protest movements of the 1960s and 1970s revealed that postwar hopes for stability in Western Europe through economic development alone were shortsighted, and in any case, the astounding rates of growth from 1945 to 1968 could not be sustained forever. The great success of these first postwar decades was the establishment of the European Common Market and the spirit of cooperation between Western European nations that had only a few years before been locked in deadly conflict.

The Eastern European revolutions of 1989 and the subsequent collapse of the Soviet Union were a revolutionary turning point, however, and posed challenging questions to those who sought to guarantee stability by continuing down the path of further integration among European nations. Like the French Revolution of 1789, the 1989 revolutions brought down not only a regime but also an empire. Like the French Revolution, they gave way to violence, and like the French Revolution, they provided no easy consensus for the peoples who were left to reconstruct some form of political and social stability in their wake. In

After You Read
This Chapter

Visit StudySpace for quizzes, additional review materials, and multimedia documents. **wwnorton.com/web/westernciv18**

REVIEWING THE OBJECTIVES

- The success of economic rebuilding after the Second World War produced a new prosperity in Western Europe. What contributed to this success, and what were its effects on daily life and mass culture in Europe?

- The postwar decades witnessed an important shift in attitudes about women and their place in society. What caused this shift, and what were its consequences for European women?

- In Europe and the United States, significant movements of social and political protest emerged in the 1960s. What were the goals of these movements, and what did they accomplish?

- The postwar economic boom ended in the 1970s, leading to a prolonged period of economic contraction. What were the consequences of this recession for governments and populations in Europe?

- In the 1980s, Mikhail Gorbachev proposed reforms for the Soviet Union, reforms that failed to prevent the collapse of the Soviet bloc in Eastern Europe. What combination of events led to this collapse?

- The first post-Soviet decade in Europe was marked by political uncertainty, economic dislocation, and violence, with war in Yugoslavia and Chechnya. What circumstances made these years so difficult for Europeans?

the former Yugoslavia, in Slovakia, and in Russia itself, the uncertainty of the post-1989 years gave fresh impetus to energetic nationalist movements. Although militant nationalism might be a useful short-term political strategy for certain politicians, such nationalism is unlikely to create stability in Europe, however, because the broad population movements of the postwar years have continued unabated, and there is no part of Europe that possesses the ethnic or cultural homogeneity demanded by hard-line nationalists. Europe's long history is one of heterogeneity, and there is no reason to think that the future will be different in this respect.

Profound differences in wealth and economic capacity between Western and Eastern Europe were the most challenging hurdle to a stable integration of the newly indepen-

dent nations of the post-Soviet empire. In the 1980s, it was possible to imagine that a relatively wealthy country like the Netherlands or Belgium might be willing to subsidize the integration of a less wealthy small country like Portugal into Europe. It has proved quite another task to convince the Dutch, the Belgians, or the Danes to help shoulder the burden for bringing large countries like Ukraine or Turkey into the European fold. Given this difficulty, can one say with confidence where Europe's outermost borders now lie? In the broader context of the global conflicts that emerged in the aftermath of the Cold War, Europe's boundaries and future remain both uncertain and linked to developments elsewhere in the world. This broader context and these global linkages are the subject of the last chapter of this book.

PEOPLE, IDEAS, AND EVENTS IN CONTEXT

- How did the wide availability of the **BIRTH CONTROL PILL** change public attitudes toward sex and sexuality in the 1960s?
- What made the **MASS CULTURE** of the postwar decades different from popular culture in previous historical eras?
- How did the struggles of the **CIVIL RIGHTS MOVEMENT** in the United States affect American efforts to promote democracy in Europe during the Cold War?
- What were the goals of **ALEXANDER DUBČEK**'s government in Czechoslovakia during the **PRAGUE SPRING**?
- How did the **1973 OPEC OIL EMBARGO** affect the economies of Eastern and Western Europe?
- How did **LECH WAŁĘSA** challenge the Polish government in the early 1980s?
- How did **MIKHAIL GORBACHEV** envision reforming the Soviet Union? What did he mean by *PERESTROIKA* and *GLASNOST*?
- What were the **VELVET REVOLUTIONS** of Central and Eastern Europe in 1989?
- What made **NATIONALISM IN YUGOSLAVIA** such a powerful force in Yugoslavia in the early 1990s, and what role did **SLOBODAN MILOSEVIC** play in the breakup of the Yugoslavian federation?

THINKING ABOUT CONNECTIONS

- The wave of protest and cultural discontent that spread throughout Europe in the 1960s encompassed both Western and Eastern Europe, in spite of the divisions imposed by the Cold War. Can one detect an echo of the revolutions of 1848 in the protests of 1968? What common concerns can one detect? What is different?
- Many observers were surprised by the resurgence of nationalism in Eastern Europe in the aftermath of the collapse of the Soviet Union. Can one compare the situation in Yugoslavia after 1989 to circumstances in that part of the world in the late nineteenth century, as Ottoman power waned and the Russian and Austrian Empires competed for influence in the region?

Before
You
Read
This
Chapter

STORY LINES

- After 1989, the trend toward globalization in the twentieth century became more visible. Improved communications and flows of money and products from one part of the world to another offered many opportunities for economic growth but also reinforced existing inequalities among the world's different regions.

- The legacy of colonialism weighed heavily on former colonies, and some became the arena for conflicts related to the Cold War, such as the end of apartheid in South Africa, civil war and ethnic conflict in Rwanda and Zaire, and postwar economic development in Japan and South Korea.

- In the second half of the twentieth century, events in the Middle East took on global significance. The Arab-Israeli conflict, bitterness against foreign interventions in Muslim countries, and frustration with the first generation of nationalist governments in the region led to the development of modern forms of Islamic radicalism aiming at revolutionary change in the Middle East and confrontation with the West.

CHRONOLOGY

1948	State of Israel formed
1948–1949	First Arab-Israeli War
1960	Formation of OPEC
1967	Israel occupies West Bank
1973	Second Arab-Israeli War
1973	Arab members of OPEC announce oil embargo
1978	Camp David Peace Accords
1979	Soviet invasion of Afghanistan
1979	Islamic revolution in Iran
1980–1988	Iran-Iraq War
1991	Persian Gulf War
1994	Genocide against Tutsis in Rwanda
1997	China reclaims Hong Kong
2001	9/11 terrorist attacks
2003	U.S. invasion of Iraq
2008	Global financial crisis
2011	Arab Spring

A World without Walls: Globalization and the West

CORE OBJECTIVES

- **DEFINE** *globalization* and understand what is new about current patterns of interconnection in the world as well as the continuities that can be seen with earlier periods of global connection.

- **EXPLAIN** the continued relevance of the colonial past in shaping the politics, economy, and society of independent states in Asia and Africa and the nature of their ongoing relationships to the societies and states of Europe and North America.

- **UNDERSTAND** the global connections that link societies in other parts of the world to the events and persistent conflicts in the Middle East.

n the twenty-first century, the world has reentered a period in which basic assumptions about the role of nation-states, the roots of prosperity, and the boundaries of cultures are changing fast. We say *reentered* because, as we have seen, a disconcerting sense of seismic and little-understood change has been central to Western culture during several different historical periods. The Industrial Revolution of the nineteenth century is an example, and just as *industrial revolution*, a term coined in the early nineteenth century, seemed to capture contemporaries' perceptions of changes in their own time, so *globalization* seems to capture ours. Globalization is not new, but our acute consciousness of it is.

We know, intuitively, what globalization means: the Internet, protests against the World Trade Organization (WTO), outsourcing of jobs and services, Walmart in Mexico, the dismantling of the Berlin Wall. All of these are powerful images of larger, enormously significant developments. The Internet represents the stunning transformation of global communication, the media, and forms of knowledge. The Berlin Wall once stood for a divided Cold War world; its fall marked a dramatic reconfiguration of international relations, an end to the ideological battle over communism, the creation of new alliances, markets, and communities. The attack on the World Trade Center in 2001 gave the term *globalization* a new and frightening meaning as well. It shattered many Americans' sense of relative isolation and security. Globalization, then, conjures up new possibilities but also new vulnerabilities.

What, precisely, does the term mean? What causes or drives globalization, and what are its effects? To begin simply, globalization means integration. It is the process of creating a rising number of networks—political, social, economic, and cultural—that span larger sections of the globe. New technologies, new economic imperatives, and changing laws have combined to make global exchange faster and, by the same token, to intensify economic, social, and cultural relationships. Information, ideas, goods, and people now move rapidly and easily across national boundaries. Yet *globalization* is not synonymous with *internationalization*, and the distinction is important. International relations are established between nation-states. Global exchange can be quite independent of national control: today trade, politics, and cultural exchange often happen "underneath the radar of the nation-state," in the words of one historian.

Globalization has radically altered the distribution of industry and patterns of trade around the world, as Asian nations in particular emerge as industrial giants and Western powers become increasingly dependent on energy resources drawn from former colonies. Globalization has forced the reorganization of economic enterprises from banking and commerce to manufacturing. Supranational economic institutions such as the International Monetary Fund are examples of globalization and also work to quicken its pace. Likewise, the International Criminal Court represents an important trend in law: the globalization of judicial power. New, rapid, and surprisingly intimate forms of mass communication (blogs, social media sites, Internet-based political campaigns, and so on) have spawned new forms of politics. International human-rights campaigns, for instance, owe an enormous debt to global communications and the communities they create. Perhaps most interesting, the sovereignty of nation-states and the clear boundaries of national communities seem to be eroded by many globalizing trends.

All these developments seem to be characteristic of our time. But are they new? For centuries, religion, empire, commerce, and industry have had globalizing impulses and effects. The East India Companies (Dutch and English), for instance, were to the seventeenth century what Microsoft is to the early twenty-first: the premier global enterprises of the time. Chartered and granted monopolies by the crown, they organized trade, investment of capi-

tal, manufacturing enterprises, and commercial agriculture. The Dutch East India Company's networks reached from Amsterdam to South Africa, through to India and Southeast Asia. The economic development of Europe in general was thoroughly enmeshed in global networks that supplied raw materials, markets, and labor. It has always been hard to strip the "West" of its global dimensions. The movement to abolish slavery was certainly transatlantic, if not global.

For another striking example, consider migration and immigration. We think of the contemporary world as fluid, characterized by vast movements of people. Mass, long-distance migration and immigration, however, peaked during the nineteenth century. Between 1846 (when the first reliable statistics were kept) and 1940, 55 million to 58 million people left Europe for the Americas, especially for the United States, Canada, Argentina, and Brazil. During that same period, 48 million to 52 million Indians and southern Chinese migrated to Southeast Asia, the Southern Pacific, and the areas surrounding the Indian Ocean (many of the Indian migrants went to other parts of the British Empire). Roughly another 50 million people left northeastern Asia and Russia for Manchuria, Siberia, central Asia, and Japan. Faster long-distance transportation (railways and steamships) made these long journeys possible; the industrialization of the receiving regions provided the economic dynamics. As the scholar Adam McKeown writes, the nineteenth century was "a world on the move, flowing into factories, construction projects, mines, plantations, agricultural frontiers, and commercial networks across the globe." The demographic, social, economic, and cultural effects of these migrations were transformative. As McKeown also points out, after the First World War, governments set out to close their gates; from the 1920s on, laborers (and refugees) found it much harder to move. If migration is a measure of globalization, our world is less "globalized" than it was a century ago.

What is more, to equate globalization with integration may be misleading. Globalizing trends do not necessarily produce peace, equality, or homogeneity. Their effects are hard to predict. During the early 1900s, many Europeans firmly believed that the world, at least the part of the world dominated by Western empires, would become harmonious, that Western culture would be exported, and that Western standards were universal. History defied those expectations. Some scholars argue that the term *globalization* should be jettisoned because it suggests a uniform, leveling process, one that operates similarly everywhere. Globalization has very different and disparate effects, effects shaped by vast asymmetries of power and wealth among nations or regions. In the last several decades, worldwide inequality has increased. Global processes encounter obstacles and resistance; they sow division as well as unity. At the level of everyday human contact, globalization has hastened new kinds of cultural blending and new forms of sociability, but it has also produced a backlash against that blending. The heady word *global* can distort our analyses or point us in the wrong direction. As one historian argues, although it is crucial to be able to think outside of "national or continental containers," it would be misleading to believe "that there is no container at all, except the planetary one."

In this chapter, we explore three subjects crucial to our early efforts to understand globalization, especially as it relates to the post–Cold War world of the twenty-first century. The first subject is the set of global changes that have accelerated the free flow of money, people, products, and ideas. The second subject is what we have come to call postcolonial politics—the varied trajectories that mark the contemporary experience of former colonies. Finally, we will consider in greater depth the complex and important role of Middle Eastern politics in contemporary global affairs. Throughout, we hope to suggest ways in which recent developments relate to familiar historical issues we have already examined in other contexts.

LIQUID MODERNITY? THE FLOW OF MONEY, IDEAS, AND PEOPLES

A key feature of late-twentieth-century globalization has been the transformation of the world economy, highlighted by the rapid integration of markets since 1970. In a series of historic changes, the international agreements that had regulated the movement of people, goods, and money since the Second World War were overturned. To begin with, the postwar economic arrangements sealed at Bretton Woods (see Chapter 27) steadily eroded in the late 1960s, as Western industrial nations faced a double burden of inflation and economic stagnation. A crucial shift in monetary policy occurred in 1971, when the United States abandoned the postwar gold standard and allowed the dollar—the keystone of the system—to range freely. As a result, formal regulations on currencies, international banking, and lending among states faded away. They were replaced with an informal network of arrangements managed autonomously by large private lenders, their political friends in leading Western states, and independent financial agencies such as the International Monetary Fund and the World Bank. The economists and administrators who dominated these new networks steered away from the interventionist policies that shaped postwar planning and recovery. Instead, they relied on a broad range of market-driven models dubbed "neoliberalism." In a variation on classic liberal economics, neoliberal economists stressed the value of free markets, profit incentives, and sharp restraints on both budget deficits and social welfare programs, whether run by governments or corporations. The new systems of lending they backed had mixed results, funding breakneck growth in some cases and bringing catastrophic debt in others. Industrial development in the globalized economy has created jarring juxtapositions of development and

"CHECKERBOARD OF POVERTY AND AFFLUENCE." Scenes of slums confronting towering skylines, such as this one from Argentina in 2000, are visible around the world as one of the side effects of development and deterioration.

The Meaning of the "Third World"

Alfred Sauvy, a French demographer, coined the term Third World in a famous 1952 article about the effects of the Cold War on international relations and economic development. The First World was the West, a world of democratic political institutions and capitalist economies. The Second World, in Sauvy's formulation, was the Soviet sphere, committed to socialist institutions. The Third World was everybody else—the world of European colonies and former colonies, marked by the history of imperialism.

Though commonly used between the 1950s and 1980s, the term Third World is less frequently encountered in the present. B. R. Tomlinson, a British economic historian, examines the ways in which the concept was rooted in the ideological world of the Cold War and looks for new vocabulary to tell the history of globalization in the contemporary world.

Alfred Sauvy, "Three Worlds, One Planet" (1952)

We speak voluntarily about two worlds today, about the possibility of war between them, about their coexistence, etc., forgetting too often that there is a third world [. . .] the collectivity called, in the style of the United Nations, the under-developed countries. . . .

[. . .]

Unfortunately, the struggle for the possession of the third world does not allow the two others to simply pursue their own path, believing it to be obviously the best, the "true" way. The Cold War has curious consequences: over there, a morbid fear of espionage has pushed them to the most ferocious isolation. With us, it has caused a halt in social evolution. What good is it to trouble ourselves or deprive ourselves, at a moment when the fear of communism is holding back those who would like to go further [on the path to equality]? Why should we consider any social reforms at all when the progressive majority is split? [. . .] Why worry about it, since there is no opposition?

In this way, any evolution toward the distant future has been halted in both camps, and this obstacle has one cause: the costs of war.

Meanwhile . . . the under-developed nations, the third world, have entered into a new phase. Certain medical techniques have now been introduced suddenly for a simple reason: they are cheap. [. . .] For a few pennies the life of a man can be prolonged for several years. Because of this, these countries now have the mortality that we had in 1914 and the birthrate that we had in the eighteenth century. Certainly, this has resulted in economic improvement, lower infant mortality, better productivity of adults, etc. Nevertheless, it is easy to see how this demographic increase must be accompanied by important investments in order to adapt the container to what it must contain. Now, these vital investments cost much more than 68 francs per person. They crash right into the financial wall imposed by the cold war. The result is eloquent: the millennial cycle of life and death continues to turn, but it is a cycle of poverty. [. . .]

Since the preparation for war is priority number 1, secondary concerns such as world hunger will only occupy our attention enough to avoid an explosion that might compromise our first priority. But when one remembers the enormous errors that conservatives have committed so many times, we can only have a mediocre confidence in the ability of the Americans to play with the fire of popular anger . . . They have not clearly perceived that under-developed nations of a feudal type might evolve more readily towards a communist regime than toward democratic capitalism. One might console oneself, if one were so inclined, by pointing to the greater advance of capitalism, but the fact remains undeniable. And maybe, in the glare of its own vitality, the first world, even in the absence of any human solidarity, might notice this slow, irresistible, humble and ferocious, push toward life. Because in the end, this ignored, exploited Third World, as despised as the Third Estate [in the French Revolution], wants to be something.

B. R. Tomlinson, "What Was the Third World?" (2003)

The term "Third World" was used frequently in histories of the societies, economies and cultures of many parts of the world in the second half of the twentieth century. [. . .] Like other collective descriptions of Africa, Asia, the Middle East, the Pacific islands and Latin America—such as the "South," the "developing world," or the "less-developed world"—the designation "Third World" was more about what such places were not than what they were. [. . .]

Those who developed a concept of the Third World around a set of measurable criteria usually relied on identifying material circumstances. . . . However, all such attempts to establish a standard measurement of relative poverty that can distinguish various parts of the world from each other run into considerable difficulties. It has often been argued that the various countries of Asia, Africa and Latin America (not to mention the Pacific islands and elsewhere) differ greatly in their size, political ideologies, social structures, economic performance, cultural backgrounds and historical experiences. These differences exist not simply between Third World countries, but within them as well. There are rich and poor people, empowered and disempowered citizens, to be found inside all states and societies in the world.

It was over broad issues of economic development that the fiercest battles for the concept of the Third World were fought. Orthodox development economists in the 1950s and 1960s had suggested that the poverty of non-western economies was the result of low levels of savings and investment, and that these problems could best be resolved by increasing external influence over them to help local élites modernize their societies (in other words, make them more like those of the West) by providing technology and education to increase productivity and output. [. . .]

To many radical critics, these ideas, and the U.S. government's development policies that flowed from them, seemed to mask a narrow political agenda that sought to justify the dominance of free-market capitalism as a model and mechanism for economic, social and cultural development. One powerful reaction to this agenda was to argue that dependence on the West had distorted the economic and social conditions of non-western societies, leading to a common process of historical change in the periphery of the world economy brought about by "a situation in which the economy of certain countries [and hence their social and political structures] is conditioned by the development and expansion of another economy to which the former is subjected." [. . .]

[. . .]

The history of imperialism has been immensely important in shaping our view of the modern world, both from the top down and from the bottom up, but the phenomenon was also historically specific, and represents only one stage in the process of understanding the interaction between the local and the global. To write the history of the "Rest," as well as of the West, we need now to move on, and to construct new narratives of global history that go beyond the models of coherent and distinct communities, nations and states, arranged into hierarchies of material achievement and cultural power, and underpinned by universal institutional ideals of participatory democracy and free markets, that dominated thinking about international and local systems in the world for much of the nineteenth and twentieth centuries. [. . .]

Sources: Alfred Sauvy, "Trois mondes, une planète," first published in *L'Observateur* 14 (August 1952), p. 5. This translation, by Joshua Cole, comes from a French reprint in *Vingtième Siècle*, no. 12 (October–December 1986), pp. 81–83; B. R. Tomlinson, "What Was the Third World?," *Journal of Contemporary History* 38, no. 2 (April 2003), pp. 307–21.

Questions for Analysis

1. In Sauvy's argument, what do the "under-developed nations" have in common? Does Tomlinson agree?

2. Sauvy calls for the First World to invest in the Third World to prevent an explosion of anger. What possible difficulties with this solution did Tomlinson identify?

3. How do Sauvy and Tomlinson see the relationship between the Cold War and the problem of understanding the "Third World?"

deterioration across entire continents and even within single cities—a phenomenon described as a "checkerboard of poverty and affluence."

At the same time, the world's local, national, and regional economies became far more connected and interdependent. Export trade flourished and, with the technological advances of the 1960s and 1980s, came to include an increasing proportion of high-technology goods. The boom in export commerce was tied to important changes in the division of labor worldwide. More industrial jobs emerged in the postcolonial world, not just among the Asian "tigers" but also in India, Latin America, and elsewhere. Although such steady, skilled manual employment started to disappear in Western nations—often replaced by lower-paying menial work—financial and service sector employment leaped ahead. The exchange and use of goods became much more complex. Goods were designed by companies in one country, manufactured in another, and tied into a broader interchange of cultures. Taken together, these global economic changes had deep political effects, forcing painful debates about the nature of citizenship and entitlement inside national borders, about the power and accountability of transnational corporations, and about the human and environmental costs of global capitalism.

Another crucial change involved not only the widespread flow of information but also the new commercial

AN AFGHAN GIRL WEEDS A POPPY FIELD, 2004. Though Afghanistan was historically a center for the silk trade, opium is its most important cash crop today. ▪ *How is this development related to globalization?*

and cultural importance attached to information itself. Electronic systems and devices designed to create, store, and share information multiplied, becoming staggeringly more powerful and accessible—none with so great an impact on the everyday lives of men and women around the world as the personal computer. By the early 1990s, increasingly sophisticated computers brought people into instant communication with each other across continents, not only by new means but also in new cultural and political settings. Electronic communications over the Internet gave a compelling new meaning to the term *global village*. The Internet revolution shared features of earlier print revolutions. It was pioneered by entrepreneurs with utopian ambitions and driven by the new network's ability to deliver personal or commercial messages as well as culturally illicit and politically scandalous material that could be published easily and informally. It offered new possibilities to social and political groups, constituting new "publics." And it attracted large, established corporate interests, eager to cash in on new channels of culture and business.

However common their use seems, the Internet and similar technologies have had wide-ranging effects on political struggles around the globe. Embattled ethnic minorities have found worldwide audiences through online campaign sites. Satellite television arguably sped the sequence of popular revolts in Eastern Europe in 1989. That same year, fax machines brought Chinese demonstrators at Tiananmen Square news of international support for their efforts. Meanwhile, leaps forward in electronic technologies provided new worldwide platforms for commercial interests. Companies such as Sony, RCA, and others produced entertainment content, including music, motion pictures, and television shows as well as the electronic equipment to play that content. Bill Gates's Microsoft emerged as the world's major producer of computer software—with a corporate profit margin that surpassed Spain's gross domestic product. At the level of production, marketing, and management, information industries are global, spread widely across the United States, India, Western Europe, and parts of the developing world. Their corporate headquarters, however, typically remain in the West and support neoliberal politics. The international media, news, and entertainment conglomerates run by the Australian Rupert Murdoch or by Time Warner, for example, are firmly allied to U.S. institutions and worldviews, edging aside state-run companies.

Like the movement of money, goods, and ideas, the flow of labor has become a central aspect of globalization. Since 1945, the widespread migration of peoples, particularly between former colonies and imperial powers, has changed everyday life around the world. Groups of immigrant workers have filled the lower rungs of expanding economies not only in Europe but also in oil-rich Arab states that attracted Asian and Filipino laborers and in the United States, where both permanent and seasonal migrations from Mexico and other Latin American nations have spread across the continent. This fusion of peoples and cultures has produced striking new blends of music, food, language, and other forms of popular culture and sociability. These seem novel until we think of Creole cultures formed in the New World from the sixteenth to the eighteenth centuries. It has also raised tensions over the definition of citizenship and the boundaries of political and cultural communities—familiar themes from modern history. As a result, cycles of violent xenophobic backlash, bigotry, and political extremism have appeared in host countries and regions, but so too have new conceptions of civil rights and cultural belonging.

As suggested earlier, sharp divides exist between the most successful global players and the poorer, disadvantaged, sometimes embattled states and cultures. In one particular area of manufacture, however, poorer postcolonial regions have been able to respond to a steady and immensely profitable market in the West. The production of illegal drugs such as opium, heroin, and cocaine is a thriving industry in countries such as Colombia, Myanmar (formerly Burma), and Malaysia. Though the trade in such substances is banned, the fragile economies of the countries where they are produced have encouraged public and private powers to turn a blind eye to their production—or even to intervene for their own profit. Other, similar forms of illegal commerce have also grown far beyond the old label of "organized crime" in their structure and political importance. Trafficking in illegal immigrants, the management of corrupt financial dealings, trade in illicit animal products, and "conflict" diamonds from several brutal postcolonial civil wars are all indicative of this trend. The organizations behind these criminal trades grew out of the political violence and economic breakdown of failing postcolonial states or from the human and commercial traffic between these parts of the world and leading Western economic powers. They have exploited cracks, loopholes, and unsupervised opportunities in the less regulated system of global trade and carved out centers of power not directly subject to the laws of any single state.

Demographics and Global Health

The developments of globalization are tied in complex ways to the evolving size and health of the world's population. Between 1800 and the middle of the twentieth century, the worldwide population roughly tripled, rising from 1 to 3 billion. Between 1960 and 2012, however, population more than doubled again, to 7 billion. Huge, if uneven, improvements in basic standards of health, particularly for young children and childbearing women, contributed to the increase—as did local efforts to improve the urban-industrial environment. Asia's population as a whole has increased nearly fourfold since 1900, to nearly two-thirds of the world's present population. Such growth has strained underdeveloped social services, public-health facilities, and urban infrastructures, increasing the potential for epidemic disease as well as for cycles of ethnic and ideological violence nursed by poverty and dislocation.

A different type of demographic crisis confronts parts of the West, where steadily shrinking populations erode social welfare systems. Longer life spans, broadened welfare programs, and rising health-care costs have contributed to the challenge. Populations in the United States and Great Britain have been stable or have been slowly expanded by immigration; in Italy, Scandinavia, and, recently, Russia, sharp drops in the birth rate have led to population decline. Declining birth rates have been accompanied by growing populations of older adults, whose health and vitality resulted from decades of improved medical standards and state-run entitlement programs. Maintaining the long-term solvency of such programs poses difficult choices for European countries in particular, as they struggle to balance guarantees of social well-being with fiscal and political realities.

GOVERNMENT EFFORTS TO CURTAIL THE SPREAD OF SEVERE ACUTE RESPIRATORY SYNDROME (SARS). In May 2003, migrant workers at a Beijing railway station line up to have their temperatures checked before boarding the trains.

José Bové, The World Is Not for Sale: Farmers against Junk Food *(2001)*

In 1999, José Bové, a sheep farmer from central France well known for his militancy, helped organize a group of activists from a local agricultural union in a demonstration against a local McDonald's restaurant. Bové claimed that McDonald's was a symbol of "economic imperialism" and his group's protest received much popular support from others in France after its action. Bové himself was imprisoned for three months after the affair and served another ten months in 2003 for destroying transgenic crops.

 ou've got to link McDonald's to the issue of hormone-treated meat. At our Congress in Vesoul in April 1999, we'd already raised the question of preparing ourselves for American retaliation against Europe's ban on the import of hormone-treated beef. In February 1998, the World Trade Organization had condemned the European Union's ban, and given it fifteen months to get its house back in order—that is to reopen its frontiers. This deadline had expired on 13 May 1999, so the American move came as no surprise. We had already envisaged linking the issue of hormones and McDonald's. What we had not foreseen, however, was that

Roquefort, the main produce of the farmers in my area, would be included in the hundred or so products affected by a 100 per cent Customs surcharge on entering the States.

In Washington, the price of Roquefort shot up from $30 a kilo to $60, effectively prohibiting its sale. Around the same time, we found out that a McDonald's was being constructed in Millau. . . .

We sell 440 tonnes of cheese annually to the States, worth 30 million francs. Given that the cost of the milk is half the value of the Roquefort, the producers are losing 15 million francs; this represents 3 million litres of milk out of the 80 million used in the annual production of Roquefort. As a result, the professional

association resorted to new measures: 10,000 pamphlets were printed and distributed across the region, including campsites and village fêtes. Posters were put up everywhere, and in Millau itself large banners proclaimed: "No to the US embargo on Roquefort." It was in the spirit of these activities that we decided, at a meeting of the SPLB, to pay a visit to McDonald's. . . .

The objective was to have a non-violent but symbolically forceful action, in broad daylight and with the largest possible participation. We wanted the authorities to be fully aware of what was going to happen, so we explained to the police in advance that the purpose of the rally was to dismantle the McDonald's. The police notified the regional govern-

---

Globalization has also changed public health and medicine, creating dangerous new threats as well as promising new treatments. Better and more comprehensive health care has generally accompanied other kinds of prosperity and has thus been more accessible in the West. In Africa, Latin America, and elsewhere, political chaos, imbalances of trade, and the practices of some large pharmaceutical companies have often resulted in shortages of medicine and a rickety medical infrastructure, making it difficult to combat deadly new waves of disease. Indeed, the worldwide risk of exposure to epidemic diseases is a new reality of globalization—a product of increased cultural interaction, exposure of new ecosystems to human development, and the speed of intercontinental transportation. By the

1970s, the acceleration of airplane travel led to fears that an epidemic would leapfrog the globe much faster than the pandemics of the Middle Ages. Such fears were confirmed by the worldwide spread of infection by HIV, whose final stage is AIDS, which first appeared at the end of the 1970s. As HIV-AIDS became a global health crisis—particularly in Africa, where the disease spread catastrophically—international organizations recognized the need for an early, swift, and comprehensive response to future outbreaks of disease. In 2003, the successful containment of an outbreak of severe acute respiratory syndrome (SARS) demonstrated the effectiveness of this planning.

Meanwhile, the work of multinational medical research firms continued to extend the ability to pre-ment, and they called back to say they would ask the McDonald's manager to provide a billboard or something similar for us to demolish. This, he said, would allow for a symbolic protest. We replied that this idea was ludicrous, and that it remained our intention to dismantle the doors and windows of the building. The police deemed it unnecessary to mount a large presence. We asked them to make sure that the site would be clear of workers, and that no tools were left lying around.

It all happened as we'd envisaged. The only odd thing was the presence of some ten plainclothes police officers armed with cameras. The demo took place and people, including kids, began to dismantle the inside of the building, taking down partitions, some doors, fuseboxes, and some tiles from the roof—they were just nailed down, and came off very easily; in fact the whole building appeared to have been assembled from a kit. The structure was very flimsy. While some people started to repaint the roof of the restau-

rant, others began loading bits of the structure on to tractor trailers. One of the trailers was a grain carrier. As soon as the trailers were loaded, everyone left the site. Children clambered on the grain wagon and used wooden sticks to bang on the sides, and the whole lot proceeded in the direction of the prefecture, seat of the regional government.

As the procession wound its way through the town, the festive atmosphere was further heightened by the cheering of local people who had gathered to watch us go by. We unloaded everything in front of the prefecture. It was a beautiful day, everyone was having a good time, and many people ended up on the terraces of Millau's restaurants. . . .

We didn't want McDonald's to be seen as the prime target. It's merely a symbol of economic imperialism. Besides, we never called for a boycott of McDonald's. The journalists grasped that pretty quickly, and most of them latched on to the ideas behind the McDonald's symbol. Our political leaders, however, tried to

talk up the anti-American element: some by playing the "typically" Gallic card, others by invoking "sovereignty" in a way that fuelled nationalism. This was the populist side of things: it's easy enough to rubbish America, to discard a problem as not being of direct concern to us, rather than to confront it. From this point of view, it was very easy for our leaders to support our actions.

Source: José Bové and François Dufour, *The World Is Not for Sale: Farmers against Junk Food* (London: 2001), pp. 3–13.

Questions for Analysis

1. Were Bové's motivations strictly economic? Was he simply protesting the surcharge on European goods entering the U.S. market?

2. What made McDonald's a tempting target for the French activists?

3. Is Bové anti-American? What precisely was the target of this protest? What did he think he was defending?

vent and treat disease. One of the most powerful tools in this endeavor was the development of genetic engineering, which stemmed from the monumental discovery of DNA in the 1950s. By the 1990s, several laboratories were engaged in the most ambitious medical research ever attempted: the mapping of the human genome—that is, the entire architecture of chromosomes and genes contained in basic human DNA. Through this process and alongside it, genetic engineers developed methods to alter the biology of living things. Infertile couples, for instance, could now conceive through out-of-body medical procedures. Genetic engineers developed—and patented—strains of mice and other laboratory animals that carried chemical markers, cells, even organs, of other species. By

1997, British researchers succeeded in producing a clone (an exact genetic copy) of a sheep. It is now possible to determine the genetic makeup of any individual human and measure their chances of developing many cancers or other life-threatening diseases and conditions. The rapidly developing field of epigenetics has been able to trace the effects of behaviors such as smoking through more than one generation, demonstrating that the choices made by a grandparent can affect the genes of their grandchildren. These developments raise provocative questions about the relationship between individual responsibility and public health, about how scientists should understand biological "defects" and diversions from genetic norms, and about the privacy of medical information. As a new form of knowledge in an age of global interconnection, genetic engineering leaped across the legal and moral boundaries of human societies. The question of who would govern these advances—nations, international bodies, or local cultural and religious communities—was opened to passionate debate. So were fresh arguments about where to draw lines between lifesaving intervention and cultural preference, between individual agency and biological determinism. Like past scientific investigations directed at humankind, genetics has raised fundamental questions about ethics, citizenship, and the measure of humanity.

Perhaps no issue raises thornier questions about the relationship among population, economic development, and public welfare than the matter of climate change. Climate scientists now largely agree that the average temperature of the planet is rising steadily as a result of increases in carbon dioxide in the atmosphere produced by the burning of fossil fuels. Every year of the twenty-first century has ranked among the fourteen hottest since records were first kept in 1880. Scientists now say that the evidence points to a pattern of global warming produced by human activity. The consequences of this warming are now thought to be substantial: a rise in sea levels as polar ice caps melt; an increase in the frequency of heat waves, droughts, rainfall intensity, coastal flooding; and possibly, increases in the frequency and severity of storms, tornados, and tropical cyclones.

Governments first sounded the alarm about climate change in the early 1990s, but it proved hard to establish a coordinated policy because individual nations worried about compromising their economic competitiveness. Energy producers and economic interests whose profits and growth depended on the burning of fossil fuels were resistant to pollution limits or requirements that they adopt expensive "clean" technologies. Few imagined that it would be easy to change the behavior of consumers in developed countries whose lifestyle depended on easy access to electric power produced by the burning of coal, manufactured goods from distant places, cheap air travel, and the automobile. Changing consumer habits, finding alternative energy sources and developing new technologies to remove carbon from the atmosphere may take years. Finding policy solutions is doubly difficult because those parts of the globe that are most closely associated with pollution caused by the burning of fossil fuels—industrialized societies in Europe and North America—are not necessarily those who will feel its effects the most acutely in the near term. Those impacted will be mainly poorer countries in the global south that have few resources to cope with the effects of climate change on their populations.

Since the 1990s, international efforts to coordinate a response to climate change focused on a UN-sponsored agreement known as the Kyoto Protocol, but the United States never joined the agreement. Current efforts are now focused on allowing market forces to generate incentives for reducing pollution through emissions trading. Under this "cap and trade" system, a central authority would allocate permits to pollute at a certain level (the "cap") and demand that industries hold the necessary permits to maintain their operations. Industries that managed to reduce their emissions could sell the permits that they did not need on the open market to other firms (the "trade"), thus generating incentives to reduce emissions on a global scale while simultaneously allowing for continued economic development. These hotly debated issues about climate change clearly illustrate the necessity of global thinking in the contemporary world.

AFTER EMPIRE: POSTCOLONIAL POLITICS IN THE GLOBAL ERA

Even after the superpower rivalry of the Cold War collapsed, another legacy of the postwar era continued to shape international relations into the twenty-first century. The so-called postcolonial relationships between former colonies and Western powers emerged from the decolonization struggles detailed in Chapter 27. Former colonies, as well as other nations that had fallen under the political and economic sway of imperial powers, gained formal independence at the least, along with new kinds of cultural and political authority. In other respects, however, very little changed for people in the former colonies. The very term *postcolonial* underlines the fact that colonialism's legacies endured even after independence. Within these regions, political communities new and old handled the legacies of empire and the postcolonial future in a variety of ways. In some cases the former colonizers or their local allies retained so much power that formal independence actually meant very little. In others, bloody independence struggles poisoned the political culture. The emergence of new states and new kinds of politics was sometimes propelled by economic goals, sometimes by the revival of cultural identities that preceded colonization, and in other cases by ethnic conflict. The results ranged from breakneck industrial success to ethnic slaughter, from democratization to new local models of absolutism. During the Cold War, these postcolonial regions were often the turf on which the superpower struggle was waged. They benefited from superpower patronage but also became the staging ground for proxy wars funded by the West in the fight against communism. Their various trajectories since 1989 point to the complex legacy of the imperial past in the post–Cold War world of globalization.

Emancipation and Ethnic Conflict in Africa

The legacies of colonialism weighed heavily on sub-Saharan Africa. Most of the continent's former colonies came into their independence after the Second World War with their basic infrastructures deteriorating after decades of imperial negligence. The Cold War decades brought scant improvement, as governments across the continent were plagued by both homegrown and externally imposed corruption, poverty, and civil war. In sub-Saharan Africa, two very different trends began to emerge around 1989, each shaped by a combination of the end of the Cold War and volatile local conditions.

The first trend can be seen in South Africa, where politics had revolved for decades around the brutal racial policies of apartheid, sponsored by the white minority government. The most prominent opponent of apartheid, Nelson Mandela, who led the African National Congress (ANC), had been imprisoned since 1962. Intense repression and violent conflict continued into the 1980s and reached a dangerous impasse by the end of the decade. Then the South African government chose a daring new tack: in early 1990, it released Mandela from prison. He resumed leadership of the ANC and turned the party toward a combination of renewed public demonstrations and plans for negotiation politics changed within the Afrikaner-dominated white regime as well when F. W. de Klerk succeeded P. W. Botha as prime minister. A pragmatist who feared civil war and national collapse over apartheid, de Klerk was well matched to Mandela. In March 1992, the two men began direct talks to establish majority rule. Legal and constitutional reforms followed, and in May 1994, during elections in which all South Africans took part, Nelson Mandela was chosen the country's first black president. Although many of his government's efforts to reform housing, the economy, and public health foundered, Mandela defused the climate of organized racial violence. He also gained and kept tremendous personal popularity among black and white South Africans alike as a living symbol of a new political culture.

NELSON MANDELA VOTES IN SOUTH AFRICA'S FIRST DEMOCRATIC ELECTIONS, 1994. He would be elected the country's president.

Mandela's popularity extended abroad, within sub-Saharan Africa and worldwide. In a number of smaller postcolonial states such as Benin, Malawi, and Mozambique, the early 1990s brought political reforms that ended one-party or one-man rule in favor of parliamentary democracy and economic reform.

The other major trend ran in a different, less encouraging direction. Some former autocracies gave way to calls for pluralism, but other states across the continent collapsed into ruthless ethnic conflict. In Rwanda, a former Belgian colony, conflicts between the Hutu and Tutsi populations erupted into a highly organized campaign of genocide against the Tutsi after the country's president was assassinated. Carried out by ordinary Hutus of all backgrounds, the ethnic slaughter left over 800,000 Tutsi dead in a matter of weeks. International pressure eventually turned local Rwandan politics against the perpetrators. Many of them fled to neighboring Zaire and became hired mercenaries in the many-sided civil war that followed the collapse of

Mobutu Sese Seko, the country's long-time dictator, infamous for diverting billions of dollars in foreign aid into his personal bank accounts. A number of ambitious neighboring countries intervened in Zaire, hoping not only to secure its valuable resources but also to settle conflicts with their own ethnic minorities that spilled over the border. Fighting continued through the late 1990s into the new century, dubbed "Africa's world war" by many observers. Public services, normal trade, even basic health and safety inside Zaire—renamed the Democratic Republic of Congo by an ineffective government in Kinshasa—collapsed. By 2008, 5.4 million people had died in the war and its aftermath, the equivalent of losing the entire population of Denmark in a single decade. As of 2013, the fighting remained unresolved.

Economic Power on the Pacific Rim

By the end of the twentieth century, East Asia had become a center of industrial and manufacturing production. China, whose communist government began to establish commercial ties with the West in the 1970s, was the world's leading heavy industrial producer by the year 2000. Its state-owned companies acquired contracts from Western firms to produce products cheaply and in bulk, for sale back to home markets in the United States and Europe. In a deliberate reversal of Europe's nineteenth-century intrusions on the China trade, Beijing established semicapitalist commercial zones around major port cities like Shanghai, a policy whose centerpiece was the reclamation of Hong Kong from Britain in 1997. The commercial zones were intended to encourage massive foreign investment on terms that left China a favorable balance of trade for its huge volume of cheap exports. In practice, they enjoyed only mixed success. Downturns in farming and a looming energy crisis hampered prosperity and economic growth inland, but Hong Kong worked to maintain its economic and cultural middle ground with the rest of the world as it had since the days of the opium trade (see Chapter 22).

Other Asian nations emerged as global commercial powers as well. Industry flourished in a string of countries, starting with Japan and extending along Asia's Pacific coastline into Southeast Asia and Oceania, during the decades after the Second World War. By the 1980s, their robust industrial expansion and their apparent staying power earned them the collective nickname of "the tigers," taken from the ambitious, forward-looking tiger in Chinese mythology. These Pacific rim states collectively formed the most important industrial region in the world outside the United States and Europe. Among them, Japan not only led the way but also became the most influential model of success, with a postwar revival that eventually surpassed West Germany's economic miracle (see Chapter 28). Japanese firms concentrated on the efficiency and technical reliability of their products: fuel-efficient cars, specialty steel, small electronic goods, and so on. Japanese diplomacy and large state subsidies supported the success of Japanese firms, while a well-funded program of technical education hastened research and development of new goods. Japanese firms also appeared to benefit from collective loyalty among civil servants and corporate managers, attitudes that were encouraged by Japan's long experience of trade guilds and feudal politics. Other East Asian nations, newer or less stable than Japan, tried to mimic its success. Some, such as South Korea and the Chinese Nationalist stronghold of Taiwan, treated the creation of prosperity as a fundamental patriotic duty. In postcolonial nations such as Malaysia and Indonesia, governments parlayed their natural resources and expansive local labor

INDUSTRIALIZATION IN CHINA, 2002. The Three Gorges Dam on the Yan River in Yichang is the largest hydroelectric dam in the world. It has been called the largest construction project in China since the Great Wall.

pools (which had made them attractive to imperial powers in earlier times) into investment for industrialization. As in China, the factories that emerged were either subsidiaries of Western companies or operated on their behalf in new multinational versions of the putting-out system of early industrialization.

The Pacific rim's boom, however, also contained the makings of a first "bust." During the 1990s, a confluence of factors resulted in an enormous slowdown of growth and the near collapse of several currencies. Japan experienced rising production costs, overvalued stocks, and rampant speculation on its high-priced real estate market. When the bubble economy burst in 1991, Japan entered a "lost decade" of economic stagnation that hit bottom in 2003. In Southeast Asia, states such as Indonesia found they had to pay the difference on overvalued industrial capital to Western lenders who set rigid debt repayment schedules. Responses to the economic downturn varied widely. In South Korea, an older generation that remembered economic catastrophe after the Korean War responded to national calls for sacrifice, frequently by investing their own savings to prop up ailing companies. Japan launched programs of monetary austerity to cope with its first serious spike in unemployment in two generations. In Indonesia, inflation and unemployment reignited sharp ethnic conflicts that prosperity and violent state repression had dampened in earlier times. This predominantly Muslim country, with a long tradition of tolerance and pluralism inside the faith, also saw outbursts of violent religious fundamentalism popularly associated with another region—the Middle East.

A NEW CENTER OF GRAVITY: ISRAEL, OIL, AND POLITICAL ISLAM IN THE MIDDLE EAST

Perhaps no other region has drawn more attention from the West in the age of globalization than the Middle East, where a volatile combination of Western military, political, and economic interests converged with deep-seated regional conflicts and transnational Islamic politics. The results of this ongoing confrontation promise to shape the twenty-first century. Here we consider three of the most important aspects of recent history in the region. First is the unfolding of the Arab-Israeli conflict. Second is the region's vital development as the global center of oil production. The third emerges from inside the Arab world, largely as

a reaction against the recent relations with the West. This is the development of a specific, modern brand of Islamic radicalism that challenges the legacies of imperialism and promises revolutionary and sometimes apocalyptic change in postcolonial nations and whose most violent elements generate a cycle of fear, anger, and ultimately direct conflict with Western governments.

The Arab-Israeli Conflict

As we saw in Chapter 27, Israel's existence was a battleground from the start. The national aspirations of Jewish immigrants from Europe fleeing the Holocaust and violent postwar anti-Semitism clashed with the motives of pan-Arabists—secular, anticolonial nationalists who urged Arab pride and self-reliance against European domination. By the late 1970s, in the aftermath of two Arab-Israeli wars, it appeared that a generation of fighting might come to an end. American mediators began sponsoring talks to prevent further, sudden outbursts of conflict, while Soviet leaders remained neutral but supportive of peace efforts. Most notably, the Egyptian president Anwar Sadat, who authorized and directed the 1973 war against Israel, decided that coexistence rather than the destruction of Israel was the long-term answer to regional conflict. Aided by the American president Jimmy Carter, Sadat brokered a peace between Egypt and Israel's staunchly conservative leader, Menachem Begin, in 1978. Leaders on both sides of the conflict believed the potential rewards were greater than the obvious risks.

Hopes for a lasting peace were soon dashed. Hostilities escalated between Israel and the Palestinian Arabs displaced by Arab-Israeli warfare, a confrontation that increasingly polarized a much larger group of people. On each side of the Israeli-Palestinian conflict, a potent blend of ethnic and religious nationalism began to control both debate and action. Conservatives in Israel played to a public sentiment that put security ahead of other priorities, particularly among the most recent Jewish immigrants, often from the former Soviet Union. On the other side, younger Palestinians, angered by their elders' failures to provoke revolution, turned against the secular radicalism of the Palestinian Liberation Organization (PLO) and toward radical Islam.

In this combustible political environment, the Palestinians living on the West Bank and in the desperately overcrowded Gaza Strip revolted in an outburst of street rioting in 1987. This rebellion—called the intifada (literally, a "throwing off" or uprising)—continued for years in daily battles between stone-throwing Palestinian youths

Media Representations of Globalization

Because the set of historical developments collectively known as *globalization* are so complex and because the local effects of these developments have often been felt as disruptions of well-entrenched habits or ways of life, debates about globalization are particularly open to manipulation through the presentation of charged imagery. Since the end of the Cold War, provocative images that capture certain aspects of the world's new interconnectedness—and the accompanying need for new kinds of boundaries—have become ubiquitous in the media. The movement of peoples and goods are variously defined as necessary to maintain standards of living or a threat to local jobs and local production. Globalization is defended as good for the economy, good for the consumer, and good for competition, but it is also blamed for hurting workers, destroying local cultures, and eroding long-standing definitions of national identity.

The images here all illustrate essential aspects of globalization. Image A shows ships waiting for loading and unloading at one of the largest container terminals in the world, in Hong Kong. Most of the shipping from China comes through this terminal. Image B shows family members separated by the border fence between the United States and Mexico in Mexicali, Mexico. In the twentieth century, Mexicali grew to be a city of 1.5 million people, in large part on the

A. Cargo ships in Kowloon Bay, 2002.

and armed Israeli security forces. The street fights escalated into cycles of Palestinian terrorism, particularly suicide bombings of civilian targets, and reprisals from the Israeli military. International efforts to broker a peace produced the Oslo Accords of 1993, which established an autonomous Palestinian Authority led by the PLO chief, Yasser Arafat. Yet the peace was always fragile at best—suffering perhaps fatal damage from the assassination of Israel's reformist prime minister Yitzhak Rabin in 1995 by a reactionary Israeli and from continued attacks by Islamist terrorists. By the turn of the twenty-first century the cycle of violence flared again, with a "second intifada" launched by Palestinians in late 2000. In the first decade

of the twenty-first century, the Israeli-Palestinian conflict has remained without a solution. The second intifada came to an end after Arafat's death in 2004 and the election of Mahmoud Abbas as the president of the Palestinian Authority in 2005. The electoral victory of a more militant Palestinian organization, Hamas, in the Palestinian parliamentary elections of 2006, however, limited Abbas's power to negotiate with Israel. Meanwhile, continued attacks on Israeli civilians by Hamas—labeled a terrorist organization by the United States and the European Union—led to an Israeli military operation against Palestinians in the Gaza strip that produced at least a three-year suspension of major hostilities along the frontier. In 2013, the UN

B. Mexican family members talk through border fence, 2003.

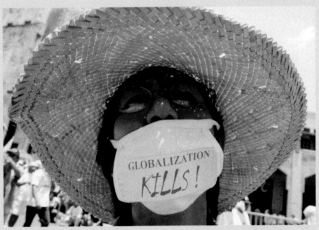

C. Filipino protester on Labor Day, 2003.

prosperity generated by sending field workers across the border to the United States. Image C shows a Labor Day protester in Manila, Philippines, at a demonstration in which globalization was blamed for amendments to the labor code favorable to employers, a ban on strikes, and antiterrorist measures that were perceived to be an infringement of personal liberties. The medical mask is a reference to the SARS epidemic.

Questions for Analysis

1. Image A is typical of images that emphasize the economic consequences of globalization. Does globalization appear to be a force subject to human control in this image? How do such images shape perceptions of China's place in the global economy?

2. Compare images A and B. Is there a connection between the accelerating

flows of money and goods between different parts of the world and restrictions on the movements of people?

3. In image C, the woman's medical mask names globalization as the enemy of Filipino workers. In so doing, who is being targeted? What does this say about the local contest over the conditions of labor in the Philippines?

General Assembly recognized the state of Palestine and granted it nonmember observer status, but a solution to the crisis is still not in sight.

Oil, Power, and Economics

The struggles between the state of Israel and its neighbors have been important in their own right. Yet one of the most compelling reasons that this conflict mattered to outside powers was material: oil. The global demand for oil skyrocketed during the postwar era and has accelerated since. Starting with the consumer boom in the Cold War

West, ordinary citizens bought cars and other petroleum-powered consumer durables, while industrial plastics made from petroleum by-products were used to manufacture a wealth of basic household items. Those needs, and the desires for profit and power that went with them, drew Western corporations and governments steadily toward the oil-rich states of the Middle East, whose vast reserves were discovered in the 1930s and 1940s. Large corporations conducted joint diplomacy with Middle Eastern states and their own home governments to design concessions for drilling, refining, and shipping the oil. Pipelines were laid by contractors based around the world, from California to Rome to Russia.

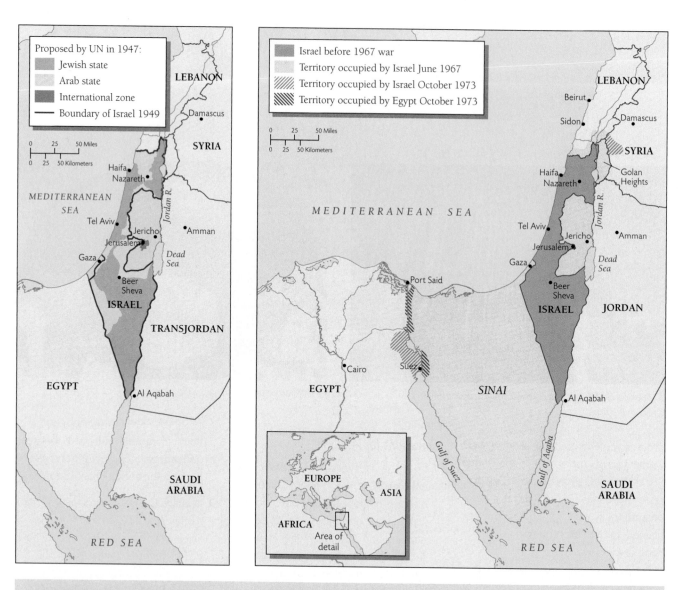

THE ARAB-ISRAELI WARS OF 1967 AND 1973. ▪ *What were the major changes in the political geography of the Middle East as a result of the Arab-Israeli conflict of 1967?* ▪ *Why did the Israelis wish to occupy the Sinai and West Bank regions at the end of the 1967 war?* ▪ *What problems did this create, and how might it have led to the conflict in 1973?*

The enormous long-term economic value of the Middle Eastern oil reserves made oil a fundamental tool in new struggles over political power. Many producer states sought to turn their resources into leverage with the West's former imperial powers. In 1960, the leading Middle Eastern, African, and Latin American producers banded together in a cartel to take advantage of this vital resource, forming the Organization of the Petroleum Exporting Countries (OPEC) to regulate the production and pricing of crude oil. During the 1970s, OPEC played a leading role in the global economy. Its policies reflected not only the desire to draw maximum profits out of bottlenecks in oil production but also the militant politics of some OPEC leaders who wanted to use oil as a weapon against the West in

the Arab-Israeli conflict. After the 1973 Arab-Israeli war, an embargo inspired by the hard-liners sparked spiraling inflation and economic troubles in Western nations, triggering a cycle of dangerous recession that lasted nearly a decade.

In response, Western governments treated the Middle Eastern oil regions as a vital strategic center of gravity, the subject of constant Great Power diplomacy. If conflict directly threatened the stability of oil production or friendly governments, Western powers were prepared to intervene by force, as the 1991 Gulf War demonstrated. By the 1990s, another new front of competition and potential conflict emerged as the energy demands of other nations also grew. In particular, the new industrial giants China and India eyed the Middle

GAMAL ABDEL NASSER AND SOVIET MINISTER ALEKSEY KOSYGIN, 1966. As the most prominent spokesman for secular pan-Arabism, Nasser became a target for Islamist critics, such as Sayyid Qutb and the Muslim Brotherhood, angered by the Western-influenced policies of his regime.

Eastern oil reserves with the same nervousness as the West. The oil boom also generated violent conflict inside Middle Eastern producer states. Oil revenue produced an uneven form of economic development. The huge gaps between or inside Middle Eastern societies that divided oil's haves and have-nots caused deep resentments, official corruption, and a new wave of radical politics. With the pan-Arab nationalists fading from the scene, the rising revolutionary force gathered instead around modern readings of Islamic fundamentalism, now tied to postcolonial politics.

The Rise of Political Islam

In North Africa and the Middle East, processes of modernization and globalization produced tremendous discontents. The new nations that emerged from decolonization often shared the characteristics of the "kleptocracies" south of the Sahara: corrupt state agencies, cronyism based on ethnic or family kinship, decaying public services, rapid increases in population, and constant state repression of dissent. Disappointment with these conditions ran deep, perhaps nowhere more so than in the seat of pan-Arabism, Nasser's Egypt. During the 1960s, Egyptian academics and cultural critics leveled charges against Nasser's regime that became the core of a powerful new political movement. Their critique offered modern interpretations of certain legal and political currents in Islamic thought, ideas linked loosely across centuries by their association with revolt against foreign interference and official corruption. They denounced Egypt's nationalist government as greedy, brutal, and corrupt.

There was a twist to their claims, however: that the roots of the Arab world's moral failure lay in centuries of colonial contact with the West. The most influential of these Islamist critics, Sayyid Qutb (*Kutb*, 1906–1966), presented these ideas in a series of essays for which he was arrested several times by Egyptian authorities and ultimately executed. His argument ran as follows. As a result of corrupting outside influences, the ruling elites of the new Arab states pursued policies that frayed local and family bonds, deepening economic divides while abandoning the government's responsibility for charity and stability. What was more, the nation's elites were morally bankrupt—their lives defied codes of morality, self-discipline, and communal responsibility rooted in Islamic faith. To maintain power, the elites lived in the pockets of Western imperial and corporate powers. From Qutb's point of view, this collaboration not only caused cultural impurity but also eroded authentic Muslim faith. This dire judgment of Arab societies—that they were poisoned from without and within—required an equally drastic solution. Arab societies should reject not only oppressive postcolonial governments but also all the political and cultural ideas that traveled with them, especially those that could be labeled "Western." After popular revolts, the Arab autocracies would be replaced by an idealized form of conservative Islamic government—a system in which a rigid form of Islam would link law, government, and culture.

In a formula familiar to historians of European politics throughout the nineteenth and twentieth centuries, this particular brand of Islamist politics combined popular anger, intellectual opposition to "foreign" influences, and a highly idealized vision of the past. By the 1970s, it began to express itself openly in regional politics. Qutb's ideas were put into practice by Egypt's Muslim Brotherhood, a secretive but widespread society rooted in anticolonial politics, local charity, and violently fundamentalist Islam. The same ideas spread among similar organizations in other urbanized Arab countries and leading Islamic universities, which were historically centers of debate about political theory and religious law. Radical Islam emerged as a driving force in criticism and defiance of autocratic Arab regimes. Secular critics and more liberal Islamists, who called for open elections and a free press, were more fragmented and thus easier to silence, whereas the new wave of fundamentalists gained concessions that allowed them to preach and publish in public as long as they did not launch actual revolts. Despite the movement's steady rise, the most dramatic turn still managed to surprise observers. Like Protestantism's emergence in the fractious German states, for example, or communism's successful revolution in Russia, radical Islam's defining moment as a political force came in an unexpected place: Iran.

IRAN'S ISLAMIC REVOLUTION

Iran offered one of the most dramatic examples of modernization gone sour in the Middle East. Despite tremendous economic growth in the 1960s and 1970s, Iranians labored with legacies of foreign intervention and corrupt rule at the hands of the shah, Reza Pahlavi, a Western-friendly leader installed during a 1953 military coup supported by Britain and the United States. In exchange for the shah's role as a friend to the West during the Cold War and for providing a steady source of reasonably priced oil, the Iranian government received vast sums in oil contracts, weapons, and development aid. Thousands of Westerners, especially Americans, came to Iran, introducing foreign influences that not only challenged traditional values but also offered economic and political alternatives. The shah, however, kept these alternatives out of reach, consistently denying democratic representation to westernizing middle-class Iranian workers and deeply religious university students alike. He governed through a small aristocracy divided by constant infighting. His army and secret police conducted regular and brutal campaigns of repression. Despite all this, and the public protests it spurred in the West, governments such as the conservative Nixon administration embraced the shah as a strategically vital ally: a key to anti-Soviet alliances and a safe source of oil.

Twenty-five years after the 1953 coup, the shah's autocratic route to an industrial state ended. After a lengthy economic downturn, public unrest, and personal illness, the shah realized he could not continue in power. He retired from public life under popular pressure in February 1979. Eight months of uncertainty followed, most Westerners fled the country, and the provisional government appointed by the shah collapsed. The strongest political coalition among Iran's revolutionaries surged into the vacuum—a broad Islamic movement centered on the ayatollah Ruhollah Khomeini (1902–1989), Iran's senior cleric and theologian, returned from exile in France. Other senior clerics and the country's large population of unemployed, deeply religious university

THE SHAH'S DOWNFALL. Two Iranians symbolically substitute a picture of the shah with one of the ayatollah Khomeini after the Iranian revolution, 1979. ■ *What did the Iranian revolutionaries who overthrew the shah have in common with the anti-colonial nationalists in other former European colonies?*

POPULAR SUPPORT FOR IRAN'S ISLAMIC REVOLUTION.
A massive crowd awaits the ayatollah Khomeini after the Iranian Revolution, 1979.

students provided the movement's energy. Disenfranchised secular protesters joined the radical Islamists in condemning decades of Western indifference and the shah's oppression. Under the new regime, some limited economic and political populism combined with strict constructions of Islamic law, restrictions on women's public life, and the prohibition of many ideas or activities linked to Western influence.

The new Iranian government also defined itself against its enemies: against the Sunni religious establishment of neighboring states, against "atheistic" Soviet communism, but especially against Israel and the United States. Iranians feared the United States would try to overthrow Khomeini as it had other leaders. Violence in the streets of Tehran reached a peak when militant students stormed the American embassy in November 1979 and seized fifty-two hostages. The act quickly became an international crisis that heralded a new kind of confrontation between Western powers and postcolonial Islamic radicals. Democratic president Jimmy Carter's administration ultimately gained the hostages' release, but not before the catalog of earlier failures led to the election of the Republican Ronald Reagan.

Iran, Iraq, and Unintended Consequences of the Cold War

Iran's victory in the hostage crisis was fleeting. During the later part of 1980, Iran's Arab neighbor and traditional rival Iraq invaded, hoping to seize Iran's southern oil fields during the revolutionary confusion. Iran counterattacked. The result was a murderous eight-year conflict marked by the use of chemical weapons and human waves of young Iranian radicals fighting the Soviet-armed Iraqis. The war ended with Iran's defeat but not with the collapse of its theocratic regime. In the short term, their long defense of Iranian nationalism left the clerics more entrenched at home, while abroad they used oil revenues to back grass-roots radicals in Lebanon and elsewhere who engaged in anti-Western terrorism. The strongest threats to the Iranian regime ultimately came from within, from a new generation of young students and disenfranchised service workers who found their prospects for prosperity and active citizenship had not changed much since the days of the shah.

The Iran-Iraq conflict created another problem for Western interests and the governments of leading OPEC states: Iraq. Various governments—including an unlikely alliance of France, Saudi Arabia, the Soviet Union, and the United States—supported Iraq during the war in an effort to bring down Iran's clerics. Their patronage went to one of the most violent governments in the region, Saddam Hussein's dictatorship. Iraq exhausted itself in the war, politically and economically. To shore up his regime and restore Iraq's influence, Hussein looked elsewhere in the region. In 1990, Iraq invaded its small, oil-rich neighbor Kuwait. With the Cold War on the wane, Iraq's Soviet supporters would not condone Iraqi aggression. A number of Western nations led by the United States reacted forcefully. Within months, Iraq faced the full weight of the United States military—trained intensively since Vietnam to rout much more capable Soviet-armed forces than Iraq's—along with forces from several OPEC states, French troops, and armored divisions from Britain, Egypt, and Syria. This coalition pummeled Iraqi troops from the air for six weeks, then routed them and retook Kuwait in a brief, well-executed ground campaign. This changed the tenor of relations between the United States and Arab oil producers, encouraging not only closeness between governments but also anti-American radicals angry at a new Western presence. It was also the beginning rather than the end of a Western confrontation with Iraq, centered on Hussein's efforts to develop nuclear and biological weapons.

Elsewhere in the region, the proxy conflicts of the Cold War snared both superpowers in the new and growing networks of Islamic radicalism. In 1979, the socialist government of Afghanistan turned against its Soviet patrons. Fearing a result like Iran, with a spread of fundamentalism into the Muslim regions of Soviet Central Asia, Moscow responded by overthrowing the Afghan president and installing a pro-Soviet faction. The new government, backed by more than 100,000 Soviet troops, found itself immediately at war with fighters who combined local

THE IRAN-IRAQ WAR. Iranian guards keep watch over Iraqi prisoners.

The Place of Islam in Modern Societies

The end of the colonial era and the impact of postcolonial migrations provided the backdrop for a renewed discussion in Europe and the Middle East about the presence of Muslim peoples in European nations and the relationship of religion to politics in traditionally Muslim societies. Among Muslim scholars and clerics, a wide range of opinions have been expressed about the place of Islam in the modern world, and the two figures here represent two distinct voices within this discussion.

Born into a family of Shi'ite Muslim religious leaders, Ruhollah Khomeini (c. 1900–1989) was recognized as the leading Iranian religious authority in the 1950s. He represented a highly conservative Islamic fundamentalism intended to unite Iranian Muslims in violent opposition to the Western-supported government of the shah of Iran and had a powerful influence on Muslims seeking an alternative to Western cultural, political, and economic domination.

Tariq Ramadan (born 1962 in Geneva, Switzerland) is a professor of religion and philosophy and a leading voice speaking for the increasingly large number of Muslims who live in Europe and North America as members of a religious minority in non-Muslim societies. He has taught at the University of Fribourg, the College de Saussure in Geneva, and St. Antony's College, Oxford. In 2004, he was forced to decline an offer to become a professor at the University of Notre Dame in the United States when the State Department denied him a visa. Ramadan argues that Muslims can and should be productive and active citizens in Western societies while remaining true to their religious beliefs.

Ruhollah Khomeini, *Islamic Government* (1979)

The Islamic government is not similar to the well-known systems of government. It is not a despotic government in which the head of state dictates his opinion and tampers with the lives and property of the people. The prophet, may God's prayers be upon him, and 'Ali, the amir of the faithful, and the other imams had no power to tamper with people's property or with their lives.[1] The Islamic government is not despotic but constitutional. However, it is not constitutional in the well-known sense of the word, which is represented in the parliamentary system or in the people's councils. It is constitutional in the sense that those in charge of affairs observe a number of conditions and rules underlined in the Koran and in the Sunna and represented in the necessity of observing the system and of applying the dictates and laws of Islam.[2] This is why the Islamic government is the government of the divine law. The difference between the Islamic government and the constitutional governments, both monarchic and republican, lies in the fact that the people's representatives or the king's representatives are the ones who codify and legislate, whereas the power of legislation is confined to God, may He be praised, and nobody else has the right to legislate and nobody may rule by that which has not been given power by God. . . .

The government of Islam is not monarchic, . . . and not an empire, because Islam is above squandering and unjustly undermining the lives and property of people. This is why the government of Islam does not have the many big palaces, the servants, the royal courts, the crown prince courts and other trivial requirements that consume half or most of the country's resources and that the sultans and the emperors have. The life of the great prophet was a life of utter simplicity, even though the prophet was the head of the state, who ran and ruled it by himself. . . . Had this course continued until the present, people would have known the taste of happiness and the country's treasury would not have been plundered to be spent on fornication, abomination and the court's costs and expenditures. You know that most of the corrupt aspects of our society are due to the corruption of the ruling dynasty and the royal family. What is the legitimacy of these rulers who build houses of entertainment, corrup-

tion, fornication and abomination and who destroy houses which God ordered be raised and in which His name is mentioned? Were it not for what the court wastes and what it embezzles, the country's budget would not experience any deficit that forces the state to borrow from America and England, with all the humiliation and insult that accompany such borrowing. Has our oil decreased or have our minerals that are stored under this good earth run out? We possess everything and we would not need the help of America or of others if it were not for the costs of the court and for its wasteful use of the people's money.

[1] "The prophet" refers to Muhammed; 'Ali was Muhammed's son-in-law and, according to the Shi'ite tradition, his legitimate heir; an amir is a high military official; and an imam, in the Shi'ite tradition, is an important spiritual leader with sole power to make decisions about doctrine.

[2] The Koran is the book of the holy scriptures of Islam; the Sunna is the body of customary Islamic law second only to the Koran in authority.

Source: Ruhollah Khomeini, *Islamic Government*, trans. Joint Publications Research Service (New York: 1979, pp. 17–19.

Tariq Ramadan, *Western Muslims and the Future of Islam* (2002)

... [W]ith the emergence of the young Muslim generation ... it has been deemed necessary to reanalyze the main Islamic sources (Qu'ran and Sunnah) when it comes to interpreting legal issues (*fiqh*) in the European context. Many of these young people intend to stay permanently in a European country, and a large number have already received their citizenship. New forms of interpretation (known as *ijtihad*) have made it possible for the younger generation to practice their faith in a coherent manner in a new context. It is important to note that this has been a very recent phenomenon. Only within the past few years have Muslim scholars and intellectuals felt obliged to take a closer look at the European laws, and at the same time, to think about the changes that have been taking place within the diverse Muslim communities ... [F]ive main points ... have been agreed upon by those working on the basis of the Islamic sources and by the great majority of Muslims living in Europe:

1. Muslims who are residents or citizens of a non-Islamic state should understand that they are under a moral and social contract with the country in which they reside. In other words, they should respect the laws of the country.
2. Both the spirit and the letter of the secular model permit Muslims to practice their faith without requiring a complete assimilation into the new culture and, thereby, partial disconnection from their Muslim identity.
3. The ancient division of the world into denominations of *dar al-harb* (abode of war) and *dar al-Islam* (abode of Islam), used by the jurists during a specific geopolitical context, namely the ninth-century Muslim world, is invalid and does not take into account the realities of modern life. Other concepts have been identified as exemplifying more positively the presence of Muslims in Europe.
4. Muslims should consider themselves full citizens of the nations in which they reside and can participate with conscience in the organizational, economic, and political affairs of the country without compromising their own values.
5. With regard to the possibilities offered by European legislation, nothing stops Muslims, like any other citizens, from making choices that respond to the requirements of their own consciences and faith. If any obligations should be in contradiction to the Islamic principles (a situation that is quite rare), the specific case must be studied in order to identify the priorities and the possibility of adaptation (which should be developed at the national level). ...

For some Muslims, the idea of an "Islamic culture," similar to the concepts of identity and community, connotes the necessity of Muslim isolation from and rejection of European culture. Such an understanding suggests that Muslims are not genuine in their desire to integrate into the society in which they live. They play the citizenship card, while trying to maintain such cultural particularities as dress code, management of space when it comes to men and women, concern about music, and other issues. For them, real integration means becoming European in every aspect of one's character and behavior. This is, in fact, a very narrow vision of integration, almost resembling the notion of assimilation. One admits theoretically that Muslims have the right to practice their religion but revokes these rights when expression of faith becomes too *visible*.

In actuality, the future of Muslim presence in Europe must entail a truly "European Islamic culture" disengaged from the cultures of North Africa, Turkey, and Indo-Pakistan, while naturally referring to them for inspiration. This new culture is just in the process of being born and molded. By giving careful consideration to everything from appropriate dress to the artistic and creative expression of Islam, Muslims are mobilizing a whole new culture. The formation of such a culture is a pioneering endeavor, making use of European energy while taking into account various national customs and simultaneously respecting Islamic values and guidelines.

Source: Tariq Ramadan, "Islam and Muslims in Europe: A Silent Revolution toward Rediscovery," in *Muslims in the West: From Sojourners to Citizens*, ed. Yvonne Yazbeck Haddad (New York: 2002), pp. 160–163.

Questions for Analysis

1. What prevents Islamic government from being despotic, according to Khomeini? Why is there no legislative branch in an Islamic government, in his view?

2. What criticism does Ramadan make of those Muslims who seek to isolate themselves from European culture while living in Europe? What does he mean by "European Islamic culture"?

3. In what ways do these two Muslim thinkers show an engagement with European traditions of political thought?

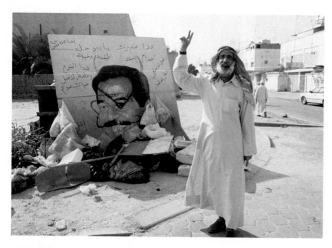

THE LIBERATION OF KUWAIT. After American forces drove out his Iraqi occupiers, a Kuwaiti celebrates with the victory sign, 1991. Behind him, a defaced poster of Saddam Hussein sits in a garbage heap.

conservatism with militant Islam and who attracted volunteers from radical Islamic movements in Egypt, Lebanon, Saudi Arabia, and elsewhere. These fighters, who called themselves *mujahidin*, viewed the conflict as a holy war. The mujahidin benefited from advanced weapons and training, given by Western powers led by the United States. Those who provided the aid saw the conflict in Cold War terms, as a chance to sap Soviet resources in a fruitless imperial war. On those terms, the aid worked; the war dragged on for nearly ten years, taking thousands of Russian lives and damaging the Soviet government's credibility at home. Soviet troops withdrew in 1989. After five years of clan warfare, hard-line Islamic factions tied to the foreign elements in the mujahidin took over the country. Their experiment in theocracy made Iran's seem mild by comparison.

VIOLENCE BEYOND BOUNDS: WAR AND TERRORISM IN THE TWENTY-FIRST CENTURY

The global networks of communication, finance, and mobility discussed at the beginning of this chapter gave radical political violence a disturbing new character at the end of the twentieth century. In the 1960s, organized sectarian terrorist tactics had become an important part of political conflict in the Middle East, Europe, and Latin America. Most of these early terrorist organizations (including the Irish Republican Army, the Italian Red Brigades, and the different Palestinian revolutionary organizations) had specific goals, such as ethnic separatism or the establishment of revolutionary governments. By the 1980s and increasingly during

the 1990s, such groups were complemented and then supplanted by a different brand of terrorist organization, one that ranged freely across territory and local legal systems. These newer, apocalyptic terrorist groups called for decisive conflict to eliminate their enemies and grant themselves martyrdom. Some such groups emerged from the social dislocations of the postwar boom, others were linked directly to brands of radical religion. They often divorced themselves from the local crises that first spurred their anger, roaming widely among countries in search of recruits to their cause.

A leading example of such groups, and soon the most famous, was the radical Islamist umbrella organization al Qaeda. It was created by leaders of the foreign mujahidin who had fought against the Soviet Union in Afghanistan. Its official leader and financial supporter was the Saudi-born multimillionaire Osama bin Laden. Among its operational chiefs was the famous Egyptian radical Ayman al-Zawahiri, whose political career linked him directly to Sayyid Qutb and other founding thinkers in modern revolutionary Islam. These leaders organized broad networks of largely self-contained terrorist cells around the world, from the Islamic regions of Southeast Asia to Europe, East Africa, and the United States, funded by myriad private accounts, front companies, illegal trades, and corporate kickbacks throughout the global economy. Their organization defied borders, and so did their goals. They did not seek to negotiate for territory, or to change the government of a specific state. Instead, they spoke of the destruction of the state of Israel and American, European, and other non-Islamic systems of government worldwide and called for a united, apocalyptic revolt by fundamentalist Muslims to create an Islamic community bounded only by faith. During the 1990s, they involved themselves in a variety of local terrorist campaigns in Islamic countries and organized large-scale suicide attacks against American targets, notably the American embassies in Kenya and Tanzania in 1998.

At the beginning of the twenty-first century, al Qaeda's organizers struck again at their most obvious political enemy, the symbolic seat of globalization: the United States. Small teams of suicidal radicals, aided by al Qaeda's organization, planned to hijack airliners and use them as flying bombs to strike the most strategically important symbols of America's global power. On September 11, 2001, they carried out this mission in the deadliest series of terrorist attacks ever to occur on American soil. In the span of an hour, hijacked planes struck the Pentagon, the headquarters of the U.S. military, and the World Trade Center towers in New York City. A fourth plane, possibly aimed at the U.S. Capitol, crashed in open farmland in Pennsylvania, its attack thwarted when the passengers fought back against their captors. The World Trade Center towers, among the tallest buildings in the world, crumbled into ash and wreckage in front of hundreds of millions of viewers on satellite television and the Internet. In these several simultaneous attacks, roughly 3,000 people died.

The attacks were at once a new brand of terror, deeply indebted to globalization in both its outlook and its method, and something older: the extreme, opportunistic violence of marginal groups against national cultures during a period of general dislocation and uncertainty. The immediate American response was action against al Qaeda's central haven in Afghanistan, a state in total collapse after the warfare of the previous thirty years. The United States' versatile professional soldiers and unmatched equipment, along with armed Afghan militias angry at the country's disarray quickly routed al Qaeda's Taliban sponsors and scattered the terrorists. The search for Osama bin Laden took a decade, during which time the United States and its allies in the war in Afghanistan faced a renewed insurrection by the Taliban beginning in 2003. U.S. forces killed Osama bin Laden at his home in nearby Pakistan in 2011. During the intervening years, the United States succeeded in disrupting, though not completely eliminating, many of the hidden networks of leadership, finance, and information that made Al Qaeda's apocalyptic terrorism possible. Meanwhile, the economic and political rebuilding of Afghanistan, a necessary consequence of American and Euro-

pean military action, began from almost nothing in terms of administration and infrastructure. These efforts were hampered by challenging political circumstances within the country, which made it difficult for the Afghan government to position itself between its U.S. ally and a population with a long tradition of mistrusting foreign powers intervening in their land. U.S. forces are scheduled to leave Afghanistan during 2013, but the stability of the nation after more than three decades of war remains an open question.

One reason for the persistent fears about such groups as al Qaeda has to do with the increasing power and availability of weapons they might use: chemical substances, biological agents that could kill millions, even portable nuclear weapons. With the end of the Cold War, methods and technologies that the superpowers employed to maintain their nuclear balance of power became more available on the margins to displaced groups with the financial or political leverage to seek them out. Other major arms races, centered, for example, around Israel or the conflicts between India and Pakistan, helped spread the availability of production sites and resources for weapons of horrific power, no longer governed absolutely by the legal conventions and deterrent strength of superpowers. Fear that the Iraqi government of Saddam Hussein was reaching for biological and nuclear capabilities helped propel the Gulf War of 1991 and active international efforts to disarm Iraq thereafter. Anxiety that states such as Iraq might transfer such weapons to apocalyptic terrorists, a fear given new life after the attacks on New York and Washington, provided the rationale for an American-led invasion of Iraq in the spring of 2003. The campaign, which used a remarkably small force both on the ground and in the air, quickly took Iraq over and deposed Hussein. No immediate evidence of recent, active weapons development programs was found, however, and in the process the United States inherited the complex reconstruction of a broken state, fractured by guerrilla violence and anti-Western terrorism. After a long struggle against a shifting insurgency that fought the new Iraqi government and the U.S.-led forces that supported it, the last U.S. troops left Iraq in 2011. Since then, continued civil conflict in Iraq has claimed thousands of lives.

A nuclear threat also remained present in North Korea. After the loss of Soviet patronage in 1991, the isolated North Korean state careened from one economic disaster to another, with verified reports of local starvation in some regions of the country and a breakdown of government into military and political fiefdoms. The North Korean government pursued the development of a nuclear arsenal as a bargaining chip against the other major states of northeast Asia and the United States. Those neighbors each understood the grim chance that North Korea might break the last and perhaps most crucial nuclear threshold, providing nuclear

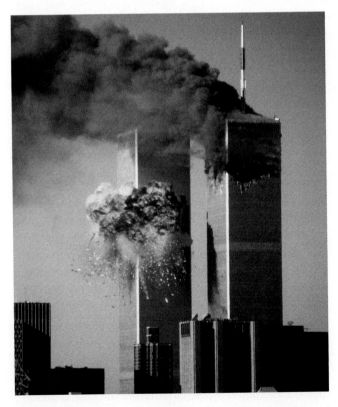

TWENTY-FIRST CENTURY TERRORISM. New York City's World Trade Center Towers under attack on September 11, 2001.

The United Nations, Report of the Fourth World Conference on Women (1995)

In September 1995, women representing 185 of the world's nations gathered in Beijing to attend the UN's Fourth World Conference on Women. Delegates to the conference adopted a platform for action that outlined the problems confronting women in the world, including poverty, violence, armed conflict, human rights violations, pollution, and differing access to medical treatment, education, economic advancement, and political power. The passage excerpted here highlights the particular burdens that poverty places on women in many societies throughout the world.

47. More than 1 billion people in the world today, the great majority of whom are women, live in unacceptable conditions of poverty, mostly in the developing countries. . . .

48. In the past decade the number of women living in poverty has increased disproportionately to the number of men, particularly in the developing countries. The feminization of poverty has also recently become a significant problem in the countries with economies in transition as a short-term consequence of the process of political, economic and social transformation. In addition to economic factors, the rigidity of socially ascribed gender roles and women's limited access to power, education, training and productive resources as well as other emerging factors that may lead to insecurity for families are also responsible. The failure to adequately mainstream a gender perspective in all economic analysis and planning and to address the structural causes of poverty is also a contributing factor.

49. Women contribute to the economy and to combating poverty through both remunerated and unremunerated work at home, in the community and in the workplace. The empowerment of women is a critical factor in the eradication of poverty.

50. While poverty affects households as a whole, because of the gender division of labour and responsibilities for household welfare, women bear a disproportionate burden, attempting to manage household consumption and production under conditions of increasing scarcity. Poverty is particularly acute for women living in rural households.

51. Women's poverty is directly related to the absence of economic opportunities and autonomy, lack of access to economic resources, including credit, land ownership and inheritance, lack of access to education and support services and their minimal participation in the decision-making process. Poverty can also force

weapons not to hard-pressed states but instead to stateless organizations. In short, by the early twenty-first century, warfare and the terrifying killing power of modern technology threatened to elude the control of national states and clearly defined political communities.

TRANSFORMATIONS: HUMAN RIGHTS

Some of the same globalizing processes have dramatically expanded our conception of citizenship, rights, and law. High school halls and college walkways are crammed with the tables of international organizations, such as Amnesty International, that promote universal human rights. How has this notion of human rights become so familiar? What older traditions has it built on or replaced?

The contemporary language of human rights is anchored in a tradition of political thought that reaches back to at least the seventeenth century. It took its present form in response to the atrocities of the First World War and, especially, the Second World War. Atrocities and people's shocked responses to them, however, did not create either a new concern with human rights or the institutions dedicated to upholding them. Enforcing *universal* human rights challenges the sovereignty of nation-states and an individual nation-state's power over its citizens. International courts and human rights organizations thus require and hasten what political thinkers call the globalization of judicial power.

women into situations in which they are vulnerable to sexual exploitation.

52. In too many countries, social welfare systems do not take sufficient account of the specific conditions of women living in poverty, and there is a tendency to scale back the services provided by such systems. The risk of falling into poverty is greater for women than for men, particularly in old age, where social security systems are based on the principle of continuous remunerated employment. In some cases, women do not fulfil this requirement because of interruptions in their work, due to the unbalanced distribution of remunerated and unremunerated work. Moreover, older women also face greater obstacles to labour-market re-entry.

53. In many developed countries, where the level of general education and professional training of women and men are similar and where systems of protection against discrimination are available, in some sectors the economic transformations of the past decade have strongly increased either the unemployment of women or the precarious nature of their employment. The proportion of women among the poor has consequently increased. In countries with a high level of school enrolment of girls, those who leave the educational system the earliest, without any qualification, are among the most vulnerable in the labour market. . . .

55. Particularly in developing countries, the productive capacity of women should be increased through access to capital, resources, credit, land, technology, information, technical assistance and training so as to raise their income and improve nutrition, education, health care and status within the household. The release of women's productive potential is pivotal to breaking the cycle of poverty so that women can share fully in the benefits of development and in the products of their own labour.

56. Sustainable development and economic growth that is both sustained and sustainable are possible only through improving the economic, social, political, legal and cultural status of women. Equitable social development that recognizes empowering the poor, particularly women, to utilize environmental resources sustainably is a necessary foundation for sustainable development.

Source: United Nations, *Report of the Fourth World Conference on Women, Beijing*, September 4–15, 1995, accessed June 2010, www.un.org /womenwatch/daw/beijing/platform.

Questions for Analysis

1. According to the UN report, why are women more likely to be poor than men?

2. What are the special challenges faced by women in developing countries?

3. What are the different challenges faced by women residing in more developed nations?

Human rights are part of the Western political tradition. So is opposition to them. The belief that rights were embedded in "nature," "natural order," or "natural law" formed a powerful strain of early modern political thought. John Locke understood natural law as the law of reason (see Chapter 15); others understood it to be the law of God. However conceptualized, it represented a higher authority to which men owed their obedience. Opponents of absolutism in seventeenth- and eighteenth-century Europe were driven by motives that were economic, religious, and social. Natural rights, however, became one of their rallying cries. The English Bill of Rights of 1689, accepted by William and Mary after the Glorious Revolution, insisted on "the true, ancient, and indubitable rights and liberties of the people of this kingdom." A century later, the American Declaration of Independence and the French Declaration of the Rights of Man more broadly proclaimed the "natural, inalienable and sacred rights of man," which in their eyes belonged to all men—not just the colonists of North America or the citizens of France. In point of fact, of course, those bold declarations of rights were not universal: women, slaves, people of color, and people of different religions were excluded, wholly or partially, and many nineteenth-century political theorists and scientists dedicated countless volumes to the proposition that these groups were *not* created equal. Which human beings might receive the "rights of man," then, was bitterly contested for the better part of the nineteenth and twentieth centuries, and only slowly did a more inclusive conception of human rights displace a narrower historical tradition of the rights of man.

As far as the history of human rights is concerned, perhaps the most important development of the nineteenth century was the rise of nationalism and nation-states. Rights, and political movements claiming them, became increasingly inseparable from nationhood. "What is a country . . . but the place in which our demands for individual rights are most secure?" asked the Italian nationalist Giuseppe Mazzini. For nineteenth-century Italians, Germans, Serbs, and Poles and for twentieth-century Indians, Vietnamese, and Algerians—to name just a few—fighting for national independence was the way to secure the rights of citizens. National sovereignty, once achieved, was tightly woven into the fabric of politics and international relations and would not be easily relinquished.

The world wars marked a turning point. The First World War, an unprecedented global conflict, almost inevitably fostered dreams of global peace under the auspices of international organizations. The Peace of Paris aimed for more than a territorial settlement: with the League of Nations it tried, tentatively, to establish an organization that would transcend the power of individual nations and uphold the (ill-defined) principles of "civilization." (Despite this commitment, the League bowed to British and American objections to a statement condemning racial discrimination.) The experiment failed: the fragile League was swept aside by the surge of extreme nationalism and aggression in the 1930s. The shock and revulsion at the atrocities of the war that followed, however, brought forth more decisive efforts. The Second World War's aftermath saw the establishment of the United Nations, an International Court of Justice at the Hague (Netherlands), and the UN's High Commission on Human Rights. Unlike anything attempted after the First World War, the Commission on Human Rights set out to establish the rights of individuals—against the nation-state.

This Universal Declaration of Human Rights, published by the High Commission in 1948, became the touchstone of our modern notion of human rights. It was very much a product of its time. Its authors included Eleanor Roosevelt and the French jurist René Cassin, who had been wounded in the First World War (and held his intestines together during a nearly 400-mile train ride to medical treatment), lost his family in the Holocaust, and had seen his nation collaborate with the Nazis. The High Commission argued that the war and the "barbarous acts which have outraged the conscience of mankind," showed that no state should have absolute power over its citizens. The Universal Declaration prohibited torture, cruel punishment, and slavery. A separate convention, also passed in 1948, dealt with the newly defined crime of genocide. The Universal Declaration of 1948 built on earlier declarations that universal-ized the rights to legal equality, freedom of religion and speech, and the right to participate in government. Finally, it reflected the postwar period's effort to put democracy on a more solid footing by establishing *social* rights—to education, work, a "just and favorable remuneration," a "standard of living," and social security, among others.

Few nations were willing to ratify the Universal Declaration of Human Rights. For decades after the war, its idealistic principles could not be reconciled with British and French colonialism, American racial segregation, or Soviet dictatorship. For as long as wars to end colonialism continued, declarations of universal principles rang hollow. (Mahatma Gandhi, asked to comment on Western civilization, replied that he thought it was a "good idea.") For as long as the Cold War persisted, human rights seemed only a thinly veiled weapon in the sparring between the superpowers. Thus decolonization and, later, the end of the Cold War began to enhance the legitimacy and luster of human rights. International institutions set up after the Second World War matured, gaining expertise and stature. Global communications and media dramatically expanded the membership and influence of organizations that, like Amnesty International (founded in 1961), operated outside the economic or political boundaries of the nation-state. Memories of the Second World War, distorted or buried by the Cold War, continue to return, and the force of those memories helped drive the creation of International Criminal Tribunals for Yugoslavia and Rwanda in 1993. Finally, as one historian points out, at a time when many feel vulnerable to the forces of globalization, human rights offers a way of talking about rights, goods, and protections (environmental, for example) that the nation-state cannot—or can no longer—provide.

It is nevertheless the case that the troubled era that began with the 9/11 attacks on the United States in 2001 has seen many challenges to the notion of universal human rights. Terrorism, no matter what the ideology of the perpetrator, is a fundamental violation of every human's right to safety and security. In their zeal to punish terrorists, meanwhile, many nations in the world have tacitly turned away from the emerging international legal structures that attempted to defend the rights of all individuals everywhere. The struggle that the United States and its allies waged against al Qaeda and Taliban leadership has raised difficult questions about the tactics used, which included torture, indefinite detention without trial, and the use of pilotless drones to kill suspected militant leaders in distant countries. The use of drone technologies make it easier to avoid U.S. casualties in operations against a dangerous enemy, but many in the United States and abroad have expressed concerns about the government's right to identify, target, and execute individuals, including in some cases U.S. citizens, based on criteria that are never subject to independent legal review. Public opinion in the United States remains strongly in favor of such tactics, but in recent years public anger in Afghanistan and Pakistan has focused on cases of mistaken identity and the deaths of family members and bystanders in drone attacks. Even within the U.S. government and military, some have expressed concern that these methods could be counterproductive.

As the U.S. and European governments pursue their interests abroad, debates about the use of military power in other parts of the world and the form that this power takes have become pressing concerns, and the issues turn on questions that have been a central part of the liberal democratic political tradition since it emerged in opposition to monarchist forms of government in the seventeenth century. How should a nation determine the balance between individual freedoms and national security? What forms of force or violence can the state legitimately use against its enemies at home or abroad? What kinds of information about its citizenry should a government be allowed to keep? Are the terrorist threats that democratic regimes routinely face today so serious that they justify the suspension of internationally recognized human rights? No easy answers to these questions exist—but the answers that governments and societies in Europe and the United States give to them will shape how people everywhere will perceive the legitimacy of the democratic political institutions that they claim to represent.

EUROPE AND THE UNITED STATES IN THE TWENTY-FIRST CENTURY

As the first decade of the twenty-first century drew to a close, the initial confidence that Europeans felt in the aftermath of the revolutions of 1989 seemed badly shaken. The process of European integration, which had contributed so much to the political stability of Europe in the decades after the Second World War, seemed to have reached its limits in the East. Although a few independent nations that were formerly a part of the Soviet Union, such as Ukraine, might be interested in joining the European Union, it is unlikely that Russia would be comfortable with this realignment toward the West. Even the future membership of Turkey, an official candidate for entry into the EU since 1999 and an associate member of the European Union since 1963, remains uncertain because of growing discomfort in many European nations about admitting a historically Muslim nation into Europe. Turkey is a modern industrial nation that has been governed by a secular government since the 1920s, participated in the Marshall Plan after the Second World War, was a member of the Council of Europe in 1949, and became a member of NATO in 1952. A 2010 poll carried out in five European countries nevertheless found that 52 percent of respondents were opposed to Turkish membership in the European Union and only 41 percent in favor.

In the economic realm, the global financial crisis of 2007–2010 caused many in Europe and North America to rethink the central assumptions of late-twentieth-century neoliberalism, especially the belief that markets were by definition self-regulating. The crisis had its origins in a classic bubble in global housing prices, which encouraged banks to make ever-riskier bets in the real estate market while also experimenting with the sale of complicated securities whose risk became difficult to gauge with accuracy. When housing prices fell, many key banks in different parts of the world found themselves unable to state clearly the value of their plummeting investments tied to real estate. Since nobody knew how much money the largest financial institutions had, banks simply stopped lending money to one another, and in the resulting liquidity crisis many businesses failed and trillions of dollars of consumer savings were wiped out. Massive government bailouts of the largest banks with taxpayer money were required to stabilize the global financial system, and popular resentment against the financial industry stimulated many nations to consider widespread reform and government regulation of banks as a result.

Contemporary debates about political integration in Europe or the benefits of free-market capitalism are closely connected with the developments that followed the end of the Cold War in the early 1990s and the period of economic globalization that followed, but they can also be seen as a continuation of debates within the traditions of political and economic liberalism that go back to the eighteenth century. In its classic formulation as put forth by liberal theorists such as Adam Smith, political and economic liberties were best defended in a nation that possessed a small and limited government. The closely related traditions of social democracy that developed in Europe in the nineteenth and twentieth century, on the other hand, arose out of a concern that limited governments in the classic liberal mold could not do enough to remedy the inequalities that emerged from modern industrial societies, and the result was the creation of welfare state institutions that aimed to use the power of the state to maintain a base level of social and economic equality. This tension between the goals of liberty and equality is a constant one within the liberal tradition, and the different trajectories of Europe and the United States in the twentieth century reflect the respective priorities of successive governments in both places.

Many Europeans, therefore, watched the election of Barack Obama in the United States in 2008 with great interest. Since the election of Ronald Reagan in 1980, the divergences between governments in the United States and Europe in their attitudes toward the role that the state might play in remedying social problems had become even more acute. With few exceptions, European governments were much more willing to use the power of the state to assist the unemployed or the aged, to support families, and to provide subsidies for education, public transportation, and national programs for health care. As we have seen, this consensus emerged in part because of a belief that the economic dislocations of the 1920s and 1930s had led directly to the emergence of destabilizing and antidemocratic extremist political movements. In the United States, on the other hand, widespread discontent with attempts by the Johnson administration in the 1960s to use the power of the federal government to end racial segregation and address broad problems such as urban poverty and environmental pollution contributed to a conservative backlash in the 1980s and 1990s. Throughout those years, conservatives in the United States called for an end to welfare programs, repeal of environmental regulations, and less government oversight in the marketplace.

Obama's election in 2008, following on the heels of the financial meltdown earlier the same year, seemed to mark a turning point of sorts in American politics, as his pragmatic campaign was predicated on a claim that government itself was not the problem facing industrial democracies at the outset of the twenty-first century. The Obama administration's ambitious plan to overhaul the health care system faced stiff opposition from many quarters, but a compromise package succeeded in passing the Congress and was signed into law in 2010. Obama's reelection in 2012 has led to the implementation of the law's first measures. The fierceness of the health care debate—which revolved around questions about the power of the state, the responsibilities of elected governments, the nature of the public good, and the balance between liberty and equality—should not obscure the fact that partisans on both sides of these controversies are using a vocabulary and a set of references that are part of the same liberal democratic political traditions that emerged in Europe and North America in the previous two centuries.

If Obama's two-term presidency has given some hope to those who see an important role for the state in solving persistent social and economic problems, the situation in Europe in the aftermath of the 2008 financial crisis has been less comforting. The European welfare state model inherited from the post–Second World War decades was based on a combination of Marshall Plan investment, European economic integration, and cooperation among representatives of labor, employers, and the state. Trade unions agreed to wage moderation in exchange for social protections from the state. Business leaders agreed to higher taxes for social protections in exchange for labor peace. Govern-

ment officials convinced their electorates to pay higher taxes in exchange for social protections such as universal health care, unemployment, and old age pensions.

This system worked well as long as the economy kept growing. When the economy flattened out beginning in the 1970s, however, businesses reduced their investments, unemployment went up, workers expressed discontent with their former restraint on wages, and European states had less revenue for social protection. In the 1980s and 1990s, European governments resorted to deficit spending to protect their welfare programs, and this system worked well enough as long as the banks that were lending the governments money were confident that they would be repaid. Faith in this system led to the creation of the eurozone as a single currency area in 2002.

After the financial crisis of 2008, however, the delicate balance in Europe between banks and governments in Europe began to crumble. European banks that were already fragile from losses in the real estate bubble demanded extraordinarily high interest rates before they would loan money to governments that were in financial trouble. The crisis was most acute in Greece, Spain, Italy, Ireland, and Portugal, where government debt reached threatening levels. So far, the solution has been for the stronger economies in the eurozone to bail out the weaker economies by providing emergency funds. To receive them, however, the indebted governments are forced to accept steep cuts in state spending, which are deeply unpopular with their populations. The ensuing political crisis has caused some to think that the eurozone might not survive in its present form and that some countries might be forced out or choose to leave of their own will. If that happens, it will mark a significant turning point in the history of European integration, which has provided a template for thinking about the European future since the years after the Second World War.

THE ARAB SPRING OF 2011

The dramatic events that began in Tunisia in December 2010 brought a wave of protest and popular insurrection to much of the Arab Middle East, overthrowing powerful dictators and presidents for life in Tunisia, Egypt, and Libya. The speed of these momentous changes surprised people living in these countries as much as they astonished foreign observers—many had long assumed that political change, when it came to these regimes, would proceed at a glacial pace. Zine al-Abidine Ben Ali of Tunisia, Hosni Mubarak of Egypt, and Muammar Qadhafi of Libya had governed for decades. Ben Ali and Mubarak were establishment figures in the international world, regularly meet-

Past and Present

The Arab Spring in Historical Perspective

With the collapse of the Berlin Wall in 1989 a relatively recent memory, many people in Europe and North America sought to compare the recent protests in the Middle East against authoritarian governments to these European events. Comparisons with 1968 (see left, the Prague Spring), 1989, or 1848 may be instructive, but it is also likely that the forms of democracy that protesters in Tunisia, Egypt (see right, protesters in Tahrir Square, Cairo), and most recently, Turkey, are striving to create will reflect their own values, rather than conform to political models borrowed from elsewhere.

 Watch related author interview on StudySpace
wwnorton.com/web/westernciv18

ing with European leaders and U.S. presidents who were among their most loyal supporters. How had this happened so suddenly? Did it mean that a wave of democratic revolution was sweeping through the Middle East?

To explain these events, many observers in Europe and the United States looked for explanations from their own histories. Some people suggested that these revolts were comparable to the movements to overthrow the dictatorial regimes of Eastern Europe that culminated in the fall of the Berlin Wall in 1989 and the collapse of the Soviet Union in 1991. The very name "Arab Spring" recalled the Prague Spring of 1968 when young people in Czechoslovakia attempted, and ultimately failed, to create a different and more democratic form of socialism in that country. Others feared that these revolts might turn out like the Tiananmen Square protests in China of 1989, which ended up in a violent repression of a democratic movement. The continued civil war in Syria is a haunting reminder of the reality of this possibility.

All of these comparisons might be instructive, but they also reveal something significant about the way that many people think about movements for democratic revolutions: there is a tendency to assume that movements for democracy all want the same thing. History shows that it is usually much more complicated than that. Great coalitions can be assembled at a moment of crisis to challenge established regimes, but success brings on new challenges. As the protests in the Middle East and North Africa unfolded in 2011, observers frequently noted how new technologies such as cell phones and new social media such as Facebook and Twitter allowed people to make their voices heard in a new way and to coordinate mass actions almost instantaneously. It remains to be seen, however, what the lasting accomplishments of this movement for change will be. How can this unity be maintained when it comes to building a new political system, a new and different society?

Prior to 2011, many people in the United States, in Europe, and in the Middle East itself had been filled with pessimism about this region of the world. Persistent conflict and the appearance of frightening movements that advocate terrorist violence caused many to give up hope. With the Arab Spring, it became clear, however, that what many people wanted was the right to build a more responsive and accountable form of government that was compatible with their core beliefs and values. Building a consensus around these values is not easy—it is the work of any society that endures. Observers in the United States might pause to remember that it took that country more than 150 years to arrive at a political system in which every adult could vote—a period that witnessed a bloody civil war and persistent violence over questions of race. For Europeans, it took generation after generation of repeated revolutionary and counterrevolutionary violence, not to mention two world wars. The nations of the Arab Middle East have been independent now for less than the lifetime of one person. The form of society that they choose will not be the same as that chosen by the French, the Poles, or the Italians. But in that effort to shape a society that conforms to their beliefs and provides them with security and sustenance, the many people who demonstrated in Tunis or in Tahrir Square in Cairo are no different from anybody else in the world.

CONCLUSION

Globalization—defined loosely as the process by which the economies, societies, and cultures of different parts of the world become increasingly interconnected—has been hailed as a solution to old problems even as it has been criticized as a source of new ones. Although some thought that the end of the Cold War in 1989 meant that economic liberalism—that is, a global free-market capitalist system unfettered by government regulations—had triumphed for good in the world, continued political instability in many parts of the globe and the global economic crisis of 2008 have called into question such optimistic interpretations of world events. In the economic realm, national states have looked for ways to reassert their control over the flow of currencies and goods and protect their populations against decisions made elsewhere by financial speculators and investors. Meanwhile, the danger of radical forms of terrorism, both foreign and domestic, has caused even strongly democratic governments in the West to create new and pervasive surveillance bureaucracies, demonstrating that global threats can have real and seemingly permanent local effects on definitions of

After You Read This Chapter

Ⓢ Visit StudySpace for quizzes, additional review materials, and multimedia documents. **wwnorton.com/web/westernciv18**

REVIEWING THE OBJECTIVES

- Globalization in the second half of the twentieth century was not new. What does globalization mean, and what was similar or different about the most recent phase of globalization in human history?

- The burden of the colonial past continued to weigh heavily on many former colonies after the 1960s. What accounts for the success of some former colonies in the global economy and the continued social and political challenges facing others?

- Since the end of the Second World War, conflicts and events in the Middle East have taken on a global significance far beyond the region's borders. What are the crucial conflicts that occupied the attention of other nations, and what events have proved to be crucial turning points in the emergence of the Middle East as a region that drives developments elsewhere?

citizenship, the permeability of borders, and extensions of state power.

In such uncertain times, it is difficult to remain consistent or to determine national priorities: is the threat of terrorism greater than the threat of a loss of liberty stemming from extensions in government power? Is it fair of the International Monetary Fund to ask developing nations to adhere to austere cuts to their social welfare spending when wealthy private investment banks receive billion-dollar bailouts for making bad bets in the financial markets because they are "too big to fail"? The complexity of the world's interconnections makes it difficult to determine definitive answers to such questions, and even if one could, any ensuing policy decisions would create winners and losers, ensuring that the political struggles implicit in such questions will endure. Globalization, therefore, is not a final destination—it is the new complex reality of human existence, the context for future struggles about the goals of political association, the meanings of liberty or equality, and the possibility of shared values.

The loss of familiar moorings makes fundamental questions about human behavior and political community difficult to answer. History offers no quick solutions. Historians are reluctant to offer what historian Peter Novick calls "pithy lessons that fit on a bumper sticker." As Novick puts it:

> If there is, to use a pretentious word, any wisdom to be acquired from contemplating an historical event, I would think it would derive from confronting it in all its complexity and its contradictions; the ways in which it resembles other events to which it might be compared as well as the way it differs from them. . . . If there are lessons to be extracted from encountering the past, that encounter has to be with the past in all its messiness; they're not likely to come from an encounter with a past that's been shaped so that inspiring lessons will emerge.

The untidy and contradictory evidence that historians discover in the archives rarely yields unblemished heroes or unvarnished villains. Good history reveals the complex processes and dynamics of change over time. It helps us understand the many layers of the past that have formed and constrain us in our present world. At the same time, it shows again and again that these constraints do not preordain what happens next or how we can make the history of the future.

PEOPLE, IDEAS, AND EVENTS IN CONTEXT

- What were the policy goals of **NEOLIBERALISM** after the 1970s, as exemplified by the activities of institutions such as the **INTERNATIONAL MONETARY FUND** and the World Bank?
- How do the **HIV EPIDEMIC** of the 1980s or the **SARS EPIDEMIC** of 2003 illustrate the new realities of public health in a globalized world?
- What was the significance of **NELSON MANDELA**'s election as president of South Africa in 1994?
- How was the **1973 OIL EMBARGO** related to the **ARAB-ISRAELI CONFLICT**, and what were its effects on the global economy?
- What did radical critics dislike about secular forms of **ARAB NATIONALISM** such as that represented by **GAMAL ABDEL NASSER** in Egypt?
- What led the United States and Britain to support the regime of **REZA PAHLAVI** in Iran, and what events brought **RUHOLLAH KHOMEINI** to power in Iran in 1979?
- What circumstances link the Soviet invasion of Afghanistan in 1979 with the origins of **AL QAEDA**?
- What made it difficult for European and North American governments to sign the UN's **UNIVERSAL DECLARATION OF HUMAN RIGHTS** in 1948? What events have occurred since 1948 that indicate that at least some nations might agree to international treaties guaranteeing human rights?

THINKING ABOUT CONNECTIONS

- Many of the global linkages between Europe and the United States, on the one hand, and the independent nations of Asia, Africa, and Latin America, on the other, were first forged during earlier periods of imperial expansion. How does this history continue to be felt in the present?
- Global networks of transport, trade, and communication have long been significant vectors for cultural change, by bringing different peoples into contact and conversation with one another. How have recent developments in technology changed the nature of this global conversation?

Rulers of Principal States

THE CAROLINGIAN DYNASTY

Pepin of Heristal, Mayor of the Palace, 687–714
Charles Martel, Mayor of the Palace, 715–741
Pepin III, Mayor of the Palace, 741–751; King, 751–768
Charlemagne, King, 768–814; Emperor, 800–814
Louis the Pious, Emperor, 814–840

West Francia

Charles the Bald, King, 840–877; Emperor, 875–877
Louis II, King, 877–879
Louis III, King, 879–882
Carloman, King, 879–884

HOLY ROMAN EMPERORS

Saxon Dynasty

Otto I, 962–973
Otto II, 973–983
Otto III, 983–1002
Henry II, 1002–1024

Franconian Dynasty

Conrad II, 1024–1039
Henry III, 1039–1056
Henry IV, 1056–1106
Henry V, 1106–1125
Lothair II (Saxony), 1125–1137

Hohenstaufen Dynasty

Conrad III, 1138–1152
Frederick I (Barbarossa), 1152–1190
Henry VI, 1190–1197
Philip of Swabia, 1198–1208 ⎫
Otto IV (Welf), 1198–1215 ⎭ Rivals

Middle Kingdoms

Lothair, Emperor, 840–855
Louis (Italy), Emperor, 855–875
Charles (Provence), King, 855–863
Lothair II (Lorraine), King, 855–869

East Francia

Ludwig, King, 840–876
Carloman, King, 876–880
Ludwig, King, 876–882
Charles the Fat, Emperor, 876–887

Frederick II, 1220–1250
Conrad IV, 1250–1254

Interregnum, 1254–1273

Emperors from Various Dynasties

Rudolf I (Habsburg), 1273–1291
Adolf (Nassau), 1292–1298
Albert I (Habsburg), 1298–1308
Henry VII (Luxemburg), 1308–1313
Ludwig IV (Wittelsbach), 1314–1347
Charles IV (Luxemburg), 1347–1378
Wenceslas (Luxemburg), 1378–1400
Rupert (Wittelsbach), 1400–1410
Sigismund (Luxemburg), 1410–1437

Habsburg Dynasty

Albert II, 1438–1439
Frederick III, 1440–1493

Maximilian I, 1493–1519
Charles V, 1519–1556
Ferdinand I, 1556–1564
Maximilian II, 1564–1576
Rudolf II, 1576–1612
Matthias, 1612–1619
Ferdinand II, 1619–1637
Ferdinand III, 1637–1657

Leopold I, 1658–1705
Joseph I, 1705–1711
Charles VI, 1711–1740
Charles VII (not a Habsburg), 1742–1745
Francis I, 1745–1765
Joseph II, 1765–1790
Leopold II, 1790–1792
Francis II, 1792–1806

RULERS OF FRANCE FROM HUGH CAPET

Capetian Dynasty

Hugh Capet, 987–996
Robert II, 996–1031
Henry I, 1031–1060
Philip I, 1060–1108
Louis VI, 1108–1137
Louis VII, 1137–1180
Philip II (Augustus), 1180–1223
Louis VIII, 1223–1226
Louis IX (St. Louis), 1226–1270
Philip III, 1270–1285
Philip IV, 1285–1314
Louis X, 1314–1316
Philip V, 1316–1322
Charles IV, 1322–1328

Valois Dynasty

Philip VI, 1328–1350
John, 1350–1364
Charles V, 1364–1380
Charles VI, 1380–1422
Charles VII, 1422–1461
Louis XI, 1461–1483
Charles VIII, 1483–1498
Louis XII, 1498–1515
Francis I, 1515–1547

Henry II, 1547–1559
Francis II, 1559–1560
Charles IX, 1560–1574
Henry III, 1574–1589

Bourbon Dynasty

Henry IV, 1589–1610
Louis XIII, 1610–1643
Louis XIV, 1643–1715
Louis XV, 1715–1774
Louis XVI, 1774–1792

After 1792

First Republic, 1792–1799
Napoleon Bonaparte, First Consul, 1799–1804
Napoleon I, Emperor, 1804–1814
Louis XVIII (Bourbon dynasty), 1814–1824
Charles X (Bourbon dynasty), 1824–1830
Louis Philippe, 1830–1848
Second Republic, 1848–1852
Napoleon III, Emperor, 1852–1870
Third Republic, 1870–1940
Pétain regime, 1940–1944
Provisional government, 1944–1946
Fourth Republic, 1946–1958
Fifth Republic, 1958–

RULERS OF ENGLAND

Anglo-Saxon Dynasty

Alfred the Great, 871–899
Edward the Elder, 899–924
Ethelstan, 924–939
Edmund I, 939–946
Edred, 946–955
Edwy, 955–959
Edgar, 959–975

Edward the Martyr, 975–978
Ethelred the Unready, 978–1016
Canute, 1016–1035 (Danish Nationality)
Harold I, 1035–1040
Hardicanute, 1040–1042
Edward the Confessor, 1042–1066
Harold II, 1066

House of Normandy

William I (the Conqueror), 1066–1087
William II, 1087–1100
Henry I, 1100–1135
Stephen, 1135–1154

House of Plantagenet

Henry II, 1154–1189
Richard I, 1189–1199
John, 1199–1216
Henry III, 1216–1272
Edward I, 1272–1307
Edward II, 1307–1327
Edward III, 1327–1377
Richard II, 1377–1399

House of Lancaster

Henry IV, 1399–1413
Henry V, 1413–1422
Henry VI, 1422–1461

House of York

Edward IV, 1461–1483
Edward V, 1483
Richard III, 1483–1485

House of Tudor

Henry VII, 1485–1509
Henry VIII, 1509–1547
Edward VI, 1547–1553
Mary, 1553–1558
Elizabeth I, 1558–1603

House of Stuart

James I, 1603–1625
Charles I, 1625–1649

Commonwealth and Protectorate, 1649–1659

House of Stuart Restored

Charles II, 1660–1685
James II, 1685–1688
William III and Mary II, 1689–1694
William III alone, 1694–1702
Anne, 1702–1714

House of Hanover

George I, 1714–1727
George II, 1727–1760
George III, 1760–1820
George IV, 1820–1830
William IV, 1830–1837
Victoria, 1837–1901

House of Saxe-Coburg-Gotha

Edward VII, 1901–1910
George V, 1910–1917

House of Windsor

George V, 1917–1936
Edward VIII, 1936
George VI, 1936–1952
Elizabeth II, 1952–

RULERS OF AUSTRIA AND AUSTRIA-HUNGARY

*Maximilian I (Archduke), 1493–1519
*Charles V, 1519–1556
*Ferdinand I, 1556–1564
*Maximilian II, 1564–1576
*Rudolf II, 1576–1612
*Matthias, 1612–1619
*Ferdinand II, 1619–1637
*Ferdinand III, 1637–1657
*Leopold I, 1658–1705
*Joseph I, 1705–1711
*Charles VI, 1711–1740
Maria Theresa, 1740–1780

*Joseph II, 1780–1790
*Leopold II, 1790–1792
*Francis II, 1792–1835 (Emperor of Austria as Francis I after 1804)
Ferdinand I, 1835–1848
Francis Joseph, 1848–1916 (after 1867 Emperor of Austria and King of Hungary)
Charles I, 1916–1918 (Emperor of Austria and King of Hungary)
Republic of Austria, 1918–1938 (dictatorship after 1934)
Republic restored, under Allied occupation, 1945–1956
Free Republic, 1956–

*Also bore title of Holy Roman Emperor

RULERS OF PRUSSIA AND GERMANY

*Frederick I, 1701–1713
*Frederick William I, 1713–1740
*Frederick II (the Great), 1740–1786
*Frederick William II, 1786–1797
*Frederick William III,1797–1840
*Frederick William IV, 1840–1861
*William I, 1861–1888 (German Emperor after 1871)
Frederick III, 1888

*William II, 1888–1918
Weimar Republic, 1918–1933
Third Reich (Nazi Dictatorship), 1933–1945
Allied occupation, 1945–1952
Division into Federal Republic of Germany in west and
    German Democratic Republic in east, 1949–1991
Federal Republic of Germany (united), 1991–

*Kings of Prussia

RULERS OF RUSSIA

Ivan III, 1462–1505
Vasily III, 1505–1533
Ivan IV, 1533–1584
Theodore I, 1534–1598
Boris Godunov, 1598–1605
Theodore II,1605
Vasily IV, 1606–1610
Michael, 1613–1645
Alexius, 1645–1676
Theodore III, 1676–1682
Ivan V and Peter I, 1682–1689
Peter I (the Great), 1689–1725
Catherine I, 1725–1727
Peter II, 1727–1730

Anna, 1730–1740
Ivan VI, 1740–1741
Elizabeth, 1741–1762
Peter III, 1762
Catherine II (the Great), 1762–1796
Paul, 1796–1801
Alexander I,1801–1825
Nicholas I, 1825–1855
Alexander II,1855–1881
Alexander III, 1881–1894
Nicholas II, 1894–1917
Soviet Republic, 1917–1991
Russian Federation, 1991–

RULERS OF UNIFIED SPAIN

Ferdinand {
    and Isabella, 1479–1504
    and Philip I, 1504–1506
    and Charles I, 1506–1516
}
Charles I (Holy Roman Emperor Charles V), 1516–1556
Philip II, 1556–1598
Philip III, 1598–1621
Philip IV, 1621–1665
Charles II, 1665–1700
Philip V, 1700–1746
Ferdinand VI, 1746–1759
Charles III, 1759–1788
Charles IV, 1788–1808

Ferdinand VII, 1808
Joseph Bonaparte, 1808–1813
Ferdinand VII (restored), 1814–1833
Isabella II, 1833–1868
Republic, 1868–1870
Amadeo, 1870–1873
Republic, 1873–1874
Alfonso XII, 1874–1885
Alfonso XIII, 1886–1931
Republic, 1931–1939
Fascist Dictatorship, 1939–1975
Juan Carlos I, 1975–

RULERS OF ITALY

Victor Emmanuel II, 1861–1878
Humbert I, 1878–1900
Victor Emmanuel III, 1900–1946

Fascist Dictatorship, 1922-1943 (maintained in northern Italy until 1945)
Humbert II, May 9–June 13, 1946
Republic, 1946–

PROMINENT POPES

Silvester I, 314–335
Leo I, 440–461
Gelasius I, 492–496
Gregory I, 590–604
Nicholas I, 858–867
Silvester II, 999–1003
Leo IX, 1049–1054
Nicholas II, 1058–1061
Gregory VII, 1073–1085
Urban II, 1088–1099
Paschal II, 1099–1118
Alexander III, 1159–1181
Innocent III, 1198–1216
Gregory IX, 1227–1241
Innocent IV, 1243–1254
Boniface VIII, 1294–1303
John XXII, 1316–1334
Nicholas V, 1447–1455
Pius II, 1458–1464

Alexander VI, 1492–1503
Julius II, 1503–1513
Leo X, 1513–1521
Paul III, 1534–1549
Paul IV, 1555–1559
Sixtus V, 1585–1590
Urban VIII, 1623–1644
Gregory XVI, 1831–1846
Pius IX, 1846–1878
Leo XIII, 1878–1903
Pius X, 1903–1914
Benedict XV, 1914–1922
Pius XI, 1922–1939
Pius XII, 1939–1958
John XXIII, 1958–1963
Paul VI, 1963–1978
John Paul I, 1978
John Paul II, 1978–2005
Benedict XVI, 2005–2013
Francis, 2013–

CHAPTER 1

Aldred, Cyril. *The Egyptians*. 3d ed. London, 1998. An indispensable, lively overview of Egyptian culture and history by one of the great masters of Egyptology.

Baines, J., and J. Málek. *Atlas of Ancient Egypt*. Rev. ed. New York, 2000. A reliable, well-illustrated survey, with excellent maps.

Bottéro, Jean. *Everyday Life in Ancient Mesopotamia*. Trans. Antonia Nevill. Baltimore, MD, 2001. A wide-ranging, interdisciplinary account.

Bottéro, Jean. *Religion in Ancient Mesopotamia*. Chicago, 2001. An accessible, engaging survey.

Dodson, Aidan. *Amarna Sunset: Nefertiti, Tutankhamun, Ay, Horemheb, and the Egyptian Counter-Reformation*. Cairo, 2009. A provocative study of the resistance to Akhenaten's religious "reformation," this book argues that Nefertiti was not only queen but also a kind of "joint-pharaoh," the mother of Tutankhamun, and the leader of the movement toward a return to traditional forms of worship.

Foster, Benjamin R. and Karen Polinger Foster. *Civilizations of Ancient Iraq*. Princeton, 2011. A critically-acclaimed survey that charts the history of this region from the earliest Sumerian civilization to the Arab conquests of the seventh c. C.E.

Geller, Markham J. *Ancient Babylonian Medicine: Theory and Practice*. Malden, MA, 2010. Makes use of previously unstudied cuneiform sources to tell a new story about the relationship between medicine and magic.

George, Andrew, trans. *The Epic of Gilgamesh: A New Translation. The Babylonian Epic Poem and Other Texts in Akkadian and Sumerian*. New York and London, 1999. A reliable translation which carefully distinguishes the chronological "layers" of this famous text; also includes many related texts.

Hodder, Ian. *The Leopard's Tale:Revealing the Mysteries of Çatalhöyük*. London and New York, 2006. The most up-to-date account of this fascinating archaeological site, written for general readers by the director of the excavation.

Kemp, Barry. *The City of Akhenaten and Nefertiti: Armana and Its People*. London, 2012. A cutting-edge study of this ancient site, based on decades of archeological research.

Leick, Gwendolyn. *The Babylonians: An Introduction*. London and New York, 2002. A wide-ranging survey of Babylonian civilization across the centuries.

McDowell, A. G. *Village Life in Ancient Egypt: Laundry Lists and Love Songs*. Oxford, 1999. A fascinating collection of translated texts recovered from an Egyptian peasant village, dating from 1539 to 1075 B.C.E.

McGregor, Neil. *A History of the World in 100 Objects*. London, 2011. Based on an acclaimed BBC Radio program, this book features a range of artifacts from the collections British Museum, embeds them in their historical contexts, and explores the ways that that still hold meaning today.

Pollock, Susan. *Ancient Mesopotamia*. Cambridge, 1999. An advanced textbook that draws on theoretical anthropology to interpret Mesopotamian civilization up to 2100 B.C.E.

Redford, Donald B., ed. *The Oxford Encyclopedia of Ancient Egypt*. 3 vols. New York, 2001. An indispensible reference work, intended for both specialists and beginners.

Roaf, Michael. *Cultural Atlas of Mesopotamia and the Ancient Near East*. New York, 1990. An informative, authoritative, and lavishly illustrated guide, with excellent maps.

Robins, Gay. *The Art of Ancient Egypt*. London, 1997. An excellent survey, now the standard account.

Shafer, Byron E., ed. *Religion in Ancient Egypt: Gods, Myths, and Personal Practice*. London, 1991. A scholarly examination of Egyptian belief and ritual, with contributions from leading authorities.

Shaw, Ian, ed. *The Oxford History of Ancient Egypt*. Oxford, 2000. An outstanding collaborative survey of Egyptian history from the Stone Age to c. 300 C.E., with excellent bibliographical essays.

Shryock, Andrew and Daniel Lord Smail. Berkeley, 2012. *Deep History: The Architecture of Past and Present*. A fascinating fusion of historical, anthropological, and scientific research on what it means to be human.

Smail, Daniel Lord. *On Deep History and the Brain*. Berkeley, 2008. A pioneering introduction to the historical uses of neuroscience and evolutionary biology.

Snell, Daniel C., ed. *A Companion to the Ancient Near East*. Oxford, 2005. A topical survey of recent scholarly work, particularly strong on society, economy, and culture.

Wengrow, David. *The Archaeology of Early Egypt: Social Transformations in North-East Africa, 10,000 to 2650 B.C.* Cambridge, 2006. An authoritative account of archeological evidence and its interpretation.

CHAPTER 2

Aubet, Maria Eugenia. *Phoenicia and the West: Politics, Colonies, and Trade*. Trans. Mary Turton. Cambridge, 1993. An intelligent and thought-provoking examination of Phoenician civilization and its influence.

Boardman, John. *Assyrian and Babylonian Empires and Other States of the Near East from the Eighth to the Sixth Centuries* B.C. New York, 1991. Scholarly and authoritative.

———. *Persia and the West*. London, 2000. A great book by a distinguished scholar, with a particular focus on art and architecture as projections of Persian imperial ideologies.

Boyce, Mary. *Textual Sources for the Study of Zoroastrianism*. Totowa, NJ, 1984. An invaluable collection of documents.

Bryce, Trevor. *The Kingdom of the Hittites*. Oxford, 1998. And *Life and Society in the Hittite World*. Oxford, 2002. An extraordinary synthesis, now the standard account of Hittite political, military, and daily life.

Curtis, John. *Ancient Persia*. Cambridge, MA, 1990. Concise, solid, reliable.

Dever, William. *Who Were the Early Israelites and Where Did They Come From?* Grand Rapids, MI, 2003. A balanced, fair-minded account with excellent bibliographical guidance to recent work.

Dickinson, O. T. P. K. *The Aegean Bronze Age*. Cambridge, 1994. An excellent summary of archaeological evidence and scholarly argument concerning Minoan, Mycenaean, and other cultures of the Bronze Age Aegean basin.

Dothan, Trude, and Moshe Dothan. *Peoples of the Sea: The Search for the Philistines*. New York, 1992. The essential starting point for understanding Philistine culture and its links to the Aegean basin.

Drews, Robert. *The End of the Bronze Age: Changes in Warfare and the Catastrophe ca. 1200* B.C. Princeton, NJ, 1993. A stimulating analysis and survey, with excellent bibliographies.

Finkelstein, Israel, and Nadav Na'aman, eds. *From Nomadism to Monarchy: Archaeological and Historical Aspects of Early Israel*. Jerusalem, 1994. Scholarly articles on the Hebrews' transformation from pastoralists to a sedentary society focused on the worship of Yahweh.

Fitton, J. Lesley. *Minoans: Peoples of the Past* (British Museum Publications). London, 2002. A careful, reliable debunking of myths about the Minoans, written for nonspecialists.

Kamm, Antony. *The Israelites: An Introduction*. New York, 1999. A short, accessible history of the land and people of Israel up to 135 C.E., aimed at students and general readers.

Kuhrt, Amélie. *The Ancient Near East, c. 3000–330* B.C. 2 vols. London and New York, 1995. An outstanding survey, written for students, that includes Egypt and Israel as well as Mesopotamia, Babylonia, Assyria, and Persia.

Marinatos, Nannos. *Minoan Kingship and the Solar Goddess: A Near Eastern Koine*. Champaign, IL, 2010. A rich new interpretation of Minoan culture and its wider connections and influence within the world of the late Bronze Age.

Metzger, Bruce M., and Michael D. Coogan, eds. *The Oxford Companion to the Bible*. New York, 1993. An outstanding reference work, with contributions by leading authorities.

Niditch, Susan. *Ancient Israelite Religion*. New York, 1997. A short introduction designed for students, emphasizing the diversity of Hebrew religious practices.

Prezioso, Donald and Louise A. Hitchcock. *Aegean Art and Architecture*. Oxford, 2000. Archaic Greek artistic forms in their broader geographic and cultural context, from the fourth millennium to 1000 B.C.E.

Redford, Donald B. *Egypt, Canaan, and Israel in Ancient Times*. Princeton, NJ, 1992. An overview of the interactions between these peoples from about 1200 B.C.E. to the beginning of the Common Era.

Renfrew, Colin. *Archaeology and Language: The Puzzle of Indo-European Origins*. Cambridge, 1987. A masterful but controversial work by one of the most creative archaeologists of the twentieth century.

Sandars, Nancy K. *The Sea Peoples: Warriors of the Ancient Mediterranean*. Rev. ed. London, 1985. An introductory account for students and scholars.

Tubb, Jonathan N., and Rupert L. Chapman. *Archaeology and the Bible*. London, 1990. A good starting point for students that clearly illustrates the difficulties in linking archeological evidence to biblical accounts of early Hebrew history and society.

Wood, Michael. *In Search of the Trojan War*. New York, 1985. Aimed at a general audience, this carefully researched and engagingly written book is an excellent introduction to the late–Bronze Age context of the Trojan War.

CHAPTER 3

Penguin Classics and the Loeb Classical Library both offer reliable translations of Greek literary, philosophical, and historical texts.

Beard, Mary. *The Parthenon*. Cambridge, MA, 2003. A book that traces the successive stages of this monument's construction, deconstruction, reconstruction, and restoration.

Boardman, John, Jaspar Griffin, and Oswyn Murray, eds. *Greece and the Hellenistic World*. Oxford, 1988. A reprint of the Greek and Hellenistic chapters from *The Oxford History of the Classical World*, originally published in 1986. Excellent, stimulating surveys, accessible to a general audience.

Brunschwig, Jacques, and Geoffrey E. R. Lloyd. *Greek Thought: A Guide to Classical Knowledge*. Translated by Catherine Porter. Cambridge, MA, 2000. An outstanding work of reference.

Buckley, Terry, ed. *Aspects of Greek History, 750–323* B.C.: A Source-Based Approach. London, 1999. An outstanding collection of source materials.

Cartledge, Paul A. *The Spartans: An Epic History*. New York, 2003. A lively and authoritative history of Sparta from its origins to the Roman conquest.

Dover, Kenneth J. *Greek Homosexuality*. Cambridge, MA, 1978. The standard account of an important subject.

Fantham, Elaine, Helene Foley, Natalie Kampen, Sarah B. Pomeroy, and H. A. Shapiro. *Women in the Classical World: Image and Text*. Oxford, 1994. Wide-ranging analysis drawing on both visual and written sources, covering both the Greek and the Roman periods.

Fornara, Charles W., and Loren J. Samons II. *Athens from Cleisthenes to Pericles*. Berkeley, CA, 1991. An excellent narrative history of Athenian politics during the first half of the fifth century B.C.E.

Garlan, Yvon. *Slavery in Ancient Greece*. Ithaca, NY, 1988. Now the standard account.

Hanson, Victor Davis. *The Other Greeks: The Family Farm and the Agrarian Roots of Western Civilization*. New York, 1995. Polemical and idiosyncratic, but convincing in its emphasis on smallholding farmers as the backbone of Greek urban society.

Havelock, Eric A. *The Literate Revolution in Greece and Its Cultural Consequences*. Princeton, 1982. A now-classic account of the wide-ranging effects of writing on Greek society.

Jones, Nicholas F. *Ancient Greece: State and Society*. Upper Saddle River, NJ, 1997. A concise survey from the Minoans up to the end of the Classical Period that emphasizes the connections between the social order and politics.

Krentz, Peter. *The Battle of Marathon*. New Haven, 2011. A fresh analysis of this landmark battle, paying special attention to the conditions in which hoplite warriors fought.

Lefkowitz, Mary, and Maureen Fant. *Women's Life in Greece and Rome: A Source Book in Translation*. 3rd ed. Baltimore, MD, 2005. A remarkably wide-ranging collection, topically arranged, invaluable to students.

Nevett, Lisa C. *Domestic Space in Classical Antiquity*. Cambridge, 2010. Reassesses what we can know about the architecture of households in antiquity through a fresh assessment of archeological evidence and material culture.

Pomeroy, Sarah B., Stanley M. Burstein, Walter Donlan, and Jennifer Tolbert Roberts. *Ancient Greece: A Political, Social, and Cultural History*. Oxford, 1999. An outstanding textbook; clear and lively.

Pomeroy, Sarah. *Goddesses, Whores, Wives, and Slaves: Women in Classical Antiquity*. New York, 1995. The first historical survey of antiquity to place women at the center of the narrative, and still unrivaled in scope.

Price, Simon. *Religions of the Ancient Greeks*. Cambridge, 1999. Concise and authoritative, this survey extends from the Archaic Period up to the fifth century C.E.

Seaford, Richard. *Money and the Greek Mind: Homer, Philosophy, Tragedy*. Cambridge, 2004. A provocative study of portable wealth and its far-reaching effects.

Strassler, Robert B., ed. *The Landmark Thucydides*. New York, 1996. Reprints the classic Richard Crawley translation with maps, commentary, notes, and appendices by leading scholars.

Thomas, Carol G., and Craig Conant. *Citadel to City-State: The Transformation of Greece, 1200–700* B.C.E. Bloomington, IN, 1999. A lucid and accessible study that examines developments at a number of different Dark Age sites.

Thomas, Rosalind. *Oral Tradition and Written Record in Classical Athens*. Cambridge, 1989. A fascinating look at how oral epic, lyric, and drama were transmitted over time.

CHAPTER 4

Penguin Classics and the Loeb Classical Library both offer reliable translations of scores of literary and historical texts from this period. Particularly important are historical works by Arrian (*Anabasis of Alexander*), Plutarch (*Life of Alexander*), and Polybius (*The Histories*).

Austin, M. M. *The Hellenistic World from Alexander to the Roman Conquest: A Selection of Ancient Sources in Translation*. Cambridge, 1981. A good collection of primary documents.

Bagnall, R. S., and P. Derow. *Greek Historical Documents: The Hellenistic Period*. Chico, CA, 1981. Another useful collection.

Borza, Eugene N. *In the Shadow of Olympus: The Emergence of Macedon*. Princeton, NJ, 1990. The standard account of the rise of Macedon up to the accession of Philip II.

Bosworth, A. B. *Conquest and Empire: The Reign of Alexander the Great*. Cambridge, 1988. A political and military analysis of Alexander's career that strips away the romance, maintaining a clear vision of the ruthlessness and human cost of his conquests.

———. *The Legacy of Alexander: Politics, Warfare, and Propaganda under the Successors*. Oxford, 2002. The most recent survey of the half century following Alexander's death and of the people who created the Hellenistic kingdoms of Egypt, Persia, and Macedon.

Burstein, Stanley M., ed. and trans. *The Hellenistic Age from the Battle of Ipsos to the Death of Kleopatra VII*. Cambridge, 1985. An excellent collection, with sources not found elsewhere.

Cartledge, Paul. *Agesilaus and the Crisis of Sparta*. Baltimore, MD, 1987. A thorough but readable analysis of the social and political challenges besetting Sparta in the fourth century B.C.E.

———. *Alexander the Great: The Hunt for a New Past*. Woodstock, NY, 2004. A compelling account of Alexander's life, times, and influences.

Green, Peter. *Alexander to Actium: The Historical Evolution of the Hellenistic Age*. Berkeley, CA. 1990. An outstanding, comprehensive, and wide-ranging history of the period.

———. *Alexander of Macedon, 356–323* B.C. Berkeley, CA, 1991. Revised edition of the author's earlier biography; entertainingly written, rich in detail and insight.

———. *The Hellenistic Age: A Short History*. New York, 2007. An authoritative synthesis that carries the history of Greek influence into the fourth century C.E.

Hansen, Mogens H. *The Athenian Democracy in the Age of Demosthenes*. Oxford, 1991. An examination of the political institutions of Athens in the fourth century B.C.E.

Holt, Frank. L. *Into the Land of Bones: Alexander the Great in Afghanistan*. Berkeley, 2012 repr. ed. A vivid, charged narrative that places the beginning of a current war in the distant past.

Lloyd, Geoffrey, and Nathan Sivin. *The Way and the Word: Science and Medicine in Early China and Greece*. New Haven, CT, 2002. An extraordinary comparative study.

McGing, Brian. *Polybius' Histories*. Oxford, 2010. A critical dissection of this influential ancient historian's techniques and historical philosophy.

Nicholas, G. L. *The Genius of Alexander the Great*. Chapel Hill, NC, 1998. A clear, authoritative, admiring account, distilling a lifetime of research on the subject.

Ober, Josiah. *Mass and Elite in Democratic Athens: Rhetoric, Ideology, and the Power of the People*. Princeton, NJ, 1989. An excellent study of the ideology of democracy in Athens that borrows from the insights of modern social science.

Pollitt, Jerome J. *Art in the Hellenistic Age.* New York, 1986. The standard account, blending cultural history with art history.

Sherwin-White, Susan, and Amélie Kuhrt. *From Samarkhand to Sardis: A New Approach to the Seleucid Empire.* London, 1993. A stimulating examination of the relationship between rulers and ruled in the vast expanses of the Seleucid Empire.

Shipley, Graham. *The Greek World after Alexander, 323–30 B.C.* New York and London, 2000. A study of the social, intellectual, and artistic changes in the Hellenistic era.

Thomas, Carol G. *Alexander the Great in His World.* Oxford and Malden, MA, 2007. A study of the contexts—familial, political, and social—that shaped Alexander's career.

Tripolitis, Antonia. *Religions of the Hellenistic-Roman Age.* Grand Rapids, MI, 2002. Survey of the variety of religious experience, ritual, and belief in the centuries before the emergence of Christianity.

Tritle, Lawrence A., ed. *The Greek World in the Fourth Century: From the Fall of the Athenian Empire to the Successors of Alexander.* New York, 1997. A wide-ranging collection of scholarly essays.

CHAPTER 5

Translations of Roman authors are available in both the Penguin Classics series and in the Loeb Classical Library.

Arnason, Johann P. and Kurt A. Raaflaub, eds. *The Roman Empire in Context: Historical and Comparative Perspectives.* Malden, MA, 2011. One of the few books to place the formation of the Roman Empire in a comparative, global perspective.

Barker, Graeme, and Tom Rasmussen. *The Etruscans.* Oxford and Malden, MA, 1998. A fine survey, from the Blackwell *Peoples of Europe* series.

Beard, Mary. *Pompeii: The Life of a Roman Town.* A fascinating, cutting-edge study of daily life.

Boardman, John, Jasper Griffin, and Oswyn Murray. *The Oxford History of the Roman World.* Oxford, 1990. Reprint of relevant portions of the excellent *Oxford History of the Classical World* (1986). Stimulating, accessible topical chapters by British specialists.

Cornell, T. J. *The Beginnings of Rome: Italy and Rome from the Bronze Age to the Punic Wars (c. 1000–264 B.C.).* London, 1995. An ambitious survey of the archaeological and historical evidence for early Rome.

Crawford, Michael. *The Roman Republic,* 2d ed. Cambridge, MA, 1993. A lively, fast-paced survey of republican Rome. An excellent place to start.

Fantham, Elaine, Helene Peet Foley, Natalie Boymel Kampen, Sarah B. Pomeroy, and H. Alan Shapiro. *Women in the Classical World.* Oxford, 1994. An expert survey of both Greece and Rome.

Garnsey, Peter, and Richard Saller. *The Roman Empire: Economy, Society, and Culture.* Berkeley, CA, 1987. A straightforward short survey.

Gruen, Erich S. *The Hellenistic World and the Coming of Rome.* 2 vols. Berkeley, CA, 1984. A massive survey, focused on the unpredictable rise of Rome to a position of dominance within the Mediterranean world.

Harris, William V. *War and Imperialism in Republican Rome, 327–70 B.C.* Oxford, 1979. A challenging study arguing that Rome's need for military conquest and expansion was deeply embedded in the fabric of Roman life.

Krebs, Christopher. *A Most Dangerous Book: Tacitus's "Germania" from the Roman Empire to the Third Reich.* A history of this ancient ethnography's transmission and reception, and especially the political uses to which was put in Nazi Germany.

Lancel, Serge. *Carthage: A History.* Trans. Antonia Nevill. Oxford, 1995. An account of Rome's great rival for control of the Mediterranean world.

Millar, Fergus G. B. *The Emperor in the Roman World, 31 B.C.–A.D. 337.* London, 1977. A classic work that showed (among much else) the importance of emperor worship to the religious outlook of the Roman Empire.

———. *The Crowd in Rome in the Late Republic.* Ann Arbor, MI, 1999. A revisionist account that emphasizes the reality of Roman democracy in the late republic, against those who would see the period's politics as entirely under the control of aristocratic families.

Ward, Allen M., Fritz Heichelheim, and Cedric A. Yeo. *A History of the Roman People,* 3d ed. Upper Saddle River, NJ, 1999. An informative, well-organized textbook covering Roman history from its beginnings to the end of the sixth century C.E.

Watkin, David. *The Roman Forum.* London, 2009. A history of the successive buildings and archeological excavations of this central Roman space.

Wells, Colin. *The Roman Empire,* 2d ed. Cambridge, MA, 1992. An easily readable survey from the reign of Augustus to the mid-third century C.E., particularly useful for its treatment of the relationship between the Roman central government and its Italian provinces.

Wiseman, T. P. *Remembering the Roman People.* Oxford, 2009. A collection of studies devoted to popular politics in the late republic.

Woolf, Greg. *Becoming Roman: The Origins of Provincial Civilization in Gaul.* Cambridge, 1998. An exemplary study of how provincial elites made themselves "Roman."

———. *Rome: An Empire's Story.* Oxford, 2012. A masterful account of Rome's reconfiguration of the ancient world and enduring impact; critically acclaimed by scholars and general readers.

———. *Tales of the Barbarians: Ethnography and Empire in the Roman West.* Malden, MA, 2011. Applies modern ethnographic methodologies to a dissection of Romans applied their own ethnographic theories to contemporary "others."

CHAPTER 6

Augustine. *The City of God.* Trans. Henry Bettenson. Baltimore, MD, 1972.

———. *Confessions.* Trans. Henry M. Chadwick. Oxford, 1991.

———. *On Christian Doctrine.* Trans. D. W. Robertson Jr. New York, 1958.

Boethius. *The Consolation of Philosophy.* Trans. R. Green. Indianapolis, IN, 1962.

Bowersock, G. W., Peter Brown, and Oleg Grabar. *Late Antiquity: A Guide to the Postclassical World.* Cambridge, MA, 1999. An authoritative compilation. The first half is devoted to essays on the cultural features of the period; the second half is organized as an encyclopedia.

Brown, Peter. *Augustine of Hippo.* Berkeley, CA, 1967. A great biography by the great scholar of late antiquity.

——. *The Body and Society: Men, Women and Sexual Renunciation in Early Christianity.* New York, 1988. A revealing study of the fundamental transformations wrought by Christianity in the late antique world.

——. *Power and Persuasion in Late Antiquity: Toward a Christian Empire.* Madison, WI, 1992. An important account of Christianity's effects on the political culture of the later Roman Empire.

——. *The Rise of Western Christendom: Triumph and Diversity, 200–1000,* 2d ed. Oxford, 2002. An evocative picture of Christianity's spread eastward and northward from the Mediterranean world.

——. *The World of Late Antiquity.* New York, 1971. Still the best short survey of the period, with excellent illustrations.

——. *Through the Eye of a Needle: Wealth, the Fall of Rome, and the Making of Christianity in the West, 350–550 AD.* Princeton, NJ, 2012. The most recent of this historian's magisterial dissections of late antiquity, focused on the relationship between religion, culture, power, and wealth (or its lack).

Cameron, Averil. *The Later Roman Empire, A.D. 284–430.* London, 1993. Now the standard account of its period, with an emphasis on imperial politics.

——. *The Mediterranean World in Late Antiquity, A.D. 395–600.* London, 1993. Masterful, with excellent, succinct bibliographical essays.

Cassiodorus. *An Introduction to Divine and Human Readings.* Trans. L. W. Jones. New York, 1946.

Chadwick, Henry M. *Augustine.* Oxford, 1986. A short introduction to Augustine's thought.

——. *Boethius.* Oxford, 1981. An intellectual biography of this important thinker.

Clark, Gillian. *Christianity and Roman Society.* Cambridge, 2004. A short, stimulating survey that places early Christianity firmly in its Roman social context.

——. *Women in Late Antiquity.* Oxford, 1993. A clear, compact account of an important subject.

Coogan, Michael, ed. *The Oxford History of the Biblical World.* Oxford, 1998. A reliable but rather traditional account of the historical events recounted in the Hebrew Bible and the New Testament.

Ehrman, Bart D. *The New Testament: A Historical Introduction to the Early Christian Writings,* 4th ed. Oxford, 2008. The standard textbook by a leading authority.

Ehrman, Bart D. and Zlatko Pleše, eds. *The Aprocryphal Gospels: Texts and Translations* Oxford, 2011. The first scholarly edition and translation of all the apocryphal gospels, including Latin, Greek, and Coptic texts.

Eusebius. *The History of the Church.* Trans. G. A. Williamson. Baltimore, MD, 1965. A contemporary account of Constantine's reign, written by one of his courtier-bishops.

——. *Eusebius' Life of Constantine.* Trans. Averil Cameron and Stuart Hall. Oxford, 1999. An admiring biography that reflects Constantine's own vision of his religious authority.

Hopkins, Keith. *A World Full of Gods: The Strange Triumph of Christianity.* New York, 1999. An imaginative study of religious pluralism in the Roman world and the context in which Christianity emerged.

Kulikowski, Michael. *Rome's Gothic Wars: From the Third Century to Alaric.* Cambridge, 2007. An authoritative and critical account.

Lawrence, Clifford Hugh. *Medieval Monasticism,* 3d ed. London, 2000. Concise, perceptive survey of monasticism from its beginnings to the end of the Middle Ages.

Pagels, Elaine. *The Gnostic Gospels.* New York, 1979. A pathbreaking study of the noncanonical gospels and the history of their exclusion from the Bible.

Potter, David. *The Roman Empire at Bay, A.D. 180–395.* London and New York, 2004. The most up-to-date account of the empire's reorganization and transformation in this era.

Rebillard, Éric. *Christians and Their Many Identities in Late Antiquity, North Africa, 200–450 CE.* Ithaca, 2012. In this book, as in his earlier works, the author argues that there was no special importance attached to being a "Christian" in late antiquity, and that religious identities are better understood as fluid and hybrid.

Sanders, E. P. *The Historical Figure of Jesus.* London and New York, 1993. A fine study of Jesus in his first-century Jewish context.

Shanks, Hershel, ed. *Christianity and Rabbinic Judaism: A Parallel History of Their Origins and Early Development.* Washington, DC, 1992. Accessible chapters written by top authorities, describing both Jewish and Christian developments from the first to the sixth centuries C.E.

Sherwin-White, A. N. *Roman Society and Roman Law in the New Testament.* Oxford, 1963. A fascinating reading of the New Testament in its historical context.

Traina, Giusto. *428 AD: An Ordinary Year at the End of the Roman Empire.* Princeton, NJ, 2011. An enlightening glimpse into the world of late antiquity, from the vantage point of a single "average" year.

Wallace-Hadrill, John Michael. *The Barbarian West,* 3d ed. London, 1966. A classic analysis of the hybrid culture of the late Roman West.

Whittaker, C. R. *Frontiers of the Roman Empire: A Social and Economic Study.* Baltimore, MD, 1994. A convincing picture of the frontiers of the Roman Empire as zones of intensive cultural interaction.

Williams, Stephen. *Diocletian and the Roman Recovery.* New York, 1997. Thorough and authoritative.

CHAPTER 7

Bede. *A History of the English Church and People.* Trans. Leo Sherley-Price. Baltimore, MD., 1955. The fundamental source for early Anglo-Saxon history.

Campbell, James, ed. *The Anglo-Saxons.* Oxford, 1982. An authoritative and splendidly illustrated volume.

Collins, Roger. *Early Medieval Europe, 300–1000.* 2d ed. New York, 1999. Dry and detailed, but a useful textbook nonetheless.

Conant, Jonathan. *Staying Roman: Conquest and Identity in Africa and the Mediterranean, 439–700.* Cambridge, 2012. An exploration of what it meant to be "Roman" and the sources of identity in this tumultuous period.

Donner, Fred. *The Early Islamic Conquests.* Princeton, NJ, 1981. A scholarly but readable narrative and analysis.

Einhard and Notker the Stammerer. *Two Lives of Charlemagne.* Trans. Lewis Thorpe. Baltimore, MD, 1969. Lively and entertaining works of contemporary biography.

Fletcher, Richard A. *The Barbarian Conversion: From Paganism to Christianity.* Berkeley, CA, 1999. Slow paced but informative and perceptive.

———. *Moorish Spain.* Berkeley, CA, 1993. The best short survey in English.

Geanakoplos, Deno John, ed. *Byzantium: Church, Society and Civilization Seen through Contemporary Eyes.* Chicago, 1984. An outstanding source book.

Gregory, Timothy E. A *History of Byzantium.* Malden, MA, and Oxford, 2005. The most accessible of the recent textbooks on Byzantium. An excellent place to start.

Herrin, Judith. *Byzantium: The Surprising Life of a Medieval Empire.* Princeton, 2009. An accessible and comprehensive history of the eastern Roman Empire.

———. *The Formation of Christendom.* Princeton, NJ, 1987. A synthetic history of the Christian civilizations of Byzantium and western Europe from 500 to 800, written by a prominent historian.

Hodges, Richard, and David Whitehouse. *Mohammed, Charlemagne and the Origins of Europe.* London, 1983. A critical analysis of the "Pirenne thesis," reexaming the relationship between the Mediterranean world and northern Europe.

Hourani, Albert. *A History of the Arab Peoples.* New York, 1992. A sympathetic and clear survey written for nonspecialists.

Kazhdan, Alexander P., ed. *The Oxford Dictionary of Byzantium.* 3 vols. Oxford, 1991. An authoritative reference work.

Kennedy, Hugh. *The Prophet and the Age of the Caliphates.* 2d ed. Harlow, UK, 2004. A lucid introduction to the political history of the Islamic world from the sixth through the eleventh centuries.

Krautheimer, Richard. *Early Christian and Byzantine Architecture.* 4th ed. New York, 1986. A classic work by one of the greatest Byzantine art historians of the twentieth century.

Little, Lester K., ed., *Plague and the End of Antiquity: The Pandemic of 541–750.* Cambridge, 2006. The first full-length scholarly history of the first global pandemic.

Mango, Cyril, ed. *The Oxford History of Byzantium.* Oxford and New York, 2002. Full of sharp judgments and attractively illustrated.

McCormick, Michael. *The Origins of the European Economy: Communications and Commerce* A.D. *300–900.* Cambridge, 2002. An astonishing reinterpretation of the evidence for the myriad contacts between Christian Europe and Islam.

McKitterick, Rosamond. *Charlemagne: The Formation of a European Identity.* Cambridge, 2008. A history of Charlemagne's career and its lasting impact by an eminent scholar of the Carolingian world.

———, ed. *The Uses of Literacy in Early Medieval Europe.* New York, 1990. A superb collection of essays.

McNamara, Jo Ann, and John E. Halborg, eds. *Sainted Women of the Dark Ages.* Durham, NC, 1992. Translated saints' lives from Merovingian and Carolingian Europe.

Murray, A. C., ed. *From Roman to Merovingian Gaul: A Reader.* Toronto, 2000. An excellent collection of sources.

Pelikan, Jaroslav. *The Christian Tradition.* Vol. II, *The Spirit of Eastern Christendom.* Chicago, 1974. An outstanding synthetic treatment of the doctrines of Byzantine Christianity.

Procopius. *The Secret History.* Trans. G. A. Williamson. Baltimore, MD, 1966. An "unauthorized" account of Justinian's reign, written by the emperor's offical historian.

Reuter, Timothy. *Germany in the Early Middle Ages, 800–1056.* New York, 1991. The best survey in English.

Treadgold, Warren. *A History of the Byzantine State and Society.* Stanford, CA, 1997. A massive, encyclopedic narrative of the political, economic, and military history of Byzantium from 284 until 1461.

Wallace-Hadrill, John Michael. *Early Germanic Kingship in England and on the Continent.* Oxford, 1971. A classic analysis of changing ideas about kingship in early medieval Europe, emphasizing the links between Anglo-Saxon and Carolingian cultures.

———. *The Frankish Church.* Oxford, 1983. A masterful account that links the Merovingian and Carolingian churches.

Watt, W. Montgomery. *Islamic Philosophy and Theology,* 2d ed. Edinburgh, UK, 1985. The standard English account.

Wemple, Suzanne Fonay. *Women in Frankish Society: Marriage and the Cloister, 500–900.* Philadelphia, PA, 1981. An influential account of changing attitudes toward marriage among the early Franks.

Whittow, Mark. *The Making of Orthodox Byzantium, 600–1025.* London, 1996. Emphasizes the centrality of orthodoxy in shaping Byzantine history. Particularly good on Byzantine relations with the peoples outside the empire.

Wickham, Chris. *Framing the Middle Ages: Europe and the Mediterranean, 400–800.* Oxford, 2007. An eye-opening history that spans the transitional periods of late antiquity and the early Middle Ages, paying careful attention to regional differences.

Wood, Ian. *The Merovingian Kingdoms, 450–751.* New York, 1994. A detailed study, but difficult for beginners.

CHAPTER 8

Amt, Emily, ed. *Women's Lives in Medieval Europe: A Sourcebook.* New York, 1993. An excellent collection of primary texts.

The Song of Roland. Trans. Robert Harrison. Penguin, 1970. A lively translation.

Arnold, Benjamin. *Princes and Territories in Medieval Germany.* Cambridge and New York, 1991. The best such survey in English.

Blumenthal, Uta-Renate. *The Investiture Controversy.* Philadelphia, 1988. A clear review of a complicated subject.

Boswell, John E. *Christianity, Social Tolerance, and Homosexuality: Gay People in Western Europe from the Beginning of the Christian Era to the Fourteenth Century.* Chicago, 1980. A pioneering account, hotly debated but highly respected.

Burman, Thomas E. *Reading the Qur'ān in Latin Christendom, 1140–1560*. Philadelphia, 2007. A fascinating account of the Qur'an's reception in medieval Europe.

Colish, Marcia. *Medieval Foundations of the Western Intellectual Tradition, 400–1400*. New Haven, CT, 1997. An encyclopedic work, best used as a reference.

Dunbabin, Jean. *France in the Making, 843–1180*, 2d ed. Oxford and New York, 2000. An authoritative survey of the disparate territories that came to make up the medieval French kingdom.

Dyer, Christopher. *Making a Living in the Middle Ages: The People of Britain 850–1520*. New Haven, 2002. A splendid new synthesis that combines social, economic, and archaeological evidence.

Fossier, Robert. *The Ax and the Oath: Ordinary Life in the Middle Ages*. Princeton, 2010. A quirky, personal, and often insightful look at the daily lives and worldview of this era by a leading French historian.

Frankopan, Peter. *The First Crusade: The Call from the East*. Cambridge, MA, 2012. Analyzes the causes and catalysts of the crusading movement.

Hicks, Carola. *The Bayeux Tapestry: The Life Story of Masterpiece*. London, 2006. An art historian's engrossing account of the making, reception, and interpretation of this amazing artifact.

Horden, Peregrine and Nicholas Purcell. *The Corrupting Sea: A Study of Mediterranean History*. Malden, MA, 2000. An extraordinary attempt to encompass the history of the Mediterranean World over a span of three millennia.

Leyser, Henrietta. *Medieval Women: A Social History of Women in England, 440–1500*. New York, 1995. Although limited to one country, this is the best of the recent surveys treating medieval women.

McLaughlin, Megan. *Sex, Gender, and Episcopal Authority in an Age of Reform, 1000–1122*. Cambridge, 2010. A new interpretation of gendered discourse and politics during the Investiture Controversy.

Miller, Maureen C. *Power and the Holy in the Age of the Investiture Conflict. A Brief History with Documents*. Boston, 2005. A stimulating approach to the eleventh-century conflicts over temporal and spiritual power, with many newly translated sources.

Moore, Robert I. *The First European Revolution, c. 970–1215*. Oxford and Cambridge, MA, 2000. A remarkable description of the ways in which European society was fundamentally reshaped during the eleventh and twelfth centuries.

Peters, F. E. *Aristotle and the Arabs*. New York, 1968. Well written and engaging.

Raffensperger, Christian. *Reimagining Europe: Kievan Rus' in the Medieval World*. Cambridge, MA, 2012. An exciting new study of early Rus' and its neighbors.

Reilly, Bernard F. *The Medieval Spains*. New York, 1993. A succinct account that covers the entire Iberian peninsula from 500 to 1500.

Reynolds, Susan. *Fiefs and Vassals: The Medieval Evidence Reinterpreted*. Oxford and New York, 1994. A detailed revisionist history of "feudalism."

Rubenstein, Jay. *Armies of Heaven: The First Crusade and the Quest for Apocalypse*. New York, 2011. An accessible narrative of the First Crusade, written for a general audience and arguing for a new interpretation of crusaders' motives.

Sawyer, Peter, ed. *The Oxford Illustrated History of the Vikings*. Oxford, 1997. The best one-volume account, lavishly illustrated.

Sheingorn, Pamela, trans. *The Book of Sainte Foy*. Philadelphia, 1995.

Stillman, Norman A. *The Jews of Arab Lands: A History and Source Book*. Philadelphia, PA, 1979. An essential resource.

Stow, Kenneth R. *Alienated Minority: The Jews of Medieval Latin Europe*. Cambridge, MA, 1992. An excellent survey.

Tierney, Brian. *The Crisis of Church and State, 1050–1300*. Toronto, 1988. An indispensable collection for both teachers and students.

Winroth, Anders. *The Conversion of Scandinavia: Vikings, Merchants, and Missionaries in the Remaking of Northern Europe*. New Haven, 2012. Argues that the peoples of Scandinavia were active participants in the cultural, economic, and political processes that accompanied their conversion to Christianity.

CHAPTER 9

Abelard and Heloise. *The Letters and Other Writings*. Trans. William Levitan. Indianapolis, 2007. A beautiful and accurate translation of the correspondence and related documents, with a full introduction and notes.

Abulafia, David. *Frederick II: A Medieval Emperor*. London and New York, 1988. A reliable biography that strips away much of the legend that has hitherto surrounded this monarch.

Baldwin, John W. *The Government of Philip Augustus*. Berkeley and Los Angeles, CA, 1986. A landmark scholarly account.

Barber, Malcolm. *The Crusader States*. New Haven, 2012. A new and comprehensive history by an esteemed historian.

Bartlett, Robert. *The Making of Europe: Conquest, Colonization and Cultural Change, 950–1350*. Princeton, NJ, 1993. A wide-ranging examination of the economic, social, and religious expansion of Europe, full of stimulating insights.

Bisson, Thomas N. *The Crisis of the Twelfth Century: Power, Lordship, and the Origins of European Government*. Princeton, NJ, 2009. A new interpretation of the evidence.

Bynum, Caroline Walker. *Holy Feast and Holy Fast: The Religious Significance of Food to Medieval Women*. Berkeley and Los Angeles, 1988. One of the most influential and important works of scholarship published in the late twentieth century.

Camille, Michael. *Gothic Art: Glorious Visions*. New York, 1996. A succinct and beautifully illustrated introduction.

Chrétien de Troyes. *Arthurian Romances*. Trans. W. W. Kibler. New York, 1991.

Clanchy, Michael T. *Abelard: A Medieval Life*. Oxford and Cambridge, MA, 1997. A great biography.

————. *From Memory to Written Record: England, 1066–1307*. Oxford, 1992. A fascinating and hugely influential account of this revolutionary shift.

Cobban, Alan B. *The Medieval Universities*. London, 1975. The best short treatment in English.

Fassler, Margot. *Gothic Song: Victorine Seqeunces and Augustinian Reform in Twelfth-Century Paris*. Cambridge, UK, 1993. The emergence of new musical genres and their cultural context.

Gillingham, John. *The Angevin Empire,* 2d ed. Oxford and New York, 2001. The best treatment by far of its subject, brief but full of ideas.

Gottfried von Strassburg. *Tristan.* Trans. A. T. Hatto. Baltimore, MD, 1960.

Hallam, Elizabeth, and Judith Everard. *Capetian France, 987–1328,* 2d ed. New York, 2001. A clear and well-organized account.

Haskins, Charles Homer. *The Renaissance of the Twelfth Century.* Cambridge, MA, 1927. A classic and influential study.

Jones, P. J. *The Italian City-State: From Commune to Signoria.* Oxford and New York, 1997. A fundamental reinterpretation of the evidence.

Jordan, William C. *Europe in the High Middle Ages: The Penguin History of Europe.* Vol. III. New York and London, 2003. An outstanding new survey.

Kaeuper, Richard W. *Chivalry and Violence in Medieval Europe.* Oxford and New York, 1999. A darker view of chivalry than Keen's.

Keen, Maurice. *Chivalry.* New Haven, CT, 1984. A comprehensive treatment of chivalry from its origins to the sixteenth century.

Lawrence, Clifford Hugh. *The Friars: The Impact of the Early Mendicant Movement on Western Society.* London and New York, 1994. The best short introduction to the early history of the Franciscans and the Dominicans.

Leclerq, Jean. *The Love of Learning and the Desire for God,* 3d ed. New York, 1982. A beautiful interpretation of twelfth-century monastic culture and the influence of Bernard of Clairvaux.

Little, Lester. *Religious Poverty and Profit Economy in Medieval Europe.* Ithaca, 1978. A fascinating study of the relationship between religious practice and economic reality.

Lopez, Robert S., and Irving W. Raymond, eds. *Medieval Trade in the Mediterranean World.* New York, 1990. A pathbreaking collection of source material.

Madden, Thomas F. *The New Concise History of the Crusades.* New York, 2005. An acclaimed and accessible survey for students.

Marie de France. *Lais.* Trans. Glyn S. Burgess and Keith Busby. Harmondsworth, UK, 1999. A compelling and entertaining prose translation.

Moore, R. I. *The War on Heresy.* Cambridge, MA, 2012. A courageous and searching revisionist history, based on decades of research and reflection. Moore argues for a radical reassessment of what "heresy" consisted of, and why those branded as "heretics" were persecuted during the Middle Ages.

Morris, Colin. *The Papal Monarchy: The Western Church from 1050 to 1250.* Oxford, 1989. An excellent scholarly survey; part of the Oxford History of the Christian Church series.

Newman, Barbara, ed. *Voice of the Living Light: Hildegard of Bingen and Her World.* Berkeley and Los Angeles, CA, 1998. An introduction to Hildegard's life and work.

Otto, Bishop of Freising. *The Deeds of Frederick Barbarossa.* Trans. C. C. Mierow. New York, 1953. A contemporary chronicle interesting enough to read from start to finish.

Smalley, Beryl. *The Study of the Bible in the Middle Ages,* 3d ed. Oxford, 1983. The standard work, gracefully written and illuminating.

Strayer, Joseph R. *On the Medieval Origins of the Modern State.* With new forewords by Charles Tilly and William Chester Jordan. Princeton, 2005. This new edition of Strayer's series of lectures places them in their scholarly context.

Swanson, R. N. *The Twelfth-Century Renaissance.* Manchester, UK, 1999. An updated survey of the intellectual developments of the twelfth century.

Symes, Carol. *A Common Stage: Theater and Public Life in Medieval Arras.* Ithaca, NY, 2007. A study of a vibrant cultural hub.

Wakefield, Walter, and Austin P. Evans, eds. and trans. *Heresies of the High Middle Ages.* New York, 1969, 1991. A comprehensive collection of sources.

Wilhelm, James J., ed. and trans. *Medieval Song: An Anthology of Hymns and Lyrics.* New York, 1971. An excellent collection of sacred and secular poetry that illustrates the connections between them.

Wolfram von Eschenbach. *Parzival.* Trans. H. M. Mustard and C. E. Passage. New York, 1961.

CHAPTER 10

Abu-Lughod, Janet L. *Before European Hegemony: The World System A.D. 1250–1350.* Oxford and New York, 1989. A study of the trading links among Europe, the Middle East, India, and China, with special attention to the role of the Mongol Empire; extensive bibliography.

Allsen, Thomas T. *Culture and Conquest in Mongol Eurasia.* Cambridge and New York, 2001. A synthesis of the author's earlier studies, emphasizing Mongol involvement in the cultural and commercial exchanges that linked China, Central Asia, and Europe.

Christian, David. *A History of Russia, Central Asia and Mongolia.* Vol. 1, *Inner Eurasia from Prehistory to the Mongol Empire.* Oxford, 1998. The authoritative English-language work on the subject.

Cole, Bruce. *Giotto and Florentine Painting, 1280–1375.* New York, 1976. A clear and stimulating introduction.

Crummey, Robert O. *The Formation of Muscovy, 1304–1613.* New York, 1987. The standard account.

Dante Alighieri. *The Divine Comedy.* Trans. Mark Musa. 3 vols. Baltimore, MD, 1984–86.

Dunn, Ross E. *The Adventures of Ibn Battuta: A Muslim Traveler of the Fourteenth Century.* Berkeley, rev. ed. 2005. Places the writings and experiences of this far-reaching Muslim traveler in their historical and geographical contexts.

Dyer, Christopher. *Standards of Living in the Later Middle Ages: Social Change in England, c. 1200–1520.* Cambridge and New York, 1989. Detailed but highly rewarding.

Foltz, Richard. *Religions of the Silk Road: Premodern Patterns of Globalization.* New York, 2nd ed. 2010. A compelling and thought-provoking study of the varieties of religious experience and cross-cultural interaction in medieval Eurasia.

The History and the Life of Chinggis Khan: The Secret History of the Mongols. Trans. Urgunge Onon. Leiden, 1997. A newer version of *The Secret History,* now the standard English version of this important Mongol source.

Horrox, Rosemary, ed. *The Black Death.* New York, 1994. A fine collection of documents reflecting the impact of the Black Death, especially in England.

Jackson, Peter. *The Mongols and the West, 1221–1410.* Harlow, UK, 2005. A well-written survey that emphasizes the interactions among the Mongol, Latin Christian, and Muslim worlds.

Jordan, William Chester. *The Great Famine: Northern Europe in the Early Fourteenth Century.* Princeton, NJ, 1996. An outstanding social and economic study.

Keen, Maurice, ed. *Medieval Warfare: A History.* Oxford and New York, 1999. The most attractive introduction to this important subject. Lively and well illustrated.

Kitsikopoulos, Harry, ed. *Agrarian Change and Crisis in Europe, 1200–1500.* London, 2011. An up-to-date collection of scholarly essays that addresses a classic and complicated set of historical questions.

Komaroff, Linda and Stefano Carboni, eds. *The Legacy of Ghenghis Khan: Courtly Art and Culture in Western Asia, 1256–1353.* New York, 2002. An informative and lavishly illustrated catalog of an acclaimed exhibition.

Larner, John. *Marco Polo and the Discovery of the World.* New Haven, CT, 1999. A study of the influence of Marco Polo's *Travels* on Europeans.

Mandeville's Travels. Ed. M. C. Seymour. Oxford, 1968. An edition of the *Book of Marvels* based on the Middle English version popular in the fifteenth century.

Memoirs of a Renaissance Pope: The Commentaries of Pius II. Abridged ed. Trans. F. A. Gragg, New York, 1959. Remarkable insights into the mind of a particularly well-educated mid-fifteenth-century pope.

Nicholas, David. *The Transformation of Europe, 1300–1600.* Oxford and New York, 1999. The best textbook presently available.

Rossabi, M. *Khubilai Khan: His Life and Times.* Berkeley, CA, 1988. The standard English biography.

Swanson, R. N. *Religion and Devotion in Europe, c. 1215–c. 1515.* Cambridge and New York, 1995. An excellent study of late-medieval popular piety; an excellent complement to Oakley.

The Travels of Marco Polo. Ed. Peter Harris. London, 2008 repr. A new edition of a classic translation.

Vaughan, Richard. *Valois Burgundy.* London, 1975. A summation of the author's four-volume study of the Burgundian dukes.

CHAPTER 11

Alberti, Leon Battista. *The Family in Renaissance Florence (Della Famiglia).* Trans. Renée Neu Watkins. Columbia, SC, 1969.

Allmand, Christopher T., ed. *Society at War: The Experience of England and France During the Hundred Years' War.* Edinburgh, 1973. An outstanding collection of documents.

———. *The Hundred Years' War: England and France at War, c. 1300–c. 1450.* Cambridge and New York, 1988. Still the best analytic account of the war; after a short narrative, the book is organized topically.

Boccaccio, Giovanni. *The Decameron.* Trans. Mark Musa and P. E. Bondanella. New York, 1977.

Brucker, Gene. *Florence, the Golden Age, 1138–1737.* Berkeley and Los Angeles, CA, 1998. The standard account.

Bruni, Leonardo. *The Humanism of Leonardo Bruni: Selected Texts.* Trans. Gordon Griffiths, James Hankins, and David Thompson.

Binghamton, NY, 1987. Excellent translations, with introductions, to the Latin works of a key Renaissance humanist.

Burke, Peter. *The Renaissance.* New York, 1997. A brief introduction by an influential modern historian.

Burkhardt, Jacob. *The Civilization of the Renaissance in Italy.* Many editions. The nineteenth-century work that first crystallized an image of the Italian Renaissance, and with which scholars have been wrestling ever since.

Canning, Joseph. *Ideas of Power in the Late Middle Ages, 1296–1417.* Cambridge, 2011. An old fashioned but nonetheless original synthesis.

Cassirer, Ernst, et al., eds. *The Renaissance Philosophy of Man.* Chicago, 1948. Important original works by Petrarch, Ficino, and Pico della Mirandola, among others.

Chaucer, Geoffrey. *The Canterbury Tales.* Trans. Nevill Coghill. New York, 1951. A modern English verse translation, lightly annotated.

Cohn, Samuel K., Jr. *Lust for Liberty: The Politics of Social Revolt in Medieval Europe, 1200–1425. Italy, France, and Flanders.* Cambridge, MA, 2006. An important new study.

Coles, Paul. *The Ottoman Impact on Europe.* London, 1968. An excellent introductory text, still valuable despite its age.

Dobson, R. Barrie. *The Peasants' Revolt of 1381,* 2d ed. London, 1983. A comprehensive source collection, with excellent introductions to the documents.

Fernández-Armesto, Felipe. *Before Columbus: Exploration and Colonisation from the Mediterranean to the Atlantic, 1229–1492.* London, 1987. An indispensible study of the medieval background to the sixteenth-century European colonial empires.

Froissart, Jean. *Chronicles.* Trans. Geoffrey Brereton. Baltimore, MD, 1968. A selection from the most famous contemporary account of the Hundred Years' War to about 1400.

Goffman, Daniel. *The Ottoman Empire and Early Modern Europe.* Cambridge and New York, 2002. A revisionist account that presents the Ottoman Empire as a European state.

Hankins, James. *Plato in the Italian Renaissance.* Leiden and New York, 1990. A definitive study of the reception and influence of Plato on Renaissance intellectuals.

———, ed. *Renaissance Civic Humanism: Reappraisals and Reflections.* Cambridge and New York, 2000. An excellent collection of scholarly essays reassessing republicanism in the Renaissance.

Hobbins, Daniel, ed. and trans. *The Trial of Joan of Arc.* Cambridge, MA, 2007. A new and excellent translation of the transcripts of Joan's trial.

Inalcik, Halil. *The Ottoman Empire: The Classical Age, 1300–1600.* London, 1973. The standard history by the dean of Turkish historians.

———, ed. *An Economic and Social History of the Ottoman Empire, 1300–1914.* Cambridge, 1994. An important collection of essays, spanning the full range of Ottoman history.

John Hus at the Council of Constance. Trans. M. Spinka, New York, 1965. The translation of a Czech chronicle with an expert introduction and appended documents.

Kafadar, Cemal. *Between Two Worlds: The Construction of the Ottoman State.* Berkeley and Los Angeles, 1995. An important study of

Ottoman origins in the border regions between Byzantium, the Seljuk Turks, and the Mongols.

Kempe, Margery. *The Book of Margery Kempe.* Trans. Barry Windeatt. New York, 1985. A fascinating personal narrative by an early-fifteenth-century Englishwoman who hoped she might be a saint.

Lane, Frederic C. *Venice: A Maritime Republic.* Baltimore, MD, 1973. An authoritative account.

Morgan, David. *The Mongols.* 2d ed. Oxford, 2007. An accessible introduction to Mongol history and its sources, written by a noted expert on medieval Persia.

Ormrod, W. Mark. *Edward III.* New Haven, 2012. A new biography of this English monarch by a leading social historian.

Saunders, J. J. *The History of the Mongol Conquests.* London, 1971. Still the standard English-language introduction; somewhat more positive about the Mongols' accomplishments than is Morgan.

Shirley, Janet, trans. *A Parisian Journal, 1405–1449.* Oxford, 1968. A marvelous panorama of Parisian life recorded by an eyewitness.

Sumption, Jonathan. *The Hundred Years' War.* Vol. 1: *Trial by Battle.* Vol. 2: *Trial by Fire.* Philadelphia, 1999. The first two volumes of a massive narrative history of the war, carrying the story up to 1369.

The Four Voyages: Christopher Columbus. Trans. J. M. Cohen. New York, 1992. Columbus's own self-serving account of his four voyages to the Indies.

CHAPTER 12

Baxandall, Michael. *Painting and Experience in Fifteenth-Century Italy.* Oxford, 1972. A classic study of the perceptual world of the Renaissance.

Castiglione, Baldassare. *The Book of the Courtier.* Many editions. The translations by C. S. Singleton (New York, 1959) and by George Bull (New York, 1967) are both excellent.

Cellini, Benvenuto. *Autobiography.* Trans. George Bull. Baltimore, MD, 1956. This Florentine goldsmith (1500–1571) is the source for many of the most famous stories about the artists of the Florentine Renaissance.

Erasmus, Desiderius. *The Praise of Folly.* Trans. J. Wilson. Ann Arbor, MI, 1958.

Fernández-Armesto, Felipe. *1492: The Year the World Began.* London, 2010. A panoramic view of the world in a pivotal year, putting the voyage of Columbus in a broad historical perspective.

Flint, Valerie I. J. *The Imaginative Landscape of Christopher Columbus.* Princeton, NJ, 1992. A short, suggestive analysis of the intellectual influences that shaped Columbus's geographical ideas.

Fox, Alistair. *Thomas More: History and Providence.* Oxford, 1982. A balanced account of a man too easily idealized.

Grafton, Anthony, and Lisa Jardine. *From Humanism to the Humanities: Education and the Liberal Arts in Fifteenth- and Sixteenth-Century Europe.* London, 1986. An account that presents Renaissance humanism as the elitist cultural program of a self-interested group of pedagogues.

Grendler, Paul, ed. *Encyclopedia of the Renaissance.* New York, 1999. A valuable reference work.

Jardine, Lisa. *Worldly Goods.* London, 1996. A revisionist account that emphasizes the acquisitive materialism of Italian Renaissance society and culture.

Kanter, Laurence, Hilliard T. Goldfarb, and James Hankins. *Botticelli's Witness: Changing Style in a Changing Florence.* Boston, 1997. This catalog for an exhibition of Botticelli's works, at the Gardner Museum in Boston, offers an excellent introduction to the painter and his world.

King, Margaret L. *Women of the Renaissance.* Chicago, 1991. Deals with women in all walks of life and in a variety of roles.

Kristeller, Paul O. *Renaissance Thought: The Classic, Scholastic, and Humanistic Strains.* New York, 1961. Very helpful in defining the main trends of Renaissance thought.

Machiavelli, Niccolò. *The Discourses* and *The Prince.* Many editions. These two books must be read together if one is to understand Machiavelli's political ideas properly.

Mallett, Michael and Christine Shaw. *The Italian Wars, 1494–1559: War, State, and Society in Early Modern Europe.* Boston, 2012. Argues that the endemic warfare of this period within Italy revolutionized European military tactics and technologies.

Mann, Charles. C. *1491: New Revelations of the Americas Before Columbus.* New York, 2006.

———. *1493: Uncovering the New World Columbus Created.* New York, 2012. Written for a popular audience, these are also engaging and well-informed syntheses of historical research.

Martines, Lauro. *Power and Imagination: City-States in Renaissance Italy.* New York, 1979. Insightful account of the connections among politics, society, culture, and art.

More, Thomas. *Utopia.* Many editions.

Olson, Roberta, *Italian Renaissance Sculpture.* New York, 1992. The most accessible introduction to the subject.

Parker, Geoffrey. *The Military Revolution: Military Innovation and the Rise of the West (1500–1800).* 2d ed. Cambridge and New York, 1996. A work of fundamental importance for understanding the global dominance achieved by early modern Europeans.

Perkins, Leeman L. *Music in the Age of the Renaissance.* New York, 1999. A massive new study that needs to be read in conjunction with Reese.

Phillips, J. R. S. *The Medieval Expansion of Europe.* 2d ed. Oxford, 1998. An outstanding study of the thirteenth- and fourteenth-century background to the fifteenth-century expansion of Europe. Important synthetic treatment of European relations with the Mongols, China, Africa, and North America. The second edition includes a new introduction and a bibliographical essay; the text is the same as in the first edition (1988).

Phillips, William D., Jr., and Carla R. Phillips. *The Worlds of Christopher Columbus.* Cambridge and New York, 1991. The first book to read on Columbus: accessible, engaging, and scholarly. Then read Fernández-Armesto's biography.

Rabelais, François. *Gargantua and Pantagruel.* Trans. J. M. Cohen. Baltimore, MD, 1955. A robust modern translation.

Reese, Gustave. *Music in the Renaissance,* rev. ed. New York, 1959. A great book; still authoritative, despite the more recent work by Perkins, which supplements but does not replace it.

Rice, Eugene F., Jr., and Anthony Grafton. *The Foundations of Early Modern Europe, 1460–1559,* 2d ed. New York, 1994. The best textbook account of its period.

Rowland, Ingrid D. *The Culture of the High Renaissance: Ancients and Moderns in Sixteenth-Century Rome.* Cambridge and New York, 2000. Beautifully written examination of the social, intellectual, and economic foundations of the Renaissance in Rome.

Russell, Peter. *Prince Henry "The Navigator": A Life.* New Haven, CT, 2000. A masterly biography by a great historian who has spent a lifetime on the subject. The only book one now needs to read on Prince Henry.

Scammell, Geoffrey V. *The First Imperial Age: European Overseas Expansion, 1400–1715.* London, 1989. A useful introductory survey, with a particular focus on English and French colonization.

CHAPTER 13

Bainton, Roland. *Erasmus of Christendom.* New York, 1969. Still the best biography in English of the Dutch reformer and intellectual.

Benedict, Philip. *Christ's Churches Purely Reformed: A Social History of Calvinism.* New Haven, CT, 2002. A wide-ranging recent survey of Calvinism in both western and eastern Europe.

Bossy, John. *Christianity in the West, 1400–1700.* Oxford and New York, 1985. A brilliant, challenging picture of the changes that took place in Christian piety and practice as a result of the sixteenth-century reformations.

Bouwsma, William J. *John Calvin: A Sixteenth-Century Portrait.* Oxford and New York, 1988. The best biography of the magisterial reformer.

Dixon, C. Scott, ed. *The German Reformation: The Essential Readings.* Oxford, 1999. A collection of important recent articles.

Duffy, Eamon. *The Stripping of the Altars: Traditional Religion in England, c. 1400–c. 1550.* A brilliant study of religious exchange at the parish level.

———. *The Voices of Morebath: Reformation and Rebellion in an English Village.* New Haven, 2003. How the crises of this period affected and are reflected in the history of a single parish.

Hart, D. G. *Calvinism: A History.* New Haven, 2013. A new survey of this leading Protestant movement from its beginnings to the present day.

John Calvin: Selections from His Writings, ed. John Dillenberger. Garden City, NY, 1971. A judicious selection, drawn mainly from Calvin's *Institutes.*

Koslofksy, Craig. *The Reformation of the Dead: Death and Ritual in Early Modern Germany.* Basingstoke, 2000. How essential rituals and responses to death were reshaped in this period.

Loyola, Ignatius. *Personal Writings.* Trans. by Joseph A. Munitiz and Philip Endean. London and New York, 1996. An excellent collection that includes Loyola's autobiography, his spiritual diary, and some of his letters, as well as his *Spiritual Exercises.*

Luebke, David, ed. *The Counter-Reformation: The Essential Readings.* Oxford, 1999. A collection of nine important recent essays.

MacCulloch, Diarmaid. *Reformation: Europe's House Divided, 1490–1700.* London and New York, 2003. A definitive new survey; the best single-volume history of its subject in a generation.

Martin Luther: Selections from His Writings, ed. John Dillenberger. Garden City, NY, 1961. The standard selection, especially good on Luther's theological ideas.

McGrath, Alister E. *Reformation Thought: An Introduction.* Oxford, 1993. A useful explanation, accessible to non-Christians, of the theological ideas of the major Protestant reformers.

Mullett, Michael A. *The Catholic Reformation.* London, 2000. A sympathetic survey of Catholicism from the mid-sixteenth to the eighteenth century that presents the mid-sixteenth-century Council of Trent as a continuation of earlier reform efforts.

Murray, Linda. *High Renaissance and Mannerism.* London, 1985. The place to begin a study of fifteenth- and sixteenth-century Italian art.

Oberman, Heiko A. *Luther: Man between God and the Devil.* Trans. by Eileen Walliser-Schwarzbart. New Haven, CT, 1989. A biography stressing Luther's preoccupations with sin, death, and the devil.

O'Malley, John W. *The First Jesuits.* Cambridge, MA, 1993. A scholarly account of the origins and early years of the Society of Jesus.

———. *Trent and All That: Renaming Catholicism in the Early Modern Era.* Cambridge, MA, 2000. Short, lively, and with a full bibliography.

———. *Trent: What Happened at the Council.* Cambridge, MA, 2012. A clear and comprehensive narrative of the Church council that gave birth to the modern Catholic Church.

Pettegree, Andrew, ed. *The Reformation World.* New York, 2000. An exhaustive multi-author work representing the most recent thinking about the Reformation.

Pelikan, Jaroslav. *Reformation of Church and Dogma, 1300–1700.* Vol. 4 of *A History of Christian Dogma.* Chicago, 1984. A masterful synthesis of Reformation theology in its late-medieval context.

Roper, Lyndal. *The Holy Household: Women and Morals in Reformation Augsburg.* Oxford, 1989. A pathbreaking study of Protestantism's effects on a single town, with special attention to its impact on attitudes toward women, the family, and marriage.

Shagan, Ethan H. *Popular Politics and the English Reformation.* Cambridge, 2002. Argues that the English Reformation reflects an ongoing process of negotiation, resistance, and response.

Tracy, James D. *Europe's Reformations, 1450–1650.* 2d ed. Lanham, MD, 2006. An outstanding survey, especially strong on Dutch and Swiss developments, but excellent throughout.

Williams, George H. *The Radical Reformation.* 3d ed. Kirksville, MO, 1992. Originally published in 1962, this is still the best book on Anabaptism and its offshoots.

CHAPTER 14

Bonney, Richard. *The European Dynastic States, 1494–1660.* Oxford and New York, 1991. An excellent survey of continental Europe during the "long" sixteenth century.

Briggs, Robin. *Early Modern France, 1560–1715*, 2d ed. Oxford and New York, 1997. Updated and authoritative, with new bibliographies.

———. *Witches and Neighbors: The Social and Cultural Context of European Witchcraft*. New York, 1996. An influential recent account of Continental witchcraft.

Cervantes, Miguel de. *Don Quixote*. Trans. Edith Grossman. New York, 2003. A splendid new translation.

Clarke, Stuart. *Thinking with Demons: The Idea of Witchcraft in Early Modern Europe*. Oxford and New York, 1999. By placing demonology into the context of sixteenth- and seventeenth-century intellectual history, Clarke makes sense of it in new and exciting ways.

Cochrane, Eric, Charles M. Gray, and Mark A. Kishlansky. *Early Modern Europe: Crisis of Authority*. Chicago, 1987. An outstanding source collection from the University of Chicago Readings in Western Civilization series.

Elliot, J. H. *The Old World and the New, 1492–1650*. Cambridge, 1992 repr. A brilliant and brief set of essays on the ways that the discovery of the Americas challenged European perspectives on the world and themselves.

———. *Empires of the Atlantic World: Britain and Spain in America, 1492–1830*. An illuminating comparative study. New Haven, 2007.

Hibbard, Howard. *Bernini*. Baltimore, MD, 1965. The basic study in English of this central figure of Baroque artistic activity.

Hirst, Derek. *England in Conflict, 1603–1660: Kingdom, Community, Commonwealth*. Oxford and New York, 1999. A complete revision of the author's *Authority and Conflict* (1986), this is an up-to-date and balanced account of a period that has been a historical battleground over the past twenty years.

Hobbes, Thomas. *Leviathan*. Ed. Richard Tuck. 2d ed. Cambridge and New York, 1996. The most recent edition, containing the entirety of *Leviathan*, not just the first two parts.

Holt, Mack P. *The French Wars of Religion, 1562–1629*. Cambridge and New York, 1995. A clear account of a confusing time.

Kors, Alan Charles, and Edward Peters. *Witchcraft in Europe, 400–1700: A Documentary History*, 2d ed. Philadelphia, 2000. A superb collection of documents, significantly expanded in the second edition, with up-to-date commentary.

Kingdon, Robert. *Myths about the St. Bartholomew's Day Massacres, 1572–1576*. Cambridge, MA, 1988. A detailed account of this pivotal moment in the history of France.

Levack, Brian P. *The Witch-Hunt in Early Modern Europe*, 2d ed. London and New York, 1995. The best account of the persecution of suspected witches; coverage extends from Europe in 1450 to America in 1750.

Levin, Carole. *The Heart and Stomach of a King: Elizabeth I and the Politics of Sex and Power*. Philadelphia, PA, 1994. A provocative argument for the importance of Elizabeth's gender for understanding her reign.

Limm, Peter, ed. *The Thirty Years' War*. London, 1984. An outstanding short survey, followed by a selection of primary-source documents.

Lynch, John. *Spain, 1516–1598: From Nation-State to World Empire*. Oxford and Cambridge, MA, 1991. The best book in English on Spain at the pinnacle of its sixteenth-century power.

MacCaffrey, Wallace. *Elizabeth I*. New York, 1993. An outstanding traditional biography by an excellent scholar.

Martin, Colin, and Geoffrey Parker. *The Spanish Armada*. London, 1988. Incorporates recent discoveries from undersea archaeology with more traditional historical sources.

Mattingly, Garrett. *The Armada*. Boston, 1959. A great narrative history that reads like a novel; for more recent work, however, see Martin and Parker.

McGregor, Neil. *Shakespeare's Restless World*. London, 2013. Based on an acclaimed BBC Radio program, this book illuminates Shakespeare's life, times, and plays with reference to specific objects in the British Museum.

Newson, Linda A. and Susie Minchin. *From Capture to Sale: The Portuguese Slave Trade to Spanish South America in the Early Seventeenth Century*. London, 2007. Makes use of slave traders' own rich archives to track the process of human trafficking.

Parker, Geoffrey. *The Dutch Revolt*, 2d ed. Ithaca, NY, 1989. The standard survey in English on the revolt of the Netherlands.

———. *Philip II*. Boston, 1978. A fine biography by an expert in both the Spanish and the Dutch sources.

———, ed. *The Thirty Years' War*, rev. ed. London and New York, 1987. A wide-ranging collection of essays by scholarly experts.

Pascal, Blaise. *Pensées* (French-English edition). Ed. H. F. Stewart. London, 1950.

Pestana, Carla. *Protestant Empire: Religion and the Making of the British Atlantic World*. Philadelphia, 2010. How the Reformation helped to drive British imperial expansion.

Roberts, Michael. *Gustavus Adolphus and the Rise of Sweden*. London, 1973. Still the authoritative English-language account.

Russell, Conrad. *The Causes of the English Civil War*. Oxford, 1990. A penetrating and provocative analysis by one of the leading "revisionist" historians of the period.

Schmidt, Benjamin. *Innocence Abroad: The Dutch Imagination and the New World, 1570–1670*. Cambridge, 2006. A cultural history of Europeans' encounter with the Americas that highlights the perspective and experience of Dutch merchants, colonists, and artists.

Tracy, James D. *Holland under Habsburg Rule, 1506–1566: The Formation of a Body Politic*. Berkeley and Los Angeles, CA, 1990. A political history and analysis of the formative years of the Dutch state.

CHAPTER 15

Beik, William. *A Social and Cultural History of Early Modern France*. Cambridge, UK, 2009. A broad synthesis of French history from the end of the Middle Ages to the French Revolution, by one of the world's foremost authorities on absolutism.

Clark, Christopher, *Iron Kingdom: The Rise and Downfall of Prussia, 1600–1947*. Cambridge, MA, 2009. A definitive account of Prussian history over nearly four centuries.

Jones, Colin. *The Great Nation: France From Louis XV to Napoleon*. New York, 2002. An excellent and readable scholarly account that argues that the France of Louis XV in the eighteenth century was even more dominant than the kingdom of Louis XIV in the preceding century.

Kishlansky, Mark A. *A Monarchy Transformed: Britain, 1603–1714.* London, 1996. An excellent survey that takes seriously its claims to be a "British" rather than merely an "English" history.

Klein, Herbert S. *The Atlantic Slave Trade.* Cambridge and New York, 1999. An accessible survey by a leading quantitative historian.

Lewis, William Roger, gen. ed. *The Oxford History of the British Empire.* Vol. I: *The Origins of Empire: British Overseas Enterprise to the Close of the Seventeenth Century,* ed. Nicholas Canny. Vol. II: *The Eighteenth Century,* ed. Peter J. Marshall. Oxford and New York, 1998. A definitive, multiauthor account.

Locke, John. *Two Treatises of Government.* Ed. Peter Laslett. Rev. ed. Cambridge and New York, 1963. Laslett has revolutionized our understanding of the historical and ideological context of Locke's political writings.

Massie, Robert. *Peter the Great, His Life and World.* New York, 1980. Prize-winning and readable narrative account of the Russian tsar's life.

Monod, Paul K. *The Power of Kings: Monarchy and Religion in Europe, 1589–1715.* New Haven, CT, 1999. A study of the seventeenth century's declining confidence in the divinity of kings.

Quataert, Donald. *The Ottoman Empire, 1700–1822.* Cambridge and New York, 2000. Well balanced and intended to be read by students.

Riasanovsky, Nicholas V., and Steinberg, Mark D. *A History of Russia.* 7th ed. Oxford and New York, 2005. Far and away the best single-volume textbook on Russian history: balanced, comprehensive, intelligent, and with full bibliographies.

Saint-Simon, Louis. *Historical Memoirs.* Many editions. The classic source for life at Louis XIV's Versailles.

Snyder, Timothy, *The Reconstruction of Nations: Poland, Ukraine, Lithuania, Belarus, 1569–1999.* New Haven, CT, 2004. Essential account of nation building and state-collapse in Eastern Europe with significant relevance to the region's contemporary situation.

Thomas, Hugh. *The Slave Trade: The History of the Atlantic Slave Trade, 1440–1870.* London and New York, 1997. A survey notable for its breadth and depth of coverage and for its attractive prose style.

Tracy, James D. *The Rise of Merchant Empires: Long-Distance Trade in the Early Modern World, 1350–1750.* Cambridge and New York, 1990. Important collection of essays by leading authorities.

White, Richard. *The Middle Ground: Indians, Empires and Republics in the Great Lakes Region, 1650–1815.* Cambridge, UK, 1991. A path-breaking account of interactions between Europeans and Native Americans during the colonial period.

CHAPTER 16

Biagioli, Mario. *Galileo, Courtier.* Chicago, 1993. Emphasizes the importance of patronage and court politics in Galileo's science and career.

Cohen, I. B. *The Birth of a New Physics.* New York, 1985. Emphasizes the mathematical nature of the revolution; unmatched at making the mathematics understandable.

Daston, Lorraine, and Elizabeth Lunbeck, eds. *Histories of Scientific Observation.* Chicago, IL, 2011. Field-defining collection of essays on the history of scientific observation from the seventeenth to the twentieth centuries.

Daston, Lorraine. *Wonders and the Order of Nature, 1150–1750.* Cambridge, MA, 2001. Erudite sweeping account of the history of science in the early modern period, emphasizing the natural philosopher's awe and wonder at the marvelous, the unfamiliar, and the counter-intuitive.

Dear, Peter. *Revolutionizing the Sciences: European Knowledge and Its Ambitions, 1500–1700.* Princeton, NJ, 2001. Among the best short histories.

Drake, Stillman. *Discoveries and Opinions of Galileo.* Garden City, NY, 1957. The classic translation of Galileo's most important papers by his most admiring modern biographer.

Feingold, Mardechai, *The Newtonian Moment: Isaac Newton and the Making of Modern Culture.* New York, 2004. An engaging essay on the dissemination of Newton's thought, with excellent visual material.

Gaukroger, Stephen. *Descartes: An Intellectual Biography.* Oxford, 1995. Detailed and sympathetic study of the philosopher.

Gleick, James. *Isaac Newton.* New York, 2003. A vivid and well-documented brief biography.

Grafton, Anthony. *New Worlds, Ancient Texts: The Power of Tradition and the Shock of Discovery.* Cambridge, MA, 1992. Accessible essay by one of the leading scholars of early modern European thought.

Jacob, Margaret. *Scientific Culture and the Making of the Industrial West.* Oxford, 1997. A concise examination of the connections between developments in science and the Industrial Revolution.

Kuhn, Thomas. *The Structure of Scientific Revolutions.* Chicago, 1962. A classic and much-debated study of how scientific thought changes.

Pagden, Anthony, *European Encounters with the New World.* New Haven, CT, and London, 1993. Subtle and detailed on how European intellectuals thought about the lands they saw for the first time.

Scheibinger, Londa. *The Mind Has No Sex? Women in the Origins of Modern Science.* Cambridge, MA, 1989. A lively and important recovery of the lost role played by women mathematicians and experimenters.

Shapin, Steven. *The Scientific Revolution.* Chicago, 1996. Engaging, accessible, and brief—organized thematically.

Shapin, Steven, and Simon Schaffer. *Leviathan and the Air Pump.* Princeton, NJ, 1985. A modern classic, on one of the most famous philosophical conflicts in seventeenth-century science.

Stephenson, Bruce. *The Music of the Heavens: Kepler's Harmonic Astronomy.* Princeton, NJ, 1994. An engaging and important explanation of Kepler's otherworldly perspective.

Thoren, Victor. *The Lord of Uranibourg: A Biography of Tycho Brahe.* Cambridge, 1990. A vivid reconstruction of the scientific revolution's most flamboyant astronomer.

Westfall, Richard. *The Construction of Modern Science.* Cambridge, 1977.

———. *Never at Rest: A Biography of Isaac Newton.* Cambridge, 1980. The standard work.

Wilson, Catherine. *The Invisible World: Early Modern Philosophy and the Invention of the Microscope.* Princeton, NJ, 1995. An important study of how the "microcosmic" world revealed by technology reshaped scientific philosophy and practice.

Zinsser, Judith P. *La Dame d'Esprit: A Biography of the Marquise Du Châtelet.* New York, 2006. An excellent cultural history. To be issued in paper as *Emilie du Châtelet: Daring Genius of the Enlightenment* (2007).

CHAPTER 17

Baker, Keith. *Condorcet: From Natural Philosophy to Social Mathematics.* Chicago, 1975. An important reinterpretation of Condorcet as a social scientist.

Blum, Carol. *Rousseau and the Republic of Virtue: The Language of Politics in the French Revolution.* Ithaca and London, 1986. Fascinating account of how eighteenth-century readers interpreted Rousseau.

Buchan, James. *The Authentic Adam Smith: His Life and Ideas.* New York, 2006.

Calhoun, Craig, ed. *Habermas and the Public Sphere.* Cambridge, MA, 1992. Calhoun's introduction is a good starting point for Habermas's argument.

Cassirer, E. *The Philosophy of the Enlightenment.* Princeton, NJ, 1951.

Chartier, Roger. *The Cultural Origins of the French Revolution.* Durham, NC, 1991. Looks at topics from religion to violence in everyday life and culture.

Darnton, Robert. *The Business of Enlightenment: A Publishing History of the* Encyclopédie, *1775–1800.* Cambridge, MA, 1979. Darnton's work on the Enlightenment offers a fascinating blend of intellectual, social, and economic history. See his other books as well: *The Literary Underground of the Old Regime* (Cambridge, MA, 1982); *The Great Cat Massacre and Other Episodes in French Cultural History* (New York, 1984); and *The Forbidden Best Sellers of Revolutionary France* (New York and London, 1996).

Davis, David Brion. *The Problem of Slavery in Western Culture.* New York, 1988. A Pulitzer Prize–winning examination of a central issue as well as a brilliant analysis of different strands of Enlightenment thought.

Gay, Peter. *The Enlightenment: An Interpretation.* Vol. 1, *The Rise of Modern Paganism.* Vol. 2, *The Science of Freedom.* New York, 1966–1969. Combines an overview with an interpretation. Emphasizes the *philosophes'* sense of identification with the classical world and takes a generally positive view of their accomplishments. Includes extensive annotated bibliographies.

Gray, Peter. *Mozart.* New York, 1999. Brilliant short study.

Goodman, Dena. *The Republic of Letters: A Cultural History of the French Enlightenment.* Ithaca, NY, 1994. Important in its attention to the role of literary women.

Hazard, Paul. *The European Mind: The Critical Years (1680–1715).* New Haven, CT, 1953. A basic and indispensable account of the changing climate of opinion that preceded the Enlightenment.

Hunt, Lynn, Margaret C. Jacob, and Wijnand Mijnhardt. *The Book That Changed Europe: Picart and Bernard's Religious Ceremonies of the World.* Cambridge, MA, 2010. Lively study of a book on global religions that came out of the fertile world of the Dutch Enlightenment in the eighteenth century.

Israel, Jonathan Irvine. *Radical Enlightenment: Philosophy and the Making of Modernity, 1650–1750.* New York, 2001. Massive and erudite, a fresh look at the international movement of ideas.

———. *Enlightenment Contested: Philosophy, Modernity, and the Emancipation of Man, 1670–1752.* New York, 2006. Massive and erudite, a fresh look at the international movement of ideas.

Munck, Thomas. *The Enlightenment: A Comparative Social History 1721–1794.* London, 2000. An excellent recent survey, especially good on social history.

Outram, Dorinda. *The Enlightenment.* Cambridge, 1995. An excellent short introduction and a good example of new historical approaches.

Pagden, Anthony. *The Enlightenment: And Why It Still Matters.* New York, 2013. Spirited history of the Enlightenment and a defense of its continued relevance.

Porter, Roy. *The Creation of the Modern World: The Untold Story of the British Enlightenment.* New York, 2000.

Sapiro, Virginia. *A Vindication of Political Virtue: The Political Theory of Mary Wollstonecraft.* Chicago, 1992. A subtle and intelligent analysis for more advanced readers.

Shklar, Judith. *Men and Citizens: A Study of Rousseau's Social Theory.* London, 1969.

———. *Montesquieu.* Oxford, 1987. Shklar's studies are brilliant and accessible.

Taylor, Barbara. *Mary Wollstonecraft and the Feminist Imagination.* Cambridge and New York, 2003. Fascinating study that sets Wollstonecraft in the radical circles of eighteenth-century England.

Taylor, Barbara and Sarah Knott, eds. *Women, Gender, and Enlightenment.* New York, 2007. Multi-author collection examining the significance of sex, gender, and politics across a wide swath of the Enlightenment world, from Europe to the American colonies.

Venturi, Franco. *The End of the Old Regime in Europe, 1768–1776: The First Crisis.* Trans. R. Burr Litchfield. Princeton, NJ, 1989.

———. *The End of the Old Regime in Europe, 1776–1789.* Princeton, NJ, 1991. Both detailed and wide-ranging, particularly important on international developments.

Watt, Ian P. *The Rise of the Novel.* London, 1957. The basic work on the innovative qualities of the novel in eighteenth-century England.

Wolff, Larry. *Inventing Eastern Europe: The Map of Civilization on the Mind of the Enlightenment.* Stanford, CA, 1994. The place of Eastern Europe in the imagination of Enlightenment thinkers interested in the origins and destiny of the civilizing process.

CHAPTER 18

Applewhite, Harriet B., and Darline G. Levy, eds. *Women and Politics in the Age of the Democratic Revolution.* Ann Arbor, MI, 1990. Essays on France, Britain, the Netherlands, and the United States.

Bell, David A. *The First Total War: Napoleon's Europe and the Birth of Warfare as We Know It.* Boston and New York, 2007. Lively and concise study of the "cataclysmic intensification" of warfare.

Blackburn, Robin. *The Overthrow of Colonial Slavery.* London and New York, 1988. A longer view of slavery and its abolition.

Blanning, T. C. W. *The French Revolutionary Wars, 1787–1802.* Oxford, 1996. On the revolution and war.

Blum, Carol. *Rousseau and the Republic of Virtue: The Language of Politics in the French Revolution.* Ithaca, NY, 1986. Excellent on how Rousseau was read by the revolutionaries.

Cobb, Richard. *The People's Armies*. New Haven, CT, 1987. Brilliant and detailed analysis of the popular militias.

Cole, Juan. *Napoleon's Egypt: Invading the Middle East*. New York, 2007. Readable history by a scholar familiar with sources in Arabic as well as European languages.

Connelly, Owen. *The French Revolution and Napoleonic Era*. 3rd ed. New York, 2000. Accessible, lively, one-volume survey.

Darnton, Robert, *The Forbidden Best-Sellers of Pre-Revolutionary France*. New York, 1995. One of Darnton's many imaginative studies of subversive opinion and books on the eve of the revolution.

Desan, Suzanne. *The Family on Trial in Revolutionary France*. Berkeley, CA, 2006. Persuasive study of the ways that women in France were able to take advantage of the revolution and defend their interests in debates about marriage, divorce, parenthood, and the care of children.

Desan, Suzanne, Lynn Hunt, and William Max Nelson, eds. *The French Revolution in Global Perspective*. Ithaca, NY, 2013. Multi-author exploration of the French Revolution's global resonance.

Doyle, William. *Origins of the French Revolution*. New York, 1988. A revisionist historian surveys recent research on the political and social origins of the revolution and identifies a new consensus.

———. *Oxford History of the French Revolution*. New York, 1989.

Dubois, Laurent. *Avengers of the New World. The Story of the Haitian Revolution*. Cambridge, MA, 2004. Now the best and most accessible study.

———, and John D. Garrigus. *Slave Revolution in the Caribbean, 1789–1804: A Brief History with Documents*. New York, 2006. A particularly good collection.

Englund, Steven. *Napoleon, A Political Life*. Cambridge, MA, 2004. Prize-winning biography, both dramatic and insightful.

Forrest, Alan. *The French Revolution and the Poor*. New York, 1981. A moving and detailed social history of the poor, who fared little better under revolutionary governments than under the Old Regime.

Furet, Francois. *Revolutionary France, 1770–1880*. Trans. Antonia Nerill. Cambridge, MA, 1992. Overview by the leading revisionist.

Hunt, Lynn. *The French Revolution and Human Rights*. Boston, 1996. A collection of documents.

———. *Politics, Culture, and Class in the French Revolution*. Berkeley, CA, 1984. An analysis of the new culture of democracy and republicanism.

Hunt, Lynn, and Jack R. Censer. *Liberty, Equality, Fraternity: Exploring the French Revolution*. University Park, PA, 2001. Two leading historians of the revolution have written a lively, accessible study, with excellent documents and visual material.

Landes, Joan B. *Women and the Public Sphere in the Age of the French Revolution*. Ithaca, NY, 1988. On gender and politics.

Lefebvre, Georges. *The Coming of the French Revolution*. Princeton, NJ, 1947. The classic Marxist analysis.

Lewis, G., and C. Lucas. *Beyond the Terror: Essays in French Regional and Social History, 1794–1815*. New York, 1983. Shifts focus to the understudied period after the Terror.

O'Brien, Connor Cruise. *The Great Melody: A Thematic Biography of Edmund Burke*. Chicago, 1992. Passionate, partisan, and brilliant study of Burke's thoughts about Ireland, India, America, and France.

Palmer, R. R. *The Age of the Democratic Revolution: A Political History of Europe and America, 1760–1800*. 2 vols. Princeton, NJ, 1964. Impressive for its scope; places the French Revolution in the larger context of a worldwide revolutionary movement.

———, and Isser Woloch. *Twelve Who Ruled: The Year of the Terror in the French Revolution*. Princeton, NJ, 2005. The terrific collective biography of the Committee of Public Safety, now updated.

Schama, Simon. *Citizens: A Chronicle of the French Revolution*. New York, 1989. Particularly good on art, culture, and politics.

Scott, Joan. *Only Paradoxes to Offer: French Feminists and the Rights of Man*. Cambridge, MA, 1997. A history of feminist engagement with a revolutionary ideology that promised universal liberties while simultaneously excluding women from citizenship.

Soboul, Albert. *The Sans-Culottes: The Popular Movement and Revolutionary Government, 1793–1794*. Garden City, NY, 1972. Dated, but a classic.

Sutherland, D. M. G. *France, 1789–1815: Revolution and Counterrevolution*. Oxford, 1986. An important synthesis of work on the revolution, especially in social history.

Tocqueville, Alexis de. *The Old Regime and the French Revolution*. Garden City, NY, 1955. Originally written in 1856, this remains a provocative analysis of the revolution's legacy.

Trouillot, Michel Rolph. *Silencing the Past*. Boston, 1995. Essays on the Haitian revolution.

Woloch, Isser. *The New Regime: Transformations of the French Civic Order, 1789–1820*. New York, 1994. The fate of revolutionary civic reform.

Woolf, Stuart. *Napoleon's Integration of Europe*. New York, 1991. Technical but very thorough.

CHAPTER 19

Bridenthal, Renate, Claudia Koonz, and Susan Stuard, eds. *Becoming Visible: Women in European History*. 2d ed. Boston, 1987. Excellent, wide-ranging introduction.

Briggs, Asa. *Victorian Cities*. New York, 1963. A survey of British cities, stressing middle-class attitudes toward the new urban environment.

Chevalier, Louis. *Laboring Classes and Dangerous Classes during the First Half of the Nineteenth Century*. New York, 1973. An important, though controversial, account of crime, class, and middle-class perceptions of life in Paris.

Cipolla, Carlo M., ed. *The Industrial Revolution, 1700–1914*. New York, 1976. A collection of essays that emphasizes the wide range of industrializing experiences in Europe.

Clark, Anna. *The Struggle for the Breeches: Gender and the Making of the British Working Class*. Berkeley, CA, 1997. Examines the process of class formation during the industrial revolution in Britain through the lens of gender.

Cott, Nancy. *The Bonds of Womanhood: "Woman's Sphere" in New England, 1780–1935*. New Haven, CT, and London, 1977. One of the most influential studies of the paradoxes of domesticity.

Davidoff, Leonore, and Catherine Hall. *Family Fortunes: Men and Women of the English Middle Class, 1780–1850*. Chicago, 1985.

A brilliant and detailed study of the lives and ambitions of several English families.

Ferguson, Niall. "The European Economy, 1815–1914." In *The Nineteenth Century*, ed. T. C. W. Blanning. Oxford and New York, 2000. A very useful short essay.

Gay, Peter. *The Bourgeois Experience: Victoria to Freud.* New York, 1984. A multivolume, path-breaking study of middle-class life in all its dimensions.

———. *Schnitzler's Century: The Making of Middle-Class Culture, 1815–1914.* New York and London, 2002. A synthesis of some of the arguments presented in *The Bourgeois Experience*.

Hellerstein, Erna, Leslie Hume, and Karen Offen, eds. *Victorian Women: A Documentary Account.* Stanford, CA, 1981. Good collection of documents, with excellent introductory essays.

Hobsbawm, Eric J. *The Age of Revolution, 1789–1848.* London, 1962.

———, and George Rudé. *Captain Swing: A Social History of the Great English Agricultural Uprising of 1830.* New York, 1975. Analyzes rural protest and politics.

Horn, Jeff. *The Path Not Taken: French Industrialization in the Age of Revolution, 1750–1830.* Cambridge, 2006. Argues that industrialization in France succeeded in ways that other historians have not appreciated, and was much more than a failed attempt to imitate the British model.

Jones, Eric. *The European Miracle: Environments, Economies and Geopolitics in the History of Europe and Asia.* Cambridge, 2003. Argues that the Industrial Revolution is best understood as a European phenomenon.

Kemp, Tom. *Industrialization in Nineteenth-Century Europe.* London, 1985. Good general study.

Kindelberger, Charles. *A Financial History of Western Europe.* London, 1984. Emphasis on finance.

Landes, David S. *The Unbound Prometheus: Technological Change and Industrial Development in Western Europe from 1750 to the Present.* London, 1969. Excellent and thorough on technological change and its social and economic context.

McNeill, J. R. *Something New under the Sun: An Environmental History of the Twentieth-Century World.* New York and London, 2000. Short section on the nineteenth century.

Mokyr, Joel. *The Lever of Riches: Technological Creativity and Economic Progress.* New York, 1992. A world history, from antiquity through the nineteenth century

O'Gráda, Cormac. *Black '47 and Beyond: The Great Irish Famine.* Princeton, NJ, 1999.

———. *The Great Irish Famine.* Cambridge, 1989. A fascinating and recent assessment of scholarship on the famine.

Kenneth Pomeranz. *The Great Divergence: China, Europe, and the Making of the Modern World Economy.* Princeton, NJ, 2000. Path-breaking global history of the Industrial Revolution that argues that Europe was not as different from other parts of the world as scholars have previously thought.

Rendall, Jane. *The Origins of Modern Feminism: Women in Britain, France and the United States, 1780–1860.* New York, 1984. Helpful overview.

Rose, Sonya O. *Limited Livelihoods: Gender and Class in Nineteenth-Century England.* Berkeley, CA, 1992. On the intersection of culture and economics.

Sabean, David Warren. *Property, Production, and Family Neckarhausen, 1700–1870.* New York, 1990. Brilliant and very detailed study of gender roles and family.

Sabel, Charles, and Jonathan Zeitlin. "Historical Alternatives to Mass Production." *Past and Present* 108 (August 1985): 133–176. On the many forms of modern industry.

Schivelbusch, Wolfgang. *Disenchanted Night: The Instrialization of Light in the Nineteenth Century.* Berkeley, CA, 1988.

———. *The Railway Journey.* Berkeley, 1986. Schivelbusch's imaginative studies are among the best ways to understand how the transformations of the nineteenth century changed daily experiences.

Thompson, E. P. *The Making of the English Working Class.* London, 1963. Shows how the French and Industrial Revolutions fostered the growth of working-class consciousness. A brilliant and important work.

Tilly, Louise, and Joan Scott. *Women, Work and the Family.* New York, 1978. Now the classic study.

Valenze, Deborah. *The First Industrial Woman.* New York, 1995. Excellent and readable on industrialization and economic change in general.

Williams, Raymond. *Keywords: A Vocabulary of Culture and Society.* New York, 1976. Brilliant and indispensable for students of culture, and now updated as *New Keywords: A Revised Vocabulary of Culture and Society* (2005), by Lawrence Grossberg and Meaghan Morris.

Zeldin, Theodore. *France, 1848–1945,* 2 vols. Oxford, 1973–1977. Eclectic and wide-ranging social history.

CHAPTER 20

Anderson, Benedict. *Imagined Communities: Reflections on the Origin and Spread of Nationalism.* London, 1983. The most influential recent study of the subject, highly recommended for further reading.

Barzun, Jacques. *Classic, Romantic, and Modern.* Chicago, 1943. An enduring and penetrating mid-twentieth-century defense of the Romantic sensibility by a humane and influential cultural historian.

Berlin, Isaiah. *Karl Marx: His Life and Environment.* 4th ed. New York, 1996. An excellent short account.

Briggs, Asa. *The Age of Improvement, 1783–1867.* New York, 1979. A survey of England from 1780 to 1870, particularly strong on Victorian attitudes.

Colley, Linda. *Britons: Forging the Nation, 1707–1837.* New Haven, CT, 1992. An important analysis of Britain's emerging national consciousness in the eighteenth and early nineteenth centuries.

Furet, François. *Revolutionary France, 1770–1880.* New York, 1970. An excellent and fresh overview by one of the preeminent historians of the revolution of 1789.

Gilbert, Sandra M., and Susan Gubar. *The Madwoman in the Attic: The Woman Writer and the Nineteenth-Century Literary Imagination.* New Haven, CT, and London, 1970. A study of the history of women writers and on examination of women writers as historians of their time.

Kramer, Lloyd. *Nationalism: Political Cultures in Europe and America, 1775–1865*. London, 1998. Excellent recent overview.

Langer, William. *Political and Social Upheaval, 1832–1851*. New York, 1969. Long the standard and still the most comprehensive survey.

Laven, David, and Lucy Riall. *Napoleon's Legacy: Problems of Government in Restoration Europe*. London, 2002. A recent collection of essays.

Levinger, Matthew. *Enlightened Nationalism: The Transformation of Prussian Political Culture 1806–1848*. New York, 2000. A nuanced study of Prussian conservatism, with implications for the rest of Europe.

Macfie, A. L. *Orientalism*. London, 2002. Introductory but very clear.

Merriman, John M., ed. *1830 in France*. New York, 1975. Emphasizes the nature of revolution and examines events outside Paris.

Pinkney, David. *The French Revolution of 1830*. Princeton, NJ, 1972. A reinterpretation, now the best history of the revolution.

Porter, Roy, and Mikulas Teich, eds. *Romanticism in National Context*. Cambridge, 1988.

Raeff, Marc. *The Decembrist Movement*. New York, 1966. A study of the Russian uprising with documents.

Sahlins, Peter. *Forest Rites: The War of the Demoiselles in Nineteenth-Century France*. Cambridge, MA, 1994. A fascinating study of relations among peasant communities, the forests, and the state.

Said, Edward W. *Orientalism*. New York, 1979. A brilliant and biting study of the imaginative hold of the Orient on European intellectuals.

Saville, John. *1848: The British State and the Chartist Movement*. New York, 1987. A detailed account of the movement's limited successes and ultimate failure.

Schroeder, Paul. *The Transformation of European Politics, 1763–1848*. Oxford and New York, 1994. For those interested in international relations and diplomacy; massively researched and a fresh look at the period. Especially good on the Congress of Vienna.

Sewell, William H. *Work and Revolution in France: The Language of Labor from the Old Regime to 1848*. Cambridge, 1980. A very influential study of French radicalism and its larger implications.

Smith, Bonnie. *The Gender of History: Men, Women, and Historical Practice*. Cambridge, MA, 1998. On Romanticism and the historical imagination.

Sperber, Jonathan. *Karl Marx: A Nineteenth-Century Life*. New York, 2013. A detailed biography examining Marx's public and private engagements, setting him in the context of his time.

Wordsworth, Jonathan, Michael C. Jaye, and Robert Woof. *William Wordsworth and the Age of English Romanticism*. New Brunswick, NJ, 1987. Wide ranging and beautifully illustrated, a good picture of the age.

CHAPTER 21

Agulhon, Maurice. *The Republican Experiment, 1848–1852*. New York, 1983. A full treatment of the revolution in France.

Beales, Derek. *The Risorgimento and the Unification of Italy*. New York, 1971. Objective, concise survey of Italian unification.

Blackbourn, David. *The Long Nineteenth Century: A History of Germany, 1780–1918*. New York, 1998.

Blackbourn, David, and Geoff Eley. *The Peculiarities of German History: Bourgeois Society and Politics in Nineteenth-Century Germany*. Oxford, 1984. Critical essays on the course of German history during the age of national unification and after.

Blackburn, Robin. *The Overthrow of Colonial Slavery*. London, 1988. Brilliant and detailed overview of the social history of slavery and antislavery movements.

Brophy, James M. *Capitalism, Politics, and Railroads in Prussia, 1830–1870*. Columbus, Ohio, 1998. Important, clear, and helpful.

Coppa, Frank. *The Origins of the Italian Wars of Independence*. London, 1992. Lively narrative.

Craig, Gordon. *Germany, 1866–1945*. New York, 1978. An excellent and thorough synthesis.

Davis, David Brian. *Inhuman Bondage: The Rise and Fall of Slavery in the New World*. New York, 2006. As one reviewer aptly puts it, "A gracefully fashioned masterpiece."

Deak, Istvan. *The Lawful Revolution: Louis Kossuth and the Hungarians, 1848–1849*. New York, 1979. The best on the subject.

Eyck, Erich. *Bismarck and the German Empire*. 3d ed. London, 1968. The best one-volume study of Bismarck.

Hamerow, Theodore S. *The Birth of a New Europe: State and Society in the Nineteenth Century*. Chapel Hill, NC, 1983. A discussion of political and social change, and their relationship to industrialization and the increase in state power.

———. *The Social Foundations of German Unification, 1858–1871*. 2 vols. Princeton, NJ, 1969–1972. Concentrates on economic factors that determined the solution to the unification question. An impressive synthesis.

Higonnet, Patrice. *Paris: Capital of the World*. London, 2002. Fascinating and imaginative study of Paris as "capital of the nineteenth century."

Hobsbawm, Eric J. *The Age of Capital, 1848–1875*. London, 1975. Among the best introductions.

———. *Nations and Nationalism since 1870: Programme, Myth, Reality*. 2d ed. Cambridge, 1992. A clear, concise analysis of the historical and cultural manifestations of nationalism.

Howard, Michael. *The Franco-Prussian War*. New York, 1981. The war's effect on society.

Hutchinson, John, and Anthony Smith, eds. *Nationalism*. New York, 1994. A collection of articles, not particularly historical, but with the merit of discussing non-European nationalisms.

Johnson, Susan. *Roaring Camp*. New York, 2000. A history of one mining camp in California and a micro-history of the larger forces changing the West and the world.

Kolchin, Peter. *Unfree Labor: American Slavery and Russian Serfdom*. Cambridge, MA, 1987. Pioneering comparative study.

Mack Smith, Denis. *Cavour and Garibaldi*. New York, 1968.

———. *The Making of Italy, 1796–1870*. New York, 1968. A narrative with documents.

McPherson, James. *Battle Cry of Freedom: The Civil War Era*. New York, 1988. Universally acclaimed and prize-winning book on the politics of slavery and the conflicts entailed in nation building in mid-nineteenth-century United States.

Pflanze, Otto. *Bismarck and the Development of Germany.* 2d ed. 3 vols. Princeton, NJ, 1990. Extremely detailed analysis of Bismarck's aims and policies.

Pinkney, David. *Napoleon III and the Rebuilding of Paris.* Princeton, NJ, 1972. An interesting account of the creation of modern Paris during the Second Empire.

Robertson, Priscilla. *Revolutions of 1848: A Social History.* Princeton, NJ, 1952. Old-fashioned narrative, but very readable.

Sammons, Jeffrey L. *Heinrich Heine: A Modern Biography.* Princeton, NJ, 1979. An excellent historical biography as well as a study of culture and politics.

Scott, Rebecca J. *Degrees of Freedom: Louisiana and Cuba after Slavery.* Cambridge, MA, 2008. Brings the lives of slaves and their owners to life during the era of emancipation in a comparative history that places the southern United States in the context of the Atlantic world.

Sheehan, James J. *German Liberalism in the Nineteenth Century.* Chicago, 1978. Fresh and important synthesis.

Sperber, Jonathan. *The European Revolutions, 1848–1851.* Cambridge, 2005. An excellent synthesis and the best one-volume treatment of the 1848 revolutions, describing the reasons for their failure.

———. *Rhineland Radicals: The Democratic Movement and the Revolution of 1848–1849.* Princeton, NJ, 1993. A detailed study of Germany, by the author of an overview of the revolutions of 1848.

Stearns, Peter N. *1848: The Revolutionary Tide in Europe.* New York, 1974. Stresses the social background of the revolutions.

Zeldin, Theodore. *The Political System of Napoleon III.* New York, 1958. Compact and readable, by one of the major scholars of the period.

CHAPTER 22

Achebe, Chinua. *Things Fall Apart.* Expanded edition with notes. Portsmouth, NH, 1996. An annotated edition of the now classic novel about colonial Africa.

Adas, Michael. *Machines as the Measure of Man: Science, Technology, and Ideologies of Western Dominance.* Ithaca, NY, and London, 1989. An important study of Europeans' changing perceptions of themselves and others during the period of industrialization.

Bayly, C. A. *Indian Society and the Making of the British Empire.* Cambridge, 1988. A good introduction, and one that bridges eighteenth- and nineteenth-century imperialisms.

Burbank, Jane, and Frederick Cooper. *Empires in World History: Power and the Politics of Difference.* Princeton, NJ, 2010. Powerful synthesis that sets European empires in the broader context of world history.

Burton, Antoinette. *Burdens of History: British Feminists, Indian Women, and Imperial Culture, 1865–1915.* Chapel Hill, NC, 1994. On the ways in which women and feminists came to support British imperialism.

Cain, P. J., and A. G. Hopkins. *British Imperialism, 1688–2000.* London, 2002. One of the most influential studies. Excellent overview and exceptionally good on economics.

Chakrabarty, Dipesh. *Provincializing Europe: Postcolonial Thought and Historical Difference.* Princeton, 2000. Sophisticated theoretical challenge to European narratives of social and political progress.

Clancy Smith, Julia, and Frances Gouda. *Domesticating the Empire: Race, Gender, and Family Life in French and Dutch Colonialism.* Charlottesville, VA., and London, 1998. A particularly good collection of essays that both breaks new historical ground and is accessible to nonspecialists. Essays cover daily life and private life in new colonial cultures.

Cohn, Bernard S. *Colonialism and its Forms of Knowledge.* Princeton, 1996. Argues that new forms of cultural knowledge were essential to the project of British imperialism in India.

Conklin, Alice. *A Mission to Civilize: The Republican idea of Empire in France and West Africa, 1895–1930.* Stanford, CA, 1997. One of the best studies of how the French reconciled imperialism with their vision of the Republic.

Cooper, Frederick. *Colonialism in Question: Theory, Knowledge, History.* Berkeley, 2005. Crucial collection of path-breaking essays on the history of colonialism.

Cooper, Frederick, and Ann Laura Stoler. *Tensions of Empire: Colonial Cultures in a Bourgeois World.* Berkeley, CA, 1997. New approaches, combining anthropology and history, with an excellent bibliography.

Darwin, John. *The Empire Project: The Rise and Fall of the British World System.* Cambridge, 2009.

Headrick, Daniel R. *The Tools of Empire: Technology and European Imperialism in the Nineteenth Century.* Oxford, 1981. A study of the relationship between technological innovation and imperialism.

Hobsbawm, Eric. *The Age of Empire, 1875–1914.* New York, 1987. Surveys the European scene at a time of apparent stability and real decline.

Hochschild, Adam. *King Leopold's Ghost: A Story of Greed, Terror, and Heroism in Colonial Africa.* Boston, 1998. Reads like a great novel.

Hull, Isabell. *Absolute Destruction: Military Culture and the Practices of War in Imperial Germany.* Ithaca, 2005. A study of the German military and its role in imperial expansion in Africa, arguing that the experience was crucial in shaping the institution as it entered the twentieth century.

Lorcin, Patricia. *Imperial Identities: Stereotyping, Prejudice and Race in Colonial Algeria.* New York, 1999.

Louis, William Roger. *The Oxford History of the British Empire.* 5 vols. Oxford, 1998. Excellent and wide-ranging collection of the latest research.

Metcalf, Thomas. *Ideologies of the Raj.* Cambridge, 1995.

Pakenham, Thomas. *The Scramble for Africa, 1876–1912.* London, 1991. A well-written narrative of the European scramble for Africa in the late nineteenth century.

Prochaska, David. *Making Algeria French: Colonialism in Bône, 1870–1920.* Cambridge, 1990. One of the few social histories of European settlement in Algeria in English.

Robinson, Ronald, and J. Gallagher. *Africa and the Victorians: The Official Mind of Imperialism.* London, 1961. A classic.

Said, Edward. *Culture and Imperialism.* New York, 1993. A collection of brilliant, sometimes controversial, essays.

Sangari, Kumkum, and Sudesh Vaid. *Recasting Women: Essays in Colonial History.* New Delhi, 1989. A collection of essays on women in India.

Schneer, Jonathan. *London 1900: The Imperial Metropolis.* New Haven, CT, 1999. Excellent study of the empire—and opposition to empire—in the metropole.

Spence, Jonathan. *The Search for Modern China.* New York, 1990. An excellent and readable introduction to modern Chinese history.

CHAPTER 23

Berghahn, Volker. *Imperial Germany, 1871–1914: Economy, Society, Culture, and Politics.* Providence, 1994. Inclusive history that seeks to go beyond standard political accounts.

Berlanstein, Lenard. *The Working People of Paris, 1871–1914.* Baltimore, MD. 1984. A social history of the workplace and its impact on working men and women.

Blackbourn, David. *The Long Nineteenth Century: A History of Germany, 1780–1918.* New York, 1998. Among the best surveys of German society and politics.

Bowler, Peter J. *Evolution: The History of an Idea.* Berkeley, CA, 1984. One of the author's several excellent studies of evolution of Darwinism.

Burns, Michael. *Dreyfus: A Family Affair.* New York, 1992. Follows the story Dreyfus through the next generations.

Clark, T. J. *The Painting of Modern Life: Paris in the Art of Manet and His Followers.* New York, 1985. Argues for seeing impressionism as a critique of French society.

Eley, Geoff. *Forging Democracy.* Oxford, 2002. Wide-ranging and multinational account of European radicalism from 1848 to the present.

Engelstein, Laura. *Slavophile Empire: Imperial Russia's Illiberal Path.* Ithaca, 2009. An examination of Russia's political culture before World War 1, with an eye toward later evolution in the twentieth century.

Frank, Stephen. *Crime, Cultural Conflict, and Justice in Rural Russia, 1856–1914.* Berkeley, CA, 1999. A revealing study of social relations from the ground up.

Gay, Peter. *The Bourgeois Experience: Victoria to Freud,* 5 vols. New York, 1984–2000. Imaginative and brilliant study of private life and middle class culture.

————. *Freud: A Life of Our Time.* New York, 1988. Beautifully written and lucid about difficult concepts; now the best biography.

Harris, Ruth. *Dreyfus: Politics, Emotion, and the Scandal of the Century.* London, 2011. A reassessment of the politics of the Dreyfus affair, with a eye toward its resonance in the culture as a whole.

Herbert, Robert L. *Impressionism: Art, Leisure, and Parisian Society.* New Haven, CT, 1988. An accessible and important study of the impressionists and the world they painted.

Hughes, H. Stuart. *Consciousness and Society.* New York, 1958. A classic study on late-nineteenth-century European thought.

Jelavich, Peter. *Munich and Theatrical Modernism: Politics, Playwriting, and Performance, 1890–1914.* Cambridge, MA, 1985. On modernism as a revolt against nineteenth-century conventions.

Jones, Gareth Stedman. *Outcast London.* Oxford, 1971. Studies the breakdown in class relationships during the second half of the nineteenth century.

Joyce, Patrick. *Visions of the People: Industrial England and the Question of Class, 1848–1914.* New York, 1991. A social history of the workplace.

Kelly, Alfred. *The German Worker: Autobiographies from the Age of Industrialization.* Berkeley, CA, 1987. Excerpts from workers' autobiographies provide fresh perspective on labor history.

Kern, Stephen. *The Culture of Time and Space.* Cambridge, MA, 1983. A cultural history of the late nineteenth century.

Lidtke, Vernon. *The Alternative Culture: Socialist Labor in Imperial Germany.* New York, 1985. A probing study of working-class culture.

Marrus, Michael Robert. *The Politics of Assimilation: A Study of the French Jewish Community at the Time of the Dreyfus Affair.* Oxford, 1971. Excellent social history.

Micale, Mark S. *Approaching Hysteria: Disease and Its Interpretations.* Princeton, NJ, 1995. Important study of the history of psychiatry before Freud.

Rupp, Leila J. *Worlds of Women: The Making of an International Women's Movement.* Princeton, NJ, 1997.

Schivelbusch, Wolfgang. *Disenchanted Night: The Industrialization of Light in the Nineteenth Century.* Berkeley, CA, 1995. Imaginative study of how electricity transformed everyday life.

Schorske, Carl E. *Fin-de-Siècle Vienna: Politics and Culture.* New York, 1980. Classic account of avant-garde art, music, and intellectual culture set against the background of mass politics in the Austrian capital.

Schwartz, Vanessa. *Spectacular Realities: Early Mass Culture in Fin-de-Siècle Paris.* Berkeley, 1998. Innovative approach to the emergence of mass culture in modern France.

Showalter, Elaine. *The Female Malady: Women, Madness, and English Culture, 1890–1980.* New York, 1985. Brilliant and readable on Darwin, Freud, gender, and the First World War.

Silverman, Deborah L. *Art Nouveau in Fin-de-Siècle France: Politics, Psychology, and Style.* Berkeley, CA, 1989. A study of the relationship between psychological and artistic change.

Smith, Bonnie. *Changing Lives: Women in European History since 1700.* New York, 1988. A useful overview of European women's history.

Stern, Fritz. *The Politics of Cultural Despair: A Study of the Rise of the Germanic Ideology.* Berkeley, 1974. Classic account of the rise of nationalist and populist politics in German-speaking lands of central Europe before World War I.

Tickner, Lisa. *The Spectacle of Women: Imagery of the Suffrage Campaign, 1907–14.* Chicago, 1988. A very engaging study of British suffragism.

Verner, Andrew. *The Crisis of Russian Autocracy: Nicholas II and the 1905 Revolution.* Princeton, NJ, 1990. A detailed study of this important event.

Vital, David. *A People Apart: A Political History of the Jews in Europe, 1789-1939.* Oxford and New York, 1999. Comprehensive and extremely helpful.

Walkowitz, Judith. *City of Dreadful Delight: Narratives of Sexual Danger in Late-Victorian London.* Chicago, 1992. Cultural history of the English capital at the end of the nineteenth century.

Weber, Eugen. *Peasants into Frenchmen: The Modernization of Rural France, 1870–1914.* Stanford, CA, 1976. A study of how France's peasantry was assimilated into the Third Republic.

Wehler, Hans-Ulrich. *The German Empire, 1871–1918*. Dover, 1997. Standard account by respected German historian.

CHAPTER 24

Aksakal, Mustapha. *The Ottoman Road to War in 1914: The Ottoman Empire and the First World War*. Cambridge, 2009. A compelling look at Ottoman involvement in the First World War.

Bourke, Joanna. *Dismembering the Male: Men's Bodies, Britain, and the Great War*. Chicago, 1996. A cultural history of the war's effects on male bodies and codes of masculinity.

Chickering, Roger. *Imperial Germany and the Great War, 1914–1918*. New York, 1998. An excellent synthesis.

Clark, Christopher. *The Sleepwalkers: How Europe Went to War in 1914*. New York, 2013. Comprehensive reassessment of the war's origins.

Eksteins, Modris. *Rites of Spring: The Great War and the Birth of the Modern Age*. New York, 1989. Fascinating, though impressionistic, on war, art, and culture.

Ferguson, Niall. *The Pity of War*. London, 1998. A fresh look at the war, including strategic issues, international relations, and economics.

Ferro, Marc. *The Great War, 1914–1918*. London, 1973. Very concise overview.

Figes, Orlando. *A People's Tragedy: A History of the Russian Revolution*. New York, 1997. Excellent, detailed narrative.

Fischer, Fritz. *War of Illusions*. New York, 1975. Deals with Germany within the context of internal social and economic trends.

Fitzpatrick, Sheila. *The Russian Revolution, 1917–1932*. New York and Oxford, 1982. Concise overview.

Fussell, Paul. *The Great War and Modern Memory*. New York, 1975. A brilliant examination of British intellectuals' attitudes toward the war.

Hynes, Samuel. *A War Imagined: The First World War and English Culture*. New York, 1991. The war as perceived on the home front.

Jelavich, Barbara. *History of the Balkans: Twentieth Century*. New York, 1983. Useful for an understanding of the continuing conflict in eastern Europe.

Joll, James. *The Origins of the First World War*. London, 1984. Comprehensive and very useful.

Keegan, John. *The First World War*. London, 1998. The best overall military history.

Macmillan, Margaret, and Richard Holbrooke. *Paris 1919: Six Months That Changed the World*. New York, 2003. Fascinating fresh look at the peace conference.

Mazower, Mark. *Dark Continent: Europe's Twentieth Century*. New York, 1999. An excellent survey, particularly good on nations and minorities in the Balkans and eastern Europe.

Rabinowitch, Alexander. *The Bolsheviks Come to Power*. New York, 1976. A well-researched and carefully documented account.

Roberts, Mary Louise. *Civilization without Sexes: Reconstructing Gender in Postwar France, 1917–1927*. Chicago, 1994. A prize-winning study of the issues raised by the "new woman."

Schivelbusch, Wolfgang. *The Culture of Defeat: On National Trauma, Mourning, and Recovery*. New York, 2001. Fascinating if impressionistic comparative study.

Smith, Leonard. *Between Mutiny and Obedience: The Case of the French Fifth Infantry Division during World War I*. Princeton, NJ, 1994. An account of mutiny and the reasons behind it.

Stevenson, David. *Cataclysm: The First World War as Political Tragedy*. New York, 2003. Detailed and comprehensive, now one of the best single-volume studies.

Stites, Richard. *Revolutionary Dreams: Utopian Visions and Experimental Life in the Russian Revolution*. New York, 1989. The influence of utopian thinking on the revolution.

Suny, Ronald Grigor, Fatma Muge Gocek, and Norman Naimark, eds. *A Question of Genocide: Armenians and Turks at the End of the Ottoman Empire*. Oxford, 2011. Multi-author work offering a comprehensive summary of research on the Armenian genocide.

Williams, John. *The Home Fronts: Britain, France and Germany, 1914–1918*. London, 1972. A survey of life away from the battlefield and the impact of the war on domestic life.

Winter, Jay. *Sites of Memory, Sites of Mourning: The Great War in European Cultural History*. Cambridge, 1998. An essential reference on the legacy of World War I in European cultural history.

Winter, Jay and Jean-Louis Robert. *Capital Cities at War: Paris, London, Berlin, 1914–1919*. Cambridge, 1997 (vol. 1), 2007 (vol. 2). Multi-author work on the demographic, social, and cultural effects of the war on civilian populations of three European capitals.

CHAPTER 25

Bosworth, R. J. B. *Mussolini's Italy: Life under the Fascist Dictatorship, 1915–1945*. New York, 2007. Comprehensive account of "everyday" fascism in Italy.

Conquest, Robert. *The Great Terror: A Reassessment*. New York, 1990. One of the first histories of the Terror, should be read in conjunction with others in this list.

Crew, David F., ed. *Nazism and German Society, 1933–1945*. New York, 1994. An excellent and accessible collection of essays.

de Grazia, Victoria. *How Fascism Ruled Women: Italy, 1922–1945*. Berkeley, 1993. The contradictions between fascism's vision of modernity and its commitment to patriarchal institutions, seen from the point of view of Italian women.

Figes, Orlando. *Peasant Russia Civil War: The Volga Countryside in Revolution, 1917–1921*. Oxford, 1989. Detailed and sophisticated but readable. Study of the region from the eve of the revolution through the civil war.

Fitzpatrick, Shelia. *Everyday Stalinism: Ordinary Life in Extraordinary Times: Soviet Russia in the 1930s*. Oxford and New York, 1999. Gripping on how ordinary people dealt with famine, repression, and chaos.

Friedlander, Saul. *Nazi Germany and the Jews: The Years of Persecution. 1933–1939*. Rev. ed. New York, 2007. Excellent; the first of a two-volume study.

Gay, Peter. *Weimar Culture*. New York, 1968. Concise and elegant overview.

Getty, J. Arch, and Oleg V. Naumov. *The Road to Terror: Stalin and the Self-Destruction of the Bolsheviks, 1932–1939*. New Haven, CT, 1999. Combines analysis with documents made public for the first time.

Goldman, Wendy Z. *Women, the State, and Revolution: Soviet Family Policy and Social Life, 1917–1936.* New York, 1993. On the Bolshevik attempts to transform gender and family.

Kershaw, Ian. *Hitler.* 2 vols: *1889–1936 Hubris,* New York, 1999; *1936–1945: Nemesis,* New York, 2001. The best biography: insightful about politics, culture, and society as well as the man.

———. *The Hitler Myth: Image and Reality in the Third Reich.* New York, 1987. Brilliant study of how Nazi propagandists sold the myth of the Fuhrer and why many Germans bought it.

Klemperer, Victor. *I Will Bear Witness: A Diary of the Nazi Years, 1933–1941.* New York, 1999. *I Will Bear Witness: A Diary of the Nazi Years, 1942–1945.* New York, 2001. Certain to be a classic.

Lewin, Moshe. *The Making of the Soviet System: Essays in the Social History of Interwar Russia.* New York, 1985. One of the best to offer a view from below.

Maier, Charles. *Recasting Bourgeois Europe.* Princeton, 1975. Now classic account of the political and social adjustments made between state and society in the interwar years throughout Europe.

McDermott, Kevin. *Stalin: Revolutionary in an Era of War.* Basingstoke, UK, and New York, 2006. Useful, short, and recent.

Montefior, Simon Sebag. *Stalin: The Court of the Red Tsar.* London, 2004. On the relations among the top Bolsheviks, an interesting personal portrait. Takes you inside the inner circle.

Orwell, George. *The Road to Wigan Pier.* London, 1937. On unemployment and life in the coal mining districts of England, by one of the great British writers of the twentieth century.

———. *Homage to Catalonia.* London, 1938. A firsthand account of the Spanish Civil War.

Payne, Stanley G., *A History of Fascism, 1914–1945.* Madison, WI, 1996. Thorough account of the origins and evolution of fascism in Europe through the end of World War II.

Paxton, Robert O. *The Anatomy of Fascism.* New York, 2004. Excellent introduction to a complex subject by a foremost historian of twentieth century Europe.

Peukert, Detlev. *The Weimar Republic.* New York, 1993. Useful and concise history of Weimar by respected German historian of the period.

Rentschler, Eric. *The Ministry of Illusion: Nazi Cinema and Its Afterlife.* Cambridge, MA, 1996. For the more advanced student.

Service, Robert. *Stalin: A Biography.* London, 2004. Updates Tucker.

Suny, Ronald Grigor. *The Revenge of the Past: Nationalism, Revolution, and the Collapse of the Soviet Union.* Stanford, CA, 1993. Path-breaking study of the issues of nationalism and ethnicity form the revolution to the end of the Soviet Union.

Tucker, Robert C. *Stalin as Revolutionary, 1879–1929.* New York, 1973.

———. *Stalin in Power: The Revolution from Above, 1928–1941.* New York, 1990. With *Stalin as Revolutionary* emphasizes Stalin's purpose and method and sets him in the tradition of Russian dictators.

Weitz, Eric D. *Weimar Germany: Promise and Tragedy.* Princeton, NJ, 2009. A valuable and thorough account that ties together the complex connections between Weimar culture and politics in this transformational period.

CHAPTER 26

The U.S. Holocaust Memorial Museum has an extraordinary collection of articles, photographs, and maps. See www.ushmm.org.

Bartov, Omer. *Hitler's Army: Soldiers, Nazis, and War in the Third Reich.* New York, 1991. A Study of the radicalization of the German army on the Russian front.

Braithwaite, Rodric. *Moscow. 1941: A City and Its People at War.* London, 2006. Readable account of one of the turning points of the war.

Browning, Christopher R. *The Path to Genocide: Essays on Launching the Final Solution.* Cambridge, 1992. Discusses changing interpretations and case studies. See also the author's *Ordinary Men: Reserve Police Battalion 101 and the Final Solution in Poland.*

Burrin, Philippe. *France under the Germans: Collaboration and Compromise.* New York, 1996. Comprehensive on occupation and collaboration.

Carr, Raymond. *The Spanish Tragedy: The Civil War in Perspective.* London, 1977. A thoughtful introduction to the Spanish Civil War and the evolution of Franco's Spain.

Davies, Norman. *Heart of Europe: The Past in Poland's Present.* Oxford, 2001. Revised edition of a classic account of Poland's place in European history, with special attention to the second half of the twentieth century.

Dawidowicz, Lucy S. *The War against the Jews, 1933–1945.* New York, 1975. A full account of the Holocaust.

Divine, Robert A. *Roosevelt and World War II.* Baltimore, MD, 1969. A diplomatic history.

Djilas, Milovan. *Wartime.* New York, 1977. An insider's account of the partisans' fighting in Yugoslavia and a good example of civil war within the war.

Fritzsche, Peter. *Life and Death in the Third Reich.* Cambridge, MA, 2009. A compelling account of the appeal of Nazi ideology and the extent to which it was embraced by ordinary people in Germany.

Gellately, Robert, and Ben Kiernan, eds. *The Specter of Genocide: Mass Murder in Historical Perspective.* New York, 2003. A particularly thoughtful collection of essays.

Graham, Helen. *The Spanish Civil War: A Very Short Introduction.* Oxford and New York, 2005. Excellent and very concise, based on the author's new interpretation in the more detailed *The Spanish Republic at War, 1936–1939.* Cambridge, 2002.

Hilberg, Raul. *The Destruction of the European Jews.* 2nd ed. 3 vols. New York, 1985. An excellent treatment of the Holocaust, its origins, and its consequences.

Hitchcock, William I. *The Bitter Road to Freedom: A New History of the Liberation of Europe.* New York, 2008. The story of Europe's liberation from Hitler's control, seen from the point of view of civilian populations.

Kedward, Roderick. *In Search of the Maquis: Rural Resistance in Southern France, 1942–1944.* Oxford, 1993. An engaging study of French guerilla resistance.

Keegan, John. *The Second World War.* New York, 1990. By one of the great military historians of our time.

Marrus, Michael R. *The Holocaust in History.* Hanover, NH, 1987. Thoughtful analysis of central issues.

Mawdsley, Evan. *Thunder in the East: The Nazi-Soviet War, 1941–1945.* New York, 2005.

Megargee, Geoffrey. *War of Annihilation: Combat and Genocide on the Eastern War, 1941.* Lanham, MD, 2006. Represents some of the new historical work on the eastern front.

Merridale, Catherine. *Ivan's War: Life and Death in the Red Army, 1939–1945.* New York, 2006. Raised many questions and insights.

Michel, Henri. *The Shadow War: The European Resistance, 1939–1945.* New York, 1972. Compelling reading.

Milward, Alan S. *War, Economy, and Society, 1939–1945.* Berkeley, CA, 1977. On the economic impact of the war and the strategic impact of the economy.

Noakes, Jeremy, and Geoffrey Pridham. *Nazism: A History in Documents and Eyewitness Accounts, 1919–1945.* New York, 1975. An excellent combination of analysis and documentation.

Overy, Richard. *Russia's War.* New York, 1998. A very readable account that accompanies the PBS series by the same title.

———. *Why the Allies Won.* New York, 1995. Excellent analysis; succint.

Paxton, Robert O. *Vichy France: Old Guard and New Order, 1940–1944.* New York, 1982. Brilliant on collaboration and Vichy's National Revolution.

Roberts, Mary Louise. *What Soldiers Do: Sex and the American GI in World War II France.* Chicago, 2013. Critical reappraisal of how sex between GIs and civilians became an issue for French and U.S. military personnel after the D-Day invasion.

Snyder, Timothy. *Bloodlands: Europe between Hitler and Stalin.* New York, 2010. Thorough and penetrating account of the methods and motives of Hitler's and Stalin's regimes.

Stoff, Michael B. *The Manhattan Project: A Documentary Introduction to the Atomic Age.* New York, 1991. Political, scientific, and historical; excellent documents and commentary.

Weinberg, Gerhard L. *A World At Arms: A Global History of World War II.* Cambridge, 2005. Second edition of a comprehensive and respected global account of the Second World War.

Wilkinson, James D. *The Intellectual Resistance in Europe.* Cambridge, MA, 1981. A comparative study of the movement throughout Europe.

CHAPTER 27

Aron, Raymond. *The Imperial Republic: The United States and the World, 1945–1973.* Lanham, MD, 1974. An early analysis by a leading French political theorist.

Carter, Erica. *How German Is She? Postwar West German Reconstruction and the Consuming Woman.* Ann Arbor, MI, 1997. A thoughtful examination of gender and the reconstruction of the family in West Germany during the 1950s.

Clayton, Anthony. *The Wars of French Decolonization.* London, 1994. Good survey.

Connelly, Matthew. *A Diplomatic Revolution: Algeria's Fight for Independence and the Origins of the Post–Cold War Era.* New York and Oxford, 2003. An international history.

Cooper, Frederick, and Ann Laura Stoler, eds. *Tensions of Empire: Colonial Cultures in a Bourgeois World.* Berkeley, CA, 1997. Collection of new essays, among the best.

Darwin, John. *Britain and Decolonization: The Retreat from Empire in the Postwar World.* New York, 1988. Best overall survey.

Deák, István, Jan T. Gross, and Tony Judt, eds. *The Politics of Retribution in Europe: World War II and Its Aftermath.* Princeton, NJ, 2000. Collection focusing on the attempt to come to terms with the Second World War in Eastern and Western Europe.

Farmer, Sarah. *Martyred Village: Commemorating the 1944 Massacre at Oradour-sur-Glane.* Berkeley, CA, 1999. Gripping story of French attempts to come to terms with collaboration and complicity in atrocities.

Holland, R. F. *European Decolonization 1918–1981: An Introductory Survey.* New York, 1985. Sprightly narrative and analysis.

Jarausch, Konrad Hugo, ed. *Dictatorship as Experience: Towards a Socio-Cultural History of the GDR.* Trans. Eve Duffy. New York, 1999. Surveys recent research on the former East Germany.

Judt, Tony. *The Burden of Responsibility: Blum, Camus, and the French Twentieth Century.* Chicago and London, 1998. Also on French intellectuals.

———. *A Grand Illusion? An Essay on Europe.* New York, 1996. Short and brilliant.

———. *Past Imperfect: French Intellectuals, 1944–1956.* Berkeley, CA, 1992. Very readable, on French intellectuals, who loomed large during this period.

———. *Postwar. A History of Europe Since 1945.* London, 2005. Detailed, comprehensive, and ground breaking, this single volume surpasses any other account of the entire postwar period.

Koven, Seth, and Sonya Michel. *Mothers of a New World: Maternalist Politics and the Origins of Welfare States.* New York, 1993. Excellent essays on the long history of welfare politics.

LaFeber, Walter. *America, Russia, and the Cold War.* New York, 1967. A classic, now in its ninth edition.

Large, David Clay. *Berlin.* New York, 2000. Accessible and engaging.

Leffler, Melvyn P. *A Preponderance of Power: National Security, the Truman Administration, and the Cold War.* Stanford, CA, 1992. Solid political study.

Louis, William Roger. *The Ends of British Imperialism: The Scramble for Empire, Suez, and Decolonization.* London, 2006. Comprehensive and wide ranging.

Macey, David. *Frantz Fanon.* New York, 2000. Comprehensive recent biography.

Medvedev, Roy. *Khrushchev.* New York, 1983. A perceptive biography of the Soviet leader by a Soviet historian.

Milward, Alan S. *The Reconstruction of Western Europe, 1945–1951.* Berkeley, CA, 1984. A good discussion of the "economic miracle."

Moeller, Robert G. *War Stories: The Search for a Usable Past in the Federal Republic of Germany.* Berkeley, CA, 2001. Revealing analyses of postwar culture and politics.

Reynolds, David. *One World Divisible: A Global History Since 1945.* New York, 2000. Fresh approach, comprehensive, and very readable survey.

Rousso, Henri. *The Vichy Syndrome: History and Memory in France since 1944.* Cambridge, MA, 1991. First in a series of books by one of the preeminent French historians.

Schissler, Hanna, ed. *The Miracle Years: A Cultural History of West Germany, 1949–1968.* Princeton, NJ, 2001. The cultural effects of the economic miracle.

Schneider, Peter. *The Wall Jumper: A Berlin Story*. Chicago, 1998. A fascinating novel about life in divided Berlin.

Shepard, Todd. *The Invention of Decolonization: The Algerian War and the Remaking of France*. Ithaca, NY, 2006. Excellent and original: a study of the deeply wrenching war's many ramifications.

Shipway, Martin. *Decolonization and Its Impact: A Comparative Approach to the End of the Colonial Empires*. Malden, MA, 2008. Accessible account emphasizing the unintended consequences of decolonization.

Trachtenberg, Mark. *A Constructed Peace: The Making of the European Settlement, 1945–1963*. Princeton, NJ, 1999. A detailed study of international relations that moves beyond the Cold War framework.

Tessler, Mark. *A History of the Israeli-Palestinian Conflict*. 2nd ed. Bloomington, IN, 2009. Updated edition of the definitive account from the 1990s.

Westad, Odd Arne. *The Global Cold War*. New York, 2005. An international history that sees the roots of the world's present conflict in the history of the Cold War.

Wilder, Gary. *The French Imperial Nation-State: Negritude and Colonial Humanism between the Two World Wars*. Chicago, 2005. Fascinating new study of the Negritude thinkers in their context.

Yergin, Daniel. *Shattered Peace: The Origins of the Cold War*. New York, 1977. Rev. ed. 1990. Dramatic and readable.

Young, Marilyn B. *The Vietnam Wars, 1945–1990*. New York, 1991. Excellent account of the different stages of the war and its repercussions.

CHAPTER 28

Bailey, Beth. *From Front Porch to Back Seat: Courtship in Twentieth-Century America*. Baltimore, MD, 1988. Good historical perspective on the sexual revolution.

Beschloss, Michael, and Strobe Talbott. *At the Highest Levels: The Inside Story of the End of the Cold War*. Boston, 1993. An analysis of the relationship between presidents Gorbachev and George H. W. Bush and their determination to ignore hard-liners.

Brown, Archie. *The Gorbachev Factor*. Oxford and New York, 1996. One of the first serious studies of Gorbachev, by an Oxford scholar of politics.

Caute, David. *The Year of the Barricades: A Journey through 1968*. New York, 1988. A well-written global history of 1968.

Charney, Leo, and Vanessa R. Schwartz, eds. *Cinema and the Invention of Modern Life*. Berkeley, CA, 1995. Collection of essays.

Dallin, Alexander, and Gail Lapidus. *The Soviet System: From Crisis to Collapse*. Boulder, CO, 1995.

de Grazia, Victoria. *Irresistable Empire: America's Advance through Twentieth-Century Europe*. Cambridge, MA, 2006. Thorough exploration of the history of consumer culture in Europe and its links to relations with the United States.

Echols, Alice. *Daring to Be Bad: Radical Feminism in America, 1967–1975*. Minneapolis, Minn., 1989. Good narrative and analysis.

Eley, Geoff. *Forging Democracy: The History of the Left in Europe, 1850–2000*. Oxford and New York, 2002. Among its other qualities, one of the best historical perspectives on the 1960s.

Fink, Carole, Phillipp Gassert, and Detlef Junker, eds. *1968: The World Transformed*. Cambridge, 1998. A transatlantic history of 1968.

Fulbrook, Mary, ed. *Europe since 1945* (The Short Oxford History of Europe). Oxford, 2001. Particularly good articles on economics and political economy. Structural analysis.

Garton Ash, Timothy. *In Europe's Name: Germany and the Divided Continent*. New York, 1993. An analysis of the effect of German reunification on the future of Europe.

Glenny, Misha. *The Balkans, 1804–1999: Nationalism, War and the Great Powers*. London, 1999. Good account by a journalist who covered the fighting.

Horowitz, Daniel. *Betty Friedan and the Making of the Feminine Mystique: The American Left, the Cold War, and Modern Feminism*. Amherst, MA, 1998. A reconsideration.

Hosking, Geoffrey. *The Awakening of the Soviet Union*. Cambridge, MA, 1990. The factors that led to the end of the Soviet era.

Hughes, H. Stuart. *Sophisticated Rebels: The Political Culture of European Dissent, 1968–1987*. Cambridge, MA, 1990. The nature of dissent on both sides of the disintegrating Iron Curtain in the years 1988–1989.

Hulsberg, Werner. *The German Greens: A Social and Political Profile*. New York, 1988. The origins, politics, and impact of environmental politics.

Jarausch, Konrad. *The Rush to German Unity*. New York, 1994. The problems of reunification analyzed.

Judah, Tim. *The Serbs: History, Myth, and the Destruction of Yugoslavia*. New Haven, CT, 1997. Overview of Serbian history by journalist who covered the war.

Kaplan, Robert D. *Balkan Ghosts: A Journey through History*. New York, 1993. More a political travelogue than a history, but very readable.

Kotkin, Stephen. *Armegeddon Averted: The Soviet Collapse, 1970–2000*. Oxford, 2001. Excellent short account.

Kurlansky, Mark. *1968: The Year that Rocked the World*. New York, 2005. An accessible introduction for nonspecialists.

Lewin, Moshe. *The Gorbachev Phenomenon*. Expanded ed. Berkeley, CA, 1991. Written as a firsthand account, tracing the roots of Gorbachev's successes and failures.

Lieven, Anatol. *Chechnya, Tomb of Russia Power*. New Haven, CT, and London, 1998. Longer view of the region, by a journalist.

Maier, Charles S. *Dissolution: The Crisis of Communism and the End of East Germany*. Princeton, NJ, 1997. Detailed and sophisticated.

Mann, Michael. *The Dark Side of Democracy: Explaining Ethnic Cleansing*. New York, 2005. Brilliant essay on different episodes from Armenia to Rwanda.

Marwick, Arthur. *The Sixties*. Oxford and New York, 1998. An international history.

Pells, Richard. *Not Like Us: How Europeans Have Loved, Hated, and Transformed American Culture since World War II*. New York, 1997. From the point of view of an American historian.

Poiger, Uta G. *Jazz, Rock, and Rebels: Cold War Politics and American Culture in a Divided Germany*. Berkeley, CA, 2000. Pioneering cultural history.

Sheehan, Neil. *A Bright Shining Lie: John Paul Vann and America in Vietnam*. New York, 1988. A study of the war and its escalation through one of the U.S. Army's field advisers.

Strayer, Robert. *Why Did the Soviet Union Collapse? Understanding Historical Change*. Armonk, NY, and London, 1998. A good introduction, with bibliography.

Suri, Jeremi. *Power and Protest*. New ed. Cambridge, MA, 2005. One of the best of the new global histories of the 1960s, looking at relations between social movements and international relations.

Wright, Patrick. *On Living in an Old Country: The National Past in Contemporary Britain*. New York, 1986. The culture of Britain in the 1980s.

CHAPTER 29

Bowen, John R. *Why the French Don't Like Headscarves: Islam, the State, and Public Space*. Princeton, NJ, 2008. An ethnographic account of this volatile debate in France.

Coetzee, J. M. *Waiting for the Barbarians*. London, 1980. A searing critique of apartheid-era South Africa by a leading Afrikaner novelist.

Epstein, Helen. *The Invisible Cure: Africa, the West, and the Fight Against AIDS*. New York, 2007. One of the best recent studies.

Frieden, Jeffrey H. *Global Capitalism: Its Rise and Fall in the Twentieth Century*. New York, 2007. Broad-ranging history for the advanced student.

Geyer, Michael, and Charles Bright. "World History in a Global Age." *American Historical Review* (October 1995). An excellent short discussion.

Glendon, Mary Ann. *A World Made New: Eleanor Roosevelt and the Universal Declaration of Human Rights*. New York, 2001. A fascinating study of the High Commission in its time by a legal scholar.

Harvey, David. *A Brief History of Neoliberalism*. New York, 2007, A critical account of the history of neoliberalism that encompasses the U.S., Europe, and Asia.

Held, David, et al. *Global Transformations: Politics, Economics, and Culture*. Stanford, CA, 1999. Major survey of the globalization of culture, finance, criminality, and politics.

Hopkins, A. G., ed. *Globalization in World History*. New York, 2002. Excellent introduction, written by one of the first historians to engage the issue.

Hunt, Lynn. *Inventing Human Rights: A History*. New York, 2007. A short study of the continuities and paradoxes in the West's human rights tradition, by one of the foremost historians of the French Revolution. On 1776, 1789, and 1948.

Keddie, Nikki. *Modern Iran: Roots and Results of Revolution*. New Haven, CT, 2003. A revised edition of her major study of Iran's 1979 revolution, with added perspective on Iran's Islamic government.

Lacqueur, Walter. *The Age of Terrorism*. Boston, 1987. An important study of the first wave of post-1960s terrorism.

Landes, David. *The Wealth and Poverty of Nations: Why Some Are So Rich and Some So Poor*. New York, 1998. Leading economic historian's account of globalization's effects on the international economy.

Lewis, Bernard. *The Crisis of Islam: Holy War and Unholy Terror*. New York, 2003. Conservative scholar of the Arab world discussing the political crises that fueled terrorism.

Mckeown, Adam. "Global Migration, 1846–1940." *Journal of World History* 15.2 (2004). Includes references to more work on the subject.

McNeill, J. R. *Something New under the Sun: An Environmental History of the Twentieth-Century World*. New York and London, 2000. Fascinating new approach to environmental history.

Merlini, Cesare, and Olivier Roy, eds. *Arab Society in Revolt: The West's Mediterranean Challenge*. Washington DC, 2012. A multi-author attempt to understand the Arab Spring of 2011

Novick, Peter. *The Holocaust in American Life*. Boston, 1999.

Power, Samantha. *The Problem from Hell: America in the Age of Genocide*. A prize-winning survey of the entire twentieth century, its genocides, and the different human rights movements that responded to them.

Reynolds, David. *One World Divisible: A Global History since 1945*. New York and London, 2000. Excellent study of the different dimensions of globalization.

Roy, Olivier. *Globalized Islam: The Search for a New Ummah*. New York, 2006. Examines changes in religious belief and practice as Islam has spread from its historic centers in the Middle East to other areas of the world, including Europe and North America.

Scott, Joan. *The Politics of the Veil*. Princeton, NJ, 2010. A leading feminist scholar analyzes the debate about the veil and the Islamic headscarf in Europe.

Shilts, Randy. *And the Band Played On: Politics, People, and the AIDS Epidemic*. New York, 1987. An impassioned attack on the individuals and governments that failed to come to grips with the early spread of the disease.

Shlaim, Avi. *The Iron Wall: Israel and the Arab World*. New York, 2000. Leading Israeli historian on the evolution of Israel's defensive foreign policy.

Stiglitz, Joseph E. *Globalization and Its Discontents*. New York, 2002. A recent and important consideration of contemporary globalization's character and the conflicts it creates, particularly over commerce and culture.

———. *Freefall: America, Free Markets, and the Sinking of the World Economy*. New York, 2010. Nobel-prize-winning economist gives account of the financial crisis of 2008.

Turkle, Sherry. *Life on the Screen: Identity in the Age of the Internet*. New York, 1995. An important early study of Web culture and the fluid possibilities of electronic communication.

Winter, Jay. *Dreams of Peace and Freedom: Utopian Moments in the Twentieth Century*. New Haven, CT, 2006. One of the leading historians of war and atrocity turns here to twentieth-century hopes for peace and human rights.

Glossary

1973 OPEC oil embargo Some leaders in the Arab-dominated Organization of the Petroleum Exporting Countries (OPEC) wanted to use oil as a weapon against the West in the Arab-Israeli conflict. After the 1972 Arab-Israeli war, OPEC instituted an oil embargo against Western powers. The embargo increased the price of oil and sparked spiraling inflation and economic troubles in Western nations, triggering in turn a cycle of dangerous recession that lasted nearly a decade. In response, Western governments began viewing the Middle Eastern oil regions as areas of strategic importance.

Abbasid Caliphate (750–930) The Abbasid family claimed to be descendants of Muhammad, and in 750 they successfully led a rebellion against the Umayyads, seizing control of Muslim territories in Arabia, Persia, North Africa, and the Near East. The Abbasids modeled their behavior and administration on that of the Persian princes and their rule on that of the Persian Empire, establishing a new capital at Baghdad.

Peter Abelard (1079–1142) Highly influential philosopher, theologian, and teacher, often considered the founder of the University of Paris.

absolutism Form of government in which one body, usually the monarch, controls the right to make war, tax, judge, and coin money. The term was often used to refer to the state monarchies in seventeenth- and eighteenth-century Europe. In other countries the end of feudalism is often associated with the legal abolition of serfdom, as in Russia in 1861.

abstract expressionism The mid-twentieth-century school of art based in New York that included Jackson Pollock, Willem de Kooning, and Franz Kline. It emphasized form, color, gesture, and feeling instead of figurative subjects.

Academy of Sciences This French institute of scientific inquiry was founded in 1666 by Louis XIV. France's statesmen exerted control over the academy and sought to share in the rewards of any discoveries its members made.

Aeneas Mythical founder of Rome, Aeneas was a refugee from the city of Troy whose adventures were described by the poet Virgil in the *Aeneid,* which mimicked the oral epics of Homer.

Aetolian and Achaean Leagues These two alliances among Greek poleis formed during the Hellenistic period in opposition to the Antigonids of Macedonia. Unlike the earlier defensive alliances of the classic period, each league represented a real attempt to form a political federation.

African National Congress (ANC) Multiracial organization founded in 1912 whose goal was to end racial discrimination in South Africa.

Afrikaners Descendants of the original Dutch settlers of South Africa; formerly referred to as Boers.

agricultural revolution Numerous agricultural revolutions have occurred in the history of Western civilizations. One of the most significant began in the tenth century C.E., and increased the amount of land under cultivation as well as the productivity of the land. This revolution was made possible through the use of new technology, an increase in global temperatures, and more efficient methods of cultivation.

AIDS Acquired Immunodeficiency Syndrome. AIDS first appeared in the 1970s and has developed into a global health catastrophe; it is spreading most quickly in developing nations in Africa and Asia.

Akhenaten (r. 1352–1336 B.C.E.) Pharaoh whose attempt to promote the worship of the sun god, Aten, ultimately weakened his dynasty's position in Egypt.

Alexander the Great (356–323 B.C.E.) The Macedonian king whose conquests of the Persian Empire and Egypt created a new Hellenistic world.

Tsar Alexander II (1818–1881) After the Crimean War, Tsar Alexander embarked on a program of reform and modernization, which included the emancipation of the serfs. A radical assassin killed him in 1881.

Alexius Comnenus (1057–1118) This Byzantine emperor requested Pope Urban II's help in raising an army to recapture Anatolia from the Seljuk Turks. Instead, Pope Urban II called for knights to go to the Holy Land and liberate it from its Muslim captors, which launched the First Crusade.

Algerian War (1954–1962) The war between France and Algerians seeking independence. Led by the National Liberation Front (FLN), guerrillas fought the French army in the mountains and desert of Algeria. The FLN also initiated a campaign of bombing and terrorism in Algerian cities that led French soldiers to torture many Algerians, attracting world attention and international scandal.

Dante Alighieri (c. 1265–1321) Florentine poet and intellectual whose *Divine Comedy* was a pioneering work in the Italian vernacular and a vehicle for political and religious critique.

Allied Powers The First World War coalition of Great Britain, Ireland, Belgium, France, Italy, Russia, Portugal, Greece, Serbia, Montenegro, Albania, and Romania.

al Qaeda The radical Islamic organization founded in the late 1980s by former mujahidin who had fought against the Soviet Union in Afghanistan. Al Qaeda carried out the 9/11 terrorist attacks and is responsible as well for attacks in Africa, Southeast Asia, Europe, and the Middle East.

Ambrose (c. 340–397) One of the early "fathers" of the Church, he helped to define the relationship between the sacred authority of bishops and other Church leaders and the secular authority of worldly rulers. He believed that secular rulers were a part of the Church and therefore subject to it.

Americanization The fear of many Europeans, since the 1920s, that U.S. cultural products, such as film, television, and music, exerted too much influence. Many of the criticisms centered on America's emphasis on mass production and organization. The fears about Americanization were not limited to culture. They extended to corporations, business techniques, global trade, and marketing.

Americas The name given to the two great landmasses of the New World, derived from the name of the Italian geographer Amerigo Vespucci. In 1492, Christopher Columbus reached the Bahamas and the island of Hispaniola, which began an era of Spanish conquest in North and South America. Originally, the Spanish sought a route to Asia. Instead they discovered two continents whose wealth they decided to exploit. They were especially interested in gold and silver, which they either stole from indigenous peoples or mined using indigenous peoples as labor. Silver became Spain's most lucrative export from the New World.

Amnesty International Nongovernmental organization formed in 1961 to defend "prisoners of conscience"—those detained for their beliefs, color, sex, ethnic origin, language, or religion.

Anabaptists Protestant movement that emerged in Switzerland in 1521; its adherents insisted that only adults could be baptized Christians.

anarchists In the nineteenth century, they were a political movement with the aim of establishing small-scale, localized, and self-sufficient democratic communities that could guarantee a maximum of individual sovereignty. Renouncing parties, unions and any form of modern mass organization, the anarchists fell back on the tradition of conspiratorial violence.

Anti–Corn Law League This organization successfully lobbied Parliament to repeal Britain's Corn Laws in 1846. The Corn Laws of 1815 had protected British landowners and farmers from foreign competition by establishing high tariffs, which kept bread prices artificially high for British consumers. The league saw these laws as unfair protection of the aristocracy and pushed for their repeal in the name of free trade.

anti-Semitism Anti-Semitism refers to hostility toward Jewish people. Religious forms of anti-Semitism have a long history in Europe, but in the nineteenth century anti-Semitism emerged as a potent ideology for mobilizing new constituencies in the era of mass politics. Playing on popular conspiracy theories about alleged Jewish influence in society, anti-Semites effectively rallied large bodies of supporters in France during the Dreyfus Affair, and then again during the rise of National Socialism in Germany after the First World War. The Holocaust would not have been possible without the acquiescence or cooperation of many thousands of people who shared anti-Semitic views.

apartheid The racial segregation policy of the Afrikaner-dominated South African government. Legislated in 1948 by the Afrikaner National Party, it existed in South Africa for many decades.

appeasement The policy pursued by Western governments in the face of German, Italian, and Japanese aggression leading up to the Second World War. The policy, which attempted to accommodate and negotiate peace with the aggressive nations, was based on the belief that another global war like the First World War was unimaginable, a belief that Germany and its allies had been mistreated by the terms of the Treaty of Versailles, and a fear that fascist Germany and its allies protected the West from the spread of Soviet communism.

Thomas Aquinas (1225–1274) Dominican friar and theologian whose systematic approach to Christian doctrine was influenced by Aristotle.

Arab-Israeli conflict Between the founding of the state of Israel in 1948 and the present, a series of wars has been fought between Israel and neighboring Arab nations: the war of 1948 when Israel defeated attempts by Egypt, Jordon, Iraq, Syria, and Lebanon to prevent the creation of the new state; the 1956 war between Israel and Egypt over the Sinai peninsula; the 1967 war, when Israel gained control of additional land in the Golan Heights, the West Bank, the Gaza strip, and in the Sinai; and the Yom Kippur War of 1973, when Israel once again fought with forces from Egypt and Syria. A particularly difficult issue in all of these conflicts has been the situation of the 950,000 Palestinian refugees made homeless by the first war in 1948 and the movement of Israeli settlers into the occupied territories (outside of Israel's original borders). In the late 1970s, peace talks between Israel and Egypt inspired some hope of peace, but an ongoing cycle of violence between Palestinians and the Israeli military have made a final settlement elusive.

Arab nationalism During the period of decolonization, secular forms of Arab nationalism, or pan-Arabism, found a wide following in many countries of the Middle East, especially in Egypt, Syria, and Iraq.

Arianism A variety of Christianity condemned as a heresy by the Roman Church, it derives from the teaching of a fourth-century priest called Arius, who rejected the idea that Jesus could be the divine equal of God.

aristocracy From the Greek word meaning "rule of the best." By 1000 B.C.E., the accumulated wealth of successful traders in Greece had created a new type of social class, which was based on wealth rather than warfare or birth. These men saw their wealth as a reflection of their superior qualities and aspired to emulate the heroes of old.

Aristotle (384–322 B.C.E.) A student of Plato, his philosophy was based on the rational analysis of the material world. In contrast to his teacher, he stressed the rigorous investigation of real phenomena, rather than the development of universal ethics. He was, in turn, the teacher of Alexander the Great.

Asiatic Society A cultural organization founded in 1784 by British Orientalists who lauded native culture but believed in colonial rule.

Assyrians A Semitic-speaking people that moved into northern Mesopotamia around 2400 B.C.E.

Athens Athens emerged as the Greek polis with the most markedly democratic form of government through a series of political struggles during the sixth century B.C.E. After its key role in the defeat of two invading Persian forces, Athens became the preeminent naval power of ancient Greece and the exemplar of Greek culture. But it antagonized many other poleis, and became embroiled in a war with Sparta and her allies in 431 B.C.E. Called the Peloponnesian War, this bloody conflict lasted until Athens was defeated in 404 B.C.E.

atomic bomb In 1945, the United States dropped atomic bombs on Hiroshima and Nagasaki in Japan, ending the Second World War. In 1949, the Soviet Union tested its first atomic bomb, and in 1953 both superpowers demonstrated their new hydrogen bombs. Strategically, the nuclearization of warfare polarized the world. Countries without nuclear weapons found it difficult to avoid joining either the Soviet or American military pacts. Over time, countries split into two groups: the superpowers with enormous military budgets and those countries that relied on agreements and international law. The nuclearization of warfare also encouraged "proxy wars" between clients of superpowers. Culturally, the hydrogen bomb came to symbolize the age and both humanity's power and vulnerability.

Augustine (c. 354–397) One of the most influential theologians of all time, Augustine described his conversion to Christianity in his autobiographical *Confessions* and articulated a new Christian worldview in *The City of God*, among other works.

Augustus (63 B.C.E.–14 C.E.) Born Gaius Octavius, this grandnephew and adopted son of Julius Caesar came to power in 27 B.C.E. His reign signals the end of the Roman Republic and the beginning of the Principate, the period when Rome was dominated by autocratic emperors.

Auschwitz-Birkenau The Nazi concentration camp in Poland that was designed to systematically murder Jews and Gypsies. Between 1942 and 1944 over 1 million people were killed in Auschwitz-Birkenau.

Austro-Hungarian Empire The dual monarchy established by the Habsburg family in 1867; it collapsed at the end of the First World War.

authoritarianism A centralized and dictatorial form of government, proclaimed by its adherents to be superior to parliamentary democracy. Authoritarian governments claim to be above the law, do not respect individual rights, and do not tolerate political opposition. Authoritarian regimes that have developed a central ideology such as fascism or communism are sometimes termed "totalitarian."

Avignon A city in southeastern France that became the seat of the papacy between 1305 and 1377, a period known as the "Babylonian Captivity" of the Roman Church.

Aztecs An indigenous people of central Mexico; their empire was conquered by Spanish conquistadors in the sixteenth century.

baby boom (1950s) The post–Second World War upswing in U.S. birth rates; it reversed a century of decline.

Babylon An ancient city between the Tigris and Euphrates Rivers, which became the capital of Hammurabi's empire in the eighteenth century B.C.E. and continued to be an important administrative and commercial capital under many subsequent imperial powers, including the Neo-Assyrians, Chaldeans, Persians, and Romans. It was here that Alexander the Great died in 323 B.C.E.

Babylonian captivity Refers both to the Jews' exile in Babylon during the sixth century B.C.E. and the period from 1309 to 1378, when papal authority was subjugated to the French crown and the papal court was moved from Rome to the French city of Avignon.

Francis Bacon (1561–1626) British philosopher and scientist who pioneered the scientific method and inductive reasoning. In other words, he argued that thinkers should amass many observations and then draw general conclusions or propose theories on the basis of these data.

balance of powers The principle that no country should be powerful enough to destabilize international relations. Starting in the seventeenth century, this goal of maintaining balance influenced diplomacy in western and central Europe for two centuries until the system collapsed with the onset of the First World War.

Balfour Declaration A letter dated November 2, 1917, by Lord Arthur J. Balfour, British foreign secretary, that promised a homeland for the Jews in Palestine.

Laura Bassi (1711–1778) She was accepted into the Academy of Science in Bologna for her work in mathematics, which made her one of the few women to be accepted into a scientific academy in the seventeenth century.

Bastille The Bastille was a royal fortress and prison in Paris. In June 1789, a revolutionary crowd attacked the Bastille to show support for the newly created National Assembly. The fall of the Bastille was the first instance of the people's role in revolutionary change in France.

Bay of Pigs (1961) The unsuccessful invasion of Cuba by Cuban exiles, supported by the U.S. government. The rebels intended to incite an insurrection in Cuba and overthrow the communist regime of Fidel Castro.

Cesare Beccaria (1738–1794) An influential writer during the Enlightenment who advocated for legal reforms. He believed that the only legitimate rationale for punishments was to maintain social order and to prevent other crimes. He argued for the greatest possible leniency compatible with deterrence and opposed torture and the death penalty.

Beer Hall Putsch (1923) An early attempt by the Nazi party to seize power in Munich; Adolf Hitler was imprisoned for a year after the incident.

Benedict of Nursia (c. 480–c. 547) Benedict's rule for monks formed the basis of western monasticism and is still observed in monasteries all over the world.

Benedictine Monasticism This form of monasticism was developed by Benedict of Nursia. Its followers adhere to a defined cycle of daily prayers, lessons, communal worship, and manual labor.

Berlin airlift (1948) The transport of vital supplies to West Berlin by air, primarily under U.S. auspices, in response to a blockade of the city that had been instituted by the Soviet Union to force the Allies to abandon West Berlin.

Berlin Conference (1884) At this conference, the leading colonial powers met and established ground rules for the partition of Africa by European nations. By 1914, 90 percent of African territory was under European control. The Berlin Conference ceded control of the Congo region to a private company run by King Leopold II of Belgium. They agreed to make the Congo valleys open to free trade and commerce, to end the slave trade in the region, and to establish a Congo Free State. In reality, King Leopold II's company established a regime that was so brutal in its treatment of local populations that an international scandal forced the Belgian state to take over the colony in 1908.

Berlin Wall The wall built in 1961 by East German Communists to prevent citizens of East Germany from fleeing to West Germany; it was torn down in 1989.

birth control pill This oral contraceptive became widely available in the mid-1960s. For the first time, women had a simple method of birth control that they could take themselves.

Otto von Bismarck (1815–1898) The prime minister of Prussia and later the first chancellor of a unified Germany, Bismarck was the architect of German unification and helped to consolidate the new nation's economic and military power.

Black Death The epidemic of bubonic plague that ravaged Europe, Asia, and North Africa in the fourteenth century, killing one third to one half of the population.

Black Jacobins A nickname for the rebels in Saint-Domingue, including Toussaint L'Ouverture, a former slave who in 1791 led the slaves of this French colony in the largest and most successful slave insurrection.

Blackshirts The troops of Mussolini's fascist regime; the squads received money from Italian landowners to attack socialist leaders.

Black Tuesday (October 29, 1929) The day on which the U.S. stock market crashed, plunging U.S. and international trading systems into crisis and leading the world into the "Great Depression."

William Blake (1757–1827) Romantic writer who criticized industrial society and factories. He championed the imagination and poetic vision, seeing both as transcending the limits of the material world.

Blitzkrieg The German "lightning war" strategy used during the Second World War; the Germans invaded Poland, France, Russia, and other countries with fast-moving and well-coordinated attacks using aircraft, tanks and other armored vehicles, followed by infantry.

Bloody Sunday On January 22, 1905, the Russian tsar's guards killed 130 demonstrators who were protesting the tsar's mistreatment of workers and the middle class.

Giovanni Boccaccio (1313–1375) Florentine author best known for his *Decameron*, a collection of prose tales about sex, adventure, and trickery written in the Italian vernacular after the Black Death.

Jean Bodin (1530–1596) A French political philosopher whose *Six Books of the Commonwealth* advanced a theory of absolute sovereignty, on the grounds that the state's paramount duty is to maintain order and that monarchs should therefore exercise unlimited power.

Boer War (1898–1902) Conflict between British and ethnically European Afrikaners in South Africa, with terrible casualties on both sides.

Boethius (c. 480–524) Member of a prominent Roman family, he sought to preserve aspects of ancient learning by compiling a series of handbooks and anthologies appropriate for Christian readers. His translations of Greek philosophy provided a crucial link between classical Greek thought and the early intellectual culture of Christianity.

Bolsheviks Former members of the Russian Social Democratic Party who advocated the destruction of capitalist political and economic institutions and started the Russian Revolution. In 1918, the Bolsheviks changed their name to the Russian Communist Party. Prominent Bolsheviks included Vladimir Lenin and Josef Stalin. Leon Trotsky joined the Bolsheviks late but became a prominent leader in the early years of the Russian Revolution.

Napoleon Bonaparte (1769–1821) Corsican-born French general who seized power and ruled as dictator from 1799 to 1814. After the successful conquest of much of Europe, he was defeated by Russian and Prussian forces and died in exile.

Boniface VIII During his pontificate (1294–1303), repeated claims to papal authority were challenged by King Philip IV of France. When Boniface died in 1309 (at the hands of Philip's thugs), the French king moved the papal court from Rome to the French city of Avignon, where it remained until 1378.

Sandro Botticelli (1445–1510) An Italian painter devoted to the blending of classical and Christian motifs by using ideas associated with the pagan past to illuminate sacred stories.

bourgeoisie Term for the middle class, derived from the French word for a town-dweller, *bourgeois*.

Boxer Rebellion (1899–1900) Chinese peasant movement that opposed foreign influence, especially that of Christian missionaries; it was finally put down after the Boxers were defeated by a foreign army composed mostly of Japanese, Russian, British, French, and American soldiers.

Tycho Brahe (1546–1601) Danish astronomer who believed that the careful study of the heavens would unlock the secrets of the universe. For over twenty years, he charted the movements of significant objects in the night sky, compiling the finest set of astronomical data in Europe.

British Commonwealth of Nations Formed in 1926, the Commonwealth conferred "dominion status" on Britain's white settler colonies in Canada, Australia, and New Zealand.

Bronze Age (3200–1200 B.C.E.) The name given to the era characterized by the discovery of techniques for smelting bronze (an alloy of copper and tin), which was then the strongest known metal.

Brownshirts Troops of young German men who dedicated themselves to the Nazi cause in the early 1930s by holding street marches, mass rallies, and confrontations. They engaged in beatings of Jews and anyone who opposed the Nazis.

Lord Byron (1788–1824) Writer and poet whose life helped give the Romantics their reputation as rebels against conformity. He was known for his love affairs, his defense of working-class movements, and his passionate engagement in politics, which led to his death in the war for Greek independence.

Byzantium The name of a small settlement located at the mouth of the Black Sea and at the crossroads between Europe and Asia, it was chosen by Constantine as the site for his new imperial capital of Constantinople in 324. Modern historians use this name to refer to the eastern Roman Empire that persisted in this region until 1453, but the inhabitants of that empire referred to themselves as Romans.

Julius Caesar (100–44 B.C.E.) The Roman general who conquered the Gauls, invaded Britain, and expanded Rome's territory in Asia Minor. He became the dictator of Rome in 46 B.C.E. His assassination led to the rise of his grandnephew and adopted son, Gaius Octavius Caesar, who ruled the Roman Empire as Caesar Augustus.

caliphs Islamic rulers who claim descent from the prophet Muhammad.

John Calvin (1509–1564) French-born theologian and reformer whose radical form of Protestantism was adopted in many Swiss cities, notably Geneva.

Canary Islands Islands off the western coast of Africa that were colonized by Portugal and Spain in the mid-fifteenth century, after which they became bases for further expeditions around the African coast and across the Atlantic.

Carbonari An underground organization that opposed the Concert of Europe's restoration of monarchies. They held influence in southern Europe during the 1820s, especially in Italy.

Carolingian Derived from the Latin name Carolus (Charles), this term refers to the Frankish dynasty that began with the rise to power of Charlemagne's grandfather, Charles Martel (688–741). At its height under Charlemagne (Charles the Great), the dynasty controlled what is now France, Germany, northern Italy, Catalonia, and portions of central Europe. The Carolingian Empire collapsed under the combined weight of Viking raids, economic disintegration, and the growing power of local lords.

Carolingian Renaissance A cultural and intellectual flowering that took place around the court of Charlemagne in the late eighth and early ninth centuries.

Carthage The great maritime empire that grew out of Phoenician trading colonies in North Africa and rivaled the power of Rome. Its wars with Rome, collectively known as the Punic Wars, ended in its destruction in 146 B.C.E.

Cassidorus (c. 490–c. 583) Member of an old senatorial family, he was largely responsible for introducing classical learning into the monastic curriculum and for turning monasteries into centers for the collection, preservation, and transmission of knowledge. His *Institutes*, an influential handbook of classical literature for Christian readers, was intended as a preface to more intensive study of theology and the Bible.

Catholic Church The "universal" (catholic) church based in Rome, which was redefined in the sixteenth century, when the Counter-Reformation resulted in the rebirth of the Catholic faith at the Council of Trent.

Margaret Cavendish (1623–1673) English natural philosopher who developed her own speculative natural philosophy. She used this philosophy to critique those who excluded her from scientific debate.

Camillo Benso di Cavour (1810–1861) Prime minister of Piedmont-Sardinia and founder of the Italian Liberal party; he played a key role in the movement for Italian unification under the Piedmontese king, Victor Emmanuel II.

Central Powers The First World War alliance between Germany, Austria-Hungary, Bulgaria, and Turkey.

Charlemagne (742–814) As king of the Franks (767–813), Charles "the Great" consolidated much of western Europe under his rule. In 800, he was crowned emperor by the pope in Rome, establishing a problematic precedent that would have wide-ranging consequences for western Europe's relationship with the eastern Roman Empire in Byzantium and for the relationship between the papacy and secular rulers.

Charles I (1625–1649) The second Stuart king of England, Charles attempted to rule without the support of Parliament, sparking a controversy that erupted into civil war in 1642. The king's forces were ultimately defeated and Charles himself was executed by act of Parliament, the first time in history that a reigning king was legally deposed and executed by his own government.

Charles II of England Nominally King of England, Ireland, and Scotland after his father Charles I's execution in 1649, Charles II lived in exile until he was restored to the throne in 1660. Influenced by his cousin, King Louis XIV of France, he presided over an opulent royal court until his death in 1685.

Chartists A working-class movement in Britain that called for reform of the British political system during the 1840s. They were supporters of the "People's Charter," which had six demands: universal white male suffrage, secret ballots, an end to property qualifications as a condition of public office, annual parliamentary elections, salaries for members of the House of Commons, and equal electoral districts.

Geoffrey Chaucer (1340–1400) English poet whose collection of versified stories, *The Canterbury Tales*, features characters from a variety of different classes.

Christine de Pisan (c. 1364–c. 1431) Born in Italy, Christine spent her adult life attached to the French court and, after her husband's death, became the first laywoman to earn her living by writing. She is the author of treatises in warfare and chivalry as well as of books and pamphlets that challenge long-standing misogynistic claims.

Church of England Founded by Henry VIII in the 1530s, as a consequence of his break with the authority of the Roman pope.

Winston Churchill (1874–1965) British prime minister who led the country during the Second World War. He also coined the phrase "Iron Curtain" in a speech at Westminster College in 1946.

Cicero (106–43 B.C.E.) Influential Roman senator, orator, Stoic philosopher, and prose stylist. His published writings still form the basis of the instruction in classical Latin grammar and usage.

Cincinnatus (519–c. 430 B.C.E.) A legendary citizen-farmer of Rome who reluctantly accepted an appointment as dictator. After defeating Rome's enemies, he allegedly left his political office and returned to his farm.

Civil Constitution of the Clergy Issued by the French National Assembly in 1790, the Civil Constitution of the Clergy decreed that all bishops and priests should be subject to the authority of the state. Their salaries were to be paid out of the public treasury, and they were required to swear allegiance to the new state, making it clear they served France rather than Rome. The Assembly's aim was to make the Catholic Church of France a truly national and civil institution.

civilizing mission An argument made by Europeans to justify colonial expansion in the nineteenth century. Supporters of this idea believed that Europeans had a duty to impose western ideas of economic and political progress on the indigenous peoples they ruled over in their colonies. In practice, the colonial powers often found that ambitious plans to impose European practices on colonial subjects led to unrest that threatened the stability of colonial rule, and by the early twentieth century most colonial powers were more cautious in their plans for political or cultural transformation.

Civil Rights Movement The Second World War increased African American migration from the American South to northern cities, intensifying a drive for rights, dignity, and independence. By 1960, civil rights groups had started organizing boycotts and demonstrations directed at discrimination against blacks in the South. During the 1960s, civil rights laws passed under President Lyndon B. Johnson did bring African Americans some equality with regard to voting rights and, to a much lesser degree, school desegregation. However, racism continued in areas such as housing, job opportunities, and the economic development of African American communities.

Civil War (1861–1865) Conflict between the northern and southern states of America that cost over 600,000 lives; this struggle led to the abolition of slavery in the United States.

classical learning The study of ancient Greek and Latin texts. After Christianity became the only legal religion of the Roman Empire, scholars needed to find a way to make classical learning applicable to a Christian way of life. Christian monks played a significant role in resolving this problem by reinterpreting the classics for a Christian audience.

Cluny A powerful Benedictine monastery founded in 910 whose enormous wealth and prestige would derive from its independence from secular authorities as well as from its wide network of daughter houses (priories).

Cold War (1945–1991) Ideological, political, and economic conflict in which the USSR and Eastern Europe opposed the United States and Western Europe in the decades after the Second World War. The Cold War's origins lay in the breakup of the wartime alliance between the United States and the Soviet Union in 1945 and resulted in a division of Europe into two spheres: the West, commited to market capitalism, and the East, which sought to build Socialist republics in areas under Soviet Control. The Cold War ended with the collapse of the Soviet Union in 1991.

collectivization Stalin's plan for nationalizing agricultural production, begun in 1929. Twenty-five million peasants were forced to give up their land and join 250,000 large collective farms. Many who resisted were deported to labor camps in the Far East, and Stalin's government cut off food rations to those areas

most marked by resistance to collectivization. In the ensuing man-made famines, millions of people starved to death.

Columbian Exchange The widespread exchange of peoples, plants, animals, diseases, goods, and culture between the African and Eurasian landmass (on the one hand) and the region that encompasses the Americas, Australia, and the Pacific Islands (on the other); precipitated by voyage of Columbus in 1492.

Christopher Columbus (1451–1506) A Genoese sailor who persuaded King Ferdinand and Queen Isabella of Spain to fund his expedition across the Atlantic, with the purpose of discovering a new trade route to Asia. His miscalculations landed him in the Bahamas and the island of Hispaniola in 1492.

Commercial Revolution A period of economic development in Europe lasting from c. 1500-c.1800. Advances in agriculture and handicraft production, combined with the expansion of trade networks in the Atlantic world, brought new wealth and new kinds of commercial activity to Europe. The commercial revolution prepared the way for the industrial revolution of the 1800s.

Committee of Public Safety Political body during the French Revolution that was controlled by the Jacobins, who defended the revolution by executing thousands during the Reign of Terror (September 1793–July 1794).

commune A community of individuals who have banded together in a sworn association, with the aim of establishing their independence and setting up their own form of representative government. Many medieval towns originally founded by lords or monasteries gained their independence through such methods.

The Communist Manifesto Radical pamphlet by Karl Marx (1818–1883) that predicted the downfall of the capitalist system and its replacement by a classless egalitarian society. Marx believed that this revolution would be accomplished by workers (the proletariat).

Compromise of 1867 Agreement between the Habsburgs and the peoples living in Hungarian parts of the empire that the Habsburg state would be officially known as the Austro-Hungarian Empire.

Concert of Europe (1814–1815) The body of diplomatic agreements designed primarily by Austrian minister Klemens von Metternich between 1814 and 1848 and supported by other European powers until 1914. Its goal was to maintain a balance of power on the Continent and to prevent destabilizing social and political change in Europe.

conciliarism A doctrine developed in the thirteenth and fourteenth centuries to counter the growing power of the papacy, conciliarism holds that papal authority should be subject to a council of the Church at large. Conciliarists emerged as a dominant force after the Council of Constance (1414–1418) but were eventually outmatched by a rejuvenated papacy.

Congress of Vienna (1814–1815) International conference to reorganize Europe after the downfall of Napoleon and the French Revolution. European monarchies restored the Bourbon family to the French throne, agreed to respect each other's borders and to cooperate in guarding against future revolutions and war.

conquistador Spanish term for "conqueror," applied to the mercenaries and adventurers who campaigned against indigenous peoples in central and southern America.

Conservatives In the nineteenth century, conservatives aimed to legitimize and solidify the monarchy's authority and the hierarchical social order. They believed that change had to be slow, incremental, and managed so that the structures of authority were strengthened and not weakened.

Constantine (275–337) The first emperor of Rome to convert to Christianity, Constantine came to power in 312. In 324, he founded a new imperial capital, Constantinople, on the site of a maritime settlement known as Byzantium.

Constantinople Founded by the emperor Constantine on the site of a village called Byzantium, Constantinople became the new capital of the Roman Empire in 324 and continued to be the seat of imperial power after its capture by the Ottoman Turks in 1453. It is now known as Istanbul.

contract theory of government A theory of government written by Englishman John Locke (1632–1704) which posits that government authority was both contractual and conditional; therefore, if a government has abused its given authority, society had the right to dissolve it and create another.

Nicholas Copernicus (1473–1543) Polish astronomer who advanced the idea that the earth moved around the sun.

cosmopolitanism Stemming from the Greek word meaning "universal city," the culture characteristic of the Hellenistic world challenged and transformed the more narrow worldview of the Greek polis.

cotton gin Invented by Eli Whitney in 1793, this device mechanized the process of separating cotton seeds from the cotton fiber, which sped up the production of cotton and reduced its price. This change made slavery profitable in the United States.

Council of Constance (1417–1420) A meeting of clergy and theologians in an effort to resolve the Great Schism within the Roman Church. The council deposed all rival papal candidates and elected a new pope, Martin V, but it also adopted the doctrine of conciliarism, which holds that the supreme authority within the Church rests with a representative general council and not with the pope. However, Martin V himself was an opponent of this doctrine and refused to be bound by it.

Council of Trent The name given to a series of meetings held in the Italian city of Trent (Trento) between 1545 and 1563, when leaders of the Roman Church reaffirmed Catholic doctrine and instituted internal reforms.

Counter-Reformation The movement to counter the Protestant Reformation, initiated by the Catholic Church at the Council of Trent in 1545.

coup d'état French term for the overthrow of an established government by a group of conspirators, usually with military support.

Crimean War (1854–1856) War waged by Russia against Great Britain and France. Spurred by Russia's encroachment on Ottoman territories, the conflict revealed Russia's military weakness when Russian forces fell to British and French troops.

Cuban missile crisis (1962) Diplomatic standoff between the United States and the Soviet Union that was provoked by the Soviet Union's attempt to base nuclear missiles in Cuba; it brought the world closer to nuclear war than ever before or since.

Cuius regio, eius religio A Latin phrase meaning "as the ruler, so the religion." Adopted as a part of the settlement of the Peace of Augsburg in 1555, it meant that those principalities ruled by Lutherans would have Lutheranism as their official religion and those ruled by Catholics must practice Catholicism.

cult of domesticity Concept associated with Victorian England that idealized women as nurturing wives and mothers.

cult of the Virgin The beliefs and practices associated with the veneration of Mary, the mother of Jesus, which became increasingly popular in the twelfth century.

cuneiform An early writing system that began to develop in Mesopotamia in the fourth millennium B.C.E. By 3100 B.C.E., its distinctive markings were impressed on clay tablets using a wedge-shaped stylus.

Cyrus the Great (c. 585–529 B.C.E.) As architect of the Persian Empire, Cyrus extended his dominion over a vast territory stretching from the Persian Gulf to the Mediterranean and incorporating the ancient civilizations of Mesopotamia. His successors ruled this Persian Empire as "Great Kings."

Darius (521–486 B.C.E.) The Persian emperor whose conflict with Aristagoras, the Greek ruler of Miletus, ignited the Persian Wars. In 490 B.C.E., Darius sent a large army to punish the Athenians for their intervention in Persian imperial affairs, but this force was defeated by Athenian hoplites on the plain of Marathon.

Charles Darwin (1809–1882) British naturalist who wrote *On the Origin of Species* and developed the theory of natural selection to explain the evolution of organisms.

D-Day (June 6, 1944) Date of the Allied invasion of Normandy, under General Dwight Eisenhower, to liberate Western Europe from German occupation.

Decembrists Russian army officers who were influenced by events in France and formed secret societies that espoused liberal governance. They were put down by Nicholas I in December 1825.

Declaration of Independence (1776) Historic document stating the principles of government on which the United States was founded.

Declaration of the Rights of Man and of the Citizen (1789) French charter of liberties formulated by the National Assembly during the French Revolution. The seventeen articles later became the preamble to the new constitution, which the assembly finished in 1791.

democracy In ancient Greece, this form of government allowed a class of propertied male citizens to participate in the governance of their polis; but excluded women, slaves, and citizens without property from the political process. As a result, the ruling class amounted to only a small percentage of the entire population.

René Descartes (1596–1650) French philosopher and mathematician who emphasized the use of deductive reasoning.

Denis Diderot (1713–1784) French philosophe and author who was the guiding force behind the publication of the first encyclopedia. His *Encyclopedia* showed how reason could be applied to nearly all realms of thought and aimed to be a compendium of all human knowledge.

Dien Bien Phu (1954) Defining battle in the war between French colonialists and the Viet Minh that secured North Vietnam for Ho Chi Minh and his army and left the south to form its own government, to be supported by France and the United States.

Diet of Worms The select council of the Church that convened in the German city of Worms and condemned Martin Luther on a charge of heresy in 1521.

Diocletian (245–316) As emperor of Rome from 284 to 305, Diocletian recognized that the empire could not be governed by one man in one place. His solution was to divide the empire into four parts, each with its own imperial ruler, but he himself remained the dominant ruler of the resulting tetrarchy (rule of four). He also initiated the Great Persecution, a time when many Christians became martyrs to their faith.

Directory (1795–1799) Executive committee that governed after the fall of Robespierre and held control until the coup of Napoleon Bonaparte.

Discourse on Method Philosophical treatise by René Descartes (1596–1650) proposing that the path to knowledge was through logical deduction, beginning with one's own self: "I think, therefore I am."

Dominican Order Also called the Order of Preachers, it was founded by Dominic of Osma (1170–1221), a Castilian preacher and theologian, and approved by Innocent III in 1216. The order was dedicated to the rooting out of heresy and the conversion of Jews and Muslims. Many of its members held teaching positions in European universities and contributed to the development of medieval philosophy and theology. Others became the leading administrators of the Inquisition.

Dominion in the British Commonwealth Canadian promise to maintain their fealty to the British crown, even after their independence in 1867; later applied to Australia and New Zealand.

Dreyfus Affair The 1894 French scandal surrounding accusations that a Jewish captain, Alfred Dreyfus, sold military secrets to the Germans. Convicted, Dreyfus was sentenced to solitary confinement for life. However, after public outcry, it was revealed that the trial documents were forgeries, and Dreyfus was pardoned after a second trial in 1899. In 1906, he was fully exonerated and reinstated in the army. The affair revealed the depths of popular anti-Semitism in France.

Alexander Dubček (1921–1992) Communist leader of the Czechoslovakian government who advocated for "socialism with a human face." He encouraged debate within the party, academic and artistic freedom, and less censorship, which led to the "Prague spring" of 1968. People in other parts of Eastern Europe began to demonstrate in support of Dubček and demand their own reforms. When Dubček tried to democratize the Communist party and did not attend a meeting of the Warsaw Pact, the Soviets sent tanks and troops into Prague and ousted Dubček and his allies.

Duma The Russian parliament, created in response to the revolution of 1905.

Dunkirk The French port on the English Channel where the British and French forces retreated after sustaining heavy losses against the German military. Between May 27 and June 4, 1940, the Royal Navy evacuated over 300,000 troops using commercial and pleasure boats.

Eastern Front Battlefront between Berlin and Moscow during the First and Second World Wars..

East India Company (1600–1858) British charter company created to outperform Portuguese and Spanish traders in the Far East; in the eighteenth century the company became, in effect, the ruler of a large part of India. There was also a Dutch East India Company.

Edict of Nantes (1598) Issued by Henry IV of France in an effort to end religious violence. The edict declared France to be a Catholic country but tolerated some forms of Protestant worship.

Edward I of England King of England from 1272 to his death in 1307, Edward presided over the creation of new legal and bureaucratic institutions in his realm, violently subjugated the Welsh, and attempted to colonize Scotland. He expelled English Jews from his domain in 1290.

Eleanor of Aquitaine (1122–1204) Ruler of the wealthy province of Aquitaine and wife of Louis VII of France, Eleanor had her marriage annulled in order to marry the young count of Anjou, Henry Plantagenet, who became King Henry of England a year later. Mother of two future kings of England, she was an important patron of the arts.

Elizabeth I (1533–1603) Protestant daughter of Henry VIII and his second wife, Anne Boleyn, Elizabeth succeeded her sister Mary as the second queen regnant of England (1558–1603).

emancipation of the serfs (1861) The abolition of serfdom was central to Tsar Alexander II's program of modernization and reform, but it produced a limited amount of change. Former serfs now had legal rights. However, farm land was granted to the village communes instead of to individuals. The land was of poor quality and the former serfs had to pay for it in installments to the village commune.

emperor Originally the term for any conquering commander of the Roman army whose victories merited celebration in an official triumph. After Augustus seized power in 27 B.C.E., it was the title born by the sole ruler of the Roman Empire.

empire A centralized political entity consolidated through the conquest and colonization of other nations or peoples in order to benefit the ruler and/or his homeland.

Enabling Act (1933) Emergency act passed by the Reichstag (German parliament) that helped transform Hitler from Germany's chancellor, or prime minister, into a dictator, following the suspicious burning of the Reichstag building and a suspension of civil liberties.

enclosure Long process of privatizing what had been public agricultural land in eighteenth-century Britain; it helped to stimulate the development of commercial agriculture and forced many people in rural areas to seek work in cities during the early stages of industrialization.

The Encyclopedia Joint venture of French philosophe writers, led by Denis Diderot (1713–1784), which proposed to summarize all modern knowledge in a multivolume illustrated work with over 70,000 articles.

Friedrich Engels (1820–1895) German social and political philosopher who collaborated with Karl Marx on many publications.

English Civil War (1642–1649) Conflicts between the English Parliament and King Charles I erupted into civil war, which ended in the defeat of the royalists and the execution of Charles on charges of treason against the crown. A short time later, Parliament's hereditary House of Lords was abolished and England was declared a Commonwealth.

English Navigation Act of 1651 Act stipulating that only English ships could carry goods between the mother country and its colonies.

Enlightenment Intellectual movement in eighteenth-century Europe, that believed in human betterment through the application of reason to solve social, economic, and political problems.

Epicureanism A philosophical position articulated by Epicurus of Athens (c. 342–270 B.C.E.), who rejected the idea of an ordered universe governed by divine forces; instead, he emphasized individual agency and proposed that the highest good is the pursuit of pleasure.

Desiderius Erasmus (c. 1469–1536) Dutch-born scholar, social commentator, and Catholic humanist whose new translation of the Bible influenced the theology of Martin Luther.

Estates-General The representative body of the three estates in France. In 1789, King Louis XVI summoned the Estates-General to meet for the first time since 1614 because it seemed to be the only solution to France's worsening economic crisis and financial chaos.

Etruscans Settlers of the Italian peninsula who dominated the region from the late Bronze Age until the rise of the Roman Republic in the sixth century B.C.E.

Euclid Hellenistic mathematician whose *Elements of Geometry* forms the basis of modern geometry.

eugenics A Greek term, meaning "good birth," referring to the project of "breeding" a superior human race. It was popularly championed by scientists, politicians, and social critics in the late nineteenth and early twentieth centuries.

European Common Market (1957) The Treaty of Rome created the European Economic Community (EEC), or Common Market. The original members were France, West Germany, Italy, Belgium, Holland, and Luxembourg. The EEC sought to abolish trade barriers between its members and it pledged itself to common external tariffs, the free movement of labor and capital among the member nations, and uniform wage structures and social security systems to create similar working conditions in all member countries.

European Union (EU) Successor organization to the European Economic Community or European Common Market, formed by the Maastricht Treaty, which took effect in 1993. Currently twenty-eight member states compose the EU, which has a governing council, an international court, and a parliament. Over time, member states of the EU have relinquished some of their sovereignty, and cooperation has evolved into a community with a single currency, the euro.

Exclusion Act of 1882 U.S. congressional act prohibiting nearly all immigration from China to the United States; fueled by animosity toward Chinese workers in the American West.

existentialism Philosophical movement that arose out of the Second World War and emphasized the absurdity of human condition. Led by Jean-Paul Sartre and Albert Camus, existentialists encouraged humans to take responsibility for their own decisions and dilemmas.

expulsion of the Jews European rulers began to expel their Jewish subjects from their kingdoms beginning in the 1280s, mostly due to their inability to repay the money they had extorted from Jewish money-lenders but also as a result of escalating anti-Semitism in the wake of the Crusades, Jews were also expelled from the Rhineland in the fourteenth century and from Spain in 1492.

fascism The doctrine founded by Benito Mussolini, which emphasized three main ideas: statism ("nothing above the state, nothing outside the state, nothing against the state"), nationalism, and militarism. Its name derives from the Latin *fasces*, a symbol of Roman imperial power adopted by Mussolini.

Fashoda Incident (1898) Disagreements between the French and the British over land claims in North Africa led to a standoff between armies of the two nations at the Sudanese town of Fashoda. The crisis was solved diplomatically. France ceded southern Sudan to Britain in exchange for a stop to further expansion by the British.

The Feminine Mystique Groundbreaking book by feminist Betty Friedan (b. 1921), which tried to define *femininity* and explored how women internalized those definitions.

Franz Ferdinand (1863–1914) Archduke of Austria and heir to the Austro-Hungarian Empire; his assassination led to the beginning of the First World War.

Ferdinand (1452–1516) **and Isabella** (1451–1504) In 1469, Ferdinand of Aragon married the heiress to Castile, Isabella. Their union allowed them to pursue several ambitious policies, including the conquest of Granada, the last Muslim principality in Spain, and the expulsion of Spain's large Jewish community. In 1492, Isabella granted three ships to Christopher Columbus of Genoa (Italy), who went on to claim portions of the New World for Spain.

Fertile Crescent An area of fertile land in what is now Syria, Israel, Turkey, eastern Iraq, and western Iran that was able to sustain settlements due to its wetter climate and abundant natural food resources. Some of the earliest known civilizations emerged there between 9000 and 4500 B.C.E.

feudalism A problematic modern term that attempts to explain the diffusion of power in medieval Europe, and the many different kinds of political, social, and economic relationships that were forged through the giving and receiving of fiefs (*feoda*). But because it is anachronistic and inadequate, this term has been rejected by most historians of the medieval period.

First Crusade (1095–1099) Launched by Pope Urban II in response to a request from the Byzantine emperor Alexius Comnenus, who had asked for a small contingent of knights to assist him in fighting Turkish forces in Anatolia; Urban instead directed the crusaders' energies toward the Holy Land and the recapture of Jerusalem, promising those who took the cross (*crux*) that they would merit eternal salvation if they died in the attempt. This crusade prompted attacks against

Jews throughout Europe and resulted in six subsequent—and unsuccessful—military campaigns.

First World War A total war from August 1914 to November 1918, involving the armies of Britain, France, and Russia (the Allies) against Germany, Austria-Hungary, and the Ottoman Empire (the Central Powers). Italy joined the Allies in 1915, and the United States joined them in 1917, helping to tip the balance in favor of the Allies, who also drew upon the populations and raw materials of their colonial possessions. Also known as the Great War.

Five Pillars of Islam The Muslim teaching that salvation is only assured through observance of five basic precepts: submission to God's will as described in the teachings of Muhammad, frequent prayer, ritual fasting, the giving of alms, and an annual pilgrimage to Mecca (the Hajj).

Five-Year Plan Soviet effort launched under Stalin in 1928 to replace the market with a state-owned and state-managed economy in order to promote rapid economic development over a five-year period and thereby "catch and overtake" the leading capitalist countries. The First Five-Year Plan was followed by the Second Five-Year Plan (1933–1937) and so on, until the collapse of the Soviet Union in 1991.

fly shuttle Invented by John Kay in 1733, this device sped up the process of weaving.

Fourteen Points President Woodrow Wilson proposed these points as the foundation on which to build peace in the world after the First World War. They called for an end to secret treaties, "open covenants, openly arrived at," freedom of the seas, the removal of international tariffs, the reduction of arms, the "self-determination of peoples," and the establishment of a League of Nations to settle international conflicts.

Franciscan Order Also known as the Order of the Friars Minor. The earliest Franciscans were followers of Francis of Assisi (1182–1226) and strove, like him, to imitate the life and example of Jesus. The order was formally established by Pope Innocent III in 1209. Its special mission was the care and instruction of the urban poor.

Frankfurt Parliament (1848–1849) Failed attempt to create a unified Germany under constitutional principles. In 1849, the assembly offered the crown of the new German nation to Frederick William IV of Prussia, but he refused the offer and suppressed a brief protest. The delegates went home disillusioned.

Frederick the Great (1712–1786) Prussian ruler (1740–1786) who engaged the nobility in maintaining a strong military and bureaucracy and led Prussian armies to notable military victories. He also encouraged Enlightenment rationalism and artistic endeavors.

French Revolution of 1789 In 1788, a severe financial crisis forced the French monarchy to convene an assembly known as the Estates General, representing the three estates of the realm: the clergy, the nobility, and the commons (known as the Third Estate). When the Estates General met in 1789, representatives of the Third Estate demanded major constitutional changes, and when the king and his government proved uncooperative, the Third Estate broke with the other two estates and renamed themselves the National Assembly, demanding a written constitution. The position of the National Assembly was confirmed by a popular uprising in Paris and the king was forced to accept the transformation of France into a constitutional monarchy. This constitutional phase of the revolution lasted until 1972, when the pressures of foreign invasion and the emergence of a more radical revolutionary movement caused the collapse of the monarchy and the establishment of a Republic in France.

French Revolution of 1830 The French popular revolt against Charles X's July Ordinances of 1830, which dissolved the French Chamber of Deputies and restricted suffrage to exclude almost everyone except the nobility. After several days of violence, Charles abdicated the throne and was replaced by a constitutional monarch, Louis Philippe.

French Revolution of 1848 Revolution overthrowing Louis-Philippe in February, 1848, leading to the formation of the Second Republic (1848–1852). Initially enjoying broad support from both the middle classes and laborers in Paris, the new government became more conservative after elections in which the French peasantry participated for the first time. A workers' revolt was violently repressed in June, 1848, and in December 1848, Napoleon Bonaparte's nephew, Louis-Napoleon Bonaparte, was elected president. In 1852, Louis-Napoleon declared himself emperor and abolished the republic.

Sigmund Freud (1856–1939) The Austrian physician who founded the discipline of psychoanalysis and suggested that human behavior was largely motivated by unconscious and irrational forces.

Galileo Galilei (1564–1642) Italian physicist and inventor; the implications of his ideas raised the ire of the Catholic Church, and he was forced to retract most of his findings.

Gallipoli (1915) In the First World War, a combined force of French, British, Australian and New Zealand troops tried to invade the Gallipoli Peninsula, in the first large-scale amphibious attack in history, and seize it from the Turks. After seven months of fighting, the Allies had lost 200,000 soldiers. Defeated, they withdrew.

Mohandas K. (Mahatma) Gandhi (1869–1948) The Indian leader who advocated nonviolent noncooperation to protest colonial rule and helped win home rule for India in 1947.

Giuseppe Garibaldi (1807–1882) Italian revolutionary leader who led the fight to free Sicily and Naples from the Habsburg Empire; the lands were then peaceably annexed by Sardinia to produce a unified Italy.

Gaul The region of the Roman Empire that was home to the Celtic people of that name, comprising modern France, Belgium, and western Germany.

Geneva Peace Conference (1954) International conference to restore peace in Korea and Indochina. The chief participants were the United States, the Soviet Union, Great Britain, France, the People's Republic of China, North Korea, South Korea, Vietnam, the Viet Minh party, Laos, and Cambodia. The conference resulted in the division of North and South Vietnam.

Genoa Maritime city on Italy's northwestern coast, the Genoese were active in trading ventures along the Silk Road and in the establishment of trading colonies in the Mediterranean. They were also involved in the world of finance and backed the commercial ventures of other powers, especially Spain's.

German Democratic Republic Nation founded from the Soviet zone of occupation of Germany after the Second World War; also known as East Germany.

German Social Democratic party Founded in 1875, it was the most powerful socialist party in Europe before 1917.

Gilgamesh Sumerian ruler of the city of Uruk around 2700 B.C.E., Gilgamesh became the hero of one of the world's oldest epics, which circulated orally for nearly a millennium before being written down.

Giotto (c. 1266–1337) Florentine painter and architect who is often considered a forerunner of the Renaissance.

glasnost Introduced by Soviet leader Mikhail Gorbachev in June 1987, *glasnost* was one of the five major policies that constituted *perestroika*. Often translated into English as "openness," it called for transparency in Soviet government and institutional activities by reducing censorship in mass media and lifting significant bans on the political, intellectual, and cultural lives of Soviet civilians.

globalization The term used to describe political, social, and economic networks that span the globe. These global exchanges are not limited by nation-states and in recent decades are associated with new technologies, such as the Internet. Globalization is not new, however, as human cultures and economies have been in contact with one another for centuries.

Glorious Revolution The overthrow of King James II of England and the installation of his Protestant daughter, Mary Stuart, and her husband, William of Orange, to the throne in 1688 and 1689. It is widely regarded as the founding moment in the development of a constitutional monarchy in Britain, while also establishing a more favorable climate for the economic and political growth of the English commercial classes.

Gold Coast Name that European mariners and merchants gave to that part of West Equatorial Africa from which gold and slaves were exported. Originally controlled by the Portuguese, this area later became the British colony of the Gold Coast.

Mikhail Gorbachev (1931–) Soviet leader who attempted to reform the Soviet Union through his programs of glasnost and perestroika in the late 1980s. He encouraged open discussions in other countries in the Soviet bloc, which helped inspire the velvet revolutions throughout Eastern Europe. Eventually the political, social, and economic upheaval he had unleashed would lead to the breakup of the Soviet Union.

Gothic style A type of graceful architecture emerging in twelfth- and thirteenth-century England and France. The style is characterized by pointed arches, delicate decoration, and large windows.

Olympe de Gouges (1748–1793) French political radical and feminist whose *Declaration of the Rights of Woman* demanded an equal place for women in France.

Great Depression Global economic crisis following the U.S. stock market crash on October 29, 1929, and ending with the onset of the Second World War.

Great Famine A period of terrible hunger and deprivation in Europe that peaked between 1315 and 1317, caused by a cooling of the climate and by the exhaustion of over-farming. It is estimated to have reduced the population of Europe by 10 to 15 percent.

Great Fear (1789) Following the outbreak of revolution in Paris, fear spread throughout the French countryside, as rumors circulated that armies of brigands or royal troops were coming. The peasants and villagers organized into militias, while others attacked and burned the manor houses in order to destroy the records of manorial dues.

Great Schism (1378–1417) Also known as the Great Western Schism, to distinguish it from the longstanding rupture between the Greek East and Latin West. During the schism, the Roman Church was divided between two (and, ultimately, three) competing popes. Each pope claimed to be legitimate and each denounced the heresy of the others.

Great Terror (1936–1938) The systematic murder of nearly a million people and the deportation of another million and a half to labor camps by Stalin's regime in an attempt to consolidate power and remove perceived enemies.

Greek East After the founding of Constantinople, the eastern Greek-speaking half of the Roman Empire grew more populous, prosperous and central to imperial policy. Its inhabitants considered themselves to be the true heirs of Rome, and their own Orthodox Church to be the true manifestation of Jesus's ministry.

Greek independence Nationalists in Greece revolted against the Ottoman Empire and fought a war that ended in Greek independence in 1827. They received crucial help from British, French, and Russian troops as well as widespread sympathy throughout Europe.

Pope Gregory I (r. 590–604) Also known as Gregory the Great, he was the first bishop of Rome to successfully negotiate a more universal role for the papacy. His political and theological agenda widened the rift between the western Latin (Catholic) Church and the eastern Greek (Orthodox) Church in Byzantium. He also articulated the Church's official position on the status of Jews, promoted affective approaches to religious worship, encouraged the Benedictine monastic movement, and sponsored missionary expeditions.

Guernica The Basque town bombed by German planes in April 1937 during the Spanish Civil War. It is also the subject of Pablo Picasso's famous painting from the same year.

guilds Professional organizations in commercial towns that regulated business and safeguarded the privileges of those practicing a particular craft. Often identical to confraternities ("brotherhoods").

Gulag The vast system of forced labor camps under the Soviet regime; it originated in 1919 in a small monastery near the Arctic Circle and spread throughout the Soviet Union. Penal labor was required of both ordinary criminals and those accused of political crimes. Tens of millions of people were sent to the camps between 1928 and 1953; the exact figure is unknown.

Gulf War (1991) Armed conflict between Iraq and a coalition of thirty-two nations, including the United States, Britain, Egypt, France, and Saudi Arabia. The seeds of the war were planted with Iraq's invasion of Kuwait on August 2, 1990.

Johannes Gutenberg European inventor of the printing press, his shop in Mainz produced the first printed book—a Bible—between the years 1453 and 1455.

Habsburg Dynasty A powerful European dynasty which came to power in the eleventh century in a region now part of Switzerland. Early generations of Habsburgs consolidated their control over neighboring German-speaking lands; through strategic marriages with other royal lines, later rulers eventually controlled a substantial part of Europe—including much of central Europe, the Netherlands, and even Spain and all its colonies for a time. In practice, the Holy Roman Emperor chosen from a member of the Habsburg lineage. By the latter half of the seventeenth century, the Austrian Habsburg Empire was made of up nearly 300 nominally autonomous dynastic kingdoms, principalities, duchies, and archbishoprics.

Hagia Sophia The enormous church dedicated to "Holy Wisdom," built in Constantinople at the behest of the emperor Justinian in the sixth century C.E. When Constantinople fell to Ottoman forces in 1453, it became an important mosque.

Haitian Revolution (1802–1804) In 1802, Napoleon sought to reassert French control of Saint-Domingue, but stiff resistance and yellow fever crushed the French army. In 1804, Jean-Jacques Dessalines, a general in the army of former slaves, declared the independent state of Haiti. (See **slave revolt in Saint-Domingue**.)

Hajj The annual pilgrimage to Mecca; an obligation for Muslims.

Hammurabi Ruler of Babylon from 1792 to 1750 B.C.E., Hammurabi issued a collection of laws that were greatly influential in the Near East and which constitute the world's oldest surviving law code.

Harlem Renaissance Cultural movement in the 1920s that was based in Harlem, a part of New York City with a large African American population. The movement gave voice to black novelists, poets, painters, and musicians, many of whom used their art to protest racial subordination.

Hatshepsut (1479–1458 C.E.) As a pharaoh during the New Kingdom, she launched several successful military campaigns and extended trade and diplomacy. She was an ambitious builder who probably constructed the first tomb in the Valley of the Kings. Though she never pretended to be a man, she was routinely portrayed with a masculine figure and a ceremonial beard.

Hebrews Originally a pastoral people divided among several tribes, they were briefly united under the rule of David and his son, Solomon, who promoted the worship of a single god, Yahweh, and constructed the first temple at the new capital city of Jerusalem. After Solomon's death, the Hebrew tribes were divided between the two kingdoms of Israel and Judah, which were eventually conquered by the Neo-Assyrian and Chaldean empires. It was in captivity that the Hebrews came to define themselves through worship of Yahweh and to develop a religion, Judaism, that could exist outside of Judea. They were liberated by the Persian king Cyrus the Great in 539 B.C.E.

Hellenistic art The art of the Hellenistic period bridged the tastes, ideals, and customs of classical Greece and those that would be more characteristic of Rome. The Romans strove to emulate Hellenistic city planning and civic culture and thereby exported Hellenistic culture to their own far-flung colonies in western Europe.

Hellenistic culture The "Greek-like" culture that dominated the ancient world in the wake of Alexander's conquests.

Hellenistic kingdoms Following the death of Alexander the Great, his vast empire was divided into three separate states: Ptolemaic Egypt (under the rule of the general Ptolemy and his successors), Seleucid Asia (ruled by the general Seleucus and his heirs) and Antigonid Greece (governed by Antigonus of Macedonia). Each state maintained its independence, but the shared characteristics of Greco-Macedonian rule and a shared Greek culture and heritage bound them together in a united cosmopolitan world.

Hellenistic world The various Western civilizations of antiquity that were loosely united by shared Greek language and culture, especially around the eastern Mediterranean.

Heloise (c. 1090–1164) One of the foremost scholars of her time, she became the pupil and the wife of the philosopher and teacher Peter Abelard. In later life, she was the founder of a new religious order for women.

Henry IV of Germany King of Germany and Holy Roman Emperor from 1056—when he ascended the throne at the age of six years old—until his death in 1106. Henry's reign was first weakened by conflict with the Saxon nobility and later marked by the Investiture Controversy with Pope Gregory VII.

Henry VIII (1491–1547) King of England from 1509 until his death, Henry rejected the authority of the Roman Church in 1534 when the pope refused to annul his marriage to his queen, Catherine of Aragon; he became the founder of the Church of England.

Henry of Navarre (1553–1610) Crowned King Henry IV of France, he renounced his Protestantism but granted limited toleration for Huguenots (French Protestants) by the Edict of Nantes in 1598.

Prince Henry the Navigator (1394–1460) A member of the Portuguese royal family, Henry encouraged the exploration and conquest of western Africa and the trade in gold and slaves.

hieroglyphs The writing system of ancient Egypt, based on a complicated series of pictorial symbols. It fell out of use when Egypt was absorbed into the Roman Empire and was only deciphered after the discovery of the Rosetta Stone in the early nineteenth century.

Hildegard of Bingen (1098–1179) A powerful abbess, theologian, scientist, musician, and visionary who claimed to receive regular revelations from God. Although highly influential in her own day, she was never officially canonized by the Church, in part because her strong personality no longer matched the changing ideal of female piety.

Hiroshima Japanese port devastated by an atomic bomb on August 6, 1945.

Adolf Hitler (1889–1945) The author of *Mein Kampf* and leader of the Nazis who became chancellor of Germany in 1933. Hitler and his Nazi regime started the Second World War and orchestrated the systematic murder of over 5 million Jews.

Hitler-Stalin Pact (1939) Treaty between Stalin and Hitler, which promised Stalin a share of Poland, Finland, the Baltic States, and Bessarabia in the event of a German invasion of Poland, which began shortly thereafter, on September 1, 1939.

HIV epidemic The first cases of HIV-AIDS appeared in the late 1970s. As HIV-AIDS became a global crisis, international organizations recognized the need for an early, swift, and comprehensive response to future outbreaks of disease.

Thomas Hobbes (1588–1679) English political philosopher whose *Leviathan* argued that any form of government capable of protecting its subjects' lives and property might act as an all-powerful sovereign. This government should be allowed to trample over both liberty and property for the sake of its own survival and that of his subjects. For in his natural state, Hobbes argued, man was like "a wolf" toward other men.

Holy Roman Empire The loosely allied collection of lands in central and western Europe ruled by the kings of Germany (and later Austria) from the twelfth century until 1806. Its origins are usually identified with the empire of Charlemagne, the Frankish king who was crowned emperor of Rome by the pope in 800.

homage A ceremony in which an individual becomes the "man" (French: *homme*) of a lord.

Homer (fl. eighth century B.C.E.) A Greek rhapsode ("weaver" of stories) credited with merging centuries of poetic tradition in the epics known as the *Iliad* and the *Odyssey*.

hoplite A Greek foot-soldier armed with a spear or short sword and protected by a large round shield (*hoplon*). In battle, hoplites stood shoulder to shoulder in a close formation called a phalanx.

Huguenots French Protestants who endured severe persecution in the sixteenth and seventeenth centuries.

humanism A program of study associated with the movement known as the Renaissance, humanism aimed to replace the scholastic emphasis on logic and philosophy with the study of ancient languages, literature, history, and ethics.

human rights The belief that all people have the right to legal equality, freedom of religion and speech, and the right to participate in government. Human rights laws prohibit torture, cruel punishment, and slavery.

David Hume (1711–1776) Scottish writer who applied Newton's method of scientific inquiry and skepticism to the study of morality, the mind, and government.

Hundred Years' War (1337–1453) A series of wars between England and France, fought mostly on French soil and prompted by the territorial and political claims of English monarchs.

Jan Hus (c. 1373–1415) A Czech reformer who adopted many of the teachings of the English theologian John Wycliffe, and who also demanded that the laity be allowed to receive both the consecrated bread and wine of the Eucharist. The Council of Constance burned him at the stake for heresy. In response, his supporters, the Hussites, revolted against the Church.

Saddam Hussein (1937–2006) The former dictator of Iraq who invaded Iran in 1980 and started the eight-year-long Iran-Iraq War; invaded Kuwait in 1990, which led to the Gulf War of 1991; and was overthrown when the United States invaded Iraq in 2003. Involved in Iraqi politics since the mid-1960s, Hussein became the official head of state in 1979.

Iconoclast Controversy (717–787) A serious and often violent theological debate that raged in Byzantium after Emperor Leo III ordered the destruction of religious art on the grounds that any image representing a divine or holy personage is prone to promote idol worship and blasphemy. Iconoclast means "breaker of icons." Those who supported the veneration of icons were called iconodules, "adherents of icons."

Il-khanate Mongol-founded dynasty in thirteenth-century Persia.

Indian National Congress Formed in 1885, this Indian political party worked to achieve Indian independence from British colonial control. The Congress was led by Ghandi in the 1920s and 1930s.

Indian Rebellion of 1857 The uprising began near Delhi, when the military disciplined a regiment of Indian soldiers employed by the British for refusing to use rifle cartridges greased with pork fat—unacceptable to either Hindus or Muslims. Rebels attacked law courts and burned tax rolls, protesting debt and corruption. The mutiny spread through large areas of northwest India before being violently suppressed by British troops.

Indo-Europeans A group of people speaking variations of the same language who moved into the Near East and Mediterranean region shortly after 2000 B.C.E.

indulgences Grants exempting Catholic Christians from the performance of penance, either in life or after death. The abusive trade in indulgences was a major catalyst of the Protestant Reformation.

Incas The highly centralized South American empire that was toppled by the Spanish conquistador Francisco Pizarro in 1533.

Innocent III (1160/61–1216) As pope, he wanted to unify all of Christendom under papal hegemony. He furthered this goal at the Fourth Lateran Council of 1215, which defined one of the Church's dogmas as the acknowledgment of papal supremacy. The council also took an unprecedented interest in the religious education and habits of every Christian.

Inquisition Tribunal of the Roman Church that aims to enforce religious orthodoxy and conformity.

International Monetary Fund (IMF) Established in 1945 to ensure international cooperation regarding currency exchange and monetary policy, the IMF is a specialized agency of the United Nations.

Investiture Conflict The name given to a series of debates over the limitations of spiritual and secular power in Europe during the eleventh and early twelfth century, it came to a head when Pope Gregory VII and Emperor Henry IV of Germany both claimed the right to appoint and invest bishops with the regalia of office. After years of diplomatic and military hostility, it was partially settled by the Concordat of Worms in 1122.

Irish potato famine Period of agricultural blight from 1845 to 1849 whose devastating results produced widespread starvation and led to mass immigration to America.

Iron Curtain Term coined by Winston Churchill in 1946 to refer to the borders of Eastern European nations that lay within the zone of Soviet control.

Italian invasion of Ethiopia (1896) Italy invaded Ethiopia, which was the last major independent African kingdom. Menelik II, the Ethiopian emperor, soundly defeated them.

Ivan the Great (1440–1505) Russian ruler who annexed neighboring territories and consolidated his empire's position as a European power.

Jacobins Radical French political group during the French Revolution that took power after 1792, executed the French king, and sought to remake French culture.

Jacquerie Violent 1358 peasant uprising in northern France, incited by disease, war, and taxes.

James I (1566–1625) Monarch who ruled Scotland as James VI, and who succeeded Elizabeth I as king of England in 1603. He oversaw the English vernacular translation of the Bible known by his name.

James II of England King of England, Ireland, and Scotland from 1685–88 whose commitment to absolutism and Catholic zealotry led to his exile to France in the Glorious Revolution of 1688.

Janissaries Corps of enslaved soldiers recruited as children from the Christian provinces of the Ottoman Empire and brought up to display intense personal loyalty to the Ottoman sultan, who used these forces to curb local autonomy and as his personal bodyguards.

Jerome (c. 340–420) One of the early "fathers" of the Church, he translated the Bible from Hebrew and Greek into a popular form of Latin—hence the name by which this translation is known: the Vulgate, or "vulgar" (popular), Bible.

Jesuits The religious order formally known as the Society of Jesus, founded in 1540 by Ignatius Loyola to combat the spread of Protestantism. The Jesuits would become active in politics, education, and missionary work.

Jesus (c. 4 B.C.E.–c. 30 C.E.) A Jewish preacher and teacher in the rural areas of Galilee and Judea who was arrested for seditious political activity, tried, and crucified by the Romans. After his execution, his followers claimed that he had been resurrected from the dead and taken up into heaven. They began to teach that Jesus had been the divine representative of God, the Messiah foretold by ancient Hebrew prophets, and that he had suffered for the sins of humanity and would return to judge all the world's inhabitants at the end of time.

Joan of Arc (c. 1412–1431) A peasant girl from the province of Lorraine who claimed to have been commanded by God to lead French forces against the English occupying army during the Hundred Years' War. Successful in her efforts, she was betrayed by the French king and handed over to the English, who condemned her to death for heresy. Her reputation underwent a process of rehabilitation, but she was not officially canonized as a saint until 1920.

Judaism The religion of the Hebrews as it developed in the centuries after the establishment of the Hebrew kingdoms under David and Solomon, especially during the period of Babylonian Captivity.

Justinian (527–565) Emperor of Rome who unsuccessfully attempted to reunite the eastern and western portions of the empire. Also known for his important codification of Roman law, in the *Corpus Juris Civilis*.

Justinian's Code of Roman Law Formally known as the *Corpus Juris Civilis* or "body of civil law," this compendium consisted of a systematic compilation of imperial statutes, the writings of Rome's great legal authorities, a textbook of legal principles, and the legislation of Justinian and his immediate successors. As the most authoritative collection of Roman law, it formed the basis of canon law (the legal system of the Roman Church) and became essential to the developing legal traditions of every European state as well as of many countries around the world.

Das Kapital (Capital) The 1867 book by Karl Marx that outlined the theory behind historical materialism and attacked the socioeconomic inequities of capitalism.

Johannes Kepler (1571–1630) Mathematician and astronomer who elaborated on and corrected Copernicus's theory and is chiefly remembered for his discovery of the three laws of planetary motion that bear his name.

Keynesian Revolution Postdepression economic ideas developed by the British economist John Maynard Keynes, wherein the state took a greater role in managing the economy, stimulating it by increasing the money supply and creating jobs.

KGB Soviet political police and spy agency, first formed as the Cheka not long after the Bolshevik coup in October 1917. It grew to more than 750,000 operatives with military rank by the 1980s.

Genghis Khan (c. 1167–1227) "Oceanic Ruler," the title adopted by the Mongol chieftain Temujin, founder of a dynasty that conquered much of southern Asia.

Khanate The major political unit of the vast Mongol Empire. There were four Khanates, including the Yuan Empire in China, forged by Chingiz Khan's grandson Kubilai in the thirteenth century.

Ruhollah Khomeini (1902–1989) Iranian Shi'ite religious leader who led the revolution in Iran after the abdication of the shah in 1979. His government allowed some limited economic and political populism combined with strict constructions of Islamic law, restrictions on women's public life, and the prohibition of ideas or activities linked to Western influence.

Nikita Khrushchev (1894–1971) Leader of the Soviet Union during the Cuban missile crisis, Khrushchev came to power after Stalin's death in 1953. His reforms and criticisms of the excesses of the Stalin regime led to his fall from power in 1964.

Kremlin Once synonymous with the Soviet government, it refers to Moscow's walled city center and the palace originally built by Ivan the Great.

Kristallnacht Organized attack by Nazis and their supporters on the Jews of Germany following the assassination of a German embassy official by a Jewish man in Paris. Throughout Germany, thousands of stores, schools, cemeteries and synagogues were attacked on November 9, 1938. Dozens of people were killed, and tens of thousands of Jews were arrested and held in camps, where many were tortured and killed in the ensuing months.

Labour party Founded in Britain in 1900, this party represented workers and was based on socialist principles.

Latin West After the founding of Constantinople, the western Latin-speaking half of the Roman Empire became poorer and more peripheral, but it also fostered the emergence of new barbarian kingdoms. At the same time, the Roman pope claimed to have inherited both the authority of Jesus and the essential elements of Roman imperial authority.

League of Nations International organization founded after the First World War to solve international disputes through arbitration; it was dissolved in 1946 and its assets were transferred to the United Nations.

Leonardo da Vinci (1452–1519) Florentine inventor, sculptor, architect, and painter whose breadth of interests typifies the ideal of "the Renaissance man."

Vladimir Lenin (1870–1924) Leader of the Bolshevik Revolution in Russia (1917) and the first leader of the Soviet Union.

Leviathan A book by Thomas Hobbes (1588–1679) that recommended a ruler have unrestricted power.

liberalism Political and social theory that judges the effectiveness of a government in terms of its ability to protect individual rights. Liberals support representative forms of government, free trade, and freedom of speech and religion. In the economic realm, liberals believe that individuals should be free to engage in commercial or business activities without interference from the state or their community.

lithograph Art form that involves putting writing or design on stone and producing printed impressions.

John Locke (1632–1704) English philosopher and political theorist known for his contributions to liberalism. Locke had great faith in human reason and believed that just societies were those that infringed the least on the natural rights and freedoms of individuals. This led him to assert that a government's legitimacy depended on the consent of the governed, a view that had a profound effect on the authors of the United States' Declaration of Independence.

Louis IX of France King of France from 1226 to his death on Crusade in 1270, Louis was famous for his piety and for his close attention to the administration of law and justice in his realm. He was officially canonized as Saint Louis in 1297.

Louis XIV (1638–1715) Called the "Sun King," he was known for his success at strengthening the institutions of the French absolutist state.

Louis XVI (1754–1793) Well-meaning but ineffectual king of France, finally deposed and executed during the French Revolution.

Ignatius Loyola (1491–1556) Founder of the Society of Jesus (commonly known as the Jesuits), whose members vowed to serve God through poverty, chastity, and missionary work. He abandoned his first career as a mercenary after reading an account of Christ's life written in his native Spanish.

Lucretia According to Roman legend, Lucretia was a virtuous Roman wife who was raped by the son of Rome's last king and who virtuously committed suicide in order to avoid bringing shame on her family.

Luftwaffe Literally "air weapon," this is the name of the German air force, which was founded during the First World War, disbanded in 1945, and reestablished when West Germany joined NATO in 1950.

Lusitania The British passenger liner that was sunk by a German U-boat (submarine) on May 7, 1915. Public outrage over the sinking contributed to the U.S. decision to enter the First World War.

Martin Luther (1483–1546) A German monk and professor of theology whose critique of the papacy launched the Protestant Reformation.

ma'at The Egyptian term for the serene order of the universe, with which the individual soul (*ka*) must remain in harmony. The power of the pharaoh was linked to *ma'at*, insofar as it ensured the prosperity of the kingdom. After the upheavals of the First Intermediate Period, the perception of the pharaoh's relationship with ma'at was revealed to be conditional, something that had to be earned.

Niccolò Machiavelli (1469–1527) As the author of *The Prince* and the *Discourses on Livy*, he looked to the Roman past for paradigms of greatness while at the same time hoping to win the patronage of contemporary rulers who would restore Italy's political independence.

Magna Carta The "Great Charter" of 1215, enacted during the reign of King John of England and designed to limit his powers. Regarded now as a landmark in the development of constitutional government. In its own time, its purpose was to restore the power of great lords.

Magyar nationalism Lajos Kossuth led this national movement in the Hungarian region of the Habsburg Empire, calling for national independence for Hungary in 1848. With the support of Russia, the Habsburg army crushed the movement and all other revolutionary activities in the empire. Kossuth fled into exile.

Moses Maimonides (c. 1137–1204) Jewish scholar, physician, and scriptural commentator whose *Mishneh Torah* is a fundamental exposition of Jewish law.

Thomas Malthus (1766–1834) British political economist who believed that populations inevitably grew faster than the available food supply. Societies that could not control their population growth would be checked only by famine, disease, poverty, and infant malnutrition. He argued that governments could not alleviate poverty. Instead, the poor had to exercise "moral restraint," postpone marriage, and have fewer children.

Nelson Mandela (b. 1918) The South African opponent of apartheid who led the African National Congress and was imprisoned from 1962 until 1990. After his release from prison, he worked with Prime Minister Frederik Willem De Klerk to establish majority rule. Mandela became the first black president of South Africa in 1994.

Manhattan Project The secret U.S. government research project to develop the first nuclear bomb. The vast project involved dozens of sites across the United States, including New Mexico, Tennessee, Illinois, California, Utah, and Washington. The first test of a nuclear bomb was near Alamogordo, New Mexico on July 16, 1945.

manors Common farmland worked collectively by the inhabitants of entire villages, sometimes on their own initiative, sometimes at the behest of a lord.

Mao Zedong (1893–1976) The leader of the Chinese Revolution who defeated the Nationalists in 1949 and established the Communist regime in China.

Marne A major battle of the First World War in September 1914, which halted the German invasion of France and led to protracted trench warfare on the Western Front.

Marshall Plan Economic aid package given to Europe by the United States after the Second World War to promote reconstruction and economic development and to secure the countries from a feared communist takeover.

Karl Marx (1818–1883) German philosopher and economist who believed that a revolution of the working classes would overthrow the capitalist order and create a classless society. Author of *Das Kapital* and *The Communist Manifesto.*

Marxists Followers of the socialist political economist Karl Marx who called for workers everywhere to unite and create an independent political force. Marxists believed that industrialization produced an inevitable struggle between laborers and the class of capitalist property owners, and that this struggle would culminate in a revolution that would abolish private property and establish a society committed to social equality.

Mary See **cult of the Virgin**.

Mary I (1516–1558) Catholic daughter of Henry VIII and his first wife, Catherine of Aragon, Mary Tudor was the first queen regnant of England. Her attempts to reinstitute Catholicism in England met with limited success, and after her early death she was labeled "Bloody Mary" by the Protestant supporters of her half sister and successor, Elizabeth I.

mass culture The spread of literacy and public education in the nineteenth century created a new audience for print entertainment and a new class of entrepreneurs in the media to cater to this audience. The invention of radio, film, and television in the twentieth century carried this development to another level, as millions of consumers were now accessible to the producers of news, information, and entertainment. The rise of this "mass culture" has been celebrated as an expression of popular tastes but also criticized as a vehicle for the manipulation of populations through clever and seductive propaganda.

Mayans Native American peoples whose culturally and politically sophisticated empire encompassed lands in present-day Mexico and Guatemala.

Giuseppe Mazzini (1805–1872) Founder of Young Italy and an ideological leader of the Italian nationalist movement.

Mecca Center of an important commercial network of the Arabian Peninsula and birthplace of the prophet Muhammad. It is now considered the holiest site in the Islamic world.

Medici A powerful dynasty of Florentine bankers and politicians whose ancestors were originally apothecaries ("medics").

Meiji Empire Empire created under the leadership of Mutsuhito, emperor of Japan from 1868 until 1912. During the Meiji period Japan became a world industrial and naval power.

Mensheviks Within the Russian Social Democratic Party, the Mensheviks advocated slow changes and a gradual move toward socialism, in contrast with the Bolsheviks, who wanted to push for a proletarian revolution. Mensheviks believed that a proletarian revolution in Russia was premature and that the country needed to complete its capitalist development first.

mercantilism A theory and policy for directing the economy of monarchical states between 1600 and 1800 based on the assumption that wealth and power depended on a favorable balance of trade (more exports and fewer imports) and the accumulation of precious metals. Mercantilists advocated forms of economic protectionism to promote domestic production.

Maria Sybilla Merian (1647–1717) A scientific illustrator and an important early entomologist. She conducted research on two continents and published the well-received *Metamorphosis of the Insects of Surinam.*

Merovingian A Frankish dynasty that claimed descent from a legendary ancestor called Merovic, the Merovingians were the only powerful family to establish a lasting kingdom in western Europe during the fifth and sixth centuries.

Mesopotamia The "land between the Tigris and the Euphrates rivers," Tigris and Euphrates where the civilization of Sumer, the first urban society, flourished.

Klemens von Metternich (1773–1859) Austrian foreign minister whose primary goals were to bolster the legitimacy of monarchies and, after the defeat of Napoleon, to prevent another large-scale war in Europe. At the Congress of Vienna, he opposed social and political change and wanted to check Russian and French expansion.

Michelangelo Buonarroti (1475–1564) A virtuoso Florentine sculptor, painter, and poet who spent much of his career in the service of the papacy. He is best known for the decoration of the Sistine Chapel and for his monumental sculptures.

Middle Kingdom of Egypt (2055–1650 B.C.E.) The period following the First Intermediate Period of dynastic warfare, which ended with the reassertion of pharonic rule under Mentuhotep II.

Miletus A Greek polis and Persian colony on the Ionian coast of Asia Minor. Influenced by the cultures of Mesopotamia, Egypt, and Lydia, it produced several of the ancient world's first scientists and sophists. Thereafter, a political conflict between the ruler of Miletus, Aristagoras, and the Persian Emperor, Darius, sparked the Persian Wars with Greece.

John Stuart Mill (1806–1873) English liberal philosopher whose faith in human reason led him to support a broad variety of civic and political freedoms for men and women, including the right to vote and the right to free speech.

Slobodan Milosevic (1941–2006) The Serbian nationalist politician who became president of Serbia and whose policies during the Balkan wars of the early 1990s led to the deaths of thousands of Croatians, Bosnian Muslims, Albanians, and Kosovars. After leaving office in 2000, he was arrested and tried for war crimes at the International Court in The Hague. The trial ended before a verdict with his death in 2006.

Minoan Crete A sea empire based at Knossos on the Greek island of Crete and named for the legendary King Minos. The Minoans dominated the Aegean for much of the second millennium B.C.E.

Modernism There were several different modernist movements in art and literature, but they shared three key characteristics. First, they had a sense that the world had radically changed and that this change should be embraced. Second, they believed that traditional aesthetic values and assumptions about creativity were ill-suited to the present. Third, they developed a new conception of what art could do that emphasized expression over representation and insisted on the value of novelty, experimentation, and creative freedom.

Mongols A nomadic people from the steppes of Central Asia who were united under the ruler Genghis Khan. His conquest of China was continued by his grandson Kubilai and his great-grandson son Ogedei, whose army also seized southern Russia and then moved through Hungary and through Poland toward eastern Germany. The Mongol armies withdrew from eastern Europe after the death of Ogedei, but his descendants continued to rule his vast empire for another half century.

Michel de Montaigne (1533–1592) French philosopher and social commentator, best known for his *Essays*.

Montesquieu (1689–1755) An Enlightenment philosophe whose most influential work was *The Spirit of Laws*. In this work, he analyzed the structures that shaped law and categorized governments into three types: republics, monarchies, and despotisms. His ideas about the separation of powers among the executive, the legislative, and the judicial branches of government influenced the authors of the U.S. Constitution.

Thomas More (1478–1535) Christian humanist, English statesman, and author of *Utopia*. In 1529, he was appointed lord chancellor of England but resigned because he opposed King Henry VIII's plans to establish a national church under royal control. He was eventually executed for refusing to take an oath acknowledging Henry to be the head of the Church of England and has since been canonized by the Catholic Church.

mos maiorum Literally translated as "the code of the elders" or "the custom of ancestors." This unwritten code governed the lives of Romans under the Republic and stressed the importance of showing reverence to ancestral tradition. It was sacrosanct and essential to Roman identity, and an important influence on Roman culture, law, and religion.

Wolfgang Amadeus Mozart (1756–1791) Austrian composer, famous at a young age as a concert musician and later celebrated as a prolific composer of instrumental music and operas that are seen as the apogee of the Classical style in music.

Muhammad (570–632 C.E.) The founder of Islam, regarded as God's last and greatest prophet by his followers.

Munich Conference (1938) Hitler met with the leaders of Britain, France, and Italy and negotiated an agreement that gave Germany a major slice of Czechoslovakia. British prime minister Chamberlain believed that the agreement would bring peace to Europe. Instead, Germany invaded and seized the rest of Czechoslovakia.

Muscovy The duchy centered on Moscow whose dukes saw themselves as heirs to the Roman Empire. In the early fourteenth century, Moscow was under the control of the Mongol Khanate. After the collapse of the Khanate, the Muscovite grand duke, Ivan III, conquered all the Russian principalities between Moscow and the border of Poland-Lithuania, and then Lithuania itself. By the time of his death, Ivan had established Muscovy as a dominant power.

Muslim learning and culture The Crusades brought the Latin West in contact with the Islamic world, which impacted European culture in myriad ways. Europeans adapted Arabic numerals and mathematical concepts as well as Arabic and Persian words. Through Arabic translations, Western scholars gained access to Greek learning, which had a profound influence on Christian theology. European scholars also learned from the Islamic world's accomplishments in medicine and science.

Benito Mussolini (1883–1945) The Italian founder of the Fascist party who came to power in Italy in 1922 and allied himself with Hitler and the Nazis during the Second World War.

Mycenaean Greece (1600–1200 B.C.E.) The term used to describe the civilization of Greece in the late Bronze Age, when territorial kingdoms like Mycenae formed around a king, a warrior caste, and a palace bureaucracy.

Nagasaki Second Japanese city on which the United States dropped an atomic bomb. The attack took place on August 9, 1945; the Japanese surrendered shortly thereafter, ending the Second World War.

Napoleon III (1808–1873) Nephew of Napoleon Bonaparte, Napoleon III was elected president of the French Second Republic in 1848 and made himself emperor of France in 1852. During his reign (1852–70), he rebuilt the French capital of Paris. Defeated in the France-Prussian War of 1870, he went into exile.

Napoleonic Code Legal code drafted by Napoleon in 1804 and based on Justinian's *Corpus Iuris Civilis*. It distilled different legal traditions to create one uniform law. The code confirmed the abolition of feudal privileges of all kinds and set the conditions for exercising property rights.

Napoleon's military campaigns In 1805, the Russians, Prussians, Austrians, Swedes, and British attempted to contain Napoleon, but he defeated them. Out of his victories, Napoleon created a new empire and affiliated states. In 1808, he invaded Spain, but fierce resistance prevented Napoleon from achieving a complete victory. In 1812, Napoleon invaded Russia, and his army was decimated as it retreated from Moscow during the winter. After the Russian campaign, the united European powers defeated Napoleon and forced him into exile. He escaped and reassumed command of his army, but the European powers defeated him for the final time at the Battle of Waterloo.

Gamal Abdel Nasser (1918–1970) Former president of Egypt and the most prominent spokesman for secular pan-Arabism. He became a target for Islamist critics, such as Sayyid Qutb and the Muslim Brotherhood, angered by the Western-influenced policies of his regime.

National Assembly of France Governing body of France that succeeded the Estates General in 1789 during the French Revolution. It was composed of, and defined by, the delegates of the Third Estate.

National Association for the Advancement of Colored People (NAACP) Founded in 1910, this U.S. civil rights organization was dedicated to ending inequality and segregation for black Americans.

National Convention The governing body of France from September 1792 to October 1795. It declared France a republic and then tried and executed the French king. The Convention also confiscated the property of the enemies of the revolution, instituted a policy of de-Christianization, changed marriage and inheritance laws, abolished slavery in its colonies, placed a cap on the price of necessities, and ended the compensation of nobles for their lost privileges.

nationalism Movement to unify a country under one government based on perceptions of the population's common history, customs, and social traditions.

nationalism in Yugoslavia In the 1990s, Slobodan Milosevic and his allies reignited Serbian nationalism in the former Yugoslavia, which led non-Serb republics in Croatia and Slovenia to seek independence. The country erupted into war, with the worst violence taking place in Bosnia, a multi-ethnic region with Serb, Croatian and Bosnian Muslim populations. European diplomats proved powerless to stop attempts by Croatian and Serbian military and paramilitary forces to claim territory through ethnic cleansing and violent intimidation. Atrocities were committed on all sides, but pro-Serb forces were responsible for the most deaths.

NATO The North Atlantic Treaty Organization, a 1949 military agreement among the United States, Canada, Great Britain, and eight Western European nations, which declared that an armed attack against any one of the members would be regarded as an attack against all. Created during the Cold War in the face of the Soviet Union's control of Eastern Europe, NATO continues to exist today and the membership of twenty-eight states includes former members of the Warsaw Pact as well as Albania and Turkey.

Nazi party Founded in the early 1920s, the National Socialist German Workers' Party (NSDAP) gained control over Germany under the leadership of Adolf Hitler in 1933 and continued in power until Germany was defeated in 1945.

Nazism The political movement in Germany led by Adolf Hitler, which advocated a violent anti-Semitic, anti-Marxist, pan-German ideology.

Neo-Assyrian Empire (883–859 B.C.E.–612–605 B.C.E.) Assurnasirpal II laid the foundations of the Neo-Assyrian Empire through military campaigns against neighboring peoples. Eventually, the empire stretched from the Mediterranean Sea to western Iran. A military dictatorship governed the empire through its army, which it used to frighten and oppress both its subjects and its enemies. The empire's ideology was based on waging holy war in the name of its principal god, Assur, and the exaction of tribute through terror.

Neoliberalism Neoliberals believe that free markets, profit incentives, and restraints on both budget deficits and social welfare programs are the best guarantee of individual liberties. Beginning in the 1980s, neoliberal theory was used to structure the policy of financial institutions like the International Monetary Fund and the World Bank, which turned away from interventionist policies in favor of market-driven models of economic development.

Neolithic Revolution The "New" Stone Age, which began around 11,000 B.C.E., saw new technological and social developments, including managed food production, the beginnings of permanent settlements, and the rapid intensification of trade.

Neoplatonism A school of thought based on the teachings of Plato and prevalent in the Roman Empire, which had a profound effect on the formation of Christian theology. Neoplatonists argued that nature is a book written by its creator to reveal the ways of God to humanity. Convinced that God's perfection must be reflected in nature, neoplatonists searched for the ideal and perfect structures that they believed must lie behind the "shadows" of the everyday world.

New Deal President Franklin Delano Roosevelt's package of government reforms that were enacted during the depression of the 1930s to provide jobs for the unemployed, social welfare programs for the poor, and security to the financial markets.

New Economic Policy In 1921, the Bolsheviks abandoned war communism in favor of the New Economic Policy (NEP). Under NEP, the state still controlled all major industry and financial concerns, while individuals could own private property, trade freely within limits, and farm their own land for their own benefit. Fixed taxes replaced grain requisition. The policy successfully helped Soviet agriculture recover from the civil war but was later abandoned in favor of collectivization.

Isaac Newton (1642–1727) One of the foremost scientists of all time, Newton was an English mathematician and physicist; he is noted for his development of calculus, work on the properties of light, and theory of gravitation.

Tsar Nicholas II (1868–1918) The last Russian tsar, who abdicated the throne in 1917. He and his family were executed by the Bolsheviks on July 17, 1918.

Friedrich Nietzsche (1844–1900) The German philosopher who denied the possibility of knowing absolute "truth" or "reality," since all knowledge comes filtered through linguistic, scientific, or artistic systems of representation. He also criticized Judeo-Christian morality for instilling a repressive conformity that drained civilization of its vitality.

nongovernmental organizations (NGOs) Private organizations like the Red Cross that play a large role in international affairs.

Novum Organum Work by English statesman and scientist Francis Bacon (1561–1626) that advanced a philosophy of study through observation.

October Days (1789) The high price of bread and the rumor that the king was unwilling to cooperate with the assembly caused the women who worked in Paris's large central market to march to Versailles along with their supporters to address the king. Not satisfied with their initial reception, they broke through the palace gates and called for the king to return to Paris from Versailles, which he did the following day.

Old Kingdom of Egypt (c. 2686–2160 B.C.E.) During this time, the pharaohs controlled a powerful and centralized bureaucratic state whose vast human and material resources are exemplified by the pyramids of Giza. This period came to an end as the pharaoh's authority collapsed, leading to a period of dynastic warfare and localized rule.

OPEC (Organization of the Petroleum Exporting Countries) Organization created in 1960 by oil-producing countries in the Middle East, South America, and Africa to regulate the production and pricing of crude oil.

Operation Barbarossa The codename for Hitler's invasion of the Soviet Union in 1941.

Opium Wars (1839–1842) War fought between the British and Qing China to protect British trade in opium; resulted in the ceding of Hong Kong to the British.

Oracle at Delphi The most important shrine in ancient Greece. The priestess of Apollo who attended the shrine was believed to have the power to predict the future.

Ottoman Empire (c.1300–1923) During the thirteenth century, the Ottoman dynasty established itself as leader of the Turks. From the fourteenth to sixteenth centuries, they conquered Anatolia, Armenia, Syria, and North Africa as well as parts of southeastern Europe, the Crimea, and areas along the Red Sea. Portions of the Ottoman Empire persisted up to the time of the First World War, but it was dismantled in the years following it.

Reza Pahlavi (1919–1980) The Western-friendly shah of Iran who was installed during a 1953 coup supported by Britain and the United States. After a lengthy economic downturn, public unrest, and personal illness, he retired from public life under popular pressure in 1979.

Pan-African Conference 1900 assembly in London that sought to draw attention to the sovereignty of African people and their mistreatment by colonial powers.

Panhellenism The "all Greek" culture that allowed ancient Greek colonies to maintain a connection to their homeland and to each other through their shared language and heritage. These colonies also exported their culture into new areas and created new Greek-speaking enclaves, which permanently changed the cultural geography of the Mediterranean world.

pan-Slavism Cultural movement that sought to unite native Slavic peoples within the Russian and Habsburg Empires under Russian leadership.

Partition of India (1947) At independence, British India was partitioned into the nations of India and Pakistan. The majority of the population in India was Hindu and the majority of the population in Pakistan was Muslim. The process of partition brought brutal religious and ethnic warfare. More than 1 million Hindus and Muslims died and 12 million became refugees.

Blaise Pascal (1623–1662) A Catholic philosopher who wanted to establish the truth of Christianity by appealing simultaneously to intellect and emotion. In his *Pensées*, he argued that faith alone can resolve the world's contradictions and that his own awe in the face of evil and uncertainty must be evidence of God's existence.

Paul of Tarsus Originally known as Saul, Paul was a Greek-speaking Jew and Roman citizen who underwent a miraculous conversion experience and became the most important proponent of Christianity in the 50s and 60s C.E.

Pax Romana (27 B.C.E.–180 C.E.) Literally translated as "the Roman Peace." During this time, the Roman world enjoyed an unprecedented period of peace and political stability.

Peace of Augsburg A settlement negotiated in 1555 among factions within the Holy Roman Empire, it formulated the principle *cuius regio, eius religio,* "he who rules, his religion": meaning that the inhabitants of any given territory should follow the religion of its ruler, whether Catholic or Protestant.

Peace of Paris The 1919 Paris Peace Conference established the terms to end the First World War. Great Britain, France, Italy, and the United States signed five treaties with each of the defeated nations: Germany, Austria, Hungary, Turkey, and Bulgaria. The settlement is notable for the territory that

Germany had to give up, including large parts of Prussia to the new state of Poland, and Alsace and Lorraine to France; the disarming of Germany; and the "war guilt" provision, which required Germany and its allies to pay massive reparations to the victors.

Peace of Westphalia (1648) An agreement reached at the end of the Thirty Years' War that altered the political map of Europe. France emerged as the predominant power on the Continent, while the Austrian Habsburgs had to surrender all the territories they had gained and could no longer use the office of the Holy Roman Emperor to dominate central Europe. Spain was marginalized and Germany became a volatile combination of Protestant and Catholic principalities.

Pearl Harbor The American naval base in Hawaii that was bombed by the Japanese on December 7, 1941, bringing the United States into the Second World War.

peasantry Term used in continental Europe to refer to rural populations that lived from agriculture. Some peasants were free and could own land. Serfs were peasants who were legally bound to the land and subject to the authority of the local lord.

Peloponnesian War The name given to the series of wars fought between Sparta (on the Greek Peloponnesus) and Athens from 431 B.C.E. to 404 B.C.E., and which ended in the defeat of Athens and the loss of her imperial power.

perestroika Introduced by Soviet leader Mikhail Gorbachev in June 1987, *perestroika* was the name given to economic and political reforms begun earlier in his tenure. It restructured the state bureaucracy, reduced the privileges of the political elite, and instituted a shift from the centrally planned economy to a mixed economy, combining planning with the operation of market forces.

Periclean Athens Following his election as *strategos* in 461 B.C.E., Pericles pushed through political reforms in Athens, which gave poorer citizens greater influence in politics. He promoted Athenians' sense of superiority through ambitious public works projects and lavish festivals to honor the gods, thus ensuring his continual reelection. But eventually, Athens' growing arrogance and aggression alienated it from the rest of the Greek world.

Pericles (c. 495–429) Athenian politician who occupied the office of strategos for thirty years and who presided over a series of civic reforms, building campaigns, and imperialist initiatives.

Persian Empire Consolidated by Cyrus the Great in 559, this empire eventually stretched from the Persian Gulf to the Mediterranean and also encompassed Egypt. Persian rulers were able to hold this empire together through a policy of tolerance and a mixture of local and centralized governance. This imperial model of government would be adopted by many future empires.

Persian Wars (490–479 B.C.E.) In 501 B.C.E., a political conflict between the Greek ruler of Miletus, Aristagoras, and the Persian Emperor, Darius, sparked the first of the Persian Wars when Darius sent an army to punish Athens for its intervention on the side of the Greeks. Despite being heavily outnumbered, Athenian hoplites defeated the Persian army at the plain of Marathon. In 480 B.C.E., Darius's son Xerxes invaded Greece but was defeated at sea and on land by combined Greek forces under the leadership of Athens and Sparta.

Peter the Great (1672–1725) Energetic tsar who transformed Russia into a leading European country by centralizing government, modernizing the army, creating a navy, and reforming education and the economy.

Francesco Petrarca (Petrarch) (1304–1374) Italian scholar who revived interest in classical writing styles and was famed for his vernacular love sonnets.

pharaoh A term meaning "household" which became the title borne by the rulers of ancient Egypt. The pharaoh was regarded as the divine representative of the gods and the embodiment of Egypt itself. The powerful and centralized bureaucratic state ruled by the pharaohs was more stable and longlived than any another civilization in world history, lasting (with few interruptions) for approximately 3,000 years.

Pharisees A group of Jewish teachers and preachers who emerged in the third century B.C.E. They insisted that all of Yahweh's (God's) commandments were binding on all Jews.

Philip II (382–336 B.C.E.) King of Macedonia and father of Alexander, he consolidated the southern Balkans and the Greek citystates under Macedonian domination.

Philip II of Spain King of Spain from 1556–98 and briefly King of England and Ireland during his marriage to Queen Mary I of England. As a staunch Catholic, Philip responded with military might to the desecration of Catholic churches in the Spanish Netherlands in the 1560s. When commercial conflict with England escalated, Philip sent the Spanish Armada to conquer England in 1588, but it was largely destroyed by stormy weather.

Philip II Augustus (1165–1223) The first French ruler to use the title "king of France" rather than "king of the French." After he captured Normandy and its adjacent territories from the English, he built an effective system of local administration, which recognized regional diversity while promoting centralized royal control. This administrative pattern would characterize French government until the French Revolution.

Philip IV of France King of France from 1285 until his death, Philip's conflict with Pope Boniface VIII led to the transfer of the papal court to Avignon from 1309 to 1378.

Philistines Descendants of the Sea Peoples who fled to the region that now bears their name, Palestine, after their defeat at the hands of the pharaoh Ramses III. They dominated their neighbors, the Hebrews, who used writing as an effective means of discrediting them (the Philistines themselves did not leave a written record to contest the Hebrews' views).

philosophe During the Enlightenment, this word referred to a person whose reflections were unhampered by the constraints of religion or dogma.

Phoenicians A Semitic people known for their trade in exotic purple dyes and other luxury goods, they originally settled in present-day Lebanon around 1200 B.C.E. and from there established commercial colonies throughout the Mediterranean, notably Carthage.

Plato (429–349 B.C.E.) A student of Socrates, Plato dedicated his life to transmitting his teacher's legacy through the writing of dialogues on philosophical subjects, in which Socrates himself plays the major role. The longest and most famous of these, known as the *Republic*, describes an idealized polis governed by a superior group of individuals chosen for their natural attributes of intelligence and character, who rule as "philosopher-kings."

Plotinus (204–270 C.E.) A Neoplatonist philosopher who taught that everything in existence has its ultimate source in the divine, and that the highest goal of life should be the mystic reunion of the soul with this divine source, something that can be achieved through contemplation and asceticism. This outlook blended with that of early Christianity and was instrumental in the spread of that religion within the Roman Empire.

poleis One of the major political innovations of the ancient Greeks was the *polis*, or city-state (plural *poleis*). These independent social and political entities began to emerge in the ninth century B.C.E., organized around an urban center and fostering markets, meeting places, and religious worship; frequently, poleis also controlled some surrounding territory.

Marco Polo (1254–1324) Venetian merchant who traveled through Asia for twenty years and published his observations in a widely read memoir.

population growth In the nineteenth century, Europe experienced a dramatic population growth. During this period, the spread of rural manufacturing allowed men and women to begin marrying younger and raising families earlier, which increased the size of the average family. As the population grew, the portion of young and fertile people also increased, which reinforced the population growth. By 1900, population growth was strongest in Britain and Germany, and slower in France.

portolan charts Also known as *portolani*, these special charts were invented by medieval mariners during the fourteenth century and were used to map locations of ports and sea routes, while also taking note of prevailing winds and other conditions at sea.

Potsdam (1945) At this conference, Truman, Churchill and Stalin met to discuss their options at the conclusion of the Second World War, including making territorial changes to Germany and its allies and the question of war reparations.

Prague spring A period of political liberalization in Czechoslovakia between January and August 1968 that was initiated by Alexander Dubček, the Czech leader. This period of expanding freedom and openness in this Eastern bloc nation ended on August 20, when the USSR and Warsaw Pact countries invaded with 200,000 troops and 5,000 tanks.

pre-Socratics A group of philosophers in the Greek city of Miletus, who raised questions about humans' relationship with the natural world and the gods and who formulated rational theories to explain the physical universe they observed. Their name reflects the fact that they flourished prior to the lifetime of Socrates.

price revolution An unprecedented inflation in prices in the latter half of the sixteenth century, resulting in part from the enormous influx of silver bullion from Spanish America.

principate Modern term for the centuries of autocratic rule by the successors of Augustus, who seized power in 27 B.C.E. and styled himself *princeps* or Rome's "first man." See **Roman Republic**.

printing press Introduced in Europe by Johannes Gutenberg of Mainz in 1453–55, this new technology quickly revolutionized communication and played a significant role in political, religious, and intellectual revolutions.

Protestantism The name given to the many dissenting varieties of Christianity that emerged during the Reformation in sixteenth-century western Europe. While Protestant beliefs and practices differed widely, all were united in their rejection of papal authority and the dogmas of the Roman Catholic Church.

provisional government After the collapse of the Russian monarchy, leaders in the Duma organized this government and hoped to establish a democratic system under constitutional rule. They also refused to concede military defeat, and it was impossible to institute domestic reforms and fight a war at the same time. As conditions worsened, the Bolsheviks gained support. In October 1917, they attacked the provisional government and seized control.

Claudius Ptolomeus, called Ptolemy (c. 85–165 C.E.) A Greek-speaking geographer and astronomer active in Roman Alexandria, he rejected the findings of previous Hellenistic scientists in favor of the erroneous theories of Aristotle, publishing highly influential treatises that promulgated these errors and suppressed (for example) the accurate findings of Aristarchus (who had discovered the Heliocentric universe) and Erathosthenes (who had calculated the circumference of the earth).

Ptolemaic system Ptolemy of Alexandria promoted Aristotle's understanding of cosmology. In this system, the heavens orbit the earth in an organized hierarchy of spheres, and the earth and the heavens are made of different matter and subject to different laws of motion. A prime mover produces the motion of the celestial bodies.

Ptolemy (c. 367–c. 284 B.C.E.) One of Alexander the Great's trusted generals (and possibly his half brother), he became pharaoh of Egypt and founded a new dynasty that lasted until that kingdom's absorption into the Roman Empire in 30 B.C.E.

public sphere Between the official realm of state activities and the private realm of the household and individual, lies the "public sphere." The public sphere has a political dimension—it is the space of debate, discussion, and expressions of popular opinion. It also has an economic dimension—it is where business is conducted, where commercial transactions take place, where people enter into contracts, search for work, or hire employees.

Punic Wars (264–146 B.C.E.) Three periods of warfare between Rome and Carthage, two maritime empires who struggled for dominance of the Mediterranean. Rome emerged as the victor, destroyed the city of Carthage and took control of Sicily, North Africa and Hispania (Spain).

pyramid Constructed during the third millennium B.C.E., these structures were monuments to the power and divinity of the pharaohs entombed inside them.

Qur'an (often Koran) Islam's holy scriptures, comprised of the prophecies revealed to Muhammad and redacted during and after his death.

Raphael (Raffaelo Sanzio) (1483–1520) Italian painter active in Rome, his works include *The School of Athens*.

realism Artistic and literary style which sought to portray common situations as they would appear in reality.

Realpolitik Political strategy based on advancing power for its own sake.

reason The human capacity to solve problems and discover truth in ways that can be verified intellectually. Philosophers distinguish the knowledge gained from reason from the teachings of instinct, imagination, and faith, which are verified according to different criteria.

Reformation Religious and political movement in sixteenth-century Europe that led to a break between dissenting forms of Christianity and the Roman Catholic Church; notable figures include Martin Luther and John Calvin.

Reich A term for the German state. The First Reich corresponded to the Holy Roman Empire (9th c.–1806), the Second Reich was from 1871 to 1919, and the Third Reich lasted from 1933 through May 1945.

Renaissance From the French word meaning "rebirth," this term came to be used in the nineteenth century to describe the artistic, intellectual, and cultural movement that emerged in Italy after 1300 and that sought to recover and emulate the heritage of the classical past.

Restoration period (1815–1848) European movement after the defeat of Napoleon to restore Europe to its pre–French Revolution status and to prevent the spread of revolutionary or liberal political movements.

Cardinal Richelieu (1585–1642) First minister to King Louis XIII, he is considered by many to have ruled France in all but name, centralizing political power and suppressing dissent.

Roman army Under the Republic, the Roman army was made up of citizen-soldiers who were required to serve in wartime. As Rome's empire grew, the need for more fighting men led to the extension of citizenship rights and, eventually, to the development of a vast, professional, standing army that numbered as many as 300,000 by the middle of the third century B.C.E. By that time, however, citizens were not themselves required to serve, and many legions were made up of paid conscripts and foreign mercenaries.

Roman citizenship The rights and responsibilities of Rome's citizens were gradually extended to the free (male) inhabitants of other Italian provinces and later to most provinces in the Roman world. In contrast to slaves and non-Romans, Romans had the right to be tried in an imperial court and could not be legally subjected to torture.

Roman Republic The Romans traced the founding of their republic to the overthrow of their last king and the establishment of a unique form of constitutional government, in which the power of the aristocracy (embodied by the Senate) was checked by the executive rule of two elected consuls and the collective will of the people. For hundreds of years, this balance of power provided the Republic with a measure of political stability and prevented any single individual or clique from gaining too much power.

Romanticism Beginning in Germany and England in the late eighteenth century and continuing up to the end of the nineteenth century, Romanticism was a movement in art, music, and literature that countered the rationalism of the Enlightenment by placing greater value on human emotions and the power of nature to stimulate creativity.

Jean-Jacques Rousseau (1712–1778) Philosopher and radical political theorist whose *Social Contract* attacked privilege and inequality. One of the primary principles of Rousseau's political philosophy is that politics and morality should not be separated.

Royal Society This British society's goal was to pursue collective research. Members would conduct experiments, record the results, and share them with their peers, who would study the methods, reproduce the experiment, and assess the results. The arrangement gave English scientists a sense of common purpose as well as a system to reach a consensus on facts.

Russian Revolution of 1905 After Russia's defeat in the Russo-Japanese War, Russians began clamoring for political reforms. Protests grew over the course of 1905, and the autocracy lost control of entire towns and regions as workers went on strike, soldiers mutinied, and peasants revolted. Forced to yield, Tsar Nicholas II issued the October Manifesto, which pledged individual liberties and provided for the election of a parliament (called the Duma). The most radical of the revolutionary groups were put down with force, and the pace of political change remained very slow in the aftermath of the revolution.

Russo-Japanese War (1904–1905) Japanese and Russian expansion collided in Mongolia and Manchuria. Russia was humiliated after the Japanese navy sunk its fleet, which helped provoke a revolt in Russia and led to an American-brokered peace treaty.

sacrament A sacred rite. In the Catholic tradition, the administration of the sacraments is considered necessary for salvation.

Saint Bartholomew's Day Massacre The mass murder of French Protestants (Huguenots) instigated by Queen Catherine de' Medici of France and carried out by Catholics. It began in Paris on 24 August 1572 and spread to other parts of France, continuing into October of that year. More than 70,000 people were killed.

salons Informal gatherings of intellectuals and aristocrats that allowed discourse about Enlightenment ideas.

Sappho (c. 620–c. 550 B.C.E.) One of the most celebrated Greek poets, she was revered as "the Tenth Muse" and emulated by many male poets. Ironically, though, only two of her poems survive intact, and the rest must be pieced together from fragments quoted by later poets.

Sargon the Great (r. 2334–2279 B.C.E.) The Akkadian ruler who consolidated power in Mesopotamia.

SARS epidemic (2003) The successful containment of severe acute respiratory syndrome (SARS) is an example of how international health organizations can effectively work together to recognize and respond to a disease outbreak. The disease itself, however, is a reminder of the dangers that exist in a globalized economy with a high degree of mobility in both populations and goods.

Schlieffen Plan Devised by German general Alfred von Schlieffen in 1905 to avoid the dilemma of a two-front war against France and Russia. The Schlieffen Plan required that Germany attack France first through Belgium and secure a quick victory before wheeling to the east to meet the slower armies of the Russians on the Eastern Front. The Schlieffen Plan was put into operation on August 2, 1914, at the outset of the First World War.

scientific revolution of antiquity The Hellenistic period was the most brilliant age in the history of science before the seventeenth century C.E. Aristarchus of Samos posited the existence of a heliocentric universe. Eratosthenes of Alexandria accurately calculated the circumference of the earth. Archimedes turned physics into its own branch of experimental science. Hellenistic anatomists became the first to practice human dissection, which improved their understanding of human physiology. Ironically, most of these discoveries were suppressed by pseudo-scientists who flourished under the Roman Empire during the second century C.E., notably Claudus Ptolomeus Ptolemy) and Aelius Galenus (Galen).

second industrial revolution The technological developments in the last third of the nineteenth century, which included new techniques for refining and producing steel; increased availability of electricity for industrial, commercial, and domestic use; advances in chemical manufacturing; and the creation of the internal combustion engine.

Second World War Worldwide war that began in September 1939 in Europe, and even earlier in Asia (the Japanese invasion of Manchuria began in 1931), pitting Britain, the United States, and the Soviet Union (the Allies) against Nazi Germany, Italy, and Japan (the Axis). The war ended in 1945 with Germany and Japan's defeat.

Seleucus (d. 280 B.C.E.) The Macedonian general who ruled the Persian heartland of Alexander the Great's empire.

Semitic The Semitic language family has the longest recorded history of any linguistic group and is the root for most languages of the Middle and Near East. Ancient Semitic languages include those of the ancient Babylonians and Assyrians, Phoenician, the classical form of Hebrew, early dialects of Aramaic, and the classical Arabic of the Qu'ran.

Sepoy Mutiny of 1857 See **Indian Rebellion of 1857**.

serfdom Peasant labor. Unlike slaves, serfs are "attached" to the land they work, and are not supposed to be sold apart from that land.

William Shakespeare (1564–1616) An English playwright who flourished during the reigns of Elizabeth I and James I, Shakespeare received a basic education in his hometown of Stratford-upon-Avon and worked in London as an actor before achieving success as a dramatist and poet.

Shi'ites An often-persecuted minority within Islam, Shi'ites believe that only descendants of Muhammad's successor Ali and his wife Fatimah (Muhammad's daughter) can have any authority over the Muslim community. Today, Shi'ites constitute the ruling party in Iran and are numerous in Iraq but otherwise comprise only 10 percent of Muslims worldwide.

Abbé Sieyès (1748–1836) In 1789, he wrote the pamphlet "What is the Third Estate?" in which he posed fundamental questions about the rights of the Third Estate and helped provoke its secession from the Estates-General. He was a leader at the Tennis Court Oath, but he later helped Napoleon seize power.

Sinn Féin The Irish revolutionary organization that formed in 1900 to fight for Irish independence.

Sino-Japanese War (1894–1895) Conflict over the control of Korea in which China was forced to cede the province of Taiwan to Japan.

slave revolt in Saint-Domingue (1791–1804) In September of 1791, the largest slave rebellion in history broke out in Saint-Domingue, an important French colony in the Caribbean. In 1794, the revolutionary government in France abolished slavery in the colonies, though this act was essentially only recognizing the liberty that the slaves had seized by their own actions. Napoleon reestablished slavery in the French Caribbean in 1802, but failed in his attempt to reconquer Saint-Domingue. Armies commanded by former slaves succeeded in winning independence for a new nation, Haiti, in 1804, making the revolt in Saint-Domingue the first successful slave revolt in history.

slavery The practice of subjugating people to a life of bondage, and of selling or trading these unfree people. For most of human history, slavery had no racial or ethnic basis, and was widely practiced by all cultures and civilizations. Anyone could become a slave, for example, by being captured in war or by being sold for the payment of a debt. It was only in the fifteenth century, with the growth of the African slave trade, that slavery came to be associated with particular races and peoples.

Adam Smith (1723–1790) Scottish economist and liberal philosopher who proposed that competition between self-interested individuals led naturally to a healthy economy. He became famous for his influential book, *The Wealth of Nations* (1776).

Social Darwinism Belief that Charles Darwin's theory of natural selection (evolution) was applicable to human societies and justified the right of the ruling classes or countries to dominate the weak.

social democracy The belief that democracy and social welfare go hand in hand and that diminishing the sharp inequalities of class society is crucial to fortifying democratic culture.

socialism Political ideology that calls for a classless society with collective ownership of all property.

Society of Jesus See **Jesuits**.

Socrates (469–399 B.C.E.) The Athenian philosopher and teacher who promoted the careful examination of all inherited opinions and assumptions on the grounds that "the unexamined life is not worth living." A veteran of the Peloponnesian War, he was tried and condemned by his fellow citizens for engaging in allegedly seditious activities and was executed in 399 B.C.E. His most influential pupils were the philosopher Plato and the historian and social commentator Xenophon.

Solon (d. 559 B.C.E.) Elected archon in 594 B.C.E., this Athenian aristocrat enacted a series of political and economic reforms that formed the basis of Athenian democracy.

Somme (1916) During this battle of the First World War, Allied forces attempted to take entrenched German positions from July to mid-November of 1916. Neither side was able to make any real gains despite massive casualties: 500,000 Germans, 400,000 British, and 200,000 French.

Soviet bloc International alliance that included the East European countries of the Warsaw Pact as well as the Soviet Union; it also came to include Cuba.

soviets Local councils elected by workers and soldiers in Russia. Socialists started organizing these councils in 1905, and the Petrograd soviet in the capital emerged as one of the centers of power after the Russian monarchy collapsed in 1917 in the midst of World War I. The soviets became increasingly powerful and pressed for social reform, the redistribution of land, and called for Russian withdrawal from the war effort.

Spanish-American War (1898) War between the United States and Spain in Cuba, Puerto Rico, and the Philippines. It ended with a treaty in which the United States took over the Philippines, Guam, and Puerto Rico; Cuba won partial independence.

Spanish Armada Supposedly invincible fleet of warships sent against England by Philip II of Spain in 1588 but vanquished by the English fleet and bad weather in the English Channel.

Sparta Around 650 B.C.E., after the suppression of a slave revolt, Spartan rulers militarized their society in order to prevent future rebellions and to protect Sparta's superior position in Greece, orienting their society toward the maintenance of their army. Sparta briefly joined forces with Athens and other poleis in the second war with Persia in 480–479 B.C.E., but these two rivals ultimately fell out again in 431 B.C.E. when Sparta and her Peloponnesian allies went to war against Athens and her allies. This bloody conflict lasted until Athens was defeated in 404 B.C.E., after Sparta received military aid from the Persians.

Spartiate A full citizen of Sparta, hence a professional soldier of the hoplite phalanx.

spinning jenny Invention of James Hargreaves (c. 1720–1774) that revolutionized the British textile industry by allowing a worker to spin much more thread than was possible on a hand spinner.

SS (Schutzstaffel) Formed in 1925 to serve as Hitler's personal security force and to guard Nazi party (NSDAP) meetings, the SS grew into a large militarized organization that became notorious for their participation in carrying out Nazi policies.

Joseph Stalin (1879–1953) The Bolshevik leader who succeeded Lenin as the leader of the Soviet Union and ruled until his death in 1953.

Stalingrad (1942–1943) The turning point on the Eastern Front during the Second World War came when the German army tried to take the city of Stalingrad in an effort to break the back of Soviet industry. The German and Soviet armies fought a bitter battle, in which more than a half million German, Italian, and Romanian soldiers were killed and the Soviets suffered over a million casualties. The German army surrendered after over five months of fighting. After Stalingrad, the Soviet army launched a series of attacks that pushed the Germans back.

Stoicism An ancient philosophy derived from the teachings of Zeno of Athens (fl. c. 300) and widely influential within the Roman Empire; it also impacted the development of Christianity. Stoics believe in the essential orderliness of the cosmos, and that everything that occurs happens for the best. Since everything is determined in accordance with rational purpose, no individual is master of his or her fate, and the only agency that human beings have consists in their responses to good fortune or adversity.

Sumerians The ancient inhabitants of southern Mesopotamia (modern Iraq and Kuwait) whose sophisticated civilization emerged around 4000 B.C.E.

Sunnis Proponents of Islam's customary religious practices (*sunna*) as they developed under the first two caliphs to succeed Muhammad, his father-in-law Abu-Bakr and his disciple Umar.

Sunni orthodoxy is dominant within Islam but is opposed by the Shi'ites (from the Arabic word *shi'a*, "faction").

syndicalists A nineteenth-century political movement that embraced a strategy of strikes and sabotage by workers. Their hope was that a general strike of all workers would bring down the capitalist state and replace it with workers' syndicates or trade associations. Their refusal to participate in politics limited their ability to command a wide influence.

tabula rasa Term used by John Locke (1632–1704) to describe man's mind before he acquired ideas as a result of experience; Latin for "clean slate."

Tennis Court Oath (1789) Oath taken by representatives of the Third Estate in June 1789, in which they pledged to form a National Assembly and write a constitution limiting the powers of the king.

Reign of Terror (1793–1794) Campaign at the height of the French Revolution in which violence, including systematic executions of opponents of the revolution, was used to purge France of its "enemies" and to extend the revolution beyond its borders; radicals executed as many as 40,000 persons who were judged enemies of the state.

Tetrarchy The result of Diocletian's political reforms of the late third century C.E., which divided the Roman Empire into four quadrants.

Theban Hegemony The term describing the period when the polis of Thebes dominated the Greek mainland, which reached its height after 371 B.C.E., under leadership of the Theban general Epaminondas. It was in Thebes that the future King Philip II of Macedon spent his youth, and it was the defeat of Thebes and Athens at the hands of Philip and Alexander—at the Battle of Chaeronea in 338—that Macedonian hegemony was forcefully asserted.

theory of evolution Darwin's theory that linked biology to history. Darwin believed that competition between different organisms and struggle with the environment were fundamental and unavoidable facts of life. In this struggle, those individuals who were better adapted to their environment survived, whereas the weak perished. This produced a "natural selection," or favoring of certain adaptive traits over time, leading to a gradual evolution of different species.

Third Estate The population of France under the Old Regime was divided into three estates, corporate bodies that determined an individual's rights or obligations under royal law. The nobility constituted the First Estate, the clergy the Second, and the commoners (the vast bulk of the population) made up the Third Estate.

Third Reich The German state from 1933 to 1945 under Adolf Hitler and the Nazi party.

Third World nations—mostly in Asia, Latin America, and Africa—that are not highly industrialized.

Thirty Years' War (1618–1648) Beginning as a conflict between Protestants and Catholics in Germany, this series of skirmishes escalated into a general European war fought on German soil by armies from Sweden, France, and the Holy Roman Empire.

Timur the Lame (1336–1405) Also known as Tamerlane, he was the last ruler of the Mongol Khans' Asian empire.

Marshal Tito (1892–1980) The Yugoslavian communist and resistance leader who became the leader of Yugoslavia and fought to keep his government independent of the Soviet Union. In response, the Soviet Union expelled Yugoslavia from the communist countries' economic and military pacts.

towns Centers for markets and administration. Towns existed in a symbiotic relationship with the countryside. They provided markets for surplus food from outlying farms as well as producing manufactured goods. In the Middle Ages, towns tended to grow up around a castle or monastery which afforded protection.

transatlantic triangle The trading of African slaves by European colonists to address labor shortages in the Americas and the Caribbean. Slaves were treated like cargo, loaded onto ships and sold in exchange for molasses, tobacco, rum, and other precious commodities.

Treaty of Brest-Litovsk (1918) Separate peace between imperial Germany and the new Bolshevik regime in Russia. The treaty acknowledged the German victory on the Eastern Front and withdrew Russia from the war.

Treaty of Utrecht (1713) Resolution to the War of Spanish Succession that reestablished a balance of power in Europe, to the benefit of Britain and in ways that disadvantaged Spain, Holland, and France.

Treaty of Versailles Signed on June 28, 1919, this peace settlement ended the First World War and required Germany to surrender a large part of its most valuable territories and to pay huge reparations to the Allies.

trench warfare Weapons such as barbed wire and the machine gun gave tremendous advantage to defensive positions in World War I, leading to prolonged battles between entrenched armies in fixed positions. The trenches eventually consisted of 25,000 miles of holes and ditches that stretched across the Western Front in northern France, from the Atlantic coast to the Swiss border during the First World War. On the eastern front, the large expanse of territories made trench warfare less significant.

triangular trade The eighteenth-century commercial Atlantic shipping pattern that took rum from New England to Africa, traded it for slaves taken to the West Indies, and brought sugar back to New England to be processed into rum.

Triple Entente Alliance developed before the First World War that eventually included Britain, France, and Russia.

Truman Doctrine (1947) Declaration promising U.S. economic and military intervention to counter any attempt by the Soviet Union to expand its influence. Often cited as a key moment in the origins of the Cold War.

tsar Russian word for "emperor," derived from the Latin *caesar* and similar to the German *kaiser,* it was the title claimed by the rulers of medieval Muscovy and of the later Russian Empire.

Ubaid culture An early civilization that flourished in Mesopotamia between 5500 and 4000 B.C.E., it was characterized by large village settlements and temple complexes: a precursor to the more urban civilization of the Sumerians.

Umayyad Caliphate (661–930) The Umayyad family resisted the authority of the first two caliphs who succeeded Muhammad but eventually placed a member of their own family in that position of power. The Umayyad Caliphate ruled the Islamic world from 661 to 750, modeling their administration on that of the Roman Empire. But after a rebellion led by the rival Abbasid family, the power of the Umayyad Caliphate was confined to their territories in al-Andalus (Spain).

Universal Declaration of Human Rights (1948) United Nations declaration that laid out the rights to which all human beings were entitled.

University of Paris The reputation of Peter Abelard and his students attracted many intellectuals to Paris in the twelfth century, some of whom began offering instruction to aspiring scholars. By 1200, this loose association of teachers had formed themselves into a *universitas,* or corporation. They began collaborating in the higher academic study of the liberal arts with a special emphasis on theology.

Pope Urban II (1042?–1099) Instigator of the First Crusade (1096–1099), who promised that anyone who fought or died in the service of the Church would receive absolution from sin.

urban populations During the nineteenth century, urban populations in Europe increased sixfold. For the most part, urban areas had medieval infrastructures, which new populations and industries overwhelmed. As a result, many European cities became overcrowded and unhealthy.

Utopia Title of a semi-satirical social critique by the English statesman Sir Thomas More (1478–1535); the word derives from the Greek "best place" or "no place."

Lorenzo Valla (1407–1457) One of the first practitioners of scientific philology (the historical study of language), Valla's analysis of the so-called Donation of Constantine showed that the document could not possibly have been written in the fourth century C.E., but must have been forged centuries later.

vassal A person who pledges to be loyal and subservient to a lord in exchange for land, income, or protection.

velvet revolutions The peaceful political revolutions throughout Eastern Europe in 1989.

Verdun (1916) This battle between German and French forces lasted for ten months during the First World War. The Germans saw the battle as a chance to break French morale through a war of attrition, and the French believed the battle to be a symbol of France's strength. In the end, over 400,000 lives were lost and the German offensive failed.

Versailles Conference (1919) Peace conference between the victors of the First World War; resulted in the Treaty of Versailles, which forced Germany to pay reparations and to give up its colonies to the victors.

Queen Victoria (1819–1901) Influential monarch who reigned from 1837 until her death; she presided over the expansion of the British Empire as well as the evolution of English politics and social and economic reforms.

Viet Cong Vietnamese communist group formed in 1954; committed to overthrowing the government of South Vietnam and reunifying North and South Vietnam.

Vikings (800–1000) The collapse of the Abbasid Caliphate disrupted Scandinavian commercial networks and turned traders into raiders (the word *viking* describes the activity of raiding). These raids often escalated into invasions that contributed to the collapse of the Carolingian Empire, resulted in the devastation of settled territories, and ended with the establishment of Viking colonies. By the tenth century, Vikings controlled areas of eastern England, Scotland, the islands of Ireland, Iceland, Greenland, and parts of northern France. They had also established the beginnings of the kingdom that became Russia and made exploratory voyages to North America, founding a settlement at Newfoundland (Canada).

A Vindication of the Rights of Woman Noted work of Mary Wollstonecraft (1759–1797), English republican who applied Enlightenment political ideas to issues of gender.

Virgil (70–19 B.C.E.) An influential Roman poet who wrote under the patronage of the emperor Augustus. His *Aeneid* mimicked the ancient Greek epics of Homer and told the mythical tale of Rome's founding by the Trojan refugee Aeneas.

Visigoths The tribes of "west" Goths who sacked Rome in 410 C.E. and later established a kingdom in the Roman province of Hispania (Spain).

Voltaire Pseudonym of French philosopher and satirist François Marie Arouet (1694–1778), who championed the cause of human dignity against state and Church oppression. Noted deist and author of *Candide.*

Lech Wałęsa (1943–) Leader of the Polish labor movement Solidarity, which organized a series of strikes across Poland in 1980. They protested working conditions, shortages, and high prices. Above all, they demanded an independent labor union. Solidarity's leaders were imprisoned and the union banned, but they launched a new series of strikes in 1988, which led to the legalization of Solidarity and open elections.

war communism The Russian civil war forced the Bolsheviks to take a more radical economic stance. They requisitioned grain from the peasantry and outlawed private trade in consumer goods as "speculation." They also militarized production facilities and abolished money.

Wars of the Roses Fifteenth-century civil conflict between the English dynastic houses of Lancaster and York, each of which was symbolized by the heraldic device of a rose (red and white, respectively). It was ultimately resolved by the accession of the Lancastrian king Henry VII, who married Elizabeth of York.

Warsaw Pact (1955–1991) Military alliance between the USSR and other communist states that was established as a response to the creation of the NATO alliance.

The Wealth of Nations 1776 treatise by Adam Smith, whose laissez-faire ideas predicted the economic boom of the Industrial Revolution.

Weimar Republic The government of Germany between 1919 and the rise of Hitler and the Nazi party.

Western Front Military front that stretched from the English Channel through Belgium and France to the Alps during the First World War.

Whites Refers to the "counterrevolutionaries" of the Bolshevik Revolution (1918–1921) who fought the Bolsheviks (the "Reds"); included former supporters of the tsar, Social Democrats, and large independent peasant armies.

William the Conqueror (1027–1087) Duke of Normandy who laid claim to the throne of England in 1066, defeating the

Anglo-Saxon King Harold at the Battle of Hastings. He and his Norman followers imposed imperial rule in England through a brutal campaign of military conquest, surveillance, and the suppression of the indigenous Anglo-Saxon language.

William of Ockham (d. 1349) An English philosopher and Franciscan friar, he denied that human reason could prove fundamental theological truths, such as the existence of God: he argued that there is no necessary connection between the observable laws of nature and the unknowable essence of divinity. His theories, derived from the work of earlier scholastics, form the basis of the scientific method.

Woodrow Wilson (1856–1924) U.S. president who requested and received a declaration of war from Congress so that America could enter the First World War. After the war, his prominent role in the Paris Peace Conference signaled the rise of the United States as a world power. He also proposed the Fourteen Points, which influenced the peace negotiations.

Maria Winkelmann (1670–1720) German astronomer who worked with her husband in his observatory. Despite discovering a comet and preparing calendars for the Berlin Academy of Sciences, the academy would not let her take her husband's place within the body after he died.

witch craze The rash of persecutions that took place in both Catholic and Protestant countries of early modern Europe and their colonies, facilitated by secular governments and religious authorities.

women's associations Because European women were excluded from the workings of parliamentary and mass politics, some women formed organizations to press for political and civil rights. Some groups focused on establishing educational opportunities for women while others campaigned energetically for the vote.

William Wordsworth (1770–1850) Romantic writer whose central themes were nature, simplicity, and feeling. He considered nature to be man's most trustworthy teacher and source of sublime power that nourished the human soul.

World Bank International agency established in 1944 to provide economic assistance to war-torn nations and countries in need of economic development.

John Wycliffe (c. 1330–1384) A professor of theology at the University of Oxford, Wycliffe urged the English king to confiscate ecclesiastical wealth and to replace corrupt priests and bishops with men who would live according to the apostolic standards of poverty and piety. He advocated direct access to the scriptures and promoted an English translation of the Bible. His teachings played an important role in the Peasants' Revolt of 1381 and inspired the still more radical initiatives of a group known as Lollards.

Xerxes (519?–465 B.C.E.) Xerxes succeeded his father, Darius, as Great King of Persia. Seeking to avenge his father's shame and eradicate any future threats to Persian hegemony, he launched his own invasion of Greece in 480 B.C.E. An allied Greek army defeated his forces in 479 B.C.E.

Yalta Accords Meeting among President Franklin D. Roosevelt, Prime Minister Winston Churchill, and Premier Joseph Stalin that occurred in the Crimea in 1945 shortly before the end of the Second World War to plan for the postwar order.

Young Turks The 1908 Turkish reformist movement that aimed to modernize the Ottoman Empire, restore parliamentary rule, and depose Sultan Abdul Hamid II.

ziggurats Temples constructed under the Dynasty of Ur in what is now Iraq, beginning around 2100 B.C.E.

Zionism A political movement dating to the end of the nineteenth century holding that the Jewish people constitute a nation and are entitled to a national homeland. Zionists rejected a policy of Jewish assimilation and advocated the reestablishment of a Jewish homeland in Palestine.

Zollverein In 1834, Prussia started a customs union, which established free trade among the German states and a uniform tariff against the rest of the world. By the 1840s, the union included almost all of the German states except German Austria. It is considered an important precedent for the political unification of Germany, which was completed in 1870 under Prussian leadership.

Zoroastrianism One of the three major universal faiths of the ancient world, alongside Judaism and Christianity, it was derived from the teachings of the Persian Zoroaster around 600 B.C.E. Zoroaster redefined religion as an ethical practice common to all, rather than as a set of rituals and superstitions that cause divisions among people. Zoroastrianism teaches that there is one supreme god in the universe, Ahura-Mazda (Wise Lord) but that his goodness will be constantly assailed by the forces of evil until the arrival of a final "judgment day." Proponents of this faith should therefore help good to triumph over evil by leading a good life, and by performing acts of compassion and charity. Zoroastrianism exercised a profound influence over many early Christians, including Augustine.

Ulrich Zwingli (1484–1531) A former priest from the Swiss city of Zurich, Zwingli joined Luther and Calvin in attacking the authority of the Roman Catholic Church.

Leon B. Alberti: "On the Family" from *The Family in Renaissance Florence*, trans./ed. by Renée Neu Watkins (University of South Carolina Press, 1969), pp. 208–213. Reprinted by permission of the translator.

Aristophanes: 300 words from *Lysistrata and Other Plays* by Aristophanes, translated with an introduction by Alan H. Sommerstein (Penguin Classics, 1973). Copyright © Alan H. Sommerstein, 1973. Reproduced by permission of Penguin Books Ltd.

Arrian: 300 words from *The Campaigns of Alexander* by Arrian, translated by Aubrey de Sélincourt, revised with an introduction and notes by J.R. Hamilton (Penguin Classics 1958, Revised edition 1971). Copyright © the Estate of Aubrey de Sélincourt, 1958. Introduction and Notes copyright © J.R. Hamilton, 1971. Reproduced by permission of Penguin Books Ltd.

Nels Bailkey (ed.): From Bailkey, *Readings in Ancient History*, 5th Edition. © 1996 Wadsworth, a part of Cengage Learning, Inc. Reproduced by permission. www.cengage.com/permissions.

Armand Bellee (ed.): *Cahiers de plaintes & doleances des paroisses de la province du Maine pour les Etats-generaux de 1789*, 4 vols. (Le Mans: Monnoyer, 1881-92), 2: 578–82. Translated by the American Social History Project, "Liberty, Equality, Fraternity: Exploring the French Revolution" by Jack R. Censer and Lynn Hunt. Reprinted by permission.

Bernard of Angers: "Miracles of Saint Foy" from *Readings in Medieval History*, 2nd Edition, edited by Patrick J. Geary (Toronto, Ont: University of Toronto Press, 2003). Copyright © 2003. Reprinted by permission of the publisher.

Henry Bettenson (ed.): "Obedience as a Jesuit Hallmark" from *Documents of the Christian Church*, 2nd Edition. Copyright © 1967, Oxford University Press. Reprinted by permission of Oxford University Press.

Gabriel Biel: "Execrabilis." Reprinted by permission of the publisher from *Defensorium Obedientiae Apostolicae Et Alia Documenta* by Gabriel Biel, edited and translated by Heiko A. Oberman, Daniel E. Zerfoss and William J. Courtenay, pp. 224–227, Cambridge, Mass.: The Belknap Press of Harvard University Press, Copyright © 1968 by the President and Fellows of Harvard College.

Jose Bove: *The World Is Not for Sale: Farmers Against Junk Food*, pp. 3–13, © Verso, 2001. Reprinted by permission of the publisher.

Walter Bower: "A Declaration of Scottish Independence," from *Scotichronicon*, Volume 7, by Walter Bower. Edited by B. Scott and D. E. R. Watt. Copyright © 1996 Aberdeen University Press. Reprinted with permission.

Boyer, Baker & Kirshner (eds): "Declaration of the Rights of Man and of the Citizen", "Napoleon's Letter to Prince Eugene" and "Circular Letter to Sovereigns" from *University of Chicago Readings in Western Civilization, Vol. 7*, pp. 238–239; 419–420; 426–427, Copyright © 1987 by The University of Chicago. Reprinted by permission of The University of Chicago Press.

Anna Comnena: 340 words from *The Alexiad of Anna Comnena*, translated by E.R.A. Sewter (Penguin Classics, 1969). Copyright © E.R.A. Sewter, 1969. Reproduced by permission of Penguin Books Ltd.

James Cracraft: "Alexander II's Decree Emancipating the Serfs, 1861," *Major Problems in the History of Imperial Russia*. Copyright © 1994 by D.C. Heath and Company.

David Brion Davis: From *Encyclopédie*, Vol. 16, Neuchâtel, 1765, p. 532 as cited in David Brion Davis, *The Problem of Slavery in Western Culture*. (Ithaca, N.Y.: Cornell University Press, 1966), p. 416. Copyright © 1966 by David Brion Davis. Reprinted by permission.

Simone de Beauvoir: From *The Second Sex* by Simone de Beauvoir, translated by Constance Borde & Sheila Malovany-Chevalier, published by Jonathan Cape, translation copyright © 2009 by Constance Borde and Sheila Malovany-Chevalier, Introduction copyright © 2010 by Judith Thurman. Reprinted by permission of Alfred A. Knopf, a division of Random House, Inc. and The Random House Group Ltd.

Geoffrey de Charny: From *The Book of Chivalry of Geoffrey de Charny: Text, Context, and Translation*, translated by Richard W. Kaeuper and Elspeth Kennedy, pp. 99. Copyright © 1996 University of Pennsylvania Press. Reprinted with permission.

Marie de France: "Equitan" in The Lais of Marie de France, translated by Gllyn S. Burgess and Kieth Burgess. Pp. 56–57. Copyright © 1985. Reproduced by permission of Penguin Books Ltd.

Bartolome de las Casas: 500 words from *A Short Account of the Destruction of the Indies* by Bartolome de las Casas, edited and translated by Nigel Griffin, introduction by Anthony Pagden (Penguin Classics, 1992). Translation and Notes copyright © Nigel Griffin, 1992. Introduction copyright © Anthony Pagden 1992. Reproduced by permission of Penguin Books Ltd.

Michel de Montaigne: From *Montaigne: Selections from the Essays*, translated and edited by Donald M. Frame (Harlan Davidson, Inc., 1973), pp. 34–38. Reprinted by permission of Harlan Davidson, Inc.

Alexis de Tocqueville: From *Recollections: The French Revolution of 1848*; trans. George Lawrence, ed. J.P. Mayer, pp. 436–437. Copyright © 1987 by Transaction Publishers. Reprinted by permission of the publisher.

Rene Descartes: From *A Discourse on the Method of Correctly Conducting One's Reason*, trans. Ian Maclean. Copyright © Ian Maclean 2006. Reprinted by permission of Oxford University Press.

Armand J. du Plessis: "Cardinal Richelieu on the Common People of France," pp. 31–32 from Hill, Henry Bertram, *The Political Testament of Cardinal Richelieu*. © 1961 by the Board of Regents of the University of Wisconsin System. Reprinted by permission of The University of Wisconsin Press.

Ecumenical Councils: "Epitome of the Definition of the Iconoclastic Conciliabulum" from *A Select Library of Nicene and Post-Nicene Fathers of the Christian Church, Vol. XIV*, eds. Schaff & Wace (Grand Rapids, MI: Wm. B. Eerdmans Publishing Company, 1955), pp. 543–544.

Frantz Fanon: Excerpt from *The Wretched of the Earth* by Frantz Fanon, copyright © 1963 by *Présence Africaine*. Used by permission of Grove/Atlantic, Inc.

Robert Filmer: "Observations upon Aristotle's Politiques" (1652), in *Divine Right and Democracy: An Anthology of Political Writing in Stuart England*, edited by David Wootton. Pp 110–18. Copyright © 1986. Reproduced by permission of Penguin Books Ltd.

Gregory L. Freeze (ed.): From *From Supplication to Revolution: A Documentary Social History of Imperial Russia*. Copyright © 1988, Oxford University Press, Inc. Reprinted by permission of Oxford University Press.

Betty Friedan: From *The Feminine Mystique* by Betty Friedan. Copyright © 1983, 1974, 1973, 1963 by Betty Friedan. Used by permission of Victor Gollancz, an imprint of The Orion Publishing Group, London and W.W. Norton & Company, Inc.

Galileo Galilei: From *Discoveries and Opinions of Galileo* by Galileo Galilei, translated by Stillman Drake, copyright © 1957 by Stillman Drake. Used by permission of Doubleday, a division of Random House, Inc.

Mohandas K. Gandhi: From *Hind Swaraj* or *Indian Home Rule* by M.K. Gandhi, p. 56, Ahmedabad: Navajivan Trust, 1946. Reprinted by permission of the publisher.

Pierre Gassendi: From *The Selected Works of Pierre Gassendi*, Edited by Craig B. Brush. (New York: Johnson Reprint Corporation, 1972) pp. 334–336. Reprinted with permission.

Joseph Goebbels: "Why are we enemies of the Jews?" from Snyder, Louis, *Documents of German History*. Copyright © 1958 by Rutgers, the State University. Reprinted by permission of Rutgers University Press.

Homer: *Iliad*, translated by Stanley Lombardo, selections from pp. 115–118. Copyright © 1997 by Hackett Publishing Company, Inc. Reprinted by permission of Hackett Publishing Company, Inc. All rights reserved.

Rosemary Horrox (ed.): From *The Black Death*, by Horrox (Trans., Ed.), 1994, Manchester University Press, Manchester, UK. Reprinted with permission.

Juvenal: 224 words from *The Sixteen Satires* by Juvenal, translated by Peter Green (Penguin Classics 1967, Revised edition 1974). Copyright © Peter Green 1967, 1974. Reproduced by permission of Penguin Books Ltd.

Nikita Khrushchev: "Report to the Communist Party Congress (1961)" from *Current Soviet Policies IV*, eds. Charlotte Saikowski and Leo Gruliow, from the translations of the Current Digest of the Soviet Press. Joint Committee on Slavic Studies, 1962, pp. 42–45. Reprinted by permission of the Current Digest of the Soviet Press.

Maureen Gallery Kovacs (trans.): Excerpts from *The Epic of Gilgamesh*, with an Introduction and Notes by Kovacs, Maureen Gallery, translator. Copyright © 1985, 1989 by the Board of Trustees of the Leland Stanford Junior University. All rights reserved. Used with the permission of Stanford University Press, www.sup.org.

Heda Margolius Kovály: *Under a Cruel Star: A Life in Prague 1941–1968*. Translated from the Czech by Franci Epstein and Helen Epstein with the author. (Cambridge, Mass.: Plunkett Lake Press, 1986), pp. 45–46.

Fritz Lang: "The Future of the Feature Film in Germany" from *The Weimar Republic Sourcebook*, edited by Anton Kaes, Martin Jay, and Edward Dimendberg (Berkeley: University of California Press, 1959), pp. 622–623. © 1994 by the Regents of the University of California. Reprinted by permission of the University of California Press.

Carolyne Larrington: "The Condemnation of Joan of Arc by the University of Paris" from *Women and Writing in Medieval Europe*, Carolyne Larrington, Copyright © 1995 Routledge. Reproduced by permission of Taylor & Francis Books UK.

Transition, pp. 120–122. Copyright © 1991. Reprinted by permission of Oxford University Press.

Martha T. Roth: Excerpts from "The Code of Hammurabi" from *Law Collections from Mesopotamia and Asia Minor*, edited by Martha T. Roth (Scholars Press, 1997), pp. 76–135. Reprinted by permission of Society of Biblical Literature.

Jean Rousseau: From *Rousseau's Political Writings: A Norton Critical Edition*, edited by Alan Ritter and Julia Conaway Bondanella, translated by Julia Conaway Bondanella. Copyright © 1988 by W.W. Norton & Company, Inc. Used by permission of W.W. Norton & Company, Inc.

Reinhard Rürup (ed.): From *Topography of Terror: Gestapo, SS, and Reichssicherheitshauptamt on the "Prinz-Albrecht-Terrain": A Documentation*, pp. 125–127. (Berlin: Verlag Willmuth Arenhövel, 1991) Reprinted with permission.

Richard Sakwa: "Stalin on Industrialism" and "The Bolsheviks Must Seize Power" from *Rise and Fall of the Soviet Union 1917–1991*, by Richard Sakwa. Copyright © 1999 Routledge. Reproduced by permission of Taylor & Francis Books UK.

Samuel the Nagid: "A Hebrew Poem in Praise of Wine." Reprinted from *Wine, Women, and Death: Medieval Hebrew Poems on the Good Life*, © 1986, by Raymond P. Scheindlin, published by The Jewish Publication Society with the permission of the publisher.

Sappho: "Fragment 16" from *The Poetry of Sappho*, translated and notes by Jim Powell, pp. 6–7. Copyright © 2007 by Jim Powell. Reprinted by permission of Oxford University Press. "Sappho to Her Pupils," translated by Lachlan Mackinnon, *Times Literary Supplement*, July 15, 2005. © Lachlan Mackinnon / The Times Literary Supplement / nisyndication.com. Reprinted with permission.

Second Congress of the Communist International: "Theses on the National and Colonial Questions" from Workers *of the World and Oppressed Peoples, Unite!: Proceedings and Documents of the Second Congress, 1920*, Volume 1, pp. 283–288. Edited by John Riddell. New York: Pathfinder Press, 1991.

Michael Sells (trans.): "81: The Overturning" from *Approaching the Qur'an: The Early Revelations*, translated by Michael Sells, pp. 48, 50. Copyright © 1999 by Michael A. Sells. Reprinted by permission of White Cloud Press.

M. C. Seymour (ed.): "The Legend of Prester John" from *Mandeville's Travels*, pp. 195-199. Copyright © 1967, Clarendon Press. Reprinted by permission of Oxford University Press.

Sidonius: Reprinted by permission of the publishers and the Trustees of the Loeb Classical Library from *Sidonius: Volume II – Letters*, Loeb Classical Library Volume 420, prepared by W.H. Semple and E.H. Warmington from material left by W.B. Anderson, pp. 127–129, 181–183, Cambridge, Mass.: Harvard University Press, Copyright © 1965 by the President and Fellows of Harvard College. Loeb Classical Library ® is a registered trademark of the President and Fellows of Harvard College.

Lewis Siegelbaum and Andrei Sokolov: "Letters from Anonymous Workers to the Newspaper Pravda" from *Stalinism as a Way of Life*, pp. 39–41. Copyright © 2004 by Yale University. Reprinted by permission of Yale University Press.

William Kelly Simpson (ed.): "The Prophecies of Neferty" from *The Literature of Ancient Egypt*, pp. 214–220. Copyright © 2003 by Yale University. All rights reserved. Reprinted by permission of Yale University Press.

Denis Mack Smith: "Building the Italian Nation" from *The Making of Italy, 1796-1870* (New York: Harper & Row, 1968), pp. 47–49, 181–182, 224–225. Reprinted by permission of the author.

St. Ambrose: "The Memorial of Symmachus, Prefect of the City" from *A Select Library of Nicene and Post-Nicene Fathers of the Christian Church, Vol. X*, eds. Schaff & Wace (Grand Rapids, MI: Wm. B. Eerdmans Publishing Company, 1955), pp. 414–415.

St. Francis of Assisi: Excerpts from *St. Francis of Assisi: Omnibus of Sources, Volume One*, edited by Marion A. Habig, © 2008 by St. Anthony Messenger Press, are used by permission. All rights reserved.

Tacitus: 480 words from *The Annals of Imperial Rome* by Tacitus, translated with and introduction by Michael Grant (Penguin Classics 1956, Sixth revised edition 1989). Copyright © Michael Grant Publications Ltd, 1956, 1959, 1971, 1973, 1975, 1977, 1989. Reproduced by permission of Penguin Books Ltd.

Simon Taylor (ed.): "National Socialist Campaign Pamphlet" from *Germany, 1918-1933: Revolution, Counter-Revolution, and the Rise of Hitler* (London: Gerald Duckworth and Co., Ltd), p. 106. We have made diligent efforts to contact the copyright holder to obtain permission to reprint this selection. If you have information that would help us, please write to Permissions Department, W. W. Norton & Company, Inc., 500 Fifth Avenue, New York, NY 10110.

Harry S. Truman: From *Memoirs, Vol. 1* (Garden City, NY: Doubleday, 1955), pp. 419–421. Reprinted by permission.

Tyrtaeus: "Exhortation to the Young Hoplite" from *University of Chicago Readings in Western Civilization, Vol. 1*, eds. Adkins & White, pp. 23–24. Copyright © 1986 by The University of Chicago. Reprinted by permission of The University of Chicago Press.

United Nations: From *Report of the Fourth World Conference on Women*, United Nations, 4–15 September 1995 and *Global Outlook 2000: An Economic Social & Environmental Perspective*, United Nations, 1993. Reprinted by permission of the United Nations.

Pontifical Commission for Sacred Archeology; **p. 184**: TopFoto/ The Image Works; **p. 185**: AKG-images/Pirozzi; **p. 189**: Gift of Martin A. Ryerson, 1922.4883. Photograph ©1997, The Art Institute of Chicago; **p. 190**: The Trustees of the British Museum; **p. 191**: The Four Tetrarchs (porphyry), Italian School/Basillica di San Marco, Venice, Italy/The Bridgeman Art Library; **p. 194 (left)**: Wikimedia Commons; **p. 194 (right)**: Wikimedia Commons; **p. 195**: The Trustees of the British Museum; **p. 197 (left)**: ©Julie Woodhouse/Alamy; **p. 197 (right)**: JAY DIRECTO/AFP/Getty Images/Newscom; **p. 198**: Erich Lessing/Art Resource, NY; **p. 201**: akg-images/ullstein bild; **p. 205**: By permission of the Houghton Library, Harvard University; **p. 208**: Scala/Art Resource, NY.

Chapter 7: p. 210: AKG-images; **p. 214 (top)**: Scala/Art Resource, NY; **p. 214 (bottom)**: Scala/Art Resource, NY; **p. 216**: Greek fire, Fol. 34v from the Madrid Skylitzes (vellum), Byzantine School, (12th century) / Biblioteca Nacional, Madrid, Spain / The Bridgeman Art Library; **p. 217**: Gianni Dagli Orti/The Art Archive at Art Resource, NY; **p. 220**: Vanni/Art Resource, NY; **p. 221**: The Art Archive/ Dagli Orti; **p. 223**: Jamal Nasrallah/epa/Corbis; **p. 225**: Frédéric Soltan/Sygma/Corbis; **p. 226**: Bildarchiv Preussischer Kulturbesitz / Art Resource, NY: **p. 228 (left)**: Galerie Bilderwelt/Getty Images; **p. 228 (right)**: NeocoreGames/Wikimedia; **p. 230 (left)**: Birmingham Museums & Art Gallery; **p. 230 (right)**: The Trustees of the British Museum/Art Resource, NY; **p. 231 (top)**: The Trustees of the British Museum; **p. 231 (left)**: The Trustees of the British Museum; **p. 231 (right)**: The Trustees of the British Museum; **p. 232**: Courtesy of Carol Symes; **p. 235 (left)**: The Granger Collection, New York; **p. 235 (right)**: The Pierpont Morgan Library/Art Resource, NY; **p. 239**: Bibliotheque Nationale, Paris, France/The Bridgeman Art Library; **p. 240**: Vatian Library: MS. Reg. Ret. 762, fol. 82r, written at Tours 800 A.D.; **p. 243**: The Granger Collection, NYC.

Chapter 8: p. 246: Bayerische Staatsbibliothek/Art Resource; **p. 249**: Berig/Wikimedia Commons; **p. 250**: Wikimedia Commons; **p. 252 (left)**: Wikimedia Commons; **p. 252 (right)**: Bayerische Staatsbibliothek/Art Resource; **p. 254 (left)**: The Art Archive / Biblioteca Nazionale Marciana Venice / Dagli Orti (A); **p. 254 (right)**: Biblioteca Riccardiana, Florence, Manuscript Ricc. 492 c. 18, with the permission of the Ministero per I Beni Culturali e Ambientali; **p. 256**: From David Nicholas, Urban Europe, 1100-1700 (Palgrave MacMillan, 2003, p.74 fig 3.3); **p. 258**: The Art Archive/British Library; **p. 260**: Wikimedia Commons; **p. 262 (top)**: French School/The Bridgeman Art Library/Getty Images; **p. 262 (bottom)**: French School/The Bridgeman Art Library/Getty Images; **p. 263**: The Granger Collection, New York; **p. 264**: Wikimedia Commons; **p. 265**: Erich Lessing/Art Resource; **p. 267 (left)**: The Bridgeman Art Library/Getty; **p. 267 (right)**: Stephen Jaffe/AFP/Newscom; **p. 270**: HIP/Art Resource, NY; **p. 276**: Giraudon/Art Resource, NY; **p. 277**: The Metropolitan Museum of Art/Art Resource, NY; **p. 278 (left)**: Sites & Photos/akg-images; **p. 278 (right)**: Album/ Art Resource, NY.

Chapter 9: p. 282: The Granger Collection, New York; **p. 284**: Giraudon/Art Resource, NY; **p. 285**: The Walters Art Gallery, Baltimore; **p. 290**: Wikimedia Commons; **p. 292**: Benito Ruiz/Newscom; **p. 293 (left)**: The Granger Collection, New York; **p. 293 (right)**: The Art Archive / Archivo de la Corona de Aragon Barcelona / Laurie Platt Winfrey; **p. 295**: Gianni Dagli Orti/The Art Archive at Art Resource, NY; **p. 297 (left)**: Scala/White Images/ Art Resource, NY; **p. 297 (right)**: Lucasfilm Ltd./Twentieth Century Fox Film Corp./Photofest; **p. 298**: Bibliotheque Sainte-Genevieve, Paris, France/ Archives Charmet/ The Bridgeman Art Library; **p. 302 (left)**: Erich Lesser/Art Resource, NY; **p. 302 (right)**: © The Metropolitan Museum of Art / Art Resource, NY; **p. 303**: Sueddeutsche Zeitung Photo / The Image Works; **p. 307**: Bayerische Staatsbibliothek, München; **p. 308 (left)**: Cliché Bibliothèque Nationale de France, Paris; **p. 308 (right)**: Cliché Bibliothèque Nationale de France, Paris; **p. 309**: Erich Lessing / Art Resource, NY; **p. 313**: Triumph of St Thomas Aquinas, detail of figure below the throne, from the Spanish Chapel, c.1365 (fresco), Andrea di Bonaiuto (Andrea da Firenze) (fl.1343-77)/Santa Maria Novella, Florence, Italy / The Bridgeman Art Library; **p. 314**: AKG-images; **p. 318 (left)**: Richard List/Corbis; **p. 318 (right)**: Richard List/Corbis.

Chapter 10: p. 322: Bibliotheque Nationale, Paris, France/ The Bridgeman Art Library; **p. 326**: Wikimedia Commons; Christie's Images/Bridgeman Art Library; **p. 327**: Wikimedia Commons; **p. 330**: Bibliotheque Nationale, Paris, France/ The Bridgeman Art Library; **p. 334**: Danita Delimont/Getty; Bibliothèque Royale Albert I, Brussels, ms. 11209, fol. 3 recto; **p. 335**: Wikimedia Commons; **p. 338 (left)**: The Granger Collection, NYC; **p. 338 (right)**: Wikimedia Commons; **p. 339**: Wikimedia Commons; **p. 340**: Cameraphoto Arte, Venice / Art Resource, NY; **p. 341**: Chris Hellier/Corbis; **p. 343**: Simone Martini/Wikimedia Commons; **p. 345 (left)**: Didier B./Wikimedia Commons; **p. 345 (right)**: Graham Bell/Getty Images; **p. 349 (left)**: akg-images/British Library; **p. 349 (right)**: Associated Press.

Chapter 11: p. 356: Réunion des Musées Nationaux / Art Resource, NY; **p. 358**: HIP / Art Resource, NY; **p. 360**: Réunion des Musées Nationaux / Art Resource, NY; **p. 361**: Réunion des Musées Nationaux / Art Resource, NY; **p. 363**: akg-images / British Library; **p. 365 (left)**: Bildarchiv Preussischer Kulturbesitz / Art Resource, NY; **p. 365 (right)**: Scala / Art Resource, NY; **p. 366**: Wikimedia Commons; **p. 371**: John Massey Stewart Picture Library; **p. 373**: Werner Forman Archive/Topkapi Palace Library, Istanbul/Art Resource, NY; **p. 375**: Bibliothèque Royale Albert I, Brussels; **p. 376**: Réunion des Musées Nationaux / Art Resource, NY; **p. 381 (left)**: The Bridgeman Art Library; **p. 381 (right)**: Associated Press; **p. 385 (left)**: Wikimedia Commons; **p. 385 (right)**: The Art Archive / British Library.

Chapter 12: p. 388: The Art Archive / Topkapi Museum Istanbul / Gianni Dagli Orti; **p. 396**: Erich Lessing/Art Resource, NY; **p. 397 (top)**: Erich Lessing/Art Resource, NY; **p. 397 (bottom)**: Réunion des Musées Nationaux / Art Resource, NY; **p. 399 (top)**: Scala/Art Resource, NY; **p. 399 (bottom)**: Ted Spiegel/Corbis; **p. 400 (top)**: Scala/Art Resource, NY; **p. 400 (left)**: Nimatallah/ Art Resource, NY; **p. 400 (center)**: Scala/Art Resource, NY; **p. 400 (right)**: Erich Lessing / Art Resource, NY; **p. 401**: Bildarchiv Preussischer Kulturbesitz / Art Resource, NY; **p. 402**: Louvre, Paris, France / Giraudon / The Bridgeman Art Library; **p. 403 (left)**: DEA

PICTURE LIBRARY/Getty Images; **p. 403 (right):** © University of Leicester/Corbis; **p. 404:** National Portrait Gallery, London, UK / The Bridgeman Art Library; **p. 406:** Bildarchiv Preussischer Kulturbesitz / Art Resource, NY; **p. 408:** Vova Pomortzeff / Alamy; **p. 409:** Museo del Prado, Madrid/ Art Archive; **p. 413:** Myriam Thyes / Wikimedia Commons; **p. 416:** Bibliotheque Nationale, Paris, France/ Giraudon/ The Bridgeman Art Library; **p. 417:** AKG-images; **p. 418:** The Art Archive / Biblioteca Nacional de Madrid / Dagli Orti.

Chapter 13: p. 422: The Art Archive / Nationalmuseet Copenhagen Denmark / Alfredo Dagli Orti; **p. 424:** Erich Lessing/Art Resource, NY; **p. 425:** Bildarchiv Preussischer Kulturbesitz / Art Resource, NY; **p. 426:** Sandro Vannini/Corbis; **p. 427:** Erich Lessing/Art Resource, NY; **p. 428 (left):** Staatsbibliothek, Bern; **p. 428 (right):** Staatsbibliothek, Bern; **p. 429 (left):** Staatliche Museen zu Berlin-Preußischer Kulturbesitz, Kupferstichkabinett; **p. 429 (right):** By permission of the British Library/Art Resource, NY; **p. 432:** Bayerische Staatsgemäldesammlungen/Alte Pinakothek, Munich; © Dietrich Rose/ Corbis; **p. 434 (left):** akg-images; **p. 434 (right):** Erich Lessing/ Art Resource; **p. 436 (left):** Erich Lessing/Art Resource, NY; **p. 436 (right):** Wikimedia Commons; **p. 441:** Alfredo Dagli Orti/The Art Archive at Art Resource, NY; **p. 443 (left):** Scala/Art Resource, NY; **p. 443 (right):** Scala/Art Resource, NY; **p. 445 (left):** Erich Lessing/ Art Resource, NY; **p. 445 (right):** Michael Cizek/AFP/Getty Images/ Newscom; **p. 446 (left):** Scala/Art Resource, NY; **p. 446 (right):** Kunsthistorisches Museum, Vienna; **p. 449:** Corbis.

Chapter 14: p. 452: Wikimedia Commons; **p. 454:** James Reeves/ Wikimedia Commons; **p. 460:** Peter Newark American Pictures/The Bridgeman Art Library; **p. 461:** Bettmann/Corbis; **p. 464:** Archivo Iconografico, S.A./Corbis; **p. 465:** British Museum/Wikimedia Commons; **p. 467 (top):** John R. Freeman & Co.; **p. 467 (bottom):** Wikimedia Commons; **p. 468:** Wikimedia Commons; **p. 471:** Giraudon/The Bridgeman Art Library; **p. 473:** The Granger Collection, NYC ; **p. 476 (top):** The National Trust Photolibrary / Alamy; **p. 476 (bottom):** Wikimedia Commons; **p. 480 (left):** Wikimedia Commons; **p. 480 (right):** Interfoto / Alamy; **p. 484 (left):** © Franz-Marc Frei/Corbis; **p. 484 (right):** Icon Entertainment International / The Kobal Collection; **p. 485 (top):** Image copyright © The Metropolitan Museum of Art / Art Resource, NY; **p. 485 (left):** Scala/Art Resource, NY; **p. 485 (right):** Wikimedia Commons; **p. 486:** Erich Lessing/Art Resource, NY; **p. 487 (top):** Wikimedia Commons; **p. 487 (left):** © English Heritage Photo Library; **p. 487 (right):** Gift of Mr. and Mrs. Robert Woods Bliss, © 1997 Board of Trustees, National Gallery of Art, Washington, D.C.

Chapter 15: p. 490: The Royal Collection © 2010 Her Majesty Queen Elizabeth II; **p. 492:** Gianni Dagli Orti/Corbis; **p. 494 (left):** The Granger Collection, New York; **p. 494 (right):** Wikimedia Commons; **p. 495 (top):** With kind permission of the University of Edinburgh / The Bridgeman Art Library International **p. 495 (bottom):** Erich Lessing / Art Resource, NY; **p. 498 (left):** The Granger Collection, New York; **p. 498 (right):** Getty Images; **p. 501:** The Royal Collection © 2010 Her Majesty Queen Elizabeth II; **p. 503:** Snark / Art Resource, NY; **p. 504:** Photo © Philip Mould Ltd, London / The

Bridgeman Art Library; **p. 507:** The Art Archive/Musee du Chateau de Versailles/Dagli Orti; **p. 509:** Interfoto / Alamy; **p. 510:** Bildarchiv Preussischer Kulturbesitz / Art Resource, NY; **p. 511:** Lebrecht Authors; **p. 513:** Courtesy Dr. Alexander Boguslawski, Professor of Russian Studies, Rollins College.

Chapter 16: p. 518: Cellarius, Andreas/The Bridgeman Art Library; **p. 521:** Jeffrey Coolidge/Getty Images; **p. 522 (left):** Private Collection/The Bridgeman Art Library; **p. 522 (right):** © Peter Ginter/ Science Faction/Corbis; **p. 523:** Erich Lessing/Art Resource, NY; **p. 525:** Stapleton Collection/Corbis; **p. 526 (left):** The Granger Collection, NY; **p. 526 (right):** Wikimedia Commons; **p. 528:** Erich Lessing/Art Resource, NY; **p. 530:** John P. McCaskey cropped by Smartse/Wikimedia Commons; **p. 531:** Rene Descartes, L'homme de René Descartes, et la formation du foetus . . . Paris: Compagnie des Libraires, 1729/"Courtesy of Historical Collections & Services, Claude Moore Health Sciences Library, University of Virginia;" **p. 535:** Wikimedia Commons; **p. 538:** Plate 20 from Metamorphosis Insectorum (1705) by Maria Sybilla Merian (1647–1717). ©The Natural History Museum, London / The Image Works; **p. 539 (right):** Bettmann/Corbis; **p. 539 (left):** Newton, Sir Isaac (1642-1727) / © Courtesy of the Warden and Scholars of New College, Oxford / The Bridgeman Art Library; **p. 540:** Bodleian Library; **p. 543:** Giraudon/Art Resource, NY.

Chapter 17: p. 546: Bridgeman Art Library; **p. 548:** Elizabeth Nesbitt Room Chapbook Collection/Information Sciences Library/ University of Pittsburgh; **p. 551:** © Ali Meyer/CORBIS; **p. 552:** The New York Public Library / Art Resource, NY; **p. 553:** Bibliotheque Nationale, Paris, France/ Lauros / Giraudon/ The Bridgeman Art Library; **p. 554:** Erich Lessing / Art Resource, NY; **p. 555:** Giraudon / Bridgeman; **p. 556:** Historisches Museum der Stadt Wien; **p. 557:** Moritz Daniel Oppenheim, "Lavater and Lessing Visit Moses Mendelssohn." In the permanent collections, Judah L. Magnes Museum. Photo: Ben Ailes; **p. 561:** Stapletib Collection/Corbis **p. 562 (left):** Sir Joshua Reynolds/Omai of the Friendly Isles/ nla.pic-an5600097/ National Library of Australia; **p. 562 (right):** William Hodges/ King of Otaheite//National Library of Australia; **p. 563:** Francesco Bartolozzi/A view of the inside of a house in the island of Ulietea, with the representation of a dance to the music of the country/nla. pic-an9184905/National Library of Australia; **p. 565 (top):** Bibliotheque Nationale, Paris, France / Bridgeman Art Library, Flammarion; **p. 565 (bottom):** © Tate Gallery, London/Art Resource, NY; **p. 570:** Bridgeman Art Library; **p. 571:** Bettmann/Corbis; **p. 573 (left):** The Granger Collection, New York; **p. 573 (right):** Bluberries/iStock Photo; **p. 575 (left):** Scala / Art Resource, NY; **p. 575: (right):** akg-images; **p. 577:** The Granger Collection, New York.

Chapter 18: p. 580: Erich Lessing / Art Resource, NY; **p. 584 (left):** AKG-Images; **p. 584 (right):** The Art Archive / Musée Carnavalet Paris / Marc Charmet; **p. 585:** Giraudon / The Bridgeman Art Library; **p. 587:** Chateau de Versailles, France / The Bridgeman Art Library; **p. 589:** Musee de la Ville de Paris, Musee Carnavalet, Paris, France / Giraudon / The Bridgeman Art Library; **p. 590:** Musee de la Revolution Francaise, Vizille, France / The Bridgeman Art Library; **p. 596:** Bibliotheque Nationale, Paris, France / The

Bridgeman Art Library; **p. 597**: Erich Lessing / Art Resource, NY; **p. 598**: Bettmann/Corbis; **p. 599**: Scala/White Images / Art Resource, NY; **p. 602 (left)**: Risma Archivo / Alamy; **p. 602 (right)**: The Art Archive; **p. 603 (left)**: Musee de la Ville de Paris, Musee Carnavalet, Paris, France/ Lauros / Giraudon/ The Bridgeman Art Library; **p. 603 (right)**: Courtesy of the Warden and Scholars of New College, Oxford / The Bridgeman Art Library; **p. 607 (left)**: The Gallery Collection/Corbis; **p. 607 (right)**: Wikimedia Commons; **p. 608**: Erich Lessing/Art Resource, NY; **p. 609**: © The Trustees of the British Museum / Art Resource, NY; **p. 612 (left)**: The Granger Collection, New York; **p. 612 (right)**: © Thorsten Strasas/Demotix/Corbis; **p. 613**: © Gianni Dagli Orti/CORBIS.

Chapter 19: p. 616: National Gallery, London / Art Resource, NY; **p. 619**: Peak District National Park; **p. 621**: Stefano Bianchetti/Corbis; **p. 622**: SSPL via Getty Images; **p. 623 (left)**: The National Archives of the UK; **p. 623 (right)**: The Granger Collection, New York; **p. 624 (top)**: Snark / Art Resource, NY; **p. 624 (bottom)**: Hulton-Deutsch Collection/Corbis; **p. 625**: Hulton-Deutsch Collection/Corbis; **p. 628**: Wikimedia Commons; **p. 631**: Hulton Deutsch Collection/Corbis; **p. 632**: HIP-Archive / Topham/ The Image Works; **p. 633**: HIP-Archive / Topham/ The Image Works; **p. 634 (left)**: © Heritage Images/Corbis; **p. 634 (right)**: © ACE STOCK LIMITED / Alamy; **p. 636 (left)**: Fotomas / Topham / The Image Works; **p. 363 (right)**: Mary Evans / The Image Works; **p. 640**: Geoffrey Clements /Corbis; **p. 641**: Constantin Guys/Wikipedia; **p. 642**: Giraudon / Art Resource, NY; **p. 643**: North Wind / Nancy Carter\North Wind Picture Archives; **p. 647**: The Granger Collection, NY; **p. 649**: The Granger Collection, NY.

Chapter 20: p. 652: Erich Lessing / Art Resource, NY; **p. 657**: Private Collection / Bridgeman Art Library, Archives Charmet; **p. 659**: Photo RMN, Paris; **p. 661**: Erich Lessing / Art Resource, NY; **p. 662**: Reproduced by the Gracious Permission of Her Majesty the Queen; **p. 665**: © The Trustees of the British Museum; **p. 661**: Michael Nicholson/Corbis; **p. 671 (left)**: akg-images; **p. 671 (right)**: Time & Life Pictures/Getty Images; **p. 672 (top)**: The Stapleton Collection / The Bridgeman Art Library; **p. 672 (bottom)**: Bettmann/Corbis; **p. 678**: Bettmann/Corbis; **p. 679 (left)**: Portrait of Mary Shelley (1797-1851) at the Age of Nineteen, c.1816 (litho) by English School (19th century), Russell-Cotes Art Gallery and Museum, Bournemouth, UK / Bridgeman Art Library; **p. 679 (right)**: Illustration from 'Frankenstein' by Mary Shelley (1797-1851) (engraving) (b/w photo) by English School (19th century), Private Collection / Bridgeman Art Library; **p. 681**: Archivo Iconografico S.A./Corbis; **p. 682**: Wikimedia Commons; **p. 683 (top)**: Wikimedia Commons; **p. 683 (bottom)**: Wikimedia Commons.

Chapter 21: p. 686: Erich Lessing/Art Resource, NY; **p. 692**: Gianni Dagli Orti / The Art Archive at Art Resource, NY; **p. 693 (top)**: Erich Lessing / Art Resource, NY; **p. 693 (bottom)**: Bildarchiv Preussischer Kulturbesitz / Art Resource, NY; **p. 695 (left)**: ullstein bild/ The Granger Collection, New York; **p. 695 (right)**: Image Source; **p. 697**: Bildarchiv Preussischer Kulturbesitz / Art Resource, NY; **p. 698 (left)**; Bildarchiv Preussischer Kulturbesitz / Art Resource, NY; **p. 698 (right)**: Corbis; **p. 700**: Imagno/Getty Images; **p. 704 (top)**: Rischgitz/Getty Images; **p. 704 (bottom)**: Scala/Art Resource, NY; **p. 706**: Charles E. Rotkin / Corbis; **p. 707**: Hulton-Deutsch Collection / Corbis; **p. 708**: Scala/Art Resource, NY; **p. 710**: Ann Ronan Picture Library / HIP / The Image Works; **p. 712**: Deutsches Historisches Museum; **p. 713 (left)**: Bildarchiv Preussischer Kulturbesitz / Art Resource, NY; **p. 713 (right)**: Bildarchiv Preussischer Kulturbesitz / Art Resource, NY; **p. 716**: Bettmann / Corbis; **p. 721**: Louie Psihoyos/Corbis; **p. 723 (top)**: Corbis; **p. 723 (bottom)**: Foto Marburg / Art Resource, NY; **p. 724**: Bettmann/Corbis.

Chapter 22: p. 726: The Granger Collection, New York; **p. 728**: Bibliotheque des Arts Decoratifs, Paris, France / Archives Charmet / The Bridgeman Art Library; **p. 732 (left)**: Ken and Jenny Jacobson Orientalist Photography Collection/Research Library, The Getty Research Institute, Los Angeles (2008.R.3); **p. 732 (right)**: Hulton Archive/Getty Images; **p. 733 (left)**: Bettmann/Corbis; **p. 733 (right)**: Punchcartoons.com; **p. 737 (left)**: The Granger Collection, New York/The Granger Collection; **p. 737 (right)**: © Janine Wiedel Photolibrary/Alamy; **p. 738**: AKG-images; **p. 741 (top)**: Oriental and India Office Collections, The British Library/Art Resource, NY; **p. 741 (bottom)**: Bettmann/Corbis; **p. 743**: Wikimedia Commons; **p. 744**: Hulton-Deutsch/Corbis; **p. 746 (left)**: Wikimedia Commons; **p. 746 (right)**: Hulton Archive/Getty Images; **p. 747 (left)**: North Wind Picture Archives; **p. 747 (right)**: Image Courtesy of The Advertising Archives; **p. 750**: Matthew Fontaine Maury, *New Complete Geography* (New York: University Publishing Company, 1906); **p. 754 (top)**: 1999 National Gallery of Art, Washington D.C.; **p. 754 (left)**: 1999 National Gallery of Art, Washington D.C.; **p. 754 (center)**: 1999 National Gallery of Art, Washington D.C.; **p. 754 (right)**: 1999 National Gallery of Art, Washington D.C.; **p. 755**: Bettmann/Corbis; **p. 757**: Bridgeman Art Library; **p. 758**: The Ohio State University Billy Ireland Cartoon Library & Museum.

Chapter 23: p. 760: AKG-images; **p. 763**: AKG-images; **p. 766**: Bildarchiv Preussischer Kulturbesitz / Art Resource, NY; **p. 769**: Hulton-Deutsch Collection / Corbis; **p. 770**: Austrian Archives/ Corbis; **p. 771**: Leemage/Getty; **p. 772 (top)**: The Hulton Deutsch Collection/Corbis; **p. 772 (bottom)**: The Hulton Deutsch Collection/ Corbis; **p. 773 (top)**: Library of Congress; **p. 773 (bottom)**: Bettmann/Corbis; **p. 774**: The Hulton Deutsch Collection/Corbis; **p. 779 (left)**: The Granger Collection, New York; **p. 779 (center)**: Charles Leandre (1862-1930) Private Collection/ The Bridgeman Art Library Nationality; **p. 779 (right)**: Rue des Archives / The Granger Collection , New York; **p. 780**: Bettmann/Corbis; **p. 783 (left)**: Universal History Archive/UIG; **p. 783 (right)**: © Charles Platiau/Reuters/ Corbis; **p. 784**: Hulton-Deutsch Collection/CORBIS; **p. 786**: Staatliche Museen zu Berlin-Preußisher Kulturbesitz; **p. 789**: From *An Autobiography: Herbert Spencer, 1904*; **p. 792**: Bettmann/Corbis; **p. 793**: © Bettmann/Corbis; **p. 794**: *Black Lines*, December 1913. Oil on canvas, 51 x 51 5/8 inches. Solomon R. Guggenheim Museum, Solomon R. Guggenheim Founding Collection, Gift, Solomon R. Guggenheim. 37.241. Vasily Kandinsky © 2007 Artists Rights Society (ARS), New York/ADAGP, Paris; **p. 795 (left)**: Erich Lessing / Art Resource, NY; **p. 795 (right)**: Scala / Art Resource, NY.

Chapter 24: p. 798: The Art Archive / Imperial War Museum; **p. 803**: Staatliche Museen zu Berlin-Preußisher Kulturbesitz;

Index

Page numbers in *italics* refer to illustrations, maps, and tables.

Edward I, king of England (r. 1272–1307), 345–47, *345*, 682

Edward II, king of England (r. 1307–1327), 346

Edward III, king of England (r. 1327–1377), 347, 348, 374, 375

Edward VI, king of England (r. 1547–1553), 442, 443

Egypt, 15, 243, 274, 1001
  Arab-Israeli conflict and, 995–96
  Arab Spring in, 1010
  Fatimid, 270, 274
  Islam in, 224, 226
  Napoleon in, 600, 605
  radical Islam and, 999, 1002
  Suez Canal project and, 727–29
  Suez crisis and (1956), 933–34

Egypt, ancient, 22–36, 42–47, 75, 213
  agriculture in, 23–24, 32
  under Alexander, 124
  archaic period of, 24–25
  art of, 29, 46–47
  astronomy in, 32
  calendar of, 32
  centrality of Nile River and, 22
  cities of, 23–24
  commerce in, 23, 131–32
  death cult of, 30–32, *32*
  decline of, 54, 58, 73
  emergence of cities and, 23
  famine in, 29
  First Intermediate Period in, 29, 34, 42
  Hellenistic Greece and, 141
  Hittites and, 48
  Hyksos domination of, 42, 43, 46
  language of, 27–28
  literature of, 31, 35–36
  Middle Kingdom in, 32, 34–36, 42
  Mitannians and, 41
  monotheism in, 47
  New Kingdom in, 42–47, *43*, 73
  Old Kingdom in, 25–34
  predynastic era of, 22–24
  Ptolemaic, 128–29, 130, 131, 138, 156, 157
  pyramids of, 28–29
  religion in, 25, 30–32, 33, 46–47
  Rome and, 160, 162, 164, 165
  science and technology in, 32, 135, 138
  Second Intermediate Period in, 42
  social structure of, 32–36, 46
  Sumerian interaction with, 15
  women's status in, 33–34
  world view of, 30–36, 42, 46
  writing in, 25–28, *27*

Eichmann, Adolf, 941

Eichmann in Jerusalem (Arendt), 940

Eiffel Tower, 745, 754, *754*, *882*

8½ (film), 954

Einhard, 240

Einsatzgruppen (death squads), 891–902

Einstein, Albert (1879–1955), 864–65

Eiriksson, Leif, 333, 336–37

Eisenhower, Dwight D. (1890–1969), 917, 922
  "military-industrial complex" speech of, 944

ekklesia, 88

Elagabalus, Roman emperor, 189–90

El Alamein, battle of (1942), 885

Elamites, 60

Eleanor of Aquitaine (1122–1204), 285, 287, 293, 309, *309*, 316, *318*, 344, 348

electricity, 763, *763*

Elements of Geometry (Euclid), 138

El Greco (Domenikos Theotokopoulos) (1541–1614), 484, *485*

Eliot, T. S. (1888–1965), 863

Elizabeth I, queen of England (1558–1603), 441, 443, 444, 455, 466, *467*, 474

Elizabeth II, queen of England (r. 1952–), *498*

Elizabeth of York, 378

Emile (Rousseau), 565, *565*, 566

Emma (Austen), 571

empires:
  European, *731*
  see also imperialism

empiricism, Bacon and, 537

encomienda system, 457–58

Encyclopedia (Diderot), 555, *555*, 558, 560, 569

Engels, Friedrich (1820–1895), 626–27, 672–73, 674, 688, 769

England, 348, 361, 362, 380, 466, 493, 505, 506, 511
  agriculture in, 254
  American colonies of, *456*, 466–68, 492, 507
  Anglo-Saxons in, 201
  Calvinism in, 437
  Christianization of, 211, 234, 237
  Civil War in (1642–1649), 474–77
  as Commonwealth, 476–77
  Crusades and, 276
  in Early Middle Ages, 232, 233, 234, 237, 241–43
  Elizabethan theater in, 482–83
  feudalism in, 284–85
  feudal monarchy in, 284–85, *286*
  France contrasted with, 288, 553
  Glorious Revolution in, 502–3, 505
  heretical movements in, 383–84, 386
  in Hundred Years' War, 347–48, 350, 357, 374, 387
  Jews expelled from, 307
  law in, 285
  as limited monarchy, 492, 501–5
  literacy in, 311
  literature of, 362
  Magna Carta and, 287
  medieval commerce in, 255, 256–57, 258
  monasticism in, 264, 442, 444
  monetary system of, 237
  national identity of, 377–78, 444, 450
  national language of, 378
  national monarchy in, 292, 377, 378

  Norman conquest of, 250, 261, 262, 284–85, 319, 362
  papacy and, 298, 441–42
  Parliament of, *see* Parliament, British
  Peasants' Revolt in, 357–58, 360, 361
  "Protectorate" in, 477, 501
  Protestantism in, 449, 465, 466, 501, 502
  Reformation in, 441–44
  reign of Charles II in, 501, *501*, 503
  reign of Henry II in, 285–87, *286*, 288
  Renaissance in, 403
  slave trade and, *460*
  Spain vs., 465–66
  unification of, 242–43, 252–53
  union of Scotland and, 503
  urban growth in, *637*
  War of the Roses in, 377
  see also Great Britain

English language:
  Arabic influence on, 280
  as national language, 378

Enheduanna, 17

Enlightenment, 546–79, 654, 677, 679
  academies in, 569
  books and literacy in, 568–69, 570–72
  colonialism and, 558, 750
  economics in, 557–58
  Encyclopedia in, 555, *555*
  foundations of, 551–52
  French Revolution and, 565, 567, 583–85, 589–90, 591, 605, 613
  humanitarianism as theme of, 556, 668
  Jews in, 557
  mercantilism in, 557
  New World colonialism and, 558, 582
  philosophes in, 552, 553–55
  popular culture in, 570–72
  public spheres and, 569–70
  religious toleration as theme of, 556
  Rousseau's influence on, 563
  salons and learned societies in, 569
  scientific exploration in, 561–62
  slave trade in, 558–60
  society and, 635, 786
  utilitarianism and, 669
  women in, 533, 569, 570
  see also scientific revolution

Entry of the Crusaders into Constantinople (Delacroix), *743*

environment:
  economy growth and, 634
  industrialization and, *634*, 639–40, *640*, 651
  problems of, 639–40, 651, 1010

Epaminondas, king of Thebes, 113, 119, 121

Ephesus, 139, *141*

Epic of Gilgamesh, 12–13

Epicureanism, 132–33, 159

Epicurus (c. 342–270 B.C.E.), 133

Epidauros, theater at, *98*

Epsom Derby, 772

Equal Rights Amendment, *956*

Erasistratus of Alexandria, 139

of High Middle Ages, 247–48, 315–16, 318–19
imperialism and, 747–52
Islamic, 226, 278–79
of Late Middle Ages, 362–63
liberalism and, 680
mass culture and, 793
naturalism in, 362–63, 405
of nineteenth-century middle class, 640–41
novel as form of, 570–71
Orientalism in, 680–81, 681
of post-Mycenaean Greece, 77–78
professional authors and, 362–63
prose, 140
Renaissance, 366, 367, 368, 369, 395, 403–4
of Roman Empire, 168–70, 177
in Roman Republic, 159
romantic, 315–16
Romanticism and, 676–80, 681
after Second World War, 937–42
stream of consciousness technique in, 863
Sumerian, 13–14
vernacular languages in, 315, 318–19, 362
"war," 834–35
women authors of, 571
Lithuania, 373, 407, 437, 492, 515, 902, 972
Litvinov, Maxim (1876–1951), 874
Livia (58 B.C.E.-29 C.E.), 169
Livingstone, David (1813–1873), 730
Livonia, 515
Livy (59 B.C.E.-17 C.E.), 240, 366
Lloyd George, David (1863–1945), 781, 816, 829–30
Loarre Castle, 292
Locke, John (1632–1704), 496, 504, 504, 541, 551–52, 553, 576, 584–85, 668, 1007
logic, 206, 311
Lollards, 384, 386
Lombard, Peter (c. 1095–1160), 311, 426
Lombard League, 288, 290
Lombards, 213, 228, 232, 235, 237
Lombardy, 699, 700, 704, 708
Loménie de Brienne, Étienne Charles (1727–1794), 586
London, 175, 359, 360, 499, 781
    environmental problems and, 640, 640
    first daily newspapers in, 568
    in High Middle Ages, 257, 316
    nineteenth-century population of, 637
    Pan-African Conference in, 751, 752–53
    as world's money market, 768
London School of Economics, 962
Lord of the Rings, The (Tolkien), 940
lordships, 259–60
Lord Thaddeus (Mickiewicz), 680
lost generation, 832, 863
Lothair I, Holy Roman emperor (840–855), 241
Louis I (the Pious), Holy Roman emperor (814–840), 237, 239, 241

Louis II (the German), king of Germany (c. 840–876), 241
Louis VII, king of France (r. 1137–1180), 285, 288, 294
Louis VIII, king of France (r. 1223–1226), 288
Louis IX (Saint Louis), king of France (r. 1226–1270), 244–45, 288, 316, 329, 340, 345
Louis XII, king of France (r. 1498–1515), 406
Louis XIII, king of France (r. 1610–1643), 473, 474, 475
Louis XIV (the Sun King), king of France (r. 1643–1675), 473–74, 475, 491–92, 493, 494, 498, 499, 505, 508, 511, 515, 553, 585–86, 585
    absolutism of, 489, 491–92, 497, 502
    administration and centralization under, 496–97, 498–99
    foreign policy of, 504, 505
    religious policies of, 499
    wars of, 506, 511
Louis XVI, king of France (r. 1774–1792), 583, 587, 588, 589, 589, 592, 596, 596, 600
Louis XVIII, king of France (r. 1795–1814), 609, 654, 655, 660
Louisiana, slave rebellion in, 665
Louisiana Purchase (1803), 613, 716
Louis Philippe, king of the French (1773–1850), 660, 687, 691, 692, 693
Lourdes, pilgrimages to, 793
Louvre, 405
Lovett, William (1800–1877), 663
Luanda, Portuguese slave trading post, 460
Lucretia, 148, 150, 152
Lucretius (98–55 B.C.E.), 159, 366
Ludd, Ned, 623
Luddites, 623
Ludendorff, Erich, 807
Luke, Book of, 165, 184
Lusiads, The, 412
Lusitania, 807, 810
Luther, Martin (1483–1546), 204, 404, 405, 423, 424, 425, 434, 438, 439, 441, 444, 445, 447, 451
    Calvin compared with, 435–37
    conversion experience of, 425
    at Diet of Worms, 430–32, 432
    indulgences campaign of, 426–30
    Ninety-five theses of, 313, 427
    printing press and, 425, 428–29
Lutheranism:
    Calvinism and, 435–37
    Catholicism vs., 424–30
    marriage and, 430
    monasticism and, 427, 434
    papacy and, 426, 428, 429, 433–34
    theological premises of, 424–30
    women and, 438–40
Luxembourg, 505
Luxemburg, Rosa (1870–1919), 770, 853
lycées, 604

Lydia, kingdom of, 64, 65, 73, 82, 85, 91, 92, 93, 94
Lyrical Ballads (Wordsworth), 677
lyric poetry, 85–87, 98

M (film), 867, 868
Ma'at (goddess), 33
ma'at (truth, order), 32, 35
MacArthur, Douglas (1880–1964), 928
MacBeth (Shakespeare), 483
Maccabees, 135, 181
Macedonia, 65, 112, 119–22, 130, 156, 978
Machaut, Guillaume de (c. 1300–1377), 405
Machiavelli, Niccolò (1469–1527), 392–93, 394–95
Macmillan, Harold (1894–1986), 924, 933
Madagascar, 891
Madeira, 414
Madison, James, 130
Magellan, Ferdinand (c. 1480–1521), 415
Magna Carta, 287, 320, 345, 501
Magyars, 241–42, 249, 250, 253, 254, 698, 699, 700, 711, 713, 715
Mahdi, 755
Mahler, Gustav (1860–1911), 715
Maids of Honor, The (Velázquez), 485, 485
Maimonides, Moses (1137–1204), 313
Maine, France, 285
Maistre, Joseph de, 668
Majorca, 331
Malacca, 412
malaria, 457
Malawi, 746, 933, 993
Malaya, 741, 933
Malay Peninsula, 412
Malaysia, 933, 989, 994
Malcolm X (1925–1965), 959
Mali, 331
Malinche, La (Cortés's consort), 417
Malory, Thomas, 392
Malthus, Thomas (1766–1834), 635, 788
Mamluk Sultanate of Egypt, 238
Manchester, 639
    Peterloo Massacre in, 661
Manchuria, 738, 742
    Japanese invasion of, 875, 877
"mandate system," 831–32
Mandela, Nelson, 993, 993
Mandeville, John de, 323, 332–33, 410
Manesse Codex, 314
Manetho, 24–25
Manhattan Project, 903, 906
Manicheanism, 192, 204
Manifest Destiny, 717
Manifesto (Marinetti), 796
maniple, 148
Mann, Thomas (1875–1955), 835
manorialism, 254–55, 260
Mansur, al-, caliph, 225
manufacturing:
    in eighteenth-century Europe, 550
    environment and, 634
    and Industrial Revolution, 617–18
    technology and, 550

Rocroi, battle of (1643), *471*
Roland, 247–48, *270*, 274
Romadonowski, Feodor Jurowicz, Prince, 512
Roman calendar, 523
Roman Empire, 22, 109, 112, 164–76, 228–29
  achievements of, 174–75
  agriculture in, 174
  architecture of, 165, 170–72, *172*, 175, *176*
  art of, 171, *177*
  borders of, 167–68, *167*, 187
  bureaucracy in, 191, 202, 203
  Christianity and, 179–80, 185–87, 190–91, 193, 194–96, 198, 208
  civil war in, 187, 190, 199
  commerce in, 174–75, 201–2
  decline of, 190, 199, 201–3, 208–9
  East-West division of, 180, 191, 198–99, 206–7, 213
  economics in, 175, 191, 202–3
  end of, 199–203
  engineering in, 171–72
  Era of Five Good Emperors in, 167, 187
  failure of, 177
  family life in, 166, 188
  Germanic invasions of, 199–201, *202*, 204
  gladiatorial combat in, 170, *172*, 187
  government in, 164–67, 174–75, 187, 190–91, 198–99
  Greek influences on, 141–43
  growth of, *163*, 167–68
  imperial succession in, 191, 198–99
  legal system of, 172–74, 175–76, 185, 186, 214–15
  literature of, 168–70, 177
  in Middle East, 167
  Neoplatonism in, 192–93
  orientalization of, 191
  Persians and, 166, 213
  philosophy in, 172, 192–93
  Principate in, 164–75
  religion in, 167, 185–87, 190, 193
  revival of, 213
  revolts in, 167, 199
  science and technology in, 171–72
  Severan Dynasty of, 187–90
  slavery in, 175, 372
  taxes in, 164–65, 191, 202, 203
  tetrarchy system of, 191, *191*, 198
  urban planning in, 174–75
  women in, 187
Romania, 722, 786, 876, 881, 887, 974
  Communists ousted in, 969–72
  Soviet influence in, 915, 917
Roman monarchy, 146, 148
Romanov dynasty, 510
Roman Republic, 145–46
  agriculture in, 148–49, 154, 157, 163
  architecture of, 146
  Carthage vs., 154–56
  commerce in, 149, 157
  Early, 148–54
  economic change in, 157–58, 162–63

  education in, 160
  Etruscans and, 146–47, 148
  expansion of, 148, *149*, 154–57, *156*, 163
  family life in, 159
  funeral rites in, 152, 153
  gladiatorial combat in, 146, 157–58
  government in, 150–51
  Greek influence on, 147, 148, 152, 157, 159
  Late, 157–63
  Latin Right privileges in, 147–48
  legal system of, 151, 152, 153
  literature of, 159
  military character of, 146, 148, 153, 154–56
  monarchy and, 146, 148
  morality in, 151–53, 208–9
  naming practices in, 153–54
  philosophy in, 159–60
  religion in, 147, 152–53, *159*, 160
  rise of, 147–48
  slavery in, 154, 156, 157–58, 160
  social struggles in, 150–51, 157–58, 160–61
  status of women in, 154, 158–59
  theater in, 159
Romanticism, 566, 677–84, *685*
  in the arts, 654, 659, *659*, 677–84
  English, 677–80
  French, 680
  gender roles and, 679–80
  German, 680, 681
  liberalism and, 680
  literature and, 677–80, 681
  music and, 681–84
  nationalism and, 680, 702
  nature as theme of, 678, 680, 682–83
  Orientalism in, 680–81, *681*
  women and, 678–80
Roma people, *see* Gypsies
Rome, 174–75, *174*, 195, 199, 341
  founding of, 146, 147–48
  papacy in, 264, 268, 379, 380
  in Renaissance, 368, 398
  unification of Italy and, 708, 709
Rome, Treaty of (1957), 924
Romeo and Juliet (Shakespeare), 483
Rome: Open City (film), 953
Rommel, Erwin (1891–1944), 885
Romulus, 146, 147, 148
Romulus Augustulus, Roman emperor (475–476), 201
Roosevelt, Eleanor, 1008
Roosevelt, Franklin D. (1882–1945), 862, 865, 883, 908
Rosetta Stone, 27, *27*, 129, 681
Ross, Helen, 820, 821
Rossellini, Roberto, 953, 954
Rossini, Gioachinno (1792–1868), 680
Rothko, Mark (1903–1970), 953
Rothschild, Jakob, 779, *779*
Rothschild family, 629, 775
Roundheads, 475

Rousseau, Jean-Jacques (1712–1778), 563–66, *565*, 566–67, 568, 569, 571, 591, 675, 676–78
Roussillon, Count of, 293, *293*
Roxane (wife of Alexander), 124, 126
Roy, Manabendra Nath (1887–1954), 840
Royal Academy of Sciences, French, 543
Royal Colonial Institute, 730
Royal Procession of Louis XIV, The (van der Meulen), *495*
Royal Society (England), 535, 540, 543, 569
Rubaiyat (Umar Khayyam), 278
Rubens, Peter Paul (1577–1640), 486, *487*
Rubicon River, 162
Rubruck, William de, 329
Rudolph II, Holy Roman emperor (1576–1612), 524
Ruhr valley, 879, 903
Rule (Saint Benedict), 207, 235, 264
Rule for Monasteries (Saint Benedict), 447
"Rule of the Master," 207
Rûm, sultanate of, 327
Rump Parliament, 476–77
Rus', 249–50, 269, 326
Russell, William Howard, 723
Russia, 226, 269, 352, *407*, 509, 577, 656, 1009
  absolutism in, 507, 510–15
  anti-Semitism in, 777, 782, 829, 859
  autocratic tradition of, 492
  Balkans conflict and (1990s), 978
  Byzantium and, 241, 373–74
  capitalism in, 784
  and Congress of Vienna (1814), 654–56, 661
  in Crimean War, 721–23
  Decembrist revolt in, 657
  economy in, after 1991, *973*
  expansion of, 513–15, *514*
  in First World War, 800, 801, 802, 803, 806, 813, *816*, 822–26, 829, 832, 838
  Greek war of independence and, 659
  imperialism of, 729, 738, 741–42, 742
  industrialization of, 782
  Industrial Revolution and, 627, 629, 631, 636
  interethnic tensions in, 782
  labor unions in, 784
  liberalism in, 656, 669, 784
  Marxism in, 782–83, 785
  Mongol invasion of, 325
  Napoleon vs., 604–5, 608–9
  nationalism in, 688, 699
  nation building in, 715–16
  October Revolution in (1905), 784, 822
  Orthodox Christianity in, 270, 373
  Ottoman empire and, 786
  Ottoman Empire's war with, 574–75
  Pan-Slavism in, 699, 713
  pogroms in, 782
  Poland's rivalry with, 374, 407
  populism in, 782
  post-Soviet, 972–74, 978
  reign of Catherine the Great in, 515

reign of Ivan the Great in, 406–8, *408*
rise of Muscovy and, 373–74, 406, *407*
Russification program in, 782
in Russo-Japanese War (1904–1905), 784
serfdom in, 513, 688, 715–16
in Seven Years' War, 573, *574*
textile industry in, 629
transformation of, under Peter I, 511–13
Troppau memorandum and, 656
see also Soviet Union
Russian Federation, 972
Russian Revolutions (1917), 822–26, *824*,
   840–41
   of February, 822–24
   of October, 824–26
   Soviets organized in, 824–26
Russo-Japanese War (1904–1905), 742, 784
Russo-Turkish War (1877–1878), 785
Rwanda, 993, 1008

Saar, 831
Sabbath, 182
sacraments ("holy rites"), power of, 342
Sadat, Anwar (1918–1981), 995
Saddam Hussein, 1001, *1002*, 1005
Sadducees, 182
Saint-Domingue, 499
   slave rebellion in, *612*
   slavery in, 664
Sainte-Chapelle (Holy Chapel), 345, *345*
St. Helena, island of, 610
Saint Jerome in His Study (Dürer), 405, *406*
St. Kitts, 507
St. Peter's Basilica, 401, *401*, *426*, 427, 484
St. Petersburg, 515
St. Thomas (São Tomé), 418
Sajo River, battle of (1241), 325
Sakharov, Andrei (1921–1989), 968
Salāh ad-Dīn (Saladin), Sultan (c. 1138–
   1193), 296
Salamanca, University of, 311
Salamis, battle of (480 B.C.E.), 96, 97
Salem, Massachusetts, 481
Salians, 253
salons, 569, *570*
Samarkand, 324
Samuel, Book of, 60, 61
Samuel (prophet), 57, 60, 61, 237
Samuel the Nagid, 279
Sand, George (1804–1876), 645, 679
San Marco Basilica, 220
San Martín, José de, 656
Sans-Culotte, A (Boilly), *603*
sans-culottes, 588, 597, 599, *603*
Sanskrit, 41
San Stefano, Treaty of (1878), 785
Santo Domingo, 759
São Tomé (St. Thomas), 418
Sappho (c. 620–550 B.C.E.), 86–87
Sarajevo, 975, 978
Sarcophagus of the Muses, *107*
Sardinia, 154, 155, 331, 700–704, 707–9,
   714
   in Crimean War, 721–22

Sargon II, king of Assyria, 60, 63, 71
Sargon of Akkad, 16–17, 57, 60
Sartre, Jean-Paul (1905–1980), 938, 939
Sassanid dynasty, 199, 213
sati, 732, *732*, 750
Satires (Juvenal), 171
Saudi Arabia, 1001–2
Saul, king of Israel (c. 1025–c. 1005 B.C.E.),
   57, 60, 61, 237
Savonarola, Girolamo, 438
Savoy, 700, 708
Saxons, 201
Saxony, 252–53, 263, 505, 656
   Crusades and, 296
Scandinavia, 241, 250, 333–34, 352, 359,
   380, 434
Schiele, Egon (1890–1918), 795, *795*
Schiller, Friedrich von (1759–1805), 680
Schleswig, 711
Schlieffen, Alfred von (1833–1913), 803, *806*
Schlieffen, Plan, 806, *806*
Schliemann, Heinrich (1822–1890), 49
scholasticism, 309, 313–14, 321, 402, 405,
   449
School of Athens, The (Raphael), *118*, *399*
Schutzstaffel (SS), 857, 890, 892–93, 896–97,
   902
science and technology:
   agriculture and, 253–54, *254*
   in ancient Egypt, 32, 129, 135, 138
   in Archaic Greece, 92
   Assyrian, 63–64
   electricity and, 763
   in Enlightenment, 551–52, 561–62
   evolutionary theory and, 786–88
   after First World War, 864–65
   genetic research and, 991
   globalization and, 988
   in Hellenistic Greece, 135–38, *139*, 141
   Industrial Revolution and, 618, 626–27
   in Islamic civilization, 277–78
   liberals and, 786
   manufacturing and, 550, 617–18
   medieval, 253–54, *254*
   missions of discovery and, 561–62, *561*
   music and, 951–52
   natural philosophy and, 530–34
   navigation and, 412
   nominalism in, 335
   Paleolithic, 5
   popular music and, 951
   of psychology, 792
   in Roman Empire, 171–72
   in second industrial revolution, 762–63
   Sumerian, 14–16, *14*, *15*
   textile industry and, 621–22
   warfare and, *14*, 15, 374
scientific revolution, 519–44
   academic societies and, 535–38
   in astronomy, 522–30
   Enlightenment and, 577
   intellectual roots of, 520–22
   mechanists and, 521, 534, *535*, 540
   philosophy and, 520, 521, 530–34

religion and, 520–22, *522*, 525–30
   Renaissance influence on, 521
Scipio Africanus (236–c. 183 B.C.E.), 155,
   156–57
Scone Abbey, 346
Scorpion, King, 25
Scotland, 201, 346–47, 361, 378, 380, 387,
   492
   Calvinism in, 437
   union of England and, 503
Scott, Walter (1771–1832), 377, 680, 681
sculpture:
   Baroque, 484
   of Hellenistic Greece, 139
   medieval naturalism in, 520
   of Renaissance, 399–401, *400*
   see also art; *specific cultures*
seals, document, 338–39
Sea Peoples, 52–54, 57, 59, 73
Sebastian, Saint, *349*
Second Punic War, 155, 156
Second Sex, The (Beauvoir), 939–40, 958
sects, 434–35
Sedan, battle of (1870), 711
Select Society of Edinburgh, 569
Seleucid Empire, 129–30, 131, 139, 157, 181
Seleucus, 129
Self-Help (Smiles), 642
Seljuq Turks, 270–71, 273, 274, 294, 327,
   370, 372
seminaries, 446–47
Senate, Roman, 148, 150, 151, 153, 155,
   160, 161, 162, 164
Senatus Populusque Romanum (SPQR), 151,
   151, 164
Senegal, 455, 744, 768, 938
Senghor, Léopold, 938
Sennacherib, king of Assyria (704–
   681 B.C.E.), 63, *63*
sensibilité, cult of, 566
Sentences (Lombard), 311
sepoys, 733
septicemic plague, 354
Septuagint, 134
Serbia, 269, 659, 786, 887, 890, 974–75,
   976
   emergence of, 659–60
   in First World War, 800–801, 804–5
serfs, serfdom, 625, 637
   abolition of, 629, 636, 688, 699, 715–16,
   716
   in High Middle Ages, 255, 258
   in Late Middle Ages, 359
   Peasants' Revolt and, 359, 360
   in Revolutions of 1848, 699, 713
   in Russia, 513, 688
service sector, in eighteenth-century Britain,
   550–51
Sesostris III, pharaoh of Egypt, *34*
Seth (Egyptian deity), 30
Sevastopol, fall of, 722
Seven Weeks' War (1866), 711
Seven Years' War (French and Indian War)
   (1756–1763), 573, *574*, 575

Treaty of Guadalupe Hidalgo (1848), 688, 758

Treaty of Nanking (1842), 738

Treaty of Paris (1783), 577

Treaty of Rome (1957), 924

Treaty of San Stefano (1878), 785

Treaty of Tordesillas (1494), 455

Treaty of Utrecht (1713), 506–7, *507*, *508*, 515, 573, *655*

Treaty of Versailles (1919), *see* Versailles, Treaty of

Treaty of Westphalia (1648), 508

Trebizond, 215

Treblinka (concentration camp), 901

trench warfare, 806, 810–13

Trent, Council of, 439, 446, *446*, 448

Trevelyan, Charles Edward, 638–39

trial by jury, 287

Tribonian, 214

trigonometry, 278

Trinity with the Virgin, The (Masaccio), 396, *396*

Triple Alliance, 800

Triple Entente, 800

Tripoli, as Crusader State, 295

triremes, *93*, 94

Tristan, Flora, 672

Tristan (Gottfried von Strassburg), 315

Triumph of the Will (film), *866*, 869

trivium, 308

Trojan War, 49

Trojan Women (Euripides), 97

Trotsky, Leon (1879–1940), 824, 825, 839, *839*, 844

Truffaut, François (1932–1984), 954

Truman, Harry S. (1884–1972), 906–7, 908, 916, 928

Truman Doctrine, 916

tsar, use of term, 406–7

Tsingtao, *816*

Tudor dynasty, 378

Tunis, 331

Tunisia, 154, 744, 885

Arab Spring in, 1010

protests in, *1011*

Turgot, Anne-Robert-Jacques, 586

Turkestan, 741

Turkey, 256, 829, 830, 831, 928

EU and, 1009

protests in, *1011*

see also Ottoman Empire

Turner, J. M. W. (1775–1851), 680, 682, *683*

Tuscany, 708

Tutankhaten (Tutankhamen), pharaoh of Egypt, 47, *47*

Tutsi people, 993

Twelve Tables, Law of, 151, 152, 153, 172

Twitter, 1011

Two Hours to Doom (Bryant), 943

Two New Sciences, The (Galileo), 530

Two Sicilies, Kingdom of, 700, 708

"Two Thousand Words" (Vaculík), 966

Two Treatises on Government (Locke), 496, 504

typhoid, 457

tyranny, Greek, 85

Tyre, 123

Tyrtaeus of Sparta, 84

Ubaid culture, 8–9

Ugarit, 48, 54

Ugaritic alphabet, 48, 55

Ukraine, 372, 373, 407, 826, 839, 887, 903, 972, 1009

ulama, 227

Ulbricht, Walter (1893–1973), 922

Ulpian, 173, 177

Ulster Volunteer Force, 781

Ulysses (Joyce), 863

Umar, caliph, 223, 225

Umar Khayyam (d. 1123), 278

Umayyad caliphate, 225–26, *225*, 236, 241, 243

uncertainty principle, 865

United Nations, 928, 930, 977, 992, 996–97, 1006–7, 1008

United Provinces, 501, 504–5, 506

United States, 577

and Americanization of mass culture, 867–68

Arab-Israeli conflict and, 931, 995

atomic bomb developed by, 865, 903, 906–7, 908

Balkans conflict and (1990s), 978

Chinese Revolution and, 927

civil rights movement in, 957–60, 962

Civil War in, 688, 717–21, *721*

in cold war, 909, 912, 914, 916–17, 942–45, *943*, 947, 964

cotton industry in, 631

film industry of, 866

in First World War, 807, 810, *810*, 821, 826, 828, *828*, 834

after First World War, 838, 839, 860–63

global economics and, 924

Great Depression in, 861–63, *862*, 875

health care reform in, 1010

immigration to, 633

imperialism of, 729, 739, 745, 758–59

industrialization of, 720

in Industrial Revolution, 621, 631

Iranian hostage crisis and, 1001

in Iraq War of 2003, 1005

in Korean War, 927–28, 964

as major power, 723

Manifest Destiny doctrine of, 717

nation building in, 716–17

in NATO, 917

New Deal in, 862–63

nineteenth century expansion of, *717*, *720*

in Persian Gulf War, 1001

racism in, 957–60, 1010

radio industry in, 865

Roman Empire compared with, 174–77

in Second World War, 883–87, *888*, 902, 908

September 11, 2001 terrorist attacks in, 1004–5, *1005*, 1008

"sexual revolution" in, 955–57

slavery in, 613, 664, 688, 716–17

in Spanish-American War (1898), 758–59

steel industry in, 762, 766

Suez crisis and (1956), 934

in twenty-first century, 1009–10

Versailles Treaty and, 875

Vietnam War and, 934–36, 960–61, 964

in war with Mexico, 688, 717

women's movement in, 956–57, *956*

women's suffrage in, 818

Universal Declaration of Human Rights, 1008

universalism, 67, 70, 133

universities:

degrees granted by, 311, 321

Lutheran Reformation and, 430

medieval, 311, *312*, 313–14, 321

1960s student movements and, 961–65

see also specific universities

Universum Film AG (UFA), 866–67

Ur, 10, 16, *16*, *17*, 18

ʿUrabi Pasha, 728

Urban II, Pope (r. 1088–1099), 271–74, 294

Urban VI, Pope (r. 1378–1389), 380

Urban VIII, Pope (r. 1623–1644), 529

urban growth, in early modern England, *637*

urbanization:

in eighteenth-century Europe, 550

in High Middle Ages, 255–59, *256*

in Industrial Revolution, 637–39, *637*

see also cities

Ure, Andrew, 626

Ur-Nammu, king of Ur, 18

Urraca, queen of Léon-Castile (c. 1080–1126), 316

Ursuline order, 448

Uruk, 9, *9*

Uruk Period (4300–2900 B.C.E.), 9–10

Ustasha (Croatian fascists), 890, 892

Uthman, caliph, 225

Utnapishtim, 40

Utopia (More), 404

utopianism, 404, 671, 795

Utrecht, Treaty of (1713), 506–7, *507*, *508*, 515, 573, *655*

Vaculík, Ludvík, 966

Valentinian II, Roman emperor, 200

Valerian, Roman emperor (253–260), 191

Valla, Lorenzo (1407–1457), 370, 404

Valley of the Kings, 45

Valois dynasty, 348, *348*

Vandals, 200–201, 202, 213

van der Meulen, Adam Franz, *495*

van der Straet, Jan (1523–1605), 416

van der Weyden, Roger (c. 1400–1464), 363, 365, *365*

Van Dyck, Anthony, *476*

Van Gogh, Vincent (1853–1890), 795

vassals, 261

Vatican City, 298

Vatican Council, Second, 448

GLOBAL SATELLITE MOSAIC

The beauty and complexity of Earth's landscape—above and below the oceans—is revealed with the Global Satellite Mosaic. The mosaic was produced for the National Geographic Society by NASA's Jet Propulsion Laboratory, using more than 500 satellite images from the National Oceanic and Atmospheric Administration. The cloud-free images show Earth in its natural colors as it would be seen from space. One can easily identify the world's major glaciers, deserts, mountain ranges, and rain forests. For example, follow the green ribbon of lush vegetation along the Nile into the stark, dry Sahara. The mountain ranges seem to rise off the map thanks to digital elevation databases from the Department of Defense. The deepest areas of the ocean realm are colored dark blue in contrast to the light blue areas highlighting continental shelves, submarine ridges, and underwater mountains.

BIOSPHERE

Thousands of satellite images are combined to show a picture of biological productivity in the oceans, red, yellow, and green indicate waters rich in phytoplankton. On land, green areas show high-potential plant productivity; tan and brown areas suffer from productivity limitations due to aridity and temperature.

THE W
SATE